Edward Vaughan Kenealy, Arthur Orton

The Trial at Bar of Sir Roger C. D. Tichborne, bart.

in the Court of Queen's bench at Westminster, before Lord Chief Justice Cockburn, Mr. Justice Mellor, & Mr. Justice Lush, for perjury, commencing Wednesday, April 23, 1873

Edward Vaughan Kenealy, Arthur Orton

The Trial at Bar of Sir Roger C. D. Tichborne, bart.
in the Court of Queen's bench at Westminster, before Lord Chief Justice Cockburn, Mr. Justice Mellor, & Mr. Justice Lush, for perjury, commencing Wednesday, April 23, 1873

ISBN/EAN: 9783337325268

Printed in Europe, USA, Canada, Australia, Japan

Cover: Foto ©Suzi / pixelio.de

More available books at **www.hansebooks.com**

INTRODUCTION

TO THE

TRIAL

OF

R. C. D. TICHBORNE, BART.

"These our actors,
As I foretold you, were all spirits, and
Are melted into air, into thin air:
And like the baseless fabric of this vision,
The cloud-capp'd towers, the gorgeous palaces,
The solemn temple, the great globe itself,
Yea, all which it inherit, shall dissolve,
And like this insubstantial pageant faded,
Leave not a rack behind. We are such stuff
As dreams are made of, and our little life
Is rounded with a sleep."—*Shakespere.*

DR. KENEALY.

THE QUEEN.

LIST OF ILLUSTRATIONS.

THE TRIAL AT BAR

OF

SIR ROGER C. D. TICHBORNE,

BART.

IN THE COURT OF QUEEN'S BENCH AT WESTMINSTER, BEFORE

LORD CHIEF JUSTICE COCKBURN, MR. JUSTICE MELLOR, & MR. JUSTICE LUSH,

FOR PERJURY,

COMMENCING WEDNESDAY, APRIL 23, 1873, AND ENDING SATURDAY, FEBRUARY 28, 1874.

TO WHICH IS PREFIXED

A BIOGRAPHICAL SKETCH OF THE DEFENDANT.

DEDICATED TO HER MAJESTY THE QUEEN;

BY

DR. KENEALY.

VIEW OF TICHBORNE HOUSE.

"ENGLISHMAN" OFFICE, BOUVERIE STREET, FLEET STREET, LONDON.

1875.

FEBRUARY 6.

DEDICATION TO THE QUEEN.

MADAM,

PERMIT me, with the greatest possible respect to your MAJESTY, to dedicate this Report of the TICHBORNE Trial to you, our most gracious Sovereign.

I do so, without having solicited your MAJESTY'S permission, because too well I know that your MAJESTY has no power to grant even the slightest favour to one of your People.

Had I entreated your MAJESTY for liberty to prefix your Name to this Dedication, and to send it forth to the world with your MAJESTY'S *imprimatur*, I should have been insolently refused by those who hold the QUEEN of this great Empire in disgraceful bondage, while they profess to do all their acts under the sanction of her Name and Authority; who, pretending to be her servants, are in reality absolute masters of her actions in all things; who assume the right to guide her as to her choice of guests, her selection of a residence, or her dismissal of a groom; who in effect have discrowned Her, and made themselves into Sultans and Shahs and Bashaws of this once-free Country.

I have, therefore, not gone through that vain ceremony; but, like one of the great lights and glories of England in the last century—I mean JUNIUS—I have ventured to approach your MAJESTY myself; and have not sought the intervention of any of the purple lacqueys who surround your Throne. These, while they hold themselves out to the Empire as being your MAJESTY'S officers, are in reality a species of mean and petty tyrants, who have usurped power for their own purposes, and have reduced our glorious Land into base submission to a most odious Despotism.

The public know little or nothing of this; they ignorantly hold your MAJESTY to be responsible for many of the worst acts of your Ministers. Hence a wild element of discontent and insubordination is daily gathering, which may burst in thunder upon us some fine day, and crumble everything into Chaos.

There are those about your MAJESTY who declare that there is no danger of such a result; but so it is always. The sycophants deceive the Sovereign—perhaps they deceive themselves—and in one moment both are swept away by the Ocean.

The story of CANUTE and his followers is as true to-day as it was a thousand years ago.

Your MAJESTY'S grandfather, King GEORGE the Third, had a certain amount of royal power. He knew and felt that he was one of the Three Estates of the Realm. He was brought up under evil auspices; but that the Constitution of England consisted of three co-equal Powers—King, Lords, and Commons—was always present to his mind.

When the even balance of any one of these Three Estates ceases, and a portion of its weight is shifted to either of the others, the condition of the Constitution is seriously altered, and evils to the People necessarily follow.

The framing of the English Constitution was the work of the wisest of men. It was moulded with a due regard to the true rights and liberties of all. It was so nicely poised and balanced that, had it not been tampered with, it would have endured for ever. The exquisite evenness of its adjustment is now lost and destroyed. The real Constitution is consequently gone; and we have substituted for it, the worst possible form of Government, an Oligarchy, which governs in the interests only of a few Great Families, and ignores the People wholly; using them but as beasts of burden.

By the fundamental Laws of this Empire, the SOVEREIGN was and ought to be a great Power in the State. By insolent usurpation, and by the covert reversal and repeal of those Laws, the SOVEREIGN is now converted into a Puppet, a Name, and a Sham.

I entreat your MAJESTY to believe that in thus speaking openly and honestly, I mean no disrespect. So far from it, I am now labouring to found and organize a Great League of Englishmen, Scotchmen, and Welshmen, to be called the MAGNA CHARTA ASSOCIATION, which shall dislodge Usurpers, destroy this rapacious, cruel, and vulture-like Oligarchy, and restore to the SOVEREIGN of our land, the jewelled crown which the SOVEREIGN alone should wear, and wear happily for the welfare of her People.

The whole patronage of the Empire is now within a dozen hands. A knot of powerful Families has arrogated, and holds it. No man, no matter what his abilities, or his merits may be, can get a public appointment unless he debases himself by flattery, by subservience, by vice mayhap, or by infamy. The Army, the Navy, the Church, the Law, the Medical profession, are all filled in their places of profit, not by the command of the SOVEREIGN, as they ought to be, but by that of political cliques, who are wholly without responsibility, and who do exactly as they please, without ever once consulting the MONARCH. She, by the true theory of the Constitution, appoints all who are entrusted with authority; she is answerable to the Country for such appointments; and in such responsibility our wise ancestors saw that there was the best safeguard that the appointments would be good, honest, and satisfactory. But all this is changed. No one is now responsible; for the Minister of to-day may be out of place to-morrow, while his base or incompetent nominee retains the appointment that he received: and by a tacit compact—which may be called a treasonable conspiracy—among public men, none of them ever interferes with the appointments so made, however bad or villainous they may be. Hence the innumerable disasters which, in your MAJESTY'S reign, have overtaken us by land and sea: hence the perpetual blunders that are made, which involve us in loss of treasure, and in national disgrace: hence the countless cases of deaths from starvation, and suicides from absolute want, which are one of the unhappy features of the present time. If any one were to go over the columns of the Newspapers, since your MAJESTY came to the Throne, and extracted all those most heart-rending narratives, he might form a volume that would thrill mankind with horror. And this *must* always be the state of affairs, and has been so from the beginning of history, in all countries where an Oligarchy like ours has usurped or grasped, or slided imperceptibly into sway.

If your MAJESTY were directly answerable to your People—as by the old Constitution you should be—for all public appointments, they would be filled by men of merit; but as no one is answerable, they are filled by bad, or unfit persons—the slaves, or relatives, or flatterers, or tools, of those Families who have robbed the Crown of its greatest possession. The MAGNA CHARTA ASSOCIATION will labour to restore to the Throne, the rights, the privileges, and the prerogatives which it has lost; and thus bring back the ancient balance of the Constitution. One of your MAJESTY'S late Ministers, Mr. JOHN BRIGHT, declared openly and publicly before the world,—and no one ever dared to contradict him, for everybody knew and felt that it was a fact,—that "the whole system of the English Government was one of out-door relief on a gigantic scale, for the members, the relations and friends of the Aristocracy." I pray your MAJESTY'S most serious attention to those remarkable words.

If your MAJESTY is treacherously advised, that words like those do not sink into the hearts of your People, and fire their souls with rage, and a terrible sense of wrong, of fraud, and of injustice, you are indeed in the hands of evil counsellors. Mr. BRIGHT spoke them when he was a MAN—but when they made him a Privy Councillor and a Cabinet Minister, he kicked the People from under him, and became a very pretty specimen of a wealthy tradesman converted into a hanger-on of the Aristocracy. He can now bow and bend and smile and scrape, and take off his hat, and perform any amount of genuflexion, as well as the best gentleman's servant out of livery that one can hire for money. He wrote and spoke against Court costume, and suggested a footman's livery—which he wears with becoming satisfaction. He is now all for the Oligarchy, and has deserted the People; whatever he may mouth at Birmingham, or

Graciously permit me to recall your MAJESTY's attention, for a few moments, to the Past. Let me mention how it was that this encroachment on royal power has insensibly grown up, increased, and assumed its present hideous dimensions; how it was that the Aristocracy secured this right of "out-door relief." The system had its origin in the reaction of the Country against the exaggerated pretensions of the STUARTS, who had some wild, papistical notion that their prerogatives were all of divine origin. For this notion they suffered, and deservedly. One lost his head: another his crown. Your MAJESTY's grandfather, GEORGE the Third, was not exempt from some high fancies of the same kind. A corrupt faction in the House of Commons unted and passed a Resolution that "the King's influence had increased, was inreasing, and ought to be diminished:" and this struck a vital blow at the most ancient prerogatives of Royalty. It was the first step by which the real enemies of the People, the Families, were enabled to filch into their own hands the rights of the SOVEREIGN, and to reduce his powers by one half. This resolution was the germ of "their gigantic system of out-door relief:" and it has produced incalculable evils.

They did this, be it remembered, not for the public benefit, but for their own.

For nearly a century it had been the object of certain great Families, Whig as well as Tory, to annihilate the SOVEREIGN, while they retained the Wearer of the Crown. They wished to make our Country their own private appanage; while they agreed to preserve the appearance of a Monarchy—but a Monarchy only for their own most selfish ends.

They tried this first with WILLIAM the Third: and only ceased when he threatened to return to Holland, and give them back their ancient King.

Alarmed by this threat, they desisted during his reign: for well they knew that JAMES STUART, or his son, would never listen to, or allow such pretensions.

GEORGE the First and GEORGE the Second were foreigners, who knew nothing about the ancient Constitution: and did not care for it a button. The first was an old man when he came to the Throne; and valued nothing but Hanover and the Duchess of KENDAL. He detested his son, GEORGE the Second, so thoroughly, that he did not heed to what abject slavery he might be reduced. He left a will alienating everything from him that he could, which that dutiful son found and burned: and so, fully justified the feeling of hatred and scorn which his father entertained towards him.

GEORGE the Second was a shrewd, sharp, artful little sensualist: who lived only for the indulgence of criminal passions. He also hated his heir apparent (and I think very properly and justly, for a more miserable fellow than "FRED" never lived), and he made a compact with his wife, that if *he* allowed *her* the appointment of the Bishops, she should never interfere with his own little peccadilloes. This compact was faithfully fulfilled by both sides: and Queen CAROLINE is known to have carried her complaisance to HIS MAJESTY in this respect to bounds which I dare not venture to recall. With such a King, WALPOLE was in reality Master of England: the great Families who surrounded and supported him were everything. The SOVEREIGN was nothing. He reigned, but did not govern: nor did he want to do so. He heeded not how miserable a slave in the future his son might be, so that his own base and selfish pleasures were for the moment secured. The existence, however, of a Pretender, in the person of the son and grandson of JAMES the Second, curbed the Great Families, and they did not then dare actually to discrown the King or usurp the whole authority of the Royal Estate.

I am no admirer of Lord BUTE; but a STUART himself, and with many of the STUART notions, he instilled into his pupil, GEORGE the Third, some true notions of what the King is and should be, according to the grand and ancient Constitution of this country.

GEORGE the Third came to the Throne with these notions, and carried them out as long and as well as he could: but the Families were too strong for him: they almost crushed him by the parliamentary Resolution to which I have already adverted; and when he became incapable of reigning, and passed away, their main object had been nearly achieved.

The Regency followed—a Regency with so many restrictions and limitations, and bonds and chains, that the Prince was hardly a Power at all. But he, like GEORGE the Second, was such a slave of passion, that he would have accepted almost any position, provided it brought him money, and gave him an opportunity for unlimited excess.

GOD preserve this country from a Prince and a reign like his; for if we had such a second voluptuary, the Vatican could buy him with its unlimited millions; and for the gratification of his sensualism could win him to almost any measures in its interest.

We know that France pensioned King CHARLES the Second. Heaven grant that the College of Propaganda may never find a King of England whom it may purchase with gold, to grant it and its Church whatever it may need, for the privilege of sweeping the lanes and alleys in search of the most debased characters, and to indulge in the most grovelling desires.

In the days of the Fourth GEORGE, the Sovereignty was again lopped of some of its most undoubted powers: and the Whig and Tory Families exulted in the prospect of its ultimate annihilation, but apparent subsistence.

But, like all base and selfish plotters, they were unwise. For the purpose of destroying the Constitution utterly, and thus making easier the destruction of the Monarchical Essence, the Whig families helped to pass the Popish Relief Bill, as it was called. They hoped by this device to get the Irish for ever on their side, and herein they have partly succeeded; but they never foresaw what has since followed: that their Allies would become their Masters, and the Masters of England; and that thenceforward they must hold power only so long as the Vatican willed that they should do so.

Probably they have since reconciled themselves to the present state of affairs, and are content to be the slaves of the Pope and the Bishops, provided they retain all the golden loaves and silver fishes of place.

But how long their Masters of the Vatican and the Romish College will allow that, no one knows: and they certainly have never done so, nor will they ever, without receiving more than an equivalent for their assistance.

It will eventually come to this: Methinks I hear the Vatican say, If you, the Oligarchs, wish to have all the material wealth of England at your disposal; to nominate yourselves and your adherents to everything, and to be the Masters of the country, its liberties and its independence, it can only be on this condition, that you help to unprotestantise it, and give us Ecclesiastical Supremacy, while you yourselves retain Political Domination.

I need not subjoin in a parenthesis, that the Ecclesiastical Supremacy, thus demanded, is the sure and certain step to Political Domination; and that the Vatican people will (if not stopped) eventually monopolise both, and be undisputed Lords of the Empire. But this is not yet—though it is in prospect.

The Whig and Tory Families are now in full possession of England, just as a majority in the House of Commons happens to be. Your MAJESTY has not power even to appoint one of your footmen. If you ventured to exercise such a right, your MAJESTY's Lord Chamberlain, or Lord Steward of the Household, or some other nobleman in plush, would very soon let you see that you were in his fetters.

The public are wickedly and fraudulently told that the QUEEN has power; at the present moment, I believe she has no more power than a snipe.

But she has the power to resume her rightful authority if she will only throw herself upon her People, and demand it at their hands. I do not believe that the reddest Republican in the land would grudge it to her, seeing in whose grasp it has been for so many years.

For, after all, she *is* our QUEEN, and represents our ancient Kings; and the blood of ALFRED and the PLANTAGENETS is in her veins, and we are loyal to our old and heroic traditions. And what care we for such people as GLADSTONE, or that apostate Jew DISRAELI, when compared with this true and noble Lady, who ought to be our QUEEN, but is not.

She has but to assume a grand course, such as MARIA THERESA of Austria would have assumed; or, greater still, our own ELIZABETH TUDOR would have taken; and issue a Manifesto calling the People of England to her side—and I will answer for them, all will follow.

Does anyone suppose that if the QUEEN had had a voice, we should have been involved in the Crimean blunder, or the Ashantee butchery?

We were inveigled into the first by the artfulness of LOUIS NAPOLEON, and that hot-headed love of a Donnybrook fight which was PALMERSTON'S hobby; and, having wasted one hundred millions sterling, and sacrificed one hundred thousand lives of British soldiers and seamen, we tore up the Treaty purchased by so much blood and gold; and sacrificing Turkey and the SULTAN, as if they were a couple of hens, we surrendered to the CZAR all that we originally refused and he demanded. We made England play the part of bully first, and fool afterwards. A Prime Minister only could do this. When a King does it, it costs him his throne or his life; as his mad expedition against Prussia cost NAPOLEON his blood-stained diadem and hellish sceptre.

As to the Ashantee massacre, it was so shabby, so cruel, so horrible a butchery, that the most wretched tyrant on the Earth would not have ventured upon the like; certainly not a QUEEN like ours. But because your MAJESTY is crownless, and has no voice in the Empire, we were led into that infamous crime also, and have returned from it with dishonour. The savages, whom we are told that we subdued, despise and laugh at us; all our "conquests" are ridiculous and without profit; and the only person who has gained is Sir GARNET WOLSELEY, whom our papers exalt into a Hero, while he is simply the BOMBASTES FURIOSO, or comical Sir HUDIBRAS, of actual life.

What can we expect for these acts but the Vengeance of GOD? And if it comes, who shall say that we do not deserve it? Nay—has it not already come? Is it not about us, over us, and in us? Let us walk through London, through Liverpool, through Manchester, through Bristol, through our other great towns and villages, and see their starving poor; children that should be bright-eyed, happy, and filled with vitality, poisoned in their blood, stunted in their growth, reduced to the condition of beggars and "street Arabs,"—for that is the accepted phrase now for the offspring of English men and English women. And we have sunk to such a pitch of slavery and debasement that we tamely endure the designation; and we do not know, feel, and express, that to find even one "street Arab" in wealthy industrious, and Christian England is the most bitter reproach and scandal of our time; and is, in fact, the punishment which Heaven justly gives for our folly in enduring the Despotism of the Oligarchs.

This miserable affair of Ashantee has also cost its millions; but your MAJESTY had no part in it. I am sure you would—if you had power—have preferred expending a hundred millions in beautifying the face of our beautiful Island: in sweeping away every lane and alley and court that contained a fever-den, or a bevy of poor little "street Arabs:" in abolishing the odious and insulting Income Tax: in getting us a free breakfast-table, and a meat dinner-table, which every one of your People ought to have: and which every household in this land *might* have, if the Rich did not dominate, and make the Laws that grind the Poor to powder. Only let us consider what a hundred millions spent in this Country, for such purposes as I have described, would accomplish. We should have public parks and gardens in every large town: we should possess picture galleries, and libraries, and museums to delight and teach the rising generation: we should be able to get rid of some of the taxes that most oppress the labouring classes: we should *for ever* be freed from the attacks of fever, blood-poisoning, and contagious diseases. The fire that purified London from the plague for centuries, would not be a more efficacious remedy than a part of this hundred millions expended for the safety of GOD'S children, instead of being wasted in powder and shot for their murder.

O GOD of Heaven! may I live to see the day when a "street Arab" shall be a thing unknown: when Englishmen will look back with burning cheeks of shame to the time when they tolerated such language from their treacherous Newspapers, and no less traitorous Leaders: when the existence of such poverty as now oppresses the People shall be regarded as proof conclusive that our whole system is at fault, and that Heaven helps us not, because we do not help ourselves: when those horrible Laws and Taxes which tend to bring up the whole rising population to an endurance of starvation all their working lives, and a workhouse at the close; to the sight of their children slowly dying before their eyes: and lunacy and idiocy spreading through the land, for want of the common necessaries of life—O GOD of Heaven, Father, Mother, Friend, and Guardian of Thy children—may I live to see those days passed and gone for ever!

And to release your MAJESTY from this dreadful and powerless condition, and to restore to you the Crown of which you have been robbed, and to make our dear Country truly prosperous, is one of the cherished objects of the MAGNA CHARTA ASSOCIATION.

WILLIAM the Fourth succeeded GEORGE—a very poor man. He could swear like any Jack Tar; but I fear his political knowledge was nothing. He was an easy prey to Earl GREY and his hungry wolf-like faction, who dared to tell him that if he did not help GREY in his measures, they would create 100 new peers, and swamp the House of Lords; and this poor gentleman, acting more like a middy than a monarch, did as he was ordered; and from that moment the SOVEREIGN of England became a nullity and a name; and the Constitution consisted only of Lords and Commons; the power and influence and standing of the first having been considerably weakened by successive outrages and insults. And I have no doubt that in your MAJESTY'S own reign, unless the people waken to a sense of their danger, the House of Lords will also be destroyed. The present "Leaders" have already pronounced its doom.

Your MAJESTY succeeded King WILLIAM, and to your great misfortune, you found for Prime Minister one of the most noted and horrible Adulterers that ever appeared in England—I mean the late Lord MELBOURNE. This man believed in no future, in no GOD, in no retribution for crimes committed in this life. Herein he resembled two of your MAJESTY'S late Ministers; it would have been better if, like GLADSTONE, he had been in fear of everlasting torment in Hell. He was as bad a man as ever directed public affairs; and he was thoroughly imbued with the Oligarch doctrine. He died with a wicked lie upon his lips. His great object was to retain place at any price, and to have the luxury of falling asleep in your MAJESTY'S presence, which he alone, I believe, of all the Ministers you ever had, dared to do. But he showed greater consciousness of power even than this; he made your MAJESTY dine with Mrs. NORTON. I am not surprised that after this they introduced Lady RADCLIFFE to your august presence. But let these trifles pass; and let us revert to MELBOURNE. He first within our own time carried out the system of raising the most disgusting and wicked Profligates to place and power. I will not recall to your MAJESTY'S memory their names. They must be familiar to you. He was followed by PALMERSTON, who, having a whole family by another man's wife, patronised all congenial Adulterers, and lifted to the Bench one of the most noted Ruffians, Swindlers, and Seducers that ever was known; and thus brought disgrace upon the Crown and Country that saw him clothed in gold and purple. One of the most remarkable men of our era, RICHARD COBDEN, never mentioned Lord PALMERSTON'S name at the Reform Club, or in private society, that he did not add "*that wicked old man.*" Yet this is he whom all England fell down and worshipped, as the old Egyptians worshipped wolves and rats, and scorpions and serpents. Only when History comes to be honestly written, will it ever be known what this Minister cost our Country. Had your MAJESTY possessed even an ounce of power, you would have expelled him from your Council room, when his forged and garbled Indian dispatches were produced and read in Parliament. That crime and falsehood ranks him for ever with the worst criminals. But your MAJESTY was utterly helpless.

If, according to the ancient Constitution of England, your MAJESTY, who is the Fountain of Honour, had the nomination—which of right belongs to you—of Judges, you would never, for your own dignity and character, have elevated open, noted, and most wicked Libertines and Adulterers to the Bench.

You would never have made men Judges merely because they had bribed constituencies, and as your present First Lord of the Treasury elegantly says, "had scattered marigolds," in perverting voters, and making men and women be guilty of perjury, and intimidation, and falsehood, and trickery of the worst kind, and personation, and the thousand other vile depravities which the Stroud, and other election trials have brought before your horrified People.

Your MAJESTY's Ministers do this, because they come and go, and pass and repass; and are no more heard of. But your MAJESTY remains; and you might well ask yourself, what would your people think of you, if you had been committed to acts like these?

Therefore it is, that I, like so many others, would rejoice to see your MAJESTY's Crown restored; and that we should have some one of character and position really responsible to Great Britain for the appointments that take place.

Certain I am that if your MAJESTY had even an atom of authority or influence in the State, we should never see such Wretches as we have, representing you in office.

Enough of this. I believe that these words will reach your MAJESTY, and that they will produce good fruit. Heaven is my witness that I pen them with pain, with shame, with sorrow; and that I would not do so, but that I am convinced that this Country is in a most perilous condition; and that it is absolutely indispensable for our honour, our safety, our liberty, and even our lives, that the present Despotism and Abomination should be so smitten that it shall be destroyed, never to revive.

Now, indeed, to use the language of the HOLY ONE, do *we see the Abomination of Desolation, spoken of by Daniel the Prophet, stand in the Holy Place.*

Our duty, however, is not to flee, but to fight against it; and we shall all gather under the banner of VICTORIA, for Virtue, for England, and for GOD.

May it please your MAJESTY:

To read this Trial carefully. Your successive Ministers have all testified to your good sense. I humbly pray you to bring it to bear upon these pages—these records—these sad, disgraceful records.

Your MAJESTY will then see to what a condition we have sunk.

Your MAJESTY will feel the deepest sympathy for those so fallen.

Your MAJESTY may probably graciously interfere to help us.

With what a splendid light to future generations the diadem of Queen VICTORIA will shine, if she does that which Justice dictates:

If she re-assumes the crown of ALFRED, and EDWARD, and ELIZABETH, and makes herself again a Power in the State.

If she dismisses those Evil Counsellors who are her worst enemies; and expels those Representatives of her functions who disgrace the Country.

Oh! how every man and woman in the Empire would bless her if she acted thus. How every mother would teach her child to invoke the treasures of Heaven upon her head for thus nobly and divinely doing; and with what a glow of honest pride every Englishman would go forth in the world, glorying in the possession of a monarch capable of an act which would rank her name and memory with that of the greatest Heroes and purest Heroines of History.

I am, with the most profound respect,
Your MAJESTY's most faithful and humble Servant,
EDWARD VAUGHAN KENEALY.

LORD COKE (Pt. 1, p. 54), on Magna Charta, says: "The damnable Judge whose prototype is RADAMANTHUS, the Judge of Hell, according to VIRGIL. First he punisheth and then he heareth, and lastly compelleth to confess, and makes and mars laws at his pleasure. Like as the Centurion in the Holy History did to St. Paul. For the text saith (Acts xxii. 24, 27) he first scourged and then examined him. But good Judges and Justice abhor these courses."

Advice to a Judge.

WHEN on the Regal Seat of Justice throned,
Bear this in mind: thou hast not been advanced
Beyond thy fellows to give loose to temper,
Or prove thyself capricious, weak, or spiteful;
But to administer the Law with truth,
And to be honest, just, and fair to all.
Sully not thy grave place with jests and jokes,
Or low buffoonery, ever on the watch
To win the thoughtless laughter of the crowd;
But be at all times decent, grave, reserved,
Dwelling alone upon the matter in hand.
Take not a cunning, subtle view of a cause,
Such as a Sophist would; but let thy mind
Contemplate it in all its bearings, broadly,
Ever regarding Equity as the Star
By which thou shouldst be guided through the maze.
For Equity is true Law; and they do wrong
Who strive to separate these heavenly twins,—
And both are as the Voice divine of God.
Lean not to Rank and Wealth, for these themselves
Are naturally strong; but rather lean
To him who is weighed down by Poverty,
Yet not so as to win that base applause
Which rises from the rabble when they see
A Judge who tramples Right to catch a cheer.
Give each man hearing with an ear attent,
Whether he be most excellent or most mean;
And talk not ever about public time,
That hackneyed phrase which hasty magistrates use
When they prejudge a cause, are tired, or wish
To go to lunch, or dinner, or are moved
To vent some petty spleen upon the Pleader,
Who, after all, seeks but to do his duty.
Think no time lost that gives thy mind new facts;
For even the humblest man may haply place
His argument before thee, in a form
That may clear up the doubt within thy mind;
But if he sees scorn in thine eye or lip,
How can he hope his mocker to persuade?
Perhaps thou dost not like him. Good my lord!
Thou wert not made a Judge to let thy likings
Bias thy judgment, but to minister right
To all who come before thee in thy court.
A Judge should be like God—far, far removed
From all the petty failings of a man.
And he should have a reverence most august
For his high office, fearing to pollute
That kingly dignity by aught debased.
And he should watch himself with wary eye,
Lest he should do some grievous giant wrong,
Because he loved this man, or hated that.
Guard thyself also from unseemly haste;
There is no virtue more becomes a Judge
Than patience—the chief jewel in his crown.
What rank injustice have I known committed,
Because the Judge would hurry on a cause,
And snub some wretched counsel into silence.
Be kind; be courteous as a king should be,
To all who come before thee.

The following skeleton Pedigree of the TICHBORNE *family shows the descent of the Baronets.*

I. **Sir Benjamin Tichborne**, Knight, Lord of Tichborne, in the county of Hants, created a Baronet on 8th March, 1620, and died 6th September, 1629, aged 90. = AMPHILIS, daughter of Richard Weston, of Skrynes, in Roxwell, co. Essex, Esq., one of the Justices of the Court of Common Pleas, survived her husband.

II. Sir RICHARD TICHBORNE, Knight, eldest son and heir, second Baronet, of Tichborne, died in April, 1652, aged 76. = SUSAN, second daughter and co-heir of William Waller, of Stoke Charity, in the county of Hants, Esq., born in 1597, and living in 1659.

Sir WALTER TICHBORNE, Knt., second son, of Aldershot, in the county of Hants, died in 1640. = MARY, second daughter and co-heir of Robert White, of Aldershot, Esq., married 7 May, 1597, and died January 31st, 1620-1.

Sir BENJAMIN TICHBORNE, Knight, third son, of West Tisted, in the county of Hants, died without issue on 21st August, 1665.

Sir HENRY TICHBORNE, Knight, fourth and youngest son, born in 1582, and died in 1667, aged 85, ancestor of Sir Henry Tichborne, Bart., created Baron Ferrard, of Ireland, in 1715, all issue extinct.

III. Sir HENRY TICHBORNE, eldest surviving son and heir, third Baronet, of Tichborne, baptized on the 24th May, 1624, and died in 1689, aged 65. = MARY, daughter of the Honorable William Arundell, of Horningsham, co. Wilts, second son of Thomas, the first Lord Arundell of Wardour, in the same county, died on 24th December, 1698.

FRANCIS TICHBORNE, of Aldershot, co. Hants, and of Frimley, co. Surrey, Esq., baptized on the 5th December, 1602, and died July 12th, 1671, aged 69. = SUSANNA, daughter of William Haws, of Brumley Hall, co. Essex, Esq., died on 21st December, 1687, aged 77.

IV. Sir HENRY JOSEPH TICHBORNE, eldest son and heir, fourth Baronet of Tichborne, died without issue male, on the 15th July, 1743. = MARY, daughter of Anthony Kemp, of Slindon, county Sussex, Esq., married in 1689, and died in 1755.

V. Sir JOHN HERMENGILD TICHBORNE, second and youngest son, fifth Baronet, of Tichborne, and a priest of the Society of Jesus, died at Ghent, on the 5th May, 1748.

WHITE TICHBORNE, of Aldershot and Frimley, Esq., baptized on 5th December, 16—, and buried on 30th August, 1700. = ANN, daughter of James Supple, of the parish of St. James, Westminster, gentleman, buried at Frimley, 14th October, 1684.

GEORGE BROWNLOW DOUGHTY, of Snarfold Hall, co. Lincoln, Esq., born in 1685, and died 24th September, 1743. = FRANCES CECILY TICHBORNE, second daughter, and one of the co-heiresses, married in 1721, and died 20th August, 1765.

MABELLA TICHBORNE, third and youngest daughter, and one of the co-heiresses, married Sir John Webb, Bart., and had issue two daughters, who both died unmarried.

MICHAEL BLOUNT, of Mapel Durham, in the county of Oxford, Esq., born 26th March, 1693. = MARY AGNES TICHBORNE, eldest daughter, and one of the co-heiresses, born in 1695, married 1715, and died 19th May, 1777, aged 82.

JAMES TICHBORNE, eldest son and heir, of Aldershot and Frimley, Esq., baptized on the 30th May, 1674, and died in 1735. = MARY, daughter of Benjamin Rudyerd, of Winchfield, in the county of Hants, Esq., married at Frimley on 30th October, 1694, and died in December, 1746.

HENRY DOUGHTY, of Snarford Hall, Esq., son and heir, born on 14th March, 1723, and died on 28th August, 1796, aged 73. = ANNA MARIA, only daughter and sole heiress of Gregory Byrne, of Hatton Garden, in the parish of St. Andrew, Holborn, Esq., married in 1762.

MARY BLOUNT, eldest daughter of Michael Blount, Esq., by his wife, Mary Agnes, eldest daughter, and one of the co-heiresses of Sir Henry Joseph Tichborne, Baronet, born 9th November, 1716, married 22nd April, 1743, and died 10th February, 1799, aged 82. = VI. HENRY TICHBORNE, of Aldershot and Frimley, Esq., baptized at Frimley, on 14th October, 1710, succeeded to the estates of Sir Henry Joseph Tichborne, fourth Baronet, under his will, proved 14th January, 1743-4, and to the baronetcy, on the death of the Rev. Sir John Hermengeld Tichborne, of the Society of Jesus, on 5th May, 1748, died 16th July, 1785, aged 75.

ELIZABETH DOUGHTY, only daughter and sole heiress, born on 9th June, 1763, and died unmarried on 8th May, 1826, aged 63. She bequeathed her estates to her cousin, Edward Tichborne, Esq., as the second surviving son of Sir Henry Tichborne, the seventh Baronet, who assumed, by royal license, the name and arms of Doughty.

VII. Sir HENRY TICHBORNE, seventh Baronet, of Tichborne, Aldershot, and Frimley, only son and heir, born September 6th, 1756, and died on 14th June, 1821, aged 65. = ELIZABETH, daughter of Edmund Plowden, of Plowden, co. Salop, Esq., born in 1757, married in 1778, and died on 24th January, 1829, aged 72.

VIII. Sir HENRY JOSEPH TICHBORNE, eldest son and heir, eighth Baronet, of Tichborne, born on 5th January, 1779, and died on 3rd of June, 1845, High Sheriff of Hants in 1831. = ANNE, daughter of Sir Thomas Burke, of Marble Hill, co. Galway, Ireland, Baronet, married on 23rd April, 1806, resided after her husband's death at Grove House Brompton, died at Woodstock, co. Oxford, on 12th August, 1853.

BENJAMIN EDMUND TICHBORNE, second son, born 2nd September, 1870, a captain in the service of the East India Company, died unmarried in China, on 8th October, 1810.

IX. EDWARD TICHBORNE (third, but 2nd surviving son), born on 27th March, 1782, assumed the name of Doughty only by Royal license, dated on 29th May, 1826, succeeded his brother, as 9th Baronet, on 3rd June, 1845, and died 5th March, 1853. = KATHERINE, daughter of James Everard Arundell, ninth Lord Arundell of Wardour, co. Wilts, born 25th August, 1795, mar. 26th June, 1827. Henry Tichborne Doughty, born 8th August, 1829, and died 30th May, 1835.

X. JAMES FRANCIS TICHBORNE, fourth son, born on 3rd Oct., 1784, succeeded his brother, Sir Edward Doughty, as tenth Baronet, on 5th March, 1853, and died on the 11th June, 1862. = HENRIETTE FELICITE, daughter of Henry Seymour, of Knoyle, co. Wilts, Esq., married on 1st August, 1827, died on 12th March, 1868, and buried at Tichborne.

ROGER ROBERT TICHBORNE, youngest son, born 15th February, 1792, died without issue on 3rd November, 1849, married Rebecca, daughter of Aaron Fernandis Nunez, of Belmont Park, co. Hants, died on 26th January, 1859.

LUCY MARY TICHBORNE, born on 22nd March, 1800, married in April, 1823, Geo. Naugle, a lieutenant on half-pay, and had issue four sons and two daughters.

1. ELIZABETH ANN TICHBORNE, born 28th May, 1807, married 5th May, 1829, to Joseph Thadeus, eleventh Lord Dormer, both living in March, 1867, having surviving issue three sons and one daughter.

2. FRANCES CATHERINE TICHBORNE, born 18th March, 1809, married 22nd September, 1829, Henry Benedict, eleventh Lord Arundell of Wardour. She died 19th April, 1836, and her husband on 19th Oct., 1862, leaving issue by this marriage two sons.

3. JULIA TICHBORNE, born 15th July, 1810, married on 2nd July, 1830, Col. Charles Thomas Talbot, who died 30 April, 1838. She married, 2ndly, on 10th Jan., 1839, Washington Hibbert, Esq. Issue by both marriages.

4. MARY TICHBORNE, born on the 28th May, 1812, and died unmarried 29th August, 1827.

5. CATHERINE CAROLINE TICHBORNE, born on 21st April, 1814, married on 22nd April, 1847, to William Greenwood, late Col. of Grenadier Guards, born 10th April, 1798, of Brookwood, near Alresford. Issue one son and two daughters.

6. LUCY ELLEN TICHBORNE, born 21st December, 1817, married 28 October, 1840, to John Towneley, Esq., second son of Peregrine Towneley, of Towneley, co. Lancaster, Esq., issue one son and four daughters.

7. EMILY BLANCHE TICHBORNE, born 18th June, 1818, married on 25th July, 1836, to John Benett, Esq., who died 26th December, 1843. She married, 2ndly, on 2nd July, 1850, Matthew Jas. Higgins, Esq., of Lowndes Square, London, no issue.

KATHERINE MARY ELIZABETH DOUGHTY, only daughter and surviving issue, born 30th April, 1834, mar., 18 Oct., 1854, to Joseph Percival Pickford Radcliffe, eldest son of Joseph Radcliffe, Bart., and has issue.

XI. Sir ROGER CHARLES DOUGHTY TICHBORNE, eldest son and heir, born at Paris on 5th January, 1829, eleventh Baronet of Tichborne.

MARY ANN BRYANT, married at Wagga Wagga, 29th January, 1865. =

ALFRED JOSEPH TICHBORNE, second and youngest son, born at Paris on September 4th, 1830, and died 22nd February, 1866, aged 26. = TERESA MARY, eldest daughter of Henry Benedict, eleventh Lord Arundell of Wardour, by his third wife, born in 1840, married 17th April, 1861.

MABELLA LOUISA, born 8th July, 1832, died on 22nd Mar., 1835.
ALICE MARY PERPETUA, born on 4th October, 1837, and died 20th October, 1839.

ROGER JOSEPH D. TICHBORNE, born at Croydon, 20th May, 1867.

JAMES FRANCIS D. TICHBORNE, born at Alresford, 30th June, 1868.

TERESA MARY AGNES, born at Wagga Wagga, 18th March, 1866.

HENRIETTA FELICITÉ, born at Brompton, Middlesex, January, 1870.

HENRY ALFRED JOSEPH TICHBORNE, a posthumous son and heir, born 28th May, 1866.

THE family of TICHBORNE is well known to be of Saxon descent, and to date the possession of their present patrimony, the Manor of Tichborne, 200 years before the Conquest. This is stated in the speech of CHYDIOKE TICHBORNE, who was executed in Lincoln's Inn Fields in the year 1586 for participation in the BABINGTON conspiracy against Queen ELIZABETH.

Positive evidence of the existence of a place called Tichborne, in Anglo-Saxon days, is to be obtained from grants made of certain portions of land to the Bishops and Church of Winchester by the Saxon kings, EDWARD the Elder, ATHELSTAN, and EDGAR.

In the Anglo-Saxon charters the name is written Ticceburna and Ticceburnam (Ticceburnam in Icenam) (Icene). Thus it may be seen the family derive their name from the place of their habitation, the river or burn of Ichen.

The family of TICHBORNE for a period after the Conquest remained in obscurity, but when the first of the Plantagenets ascended the throne, and the Saxons resumed their wonted places of honour, Chronicles tell of a Crusader named Sir ROGER DE TYCHEBURNA who went to the Holy Wars, and was rewarded with the hand of the fair lady MABELLA, the heiress of RALPH DE LYMERSTON, Lord of Lymerston, in the Isle of Wight.

This circumstance is alluded to here, on account of the statement made by the Claimant when he was making his will in Australia, of the family having property in the Isle of Wight.

The Lady MABELLA above alluded to, founded the celebrated Tichborne Dole, of which mention will be made hereafter.

The institution of the Dole may be shortly stated to be as follows:—

When the Lady MABELLA, worn out with age and infirmities, was lying on her death-bed, she besought her loving husband, Sir ROGER DE TYCHEBURNA, as her last request, that he would grant her the means of leaving behind her a charitable bequest, in a dole of bread to be distributed to all who should apply for it, annually, on the feast of the Annunciation of the VIRGIN MARY. Sir ROGER readily acceded to the request, by promising the produce of as much land as she could go over in the vicinity of the park while a certain brand or billet was burning; supposing that from her long infirmity (as she had been bedridden for some years) she would be able to go round a small portion only of his property. The venerable dame, however, ordered her attendants to convey her to the corner of the park, where, being deposited on the ground, she seemed to acquire a renovation of strength, and, to the surprise of her anxious and admiring lord, who began to wonder where this pilgrimage might end, she crawled round several rich and goodly acres. The field which was the scene of Lady MABELLA's extraordinary feat and final exertions retains the name of "The Crawls" to this day.

It is situated near the entrance of the park, and contains an area of twenty-three acres. Her task being completed, she was re-conveyed to her chamber, when, summoning her family to her bedside, she predicted the prosperity of the family while that annual dole existed, and left her malediction on any of her descendants who should be so mean or covetous as to discontinue it, or divert her bounty from the pious purposes to which she had devoted it: prophesying, with her expiring breath, that when this happened the whole house would fall, the name should cease, and the family become extinct from the failure of heirs male, and this would be foretold by a generation of seven sons, being followed immediately after by a generation of seven daughters and no son.

So the Lady MABELLA was gathered to her fathers, her bones resting in peace within the chancel of the parish church of Tichborne, erected by the piety and liberality of her husband. Centuries rolled on, and the pious ceremony she instituted continued to be observed. The 25th March became the annual festive day of the family, and the friends and different branches of the house of Tichborne came from far and near to witness and assist at the performance of the good Lady MABELLA's legacy. So important a feature was it in the annals of the family, that in the year 1670 Sir HENRY TICHBORNE, the third Baronet, employed GILES TILBURY, an eminent Flemish painter, to represent the ceremony of the distribution of the bread. The commission was admirably executed. The picture, in addition to the interest acquired by presenting so many family portraits, is highly valuable as giving a faithful representation of old Tichborne House as it stood in the days of Charles II., which CAMDEN, nearly a century previous had declared to be a "very antient house."

The Estate of Lymerston continued in the possession of the TICHBORNE family till after the middle of the last century, when the great grandfather of the present Baronet sold it to GEORGE STANLEY, Esquire, and it is now in the possession of SLOANE STANLEY, Esquire, of Paultons, in the County of Hants.

From the time of HENRY II. till 1620 the principal representatives of the family were knights, but when Queen ELIZABETH died, Sir BENJAMIN TICHBORNE, Knight, who was at the time sheriff of the county, acting on his own responsibility, went directly to Winchester, and there proclaimed JAMES VI. of Scotland her successor as King JAMES I. of England.

After the Monarch had been settled on his throne he never forgot his champion in Hampshire, and Sir BENJAMIN TICHBORNE was created a baronet in 1621, and his four sons received the honour of knighthood. He was made Custodian of the Castle of Winchester, which was settled upon him in fee farm.

The baronetcy has come down in lineal descent to the present time. The late Sir HENRY TICHBORNE, seventh Baronet of Tichborne, Aldershot, and Frimley (see No. 7 in the Pedigree) died in 1821, and was succeeded by his eldest son, Sir HENRY JOSEPH TICHBORNE, who thereupon became eighth Baronet. He died in June, 1845, and was succeeded by his brother, EDWARD TICHBORNE, who had in 1826, by royal licence, taken the surname of DOUGHTY only, pursuant to the will of his cousin ELIZABETH DOUGHTY, proved in June, 1826, and under which will the Doughty estates came into the Tichborne family. Sir EDWARD DOUGHTY, the ninth Baronet, died on the 5th March, 1853, leaving only one daughter surviving, who was born in April, 1834, KATHERINE MARY ELIZABETH DOUGHTY, and now the wife of JOSEPH PERCIVAL PICKFORD RADCLIFFE, eldest son of Sir JOSEPH RADCLIFFE, Baronet. She was married on the 18th October, 1854. Upon the death of Sir EDWARD DOUGHTY, JAMES FRANCIS TICHBORNE, his only surviving brother, and one of the sons of the seventh Baronet, and the father of ROGER TICHBORNE, succeeded to the title and estates. By royal licence, dated 20th April, 1853, he obtained permission for himself and his issue to use the name of DOUGHTY before that of TICHBORNE.

Sir JAMES FRANCIS DOUGHTY TICHBORNE, the last Baronet, was born in 1784, and died on the 11th June, 1862. He married (as will be seen by the Pedigree) HENRIETTE FELICITE, daughter of Mr. HENRY SEYMOUR, of Knoyle, in the county of Wilts, the marriage taking place at St. George's, Hanover-square, on 1st August, 1827. They had issue, ROGER CHARLES TICHBORNE, who was born in Paris, on the 5th January, 1829, now eleventh Baronet of Tichborne, and ALFRED JOSEPH TICHBORNE, who was born on the 4th September, 1839, and died on February 22nd, 1866, aged 26, having married TERESA MARY, eldest daughter of the eleventh Lord ARUNDELL, and left a posthumous child (HENRY ALFRED JOSEPH TICHBORNE), and there were also two daughters, issue of the marriage of JAMES FRANCIS TICHBORNE, and HENRIETTE FELICITE, his wife, who died during infancy.

When Sir JAMES FRANCIS TICHBORNE became a baronet in 1853, his eldest son, ROGER CHARLES, the Claimant, was 24 years of age, and his younger brother, ALFRED JOSEPH, was 14.

The Tichborne family estates, one of which was the subject of the great trial, consist of Tichborne Park, and the greater part of the parish of Tichborne, containing 2,290 acres; the manor of Tisted, near Tichborne; the manors of Priors Dean and Colemore, and lands and farms at Cheriton, Hawkley, Froxfield, Ovington, Ropley, and Alresford. The estates in the County of Hants are so extensive that they extend in one direction a distance of between thirteen and fourteen miles.

The Doughty property was inherited by the Tichborne family from the before-mentioned ELIZABETH DOUGHTY, who was, at the dates of her will and codicil, seized of an estate of inheritance in fee simple in possession in the several counties of Middlesex, Surrey, Lincolnshire, and Buckinghamshire. They are generally called the Doughty estates, and consist of property in Bedford-row, King's-road Terrace, Gray's Inn-lane, Great James-street, Little James-street, Theobald's-road, Brownlow-street, Holborn, Warwick-place, King's-road, John-street, Upper North-place, Guildford-street, Doughty-street, Henry-street, Brownlow-mews and Doughty-mews, all in London; and of property in Snarford, Lincolnshire, West Barkwith, and Chesham, Buckinghamshire; and also property in Surrey, and the Manor House and park and grounds called Upton Park, with lands and farms adjoining in the County of Dorset.

To return to the family history: it is necessary to state that the family have been Roman Catholics from time immemorial, and like the rest of Roman Catholic families, had to submit to all the restrictions of the penal laws, and were, from the time of CHARLES II., precluded from holding offices of trust or position either in the army or navy, or from acting in the capacity of county magistrates, or taking any part whatever in the management of county or local affairs.

The penalties on Roman Catholics were, up to the Emancipation Act of 1829, so great, that they were obliged to live in the utmost seclusion, and during the greater part of that time were not allowed to keep a horse over the value of £5. Most of their neighbours looked upon Romanist families with the greatest suspicion, consequently their circle of acquaintances was extremely limited. They were obliged to send their children abroad for education, and then under an assumed name, as otherwise they were liable to be disinherited, and any son turning Protestant could disinherit his father or elder brother or brothers.

Sir HENRY JOSEPH TICHBORNE, the eighth Baronet, was the first member of the family who, after the time of CHARLES II., held any public appointment, and was the first Roman Catholic who was made High Sheriff after the passing of the Emancipation Act. He also was at that time made a county magistrate. He was a man of very simple habits; all his amusements and attention being confined to farming pursuits, and from his regular associations was in point of fact little better than a local farmer. He was a stout, thickset man. His brother EDWARD allowed him £1,000 a year, after succeeding to the Doughty property. He had a family of seven daughters, but no son. He always evinced a strong dislike to his brother JAMES and his children.

His brother Mr. EDWARD TICHBORNE, afterwards Sir EDWARD DOUGHTY, the ninth Baronet, was of a different stamp altogether, having in early life gone to Jamaica, where he managed some Sugar Estates for the Duke of BUCKINGHAM, and having married

PORTRAIT OF LADY TICHBORNE.

a daughter of Lord ARUNDEL, he was much more of an aristocrat than any preceding or then living member of his family. He was always lame, and in later years a complete cripple. When he returned from Jamaica he was exceedingly thin, but afterwards became a large, stout, heavy man.

Sir JAMES FRANCIS TICHBORNE, the father of Sir ROGER, the Claimant, and the tenth Baronet, being the third son, was allowed a small stipend by his brother Sir HENRY; according to the statement of the Claimant it was only £150 a year. On his marriage, as before mentioned, with Miss SEYMOUR, he and his wife resided the greater part of their time in Paris, where their son ROGER CHARLES, the Claimant, was born. Mr. JAMES FRANCIS TICHBORNE was a person of very irascible disposition. He never could agree with his brothers or sister and whenever he visited them, the visit usually ended in a quarrel or a row. It can be said that he never had during his life a friend with whom he did not quarrel at one time or another, and generally from some very unreasonable cause. His domestic life was one of continual storm and dispute. His wife, HENRIETTE FELICITE (as before mentioned), the daughter of Mr. SEYMOUR of Knoyle, and consequently half-sister of the two Seymours, HENRY and ALFRED (both known in political life), was a person of great personal attractions; though of timid and retiring, yet pleasing and obliging disposition; and acted with the utmost forbearance. Notwithstanding these attributes, the domestic life of Mr. JAMES FRANCIS TICHBORNE and his wife was of the most turbulent character, for although he doted upon her almost to madness, yet his outbursts of passion were so great and so frequent, as to be a severe trial to those who had to live under the same roof.

It may therefore be well imagined how anxious their eldest son (the Claimant) was to get away from such scenes of contention.

It was the habit of Mr. JAMES FRANCIS TICHBORNE to resort daily when in Paris to an Hotel, where he received visitors, read his papers, and saw his friends. His eldest son (the Claimant) was provided with a tutor named CHATILLON, who, instead of directing attention to his education, used to take him about the streets and gardens, lounging about, wasting his time, and encouraging him in bad habits.

ROGER and CHATILLON took a tour into Brittany when he was

about fourteen years old, and at a town on the Coast called Pornic ROGER fell upon a rock and cut the back of his head; Dr. LIPSCOMB, of Alresford, the Family Surgeon, heard of the occurrence at the time, and swears in his affidavit that he has examined Sir ROGER's head since his return to England, and finds upon the back of it a very old scar. CHATILLON afterwards opposed Sir ROGER, but he mentioned the fact of the fall at an interview with him in Paris in January, 1867; and when told of the existence of the scar, asserted that no blood came from the wound, and therefore no scar would be left. His younger brother ALFRED, who was ten years his junior, was made much of by his father, and every possible slight and contumely heaped on the eldest son, owing, it is conceived, principally to his tendency to take his mother's part in the serious quarrels which arose at every meal, and made the house, as Sir ROGER described it in 1846, to Mr. HOPKINS, "a perfect hell."

We insert here the affidavit of Dr. LIPSCOMB:—

I, JOHN KEPPLEY LIPSCOMB, of New Alresford, in the County of Southampton, Surgeon, make oath and say as follows:—

1. I am a member of the Royal College of Surgeons, and a Licentiate of the Apothecaries' Company of London. I passed both the College and the Hall in the year 1837. I first came to reside and practise in New Alresford in the year 1838, having in that year bought the business of a Mr. RENNIE, then recently deceased, who formerly carried on practice there, and I have continued to reside and practise as a surgeon in New Alresford ever since. I am medical officer of one of the districts of the Alresford Poor Law Union, and have been so since the year 1838. Tichborne Park, the family seat of the TICHBORNES, is within three miles of New Alresford.

2. I well knew the late Sir HENRY JOSEPH TICHBORNE, also the late Sir EDWARD DOUGHTY, and also the late Sir JAMES FRANCIS TICHBORNE, all formerly of Tichborne Park (now severally deceased) both before and after they severally came into the possession of the Tichborne estates, extending over a period of several years, and during that time I very frequently saw and conversed with them. I attended the said Sir EDWARD DOUGHTY professionally almost daily for about three years and a half. I have also dined with the said Sir JAMES FRANCIS TICHBORNE. I was perfectly acquainted with the persons, characters, and habits of the said Sir HENRY JOSEPH TICHBORNE, Sir EDWARD DOUGHTY, and Sir JAMES FRANCIS TICHBORNE. I also knew the present Dowager Lady TICHBORNE, the widow of the said Sir JAMES FRANCIS TICHBORNE.

3. I also well knew ROGER CHARLES TICHBORNE, the eldest son of the said Sir JAMES FRANCIS TICHBORNE. He occasionally came to Tichborne Park during the life of the said Sir EDWARD DOUGHTY. To the best of my recollection, I first became acquainted with the said Mr. ROGER CHARLES TICHBORNE some time in the year 1850, and I continued to be well acquainted with him whenever he visited Tichborne from that time until he went abroad in the year 1853.

4. I well recollect a serious illness which Sir EDWARD DOUGHTY had in the year 1851-2. I attended him professionally during that illness, which lasted several months. I frequently slept at Tichborne House. The said Mr. ROGER CHARLES TICHBORNE was staying there at that time, and became very anxiously excited about his uncle's illness, and obtained no sleep for some nights, and Lady DOUGHTY requested me to attend professionally upon him, which I did. I got him to bed and sat by his bedside for some time, until he slept. I very frequently saw and conversed with the said Mr. ROGER CHARLES TICHBORNE, and during the time I stayed at Tichborne House I was accustomed in the evening to go to his room to chat and smoke with him. I also saw him again about August 1852, at Tichborne House, when he was about to sell out of the army, and he then used to talk about travelling abroad for the sake of wild sports, and he produced to me several books on sports that the different countries afforded. I also attended the said Mr. ROGER CHARLES TICHBORNE professionally in February, 1853, for relaxed and inflammatory sore throat. After many conversations he told me that he meant going to South America to shoot black panthers and hunt wild horses, as he thought no sport equal to catching and riding wild horses; he also said he should not have sold out of the army if their going to India had not been countermanded.

5. I had thus frequent opportunities of noticing, and I often noticed and well remember, the person, shape of head, and expression of countenance of the said Mr. ROGER CHARLES TICHBORNE, and also a peculiarity about his eyes which consists of a certain involuntary twitching of the muscle called the *orbicularis palpebrarum* and extreme mobility of the eyebrows, which were particularly developed.

6. On the 23rd day of February, 1867, I called at the Swan Hotel, Alresford, and there saw and spent a short time with the above-named Plaintiff, who, I was informed, had then recently returned to England from Australia. I recognised in him the several peculiarities I have hereinbefore referred to, and also the general expression of face of the said Mr. ROGER CHARLES TICHBORNE. He then referred to various circumstances which I well remembered relating to his family. I desired, however, to have another interview with him. Accordingly, on Saturday, the 23rd March, 1867, I again went to the Swan Hotel, Alresford, and then spent several hours and dined with the plaintiff. I have no hesitation in stating, and do positively state, that the plaintiff is the same person as the Mr. ROGER CHARLES TICHBORNE whom I formerly knew and attended. He had then recently suffered from relaxed sore throat, and at his request I have carefully examined his throat, and he had been and still was suffering slightly from the same kind of sore throat which he had in February, 1852, and he remarked that he had not had anything of the sort in Australia: a circumstance which is very likely to happen from the influence of climate, but it serves to a certain extent to identify the Plaintiff, inasmuch as it is a circumstance often observed, that on the return of persons to the climate from whence they had emigrated, the same diseases are found to again attack them, and at the same time of year, too, which they were before afflicted with. Upon that occasion I examined a cicatrix at the back of the Plaintiff's head, which is undoubtedly a very old scar. When the Plaintiff was a boy I remember hearing that he had met with an accident to his head, occasioned by a fall, and the cicatrix, in my opinion, would be the result of an injury sustained about that time. And I find the peculiarities I have before referred to most marked in him. The contour of his head is that of a TICHBORNE, and his face greatly resembles the expression of his late brother ALFRED, whom I knew intimately, and I have no doubt whatever that he is the eldest son of the late Sir JAMES FRANCIS TICHBORNE, whom I formerly knew.

7. I have again seen and talked with the Plaintiff to-day, and am convinced as to his identity.

8. The statements hereinbefore made, are within my own knowledge.

JOHN K. LIPSCOMB.

Sworn at New Alresford, in the County of Southampton, this first day of July, 1867—Before me

JNO. FRAS. ADAMS,

A Commissioner to administer oaths in Chancery in England.

It was in this year, owing to the unexpected arrival of Mrs. JAMES TICHBORNE at Tichborne Park, and her being denied entrance into the house where her husband and son were staying, that led to the Claimant's first visit to Mr. HOPKINS' house at Alresford, of which Mr. HOPKINS swears he gave him the particulars in his first interview on his return to England, on the 2nd of February, 1867.

The marriage of Mr. JAMES FRANCIS TICHBORNE with Miss SEYMOUR was very much condemned by the whole of the then existing TICHBORNE Family. The principal objection was on account of her illegitimacy, to which Mr. EDWARD (afterwards Sir EDWARD) DOUGHTY especially objected; and secondly, it was considered that having passed the middle of life, there was no necessity for Mr. JAMES FRANCIS TICHBORNE to get married at all. In consequence of these reasons, the family looked down upon and cold-shouldered Mrs. TICHBORNE, the Claimant's mother, to such a degree as could not fail to be painful to her. She seldom visited any of the TICHBORNES, and spent the greater part of her time in Paris. When she did visit at Tichborne or elsewhere, she was treated with great contumely, and consequently went as little as possible. The family never attempted to conceal their dislike and enmity to her. In consequence of this, Lady TICHBORNE imbibed an idea that the family, being against her, would naturally be biassed against her children, and she regarded any overtures from them respecting her children with suspicion and dislike.

The Claimant himself states, during his recollection of his childhood, that whenever he came to England to see any of his relatives, especially from the time of his going to Stonyhurst in 1845, every one of his relatives in England endeavoured to set him against his mother.

According to Sir ROGER's statement, his mother refused to allow him to go to England to be educated, although both his father and his grandfather SEYMOUR continually urged her to permit it. The stratagem employed to get him away was to take him to attend his uncle's (Sir HENRY TICHBORNE'S) funeral, from whence within a short time he was sent to Stonyhurst. He was then a boy who had never been to school in his life, or had anything like training, and his tasks and lessons appear to have been limited to lounging about Paris and the neighbourhood with CHATILLON.

It may be conceived that a boy perfectly undisciplined up to the age of sixteen and a half, who had received nothing that could be called education, would not be a very tractable pupil, or fail to consider College life irksome and distasteful. His preceptors did not even succeed in giving him a knowledge of English Grammar—the very object for which he was sent there. His letters to his father and mother and to Mr. HOPKINS, from the time of his leaving Stonyhurst, prove the deficiency of the education he there received, or of being able to speak or write correctly. His deficiency of education is also testified by the letter to his grandfather SEYMOUR, dated 29th November, 1848.

When he went to Stonyhurst he was parlour-boarder, and therefore allowed much greater liberties than other students who had not the same privileges; and this no doubt encouraged him in his own waywardness, and was looked upon as quite a character, so that it was with the greatest difficulty, if at all, that his preceptors could get him to give his mind to any kind of study. His French habits and his foreign gibberish made him a sort of butt with everybody; and as his associates could not speak French, and he could not speak English, he lived very much alone, and passed the greater portion of his time in smoking: his use of tobacco became almost unlimited. He frequently resorted to Preston, and was known there in certain places to which vestal virgins do not belong. He had not long been at Stonyhurst before his mother wrote to the Rector to complain of his not having written home, and desiring the Rector, the Reverend Mr. WALMESLEY, to inculcate principles of filial love and duty in him. Upon this he appears to have made excuses for not writing, as appears by the letter from Mr. WALMESLEY.

Whilst at Stonyhurst he visited at the residence of Mr. TOWNELEY, whose brother had married his cousin LUCY TICHBORNE, one of the daughters of Sir HENRY JOSEPH TICHBORNE, whom he met on one occasion there. He also, before leaving Stonyhurst, during the year 1848, spent one of his vacations at Burton Constable, near Hull, in Yorkshire, the seat of the late Sir CLIFFORD CONSTABLE, and spent his time in companionship of the then young Mr. CLIFFORD CONSTABLE, with whom he used to play in Paris, and whom he had then not seen for three years. This is fully described in that gentleman's affidavit:—

I, FREDERICK AUGUSTUS TALBOT CLIFFORD CONSTABLE, of Burton Constable, in Holderness, in the County of York, Esquire, but now residing at Kingston-upon-Hull, Deputy-Lieutenant of the East Riding of Yorkshire, and formerly Major of the East York Militia, make oath and say as follows:—

1. I am about forty years of age, and the only son of Sir THOMAS ASHTON CLIFFORD CONSTABLE, Baronet, of Burton Constable aforesaid. From the time when I was about five years of age, I remember that I used frequently to accompany my parents to Paris, where we used to pass the summer months. During our sojourn there I used to be constantly with ROGER CHARLES TICHBORNE, the eldest son of Mr. JAMES FRANCIS TICHBORNE—he was, in fact, my playmate. This continued until about the year 1845, when he was sent to England for education. I also well remember that he came on a visit to Burton Constable in or about the year 1848, and spent his vacation with us. We were constantly together as companions. I know and well recollect the room in which he slept at Burton Constable. I also remember that one day he employed himself in cutting down a hedge in a particular field, and went without his luncheon. I was with him in the field, but employed myself in spreading manure. I remember that on one occasion when at dinner, in the absence of the butler he rose from the table, went to the sideboard, and put the wine on the table; and I recollect his purchasing for me a black mare of Mr. HENRY LAMBERT, who at that time lived at Keringham.

2. I do not remember having seen the said ROGER CHARLES TICHBORNE after his aforesaid visit to Burton Constable until the 14th of May, 1868, when I called upon him at the Royal Station Hotel, Hull. I invited him to my house, and took him to Burton Constable. I spent many hours in conversation with him. On the 15th, 16th, 17th, and 18th days of the same month I saw and conversed with him, he spending many hours at my house and in my company. The peculiar twitching of his eyes and eyebrows, the upper part of his face and downcast look, and his voice when reading, recalled to my mind the said ROGER CHARLES TICHBORNE, notwithstanding the very great alteration in his personal appearance. I took him through several of the bedrooms at Burton Constable, and he recognised one of them as the bedroom he occupied—which, in fact, it was—and drew my attention to the window through which we used to pass into the garden to smoke; and when in another room he said he recollected that particular room—and it was, in fact, my own room. He told me the name of the field, and the circumstance of his cutting down the hedge, of his going without his luncheon, and of my spreading manure over the field. We walked into the field, and he then and there pointed out the exact spot where the hedge grew that he cut down, and pushed aside the grass to see if he could find the stumps of the said hedge; and I well remember that when he cut it down he did leave the stumps in the ground as he stated. He also remarked that in the same field a shed attached to the engine-house had been removed, and a square hedge or fence that was standing there when he was staying at Burton Constable was also gone; and such is actually the case. He also mentioned to me the circumstance of his putting the wine on the table at dinner, and how it happened that he did so, also of his buying for me the black mare of Mr. LAMBERT.

3. The result of my interviews with the Plaintiff, of my conversations with him, the facts and occurrences that he mentioned, and his general demeanour, have led me to form the opinion, and I do verily believe that he is the same ROGER CHARLES TICHBORNE whom I formerly knew.

4. The several statements herein contained are within my own knowledge.

F. A. T. C. CONSTABLE.

Sworn at the Town of Kingston-upon-Hull, this 2nd day of June, 1868—Before me,

WM. WATSON,

A Commissioner to administer oaths in Chancery in England.

After that long visit in 1848, he appears never to have communicated with his friends the CONSTABLES, either by writing or otherwise, until after his return from Australia, in 1868. This shows the negligent disposition of the boy, exemplified so much to his disadvantage throughout his career. Before he left Stonyhurst he visited his uncle ROBERT TICHBORNE at Bath. It was here that the companionship between ANTHONY BIDDULPH, Esq. and his cousin ROGER was carried on, as is shown in the affidavit of the former:—

I, ANTHONY JOHN WRIGHT BIDDULPH, of Burton Park, in the County of Sussex, Esquire, a Justice of the Peace for the said county, make oath and say as follows:—

1. I am the second cousin of the above-named Plaintiff; his grandfather, Sir HENRY TICHBORNE, the seventh Baronet of Tichborne, and my grandfather, ANTHONY WRIGHT, Esq., having each married a daughter of EDMUND PLOWDEN, of Plowden, in the County of Salop, Esq.

2. An intimate acquaintance was always kept up in former years between my family and the Tichbornes, and in or about the year 1848 or 1849 ROGER CHARLES TICHBORNE, the eldest son of the late Sir JAMES FRANCIS DOUGHTY TICHBORNE (then JAMES FRANCIS TICHBORNE, Esq.), was at Bath, where I was also then residing with my family, being then under age. He remained at Bath for about a fortnight or more on a visit to his uncle, ROGER ROBERT TICHBORNE (since deceased), and I saw the said ROGER CHARLES TICHBORNE almost daily whilst at Bath. He used to smoke a pipe with a death's head on it, and I was on intimate terms with him. I was on terms of intimacy with his uncle, Sir EDWARD DOUGHTY, and his family.

3. I did not see the said ROGER CHARLES TICHBORNE after such above-named period, but knew of his entering the army, and of his afterwards leaving the service and going abroad, and of his supposed loss at sea. When I knew the said ROGER CHARLES TICHBORNE, he was very peculiar in his manner, and very shy, and, I should say, sensitive to a degree.

4. On the 18th day of May last I went to No. 2, Wellesley Villas, Wellesley-road, Croydon, where the Plaintiff is residing, and I believe my visit was unexpected by him. I so went, on being applied to for the purpose of judging whether or not he was the ROGER CHARLES TICHBORNE, my cousin. My impressions towards the Plaintiff previous to such visit were of the most unfavourable kind, and I expressed myself to the effect that the Plaintiff was not the person that he represented himself to be.

5. I went to Croydon, accompanied by Mr. NORRIS, my solicitor, and remained about two hours in the Plaintiff's company. After I had been some little time there, during which I watched every movement of his countenance, I said before him that I discovered a likeness in the upper part of his face to the ROGER CHARLES TICHBORNE, whom I had known so long before; and there was something in his voice which, to the best of my recollection, also reminded me of him. The Plaintiff seemed to be well acquainted with different circumstances connected with his family which had occurred before the departure of the said ROGER CHARLES TICHBORNE from England, and answered my questions quite naturally, and without any hesitation of manner, and left the strong impression on my mind that he was speaking the truth.

6. For these reasons I am of opinion that the Plaintiff is Sir ROGER CHARLES DOUGHTY TICHBORNE, Baronet, the eldest son of the late Sir JAMES FRANCIS DOUGHTY TICHBORNE, and is, I believe, the same person as the ROGER CHARLES TICHBORNE who was supposed to have been lost at sea.

A. J. W. BIDDULPH.

Sworn at Petworth, in the County of Sussex, this 13th day of July, 1867—Before me,

RICHARD BLAGDEN,

A Commissioner to administer oaths in Chancery in England

After Roger left Stonyhurst he visited his grandfather SEYMOUR at Knoyle, and he also paid a visit to Wardour Castle—the residence of Lord ARUNDEL. He, however, spent his vacations principally at Tichborne, where he learned to ride and shoot.

At the close of his Stonyhurst career, during his visit to Tichborne, his uncle Sir EDWARD DOUGHTY, not liking his propensities for smoking (which were inveterate) and other reprehensible habits, two rooms were built for him at the end of one of the corridors in Tichborne House, so that he might smoke in the house, and live as it were separate from the family. In one of these rooms he used to sleep in a hammock slung from the ceiling, and had his pipes hung up by the side of his hammock so that he could smoke in bed. After leaving Stonyhurst, owing to his dirty habits and general want of personal cleanliness and negligence of dress, it was resolved to send him into the army, in order that he might become something like a gentleman. As a regulation had just then been issued that all persons applying for commissions should undergo an examination, it created great consternation in the family, as they had scarcely any hopes they could get him to pass such an examination; but the thing being inevitable, they obtained the assistance of Colonel GEORGE GREENWOOD, who then lived at Brookwood, near Tichborne, and who was formerly in the Life Guards, to coach him up.

He was then sent to London to stay at his uncle SEYMOUR'S, in Grosvenor-street, where he had a tutor who taught him fortification, and other subjects necessary for his passing the examination. Mr. TILT, the priest of Tichborne, attempted without success to coach him up in arithmetic—for he failed to pass in this qualification; and ultimately, in July 1849, he went up to Sandhurst to be examined—which, being the first examination of this kind ever held, was by no means formidable. The books at Sandhurst contain a record of the subjects in which he passed, and did not pass, and also a record that his height was 5-ft. 8¾in., he being then nineteen years of age. He was gazetted on the 6th July, 1849, and obtained leave of absence until the end of October. He then proceeded to obtain his outfit and accoutrements; ANDREWS, of Pall Mall, equipped him, and amongst other things made his helmet for him and his forage-cap. The measurement of his head for the helmet is set down in ANDREWS' books—8 by 6½. It may be here noticed that in December, 1867, he went, at the request of his solicitor, Mr. HOLMES, to ANDREWS' shop to have his head measured, and the said measurement was handed to him in writing, and it was found exactly to correspond with the measure in ANDREWS' books of 1849. At the expiration of his leave of absence he went from Tichborne to Dublin, and joined his regiment at Portobello barracks on the 26th October, 1849; and the Claimant was afterwards recognised as being the same man by Colonel CUSTANCE, as is proved by that gentleman's affidavit:—

I, WILLIAM NEVILLE CUSTANCE, of Fryern Court, Fordingbridge, in the County of Hants, Companion of the Bath, and Lieutenant-Colonel (Brevet-Colonel), half-pay unattached, make oath and say as follows:—

1. I was captain in the 6th Dragoon Guards (Carabineers) when Mr. ROGER CHARLES TICHBORNE joined that regiment as a cornet in the year 1849, and was major of that regiment when he retired in the year 1853. I was frequently quartered with him at the same barracks in Ireland. During the period which extended over three years that he was in the regiment, I frequently messed at the same table, and saw and conversed with Mr. ROGER CHARLES TICHBORNE, and had ample opportunity of knowing him well.

2. On the 10th of October, 1867, I received a letter signed R. C. D. TICHBORNE, asking me to meet the writer on the 12th of that month at the Three Swans Hotel, and see for myself whether he was not really Mr. ROGER TICHBORNE, my old brother officer. Before the receipt of such letter I was greatly prejudiced against the Plaintiff's identity, because of statements I had read in the press from time to time, and from conversations with and letters from various persons. I, however, determined to go and see the writer of such letter, and judge for myself as to his identity. Accordingly on Saturday, the 12th day of October, 1867, I went to the Three Swans Hotel, Salisbury, where I saw the above-named Plaintiff. He had grown very stout since I last saw him in the Carabineers. I had a long conversation with him, and he was easy and natural in his replies to my questions.

3. I recognised the Plaintiff by his eyes and the upper part of his face, and the more I looked and talked with him, the more I felt convinced he was the same person as the Mr. ROGER CHARLES TICHBORNE who was my brother officer in the 6th Dragoon Guards; and I have no hesitation in deposing that, to the best of my belief, he is the said ROGER CHARLES TICHBORNE. In fact, I told him at our interview, after I had satisfied my mind that he really was not an impostor, that I felt bound to and would do everything I could to assist in establishing his just rights.

W. N. CUSTANCE, Colonel.

Sworn at Fordingbridge, in the County of Southampton, this 7th day of November, 1867—Before me,

R. M. DAVY,

A Commissioner to administer oaths in Chancery in England.

Colonel CUSTANCE, who is now a general, gave evidence for Sir ROGER at the trial in the Common Pleas, but declined to do so when he was tried in the Queen's Bench. But the affidavit of Colonel NORBURY is of greater weight than that of CUSTANCE; and we insert it here:—

I, THOMAS CONINGSBY NORBURY NORBURY, of Sherridge, near Malvern, in the County of Worcester, Major of the Worcester Militia, late Captain of the Carabineers, a Justice of the Peace for the Counties of Hereford and Worcester, and Deputy Lieutenant for the County of Worcester, make oath and say as follows:—

1. I became a cornet in the 6th Dragoon Guards (Carabineers) about the month of January, 1849, and I remember Mr. ROGER CHARLES TICHBORNE joining that regiment in the same year. He left it about the beginning of 1853. I did so in the year 1856. I knew and was perfectly well acquainted with Mr. ROGER CHARLES TICHBORNE during the time he and I were brother officers in that regiment.

2. On the 15th day of July, 1867, I saw and had several hours' conversation with the above-named Plaintiff, and I firmly believe that he is the same person as the said Mr. ROGER CHARLES TICHBORNE, my brother officer, whom I formerly knew. He has grown very stout since we last saw each other, and so have I. I recognise him by his general appearance, voice, manners, and from the conversations I have had with him.

3. I have also seen him again this 16th day of July, 1867, for several hours, and I still retain the same opinion.

4. The statements herein contained are within my own knowledge.

T. C. N. NORBURY.

Sworn at Great Malvern, in the County of Worcester, this 16th day of July, 1867—Before me,

WM. WILKES CAWLEY,

A Commissioner to administer oaths in Chancery in England.

The military evidence advanced in favour of the Claimant would have been crushing and overwhelming to his opponents, if anything like justice had been done him; but the testimony of honourable gentlemen, like the Colonel, was thrown overboard by the prosecution as if it had been of no value at all.

During ROGER's service with the Carabineers he was the object of much ridicule by his brother officers, and the subject of practical jokes; consequently, he used to mix but little with them, and spent most of his time in his own room, smoking. The officers who were most intimate with him appear to have been Major NORBURY, Captain MORTON, and Captain PINKNEY, though of course he was brought into much communication with the others. At Stonyhurst ROGER obtained the nickname of "Frenchy" and "Froggy;" and up to the time of his arrival at that college, he could speak nothing but French, and one of the principal objects of his being sent to that college, was that he might get rid of his French, and learn English. This he did in a very imperfect degree, so that when he joined the Carabineers he spoke much more like a Frenchman than an Englishman; speaking broken English on all occasions, and never was able to join in any running conversation at the mess-table or other places. His writing and spelling were so absurd and imperfect, that it is said that one of his letters, which was laid hold of by his brother officers, was hung up for a long time in the mess-room as a curiosity. When it was his duty to fill up returns and make reports, &c., it is known that he would waste many of the forms before he could make one perfect enough to send in, and when sent in they were frequently returned to him on account of blunders and inaccuracies.

During the year 1844, certain family settlements were made in order to prevent the Tichborne Estates going out of the family. This arrangement was made in contemplation of cutting off the Doughty Estate entail, on ROGER TICHBORNE coming of age. This could only be done in the lifetime of Sir EDWARD DOUGHTY and JAMES FRANCIS TICHBORNE, his brother, and the Claimant himself. It was deemed desirable to have all the deeds prepared and executed the day after his coming of age.

Some six or seven months before he came of age, Mr. HOPKINS, the Solicitor at Alresford, communicated with him at the request of his father, in order to get the deeds ready, but he, instead of so doing and carrying out these wishes, wrote to Mr. HOPKINS and said, that as it would be four months and a half before he came of age, he should require that time to make up his mind, in order that he might do nothing he might hereafter have to repent of; and thus shelved the matter completely.

When he came of age, Mr. HOPKINS could do nothing with him, although he had several interviews with him at that time, and Mr. HOPKINS had drafted the deeds for this purpose, but he refused to sign, as the drafts did not carry out his intention in every respect. A correspondence upon this ensued, but so tardy was he in making up his mind, that his father was obliged to go over to Cahir to see him, and it was not until the month of May, 1850, that Mr. HOPKINS succeeded in getting him to execute these deeds. For this purpose Mr. HOPKINS himself was obliged to go to Ireland; and in these deeds he is described as "ROGER CHARLES TICHBORNE, Esq., a Cornet in Her Majesty's Sixth Dragoon Guards, eldest son and heir apparent of JAMES FRANCIS TICHBORNE, Esq."

Some time after this he made other deeds relating to the disposal of his mother's portion, and also to raise the money for the purchase of his Lieutenancy. He obtained his lieutenant's commission on 22nd November, 1850.

Shortly after he joined the Carabineers his Uncle ROBERT TICHBORNE died, but he was unable to attend his funeral. His first absence from the Carabineers appears to have been without leave, when he went to Tichborne to keep his majority, and he was absent on this occasion for about a week or ten days. Miss BRAINE saw ROGER during this time, and she afterwards identified the Claimant as being the same person, as the following affidavit testifies:—

I, ANNA MARY BRAINE, late of Ridgway, in the County of Devon, but now residing at Ladbrook-terrace, Notting-hill, in the County of Middlesex, spinster, make oath and say as follows:—

1. In the latter part of the year 1849, and during the greater part of the year 1850, I resided at Tichborne Park, the seat of Sir EDWARD DOUGHTY, Baronet, as governess to his only daughter, Miss CATHERINE MARY ELIZABETH DOUGHTY. Mr. ROGER CHARLES TICHBORNE, an officer in the 6th Dragoon Guards or Carabineers, and nephew of the said EDWARD DOUGHTY, was a guest at Tichborne House, and was there in January, 1850. On the 5th day of that month the said Mr. ROGER CHARLES TICHBORNE attained his age of twenty-one years. There were great rejoicings on that day at Tichborne Park. A ball was given to the servants and tenantry, and very many friends were invited to it. At this time I was also in the house, and during his visit, which lasted several days, I saw and was in the company of the said Mr. ROGER CHARLES TICHBORNE very often. I had continual opportunities of seeing and speaking to him, and he to me, and a good deal of conversation did pass between us. I took particular notice of his features, personal appearance, manners, peculiarities, voice, and manner of speaking, and I have ever retained a perfect recollection of them.

2. In 1854 I heard of the loss of the "Bella," and that he was supposed to have perished at sea with that vessel. Afterwards I heard rumours of his having been seen or heard of as still alive, and living in Australia. In the year 1866, I accidentally heard at the house of a friend in the West of England that "ROGER TICHBORNE had turned up in Australia, having been seen there by Mr. TURVILLE, and that he was probably then on his way to England;" and towards the latter part of 1867, having occasion to write on business matters to a friend at Alresford, in Hampshire, I asked at the end of my letter whether the TICHBORNE question was all arranged satisfactorily. My correspondent replied that there was no doubt whatever as to the Claimant being the real baronet, as he had been seen and recognised by almost every one in the neighbourhood who had known him in former years, but that there was still great opposition to his claims on the part of some of his relatives. I felt anxious after this to see

the gentleman in question, for the sake of satisfying my mind as to whether or not he was the Mr. ROGER CHARLES TICHBORNE whom I formerly knew and so well remembered, and should certainly know again if I saw him.

3. In the beginning of the year 1868, I received a letter, signed R. C. D. TICHBORNE, in which the writer asked me to call upon him at his residence, in Croydon. Accordingly on Thursday, the 16th day of January, 1868, I went to No. 2, Wellesley-villas, Croydon, for the express purpose of seeing the above-named Plaintiff. I had not seen him since his return from Australia, and he did not expect to see me on that day. He and his family were from home at the time I called, but I waited for his return. The Plaintiff on his return home came into the room to see me immediately. I was astonished to see so stout a man instead of the slight youthful figure I had in my mind's eye. I asked him to come towards the light, so that I might scrutinise his countenance. He did so, and I requested him not to speak until I had studied his features. After examining and looking well at his features, I enquired how he got the scar I noticed between his eyebrows, which I had not seen before, and he explained that it was the result of a fall from horseback he had met with in Australia. I then told him that I fully recognised him by his eyes, eyebrows, and by his hair, and the falling of a lock of it over his forehead, to be the same Mr. ROGER CHARLES TICHBORNE I formerly knew, and had seen at Tichborne House. I also recognised his hands, and his voice, his peculiarity of articulation, also his accent and imperfect English speaking. I spent upwards of two hours in his company that day in conversation with him. I found that he knew the various occurrences I questioned him upon, and was most free and easy in his conversation with me. I had not so much as a shadow of a doubt as to his identity after the first few minutes I was with him.

4. On the following day (January 17th, 1868) I called on him again, about 12 o'clock, and remained in his company in conversation with him till about nine in the evening. Since the 16th and 17th days of January, 1868, I have seen and visited the Plaintiff on several occasions, and have spent many hours in his company, and in conversation with him, my last interview being on the 20th day of March, 1868, on which day, at his residence in Croydon, I spent upwards of five hours in his company.

5. The result of my several interviews has convinced me more and more of his identity, and without any hesitation whatever I do distinctly and absolutely swear that the Plaintiff is the same Mr. ROGER CHARLES TICHBORNE whom I formerly knew as the nephew of the late Sir EDWARD DOUGHTY, Baronet, deceased, as aforesaid.

6. The statements herein contained are within my own knowledge.

ANNA M. BRAINE.

Sworn at 4, Orchard-street, Portman-square, in the County of Middlesex, this 30th day of March, 1868—
Before me,

RICHD. NATION,
A London Commissioner to administer oaths in Chancery.

The following memorandum from the Horse Guards, furnished in reply to a letter from Mr. HOLMES, Sir ROGER's solicitor, shows officially his movements with the Carabineers, that he retired on the 4th February, 1853, and his various leaves of absence:—

Horse Guards, 26th March, 1867.

Memorandum,

Mr. ROGER C. TICHBORNE was appointed Cornet in the 6th Dragoon Guards on 13th July, 1849, and joined the regiment at Portobello Barracks, Dublin, on 26th October following.

In April 1850 the regiment was removed to Cahir, Limerick, and Gort, and he was stationed at the Head Quarters at the first-named station.

Promoted Lieutenant 22nd November, 1850.

He proceeded on 9th April, 1851, with a troop of the regiment from Cahir to Clonmel.

The troop to which he was attached marched on 17th July, 1851, from Clonmel to Waterford, but he appears to have remained at Clonmel with the troop that arrived there from Cahir until October, when he rejoined his former troop at Waterford.

Lieutenant TICHBORNE obtained leave of absence on his private affairs, from 15th December, 1851, to 14th February, 1852, in which latter month he rejoined the troop stationed at Clonmel.

In the month of March, 1852, the whole regiment was assembled at Dublin, the troop from Clonmel marching on the 13th of the month.

The regiment embarked at Dublin on the 1st June, 1852, on board the "Duke of Cornwall" steamer, and disembarked on the 4th of the same month at Herne Bay, and marched to Canterbury.

Lieutenant TICHBORNE proceeded on leave of absence on his private affairs, from 28th October to 30th December, 1852, and again from 24th January, 1853, until his retirement from the service, which took place on 4th February, 1853.

(A true Copy.) W. PAULET, A.G.

When absent on leave he generally spent his time at Tichborne, where he became very intimate with his cousin KATHERINE, the only daughter of his uncle Sir EDWARD DOUGHTY, and being a great deal in her society, an attachment sprang up between the two, and efforts were made by Lady DOUGHTY, Mr. VINCENT GOSFORD (who was then agent to the estate) and others, to bring about a marriage between ROGER and Miss DOUGHTY, which would have kept her fortune in the family. When Sir EDWARD DOUGHTY heard of this he was decidedly opposed to it, and on one occasion became excessively angry, and Mr. ROGER TICHBORNE had to leave the house hastily, and, as his aunt, Mrs. ROBERT TICHBORNE, who was staying on a visit, said, "was sent away with less ceremony than a footman."

It appears that the principal reason of ROGER TICHBORNE's having a great regard for his cousin KATE DOUGHTY was because she was the only member of the family who did not try to set him against his mother. His other relatives took every opportunity of so doing.

That there had been some strong attachment between ROGER TICHBORNE and his cousin KATE (as she was commonly called) is evidenced in many ways, but especially by his Will. In that he gives the Doughty property to her in preference to the daughters of his brother ALFRED. It is further instanced by his leaving her (as long as she remained unmarried) the privilege of residing at Upton House, in Dorset.

The circumstances under which the Will was made are as follows, and instance the secretive nature of the young man—since the fact was carefully concealed from his father and relatives:—Whilst he was in Ireland he opened a correspondence by a letter dated 1st February, 1851, with Mr. SLAUGHTER, who was a particular friend of the Tichborne family and the solicitor of Sir EDWARD DOUGHTY, but not of JAMES FRANCIS TICHBORNE, his father. The correspondence commenced in Ireland, and at the end of about eighteen months the Will was finally prepared, but the instructions for it were singularly enough sent from Tichborne, and are evidently such as he himself could not have given. This probably arises from the fact that Mr. GOSFORD, who was the agent of the Tichborne property, was resident there, and helped him to draw the instructions. Mr. GOSFORD had taken great pains to ingratiate himself with the heir expectant, and obtained such influence over him, that he was made co-executor of this clandestine Will with Mr. SLAUGHTER. The circumstance of his making this Will was kept a profound secret, in accordance with his own wish and expressed in the correspondence, and after the report of his being lost in the "Bella" reached England, his father was greatly astounded and much cut up at finding this Will had been made without his knowledge, and thereupon instructed Mr. HOPKINS to demand particulars of the circumstance from Mr. SLAUGHTER, under which the Will was made, together with a copy of all the correspondence.

It was only by information communicated by Mr. HOPKINS that these particulars have become known.

Shortly afterwards Sir JAMES FRANCIS TICHBORNE filed a Bill in the Court of Chancery for the purpose of setting aside Messrs. GOSFORD and SLAUGHTER as Trustees of the Will, and appointing two others in their places, the substituted persons being Sir PYERS MOSTYN and Mr. TURVILLE. Subsequently to this Mr. TURVILLE going abroad after Sir JAMES' death, WILLIAM MOSTYN, brother of Sir PYERS MOSTYN, was appointed in his place.

The affair with KATE DOUGHTY, and other circumstances of a similar nature (for his relatives were always importuning him to get married and perpetuate the line), irritated him excessively, and probably caused, with the quarrels arising therefrom and disputes with his father, his determination to get out of the whole thing; and, coupled with the fact that his mind had been inflamed by reading books of foreign sports and travel, and his excessive love of field sports, determined him to go abroad.

There were also other reasons for his dislike of a civilised life, such as he was then leading. Although he had been three years and a half in the army, he had not succeeded in learning his drill, and he was not therefore able at any time to remember and give properly the words of command. He had acquired no proper knowledge of military language, and he in fact was never dismissed his drill up to the time of his retirement. In consequence of this, his military life had become very distasteful to him. It is usual for officers in Dragoon regiments to be dismissed their drill in about six months. The difficulty in his case was that although he was a good horseman—that is, could stick on a horse however wild or restive—he could not be taught to acquire a good seat or military bearing in the saddle.

It appears that he had weak hands, and the evidence will show that he had very indifferent health, and was subject to spasms of the heart. He was then very thin, weighing perhaps only between nine or ten stone, but with broad shoulders and a frame that was subsequently explained by Dr. LIPSCOMB, which would develope under the influence of a genial climate into the corpulent person he now is.

It should be observed that all his family have become stout men on attaining middle life.

Whilst he was quartered at Canterbury he was suddenly taken ill with spasms of the heart, and became insensible. His then regimental servant, McCANN, ran for the doctor of the regiment, a person named MOORE, who arrived just in time to save his life, which he did by bleeding him in the ankle. This incident is described in the evidence of McCANN as follows:—

"The moment Mr. MOORE came into the room he tried to bleed Lieutenant TICHBORNE in both arms, but blood would not come. He then ordered me to strip off his boot and sock, and seizing his foot—I think it was his left foot—he forcibly struck the lancet across it below the ankle, giving a rough gash, upon which blood came in both arms, and Mr. TICHBORNE's life was saved." The marks, both of the bleeding in the arms, and of the gash across the ankle, are testified in the medical evidence, which will be hereafter commented on. (This incident is here mentioned as being remarkable in its way, and by the evidence with which it will be supported, can leave no doubt of the identity of the Plaintiff with the ROGER CHARLES TICHBORNE of the 6th Dragoon Guards, Carabiniers.)

I, JAMES MCCANN, of No. 6, Alexander-terrace, Maidstone, make oath and say as follows:—

1. I am fifty-two years of age. I went into Her Majesty's 6th Dragoon Guards (Carabiniers) in August, 1839, having joined the regiment as a private soldier, and remained with the regiment from that time until long after the year 1854.

2. I well remember Mr. ROGER CHARLES TICHBORNE, who joined the regiment as Cornet at Portobello Barracks, Dublin, in the year 1849. I was there at that time.

3. In the year 1850, a person named CLARKE, who was then servant to Mr. TICHBORNE, was run away with upon a horse of his master's upon the road from Clonmel to Cahir, and died a few hours afterwards from the accident. I then became regimental servant, by order of Colonel HAY to Mr. TICHBORNE, and I continued with him in that capacity until he left the regiment, about the end of 1852 or beginning of 1853. I waited upon and was with him in his rooms for the period of nearly three years that I served him, and I had the most ample opportunity of knowing him, and I well knew and remember all his ways and peculiarities. He spoke with a broken accent, and had a peculiar twitching of the eyebrow. He was very fond of horses and hunting, and smoked a great deal, and his principal amusement was hunting. He had two dogs named "Pyecrust" and "Spring."

4. The troop Mr. TICHBORNE belonged to changed from Cahir to Clonmel, and from Clonmel to Dublin, and thence to Herne Bay and Canterbury while I was with him. The cart-horses were sold in Dublin, and the regiment landed at Herne Bay, and marched into Canterbury on foot. It had been ordered to India before it left Dublin, and Mr. TICHBORNE was pleased at the idea of going abroad.

5. While the regiment was at Canterbury, and in the year 1852, Mr. TICHBORNE was attacked with what I believe were spasms of the heart. Speech left him, and blood apparently ceased to flow. The regimental assistant, Surgeon MOORE (who has since, as I believe, been killed in India) attended him, and tried to bleed him from either arm, but no blood came. It did, however, after the surgeon had pierced his ankle. Dr. TAYLOR, of the regiment, came in shortly afterwards, and said that all Mr. MOORE had done was correct. Mr. TICHBORNE was ill at that time for about two weeks, and I nursed him all the while, and another man was employed to look after his two chargers, and a groom named THOMAS CARTER attended to Mr. TICHBORNE's other two horses, which he drove in a dog-cart.

6. Mr. TICHBORNE was a kind, liberal, and good master to me, and I was a great favourite with Captain MORTON, the captain of his troop; but he was shy, and did not associate much with his brother officers. When Mr. TICHBORNE left the regiment, he was lieutenant, and had been for some time previously. When Mr. TICHBORNE left the regiment, I became regimental servant to Mr. FORMBY, who was then cornet, and remained with him about twelve months. I then filled a similar capacity to Cornet WIGHT until the regiment went to the Crimea. I was then an invalid, and remained at home with the depôt at Hounslow. About the year 1860, Colonel GIBSON was kind enough to get me changed into the 17th Lancers, and in that regiment I served the last two years of my time, and was discharged after completing my full term of twenty-four years in the army, about four years ago. I am now in receipt of my pension of 1s. 1d. per day.

7. From the time Mr. TICHBORNE left the regiment at Canterbury, until the 5th March, 1867, I had not seen him, and I had heard whilst at the depôt at Hounslow that Mr. TICHBORNE had gone to a foreign country soon after he had left the regiment, and that there was a rumour that a ship in which he was a passenger had been lost at sea with all on board.

8. On the 2nd March, 1867, THOMAS CARTER, who was formerly Mr. TICHBORNE's groom, called upon me at Maidstone, and told me that our old master, Mr. TICHBORNE, had returned to England, and wished to see me at Croydon. I was very much surprised to see CARTER, and to hear that Mr. TICHBORNE was alive; and I asked CARTER whether he had seen him, and he replied that he had seen him several times lately, and knew him perfectly well again. I then said that I was quite sure that I should know him, and I at once agreed to meet CARTER in London that he might take me to see Mr. TICHBORNE at Croydon. Accordingly, on Tuesday, the 5th March, 1867, I went with CARTER to Essex Lodge, Croydon, and there saw the above-named Plaintiff, who is my old master, Mr. ROGER CHARLES TICHBORNE. I found him very much altered in his personal appearance, being stouter than when he was with the regiment, but I recognised him by his eyes and eyebrows, forehead and head. Mr. TICHBORNE conversed with me upon things which happened while I was in his employ, until I was convinced he was indeed my old master.

9. I slept at the Prince of Wales Hotel, at Croydon, that night, and went to see the Plaintiff at his house on the next day, Wednesday, the 6th March, 1867, and remained talking with him for some hours, and I was then confirmed in my previous opinion as to his identity, and I have no hesitation whatever in asserting, and do positively swear, that the Plaintiff is the Mr. ROGER CHARLES TICHBORNE whom I formerly served in the Carabineers.

10. About the end of March last a man called upon me at Maidstone, and told me his name was BRADON, and that he came down from London to see me as a friend, and to tell me not to have anything to do with the Plaintiff, whom he had had an interview with, and who, he declared, was not Sir ROGER TICHBORNE. I explained to BRADON that I knew the Plaintiff well, and was perfectly sure he was my old master, Mr. TICHBORNE.

11. On the 1st April last I received by post the letter signed "F. BOWKER," now produced to me, and marked "M., No. 1." I had no previous communication with, nor did I know the writer, but I had been informed and believe that he is the solicitor for the two first-named Defendants. I sent such letter to Mr. HOLMES, the Plaintiff's solicitor, and told him of BRADON's visit, and that I never thought my old master had so many enemies.

12. Yesterday, and the day before, and to-day, I have again seen and conversed with the Plaintiff, and have no doubt as to his identity.

13. The statements hereinbefore contained are within my own knowledge. JAMES MCCANN.

Sworn at my office, No. 3, Church-court, Old Jewry, in the City of London, this 27th day of June, 1867—Before me,

JAS. CROSBY,

A London Commissioner to administer oaths in Chancery.

It appears, from the reasons before mentioned, he had determined to sell out of the army long before his regiment was ordered to India, but shortly after the regiment was ordered to India he changed his intention, as he wished to go to that country for the sake of wild sports. Not long afterwards this order was countermanded, and he thereupon finally resolved to sell out, which he did on the 2nd February, 1851. His commission was purchased by Mr. MYLES FORMBY.

As we have mentioned the name of Mr. FORMBY here, we think it well to insert a memorandum, which appeared in the *Englishman* for December 5, 1874, being No. 35. This memorandum was written by Mr. GUILDFORD ONSLOW:—

REMINISCENCES OF SIR ROGER TICHBORNE.

Whilst Sir ROGER TICHBORNE, the Claimant, was staying at the Inns of Court Hotel in Holborn, previous to his first trial in 1871, he happened to be smoking his cigar with a few friends in the great glass hall of that establishment, when two gentlemen came in to smoke and have a glass of brandy and water. They sat immediately opposite Sir ROGER and his friends on the divan. Sir ROGER looked at them for some length of time, when suddenly he said to his friends, "I verily believe that one of those gentlemen, the tallest, was the very man to whom I sold my commission when I left the 6th Dragoon Guards, and, if so, his name is F——." Upon hearing this, one of his friends, on seeing these two gentlemen depart, followed them out into Holborn, and said to them, "Were either of you two gentlemen in the army." Upon which they said "No." The friend then said, "Did you observe that stout gentleman opposite to you in the room you have just left?" They said, "Yes, we did." "Did you know him?" Reply, "No. Never saw him before in our lives. Who is he?" The reply was, "He is Sir ROGER TICHBORNE, the Claimant, and he says," pointing to the tallest gentleman, "that you are the gentleman to whom he sold his commission when in the 6th Dragoon Guards, and that your name is F——." Upon which the gentleman replied, "Strange to say, my name is F——, and my brother was in the 6th Dragoon Guards, and he did purchase his commission of Mr. ROGER TICHBORNE. He died eight years ago, and I and my brother were so much alike our own mother never knew us apart."

Somewhere about this period, whilst Sir ROGER was at the same hotel, smoking in the same place, a perfect stranger walked in and called for something. After Sir ROGER had looked at him, he said to a friend with him, "I have not seen that person (pointing to the stranger) for over twenty years, and yet I think I recognise him; his name is E——. He is the land agent of Colonel TOWNLEY, in Lancashire." The friend present went up to the stranger, and found his name was correct, and he was the person Sir ROGER had declared him to be.

Scarcely less remarkable is the following, which Mr. ONSLOW communicated to the *Englishman* for November 14, 1874, being No. 32:—

TO THE EDITOR OF THE "ENGLISHMAN."

SIR,—Some months previously to the first TICHBORNE Trial I happened to call on the Claimant at the Waterloo Hotel in Jermyn-street, and I found him having luncheon with his solicitor and his friend and former acquaintance, Mr. BAIGENT, of Winchester. After the luncheon was over, I took my leave, and as I was about to quit the room the Claimant called out my name, and asked if I knew Mr. D——E R——FFE. I said, "Yes, very well." He said, "Tell him I want to see him; he was once a friend of mine." *I said, "I know he is not in London:* for I have just come from his club in St. James's-street, and I hear *he is not in town.*" Upon which the Claimant said, "Do you mind writing to him? He lives——" mentioning his place in Hertfordshire. I assured him I would not forget his request. I had hardly left the Hotel half a minute before turning down Duke-street, I met Mr. D——E R——FFE, and I said to him, "There are more than 3,000,000 inhabitants in London, and I am looking for you, therefore it was over 3,000,000 to 1 I found you." I said, "Within fifty yards of where we are now standing is the Claimant to the Tichborne estates, and less than three minutes ago he expressed a wish to see you. 'Will you come and see him? He cannot bite you."

Mr. D——E R——FFE said, "With all my heart."

I immediately observed, "This will be a capital test for the Claimant, because *you* are the last man in the world he will expect to see, as only a few minutes ago I told him you were *out of town*."

We proceeded arm-in-arm to the Waterloo Hotel, and refusing to allow the waiter to announce our names, we went into the room suddenly where I had left the Claimant only a few minutes before.

I said, "I have returned to ask you if you know *this* gentleman," pointing to Mr. D——E R——FFE, who was standing in the middle of the room with his hat in his hand; upon which the Claimant immediately, and without the slightest hesitation, said, "Why, of course—"D——E R——FFE;" and put out his hand to shake. I left them alone some minutes, whilst I and Mr. BAIGENT walked up and down Jermyn-street. On our return I asked Mr. D——E R——FFE what he thought of him. He said, "Of course he is so much altered, I cannot say. It is a most extraordinary fact, he asked me about our mutual friend, little PHILLIMORE, and although I cannot say I recognise him, he may be the man for all that."

I would add that I received a letter from this gentleman about a year ago, in which he admitted what I have now stated to be correct.

Sir ROGER TICHBORNE, the Claimant, said to me afterwards, "Although I instantly recognised my friend D——E R——FFE, I observed he had lost an eye since I knew him, which accounts for a difference in his appearance."

Previously to his selling out, he had a long leave of absence, which he spent at Upton House, which was placed at his disposal by his uncle Sir EDWARD DOUGHTY. Here it was that he became acquainted with the various witnesses in the neighbourhood of Poole who swear to his identity. He was living here by himself, with a few servants, and spent his time in boating, and shooting, and fishing. JAMES SCOTT, Esq., gave most valuable testimony in his favour, as witness his affidavit:—

I, JAMES WINTER SCOTT, of Rotherfield Park, in the County of Southampton, Esquire, a Magistrate for the said county, make oath and say as follows:—

1. I knew Mr. ROGER CHARLES TICHBORNE previously to his leaving England about the year 1853. I well knew his father, uncle and family.

2. I have had an opportunity of seeing and conversing with the above-named Plaintiff since his return to this country. I am quite satisfied as to the identity of the Plaintiff, from his voice, manner, and face, and recognise him as the Mr. ROGER CHARLES TICHBORNE I formerly knew as the son of the late Sir JAMES DOUGHTY TICHBORNE, Baronet.

3. The statements herein contained are within my own knowledge. JAMES WINTER SCOTT.

Sworn at Rotherfield Park, East Tisted, in the County of Southampton, this 12th day of July, 1867—Before me,
JNO. FRAS. ADAMS,
A Commissioner to administer oaths in Chancery in England.

Just previous to ROGER's selling out, he made arrangements for proceeding to South America, where he intended to travel for some years. For this purpose he opened an account with Messrs. GLYN and Co., on 26th January, 1853, for the purpose of obtaining letters of credit in South America. He went to GLYN's Bank for this purpose, was introduced to Mr. GLYN, the senior partner, and signed his name in the books on the day above named. He then went to Paris to wish his father and mother good-bye, and on his return visited Tichborne to take a farewell of his relatives there; he finally left London (his lodgings were in St. James's-place, kept by a man named THOMPSON) on the 2nd March, 1853, for Southampton, where he embarked for Havre, whence he sailed, accompanied by his servant, JOHN MOORE, in the "Pauline" for Valparaiso. The captain of the "Pauline" is dead, but there were, so late as two or three years ago, four sailors, Frenchmen, who went the voyage with Roger Tichborne, alive, and who are probably still alive.

ROGER TICHBORNE arrived at Valparaiso in the "Pauline" at the end of June, 1853. His letter dated 29th June, 1853, from Valparaiso to his father, shows that ROGER TICHBORNE, on arriving out there, first heard of the death of his uncle, Sir EDWARD DOUGHTY. This should be borne in mind, because the public impression is that ROGER TICHBORNE was the son of a baronet, and entitled to great possessions when he went out in 1853, whereas the real fact is that he was only the son of Mr. JAMES FRANCIS TICHBORNE, and there were two lives between him and the baronetcy. Up to the time of ROGER TICHBORNE's embarkation on board the "Bella," his travels are traced by independent evidence, and his identity is undenied and beyond question. From the time of his embarkation and shipwreck we have to depend on information supplied by himself and verified, or otherwise by evidence since obtained. At the time of his embarkation his family ties may have been considered to be of the weakest description. His father's residence, and even presence, was distasteful to him, his English relatives were, before his departure, pressing him to marry, he had a predominant love of self-will and secresy, and a great dislike to being watched or reported on, or of any one knowing what he was doing or going to do.

The last letter which he wrote to his mother from Buenos Ayres evidences his disregard of home ties, and is worth an attentive perusal. The following is an accurate description of the character and personal appearance of the young man, as he was in France and England up to the time of his departure for South America:—He was very slovenly, untidy, wayward, and intractable, awkward in the movement of his limbs, and had not the slightest appearance of a gentleman about him. The peculiarity in his legs was very great, one knee was bent inwards and the calf of the leg turned outwards, which gave him a peculiar gait, much noticed by the regimental witnesses hereafter alluded to. The TICHBORNES are noticeable in their walk, all that family having a peculiarity in this respect.

The peculiarity in his walk has been perceived in other members of the TICHBORNE family, so that when he first appeared in 1868 in Alresford, people observed—"that is the TICHBORNE walk."

As before stated, he spoke broken English, and had no knowledge whatever of grammar or spelling. He had an objection and great aversion to letter writing; was of a shy and retiring disposition; and took every opportunity he could of withdrawing from society. He preferred the company of those persons below him who he thought would not make remarks upon his peculiarities, manners or conversation, and broken language. He was an inveterate smoker and snuff-taker, and chewed tobacco. He had a reprehensible habit of making and breaking appointments—a habit he has preserved to this day—to his great detriment and disadvantage.

In addition to these peculiarities, he was excessively indolent and very fond of drinking whiskey; yet with all these bad characteristics, when forced into the presence of ladies, his French manners and politeness in society were very remarkable.

The favourable points in his character were his consideration towards servants, and his fondness for horses, dogs, and other animals. He used to talk of stocking Tichborne Park with kangaroos—a circumstance the memory of which was recalled by Mrs. GREENWOOD after his return from Australia, and his repeating accidentally the intention which he had formed before his departure.

During his travels in South America he wrote several letters to his father and mother, and also to Mr. VINCENT GOSFORD, and as he has stated in his examination at the Law Institution, one to his grandmother, Mrs. SEYMOUR, now deceased.

The first of his South American letters is dated June 29th, 1853, from Valparaiso, in which, as before mentioned, he states to his father that he has first heard, by a letter from Lady DOUGHTY, of his uncle Sir EDWARD DOUGHTY's death, on his arrival at Valparaiso. In this letter he gives a brief account of his voyage, and in describing the extreme cold, states that it was so intense that any water falling on deck was "frosten up." The peculiarities in this letter should be carefully studied, as tending to show how imperfectly he was educated; and yet he possessed evident powers of description which show that he was not then wanting in mental capacity.

One of the principal incidents of the South American travels before alluded to, is described in one of the letters dated Lima, August 25th, 1853. There his servant, JOHN MOORE, who was the son of the old butler at Tichborne House, whom, as before stated, he took out with him in the "Pauline," was taken ill in the night at Santiago, and the doctor having pronounced him to be unfit to travel, Mr. TICHBORNE "settled all about with him" and left him there, and then left on his way to Valparaiso, where he subsequently hired another servant. This servant became sick at Lima, and he was obliged to leave him there. He then hired another man of the name of JULES BARRATT, who continued in his service up to the short time of his embarkation on board the "Bella."

It should be observed in the letter just quoted there is the following paragraph:—"My health has been remarkably good ever since I left Europe. I have not had a single moment of any kind of illness of any kind whatsoever ever since that time."

The next letter written from South America is dated December 31st, 1853, in which he alludes to the long time (four months) "which has taken place" since he last wrote. He describes, in very extraordinary language and spelling, the country through which he has passed and is going to travel, and gives a short description of what he has seen and gone through.

The last letter which is preserved is dated from Buenos Ayres, March 1st, 1854, and is the one above alluded to. He complains of his mother's constantly desiring his attention to the duties of a son, and instances great impatience that he should thus be lectured; and he states that if she is always determined to think that he is ill or sick when he tells her in his letters that he is very well, it is perfectly useless for him to write to her at all. In this letter he states that the servant he took at Lima suits him very well (this was JULES BARRATT), and that he intends him to continue on his travels and return with him to England, but adds that it is impossible for him to fix, in any kind of way, the time of his return to England, as the life which he is following, suits his tastes too well to leave it in a hurry, especially as his health is remarkably good, and promising to keep so for a long time to come. The rest of the letter is a description of his journey from Santiago to Buenos Ayres, and desiring his mother to direct her next letter to the Post Office, Kingston, Jamaica, West Indies, where he intended to call to get his letters on his way to Mexico.

It was between the time of his leaving his servant MOORE at Santiago, or the 5th July, and the 27th July, 1853, when he sailed from Valparaiso for Arica, that he visited Melipilla, which has become so [illegible]nent a place in this eventful history.

There i[illegible] [illegible]dependent record of his visit to Melipilla; all that is known i[illegible] [illegible]s himself stated at the Law Institution in his affidavits [illegible] the statement before alluded to, together with the comments w[illegible] [illegible]h has made on the evidence taken in the Chilian Commission. The principal description of the time he passed at Melipilla is [illegible]ntained in his affidavit, where he gives the distances between Santiago and Melipilla, and Melipilla and Valparaiso, with his mode of travelling, and how he became introduced to TOMAS CASTRO, and how he employed himself during the thirteen or fifteen days he visited in that locality. His character at this time may be judged by a letter received from Valparaiso, and set out in his Answer to the Bill in Chancery of Lady TERESA TICHBORNE, in which Mr. WATSON, the writer, describes him as follows:—"In December of the year 1853 I was pa[illegible]ger by one of the British steamers that ply between this port and that of Valparaiso, and there was also passenger on board of the same vessel a Mr. TICHBORNE, a young man whose appearance I remember perfectly well; he was, I should think, a year or two younger than myself. I had then completed my twenty-fifth.

"This gentleman I have described was certainly one of the last I should ever have imagined could keep a shop, as the present Claimant to his name is said to have done. He appears to me to be a person utterly incapable of devoting his attention for five minutes together to any kind of business. The object of his existence appeared to be the satisfaction of a desire for excitement, obtained at no matter what cost, either in health, comfort, or money.

"The Mr. TICHBORNE I knew, was a slim, smooth-faced young man of medium height, possessing, if I am not mistaken, a knowledge of French. He landed at Valparaiso, and the last time I saw him he was equipped for riding with the mail post across the Andes to Buenos Ayres, which I believe he did, for I saw no more of him."

However unfortunate this circumstance may be, it is not surprising that with the distance of time between the visit in 1853 and the time of his letter of the 28th day of August, 1867, to TOMAS CASTRO and the subsequent commission, that the circumstances of his visit of thirteen or fifteen days should have been

"THE BELLA."

entirely forgotten by the residents, whilst the recollection in the visitor's own mind might naturally be quite vivid, both as to names and places.

When ROGER TICHBORNE returned to Valparaiso from Arica and Lima, he caused various articles which he had obtained in the course of his travels, consisting of silver spurs, bridles and stirrups (all of a massive character), skins of birds and beasts, a number of pictures, antique vases, church candles (many of them painted), and other curiosities, to be sent home to Tichborne, and addressed the box to Mr. GOSFORD, the agent, who was then residing at Cheriton, near Tichborne. This circumstance is merely mentioned on account of the reference to it in the evidence of Mr. COOPER, of Alresford, and of his mother, the Dowager Lady TICHBORNE, which will be hereafter commented on.

JULES BARRAUT's statement, which is the last independent evidence obtained of the movements of ROGER TICHBORNE up to the time of his embarkation on board the "Bella" must be received with grave suspicion, for when it was made JULES BARRAUT fully believed that his master was drowned, and no doubt made out a statement to suit his own purposes, which, amongst other things, appears to have been an appropriation of all his master's effects not taken on board the "Bella."

It appears to have been well known at Rio that at the time ROGER TICHBORNE went on board the "Bella" he was intoxicated. He states that he had been drinking cana or aguardiente, which is fire-water, a kind of white brandy distilled from the skin of the grape after fermentation, and very fiery and intoxicating.

During his examination at the Law Institution the Defendant's Counsel pressed the Claimant very hard to know in what state he was when he went on board the "Bella," but did not venture to ask him directly. At last the Claimant said, "Well, I was drunk; now you have it: you might as well have asked me at once."

The Claimant states that whilst he was at Rio, he received an angry letter from his father, ordering him to come home at once, and reproaching him for undutiful conduct, so that when he went on board the "Bella," which was destined for Kingston and New York, he had not any great incitement to return to England, and this, in addition to the evidence which is possessed as to his resolution never to return during his father's lifetime, shows that even had not the "Bella" been wrecked, the family might not have seen him for years.

When the news of the loss of the "Bella" reached England in 1854, Sir JAMES TICHBORNE consulted his solicitor, Mr. HOPKINS, of Alresford, on the subject. We refer the reader to Mr. HOPKINS' affidavit.

Messrs. GOSFORD and SLAUGHTER proceeded in July, 1855, to prove the Will, which was left in Mr. SLAUGHTER's custody, by an affidavit that ROGER CHARLES TICHBORNE died on or about the 26th day of April, 1854, but without stating any circumstances upon which such Affidavit was founded, without giving any particulars as to the cause of his death. The Will was proved under the old system of proving before the Commissary, the Archbishop of Canterbury, and before the institution of the new method adopted by the Probate Court, otherwise it could not have been done, as a more circumstantial proof of death would have been required.

It should here be observed that each of the executors, GOSFORD and SLAUGHTER, received a legacy of £500, which they of course immediately paid themselves out of the first proceeds of the Estates.

Although it was believed by the Dowager Lady TICHBORNE, and other members of the family, that ROGER CHARLES TICHBORNE might still be alive, no advertisements were for a time inserted in the newspapers, or enquiries set on foot, to ascertain whether he was in existence or not, and notwithstanding the proof of the Will, the disbelief of his death was very general in Hampshire. It was always expected that he would turn up after the death of his father, because he had said he would never return whilst he was alive.

We have now got the statement of the Claimant to rely upon, for the further continuation of this history. On the 29th January, 1865, whilst at Wagga-Wagga, the Claimant married MARY ANN, daughter of JOHN and MARY ANN BRYANT, a native of Australia, and of humble origin, and on 18th March, 1866, two months after his first letter to his mother was written, he became the father of a daughter (christened TERESA MARY AGNES TICHBORNE). Mr. GIBBES, in his evidence, alludes to the fact of the expected birth of this child to have been one of the assistant causes in inducing the Claimant to write home.

On 1st June, 1866, the Claimant left Wagga-Wagga for Goulburn, en route for Sydney, leaving his wife and infant child at Goulburn, to be taken care of by her mother. Leaving them at Goulburn, he went to Sydney, in the first instance by himself. He called upon

PORTRAIT OF ROGER TICHBORNE. (FROM THE CHILI DAGUERREOTYPE, 1851.)

Mr. FORD, the manager of the Australian Bank in that City, with a letter of introduction from Mr. COTTEE, Banker at Wagga-Wagga. Mr. FORD spoke highly of Mr. CUBITT, the advertising agent, and induced him to call upon him. GIBBES had, from motives of jealousy, spoken ill of CUBITT, and recommended the Claimant not to do so. It should be mentioned that Mr. CUBITT, the advertising agent, and Mr. GIBBES, had had a long correspondence, which shows the means taken by the Dowager Lady TICHBORNE to discover the whereabouts of her long-lost son; also a memorandum of the day she saw CUBITT's advertisement in the *Times* newspaper, of his agency, and of her writing to him. The Claimant called upon Mr. CUBITT, and he states in his evidence in the Australian Commission, "That the Claimant gave him various details relative to the family and estates, mentioning the names of HOPKINS, GOSFORD, and DOUGHTY, and other particulars." Owing to Mr. GIBBES not making a remittance, as provided for, and promised to his wife during her residence at Goulburn, the Claimant was obliged to retrace his steps from Sydney to Goulburn, and there entered into the bonds of matrimony for the second time with his wife, the ceremony being performed by the Catholic Priest at that place.

It was here for the first time that the Claimant's wife learnt that her husband TOMAS CASTRO was Sir ROGER CHARLES TICHBORNE.

After this, he returned with his wife and child to Sydney, and his arrival at the Metropolitan hotel was announced in the Sydney newspapers. A nurseryman named GUILFOYLE, who, as before stated, was formerly gardener at Tichborne Park, and living near Sydney, seeing this notice in the *Sydney Morning Herald*, called upon him in company with his wife on the following Sunday morning. They met in the street near the hotel, and GUILFOYLE, according to the Claimant's statement in his letters to his mother, identified him. Some few days after this, BOGLE, the black servant of the late Sir EDWARD DOUGHTY, and who had been residing in Sydney for many years, waited upon the Claimant at the hotel (under the circumstance detailed in his evidence), and was recognised by the Claimant, and entered into communication with him.

About this time Mr. JERVIS MORANT LONG, the second grandson of Mr. WALTER JERVIS LONG, of Preshaw Park, near Tichborne, a well-known Hampshire family, hearing the Claimant's name [illegible] at a shop in Sydney, enquired for his address, and [illegible] him at his hotel, and was at once satisfied of his identity.

We [illegible] the Affidavit of that gentleman, which we transcribe from the [illegible] of July 25, 1874, being No. 16:—

I, JERVIS MORANT LONG, second son of WALTER JERVIS LONG, of [illegible] House, near Bishop's Waltham, in the County of Hants, Esquire, [illegible] and swear as follows:—

I am the [illegible] grandson of WALTER LONG, of Preshaw House, near Bishop's Waltham, in the same county, Esq. I am twenty-five [illegible] January. My father and grandfather live [illegible] of Tichborne Park, near Alresford, the family seat of the Tichbornes, and our family knew the family of the late Sir EDWARD DOUGHTY, and the late Sir JAMES FRANCIS TICHBORNE [illegible]. I remember hunting with the Hampshire Hounds, known as the "H.H." pack, and with the Hambledon Hounds, formerly kept by my father, when I was a boy about [illegible]. I used to wear a scarlet jacket, and ride a Shetland pony. A man ran by the side of me. In February, 1861, I left England for Australia, and I have been for the last [illegible] years in Queensland, engaged in obtaining experience in stock-keeping and sheep farming.

In August, 1866, I was in Sydney, and being in a shop there, I overheard a conversation respecting the arrival of Sir ROGER CHARLES TICHBORNE in Sydney. The supposed death of Mr. ROGER CHARLES TICHBORNE had been the subject of conversation at my father's and grandfather's tables, and shortly before I left England, I remember a discussion taking place at Preshaw upon it, that it was suggested that he was still alive, and would turn up some day; and the fact of his mother's disbelief in his death was alluded to most particularly. When I heard in Sydney the name of TICHBORNE mentioned, I enquired of the shop-keeper for his address, and was referred to the Metropolitan Hotel. I went there accordingly the next day, and was shown into a room, where I saw the Plaintiff and a lady and child, who were, as I believe, his wife and daughter. I made myself known to the Plaintiff, and we [illegible] into conversation respecting Tichborne Park, Preshaw, and the neighbourhood. The Plaintiff enquired after my father and grandfather, and remembered and referred to my hunting in a scarlet jacket, and on a Shetland pony with a man at my side. He very well knew and stated the places where the different packs of hounds used to meet, and evinced so much knowledge of localities and persons known to me in Hampshire, that I had no hesitation in believing him, and do firmly believe him, to be in reality Sir ROGER CHARLES DOUGHTY TICHBORNE. I spent several days with the Plaintiff in Sydney, and I saw him and his family on board ship when they left for England, in September, 1866, and so convinced was I of his identity, that I advanced to the Plaintiff £200 towards the expenses of his voyage, and I wrote to my father explaining that I had met Sir ROGER CHARLES TICHBORNE, and that he was then returning home. I left Sydney January, 1867, and arrived in England in April following. I have been twice for several days upon a visit with the Plaintiff at his house in Croydon. The statements hereinbefore contained, are within my own knowledge. JERVIS MORANT LONG.

As before mentioned, he also saw Mr. TURVILLE (who had been the trustee of his clandestine Will), and the result of Mr. TURVILLE'S interview was that Mr. TURVILLE wrote to his friends in England to say that he had no doubt the real ROGER TICHBORNE had turned up.

The Claimant's interview with GUILFOYLE deserves particular notice. There can be no doubt that from the time of the Claimant's refusal or neglect to attend the dinner which Mr. GUILFOYLE had got up for the special purpose of doing him honour, a feeling of rancour and antagonism was roused, and these feelings culminated in the letter which Mr. GUILFOYLE wrote after seeing Mr. MACKENZIE, the Defendant's agents, on 23rd June, 1867. From the tenor and animus shown in the letter, it was anticipated that at one time Mr. GUILFOYLE would have been brought over by the Defendants as a witness against the Claimant, but this was not the case, and the latest intelligence possessed of Mr. GUILFOYLE was, that he was seen by Mr. ARTHUR SCOTT, son of Mr. JAMES WINTER SCOTT, of Rotherfield Park, Hants, at Sydney (who had just returned from that place), and was understood to have stated that Mr. GUILFOYLE was doubting whether the Claimant was ROGER TICHBORNE or not.

In the Claimant's statement he describes his meeting with ANDREW BOGLE, who is said by the Defendants to have been the prime mover in what they alleged was an attempt to obtain for an impostor the Tichborne estates and baronetcy. ANDREW BOGLE was [illegible] servant of Sir EDWARD DOUGHTY for more than thirty years, and received a pension of £50 a year from Lady DOUGHTY. [illegible] conversation with BOGLE would satisfy the most sceptical of his honesty and truthfulness.

Up to the time of BOGLE'S embarkation for England with the Claimant, he states in his proof that having been informed by Lady DOUGHTY herself that there was a probability that ROGER TICHBORNE had been carried to Australia after the wreck of the "Bella," he never allowed a stranger to pass him in the streets without scrutinising him for the purpose of discovering the lost heir. BOGLE'S proof is so precise and particular, that it need not be commented on here; suffice it to say that the allegations which have been made against him were entirely without foundation. His conviction from the time he first saw him in Sydney, that the Claimant was the real ROGER CHARLES TICHBORNE, has never been shaken during his intercourse with the Claimant, which extended over five or six years. In the Claimant's statement, and also in BOGLE'S evidence, it will be seen that it was BOGLE'S own desire to come to England with the Claimant, and that it had been his desire long before he met him, and that the Claimant complied with it at very serious inconvenience.

ANDREW BOGLE, acting in the full belief that the Claimant's relatives would be glad to hear that he was alive, and had been recognised by one who knew him so well, wrote a letter to Lady DOUGHTY, informing her of the fact that Sir ROGER and himself were about to embark for England. This letter is set out in paragraph 12 of BOGLE'S Affidavit, and was received by Lady DOUGHTY in course of post in October, 1866. From that moment BOGLE'S pension was stopped, and Lady DOUGHTY refused not only to see him, but never even replied to his letters, thus condemning him unheard, as well as depriving him of his pension.

I, ANDREW BOGLE, at present residing at Croydon, in the County of Surrey, make oath and say as follows, viz:—

1. I am a native of Jamaica in the West Indies, and am now in my sixty-first year.

2. When I was about eleven years of age, Mr. EDWARD TICHBORNE, who afterwards became Sir EDWARD DOUGHTY, was in Jamaica, having gone to the West Indies to manage the estates there of the then DUKE of BUCKINGHAM. Mr. TICHBORNE took a fancy to me then, and I became his page boy, and he brought me to England with him, in or about the year 1825 or 1826. I remained with him in England for about six months, staying principally at Tichborne Park, near Alresford, in the County of Southampton, the family seat of the Tichbornes, Sir HENRY JOSEPH TICHBORNE, the brother of my master Mr. EDWARD TICHBORNE, being then in possession. I then returned to the West Indies with my said master, and resided with him for about eighteen months at the Hope Estate, belonging to the said Duke, and situated about seven miles from Kingston, in the Island of Jamaica. At the end of that time Mr. EDWARD TICHBORNE gave up the management of the Duke's estates and returned to England, taking me with him. He had only been back a few weeks before his cousin Miss ELIZABETH DOUGHTY died, leaving him very large property in Middlesex, Buckinghamshire, Lincolnshire, and Surrey, called the Doughty Estates, and he, upon coming into possession of it, took the name of DOUGHTY, instead of the name of TICHBORNE, and was always afterwards, during his life, called, first Mr. EDWARD DOUGHTY until the death of his brother Sir HENRY, and then Sir EDWARD DOUGHTY.

3. I was constantly in close personal attendance upon my said master from the time he so engaged me in Jamaica, until his death at Tichborne Park on the 5th March, 1853, and for the last twenty years of his life I was his valet, and never left him but for about one month during the whole time. I accompanied him and his wife, the Honourable KATHERINE DOUGHTY upon their wedding tour to Paris, Naples, Rome, and other parts of the Continent, and lived with the family at Upton, in Dorsetshire, London, Tichborne, and everywhere they happened to be. I knew the son of Sir EDWARD and LADY DOUGHTY, who died, from his cradle to his grave, and was present at his funeral. I also knew and was personally well acquainted from her birth, with the above-named defendant KATHERINE RADCLIFFE, formerly KATHERINE DOUGHTY, the only daughter of Sir EDWARD and Lady DOUGHTY, and I was personally well acquainted with Sir HENRY JOSEPH TICHBORNE and his mother, who was a PLOWDEN, and also his seven daughters, Lady DORMER, Lady ARUNDEL, Mrs. GREENWOOD, Mrs. HIBBERT, Mrs. TOWNLEY, Mrs. HIGGINS, and Miss MARY who died; also Sir EDWARD'S only sister, Mrs. NANGLE, and his brother, Mr. ROGER ROBERT TICHBORNE, who lived for some years at Bishop Sutton, near Alresford aforesaid, and afterwards at Bath; likewise Sir EDWARD'S brother JAMES FRANCIS TICHBORNE and his wife, the present Dowager Lady JAMES TICHBORNE, the father and mother of the above-named Plaintiff, Sir ROGER CHARLES DOUGHTY TICHBORNE; also their second son ALFRED JOSEPH TICHBORNE, and in fact every member of the TICHBORNE family living, during the time I was so in the service of the said Sir EDWARD DOUGHTY, and who visited him.

4. I first saw the above-named Plaintiff, Sir ROGER CHARLES DOUGHTY TICHBORNE, Baronet, as an infant child, upon his visiting Sir EDWARD DOUGHTY at Upton, with his parents, and I remember him and his nurse, SARAH PASSMORE, for I used to walk out with them. I saw him occasionally when he visited my said master, from that time until he went to school at Stonyhurst, and also when he spent his holidays at Tichborne, where Sir EDWARD took up his residence in the year 1845, after the death of Sir HENRY. I have a distinct memory of the Plaintiff as a youth coming home from school, and of his growing up to manhood, and up to the day he left England in March, 1853. Both while he was at college, and in the army, he made Tichborne his home, and constantly lived there during his vacations and while he was on leave of absence. His bedroom and mine at Tichborne were adjoining each other, and for about nine years we were constantly in the company of each other, shooting, fishing, and otherwise amusing ourselves during his visits to Tichborne, which were generally about three or four times in each year, and sometimes extended over two months at a time.

He was very fond of hunting and field sports, was a great smoker, not fond of company, and of a shy and retired disposition, seeming to prefer the society of gamekeepers, grooms, and his inferiors rather than that of his equals. He was never partial to reading or writing, and when in his room occupied himself very often in playing the French horn. He spoke English with a foreign accent, but so as to be easily understood, and had much improved in his English speaking before he went away in 1853.

5. Upon the death of Sir EDWARD DOUGHTY, I remained at Tichborne and entered the service of the Plaintiff's father, the said Sir JAMES FRANCIS DOUGHTY TICHBORNE, with whom I stayed about four months. The above-named Defendant VINCENT GOSFORD, who had been for some years steward to Sir EDWARD DOUGHTY, and was then steward to Sir JAMES, told me that a great alteration was to be made in the establishment, and after a conversation with Sir JAMES, I left his employ, and went to London with my son ANDREW, where we remained about eight months, and I married my second wife, who was formerly JANE FISHER, the schoolmistress at Tichborne. My first wife was Miss YOUNG, nurse to Lady DOUGHTY, by whom I had two sons, JOHN and ANDREW, both of whom are now in Sydney.

6. During Sir EDWARD DOUGHTY's life, he frequently told me that he had left me £50 a year for life as a reward for the many years I had been in his service. My second wife and myself resolved to go to Australia, and I told Lady DOUGHTY of it, and she very kindly provided us with the passage money. Myself, my wife and son ANDREW, left England for Sydney in the spring of 1854 by the sailing ship "Africa," and we arrived there about the month of August in that year. I wrote to the said Lady DOUGHTY directly on my arrival, and in reply received from her the letter dated January 1, 1855, now produced to me and marked B No. 1. It is in her handwriting, which I know from having very frequently seen her write. In such letter the following passage occurs, viz.:—"Then poor dear ROGER TICHBORNE at Rio Janeiro embarked on board a merchant vessel, the 'Bella,' for New York, on the 20th April, and on the 26th it was seen a wreck by the 'Kent,' but no bodies found. The banker at Rio wrote to GLYNN that ROGER embarked, and hope has been held out that they might have been picked up and taken to Australia or elsewhere; but all hope is gone—it is dreadful; pray hard for him." That was the first and only information I ever received of the supposed death of the Plaintiff, or of where it was likely he would be conveyed to, supposing he had been picked up at sea, except that in another letter of Lady DOUGHTY to me, dated 4th January, there occurs this passage, viz.:—"I have just read a letter from JOHN MOORE to his brother, Rev. HENRY MOORE, dated October 28. He was much grieved at hearing about Mr. ROGER TICHBORNE in letters from England. I give you John's direction in case you ever like to write to him: 'E. C. SARL, Calle de los Uaspanos, Santiago, de Chili.' He says, if he could have got a hope of finding Mr. ROGER TICHBORNE, he would have gone to Australia or anywhere to find him. No, there is none, I fear. God's will be done." Such last-mentioned letter is also in the handwriting of the said Lady DOUGHTY, and it is now produced by me and marked B No. 2. The JOHN MOORE therein mentioned, is the valet who accompanied the Plaintiff when he left England, in 1853.

7. When I had been in Sydney a few days, I called upon MICHAEL GUILFOYLE, who was settled there with his wife and family and carrying on the business of a nurseryman. He had been for some years previously, gardener to my master, the said Sir EDWARD DOUGHTY, at Tichborne aforesaid, and I knew him and his wife and children intimately. GUILFOYLE and his wife knew the Plaintiff very well indeed, from having frequently seen him at Tichborne, and when I received the letters above mentioned from Lady DOUGHTY, I told him the news they contained as to the Plaintiff's supposed loss at sea, and that he might have been picked up, and conveyed to Australia.

8. From 1854 to 1866, a period of twelve years, I lived in Sydney, where my second wife died in the year 1858. During those years I frequently wrote to Lady DOUGHTY, and she to me, and from 1854 to March 1866, I regularly received from her, through the Union Bank at Sydney, the £50 each year which Sir EDWARD DOUGHTY had promised to leave me. This, with what business I was able to do, was the means by which I supported my wife and family.

9. During the time I was in Sydney, and after receiving the said first letter from Lady DOUGHTY, I was in the habit of taking particular notice of every man I met, to see if he was the Plaintiff, because her ladyship stated that he might have been picked up and carried to Australia.

10. My son, ANDREW BOGLE, has carried on the business of a barber in Sydney for about seven years past, and he does so now. He was in the habit of shaving an invalid gentleman at Belmain, near Sydney, named, I think, Captain DE LOITE, and about the middle of August, 1866, he was doing so, and the captain's lady asked my said son if he had seen in the newspapers the advertisement which frequently appeared for Mr. ROGER CHARLES TICHBORNE, and on his replying that he had, she further inquired whether my said son knew that the person sought for, had been discovered and was then in Sydney on his way home. My said son informed her that he had not known the circumstances and she then showed him a Goulburn newspaper, stating the fact, and allowed him to cut out the part relating to it, which my said son ANDREW brought to me, and I, in the evening of that day, made inquiries, and found that the Plaintiff was in Sydney and staying at the Metropolitan Hotel. I went there on the following morning about twelve o'clock, and inquired if Mr. ROGER TICHBORNE was there, and was told that he was, but was out. I sat down and waited for him in the gateway for about half an hour, at the end of which time two gentlemen came through a doorway on the opposite side of the gateway; they crossed over to go into the hotel, and one of them, on seeing me, stopped and looked hard at me as if he knew me. I looked hard at him and smiled, for I instantly knew him to be the above-named Plaintiff. He came up to me and said, "Halloo, BOGLE, is that you?" and I said, "Yes, sir. How do you do? how very stout you've got." He then went to his room in the hotel, and a waiter came directly to me and asked me to go with him. I accordingly went up stairs to a room where I saw the Plaintiff, and upon my remarking how stout he had got, he replied, "Yes, BOGLE, I am not that slender lad I was when I left Tichborne;" and he then asked me how long I had been in Sydney, and made inquiries after my family, and about my wife, and my sons JOHN and ANDREW, all of whom he knew at Tichborne. He also asked me if his father, Sir JAMES TICHBORNE, was living at Tichborne when I left, and why I left; and upon my telling him that the Steward had suggested it, he asked whether I meant Mr. GOSFORD. I told him I did. I had not mentioned Mr. GOSFORD's name to him. He talked about Tichborne, and asked whether the two Brothers GODWIN were alive. The GODWINS were farmers living near Tichborne, and one of them rented a farm belonging to the Tichborne estate. The Plaintiff also asked me if old Mrs. MARTIN, the nurse, was alive, and I told him she was when I left. He also inquired after two brothers living in Tichborne village, named "GUYS." Likewise about ETHERIDGE, the old blacksmith, and if I remembered going rabbit-shooting with himself and BRAND, the gamekeeper, and the Plaintiff evinced a perfect knowledge respecting Tichborne and the people residing about it, at and before the time he left, in 1853. The Plaintiff told me that he was going back to England almost directly, and I said that many people would be glad to see him back there after his long absence, and that I wished I was going with him, to which he replied, "I will take you, if you like." I thanked him, and said, "I should be very glad to go."

11. Upon leaving the Plaintiff after such interview, I immediately went to Mr. GUILFOYLE, who told me that he had recently seen and conversed with Sir ROGER (meaning the Plaintiff) several times, and was quite certain that he was the Mr. ROGER TICHBORNE he knew formerly in England, as the eldest son of Sir JAMES TICHBORNE.

12. I called upon and saw the Plaintiff again several times in Sydney, and had further conversations with him respecting the TICHBORNE family and neighbourhood. My son ANDREW, who had known him as a boy, also saw and recognised him. I asked the Plaintiff whether I had better write to England and say I was coming, and he said, "Yes, you should write to my aunt, Lady DOUGHTY, and tell her I am going with you." I accordingly got my son JOHN to write and post a letter to Lady DOUGHTY, which I believe was as follows:—

"MY LADY,— "Sydney, August 29th, 1866.

"I hope these few lines will find your Ladyship, Mr. and Mrs. RADCLIFFE and family quite well. I send your Ladyship these lines to inform your Ladyship that Sir ROGER and Lady TICHBORNE are in Sydney, also one little girl six months old, that they leave Sydney by the mail (Panamá and New Zealand) on the first proximo, and I am going with them. Sir ROGER goes direct to Paris to his mother, and I am going to take her Ladyship from Southampton to Upton. Her Ladyship is a native of Australia, twenty-two or twenty-three years of age. We have had an extremely cold winter this year, and I have had my rheumatics very bad in consequence. My family are all quite well, and I am bringing the youngest with me to England. I shall be glad to see your Ladyship once more, a pleasure which I thought I should not enjoy again; but, please God, in two months' time I shall set foot on Old England, and see all my friends once more. With my duty to your Ladyship, I beg to remain your Ladyship's humble servant, ANDREW BOGLE."

On the Thursday previously to our leaving Sydney on the following Sunday, the Plaintiff told me that he could not take me with him to England, as he was short of money to pay my passage, and he desired me to see him the next day, which I did, and he then told me that he had made the necessary arrangements for my going with him. I accordingly left Sydney with the Plaintiff and his family and servants on the 2nd September, 1866, by the steamship "Rakaia" to Panamá, and from thence by the steamer "Henry Chancey" to New York, and thence by the "Cella" to London, where we arrived in the Victoria Docks on Christmas-day, 1866.

13. Within a few days of my arrival in England, I wrote to Lady DOUGHTY and informed her of the fact, and that the Plaintiff and his family had arrived safely also. I never received any reply to such letter.

14. On the 31st December, 1866, in consequence of a telegram I received at Ford's Hotel from the Plaintiff, I went to Alresford and joined him there, and the next day I visited Tichborne and saw the said Mrs. GREENWOOD, the Plaintiff's cousin, and told her of his return, and I likewise saw Mrs. NOBLE, who told me she

had then recently seen him with Mr. Rous, and was quite sure about him. I understood the Plaintiff did not then wish to make himself known. I believe he sent for me to Alresford because it was reported in that neighbourhood that I was dead.

15. On the 12th day of January, 1867, in consequence of a telegram I received from Mr. Holmes, the Plaintiff's solicitor, I went to Paris, and upon arriving at the Hotel de Lille et d'Albion, in the Rue St. Honoré, I was shown into a room in which there were about six or seven ladies, and was told to see if I knew either of them. I looked round the room and went directly up to the Plaintiff's mother, the Dowager Lady James Tichborne, and asked her how she did. I had not seen her for about twelve years previously, but I knew her again instantly.

16. About the end of February last, I called at No. 3, Kensington-square, the residence of the said Lady Doughty, and ascertained that she was at home, and asked to see her. The butler, named Sansom, took in my message to her ladyship, and returned with a reply that she declined to see me until after the law affair respecting Sir Roger was settled, let it end which way it may, or words to that effect.

17. I have not received my annuity of £50 per annum from the said Lady Doughty since March, 1866, although I have written to her.

18. Since my arrival in England, both myself and my son Henry, a lad of eleven years of age, have been entirely supported by the Plaintiff. I was very ill with rheumatism during the whole of the voyage home, and confined to my bed, and was carried about from place to place. I also had a bad attack in Paris, and have suffered very much since, and am entirely unable to follow any occupation for the purpose of earning a livelihood.

19. From the first time I so saw the Plaintiff in Sydney, as aforesaid, I never had, and have not now, the least doubt but that he is Sir Roger Charles Doughty Tichborne, Baronet, the eldest son of the late Sir James Francis Doughty Tichborne, Baronet, and the nephew of my said late master Sir Edward Doughty, whom I formerly knew.

20. On the 16th day of June instant, I received a letter from my said son, Andrew Bogle, in Sydney, enclosing me the letter from Lady Doughty, dated 8th December, 1866, now produced and shown to me, and marked B No. 3.

21. The several statements hereinbefore contained are within my own knowledge, except as hereinbefore appears, and in such last-mentioned cases, are believed by me to be true on the grounds therein appearing. Andrew Bogle.

Sworn at No. 7, Walbrook, in the City of London, this 27th day of June, 1867—Before me,

Jas. H. Linklater,

A London Commissioner to administer oaths in Chancery.

That Lady Doughty, however, was at this period fully convinced of the identity of the Claimant with Roger, is made manifest by the following letter, which appears in the *Englishman* for September 19th, 1874, being No. 21:—

LADY DOUGHTY TO MR. BAIGENT.

23, Kensington Square, Kensington.
Oct. 20th, 1866.

Dear Sir,—I am sorry to have delayed answering your letter, but I have been very unwell ever since my return, a fortnight ago, and this, with the number of letters I have had to write and answer, has caused this delay; and unfortunately I have mislaid your letter, but I remember that I had not seen the publication you named, and should be thankful if you ordered it to be sent to me. I did secure the old journal of Sir Henry, and tho' I should be quite willing to allow you to look it over and compare with your copy some day you may be *in town*, and should prefer that arrangement to sending it anywhere. *The mass of evidence I have now seen from different persons from Australia, together with what the Dowager Lady* Tichborne *admits, leave no doubt this person must be* Roger, *but the circumstances altogether make it a painful event in the family.*

I remain, Dear Sir,
Yours obliged,
K. Doughty.

The Dowager Lady Tichborne, not having sent the £100 which the Claimant asked for in his first letter, he was obliged to borrow money in Sydney for the purpose of enabling him to return home with his family and servants. Having done this, and having also (foolishly, but as the event turned out, profitably) entered into an extensive speculation for the purchase of the Metropolitan Hotel at Sydney, he embarked from Sydney in September, 1866, on board the "Rakaia," bound for Panama. The "Rakaia" called at Wellington, New Zealand, and the Claimant went ashore and enquired for Mr. Frederick Weld, Prime Minister of that Colony, whom he had known in former years in England, but finding that he lived at a considerable distance, and that the duration of the ship's stay would not allow him to go so far, the Claimant wrote him a letter, mentioning his disappointment in being unable to see him, and that he was on his way to England. Mr. Weld wrote a letter to him, and addressed it to Tichborne Park, and it was received by the Claimant soon after his arrival in England. It is as follows:

Brackenfield, Canterbury, New Zealand.
October 17th, 1866.

My Dear Tichborne,—Many thanks for your note. I have often thought of you since we last met, and wondered if you were alive.

I hope you will keep up the credit of the old name and restore the Dole.

I shall most probably return to England in a year or so, when, perhaps, we may meet at Tichborne. In the meantime,

Believe me yours very truly,

Sir R. Tichborne, Bart., Tichborne. Fredk. A. Weld.

P.S.—I am very glad you took Bogle home. Remember me to him.

The reader will observe that Mr. Weld, who knew the handwriting of Roger perfectly well, does not express the least doubt that the writer of the note to him was his old friend—a thing which he could not have failed to do, had he not recognised the writing as being the same (though altered) which he had been perfectly acquainted with in olden times.

On his arrival at Panamá he resolved to wait for the French boat, for the purpose of taking a passage to St. Nazaire. This delayed him a month at Panamá, but the French boat not arriving, and his family becoming sick, he took a passage to New York.

When he arrived at New York he determined to see as much as possible of the United States, so he stayed there a month, and had to raise funds in New York to enable him to reach England, and finally arrived in the afternoon or evening of Christmas Day, 1866, at the Victoria Docks, Limehouse. Whilst the Claimant was in New York, he saw a paragraph copied from an English paper, repudiating his identity, and stating that he was an impostor.

It is necessary here to advert to proceedings in England between the time of the Claimant's last letter from Sydney, and his arrival from New York. In the month of March, 1866—soon after his first letter from Wagga-Wagga arrived—rumour in England stated that Sir Roger Tichborne had been discovered in Australia, and that his mother had received a letter from him, desiring her to send out a sum of money to enable him to return. This rumour, confirmed by the letter, caused great consternation in the family, and great efforts were made to dissuade the Dowager Lady Tichborne from taking any steps in the matter.

Upwards of three years had elapsed since the death of his father, Sir James Francis Doughty Tichborne, and as his son Alfred had succeeded to the title and been in possession of the estates (which he had anticipated before his accession), almost everyone had given up the notion of the Claimant being alive, notwithstanding the reports of his having been found in Australia. The letter before alluded to from Mr. Turville, one from Mr. Scott (second son of Mr. Scott, of Rotherfield), who is, with his brother, one of the largest landed proprietors in Australia, and various others detailing various circumstances connected with the discovery and the individuality of the Claimant, produced a deep impression, so that many persons, including members of the family, wavered in their incredulity. Amongst these was Lady Doughty, whose letter has before been quoted, in which she states—"This person must be Roger; but the circumstances altogether make it a painful event in the family." The arrival of the lost heir was anxiously expected, and it was anticipated that he would come some time about October, 1866.

Towards the end of September, or the beginning of October, a photographic portrait, taken in Sydney, had been sent either by the Claimant or Mr. Turville, or both, to the Dowager Lady Tichborne. There were other copies made and circulated from the one given by the Claimant himself to Mr. Turville, who sent it to England, and it was seen by members of the family, Lady Doughty being amongst the number. This photograph being a very unsatisfactory portrait, taken with a faulty lens, was so unlike Roger Tichborne when he left England, in 1853, that little or no resemblance could be traced; and Lady Doughty, in a letter, pronounced it to be "so totally unlike Sir Roger, that it seems impossible to be him." A copy of this photograph was sent to Brookwood, the residence of Colonel Greenwood and his wife, Mrs. Greenwood (formerly Catherine Tichborne, daughter of Sir Henry Joseph Tichborne). This tended to perplex the Greenwood family, who, however, admitted that there was some likeness in the upper part of the face; and the same opinion was expressed by Mr. James Morley, an old servant of the Tichborne family, and one of the witnesses, in the presence of Lord Arundel.

We transcribe his Affidavit.

I, James Morley, of Hinton Ampner, in the County of Southampton, Farmer and Maltster, make oath and say as follows:—

1. I am sixty years of age. I have known the Tichborne family all my life. When a boy I entered the service of Sir Henry Tichborne, the seventh baronet, and lived in Tichborne House and in his service up to the time of his death in 1821. I then entered the service of his son, Sir Henry Joseph Tichborne, and continued in his service as butler up to the year 1838, when I married and became a farmer and maltster at Hinton Ampner, a village about three miles from Tichborne, and have resided there ever since. I well knew every member of the Tichborne family, who resided at, or visited Tichborne during the last fifty years. After I left Tichborne House I continued on friendly terms with the family, whom I frequently saw, and was upon conversational terms with the several members of the family who have resided or visited Tichborne House since the year 1815.

2. I also well knew Mr. Roger Charles Tichborne, and Mr. Alfred Joseph Tichborne, the two sons of the late Sir James Francis Tichborne.

3. I remember the Plaintiff, then Master ROGER CHARLES TICHBORNE, the eldest son of the aforesaid Sir JAMES FRANCIS DOUGHTY TICHBORNE, when a boy, coming to Tichborne at different times, and that he was often at Tichborne during Sir EDWARD DOUGHTY's residence there, and I frequently saw and spoke to him; in fact I knew him as he grew into manhood and up to the time of his leaving England in 1853. I well remember his personal appearance, manners, and walk.

4. On the 13th day of October, 1867, I went to the Swan hotel at Alresford, for the express purpose of seeing the Plaintiff, whom I had not seen since he left England in the year 1853. I did see the Plaintiff, who at once recognised me, but I myself did not recognise the Plaintiff at first sight, he having grown very stout since I last saw him, but after a few minutes' conversation, during which I watched the movement of his features, I fully recognised him as the Mr. ROGER CHARLES TICHBORNE I had formerly known; and I noticed in the Plaintiff's features that same expression of face and movement of the eyes which I knew and recollected he had when a boy, and as he grew up into manhood, and in after years, and the longer I talked to him, and the more I looked at him, the more I was convinced as to his identity. His eyes and eyebrows, and the general expression of his face, and his voice, are unmistakeable, and I was particularly struck by the strong likeness and resemblance he now bears to his uncle, the late Sir HENRY JOSEPH TICHBORNE, my old master. I remained in conversation with the Plaintiff for some hours, during which he freely conversed with me about Tichborne and its neighbourhood, and about his family and other matters well known to me.

5. I have seen and conversed again on the 30th day of November, with the Plaintiff, and am certain and positive as to his identity, and have no hesitation whatever in declaring, and do distinctly swear that he is the Mr. ROGER CHARLES TICHBORNE whom I formerly knew, the eldest son of the late Sir JAMES FRANCIS DOUGHTY TICHBORNE, Baronet, deceased, and Dame HENRIETTE FELICITÉ, his wife.

6. The several statements herein contained are within my own knowledge.

JAS. MORLEY.

Sworn at New Alresford, in the County of Southampton, this 7th day of December, 1867—Before me,
JNO. FRAS. ADAMS,
A Commissioner to administer oaths in Chancery in England.

Soon after this, two or three Australian newspapers reached England, containing an account of the Claimant and the life he had been leading, of his marriage, and the humble position of his wife's family. These paragraphs were first reprinted in the *Hampshire Chronicle*, and a few days afterwards were transferred—through the agency of HIGGINS, otherwise Jacob Omnium—to the country and various local and London newspapers; so that the paragraphs obtained circulation all over England. These produced indignant feelings in the minds of members of the Tichborne family, who felt annoyed that their name should be brought into notice and disgraced by such details. Their pride being deeply wounded, the inveterate dislike to ROGER TICHBORNE's mother, and the old spirit of family disunion were brought out afresh, and they made up their minds, not only to repudiate the Claimant before seeing him, but to prevent, if possible, his recovering the estates, on the pretext that he had rendered himself unworthy of them, and that it would be far better for the estates to remain in the hands of the posthumous son of his brother ALFRED—there being the comforting assurance that if the child should die, a grandson of Sir HENRY JOSEPH TICHBORNE (Major DORMER, the second son of Lord DORMER, and nephew of Mrs. GREENWOOD, of Brookwood), would, according to the deeds of settlement, enjoy the Tichborne property, and the grandson of Sir EDWARD DOUGHTY, the Doughty estates.

At the time these paragraphs appeared in the newspapers, there was inserted in the *Hampshire Chronicle* a letter written by ANDREW BOGLE to Lady DOUGHTY (and subsequently in many of the London and local papers) taken from a copy which was sent to Mrs. GREENWOOD, of Brookwood Park, announcing that he (ANDREW BOGLE) had seen ROGER TICHBORNE, and would accompany him to England. This letter produced some sensation; but owing to the circumstances of its being a matter of doubt whether it was written by *the* ANDREW BOGLE, valet for many years to Sir EDWARD DOUGHTY, who knew ROGER TICHBORNE quite well; or by his son, ANDREW BOGLE, who had left England a mere boy, and consequently was not in a position to judge as to his identity, the letter was viewed with suspicion, which did not tend to allay the irritated feelings caused by the publication of the Australian paragraphs. Lady DOUGHTY was annoyed by BOGLE's letter, and in a letter printed in the *Hampshire Chronicle*, November 3rd, 1866, intimated that it was done so without her knowledge or permission, and that moreover the whole affair at present seemed very questionable. BOGLE's letter, however, having given the date of the intended departure of himself and the Plaintiff from Australia, enabled the expectants to fix the time of their probable arrival in England; consequently it was anticipated they would arrive by the steamer "Shannon," due at Southampton by the end of October, 1866. This vessel arrived without them; but it was ascertained on board the steamer that Sir ROGER and BOGLE were left at Panamá, with the view of continuing their journey either by a French boat, or viâ New York. This was interpreted as being suspicious, and raised the hopes of the family that an imposition was really being practised. Weeks passed over without further intelligence, doubts increased, and soon afterwards bills amounting to upwards of £10,000 were presented at DRUMMOND's Bank for payment. The fact of the Claimant never having had a banking account at DRUMMOND's, and yet drawing bills payable at that bank, was set down as a proof of the scheme being one for extortion only, and it was then circulated that the lost heir would never make his appearance in England. The Claimant's explanation of the drawing on DRUMMOND's is, that he stipulated the bills should not be put in circulation, and he fully expected to have been put in possession of his property long before they were payable, and intended to meet them at DRUMMOND's at the time of presentation.

The members of the family, and the newspaper writers, freely expressed their opinions that the Claimant was nothing more than an impostor, and that the whole affair was an impudent fabrication of some persons either in England or Australia.

During the time the Claimant was in New York, he sent a telegram to his mother, for which he paid £20 or upwards, which, however, never reached her.

The Claimant and his family left New York in the steamer "Cella," for England, and arrived at the Victoria Docks, Limehouse, as before stated, on the afternoon of Christmas-day, 1866, and they went direct to Ford's Hotel, Manchester-street, Manchester square, a well-known Roman Catholic Hotel.

With regard to the young man named BUTTS (son of the Imperial Hotel keeper at Sydney), whom he had engaged at Sydney as a Secretary, at a salary of £300 a year, it is necessary to state that BUTTS was left at Ford's Hotel when the Claimant and his family went to the Clarendon Hotel at Gravesend. The day after the Claimant departed for the Clarendon, several persons called at Ford's Hotel, for the purpose of seeing him. Some of them spoke to BOGLE, one of them being a Mr. FITZGERALD, a nephew of Lady DOUGHTY's, and who shortly afterwards called again with Mr. CULLINGTON, the solicitor. Mr. FITZGERALD told BOGLE, in a most insulting tone, that if it were not for him, there would be no Sir ROGER, but Mr. CULLINGTON, more diplomatic, attempted to get on good terms with young BUTTS, the secretary, with whom he very freely conversed. CULLINGTON got young BUTTS to dine with him several times. It was in consequence of this, that the Claimant discharged young BUTTS, who returned to Sydney.

There were others who called the day after, at Ford's Hotel, to see BOGLE; amongst these was Mr. BLOUNT, since deceased, and Mr. NANGLE, the uncle of the Claimant by marriage, who told him he had been sent there by Lady DOUGHTY, to see if he was BOGLE. Mr. NANGLE said he would swear to him anywhere, and that he should write to Lady DOUGHTY, to say so. This is mentioned for the purpose of showing that Lady DOUGHTY ought in fairness, at any rate, to have seen BOGLE, and heard his statement and opinion, about the identity of the Claimant.

The Claimant, after his arrival at Gravesend, wrote to his mother at Paris, asking her to come over to see him. This letter unfortunately cannot be found.

Knowing that it would take three or four days before he could get an answer, he resolved to go down and have a look at Tichborne, wishing to ascertain if the house was in the occupation of his relatives, and also to see the whole place. He arrived at Alresford, on Friday evening, the 28th December, 1866, by the train due there at 7.10. He went to the Swan Hotel, and afterwards sent for the landlord, Mr. ROUS, to smoke and have a chat with him. He made enquiries about the places in the neighbourhood, and as to who was living at Tichborne House. The next day he went to Tichborne, in company with ROUS, and seemed very anxious not to be recognised, invariably covering the lower part of his face when any one approached. On their arrival at the Dairy, close to Tichborne House, he walked round the back of the house with evident curiosity and interest, and afterwards drove round to Cheriton, and then to Alresford. In the afternoon of the same day, he walked to Tichborne, looking round the Park and other property.

The following is the Affidavit of Mr. ROUS:—

I, EDWARD ROUS, of New Alresford, in the County of Southampton, hotel-keeper, make oath and say as follows:—

1. I am of the age of 48 years, and have resided at Alresford nearly all my life. I was upwards of 25 years a clerk in the office of Messrs DUNN, HOPKINS and Co., Solicitors, Alresford. During that time I had opportunities of seeing clients who came to the office. I remember on one or two occasions, seeing the above-named Plaintiff, then Mr. ROGER CHARLES TICHBORNE, come there on business visits to Mr. HOPKINS, who was his professional adviser, and from what I saw of him at those times I have a strong recollection of his features, particularly the upper part of his face. I well knew the late Sir HENRY TICHBORNE, Sir EDWARD DOUGHTY, Sir JAMES FRANCIS TICHBORNE, and the Plaintiff's brother, the late ALFRED JOSEPH TICHBORNE, Esquire.

2. On the 28th day of December, 1866, the Plaintiff arrived at my hotel by the train from London, which reached Alresford at 7·10, and about 9 o'clock the same evening he sent for me to his private room. Upon entering he accosted me as Mr. ROUS, and said he supposed I did not recollect him, that he was some years since on a visit in the neighbourhood, and had been to Alresford before, and he invited me to sit down and take a cigar with him, which I did.

3. Our conversation commenced by his asking me, if I knew

whether any one could get a view of any of the gentlemen's halls in the neighbourhood? I told him I did not think they could, as they were all occupied. I told him that the Grange was occupied by Lord [illegible], and Tichborne House was occupied by Colonel Lushington. This commenced the subject of Tichborne, and after conversing about the late Sir Alfred Tichborne, the Plaintiff told me that Sir Roger Tichborne had arrived in England on Christmas-day, having landed at Gravesend on the evening of that day, and that he had come over with Sir Roger from Australia, and represented to me that he was himself connected with the press, and had come down to take notes relative to the Tichborne estate; but I formed my own opinion from the great resemblance of the Plaintiff to the Mr. Roger Charles Tichborne, and from his conversation relative to the Tichborne family and estates, that my visitor was no other than Sir Roger Tichborne himself, and I consequently particularly scrutinised his features and appearance generally, and I discovered a great resemblance to his late brother, and also to his late uncle Sir Henry Tichborne. The Plaintiff asked me if I could let him have a saddle-horse the next morning to ride over to Tichborne, but I told him I had not got one that I could depend upon carrying him safely, but that as I should be driving over to the Farm at Tichborne in the morning, I would take him with me, and he could then see Tichborne House, to which he consented.

4. The next morning, Saturday, the 29th December, 1866, I drove the Plaintiff to Tichborne, and whilst at the back entrance to Tichborne House, the Plaintiff got out of the carriage and looked round that part of the house where, I understood, his room used to be (but which has since been pulled down). I afterwards drove him through the village, and thence to Cheriton, and in our conversation he frequently, whilst talking of the late Sir James Tichborne, and the Dowager Lady Tichborne, and the late Sir Alfred Tichborne, spoke of them unconsciously as his "father," his "mother," and his "brother," but always checked himself immediately he found he had slipped out those words. In passing through the village he asked me if the Dole was distributed as usual; and, on my telling him I thought not, he said, Didn't "my brother" give it? His knowledge of different places we passed, and the result of his conversation during our drive, further confirmed my opinion that he was Sir Roger Tichborne.

5. It had been customary for the occupiers of Tichborne House for the time being, during my recollection, until the death of the Plaintiff's father, Sir James, and I have been informed and believe that it was an ancient custom, for the occupiers of Tichborne House to distribute alms, which was commonly known as "The Tichborne Dole."

6. On the following morning, 30th December, whilst walking in my garden with the Plaintiff, I asked him if I was not then talking to Sir Roger himself. He enquired of me why I thought so? and I told him, I had suspected who he was from the first half-hour I saw him, as he was so much like Sir Roger Tichborne and his brother Alfred, about the eyes and upper part of his face. He replied, "I am Sir Roger, but I do not want any one to know it for a few days;" he said he was going to Paris to see his mother, and he did not wish to see any one before he had first visited her. Whilst walking or riding with the Plaintiff, he appeared very anxious that no one should recognise him, and always placed his handkerchief to his mouth to hide his face whenever he saw any one approaching him.

7. The Plaintiff stayed at my house till Tuesday, the 1st of January, and left by the evening train. When taking leave of me, he said, "I shall be down again in a few days with either my mother or my solicitor, and I shall want apartments, and when I come again I shall not be ashamed to be known as Sir Roger Tichborne, not that I am ashamed now, but I have a motive."

8. I have seen and talked to the Plaintiff several times since, and feel perfectly satisfied that he is the same person I formerly knew, as Roger Charles Tichborne, the eldest son of the late Sir James Francis Doughty Tichborne.

9. The several statements herein contained, are within my own knowledge, except as hereinbefore appears, and in such last-mentioned cases are believed by me to be true, on the grounds herein appearing.

Edward Rous.

Sworn at New Alresford, in the County of Southampton, this 1st day of July, 1867—Before me,
Jno. Fras. Adams.
A Commissioner to administer oaths in Chancery in London.

On the 9th of January, the day after his interview with Gosford, hereafter described, the Claimant wrote to his mother the following touching letter, which is here inserted because it alludes to his visit to Tichborne, and unhesitatingly tells her that his identity had been denied by Vincent Gosford:—

International Hotel (late Terminus), London-bridge, S.E.
January 9th, 1867.

Dear and Beloved Mamma, I am here, and am prevented by circumstances from coming to see you. O do come over and see me at once, and i will not go out of the Hotel until you come. I have been down to tichborne, and had a look at the dear old place once more, and it made my heart bleed to look at the destruction there has been made there, but has my poor brother is dead we will not mention that subject again: let the past be past and no more about it. I have seen Mr. Gosford; he seems very much change to what he use to be. He came down in the train from Gravesend last night. I had a long talk with him, and he se ms to deny everything I put him in mind of. He says he do not remember me coming down in the coach from London with me to Tichborne. I had a hours conversation with him about different things, mamma, that nobody in the world could have told him but me. I even told him under what circumstances Moore came left me. You must remember, mamma, I wrote to him from almost every place. Cullington and a lot more would insist on seeing me at Gravesend when they came, and because I did not wish to see them until i had seen you, they where very angry. Oh do come at once to the Hotel, Mamma, and i will not go out until you come. Everything will be explained when you come. It dangerous for me to go out has some of the Bills i drew in Sydney are due, and i believe they intend to arrest me if I attemp to leave England; so do come at once, Mamma.

I did not receive an answer to the telegram i sent from New York.

Hoping i will not have to wait long before i see you.

I remain, your ever affectionate Son,
R. C. Tichborne.

On Sunday, the 30th of December, 1866, he stayed at the hotel in the morning, but appears to have gone to Tichborne at the time the people were leaving the Protestant church. On this day Mr. Rous, the landlord, states in his affidavit, that he asked him if he was not Sir Roger Tichborne. He admitted that he was, but stated he did not desire it to be known, the landlord understanding that he had promised to see no one until he had seen his mother. It appears that it was generally believed in England, especially at Alresford, that Andrew Bogle, the valet of the late Sir Edward Doughty, was dead, and this rumour having reached the ears of the Claimant whilst at Alresford, on the 31st of December, 1866, he telegraphed to Bogle at Ford's Hotel, desiring him to come to Alresford by the train, which was due at ten minutes past seven.

The next morning, Tuesday, January 1st, 1867, being a Day of Obligation (on a par with the Sunday amongst Catholics), Andrew Bogle, who is, like the Claimant, a Catholic, attended divine service at the domestic chapel attached to Tichborne House. He was there seen and spoken to, by Mrs. Greenwood, of Brookwood Park (the Claimant's first cousin), and he answered freely every question put by her concerning himself and the Claimant. He also spoke to Mr. and Mrs. Noble, the bailiff and his wife, and others whom he had known years ago.

The same day Mrs. Greenwood communicated the circumstance that she had seen Bogle at chapel, to her sister and brother-in-law, Mr. and Mrs. Higgins, who resided in London until the death of Mr. Higgins (Jacob Omnium). Mr. Higgins thereupon wrote an article, which appeared in the *Pall Mall Gazette*, speaking in anything but complimentary terms of the Claimant, and conveying the impression that he was an impostor, but vouching for the identity of Andrew Bogle. This article was reprinted in the local and London newspapers.

On the same day, Tuesday, January 1, 1867, Mr. Frederick Bowker, of Winchester, a solicitor, employed by the late Mr. Alfred Tichborne, having heard of the Claimant and Bogle being at Alresford, went to the Swan hotel, and asked the servant which was the room the gentleman was staying in, and in the absence of the landlord, pushed himself past the maid servant, and tried to obtain forcible entry into the room in which the Claimant was seated. The Claimant hearing a violent noise at the door, which he had fastened to prevent intrusion, went and opened it, when Mr. Bowker entered, and the Claimant asked him what was his business. Mr. Bowker said he had come to see him, understanding that he had something to do with Sir Roger Tichborne, for that as he (Bowker) had the management of the estate and affairs in his hands, he wished to know who he (the Claimant) was, adding that he had better mind what he was about. The Claimant naturally felt annoyed at such an intrusion, and asked Bowker if he knew to whom he was speaking, stating that he was Sir Roger Tichborne himself, and adding, "How dare you speak to me in such a manner?" He then ordered him to leave the room, but Bowker spoke in the following words:—"I beg your pardon, sir, I shall be very glad, as I know all about the estate, to give you any assistance, and place myself at your service." The Claimant thereupon said, "I don't require any assistance, and if I did I would not go to you"; and taking off the mantelpiece a catalogue of the sale of furniture at Tichborne House, which had occurred after the death of his father, said, "Sir, if you had anything to do with this, you will have enough to do to look after yourself, as neither you nor they had any right to sell the furniture and fixtures even if I was dead." Bowker felt confused at this, and took up a newspaper to hide his embarrassment. The Claimant then ordered him to leave the room, which he accordingly did.

The above description of the interview between the Claimant and Bowker, is obtained from independent evidence to that of the Claimant himself, but his own description of the interview will be found in his cross-examination.

The Claimant returned to Gravesend, and Bogle to Ford's Hotel that evening by the 7.20 train.

On his return from Alresford to Gravesend, he appears to have stayed a night at the International Hotel, London Bridge, where he made the acquaintance of Mr. Leete (under singular circumstances) and through whose instrumentality he was introduced to Mr. Holmes his first solicitor, and the following is a description of the interview as related soon after, by Mr. Leete himself:—

The Claimant went into the smoking-room of the hotel and called for a glass of brandy. He sat down. There were only two gentlemen in the room beside himself. These two gentlemen were holding a lively conversation in French, one of them being Mr. LEETE, and the other a Belgian who had come over to England on business, and had been staying a few days with Mr. LEETE at Norwood, as a visitor. He had come up to London for the purpose of proceeding to Paris early the next morning.

There appears to have been a pause in the conversation between Mr. LEETE and his friend, and the Claimant addressed himself to Mr. LEETE, saying as he (Mr. LEETE) spoke French so very fluently he would be glad if he would tell him the best means to proceed to Paris, whether by Dover or Folkestone, adding that he had been fourteen years out of the country, and did not know which was the best route. Mr. LEETE replied, "My friend here is going to Paris by the 7 o'clock train to-morrow, and you cannot do better than accompany him." The Claimant replied, "I thank you much, it will give me great pleasure to do so." Mr. LEETE then asked him if he could speak French, having noticed that he had more than once smiled during his conversation with his Belgian friend. He replied, "I could once speak it as fluently as you do, but I have not heard a word of it spoken for the last twelve or thirteen years, and I have lost all command of my tongue over it." Mr. LEETE, struck by his enquiry as to the best route to Paris, and noticing his dress, asked him if he had come from one of the colonies, or was colonial born. "No, I was born in Paris." Asking the following question, "Do you know anything of Paris?" Mr. LEETE replied, "That he was often there, and knew it well." The Claimant then asked him if he knew Mr. BLOUNT, a banker there; Mr. LEETE said, "No, I do not." He then asked him if he remembered Mr. CALLAGHAN, a banker, and two or three other persons whom he named, to which Mr. LEETE gave the same answer. The Claimant then said, "Do you know Lady TICHBORNE?" Mr. LEETE said, "No;" but he knew the name very well, as a friend of his had sued the late Sir ALFRED TICHBORNE for a debt, and when he (LEETE) was at Frankfort a short time ago, one of his clerks had sent him a cutting from a newspaper about the return of a Sir ROGER TICHBORNE. Sir ROGER thereupon said, "I am Sir ROGER TICHBORNE, and am going to Paris to see my mamma." Mr. LEETE being struck with the oddity of the affair, said he hoped he was acting under advice. He said he had no one to advise him: but Mr. LEETE said he should not act without advice. The Claimant said he perfectly agreed with him, but could not help himself, as a friend of his in Australia (Mr. TURVILLE) had given him the address of a London solicitor, but he had unfortunately lost the card. Mr. LEETE then gave him the address of his own solicitor, Mr. JOHN HOLMES, of 25, Poultry, writing it on the back of his card, and on his doing this the Claimant looked at the name and said, "Well, then I will not go to Paris to-morrow, but will call and see this gentleman."

Accordingly, on Thursday the 3rd January, the Claimant called at Mr. HOLMES'S office, 25, Poultry, handed in Mr. LEETE'S card, and told Mr. HOLMES who he was, giving some particulars of his career, and instructed him to put himself in communication with Mr. VINCENT GOSFORD, who knew him and his estates well, and that he (HOLMES) was to act with Mr. GOSFORD.

On the 5th January, 1867, he again called on Mr. HOLMES, and showed him a letter from his mother, which letter insisted on his coming to Paris immediately.

There being some hesitation in his manner, Mr. HOLMES asked him if he was in want of money. He said it was the truth, and that he had not the means wherewith to go to Paris. Mr. HOLMES thereupon advanced him £20, which he accepted, saying that he would first have to buy a few things, and then that he would go to Gravesend to wish his wife goodbye, and then start to Paris.

On the Claimant's arrival at the Clarendon Hotel, Gravesend, whilst he was proceeding up stairs, three persons came rushing in a very unceremonious manner after him; one of them called out loudly to him; and he not liking such behaviour proceeded to his room, where he learnt from Lady TICHBORNE that these gentlemen had been trying to force themselves into her presence, upon which he was much annoyed.

Presently the waiter informed him that Mr. GOSFORD was waiting below to speak to him, and he sent out word that he could not see him until he had seen his mother; Mr. GOSFORD sent a reply stating he should stop until he had seen him. The Claimant then sent him back a note by the waiter, which they ridiculed. Not succeeding in getting an interview, Mr. GOSFORD, Mr. CULLINGTON, and Mr. PLOWDEN addressed some observations to the landlord of the hotel, that he had better look out for his bill, and they then left the hotel. In consequence of this communication, the landlord made out his bill, amounting to £22, and sent it up to the Claimant desiring him to pay at once. The Claimant emptied his purse upon the table, and gave the waiter £18 odd, all the money he had got. The waiter appears to have been much moved at the harsh treatment thus accorded to him, for he has stated that if he had possessed the money he would have cheerfully lent it to him, in order that the bill might be defrayed; so satisfied was he that the Claimant was a gentleman in every sense of the word. Imagine the painful position of the Claimant at this time: night time, snow on the ground, with a wife and infant child, and nurse dependent upon him; without a friend, and without a penny, not knowing what to do or which way to turn, and this brought about by one (GOSFORD) whom he had so fully trusted in former years, and wished still to trust and treat as his friend.

At the time the bill was sent up it was about eight o'clock, and the night was dark and snowy; so that there was no possibility of his moving that night. The Claimant borrowed a penny stamp of the waiter, with which he posted a letter to Mr. HOLMES, who came down on Monday morning, the 7th January, 1867, to see him.

The above circumstances are minutely repeated, in order that it may be seen what measures were taken by Mr. VINCENT GOSFORD and his friends to force the Claimant out of the country before he had time to be seen by any one else, and to throw every difficulty in the way of his obtaining his title and estates.

Mr. HOLMES, on the 7th January, 1867, thinking that the evident object of Messrs. GOSFORD, CULLINGTON and PLOWDEN, by driving him to extremities, was to prevent him obtaining access to his mother in Paris, consulted with Mr. LEETE, who accompanied him to Gravesend, and after seeing the Claimant, arranged to accompany him to Paris in order to prevent further interference.

It was decided that they should leave Gravesend the following day, that they should all go to Croydon, and that Lady TICHBORNE, with her nurse and child, should stay at Mr. HOLMES'S house, whilst the Claimant went to see his mother.

On Tuesday, the 8th January, Mr. HOLMES again went to the Clarendon Hotel, Gravesend, for the purpose of taking the Claimant's family to Croydon. Preparations for removal were being made, when Mr. GOSFORD arrived, and on learning that the Claimant was still there, sent a message that he wished to see the Claimant. The Claimant felt annoyed, and said he would neither see nor speak to him, as he had already told him he wished to see his mother first. Mr. HOLMES told the Claimant he had better see him, but to this the Claimant objected, in consequence of the promise he had made to his mother.

After some pressing, the Claimant said, "Mr. HOLMES, you are my solicitor; if you insist on my seeing him, I will, though I don't think I ought to do so yet."

He then accompanied Mr. HOLMES to a private room, where Mr. GOSFORD was shown in, and where they all three remained nearly two hours, Mr. GOSFORD asking the Claimant a number of questions on various matters, persons, and places, all of which the Claimant readily answered, and it was apparent to Mr. HOLMES that they well knew each other, and were conversant with the subjects discussed.

Mr. GOSFORD accompanied the Claimant and Mr. HOLMES, together with Lady TICHBORNE and their family, to the railway station, and the Claimant, Mr. HOLMES, and GOSFORD entered the compartment of a first-class carriage, of which they were the only occupants, and where they conversed freely with each other until the train arrived in London.

The train was delayed in the snow, and they were over two hours and a half getting to London. During the whole of this time the Claimant and Mr. GOSFORD talked, Mr. HOLMES refraining from conversation.

On the arrival of the Claimant, Mr. HOLMES, and Mr. GOSFORD, at the London Bridge Station, Mr. CULLINGTON and others were there awaiting the return of Mr. GOSFORD from Gravesend.

There was considerable excitement at the station; caused by the desire of people to see the gentleman who was termed the "Tichborne Impostor;" but the Claimant states in his account of this interview that Mr. GOSFORD addressed him as Sir ROGER, during his four hours' conversation, and shook hands with him on his parting at the London Bridge Station, saying, "Good night, Sir ROGER."

On Thursday, 10th January, the Claimant, Mr. HOLMES, and Mr. LEETE, started for Paris. They arrived there between nine and ten o'clock in the evening of that day, and went to the Hotel de Lille d'Albion, Rue St. Honoré.

Soon after their arrival they went into the coffee-room and had dinner. Whilst so engaged a lady came in, accompanied by a gentleman, muffled up with a scarf around the neck. They took a seat not far from the Claimant and his party, and looked intently at him; presently after they got up and left the room, passing near the Claimant, and in so doing looking right at him. This directed his attention; he looked at the lady's features as she passed by on her way out of the room, and as soon as they had left the room he said to his two friends, "I know that lady; she is a distant relative of mine, but I cannot recollect her name. I knew her here in Paris."

In a few minutes after this the lady and gentleman both came in again, and sat down in a different place, evidently for the purpose of taking another scrutiny of the Claimant's features. After sitting a few minutes they left the room, the lady making an observation in French as they passed out. The Claimant being nearest to the lady, was asked by Mr. HOLMES and Mr. LEETE if he had caught the lady's remark. He said, "Yes, that is him; I know him by his eyes." Several months afterwards the Claimant met with his cousin Count ERNEST DE LOUSADA, and on seeing him, immediately said, "Why, it was your mamma that came in and stared at me the first night I was in Paris." The Count said, "You are quite right; my mother, the Marchioness DE LOUSADA told me the same night that she had done so, and recognised you, and that she had gone there with the ABBE ROGERSON."

The affidavit of Count ERNEST DE LOUSADA, above alluded to, is as follows:—

I, Count ERNEST DE LOUSADA, at present residing at No. 6,

Arlington-street, in the County of Middlesex, make oath and say as follows:—

1. My mother, MARIANNE, Marquise DE LOUSADA, was the daughter of Sir CHARLES WOLSELEY, and the above-named Plaintiff, Sir ROGER CHARLES DOUGHTY TICHBORNE, Baronet, is therefore my cousin.

2. During the last six months I have frequently seen and conversed with the said Plaintiff, and have been in his company with his mother, the late Dowager Lady JAMES TICHBORNE, at Howlett's Hotel during that time, and I have no hesitation whatever in deposing to the best of my belief that the said Plaintiff is without doubt my cousin, Sir ROGER CHARLES DOUGHTY TICHBORNE, Baronet, the eldest son of the late Sir JAMES FRANCIS DOUGHTY TICHBORNE, Baronet, deceased.

3. The statements herein contained are within my own knowledge.

ERNEST DE LOUSADA.

Sworn at No. 5, Walbrook, in the City of London, this 6th day of April, 1868.—Before me,

JOHN BIGGENDEN,

A London Commissioner to administer oaths in Chancery.

It should be further noted that Mr. JAMES BOWKER, a London practitioner, who had been acting as solicitor for the Dowager Lady TICHBORNE, preceded the Claimant to Paris, and with the aid of Mr. HENRY HEYSHAM, did all they could to prevent the Dowager from seeing the Claimant.

A draft affidavit was prepared for the Marchioness DE LOUSADA detailing these circumstances as taken down from the lips of her son, but there was some difficulty in getting it to Paris.

On the morning of January 11th, 1867, the Dowager Lady TICHBORNE sent her man-servant to the Hotel de Lille d'Albion, where the Claimant was staying, to enquire if her son had arrived, stating she was anxiously expecting him at her apartments, No. 27, Place de la Madeleine, and if so, he was to be conducted there. A message was sent in reply that Sir ROGER had arrived and would shortly come to see his mother. He immediately dressed for the purpose, but when ready to start became so affected, that seeing some delay inevitable, Messrs. HOLMES and LEETE accompanied the servant to Lady TICHBORNE's and explained that Sir ROGER was not very well, but would probably be able to see her in an hour's time, and it was arranged by Lady TICHBORNE that they should accompany him. Mr. HOLMES and Mr. LEETE returned to the hotel, and another attempt was made by Sir ROGER, but his emotion became so great that it was impossible for him to leave the hotel. He was unable to stand or hold up his head. Some time having elapsed, Lady TICHBORNE again sent an urgent message for him. Mr. HOLMES desired her servant to ask her to come to the hotel. Accordingly, about half-past one o'clock in the afternoon, Lady TICHBORNE came to the hotel, and was taken by LEETE and HOLMES to a bedroom where Sir ROGER was lying dressed on the bed facing the light, the room being fully lighted by two large windows.

Sir ROGER having to keep the glare from his eyes, placed a white pocket-handkerchief over his face. Lady TICHBORNE immediately went up to him, and, lifting up the pocket-handkerchief, looked intently at him for a few seconds, and then exclaimed, "Oh, my dear ROGER, is it you?" upon which he burst out crying, and Lady TICHBORNE, without waiting, said, "Oh! where is your wife and child—what is your little girl's name?" Sir ROGER then said, "Oh, mamma, I did not think you would care to see them." To which Lady TICHBORNE rejoined, "They are yours, and therefore they are mine; they are dear to me;" upon which he sobbed aloud. Lady TICHBORNE seeing what a state he was in, directed that Sir JOSEPH OLLIFFE and Dr. SHRIMPTON, two eminent and well-known physicians, should be sent for, and tried all she could to soothe him. The two doctors arrived at the hotel about two or three o'clock in the afternoon, and were informed of the circumstances of the case. Finding that Sir ROGER was labouring under great nervous excitement, they prescribed for him, and in answer to their enquiries, Lady TICHBORNE assured them that he was her son Sir ROGER TICHBORNE, that she knew him perfectly well again, and had no difficulty in recognising him, although he was much stouter than when she saw him last. She stated that his features and hair were the same, and made no hesitation in identifying the Claimant as her son, as the following affidavits of Sir JOSEPH OLLIFFE and Dr. SHRIMPTON will show:—

"H 2."

We, Sir JOSEPH FRANCIS OLLIFFE, Knight, of Number 2, Rue St. Florentin, in the City of Paris, Physician to the British Embassy in that city, and Doctor of Medicine of the Faculty of Paris, and Fellow of the Royal College of Physicians, London; and CHARLES SHRIMPTON, of No. 17, Rue d'Anjou St. Honoré, Paris, Doctor of Medicine of the Faculty of Paris, do solemnly and sincerely declare that, on Friday, the 11th day of January, 1867, we received a message to attend upon a gentleman who was lying ill at the Hotel de Lille et Albion, Rue St. Honoré, in the said City of Paris, and accordingly went to the said hotel between the hours of two and three o'clock in the afternoon of that day, and were shown into a bedroom, where upon the bed lay the gentleman whose photographic likeness is now shown to us, and marked with the letter "C" and also with our initials. There were present in the said bedroom when we entered it, the lady whose photographic likeness is now shown to us, and marked with the letter "D," and also with our initials, and who was introduced to us as the Dowager Lady TICHBORNE, and two gentlemen, who introduced themselves to us, one as Mr. JOHN HOLMES, of No. 25, Poultry, London, Solicitor, and the other as Mr. JOSEPH LEETE, of the firm of LEETE and BAILLON, of No. 36, St. Mary-at-hill, London, Merchants. The gentleman on the bed was dressed, and we were informed that he was Sir ROGER TICHBORNE, the eldest son of the lady, that he had left England nearly fourteen years ago, was supposed to have been lost at sea, and had not been heard of until recently, but was now returned to see his mother and claim his estates. Sir ROGER was labouring under great nervous excitement, and after consultation, we prescribed for him. In reply to our questions, addressed at that time, and while we were in the said bedroom, to Lady TICHBORNE, she informed us that the said gentleman on the bed was her son Sir ROGER, that she knew him perfectly well again, and had no difficulty in recognising him, although he was much stouter then when she last saw him; but his features and hair were the same; she made no hesitation, whatever, about his identity as her son Sir ROGER. And we lastly declare that on Thursday, the 17th day of January, 1867, we again saw the said Lady TICHBORNE, Sir ROGER TICHBORNE, JOHN HOLMES, and JOSEPH LEETE at the said hotel, but in a sitting-room; and and in answer to our questions put to Lady TICHBORNE, she stated that she had been with her son every day since the preceding Friday, and was perfectly satisfied that he really was her son Sir ROGER CHARLES TICHBORNE. All the parties herein named, are now present at the time of our making this declaration. And we make this solemn declaration conscientiously, believing the same to be true, and by virtue of the provisions of an Act made and passed in the session of Parliament of the 5th and 6th years of the reign of His late Majesty King WILLIAM the Fourth, intitled "An Act to repeal an Act of the present session of Parliament, intitled an Act for the more effectual abolition of oaths and affirmations taken and made in the various departments of the State, and to substitute declarations in lieu thereof, and for the more entire suppression of voluntary and extra judicial oaths and affidavits, and to make other provisions for the abolition of unnecessary oaths."

J. F. OLLIFFE, M.D.

CHARLES SHRIMPTON, M.D.

Subscribed and declared by the said JOSEPH FRANCIS OLLIFFE, and CHARLES SHRIMPTON, at Paris, in the Empire of France, this 19th day of January, 1867—Before me,

FALCONER ASKE,

Her Britannic Majesty's Consul in Paris.

From this time until the 19th day of January, 1867, Lady TICHBORNE spent the greater part of each day, and until late in the evening, at the hotel with her son the Claimant, and Messrs HOLMES and LEETE, always manifesting the greatest maternal affection and solicitude for him.

We insert here the affidavits of the Mother, and of Messrs. HOLMES and LEETE:—

I, Dame HENRIETTE FELICITÉ TICHBORNE, at present residing at No. 2, Dorset-street, Manchester-square, in the County of Middlesex, widow, make oath and say as follows:—

1. On the 1st day of August, 1827, I intermarried with the late Sir JAMES FRANCIS DOUGHTY TICHBORNE, Baronet, late of Tichborne, in the County of Southampton, then JAMES FRANCIS TICHBORNE, Esquire (now deceased). My said marriage was solemnised at St. George's, Hanover-square, and at the Roman Catholic Chapel, Chelsea, both in the County of Middlesex. There was issue of the said marriage four children and no more, namely—(1) The above-named Plaintiff, our first-born son, who was born at Paris on the 5th day of January, 1829; (2) MABELLA-LOUISA, who was born on the 8th day of July, 1832 (now deceased); (3) ALICE MARY PERPETUA, who was born on the 14th day of October, 1837 (now deceased); and (4) ALFRED JOSEPH TICHBORNE, who was born at Paris on the 4th day of September, 1839 (now deceased).

2. Upon the death of the late Sir EDWARD DOUGHTY, my husband became Sir JAMES FRANCIS TICHBORNE, 10th Baronet of Tichborne, and entered into, and thenceforth down to his death, continued in the possession, or receipt of the rents and profits of the Doughty estates, referred to in the Plaintiff's bill, filed in this cause, as tenant for life under the limitations created in his favour, as in the said bill mentioned.

3. By royal license, dated the 26th day of April, 1853, Her MAJESTY granted unto my husband licence and authority that he and his issue might thenceforth use the surname of DOUGHTY in addition to and before that of TICHBORNE, and that he and they might bear the arms of DOUGHTY quartered with those of TICHBORNE, and in exercise of the said license, my late husband thenceforth continued down to his death to use the surname of DOUGHTY in addition to and before that of TICHBORNE, and also to use the arms of DOUGHTY.

4. My husband died on the 11th day of June, 1862, leaving the Plaintiff, his eldest son and heir-at-law, and the said ALFRED JOSEPH TICHBORNE, his second son, his only issue him surviving.

5. Upon the death of my husband, the Plaintiff became the 11th Baronet of Tichborne. He attained his age of 21 years on the 5th day of January, 1850.

6. The Plaintiff's brother, the said ALFRED JOSEPH TICHBORNE, being then a bachelor, intermarried on the 17th day of April, 1861, with the above-named Defendant, the said Honourable TERESA MARY JOSEPHINE TICHBORNE, daughter of the Right

Honourable HENRY BENEDICT, 11th Lord ARUNDEL, of Wardour.

7. The said ALFRED JOSEPH TICHBORNE died on the 22nd day of February, 1866, having had issue one son, born in his lifetime, namely, EDWARD FRANCIS TICHBORNE, who died in early infancy, and no other son born in his lifetime, but his wife was *enceinte* at the time of his decease, and on the 28th day of May, 1866, she gave birth to the above-named Defendant, HENRY ALFRED JOSEPH TICHBORNE.

8. My husband and myself resided for many years before he succeeded to the baronetcy, at Paris, and the Plaintiff resided with us at Paris, where he was born, from the date of his birth until the year 1845, when he was brought over to this country, and was shortly afterwards placed at Stonyhurst College, Lancashire, where he received his English education.

9. In the month of July, 1849, the Plaintiff was appointed Cornet, and subsequently Lieutenant, in Her MAJESTY'S 6th Dragoon Guards (Carabineers). He joined that regiment in the month of October, 1849, at Dublin, where it was then quartered, and was on duty with the regiment until the month of January, 1853, except during temporary leave of absence. The Plaintiff retired from the regiment in the month of February, 1853.

10. During his vacations from college, and whilst on leave of absence from his regiment, the Plaintiff usually resided, from the year 1845, until he left this country to travel in foreign parts, as hereinafter mentioned, with his late uncle, the said Sir EDWARD DOUGHTY, at Tichborne Park, the family seat of the TICHBORNES, and was in the habit of shooting over the Tichborne estates, and hunting in that neighbourhood, and gave up much of his time to field sports and the management of horses.

11. The Plaintiff frequently expressed a strong desire to travel in foreign parts, and he left his regiment with the object of travelling for some years in distant parts, and in the first instance he determined to proceed to South America.

12. In the month of March, 1853, the Plaintiff took passage on board a ship bound for Valparaiso, and from letters which I subsequently received from him, I was informed and believe that he arrived there in due course, and from the like source of information, I knew that he was engaged in travelling in various parts of South America, and enjoyed the wild sports of the field until about the month of April, 1854.

SIR ROGER TICHBORNE, BART.

13. After the death of Sir EDWARD DOUGHTY, my husband and I took up our residence at Tichborne House, where we continued to live, down to the date of his death. During the Plaintiff's stay in South America, he sent home to Tichborne some birds, which I understood he had killed, and also some pictures, and two pairs of very large and peculiar silver-plated spurs and stirrups.

14. Some time afterwards, and in the course of the year 1854, intelligence reached Tichborne that the Plaintiff had taken passage in the month of April, 1854, at Rio de Janeiro on board a ship called the "Bella," bound for New York, and that she foundered at sea, and that the owners of the ship and the underwriters at Lloyd's treated her as having been lost, but no tidings reached us as to the fate of her crew, except that one boat belonging to the "Bella" had been met with at sea, with no one on board, and it was feared all the crew were drowned.

15. I clung to the belief that my son was saved, and I had a settled presentiment that some day I should see him again. I thought it probable he might have been picked up at sea, and I never ceased to express that belief to my husband, and various members of the family, and also to Mr. FRANCIS JOSEPH BAIGENT, of Winchester, an old friend of the family and a frequent visitor at Tichborne, and to other persons.

16. In, or about, the year 1858 a sailor, whose name is unknown to me, solicited alms at Tichborne Park whilst I was living there with my husband, and represented that he had come from Australia, and I had a conversation with the sailor, and made enquiries of him as to whether he had ever heard of the "Bella" or of any of her crew having been saved. The sailor replied that he had heard, when in Australia, of some of the crew of a ship which he thought was the "Bella" having been picked up at sea and

brought to Melbourne, but no further or more definite information as to the "Bella" or her crew could be obtained from the sailor.

17. I communicated to my husband the statement made by the sailor, but he expressed the opinion that it was not worth notice, and no further notice was taken of such statement in his lifetime, save that I frequently referred to it, and when the marriage between my younger son and the Honourable TERESA MARY JOSEPHINE TICHBORNE was in contemplation, I stated that I had still the presentiment that the Plaintiff was not lost, and my husband and I sent the Defendant VINCENT GOSFORD from Tichborne to Wardour Castle, to Lord ARUNDEL, before her marriage, to explain that whenever the Plaintiff returned, the title and estates would belong to him, and not to ALFRED.

18. After the death of my husband, and in the year 1863, I caused advertisements for the Plaintiff, in the English, French, and Spanish languages, to be inserted in the *Times* newspaper.

19. I sometime subsequently communicated with Mr. ARTHUR CUBITT, of the "Missing Friends' Office," Bridge-street, Sydney, New South Wales, advertising agent, and the said Mr. CUBITT, by my direction, caused advertisements to be inserted in various newspapers published at Melbourne and elsewhere, announcing the death of the Plaintiff's father, and giving a description of the Plaintiff, and offering a reward for his discovery.

20. Ultimately, and in or about the month of March, 1866, I received a letter from the Plaintiff, dated from Wagga-Wagga, New South Wales, in which he told me that he had made up his mind to face the sea once more, and requesting that funds might be sent out to him to defray his voyage home. I replied, urging his immediate return home, and I afterwards wrote him a letter, and remitted to him a draft for £400. I had been previously in communication with Mr. GIBBES, of Wagga-Wagga, and the said Mr. CUBITT, and had urged them to be very careful of the Plaintiff's identity, and to be sure that he was my son before they allowed him to come home; and I gave them certain information respecting the Plaintiff, upon which they could question him and test his identity. I have been informed and believe that the Plaintiff left Australia before such letter arrived there, and I have since received the £400 back.

21. I expected that the Plaintiff would arrive by the French packet from Australia to St. Nazaire, in France, and I went to Paris in November, 1866, to meet him. He did not however come by that route. I received a letter from him in the early part of January, 1867, announcing that he had arrived in England with his wife and child, and that he would be at the Hotel de Lille et d'Albion, in the Rue St. Honoré, Paris, on Thursday, the 10th day of the same month.

22. I sent my servant on the following Friday morning to the hotel he had named, to enquire if Sir ROGER TICHBORNE had arrived, and a message was returned to me to the effect that he had arrived, but was too unwell to go out. I then went to the hotel and was shown into a room, where I saw the Plaintiff. He was dressed, but lying down upon the bed, and was much overcome by emotion at seeing me. I instantly recognised him as my first-born son, Sir ROGER CHARLES TICHBORNE.

23. I expressed my happiness at seeing him, and did all I could to soothe him; but he became so ill that I sent for Sir JOSEPH OLLIFFE, physician to the British Embassy at Paris, and Dr. SHRIMPTON, of that city, to attend upon him. I waited until they arrived, and in the presence of the Plaintiff, and of the said Sir JOSEPH OLLIFFE and Dr. SHRIMPTON and Mr. HOLMES, the Plaintiff's solicitor, and Mr. JOSEPH LEETE, a friend of the Plaintiff, I declared that the Plaintiff was, as in fact he is, my first-born son.

24. From that time until the 19th day of January, 1867, I spent the greater part of each day with the Plaintiff. By that time he had sufficiently recovered to return to England, and he did return on that day, and a few weeks subsequently I rejoined him, the Plaintiff, and his wife and daughter. I resided with them at Essex Lodge, Croydon, where they then lived from the 15th day of February to the 25th day of April last, when I left Croydon because it did not agree with my health, and came to live in London. Since the last-mentioned day I have frequently visited and written to the Plaintiff, and I have made and paid him an allowance at the rate of £1,000 per annum, to support his family until he obtains possession of his estate.

25. I am as certain as I am of my own existence, and distinctly and positively swear that the Plaintiff is my first-born son, the issue of my marriage with the said Sir JAMES FRANCIS DOUGHTY TICHBORNE (deceased). His features, disposition, and voice are unmistakeable, and must, in my judgment, be recognised by all impartial and unprejudiced persons who knew him before he left England in the year 1853.

26. Since he returned, we have constantly talked over many private family matters which occurred in his youth, and up to the time of his leaving England, upon all of which he has a perfect recollection, and he has reminded me of his having sent over from South America, the birds, pictures, spurs, and stirrups hereinbefore referred to. I had forgotten the circumstance of his having sent the spurs and stirrups. After the loss of the "Bella" was reported, I ordered that all his military accoutrements should be placed within a large box, which was accordingly done, and, to the best of my knowledge and belief, such box has not been opened for some few years, until it was searched as hereinafter mentioned. I had the box sent to me at Essex Lodge, Croydon, aforesaid, and opened it, and in the box I found the spurs and stirrups which the Plaintiff immediately recognised as those he had sent home from South America. The box also contained the Plaintiff's two military cloaks, three-cornered hat, gauntlets, cap, coat, trousers, epaulettes, and other articles. The hat, cap, cloaks, and gauntlets fitted him directly they were taken out of the box, and he put them on, while the other garments seemed to have been made for a man of the same height and length of arm as the Plaintiff, but thinner in person than he now is. The evidence I have had that the Plaintiff is my first-born, is most positive and conclusive, and it is impossible I can be mistaken.

27. Whilst the Plaintiff was staying with me at Paris, the said TERESA MARY JOSEPHINE TICHBORNE wrote and sent to me a letter enquiring of me whether I was perfectly satisfied that the Plaintiff was my son. I immediately upon the receipt of such letter, wrote and sent to the said TERESA MARY JOSEPHINE TICHBORNE from Paris a letter in reply, informing her in the most positive terms that the Plaintiff was my son.

28. I believe that the last-mentioned letter was received by the said TERESA MARY JOSEPHINE TICHBORNE in the course of post, and in the month of January, 1867. Since then she has had no communication whatever with me, although previously we had been on terms of close intimacy and affection with each other, and in particular since the death of my son, ALFRED JOSEPH TICHBORNE, I have shown her many, and repeated marks of kindness and affection.

29. The several statements, hereinbefore contained, are within my own knowledge, except as hereinbefore appears, and in such last-mentioned cases are believed by me to be true, on the grounds herein appearing.

HENRIETTE F. TICHBORNE.

Sworn at the Record and Writ Clerks' Office, Chancery Lane, in the County of Middlesex, this 27th day of June, 1867—Before me,

FREDERICK BEDWELL

I, JOHN HOLMES, of No. 25, Poultry, in the City of London, Solicitor for the above named Plaintiff, make oath and say as follows:—

1. On the 3rd day of January, 1867, the Plaintiff, whom I had not previously known, called at my office and presented me with the card of my clients, Messrs. LEETE and BAILLON, of St. Mary-at-Hill, in this city, merchants, and told me that he knew Mr. LEETE, of that firm, who had strongly advised him to place his affairs in my hands. Mr. LEETE is the continental agent for Messrs. SAMUEL ALLSOPP and SONS, of Burton-upon-Trent, and I am the London solicitor of that firm. The Plaintiff informed me that he was Sir ROGER CHARLES TICHBORNE, the eldest son of the late Sir JAMES FRANCIS TICHBORNE, deceased, and was entitled to large estates, and gave me other particulars. He also informed me that he had been away from England, for some years, and did not know what had been done with his property, and that he wished me to look after his rights. He also instructed me to put myself in communication with the above-named Defendant, VINCENT GOSFORD, who, he said, was formerly agent for his uncle, the late Sir EDWARD DOUGHTY, deceased, and knew him and his estates well, and that I was to act with Mr. GOSFORD. The Plaintiff also told me that he expected a letter from his mother, from Paris, and that he should immediately go to see her. Much conversation took place between us, and he entered into full particulars of his history, and the Plaintiff having fully satisfied me as to his identity, I accepted his retainer.

2. On Saturday, the 5th day of January, 1867, the Plaintiff called upon me again and showed me a letter, which he informed me, as I believed the fact was, he had received from his mother, the Dowager Lady JAMES TICHBORNE, and at his request I advanced him money to defray the expenses of his journey to see her, and it was his intention, as I well knew from his statements to me, to leave for Paris immediately. He was then staying at the Clarendon Hotel, Gravesend. On the Monday following, however, I received a letter from the Plaintiff from Gravesend, in which he informed me, as I believe the facts were, that upon returning to his hotel at Gravesend, after his interview with me on the previous Saturday, he found there Mr. PLOWDEN, Mr. CULLINGTON, and Mr. GOSFORD, in the Plaintiff's Bill of Complaint filed in this cause respectively named, and that the landlord of the hotel had informed him that they had made statements which induced him, the landlord, to require immediate payment of his bill, and that he, the Plaintiff, was consequently left without any means whatever to take him to Paris. I felt great sympathy for his position, and Mr. LEETE and I went to Gravesend that evening, and we arranged ourselves to accompany the Plaintiff to Paris, in order that no further obstacles should be thrown in the way of his seeing his mother, which he was very anxious to do.

3. On the following day, Tuesday, the 8th day of January, 1867, I again went to the Clarendon Hotel, Gravesend, and saw the Plaintiff. As we were leaving the hotel a message was brought to me that the Defendant VINCENT GOSFORD wished to see the Plaintiff, and the Plaintiff and myself immediately saw the said VINCENT GOSFORD in a private room, and remained together for nearly two hours, and the said VINCENT GOSFORD subsequently, and on the same day accompanied the Plaintiff and myself in a first-class railway carriage to London, the journey occupying

about two hours, and no other person entered the carriage. During those interviews the Plaintiff and the said VINCENT GOSFORD, in my presence and hearing, asked each other various questions respecting the TICHBORNE family and the neighbourhood of Tichborne. The impression left upon my mind was, that they were talking of matters familiar to them both, and that they well knew each other.

4. Mr. LEETE and I accompanied the Plaintiff to Paris on the 10th day of January, 1867, and we were both present at an interview which took place between the Plaintiff and his mother, Lady JAMES TICHBORNE, on the following day. The said Lady JAMES TICHBORNE instantly recognised the Plaintiff, in the presence of Mr. LEETE and myself, as her first-born son. We remained in Paris for ten days, and before leaving that city I prepared and caused to be taken and declared at the British Embassy, the declarations of Lady TICHBORNE, Sir JOSEPH OLLIFFE, Dr. SHRIMPTON, JOSEPH LEETE, and myself, now produced, and marked respectively, "H 1," "H 2," and "H 3." The statements contained in such declarations are, as I verily believe, true in all respects, and the facts therein declared to, are within my knowledge, so far as they occurred in my presence. During our stay in Paris, Monsieur CHATILLON, who I believe was the Plaintiff's tutor when he was a boy, called and saw the Plaintiff, and in my presence, and in that of Mr. LEETE and Lady TICHBORNE, the said Monsieur CHATILLON stated that the Plaintiff in his boyhood had met with an accident which caused a wound on the back of his head. The said Mr. LEETE and myself examined the Plaintiff's head, and on the back of it we found a scar.

5. On the 9th day of March, 1867, the said VINCENT GOSFORD called at my offices and informed me that Mr. and Mrs. RADCLIFFE and Mrs. TOWNLEY (the two latter being, as I have been informed, and believe, cousins of the Plaintiff) had had an interview with the Plaintiff on the previous day at his then residence at Croydon, and that Mrs. RADCLIFFE recognised the Plaintiff as her cousin by his eyes, eyebrows, and the shape of his forehead, and that certainly none of the party could declare that it was not Sir ROGER.

6. The exhibits now produced to me, and marked respectively "H 4" and "H 5" and "H 6," are true copies of letters which have been written and sent by me to Mr. F. BOWKER, Messrs. DOBINSON and GEARE, and Messrs. SLAUGHTER and CULLINGTON, in the said Bill respectively named, and the documents now produced and marked "H 7," "H 8," "H 9," "H 10," "H 11," "H 12," "H 13," "H 14," "H 15," "H 16," "H 17," and "H 18," are original letters received by me from the same parties.

7. Speaking for myself positively, and to the best of my information and belief as to the acts of other persons, I say that the several statements contained in my said letters are true in all respects.

8. The matters hereinbefore referred to, are within my own knowledge, save as hereinbefore appears.

JOHN HOLMES.

Sworn at the Record and Writ Clerks' Office, Chancery Lane, in the County of Middlesex, this 3rd day of July, 1867—Before me, FREDK. BEDWELL.

DECLARATIONS REFERRED TO IN AFFIDAVIT OF JOHN HOLMES.

"H. 1."

I, HENRIETTE FELICITÉ TICHBORNE of No. 27, Place de la Madeleine in the City of Paris, and also of No. 31, Blandford Street, Portman Square, London, widow of the late Sir JAMES FRANCIS DOUGHTY TICHBORNE, Baronet, of Tichborne Hall, in the County of Hants, do solemnly and sincerely declare that I was married to my said husband at St. George's, Hanover Square, and at the Catholic chapel, Chelsea, I believe in the year 1827, and that the eldest son of my said marriage was ROGER CHARLES, who is named in the extracts now shown to me and marked respectively with the letters "A" and "B," and that the photographic likeness now shown to me and marked with the letter "C" and with my initials is a photographic likeness of my said son ROGER CHARLES, and of the same person as the "ROGER CHARLES" mentioned in the said extracts, and whom I saw at the Hotel de Lille et d'Albion as hereinafter mentioned, and who is now present at the time of my making this declaration. The photographic likeness now shown to me and marked with the letter "D" and with my initials is a photographic likeness of myself. My said son is now Sir ROGER CHARLES DOUGHTY TICHBORNE and takes the name of DOUGHTY by virtue of Royal Letters Patent. He left England for South America in the early part of the year 1853. I believe he wrote me from Rio de Janeiro about April, 1854, but I have not his letter here, in Paris. I heard nothing of him for several years afterwards, and he was commonly reported to have been lost at sea, but I did not believe it, and have used every means in my power, by advertising and making enquiries, to discover his whereabouts. I have frequently informed the wife of his late brother ALFRED and members of her family that I believed Sir ROGER was not dead and would certainly return. My said husband and myself sent Mr. GOSFORD from Tichborne to Wardour Castle to Lord ARUNDEL, the father of my late son ALFRED's wife, before her marriage, to explain that whenever Sir ROGER returned, the title and estates would belong to him and not to ALFRED. In or about March last I received a letter from my said son Sir ROGER, dated from Wagga-Wagga in Australia, asking me to send him money for the purpose of bringing him home. I recognised his handwriting and remitted £400 to Australian bankers with that object, but he had embarked on his voyage before it arrived there, and the money has since been returned to England. I expected he would arrive by the French packet from Aspinwal to St. Nazaire, in France, and I went to Paris last November to meet him. He, however, did not come by that route. I received a letter from him last week, stating that he would be at the hotel de Lille, et d'Albion, Rue St. Honoré, Paris, on Thursday, the 10th day of January, 1867. On the next day, Friday, after having sent my servant to inquire if Sir Roger had arrived, and being informed that he had, but was too unwell to go out, I went to the said hotel, and was there shown into a bedroom, where upon the bed lay my said son, Sir ROGER. He was dressed, but overcome by emotion. I knew him again immediately, although he had grown much stouter, but his look, features, and hair were, and are the same, as when I last saw him, making allowance for the difference of his age. I expressed my happiness at seeing him, and I did all I could to soothe him, but as he became worse, Sir JOSEPH OLLIFFE and Doctor SHRIMPTON were sent for, and when they came I told them, in reply to their questions put to me, that he was indeed my son Sir ROGER, and I had no difficulty in recognising him. From that time until this 19th day of January, 1867, I have spent the greater part of each day and dined with my said son, Sir ROGER, in company with Mr. JOHN HOLMES and Mr. JOSEPH LEETE, and I have no hesitation, or doubt, respecting his identity as my said son. And I make this solemn declaration conscientiously believing the same to be true, and by virtue of the provisions of an Act, made and passed, in the session of Parliament of the fifth and sixth years of the reign of His late Majesty King William the Fourth, intituled "An Act to repeal an Act of the present session of Parliament, intituled, An Act for the more effectual abolition of Oaths and Affirmations taken and made in various departments of the State, and to substitute Declarations in lieu thereof, and for the more entire suppression of voluntary and extra-judicial Oaths and Affidavits, and to make other provisions for the abolition of unnecessary Oaths."

HENRIETTE FELICITÉ TICHBORNE.

Subscribed and declared at Paris, in the Empire of France, this 19th day of January, 1867—Before me,

FALCONER ASKE,

Her Britannic Majesty's Consul at Paris.

"H. 3."

We, JOHN HOLMES, of No. 25, Poultry, in the City of London, Solicitor, and JOSEPH LEETE, of the firm of LEETE and BAILLON, of No. 36, St. Mary-at-Hill, in the City of London, Merchants, do solemnly, and sincerely declare, that on Thursday, the 10th day of January, 1867, we accompanied the gentleman whose photographic likeness is now shown to us and marked with the letter "C," and also with our initials, from London to Paris, in which latter city we arrived the same evening and occupied apartments in the Hotel de Lille et d'Albion, Rue St. Honore. On the following morning we were waited upon by a manservant, who said that his mistress, Lady TICHBORNE, wished to know if her son Sir ROGER had arrived, as she was anxiously expecting him at her apartments, No. 27, Place de la Madeleine, whither Sir ROGER and ourselves were to be conducted. The said gentleman was up and dressed for the purpose of going there; but his emotion became so great that it was impossible for him to leave the hotel, and therefore we, in company with the said servant, proceeded to No. 27, Place de la Madeleine, and there saw the lady whose photographic likeness is now shown to us and marked with the letter "D," and also with our initials, who informed us, that she was the Dowager Lady TICHBORNE, and was most anxiously waiting to see her son, Sir ROGER. We explained that the said gentleman was not well, but would probably be able to see her in an hour; and it was arranged that we should take him to her. We returned to the hotel and found the said gentleman much worse and lying on the bed in his room, he was unable to stand, or hold up his head. Her ladyship having sent again an urgent message for him, we desired her servant to ask her to go to the said hotel, as the said gentleman was so ill. Accordingly, about half-past one o'clock in the afternoon of Friday, the 11th day of January, 1867, the said Dowager Lady TICHBORNE arrived at the said Hotel de Lille et d'Albion, and entered with us into the bedroom where the said gentleman lay, and immediately said to him "Oh, my dear ROGER! I am so happy to see you. Where is your wife and little girl? Did you bring them with you?" to which he replied in sobs, "Oh, my dear mamma! I did not know you would receive them." We asked her ladyship if she knew the said gentleman? and she answered "Oh, yes! It is my son ROGER. I know him by his look, features, and his hair; no one could mistake them who knew him before he went away; but he is much stouter," or words to that effect. She made no difficulty, whatever, in recognising him as her son. Sir ROGER complained of pain in his head, and at her ladyship's request we sent for English doctors, and between two and three o'clock of the same day, Sir JOSEPH OLLIFFE, Physician to the British Embassy in Paris, and Doctor SHRIMPTON arrived at the said hotel and saw the said Lady TICHBORNE, and Sir ROGER, with ourselves in the said bedroom, and prescribed for him. In answer to their questions then addressed by them to her, Lady TICHBORNE stated that the said gentleman on the bed was her son Sir ROGER, and she had no difficulty in recognising him again.

From that time until this 19th day of January, 1867, her ladyship has spent the greater part of each day, and until late in the evening, at the said Hotel de Lille et d'Albion, in company with her said son Sir ROGER, and ourselves, and has manifested the greatest maternal solicitude and affection for him, and has frequently told us of traits in his character, and pointed out peculiarities of his manner, which she said were the same as those he had before he left England; and in reply to our repeated questions she has continually assured us that the said gentleman was her son Sir ROGER. We were both present with SIR ROGER at the studio of PAUL BERTHIER, No. 15, Quai Malaquais, Paris, when the said Sir ROGER sat for the said photographic likeness marked "C," and I, the said JOSEPH LEETE, for myself alone, do solemnly and sincerely declare that on Saturday last I obtained from the parish church of the Madeleine, in the said city of Paris, the extract from the Register of the Acts of Baptism kept there, now shown to me and marked with the letter "A," and that I did on the following Wednesday obtain from the Prefecture of the Department of the Seine, the extract from the Register of the Acts of Birth kept there, now shown to me and marked with the letter "B." And lastly, that I was present on Thursday last with Lady TICHBORNE at the said PAUL BERTHIER'S studio when she sat for the photographic likeness marked "D." And we make this solemn declaration conscientiously believing the same to be true, and by virtue of the provisions of an Act made and passed in the Session of Parliament of the fifth and sixth years of the reign of His late Majesty King WILLIAM the Fourth, intituled "An Act to repeal an Act of the present Session of Parliament, intituled, An Act for the effectual abolition of Oaths and Affirmations taken and made in various departments of the State, and to substitute Declarations in lieu thereof, and for the more entire suppression of voluntary and extra-judicial Oaths and Affidavits, and to make other provisions for the abolition of unnecessary Oaths.'

JOHN HOLMES,
J. LEETE.

Subscribed and declared by the said JOHN HOLMES' and JOSEPH LEETE, at Paris, in the Empire of France this 19th day of January, 1867—Before me,

FALCONER ASKE,
Her Britannic Majesty's Consul at Paris.

During all this time their movements were watched by Mr. JAMES BOWKER, HENRY HEYSHAM, and other emissaries.

Soon after the arrival of the Claimant in Paris, he was called upon by M. CHATILLON. Lady TICHBORNE did not wish to give him an interview, because she had been informed by the Abbé SALIS that he (CHATILLON) did not intend to acknowledge Sir ROGER, even if he did recognise him. However, an interview was brought about.

During Sir ROGER'S stay in Paris, he and his mother, Lady TICHBORNE, both had their portraits taken in the studio of PAUL BERTHIER, photographer. Copies of these photographs were preserved by Mr. HOLMES, attested by the signatures of the Dowager Lady TICHBORNE, Sir JOSEPH OLLIFFE, and Dr. SHRIMPTON, and the officials at the British Embassy, and they were attached as exhibits to the Declaration made by the Dowager Lady TICHBORNE, Sir JOSEPH OLLIFFE, and Dr. SHRIMPTON.

During Sir ROGER'S stay in Paris, Lady TICHBORNE received a letter from the Honourable Mrs. TERESA TICHBORNE (the widow of the late Mr. ALFRED TICHBORNE). This letter, as well as one dated December 15th, 1866, is material.

We insert these letters here:—

My dear Mamma,—As you have always been so kind to me in my troubles, I feel sure you will not take it amiss my writing to you in my present difficulty, as it seems there is a possibility of my fortune being stopped until ROGER has arrived.

Therefore, you will oblige me very much if you will inform me when you expect him to arrive, and if you still feel quite certain of his joining you in France,—Excuse haste, dear Mamma. Your affectionate daughter, TERESA TICHBORNE.

Hyde House, Brimpton, Reading,
December 15, 1866.

Extract from letter written by the same, dated January 19, and enclosed in envelope bearing the post-mark of January 19, 1867:—

My dear Mamma,—As I have not heard from you lately, I hope you are not ill with this cold weather. I hear so many reports, and so different, that I am going to ask you to let me have a line to say whether you recognised ROGER. As soon as you can, please, as I feel so anxious to know.—I remain, my dear Mamma, your affectionate daughter, TERESA TICHBORNE.

Letter from the Dowager Lady TICHBORNE to her daughter-in-law at Paris, January 21, 1867:—

My dearest TERESA,—Many thanks for your kind letter, which I received yesterday. I have not written to you lately because my time was much taken up with attending on my dear son, ROGER. I have fully recognised him—as it is really him—and I cannot conceive those who knew him very well and will not recognise him.

I told ROGER yesterday I was in hopes that one day I might hold my dearest little grandson (HENRY ALFRED) in one hand, and my dear little grand-daughter (AGNES) in the other.

He said he hoped so.

I would go back to London immediately, only I am not very well.—Your affectionate and devoted Mother,

H. F. TICHBORNE.

It is the fact that these expressions about holding a grandchild in each hand caused great offence to Mrs. TERESA TICHBORNE and the family, and from that moment they refused to have any more communication with her.

To show the vigilance of the family, it is known and has been proved, that the news that Lady TICHBORNE had recognised and acknowledged the Claimant was known in London by the 15th of January, before her letter to Mrs. TERESA TICHBORNE had been written, and it is presumed that it was in consequence of her desiring to get a proof from the Dowager that the letter of the 19th January was written.

It appears that during the Claimant's stay in Paris the Dowager had expressed a wish to see BOGLE, so Mr. HOLMES telegraphed for him, and although suffering greatly from rheumatism, he undertook the journey. Soon after his arrival he was shown into a room where there were six or seven ladies, several of whom were dressed in black.

He was asked if he knew any of them, when he immediately went up to the Dowager Lady TICHBORNE, and asked her how she did.

BOGLE was so ill, that he was unable to leave his room during his stay in Paris.

On the 20th January, 1867, the Claimant, with Mr. HOLMES, Mr. LEETE, and BOGLE, left Paris for England, and arrived in London in the evening of the following day.

On the 22nd January, 1867, Mr. HOLMES wrote a letter to the *Times*, and by that letter all the family had a public notification of the fact that the Claimant had been recognised by his mother, and that proceedings would be taken to reinstate him in his title, and property.

Mr. HOLMES, by letter dated 22nd January, 1867, informed Messrs. DOBINSON and GEARE, the Defendants' solicitors, that the Claimant had been identified by the Dowager Lady TICHBORNE, his mother, they having stated in a former letter (7th January) "that on his identity being established, his family would doubtless receive him with open arms." The intimation of his mother's recognition (and who was, or could be more qualified to identify him in the first instance than his own mother?) received the following reply:—

57, Lincoln's Inn Fields: 25th January, 1867.

SIR,—Our instructions are to deny emphatically that your client is the person he represents himself to be, and to leave him to adopt such measures as he thinks proper.—Yours obediently.,

DOBINSON and GEARE.

JOHN HOLMES, Esq., solicitor, 25, Poultry.

Mr. HOLMES, acting upon the instructions of the Dowager Lady TICHBORNE, who intended to come over to England to reside with her son, procured a house for the Claimant and family at Croydon, called Essex Lodge, and this is alluded to fully, in the Claimant's statement.

Mr. HOLMES not knowing anyone at Alresford, sent for Mr. ROUS, the landlord of the "Swan," who had formerly been clerk to Mr. HOPKINS, the TICHBORNE family solicitor, and whom he knew had seen the Claimant.

Mr. ROUS suggested that Mr. HOPKINS should be communicated with, and accordingly, on the 31st January, Mr. ROUS saw Mr. HOPKINS, who said that if the Plaintiff wrote him a letter such as he would receive from the Mr. ROGER TICHBORNE he had known, asking for an interview, or mentioning some circumstances only known to themselves, or anything of a personal nature so as to identify him, he would accede to his wish. Mr. ROUS intimated this by letter to Mr. HOLMES, and the Claimant wrote to Mr. HOPKINS a letter, of which the following is a copy:—

1st February, 1867. Essex Lodge, Thornton Heath,
Croydon.

My Dear Friend, —You will no doubt think it strange that i did not call on you when at Alresford. I should have done so with pleasure, had i not been under a promise to Mamma not to converse with anybody i know, until i had seen her. I now know her reasons, and am very glad i kept my promise. I suppose you have heard how i have been served by GOSFORD and others since I have been away. I should not have gone to Alresford, only i thought nobody would know me, has i had grown so stout, so i thought i would have a quite look round. I know you and Dr. LIPSCOMBE are old friends, so praps you will kindly tell him the reason I did not call on him likewise. If Mamma does not send for me to meet her, most likely i will come down with Mr. HOLMES to-morrow. Hoping, my dear HOPKINS, the old friendship that once existed between us may again be renewed, and that i may have the pleasure of again receiving your advice how to act.

I suppose you remember having heard of a Miss BELLEW in Ireland, runnour only. Hoping to have the pleasure of meeting you before long, I remain, Yours Faithfully,

R. C. D. TICHBORNE, B.

E. HOPKINS, Esq., Alresford, Hants.

This letter Mr. HOPKINS received on the 2nd of February, and on the same day Mr. HOLMES arrived at Alresford, and had an interview with Mr. HOPKINS.

It appears that on the 31st of January Mr. HOPKINS, in

anticipation of this visit, wrote to Mr. FRANCIS JOSEPH BAIGENT, of Winchester, and asked him to come to Alresford, as he wished to consult him (Mr. BAIGENT) on the subject. Mr. BAIGENT, in consequence of this, went to Alresford on the 1st February, and spent several hours in communication with Mr. HOPKINS as to arrangements to be made of what to do in the event of the Claimant making an application for an interview.

On Mr. HOLMES' arrival, Mr. HOPKINS telegraphed to Winchester for Mr. BAIGENT, who came by the next train.

Mr. HOPKINS went to the railway station and met Mr. BAIGENT, and told him that Mr. HOLMES was at his house, and showed him a letter which the Claimant had sent him, containing an allusion to a Miss BELLEW, by which he (Mr. HOPKINS) said he understood well what was meant. Mr. HOPKINS informed Mr. BAIGENT that the Claimant was due by the next train, and it was then settled that Mr. HOPKINS should invite the Claimant to dine with him in order to have an opportunity of finding out if he was the person he professed to be.

Mr. HOPKINS then returned home in company with Mr. BAIGENT, and introduced him to Mr. HOLMES.

After some conversation, and showing him the photographic likenesses of the Claimant which had been taken in Paris, Mr. HOPKINS handed to Mr. HOLMES a note from the Claimant, inviting him to dine that evening.

Mr. BAIGENT then left with Mr. HOLMES for the Swan Hotel, where the Claimant had arrived.

Mr. HOLMES had an interview with him, delivered Mr. HOPKINS' note, and soon afterwards Mr. BAIGENT was brought into the room to see him. Mr. BAIGENT had not seen him since the year 1853 (except on the 31st December, when he and Mr. HOPKINS saw him, but not near enough to see his features on that occasion).

After interchanging a few words, Mr. HOLMES left the room, leaving the Claimant and Mr. BAIGENT together. After conversing some little time, the Claimant, having dressed for dinner at six o'clock, accompanied Mr. BAIGENT to Mr. HOPKINS' house, where they dined.

Mr. HOLMES had previously arranged to call for the Claimant about nine o'clock. He left soon after, in his company, Mr. HOPKINS having during the interview fully satisfied himself and convinced beyond a doubt of the identity of the Claimant with Sir ROGER TICHBORNE, his former client.

We here insert the Affidavit made by Mr. BAIGENT:—

I, FRANCIS JOSEPH BAIGENT, of Winchester, in the County of Hants, Associate of the British Archæological Association, make oath and say as follows:—

1. I was born at Winchester in the year 1830, and have resided there all my life.

2. My acquaintance with the TICHBORNE family commenced in my earliest infancy. No name or family has been so associated with my earliest recollections, and in that family, its members, and its history, past and present, I have ever continued to take the greatest interest.

3. My godmother was the Right Honourable Lady FRANCIS CATHERINE ARUNDEL, wife of the late Lord ARUNDEL of Wardour, and second daughter of the late Sir HENRY JOSEPH TICHBORNE, eighth baronet of Tichborne; and I have still in my possession her letter expressing her desire that I should be christened FRANCIS JOSEPH.

4. In the year 1845 I turned my attention to antiquarian pursuits of an ecclesiological and genealogical character, and in 1846 I was elected an Associate of the British Archæological Association, and for many years past I was a member of the Council or governing body of that association. Since 1847 I have been a frequent contributor to the *Archæological Journal*, and have contributed, from time to time, papers relating to the TICHBORNE family. The undermentioned, among other papers in that journal, are from my pen, namely:—Vol. V. (1849) "A notice of the Font in Tichborne Church, and an account of a curious Coffin Lid found in the same Church." Vol. VII. (1851) "Remarks on the WANDESFORDS and their alliance with the family of TICHBORNE;" also a paper on "The Family of LYMERSTON and its Heiress, the Foundress of the TICHBORNE Dole," which was read at the Congress of the Association held at Newport, in the Isle of Wight, in August, 1855, and was published in the *Archæological Journal* in December, 1855 (Vol. XI.), with several illustrations, including a *fac-simile* of a charter of Sir ROGER DE TICHBORNE, executed about the year of our Lord 1160, and several shields of the armorial bearings and early seals of the TICHBORNES. Other articles on the TICHBORNE family also appear in the *Archæological Journal* of the following year (Vol. XII.), and in the *Herald* and *Genealogist* of last year, which are from my pen. From the year 1847 to the present time I have paid very great attention to the history of the TICHBORNE family, and have accumulated voluminous collections for materials towards compiling a history of the family. I have searched for this purpose the several archives of the bishopric of Winchester, of the cathedral and college, and have investigated the archiepiscopal records at Lambeth Palace, the old wills at Doctors' Commons, and very many documents in the public Record Office, and manuscripts in the British Museum. My researches have been well known to the TICHBORNE family, and I have often been introduced to the visitors at Tichborne House as one who knew more of the family than even the members of the family themselves, and I have generally had to reply to queries sent to the family by the author of "Burke's Peerage" and "Baronetages," and others engaged in the publication of similar works.

5. I knew the late Sir HENRY JOSEPH TICHBORNE, his wife, and daughters. Sir HENRY JOSEPH died on the 3rd day of June, 1845, from the effects of an accident, having broken his collar-bone by a fall from his horse, and been dragged along with his foot entangled in the stirrup. I well recollect the spot where the accident occurred.

6. On Sir HENRY JOSEPH TICHBORNE'S death, his widow, who died at Woodstock in the year 1853, remained at Tichborne House till 1846, and in or about the summer of that year the late Sir EDWARD DOUGHTY (now deceased) took up his residence at Tichborne House. I well remember that, upon the occasion of Sir EDWARD DOUGHTY taking possession, the domestic chapel attached to the house and its pictures were cleaned up, and I remember being at Tichborne on the reopening of the chapel.

7. To the best of my recollection and belief, the first time I saw the above-named Plaintiff, then Master ROGER CHARLES TICHBORNE, the eldest son of the late Sir JAMES FRANCIS DOUGHTY TICHBORNE and Dame HENRIETTE FELICITÉ his wife, was at Tichborne in the lifetime of his uncle, the said Sir HENRY JOSEPH TICHBORNE, when the Plaintiff was about fourteen years of age.

8. In 1845, and I think in the month of July, the Plaintiff went to Stonyhurst College, Lancashire, and generally spent some portion of his Christmas and Midsummer vacations at Tichborne, and on those occasions I often saw and conversed with him both at Winchester and Tichborne.

9. The said Sir EDWARD DOUGHTY resided at Tichborne from the year 1846 until his death, which occurred on the 5th day of March, 1853, with the exception of an occasional temporary visit at Upton House, near Poole, Dorsetshire, and in Scotland. During the period Sir EDWARD DOUGHTY resided at Tichborne House, I was there frequently. I well recollect that I was at Tichborne House in the month of October, 1848, and that I was present at the funeral of the late ROGER ROBERT TICHBORNE (deceased) in the month of November, 1849, and that the Plaintiff's father was also present on that occasion. I was also at Tichborne House in the month of January, 1850, when the Plaintiff became of age, and I believe his father was there also; and I was also at Tichborne House, for several days at a time, at various other periods, and I very frequently saw and conversed with the Plaintiff, and participated in some of his amusements. On one occasion in particular, I remember his coming to my own room to have explained to him, how it was that the BLOUNTS, of Mapel, Durham, became connected with the TICHBORNE family, and this occupied some considerable time. On various occasions I rode into Winchester in his company in his uncle's carriage, and have smoked with him; and I well recollect being with the Plaintiff in February, 1853, before he left England. Being the heir to the family estates, I took especial interest in the Plaintiff, and have always entertained the kindest of feelings towards him, and did anything I could for him.

10. I was present at the funeral of the said Sir EDWARD DOUGHTY in the month of March, 1853, on which occasion I again met the late Sir JAMES FRANCIS TICHBORNE, who was delighted to see me, and said he hoped I would often come to Tichborne. I was at Tichborne House during the last few weeks. Dame KATHERINE DOUGHTY, the widow of the said Sir EDWARD DOUGHTY, stayed there. I saw the monument to her husband's memory fixed in the family chantry, and at her request, arranged with the incumbent for its admission into the church. I accompanied her to the church on her going to see it. Also at her particular request, I stayed in the house until she actually left it, which she did on or about the month of May, 1853. I also remember that one of the last requests she then made to me was, that I should take an interest in the Plaintiff's younger and only brother ALFRED JOSEPH TICHBORNE, now deceased, and that I should try to get him to take an interest in the family history, and in all such pursuits.

11. Shortly after Dame KATHERINE DOUGHTY left Tichborne, the said Sir JAMES FRANCIS DOUGHTY TICHBORNE took up his residence at Tichborne House, he called upon me, and again said how happy he should be to see me at any time at Tichborne, and about the end of July, 1853, I paid him a visit at Tichborne House, and was introduced to his wife Dame HENRIETTE FELICITÉ TICHBORNE, commonly called the Dowager Lady JAMES TICHBORNE, the Plaintiff's mother. I saw Sir JAMES and his lady on several occasions during that year, and was a frequent guest at their house.

12. For ten days or a fortnight in the month of June or July, in the year 1854, I was staying at Tichborne House, and I was there when the news arrived of the loss of the "Bella." The said Sir JAMES FRANCIS DOUGHTY TICHBORNE, and Dame HENRIETTE FELICITÉ his wife, always treated me in the kindest manner. I was very fond of the said ALFRED JOSEPH DOUGHTY TICHBORNE, and previous to his marriage was, as I believe, his greatest confidant.

13. I was a very frequent visitor at Tichborne House during the said Sir JAMES FRANCIS DOUGHTY TICHBORNE'S lifetime, and stayed there many days at a time. I was staying there in August, 1856, and was there on the 24th day of that month, when the news arrived of the death of Sir JAMES FRANCIS TICHBORNE'S Nephew, BERTRAM, the seventeenth Earl of Shrewsbury.

I was also at Tichborne on the 4th December, and remained until the 13th day of the same month. In the year 1857, I was there on the 27th day of July, and remained there until the 18th day of August, and on the 17th day of September, and remained until the 26th, and on the 29th of November, and remained until the 5th of December. In 1858, I was there on the 2nd, and remained until the 10th day of February, and on the 28th day of June, and remained until the 17th July. I give these dates to show the frequency and length of my visits at Tichborne House; but they are by no means the only times I was there during those years, and in other years I was there almost as often.

14. I received many letters from the Plaintiff's brother ALFRED JOSEPH DOUGHTY TICHBORNE (some of which I have kept); he usually addressed me as "My dear FRANCIS," two of such letters now are produced and marked B 1 *a*, and B 1 *b*.

15. I also received many letters from the said Sir JAMES FRANCIS DOUGHTY TICHBORNE (some of which I have kept), in which he addressed me as "My dear FRANCIS BAIGENT." One of such letters is now produced and marked B 2.

16. My intercourse with the said Sir JAMES FRANCIS DOUGHTY TICHBORNE, and Dame HENRIETTE FELICITÉ his wife, and with the said ALFRED JOSEPH DOUGHTY TICHBORNE was of a very intimate nature, and I was wont to hold long conversations with Dame HENRIETTE FELICITÉ TICHBORNE, who was always impressed with the idea that her son ROGER CHARLES TICHBORNE, the Plaintiff, had been picked up by some vessel, and that he was still alive, and very frequently spoke to me about it, and even asked me more than once if I would consent to go to Australia and make enquiries and try to find him; so firmly was the impression fixed in her mind that she frequently remarked to me, "You will see that he will come home some day. I know my poor dear ROGER is alive."

17. The said ALFRED JOSEPH DOUGHTY TICHBORNE often told me that he could not dismiss from his mind that his brother would some day return. I remember in particular on one occasion in in the year 1858, when he was unwell and lying in bed, I was talking to him, he said "I cannot help feeling that my brother is still alive and may come back, and then I should be obliged to go into the army." In the year 1862, when he was in trouble about his bankruptcy, he said to me "Oh, how I wish ROGER would come back." I was on friendly terms with the said ALFRED JOSEPH DOUGHTY TICHBORNE up to the time of his death, and was present at his funeral at Tichborne, on the 2nd March, 1866.

18. I well recollect in or about the year 1858, whilst I was on a visit at Tichborne House, Dame HENRIETTE FELICITÉ TICHBORNE requested me to see a sailor who had called at the house, and I accordingly saw and had a conversation with the sailor, who told me that he had then recently come from Australia, and that he heard when in Australia, of some of the crew of a ship which he thought was called the "Bella," having been picked up at sea and brought to Melbourne. I enquired very particularly of the sailor for further particulars; but was unable to learn anything more from him touching the "Bella," or the crew of that ship. The probability of the Plaintiff's return has been most frequently talked about at Tichborne House, and elsewhere, since 1854, in my presence, and since the death of his father, the late Sir JAMES FRANCIS DOUGHTY TICHBORNE, which occurred on the 11th day of June, 1862, in particular reports have been continually abroad as to the Plaintiff being still alive.

19. On or about the 21st day of March, 1866, the said Dame KATHERINE DOUGHTY wrote and sent to me a letter, in which she stated "I heard the Dowager (meaning Dame HENRIETTE FELICITÉ TICHBORNE) was consulting her lawyer whether to forward money for some communication made from Australia. What the lawyer thinks I do not know; the person who named it, thinks it was only a person trying to get money from her." Such letter is now produced marked B 4.

20. On or about the 24th day of September, 1866, I received a letter from Mr. SCOTT MURRAY, of Danesfield, county Bucks, in which he stated as follows:—"You will now have to add a new and most astounding chapter to your Tichborniana, if, as I have heard to-day, on what seems reliable authority, Sir ROGER TICHBORNE is found, and is likely to appear shortly in England with a wife and child. How fortunate that the child 'Sir HENRY ALFRED JOSEPH' is too young to feel the loss of position and estate." The last mentioned letter is now produced and marked B 4.

21. Other reports of the like nature reached me, and I wrote to the Plaintiff's aunt, Dame KATHERINE DOUGHTY, on the subject, and on or about the 19th day of October, 1866, I received a letter from her in reply, in which she states as follows:—"The mass of evidence I have now seen from different persons writing from Australia, together with what the Dowager Lady TICHBORNE admits, leaves no doubt this person must be ROGER; but the circumstances altogether make it a painful event in the family." Such letter is now produced and marked B 5.

22. About the same time I heard that ANDREW BOGLE, an old servant of the family, had met the Plaintiff in Australia and recognised him as the eldest son of the late Sir JAMES FRANCIS DOUGHTY TICHBORNE, and had written to the said Dame KATHERINE DOUGHTY a letter informing her of the fact, and that the Plaintiff, his wife and child, were about to leave for England, and that BOGLE would accompany them.

23. On the 25th day of October, 1866, Mr. HOPKINS, of Alresford, who was, I well knew, formerly the solicitor of the said Sir JAMES FRANCIS DOUGHTY TICHBORNE, and also the solicitor of the Plaintiff, before he left England, called upon me to discuss the probabilities of the Plaintiff's return, and what we ought to do in the matter, and on the 27th day of the same month, Mr. HOPKINS came to see me again, and we held a long discussion, and looked upon the question from every point of view. We both felt that if the Claimant really was Sir ROGER he ought to be in good hands and well advised, and I on the last-mentioned day wrote to my brother WILLIAM at Southampton, asking him to board the Panama mail steamer the "Shannon" on her arrival (it having been reported that the Plaintiff was expected by that vessel), and to see if Sir ROGER and party were on board.

24. On the same evening (October 27th) I saw in the *Hampshire Chronicle* various paragraphs relating to the Plaintiff, some purporting to be extracts from Australian newspapers, and another purporting to be copy of the letter dated Sydney, the 20th August, 1866, addressed by the said ANDREW BOGLE to Dame KATHERINE DOUGHTY.

25. I considered BOGLE's letter entitled to great weight, and that if it was authentic and actually written by BOGLE, there would be but little room for doubt, as I knew BOGLE to be trustworthy, and a man of whose acts I could entertain no suspicion. I accordingly wrote to Dame KATHERINE DOUGHTY a letter to ask if she were certain that the letter was old BOGLE's writing, but I could get nothing definite from her upon the point.

26. On or about the 28th day of October, 1866, I had sent to me a letter from Miss WELD (daughter of the late JAMES WELD, Esq., a brother of the late Mr. JOSEPH WELD, of Lulworth Castle, county Dorset) who are well known to the TICHBORNE family, and one of whom was I believe trustee of certain of the Tichborne estates, dated Lulworth Castle, Wareham, October 29, 1866, in which she stated as follows:—

"It seems that BOGLE has recognised Sir ROGER TICHBORNE, has written to that effect, and is coming over with him. They are to arrive in a few days. Lady DOUGHTY has no doubt at all on the subject.

"You know that BOGLE was the servant of Sir EDWARD DOUGHTY and knew ROGER perfectly."

27. On the 29th day of October, 1866, Mr. HOPKINS again came to see me by appointment on this question, and whilst he was with me I received a letter from my brother WILLIAM, which I opened and read to him, in which my brother informed me the "Shannon" had arrived, and that Sir ROGER was not on board, but that he learnt Sir ROGER was left at Panama, and would probably come *viâ* New York by one of the Cunard line of steamers, or by the boat that would arrive here in a fortnight's time; and on the 29th day of November, 1866, my brother sent me word from Southampton to say that the Plaintiff had not come by the Panama mail, which had just arrived, and I did not therefore know when to expect the Plaintiff's arrival in England.

28. On the 31st December, 1866, I went to Alresford, having received a note from Mr. HOPKINS. He met me at the railway station, where I had a talk with Mr. EDWARD ROUS, the landlord of the Swan Hotel at Alresford, as to the visitor, whom I learnt was staying at his house, and whom I had not then seen.

29. We were told that BOGLE was expected by the next train, due in about a quarter of an hour, and Mr. HOPKINS and myself took a short walk to occupy the time, and turning back to go to the station, when about one hundred yards from the back entrance to the Swan Hotel, a person came out of that entrance, and Mr. HOPKINS said, "This is Sir ROGER." He stood still and looked at us as we approached nearer and nearer to him. He looked so pointedly at us, that Mr. HOPKINS remarked, "Depend upon it, he knows us both." When we came up within a few yards he turned round and walked on, holding a handkerchief before the lower part of his face, whilst a cap, with a projecting peak, shadowed the upper part. We walked behind him for several yards—only two or three yards from him—and at last he moved off the path at an angle, and thus allowed us to pass on.

30. We remarked that although much increased in size his height was just about that of the Mr. ROGER CHARLES TICHBORNE we had known formerly. We could easily have spoken to him, but as we had learnt from ROUS that he wished to be incog.; we felt bound to pay due respect to his wish. ROUS had also told us he had recognised the gentleman, and that he did not wish to be seen until he had seen some one in particular, and this individual, ROUS told us, he believed was his mother the Dowager Lady JAMES TICHBORNE.

31. On reaching the station the train arrived, but old BOGLE did not appear. We then had another talk with ROUS, and I afterwards went home with Mr. HOPKINS. I had not then had an opportunity of seeing the face of the gentleman close enough to discern his features, and the whole circumstances of the case were so remarkable that I could not at that time really bring my mind to believe it was Sir ROGER, and I recollect so expressing in divers letters.

32. I left Alresford by the 7h. 10m. train, and just as I was getting into the carriage the guard called my attention to old BOGLE who had just got out of the same train. I went and spoke to him and saw in an instant that there was no mistake as

to his being the same man who was so many years servant to the late Sir EDWARD DOUGHTY. I had to jump into the train immediately and proceed to Winchester, but finding it was really old BOGLE, I felt my misgivings altogether shaken.

33. On the 16th day of January, 1867, I learnt that the Dowager Lady JAMES TICHBORNE had seen and acknowledged the Plaintiff to be her son, and on the 23rd of the same month I saw the letter of Mr. HOLMES, the Plaintiff's solicitor, in the *Times*. The identification by his mother, by the old servant BOGLE, and by ROUS, seemed to be conclusive in spite of all improbabilities that the gentleman from Australia was actually Sir ROGER CHARLES TICHBORNE.

34. On the 2nd of February, 1867, having received a telegram, I went to Alresford by the three o'clock train. Mr. HOPKINS met me at the station and took me to his house, where I found Mr. HOLMES, the Plaintiff's solicitor, whom I had never before seen. I was shown a large photograph portrait, and, recognising the features, I instantly said—"That is ROGER TICHBORNE and no mistake about it." I covered over the lower part of the face with a piece of paper, and looking at the uncovered part, I exclaimed—"There he is, unaltered, just as he was fourteen years ago. He has had a blow or accident to the upper part of his nose which is certainly widened," and I have since heard that this was actually the case.

35. The Plaintiff was expected at Alresford that day, 2nd February, and Mr. HOPKINS wrote a note inviting him to dinner that evening, it being felt by Mr. HOPKINS, Mr. HOLMES and myself, that the Plaintiff could not be in the company of Mr. HOPKINS and myself for a few hours without our being able to satisfy ourselves whether or not he was the ROGER CHARLES TICHBORNE we formerly knew. I then left with Mr. HOLMES, and accompanied him to the Swan Hotel, and, on entering the large room facing the street, I there saw the Plaintiff, whom I recognised instantly as the eldest son of the late Sir JAMES FRANCIS DOUGHTY TICHBORNE whom I formerly so well knew; his eyes, the upper part of his head and his ears were unmistakeable, but his voice had quite an effect upon me—that alone was quite enough to convince me that I was speaking to ROGER CHARLES TICHBORNE.

36. The Plaintiff at once recognised me and addressed me as he used to do years ago. I chatted with him till close upon six o'clock, and I then took him to Mr. HOPKINS, when the Plaintiff and myself dined together with Mr. and Mrs. HOPKINS. Mr. HOLMES was not present.

37. After Mrs. HOPKINS had left the table, Mr. HOPKINS and myself commenced questioning him upon matters of the most private and personal character with the view to test his knowledge of past events which occurred before he left England in 1853. His answers were clear, straightforward, and convincing. His memory of old events astonished us both.

38. Mr. HOPKINS and myself, with our intimate knowledge of his family matters, tested him with questions no other persons could have put, and no one but the Plaintiff could have answered. Amongst other things, to test the Plaintiff's accuracy and identity, I took a letter from my pocket and folded it up so that he could only see the middle portion, and showing it to him, said—"Do you know whose writing that is?" Looking at it, he answered almost immediately, "My Papa's." It was in fact his father's handwriting. Such letter is now produced and marked B. I had had that letter in my possession, from the time it was first received by me. I had never before shown it to the Plaintiff, nor had I given him the slightest intimation that I intended to put the question to him or to produce any letter to him, and I am certain that the Plaintiff was utterly ignorant that such letter was in existence, until I produced it to him at the last-mentioned interview.

39. Subsequently and at the same interview a letter, which was written by the Plaintiff in the year 1849 and addressed from 39 Upper Grosvenor Street, was put into his hands, and as soon as he caught sight of the heading he exclaimed "Why I wrote this at Mr. SEYMOUR'S." I believe it to be the fact that such letter was written by the Plaintiff at the then residence of Mr. SEYMOUR, No. 39, Upper Grosvenor Street, London.

40. About nine o'clock in the evening of the same day, as previously arranged with Mr. HOLMES, he called for the Plaintiff and remained for some little time. The Plaintiff and Mr. HOLMES then left, and Mr. HOPKINS and myself discussed together for an hour or so all that had passed, and we felt perfectly satisfied that the gentleman with whom we had conversed was ROGER CHARLES, the eldest son of the said late Sir JAMES FRANCIS DOUGHTY TICHBORNE, and that it was impossible we could be deceived or that he could be any one else.

41. I left Mr. HOPKINS soon after ten o'clock, and rejoined the Plaintiff and Mr. HOLMES at the Swan Hotel at Alresford, and continued in conversation with them till twelve o'clock that night.

42. In the afternoon of the next day I went with the Plaintiff again to Mr. HOPKINS, and they had a walk together. In the evening, the Plaintiff and Mr. HOLMES left for London and I returned to Winchester. On reaching home, I immediately wrote to Dame KATHERINE DOUGHTY and to others on the following day, announcing the fact that the Plaintiff was undoubtedly ROGER CHARLES TICHBORNE, the eldest son of the late Sir JAMES FRANCIS DOUGHTY TICHBORNE.

43. Since the 2nd day of February, 1867, I have been in frequent communication verbally and by letter with the Plaintiff, I met and dined with him on the 8th day of the same month at Mr. HOPKINS' house at Alresford, and I have been to Croydon and visited him and his mother, the Dowager LADY JAMES TICHBORNE, for several days together, on more than one occasion.

44. I have thus had ample opportunities of forming a correct judgment as to the Plaintiff's identity. I have observed him most closely and have conversed with him for many hours together about the neighbourhood of Tichborne and the TICHBORNE family and affairs, and as to events which occurred prior to his leaving England in the year 1853, and I am certain that the Plaintiff is Sir ROGER CHARLES DOUGHTY TICHBORNE whom I formerly knew as the eldest son of the late Sir JAMES FRANCIS DOUGHTY TICHBORNE and Dame HENRIETTE FELICITÉ his wife. In fact I have no more doubt about it than I have of my own existence. This is a careful and deliberate decision, founded on facts and upon my own independent judgment and knowledge of him in former days.

45. The several statements hereinbefore contained, are within my own knowledge except as hereinbefore appears, and in such last-mentioned cases are believed by me to be true, on the grounds hereinbefore in that behalf appearing.

FRANCIS JOSEPH BAIGENT.

Sworn at New Alresford, in the County of Southampton, this 2nd day of July, 1867—Before me,

JNO. FRAS. ADAMS,

A Commissioner to administer oaths in Chancery in England.

We insert also the affidavit of his father.

I, RICHARD BAIGENT, of the City of Winchester, artist and professor of drawing to Winchester College, make oath and say as follows:—

1. I am now in the sixty-eighth year of my age, and have resided at Winchester ever since the year 1820.

2. I first became acquainted with the TICHBORNE family in the year 1822 or 1823. I knew very well the Dowager Lady TICHBORNE, mother of the late Sir HENRY JOSEPH TICHBORNE, also Sir HENRY JOSEPH TICHBORNE and Lady TICHBORNE. Their seven daughters were pupils of mine for several years, and I knew them intimately, as well as the late Mr. EDWARD TICHBORNE (afterwards Sir EDWARD DOUGHTY), the late Sir JAMES F. TICHBORNE, and the late Mr. ROGER ROBERT TICHBORNE (brothers of Sir HENRY JOSEPH TICHBORNE), also their sister, Mrs. NANGLE, and the late Mr. ALFRED JOSEPH TICHBORNE.

3. I also well knew Mr. ROGER CHARLES TICHBORNE, the eldest son of the late Sir JAMES FRANCIS DOUGHTY TICHBORNE, and Dame HENRIETTE FELICITE, his wife, and saw and conversed on several occasions, between the years 1845 and 1853, with the said Mr. ROGER CHARLES TICHBORNE.

4. On Friday, the 22nd day of March, 1867, I saw the above-named Plaintiff at the Swan Hotel, Alresford, and I immediately recognised him. I entered into conversation with him, and spent several hours in his company, and I have no hesitation whatever in declaring that the Plaintiff is the Mr. ROGER CHARLES TICHBORNE I formerly knew, the eldest son of the late Sir JAMES FRANCIS DOUGHTY TICHBORNE, baronet, deceased.

RICHARD BAIGENT.

Sworn at New Alresford, in the County of Southampton, this first day of July, 1867—Before me,

JNO. FRAS. ADAMS,

A Commissioner to administer oaths in Chancery in England.

On the following day, viz., Sunday, February 3rd, 1867. Mr. HOPKINS wrote a letter to Lord ARUNDEL, of which no copy was kept.

He also wrote to Mr. HENRY DANBY SEYMOUR a letter, of which no copy was kept, and both letters were to the effect that he had recognised the Claimant as Sir ROGER TICHBORNE. He also wrote a letter to the Claimant inviting him to come to his house as a guest.

The severe testing and ordeal which the Claimant underwent at the hands of Mr. HOPKINS, and Mr. BAIGENT, entailed upon him a very severe headache and illness, so that he was thoroughly knocked up. In consequence of this he was unable to go to Mass at Tichborne Chapel, as settled upon before he left Mr. HOPKINS' house the previous night.

Mr. BAIGENT, however, went to the Claimant, who requested him to tell Mrs. GREENWOOD how unwell he was, and utterly unable to go to chapel.

He also desired him to add that he should be glad if she would call upon him on her way home to Brookwood Park. Mr. BAIGENT reached Tichborne Chapel shortly after the commencement of the service, and on entering a vacant seat, found Mrs. GREENWOOD was occupying the next one in front. She immediately glanced round, and seeing Mr. BAIGENT became agitated, and turning round said: "Have you come from Winchester?" Mr. BAIGENT motioned her not to speak as the service was going on. She turned round two or three times and looked in his face, as if she expected to read something from it, and was evidently uneasy.

After the service was over, Mr. BAIGENT told Mrs. GREENWOOD that he wished to speak to her outside the chapel. She came out much agitated, and said: "What is the matter?"

Mr. BAIGENT said: "I am afraid you will regard me as a sort of "black crow," but I have no unpleasant news to communicate. I have seen the gentleman who has come from Australia, and who is now at the Swan Hotel, Alresford. I dined with him last night at Mr. HOPKINS's, and I can assure you he is Sir ROGER TICHBORNE." Mr. BAIGENT added "that Mr. HOPKINS is as certain of it as I am." Upon which Mrs. GREENWOOD turned pale and said: "It cannot be him because we know who he is—he is an impostor; we know all about him; he is a son of——" (Name not recollected.) Mr. BAIGENT said, "It is unkind of you to go on in this way: he is now, as I told you before, at the Swan Hotel, and I have a carriage here. Come and see him, and judge for yourself. Were he not very unwell this morning he would have been here himself, and I should not have had to ask such a favour of you. Mrs. GREENWOOD replied, "He is an Impostor, therefore I will not go." Mr. BAIGENT then said, "Shall I bring him to Brookwood?" She replied, "No: neither I nor Colonel GREENWOOD would have the Impostor at Brookwood for all the world; we have made up our minds about that." Just then Colonel LUSHINGTON came up, and as soon as a word or two in recognition had passed between him, Mrs. GREENWOOD, and Mr. BAIGENT, Mrs. GREENWOOD, in an agitated manner, said, "Oh! Colonel LUSHINGTON, Mr. BAIGENT has seen the man from Australia, and will have it that he is ROGER TICHBORNE; whereas we know that he is an Impostor." Mr. BAIGENT then said, "I don't think you ought to use such a word. It is unkind of you to treat it in this manner." Colonel LUSHINGTON said, "I beg your pardon, Mrs. GREENWOOD. May I ask you if Mr. BAIGENT knew ROGER TICHBORNE before he went away?" She then replied, raising her eyebrows with an expression of astonishment at the question, "Oh! yes." Mr. BAIGENT said, "Did I not know him as well as yourself?" To this she assented; and Colonel LUSHINGTON said, "Well, Mrs. GREENWOOD, I think, considering that Mr. BAIGENT has seen him, and you have not, you should pay some deference to his statement." Mr. BAIGENT then said, "Mrs. GREENWOOD has no right to keep on telling me that he is an Impostor; especially when I have told her that Mr. HOPKINS has also recognised him as ROGER TICHBORNE, and that we both dined with him yesterday." Colonel LUSHINGTON then said, "We had better go into the house, and talk about it." On her way in, she said to Mr. BAIGENT, "Is his hair darker than yours? His hair was much darker. Are his eyebrows more arched than ALFRED's?" Mr. BAIGENT said, "Never mind about the colour of his hair or eyebrows. All I wish you to do is to come and see him, and judge for yourself." Mrs. GREENWOOD, Colonel LUSHINGTON, and Mr. BAIGENT sat down in the drawing-room, and continued to converse on the subject. Mrs. GREENWOOD was greatly excited, and continued to use the word "Impostor" most freely. Colonel LUSHINGTON did all he could to impress upon her the impropriety of such expressions, as Mr. HOPKINS and Mr. BAIGENT were satisfied that he was ROGER TICHBORNE, and that she had not herself had an opportunity of seeing him; and pressed upon her the reasonableness of Mr. BAIGENT's wishes, that, if she would not go to Alresford to see him, to allow him to come to Brookwood and see him there; notwithstanding the reiterated assertion of Mrs. GREENWOOD that they would not have him there for all the world, and certainly would not see him if he called, Colonel LUSHINGTON said it was very unreasonable behaviour, and they ought to give him the opportunity of going there, as no Impostor would venture to go to Brookwood; and said, "Well, then, see him in this house. Mr. BAIGENT shall take him an invitation to come and dine here, which would give you, Colonel GREENWOOD, and his brother, an opportunity of seeing him; as the sooner the truth is arrived at the better, and it is what no Impostor would be induced to do." Mrs. GREENWOOD would not hear of this proposal, and continued to maintain that he was an Impostor.

After much talk and a deal of pressing, Mr. BAIGENT, wishing her to consent to see him at Brookwood in case he should find him well enough on his return to Alresford to go to Brookwood, at last and with much reluctance Mrs. GREENWOOD said, "If he comes I will see him, but I wish it distinctly understood, Mr. BAIGENT, that we don't invite him to Brookwood." Mr. BAIGENT said he was satisfied, and that if he could manage it he would be at Brookwood somewhat about 3 o'clock.

On Mr. BAIGENT's return to the Swan at Alresford he found Sir ROGER looking still more unwell, and not by any means fit to go; still, in his anxiety that his visit to the GREENWOODS should not be delayed, he gave Sir ROGER to understand that he was expected there, and acted as if Mrs. GREENWOOD's behaviour had been just the reverse of what it was; as he felt certain that if Sir Roger had the slightest notion or idea of the way in which Mrs. GREENWOOD behaved and had spoken of him, no power on earth would ever have induced him to go to Brookwood. Mr. BAIGENT pressed his determination to get him to Brookwood to the utmost extent, and on getting a refusal took up his hat and said, "Well, then, if you won't go, I will say good morning and take my departure." Mr. HOLMES, who was in the room, then said, "Mr. BAIGENT, you see he is not in a fit state to go anywhere." Mr. BAIGENT said, "Still for all that, I wish him to go to Brookwood." Sir ROGER then said to him, "I will write KATTY a note if you like." Mr. BAIGENT said, "Well, if you will do that, I shall be quite satisfied," and then put his hat down. Sir ROGER without saying another word opened his blotting-case and wrote a note, and placing it in an envelope was about to fasten it down, which Mr. HOLMES observing, said, "You will allow Mr. BAIGENT to see it before sealing it up." Sir ROGER said, "I beg your pardon, I quite forgot myself," and handed the note to Mr. BAIGENT, who read it, and was the only person who read it; it was then placed in the envelope and despatched by a special messenger to Brookwood Park; the messenger subsequently returned and said he had duly delivered it.

Mr. BAIGENT was so struck with the natural simplicity of its language and its general tone, that he thought that the note alone would be quite sufficient to convince the GREENWOODS that the writer was indeed Sir ROGER TICHBORNE.

Shortly after the sending of this letter, Mr. BAIGENT, in accordance with an arrangement made the previous night, accompanied Sir ROGER to Mr. HOPKINS's. They saw Mr. and Mrs. HOPKINS, and had some conversation. Mr. HOPKINS told Sir ROGER that he was to be perfectly easy in his mind, as he knew him to be Sir ROGER CHARLES TICHBORNE, and as a proof of it, better than words, he had to say that he had already written and posted two letters, one to Lord ARUNDEL and the other to HENRY DANBY SEYMOUR, telling them that he was Sir ROGER TICHBORNE. This was the first intimation Sir ROGER had that either Mr. HOPKINS or Mr. BAIGENT had identified him—We insert here the Affidavit of Mr. HOPKINS:—

I, EDWARD HOPKINS, of New Alresford, Hants, lately a Solicitor, but now retired from practice, make oath and say as follows:—

1. I am now in the sixty-fourth year of my age. I knew and was for many years intimately acquainted with the late JAMES FRANCIS TICHBORNE, afterwards Sir JAMES FRANCIS DOUGHTY TICHBORNE, now deceased. On the disentailing and resettlement of the Tichborne estates in 1844, he was my client. The resettlement proceeded on the assumption that on his eldest son, ROGER CHARLES TICHBORNE, attaining the age of twenty-one years, certain estates, known as the Doughty estates, of which he was tenant in tail, expectant on the decease of the late Sir EDWARD DOUGHTY without issue male, should be disentailed and resettled. The above-named Plaintiff, now Sir ROGER CHARLES DOUGHTY TICHBORNE, is such eldest son.

2. In the year 1849, I prepared a statement for the opinion of Mr. BRODIE as to the re-settlement of the Doughty estates. Mr. BRODIE's opinion and suggestions were submitted by me to the Plaintiff, but he then objected to act on them. I had before this and subsequently several interviews with the Plaintiff, and a correspondence with him which resulted in his ultimately acceding to a scheme which in effect realised the intentions entertained in the year 1844.

3. The Plaintiff entered the army as a cornet in the 6th Dragoon Guards in 1849, and attained his age of twenty-one years in 1850. The requisite deeds of disentailment and resettlement of the Doughty estates were prepared, I acting as the solicitor of the Plaintiff and his father on the occasion, and in the month of May or June, 1850, went specially to see the Plaintiff at Cahir in Ireland, when he executed such deeds in my presence, being the deeds of the 8th, 9th, and 10th May, 1850, referred to in the Plaintiff's Bill of Complaint filed in this cause.

4. Subsequently, and whilst the Plaintiff was in Ireland with his regiment, I had a correspondence with him respecting the purchase of his lieutenancy and other affairs, and after his arrival in England, and in the month of October, 1852, whilst he was with his regiment at Canterbury, I received letters from him. The Plaintiff once dined at my house at Alresford, and subsequently dined with me at a club in London, and I have met him at dinner at Tichborne House, and on one occasion in particular, he spent some time in my house, when I had some anxious conversation with him. After he left the army in 1853 I do not recollect to have seen him before he left England for South America.

5. In the year 1854, shortly after the report of the loss of the ship "Bella," the said Sir JAMES FRANCIS DOUGHTY TICHBORNE, Baronet, consulted me on the subject, and as to the steps which should be taken, it having been discovered, that before leaving England, his said son, the Plaintiff, had made a will and deposited the same with Mr. SLAUGHTER (now deceased), whom he had appointed conjointly with Mr. VINCENT GOSFORD, trustees and executors of the will. Sir JAMES was much astonished that any will was in existence, and informed me that he was in utter ignorance that his son had made, or contemplated making, any will, and he was desirous that other trustees should be appointed.

6. I advised Sir JAMES to investigate the reported loss of the "Bella" and her crew, and to get such evidence, if possible, as would establish the fate of the ship and crew; and acting under the advice of counsel, a suit was instituted in this Honourable Court in Trinity term, 1855, being the suit of TICHBORNE v. GOSFORD, referred to in the Plaintiff's said Bill of Complaint, filed in this cause, for the purpose of administering the trusts of the said will, and of having new trustees thereof appointed. The original Bill of Complaint in TICHBORNE v. GOSFORD, was amended by striking out the prayer for administering the trusts, and the order of the 5th December, 1857, referred to in the Plaintiff's Bill of Complaint, filed in this cause, was made in the said suit of TICHBORNE v. GOSFORD. My then firm of Messrs. DUNN, HOPKINS, BLACKMORE and CARTER acted as the solicitors of the Plaintiff in the suit of TICHBORNE v. GOSFORD. Such inquiries were made touching the loss of the "Bella" and her

crew, as mentioned in the said Bill of Complaint in TICHBORNE v. GOSFORD, with such results as therein mentioned, from which it appeared that the "Bella" was lost at sea, and, as I believe, no tidings reached England at that time of any of the crew having been saved.

7. I was surviving trustee of the DOUGHTY estates for raising £100,000, and, acting upon the assumption that the Plaintiff was lost in the "Bella," and conceiving that Sir JAMES FRANCIS DOUGHTY TICHBORNE, as the survivor, had in himself the power to appoint new trustees, I resigned my trusteeship; indeed I acted generally until the year 1866, on the assumption that the Plaintiff was dead.

8. Having heard the various reports that the Plaintiff was alive, and intending to return to England, I expressed to Mr. FRANCIS JOSEPH BAIGENT that having had the Plaintiff's confidence on the disentailment and resettling of the DOUGHTY estates, I should be willing to render him any assistance in my power, and having been requested by the Plaintiff's solicitor, Mr. HOLMES, to see the Plaintiff for the purpose of satisfying myself as to his identity, I invited the Plaintiff to dine at my house on the 2nd day of February, 1867, in company with the said Mr. FRANCIS JOSEPH BAIGENT, and they did dine at my house on that day.

9. In a conversation of two or three hours' duration, which I had with the Plaintiff on that occasion, the Plaintiff evinced an intimate acquaintance with the state of the garden and grounds about Tichborne House before the alterations, since the year 1853, a knowledge of the name of a particular cottage at Tichborne and its inmates, of the names of his deceased uncles and of their wives and families, and of various particulars relating to them, a perfect recollection of his being in my house in 1846, and the circumstances leading to it, a recollection of interviews with me when he was my client in 1849, 1850, 1851, and 1852, and his conduct thereon. These and other facts which transpired in conversation so satisfied me, that he was in fact my old client, Mr. ROGER CHARLES TICHBORNE, the eldest son of the said Sir JAMES FRANCIS DOUGHTY TICHBORNE and Dame HENRIETTE, his wife, that on the following day I wrote to the Plaintiff, inviting him to stay at my house on a visit. On the same day I wrote to Lord

PORTRAIT OF MR. HOPKINS.

ARUNDELL of Wardour, and to HENRY DANBY SEYMOUR, Esq., and on the 4th day of February, I wrote to Messrs. CULLINGTON and SLAUGHTER, Solicitors of certain of the Defendants, as follows:—

Alresford, 4th February, 1867.

DEAR SIR,—I think it right to tell you I received a letter from Sir ROGER CHARLES TICHBORNE on Saturday, and he dined at my house on that day, that on the following day (yesterday) I had a walk and talk with him, and I have no doubt whatever he is the ROGER CHARLES DOUGHTY TICHBORNE who was my client on my disentailment of the Estates. I received a letter from Mr. GOSFORD of the 9th day of January, and purposely abstained from replying to it, and glad I am I so acted. I have left my business for more than a year; this, however, will not preclude me from rendering such services to Sir ROGER CHARLES TICHBORNE as I am able, in acknowledgment of the confidence reposed in me when he was my client. Yours truly,

EDWARD HOPKINS.

Messrs. CULLINGTON & SLAUGHTER.

10. The Plaintiff accepted my invitation, and came on a visit to my house on the 8th day of February, 1867, and remained for five days in my house, and during that time he associated with myself and the members of my family as any ordinary visitor. Since then he has breakfasted in my house, and I have received letters from him.

11. The communications, written and verbal, which I have had with the Plaintiff, confirm me in my first conviction that the Plaintiff is my former client, the eldest son of the late Sir JAMES FRANCIS TICHBORNE, and Dame HENRIETTE FELICITÉ, his wife; and though I cannot recall to my recollection the expression of his features, I entertain no doubt whatever as to his identity.

12. The several statements hereinbefore contained, are within my own knowledge, except as hereinbefore appears, and in such last-mentioned cases are believed by me, to be true on the grounds herein appearing.

EDWARD HOPKINS.

Sworn at New Alresford, in the County of Southampton, this 1st day of July, 1867—Before me, JNO. FRAS. ADAMS, A Commissioner to administer oaths in Chancery in England

After this intimation, Mr. HOPKINS took the Claimant for a walk in his garden, known as the Weir Gardens, through which a trout-stream runs. Here the Claimant pointed out to Mr. HOPKINS alterations which had been made since he was there before.

Mr. HOPKINS subsequently entertained the Claimant as a visitor, gave him the privilege of fishing, which he had denied to his dearest friends before, and testified on every occasion of his life his full belief of the identity of the Claimant with his former friend ROGER CHARLES TICHBORNE.

Mr. HOPKINS died at Bath, on Monday, 5th October, 1868, and was buried at Alresford, on Saturday, 10th of that month. His loss to the Claimant has been of the most disastrous description. Mr. HOPKINS married the sister of the late Lord Justice MARKHAM GIFFARD. He (Mr. HOPKINS) had often consulted MARKHAM GIFFARD on the family affairs of the TICHBORNES, and in this instance he also made him his confidant. Mr. GIFFARD appeared for the Claimant in the Vice-Chancellor's Court on several occasions, and stated to Mr. GUILDFORD ONSLOW, and others, that he was as certain the Claimant was the real ROGER TICHBORNE, as that he was sitting in the chair from which he spoke.

Mr. HOPKINS had been Solicitor to Sir HENRY JOSEPH TICHBORNE, as well as to the Claimant's father, Sir JAMES FRANCIS DOUGHTY TICHBORNE. He acted for the Claimant and his father as before mentioned, in the cutting off of the entail and re-settlement of the DOUGHTY estates, and he visited the Claimant for the purpose of their execution, when he was quartered in Ireland. Mr. HOPKINS admitted to Mr. BAIGENT that the Claimant had disputed with him, about the execution of certain deeds, which had escaped his recollection, and in which circumstance the Claimant turned out to be right.

It should be noticed that exception was taken by the TICHBORNE family to the last paragraph of Mr. HOPKINS's affidavit, in which he states he cannot recall to his recollection the expression of the features of ROGER CHARLES TICHBORNE, although he entertains no doubt whatever as to his identity. Long before Mr. HOPKINS saw the Claimant, he told Mr. BAIGENT that he could not call to mind the features of his friend ROGER TICHBORNE, and only remembered he was something like his mother, the Dowager Lady TICHBORNE. He had a peculiar defect of being unable to recollect the features of any person for a length of time, and had frequently to ask the names of persons with whom he was well acquainted. This will explain the paragraph in the Affidavit which was considered detrimental to the Claimant's interest, but confirms the character which Mr. HOPKINS had, of being a thoroughly conscientious and upright man, who was incapable of straining a point, even in a matter of vital importance, like the above.

Mr. HOPKINS had at this time retired from practice, and was a person of considerable means; the personalty under his will was proved under £30,000, and he had real property besides.

On the 8th February the Claimant, by special invitation from Mr. HOPKINS, went and stayed at his house in Alresford. On his arrival, having told Mr. HOPKINS that his footsteps were dogged by detectives, he (Mr. HOPKINS) was much annoyed at the circumstance, and immediately wrote the following letter to Captain HARRIS, one of the Commissioners of the London Police:—

My dear Sir,— Alresford, 8th Feb., 1867.

I had the pleasure of knowing you when at Winchester, and think you may remember my name. Sir ROGER CHARLES TICHBORNE is at this time a guest in my house, having just come to me from his residence, Essex Lodge, Thornton Heath, Croydon. He tells me he is watched by detectives, as if he were a malefactor. As I have not the shadow of a doubt that the gentleman in question I speak of, is Sir ROGER TICHBORNE, I think it due to him, to give you this voucher of the fact, and you are welcome to show it to any one, on whose application or authority, Sir ROGER is so molested. I am not taking a professional interest in the affair, for I have retired altogether from my business; but, convinced of the truth of his being Sir ROGER CHARLES TICHBORNE, who was formerly a client of mine, I feel it is due to him, due to the cause of truth and justice, and to the TICHBORNE family to give him the benefit of such services as I can. I feel sure you will pardon this communication—I am, dear Sir, yours faithfully, EDWARD HOPKINS.

Captain HARRIS, Com. Police, Scotland Yard.

The Claimant remained at Mr. HOPKINS's house till the 13th of February, 1867, and then returned to Croydon; and it was during this stay at Alresford, that he first saw some of his old friends who identified him.

It was also during this visit, that occurred the celebrated interview with Mr. HENRY DANBY SEYMOUR, and BURDEN, the former servant of the Claimant's father. It was during this visit also, that the Claimant first saw Colonel LUSHINGTON, and paid a visit to Tichborne House, all of which is set forth in Colonel LUSHINGTON's affidavit, which is as follows:—

I, FRANKLIN LUSHINGTON, of Tichborne Park, in the County of Southampton, Companion of the Bath, and late a Lieutenant-Colonel of the Scots Fusilier Guards, make oath and say as follows:—

1. I reside at Tichborne House, the family seat of the TICHBORNES, of which I have a lease. I did not know the above-named Plaintiff until this year, 1867. In the early part of this year, I heard that the eldest son of the late Sir JAMES FRANCIS DOUGHTY TICHBORNE, and who had not been heard of for some thirteen years, had recently returned from Australia to England. I was very anxious to get him to Tichborne House in order that I might form my own judgment of his identity. Before his visit there, I confess to having freely expressed my doubts that he was not the person he represented himself to be.

2. In February, 1867, the Plaintiff was upon a visit to Mr. EDWARD HOPKINS, of Alresford, and I was introduced to him. He walked over to Tichborne with me, and on entering the dining-room he was so much affected that he was obliged to sit down. He immediately recognised the portrait of Lady JAMES TICHBORNE which hangs up in the dining-room, and when he stood by it his likeness to her was unmistakeable and most striking. He said I don't remember the picture next to it, and seemed surprised; but it was the portrait of my father which he had not seen before, and it was the only picture on that side of the room which did not belong to the TICHBORNE family. He observed that the "Dole" picture was brighter than he had ever seen it before, and the fact is, that such picture had been then lately cleaned and revarnished. In speaking to me of the chapel which adjoins the house, he mentioned a door leading into the gallery of the chapel, which I had blocked up since I took the house.

3. In an unfinished wing to the house there was the skin of a bird and a picture, which the Plaintiff told me he had sent over from South America, and he took up the skin and showed me how it was cured by friction. He said the picture was the largest of a number he had sent home. He also recognised a French horn as belonging to him, and being the one upon which he used to play.

4. In the house there was a brass helmet in a japanned case, with the name of R. C. TICHBORNE upon it. I took the helmet when I went to see Plaintiff at Mr. HOPKINS' and he knew it again directly, and upon placing it upon his head, it was found to fit him.

5. All these circumstances coupled with his general demeanour quite satisfied me that the Plaintiff was the man he represented himself to be; and I have since been a firm believer in his identity, although the fact of his turning up again is adverse to my interest, for I have spent over £1,000 on the house and grounds; and I believe his return makes my lease worthless.

6. The statements herein contained are within my own knowledge. FRANKLIN LUSHINGTON.

Sworn at New Alresford, in the County of Southampton, this first day of July, 1867—Before me,

JNO. FRAS. ADAMS,

A Commissioner to administer oaths in Chancery in England.

Before leaving the subject, it should be mentioned that both Mr. HOPKINS, and Colonel LUSHINGTON made overtures to the GREENWOODS either to meet the Claimant at Tichborne House or at Mr. HOPKINS's, house, or to take the Claimant over to Brookwood, all of which overtures were declined by the GREENWOODS.

On his return from Alresford to Croydon, he was joined by his mother, the Dowager Lady TICHBORNE, who resided with him at Essex Lodge, Croydon, from the 15th February to 25th April, 1867. She then left Croydon, on account of the air not agreeing with her; but continued on the most affectionate terms with her son, as is amply proved by the correspondence with him; seeing him, or writing to him daily—almost up to the very last hour of her existence.

A perusal of the correspondence between the Claimant and his mother, will be as strong a confirmation, that the relative positions of parent and child existed between these two persons as anything that can be adduced. From the time of Lady TICHBORNE's recognition of the Claimant as her son, she discontinued the allowance which she had been making of £1,000 a year to Mrs. TERESA TICHBORNE, and transferred it to the Claimant, paying in addition to this £1,000 a year, the house rent, servants' wages, and taxes, during the time of the Claimant's residence at Croydon.

One of the extraordinary devices to which the family, or their friends resorted, while Lady TICHBORNE lived with her son at Croydon, is related by Dr. KENEALY in the *Englishman* for April 18th, 1874, being the second number of that journal:—

"In the consultations which Dr. KENEALY necessarily had with his Client—and it may here be stated that Dr. KENEALY never was in his company but professionally; we mean no social intimacy existed between them—hardly five minutes ever passed in which, unconsciously to the speaker, incident after incident, bearing the unmistakable stamp of truth, did not take place which carried conviction to the mind of his listener that he was the true man. At one of these consultations Sir ROGER related the following anecdote: the melancholy tones in which he did so, still ring in the ears of those who hearkened, and the deep and impressive earnestness with which he spoke, will ever be recollected, while his eyes were at times half suffused with tears, as he remembered the undying, tender, sacred affection of that gentle mother, who endured such terrible persecution in his cause, upon whom such appalling priestly influences were brought to bear, and who finally died, heart-broken and despairing, a martyr to the holy promptings of maternal love. The reality of the scene described was fully apparent to the mind of Dr. KENEALY, in consequence of this great fact, that never once during the whole course of the Trial did TICHBORNE, tell him a single word which was ever found to be untrue.

One morning at Croydon, he (Sir ROGER) returned home unexpectedly, and not finding his mother in her usual room, he inquired for her. He was told that she was engaged in conversation with a gentleman. After about half-an-hour, the hall door was heard to close, and Lady TICHBORNE appeared. She seemed in a most dreadful state of agitation. Her melancholy and most expressive face was white almost to ghastliness; she trembled all over, and with faltering footsteps tottered along until she fell into a chair. Her heart was beating violently; her feelings, which were sensitive to the highest degree, seemed to overmaster her, so that her whole frame trembled like an aspen. In broken accents, amid tears and sobs, she told her son that the person with whom she had been having an interview was a Jesuit-father, who had called to her and asked her to confess. Being informed by her that she would prefer confessing to her own priest, the Jesuit-father informed her that he had come to her with only one object, the welfare of her immortal soul; that, to all appearance, she had only a few short weeks or months in which she could hope to survive; that she belonged to a Church which held the keys of heaven and hell, and which, having been founded by God Himself, commanded and spoke to all its members with the voice and authority of the Lord of the Universe. That, as everlasting damnation must be the sure punishment of those who disobeyed the Church, so a state of eternal happiness with the angels was marked out for those who were its docile servants, ready to yield obedience like little children, and rejecting their own thoughts or feelings at the bidding of their spiritual directors. That the Old Testament had recorded a brilliant example of the divine virtue of ready obedience. Remember ABRAHAM, he said. In obedience to the command of GOD, he went forth to sacrifice his loved, his only son. He bound him, and was prepared to offer him up as a victim; and glorious has been the reward of that holy Patriarch. In the name of that Church, he added, which is the representative of GOD on earth, I also command you to follow the example of that divine servant of heaven, and I adjure you to sacrifice your son without a murmur, at the bidding of our holy Church. If you do this, great shall be your reward in heaven; but if you fail to do it, equally terrible shall be your fate in hell.

Such was the proposal which this man dared to make. He never once pretended to think that her son was an impostor, or that she was the victim of a delusion or a dream. He took it and treated it as an accepted fact, that no mother could be deceived by an impostor, under whose roof she was actually residing, into the belief that he was her eldest, long-sought, dear-loved son. He wore no mask of that kind, for he knew it would be absurd to argue with a woman of her sagacity—and it should be known that a more keen, cautious, and even suspicious woman than Lady TICHBORNE never lived—that her own son was not her son at all. He owned, as it were, what we believe every one of those priests and Jesuits owns and believes, that the Defendant was the real and undoubted ROGER; but, owning this, he besought her to abandon him, because the Church commanded her to do so. We need not add that the answer to this was such as might have been expected. The Jesuit-father begged, and prayed, and threatened; but was obliged to leave the house, his object unattained, his last words being a sort of imprecation on her whom he had thus sought to make his guilty dupe.

The most astounding influences have however been brought to bear in all quarters, as witness the following narrative, communicated by Mr. GUILDFORD ONSLOW to the *Englishman* for Dec. 5, 1874, being Number 35:—

To THE EDITOR OF THE "ENGLISHMAN."

SIR,—The following circumstance relating to the Claimant to the Tichborne estates may interest your readers. In the summer of 1872 I accompanied Sir ROGER TICHBORNE to Liverpool, to hear him address a Liverpool audience in the Amphitheatre of that city. We arrived about four o'clock in the afternoon at the great railway hotel—I think the "Queen's." We were met by thousands of people of all classes, who accompanied Sir ROGER TICHBORNE to his hotel. After receiving a deputation from Liverpool, and after a deal of shaking of hands, Sir ROGER wished to be left alone, and desired it to be known that no more visitors could be received. There were present with Sir ROGER TICHBORNE, Mr. GUILDFORD ONSLOW, Captain HUNT, and another gentleman. It was agreed to lock the door and admit no one until after dinner. Sir ROGER TICHBORNE threw himself on the sofa, and lit his cigar. Mr. ONSLOW and Captain HUNT occupied themselves in writing at the table; in about ten minutes he heard a knock at the door, which was repeated, when I was requested to open it by Sir ROGER and see who it was. On opening the door I was accosted by a very good-looking lady in morning costume—a blue satin dress and black lace. She said she wished to speak to Sir ROGER TICHBORNE. I said it was impossible, as he was very tired, and was on the sofa. I asked her name. She said she was related to Sir ROGER TICHBORNE, that her name was Mrs. VANSITTART, that she was living in Maid of Honours-row, Richmond, that she was in Liverpool about some new invention for propelling vessels of her own, and that she had some extraordinary information to convey to Sir ROGER; that she was residing in the hotel with her husband, and that she had come to speak to Sir ROGER against the wishes of her husband, but that she was determined to see him and tell him the important information she had to convey.

I returned to Sir ROGER and told him a very pretty woman, a Mrs. VANSITTART, wished to see him; that she was in fact related to him. Upon which Sir ROGER TICHBORNE said, "Oh, pray let her come in." The lady immediately came, and shook hands with Sir ROGER, and took a chair by his side, and as well as I can remember told the following story: first, that she was related to him through the SEYMOURS, that none of her family (the Duke of SOMERSET) had spoken to her because of her marriage, that it was against her husband's wish she had to inform Sir ROGER that she had in her possession documents given to her by her grandfather, or rather, which he had made in Melbourne, in Australia, about the arrival of Mr. ROGER TICHBORNE, and his antecedents for some years after, about his being saved from the "Bella," and full particulars which would vouch for all the Claimant had said of his life in Australia, of which her relative was cognisant and which could be amply proved by the documents in her possession, and which, in spite of the entreaties of her own family, she was prepared to hand over to Sir ROGER.

Sir ROGER TICHBORNE replied very courteously, but expressed his surprise that anyone without his knowledge could have known of his arrival and antecedents in 1854 in Australia; and he begged Mrs. VANSITTART not to hand over the documents to him, but to enclose them to his friend, Mr. ONSLOW, giving her that gentleman's address in Hampshire. Mrs. VANSITTART promised to do so in a few days, as soon as she had returned to her home at Richmond; and the lady took her departure. That same evening Sir ROGER appeared at the Amphitheatre, which was crowded to overflowing, and made a long and excellent speech. About eleven o'clock, he was accompanied by thousands to his hotel—in fact, the stairs were crowded with Liverpool people to shake hands with the Claimant. Shortly before twelve, when only a few remained, Captain HUNT called my attention to Mrs. VANSITTART, who appeared to be waiting for us at our landing-place; she, seeing me coming, immediately advanced to speak, and held in her hand a letter, with a ducal coronet on it in gold, and said, "Although my family have never spoken to me since my marriage, I have just received this letter" (holding one in her hand), which she said, to her intense surprise and astonishment, came from one of the heads of her family, the SEYMOURS. It requested her, on no account whatever, to see or call on the Claimant, and not to give him, or show him, or tell him that she had documents in her possession about the arrival of Sir ROGER TICHBORNE in Melbourne, as the Claimant was an impostor, and those documents related only to Sir ROGER TICHBORNE, and not to him.

Upon hearing this, I asked her what her intentions were. She said immediately, "Why, to fulfil my promise to send the documents, as I agreed, to Mr. ONSLOW;" upon which I commended her, and said, "Always speak the truth—out with it. It's the best, after all, in the long run." She expressed her fears she might get into trouble, as the communication was forbidden by her husband; but she had made up her mind, and was resolved what to do. We parted, and never met again; but I understand Mr. ONSLOW, on not getting the promised documents, wrote to Mrs. VANSITTART several letters; and at last she replied, refusing to give up the documents, as she was afraid of the consequences.

The Dowager Lady TICHBORNE'S great affection for her second son, ALFRED TICHBORNE, is manifested by the 200 or 300 letters from him, found among her papers after her decease, and the letters written to her by Mrs. TERESA TICHBORNE, manifested her deep affection and interest in her welfare as well.

In the beginning of March 1867, occurred the celebrated interview between Mr. and Mrs. RADCLIFFE (the KATE DOUGHTY of former days) and the Claimant. It was preceded by Mr. HOLMES (the Claimant's then solicitor), having been at Alresford where he had a lengthy interview at the office of Mr. ADAMS, Solicitor of Alresford, with Mrs. GREENWOOD and Mr. and Mrs. RADCLIFFE.

It was a long interview, during which time Mr. HOLMES told them as much as ought to have satisfied them that his client was Sir ROGER TICHBORNE and the result of the interview was, that it was arranged that Mr. RADCLIFFE on the part of himself, his wife, and Mrs. GREENWOOD should call on the Claimant at Croydon. Mr. RADCLIFFE and the ladies undertaking that the Baronet should be treated with courtesy and respect, and no unfair advantage should be taken of the interview.

On the 2nd March the interview took place. The party came suddenly and without arrangement, entirely with a view to take him by surprise.

The ruse employed by Mr. RADCLIFFE on his first entering the house, by attempting to pass off Mrs. TOWNLEY as his wife, and his rude behaviour to the Dowager Lady TICHBORNE by shutting the door in her face, shows the gross injustice and impropriety with which the family were prepared to act and did act. Mr. RADCLIFFE positively denied both facts at the trial.

After an hour's conversation the ladies left, shaking the Claimant warmly by the hand, and asking if they might come again to see him. He replied, "Yes, certainly; but it could not be in that house on account of Mr. RADCLIFFE'S conduct to my mother." Mr. RADCLIFFE did not shake hands, as the Claimant did not offer to do so.

On the same day Mr. RADCLIFFE wrote to Mr. HOLMES in the following words:—"Mrs. TOWNLEY, Mrs. RADCLIFFE and myself went down yesterday afternoon to see your client; we regret to say that we do not feel satisfied with our interview; we should require some further conversation before we can be quite certain he is the ROGER TICHBORNE we formerly knew."

What can be more significant than this expression which is here repeated?—"We shall require some further conversation before we can be quite certain he is the ROGER TICHBORNE we formerly knew."

This is an admission that they evidently were not satisfied he was the impostor they had been prepared to see.

The party then asked for another interview. Mr. HOLMES wrote back to say that he was glad they had been to Essex Lodge, as he felt the more the Baronet saw of his relatives the sooner a satisfactory settlement of the doubts and uncertainties would be arrived at, but that Sir ROGER had said it was most painful to him their declining to see his mother.

Mr. HOLMES promised to see the Claimant, and arrange another interview.

On the next day Mr. HOLMES wrote to say that the doctor deemed it inexpedient for the Claimant, who was then seriously ill, to go out in the then inclement weather, and added that the Claimant was placed in a most painful position with his mother by the gross treatment which she had received at the hands of Mr. RADCLIFFE.

Mr. HOLMES further proposed that Lady DOUGHTY, Sir ROGER's aunt, and his cousins, Mrs. TOWNLEY and Mrs. RADCLIFFE, should meet him (the Claimant) at Mr. HOLMES's house, 3. Sydenham-road, Croydon, which he would freely place at their disposal whenever Mr. RADCLIFFE pleased to appoint, and intimated that he (Mr. HOLMES) would not be present at such an interview.

This letter was sent by THOMAS CARTER (the Claimant's groom and former servant during the last fifteen months previous to the year 1853, when he left England), and intimated that THOMAS CARTER was there for the purpose of Mr. RADCLIFFE asking him any questions that he might think proper. Mr. RADCLIFFE replied that he would see the ladies, so as to arrange a meeting as Mr. HOLMES proposed. Next day Mr. RADCLIFFE wrote to say, that he had seen the ladies respecting the next proposed meeting with the Claimant, and that they agreed with him in the propriety of another interview in company with their aunt (Lady DOUGHTY). They proposed to go to Croydon by the two o'clock train, and Mr. HOLMES wrote back to say that the Claimant would be glad to see his aunt Lady DOUGHTY, and cousins, at Mr. HOLMES's house, the next day at three o'clock, as proposed. Mr. RADCLIFFE sent back word that there was some mistake, as the day named was Wednesday, not Tuesday, and that the appointment must stand for the former day, as the ladies had engagements for Tuesday. Mr. HOLMES replied that Mr. RADCLIFFE had named no day for the meeting, but only asked him to give the bearer a reply. He enclosed Mr. RADCLIFFE a copy of his letter in proof of the same, and promised to let him know whether Wednesday would suit. Notwithstanding this, on Tuesday, March 12th, Mr. RADCLIFFE and three ladies suddenly made their appearance at Mr. HOLMES's house, demanding to see the Claimant, who, of course, was not there, being at his home, Essex Lodge, a distance of more than a mile off.

Mrs. HOLMES offered to send for the Claimant; but Mr. RADCLIFFE preferred going for him himself. During his absence on this errand, the ladies remained with Mrs. HOLMES in conversation. One of the ladies was Mrs. TOWNLEY, the others were Mrs. and Miss NANGLE, and their remarks were anything but complimentary; they told Mrs. HOLMES that the Claimant was an impostor, an Australian navvy, and freely indulged in similar aspersions on one they had not even seen, thus showing the spirit which animated them.

The Claimant accompanied Mr. RADCLIFFE and was told by Mr. RADCLIFFE he was going to see his aunt, Lady DOUGHTY, her daughter CATHERINE (his wife), and Mrs. TOWNLEY, who were waiting for him at Mr. HOLMES's house.

On entering the dining-room, Mr. RADCLIFFE, in an excited manner, ordered Mrs. HOLMES to leave the room, notwithstanding that it was her own room; then, turning round to the Claimant, he demanded of him the name of the lady who was sitting in the chair.

The Claimant looked round, and, not seeing Mrs. RADCLIFFE and rendered wary by the former ruse of exchanging names, seeing a lady who was thickly veiled and sitting down, desired her to remove it and stand up. On her doing so, the Claimant said he did not know her, though he immediately saw that it was not his aunt, Lady DOUGHTY. He was then asked if he knew the other strange lady; he, almost without looking at her, said "No, I do not." On this, the party commenced a tirade of uncomplimentary language.

The interview was so short that Mrs. HOLMES had not got to the top of the stairs before she was called down by Mr. RADCLIFFE, and on making her appearance, she was told by the party that her husband's client was "a rank impostor," and other coarse language. As soon as Mr. HOLMES heard of this interview, he wrote to Mr. RADCLIFFE, as follows:—

"The way in which you, and three ladies who were with you yesterday, behaved for the very few minutes Sir ROGER TICHBORNE condescended to see you, was an entire breach of the arrangement we made at Alresford, and can only result in his withdrawing himself. I regret it very much, because after what Mr. GOSFORD told me on Saturday, it is certain that if Sir ROGER had been treated by you and your party with common civility, the litigation which must ensue would have been entirely avoided. However, neither myself, nor my client can now be blamed. You did wrong in going to my house without a previous appointment, or in taking anyone there, respecting whom we had not arranged.

"My wife was surprised that neither of the three ladies favoured her with their names. Their remarks (whilst Mr. RADCLIFFE was gone to fetch Sir ROGER) were altogether unjustifiable; for they had not then seen him. I am very sorry indeed to find that your attempted surprise on Sir ROGER, and manner of treating him, were as unfair as the conduct pursued towards him by his family since his arrival in England; but the same spirit evidently animates all those whose interest it is he should not succeed.

"It is, however, a great satisfaction for Sir ROGER to know that the Court will disapprove the conduct complained of, and in the end his rights, which are founded on truth, must prevail."

On the same day Mr. HOLMES wrote a letter to Messrs. SLAUGHTER and CULLINGTON, Solicitors of the Honourable Lady DOUGHTY and Mr. and Mrs. RADCLIFFE, Mr. GOSFORD, and others, from which the following is an extract:—

"The result of a long discussion which took place between Mr. and Mrs. RADCLIFFE and Mrs. GREENWOOD and myself, at Alresford, was that it was agreed that my client should be treated with every consideration by them, and they should meet him at Tichborne.

"Sir ROGER's health prevented him from going there, and Mr. and Mrs. RADCLIFFE and Mrs. TOWNLEY called and spent an hour with him on March 8th, at Essex Lodge, Croydon, where he was living with his mother, the Dowager Lady JAMES TICHBORNE.

"Unfortunately for my efforts with a view to peace, Mr. and Mrs. RADCLIFFE and Mrs. TOWNLEY refused to see her Ladyship, and Sir ROGER was placed in consequence, in a most painful position. The next day Mr. RADCLIFFE wrote to me a letter in which, so far from denying, he tacitly admits, that my client is Sir ROGER TICHBORNE, and asked for another interview for himself and the two ladies, in order that they might be quite certain.

"Mr. GOSFORD, who went to Croydon with them, but did not go to the house, called upon me on the 9th instant, and told me that Mrs. RADCLIFFE recognised Sir ROGER by his eyes, his eyebrows, and shape of his forehead, &c., and that certainly none of the party could declare it was not him.

"I promised Mr. GOSFORD to bring about an interview between himself and Sir ROGER as soon as possible.

"I replied to Mr. RADCLIFFE's note, and stated that Sir ROGER would be happy to see his aunt, Lady DOUGHTY, as well as the other two ladies, and I placed my house at their disposal to meet at, so as to avoid the unpleasantness of their refusing to see the Dowager, and intimated that I should not be present.

"I sent the letter by THOMAS CARTER, who was Sir ROGER's groom up to within a few days of his leaving England, in 1853, and offered that any questions might be put to CARTER.

"Mr. RADCLIFFE wrote to me on the 11th instant, and said that the ladies would go again to Croydon, in company with Lady DOUGHTY, and asked me for an appointment. I answered, fixing the next day, at 3.

"On that morning Mr. RADCLIFFE sent me another letter, stating that the ladies would not go until Wednesday. I therefore sent a telegram to Sir ROGER, and postponed the appointment.

"To my great surprise, however, when I arrived home on Tuesday evening, I found that Mr. RADCLIFFE and three ladies went to my house in the afternoon of that day, and insisted upon seeing Sir ROGER. Of course, he was not there; but my wife offered to send for him.

"Mr. RADCLIFFE himself went to Essex Lodge, and Sir ROGER directly accompanied him to my house for the purpose, as he thought, of seeing Lady DOUGHTY and his cousins, Mrs. RADCLIFFE and Mrs. TOWNLEY. To his amazement, however, when he entered my dining-room, Mr. RADCLIFFE became very excited, requested my wife to retire, and asked him who the eldest lady in the room was. She was closely veiled, and Sir ROGER said he could not see her face; when, at his request, she put her veil back, and stood up. He stated he did not know her; when the whole party commenced a tirade of abuse at Sir ROGER, and he, after expressing his astonishment at such conduct following upon the arrangement Mr. RADCLIFFE made with me, at once left the room, declining to submit to such treatment. The interview, therefore, only lasted a few minutes. Mrs. RADCLIFFE was not present at it, but called after all parties had left. The three ladies had not the common politeness to announce their names to my wife, although they were with her more than half-an-hour, and during the time Mr. RADCLIFFE was gone for Sir ROGER, they freely indulged themselves in calling him an impostor, and assured Mrs. HOLMES that he was an Australian navvy.

"The youngest lady could only have been a girl when Sir ROGER left England. My wife told the eldest that she was thickly veiled, and no one could see her features.

"The third lady was Mrs. TOWNLEY.

"Mr. RADCLIFFE wrote me a letter yesterday, and I replied, complaining of the trick he had practised, and of his breaking faith with me. Copies of these letters are enclosed for your perusal. I need not say how sincerely I regret, for the sake of all parties, that such improper conduct has been pursued towards my client, but I am sure the Court will condemn it.

"Every disinterested witness who has seen and conversed with him (and they are now very numerous) is perfectly convinced that he is Sir ROGER TICHBORNE.

"I had no hesitation whatever in permitting interviews with Mr. and Mrs. RADCLIFFE, Lady DOUGHTY, and Mrs. TOWNLEY, but certainly did not expect any trick would be attempted, or my confidence abused.

"Mr. and Mrs. and Colonel GEORGE GREENWOOD have had invitations to meet Sir ROGER, but they have not responded to them. (Signed), JOHN HOLMES."

After this correspondence no further attempt was made to obtain an interview with the Claimant, with the exception of the call of Mr. WALTER NANGLE, and no efforts were afterwards made by the Claimant to see any members of his family who had treated him so harshly, and with such disrespect.

The Claimant had an interview with Mr. GOSFORD, the importance of which cannot be exaggerated. In this interview the Claimant again expressed his wish to see his Aunt DOUGHTY, notwithstanding the imposition practised upon him at Croydon.

On the 2nd May, 1867, the Claimant's second child was born. It was a boy, and christened ROGER JOSEPH DOUGHTY TICHBORNE. A notification of the birth was inserted in the *Times*, and thereupon Messrs. DOBINSON and GEARE published in the *Times* of 24th May, 1867, a letter of which the following is a copy:—

THE TICHBORNE BARONETCY.

To the EDITOR of the "TIMES."

SIR,—Your impression of Tuesday last contained an advertisement of the birth of a son to Sir ROGER CHARLES DOUGHTY TICHBORNE, Baronet. As representing the infant Baronet Sir HENRY ALFRED JOSEPH DOUGHTY TICHBORNE (only child to the late Sir ALFRED TICHBORNE, will you allow us to say that the guardians of the person and estate of the infant appointed by the Court of Chancery utterly deny the right of the person calling himself Sir ROGER CHARLES DOUGHTY TICHBORNE to bear the name and title he has unwarrantably assumed, and that should he venture to put forward any claim in a tangible shape, the guardians will be prepared to prove it wholly without foundation.

We have the honour to be, Sir, your obedient Servants,
(Signed) DOBINSON & GEARE.

57, Lincoln's Inn Fields, May 23rd.

It should be observed that this letter was written with the knowledge that the Dowager Lady TICHBORNE, his mother, had acknowledged the Claimant, and that he had been recognised by Mr. HOPKINS, the Solicitor, by Dr. LIPSCOMB of Alresford, the family surgeon, and numerous other friends and former acquaintances. Moreover, shortly after this, the Claimant's claim was put forward in a tangible shape.

The following letter, written by Mr. HOLMES to the TICHBORNE Family's Solicitors, supports this and gives particulars:—

34, Clement's Lane, Lombard-street, E.C.
London, June 2nd, 1868.

TICHBORNE *v.* MOSTYN—TICHBORNE *v.* TICHBORNE.

DEAR SIRS,—The following reference to the dates of proceedings in these suits will show how the Defendants have caused my client delay:—

27th June, 1867—Bill filed by Plaintiff.
3rd and 17th July, 1867—46 Affidavits filed by Plaintiff.
20th December, 1867—Last Answer filed by Defendants six months after Bill, and not until attachment issued.
17th February, 1868—Order on Summons adjourned into Court by Defendants binding the Infant Henry A. J. D. TICHBORNE.
3rd March, 1868—Plaintiff amended his Bills in consequence.
6th April, 1868—Plaintiff served Notice of Motion for Decree, and filed 48 additional Affidavits.
16th and 19th May, 1868—Defendants filed three Affidavits in reply in each suit. It is now eleven months since the Bills were filed, and the Defendants have consumed seven and a-half of that time merely to file their Answers and six Affidavits.

The Plaintiff's Counsel advises that the only Decree which the Court can now make on the hearing of these causes will be to retain the Bills, giving the Plaintiff liberty to take proceedings at law to establish his title, and restraining the Defendants from setting up outstanding terms, reserving further consideration and costs, with liberty to apply. I therefore enclose you minutes of such a Decree, and am quite willing, upon hearing that they meet your approval, to have the causes heard as short, and a Decree made in accordance with them.

It may be necessary for the Plaintiff to cross-examine the Defendants upon their recent Affidavits, and therefore I have served the usual notices.

If an early appointment cannot be procured from Mr. OTTEN, I presume you will consent to a motion, which I will at once make for the appointment of Mr. CHARLES ROUPEL as Special Examiner, so that no delay whatever will take place.—I am, yours truly,
JOHN HOLMES.

Messrs. DOBINSON & GEARE.

On the 30th June, 1867, the Claimant filed two Bills in Chancery, one known as TICHBORNE *v.* TICHBORNE, and the other as TICHBORNE *v.* MOSTYN, the first relating to the TICHBORNE estate only, and the second to those known as the DOUGHTY estate.

On the 2nd July he filed 37 Affidavits as to identity, with many others, subsequent filed.

Upon this the enemy, through the *Pall Mall Gazette*, with which Mr. HIGGINS (JACOB OMNIUM) was connected, opened fire upon him, and in such virulent language, that a complaint was made before Vice-Chancellor WOOD, and the Editors of the *Pall Mall Gazette*, and the *Times*, and *Morning Post*, were obliged to make an ample apology, and to pay the Claimant's costs. One of the paragraphs in the *Pall Mall Gazette* of July 17th, 1867, upon which these proceedings were taken, contains the following remarks:—

"Many of them (the Affidavits) are important enough, if the deponents can endure cross-examination in the witness-box. Many are obviously false, absurd, and worthless, being those of persons who, never having seen the Plaintiff before he left England, are nevertheless convinced that he is the person that he claims to be."

At this point, it is advisable to give a list of the various aliases which the Defendants, in their ingenuity, have given to the Claimant:—

1. JOHN MOORE, formerly servant to Mr. ROGER C. TICHBORNE.
2. SMITH, son of the old Bailiff.
3. A sailor, who left Poole.
4. Illegitimate Son of ROBERT TICHBORNE.
5. An Illegitimate Son of Mr. JAMES TICHBORNE.
6. An Illegitimate Son of Mr. EDWARD DOUGHTY.
7. DAVID CASE.
8. Servant of the late Sir EDWARD DOUGHTY at Tichborne.
9. An Australian Navvy.
10. An Australian Prizefighter.
11. ARTHUR ORTON. HENRY ORTON.
12. EDWARD HORTON.
13. A Chilian, who used to attend to Don CASTRO's horses.
14. A Whitechapel Butcher.
15. An Illegitimate Son of the Dowager Lady TICHBORNE.
16. An old Carabineer Soldier.
17. An old Servant of Mr. JAMES TICHBORNE.
18. Son of a woman, an Australian, well known there.

The Claimant himself alluded to the presence of a Mrs. CASE and somebody else, and a Miss ASHFORD, from Swanage; also three men named CURTIS, KING, and MITCHELL, who were all brought up by the Defendants to identify the Claimant as one DAVID CASE (No. 7 on the above list), son of Mrs. CASE, and who had not been heard of for some years. However, it turned out to be a lamentable failure, as described by the Claimant. Nothing was heard of the ORTON theory until after Mr. MACKENZIE, who had been dispatched to Australia in the beginning of the year 1867, wrote to England.

The next occurrence of any importance was the death of the Dowager Lady TICHBORNE, the Claimant's mother, who died suddenly, at Howlett's Hotel, in Manchester-square, on the 12th of March, 1868.

About an hour before her death she wrote a letter, dated 12th of March, 1868, to Mr. ROTS, the landlord of the Swan Hotel, at Alresford, who was then staying at Croydon with the Claimant, evincing great interest in the welfare of the Claimant, whom she designated in that letter, "My poor dear Son," who was then pressed by many troubles.

By the desire of the Claimant, a *post-mortem* examination was made, and an inquest held on the body of the Dowager Lady TICHBORNE, on 14th of March, 1868, when the Jury found a verdict that she died from disease of the heart. The Claimant's description of the occurrences at the funeral, and the efforts made to crush him at this momentous period of his career, and his description of the scandalous scenes enacted at that funeral, at Tichborne House, show clearly the feelings of his own relatives towards him.

We insert here from the *Morning Advertiser* of Monday, March 16th, 1868, the following account of the

INQUEST ON LADY TICHBORNE.

The difficulties which surrounded the settlement of the question of succession to the TICHBORNE baronetcy are likely to become still more complicated by the sudden and unexpected death of Lady HENRIETTE FELICITÉ TICHBORNE, upon whom an inquest was held on Saturday, by Dr. LANKESTER, at the request of the Claimant to the family estates, who made a very serious statement upon oath, from which it would seem that he had suspected the death to have been caused by unfair means. It may, perhaps, be necessary, for the purpose of rendering the case complete, to recal attention to the fact that recently a gentleman suddenly appeared in England who claimed to be ROGER CHARLES DOUGHTY TICHBORNE, tenth baronet, and heir to the title and estates connected with the TICHBORNE family. He stated that, after meeting with the various misfortunes consequent upon a voyage he had undertaken thirteen years ago, he reached Australia, and had remained there up to the time of his leaving for England last year. He was admitted by the deceased lady to be her son, and was in intimate and friendly relations with her up to the time of her death, but his identity was denied by the other members of the family interested in the disposal of the property, and the case yet pends the decision of the Lords Justices.

Upon the opening of the Coroner's Court, on Saturday, at Howlett's Hotel, Manchester-street, Manchester-square, Mr. LOCOCK WEBB stated that he appeared on behalf of Sir ROGER CHARLES DOUGHTY TICHBORNE.

Mr. ALFRED SEYMOUR, 39, Upper Grosvenor-street, sworn and examined, said—I am half-brother of the deceased. I believe she was born in 1804, and was at the time of her death 64 years of age. She was the widow of Sir JAMES FRANCIS DOUGHTY TICH-

BORNE, but I have no reason to suppose that she came to her death by any other than natural causes.

Coroner:—I believe the son of the deceased is present?

Mr. DOBINSON, of the firm of DOBINSON and GEARE, Lincoln's-Inn:—As the agent of the estate, I dispute that this gentleman is her son.

Coroner:—That does not matter, so far as this inquiry is concerned, if he swears that he is her son.

The gentleman in question, who had only been referred to by gesture, here stepped forward, and having been sworn by the coroner, said—My name is ROGER CHARLES DOUGHTY TICHBORNE. I am the son of the deceased. I saw her last alive this day week. She appeared to me to be in good health. I heard of her death about ten minutes past two on Thursday last, or rather I was summoned to come to London from Croydon, immediately at that time. I found her dead a little after four.

Coroner:—Do you know how she came by her death, or do you suspect any one of causing her death?

Witness (after a long pause, during which he seemed struggling to control his feelings)—I do not know how she came by her death, but I wished the *post-mortem* examination to be made, because I am fully aware that one of my servants was offered £1,000 to put me out of the way.

At the request of a juror, this statement was repeated.

Coroner:—We cannot go into that question here, although, if you can bring evidence in support of what you state, you can take action in another court.

The next witness was then called.

EDWARD HURST, a waiter at Howlett's Hotel, deposed:—Her ladyship had been living there for five months. She had been in general good health all that time. I found her dead on Thursday morning, at 25 minutes past eleven, in her room, with her body on the floor by the fire-place, and her head on the sofa. She had her dressing-gown on. I had not seen her till then since the morning before, when she went to Croydon. Her maid and her footman were both with her the morning she died.

CATHERINE BARRETT:—I was her ladyship's maid, and saw her on last Wednesday night. She was in her usual health. She got up at half-past six on Thursday morning, and went into the drawing-room, and said to me, "You have not yet lighted my fire." She appeared in her usual health still. She went back to her bed-room, and slept till seven o'clock. She came into the drawing-room again, and took two cups of tea. I was called to her about half-past nine, and had some conversation with her. I saw her again at a quarter-past eleven, when she had a newspaper in her hand. I never saw her again alive. She was not dressed. She never dressed till twelve.

Mr. HENRY TIMES, M.R.C.S:—I was called to deceased at half-past eleven on Thursday morning. She was quite dead. She had been dead a very few minutes, and was quite warm. I could not detect anything in the room like poison. Her body was moderately nourished. I found extensive congestion of the brain. There was a little fluid, but not enough to account for death. There was some also in the ventricle. I opened the chest and found the lungs congested; and there was evidence of long-standing disease. There was very little fluid in the precordium. The heart was very small and shrunken. The right wall was very thin. The left wall was thicker, but the fibrous substance was easily broken in. There was fatty degeneration of the heart. The right cavities were full, and there was a slight quantity of fluid blood in the left. The valves were healthy. The stomach had a little fluid in it, which I have preserved. I did not perceive any indications of poison. Mr. TIERNAN and several other medical gentlemen, who were with me when I made the post-mortem examination, agreed with me. Mr. TIERNAN said all the organs were healthy, except the heart. The cause of death was fatal syncope from a feeble heart.

The Coroner said that was a very common cause of death in persons of from 60 to 70. The heart naturally shrunk from its natural size, and suddenly failed altogether. There were circumstances connected with the case that might lead them to suspect unfair play, but there was an entire want of evidence to support any suspicion. Everything seemed to be going on properly in the hotel, and they could not suspect deceased's servants. If, however, the Jury thought there was the slightest reason to suppose that she had taken, or had had administered to her any poison, they must adjourn, and send the contents of the stomach to undergo careful analysis.

After some conversation on the subject of further medical evidence, in the course of which the Coroner said the Middlesex magistrates frequently hampered him by making him liable to pay for extra medical evidence out of his own pocket, and would do any injustice to save a few shillings, Mr. LEWIS, M.R.C.S., corroborated the evidence of Mr. TIMES.

Mr. TIMES, in answer to the foreman of the Jury, said, that death might have been hastened by abstinence from food. Deceased was a strict Catholic, and might have been fasting, but she had not asked for certificates lately.

After a short deliberation in private, the Jury returned a verdict, "That deceased was found dead, and that death was caused by atrophy and fatty degeneration of the heart."

This comment may be closed by a quotation from a poem which was written by a Hampshire farmer, and published after the funeral, with the following distich:—

"Over the ashes of the dead
No peace was brought about,
But all with bitterness turned back
To fight the Battle out."

The Claimant having been left destitute by the death of his mother, his friends immediately after the funeral assembled in the dining-room at Tichborne House, spontaneously; and, without preconcert, subscribed £1,400 to form a fund for the maintenance of himself and family, and they also expressed their desire that he and his family should come to reside at Alresford, to be near his estates. This desire was carried out, and the Claimant went to reside at Alresford in April, 1868, where he continued to reside until March, 1869, and during his residence there he had continual opportunities of seeing and conversing with his old friends.

The evidence as to his identity was then procured from various parts of the country.

Within a few days after the death of the Dowager Lady TICHBORNE, it was rumoured that the Defendants intended to apply for commissions to examine witnesses in Australia and Chili, but no steps were taken, until the Claimant had taken proceedings in the Court of Probate, to administer to the effects of his late mother; and Lord PENZANCE had given notice that he would fix the day of trial on a particular day.

On the day before the day appointed for fixing the time of trial the Defendants applied for the Commission, thus deferring the application to the latest possible moment.

The Defendants filed a Bill against the Claimant in the name of TOMAS CASTRO, with two objects: First, to obtain possession of his mother's private letters and papers, and 2ndly, for the sake of annoyance.

When the Claimant was married, in January, 1865, at Wagga-Wagga, he weighed 11 stone 4lb. His weight afterwards increased to nearly 27 stone.

The rate of increase, which is almost astounding, will be seen in the following table:—

SIR ROGER TICHBORNE'S WEIGHT.

In January, 1865, when married, 11st. 4lb.
" 24th August, 1866, at Sydney, 13st. 6lb. (Record in London)
" March or April, 1867 (at Croydon Steeple Chases) 19st. 11lb.
" 13th June, 1867 (weighed at the Crystal Palace) 21st. 4½lb.
" August, 1868 do. do. 24st. 7½lb.
" September, 1870 .. .. 27st. 10lb.

Afterwards his troubles and anxiety reduced him to something under 24 stone.

It will easily be imagined that such increased bulk, ill-adapted him for another journey round the world, so that when the Commissions were applied for, he was naturally averse to accompany them; he was strongly dissuaded (by the most powerful of his Hampshire friends, Mr. SCOTT, of Rotherfield Park, Major MARX, and others), who entreated him to stay at home at all risks; but the pressure of his legal advisers caused him finally to resolve on a voyage to Chili; and his description of the steps taken for that purpose, and his reason for returning from Cordova, are thoroughly satisfactory to any unprejudiced person.

We insert Major MARX's Affidavit:—

I, FRANCIS JOSEPH PETER MARX, of Arlebury House, Alresford, in the County of Southampton, Esquire, a magistrate for the county, make oath and say as follows:—

1. I knew Mr. ROGER CHARLES TICHBORNE previously to his leaving England, about the year 1853. I well knew his father, uncle and family.

2. I had an opportunity of seeing and conversing with the above-named Plaintiff since his return to this country. I am quite satisfied as to the identity of the Plaintiff from his voice, manner, and face, and recognise him as the Mr. ROGER CHARLES TICHBORNE I formerly knew as the son of the late Sir JAMES DOUGHTY TICHBORNE, Baronet.

3. The statements herein contained are within my own knowledge. FRANCIS J. P. MARX.

Sworn at New Alresford, in the County of Southampton, this 12th day of July, 1867—Before me,
JNO. FRAS. ADAMS,
A Commissioner to administer oaths in Chancery in England.

The precarious state of his health was testified by Dr. THORP, surgeon of the ship "Oneida" (in which he sailed from Southampton to Rio) as well as by Mr. PARKES, the chief officer of that ship; and in his return voyage by Dr. HEALEY, the surgeon of "The City of Brussels" (in which vessel he returned from Buenos Ayres to Falmouth).

The next Affidavit is that of ROBERT CHERRETT, of Lytchett, near Poole, Dorsetshire, who died on the 10th of June, 1868, and is buried at Lytchett, in Dorsetshire.

I, ROBERT CHERRETT, of Lytchett, near Poole, in the County of Dorset, Carpenter, make oath and say as follows:—

1. I am fifty-one years of age. I knew Mr. ROGER CHARLES TICHBORNE when he was living at Upton, in the years 1852 and 1853. I made for him some packing-cases and models of axes for him to take to America. I spoke to him often upon them, and had frequent opportunities of seeing him.

2. On the 15th October, 1867, I saw the above-named Plain-

tiff at Poole aforesaid, and had some talk with him. I recognised him by his eyebrows and upper part of his face to be the same person as the said Mr. Roger Charles Tichborne whom I formerly knew as aforesaid, and I have no hesitation in deposing to his identity.

3. The facts herein stated are within my own knowledge.

R. Cherrett.

Sworn at Upton, near Poole, in the County of Dorset, this 19th day of December, 1867—Before me,

H. W. Dickinson,

A Commissioner to administer oaths in Chancery in England.

The next Affidavit is that of John McCourt, the only Catholic Sergeant in the 6th Dragoon Guards, Carabineers, at the time Mr. Tichborne left, in 1853.

I, John McCourt, of No I, Victoria-terrace, Mortlake, in the County of Surrey, late a troop sergeant-major in the 6th Dragoon Guards, or Carabineers, make oath and say as follows:—

1. I am forty-eight years of age. In the year 1840 I enlisted in the 6th Dragoon Guards, or Carabineers, and about the year 1846 I became a sergeant in the said regiment, which rank I continued to hold until the year 1855, when I was promoted to the rank of troop sergeant-major, and I remained in the regiment as troop sergeant-major until the year 1864, when I obtained my discharge on a full pension.

2. I well remember Mr. Roger Charles Tichborne joining the 6th Dragoon Guards as cornet at Portobello Barracks, Dublin, about the end of October, 1849, and that he was appointed a lieutenant in the following year. I knew him well from the time of his joining the regiment in 1849 until his retirement therefrom at Canterbury in February, 1853. I had, whilst he was on duty with the regiment, opportunities of seeing him daily, and was with him for hours at a time. On Sundays I was under his immediate command, being the only Catholic sergeant in the regiment at that time who accompanied the men to chapel. I distinctly recollect his features and personal appearance, his large eyes and eyebrows, and the upper part of his face, a peculiarity in the parting or arrangement of his hair, and its colour. I also recollect his voice, which was peculiar and broken. He spoke more like a foreigner than an Englishman, and his manners were also peculiar, and he was of a most kind, liberal, and considerate disposition, all of which had continued firmly impressed on my memory.

3. I had not seen the said Mr. Roger Charles Tichborne from the time he left the regiment in 1853, until Saturday, the 14th day of March, 1868, when I went into a room at Howlett's Hotel, Manchester-street, London, for the express purpose of seeing the above-named Plaintiff. I did see the Plaintiff, and I knew him again the instant I saw his features. I recognised him by the upper part of his face, eyes, and eyebrows, by his hair and by his voice, as soon as he spoke, to be the same Mr. Roger Charles Tichborne, whom I so well knew and recollected as an officer in the 6th Dragoon Guards (or Carabineers). I entered into conversation with him, and he answered accurately the several questions I put to him. I told him I would, and was ready, to swear to him anywhere, as there could be no mistake about his identity whatever. His voice, I noticed, was more firm and less broken than when I knew him in the Carabineers; but on hearing him read, I found his accent and pronunciation to be exactly as it was when he was an officer in the Carabineers.

4. I again saw and conversed with the Plaintiff on the 24th day of March, 1868, and I am certain of his identity, and I do distinctly and positively swear that he is the same Mr. Roger Charles Tichborne whom I formerly knew, and well remember as an officer in the 6th Dragoon Guards or Carabineers, as aforesaid.

5. The statements herein contained are within my own knowledge.

John McCourt.

Sworn at No. 5, Wallbrook, in the City of London, this 27th day of March, 1868.—Before me,

John Biggenden,

A London Commissioner to administer oaths in Chancery.

This witness died at Mortlake, Surrey, on 11th June, 1870.

It may be well to state the circumstances under which this witness was heard, of the Claimant having employed Mr. Garstin, of Welbeck-street, a well-known undertaker, to conduct his mother's funeral, was informed by Mr. Garstin, the next day, that there was living, near his residence at Barnes, an old Carabineer of the name of McCourt. The Claimant thereupon asked Garstin to request McCourt to call upon him, which he did on the following day, and the result is set forth in the Affidavit.

The next Affidavit is that of John Waddington, of the Royal Military College Sandhurst, who died in February, 1870, and was buried on the 7th of that month.

I, John Waddington, now stationed at the Royal Military College, Sandhurst, as gatekeeper, make oath and say as follows:—

1. I am 61 years of age. I was in 1849 in Her Majesty's 6th Dragoon Guards (Carabineers) corporal and assistant in the riding-school, of which Mr. Phillips was riding-master. I remember Mr. Roger Charles Tichborne joining the regiment in that year at Portobello Barracks, Dublin. I knew him from that time until he left the regiment, about the end of 1852. I was sergeant in the riding-school when Mr. Tichborne left. While he was in the regiment I saw Mr. Tichborne every day, or nearly so, and I gave him riding lessons. He was very heavy at his drills, and difficult to teach; and he had extra riding and drills. He was a good horseman—that is, he had a good seat, and could stick well upon a horse; but I remember in Cahir his horse shook his bridle off his head, and Mr. Tichborne jumped off.

2. Some time after Mr. Tichborne left the regiment I heard that he was supposed to be lost at sea.

3. On Monday, the 25th March, 1867, Thomas Carter, who was formerly a groom to Mr. Tichborne, called upon me at Sandhurst, and, at his request, I came to London on the 27th March, 1867, and went to the offices of Mr. Holmes, 25, Poultry. I was shown into a room there, where sat the gentleman whom I formerly knew in the Carabineers as Mr. Roger Charles Tichborne. I had an hour's talk with him, and during that time he asked me particularly after Major Norbury, who was a brother officer of his in the regiment, and other officers, and also named to me things which I well remember to have taken place while he was in the regiment. I am quite certain that the Plaintiff, being the gentleman whom I saw and conversed with at Mr. Holmes's office, as aforesaid, is the Mr. Tichborne I formerly knew in the Carabineers. I recognise him particularly by the upper part of his face and the movement of his eyebrows, and by his voice. I was formerly so often and so long with him that I am perfectly sure I am not mistaken. He is the right height.

4. No one was present at the last-mentioned interview except the Plaintiff and myself.

5. I have again seen and conversed with the Plaintiff on Saturday last and to-day, and have no doubt as to his identity.

6. The statements hereinbefore mentioned are within my own knowledge.

J. Waddington.

Sworn at New Alresford, in the County of Southampton, this 1st day of July, 1867,—Before me

Jno. Fras. Adams,

A Commissioner to administer oaths in Chancery in England.

I, Andrew McEleny, bandmaster of Her Majesty's 44th regiment, now stationed at Aldershot, in the county of Hants, make oath and say as follows, videlicet:—

1. My father, who is now dead, was bandmaster of the 6th Dragoon Guards (Carabineers), during the time Mr. Roger Charles Tichborne was an officer in that regiment, and I was band-sergeant of the same regiment during the latter part of that time. My father used to teach the said Mr. Tichborne the French horn, and he came to my father's rooms to take lessons. I had ample opportunity of knowing, and did well know, and do distinctly remember the features and personal appearance of the said Mr. Roger Charles Tichborne.

2. On the 8th day of October, 1867, I saw, and had a long conversation with the above-named Plaintiff. I recognise him particularly by the upper part of his face, his expression of countenance and his walk, to be the same person as the said Mr. Roger Charles Tichborne whom I formerly knew as an officer in the Carabineers, and I have not the least doubt respecting his identity. We conversed about my father and the French horn, and he quite satisfied me by his answers to my questions.

3. The facts herein stated are within my own knowledge.

A. McEleny.

Sworn at Brentford, in the County of Middlesex, this 19th day of December, 1867—Before me,

Thos. A. Woodbridge,

A London Commissioner to administer oaths in Chancery

I, William O'Ryan, late of Bansha Castle, in the County of Tipperary, in the kingdom of Ireland, Esquire, but now residing at Winchester, in the County of Southampton, and formerly a lieutenant in the Tipperary Artillery, make oath and say as follows:—

1. I am thirty-five years of age, and am the eldest surviving son of the late Edmund O'Ryan, of Bansha Castle, in the County of Tipperary, Esquire, a justice of the peace for the said county. My father died when I was about four years of age, and I became a ward of Chancery. My mother subsequently intermarried with John Chatfer, Esquire, of Park View, J.P. His house was my home, and I resided there with my brothers and sisters from the time of my childhood until about the year 1854.

2. I well remember the 6th Dragoon Guards (Carabineers) coming to Cahir about the month of June, 1850, and that the regiment remained there for eighteen months or more, to the best of my belief. The Officers of the Carabineers were upon visiting terms at my own house, and I have a distinct remembrance of several of them, and in particular I remember among others, Mr. Roger Charles Tichborne, who used to visit us, and that I myself dined on several occasions at the Carabineers mess. I often saw the said Mr. Tichborne during his visits to our house and elsewhere in the neighbourhood, and knew him well. I recollect his features and personal appearance, that he smoked a great deal, was rather shy and retired in his manners, and spoke with a broken accent and hesitation. On one occasion, I distinctly remember his testing my strength in Mr. Sarjent's dining-room, by wrestling with me, and that for that purpose we removed the chairs and table from the centre of the room.

3. In the early part of November, 1867, at Winchester, a conversation arose in my presence and hearing about the return of Mr. Roger Charles Tichborne. As soon as I heard the name of Tichborne mentioned, and that he was formerly an officer of

the Carabineers, I immediately said: "I knew Mr. TICHBORNE, who was in the Carabineers, quite well. He used to visit our house when they were quartered at Cahir, and I am sure I should know him again," or words to that effect. I expressed a wish to see the gentleman in question, and as the result of subsequent inquiries, I went to the Swan Hotel, Alresford, on the 30th day of November, 1867, for the purpose of seeing the Plaintiff, and judging for myself whether or not he was the same person whom I formerly knew as an officer in the 6th Dragoon Guards, or Carabineers. I did see the Plaintiff, when I instantly recognised him by his features, to be the same Mr. TICHBORNE whom I knew as an officer in the Carabineers at Cahir, as aforesaid. I entered into conversation with the Plaintiff, and he answered correctly every question I put to him about Cahir and its neighbourhood, and about the different families living there, and in the immediate neighbourhood. He well remembered my wrestling with him, and gave particulars relating to it, and he recalled to my mind many circumstances which occurred in my presence, and also mentioned the names of those who were with us on those occasions, and gave me ample evidence of an intimate acquaintance with Cahir and its neighbourhood. I also recognised him by his manner, and I do distinctly and absolutely swear that the Plaintiff is the same person as the Mr. ROGER CHARLES TICHBORNE whom I knew as an officer in the 6th Dragoon Guards, or Carabineers.

4. The statements herein contained are within my own knowledge. WILLM. O'RYAN.

Sworn at New Alresford, in the County of Southampton, this 30th day of November, 1867—Before me,

JNO. FRAS. ADAMS,

A Commissioner to administer oaths in Chancery in England.

It may be desirable here to mention, that, although the Claimant was frequently pressed to go over to Ireland to see Cahir and the neighbourhood, and to call on his former friends, he never did so, giving as a reason, that had he consented, his enemies would have suggested he had done it for the purpose of picking up information as to localities and persons. His power of description is very great, and he to the satisfaction of Carabineers, sketched the position of his room at the Barracks at Cahir, and other particulars, which satisfied them of his identity. For the same reason, he stedfastly refused to go to Canterbury, which place he has never seen since he left in 1853, yet his power of description, and whole knowledge of that place, and of the Barracks in which they were quartered, is surprising, considering the lapse of time.

The next Affidavit is of an importance which cannot be overstated: that of JOHN WYATT CATER:—

I, JOHN WYATT CATER, of No. 29, Henry-street, Pentonville in the county of Middlesex, master baker, but now out of business make oath and say as follows:—

1. I lived in the town of Wagga-Wagga, New South Wales, during the year 1865, and until May, 1866, when I left to return to England. During the time I so resided in Wagga-Wagga I carried on business as a baker, and there knew, and was pertectly well acquainted with, the above-named Plaintiff, who was then passing by the name of TOM CASTRO. I served him with bread daily for twelve months. He was, during the greater part of the time, employed as manager by ROBERT HIGGINS, who then carried on business in Wagga-Wagga as a butcher and hotel-keeper, and in the same employ and at the same time, there was another man whom I well knew by the name of ARTHUR ORTON, and whose face was pitted with small-pox.

2. Since my return to England, I have frequently seen and conversed with the above-named Plaintiff, and I say he is the same person whom I knew under the name of TOM CASTRO in Wagga-Wagga, as aforesaid, and another and totally distinct person from the said ARTHUR ORTON. JOHN WYATT CATER.

Sworn at 21, Abchurch-lane, in the City of London, this 28th day of May, 1868—Before me,

THOS. PRICE,

A London Commissioner to administer oaths in Chancery.

Great efforts were made by the Clamant in the hopes of inducing him to remain in England to give evidence at the Trial, but the Trial not being then fixed, and its possibility of coming on at all, being then doubted, Mr. CATER decided to return to Australia.

The importance of this witness's evidence is derived from the fact that the Claimant knowing that CATER was about to leave Wagga-Wagga for England, gave him in the beginning of April, 1866, a sealed letter, with instructions not to open it until at sea. These instructions were written on the envelope, and enforced by a promise which the Claimant obtained from CATER, previous to delivery. This letter is dated 2nd April, 1866.

COPY LETTER.

Wagga-Wagga, April 2nd, 1866.

At any time when you are in England, if you should feel inclined for a month's pleasure, go to Tichborne in Hampshire, enquire for Sir ROGER CHARLES TICHBORNE, Tichborne Hall, Tichborne, and you will find one that will make you a welcome guest, but on no account mention the name of CASTRO, or allude to my being a married man, or that I have been a butcher. You will understand me, I have no doubt.—Yours truly,

THOMAS CASTRO.

I sail by the June Mail.

Mr. CATER sailed for England the same month, and never thought of the matter until he was reaching England, when turning over his boxes, the letter appeared.

The contents of this letter naturally surprised him greatly. After he had been in England a few months, he was anxious to know if his unexpected friend was actually a TICHBORNE, and wrote a letter to him there. In consequence of this, in the early part of December, 1866, he wrote to the Postmaster at Alresford, inquiring the address of SIR ROGER TICHBORNE. The Postmaster showed the letter to Mr. HOPKINS of Alresford, who immediately took it to Winchester, and showed it to Mr. BAIGENT. It was then resolved to open communication with Mr. CATER and ascertain what he knew of the person in question. Mr. HOPKINS accordingly wrote to the address given, but after waiting several days, and having no reply, he suggested that Mr. BAIGENT should also write, which he accordingly did.

The letter had only been posted a few hours, when a message was received from Mr. HOPKINS, telling Mr. BAIGENT he had just got a letter, and asking him to come to Alresford to see it.

Shortly after the Claimant's return, hearing of this correspondence, he communicated with Mr. CATER, who accordingly came to see him at Croydon.

On seeing him at Croydon, he said he was so altered in appearance, that he hardly knew him again, although only ten months had elapsed since they parted at Wagga-Wagga.

The importance of the letter consists in its date (the 2nd April, 1866), which was before the Claimant received his mother's reply to his first letter, which was dated January 17th in the same year. His mother's letter in reply to it, was dated February 25th, 1866, and would not reach Wagga-Wagga until the expiration of forty-five days, which would be after the 2nd April, 1866.

The date of the receipt of the Dowager's letter is fixed in the evidence of CUBITT. It is evident that when this letter was written, so confident was the Claimant, and so little doubt did he entertain of being recognised and acknowledged, that he did not hesitate to ask a brother colonist to his mansion house in England. It should also be observed that he named the day of his departure from Sydney, irrespective of the result of his letter to his mother.

Before commenting on the local evidence, the following very able letter, written by the Reverend Mr. BISHOP, who from 1839 to 1852 was perpetual Curate of the Parish of Tichborne, and who consequently intimately knew all the members of the family of TICHBORNE, and who was afterwards Rector of Brandean, a parish only four miles from Tichborne, deserves attentive perusal:

DEAR SIR,—Having been for many years curate of Tichborne, and knowing with some degree of intimacy the three baronets of the last generation—Sir HENRY, Sir EDWARD, and Sir JAMES TICHBORNE (the father of the Claimant), I naturally took a deep interest in the question at issue from the first, and my long and close friendship with the legal adviser of the late Sir JAMES TICHBORNE—Mr. HOPKINS, of Alresford—gave me ready access to the evidence and proofs which finally convinced him of the Claimant's identity. Mr. HOPKINS was cautious and deliberate in adopting the supposition that ROGER TICHBORNE had re-appeared, and after he had learnt enough to warrant an investigation on his own part, he received the Claimant at his table, and eventually at his house; and in long repeated familiar conversations, as little catechetical as possible, and studiously suited to place the Claimant at his ease and off his guard, Mr. HOPKINS came to the conviction, without the shadow of a remaining doubt, that his guest was the person he professed to be. From time to time, as the proofs accumulated, they were laid before me at my interviews with Mr. HOPKINS, and I have at length drawn the same conclusion as himself.

The evidence on which this conclusion is based may be ranged under three heads:—

I. Physical Proofs.—The Claimant measures exactly the same height as ROGER TICHBORNE; his head is the same size; and his foot the same length; which is the more remarkable as the comparison is between a man of twenty-four stone and a man of ten. Moreover, he has identifying marks from top to toe: a scar in the hair behind the ear; a birth-mark on the side; the scar of a lancet on his ankle. There is also a mark on the arm, which indicates French vaccination (the *stigmata* being different from ours), and though this does not identify, yet it agrees perfectly with the theory of his being TICHBORNE, and not at all with the theory of his being ORTON. Under this head I also class the evidence of his letters. I do not say handwriting, because there is some difference between that of ROGER TICHBORNE'S, in the dozen or more letters he wrote Mr. HOPKINS before leaving the Army, and that of the several letters which the Claimant wrote to him since his appearance at Alresford. But this difference is no more than you might expect after fourteen years of bush life. The hands are not so different in character that the one could not well have become the other. But there is, on the other hand, a very striking identity in the turn of expression, and in the repetition of old solecisms and peculiarities. I have compared the letters more than once, and was struck with this point of resemblance. Any designed conformity would have been directed, first to the handwriting. I remember Mr. HOPKINS pointing out to me that the initial signatures of the recent letters exactly corresponded with those of the earlier correspondence; which was the more remarkable, as whenever the Claimant was mentioned in the public papers, his name was not stated in conformity with these, his invariable signatures.

I must add another proof, which is to me very convincing—his familiarity with the fly-rod, the saddle, and the gun. The two latter would be within reach, probably, of every colonist, but not so the former. One must serve an apprenticeship from one's youth ever to make an expert fly-fisher. It would be quite natural that ROGER TICHBORNE, who passed some years on the banks of the Itchen, should be able to throw a fly, and should be acquainted with the likely places of the river; but exceedingly unlikely that a butcher's son should acquire the art at Wapping, or perfect it in Australia, where there are neither the fish nor the flies.

II. I next come to another class of evidence—Testimony; and as this is now *litera scripta*, I need not enter into the specific depositions which are to be found in the several affidavits. Those which most swayed my mind are the statements of Mr. HOPKINS, Mr. BAIGENT, GREENWOOD the tailor, JOHN MANSBRIDGE, the under keeper, Major HEYWOOD, MORLEY, Dr. LIPSCOMBE, Mr. SCOTT, and I might add many others; and I would remark that what would make it next to impossible, even for the most clever impostor to be primed effectually for the various conversations he must encounter in setting up this claim, is the fact that there are so many distinct worlds into which he is thrown in the process of identification:

1. There is the little world of Tichborne, where he used to pass his holidays and intervals of leave. The house at his first entering it is familiar to him; he remarks on various alterations of doors and windows in the rooms; speaks of the old family picture as "looking brighter than ever he had known it"—just lately done up; ascends familiarly to the lumber-room, sees some pheasant skins there, which he immediately recognised as those he had sent from South America, and at once explains the process of their preservation; recognises several of the old servants, and converses freely with them severally on all the little incidents which connected them with him; how one man caught him spear-

PORTRAIT OF ALFRED JOSEPH TICHBORNE.

ing the fish, chased him and overtook him in "the hassock, on Tichborne Down;" how another used to hold up his music while he practised the key-bugle, &c.

In all these conversations, it is noticed that he never says the right thing of a wrong person; but the sight and name and presence of each person seems to draw out naturally the old circumstances associated with each. Supposing that there was some-one at the Claimant's elbow prompting him for some of these conversations, and that he himself was clever enough to draw from one man's conversation things which would prepare him for another's, yet how could the informant who could help him at Tichborne be competent for the other totally different scenes of ROGER TICHBORNE's life?

2. At Poole, where he spent some months at his uncle's empty house, between his leaving the service and going abroad, he mixed constantly with the fishermen of the place. He went there expressly to indulge his love of sports a little out of the usual way. The Claimant can tell, and does tell, the very respectable man, whom Mr. SEYMOUR sent to give an affidavit against him, all the little incidents and particulars which occurred between them in their fishing at night, to the thorough conviction of the man in question that this must be his former companion by the token of his knowing things which only they two could know anything about.

3. Then there is another distinct scene with which the Claimant's prompter must be no less familiar—the quarters of his regiment. He can converse with brother officers without committing himself, avoid the traps they laid purposely to test him, and put in his word in the conversation in a way which absolutely proves participation in the circumstances referred to. If I reject the testimony of all these persons who actually identify the Claimant, or believe in his identity, then I must suppose that his mother was mistaken as to her son, the lawyer who settled most important family affairs with him was mistaken as to his client, the surgeon who attended him, as to his patient, many old servants of Tichborne House as to the heir, gentlemen of the

county as to the son of their old friend, scores of officers and non-commissioned officers and privates of his former regiment as to their comrade. In Australia, before he comes over, the Claimant tells Mr. LONG, grandson of my old friend Mr. LONG, of Preshaw, the names of the different meets of the H. H., where he had met him in hunting. He tells his tailor what was the last coat he had made for him thirteen years before; he tells Mr. HOPKINS various details of family affairs in which they had both been concerned, and points of business in which Mr. HOPKINS had acted between him and his father; he singles out at Burton Constable the bed-room he used to occupy (one out of thirty), and tells his friend Major CONSTABLE on the spot, "Here we used to smoke on the grass plat," "There we grubbed a thorn." &c.; he names to the under-keeper the different dogs with which he was used to shoot, and details endless incidents of their sporting companionship; he can do the same at Poole; he can do the same in Ireland. He never flinches from conversation with those whom he has formerly known, and often corrects them when they mis-state things accidentally or intentionally. Altogether there is an air of lazy self-reliance about him quite incompatible with imposture, and a total absence of rising to take the bait when there is an opportunity to strengthen his own case by doing so. Let me give an instance:—"That ring on your hand is the one your uncle gave you on your birthday, I suppose," said Mr. HOPKINS to him one day, at his table. Now as this would have been a very strong mark of identification, and would have tended to persuade the person who put the question, no impostor in the world but would have followed this lead. The Claimant's answer was simple and natural. "Oh, no! I lost that. This is one I had made for me in Sydney."

I pass to a third kind of evidence, which has drawn me to the conclusion I have come to of the Claimant's identity—the agreement of various phenomena with the theory:

1. As to his language. On my first interview with him I was so surprised by the vulgarity of his dialect and expressions, that my immediate prepossession was strong against him. But in the course of conversation I was enabled to analyse it a little, and I found the following components in it, altogether forming a very strange mixture, but exactly such as would correspond with the circumstances of TICHBORNE's life, and with the presumption that this is TICHBORNE. You have, in his language, a quantity of common words miscalled and ill-pronounced (such as howsomedever for howsoever or however); these savour of low life in the bush. Yet there was a remarkable fluency in the use of words such as you do not find in men of the lower class (unless here and there in a man talented enough to be a demagogue); then thirdly, there was in his language a little perceptible French accentuation, and a little easy action and gesticulation of the hands, foreign, or else confined to the educated classes. Now all this exactly fits the case of a man who was bred in France up to sixteen years of age, never afterwards perfectly masters English, goes to a colony with the intention of burying himself there, and associates with a class beneath him. The shock I received at first hearing him speak wore off in a few minutes' conversation, and I may add that there is scarcely an instance of any one continuing doubtful of his identity after an hour's conversation with him.

2. Another of the phenomena as to eccentricity. In the original ROGER TICHBORNE it was marked. As a youth in the army his whole reading was of wild sports and adventures. The moment he can do so he quits the service and goes in quest of adventures. He prefers the amusement of deep-sea fishing to the ordinary life and pleasures of TICHBORNE. He told his brother ALFRED to marry and keep up the line, as he would not be heard of again. It is an undeniable fact that his brother ALFRED, when he married, impressed in a very honourable way on his cousin and bride, "that ROGER might appear any day."

When, therefore, the Claimant does appear, in a very eccentric way, after an equally eccentric disappearance, this is all in harmony with the same character. It is quite consistent that a man who wished to be lost sight of should not draw his allowance, should drop correspondence with home, should marry beneath him, and should live by his own labour; and it is part and parcel of the same eccentricity that when he returned he should pay a furtive visit to the old tenants and disclose himself by degrees instead of at once.

3. Another of the phenomena—personal resemblance. ROGER TICHBORNE, as a boy, was not often before me, and what imperfect recollection I have of him does not enable me to recognise the Claimant as the man; others who knew him better can do so. I can see an exact resemblance of him to his mother's portrait in a very peculiar dropping of the outer corners of the eyes, and in the whole *contour* of the upper part of the face. Many who have seen his children say that they are TICHBORNE all over, and I, who remember the three old baronets, certainly consider that, in so far as the Claimant departs from the stature and lines of young ROGER, he assimilates himself proportionately to the old members of the family. Taking the opponents' ground "that there is not the slightest resemblance between this man and the real Sir ROGER," one cannot but wonder how so many old servants could see a likeness, and how those who set up an impostor could have added so materially to their own difficulties by selecting a man who refuted his claims in his own appearance.

I will end this lengthened letter with a few words on the objections which I hear most commonly in this neighbourhood from those who disavow the Claimant.

The first is as to his failing memory. He forgets a great deal he ought to remember—names of relatives, of schoolfellows, of tutors. In my judgment, one little incident remembered outweighs a score forgotten. Any man may forget—all do forget; but no one can make a happy guess of the thousands of things which the Claimant has deposed to.

The next objection is as to his not going at once to Colonel GREENWOOD's (Brookwood), and openly proclaiming himself to the cousin he was so intimate with.

The explanation is twofold: first, Colonel and Mrs. GREENWOOD were as unwilling to go to Alresford to meet the Claimant at Mr. HOPKINS' house, though earnestly requested to do so, as the Claimant was to go to Brookwood. The hesitation of the latter rose out of the following circumstances. Long before he left Australia, a character of him had been sent home, in the public papers and by private communications. Mr. HOPKINS was fully convinced, and more than once stated to me the conviction, that it was a religious movement which was at the bottom of the statements to his prejudice—that the Claimant was looked on as very lax in his views, and no true member of the Romish Church. Whether this was so I know not; but immediately on his landing at Gravesend, Mr. GOSFORD, the agent for the Tichborne estates, was sent down by the CULLINGTON family to meet him, or went of his own accord. Before Mr. GOSFORD had seen him he proclaimed him to the master of the inn as an impostor, and induced him to send in his bill at once. I have seen the letters which subsequently passed from Mr. GOSFORD to Mr. HOPKINS, and I regarded them as the letters of an uncandid man, who was gradually taking his line as would best serve his own ends, and the prepossessions of the family. Such proceedings would very naturally indispose the Claimant to present himself where it was likely his identity would be rather doubted than surmised. However incorrectly he would naturally look on Mr. GOSFORD's reception of him as an index of what he might expect from the family, and though I am fully convinced he would have met with fair play from my friends Colonel and Mrs. GREENWOOD, who are both thoroughly honourable and honest in their opposition, yet I am not surprised at his reluctance to trust himself in a house which he would have entered (in their eyes) in a very doubtful character. Mr. SEYMOUR's proceedings at Alresford and in London widened the breach, and made it more impossible for the Claimant to go to Brookwood.—I am, dear Sir, yours very truly,

A. BISHOP.

Brandean House, Alresford, Hants: 18th October, 1870.

P.S.—I did not attend the funeral of the Claimant's mother, Lady TICHBORNE, but many of my friends and neighbours did. Their accounts of the incidents of the day are very consistent, and have led me to the conclusion that no impostor could have aped the sorrow, nor assumed the dignity and self-possession which were conspicuous in your client on that occasion.

An affidavit by the writer follows:

I, the Reverend ALFRED CÆSAR BISHOP, of Bramdean, in the County of Southampton, clerk, Rector of Bramdean aforesaid, make oath and say as follows:—

1. I was formerly curate of the parish of Tichborne, in the said county, and well knew the late Sir EDWARD DOUGHTY, and his brother, the late Sir JAMES FRANCIS DOUGHTY TICHBORNE, during their respective residences at Tichborne House, the family seat of the TICHBORNES. Also knew the Plaintiff and the late ALFRED TICHBORNE, his brother, the two sons of the said Sir JAMES TICHBORNE.

2. Since the Plaintiff's return to England I have seen and conversed with him, and I verily believe that he is the Mr. ROGER CHARLES TICHBORNE, the eldest son of the said late Sir JAMES FRANCIS DOUGHTY TICHBORNE, deceased, whom I formerly knew previously to his leaving this country in the year 1853.

3. The facts herein stated are within my own knowledge.

ALFRED CÆSAR BISHOP.

Sworn at New Alresford, in the County of Southampton, this 1st day of July, 1867—Before me,

JNO. FRAS. ADAMS,

A Commissioner to administer oaths in Chancery in England.

The following sketch of the life of Sir ROGER TICHBORNE was prepared by another hand. We insert it here, as it contains many things which are not embraced in the foregoing:—

BIOGRAPHICAL SKETCH OF SIR ROGER CHARLES DOUGHTY TICHBORNE, BARONET.

The late Sir HENRY TICHBORNE, Seventh Baronet of Tichborne, Aldershot, and Frimley, died in 1821, and was succeeded by his eldest son, Sir HENRY JOSEPH TICHBORNE, who thereupon became the eighth baronet. He died in June, 1845, and was succeeded by his brother EDWARD, who had by royal license taken the name of DOUGHTY, pursuant to the will of his aunt, ELIZABETH DOUGHTY, proved in June, 1826, and under which will the Doughty estates came into the TICHBORNE family.

Sir EDWARD DOUGHTY, the ninth baronet, died on the 5th March, 1853, leaving only one daughter surviving, who was born in April, 1831, and is now KATHERINE MARY ELIZABETH RADCLIFFE, the wife of JOSEPH PERCIVAL PICKFORD RADCLIFFE, eldest son of Sir JOSEPH RADCLIFFE, Baronet. She was married on the 18th October, 1851.

Sir JAMES TICHBORNE married on the 1st August, 1827, at St. George's, Hanover-square, and at the Roman Catholic Chapel,

Chelsea, HENRIETTE FELICITÉ, an illegitimate daughter of HENRY SEYMOUR, Esq., of Knoyle, Wiltshire, the father of HENRY DANBY SEYMOUR, late Member for Poole, and ALFRED SEYMOUR, late Member for Totnes. Her mother was a French lady, and HENRIETTE was born and brought up in Paris, and up to her death had a greater partiality for France than England. Previously to his marriage, JAMES TICHBORNE had the very slender income of about £150 per annum allowed him by his brother, Sir HENRY, who had seven daughters to provide for. The seventh baronet had, through gambling, disposed of Aldershot, Frimley, and other portions of the estate, and reduced the income to about £4,000 per annum. Sir HENRY JOSEPH, in addition to making an allowance to his brother JAMES, did the same to his brothers EDWARD and ROGER ROBERT, and his sister LUCY, until in 1826, EDWARD became possessed of the Doughty Estate, when he allowed Sir HENRY JOSEPH £1,000 per annum, and also assisted his other brothers and sister. EDWARD TICHBORNE went out to Jamaica as a young man, and managed some sugar estates. He brought with him to England from Kingston a black servant named ANDREW BOGLE, who was his valet for forty years previously and up to his death.

HENRY SEYMOUR settled upon his daughter HENRIETTE £12,000 at the time of her marriage. On the deaths of herself and husband, the fund was divisible among their children. By one of the deeds executed by ROGER TICHBORNE in 1850, hereinafter mentioned, he gave up his share for the benefit of his brother ALFRED and his children.

JAMES TICHBORNE and his wife lived in Paris from 1827 to 1853, continually changing their apartments. They had four children, all born in Paris, viz.: ROGER CHARLES, born 5th January, 1829; MADELLA LOUISE, born 8th July, 1832, and died in infancy; ALICE MARY PERPETUA, born 14th October, 1837, and died in infancy; ALFRED JOSEPH, born 4th September, 1839, and died 22nd February, 1866.

ROGER had a French tutor, named CHATILLON, but being a delicate youth, and disliking study, he made little progress in acquiring a knowledge of that language, and, although it was his native tongue, could never speak or write it correctly.

HENRIETTE'S father and husband, as appears by their letters, urged her to have ROGER educated in England, which she resisted for a long time. However, in June, 1845, when ROGER was sixteen and a half years old, he came over to the funeral of his uncle, Sir HENRY, and was then sent to the Roman Catholic College at Stonyhurst, Lancashire, for the purpose of being educated in the English language. The following letter from Father WALMESLEY to his mother, shows how backward ROGER then was, and his disinclination to writing:—

Stonyhurst, Preston, Lancashire: April 1st, 1846.

Dear Madam,—Your letter of anxious inquiry after your son came to hand yesterday, and I hasten to relieve your uneasiness in his regard.

He had already been enjoined to write to you according to your desire, and the affectionate interest which he ought the more especially to show towards his parents in their separation from him. He speaks most affectionately and dutifully of you, but pleaded as an apology for any seeming neglect towards yourself, that he had already twice, I think, written to you without receiving any reply. He will write now immediately, and expressed great willingness to write once a month, or as often as you might wish him to do so.

He is very well in health, and very happy; and advancing in his studies, but slowly yet, from the forward age at which he has begun for the first time, to apply to study. He seems very anxious to do well, and gives great satisfaction to his superiors by his general good conduct.

You do us, I hope, no more than justice when you presume that we desire to cherish the natural good feelings of children towards their parents, and upon inquiry I find that Master ROGER has been continually reminded of his duty to write home. He has sent many letters, and perhaps they have failed to reach their destination.

Mr. TICHBORNE'S wishes, expressed in his letter to Mr. SEYMOUR, shall be attended to. They gave me the occasion of speaking to ROGER, and I was much pleased with the very proper manner in which he seemed to feel in regard of both his parents. I hope, dear Madam, that this short account, which I have made the shorter to avoid delay in satisfying your inquiries, will be a comfort to your uneasiness, and either be accompanied, or immediately followed, by an affectionate letter from your son. He is engaged to-day in preparing his letter for you.

With every wish for your happiness in your son, believe me, dear Madam, truly yours, HENRY M. WALMESLEY.

P.S.—It is sometime since he was enjoined to sign himself by his name of ROGER.

Mrs. TICHBORNE, 49, Via di Pontifice, Rana.

From June, 1845, ROGER TICHBORNE never resided permanently with his father and mother. They led a very disturbed domestic life, as can easily be proved, and is evidenced by letters from the father to the mother, found among her papers, and ROGER escaped their broils by only paying them occasional visits for a few days together, and passing his leisure time principally at his uncle's, Sir EDWARD DOUGHTY'S, at Tichborne Park, enjoying field sports and the society of his cousin, KATHERINE. He left Stonyhurst College at the end of 1848 or early in 1849. His grandfather, HENRY SEYMOUR, in a letter to his mother, dated 29th November, 1848, thus describes him at the period:—

"Your husband left here last week with ALFRED and his nurse, and ROGER went away on Sunday to Wardour Church, and was to stay there the week; then to go to some of his numerous friends. He is now nearly twenty years of age, and a very good fellow, but does not like reading, and therefore ignorant of a very great variety of things he ought to know. It is a sad disadvantage to him I am very sorry to witness every day, for it keeps him silent, as he has very good sense and excellent heart."

On the 13th July, 1849, ROGER CHARLES TICHBORNE was appointed a Cornet in the 6th Dragoon Guards (Carabineers). His schooling had produced such a small amount of knowledge in him that he had to be coached by tutors for several months prior to his passing the very simple examination at the Royal Military College, Sandhurst, which it had only just then become requisite for an officer to go through, before he obtained his commission. The books at Sandhurst show, that on the 2nd July, 1849, ROGER CHARLES TICHBORNE passed the examination in History, Geography, English, French, and Fortification. He was not examined in Latin or German, and failed to pass in arithmetic. His height is recorded as 5ft. 8½in. His style of composition at this period will be best judged by referring to copies of his letters to his mother and father in the year 1849, the originals of which were found among his mother's papers. They show conclusively that he was essentially an unlearned young man. Simple as the examination then was, great fears were entertained among his family and friends that he would not be able to pass through it.

Mr. ROGER CHARLES TICHBORNE joined his regiment at Portobello Barracks, Dublin, on the 26th October, 1849, and became Lieutenant, by purchase, on the 22nd November, 1850, vice HEYWOOD, promoted to a captaincy. This gentleman, who is now retired from the army, and is a Deputy-Lieutenant and Justice of the Peace for Herefordshire, deposes to Sir ROGER TICHBORNE'S identity.

Mr. ROGER CHARLES TICHBORNE entered the army when he was twenty and a half years old, and quitted it after a service of three years and a half, when he was twenty-four years old. He was present actively serving with his regiment during the greater part of such three years and a half, and only had occasional leave of absence. Obviously, therefore, the best witnesses to his identity must of necessity be his brother officers, and the men with whom he associated day by day during such service. He was very little with his father and mother during the time, and still less with his cousins, the seven daughters of his uncle, Sir HENRY, most of whom were married, and only had an opportunity of knowing him by casually meeting him when he visited Sir EDWARD DOUGHTY at Tichborne, or his aunt, Lady ANN, at Grove House, Brompton. His cousin, Mrs. CAROLINE GREENWOOD, the wife of Colonel WILLIAM GREENWOOD, who resides at Brookwood, near Tichborne, had more opportunity of knowing Mr. ROGER CHARLES TICHBORNE than any of her six sisters, arising from her near residence to Tichborne Park. Of course KATHERINE DOUGHTY, the only daughter of Sir EDWARD, was perfectly well acquainted with him.

The steward and agent for Sir EDWARD DOUGHTY was a Mr. VINCENT GOSFORD, who always took great pains to ingratiate himself into the favour of ROGER TICHBORNE, as the expectant heir to the estates, and he acquired such an influence over him as to get himself appointed executor to the clandestine will which ROGER TICHBORNE made before leaving England, without the knowledge of his parents. Upon the death of Sir EDWARD DOUGHTY, and the succession of Sir JAMES TICHBORNE to the baronetcy, Mr. GOSFORD left Tichborne, and became steward to Sir PYERS MOSTYN, in Wales.

The life of Mr. ROGER CHARLES TICHBORNE in the army was a very unpleasant one indeed. He spoke broken English, and was an object of ridicule, and the laughing stock of both officers and men from his peculiarities. His brother officers continually played practical jokes upon him, and more particularly did Captain PINCKNEY, who now recognises and deposes to his identity. So dense was his capacity that, although he was three years and a half in the regiment, and had drilling lessons almost every day, he never acquired a proper knowledge of it, and, in military language, was never dismissed his drill up to the time of his retirement. Among the deponents to his identity will be found almost every surviving non-commissioned officer and private who endeavoured to instruct him.

One of the riding-masters especially states that Mr. ROGER TICHBORNE was frequently sent back from the riding-school to comb his hair. His leisure time was mostly taken up with his dogs and horses, and he is represented to have been a good horseman, with a firm seat in the saddle, but weak hands. He had very indifferent health, was subject to spasms of the heart, and was a very thin young man, weighing only, perhaps, nine or ten stone. But he had a bodily frame, which, as explained by Dr. LIPSCOMBE, would develope under the influence of a genial climate into the corpulent person he now is. All his ancestors have been stout men on attaining middle life.

For many generations past the TICHBORNES have been strict Roman Catholics, and have so intermarried with their cousins that their intellectual capacity has sunk to a very low standard.

Mr. ROGER CHARLES TICHBORNE attained the age of twenty-one on the 5th January, 1850, upon which occasion a ball was given at Tichborne by Sir EDWARD DOUGHTY. During his visit upon that occasion, he became acquainted with Miss BRAINE, who was the governess to KATHERINE DOUGHTY, then seventeen years of age. Miss BRAINE was of a very good family, and had become a convert to the Roman Catholic faith, and was for some time governess in the family of Lord ARUNDEL of WARDOUR. Her remembrance of ROGER TICHBORNE, his shyness of manner, and singular peculiarities are very vivid. He used to sleep in a hammock, in a bedroom at Tichborne House, with a smaller one by his side, containing pipes and tobacco, for he was a great smoker. His habits were anything but cleanly. He was fond of horses, and engaged very much in shooting and field sports, but had a great dislike to reading and society.

In May, 1850, various deeds were executed between Sir EDWARD DOUGHTY, Mr. JAMES FRANCIS TICHBORNE, and ROGER CHARLES TICHBORNE, by which the Doughty estates were re-settled, so as to devolve, after the death of Sir EDWARD, upon Mr. JAMES TICHBORNE, with remainder in fee to ROGER CHARLES TICHBORNE, subject to a charge of £100,000 for various purposes. Under one of them, dated May 9th, 1850, ROGER CHARLES TICHBORNE was secured £500 per annum, during the lives of his uncle and father, and £1,000 per annum on his father succeeding to the estates. These deeds are all set forth in the Bill of Chancery filed by Sir ROGER TICHBORNE against Sir PYERS MOSTYN to recover the Doughty estates.

Mr. EDWARD HOPKINS, of Alresford, acted as the solicitor of JAMES and ROGER TICHBORNE with reference to these deeds, and took them to Ireland to obtain their execution by the latter. Mr. HOPKINS had been all his life on the most intimate terms with the TICHBORNES. Mr. SLAUGHTER, now deceased, was the solicitor of Sir EDWARD DOUGHTY in that business.

Mr. ROGER TICHBORNE, being tired of the life he was leading, and inflamed by reading books on foreign travel, resolved to sell out of the army for the purpose of going abroad to hunt and shoot. He obtained leave of absence from his regiment in October, 1852, and resided by himself for two months at Upton, near Poole, a seat belonging to Sir EDWARD DOUGHTY, which was placed at his disposal. There he remained with two or three servants, and occupied himself with boating and shooting, in the company of WILLIAM GOULD, a fisherman. ROGER TICHBORNE took leave of his cousin KATHERINE DOUGHTY, having previously left in the hands of VINCENT GOSFORD a document sealed up, giving directions as to what should be done respecting her if a certain event happened. Actuated by the most honourable motives, Sir ROGER refused since his return to England to give any information respecting the contents of this document to any person whomsoever until GOSFORD, upon his cross-examination, stated he had destroyed it. Sir ROGER was then compelled, upon the especial request of his counsel, Mr. Serjeant BALLANTINE, and Mr. Justice HANNEN, to, and he wrote out a statement of its contents on the following morning, but of course, too late to be used for the purpose of examining GOSFORD upon. In an interview which took place between Mr. GOSFORD, Sir ROGER TICHBORNE, Mr. BULPETT, Mr. WHITE, and Mr. HINGSTON, at the Grosvenor Hotel, in June, 1867, GOSFORD stated that he had a certain document sealed up, which if he had known he was going to meet Sir ROGER, he would have brought with him; but he afterwards swore upon cross-examination that he had destroyed the document some years previously. ROGER TICHBORNE paid a farewell visit to his father and mother in Paris for a few days, and about the 10th day of March, 1853, sailed from Havre on board the French ship "La Pauline," in company with one man-servant named JOHN MOORE, touched at Falmouth, and arrived at Valparaiso in June of that year. There were no other passengers on board. Enquiry has elicited that the captain is dead, but there are a few sailors who went the voyage still alive, and residing in France; Sir ROGER has not, however, seen them. The letter, dated 29th June, 1853, from Valparaiso to his father, shows that ROGER TICHBORNE, on arriving out there, first heard of the death of his uncle, Sir EDWARD DOUGHTY. This is important to be borne in mind, because the public impression is that ROGER TICHBORNE was the son of a baronet, and entitled to great possessions when he left England, whereas the real fact is that he was only the son of Mr. JAMES TICHBORNE, brother of Sir EDWARD DOUGHTY, and there were, consequently, two lives then in existence between him and the baronetcy.

ROGER TICHBORNE dismissed his servant MOORE at Valparaiso, and went in the same ship to Lima. From thence he returned to Valparaiso, and afterwards made the acquaintance of Don TOMAS CASTRO, of Melipilla, in Chili, whose hospitality he partook of for about a month, and was introduced to his relations and friends. He then went to Santiago, and crossed the mountains to Buenos Ayres, where he arrived in March, 1854.

From Buenos Ayres ROGER TICHBORNE went to Rio Janeiro, where he seems to have had a servant named JULES BARRAUT.

About the 20th day of April, 1854, ROGER TICHBORNE embarked on board the ship "Bella," of Liverpool, then lying in the harbour of Rio de Janeiro, and sailed for New York. He was the only passenger, and, according to his own statement, was carried on board drunk. There is no official entry in Rio or anywhere of his having gone on board the ship at all. His servant was too late with the bulk of his luggage, and was left behind with it.

His expenses were defrayed by means of letters of credit, which he took with him, and obtained from England as his necessities required.

The crew of the "Bella" consisted of Captain BIRKETT and about sixteen sailors. All went on well until the 4th day after she left the port of Rio, and was far out of sight of land, but on the morning of that day the mate reported to the captain that she had sprung a leak, and all hands were instantly set to work at the pumps, and every effort was made to save the ship, but without effect. Very shortly after the mate reported the leak it became apparent that the vessel was fast filling with water, and the captain announced that all further efforts to save the ship were useless, and all on board must instantly take to the boats.

The "Bella" carried a longboat on deck, and two smaller boats, one of which was slung from the davits on each quarter. One of the small boats was stove in and rendered useless, but the crew succeeded in safely lowering upon the sea the longboat and the larger of the two smaller ones (called here for distinction the second boat), and in stowing some provisions and casks of water into them. Mr. ROGER TICHBORNE and eight of the crew got into the second boat, and the captain and the rest of the crew into the longboat, and immediately pushed off from the "Bella," which soon afterwards sunk. The captain, who had in the longboat the ship's charts, ordered that the second boat, which contained Mr. ROGER TICHBORNE and others, should keep in sight of the longboat, which was done for two days, but in the night of the second day a high wind and storm came on, and the boats were soon out of sight of each other, and the longboat was not again seen by those in the second boat. The man who had command of the second boat then determined to let her drift with the wind. On the morning of the fourth day after the "Bella" had sunk, the crew of the second boat descried a ship in the distance, and used every means to reach her and to attract notice, and for that purpose a red flannel shirt, which one of the crew of that boat wore, was attached to an oar and hoisted as a signal. Ultimately a signal was made in reply, and the crew of the second boat rowed to the ship, and ROGER TICHBORNE and the whole of the crew on board the second boat were thus saved, after they had been three days and three nights at sea in an open boat. Mr. ROGER TICHBORNE was in a very exhausted state when he was rescued, and was for some time seriously ill on board the ship that saved him, but he was landed at the port of Melbourne, in Australia, about the end of July, 1854. He had saved nothing from the "Bella" except the clothes he wore, and a signet ring, which he sold for a few shillings, and when he landed at Melbourne, in Australia, he had no means whatever for his support.

On the first day Mr. ROGER TICHBORNE landed at Melbourne the captain of the ship which brought him there took him to an office, which he believes was the Custom-house, and had a conversation with some person as to what should be done for him, but nothing was arranged except that he should be allowed to sleep on board the ship that night, which he accordingly did. Before returning to the ship, the captain and ROGER TICHBORNE called at an office and made inquiries, for the purpose of ascertaining how he could get a passage to England, but without any useful result.

Melbourne was then in a very unsettled state, in consequence of the gold mania; the crews of ships as they arrived very frequently deserted for the gold diggings, and there was consequently great difficulty in procuring a passage to England.

On the day after Mr. ROGER TICHBORNE landed in Melbourne, he was strolling about the town, and went into a yard called Row's yard, situate in Burke-street, where a large number of horses were being sold. He was much attracted by what was taking place, and a person named Mr. WILLIAM FOSTER, an extensive stock-keeper of Gippsland, spoke to him, and after ascertaining that he was a good rider, offered to take him with him to Gippsland. ROGER TICHBORNE accepted such offer, and not desiring to disclose his family name, assumed the name of TOMAS CASTRO (after that of his friend, Don TOMAS CASTRO, of Melipilla, in Chili). He thenceforward continued to use, and was known in Australia by the name of TOMAS CASTRO until shortly prior to his return to England. Mr. FOSTER immediately afterwards left Melbourne with his horses, and proceeded with ROGER TICHBORNE as TOM CASTRO, to his station at Boisdale, in Gippsland, on the Avon River, nearly 300 miles from Melbourne, where ROGER remained about nineteen months. Mr. FOSTER then gave him charge of Dargo Station in the Australian Alps, about 115 miles further inland, where he remained for about eighteen months, and then returned to Boisdale, where, after staying for about three months, he went about twenty miles off to Sale or Flodden Creek, on the River Latrobe, where he remained about six months. From that place he proceeded to NORMAN McLEOD's station on the Mitchel River, about sixty miles from Sale, where he entered into partnership with one FREDERICK BURROWS, and remained there about four months. He then went from that place to the Omeo diggings, where he remained about four months; and from there to Deniliquin, where he remained about thirteen months; and from thence he proceeded to Hay on the Murrunbidgee River, and remained there about nine months, and from thence he proceeded to Wagga-Wagga, and then to Boree and Narrandra, where he remained four months; and then to Nangus for about four months; then to Melbourne, with cattle; thence to Bendigo where he remained about two months; then to the town of Tumut, where he remained seven months; and from thence to Guadagay, and remained there about one month; then to Wagga-Wagga, where he lived about four years. On the 29th January, 1865, ROGER TICHBORNE intermarried with MARY ANN, daughter of JOHN and MARY-ANN BRYANT, spinster. Both he and his wife being Roman Catholics, and he being desirous to conceal his real name, refused to attend the confessional previously, according to the practice of that Church. The priest, therefore, refused to perform the ceremony, which was accordingly solemnised by the Rev. FREDERICK BRENTNANT, a minister of the Wesleyan Church, in the house of Mrs. ROBINSON of Wagga-Wagga.

Towards the end of the year 1865, Sir ROGER TICHBORNE, then being in the employ of a butcher at Wagga-Wagga, and living in a wooden hut with his wife, saw an advertisement in the Australian newspaper, inserted by Mr. CUBITT, his mother's agent, of which the following is a copy:—

"A handsome reward will be given to any person who can furnish such information as will discover the fate of ROGER CHARLES TICHBORNE. He sailed from the port of Rio Janeiro on the 20th April, 1854, in the ship "La Bella," and has never been heard of since; but a report reached England to the effect that a portion of the crew and passengers of a vessel of that name were picked up by a vessel bound to Australia—Melbourne, it is believed. It is not known whether the said ROGER CHARLES TICHBORNE was amongst the drowned or saved. He would, at the present time, be about 32 years of age, of a delicate constitution, rather tall, with very light brown hair with blue eyes. Mr. TICHBORNE is the son of Sir JAMES TICHBORNE, Baronet (now deceased), and is heir to all his estates. The advertiser is instructed to state that a most liberal reward will be given for information that may definitely point out his fate. Gentlemen in a position to refer to shipping reports may be able to find some record of the saving of the shipwrecked passengers from "La Bella," and a very careful search, if with a successful result, will amply repay any one who will take the trouble to investigate the matter. All replies to be addressed to Mr. ARTHUR CUBITT, Missing Friends Office, Bridge-street, Sydney, New South Wales.

August 4, 1865."

This was the first intimation that he had of his father's death, and that he had succeeded to the baronetcy. He had not written home to England since 1854, a period of twelve years, but he at length resolved to, and did write on the 16th January, 1866, to his mother, a letter, informing her that he had made up his mind to face the sea once more and return home. Mr. GIBBES, mentioned in this letter, is a solicitor, residing at Wagga-Wagga, who knew Sir ROGER as THOMAS CASTRO, but whose wife was mainly instrumental in discovering him to be living under an assumed name.

The correspondence between Mr. GIBBES and Mr. CUBITT, of Sydney, and Lady TICHBORNE, shows the steps which led to Sir ROGER's discovery in Australia. Mr. ARTHUR CUBITT advertised in the *Times* that he kept an Enquiry Office in Sydney, for the purpose of seeking out missing friends. Lady TICHBORNE saw it and wrote over to him, with a description of her son ROGER, and engaged his services. Lady TICHBORNE appears to have replied to Sir ROGER's first letter from Australia as soon as she received it on the 25th February, 1866. He, however, has not the reply, for he left it, with several other letters, in the possession of his solicitor, Mr. DAWSON, of Sydney. Sir ROGER wrote again to his mother from Wagga-Wagga on the 24th May, 1866 and says that fate had a great deal to do with his not writing to her for so long a period, and expressing his sorrow to hear of his father's and brother ALFRED's death. Without waiting for a remittance from his mother, Sir ROGER TICHBORNE left Wagga in June, 1866, and proceeded to Sydney.

On the 9th July, 1866, he went again through the ceremony of marriage with his wife, and this time under his proper name of ROGER CHARLES TICHBORNE, at the Roman Catholic Church of St. Peter and St. Paul, at Goulbourne, New South Wales, the ceremony on that occasion being solemnised by the Reverend Father MACILLROY, a priest of that church.

While Sir ROGER TICHBORNE was remaining in Sydney, previously to embarking for England, he accidentally met a person named GUILFOYLE, who was for many years in the employ of his uncle Sir EDWARD DOUGHTY, and is now carrying on business there as a nurseryman. Both GUILFOYLE and his wife knew him very well before he left England in the year 1853, and immediately recognised him in Sydney as the eldest son of the late Sir FRANCIS JAMES TICHBORNE.

Sir ROGER TICHBORNE also met there ANDREW BOGLE, the black servant of his uncle, Sir EDWARD DOUGHTY, who had known him from infancy, and recognised him as the eldest son of the late Sir JAMES FRANCIS TICHBORNE, and begged to be allowed to go with him to England. Previous to their embarkation, ANDREW BOGLE, acting in the full belief that Sir ROGER TICHBORNE's relatives would be glad to hear that he was alive, and had been recognised by one who knew him well, wrote a letter to Sir ROGER's aunt, Dame CATHERINE DOUGHTY, informing her of the fact that Sir ROGER and himself were about to embark for England. The letter is set out in paragraph 12 of BOGLE's affidavit, and was received by Lady DOUGHTY in course of post, in October, 1866. She no doubt communicated its contents to TERESA TICHBORNE, KATHERINE RADCLIFFE, and many relations and friends of the TICHBORNE family.

In the month of September, 1866, Sir ROGER TICHBORNE, his wife, and child, embarked at the port of Sydney, on board the steamship "Rakaia," and going by way of Panama and New York, arrived in the Victoria Docks, Limehouse, London, on board the steamship "Cella," on the Christmas-day of 1866. He proceeded at once to Ford's Hotel, Manchester-square, where he had been in the habit, previously to his leaving England, of staying with his father and uncle, but finding that many inquiries were being made for him, he removed to the Clarendon Hotel, Gravesend, which had been recommended to him in New York.

Being desirous of seeing Tichborne again before going to his mother in Paris, Sir ROGER went there on the 28th December, 1866, and put up at the Swan Hotel, Alresford. The servant asked his name, and as his portmanteau was marked R. C. T., he said, "Oh, anything; say TAYLOR."

Sir ROGER returned to Gravesend, and on the 5th January, 1867, VINCENT GOSFORD, Mr. PLOWDEN, and Mr. CULLINGTON called at the hotel and endeavoured to speak to him, but as his mother had requested him not to see anyone before he saw her, he declined giving them an interview. They then represented to the landlord that he was an impostor, and the landlord therefore required payment of his bill. Sir ROGER had only £18 out of £20, which his solicitor, Mr. HOLMES, had that morning advanced him for the express purpose of paying his expenses to Paris to see his mother, and he was obliged to part with that. He was thus left penniless, but Mr. HOLMES went to Gravesend on the 7th January, 1867, immediately on hearing of the circumstance, and resolved to pay the balance of the hotel bill and give Sir ROGER and his family the shelter of his own house at Croydon, so that he might be unmolested until he could see his mother.

On the 8th January, 1867, VINCENT GOSFORD again called upon Sir ROGER TICHBORNE, at Gravesend, and (Mr. HOLMES being present) had a prolonged interview with him at the Clarendon Hotel, and accompanied him in the train to London.

During such interview, Sir ROGER TICHBORNE and VINCENT GOSFORD discussed a variety of matters and circumstances relating to the TICHBORNE and DOUGHTY families, and the neighbourhoods of Tichborne and Upton, with which they were both familiar.

At this interview both Sir ROGER and his solicitor, Mr. HOLMES, first learned that Sir ROGER's will, which was left in Mr. SLAUGHTER's hands, had been proved, and Sir ROGER expressed his surprise that such a thing should have been done when he was not dead. Search was made on the following morning at the Probate Court Office, and it was found that GOSFORD and SLAUGHTER had proved the will, on the 17th day of July, 1855, upon the common affidavit, simply stating that the deceased died on or about the 26th day of April, 1854, without mentioning any special circumstances connected with his death, or any evidence on which it was supposed he was lost at sea.

Since Lady TICHBORNE's death the following letter was found, among her papers, from her stepmother:—

39, Upper Grosvenor-street: Saturday, July 23rd, 1854.

Dearest Harriet,—I am so glad you have this reasonable hope to cheer you, for indeed this account you send me has an air of much probability, and we must not allow ourselves to despair.

Thank you for writing to us; we shall all rejoice with you and Sir JAMES, if at last we hear of him ever from Australia.— Ever your affectionate,

In haste. JANE SEYMOUR.

Sir ROGER remained in Paris for ten days with his mother, and during his stay there his sister-in-law, TERESA TICHBORNE, wrote to her a letter, of which the following is a copy:—

Hyde House, January 19, 1867.

My dear Mama,—As I have not heard from you lately, I hope you are not ill with this cold weather. I hear so many reports, and so different, that I am going to ask you to let me have a line to say whether you recognised ROGER, as soon as you can please, as I feel so anxious to know. Poor Sir JAMES FITZGERALD is dead. BLANCHE was with him, but he did not regain his senses at all, but died quite quietly at the last. R.I.P. Mrs. WELD BLUNDELL is going to have another baby in April. She will have a large family—twelve, I think. GERTRUDE enjoyed herself much at Wardour. I am happy to say baby is very well indeed; your namesake, you know—HENRY. Hoping to hear soon from you,—I remain, always your most affectionate daughter,

TERESA TICHBORNE.

In reply to this the Dowager Lady TICHBORNE sent to TERESA TICHBORNE a letter, of which the following is a copy:—

My dearest Tessie,—Many thanks for your kind letter, which I received yesterday. I have not written to you lately as my time was much taken up with attending on my dear son ROGER. I have fully recognised him, and it is really him, and I cannot conceive those who knew him very well, and who will not recognise him. BOGLE has been here, but he is much troubled with rheumatism, and I am afraid he has not seen much of Paris beyond his bedroom; however, he is much better. I told ROGER yesterday that I was in hopes that one day I might hold my dearest little grandson in one hand and my dear little granddaughter AGNES in the other. He said he hoped so. I would go back to London immediately, only I am not very well, and the Paris water disagrees with me very much. I am obliged to wait a little, as the weather is so cold at present that it would make me worse. As soon as I can, however, I will go back to London. You do not mention whether my dearest little Henry's hair begins to grow; I shall be so glad to see him when I go back to England. I suppose Mrs. Weld Blundell and her daughter will be confined at the same time. With every kind love to yourself, and kind regards to Lady Arundell, ever believe me, your affectionate and devoted Mother, H. F. Tichborne.

21st January, 1867.

After the receipt of this letter, Teresa Tichborne had no further communication with the Dowager Lady Tichborne, although the latter always affectionately enquired after her and her son up to the day of her death.

During Sir Roger's stay in Sydney, he resided at the Metropolitan Hotel, which was kept by Mr. Stephen Butts. This person appears to have acquired great influence over Sir Roger, who, at his instigation, entered into a contract for the purchase of the hotel for £10,000; and accepted bills for the amount, payable at Messrs. Drummond's, Charing-cross. The purchase, of course, has never been completed, and the bills were returned dishonoured.

Sir Roger engaged Truth William Butts, a youth of sixteen years of age, and son of Stephen Butts, as his private secretary, at a salary of £500 per annum, and brought him to England. But Sir Roger, having found that Truth Butts was assisting Mr. Cullington, declined to have anything further to do with him. A formal agreement was entered into in Sydney between Sir Roger and Stephen Butts, the father, by which the former engaged to keep Truth Butts until he took him back to Sydney.

Mr. Cubitt, the advertisement-agent, procured Sir Roger's acceptance to a bill for £1,000 as a reward for inserting the advertisement, and making enquiries which led to his discovery. This bill has passed into third hands, and judgment obtained upon it in England.

Mr. Gibbes also obtained a bill for £500 from Sir Roger before he left Wagga-Wagga. Altogether, the liabilities contracted by Sir Roger during the year 1866, before he left Australia, amount to about £11,000. The bills were made payable at Messrs. Drummond's Bank, Charing-cross, upon the suggestion of some of the parties in Sydney. Sir Roger explains that he thought he would have sufficient money to pay these bills from the twelve years' accumulations of his annuity of £1,000 per annum, under the deed of 9th May, 1850, and which he expected would be standing to his credit at his bankers, Messrs. Glyn & Co.; and that he would have nothing to do on his arrival in England but simply to draw out the money and pay them off.

Mr. Hopkins having identified Sir Roger, was good enough to assist his solicitor, Mr. Holmes, with very valuable information and copies of documents. It was thus ascertained that shortly after news reached England, of the longboat of the "Bella" being picked up by the ship "Kent," of Baltimore. Mr. Hopkins, on the part of Sir James Tichborne, made inquiries at Rio de Janeiro to prove the supposed death of Sir Roger Tichborne, and collected the affidavits which were made use of in a suit of Tichborne v. Gosford, instituted by Sir James Tichborne against Gosford and Slaughter, to remove them from the trusteeship of Sir Roger's will, and for the appointment of new trustees in their stead. A correspondence took place between Mr. Hopkins and Mr. Slaughter upon the subject of Roger Tichborne's will, after the loss of the "Bella," from which the fact of the existence of such will became, for the first time, known to his parents, and caused them great surprise and indignation. If Roger Tichborne had died in his father's lifetime, without making a will, his father, as heir-at-law, would have been entitled to the fee simple of the Doughty estates (subject to the £100,000), and could have dealt with it as he pleased. He therefore was intensely annoyed to find that Gosford and Slaughter, who probably acted under the instigation of Sir Edward and Lady Doughty, had deprived him of such a right.

In the Bill against Sir Pyers Mostyn, this will is set out. It appoints Gosford and Slaughter executors, and gives them a legacy of £500 each, gives Alfred an annuity of £500 per annum, and, after his death, £1,000 per annum to his widow, and settles the estates upon Alfred's children, and, in default, upon Katherine Doughty, and her issue.

The present trustees of this will are Sir Pyers Mostyn, and William Mostyn, who are acting under an order of the Court of Chancery, in the suit of Mostyn v. Emanuel.

The present trustee of the Tichborne Estate is Renfric Arundell, who is also acting under an order of the Court of Chancery in a suit of Tichborne v. Arundell.

Both these suits were in existence at the time Sir Roger came to England, therefore he had to file Bills in Chancery, praying for leave to bring actions of ejectment.

Sir James Tichborne died on the 11th June, 1862, and thereupon Sir Roger's younger brother, Alfred Joseph Tichborne, assumed the title of Baronet, believing his brother Roger to be dead. He thenceforth received the rents of the Tichborne Estate, and the annuity of £3,000 per annum, under Sir Roger's supposed will.

Alfred Tichborne died suddenly on the 22nd February, 1866, at the early age of twenty-six. He had married a daughter of Lord Arundell of Wardour. The only surviving issue of such marriage is an infant son, Henry Alfred Joseph Tichborne, born after his father's death, on the 28th May, 1866. It was between the guardians of this Infant and Sir Roger Tichborne, that the contest for the family estates really lay. If the career of Sir Roger Tichborne has been extraordinary, that of his brother Alfred was no less remarkable. The greatest difficulty was experienced in educating Alfred, and he was turned out of several schools to which he was sent. He was a man of low and vulgar tastes and habits; he was constantly in the habit of associating with grooms and stable boys; was even photographed in their company, he and his friends being depicted with pipes in their mouths; he has been known to have had a calf brought up to the stables near Tichborne House, to be slaughtered by his own hand—for he delighted in feats of butchery; and on the day of his marriage he was so drunk that he had to be carried by two servants from the breakfast room into the travelling chariot, where he was deposited at the feet of his youthful bride. Soon after he attained twenty-one, he was so much involved in debt that all his father's savings—amounting, it is believed, to over £20,000—had to be spent to pay them off and keep him out of prison. After the death of his father, Alfred's drunkenness and dissipation became so uncontrollable that he incurred liabilities approaching £40,000, and was adjudicated bankrupt in 1863. The schedule of his debts, which can be seen the Bankruptcy Court, tells the woful tale of a dissolute young spendthrift. He cared not what he spent in horses. He had singular peculiarities, and among them was that of having a steam-lathe fixed in the dining-room of Tichborne House. He perpetually tried to make a perfect sphere. He was a more educated and polished man than his brother Roger, because he never quitted good society for any length of time. He was, however, really half insane; having in one of his drunken fits contracted for the building of a yacht which was to cost £200,000, the floors and decks were to be inlaid mosaic, and the doors covered with mother o'pearl and ebony. He once half hanged himself in the Albany, and got himself cut down by a servant in the plot, which was to extract money from Sir James to pay his debts. Any wretched or ruffianly picture that pleased his fancy, he bought at any cost. In fact, *he knew* that his brother was alive, and he did not care what debts he contracted, as he believed that when his brother came back, the estate would be freed from any liability for them, he having, of course, no legal power to bind it, his elder brother being alive. Nearly all his mad extravagance can be accounted for on this principle. Hence his appearance at last in the Bankruptcy Court. The bankruptcy proceedings lasted for two years, but the scandal of them was put an end to by the Star Life Office lending £10,000 upon Alfred's supposed interest in the estates. This office has this interest against the Claimant. The bankruptcy was thereupon annulled, and all the creditors paid in full. Alfred's mortgagees cut down and sold all the timber they could in Tichborne Park. Notwithstanding his numerous promises of reformation and the difficulties he had escaped, Alfred was no sooner free from the Bankruptcy Court than he launched out again in wantonness and extravagance, and in the short space of a few months he had again incurred debts to the extent of £12,000, and then was obliged to make an assignment for the benefit of his Creditors. Subsisting upon an allowance from his mother, but enfeebled in body and weakened in mind by his dissipated and vicious career—excluded from society, and bankrupt in reputation as well as in purse, Alfred burst a blood-vessel, and expired at a little cottage in Yorkshire, in February, 1866, but three days before the first letter from Sir Roger, in Australia, reached his mother. Alfred was buried in the family vault at Tichborne; but none of his relations attended the funeral, which was conducted in the most poverty-stricken manner by Mr. Bowker, the solicitor, of Winchester, who acted for the trustees under the assignment, and had much to do with that unfortunate and misguided young man.

The cheque-books of the Dowager Lady Tichborne show that from the time of her son Alfred getting into difficulties she allowed him £20 per week, and continued the same to his Widow Teresa, after his death, and also made Sir Roger Tichborne the same allowance upon his return to England. While negotiations for a loan to Alfred Tichborne were pending in 1863, his mother inserted in the *Times* newspaper an advertisement in English, French and Spanish, for her son Roger.

This, of course, caused great consternation to Alfred and his advisers, and nearly prevented the completion of the loan; and she was with difficulty induced to countermand future insertions. It was, however, well-known among the members of the Tichborne family that she never would believe her son Roger was dead. She was a most pious and devout Catholic, and had masses and prayers continually offered up for his safe return. Her charity to the poor was only bounded by her means, and she was so self-denying that she gave away to them and the priests all she possessed.

In consequence of her firm belief in Sir Roger's existence, and of her French proclivities, she was not upon favourable terms with the members of the Tichborne family. It was, of course, very unpleasant to them to be continually told that Roger would come home and deprive them of their expectations. She was so careful that at her death upwards of 3,000 letters were found in her boxes, and very many drafts and copies in her own handwriting. This is particularly the case in reference to her letters to Mr. Cubitt, Mr. Gibbes, and others, respecting the discovery of Sir Roger. Such was her maternal solicitude for him when he came to England, that she either saw or wrote to him every day. He had 165 of her letters written to him during the year 1867, and up to the 12th March 1868, when she died suddenly at Howlett's Hotel, Manchester-street, of diseased heart. She was at his house in Croydon the previous evening until 9 o'clock.

Sir ROGER TICHBORNE, instead of finding upon his return to England that he had nothing to do but quietly take possession of his property, found it in the hands of strange trustees, and that his identity was denied by them and his deceased brother ALFRED's wife, whom he had never seen or even known but, if at all, only as a little girl.

An interview was brought about between Sir ROGER and his cousin KATHERINE RADCLIFFE, at Croydon, as stated in the correspondence between Mr. HOLMES and Messrs. DOBINSON and GEARE.

Since his arrival in England, until the trial for perjury, Sir ROGER has, at great labour, been continuously occupied in renewing the acquaintance of his military friends, and all those disinterested witnesses who have voluntarily sworn to his identity.

Considering the prejudice created against him by the Press, the active efforts made by Mr. BOWKER and his other opponents to poison the mind of every one of his witnesses before he saw them, the natural distaste of Sir ROGER for society, the bad state of his health since his return to England, and his great increase in size, it is very satisfactory that so many persons have been obtained to volunteer their testimony to the undeniable fact of his identity.

Sir ROGER TICHBORNE does not speak French, and this circumstance is relied upon by his opponents as being most fatal to his claims. A review however of the events of his life as affecting his language will clear up any difficulty upon this point.

French was unquestionably his native tongue, and he spoke it until he was sixteen years of age, but he acquired no knowledge of the grammar of that language.

From the age of sixteen every effort was, according to the wish of his uncles and father, made at Stonyhurst for a period of between three and four years to convert him from a French youth into an English one, and to drive the English language into him and the French out. A little Latin also was added.

Speaking broken English from the age of sixteen to the time he left England, at the age of twenty-four, he went away attended by an English servant and travelled in Chili, Peru, and Brazil for twelve months, and acquired some knowledge of the Spanish language spoken in those countries, and which to some extent he now retains.

Landing in Australia in 1854, and passing his life for twelve years among uneducated stockmen, drivers, horse-dealers, butchers, and people of that class, their manner of speaking and writing became his, so that upon Sir ROGER's return to England in 1866 he spoke and wrote the most ungrammatical English, and used pronunciations and expressions which are only met with among vulgar and uneducated persons of the lowest class.

When these facts are remembered, and it is borne in mind, that Sir ROGER TICHBORNE only spoke French as a boy, that he had at the most (excluding holidays), but little over two years' schooling in English, which he was endeavouring to speak and write from the age of sixteen, and that he did not hear or speak one word of French for the twelve years he was in Australia, surely it is not to be wondered at that he should have forgotten *the little French* he ever knew. When, however, he now reads aloud, he does so with a French accent, just as a Frenchman would.

It is worth noticing that only two of Sir ROGER TICHBORNE's letters in French to his mother, when he was a boy, have been found. All his letters from 1849 to 1851 to his father and mother are written in English, without the introduction of a single French word. A perusal of these letters will show that Sir ROGER TICHBORNE never acquired any accurate knowledge of English composition, and was a very bad writer. A comparison of them with the *fac-similes* of the letters which he wrote to his mother from Wagga-Wagga and Sydney in 1866, have convinced very many persons that the handwriting of each is the same in character, and were written by identically the same individual, although some of the words are formed differently, which might be expected to arise from the writer being out of practice for a considerable time.

In some of his letters, written in 1867, shortly after his return to England, Sir ROGER TICHBORNE uses a small "i," and spells very badly, but it is curious to observe that in them he frequently spells the same word correctly and incorrectly. The omission to use the capital "I" is no doubt founded upon his early French teaching, and perhaps from having seen letters of uneducated persons so written. But, like many of his ancestors in days gone by, Sir ROGER TICHBORNE has a supreme contempt for reading, writing, and correct spelling.

With reference to the ORTON theory, we append the following proofs prepared (among others) for the trial in the Common Pleas: the evidence as briefed was taken down from the lips of the witnesses themselves. Dr. KENEALY did not call them at the present trial, for reasons satisfactory to his own mind, and to all the best friends of Sir ROGER.

ELIZABETH JURY says:—I am the wife of Mr. GEORGE JURY, of No. 69, Mansell-street, Goodman's-fields, Middlesex, Captain in the Merchant service.

I am now forty-nine years of age, and am the eldest daughter of the late Mr. GEORGE ORTON, of High-street, Wapping, butcher. I had eight brothers and three sisters, viz.:—THOMAS, CHARLES, GEORGE, WILLIAM, ROBERT, ALFRED, EDMUND, and ARTHUR, and MARGARET ANNE, MARY ANNE (now MARY ANNE TREDGETT) and MATILDA. Four of my brothers, THOMAS, WILLIAM ROBERT, and ALFRED are dead; CHARLES now resides in London; GEORGE is now in India; EDMUND, I believe, is in Chili, and ARTHUR in Australia. My two sisters MARGARET ANNE JURY and MARY ANNE TREDGETT are now living, and reside in London; my sister MATILDA died in infancy. The circumstances under which I became acquainted or heard of the TICHBORNE Case were as follows:—

On Christmas-day, in the year 1866, I was residing at No. 55, Litchfield-road, Tredegar-square, Bow; my sister, MARY ANNE TREDGETT, resides with my sister MARGARET ANNE JURY, at No. 31, Ann's-road, South Hackney. On the above day my sister, MARY ANNE TREDGETT, dined and spent that and part of the following day with me.

My sister MARY ANNE subsequently told me that while she was with me on the Christmas-day, a person called at the house, but finding the house shut up, had been referred by the neighbours to her sister-in-law, Mrs. PARNELL, to whom the person referred to stated, that he wished to see MARY ANNE ORTON, and also requested to know if my said sister, MARY ANNE TREDGETT, was that person, to which she, Mrs. PARNELL, replied that she was, and after some enquiries as to the family, he left, saying he would call on Mrs. TREDGETT in the morning; before he left he said his name was STEVENS.

My sister informed me, that the said Mr. STEVENS accordingly called at my sister's house, who was still from home, in consequence of which he again called on Mrs. PARNELL, and left a letter for my sister, which he said came from ARTHUR ORTON, whom he had known in Australia, and also that if my said sister wished to communicate with him, a letter addressed to him at the Post Office, Gravesend, would reach him.

My sister MARY ANNE TREDGETT, accordingly wrote to the address, saying she had received the letter from her brother, for which she was obliged, and also that she would be very pleased if he STEVENS would favour her with a call, to which she received a reply, saying that in consequence of his being compelled to go to Ireland, he was about leaving for Liverpool to proceed there, and therefore could not spare the time to see her (Mrs. TREDGETT).

A short time after the receipt of the letter, I wrote to the Post Office at Liverpool, requesting Mr. STEVENS to forward my brother's address in Australia.

I recollect about a year prior to my father's death, a Mr. RICHARDSON, a brother of an old neighbour of ours, called on my father with a letter he had received from a person signing himself as TOMAS CASTRO or TOM CASTRO, from Australia, wishing to know if he, RICHARDSON, knew of the whereabouts of my brother ARTHUR, and, if he did, requesting him to communicate the same to him (CASTRO). My father answered saying, my brother ARTHUR was not in England, and that he did not know of his whereabouts, and asking the said TOM CASTRO (if he ever heard or saw my brother ARTHUR) to request him to communicate with his family, as we were most anxious to hear from him.

I never heard, nor did I believe any of my family ever heard, from the said TOM CASTRO again.

It was only from the fact of my reading the name of CASTRO or DE CASTRO in the papers in connection with Sir ROGER TICHBORNE and that Sir ROGER had just returned from Australia, after some years' stay there, that it struck me that if Sir ROGER was not the TOM CASTRO or DE CASTRO, who had written to Mr. RICHARDSON, he would most likely know something of him; and it was only in the hope that I should hear something of my brother ARTHUR, that I communicated with Sir ROGER.

I left London for Cardiff in September, 1867, and previous to my leaving London, having seen Sir ROGER's address at Croydon, in the papers, I went to Croydon for the purpose of seeing him; but when I arrived there, in reply to my question whether I could see Sir ROGER TICHBORNE, the servant told me that Sir ROGER was very unwell and could not see anyone that day; upon which I requested her to take my card up to him; she did so and brought down the answer that Sir ROGER was very unwell at that time, that he could not see me, but that he should be very happy to do so at any other time, and on that occasion of my visit, I did not see any one but the servant girl who answered my enquiries.

From that time until I went to Cardiff, just previous to sailing for Bombay with my husband, who was captain of a merchant vessel, I troubled myself no more about the matter, except writing one letter from Cardiff to Sir ROGER TICHBORNE, to try and ascertain the address of my brother, I being naturally desirous of communicating with him if possible.

We left England, or rather Cardiff, on the 28th October, and arrived at Bombay on the 4th April, 1868, where I continued until the 28th May, when, through the sickness of my husband, I was compelled to leave India and return home by the overland route, arriving in England on the 28th of June, 1868.

While in Bombay, I had several letters from my daughter EMILY in England, in one of which she stated that a detective was going about Bow and the neighbourhood saying, that the Claimant, Sir ROGER TICHBORNE, was my brother ARTHUR. Before leaving Cardiff Sir ROGER TICHBORNE answered my letter, saying he was a friend of my brother's, and enclosed a name and address which he said would find him in Australia; and before leaving Bombay, I wrote to my brother at that address, but had no reply to it, nor did I get the letter back through the Post Office. I believe, from what Mr. JOHN HOLMES (the former solicitor of Sir ROGER TICHBORNE) stated that the letters had been opened and read in Australia, this being confirmed by Mr. HOLMES reading me extracts from the said letters, which I recognised as what I had written.

On our return to England, I wrote a note to Sir ROGER, telling him we had returned to England, and that if he wished to see me he would find me at the address given in the letter.

The reason I wrote the letter was, I wished, if possible, to have an interview, and to ascertain if Sir ROGER TICHBORNE was really my brother.

Some little time after I had dispatched the above letter, I had a reply from Sir ROGER TICHBORNE, requesting him to meet me at the office of his solicitor, Mr. JOHN HOLMES, 34, Clement's-lane, Lombard-street, at which place I attended; and after seeing a gentleman there who was said to be my brother ARTHUR, I made the following declaration:—

"I, ELIZABETH JURY, wife of Captain GEORGE JURY, late commander of the 'Eastern Empire,' now temporarily residing at 23, East India Dock-road, say I am a daughter of the late GEORGE ORTON, of High-street, Wapping. One of my brothers was named ARTHUR. He went to sea about sixteen years ago. I think I gave him his bedding to go. I last heard from him at Hobart Town about fourteen years ago. I left the letter at Bombay. He said in it he would not come back to England again.

"Having heard it said that a gentleman named Sir ROGER CHARLES DOUGHTY TICHBORNE, who had come from Australia last year, was, in fact, my said brother ARTHUR who had returned, and claiming the Tichborne and Doughty estates, I met the said gentleman by appointment, this 16th of July, 1868, at the office of Mr. JOHN HOLMES, 24, Clement's-lane, London. I solemnly declare that the said Sir ROGER CHARLES DOUGHTY TICHBORNE is not my said brother ARTHUR, nor any relation whatever of mine; and I have never, up to the said meeting, seen the said Sir ROGER TICHBORNE previously. I last heard from my brother EDMUND, in Mexico, about six years back. He is a dark man. My brother GEORGE is living in Singapore. My brother CHARLES is living in Peckham. ELIZABETH JURY."

Since making the said declaration, I have seen Sir ROGER TICHBORNE's solicitors at their office, on several occasions, and on one or two of the occasions I have also seen Sir ROGER TICHBORNE, or rather, the gentleman I saw at Mr. HOLMES's office, although not to speak to him, and I feel more and more confirmed in my opinion that he is not my brother ARTHUR, nor, to my knowledge, have I ever seen him before in my life, except so before mentioned.

In consequence of various enquiries being made for the address of my sister, MARY ANNE TREDGETT, who was on a visit to me, I went with her to the office of Messrs. DOBINSON and GEARE, in Lincoln's Inn-fields, where I saw a gentleman (Mr. DOBINSON) whom I asked what was wanted with my sister. He replied that he had not sent for her; but that he was ready to see her. On my asking him what he meant, he simply made the same reply—"I am ready to see her." He also asked me various other questions, amongst others "Why had I scolded my brother CHARLES for saying the Claimant was his brother?" to which I replied, that the only thing I scolded my brother for was that he had seen the Claimant and signed a statement in the presence of three or four gentlemen, stating most positively that the Claimant was not his brother, and although he had not seen him since, he turned round and said the Claimant was his brother.

Mr. DOBINSON then said: "If you are the daughter of GEORGE ORTON, the butcher of Wapping, so sure as there is breath in your body this person is your brother ARTHUR, and you will come to grief, and all who have to do with it." To which I replied, "So sure as the breath is in my body, he is not my brother ARTHUR, and that I cannot come to grief through speaking the truth."

In the year 1852 or 1853, I remember my brother ARTHUR being, on his return from South America, laid up with the small-pox. My sister, Mrs. TREDGETT, nursed him, and afterwards he was marked in the face from the effects of the small-pox.

I remember he had the marks "A. O." on his arm. I also well remember his ears having been pierced, and his wearing small gold rings. Mrs. ELIZABETH JURY.

69, Mansfield-street, Goodman's-fields.

MARGARET ANNE JURY says:—I am the wife of ROBERT JURY, late of Victoria Park, but am living apart from my husband.

I am the second daughter of the late Mr. GEORGE ORTON, butcher, of High-street, Wapping, and I am in the forty-sixth year of my age.

I had eight brothers and three sisters, viz., THOMAS, CHARLES, GEORGE, WILLIAM, ROBERT, ALFRED, EDMUND, and ARTHUR; and the sisters were ANNE, ELIZABETH, MARY ANNE, and MATILDA, who died in her infancy. Four of my brothers, viz., THOMAS, WILLIAM, ROBERT, and ALFRED, are dead. CHARLES now resides in London, GEORGE is now in India, EDMUND, I believe, is in Chili, and ARTHUR in Australia. My two sisters, ELIZABETH JURY and MARY ANNE TREDGETT, are now residing in London. I was married to ROBERT JURY, and resided in the neighbourhood of Victoria-park for some years. Shortly after my marriage, in consequence of differences arising between my husband and myself, we separated, and have since lived apart. My brother ARTHUR left England about eighteen years ago, and I heard that he had been in England in 1860, but only stayed a few days, after which he sailed for Australia. Since the death of the husband of my sister MARY ANNE I have resided with her. I recollect, previous to my father's death, a Mr. RICHARDSON—a brother to an old neighbour of ours, called at my father's house in Wapping and read a letter he had received from a person signing himself TOM or THOMAS DE CASTRO, from Australia, making enquiries for my brother ARTHUR, and requesting my father, in the event of his knowing ARTHUR's whereabouts, to let him know, as he wished to communicate with him. I saw that letter, and also the answer that was written by my father to the effect that ARTHUR was not in England, and that he (my father) would be only too glad to know of ARTHUR's whereabouts, and asking the correspondent (DE CASTRO) to communicate with my father in the event of his obtaining any tidings of ARTHUR. From the time Mr. RICHARDSON received that letter from DE CASTRO mentioning my brother ARTHUR's name, I never heard anything of or from him until the day after Christmas-day, 1866, at which time I was residing with my sister MARY ANNE at Victoria Park. We left home on Christmas morning to pass the the Christmas and following day at the house of a friend, and on my return with my sister I learnt that a gentleman had called and made inquiries about our family, and had left a letter, addressed to my sister MARY ANNE, in her maiden name, from my brother ARTHUR. The purport of the letter was that the bearer was a friend of his, and requesting us to show him what hospitality we could and assist him in every way in our power.

I was informed that the gentleman who left the letter called first on Christmas-day, and, not finding us at home, he made inquiries as to our whereabouts, and was referred by the neighbours to Mrs. PARNELL, who is a sister-in-law of my sister MARY ANNE, and also that the said gentleman called again on the day following Christmas-day, and he then handed the letter to the said Mrs. PARNELL, who delivered it to my sister MARY ANNE, on our return home. The gentleman also left the following address with Mrs. PARNELL, viz: "Mr. STEVENS, Post Office, Gravesend," saying that if my sister wished to communicate with him, a letter to that address would reach him. My sister accordingly wrote (I believe) two letters, and she received an answer stating that he (STEVENS) was about to leave England for Ireland, on important business, so that he could not call upon her again then, but that on his return he would in all probability pay her a visit. Some short time after this correspondence, I read in the newspapers about the Tichborne baronetcy case, and amongst other names mentioned, I noticed the name of DE CASTRO, which at once brought to my recollection the letter received by Mr. RICHARDSON from Australia; and in consequence of that circumstance, and, in addition thereto, the fact of the letter recently received per Mr. STEVENS, I thought, it must, at any rate, be someone who would be able to give some tidings of my brother ARTHUR. My sister MARY ANNE accordingly wrote, and I read the letter addressed to Mr. JOHN HOLMES, the then Solicitor for Sir ROGER TICHBORNE, asking him to forward it to Sir ROGER, the letter containing a request that Sir ROGER should grant us an interview, we having an impression that Sir ROGER was our brother ARTHUR. A reply to that letter was sent by Sir ROGER, who stated that he knew ARTHUR, and was a friend of his, and that if we sent him a letter for ARTHUR he would forward it in a letter he himself was going to write to him. I believe Sir ROGER's letter was burnt by my sister MARY ANNE. Soon afterwards, I received a letter from Mr. HOLMES, saying that Sir ROGER and he would call upon us, to see if we could identify our brother ARTHUR with the supposed Sir ROGER TICHBORNE. Mr. HOLMES accordingly called, with a gentleman whom he introduced as Sir ROGER TICHBORNE. We had a long conversation with him (lasting about an hour-and-a-half), and we observed him very closely, and we then were, and still are, perfectly certain that he is not our brother ARTHUR, nor could we detect any similarity in appearance between Sir ROGER and ARTHUR.

Before my brother left England, in 1852, I remember his having the small-pox, and that my sister MARY ANNE nursed him. After his recovery he carried the marks of the small-pox.

My brother ARTHUR had the marks "A. O." on his arm. He had also his ears pierced.

Affidavit of Mrs. MARGARET ANNE JURY, and Mrs. MARY ANNE TREDGETT.

We both say we are daughters of GEORGE ORTON, late of 69, High-street, Wapping, deceased, who lived and carried on business there as a wholesale and shipping butcher, for upwards of fifty years. He had eight sons and four daughters, viz.:—THOMAS, CHARLES, GEORGE, WILLIAM, ROBERT, ALFRED, EDMUND, and ARTHUR; and ELIZABETH, MARGARET ANNE, MARY ANNE, and MATILDA. THOMAS, ROBERT, ALFRED, WILLIAM, and MATILDA are all dead. CHARLES is still living and in London. GEORGE is captain of the steamship "Chowphya," and stationed in Singapore. EDMUND left this country about eighteen months ago as a sailor, having been apprenticed on board the ship "Niagara." We last heard from him about two years ago, and he was in Guy Map, New South Mexico; and we have heard from our brother GEORGE that he has had a letter from EDMUND, during the year 1867. Our other brother, ARTHUR, left England about fifteen years ago: he was then about sixteen years old. He went to sea. He was never brought up or apprenticed to any trade, or taught any business. ARTHUR was in England about seven years ago; and I the said MARY TREDGETT for myself say, I saw him then. Since that time he has written to me from Wagga-Wagga in Australia, about two years ago; and about August, 1867, he sent me a letter from Fremantle, on the Swan River, Western Australia, which I received in October, 1867. We both say that both these letters were sent soon, after their receipt by us, to our brother GEORGE, in Singapore, and we have written him to return them.

2. We both say that about the month of September, 1867, a man marked with small-pox called upon us, and asked if we were daughters of Mr. ORTON, of Wapping, and whether we had heard of anything, and said he was inquiring for our brother HENRY, who had killed cattle in Newgate Market, and kept fancy dogs. We said we never had a brother of that name, nor anyone who had lived or been employed in Newgate Market. His manner was strange; and in reply to our inquiries, he said if we were of the same family we should come into a great deal of property. We believe this person was a detective named WHICHER. The next day he came again, and brought a photographic likeness of a man, and asked us to look well at it, to see if it was the likeness of either of our brothers. We did so; and said it was not. He also brought an envelope, and asked if we knew the writing; but we did not. He asked if HENRY had not been to see us within a few months, and we said we had no brother of that name. He tried to borrow EDMUND's likeness, but we would not lend it, and brought him back from the gate with it. He asked if we would go to Lincoln's Inn-fields, to see some gentlemen, and that our expenses would be paid; but we said if they wanted to see us they could come to our house. Two days afterwards, the same person came with two gentlemen, one of whom was tall and thin, about 50 years of age, and the other was a fair man. They gave no names; but in answer to our inquiries said it was a question of property. They inquired about our brothers. They were very mysterious. Since then we have been told by Miss CORSAN, of Belgrave-street, Commercial-road, that inquiries had been made of her respecting our family; also of Miss REDOUT (now Mrs. FRIBORNE), of Mrs. EAST, of Mr. EDWARDS, of Mr. RAYMOND, of Mr. LANE, of Miss LOADER, of Mrs. LAWS, of Mr. PANNEL, of Mrs. JOYCE, Mrs. TEES, Mrs. SMITH, Mrs. GOSCHEN, of Mr. CRONIN, Miss COCKBURN, and others in the neighbourhood of Wapping, in reference to our brother ARTHUR; and statements have

ROGER TICHBORNE, ELDEST SON OF SIR R. C. D. TICHBORNE, BART.

been, we believe, made that ARTHUR had recently come to England and claimed the Tichborne baronetcy. Many of these persons, we believe, have been to an office in Lincoln's Inn-fields upon the matter.

3. ROBERT JURY, the husband of this deponent, MARGARET ANNE JURY, called upon us lately, and said that he had been to Mr. DOBINSON's office, in Lincoln's Inn-fields, and was shown a photographic portrait, but he said he did not know the man. They paid him 5s. ROBERT JURY told this deponent, MARY ANNE TREDGETT, that he understood, from what the detective said, there was £2,000 hanging to the business for him.

4. I, the said MARY ANNE TREDGETT, for myself say that having read in the newspapers what appeared respecting the Tichborne Case, and having so learnt the name and address of Mr. HOLMES, 25, Poultry, I went to see him.

5. We both say that on the 17th day of April, 1868, the abovenamed Plaintiff, Sir ROGER CHARLES DOUGHTY TICHBORNE, baronet, called upon us at our house. We distinctly and positively say he is not our brother ARTHUR, nor any relation of ours, and that we never saw him previously. We have no hesitation whatever upon the subject, and are willing to swear to the fact in any Court in the country.

6. ARTHUR ORTON, our brother, had small-pox when he was young, and was marked with pits on the face.

7. The facts herein deposed to are within our own knowledge respectively.

MARGARET ANNE JURY.
M. A. TREDGETT.

Sworn by the deponents, MARGARET ANNE JURY and MARY ANNE TREDGETT, at No. 31, Anne's-road, South Hackney, in the County of Middlesex, this 28th day of May, 1868,—Before me, F. A. LEWIS,
A London Commissioner to administer Oaths in Chancery.

The following correspondence will show the way Messrs. DOBINSON and GEARE proceeded to get up evidence:—

Letter from Mr. COTTEE, manager of the Australian Union Bank, at Wagga-Wagga:—

Wagga-Wagga, New South Wales, April 25, 1868.

JOHN HOLMES, Esq., 31, Clement's-lane, Lombard-street, London, E.C.

TICHBORNE.

Dear Sir.—Your favours of 27th January and 26th February were duly received some weeks since. I learned from very good authority that Captain ANGEL, of the ship "Glen Osmund," that arrived in Adelaide, South Australia, early in February last, had, immediately before leaving England, made an affidavit for Messrs. CULLINGTON and SLAUGHTER, identifying a portrait of Sir ROGER TICHBORNE as that of one ARTHUR ORTON, whom he had known years before at Hobart Town, and also in London. With a view to test the accuracy of this information, I wrote to a gentleman in Adelaide, requesting him to see ANGEL, and to ascertain if he did make such affidavit, and to let me know the result. I give you the following extract from the letter received in reply to my inquiries: "Captain ANGEL states that he knew ARTHUR ORTON well. He was English, being the son of a butcher at Wapping. He knew him as a child, and lived in the same house. Took him and his mother as passengers from London to Bridport. Last saw him at Hobart Town thirteen years ago; his age was then about seventeen. He came down to the ship, hearing that ANGEL was in command. Stayed a short time and talked of old times. He said he was stock-keeping and butchering. He was stout and of middle height. He did not speak French and Spanish. Captain ANGEL did make an affidavit in England to the effect that to the best of his knowledge and belief a photograph, said to be the likeness of Sir ROGER TICHBORNE, was the likeness of ARTHUR ORTON he had formerly known. Although ORTON was dressed as a gentleman, he recognised the likeness at once." I give you the foregoing for what it may be worth. It may be of some service. I may mention that Mr. MACKENZIE has taken, or rather, has said that he has taken, affidavits from several persons reflecting upon the usual character of Sir ROGER's wife. Every possible circumstance connected with the career of Sir ROGER or his wife at all adverse to them appears to have been collected by Mr. MACKENZIE, so that you may expect he will paint them as dark a colour as he can. I was in company of a learned Judge of our Supreme Court the other evening, and also of a leading barrister, and they both think that the present Claimant is the right man, and expressed themselves thoroughly satisfied of it. The ORTON mystery, no doubt, Mr. BERLINER will be able to unravel. There appears to me no doubt that Sir ROGER did use the name of ORTON, at one time, in Gipp's Land and elsewhere. Mr. BERLINER and Mr. ALLPORT are expected in this district very shortly, when every aid I can give them they shall have. I was in Melbourne a few weeks since, and saw Messrs. SEDGEFIELD and ALLPORT, and they wish me to make an affidavit as to Mr. MACKENZIE's statement, when he said that he had come under the sanction of the Lord Chancellor, &c. This I have promised to do. I have to thank you for the copies of the affidavits, which reached me safely by last mail. —I am, dear Sir, yours truly, W. A. COTTEE.

On Friday, July 3rd, 1868, an interview took place at Mr. HOLMES's Office, between Sir ROGER TICHBORNE and CHARLES ORTON, in the presence of Colonel LUSHINGTON, who asserted that he did not know Sir ROGER, that he was no relative whatever to him, and that he had never seen him before until that moment. There was also present Captain HENRY ANGEL, who also declared that Sir ROGER was a perfect stranger to him, and that he had never before seen him. Captain ANGEL told Sir ROGER and Colonel LUSHINGTON, that about twelve months ago, two persons, DOBINSON and another, came to see him on board his ship, and asked him if he knew a person named ARTHUR ORTON. He said "Yes, he had known him nearly all his life, having for years lived in the same house with him, and they had also been shipmates." They then asked him when he last saw ARTHUR ORTON. He replied, "About thirteen years ago, at Hobart Town;" and they then asked him if he would know his likeness, or portrait, if he saw it. He said he thought he should. DOBINSON then told him that ARTHUR ORTON had made a will in New Zealand, and left him Captain ANGEL his executor, and showed him a piece of writing, which he said was an extract from the will. Next day DOBINSON and friend called again and showed him a photograph portrait. Captain ANGEL said, "He thought he could see a resemblance, and he thought it was ORTON's Portrait." They then requested him to go to their office in Lincoln's Inn-fields with them, which he did, and they then and there got him to swear an affidavit, which he did, under the impression and belief that it was in connection with his duty as executor to ORTON's will, and to enable him to act, &c.

To Mr. JOHN HOLMES. London, August 4th, 1868.

Dear Sir,—Before taking my departure for Australia, you will perhaps feel obliged if I write my opinion concerning Sir ROGER TICHBORNE. When first introduced to your client, and expecting, as I did, to see my guardian friend ARTHUR ORTON, I was astonished in beholding the face of a stranger. Subsequently I have perceived a likeness to ARTHUR ORTON, or to the ORTON family, but not sufficiently strong for me to say I am certain this is ARTHUR ORTON.

Having never had the pleasure of seeing Sir ROGER TICHBORNE before he left England, I cannot of course recognise him as such, but bearing as he does a likeness to ARTHUR ORTON, I can only fancy that he may be ARTHUR ORTON.—Yours respectfully,

H. R. ANGEL.

The following is a copy of a letter received by Mrs. JURY, from her brother GEORGE ORTON, from Singapore, returning a photographic likeness of Sir ROGER.

This photograph corresponds with that marked D 7, of the Australian exhibits not enlarged.

On the front of the carte-de-visite returned (which is in the custody of Mr. MOOJEN) is the following observation:—"Not ARTHUR likeness.—G. O."

On the back:—"This carte-de-visite is not like my brother ARTHUR. I cannot see any likeness of him in it."

"GEORGE ORTON, Singapore, April 17th, 1869."

Singapore, April 27, 1869.

My dear Sister,—I have returned the carte-de-visit. I cannot see any likeness of my brother ARTHUR in it. ARTHUR had is name marked on is arms, and likewise holes in is ears. if you can remember he use to ware small gold earrings in is ears, but it is not ARTHUR, and not the least like him: but surely, my dear sister, if you see him and speak to him you ought to know if it is ARTHUR, and I cannot see anything like him in the likeness.

Give my love to GEORGE and the children, and all, and remain your affectionate brother, GEORGE ORTON.

ADELAIDE send her love to all.

We insert here EDMUND ORTON's letter to his sister, Mrs. TREDGETT, which utterly annihilates the possibility of the Claimant being ARTHUR ORTON:—

My dear Sister,—I have not received a letter from you for a year. I have written two or three times to you but have not received an answer. I get a Cornish paper once in a while. I see the Claimant has been prosecuted, and also he is trying to get a new trial. Now if you think that this letter will assist him, you can get some one to dictate and publish it with my name, and I will hold myself responsible for it. I did not know that my name was mentioned, or that I was wanted in England, or I would have come home. If he gets a new trial, I will come home on condition that they send for me, and send me money to come with. Where I am living is 300 miles from the nearest seaport, which is Matfeland, to take the steamer. I saw some few papers during the trial. The witnesses that were examined as to ARTHUR's playmates could not have been ARTHUR's playmates without being my playmates. We were the last two to leave home. We went to school together. We played together. We slept in the same bed together. And his playmates—I must have known them. But out of the many witnesses there was but one that I knew, and that was ROBERT or JOHN WHITE. The rest of them that I saw [the statements of] I pronounce as false from beginning to end. By their evidence they could not have known ARTHUR, or they would have given a very different statement. If I had been in England, I do not think that one in twenty would have dared to come into Court. As for ARTHUR having any marks on his body, I will swear his body was as clear as could be. If he had any marks, I, above all, must have seen them, as our sleeping together and bathing together at the bath-house on the New-road, very near every Sunday. To the best of my recollection, ARTHUR's eyes were a light blue, I am confident they were not black. It's a paper a few days ago, with CHARLES's statement in it,* which has caused me to write this. I cannot think how he could have the impudence to write such a false statement. I pronounce it as lies, from beginning to end, of the blackest dye. As regards the family, he said I was born in the year 1828. That is false; I was born on the 1st of March, 1831. He said I was in New Mexico. He said I had my ears pierced the last time I was in England. I never had my ears pierced when I was in England, and I never wore gold earrings in my life. The statement he made about my brother WILLIAM is false, every word of it. He (WILLIAM) never reached California. He died on the passage from Ruamar to San Francisco. After the false statements he has made about our family, I would not believe him under oath. It is hard words to say about a brother, but after such slander I do not acknowledge him as a brother, and I do not want to put my eyes on him again while we live, as I cannot be responsible for what may happen. No doubt if I had seen [the report of] all the trial, I could write a good deal more. I do not think CHARLES would dare to face me in Court with such false statements.—I remain, your affectionate brother, EDMUND ORTON.

Promontora, Nov. 26th, 1871.

We next insert the Claimant's cross-examination in Chancery, 30th July, 1867, before Mr. ROUPELL, by Mr. CHAPMAN BARBER. Its unfair spirit needs no comment. We supplement it with that of Mr. GOSFORD:—

SIR ROGER CHARLES DOUGHTY TICHBORNE, Sworn. Cross-examined by Mr. CHAPMAN BARBER, on his affidavit of the 3rd July, 1867.

Q. You have stated in your affidavit that you landed at the Port of Melbourne, in Australia, about the end of July, 1851. Do you remember the day when you landed?

A. Excuse me; I will speak to my counsel.

The Examiner. No, no; we cannot allow that.

The Witness. I want to know if this is a private examination?

The Examiner. It is in my discretion whether it should be a private or a public one. I see no reason for making it private.

---

* This is the statement which appeared in the *Daily Telegraph* soon after the late trial, and for which CHARLES ORTON says he was promised £500, but only got £5.

The Witness. I understood it was to be a private examination. I wanted an examination in Court.

The Examiner. The Court has deputed to me the duty of taking the examination.

Mr. Serjeant BALLANTINE. There is no question about it. [To the witness.] You had better attend and answer the questions.

The Witness. I am agreeable.

Q. (By Mr. C. BARBER.) I asked you, do you remember the exact day in July, 1854, when you landed at Melbourne?

A. No, I do not.

Q. How long did you stay in Melbourne?

A. On my first arrival?

Q. Yes?

A. Two days.

Q. Where did you go to from Melbourne?

A. To Gippsland.

Q. You state in your affidavit that you changed your name.

A. I did.

Q. When did you do that?

A. On the morning I started from Gippsland, or rather on the previous evening.

Q. The name you took was TOMAS CASTRO.

A. Yes.

Q. (By the Examiner.) You took the name of TOMAS CASTRO?

A. Yes.

Q. Thomas without an *h*?

A. Sometimes one and sometimes the other.

Q. (By Mr. C. BARBER.) Was CASTRO an Englishman?

A. No, he was not; he was a Chilian.

Q. What induced you to select that particular name?

A. Private reasons.

Q. What reasons?

A. Because it suited me to do so.

Q. What reasons?

A. Because I did so.

Q. Can you give the particular reasons which induced you to change your name?

A. I do not know how I could, no more than I thought it would be better than using my own name; I did not want to make my own name public.

Q. You did not want to make your own name public?

A. That is to say, I went down to Gippsland as a stock-man, and I did not wish to go under my own name.

Mr. Serjeant BALLANTINE. There may be a great deal of embarrassment to a witness if persons are introduced into the room to stare at him while he is under cross-examination; that is the course which is pursued by the parties behind my friend.

The Examiner. I think as long as they conduct themselves properly they may remain.

Mr. Serjeant BALLANTINE. They are whispering and staring at the witness.

The Witness. I consider it unfair.

Mr. Serjeant BALLANTINE. This is not a place where ladies have a right to come to and stare at a witness; there are plenty of places where they can identify him; I will call attention to any one whom I see acting in an improper way.

Q. (By Mr. C. BARBER.) Did you give your own name on board the ship which took you to Melbourne?

A. Most undoubtedly.

Q. Did you make any arrangement with Mr. FOSTER as to wages or otherwise on going to Gippsland?

A. I did.

The Examiner. We have have not heard of Mr. FOSTER.

Mr. C. BARBER. Perhaps it had better be put in this way, "With reference to the 36th paragraph of my affidavit, I say I made an arrangement with Mr. WILLIAM FOSTER there mentioned as to wages."

Q. What wages were you to receive?

A. Thirty shillings a week.

Q. Was there any definite time fixed for the engagement?

A. No.

Q. Did you take any horses from Melbourne?

A. The station horses went back.

Q. How many?

A. I think there was eight or nine; there was several of us together.

Q. (By Mr. Serjeant BALLANTINE.) You were accompanied by eight or nine horses?

A. That is to say, they had previously brought horses for sale.

Q. We should call them return-horses?

A. Yes.

The Examiner. "I was accompanied by eight or nine station or return horses from Melbourne to Boisdale."

Q. (By Mr. BARBER.) Mr. FOSTER and others went with you?

A. Yes.

Q. You say you remained there about nineteen months?

A. Yes.

Q. Did you continue at the same rate of wages?

A. No; I received £2 a week after I had been there about six months.

Q. Then did you go to another station?

A. Yes.

Q. How far off was that?

A. It is a little over 100 miles; I cannot say exactly. I should imagine about 140 or 150 miles.

Q. Then you went back to Boisdale?

A. Yes.

Q. (By the Examiner.) From the other station you went back to Boisdale?

A. Yes, to another station named Dargo. I returned from Dargo to Boisdale, and stayed there about three months.

Q. (By Mr. C. BARBER.) Did you quit Mr. FOSTER's employment at that time?

A. It was all in the same employment up to that.

Q. It was all in the same employment up to that time?

A. Yes.

Q. (By the Examiner.) That is to the end of the three months?

A. Yes.

Q. (By Mr. C. BARBER.) Into whose employment did you next go?

A. I was breaking-in horses in the township of Flodden Creek, on my own account.

The Examiner. That is, "After the three months expired I then commenced breaking-in horses on my own account at Flodden Creek."

Q. (By Mr. C. BARBER.) How long did you remain there?

A. About six months.

Q. What did you do after that?

A. I went to the Mitchell Station on the Mitchell River.

Q. In what capacity?

A. As a horse-breaker, breaking-in horses, Norman McLeod –

The Examiner. "I then went to the Mitchell Station (Norman McLeod), on the Mitchell River, and broke-in horses."

Q. (By Mr. C. BARBER.) You entered into partnership there with a Mr. BURROWS?

A. Yes.

Q. Was that in the same business?

A. Yes. You must understand I mean by partnership we worked together, there was no legal partnership.

Q. After a time you gave up breaking horses, did you not?

A. Yes; some time after.

Q. How long afterwards?

A. About nine months.

Q. What did you do then?

A. That is to say, I ceased to break-in horses with him, but I did not cease to break-in horses.

Q. (By the Examiner.) Nine months afterwards?

A. Nine months afterwards we parted, you know.

Q. (By Mr. BARBER.) When did you give up breaking horses altogether?

A. I broke-in horses almost up to the time I left Australia.

Q. That was not the only business you carried on in Australia?

A. No.

Q. What other trades did you carry on in Australia?

A. Several.

Q. Be so good as to mention them?

A. Put your question, and I will answer it.

Q. I do ask you the question; I want to know what trades you carried on in Australia?

A. I had been travelling with stock; I had been carrying on a butcher's establishment; I have done Her Majesty's mails.

Q. You drove Her Majesty's mails?

Mr. Serjeant BALLANTINE. No, rode; they do not drive there.

Q. (By Mr. C. BARBER.) Did you carry on the business of a butcher on your own account?

A. I did for a short time.

Q. How long?

A. I could not exactly say how long.

Q. Cannot you tell how long?

A. I think seven months in one place, and a couple or three months in another.

Q. At what places?

A. At Tumut; I was there seven months, about that; and two or three on my own account in Wagga-Wagga.

Q. Did you carry on the business of a butcher all the time you were at Wagga-Wagga, or only part of it?

A. Part of it.

Q. How long?

A. Oh, a very short time; I was breaking-in horses for a short time, about a couple of months, or so.

Q. During all this time were you in good circumstances?

A. Yes, I was, at least the principal part of the time.

Q. Did you ever fail?

A. Well, I closed my establishment, if you call that failing.

Q. (By the Examiner.) Once?

A. Twice.

Q. (By Mr. C. BARBER.) Did you pay your creditors?

A. I paid some of them, some of them are not paid.

Q. When did you marry?

A. On the 29th January, 1865.

Q. What was your wife before her marriage?

A. A domestic servant.

Q. Was she an educated person?

A. No, not to say very.

Q. Could she write?

A. She can a little.

Q. Could she write then?

A. Well, I cannot say, yes; it is very little, if she can at all now.

Q. Surely you know whether she can write or not?

A. If she can write at all, it is but little now.

Q. I think you are described as a butcher in your marriage certificate?

A. I cannot say whether I am or not.
Mr. Serjeant BALLANTINE. You know the certificate will speak for itself, at least that is our rule.
Q. (By Mr. C. BARBER.) Were you a butcher at that time?
A. Yes, I was managing a butchery at that time.
Q. When you landed in Australia in July, 1854, did you write to England?
A. No, I did not.
Q. When did you first write to England?
A. I first wrote to England in January, I think, 1866.
Q. Can you give any reason for not writing in the meantime?
A. I did intend to write when I first went down; I put it off from time to time. I have not any particular reason, no more than I did not wish any one to know where I was.
Q. But why should you not wish persons to know where you were?
A. Because I was not inclined to do so.
Q. Do you remember when was the last time you wrote to England before you landed at Melbourne?
A. Yes, but I do not know exactly about the date; I know it was somewhere about the middle of April.
Q. (By Mr. Serjeant BALLANTINE.) April in what year?
A. 1854, from Rio.
Q. (By Mr. C. BARBER.) To whom did you then write?
A. I think I wrote to my father, and to VINCENT GOSFORD.
Q. Did you write to anybody else?
A. Not that I remember now.
Q. (By the Examiner.) The question was, the last time you wrote?
A. That is previous to arriving in Melbourne.
Q. (By Mr. Serjeant BALLANTINE.) That was from Rio?
A. Yes.
Q. (By Mr. BARBER.) Do you remember when you first heard of Sir EDWARD DOUGHTY's death?
A. I do.
Q. When was it?
A. It was when I arrived at Valparaiso.
Q. Then you knew when you were at Valparaiso that Sir JAMES FRANCIS TICHBORNE had succeeded to the title?
A. Certainly I had.
Mr. Serjeant BALLANTINE. That is, his father; you had better put it in that way.
The Examiner. I should think so.
Q. (By Mr. BARBER.) Then when you landed destitute at Melbourne, did it not occur to you to write to Sir JAMES TICHBORNE?
A. If I had remained any time at Melbourne, I should have done so.
Q. Did it not occur to you when you arrived destitute at Melbourne, to write to Sir JAMES TICHBORNE?
A. It might have occurred to me, I cannot say what might have occurred to my mind that long period ago. I should have done so had I not have gone down to Gippsland.
Q. Have you no other reason to give for not writing to Sir JAMES TICHBORNE?
A. No.
Q. Had there been any quarrel between you?
A. Well, I think you might leave that out.
Q. I do not mean to leave it out.
A. Then I shall decline to tell you whether there was or not.
Q. I request to know, and must know?
Mr. BARBER. You had better take down this question and answer.
[The short-hand writer read his note commencing with the question: "Did it not occur to you, when you arrived destitute at Melbourne, to write to Sir JAMES TICHBORNE?" to the words "I request to know and must know."]
The Examiner. The Counsel says, he requests to know and must know. Witness will answer the question.
A. No; I will not.
Q. (By Mr. BARBER.) Did it not occur to you to write to Lady TICHBORNE?
A. It might have done so.
Q. Had you any quarrel with her?
A. I decline to answer that question.
Q. Did it occur to you to write to Mr. ALFRED TICHBORNE?
A. I cannot say that it did; it is impossible for me to remember what occurred to my mind at that time.
Q. You remember some things very well—you have gone into details in your affidavit?
Mr. Serjeant BALLANTINE. His brother was fourteen at that time.
Q. (By Mr. BARBER.) You said that you did not write to England during the time you were in Australia; did you make any application, by letter or otherwise, for pecuniary assistance to any member of the TICHBORNE family while you were in Australia?
A. I did not—that is to say, not till I wrote home in January, 1866.
Q. Can you give us the name of the vessel which landed you in Melbourne?
A. I am under the impression it was the "Osprey."
Q. You do not know for certain?
A. No, I do not.
Q. Can you give us the name of the captain?
A. It was either OWEN LEWIS or LEWIS OWEN.
Q. Have you ever seen him since?
A. No; I have not.
Q. Have you had any communication with him since?
A. No.
Q. Did you tell him you were the eldest son of a baronet?
A. I cannot say whether I did or not.
Q. Did you make any promises to him for saving your life?
A. No: I did not.
Q. Do you remember the names of any of the officers on board the ship?
A. I cannot say that I do to a certainty.
Q. Can you guess?
A. No; I am not going to guess—I am on my oath.
Q. Do you remember the names of any of the crew?
A. No; I should not be likely to know them; I do not know them.
Q. Is there any log-book of the vessel in existence, as far as you know?
A. Not as far as I know.
Q. You remember, of course, when you left England?
A. I do.
Q. What port did you start from?
A. From Southampton.
Q. Where did you go to from Southampton?
A. To Havre.
Q. Was there any particular reason for your selecting Havre as a starting point?
A. There might be, but I am not likely to remember it now.
Q. What was the name of the vessel you left in?
A. From where?
Q. From Havre?
A. "La Pauline."
Q. Do you remember the name of the captain?
A. No; I do not.
Q. Were there any passengers on board besides yourself?
A. Yes; there were passengers on board.
Q. How many?
A. Well, I really do not remember how many now.
Q. Give some sort of notion—were there a dozen?
A. I tell you I do not remember.
Q. You must give some notion.
A. You would like me to say anything?
Q. No; I would not.
A. Well, I am not going to do it. I tell you, I do not remember.
Q. Were there two?
A. I have given my answer—I do not remember.
Q. Were there two—you said *passengers*?
A. Yes; there was two.
Q. Were there three?
A. I do not know about that—I say there was two passengers on board the vessel.
Q. Who were those two passengers?
A. I do not remember.
Q. Two besides yourself?
Mr. Serjeant BALLANTINE. He does not confine himself to two.
Q. (By Mr. BARBER.) At least two—you say that there were at least two besides yourself?
A. I said there were two passengers on board the ship.
Q. (By Mr. Serjeant BALLANTINE.) Besides yourself?
A. I do not say besides myself.
Q. (By Mr. BARBER.) Which do you mean to say?
The Examiner. There were at least two passengers on board—that would include himself.
Mr. BARBER. Then I ask him if there were two besides himself.
Q. Surely you must remember that?
A. I told you before, I do not remember how many passengers there were.
Q. You must surely be able to remember whether there were two passengers besides yourself?
A. I do not remember correctly, and therefore I say I do not remember.
[The short-hand writer, at the request of the Examiner, read his note as follows:—"Were there two—you said passengers? A. Yes; there was two. Q. Were there three? A. I do not know about that; I say there was two passengers on board the vessel. Q. Who were those two passengers? A. I do not remember."]
The Witness. "I do not remember"—that is not right; I do not understand that question—there was myself and servant.
[The short-hand writer continued reading his note, commencing with the question, "Q. Two besides yourself?" to the words "and therefore I say I do not remember."]
Q. (By Mr. BARBER.) Now I understand you to say the two passengers were yourself and servant?
Mr. Serjeant BALLANTINE. That is, the two passengers I positively speak to are myself and servant.
Q. (By Mr. BARBER.) Surely you must be able to tell whether there was another passenger besides your servant. I did not refer to a servant when I asked you about other passengers.
A. I suppose a servant is a passenger?
Q. In a sense.
A. You would want to know something differently if I told you differently.
Q. You must answer me, yes or no. Were there any other passengers in that vessel besides yourself and servant?
A. I have told you, I do not remember.
Q. What language was generally spoken on board the vessel?
A. French.
Q. Did you speak French as well as the rest?
A. I could.
Q. Did you?
A. I did.

Q. How long did you stay at Valparaiso?
A. The first time?
Q. Yes.
A. About five weeks.
Q. Where did you go from Valparaiso?
A. I went to Callao.
Q. Did you go to Lima?
A. Yes.
Q. (By the Examiner.) From Callao to Lima?
A. Yes.
Q. (By Mr. C. BARBER.) Where did you go from there?
A. I went into the interior, shooting.
Q. Where did you go from thence?
A. Back to Valparaiso.
Q. And from there?
A. To Cassa Blanca.
Q. Where is that?
A. A short distance from Valparaiso.
Q. Is it on the coast, or inland?
A. Inland.
Q. From where?
A. I suppose you do not want me to give you the name of every small town I went to?
Q. Not every small place.
A. Well, I went from there to St. Iago.
Q. And from St. Iago?
A. To Mendoza.
Q. Where is that?
A. It is on the reverse side of the River Constant.
Q. And from there where did you go?
A. To Santa Fé, and from there to Buenos Ayres.
Q. And from there?
A. To Monte Video.
Q. From thence?
A. To Rio.
Q. When you left Australia, you went from Australia to Panamá?
A. Yes.
Q. And from there you went to New York?
A. To New York.
Q. Had you any particular reason for going to New York?
A. Yes, I had.
Q. What was the reason?
A. Because I could go nowhere else—at least, at that time; I could go the other way to California.
Q. I quite understand you; if you wanted to go eastward, you had no other way than to go to New York.
Q. (By the Examiner.) "When I left Australia I went to Panamá, and from there to New York; I had a particular reason for going to New York, which was that I could go nowhere else."
A. I was waiting for the French boat, and she never arrived up to her time of sailing; I had been three weeks in Panamá, and I was not inclined to stay any longer.
Q. I will put "The boat was overdue three weeks."
A. She was not overdue three weeks; her time for sailing had passed, and she had not even arrived.
Q. (By Mr. C. BARBER.) You went to New York from there?
A. Yes, my family was getting sick, and, of course, I did not wish to remain any longer.
Q. I believe you stated that you had been at Panamá altogether three weeks?
A. Yes, I did.
Q. How long did you stay in New York?
A. One month, I think; I am not certain to a day, you know.
Q. Do you remember where you stayed there?
A. Yes, I do.
Q. Where?
A. At the Clarendon Hotel, Fourth Avenue.
Q. Did you draw some bills on Messieurs DRUMMONDS?
A. I did.
Q. Was it from New York you drew the bills?
A. Yes, from there.
Q. (By the Examiner.) DRUMMONDS, the London Bankers?
A. Yes.
Q. (By Mr. C. BARBER.) What induced you to draw these bills?
A. What induced me to draw the bills?
Q. Yes.
A. I do not exactly understand your question. I drew these bills with the intention of paying them when I arrived here.
Q. But you drew them on DRUMMONDS'?
A. I know.
Q. Had you any account with DRUMMONDS'?
A. No; but I should have had if I had had my own when I returned to England. Of course I should have remitted the money to them to pay them.
Q. Do you mean that you drew on DRUMMONDS'?
A. I made the bills payable at DRUMMONDS'—that was it. I did not draw on DRUMMONDS'; of course not.
Q. You drew the bills on DRUMMONDS' for them to accept, did you not?
A. I made the bills payable at DRUMMONDS'.
Q. Upon whom were they drawn?
A. I do not exactly understand the meaning of your word.
Q. You know what a bill of exchange is, don't you?
A. Yes. They were drawn on DRUMMONDS'.

Mr. Serjeant BALLANTINE. It is all confusion. That is not what he means.
Q. Do you remember the form?
A. No; I do not. I do not think I ever looked at it. Of course it was not drawn in a way that DRUMMONDS would pay till I paid the money in.
Mr. C. BARBER. That would speak for itself?
The Witness. Of course it would.
Q. Had DRUMMONDS ever been your bankers?
A. No; certainly not.
Q. Did you discount any of these bills?
A. Yes; I discounted some of them. One or two of the smaller ones, I think.

(Adjourned for half an hour.)

Q. Who did you discount them with?
A. Really I could not tell you; but if you wish to know the names, my solicitor, I have no doubt, can find out.
Q. No, no. I wish to know from you. The bills, in fact, were not paid.
A. Some of them are not paid.
Q. No. Were not paid? I mean at the time they became due?
A. No; they were not paid when they became due.
Q. (By the Examiner.) Some of the bills were presented at maturity and were not paid?
A. The bills, when they became due, were not paid. Some were not; some were. I don't know whether the bills I paid were paid when they became due.
Mr. Serjeant BALLANTINE. It is only a question of hearsay?
The Witness. That is all.
Q. (By Mr. C. BARBER.) Were you sued on any of the bills?
A. Yes. I believe I have been sued on all the bills. I will not say all; I think so. I cannot say.
Mr. Serjeant BALLANTINE. That does not affect his identity at all.
Mr. C. BARBER. Perhaps not.
Q. Do you remember any circumstance connected with yourself occurring on board "La Pauline"—any special circumstance?
A. Nothing of a very serious character. I think not. I met with a slight accident from an albatross, or something of that sort, I received a slight cut in the eye.
Q. From the beak or wing?
A. From the wing? I think it was. I do not remember which it was.
Q. Was the bird on the wing?
A. No; it was on the deck of the ship. We had caught the bird; it was pulling him in by the line.
Q. That was a slight accident and passed away in no time?
A. Yes; that was all.
Q. Do you recollect anything else of importance or singularity, which occurred on board the "Pauline"?
A. No.
Q. Can you give us a description of the shipwreck?
A. Yes; and I will answer every question you put to me.
The Examiner. You are now going back to the "Bella," I presume?
Mr. C. BARBER. Yes.
The Examiner. "Can you give a description of the shipwreck?" is the question.
The Witness. I hope the learned gentleman does not want me to make a speech, it is next door to it.
Q. (By Mr. C. BARBER.) You see your affidavit contains a long statement connected with this shipwreck; can you repeat that in substance?
A. Most undoubtedly I can; but I tell you again, I will answer any question that you put to me.
Q. Well, I ask you to be so good as to repeat the statement of the shipwreck?
A. It would be very amusing, I have no doubt, for you all, but I am not going to do it; I am here to answer any question you put to me.
Q. You must do more that that.
A. Perhaps you would like me to commence from my sailing from England?
Q. Not the least.
A. You may as well ask me the one as the other.
Mr. Serjeant BALLANTINE. I do not think that any counsel can tell a witness to give a description of a shipwreck.
Mr. C. BARBER. If he declines to do it there is an end of it.
Mr. Serjeant BALLANTINE. It must be understood that he does not decline to answer any questions in relation to the shipwreck.
Q. (By Mr. C. BARBER.) At what time of the day were the boats hoisted out?
A. I should think it would be about half-past ten.
Q. (By the Examiner.) Forenoon or night?
A. In the morning.
Q. (By Mr. C. BARBER.) You said one of the boats was destroyed—which of the two was it?
A. Well, if you tell me the particular names of the three, I will tell you.
Q. Which side of the vessel?
A. On the left-hand side.
Q. (By the Examiner.) The boat that was destroyed was on the left-hand side of the ship?
A. That is the counsel's words. It was on the left-hand side,—that is, if you look at the ship's head.
Q. The boat that was destroyed was on the port side?
A. No; the left-hand side.
Q. (By Mr. C. BARBER.) On what tack was the ship, do you know?

A. No; I don't know anything about the ship.
Q. Can you give any description of the ship?
A. Can I give any description of the ship?
Q. Yes; the ship in which you were saved?
A. In which I was saved?
Q. I mean the "Bella."
A. Then you say one thing and mean another?
Q. I do.
A. I cannot exactly tell you much about it, for I was never much upon deck till the time of the leak.

Mr. Serjeant BALLANTINE. Three people have been planted by that window to stare at my client. He will be perfectly ready to allow any person to see him, without their staring him out of countenance, while he is under examination.

Mr. C. BARBER. I have not the least desire that he should be, in the slightest degree, inconvenienced in any way.

Mr. Serjeant BALLANTINE. They had better go to the bottom of the room, instead of standing there staring at the witness; it would not be allowed in a Court of Justice.

The Examiner. Probably they have seen the witness by this time and will not oppress him any further by their presence.

Q. (By Mr. C. BARBER.) Are you subject to sea-sickness?
A. Yes; sometimes.
Q. Were you at that time?
A. No; I was not at that time.
Q. What made you stay below all the time?
A. Because I was tipsy; now you have got the answer; you might just as well have asked it before.
Q. Were you tipsy all the time; the four days?
A. I was on and off; I was recovering: I was getting myself right.
Q. Were you tipsy when you went on board?
A. Yes: I was.
Q. Had you recovered when you discovered the leak?
A. That was the first morning I came upon deck.
Q. Where was the leak?
A. I did not happen to be exactly at the bottom of the ship to see that.
Q. (By the Examiner.) No; but do you know where it was?
A. No; I do not, it is a curious question.
Q. (By Mr. C. BARBER.) It is generally known, somewhere, where a leak is?
A. I very much doubt whether the captain himself knew.
Q. What sort of a ship was it?
A. What sort of a ship?
Q. (By the Examiner.) Was she, a schooner or what?
A. I think they called her a ship; whether there was any other technical name for her I don't know.
Q. (By Mr. C. BARBER.) Do you know how she was rigged?
A. Not exactly.
Q. You have been a good deal at sea?
A. Yes; I have been a good deal at sea, but I did not see much of her, though I believe she was ship-rigged, whatever that is.
Q. How many officers were there?
A. There were two, I think.
Q. Two, besides the captain?
A. Well, that I could not say; you might call the cook an officer, perhaps.
Q. No; I should not.
A. Well, I do not know exactly how many.
Q. Do you know the number of the crew?
A. I should think from 16 to 17; let me see,—(a pause)—Yes; I should think from 16 to 17.
Q. Have you ever seen or had any communication whatever with any of the officers or crew?
A. Since the wreck?
Q. Yes.
A. No; I have not.

Mr. Serjeant BALLANTINE. You do not mean in the boat, after they left the ship?

Mr. C. BARBER. No; except that.

The Witness. Except after my arrival at Melbourne.

Q. Have you ever made any attempt?
A. I have—every attempt that possibly could be made.
Q. (By the Examiner.) To do what?
A. To find them out, and I have spent a large sum of money in so doing.
Q. (By Mr. C. BARBER.) Will you be so good as to state what attempts you have made?
A. I cannot exactly tell you that, not from memory.
Q. State some of them.
A. You must be well aware that all such things as that are conducted by my solicitor, not by me.
Q. That is another point entirely.
A. It means the same thing.
Q. My question is—Have you made any attempts yourself?
A. That is the attempt; of course I have paid for it; I have engaged a man to go round England and Scotland to try and find them.
Q. All that has been since you landed in England?
A. Yes; it has been since my arrival.
Q. Do you remember what provisions were placed in the boats?
A. Yes; there were some bags of biscuits, and some barrels of biscuits, and some water, and some preserved provisions.
Q. Anything else?
A. Water.
Q. Any wearing apr[illegible] you were th[illegible] besides what you [illegible]?

A. No, none.
Q. Were you in your cabin at the time the leak was sprung?
A. No: I had just come up on deck.
Q. (By the Examiner.) You had just come on deck when you heard of the leak?
A. Yes.
Q. (By Mr. C. BARBER.) Did you make any attempt to save anything you had on board?
A. No; I did not; I was too excited in looking out. I never returned to the cabin at all.
Q. Had you any money in the cabin?
A. Yes; there was a little.
Q. Do you remember how much?
A. Only some £20 or £30. I do not remember exactly what the amount was.
Q. Any bills?
A. Yes; there were some bills, I think, but I will not be positive; I think I had one bill.
Q. Who was it drawn on?
A. GLYN's agents at New York, a bill or letter of credit. I do not know what you call it.
Q. Do you remember the amount of it?
A. No; I do not.
Q. Give us the amount as near as you can?
A. I have told you the plain truth, that I do not remember, and what else can you want me to say?
Q. Was it £100 or £1,000?
A. I could not say whether it was £100.

Mr. Serjeant BALLANTINE. Do not get excited, but keep yourself quite cool.

The Witness. But when I tell the gentleman that I do not remember what the amount is, what does he want to ask me any more about it for?

Mr. Serjeant BALLANTINE. You do not know how troublesome lawyers are; you must remember that all this is taken down, and if you answer anything hastily, it may appear as if you are not cautious in what you have stated.

Q. (By the Examiner.) Let me read to you what you have said. "I had some money in my cabin, some £20 or £30."
A. Perhaps you would say "pounds' worth of money," I do not exactly mean sovereigns, money to the value of £20 or £30.

The Examiner. Very well, I will put that. "I do not remember the amount of the bill, or letter of credit," is the last.

Q. (By Mr. C. BARBER.) Be so good as to try and remember.

Mr. Serjeant BALLANTINE. It is quite right you should be asked the question.

A. But I do not remember.
Q. Try.
A. If I remembered, of course I would say at once.
A. (By Mr. C. BARBER.) I do not ask you to tell me the exact sum, but only whether it was £100 or £1,000?
A. It was a very trifling sum, not more than £300, I know.
Q. Where did you receive that bill or letter of credit?
A. In New York.
Q. At what place had you received it, I ask you?
A. What place had I received it?
Q. Where were you when you received it?
A. In Rio.
Q. You received it at Rio?
A. I think it was Rio.
Q. Had you written to England for it?
A. No; I wrote to England for them to send me £1,000 to New York.
Q. How did it happen that you got a bill in New York, unless you wrote for it?
A. It was for what money I had instead of taking the gold. It was merely a pass from one bank to another.
Q. Where did you get the letter of credit from?
A. From my agents in Rio.
Q. You said GLYN's agents.

Mr. Serjeant BALLANTINE. No, no; it was a draft on GLYN's agents.

The Examiner. He said there was a bill or letter of credit on GLYN's agents in New York in his cabin.

Q. (By Mr. C. BARBER.) Did you get this from GLYN's agents at Rio?
A. Yes; I think it was GLYN's agents; I will not be sure of that. It was a man of the name of YOUNG, or some such name as that, but you had better not put that down, for I do not quite remember.
Q. How did you pay the expenses of travelling when you were in South America?
A. In cash.
Q. Where did you get the money from?
A. Money that I took with me, and money that I received at different times.
Q. Who did you receive any money from?
A. Who from?
Q. Yes.
A. I received it from GLYN's bank.
Q. Were GLYN's your bankers?
A. They were before I left England.
Q. You mean you had a regular account there?
A. Yes; I had a regular account.
Q. When you came back to England did you go to GLYN's?
A. I did not.

Q. (By the Examiner.) You mean the bankers'?
A. Yes; I did not go to the bankers. I did not call on them.
Q. (By Mr. C. BARBER.) Do you know whether there was any balance in your favour standing at GLYN's?
A. Yes; of course there would be a balance. I suppose there would be £1,000.
Q. Is it not very strange that you did not go and ask them for the money?
A. If I choose to do strange things it has nothing to do with you. If you ask me questions I will answer them.
Q. (By the Examiner.) Was there a credit in your favour, do you mean?
A. Yes.
Mr. Serjeant BALLANTINE. What he means to imply is, that Mr. BARBER's comment at present is out of place.
The Witness. If you ask me why I did not go there I can tell you.
Q. (By Mr. C. BARBER.) Then tell me why.
A. My reason was, that I was run down as an impostor and branded as an impostor in all the newspapers before I arrived in England.
Q. Did you personally know any of the members of GLYN's house?
A. Yes; I knew Mr. GLYN.
Q. Do you know which Mr. GLYN?
A. No; I do not recollect exactly.
Q. (By the Examiner.) I knew a Mr. GLYN?
A. One of them.
Mr. Serjeant BALLANTINE. One of the partners, is what I conclude he means.
Q. (By Mr. C. BARBER.) The Mr. GLYN you knew was a member of the firm?
A. Certainly; he was a banker.
Q. Were you in the habit of drawing cheques on the firm?
A. Yes; before I left England.
Q. Did it ever occur to you to draw a cheque on them?
A. No.
The Examiner. After he left England?
Mr. C. BARBER. No; since he came back.
The Witness. I should not think of doing so without going to see him first.
Mr. Serjeant BALLANTINE. Probably if he had he would have been taken up for forgery.
Q. (By Mr. C. BARBER.) I suppose when you were in Australia you knew you had this balance standing to your credit at GLYN's?
A. Of course; I knew very well I had £1,000 coming in to me. Of course I expected that it would be paid in to GLYN's to my credit year after year.
Q. Did it ever occur to you, when you were in difficulties in Australia, to send over to GLYN's for some money?
A. No, it did not; because I never intended to do so.
The Examiner. I will read to you, Witness, the last two or three questions and answers which were given yesterday. The question was,—"When you were in Australia, did you know you had then a balance at GLYN's" and your answer was,—"I knew I had a thousand pounds coming to me, and I expected it would have been paid to my account at GLYN's year after year. Q. When you were in difficulties in Australia, did it ever occur to you to send over to GLYN's for some money? A. No, it did not, because I never intended to do so."
Q. (By Mr. C. BARBER.) Were you ever in gaol in Australia?
A. I was never.
Mr. Serjeant BALLANTINE. This is what you call cross-examination as to character, I suppose?
Mr. C. BARBER. No; that is not at all the object of it.
Q. What business did you follow besides that of breaker-in of horses and a butcher in Australia?
A. None, excepting that I rode the Mail.
Q. Were you not a sawyer?
A. No.
The Examiner. You drove the Mail?
A. I rode the Mail.
Q. (By Mr. C. BARBER.) You were not a sawyer?
A. Never.
Q. When you were a butcher did you act as slaughterman?
A. Sometimes, if there was nobody else handy to do it.
Q. Did you ever mention the story of the shipwreck to any person in Australia before 1865?
A. I do not know that I did, I could not say whether I had or not.
Q. Did you detail it to Mr. FOSTER?
A. I think most likely I have done so, but I do not remember doing so.
The Examiner. "I may have done so to Mr. FOSTER."
A. I may have done so, but I do not remember.
Q. (By Mr. C. BARBER.) You do not remember whether you did or not?
A. No, I do not.
Q. Can you state distinctly whether you ever mentioned it to anybody but Mr. FOSTER before 1865?
A. No.
Mr. Serjeant BALLANTINE. That implies that he mentioned it to Mr. FOSTER, which he has not positively said.
The Examiner. "I do not remember whether I ever mentioned it to Mr. FOSTER, but I may have done so."
Mr. Serjeant BALLANTINE. Being in a narrative form, it would convey a false impression, that he had mentioned it positively to Mr. FOSTER.
Q. (By the Examiner.) You may have done so?
A. Yes, I may have done so.
Q. (By Mr. C. BARBER.) Did you ever mention it to anybody else?
A. Previously to 1865?
Q. Previously to 1865?
A. I do not remember that I did.
Q. Did you mention it to your wife before your marriage?
A. Yes, I think I did, to her and her brother-in-law, but I did not give any names, you know, or full particulars.
Mr. Serjeant BALLANTINE. Her brother-in-law or yours?
A. He was married to her sister.
Q. I think you said you did not give any names?
A. No, her brother-in-law.
Q. (By Mr. C. BARBER.) Did you tell your wife before your marriage that you were Sir ROGER TICHBORNE?
A. No, I did not.
Q. Did you seek out Mr. CUBITT, or did Mr. CUBITT seek out you?
A. Well, I do not know how that would be, I am sure; I did not seek Mr. CUBITT.
The Examiner. I suppose Mr. CUBITT is mentioned in the affidavit?
Mr. C. BARBER. Yes, as an advertising agent.
Q. (By the Examiner.) Did he seek you out?
A. No, I was given to understand that Mr. CUBITT was a man of not a very good character, and therefore I never sought him out; but when I arrived in Sydney the manager of the City Bank told me differently, and that Mr. CUBITT was a respectable man; and with that I gave him permission to tell Mr. CUBITT to call on me, and Mr. CUBITT did so. That is my relation with Mr. CUBITT.
Mr. CRACKNALL. CUBITT is mentioned in paragraph 43 of the Plaintiff's affidavit.
The Examiner. Thank you.
Q. "I did not originally seek him out because I heard matters against him; afterwards I heard the contrary and went to him."
A. The manager of the City Bank sent down, wrote to him to call on me.
Q. (By Mr. C. BARBER.) When did you first hear of the advertisements in Sydney?
A. I think it was in September.
Q. (By the Examiner.) What year?
A. 1865.
Q. (By Mr. C. BARBER.) Where were you at that time?
A. I was at Wagga-Wagga.
Q. What did you do when you first heard of these advertisements?
A. What did I do in regard of the advertisements?
Q. Yes?
A. Nothing at all.
Q. How long did you continue at Wagga-Wagga afterwards?
A. Till the following June.
Q. Where did you go then?
A. To Goulburn.
Q. What induced you to go to Goulburn?
A. I went to Goulburn on my road to England, with the intention of starting, you know, not direct.
Q. Where did you go from Goulburn?
A. To Sydney.
Q. Who paid the expenses of the journey?
A. Myself.
Q. Out of what funds?
A. Out of funds, of course, that I had in my pocket.
Q. Your own money?
A. Yes, of course.
Q. The proceeds of your own business?
A. I am not going to tell you all that.
Q. But you must.
A. Some money I had in my pocket.
Q. I desire to know how you got it?
The Examiner. You must not go so fast. The last is, "I am not going to tell you how I came by the funds."
The Witness. I have no objection to tell you if you want to know. It was advanced to me by Mr. COTTEE, or by Mr. GIBBES, I should say; he came from COTTEE.
Q. Through Mr. GIBBES from Mr. COTTEE?
A. Yes.
Q. (By Mr. C. BARBER.) I asked you yesterday to give me a description of the "Bella;" can you give me any description of the "Osprey"?
A. Yes; the "Osprey" was a large vessel.
Q. How was she rigged, as far as you know?
A. I do not know, I am sure, what they would call her rig.
Q. How many masts had she?
A. Three, I think.
Q. You said yesterday that you were under the impression that the name of the vessel which saved you was the "Osprey;" cannot you be certain of the name of the vessel?
A. No, I cannot.
Q. You were on board this ship many months?
A. Yes, I was on board a good while.
Q. Can you tell me what port she belonged to?
A. No, I cannot.
Q. Had she any boats on deck?
A. Yes.
Q. You must have seen her name often enough, then?
A. It appears that you want to tell me what I must have done;

I am telling you what I did do; I tell you I am under the impression it was the "Osprey," and I cannot tell you anything more.

Q. How many boats had she on deck, I ask you?

A. That I do not know.

Q. You cannot even now tell me the names of any of the officers, or any of the crew, on board the "Osprey"?

A. No, I cannot, except so far as I have mentioned my impression as regards the captain's name.

The Examiner. That it was LEWIS OWEN or OWEN LEWIS?

A. Yes.

Q. (By Mr. C. BARBER.) Did you see any of the newspapers at Melbourne on your arrival there?

A. No, I do not think I did.

Q. Did you ever hear that there was any report of the wreck, and of your being saved and brought to Melbourne, in any of the papers?

A. No, no further than Mr. COTTEE told me he remembered seeing something of the kind.

The Examiner. "Except that Mr. COTTEE told me."

Mr. C. BARBER. He said he remembered seeing something of the kind.

The Witness. Some report of it.

Mr. HAWKINS. There is a particular reason for that gentleman, who is sitting by the side of the witness, moving away from the table.

Mr. Serjeant BALLANTINE. In my opinion there are a good many particular reasons for all your witnesses sitting a little way back.

Mr. HAWKINS. I only desire that that gentleman should not be near the witness, who is being examined.

[The gentleman referred to withdrew to another part of the room.]

Q. (By Mr. C. BARBER.) When did you hear this from COTTEE?

A. I think it was in the month of May.

Q. What year?

A. 1866.

Q. Mr. COTTEE told you he thought he remembered seeing something of the kind?

A. Well, I was telling Mr. COTTEE of it; he said he remembered reading something of the sort.

Q. Did he tell you the paper he read it in?

A. No, he did not; but he has tried to find the paper, and he is still trying.

Q. I asked you yesterday about the "Pauline." Have you been able to remember since yesterday, whether there was any other passenger, besides yourself and your servant, on board the "Pauline"?

A. No, I do not.

The Examiner. You do not remember?

A. No, I do not remember.

Q. (By Mr. C. BARBER.) Were there any English persons on board, besides yourself and the servant?

A. Not that I remember.

Q. How did you pass your time on board?

A. Oh! various amusements.

Q. Did you read much?

A. Yes; I used to read a good deal.

Q. Do you remember any books that you read?

A. The idea of asking me such a question as that!

Q. Perhaps you will be so good as to answer it?

A. No, I do not think I can.

Q. Were they novels?

A. I told you I do not remember.

Q. Can you remember any one book you read on that voyage?

A. No, I cannot.

Q. Had you many books with you?

A. I do not remember what was the number I had.

Q. Did you go direct from Havre to Valparaiso?

A. Yes, I think so.

Q. Can you be certain?

A. No, I am not certain; they might have turned the ship round, and come back a little way, for aught I know.

Q. Did you touch at any place between Havre and Valparaiso?

A. [After a short pause.] No, I do not remember doing so.

The Examiner. You do not remember touching at any intermediate port?

A. No.

Q. (By Mr. C. BARBER.) Now I am going to quite a different subject. Before you left England you made your will?

A. I did.

Q. Who was your solicitor?

A. Mr. SLAUGHTER.

Q. In what way did you give instructions to him for the will, verbally or in writing?

A. In writing.

Q. Did you have correspondence with him on the subject of the will?

A. I did—a good deal.

Q. Where were you at the time?

A. Sometimes at one place and sometimes at another.

Q. Be so good as to tell me the different places.

A. I think it commenced from Portobello.

Mr. Serjeant BALLANTINE. Do you mean in Scotland?

A. No, near Dublin.

The Examiner. "I made my will before I left England. My then solicitor was Mr. SLAUGHTER. I gave him instructions for it in writing; I corresponded with him a good deal on the subject. I think that commenced from Portobello, near Dublin."

Q. (By Mr. C. BARBER.) Did you see Mr. SLAUGHTER in London on the subject of the will?

A. I did.

Q. Did Mr. SLAUGHTER fully explain to you the nature of your interests in the various estates?

A. He did.

Q. You said you had some correspondence with Mr. SLAUGHTER?

A. Yes.

Q. I suppose Mr. SLAUGHTER wrote to you, as well as you wrote to Mr. SLAUGHTER?

A. Yes, he did.

The Examiner. "In the various estates"; it stops rather vaguely.

Mr. C. BARBER. "In which you were interested," say.

Q. Have you got any of the letters that Mr. SLAUGHTER wrote to you?

A. No, I have not.

Q. Do you know what became of them?

A. No, I do not, unless they were stolen with the rest that were stole from my mother's trunks at Winchester. There is a gentleman in the room could tell you more about them than I could.

Q. Then you left the letters in England?

A. I did, to the best of my belief.

Q. Do you know whether the will was settled by counsel, or not?

A. It was.

Q. Do you know by what counsel?

A. I know the counsel is now living in the same town as myself, but I do not know his name. Yes, "BURROWS," or some such name as that.

Q. (By the Examiner.) "He is still living in the same town as myself?"

A. Yes, I saw him at Croydon the other day.

Q. (By Mr. C. BARBER.) Did you have any conference with Mr. BURROWS on the subject of this will?

A. I did.

Q. You state in your affidavit that you were born in Paris?

A. Yes.

Q. Where were you residing in Paris when you first remember?

Mr. Serjeant BALLANTINE. You must not take it that he positively swears he was born in Paris.

Mr. C. BARBER. He states so in his affidavit.

Q. (By Serjeant BALLANTINE.) I suppose you do not remember that event?

A. No, I do not.

Q. (By Mr. C. BARBER.) Where were you residing in Paris when you can first remember?

A. In the Rue de Madeleine.

Q. You continued to reside in Paris, as you have stated, until you were fifteen or sixteen?

A. Yes.

Q. Did you continue to reside in the same house?

A. No.

Q. Can you mention where else you resided in Paris?

A. No, I cannot; I do not remember the exact places.

Q. Can you mention any one of them?

The Examiner. Wait a moment.

Q. You say you were fifteen years in Paris?

A. Yes, I remained in Paris until I was fifteen years of age.

Q. But you cannot exactly remember what other houses you lived in besides the house in the Rue de Madeleine?

A. No.

Q. (By Mr. C. BARBER.) You surely must remember?

A. I can tell you one, and if I tell you one, you will want me to tell you twenty; so you go on.

Q. (By Mr. Serjeant BALLANTINE.) Try if you can satisfy the gentleman.

A. Rue St. Honoré, near the Louvre.

Q. (By Mr. C. BARBER.) Do you remember the number?

A. No; I do not remember the number.

Q. Was that the last residence you were in in Paris?

A. I think it was, to the best of my remembrance; but I will not be certain of that.

The Examiner, "I think, but I will not be certain, that the house in the Rue St. Honoré was—"

The Witness. Was the last house where I resided in Paris.

Mr. Serjeant BALLANTINE. Near the Louvre, he said.

Mr. CHACKNALL. He said in the Rue St. Honoré, near the Louvre.

Q. (By Mr. C. BARBER.) Did you go to school in Paris?

A. No.

Q. Did you have a tutor?

A. I did.

Q. What was his name?

A. CHATILLON.

Q. A Frenchman, I presume?

A. Yes.

Q. Could he speak English?

A. Not sufficient to say so far that he could speak English. He could just a little; a few words.

Q. His communications with you, I suppose, were in French?

A. They were.

The Examiner. "He and I communicated in French?"

A. Yes.

Q. (By Mr. C. BARBER.) How old were you when he became your tutor?

A. Well, I cannot say exactly.
Q. Give me some idea?
A. You want me to guess, perhaps.
Q. No, I want you to state the fact.
A. I tell you I cannot say.
Q. Were you seven?
A. I tell you I cannot say what age I was.
Q. Were you seven?
A. I tell you that I cannot say.
Q. Were you seven?
A. I tell you I cannot tell you what age I was, because I do not remember.
Q. Then I will ask you, were you eight?
A. I do not remember.
Q. Were you nine?
A. I do not remember; it must have been previous to that, I think.
Q. Before you were nine?
A. Yes.
Q. Was he your tutor during the whole of the time from that time till you left Paris?
A. Yes, pretty nearly; I cannot say the whole of the time.
Q. (By the Examiner.) "He was my tutor the whole of the time I was in Paris."
A. He asked me if he was.
Q. Was he your tutor up to the end of your stay in Paris?
A. Yes.
Q. (By Mr. C. Barber.) Did he reside in the house with you, or elsewhere?
A. No, he did not reside in the house; I think not; I do not recollect.
Q. Had you any other instructor up to the time when M. Chatillon came?
A. I do not remember.
Q. What did he teach you?
A. He taught me to read and write.

PORTRAIT OF HENRY ALFRED TICHBORNE, ELDEST SON OF THE LATE SIR ALFRED.

Q. In French?
A. Yes.
Q. Did he teach you Latin?
A. Yes, I think so.
Q. (By the Examiner.) You think he taught you Latin?
A. Yes, a little.
Q. (By Mr. C. Barber.) Did he teach you any Greek?
A. Really I do not remember.
Q. Did he teach you any mathematics?
A. Yes, of course; I received general school education.
Q. But I want to know particularly what he taught you?
A. If you ask me the question at once, I will answer you.
Q. Do you remember any of the Latin books you read?
A. No, I do not.
Q. I suppose he taught you arithmetic?
A. Yes.
Q. Did he teach you algebra?
A. Well, I really do not remember what he did teach me.
Q. During your residence in Paris, did you and your family go backwards and forwards to England or not?
Mr. Serjeant Ballantine. Do you mean his mother by his family?
Mr. C. Barber. I will hear what he says in answer to my question.
The Witness. Sometimes, I think; not very often.
Q. Who went?
A. I am sure I cannot tell you all of them, so many years ago.
The Examiner. "During my residence in Paris my family went sometimes to and fro from England."
Q. (By Mr. C. Barber.) Did your mother go?
A. That I do not remember.
Q. Did your father go?
A. He might have gone.
Q. Can you call to mind any particular occasion on which you went with your family?
A. What year do you mean?

Q. At any time whatever, when you were resident in Paris, can you remember making a visit to England with your father or mother, or either, or both of them?

A. No, I do not now, except at my uncle's death; I came over with my father in the year 1845.

Q. But my question is, as to your going to England and back again to Paris in the interval?

A. I do not remember any particular occasion.

Q. I want to know whether you did, in the interval between 1829 and 1845, go to England and back again to Paris?

A. Certainly, on several occasions, as a child; but, of course, you do not expect me to remember that.

Q. But I do.

A. Then if you do, I do not remember it.

Q. (By the Examiner.) The question is, "Did you, in the interval between 1829 and 1845, go to England and back again to Paris?"

A. Yes: I remember that I went on several occasions; but I cannot state when or who with.

Q. (By Mr. C. BARBER.) Where did you go when you went to England?

A. I think principally, the first time I went, would be to Upton and Tichborne.

Q. Do you remember the time of year when you went?

A. No, I do not.

Q. Was it winter or summer?

A. I cannot tell you.

Q. Did they have any juvenile parties when they went over?

A. That I really do not remember.

Q. Do you remember seeing any member of the family when you went to England; any one in particular on any one of the occasions?

A. Yes; I generally saw all of them.

Q. Who did you see?

A. I cannot remember on any particular occasion. I can tell you who I would be likely to see.

Q. I could tell you that, but I want to know who you did see?

A. I do not remember any particular persons. I could not tell you.

Q. (By the Examiner.) "I do not remember any particular persons that I saw on my visits to England."

A. I would be sure to see them all, of course.

Q. (By Mr. C. BARBER.) Did you go to the theatre in England when you came over here?

A. I really do not remember whether I did or not.

Q. Do you remember taking any tour in any part of France with your tutor?

A. Yes, I know we went.

Q. Where did you go?

A. I do not remember the names of the places.

Q. (By the Examiner.) You do remember making a tour with Mr. CHATILLON in France?

A. Yes.

Q. (By Mr. C. BARBER.) How long were you away; do you remember?

A. No; I cannot say.

The Examiner. On that tour?

Mr. C. BARBER. Yes.

The Witness. No; I do not remember exactly how long.

Q. Was it a tour of a month or two, or of six months.

A. I think it was only some fortnight or three weeks?

Q. Surely you can remember where you went if it was only for a fortnight or three weeks?

A. I tell you I do not remember the names of the places.

Q. What part of France was it?

A. That I do not remember.

Q. Cannot you tell me the name of one single place?

A. No.

Q. Do you remember any particular circumstance occurring in the course of the tour.

A. No.

Q. You do not remember anything occurring?

A. No.

Q. Was anybody with you besides the tutor?

A. Well, I really do not remember.

Q. (By the Examiner.) "I do not remember whether there was any third person with us."

A. I do not remember whether there was or not.

Q. (By Mr. C. BARBER.) You cannot tell me any place you went to?

A. No; I do not remember any.

Q. Did you stay at hotels, or did you go to private houses?

A. Upon my word I do not remember where we slept exactly.

Q. How did you travel?

A. Upon my word I do not remember; it is many years ago.

Q. Can you tell me a single thing that you saw, or a single thing that you did on that tour?

A. No, I cannot.

The Examiner. If you would like to retire at any time, mention it to me, witness.

The Witness. I should, if you please.

The Examiner. Now?

The Witness. Yes; I feel the heat very much.

The Examiner. Then we will adjourn for half an hour.

(Adjourned for half an hour.)

Mr. Serjeant BALLANTINE. Unless those ladies [alluding to two ladies seated by the window] sit out of the way, I shall not allow the examination to go on.

Mr. C. BARBER. What objection do you raise?

Mr. Serjeant BALLANTINE. To those ladies sitting there staring at the witness.

Mr. C. BARBER. One of them is a witness.

Mr. Serjeant BALLANTINE. That is no reason why they should sit opposite another witness, and stare him out of countenance. If they are witnesses, I desire they may leave the Court. I desire that every witness intended to be called may leave the Court.

Mr. C. BARBER. There is no witness intended to be called.

Mr. Serjeant BALLANTINE. I shall take on myself to decline to allow this examination to go on, unless those ladies move from that window to another part of the room.

The Examiner. I would suggest that they should accede to the counsel's request.

Mr. C. BARBER. I must ask you to make a note of this, Sir, Lady TICHBORNE being one of the parties. I do not know who the other is.

The Examiner. I do not object to their being here.

Mr. C. BARBER. It is the very object that they should be in front.

Mr. Serjeant BALLANTINE. I know it is yours, but it is an object which I shall not allow.

Mr. HAWKINS. The gentleman who is sitting by you had also better retire to another part of the room.

Mr. Serjeant BALLANTINE. You have already ordered him from one part.

Mr. HAWKINS. I did not order him to sit immediately opposite the witness.

[The two ladies then retired to another part of the room.]

Mr. C. BARBER. I must press you, sir, to take a note of this objection on your notes.

Mr. Serjeant BALLANTINE. What is the note you wish taken?

Mr. C. BARBER. That Mr. Serjeant BALLANTINE objects to the witnesses sitting in a particular part of the room.

Mr. Serjeant BALLANTINE. That Mr. Serjeant BALLANTINE objects to two ladies sitting in front of the witness and staring him out of countenance.

The Examiner. I am very anxious to give a correct account of what transpires; but, at the same time, I have never yet put down skirmishes like this.

Mr. C. BARBER. It is most important that the Court should know that the witness does not like members of his own family, according to his story, to be present.

The Witness. I know the ladies perfectly well. I have no objection to their being present.

The Examiner. I have heard, on two different occasions, an objection taken as to persons being in Court and staring the witness out of countenance. I do not say these ladies have been doing so; indeed, I should imagine they have not: but that objection has at once been acquiesced in.

The Witness. I do not accuse Mrs. GREENWOOD of doing so. It is my brother's wife whom I accuse.

Mr. Serjeant BALLANTINE. I mentioned the matter privately; and it was very unwillingly that I said anything about it in public.

The Examiner. We were upon the tour in France. "I do not remember whether we went to hotels or stayed at private houses; it happened many years ago. I cannot tell you a single thing that I saw, or a single thing that I did on that tour."

Q. (By Mr. C. BARBER.) Do you remember who were your associates or playmates while you were in Paris?

A. I do not remember. You must remember, anything that I am not positive upon, I am going to say that I do not remember.

Q. But that will not do.

A. But it will do, because I am on my oath, and unless I remember a thing and am positive about it, I am going to say I do not remember.

Q. (By the Examiner.) "I do not remember any of my playmates or associates when I was in Paris. When I say I do not remember, I mean I am not positive?"

A. That is right.

Q. (By Mr. C. BARBER.) Cannot you tell me the name of a single one of your associates or playmates in Paris?

A. I do not remember just at the present time.

Q. But try and remember.

A. This is no place to remember.

Q. Yes; it is indeed.

A. Then I don't remember.

Q. You cannot tell me the name of one?

A. No, I cannot.

The Examiner. "I do not remember the name of a single one of my associates or playmates in Paris. This is not the place to remember."

Mr. Serjeant BALLANTINE. That was rather in answer to a question of my friend's, who told him to try and remember.

Mr. C. BARBER. Then we will have this question and answer, if you please.

The Examiner. Do you wish it, or shall I strike out, "This is not the place to remember"?

Mr. C. BARBER. No, I wish to have that down.

[The shorthand writer, at the request of the Examiner, read from the question beginning "Cannot you tell me the name of a single one of your associates or playmates in Paris?" to the answer, "No, I cannot."]

Q. Cannot you remember any boy that you used to play with?

A. I have answered that question before.

Q. Did you learn to dance?

A. Yes, I learned to dance a little.

Q. Cannot you tell me the name of any young lady you danced with in Paris?

A. If I could, I should not.

Q. Why not?

A. Because I object to it. Why should I mention the names of the ladies here in public court?

Q. You will be obliged to.

A. Then I won't do it.

Q. Suppose you tell us the Christian name of any young lady you danced with, without telling her surname?

A. [After a pause.] I have answered the question. I do not consider it has anything to do with the case. That is my objection for not answering. If this gentleman can point out to me in my affidavit that there is reason for that question to be answered, of course I will answer it.

The Examiner. Your own counsel will tell you this is quite within the proper limits of cross-examination.

Q. Can you tell us her Christian name?

A. I have answered that question.

Q. (Mr. C. BARBER.) Do you remember?

A. No, I do not.

Q. Do you remember the names of any of the servants in the establishment?

The Examiner. In M. CHATILLON's establishment?

Mr. C. BARBER. No, in his father's house.

Q. Do you remember the names of any of the servants in either of your father's residences at Paris?

A. I only remember the name of one, that is WILLIAM BURDEN.

Q. (The Examiner.) How do you spell it?

A. B-U-R-D-E-N, I think, but I am not sure.

Mr. C. BARBER. You do not know how he spells his name?

The Examiner. "I now recollect the name of one, but I am not certain."

Mr. Serjeant BALLANTINE. Do you mean you are not certain about the spelling, or about the name?

A. I am not certain about the spelling of the name.

Q. You are certain about the sound of it?

A. Oh! yes.

Q. (By Mr. C. BARBER.) You cannot remember the name of any servant but this one?

A. No, I cannot, not just now.

Q. Not just now?

A. No.

Q. Do you remember the name of your nurse?

A. No.

Mr. Serjeant BALLANTINE. Which do you mean, Christian name or surname?

Mr. C. BARBER. I said the name.

The Witness. I do not remember what her name was.

Mr. Serjeant BALLANTINE. Which nurse do you mean—the wet nurse?

Mr. C. BARBER. I have put my question and I have got an answer.

Mr. Serjeant BALLANTINE. It would be *Bonne*, most likely, I should think.

Q. (By Mr. C. BARBER.) When you were a boy did you not walk about the Tuileries Gardens and places of that sort in Paris?

A. Very likely.

Q. Who did you walk with?

A. That is really such a ridiculous question that I cannot answer it.

Q. I do not consider it ridiculous, and must trouble you to answer it.

A. Then I do not remember?

Q. Do you remember the name of any single person with whom you had any conversation in Paris, besides your father and your mother and M. CHATILLON?

A. Yes.

Q. Who?

A. If you ask me, I could tell you hundreds.

Q. Tell me some?

A. I do not remember any just at the present time.

Q. Can you tell me the name of any person whom you saw in Paris besides your father and mother and M. CHATILLON?

A. If you say who you want to know the name of, I will tell you.

Q. I want an answer to my question.

A. The question is so ridiculous.

Q. Never mind that—I want an answer.

A. A person might see 500 people.

Q. The question is a very simple one.

A. It is simple, but it is very ridiculous.

Q. Will you answer it?

A. Yes; I have seen Mr. BLUNT, I have seen Mr. CALLAGHAN.

Q. Is Mr. BLUNT living or dead?

A. I do not know.

Q. Is Mr. CALLAGHAN living or dead?

A. I think young Mr. CALLAGHAN is living.

Q. What are they in Paris?

A. They are bankers.

Q. Who are Mr. BLUNT and Mr. CALLAGHAN?

A. I say I think they are bankers.

Q. You saw both these gentlemen in Paris before 1845?

A. Yes; and Mr. TURVILLE.

Mr. Serjeant BALLANTINE. Spell it.

A. T-U-R-V-I-L-L-E.

Q. (By Mr. C. BARBER.) What is Mr. TURVILLE?

A. He was a friend of my father's; I don't know what he was.

Q. Was he a resident in Paris?

A. I cannot tell you whether he resided there permanently or not.

Q. Did you visit any house in Paris?

A. Plenty.

Q. Did you visit any house in Paris?

A. Sometimes.

Q. Can you name the house of any person?

A. No; I do not remember just now.

Q. You said that when you came over to England, in 1845, you went to Stonyhurst?

A. Yes.

The Examiner. The College, is it not?

A. Yes.

Q. (By Mr. C. BARBER.) For how many years?

A. For three years.

Mr. Serjeant BALLANTINE. It is a Jesuit college, is it not?

A. Yes.

Q. (By Mr. C. BARBER.) Under whose care were you at that college?

A. I am not aware that I was under anybody's particular care, as I know of.

Q. Do you remember the names of any of the masters?

A. No; I do not just now.

The Examiner. What was that?

Mr. C. BARBER. He says he does not remember the names of any of the masters.

The Witness. Not just now.

Q. I suppose there is a principal or head master at Stonyhurst?

A. Yes; I think there was.

Q. Who was the principal or head master when you were there?

A. Well, I do not remember just now.

Q. Did you learn Latin at Stonyhurst?

A. A little.

Q. What books did you read?

A. I do not remember.

Q. Not any one of the books?

A. No; none of them.

Q. Who was the Latin master; do you remember the name of the Latin master?

A. No; I do not remember.

Q. Did you learn any Greek at Stonyhurst?

A. I do not remember whether I did or not.

Q. What mathematics did you learn at Stonyhurst?

A. I do not remember.

Q. Did you do Latin exercises?

A. Yes, of course; I went through the general course of College education.

Q. What was the course?

A. I do not remember.

Q. Were there examinations at the college?

A. There were.

Q. How often?

A. I do not remember.

Q. What was about the number of students at the time you were there; I do not want an accurate answer, but a general one; how many do you suppose?

A. Well, I really cannot say exactly how many.

Q. Were the students divided into classes?

A. Yes.

Q. How many were there in your class?

A. I do not remember.

Mr. Serjeant BALLANTINE. I must say I have never in the whole course of my professional career seen such indecency exhibited as I have seen in the progress of this case; look at that man pressing forward against the witness!

Mr. C. BARBER. I am informed this gentleman is your own friend.

Mr. Serjeant BALLANTINE. I don't care who he is; I never saw such indecency.

Mr. DOBINSON. There has been no intention of such on our part; we should be the last to countenance it.

Mr. Serjeant BALLANTINE. Then I wish you would manage at the next meeting to prevent it; you can prevent all those people crowding round and staring at the witness.

Mr. DOBINSON. We have never desired it; I should not consider it proper respect to the Special Examiner.

Q. (By Mr. C. BARBER.) Can you remember any particular person who was in your class?

A. No.

Q. Can you remember the name of any of the students?

A. Of course, I can remember the name of some students.

Q. Name them?

A. I do not remember.

Mr. Serjeant BALLANTINE (to the witness). Remember the whole of this matter is intended to be used either for or against you hereafter; just reflect, and, if you remember people, say so; do not allow any feeling of obstinacy or annoyance to prevent you doing yourself justice.

The Witness (after a pause). I remember PETRE and ARUNDELL.

Q. (By Mr. C. BARBER.) Do you mean Lord PETRE?

A. I do not know whether it is the present Lord PETRE or not.

Q. (By the Examiner.) Were they in your class, or were they in the college generally?

A. They were in the college.

Mr. Serjeant BALLANTINE. I hope you will take a note, Sir, of what I say: that, after talking about it to my friend, Mr.

HANNEN, I do not consider this examination to be one by which this witness ought at all to be tested.

Mr. C. BARBER. You are at perfect liberty to say that if you please, but it is for the Court to decide.

Mr. Serjeant BALLANTINE. I do say it; I do not believe any man, however calm his temperament may be, could undergo an examination of this kind, in this room, with all these people staring at him.

Mr. C. BARBER. I think you are rather making a speech now.

Mr. Serjeant BALLANTINE. If I choose to make a speech I shall, without your leave.

Mr. C. BARBER. I cannot prevent you, of course.

Mr. Serjeant BALLANTINE. I know you cannot. I shall ask you, Sir, to take a note of the solemn protest which I make against the mode in which this witness is treated; I never saw such a scene; it is more like what one hears of as taking place in an American Court than in an English Court of Justice; it is perfectly scandalous; it is very much like what one reads of in the backwoods of America.

The Examiner. As I understand, the ground of your objection is that the witness is crowded?

Mr. Serjeant BALLANTINE. Crowded, pressed on, and people staring at him; besides, it puts a man out of temper.

Mr. HANNEN. You will allow me, Sir, also to add my solemn protest against it.

Mr. DOBINSON. We are just as willing as you are for nobody to look at the witness.

Mr. HANNEN. That man whom Serjeant BALLANTINE spoke about was leaning right forward in front of the witness.

Mr. Serjeant BALLANTINE. Nobody would impute to you that you would act willingly in such a way.

Mr. C. BARBER. As I am told, that gentleman is one of your friends.

Mr. Serjeant BALLANTINE. Then I can only say, "Preserve me from my friends."

Mr. HANNEN. If he was our friend, it was very odd he did not come on our side.

The Witness. He was a friend to me in Valparaiso, but I cannot say he is at the present time.

Mr. HOLMES. There is not a friend of his on that side of the room.

Mr. Serjeant BALLANTINE. You may depend upon it this is a matter that will not be endured in the Courts of this country.

Mr. C. BARBER. Then perhaps we had better adjourn, and begin again.

The Examiner. Oh, no! The last I have is, "I remember the names PETRE and ARUNDELL as being the names of two young men in the college."

Q. (By Mr. C. BARBER.) And you do not know whether it is the present Lord PETRE, and the present Lord ARUNDELL, or not?

A. No, I do not; I have had no opportunity of seeing them since I have been in England: I have been too busy.

Q. (By the Examiner.) I have not had time since I have been in England to make the inquiries."

A. That is to say, I have not been composed enough; I have had to work about my own affairs.

Q. "I have not inquired into it," I will say?

A. Yes; WALMESLEY was the name of one of the priests.

Q. "One of the priests who was there, at the same time that I was, was named WALMESLEY?"

A. Yes.

Q. (By Mr. C. BARBER.) Who did you write to from South America, besides your father and VINCENT GOSFORD?

A. I wrote to Mrs. SEYMOUR; and my last letter to Mrs. SEYMOUR was from Buenos Ayres.

Q. Did you write to anybody else?

A. I do not remember just now.

Q. (By the Examiner.) "When in South America, I wrote, not only to my father and Mr. VINCENT GOSFORD, but to Mrs. SEYMOUR; my last letter to her was from Buenos Ayres?"

A. My last letter to her? I think you have it from her?

Q. "My last letter to her was from Buenos Ayres?"

A. That is right.

Mr. C. BARBER. That is all I have to ask.

The Examiner. Who do you appear for, Serjeant BALLANTINE?

Mr. Serjeant BALLANTINE. For Sir ROGER TICHBORNE, the Claimant.

Mr. C. BARBER. The Plaintiff?

Mr. Serjeant BALLANTINE. Yes; if you would let me, I should wish to postpone my re-examination until another day. There are some documents which I think it not unlikely I shall have to produce, and some letters.

The Examiner. It must rest with you.

Mr. CRACKNALL. In form, you must begin the re-examination after the closing of the cross-examination.

Mr. C. BARBER. Yes, the re-examination must follow immediately upon the cross-examination.

Mr. CRACKNALL. One question will do if you want to adjourn.

Mr. Serjeant BALLANTINE. Then I will ask one or two questions to-day and finish to-morrow.

RE-EXAMINED by Mr. Serjeant BALLANTINE on behalf of the Plaintiff.

Q. You stated that when you got to Australia, you changed your name to CASTRO?

A. Yes.

Q. Had you known any person of that name?

A. I had.

Q. Had you been intimate with him?

A. Very.

Q. What was his Christian name?

A. TOMAS.

Q. Where had you met with him?

A. In Melipilla.

Q. Where is that?

A. It is about 23 leagues from Valparaiso; it is about 50 or 60 miles from Valparaiso.

Q. Had you seen much of him?

A. Yes, I was his guest for a while.

Q. Where was that at?

A. At Melipilla.

Q. At the place you have already mentioned?

A. Yes.

Q. Is that in Chili?

A. In Chili.

Q. You say you had been his guest?

A. Yes.

Q. Do you mean by that you have stayed at his house?

A. That is to say there are no hotels in Melipilla, and he was very kind in inviting me to stay with him.

Q. For how long did you stay with him?

A. I think somewhere about three weeks.

Q. Is there any person that you know who was also an acquaintance of Signor CASTRO?

A. Yes, there is; but if you will excuse me, I will not mention his name, because there are persons in this room, who, I know, have been tampering with my witnesses, and if I mention the gentleman's name they will, no doubt, go and try to tamper with him.

Mr. C. BARBER. We will have that down, if you please, Sir.

The Witness. I should like to have it down, because I can prove it.

Q. (By Mr. Serjeant BALLANTINE.) You had better keep quite cool; you have done so very well up to the present time. You say there is a person who is acquainted with your intimacy with CASTRO?

A. No, not that is acquainted with my intimacy with CASTRO, but who has likewise been a guest of CASTRO's.

The Examiner. Do you want that down about tampering with witnesses?

Mr. Serjeant BALLANTINE. No, I think not; of course, as far as the solicitors are concerned, they would not think of such a thing.

Q. (The Examiner.) "There is a person whom I know who has likewise been a guest of Signor CASTRO."

A. He was in the room a few minutes ago. I do not see him just now.

Mr. Serjeant BALLANTINE. Never mind looking for him. I dare say he has had a good look at you.

A. I dare say. I hope I will have a good look at him before I have done with him.

Q. Your wife is with you in this country?

A. Yes.

Q. She came over with you?

A. Yes.

Q. And a couple of children?

A. One child, and the other was born in Croydon.

Q. You have two children now?

A. Yes.

Q. One of them came over with you.

A. Yes.

Q. And another was born since you have been in this country?

A. Yes.

Q. I may have to ask you a question or two more on this hereafter, but when you were in Australia used you to ride a great deal?

A. Yes; I was a great deal in the saddle.

Q. Was there any hunting there of any kind?

A. Yes; there was very good hunting.

Q. Hunting of what?

A. Kangaroo, emeu, and the native dog—the dingo.

Q. Were you always very fond of sport of that kind?

A. Yes; very much so.

Q. Were you a good shot?

A. Yes; very.

Q. And used you to go out for hunting and shooting excursions into the interior?

A. Yes; very often. I used to go out by myself for months at the time.

Q. (By the Examiner.) You went out by yourself, did you say?

A. Yes.

Mr. Serjeant BALLANTINE. When you say by yourself, how do you mean?

A. I have been four months in the mountains without seeing the face of a human being of any description.

Q. Were you on horseback?

A. Yes, on horseback.

Q. And you have frequently been alone into the interior?

A. Oh! yes; very often.

Q. Were they occupations that attracted much of your time and attention?

A. Yes.

Q. Were you very fond of them?

A. Yes, I was; they were my principal hobby.

Q. Excuse my asking the question, but were you a man of temperate habits? When you went on board at Valparaiso?

A. At Rio?

Q. You were rather queer there, were you not?

A. Yes.

Q. Were you a person of ordinary temperate habits?

A. Very much so after my arrival in Australia. I have been for years. I have never tasted wine or spirits for years.

Q. Previously to reaching Australia had your habits been temperate, or the reverse?

A. Sometimes, of course, I would drink a glass too much.

Q. You were not ordinarily intemperate?

A. No; I was not.

Q. During any of these excursions did you meet with any serious accident?

A. I met with so many, I do not know any in particular.

Q. I suppose in a life of that kind you do meet with a good many adventures and accidents. Did you meet with any accident while you were out on these expeditions in Australia?

A. No, I think not while I was out on any expedition.

Q. Did you at any time?

A. Yes; I met with a great many.

Q. Did you at any time meet with an accident to your head?

A. Yes.

Q. When was that?

A. I can tell you the day, I think; it was the 24th December, 1864.

Q. What was the nature of that accident?

A. I came home in a hurry and gave some instructions to one of the men—

Q. (By the Examiner.) You came home in a hurry?

A. I found that certain things that I had ordered to be done had not been done, and I went out in a passion and jumped on my horse and forgot that my girths were undone. I loosened the girths for to let the horse, in fact, get cool.

Q. (By Mr. Serjeant BALLANTINE.) You came home in a hurry, found that certain orders you had given had not been carried out, and jumped on your horse without remembering to tighten the girths?

A. Yes.

Q. What happened?

A. A person came racing by me, and my horse bolted. I went to pull him up, and pulled myself, of course, over his head, and I came down on a newly-metalled road.

Q. You went over his head?

A. Yes.

Q. Where did your head go?

A. Down on the ground. My horse, as soon as he found the saddle had gone, commenced bucking.

Q. Did you fall on your head?

A. Yes; I came on my head. That is the position of a bucking horse (handing a photograph to Serjeant BALLANTINE.)

Q. Is this your own drawing?

A. No; it is a photograph of a thing like that. You can fancy the saddle being loose.

Q. You went over its head, you say?

A. Yes.

Q. What did you go down on?

A. It cut my face from here to here (pointing).

Q. There is the mark, is there not?

A. Yes; and there were two bones taken from my nose.

Q. (By the Examiner.) I will say, "I fell on a stone and cut my face, and broke the bridge of my nose, from which two bones were extracted."

A. Yes; by Dr. ROBINSON.

Q. Two pieces of bone, I presume?

A. Yes; pieces of bone, by Dr. ROBINSON, of Wagga-Wagga.

Q. (By Mr. Serjeant BALLANTINE.) I do not propose, in the present stage of things, to go on to the effect that had on you, but had it a very serious effect on your head?

A. Yes; it had a little.

Q. What you call a little effect?

A. Yes; of course, I was ill for a long while after.

Q. I do not mean whether it cut your head, but did you find it affect your head?

A. Mentally?

Q. Yes.

A. No; not that.

Q. (By Mr. CRACKNALL.) I think you said you were ill?

A. Yes, I was ill; for I felt the effects of it. I was not laid up.

Q. (By Mr. Serjeant BALLANTINE.) Did you have any other accident which at all affected your head?

A. No; my head was affected a good deal after the wreck.

Q. As you have mentioned it, I may as well ask you—you mean the wreck of the "Bella"?

A. Yes.

Q. Can you tell me what latitude you were in when this occurred?

A. It must have been very nearly—I have no idea what it was—whether it was 1 or 1,000; I have no idea at all.

Q. (By Mr. CRACKNALL.) I understand you to say you do not know whether the latitude was from 1 to 1,000?

A. That means, I do not know at all.

Q. (By Mr. Serjeant BALLANTINE.) Can you tell whether it was hot weather or not—I mean peculiarly so? Of course it was warm.

A. Yes; it was warm weather.

Q. How do you say you were affected after the wreck?

A. Why, because I was very often out of my mind.

Q. Can you give me any idea of how long you were at sea in the boat?

A. Oh! yes.

Q. How long?

A. It was in the morning of the fourth day that we was picked up.

Q. Was there any difficulty in keeping the boat afloat?

A. No; there was no particular difficulty in keeping the boat afloat any more than that she had to be bailed out, you know.

Q. How was that done?

A. It was done by throwing the water out of her.

Q. With any vessels that there might be at hand?

A. No; I think it was done with one of the preserved meat cans; I happen to remember exactly what that was, because I generally did it myself.

Q. Some questions have been put to you about the "Osprey"; was the "Osprey" larger or smaller than the "Bella"?

A. She was larger than the "Bella"—that is to say, she had the appearance of being larger, you know.

Q. I do not know whether you told my friend; but do you remember what the tonnage of the "Bella" was?

A. No, I do not.

Q. The "Osprey" appeared to be larger, did it?

A. Yes.

Q. When you had got on board the "Osprey," did you suffer from what you had gone through the three preceding days and nights?

A. I was on board several days before I ever knew anything about it.

Q. (By the Examiner.) Before you knew anything about what had occurred?

A. Yes.

Q. (By Mr. Serjeant BALLANTINE.) When you say you do not remember anything that occurred, do you mean the mode of getting on board?

A. I remember the signal going up for her to see us; the vessel had passed us a good bit, and we were afraid we should not make ourselves seen.

Q. (By the Examiner.) The "Osprey" had passed when you saw her?

A. She had passed us a good bit, and the sailors had given over rowing, for they thought they could not overtake her; then all at once, one of them took off his shirt and put it on the top of one of the oars, and then she saw it.

Q. The "Osprey" observed that?

A. Yes.

Q. (By Mr. Serjeant BALLANTINE.) And lay-to?

A. Yes; I expect so.

Q. After the signal was hoisted, you mean you do not know what occurred?

A. No, I do not.

Q. You have been asked questions about Stonyhurst, and I observed my friend stopped when you were giving us some of the names; you have mentioned the names of PETRE, ARUNDELL, and TURVILLE?

Mr. C. BARBER. No; TURVILLE was at Paris.

Mr. Serjeant BALLANTINE. Yes you are right.

Q. Can you recollect the names of any of the other priests or any of the pupils at Stonyhurst? do not be in a hurry, but give yourself time.

A. No; I do not just at present; it was only the other day I was talking of the whole.

Q. You remembered them the other day, but at the present moment you cannot?

A. No.

Q. Then I will give you an opportunity of doing so to-morrow.

The Examiner. Shall I take that down?

Mr. Serjeant BALLANTINE. If you please. "At present I do not remember the name of any one of the other priests or students at Stonyhurst. It was only the other day I was speaking of them, but I do not remember their names at this moment."

Q. Have you seen any of them here—any that you have recognised?

A. No, I have not.

The Examiner. By "here" you mean in this room?

Mr. Serjeant BALLANTINE. Yes—since he has been under examination.

The Witness. No, I cannot say that I remember any of them.

Q. Have you seen anybody in this room that you recognise as having known them in former days?

A. Yes; there are plenty.

Q. That you remember to have met before you left England?

A. Yes.

Q. (By the Examiner.) You have seen plenty in this room?

A. I have seen several.

Mr. Serjeant BALLANTINE. Name me any person that you have so recognised.

A. Mrs. GREENWOOD.

Q. Had you seen her since the time you left England, before you saw her in this room?

A. No.

Q. (By the Examiner.) Since you left England for South America?

A. Yes.

Q. Mr. Serjeant BALLANTINE. Anybody else?

A. Yes; I see Quartermaster FRASER a little time ago.

Q. Had you seen him before to-day?

A. No, I have not.

Q. Not since you left England?

A. No, I have not.

The Examiner. For South America—is that what you mean?

A. Yes.

Mr. Serjeant BALLANTINE. Had you any reason to suppose you would see them here to-day?

A. None whatsoever. He was along with Captain POLLHAL.

Q. You said Quartermaster FRASER was with somebody?

A. He was with POLLHAL.

Q. Who is POLLHAL?

A. He was a captain.

Q. In the Carabineers?

A. Yes.

Q. Any one else?

A. Yes, there is. Since I have been in England, I have seen MOORE, who went out a servant with me.

Q. Do you know what his Christian name is?

A. Yes; JOHN.

Q. He is the man who went out with you in the "Pauline"?

A. Yes.

Mr. Serjeant BALLANTINE. I shall not have to occupy much more time, but there are some few questions I would rather ask to-morrow.

The Examiner. If you please.

The Witness. There was a person with MOORE who lived on Admiral's Island, in Valparaiso.

Q. (By Mr. Serjeant BALLANTINE.) When you were in Valparaiso he was living there?

A. Yes.

Q. (By the Examiner.) Was it to-day you saw him, or yesterday?

A. To-day.

Q. (By Serjeant BALLANTINE.) He was with MOORE, you say?

A. Yes, he was.

Q. Just answer me this: Did anybody point out to you, or have you seen him at all since he was on board the "Pauline" with you?

A. Yes; I have seen him once.

Q. Where?

A. At Croydon.

Q. There is one question which occurs to me, and I may as well ask you it. You mentioned some barrister who was consulted about making your will?

A. Yes.

Q. You say you saw him at Croydon?

A. Yes; I saw him coming out of the train one day.

Q. And you remembered him?

A. Yes; I thought he was the same person.

Q. That is since your return to England, of course?

A. Yes.

Q. Mr. BURROWS?

A. Yes; BURROWS. I will not be certain that it is the same person.

Q. The person that you believed to be him?

A. Yes; I did not speak to him, and therefore, of course, I cannot say for certain.

The Examiner. "A person whom I believed to be the Mr. BURROWS who had to do with my will."

Mr. Serjeant BALLANTINE. Did you point him out to any one?

A. I do not remember whether I did or no. I think not.

Q. You have had no communication whatever with him?

A. No; none whatever.

Q. You have been asked about letters received from Mr. SLAUGHTER, and you say you do not know what has become of them, unless they were stolen out of your mother's box at Winchester?

A. Yes.

Q. Just explain what you mean by that?

A. I merely mean to say by that, that my mother's boxes were opened and a package of letters, which she had with several other things, was taken out; a watch that I left her to take care of and my father's watch was stolen.

Q. Is it known by whom?

A. Yes; we know who has taken them. It was done under the authority of VINCENT GOSFORD, and BOWKER, the solicitor, has exhibited some of the letters in Winchester; therefore we know he is in possession of some of them.

Q. You have heard that the box has been opened?

A. We can prove it.

Q. And you say there were papers and documents in that box?

A. Yes.

Mr. C. BARBER. He says he has heard there were.

Mr. HAWKINS. That cannot, by possibility, be evidence.

Mr. Serjeant BALLANTINE. I beg your pardon.

Mr. HAWKINS. I object to it.

Mr. Serjeant BALLANTINE. It is sufficient for me that he says he knows there were papers and documents in one of his mother's boxes at Winchester.

The Witness. Yes; my mother said so.

Q. You know it from your mother?

A. Yes.

Mr. Serjeant BALLANTINE. Then, perhaps, it is not evidence.

Mr. HANNEN. Except that there were letters that were stolen.

Mr. C. BARBER. What he calls stolen.

Mr. Serjeant BALLANTINE. He left them there, and he cannot find them; and I have no doubt Mr. GOSFORD will exhibit them to his affidavit.

The Witness. I do not mean to say that VINCENT GOSFORD is the person who took them, but he gave some other person authority to go there for other things, and he took these.

Q. (By Mr. C. BARBER.) You know nothing about this?

A. I can prove it.

Mr. C. BARBER. Mr. Serjeant BALLANTINE, the other two witnesses in TICHBORNE v. TICHBORNE are Lady TICHBORNE and Mrs. STOURTON.

The Examiner. At present we are limiting ourselves to TICHBORNE and TICHBORNE, and only certain of the parties have applied for leave to cross-examine before me.

Mr. Serjeant BALLANTINE. We will take those witnesses to-morrow, and finish the little I have to ask of this witness.

The Examiner. Only those can cross-examine who have applied in TICHBORNE and TICHBORNE for leave to cross-examine before me.

Mr. L. WEBB. Except that you were appointed General Examiner in the cause, for the purpose of taking the cross-examination generally of those witnesses who have made affidavits, and any other witnesses; it certainly was so intended, and we assented to the Order on that distinct impression.

Mr. C. BARBER. I do not exactly see the point.

The Examiner. In TICHBORNE v. TICHBORNE the cross-examination must be limited to those counsel who applied for leave to cross-examine.

Mr. C. BARBER. Nobody asks that it may be otherwise.

Mr. L. WEBB. Only, the Order is general.

Mr. C. BARBER. Nobody proposes to cross-examine.

The Examiner. Very well, then, we are beating the air.

Mr. L. WEBB. But, if any one of the defendants wishes to cross-examine, he would have a perfect right to cross-examine.

The Examiner. I doubt that, but it will not arise.

Mr. Serjeant BALLANTINE. We will not ask you to settle the question, then, till it does.

Mr. HOLMES. I suppose, Mr. DOBINSON, the motion had better stand over to-morrow?

Mr. DOBINSON. If it is distinctly understood now.

Mr. L. WEBB. It is quite clear we can do nothing in it.

Mr. DOBINSON. When shall it stand over to?

Mr. L. WEBB. The last day of the sittings.

Mr. C. BARBER. We have no power to do that, you know.

Mr. DOBINSON. It is distinctly understood that neither motion will be mentioned in Court to-morrow.

Mr. L. WEBB. Except for the purpose of allowing them to stand over until the last day of the sittings.

(Adjourned till 12 o'clock next day.)

SIR ROGER C. D. TICHBORNE recalled.

Re-examination (continued) by Mr. Serjeant BALLANTINE.

The Examiner. The last sentence I have is:—"Since my return to England I have seen a person whom I believe to be the Mr. BURROWS who had to do with my will—I saw him get out of the train at Croydon. I have had no communication whatever with him."

Mr. Serjeant BALLANTINE. Will you allow us five minutes?

[Mr. Serjeant BALLANTINE, Mr. HANNEN, and Mr. HOLMES, then retired for a short time.]

Mr. Serjeant BALLANTINE. Now, Sir, if I might give you the trouble of again reading the last three or four sentences?

The Examiner. "FRASER was here with POLLHAL, who was a Quartermaster in the Carabineers; I have seen here JOHN MOORE—he went out with me from Havre in 'La Pauline.' There was a person here with MOORE, who was in Valparaiso when I was there. MOORE I saw at Croydon, since I returned to England."

The Witness. I said FRASER was the Quartermaster in the Carabineers—as you read it there, it would be POLLHAL.

The Examiner. Yes, it looks as if POLLHAL was. You have no objection, I suppose, Mr. BARBER?

Mr. C. BARBER. None at all. He said Quartermaster FRASER.

Q. The Examiner. "FRASER was here with POLLHAL. FRASER was a Quartermaster in the Carabineers." Is that right?

A. Yes.

Q. Then I have got, "MOORE I saw at Croydon since I returned to England."

A. Yes, that is right.

Q. "Since I returned to England I saw a person whom I believed to be the Mr. BURROWS who had to do with my will. I saw him get out of the train at Croydon. I have had no communication whatever with him."

A. Yes, that is right.

Mr. Serjeant BALLANTINE. It is only my intention to cross-examine Mr. GOSFORD. There are some other witnesses who have been summoned here for cross-examination, but I shall not trouble them.

Mr. C. BARBER. You do not intend to cross-examine Lady TICHBORNE?

Mr. Serjeant BALLANTINE. No, not Lady TERESA.

Mr. C. BARBER. Then Sir PYERS MOSTYN need not stay?

Mr. Serjeant BALLANTINE. No; they may all leave, with the exception of Mr. GOSFORD.

Q. You mentioned a gentleman yesterday of the name of CHATILLON; he was your tutor at Paris, was he?

A. Yes.

Q. I forgot whether you told me yesterday up to what time he had charge of you?

A. Principally up to the time that I lived there.

Q. (By the Examiner.) That we have got, I think?

A. Yes; that you have got.

Q. (By Mr. Serjeant BALLANTINE.) You also told us that you went a little trip with him, but you could not remember where you went to?

A. No.
Q. Did you see Monsieur CHATILLON in Paris since your return?
A. Yes, I did.
Q. Was that in the presence of Lady TICHBORNE?
A. Yes; Lady TICHBORNE, my mother.
Q. I cannot ask you what the nature of the conversation was, but, recalling your memory to it, can you tell me where you went to with Monsieur CHATILLON?
A. Yes, I can.
Q. Where?
A. Brittany.
Q. (By the Examiner.) You now recollect that the tour you took with Monsieur CHATILLON was in Brittany?
A. Yes.
Q. (By Mr. Serjeant BALLANTINE.) Do you recollect any accident that occurred to you while you were upon that tour?
A. Yes; I remember that I was climbing some rocks, and I fell down and cut my head.
Q. Where was that?
A. At Ponnic.
Mr. C. BARBER. Will you spell it?
A. I do not know that I can.
Q. (By Mr. Serjeant BALLANTINE.) Something sounding like Ponnic?
A. Yes.
Mr. HAWKINS. Some place the name of which begins with P, is that what you mean?
A. Yes.
Q. (By Mr. Serjeant BALLANTINE.) Sounding like Ponnic?
A. Yes.
Mr. C. BARBER. Will you tell me, Mr. Examiner, how you propose to spell it?
Mr. Serjeant BALLANTINE. P-o-n-i-c.
The Examiner. Two n's would give the accent which he gave to it—Ponnic.
Mr. Serjeant BALLANTINE. Yes.
Q. Is there any mark upon your head, the result of that fall?
A. Yes, there is.
Q. Did you point out that mark to Monsieur CHATILLON at the interval with him to which you have alluded?
A. Well, I pointed out the place to him, but we could not find the mark. It was found by the perfumer the next morning.
Q. You pointed out the place?
A. Yes; I told him the mark was there.
Mr. HAWKINS. We cannot have what you told him.
The Witness. I pointed out the place where the mark would be.
The Examiner. I pointed out to Monsieur CHATILLON where I said the mark was.
Mr. Serjeant BALLANTINE. Where I believe the mark to be—that is strictly evidence, and where he said he felt it.
Mr. C. BARBER. But it could not be found, he said.
Mr. Serjeant BALLANTINE. He did not say that.
Q. As a matter of fact, is that mark present on your head now?
A. It is.
Q. I believe that mark has been seen since by some medical gentleman?
A. It has.
Q. I do not wish to trouble you further on that point. Have you carried back your recollection to the period when you were at college, since you were examined yesterday?
A. Yes.
Q. You have carried back your memory to the days you passed at college?
A. Yes; and I remember some of the clergymen.
Q. Are you able to mention any more names than those you mentioned yesterday?
A. Yes; I think so.
Q. Just mention them, and speak loud enough for us all to hear you?
The Examiner. "I have carried my memory back to that period when I was at college."
Q. You say you remember the names of more fellow collegians, and of more priests than you did yesterday?
A. Yes; of the priests.
Q. (By Mr. Serjeant BALLANTINE.) Just mention them?
A. I remember McCANN.
Q. (By Mr. HAWKINS.) With an *n* or an *m*?
A. Two *n's*, I think; I will not be certain.
Q. (By the Examiner.) Any one else?
A. Yes; there was.
Q. (By Mr. Serjeant BALLANTINE.) Was he a priest?
A. Yes; he was.
Q. Any one else?
A. There was CLOUGH; I think that is the name.
Q. Was he a priest?
A. Yes, he was; I will not be certain of the way you spell it.
Q. How did it sound?
A. *Clo'.*
Q. Any one else?
A. There was two brothers of the name of COOPER.
Q. They were scholars,—pupils?
Mr. HAWKINS. Just ask him what they were, Mr. Serjeant BALLANTINE, and do not put the words into his mouth.
Q. (By Mr. Serjeant BALLANTINE.) Were they scholars?
Mr. HAWKINS. You will please take this, Sir, question and answer.
The Examiner. Do you wish it taken down?
Mr. Serjeant BALLANTINE. I have no objection.
Q. Were they scholars or priests?
Mr. HAWKINS. That was not your question.
Mr. Serjeant BALLANTINE. That does not matter at all; I have a perfect right to amend my question.
The Examiner. If it is required I will ask the short-hand writer to read it, and I will take down the exact words.
Mr. HAWKINS. If you please, Sir.
Mr. Serjeant BALLANTINE. May I ask my friend, Mr. HAWKINS, who he appears for?
Mr. HAWKINS. Some of the defendants.
Mr. Serjeant BALLANTINE. Which? You stated yesterday you did not appear for anybody in TICHBORNE v. TICHBORNE.
Mr. HAWKINS. I did not state that at all.
Mr. Serjeant BALLANTINE. I object to Mr. HAWKINS's interference.
Mr. HAWKINS. I appear for Mr. ARUNDELL.
Mr. Serjeant BALLANTINE. You said yesterday you did not appear for anybody in this suit.
Mr. HAWKINS. Do not say that, because it is not true, and you know it is not true.
Mr. Serjeant BALLANTINE. Now, Sir, I propose to alter my question by saying, Were they scholars or priests?
Mr. HAWKINS. I must ask you to take down the very question as it was put originally, not as it is moulded after the witness has had a suggestion given to him.
(The short-hand writer, at the request of the Examiner, read the question, "They were scholars, pupils?")
Mr. Serjeant BALLANTINE. Then I suppose you will put that that question is objected to?
The Examiner. Yes.
Mr. Serjeant BALLANTINE. Then I amend my question by asking, were they scholars or priests?
Q. (By the Examiner.) Were they scholars or priests?
A. I do not remember, but I think they were priests.
Q. (By Mr. Serjeant BALLANTINE.) Are there any other names that you recollect?
A. Yes; there was a foreigner there of the name of GLENDERELL, or GLUNDERELL, or some such name as that.
Q. A foreigner?
A. Yes.
Q. What name did you say?
A. GLUNDERELL, or some such name.
Q. (By the Examiner.) GLUNDERELL or GLUNDERO?
A. GLUNDERELL; he was an Italian.
Q. (By Mr. Serjeant BALLANTINE.) Have you recalled the names of any of the persons that you knew in Paris?
A. No more than Mr. TALBOT CONSTABLE; did I mention him yesterday?
The Examiner. No; I do not think you mentioned anybody of the name of CONSTABLE.
The Witness. There was a Spanish gentleman there, a very great friend of my father's, but I do not remember his name just now.
Q. In Paris?
A. Yes.
Q. I will say, "There was a Spanish gentleman, who was a friend of my father's, but I forget his name."
A. Yes.
Mr. Serjeant BALLANTINE. That is all I have to ask, Sir.
The Examiner. Does any other defendant, who has joined in this application for leave to cross-examine, wish to cross-examine the plaintiff?
Mr. C. BARBER. No; I think not.
The Examiner. Then it is my duty to read the whole of this over. Witness, Serjeant BALLANTINE having no more questions to ask you, it is my duty to read over to you the evidence you have given; and the object of that is that you should see that it is quite accurate. If you think the words I have taken down do not convey your meaning, you will please to mention it, and I will make such addition as is necessary. Do you understand me?
The Witness. Yes; I understand.
(The Examiner proceeded to read over the deposition to the witness, and on coming to the following words, "From there I went to Santiago, and from thence to Mendoza.")
The Witness said, I beg your pardon, but I wish you to take notice that the counsel said he did not require me to give the names of all the towns I went through, and therefore I omitted Melipilla.
The Examiner. Yes, Mr. BARBER, you did tell him that.
The Witness. Therefore I omitted to mention Melipilla, where I went on my journey to Santiago.
The Examiner. By the consent of both sides I can insert that here.
Mr. C. BARBER. You had better put it in at the end.
Mr. HANNEN. Or in the margin.
Mr. C. BARBER. I do not think that would be regular.
Mr. HANNEN. Yes, I have known it done, and quite recently.
Mr. C. BARBER. Where does Melipilla come?
A. It lies off Casa Blanca.
Q. (By the Examiner.) Where did you go to from Melipilla?
A. I went from Casa Blanca to Santiago, by way of Melipilla; that will denote the two roads, the one a straight road and the other not.
(The Examiner read a further portion of the deposition to the words, "There were in the boat some barrels of biscuits and some water.")
The Witness. I said some bags of biscuits and casks of biscuits; I said some casks and some bags, both.
Q. (By the Examiner.) There were bags and casks?
A. Yes; I think the word I said was barrels, likewise.

The Examiner. I will put that in.

(The Examiner proceeded to read a further portion of the deposition to the words, "I did not see any newspaper while I was at Melbourne.")

The Witness. I mean I had not read any of the papers myself; I might have seen papers in people's hands; so long as it does not misconstrue my meaning.

The Examiner. No; I think it is all right.

(The Examiner read a further portion of the deposition to the words, "I saw him get out of the train at Croydon.")

Mr. Hawkins. I do not know whether you have a note, Sir, of the times of the adjournment, and the time of our meeting again, so as to show the break in the re-examination.

The Examiner. I have put here, "The re-examination was continued to-day."

Mr. Hawkins. I did not know whether you had a note of the different days.

Mr. Serjeant Ballantine. My question would almost show it. I began, "Since yesterday."

(The Examiner read the remainder of the deposition to the witness.)

Mr. C. Barber. I have not observed that you noticed that you adjourned for half an hour each day, one day at one o'clock, and another day at half-past.

Mr. Hawkins. No; if you could turn, Sir, to the period when that was, I should be much obliged if you would notice it.

Mr. Serjeant Ballantine. If that is customary, of course, I cannot have any objection; but if it is not, it is rather accusing us of tampering with the witness.

The Examiner. I have never been asked to do such a thing before.

Mr. Serjeant Ballantine. You might just as well put down what we had for lunch.

The Examiner. I would rather not notice it.

Mr. C. Barber. Very well, Sir.

The Examiner. There was a solemn protest of yours, Mr. Serjeant Ballantine, which you desired me to notice; what shall I say about that?

Mr. Serjeant Ballantine. There has been no renewal of it, and I do not know that I care about your noticing it.

(The Witness then signed the deposition.)

Mr. Serjeant Ballantine. There was one question which I forgot to put. I will tender the question for you to put, Sir; it is whether, during the last two or three years, he has changed very much in size?

Mr. C. Barber. I have no objection to that.

Q. (By the Examiner.) Have you increased very much in bulk during the last two or three years?

A. Yes; very much.

Mr. Serjeant Ballantine. From what time?

A. From the year 1865.

Mr. Hawkins. That does not arise out of the cross-examination.

The Examiner. No; it is put through me, as it were.

Mr. C. Barber. We have no objection.

Mr. Hawkins. No; it is immaterial.

Mr. Barber. Do you object, Mr. Serjeant Ballantine, to this evidence being read in Tichborne v. Mostyn, as if it had been taken in that cause?

Mr. Serjeant Ballantine. No, I do not think I ought to object to that.

(Adjourned at ten minutes past one o'clock for half an hour.)

Mr. VINCENT GOSFORD, Sworn.

Cross-examined by Mr. Serjeant Ballantine on behalf of the Plaintiff.

Q. What are your names?

A. I have only one Christian name, Vincent.

Q. What are your names?

A. Vincent Gosford is the name I go by. I believe I have another name, but I do not feel conscious of it, and I have never used it in my life.

Q. I shall trouble you with very few questions. When Mr. Roger Tichborne left England did he leave a written paper sealed up in your possession?

A. Before I reply to that question I should like to ask my counsel, and if he says I am to answer it, I will.

The Examiner. I will take this question and answer.

Mr. Hawkins. You may answer the question.

The Witness. Do you wish me to answer now?

Q. (By Mr. Serjeant Ballantine.) I ask you, Sir.

A. He left a paper in my hands when he left England, but it had been deposited with me some time before.

Q. He left a paper in your hands when he left England, but it had been deposited with you some time before?

A. Yes.

Q. Was it written in your presence?

A. It was.

Q. When deposited with you was it sealed up?

A. It was.

Q. Have you since opened it?

A. I have.

Q. That, I presume, was after news came of the foundering of the "Bella"?

A. Yes: probably a year and a half after.

Q. That is your answer, is it.

A. Yes. I had no curiosity about it, inasmuch as I saw it written.

Q. Have you got it in your possession now?

A. (Addressing Mr. Hawkins.) Am I to answer that?

Mr. Hawkins. Say yes or no.

The Witness. No.

Q. (By Mr. Serjeant Ballantine.) Where is it?

A. (No answer.)

Q. Where is it?

A. I destroyed it.

Q. When?

A. Some year and a half; about the time it was decided that Mr. Roger Tichborne was lost.

Q. (By the Examiner.) About a year and a half after the wreck of the "Bella"?

A. About the time when it was finally decided that the vessel was lost.

Q. (By Mr. Serjeant Ballantine.) You had an interview with the Plaintiff at Gravesend, had you not?

A. I had.

Q. And also at the Grosvenor Hotel?

A. I had.

Q. Was Mr. Bulpett present at the interview?

A. He was.

The Examiner. At both those interviews?

Mr. Serjeant Ballantine. No; at the Grosvenor Hotel.

Q. Mr Bulpett is a banker, is he not, at Winchester?

A. Yes, at Winchester.

Q. And had known Mr. Tichborne before he left England?

A. As to knowing him, I doubt it very much; for, I should think, he never spoke to him in his life.

Q. Did you at that interview say that you had got this document in your desk at home?

A. I did not.

Q. Or words to that effect?

A. No, not to that effect.

Q. Did you convey the idea that the document was in existence?

A. I did not, further than by the remark I made.

Q. What was that?

A. If you wait a moment I will repeat the whole conversation; that was in reply to a question. If I repeat my answer, I must repeat the question.

Q. There were other persons present, were there not: Mr. Hingston and Mr. White?

A. Yes, those were the names of the gentlemen present.

Q. The Examiner. "At that interview, besides Mr. Bulpett, there were two other persons present who gave their names—Hingston and White?"

Mr. Hawkins. Whose names were given as Hingston and White?"

The Witness. Yes, Hingston and White.

Q. (By Mr. Serjeant Ballantine.) Give us your own version of what took place in relation to that document.

A. When I had mentioned the document privately to the Claimant, we returned to the table. I had had a private conversation with him. Am I to give it in my own words, or merely the effect, or how much of it?

Q. You have sworn to tell the whole truth, and I suppose you will tell the whole truth?

A. Certainly I will. I had had a private conversation with the Claimant about this document. I had asked him if he remembered leaving it with me, and what were the contents? He could give me no intelligence whatever as to its contents. I led up to the circumstance to which it referred without naming the person, and he then could give me no answer.

Q. What did you say about the document?

Mr. Hawkins. Do not interrupt him in the middle of what he is telling you.

The Examiner. I thought he had come to a finish.

Mr. Serjeant Ballantine. And I.

The Witness. I shall be very happy to answer either gentleman.

Mr. Hawkins. State exactly what took place.

The Witness. We were then rejoined by the other gentlemen, Mr. Bulpett and the two others. At the moment they joined us we were discussing irrelevant topics, and Mr. Bulpett said, "I do not want you to talk about this: I want you to talk about things that you remember." Is this to be written down?

The Examiner. The shorthand writer is taking it all down, and will read it to me presently.

The Witness. I then said: "I have just asked him a question. I have asked him the nature of a document which he left in my hands when he went abroad," and Mr. Bulpett turned to him, and said, "That is a straightforward question; what is your answer?" and he could not reply a word.

Q. (By Mr. Serjeant Ballantine.) You have told us a long story, which I expected you would. I ask you, upon your solemn oath, whether you did not say that that document was in existence and in your possession?

A. I will swear, on my positive oath and existence, that I did not say so. I have not told you what I did say.

Q. Then do tell us.

A. Mr. Bulpett said, "Where is it?" I said, "No matter where it is."

Q. Mr. Bulpett said, "Where is it?" and you said, "No matter where it is."

A. Yes.

Q. Now, I ask you whether, in the presence of the whole of

those four persons, you did not state that that document was in existence and in your possession?

A. I state most positively that I did not: but in the presence of all those four gentlemen I stated that I had a large number of his letters in my possession.

Q. I do not want anything about other letters.

A. You shall have the whole of it.

Q. But I mean to have a distinct reply to that question.

A. You have had it.

Q. I understand you to swear that you did not say that that document was then in existence and in your possession?

A. Most positively not.

Q. You had some letters of Mr. ROGER TICHBORNE in your possession?

A. I had.

Q. Letters directed to his mother?

A. Not one.

Mr. HAWKINS. To whom they are addressed will appear by the letters themselves.

Q. (By Mr. Serjeant BALLANTINE.) Did you get possession of any papers from a box at Winchester?

A. I never was aware that a box belonging to Lady TICHBORNE was deposited at Winchester, and I never had any letters or contents from it whatever.

Q. Have you obtained possession of any letters since the Claimant's return to England?

A. Have I retained, or obtained, do you say?

Q. Obtained.

A. Have I obtained any letters?

Q. Have you obtained possession of any papers connected with the Claimant since his return?

A. Not a scrap of any description.

Q. Have you obtained possession of any papers relating to Mr. TICHBORNE?

JAMES FRANCIS DOUGHTY TICHBORNE, SECOND SON OF SIR R. C. D. TICHBORNE, BART.

A. Have I obtained?

Q. Yes.

A. Since the Claimant's return?

Q. Yes.

A. Not a paper of any kind whatever.

The Examiner. "Connected with the Claimant, Mr. ROGER TICHBORNE."

Mr. HAWKINS. No, not the Claimant, Mr. ROGER TICHBORNE. Mr. GOSFORD does not admit that he has anything relating to the Plaintiff at all.

Mr. Serjeant BALLANTINE. The answer was, Nothing relating to Mr. TICHBORNE.

Q. Have you heard of any papers having been taken from any box at Winchester belonging to the Dowager Lady TICHBORNE?

A. Yes; I have heard the statement made, certainly.

Q. Am I to understand that you know nothing, in all its terms, about such a transaction?

A. As far as I am personally concerned, nothing.

Q. I ask you whether you know nothing of such a transaction?

A. I know nothing except what I have heard stated, which I shall be happy to tell you.

Q. Have you seen any papers?

A. Not one.

Q. Did you authorise anyone to search any boxes?

A. Yes, I authorised a person to search boxes at Winchester, certainly. I should like to correct that; you may put it down, but I should like to correct it afterwards.

The Examiner. You will have plenty of opportunity.

Q. (By Mr. Serjeant BALLANTINE.) Who was that person?

A. I gave, or rather I signed, an authority—

Mr. HAWKINS. That is, in writing.

Q. (By Mr. Serjeant BALLANTINE.) Who was the person?

A. I signed an authority which was sent to me, as executor of Sir JAMES TICHBORNE, by the solicitor of the executors, Mr. CULLINGTON.

Q. Who was it you authorised to search that box?

A. I shall arrive at the answer in time.

Q. You will arrive at it at once by telling me the name.
A. I authorised no one verbally.
Q. Whom did you authorise?
Mr. HAWKINS. I object to that question; he says he authorised no one verbally; therefore the writing will speak for itself.
Mr. Serjeant BALLANTINE. I have a perfect right to ask one of the parties to the suit what he wrote.
The Witness. Let me answer the question; I am quite ready to do so; there is no mystery about it.
Q. (By the Examiner.) Who was it you authorised to search the boxes?
A. I authorised no one further than by returning that authority to Mr. CULLINGTON, who sent it, so far as I know, to the person with whom the boxes were deposited, an upholsterer at Winchester, of the name of MORRIS.
Q. (By Mr. Serjeant BALLANTINE.) Was that document an authority to search the box?
A. So far as I remember its contents, it was an authority to open certain boxes which had been deposited with him by the executors.
Q. Whose boxes?
A. They contained—
Q. Whose boxes?
A. Boxes deposited by the executors.
Q. Whose boxes?
A. I have no idea whose boxes they were, except—
Mr. Serjeant BALLANTINE. Wait a moment, we will have that—
The Witness. Allow me to finish.
The Examiner. Yes, you shall.
Q. You have no idea whose boxes they were?
A. Except so far as they contained the property of Sir JAMES TICHBORNE, and, therefore belonged to the executors; I have not quite done with my answer.
Q. No, I am only taking it down.
A. I had no knowledge whatever that any boxes of Lady TICHBORNE, or of any other person, were in his possession.
Q. "Or of any other person"?
A. Yes.
Q. (By Mr. Serjeant BALLANTINE). Did you learn afterwards that there were boxes belonging to Lady TICHBORNE that had been searched?
A. Not very—
Q. Never mind that, answer the question.
A. But it is important.
Q. You may add it, then. Did you afterwards learn that boxes belonging to Lady TICHBORNE had been searched?
A. I did.
Q. Did you also learn that papers had been extracted from them?
A. I learnt that a statement was made to that effect.
Q. Did you learn from the persons whom you employed that the papers had been taken from them?
A. Certainly not from the persons that I employed.
Q. Did you learn from Mr. CULLINGTON that the papers had been taken from them?
A. I did; he informed me that a solicitor (Mr. NORRIS) had received her Ladyship's instructions to proceed against me for having searched her boxes, and for having abstracted—or authorised some one to abstract—her letters and certain watches. He also asked me if I had been written to by Mr. NORRIS on the subject, and, being in town, I threatened at once to go and see Mr. NORRIS, and inquire what it meant?
Q. (By the Examiner.) And learn what it meant?
A. And learn what it meant.
Q. (By Mr. Serjeant BALLANTINE.) Is that all?
A. He rather dissuaded me, and said it was not worth while, and I did not call on Mr. NORRIS; he rather dissuaded me. I could have gone if I liked, but I looked upon it as so ridiculous a thing that I did not think it worth while to contradict it.
Q. Were there two watches?
A. I have not the slightest idea or knowledge whether there were or not; I heard it then stated that her Ladyship had said so.
Q. Is that all you know about the watches?
A. Everything about it, except that I heard this rumour.
Q. Did not Mr. CULLINGTON tell you there were two watches?
A. No further than, I think, but I will not be positive, he may have said that that was what her Ladyship accused me of. I think it was only one watch—Sir JAMES's gold watch, if I remember right.
Q. Did he tell you he had taken one watch?
A. That who had?
Q. Did he tell you that there was one watch?
A. He told me of this statement made with regard to me.
Q. Did you ask him whether it was a watch or not?
A. Certainly not.
Q. You made no inquiry?
A. Certainly not of him.
Q. He was the person to whom the authority was given?
A. I beg your pardon; you are referring to a totally different thing.
Q. Then who was the person to whom the authority was given?
A. I returned it to Mr. CULLINGTON.
Q. Then Mr. CULLINGTON was the person to whom the authority was given?
A. Unquestionably, so far as it was returned to him by me with my signature.
Q. Have you seen those papers that were taken out of that box?
A. I am not aware that any papers were taken out, and I have not seen any papers that were taken out.

Q. I suppose you had some motive in having the boxes searched. Had you any motive in having the boxes searched?
A. Yes; clearly.
Q. Then, have you not asked CULLINGTON the result?
A. No; because I do not believe he ever saw the contents of the boxes.
Q. Have you asked anybody who did?
A. No; I have not troubled about it. I think we are alluding to different boxes altogether. That is my opinion.
Q. Just endeavour to answer me this question. Who, to the best of your belief, was the person who searched Lady TICHBORNE's box?
A. I have no belief or knowledge on the subject, further than when this question arose some month or two ago—I do not think longer—then I made further inquiry as to whether the boxes of her Ladyship had been opened or not. I wish further to explain the circumstance by stating that this authority that I sent must have been some years ago.
Q. (By the Examiner.) That it must have been some years ago when you signed the authority?
A. Yes. As for my motive of doing it, it was for the purpose of returning back to Tichborne House certain articles which had been removed about the time that Sir ALFRED left, and which, as I understood, were claimed by the present tenant of the house as being part of his inventory, and therefore that he had a right to have them.
Q. And as contained in the inventory?
A. Yes. I do not know how much of it. Certain articles that he claimed.
Q. To which he claimed to be entitled?
A. Yes; as forming part of the fixtures of the house. I never knew when I signed the authority that Lady TICHBORNE had anything whatever in the hands of the upholsterer.
Q. (By Mr. Serjeant BALLANTINE.) Who did search the box?
A. I do not know, of my own knowledge.
Q. Whom do you believe searched the box?
A. I do not know, of my own knowledge.
Q. Whom do you believe searched the box?
A. I believe they were searched; the word "search" should not have been used; it should have been "opened."
Q. Well, "opened" and "looked into it," if you like.
A. Certainly, and things taken out.
Q. Who did it?
A. As far as I know—and I have been to inquire since this question arose, within the last month or two—I have inquired of one person, and think his statement was that he and Mr. MORRIS, the upholsterer, opened these boxes; but what they removed or took out I know nothing of.
Q. Who is he?
A. A person of the name of BURDTS.
Q. Who, in company with the upholsterer, searched the boxes?
A. "Opened" the boxes. I should use the word "opened."
Q. I suppose "opening" and looking into a box would be searching?
A. Well, perhaps it would.
Q. Who is BURDTS?
A. He was formerly resident at Tichborne, as agent to Sir JAMES; afterwards as agent and secretary to Sir ALFRED—general manager.
Q. Where does he live now?
A. In London. I do not remember his address at this moment; it can easily be obtained; at least, he did when I made this inquiry, a month or two ago.
Q. Did you make the inquiry of him?
A. Yes; I sent to him specially.
Q. Then you knew where he lived?
A. Yes; exactly.
Q. Where?
A. Over the water, by Camden Town.
Q. What do you mean—"Over the water by Camden Town"?
A. Camberwell, I mean: he lives down the Kennington direction.
Q. You know where you sent for him, I suppose?
A. I knew, because I had his written address. He had lived up to that time at Chelsea, and he had recently moved somewhere to Camberwell. I shall be most happy to furnish you with the address to-morrow. The last time I saw him was in Mr. BULPETT's presence.
Q. He is none the worse for that.
A. No; Mr. BULPETT might refer to the time; I have not quite done with that subject, if you are not tired with it.
Q. Oh, no; I am not tired.
A. I was going to add, that I believe that at that very time I complained of this topic to Mr. BULPETT, or, rather, discussed it over with him.
Q. When was the search?
A. I have not any idea: I should fancy that the opening, or search, must have taken place several years ago; more than a year ago, at all events, I should imagine.
Q. More than a year ago, and several years ago, are two very different things.
A. I have some idea when I signed the authority; but when they made use of it, I do not know.
Q. Have you never heard when they made use of it?
A. As far as regards the exact time, I have not.
Q. Within six months, then?
A. If you ask me within six months, I should say it was made use of at the time it was signed, or soon after.

Q. When was that?

A. I cannot positively tell you, but certainly not within the last twelve months. I should think eighteen months or two years ago, or possibly longer than that.

Q. You swear positively that it was not within the last twelve months?

A. Certainly not, so far as I know.

Q. But I want to have a positive answer. Will you swear it was not within the last twelve months?

A. I will swear I do not know it was within the last twelve months.

Q. Will you swear that you do not know that the search was made after the Claimant came to England?

A. Oh, most positively.

Q. You swear that positively?

A. Most positively—without the slightest hesitation.

Q. (By Mr. HAWKINS.) "But I do not know it"?

A. But I do not know it.

Q. (By Mr. Serjeant BALLANTINE.) "I most positively swear that I do not know the search was made since the Claimant came to England."

A. Yes.

Q. Or since he was heard of?

A. Or since he was heard of? I cannot connect his name with the boxes or the search in any way.

Q. Since he was heard of by you?

A. Certainly.

Q. You say that positively?

A. Yes; that I do not know that any search whatever has been made since he was heard of by me.

Q. That is your answer?

A. That is my answer—I have nothing to add to it.

Q. You heard that there was a gold watch, which I presume, if it was Sir JAMES's, would belong to Lady TICHBORNE?

A. The gold watch that I heard of was Sir JAMES's watch—I inquired what had become of it, and I understood it had been retained by her Ladyship, which I believe is the case.

Q. That it was not in the box?

A. I have no idea.

Q. If you mean that it was retained by her Ladyship in the sense that it was in the box before it was opened, I agree with you. Do you mean to represent it was not in the box?

A. I mean to state that at Sir JAMES's death her Ladyship retained it.

Q. Do you mean to represent that when this box was broken open by your agent——?

Mr. HAWKINS. He has never said yet that this box was broken open by his agent.

Q. (Mr. Serjeant BALLANTINE.) Do you mean to represent that you do not believe there was a watch in that box?

A. I do not believe or disbelieve it further that this, that it was stated to me that her Ladyship accused me of opening the box and retaining the watch.

Q. I am to take that as your answer, am I?

A. If her Ladyship says she had a watch in the box, I would believe her.

Q. What do you believe?

A. I believe neither the one way nor the other. If her Ladyship states that she deposited the watch in the box, I believe her, but I have no knowledge.

Q. Your mind is in a state of doubt?

A. Not at all. I am only stating that I have no personal knowledge whether there was a watch in the box or not.

Q. Your mind is in doubt on the subject?

A. Just this way, that if her Ladyship said she had deposited the watch in the box, I would believe her.

Q. You know she has said so?

A. No, I only know this rumour.

Q. You know the person who opened the box, to use the mildest term?

A. You are confusing the boxes: excuse me.

Q. Have you not inquired of BURDUS whether there was a watch?

A. Yes; I asked BURDUS what had become of Sir JAMES's gold watch.

Q. Well, what did he say?

A. He said her Ladyship had got it.

Q. Did you not hear that there were some letters from TICHBORNE to his mother?

A. I heard that stated just as I have told you before.

Q. Did you not hear from this gentleman, Mr. BURDUS?

A. Certainly not.

Q. Did you hear there were any letters?

A. I think he made a statement that there were boxes of letters left by Sir JAMES.

Q. What has become of those letters?

A. I have not an idea. They went into Sir ALFRED's possession.

Q. Did he not tell you that there were letters from TICHBORNE to his mother?

A. Who, BURDUS?

Q. Yes.

A. No, I am quite sure he never told me, or that he could have known what the letters were, further than that they were boxes of letters.

Q. Am I to understand that he never told you that there were letters from TICHBORNE to his mother?

A. I will not be positive whether we mentioned the name of Mr. ROGER TICHBORNE at the time or not. I know the conversation that passed as to these letters was, that there were boxes containing letters when Sir JAMES died.

Q. Really there can be no doubt about my question. Will you pledge your oath that he did not tell you that there were letters from TICHBORNE to his mother in some of those boxes?

A. I will certainly swear that I have not the least recollection of his telling me that.

Q. Will you swear he did not?

A. I will swear I do not remember it.

Q. You will not swear positively that he did not?

A. No; I will not swear positively that he did not, because I have no recollection on the subject.

Q. Do you know Mr. BOWKER?

A. Which? I know two.

Q. The solicitor?

A. They are both solicitors.

Q. He is a solicitor at Winchester.

A. Yes, I know him.

Q. Do you know whether he has got any of these letters?

A. I do not know anything on the subject.

Q. (By the Examiner.) You do not know whether he has got any of these letters?

A. No, I do not.

Q. (By Mr. Serjeant BALLANTINE.) Do I understand you to say that when you saw this Mr. BURDUS about a month ago, you do not remember whether ROGER TICHBORNE's name was mentioned or not?

A. Oh dear, no! I said nothing of the kind, for his name was mentioned in our conversation very frequently.

Q. Was anything said about these letters?

A. I do not remember whether we mentioned his letters or not. It was the general letters of her Ladyship that we talked about, and that would naturally include some of his; but I have no distinct recollection of his letters being spoken of in particular.

Mr. Serjeant BALLANTINE. That is all I ask, Sir.

Mr. HAWKINS. I have a few questions to ask.

The Examiner. For whom do you appear, Mr. HAWKINS?

Mr. HAWKINS. I am going to re-examine for Mr. GOSFORD, who is a Defendant himself.

Mr. L. WEBB. He is not a Defendant to the TICHBORNE suit.

Mr. C. BARBER. We are now on TICHBORNE v. MOSTYN.

Mr. L. WEBB. I beg your pardon.

Mr. C. BARBER. Mr. HAWKINS appears for Sir PYERS MOSTYN, WILLIAM MOSTYN, and VINCENT GOSFORD.

Re-examined by Mr. HAWKINS on behalf of Sir PYERS MOSTYN, WILLIAM MOSTYN, and VINCENT GOSFORD.

Q. Was Mr. CULLINGTON the successor to Mr. SLAUGHTER?

A. He was the partner and successor.

Q. Was Mr. SLAUGHTER the TICHBORNE family solicitor?

A. Yes, he was for many years.

Q. Was the authority which you have mentioned for the opening of this box a written authority, which Mr. CULLINGTON sent to you?

A. It was entirely; it was only a sheet of paper, and I have not the least recollection what was upon it. I understood there was an authority to MORRIS to open the box, and to return the contents to Tichborne; it had no reference to anything belonging to Lady TICHBORNE; that was the last thing I should have thought of touching.

Q. That was the only authority you gave?

A. Yes; it must have been about the time when Tichborne House was being refitted ready for further occupation. I cannot recollect the date; if you ask me to-morrow I have no doubt I can ascertain it; the paper was sent to me to sign as executor to Sir JAMES.

Q. And in your character as executor you signed it?

A. Yes.

Q. (By the Examiner.) You signed it in that capacity?

A. Yes, as executor.

Q. (By Mr. HAWKINS.) Solely for the purpose you have mentioned?

A. Yes.

Q. You have spoken of a conversation that you had with the present Plaintiff?

A. Yes.

Q. Was there other conversation which took place at that time which has not been made the subject of inquiry to-day?

A. Yes.

Q. (By Mr. Serjeant BALLANTINE.) That was at the Grosvenor Hotel?

A. I do not know whether Mr. HAWKINS was speaking of the Grosvenor Hotel or at Gravesend.

Mr. HAWKINS. The Grosvenor Hotel.

Q. During the interview which you have spoken to at the Grosvenor Hotel, was there other conversation that has not been referred to to-day?

A. Yes, very much.

Q. So that, on your cross-examination, in the answers to the questions put to you, you have not professed to give the whole of what took place?

A. Oh no, not nearly.

Q. I am not aware that it has any bearing on the present case;

but, with reference to the document which you say you destroyed, when it was finally determined that the "Bella" was lost, are you prepared, whenever any question arises on it, to explain thoroughly the nature of that document, and your reasons for destroying it?

A. Perfectly.

Q. I do not want to go into it, for I do not understand that it has any bearing on this case; but are you ready to give all your reasons?

A. Perfectly.

Q. You have nothing to conceal in the matter?

A. Nothing whatever.

Q. Tell me, was the document that was destroyed a paper which you had any reason at all to believe could be of any possible use afterwards?

A. After the loss of the "Bella"?

Q. Yes.

A. Certainly not.

Q. It was a paper which from that time was considered utterly useless?

A. Yes, and there were other circumstances which rendered it useless.

Q. But nothing connected with this suit?

A. No; not in any shape or way. I made use of the document for the purpose of satisfying myself whether the Claimant could give any answer or not.

Q. You are alluding to the conversation which took place at the Grosvenor?

A. Yes.

Q. I am speaking of the time when you destroyed it.

A. Yes.

Q. At that time was the document, as far as you knew, perfectly useless?

A. Perfectly. My reason for destroying it was simply because I destroyed it in common with a vast number of other private papers of Mr. ROGER TICHBORNE; private and confidential papers which I did not think it was proper should fall into other hands, or under other eyes.

Q. You were about removing into Wales at that time?

A. I forget, almost; what time was the "Bella" lost? In 1854, was it not? No; I did not move into Wales till after then. I beg your pardon. Do you mean when I destroyed the papers?

Q. Yes.

A. Oh, yes. I have said so before.

Mr. HAWKINS. That is all I have to ask.

Mr. C. BARBER. I do not put any questions to him.

(The Examiner proceeded to read the deposition to the witness to the words "the 'Bella' was lost.")

The Witness. I should correct that statement. I think it would be near the time when I went into Wales.

Q. (By the Examiner.) The words I have are, "about the time when it was decided the 'Bella' was lost."

A. It was some time after, because it was when I was packing up my things to take into Wales.

Mr. HAWKINS. I think the expression was, "I destroyed it when it was finally decided the 'Bella' was lost"?

The Witness. Yes.

The Examiner. I will read over the rest, and then you can add anything you like at the end.

(The Examiner read over the rest of the depositions to the witness.)

The Witness. One small circumstance has just occurred to me, which I think I ought to name. I think, in all probability, the authority to search the boxes was also signed by my co-executor, Mr. WILLIAM MOSTYN. I had no knowledge of it, but it would naturally be signed by both executors, and therefore I think, in all probability, it was signed by him as well as me. That can be ascertained in a moment.

The Examiner. I do not think it is very important.

The Witness. I think it is important for this reason: that it would show it could not have been an authority having any reference to Lady TICHBORNE's property.

Mr. HAWKINS. You have stated that positively yourself. It may be desirable, Sir, that you should have this for this reason, that in case the authority is produced, and purports to be signed by the two, it will show it was a suggestion of Mr. GOSFORD'S.

The Witness. I think it is very probable it was signed by Mr. MOSTYN. I think it would naturally have been signed by both.

The Examiner. The suggestion is, Serjeant BALLANTINE, that I should add, "in all probability the authority to search the boxes was signed by the other executor."

Mr. Serjeant BALLANTINE. That is only guessing. There will be no contradiction if it turns out that it was signed by the other. He does not say that he was the only person who signed it.

The Examiner. Yes; I feel disinclined to put it in.

Mr. HAWKINS. I do not care about it.

The Examiner. Now, as to rectifying that matter which you mentioned just now. I have—"It was after the news had arrived, probably a year and a half." You say that is not the fact.

The Witness. No; I only say that I recollect perfectly well having made the statement previously. I destroyed it when I went down into Wales, or when I was packing up my papers to go into Wales, and I destroyed this with a lot of other papers of Mr. TICHBORNE'S; I mean that it is a document which has been destroyed years ago, having no reference to this suit.

The Examiner. Cannot you fix the time when you were packing up?

A. No, I really cannot; because it would be very likely during six months I was packing and preparing. I do not think it is of any consequence.

(The Witness signed the depositions.)

The Examiner. You have undertaken to produce that address to-morrow morning. Perhaps you will send it to your solicitors.

Mr. Serjeant BALLANTINE. Yes, and we will get it from them.

The Witness. If there is a London Directory in the room I could tell you in a minute.

Mr. Serjeant BALLANTINE. If you will be good enough to furnish it to your solicitors, that will be the best way.

The Witness. Yes, I have no hesitation whatever in furnishing it.

Mr. Serjeant BALLANTINE. I treat it as if you had already given me the address. Are we to treat this, Mr. BARBER, as being an examination in the other suit?

Mr. C. BARBER. No, I think not.

Mr. Serjeant BALLANTINE. Why not?

Mr. C. BARBER. There is no affidavit of Mr. GOSFORD in the other suit.

Mr. Serjeant BALLANTINE. Oh, no; I beg your pardon.

During the whole of this examination, Lady TICHBORNE sat by the side of the Claimant; and often threw her arms around him in open Court, and kissed him: manifesting in every possible way, the most devoted love that can be imagined, of a Mother towards her long-lost Son. She fastened her eyes upon him, as if she could never behold him enough. In the presence of her brothers, the SEYMOURS, and many other members of the family, she over and over again testified in the most devoted, moving, and solemn manner, that he was her son—her dearly-loved and first-born son; the wild Prodigal who had returned to home—and to hostile relatives and friends. She begged to be cross-examined; but her prayer was refused. They dared not leave on record the further testimony which she could present: the testimony of as true and noble a lady as ever lived.

Our readers may have noticed in page 64, the remarkable questions put by Mr. Serjeant BALLANTINE to GOSFORD: What are your *names*? &c. There was only one man living to whom GOSFORD ever mentioned that he had two Christian names, and that man was ROGER TICHBORNE. Nobody else ever knew it: GOSFORD appears to have forgotten it. The Claimant informed his Counsel of those initials: and GOSFORD half, if not wholly, admits that it was correct. This singular little fact *alone* ought to have shown that the Claimant was ROGER. Its very triviality was enough to prove the fact. But Fate seems to have been against him in all things. His enemies were wilfully blind, or intentionally obstinate, against even the most positive proof that he could offer.

The examination in Chancery having closed, the next move which the Defendants made was for a Commission to the Antipodes, to find out who the Claimant was. They procured an order for the examination of witnesses in South America, and in Australia; calculating probably on the chapter of accidents turning something up that would impede the Claimant in his efforts for justice. This we know happened in the sudden death of Lady TICHBORNE, the Claimant's mother: thus depriving the unhappy gentleman of the very right arm of his claim. In January, 1868, they caused to be inserted the following advertisement in all the London papers. It is beyond dispute that the Claimant had no hand in this publication:—

"BELLA.—Any of the crew saved from the ship Bella, lost off Rio in 1854, are requested to communicate with Mr. POLLAKY, Private Inquiry Office, 13, Paddington-green, W."

It affords matter for curious speculation whether, if any of the crew had turned up, Mr. POLLAKY would have sent them to the Claimant, or his advisers. One or two persons pretending to be survivors of the wreck did come; but they were detected by the Claimant, and very summarily dismissed. We often wonder whence they came?

The death of Lady TICHBORNE, which occurred in March, 1868, realised many of the hopes and expectations of the Family. HIGGINS, of the *Pall Mall Gazette*, and half a dozen other equally bribable prints, published a garbled account of the funeral; which called forth from the *Southampton Times* of March 28th, the following statement:—

THE TICHBORNE SUCCESSION.

The *Pall Mall Gazette* of the 20th inst. published an account of the funeral of the Dowager Lady TICHBORNE, which took place on the previous day, as recorded in our last, and gave the following version of what occurred on that occasion:—As soon as the service for the dead had been performed, and a short sermon preached, the bearers raised the coffin, and proceeded to carry it to the parish church, distant about a quarter of a mile, and Lord ARUNDEL and Mr. SEYMOUR assumed their position as chief mourners, from which, however, they were summarily extruded by the Australian Claimant, a large and corpulent man, supported by a Jamaica negro named BOGLE, whose jet black head and face, and snow-white goatee, imparted to his interference a startling character. Lord ARUNDEL and Mr. SEYMOUR instantly gave way, and withdrew from the procession, as did all the other relatives and connections of the family, and walked on to Tichborne Church, where, through the courtesy of the rector, the Rev. Mr. HUBBARD, they were provided with seats, from whence they could witness the conclusion of the ceremony secure from molestation.

The following letters, referring to the preceding statement, from Mr. HOLMES, the Solicitor to the Claimant, appeared in Monday's *Times*:—

"To THE EDITOR OF THE 'TIMES.'

"SIR,—I beg to enclose copy of a letter I have this morning addressed to the Editor of the *Pall Mall Gazette* in reference to the article in his paper of yesterday, which you have copied into yours of to-day. I trust to your sense of justice for its insertion.

"Instead of Mr. ALFRED SEYMOUR and the other opponents of my client rushing into print for an obvious purpose, it would be much more satisfactory if they would join in consenting at once to try whether a British jury will believe them or the 85 disinterested witnesses who have voluntarily sworn that my client is the eldest son of the late Sir JAMES TICHBORNE and the recently deceased lady, Dame HENRIETTE FELICITE, his wife.

"I am, Sir, your obedient servant, JOHN HOLMES,
"Solicitor for Sir R. C. D. TICHBORNE, Bart.

"25, Poultry: March 21."

"THE TICHBORNE SUCCESSION.

"TO THE EDITOR OF THE 'PALL MALL GAZETTE.'

"25, Poultry, London, E.C: March 21.

"SIR,—The article under this head in your paper of yesterday contains an untrue account of proceedings at the funeral of the late Dowager Lady TICHBORNE, and is so worded as to prejudice the case of my client. I will, therefore, thank you to give this letter a place in your columns.

"The late Dowager Lady TICHBORNE not only acknowledged, but evinced up to the last moment of her life the utmost maternal affection for, her son, Sir ROGER CHARLES DOUGHTY TICHBORNE. Only a few minutes previously to her death she wrote a letter exhibiting the greatest anxiety for his welfare. None of her relations except her son gave any orders respecting the inquest or her funeral, and the preparations entirely devolved upon him.

"Through the kindness of Colonel LUSHINGTON, who occupies Tichborne House, Sir ROGER TICHBORNE and his numerous friends were received as guests at the family mansion, from whence they proceeded to the chapel, where Sir ROGER TICHBORNE took, without any opposition, the seat assigned for the chief mourner, and next him was his cousin, the Count LOUSADA. After the service was over, Lord ARUNDEL and Mr. ALFRED SEYMOUR left their seats and placed themselves next to the Abbé VASSEUR, the deceased lady's confessor, but before the body; the priests, however, explained that they were in the wrong place, and they stood aside. Sir ROGER TICHBORNE walked immediately behind the body, followed by his cousin and friends, but when they came by Lord ARUNDEL and Mr. SEYMOUR in the chapel those two gentlemen endeavoured to displace him, but did not succeed. Mr. SEYMOUR's party then left the chapel, and did not join in the funeral procession, but made a detour through the park to the parish church. There they occupied a pew in the same way as the crowd of other persons did. Poor ANDREW BOGLE, the faithful and much-respected black servant of the late Sir EDWARD DOUGHTY, was not near Sir ROGER when Lord ARUNDEL and Mr. SEYMOUR made their unsuccessful endeavour to displace him.

"A concourse of nearly 500 persons witnessed the funeral, many of whom saw Sir ROGER TICHBORNE for the first time since his return to England, and openly expressed their recognition of and sympathy for him.

"The important question of identity could be speedily settled and the public mind set at rest, if my client's opponents would accept the challenge he made through his counsel, the present Lord Justice SELWYN, last November, and which he instructs me publicly to repeat, that he is ready to concur in waiving all technical legal objections and go at once before a jury of his countrymen, for the purpose of fairly trying the matter out.

"I am, your obedient servant,
"JOHN HOLMES,
"Solicitor for Sir R. C. D. TICHBORNE, Bart."

The *Pall Mall Gazette* comments as follows upon this communication:—"We received on Saturday last, too late for publication, a letter from Mr. HOLMES, Solicitor to the Claimant of the TICHBORNE title and estates, denying the accuracy of the report published on Friday last in our columns, of the proceedings at the funeral of the late Lady TICHBORNE. This letter, published in to-day's *Times*, professes to be merely a correction of our report, but is unquestionably calculated to produce the very effect on the case of the infant baronet which Mr. HOLMES says our remarks were calculated to produce on the case of the Australian Claimant. The points upon which Mr. HOLMES calls in question the accuracy of our reporter are as to the extrusion of Lord ARUNDEL of Wardour and Mr. ALFRED SEYMOUR from the position they had assumed in the procession as chief mourners; as to the wish of the TICHBORNE family to have conducted the funeral themselves; and as to the Claimant having been supported on the occasion by a Jamaica negro named ANDREW BOGLE. On turning to the three local papers that have described the transaction, we find that they entirely corroborate our reporter's account of it. The *Southampton Times* says that:—

"'Messrs. GUDGEON, of Winchester, the undertakers engaged on behalf of the family, had hung the chapel at Tichborne with the customary black, which, however, was entirely covered by other draperies brought from London by Messrs. GAUSTIN, the undertakers employed by the Claimant. . . . On the corpse being removed from the bier, Mr. SEYMOUR took his place next to the coffin as chief mourner, but the Claimant having also occupied that position, the family withdrew from the procession and walked by themselves to the church to witness the interment of their lost relative.'

"The *Hampshire Chronicle* says:—

"'On the corpse being removed from the bier, Mr. SEYMOUR took his place next the coffin as chief mourner, when he was displaced by the Claimant, and a son of Mr. BAIGENT, a stationer in Winchester, took the next position. To prevent any unseemly conduct and results, the family withdrew from the procession, and walked by themselves to the church to witness the interment of their lost relative. Except this incident, matters passed quietly and with decorum.'

"And the *Hampshire Advertiser*, although it omits the names of Lord ARUNDEL of Wardour, of Mr. ALFRED SEYMOUR, and of every other relative and connection of the deceased who were present at the funeral, devotes a special paragraph to 'the interesting appearance of Mr. ANDREW BOGLE.' Mr. HOLMES affirms in his letter that the Claimant was accompanied by 'his cousin, the Count LOUSADA,' as chief mourner, which, for all we know, or have stated, may have been the case, the name and style of Count LOUSADA being entirely new to us."

The Solicitors to the infant baronet and his guardians reply to Mr. HOLMES's statement as follows:—

"TO THE EDITOR OF THE 'TIMES.'

"SIR—Had Mr. HOLMES, in his letters to you and the editor of the *Pall Mall Gazette*, which appears in your paper to-day, limited himself to comments on what passed at the funeral of the Dowager Lady TICHBORNE, we should not have thought it at all necessary to notice his communication, but as his letters insinuate that those whom we represent are imposing delays in the way of his client bringing his case before a jury, we must request the favour of your allowing us to state that such insinuation is wholly unwarranted by anything which has hitherto occurred in the course of the litigation. The matter is not yet ripe for a trial by jury. We are as anxious as the Claimant or his solicitor can be that the question should be tried at the earliest possible moment.

"We abstain from noticing the parade of witnesses who are stated to have come forward on the Claimant's behalf, it being in our judgment the height of impropriety to attempt to prejudge the case by such means. We will only state that, notwithstanding the affidavits which have been made in support of the Claimant's case, his identity with the late ROGER CHARLES TICHBORNE will, at the proper time, not only be plainly disproved, but we shall prove who the Claimant really is.—We are, sir, your obedient servants, DOBINSON AND GEARE,

"Solicitors for Sir H. A. J. D. TICHBORNE and his Guardians

"57, Lincoln's-inn-fields: March 23rd."

On the other hand, Mr. GUILDFORD ONSLOW, M.P. for Guildford, who was present at the funeral, denies the accuracy of the account given of it by the *Pall Mall Gazette*, and expresses his firm belief that the Claimant is the real baronet. We append his letter:—

"TO THE EDITOR OF THE 'TIMES.'

"SIR,—I have read a paragraph in the *Times* of to-day—a statement copied from the *Pall Mall Gazette*—calculated to mislead, and, therefore, unfair and unjust, as to what took place at the funeral of the late Dowager Lady TICHBORNE. By the invitation of the Claimant to the title and estates—who I firmly believe to be the real baronet—I made a point of attending, and a more quiet, attentive, and orderly assembly I never witnessed. After the coffin was removed, I observed Mr. SEYMOUR immediately attempt to occupy the place of chief mourner, and, although Sir ROGER TICHBORNE was overwhelmed with grief, and in tears, he quietly, and not offensively, put Mr. SEYMOUR aside, and placed himself in that position which his deceased mother would have wished he should occupy. Mr. SEYMOUR and his friends then left in a body, to reappear in the village church. I avow this is the plain, unvarnished truth of what did really occur on Thursday morning last at Tichborne Park. As to anyone being 'summarily extruded,' insulted or abused, I utterly deny.—I have the honour to remain, your obedient servant, GUILDFORD ONSLOW.

"The Grove, Ropley, Hants: March 21."

Another correspondent who was present at the funeral writes thus to the *Times* in favour of the Claimant's case:—

"SIR,—My attention has been directed to a letter which appeared in the *Pall Mall Gazette* a few days ago, giving a detailed account of the funeral of the late Dowager Lady TICHBORNE, in which the writer, with, perhaps, more zeal than discretion, insinuates that the friends of Sir ROGER TICHBORNE had no business there, and occupied places to which they were not entitled. As my name is mentioned as one of the intruders, I think it due to myself, as well as to Sir R. TICHBORNE, to say that I was there at his earnest request, and took up the position which was assigned to me. I also beg to explain the reasons which have induced me to take the view which I do of this extraordinary case.

"It appears to me utterly improbable, not to say impossible, that any lady should acknowledge as her son a person she has never seen, and not only acknowledge him, but share her income with him. I think it incredible that a number of gentlemen, many of them magistrates, and fully understanding the obligations and solemnity of an oath, with no possible interest in the result, should volunteer their affidavits to prove Sir ROGER TICHBORNE's identity. I think it equally incredible that several of his brother officers, non-commissioned officers, and privates, who served in the same regiment with Sir ROGER, should also swear to his identity. I think it impossible that his father's tenants, servants, and tradespeople should recognise him at once, and yet be mistaken. And, lastly, I think it strange that, after a two hours' conversation, in which Sir ROGER answered my questions with perfect simplicity and good faith, mentioning circumstances which no person but himself could have known, I should have come to a wrong conclusion.

"I cannot close these observations without expressing my great regret that I feel compelled to take a view of the case in opposition to that taken by some of my earliest and best friends. I should have had much greater pleasure in taking the opposite view, had truth, justice, and honour permitted me to do so.—I am, sir, your most obedient servant, J. W. SCOTT.

"Rotherfield Park, Alton, Hants: March 24."

This writer, HIGGINS, had, as we know, done everything to corrupt the public mind upon the TICHBORNE Case before it came into Court. So early, indeed, as May, 1867, he had appeared publicly, as appears in the following most improper correspondence—a correspondence, it should be noted, of which the Claimant's Counsel, Dr. KENEALY, never heard during the Trial, or he would certainly have cross-examined General JONES upon it:—

THE TICHBORNE SUCCESSION.

TO THE EDITOR OF THE "PALL MALL GAZETTE."

SIR,—The following correspondence will speak for itself. Having the honour of being nearly connected with the TICHBORNE family, it occurred to me that an opportunity would offer itself during the Derby week for effectually clearing up the doubt which in many persons' minds attaches itself to the identity of the person who states himself to be Sir ROGER DOUGHTY TICHBORNE, returned to England after a self-imposed exile of thirteen years. I accordingly addressed the following letter to Mr. HOLMES, of 25, Poultry, E.C., the solicitor who has undertaken the establishment of Sir ROGER's claims:—

"71, Eaton-square: May 23, 1867.

"SIR,—General RICHMOND JONES, who was in the 6th Dragoon Guards while the late Cornet ROGER DOUGHTY TICHBORNE served in that regiment, is now in London, and he has authorised me to say that if it will be agreeable to your client, who claims to be Sir ROGER DOUGHTY TICHBORNE, he will wait upon that gentleman at any time and place that may be most convenient to him, taking with him those amongst the officers of the Carabineers who were most intimate with Cornet TICHBORNE. Should your client be disposed to receive General JONES's visits, all questions as to his identity will probably be disposed of one way or the other. As soon as I hear from you I will make arrangements for the meeting. Many of the officers of the regiment are now in London, and are likely to remain here until after Ascot races.—I am, sir, your obedient servant, M. J. HIGGINS.

"J. HOLMES, Esq., 25, Poultry, E.C."

In due course of post I received the following reply from Mr. HOLMES:—

"25, Poultry, London, E.C: May 24, 1867.

"SIR,—I am much obliged by your note of yesterday's date, stating that General RICHMOND JONES is now in London, and would visit my client, Sir ROGER DOUGHTY TICHBORNE, if agreeable, taking with him those amongst the officers in the Carabineers who were most intimate with him when a cornet in that regiment. If I mistake not, General RICHMOND JONES is now or recently has been staying with Sir ROGER's sister-in-law, the Hon. TERESA TICHBORNE, or has been in correspondence with her and her mother, and the General will probably have learnt that shortly after Sir ROGER's return to England she wrote to his mother, the Dowager Lady JAMES TICHBORNE, to inquire whether he was in fact her son, and received a reply from her conveying the most positive assurance that he was. Consequently, the Hon. TERESA TICHBORNE can have no doubt whatever as to my client's identity, nor can I concur that the General sees any room to question it. I have not as yet had an opportunity of seeing my client since the receipt of your note; but I cannot advise him to accept the honour of receiving the gentlemen you refer to upon the ground mentioned in your note—namely, that his identity is questioned. At the same time, I doubt not that it will give him much pleasure to renew the acquaintance of his old military friends; and I have therefore to request you to be good enough to give me the names and addresses of the officers to whom you refer, as well as the present address of General RICHMOND JONES.—I am, sir, yours obediently, JOHN HOLMES.

"M. J. HIGGINS, Esq., 71, Eaton-square."

The only comment I shall make on Mr. HOLMES's letter is, that he is entirely mistaken in supposing that "General JONES is now, or has recently been staying with Sir ROGER's sister-in-law, the Hon. TERESA TICHBORNE (widow of the late and mother of the present baronet), or that he has been in correspondence with that lady or her mother." General JONES assured me yesterday, not only that he was not personally acquainted with those ladies, but that he has, up to the present moment, never communicated with either of them, directly or indirectly, on this or any other subject. Nor can General JONES have any preconceived impressions concerning the identity of the person who claims to be Sir ROGER TICHBORNE—for he has never seen him. General JONES, however, is fully convinced that he and his brother officers will have no difficulty in identifying their old comrade, if Mr. HOLMES's client indeed be he; as it is but thirteen years since they parted, and as, for nearly four years prior to his embarkation for South America, they lived with him on the most friendly and familiar terms. During the time of Cornet TICHBORNE's service in the Carabineers he was seldom absent on leave, and but for short periods, consequently his person and habits were even better known to the officers of that corps than to the members of his own family—none of whom, save and except his mother, have been able to discern in the Claimant to the succession the slightest resemblance to their long-lost relative.

I may as well add that up to the present moment no steps have been taken by Mr. HOLMES to assert his client's alleged rights legally.—I am, sir, your obedient servant, M. J. HIGGINS.

71, Eaton-square: May 26, 1867.

The next move of the Family was to put off the trial of the Probate of Lady TICHBORNE's Will, which was likely to come on before the Judge Ordinary. We subjoin the Report of their proceedings:—

COURT OF PROBATE, WESTMINSTER HALL—

MAY 5th, 1868.

BEFORE THE JUDGE ORDINARY.

TICHBORNE v. TICHBORNE.—TRANSCRIPT OF MR. TOLCHER'S SHORT-HAND NOTES.

Dr. TRISTRAM: In this case I appear for the Plaintiff, Sir ROGER TICHBORNE, who has filed a declaration in which he alleges that his mother, the late Lady TICHBORNE, died on the 12th of March, 1868, a widow, and intestate, leaving him her natural and lawful son by the late Sir JAMES TICHBORNE. The Defendant appears by his Guardian, he being an infant, and he denies that the Plaintiff is the natural and lawful son of the late Lady TICHBORNE. Upon that, issue has been joined on behalf of Sir ROGER, and I have to ask your lordship to direct the question at issue to be tried by a Special Jury.

Mr. COLERIDGE: I appear on the other side, and I have to ask your lordship not to make the order, upon this ground—that the case has already gone before the Court of Chancery, and the question and the only question to be determined in all these suits is the personal identity of the Claimant. If he is Sir ROGER TICHBORNE, he is entitled to all that he claims; if he is not Sir ROGER, he is not entitled. That is the simple issue in the whole case. The cause was set down for hearing before the late Vice-Chancellor WOOD, and I am told that it stands for hearing on the first day of Trinity Term. The Claimant has, I understand, filed as many as 95 affidavits. We have filed no affidavits in answer. The Claimant has been cross-examined to some extent, but we have thought it not right to file affidavits on our side in Chancery. We propose that the moment the case comes before the Court of Chancery, to say that we shall reserve all we have to say for the trial of the cause at law, where it must ultimately go to be tried, either upon an issue directed or an ejectment. And my application is, that no proceedings should be taken in this cause until the matter before the Court of Chancery has been decided one way or the other. In the suit in the Court of Chancery the property to be affected may be roughly stated at about £20,000 a-year; the property to be affected by the suit before your lordship may be roughly stated at £1,500—therefore, it seems to me utterly unreasonable to incur the enormous expense of going into a trial before your lordship upon the same identical question as to £1,500 which must inevitably be raised and tried in an issue directed by the Court of Chancery, or some other form of procedure, where the sum of £20,000 a-year is at stake—the question, as I said before, being simply one of identity. The statement of the supposed Sir ROGER is one of a certainly somewhat romantic character, and he has given us an opportunity of testing the truth of his statements. He says that on a particular day, when on a voyage from this country to some distant place, the ship on which he was on board went down; that he was picked up by another vessel, and taken to Melbourne; that there he served in certain capacities; and he gives, in short, a history of his life afterwards, which is set out in the 28th and following paragraphs of the Bill in Chancery; and the very first thing that will be done, either before the Court of Chancery or a Court of Common Law, will be to apply for a Commission to go out to Chili, to Valparaiso, and these other places which he names, and test the truth of the statement made by the supposed Sir ROGER in his claim. I need not say anything about the expenses which will certainly be incurred in these suits. One does not like to be confident of anything; but of this I think I may be confident—that we have a complete answer to the claim of the present Sir ROGER; but it will take a great deal of time to make out, and must be made out by the means of a Commission to collect a vast quantity of evidence. There is but one point in issue—the identity of the supposed Sir ROGER; and if he succeeds in the Court of Chancery, or before a jury, he will be entitled to the £20,000 a-year; and if so, it would be idle and childish to contend before your lordship that he is not entitled to the £1,500. Therefore the whole matter will be decided in a suit which is substantially at issue, and will be sent to a Court of Law in the course of a very few weeks. Under these circumstances I trust your lordship will make no order as to this suit, but will allow the case to go on before the Court of Chancery, we pledging ourselves that we will do all in our power to advance the trial of the cause in that Court or before a Court of Law, so that the whole matter may be decided.

The Judge Ordinary: The question before the Court is not when the case may be tried, but how it shall be tried. The Court would have no hesitation on the statement of Dr. TRISTRAM, and still less after the statement you have made, in saying the right way to try such a case would be by a jury, and the Court has no hesitation to make the order. That may be coupled with any order staying the proceedings that you think right. You say the suits cannot be decided without a Commission.

Dr. TRISTRAM: I have some affidavits that I should like to read to the Court. I should resist the application upon two grounds—that, first, it is contrary to the practice of this Court when an issue is raised in a suit pending in this Court to direct it to stand over or delay the hearing of it until an issue before some other Court may have been tried. Secondly, I object to it on the ground that the real object of this application is not for the furtherance of justice, but for the purpose of harassing Sir ROGER with vexatious delay. I have two affidavits before me, one of them by Sir ROGER himself, which I will briefly state to your lordship. This is only one of a series of applications that will be made by the other side to interpose every possible obstacle in the way of the trial of this issue. The first affidavit is that of Mr. HOLMES, the Solicitor for Sir ROGER. The original has been handed to the Registrar, and he says that the way in which he became acquainted with the Claimant was that he was introduced to Sir ROGER by Messrs. LEETE and BAILLOT, merchants in the City, who were clients of his, and that, in consequence of the certainty of his identity being doubted, he accompanied Sir ROGER to Paris.

The Judge Ordinary: I am not going to try this question upon affidavits.

Dr. TRISTRAM: My friend has made certain statements.

Mr. COLERIDGE: Are any of them untrue?

The Judge Ordinary: I consider that what Mr. COLERIDGE has said amounts to this—that there is one question, and one only, in all these proceedings—as to the identity of your client, which question is in the course of litigation in the Court of Chancery. That your client has, in the course of those proceedings, made certain statements as to the proof of his identity with respect to his whereabouts, at certain times, in certain foreign lands, that whenever that question of identity comes to be tried it will be material that evidence should be brought forward to show how far those statements are true; and Mr. COLERIDGE says, as it is the same question that arises in both Courts, he is desirous that the proceedings in this Court should be stayed. He has said nothing more; if he did it has escaped me.

Dr. TRISTRAM: My friend made a very positive statement.

The Judge Ordinary: Yes; he said he felt certain that he should succeed.

Mr. COLERIDGE: Then pray let that be considered as not said by me.

The Judge Ordinary: I will not entertain any of the affidavits upon this issue; I am not trying the issue. I think it is very much to be deprecated when a question is going to be submitted to some tribunal, which I assume to be competent to try it, that parties should attempt to get up a representation on the one side or the other. I totally object to entering into the question of who is right, and I will not allow it to be done indirectly if it cannot be done directly. You may make a statement to be put into the other scale against Mr. COLERIDGE that you are quite certain you are right, and that there is no pretence whatever for his statement.

Dr. TRISTRAM: Not only so, but there are the statements of the gentlemen of the county.

The Judge Ordinary: Never mind those.

Dr. TRISTRAM: And Sir ROGER is prepared to go to trial at once, and produce his 93 witnesses.

The Judge Ordinary: They may know nothing about it when they come. That is another attempt to get up a representation which I entirely deprecate. Wherever this question is to be tried, it is obviously to the interest of both parties that it should only be tried once.

Dr. TRISTRAM: The reason that I wish to have it tried here is, that in the Court of Chancery my friend's clients will resort to all sorts of contrivances and tricks to delay the trial of the cause. They have done so already.

Mr. COLERIDGE: That is entirely and utterly untrue. There is not one single word of truth in it.

Dr. TRISTRAM: I am prepared to prove it from the affidavit, if your lordship will kindly listen to me. One of your clients refused to put in an answer for five months. At any rate I submit that I am entitled to this—that this issue being raised in this Court, I am entitled, by the practice of the Court, to have it tried here by a special jury. My friend has produced no case, no precedent for your lordship delaying the trial, and under those circumstances I appear on behalf of Sir ROGER TICHBORNE, and claim it as a matter of right.

The Judge Ordinary: You take a little too high ground there. This Court in practice will always stay the proceedings for a time, if they think by so doing they may serve the ends of justice. What appears plain in the present case is this—that there ought to be but one trial, and that that trial ought to be as speedily as may be. Those points, I think, are clear. Whether the parties will agree to have one trial is a matter over which I have no control. As no answer is made to that suggestion, I suppose they will not.

Mr. COLERIDGE: As to that, I should only say that if they succeeded on a proper trial in ejectment or otherwise as to the £20,000 a year, it would be perfect madness to contest a matter of £1,500. I am not instructed to say anything more.

The Judge Ordinary: The parties at present have not come to any agreement of that character. If there is an issue joined between them on this one fact, the finding in whatever Court it is tried may be conclusive on the other party. Practically there may be but one trial. That is a thing to be desired. Time was when the Courts in Westminster Hall used to say, you may go straight on and not listen to the proceedings in any other Court. I think that time has gone by. I think it is time for one branch of Westminster Hall to take notice of what is going on in another, so far as that information may tend to render its own proceedings satisfactory to justice, economy, and a speedy issue of the trial. The question resolves itself into this—whether the trial in the Court of Chancery, or an issue directed by that Court, would take place before the parties could go to trial here. If they are satisfied to try the case here, I cannot see a reason why they should not try it here, because a larger amount of money is involved in a suit in another Court. It is simply a question where they can try it first.

Mr. COLERIDGE: The case has been a considerable time in the Court of Chancery; so far as I know, we shall not file any but formal affidavits there, and make no contest in that Court. The Vice-Chancellor, as a matter of course, will either direct an issue or an ejectment to be brought.

The Judge Ordinary: When might you expect to get to trial under such an issue?

Mr. COLERIDGE: We have to the 20th of May to file our proofs. Those will be mere formal proofs. When the case is at issue before the Vice-Chancellor, the immediate consequence will be that it will be sent to a trial at law, upon which a Commission will issue at once for the purpose of collecting such evidence as may be necessary to test the truth of the statements which this gentleman, whatever he may be, called the Claimant, has made in certain paragraphs of his Bill. By setting out a sort of history of his life, he has given us the means of ascertaining where he was, and whether there is a word of truth in the statement he has made. He makes certain statements as to his having been at Melbourne.

Dr. TRISTRAM: If my friend is allowed to read this, I ought to be allowed to do so.

Mr. COLERIDGE: I do not read them to impugn them; they may all possibly be true. He makes certain statements, in order to test the truth of which it will be necessary to send to Melbourne, to Wagga-Wagga (wherever that may be), to Rio, Chili, and other places in South America. For the purpose of testing the truth of his statements it will be necessary to send a Commission to those places to take evidence. That will be the course of procedure in the suit, wherever it is tried. If it is an issue here, the application will be made here for a Commission to those places. Therefore the question of its being tried now or next term is simply childish. We cannot get a Commission to Rio and back in a week. The thing is absurd. It must take a considerable time. Whether your lordship direct it, or whether the Court of Chancery direct it, is a matter perfectly immaterial. The case cannot come on for trial for some months, at all events. It has been a long while in the Court of Chancery. They are possessed of it; it will be again before that Court in the course of another fortnight, and without saying that because one suit involves £1,500, the other £20,000, that that is in itself a reason for what we ask. Where your lordship sees there is a proceeding pending in another Court in which the very same question arises, which, if decided, will, of course, decide the minor question in point of value: there I submit your lordship will stay your hand until the issue from the Court of Chancery is tried. I do not say that the finding in the one case may necessarily bind the other, but it is ninety-nine to one that it will. As a matter of sense and reason, no one would dispute the propriety of that. As an order has been made for a Receiver in this very matter, no question can arise about the man getting his money, therefore the money cannot be touched until the issue in the cause is decided one way or the other. I do not object to my friend's application, which asks that it should be decided by a special jury. It is a very fit case for a special jury; but I trust that your lordship will stay your hand until you see what has been done. If your lordship should think that the making an order absolutely staying the matter is too large, perhaps you will stay your hand until after the 20th of May, when the case comes on in the Court of Chancery. If we interpose any vain objections, or are at all fighting for the purposes of delay and troubling this gentleman with improper objections, then it will be quite open to them to ask your lordship to try the case here.

Mr. BAYFORD: It appears that originally the Plaintiff had the option of trying the case here, instead of in Chancery. There was a Will of the late baronet, which has been proved, and they had an opportunity of coming here for a revocation of the probate. Instead of that, they have chosen to go to the Court of Chancery, and when the suit is ripe for hearing they come here. In the affidavit of Mr. HOLMES, he says, "In the month of March, 1867, I laid a case before Dr. SPINKS, to advise the Plaintiff as to what steps should be taken to obtain a revocation of such probate, and was advised to make an application for that purpose;" so that this is no new thing which has occurred since the death of this lady.

Dr. TRISTRAM: The sole object of Sir ROGER coming here is that he thinks he shall get a trial here much earlier than in the Court of Chancery. The Bill was filed in June, 1867. He filed his first batch of affidavits in July, 1867, and further affidavits in April this year. I understand that in November last his leading counsel offered to go to a jury. The Defendants have had time to file affidavits up to the 20th of May.

Mr. COLERIDGE: If you are instructed to state that as what passed in Court, I understand you are misinstructed.

Dr. TRISTRAM: They had time to file affidavits to the 20th of

May. They may then ask for further time, and the case would be set down for hearing. Then we should have to wait for it to be argued before the Vice-Chancellor, which might not take place for eight or nine months. Then he might direct an issue, and there would be an application for a Commission. If your lordship directs the case to be tried here, the Commission may issue at once.

The Judge Ordinary: Do you object to consent that any evidence taken under a Commission should be used in the Court of Chancery?

Dr. TRISTRAM: The case may be disposed of at a very much earlier period here.

The Judge Ordinary: The Court has already pointed out that the two things to be desired are—first, that there should be one trial; that the Court has no power over, though, probably, the parties would consult their own interest by agreeing to that. The second point is that the trial may be had as soon as possible. The Court, therefore, makes an order for the trial of this cause by a special jury, but at present makes no order to delay the hearing of the cause. It is quite plain that the case cannot be tried within a very short time, because it has been intimated upon good grounds that it will be necessary to send a Commission abroad. For that very reason it would be very desirable that the Court should *not* stay the proceedings, because the Commission may at once be sent out. As long as I find that the gentleman who claims to be Sir ROGER TICHBORNE makes no opposition to the proceedings taken in this Court being usable in the Court of Chancery or at Common Law, and gives his consent to their being so used, I should allow the cause to be going on. If I find him throwing any impediment in the way, I shall take another course. I shall allow the cause to go on, subject to this—that the Chancery proceedings being first commenced, if I find it is shown on affidavit that, in consequence of the proceedings arising out of them, a trial is likely to be had, or will be had, within any period corresponding to the time it may be tried here, I should prefer its being tried in Chancery, where the proceedings first commenced. If, on the other hand, I find that those proceedings will delay the trial, and that it may be tried here first, I see no reason for suspending the Claimant's proceedings here, for he is as much entitled to the administration of his mother, if he is her son, as he is entitled to the estates which devolve upon him by settlement. At present it would seem to meet the justice of the case by making no order further than that I direct the case to be tried by a special jury.

Dr. TRISTRAM: Your lordship will direct it to be tried by a special jury in this Court?

The Judge Ordinary: Yes; and the remarks I have thrown out will be for the guidance of the parties.

The tactics of delay having so far succeeded, the Family repeated the same play a third time in the Probate Court. The friends of the Claimant having resolved to dispute probate of the Will to which GOSFORD and SLAUGHTER were executors, a suit was commenced before the Judge Ordinary to try whether the Testator was alive or dead. This also the Family laboured to put off. We append the report:—

IN THE PROBATE COURT.

WESTMINSTER HALL, JUNE 17, 1868.—Before Sir J. P. WILDE.

TICHBORNE v. TICHBORNE.

Mr. COLERIDGE: My Lord,—In this case I have to apply to your lordship for the issuing of a Commission in the two cases of TICHBORNE v. TICHBORNE to take evidence both in South America and also in Australia: and, my lord, it is for the purpose of examining witnesses upon an affidavit of Mr DOBINSON, the attorney for the Defendant in the suit, who says "that I am advised and believe it will be necessary on the part and behalf of the said infant to examine numerous witnesses permanently residing in various parts of Australia, New South Wales, and South America, and amongst others ROBERT JOHN HIGGINS, of Wagga-Wagga, in the colony of New South Wales, squatter; PETER JOHN HARTNETT, of Ryamber, County Wynyard, New South Wales, aforesaid; CONSTABLE WILLIAM MONTGOMERY, of 'The Heart,' near Sale, Gippsland, Australia, squatter; and MATTHEW MACALISTER, of Sale aforesaid, gentleman; SAMUEL BENDALL, of Hobart Town, in the colony of Tasmania, butcher; ROBERT KENT, of Melbourne, Victoria, commission agent; MICHAEL GUILFOYLE, of Double Bay, Sydney, New South Wales, nurseryman; Don JUAN HALLEY, of Melipilla, in Chili, in South America, doctor of medicine, and Dona CLARA, his wife, of the same place—that none of the before-mentioned persons are likely, to the best of my knowledge, information, and belief, to be within the jurisdiction of this Court at any time previous to or during the trial of the said causes. Fourthly, that I am advised and believe all the last-named persons and numerous other persons, residing as aforesaid in various parts of Australia, New South Wales, and South America, are material and necessary witnesses for the said infant, and that he cannot with safety proceed to the trial of the issues in these suits without having the benefit of the evidence of such persons. Fifthly, that I am informed and believe many of such witnesses in Australia and New South Wales reside several hundred miles apart from each other, and that a considerable period of time must necessarily and unavoidably be occupied in communicating with them and in making necessary arrangements, and in taking their evidence under Commission." And the application is not made for delay. Your lordship knows, from other matters that have been before you, what is the point in the case here. It is simply a question, as I had occasion before to say, whether this gentleman, who claims to be Sir ROGER TICHBORNE, is or is not the person he claims to be. He, in the proceedings in Chancery, has set out a certain portion of his life in considerable detail, pointing to residences at these various places in Chili and various parts of New South Wales, and it is essential to the interest of the infant in the suit that we should examine witnesses to ascertain whether or not what he states on the part of himself is correct. If it is correct, it is a strong confirmation of his story; if not correct, I need not point out it is most material evidence for the infant; and I do not quite know what my learned friend's objection is.

Mr. Serjeant BALLANTINE: My learned friend has scarcely been instructed in all the matters that have occurred in this case, which is undoubtedly one of the most important causes that has arisen in our courts of justice; and I venture to call your lordship's attention to some of the dates of the transactions that have taken place. The original Bill was filed as far back as June, 1867. A variety of proceedings have taken place during that time—among others, the Plaintiff has from time to time been filing affidavits, amounting in the whole, I believe, to something like 100 affidavits, as to the identity of this gentleman with Sir ROGER TICHBORNE, whom he claims to be; that since that period—that is to say, since towards the end of June—no further affidavits relating to his identity have been filed, and no new matter of any kind whatever has arisen or is likely to arise, in this extremely important suit. At the very moment the bills and the affidavits were filed, showing the nature and the character of the claim, and the nature of the evidence in support of that claim, it would have been in the power of those who represent the adverse party to apply to the Court of Chancery for the Commission for which they are now applying to your lordship. During the great delays that have been created—certainly not by the fault of Sir ROGER TICHBORNE or his advisers, because they have been most desirous of bringing it to an issue, but every conceivable difficulty and delay has been thrown in the way of preventing the issue being fairly raised—during that period the death of the lady occurred, which brings the matter into your lordship's Court; and it is notorious, at any rate it is said in the affidavits, that this lady was among those who recognised Sir ROGER TICHBORNE, and dealt with him as if he were her own son. Sir ROGER TICHBORNE himself has undergone, in his early days and during his life in New South Wales, a considerable amount of hardship. His life is one that cannot be relied on, and every day's delay is a delay which I venture to think has a tendency to interfere with the course of justice. My friend's affidavit mentions a variety of people in New South Wales whom he wants to examine. An affidavit of Mr. HOLMES, the attorney who is instructing me, states that an agent has been in Australia, as he has been informed and believes, on the part of the Defendants in these suits, for nearly twelve months, and investigations have been conducted by that agent. Now, in the affidavit that my learned friend has produced it is not suggested for what purpose the Commission is to be issued. They do not say what they desire to find out. In the affidavit of Mr. HOLMES, he refers to a person of the name of HORTON, it having been common rumour that the allegation was that Sir ROGER TICHBORNE was not Sir ROGER TICHBORNE, but a person of the name of HORTON, and a number of persons, every one of whom knew Mr. HORTON, have been spoken to. There are at least 60 or 70 of those persons in England at present; and if, therefore, the suggestion is that Sir ROGER TICHBORNE is Mr. HORTON, there is abundant means to show at once, and without any Commission, that their theory on that subject is correct. But if your lordship will look at the parties they name, and the character of the persons they name in Australia, in conjunction with the observation I have submitted to you—that there has been an agent in New South Wales for a considerable period—there is not one of these persons who might not, with the utmost facility, and at much less expense than the issuing of a Commission, have been brought over to this country long ago, if it were desirable, for they are not in a position likely to resist any endeavour on the part of those who are ready to pay their expenses, and there is no excuse whatever made for their not being here, and there is no assertion in the affidavit that the slightest endeavour has been made. Although the agent is there to bring every one of these witnesses forward, I know at the earliest period it was a matter, and it is a matter which I was consulted upon at the very earliest period, and I had an opportunity of forming certain opinions very early on the subject. This gentleman has been denounced as an impostor, and he has been struggling by every means in his power to bring this matter to an issue.

Sir J. P. WILDE: Why did he not bring an ejectment at once?

Mr. Serjeant BALLANTINE: There were outstanding terms which prevented his doing it, and the whole estate is in Chancery, and he has been struggling really to bring this matter forward. At last the opportunity arose from the death of his mother, of bringing the matter into your lordship's Court, where no doubt, although it is a small question that is in issue here—no doubt whatever, if this is an honest proceeding on the part of Sir ROGER TICHBORNE, and if it be an honest defence on the part of those who opposed him, there will be an opportunity by means of a special jury of trying this issue, and, in all human probability, of preventing an enormous expense, by which the property, whatever it is, is likely to be seriously damaged. One further observation, that in opposing this matter, of course your lordship's directing of a Commission, or ordering what should be done in this Court, would not bind any of those against whom actions might be brought in relation to other portions of the property; and if the Commission is granted, there appears to be a litigation in prospect that will far exceed the term of Sir ROGER TICHBORNE'S life, and render this cause almost a disgrace to the Courts of this country.

Mr. COLERIDGE: Whether it will be a disgrace to the Courts of this country or not, I will not pretend to argue. This, I contend, is a matter of course, and I cannot see that my learned friend has made any observations to show your lordship should not grant the order, which is, as I say, almost a matter of course.

Sir J. P. WILDE: Can you refer me to that passage that you did refer to before about this man's life in Australia? It is in answer to the Bill, or in the Bill itself.

Mr. COLERIDGE: It is set out in considerable detail in his own Bill. It is the 54th, 55th, and 56th paragraphs of this Bill.

Mr. Serjeant BALLANTINE: It is in the Plaintiff's affidavit.

Mr. COLERIDGE: This will do just as well. "On the day after he first landed at Melbourne, the Plaintiff was strolling about the town, and went into a yard, called Row's-yard, situate in Burlee-street, Melbourne, where a large number of horses were being sold. He was much attracted by what was taking place, and a person, whom the Plaintiff afterwards discovered to be Mr. WM. FOSTER, an extensive stock-keeper, of Gippsland, spoke to him, and, after ascertaining that he was a good rider, offered to take the Plaintiff with him to Gippsland, where there was good hunting and shooting. The Plaintiff accepted such offer, and, for family reasons, assumed the name of TOMAS CASTRO (after that of a friend named Don TOMAS CASTRO, whose acquaintance he had made in Melipilla, Chili), and the Plaintiff continued to use, and was known in Australia by the name of TOMAS CASTRO, until shortly prior to his return to England, as hereinafter mentioned. The Plaintiff immediately afterwards left Melbourne with Mr. FOSTER and his horses, and proceeded to Mr. FOSTER'S station at Boisdale, in Gippsland, on the Avon river, nearly 300 miles from Melbourne, where he remained about nineteen months; Mr. FOSTER then gave him charge of the Dargo Station, in the Australian Alps, about 115 miles further inland, where the Plaintiff remained for about eighteen months, and then returned to Boisdale, where, after staying for about three months, he went about 20 miles off to Sale, or Flodden Creek, on river Latrobe, where he remained about six months. From that place the Plaintiff proceeded to NORMAN MCLEOD'S station on the Mitchell river, about 60 miles from Sale, where he entered into partnership with one FREDERICK BURROWS, and remained there about four months, and was well known to Mr. SMITH, of the Lindnio Station. Plaintiff went from that place to the Omeo diggings, where

THE CLAIMANT'S HUT IN AUSTRALIA.

he remained about four months, and from there to Deniliquin, in New South Wales, where he remained for about 13 months, and from thence he proceeded to Hay, on the Murrumbidgee river, and remained there about nine months, and from thence he proceeded to Wagga-Wagga, and then to Beree and Narrandra for about four months, and then to Mr. JENKIN'S station at Naugus for four months, and then to Melbourne with cattle belonging to one Mr. JOHNSTONE, and from there to Bendigo, where he remained for about two months, and then to the town of Tumut, where he remained for about seven months, and from thence to Gundaigai, staying there about one month, and then returned to Wagga-Wagga, where he lived about four years." Then he afterwards intermarried with MARY ANN BRYANT.

Sir J. P. WILDE: How long ago was that?

Mr. COLERIDGE: This was filed the 27th of June.

Sir J. P. WILDE: How long was it that he stated he went abroad?

Mr. Serjeant BALLANTINE: July, 1854, my lord, down to 1865.

Mr. COLERIDGE: From 1854 to 1865.

Sir J. P. WILDE: I think there can be no doubt whatever you are entitled to a Commission. Speed is all very well, and nobody is more inclined than I am to see that justice is pushed forward as far as propriety would allow, but the case cannot be tried without the proper evidence, and if the question is the identity of this man, and he has passed a great number of years in Australia, and he gives the details of his own life in Australia in order to fortify the assertion of his own identity, I think it would be monstrous that the other side should not have the opportunity of testing this statement, and ascertaining from witnesses in Australia what his life has been. Then as to the affidavit, it states what all affidavits do which are ordinarily made for issuing commissions—namely, the names of witnesses, that they are material and necessary, and the application is not for delay. The only question is, inasmuch as it is impossible to try this cause without this evidence, whether there is anything in the suggestion that the witnesses might be brought here. That only depends on whether they are willing to come, and that we do not know, and the Court has never asked for an affidavit positively that a man is unwilling to come here. I think the Commission should go. Then the practical question is, where it shall go to? Where do you desire to send it?

Mr. COLERIDGE: To Chili, and also these places.

Sir J. P. WILDE: But it should be to go from place to place in Australia.

Mr. COLERIDGE: I should think there ought to be two Commissions, at least one to Chili.

Sir J. P. WILDE: But I mean in Australia; these places, I understand, are several hundred miles apart.

Dr. TRISTRAM: It might be a *mandamus* to the Supreme Court

of the different colonies, and they might compel the witnesses to attend.

Mr. COLERIDGE: This is a matter of procedure as to the power of the Commissioners. It would be better to have one Commission directed to Melbourne, where the greater body of the witnesses would be, with power to go to other places if necessary.

Mr. Serjeant BALLANTINE: Not to Chili?

Mr. COLERIDGE: No; there must be two Commissions, one to South America and the other to Australia.

Sir J. P. WILDE: And you should also have power to examine *vivâ voce* in a case like this.

Mr. Serjeant BALLANTINE: That I should ask.

Sir J. P. WILDE: I think it should be *vivâ voce*, because you do not know until you get there what questions it will be necessary to put.

Dr. TRISTRAM: I am told that some of these witnesses, for instance at Wagga-Wagga, reside about 300 miles from Melbourne, and Sale is about the same distance. There is railway communication over a greater part of the distance between these places, and if your lordship were to issue a *mandamus* to the Supreme Court of Melbourne, the witnesses might be compelled to come to Melbourne and be examined there, and it would save a great deal of time. What we object to is a roving Commission. It is a very common thing to send out a *mandamus* to a Supreme Court.

Sir J. P. WILDE: It used to be very common to send a *mandamus* to India, but that is pretty well superseded by the Statute of WILLIAM, under which Commissions were issued.

Mr. COLERIDGE: I should think the two Commissions, one to South America and one to Australia, directed in the first place to Santiago, which is the capital of Chili, and the other to Melbourne, with power to go, I will not say to any place, but to the other places that may be agreed upon between the parties.

Sir J. P. WILDE: That will be the best way, if not agreed upon. Then the only place must be Melbourne. Now the Court must do all that it can to insist upon the speedy issuing of the Commission, and its speedy return.

Mr. Serjeant BALLANTINE: I was going to ask your lordship to limit the period of the Commission.

Sir J. P. WILDE: How soon can you get a Commission out? Interrogatories have not got to be prepared; it ought to go out by the next mail.

Mr. Serjeant BALLANTINE: That is in about a week or ten days from now, the 2nd of July. Friday is the next Melbourne mail, I am told.

Sir J. P. WILDE: They can hardly get ready by then.

Mr. COLERIDGE: That is unreasonable.

Sir J. P. WILDE: The next after that?

Mr. Serjeant BALLANTINE: It will be a long time, probably, before they can get anybody to go there.

Sir J. P. WILDE: The next mail after?

Mr. Serjeant BALLANTINE: Will this Commission be directed to anyone?

Sir J. P. WILDE: Commissioners fixed upon by the parties, or named by the Court if they do not agree. Generally each party names a Commissioner.

Mr. COLERIDGE: Perhaps I ought to draw your lordship's attention to this. It appears from the affidavit that on Saturday this case will be heard as a short cause in Chancery. The inevitable result will be this—the direction of an issue, or leave to bring an ejectment.

Mr. Serjeant BALLANTINE: I think I may say we have the power of bringing ejectment now, and, if the Commission is to issue, it will be probably desirable that the Commission should not actually go until we have the power to join the Common Law as well in the Commission.

Sir J. P. WILDE: You have not all the parties here. You mean you have somebody else to deal with.

Mr. COLERIDGE: It will be extremely inconvenient to have two sets of Commissions.

Sir J. P. WILDE: It will be monstrous.

Mr. COLERIDGE: It is actually set down as a short cause for Saturday, which is the first short cause day.

Sir J. P. WILDE: One term of the order should be that between the same parties the evidence taken under that Commission shall be used in any suit.

Mr. Serjeant BALLANTINE: They cannot bind others.

Sir J. P. WILDE: But it may go so far.

Mr. COLERIDGE: We have no objection to that.

Sir J. P. WILDE: We cannot meet the whole matter, but it is right to do that.

Mr. COLERIDGE: We only wanted your lordship to know we are close on the issue in Chancery, it being set down as a short cause on agreed minutes in Chancery for Saturday.

Sir J. P. WILDE: That they must settle. All I can do is, in granting the Commission, to bind the parties to admit the evidence in any proceedings between them.

Mr. COLERIDGE: Only I mean it would be a pity to enforce the issuing of any Commission so as to compel a second to go out.

Sir J. P. WILDE: They are as alive to that as you are. I must make the order independent of that.

Mr. Serjeant BALLANTINE: I am not acquainted with how long these matters will take. My client tells me, if the issuing of the Commission is postponed for a week, that we shall be enabled to join the two Commissions.

Mr. COLERIDGE: Then so be it.

Sir J. P. WILDE: What is the arrangement?

Mr. COLERIDGE: It is agreed that the issuing of the Commission shall stand over for a fortnight. In the meantime the ejectment shall be brought in Chancery, and then they shall be issued separately, but to the same persons.

Sir J. P. WILDE: Now, about the return.

Mr. Serjeant BALLANTINE: We must give them six months, I am afraid.

Mr. COLERIDGE: It cannot be done in six months. It takes two months to go there and two months to come back.

Sir J. P. WILDE: Two months ought to be sufficient to examine the witnesses. Make Commission returnable in six months, and stay the cause until then, and you can apply again if the time is required to be extended.

Mr. COLERIDGE: Six months from the time of issuing?

Sir J. P. WILDE: Yes, and then apply again if need be.

We shall notice only one more of their devices for delay, which we copy from the *Hampshire Chronicle* of January 25th, 1871:—

THE TICHBORNE BARONETCY.

On Wednesday, January 25th, 1871, an application to postpone this Trial to a later date was made to Lord Chief Justice BOVILL, sitting in his private room at Westminster.

The Solicitor-General said that he had to apply, on behalf of the Defendants, that the Trial be further postponed, on the ground that several witnesses, whose evidence would be material to the issue, were absent in Paris. A great deal, no doubt, would depend upon the manner in which the Claimant had resided in Paris. He was substantially a Parisian until he was sixteen years of age. His father and mother lived there, and there were many persons in that city who were relations and intimate friends of the family. All, with the exception of one who was in the French army, were supposed to be shut up in Paris. There could be no doubt now that the siege was approaching its termination; but it was plain that a considerable time must elapse before the Solicitor for the Defendants could communicate with his witnesses. Taking all responsibility on himself, he (the Solicitor-General) had expressed an opinion that in their absence it was not safe or right that the Defendants should proceed to Trial. He named one witness, and did not think his lordship would consider it reasonable that he should give the names and addresses of the other persons in a case of this kind. The Solicitor-General said it was a matter of course. The terms he left to his lordship.

Mr. Serjeant BALLANTINE, who is retained for the Plaintiff, said that he was not in a condition to dispute some of the assertions of his learned friend. There could be no doubt that the presence of witnesses was material for the purpose of rebutting, if possible, any statement which Sir ROGER had made, but whether they were in existence at the present time must be a matter extremely vague and speculative. The capitulation of Paris was imminent, and there was little doubt that the presence of the witnesses could be secured before the Trial came to a termination. At all events, if it was further postponed a grave and serious hardship would be inflicted upon Sir ROGER. Five or six years had elapsed since he arrived in this country. He took, as it would be remembered, immediate measures for recovering his rights. By the death of his mother, Lady TICHBORNE, he had lost a most material witness in his favour. Since the time that Sir ROGER first made his claim, as many as ten of his witnesses had died.

The Solicitor-General: Seventeen of ours are dead already, so that the statement tells both ways.

Mr. Serjeant BALLANTINE: There were others who were extremely unwell—two of them being in a most perilous condition—and under these circumstances he apprehended that his learned friend ought to be compelled to make out most urgent grounds for a postponement. The Claimant had at least a hundred witnesses at present, whom it would be necessary to examine, and there would be, in addition, the examination of Sir ROGER himself, whose career would have to be most minutely inquired into. He would be subjected, no doubt, to an extremely long cross-examination, and the Trial might occupy a longer time than was expected. If the witnesses for the Defendant were in existence, he apprehended in the present state of Paris there would be no difficulty in bringing them forward before the action had terminated. There was another matter of very serious import to Sir ROGER. When he found that his identity was denied, he became pauperised, as it were, and it was only through the kindness of friends who recognised him, that money was placed at his command. Of course, there must be a certain limit to their kindness; and he was instructed to say that Sir ROGER was now in a state of difficulty. There was a pressure upon him which made it most important that no further delay should take place.

The Lord Chief Justice did not see there was any difference between the state of things now and when the last application was made in November. At that time it was expected—certainly in this country—that the siege of Paris would be over long before this. The application then was at the instance of the Plaintiff, and it was strongly resisted at the time by the counsel for the Defendants, but both sides expressed their anxiety to proceed to Trial with as little delay as possible. He must take it there were material witnesses to be examined on behalf of the Defendants. The whole history of the Plaintiff's life would have to be inquired into; they might have to go into every-day occurrences, and the Trial might occupy a longer time than was expected. Under all the circumstances, therefore, he thought the application a reasonable one, and that the Trial must be postponed; for (said his lordship) if he were to let the case proceed, and there were witnesses not forthcoming in consequence of their being detained in Paris, all the expenses incurred would be thrown away; therefore he had no alternative. It was the ordinary case of the absence of a material witness, and it was not the default of the Defendants; therefore the cause must be postponed. The only question was time and terms.

His lordship, after some further conversation, withdrew in order to consult the Judges of the Common Pleas as to the most convenient day for commencing the Trial, which, it was believed, would occupy many weeks. On his return,

The Lord Chief Justice said that their lordships had named the 9th of May, the first of the sittings after Easter Term, as the most suitable day for the Court, and that he was ready to give up the six days that were looked upon as a relief to the Judges, and that he should have no objection to sitting on during the term, thus securing nine or ten weeks for the Trial. And as the jury fund of the Court, if this time lasted any time, would be bankrupt, therefore there ought to be some arrangement about the payment of the jury. There would be twelve jurymen, who would be entitled to £1. 1s. per day by law, and his lordship thought the Defendants should bear a part.

To this the Solicitor-General assented.

On the part of the Plaintiff, it was urged that the Plaintiff had not six guineas a day to pay, on which

His lordship observed that could not be, because the case was not brought into Court at the expense of six guineas a day. According to Serjeant BALLANTINE's statement, the Plaintiff was bankrupt, and the same people who brought the case into Court could provide the jury expenses. It was quite clear that a case of this sort could not be fought except at a great expense, and part of that expense was a jury.

Serjeant BALLANTINE having expressed himself ready to obey whatever his lordship suggested,

An order was then made for the Trial to be postponed, each party consenting to the Trial proceeding beyond the usual time of sitting, and that the fees to the jury should be borne equally between them. The Plaintiff and Defendants were also ordered to pay their own costs of postponement, as also those incurred on the former occasion—the order of the Judge, so far as it related to costs, on the 2nd of November being rescinded by his lordship.

But we confess we are wearied out by a contemplation of "the law's delay," and the course of the Family in these proceedings. We hasten on to the Trial in the Common Pleas, which began on May 11th, 1871, and collapsed on March 7th, 1872. With that Great Issue we do not, of course, propose to deal. The number of actual sittings was 102; the witnesses for the Plaintiff were 85 in number, comprising the depositions and evidence of Lady TICHBORNE (the Mother), the Family Solicitor, Mr. HOPKINS; one baronet, six magistrates, one general, three colonels, one major, two captains, 36 non-commissioned officers and privates, four clergymen, seven tenants on the estate, sixteen servants of the Family, and twelve general witnesses, who all swore to his identity as Sir ROGER TICHBORNE. The claim was denied by the evidence of only 17 witnesses. After hearing these the Jury said they had no desire to hear any more; and Serjeant BALLANTINE having thereupon elected to be nonsuited, Lord Chief Justice BOVILL spoke as follows:—

"After the opinion expressed by the jury, and expressed after mature consideration and deliberation, in this case, and after the Plaintiff has elected to be nonsuited, the question arises—what course I should take under the Act of Parliament. The opinion of the jury is now placed beyond all doubt by what they have stated in answer to the observations which my brother BALLANTINE has made, and the questions that have been addressed to them. Although it may be my duty, on an occasion like this, to come to a conclusion as to the truth or falsehood of the Plaintiff's story, yet, of course, in the exercise of my discretion, I should be governed in a great degree by the finding of the jury. Substantially, that finding is a verdict for Defendant, because it has afforded my brother BALLANTINE an opportunity of electing to be nonsuited. He then elected to be nonsuited in consequence of the opinion expressed by the jury. In that opinion I entirely concur; and *I feel that I may as well state at once that it has appeared, and it does appear to me, that the Plaintiff has been guilty of wilful and corrupt perjury in his examination, taken on oath before me, and, therefore, that there is reasonable ground for directing him to be prosecuted on this charge; and I do direct that such prosecution be instituted, and that the Plaintiff be prosecuted accordingly.* In pursuance of the Act of Parliament, which imposes the duty of considering that question on the Judge, I think it necessary to give effect to what I have said by committing the Plaintiff, and I do order him to be imprisoned and detained in the common gaol until the next session of the Central Criminal Court, unless the Plaintiff enters into and finds bail on his own recognisance in the sum of £5,000, and two sureties of £2,500 each, or four sureties of £1,250 each, to answer in person the charges brought against him. . . . There is one other subject to which I would refer. I think it right to express my entire belief in the evidence of Mrs. RADCLIFFE; not depending upon her own testimony alone, but confirmed by testimony, letters, correspondence, and all other evidence in the case."

Language like this, uttered from the Bench, against a man who was subsequently to be put upon his Trial, is wholly without precedent, and can neither be justified nor excused. It was a prejudgment of the issue which the Jury to be subsequently empanelled were to try; and could not fail to have the greatest effect upon their minds. If BOVILL had stopped short with his previous words, it might be pleaded for him that he only read the words of the Act of Parliament which gave him authority to commit; but when he exonerated Mrs. RADCLIFFE, he went out of his way to injure, and even to help in the conviction of, the Defendant. BOVILL afterwards lived to repent his course; and we have heard from the best authority that, about six weeks before he died, in answer to a friend who asked him what he thought of the TICHBORNE case, he put his hand to his head, and said, brokenly: "Don't mention it. It weighs on me—it weighs on me."

As soon as the Judge had issued his warrant for the apprehension of the Claimant on the charge of perjury, it was at once placed in the hands of Superintendent WILLIAMSON, of the detective department. Owing to the opinion expressed by the Jury on the Monday, and the probable result of the case, the detective department was already on the alert, and the Claimant's movements were tolerably well known. Superintendent WILLIAMSON, therefore, accompanied by Chief-Inspector CLARKE and Inspector DENNING, instead of going to the Claimant's house, at the Boltons, Brompton, where it was natural to suppose him to be, at once went to the Waterloo Hotel, where, on inquiring for Sir ROGER, they were shown into his private sitting-room. Superintendent WILLIAMSON then acquainted the Claimant with the object of his visit, and read the warrant over to him. The Claimant for a minute or two looked serious, but maintained himself perfectly composed. At last he said, "Well, it is very unfortunate, as it will put me to considerable personal inconvenience if I am arrested now." Of course, there could be no delay, and he seemed determined to put the best appearance on the matter possible. The coach in which he had so often ridden to Westminster was once more ordered, but this time to convey him to Newgate. The affair at the hotel created a great sensation, as soon as it was known that the three gentlemen visitors were detective police. The visitors at the hotel crowded round to take a last look, and numbers of persons ran after the carriage, the crowd increasing all along the road, till Newgate was reached. He was placed in an ordinary cell, and, though serious, and apparently contemplating with little satisfaction the change of scene, he was yet perfectly calm and composed.

But though we do not enter upon any discussion of that Trial, we think it right to subjoin the following summary of evidence given on behalf of the Plaintiff; and we simply ask of our readers what they think of a Jury who, in the face of such testimony, absolutely stopped the case, upon the swearing of some dozen and a half such persons as swore against TICHBORNE?

JAMES M'CANN: "I entered Her Majesty's 6th Dragoon Guards in 1830. . . . I remember Mr. R. C. TICHBORNE joining. . . I became his servant. . . I was with him continually, and I remember him well. . . I saw him about the beginning of 1853."

"The next time I saw him was in 1867. . . I recognised him at first, without any trouble whatever. . . I knew him thoroughly well. . . The more I saw of him the more I became convinced he was the man. . . I have really no doubt whatever about his being the same man."

Colonel NORBURY, of the Forest, near Malvern, a Lieutenant-Colonel of the Worcester Militia, and Justice of the Peace for the County of Hereford: "I was formerly in the Carabineers. . . I joined as cornet in 1847, the same year as ROGER TICHBORNE joined. I saw him continually."

"I am still of the same opinion I expressed at the commencement of my examination, that he is the ROGER TICHBORNE. . . I am fully convinced he is the same ROGER TICHBORNE."

Major HEYWOOD: "In February, 1847, I became lieutenant in the Carabineers. I remember R. C. TICHBORNE joining the regiment in 1849. . . In November of that year I was gazetted captain, and TICHBORNE succeeded me as lieutenant. I frequently went to the head-quarters at Cahir, and saw him often, both there and at Clonmel. I last saw him there late in the summer of 1851."

"I next saw him at Alresford in July, 1867. . . I recognised him as my old brother officer. I saw him repeatedly. I was staying in the neighbourhood. I have satisfied myself that he is my old brother officer."

GEORGE WILDE: "I was the officers' batman in the 6th Dragoon Guards when Mr. ROGER TICHBORNE joined the regiment in 1849. . . I knew him till he left, in 1853. . . I saw a good deal of him. . . Occasionally I attended him in his rooms."

"In 1867 I saw the same gentleman. . . In my opinion the Claimant is the same man that I knew in the regiment when I was in it. I have not the least doubt about it."

Major-General WILLIAM NEVILLE CUSTANCE, C.B.: "I was a captain in the 6th Dragoon Guards when ROGER TICHBORNE joined the regiment, and I became major before he left. We were quartered in the same barracks in Ireland. . . I messed with him from the spring of 1852 to 1853."

"From 1853 I saw nothing of him until he came to see me at Salisbury on the 12th of October, 1867. . . When he sat down with his face to the light I recognised him immediately. . . The more I looked at him and talked with him the more I was convinced he is the man. . . Most undoubtedly he is the man. . . My deliberate opinion is that he is the man."

Sergeant-Major WILLIAM QUINN: "I live in the city of York. I was formerly sergeant-major of the 6th Dragoon Guards. I have retired on a pension, after twenty-six years' service. . . I left the regiment with a full pension. . . I remember ROGER C. TICHBORNE joining the regiment. I had as good opportunity for seeing him as any man in the regiment. . ."

"In 1867 I saw him at Croydon. . . I really believe he is the Mr. R. C. TICHBORNE. I don't know anything about Sir ROGERS, or D's or P's, but he is the same man who served in my regiment."

Captain JOHN DAVID SHERSTON: "I am a Justice of the Peace for the County of Lincoln. I was formerly an officer of the 6th Dragoon Guards. I was a lieutenant at the time Mr. TICHBORNE joined. I was well acquainted with him, and continued so until he left. He was in the habit of visiting at my house at Waterford and Canterbury. . ."

"I received a letter from him in the year 1867. I called on him at the White Horse Hotel, Romsey. . . I arrived at the conclusion that he was the officer I knew in the regiment. I came to that conclusion very firmly. . . I have not the slightest hesitation in recognising him as my old brother officer. . . My deliberate judgment is that he is my old brother officer."

Mrs. SHERSTON (wife of Captain SHERSTON): "I lived with my husband at Waterford and Canterbury. ROGER C. TICHBORNE frequently visited our house and dined with us. . . I knew his features perfectly. . ."

"I saw the present Claimant on the 25th of November, 1867. The moment he spoke I recognised him. . . My deliberate judgment and belief is, that he is the ROGER TICHBORNE I knew in 1851. . . I have not the least doubt about it."

WILLIAM FRY: "I am now employed as mess-waiter in the Staff College at Sandhurst. I was in the Carabineers between 1849 and 1861. I remember Mr. ROGER TICHBORNE joining the regiment, and I saw him often, and waited on him at mess. . ."

"I saw the Claimant first, since his return to this country, at Alresford, about three years ago. . . I knew him at once. I have not the least doubt he is the Sir ROGER TICHBORNE I knew and waited on in the regiment. . . I should think no one who knew ROGER TICHBORNE in 1853 could mistake him after seeing him a short time."

JOHN MOORE: "I am fifty-one years of age. . . My father was a servant for more than 25 years in the DOUGHTY family. . . I had a letter from my father stating that Mr. ROGER TICHBORNE wanted a servant. . . I engaged with him near the end of 1852. . . On the 1st of March, 1853, I embarked with him on board the 'Pauline' as his servant. . ."

"I arrived at the decided conclusion he is Sir ROGER TICHBORNE. My conviction and judgment are the same they were three years ago. I am perfectly confident he is no other than ROGER TICHBORNE."

Colonel CHARLES SAWYER: "I was a Colonel in the Carabineers, and retired on half-pay in 1863. I was in the regiment in 1849, and remember ROGER TICHBORNE being in the regiment. . . I remember him up to 1853. During that time I saw him every day. I frequently dined at mess with him."

"In 1867 I went to the Claimant at a hotel at Brighton on the 10th of November. . . After conversing with him some time I felt sure he was the ROGER TICHBORNE whom I had known before. . . I felt sure he was the same man."

ANTHONY JOHN WRIGHT BIDDULPH, Esq.: "I am a Justice of the Peace for the County of Sussex, and a second cousin of ROGER TICHBORNE. . . About 1818 or 1819 I was a good deal with him; for a fortnight I was with him every day."

"I saw the Plaintiff after his return, in the summer of 1867, at Croydon. . . I had formed a strong prejudice against him, and denounced him as an impostor. . . I have seen him from time to time since my first interview. . . My deliberate judgment is that he is my cousin, or I would not have stood up for him as I have done. The more I see him the more I am convinced he is my cousin."

JAMES WINTER SCOTT, Esq.: "I am a Justice of the Peace and Deputy-Lieutenant for the County of Southampton. . . I knew Sir ROGER TICHBORNE before he left England. . ."

"I first saw him, after his return, at my house, Rotherfield Park (which adjoins the TICHBORNE estate). . . I then said, 'Now that I have had an interview with you, I have no objection to give you my affidavit.' . . I have seen him several times since then, and have no more doubt about his being Sir ROGER TICHBORNE than I have of my own existence."

Miss ANNA MARY BRAINE: "I am living at Brompton just now, but I reside in Devonshire. I was living as governess to Miss KATE DOUGHTY in 1849. I lived there, I think, till October or November, 1850. I was there for the greater part of a year. During that time Mr. R. C. TICHBORNE visited the house. He was there on his birthday. There was a ball given to the servants and tenantry. I saw him a great part of every day during that period, and I have a perfect recollection of his features, manners, and appearance."

"In 1868 I received a letter signed TICHBORNE, and in consequence of that letter I went to Croydon. . . I have seen Sir ROGER repeatedly since, and have lived for weeks in his house. . . My opinion is that he is the same ROGER TICHBORNE whom I knew in 1850. I am as certain about his identity as I am of my own. . . My brother, who is abroad, was a Member in Parliament."

Mr. JOHN GREENWOOD: "In 1849 I was tailor to the 6th Dragoon Guards, and remember Mr. ROGER TICHBORNE joined the regiment. . . I constantly saw him. . . My dealings with him lasted the whole time he was in the regiment. . ."

"I am quite certain, and I positively swear that the Plaintiff is the same person whom I formerly knew by the name of ROGER CHARLES TICHBORNE; and have not the shadow of a doubt as to his identity, as it is a matter of positive certainty."

Mr. JOHN GREENWOOD, Jun.: "I am the son of the last witness called. I succeeded him in his business in 1867. The books were then handed over to me, and they have since been in my keeping. They were never out of my custody until I sent them to my father. I looked for the entry of the jacket; that was at Canterbury, and I found it."

GEORGE ALLEN: "I live at Bath. I was butler to Mr. ROBERT TICHBORNE. For sixteen years I was in his service. He left my family a legacy. I knew Mr. ROGER TICHBORNE at Bath, but I remember him better at Tichborne Park. He was not at Bath more than four or five times." . . . "I saw him at the Royal Hotel, Bath, on October 10, 1867. . . I had an interview with him. I have no doubt whatever as to his identity. . . I had a conversation with him which lasted probably three or four hours. After that conversation, the conclusion at which I arrived was that I had no doubt at all about his being ROGER TICHBORNE. That is my opinion now."

THOMAS CARTER: "I was private servant in the army to Captain MORTON in the Carabineers. . . I remember first seeing Mr. TICHBORNE at Cahir in 1846. I was then in Captain MORTON'S service. . . I was afterwards in the service of Mr. TICHBORNE in 1852 and 1853 till he left the regiment. I am not in his service now. I left him on the 10th of December last."

"I first saw him after his return, in February, 1867."

"From what I saw then and since, I have not the slightest doubt the Claimant is Sir ROGER TICHBORNE. When I had satisfied myself he was the person he represented himself to be, I was ready to enter his service."

Sergeant-Major MOODIE: "I enlisted in the Carabineers in January 1844, and remained in the regiment till January, 1851."

"I remember Mr. R. C. TICHBORNE joining the regiment at Portobello Barracks, Dublin. When at Cahir he became an officer of the troop to which I belonged, and I had daily opportunities of knowing him and speaking to him. . ."

"I saw him, I believe, on the morning I left the regiment in December, 1851."

"I did not see him again till January, 1868. . . He recognised me first, and called me by my name. . . I had not the slightest doubt then that he was Mr. TICHBORNE. . . I have not the slightest doubt about the Claimant being Sir ROGER TICHBORNE. I can stand in this box, in front of the ladies and gentlemen here, and say without the slightest doubt that the Claimant is Sir ROGER TICHBORNE."

Sergeant THOMAS DUNNE: "I was in the 6th Dragoon Guards in 1847 until 1852. I am now in the 4th Dragoon Guards. I knew a gentleman called TICHBORNE who joined the regiment. I frequently saw him when he was orderly officer. The last time I saw him was in 1851."

"The next time I saw him was in 1867. . . I knew him after a few moments' observation of his features. . . I have no doubt he is the same man who was serving in the Carabineer regiment to which I was attached."

JOHN LESSWARE: "I reside at Liverpool. I am a Custom House officer. I formerly enlisted in the 6th Dragoon Guards, and became trumpet-major in the regiment, and continued so until 1851. . . I remember Mr. TICHBORNE joining the regiment at Portobello Barracks and subsequently becoming lieutenant in the same regiment. . . I delivered letters to him—the first on the 28th of October, 1849, and the last on the 4th of April, 1851. . . The Plaintiff then left for Clonmel, and I never saw him until April, 1868."

"I came to the Victoria Hotel, Liverpool, and saw Mr. TICHBORNE there. . . I was with him about four hours. . . I have not the slightest doubt he is the man. . . Looking at him now, I have not the slightest doubt as to his identity."

ANN LESSWARE: "I was married in the year 1841 to the last witness, and lived with him whilst he was in the regiment. I recollect Mr. ROGER TICHBORNE. I have frequently seen him in conversation with my husband, and I have a good recollection of his face and features. . ."

"I saw him again in 1868, at the Victoria Hotel, Liverpool. . . I had some conversation with him, and I am now perfectly certain he is Mr. TICHBORNE. I have not the slightest doubt about his identity. I had no serious doubt from the first when I met him in the passage. . . There is a strong resemblance, but he is much stouter."

THOMAS AUSTEN: "I am coachman to Mr. BOWYER, of New Brighton, in Cheshire. I remember entering the service of Mr. EDWARD DOUGHTY in 1842, at Upton. I lived with him seven years. I knew Mr. TICHBORNE after he left Stonyhurst. He was at his uncle's. I had to look after his horse. . . I remember coming to town when Mr. TICHBORNE was stopping at 39, Upper Grosvenor-street. I subsequently went with him to Knoyle, and afterwards to Tichborne Park. I was his groom and valet. I remember his first going to the regiment."

"I next saw the Plaintiff about a month ago. . . I had heard that he was an impostor, and expected to find him so. . . I now believe that he is Sir ROGER TICHBORNE. My deliberate belief on my oath is, that he is Sir ROGER TICHBORNE."

WILLIAM GOULD: "I have lived in Poole all my life. I was

acquainted with the late Sir E. DOUGHTY. I remember Sir ROGER. I knew him well, and have spent many days with him. I am a fisherman, and he, being fond of fishing and boating, used to go about with me. . ."

"On the 14th of October, 1867, I had a conversation with Mr. HENRY SEYMOUR. In consequence of what that gentleman told me, I went to the train which comes in in the afternoon. When the train arrived I saw Mr. TICHBORNE get out. I would swear to him anywhere. . . Any one who had known Sir E. DOUGHTY would know the Claimant."

MARIA GOULD (wife of the last witness): "I knew ROGER TICHBORNE about 1852 or 1853. My husband used to go shooting and fishing with him, and I saw him frequently. He sent for me after his return to England. I was ill, and could not go. He afterwards came to my house, and I recognised him among three gentlemen who were with him in a carriage. I am quite certain that the Claimant is Sir ROGER TICHBORNE. I knew him from his general appearance, and particularly his walk, his eyes, and his speech. . . I should have known him by his likeness to Sir EDWARD DOUGHTY: when you see Sir ROGER you see Sir EDWARD."

MARTHA LEGG: "I was living at Upton when Mr. R. C. TICHBORNE went there before going abroad. I did some laundry work for him, and saw him from time to time while staying there. I saw him at the Catholic church occasionally. I first heard of his having been lost at sea by hearing him prayed for in church. . ."

"After his return I saw him at the Lion Hotel in Poole. I went into a room in which I saw two gentlemen. . . I went over to one of them and said, 'How do you do, Sir ROGER?' . . . My opinion is that he is Sir ROGER, and that no other person could have said to me what Sir ROGER said when I went into the room.'"

The Rev. ROBERT GUY: "I am a priest of St. Anne's Catholic Church, Liverpool, and was educated at St. Gregory's full fifteen to seventeen years ago. Mr. ALFRED TICHBORNE was a pupil there for five years. I saw him just before he was married. He died. I only saw ROGER once; when he came to take leave of his brother. . ."

"I saw the Claimant on the 9th of October, 1867, at the railway-station at Winchester, and saw there was a likeness. I have seen him often since, and believe he is the brother of ALFRED—Sir ROGER. I have seen the Claimant on two or three occasions."

The Rev. RALPH COOPER, Incumbent of St. Augustine's Catholic Church, Liverpool: "I was president of a college in Yorkshire. I remember having met Mr. ROGER TICHBORNE at Mr. ROBERT TICHBORNE's at Bath. According to my recollection that was about 1848. I saw him at Mr. ROBERT TICHBORNE'S. I saw him in the street and elsewhere. I am under the impression that I saw him at Lord ARUNDEL's. That was in 1851 or 1852. I have a recollection of his appearance. It is not a strong recollection, but I had a reason for his appearance being impressed on my mind."

"I first saw him, after his return, in 1868. At that time I had formed a strong impression against him. My deliberate judgment now is that he is Sir ROGER."

Sir FREDERICK AUGUSTUS TALBOT CLIFFORD CONSTABLE: "I am Deputy-Lieutenant of the East Riding of Yorkshire. When young I used frequently to go to Paris with my parents. . . I used frequently to be associated with young ROGER TICHBORNE. I remember his coming on a visit to Burton Constable to spend the vacation. We were constant companions."

"It was about three years since I saw him again. That was at the Royal Station Hotel, at Hull. I took him to Burton Constable. He was there four or five days in my company. . . I afterwards arrived at the conclusion that the Claimant was ROGER TICHBORNE. . . From all I have observed I have no doubt but the present Claimant is the same ROGER TICHBORNE. . . I used to play with him when I was a boy. . . Formerly TICHBORNE and I were friends."

JOHN KERSLEY LIPSCOMBE: "I live at New Alresford, and am by profession a surgeon and a member of the Royal College of Surgeons. I have practised at Alresford for thirty-three years, and I am one of the medical officers of the Poor-law Board. Tichborne Park, the family seat of the TICHBORNES, is within three miles of my residence. I have been acquainted with them for years, and have attended the Family for years. I was acquainted with Mr. ROGER C. TICHBORNE. . . I saw him occasionally. I saw him in the hunting-field with the Hampshire hounds, and during his visit to the house on the occasion of Sir E. DOUGHTY's illness, I frequently saw him. . . I saw him twenty or thirty times altogether. . ."

"I saw the Claimant at Alresford at the end of February, 1867. . . I saw him on the 23rd of March, 1867. I passed several hours with him, and dined with him. . . I believe, undoubtedly, that he is the ROGER TICHBORNE whom I knew in 1852. . . Every time I have seen him my opinion as to his identity has been strengthened."

THOMAS COLE: "I was groom and footman to the late Sir HENRY JOSEPH and Lady ANN TICHBORNE. I was in their service for upwards of eighteen years. After the death of Sir HENRY, Lady ANN removed removed to Grove House, Brompton, and I remained in her service as butler. I remember Mr. R. C. TICHBORNE, and his visiting his aunt at Brompton. He stayed there for a considerable time, and used to come into the servants' hall to smoke his pipe after the ladies had retired to bed. . ."

"I remember seeing him again at Alfresford in 1867. . . Sir ROGER spoke to me before I recognised him. He said, 'Good morning, COLE; Do you recognise me?' and I said, 'Yes, sir, I do.' . . I felt his legs to see if the knee was turned in, and then I said, 'You are ROGER TICHBORNE.' . . I have not conversed with him since my affidavit was signed, about four years ago. I have not the least doubt that he is the ROGER TICHBORNE I knew at Lady ANN's."

FRANCIS J. P. MARX, Esq., of Arlbury House, near Alresford, Hampshire (within two miles of Tichborne Park): "I am a Justice of the Peace for the County, and Major of the Volunteers. I recollect seeing ROGER TICHBORNE when he was staying at Tichborne House. I remember him well in the hunting seasons of 1851 and 1852. . . I have a distinct recollection of his appearance, manner, and demeanour. Before his going abroad, I had two serious conversations with him about his going away. He said he was not comfortable at home, and that he should not return until his father died. . ."

"I have seen him since his return. He came to my house in June or July, 1867. My wife and my sister were present. . . I thought his face was familiar to me. I had a conversation with him. . . I have no doubt about his identity. . . I should call his manners that of a gentleman. His language was not that of society. . . I have heard of Wapping. His demeanour was not such as I should expect of a person from that neighbourhood."

NINIAN TERTIUS LOCKHART: "I am a flax-spinner, living at Kirkaldy. I went to Melbourne in 1853, and entered the firm of LUMSDEN and LOCKHART as shipowner. It was my duty to board all vessels on their arrival. I lived at Williamstown, and used to come up every day. . . I recollect going to Melbourne with Captain CARDEN in May, June, or July, 1854. . . Captain CARDEN pointed out some persons to me who were passengers like myself from Williamstown to Melbourne, a distance of about ten miles. . . They were like sailors coming off a ship. . . I saw no boxes or chests with them. . . A captain was not bound to report his arrival at Melbourne."

J. MOORE: "I have met the Claimant in the passage of the Court, but nowhere else [since the previous examination]. . . I have not the least doubt he is my old master. I swear that I never said to any one after the examination at the Law Institution that he was an impostor. If I expressed myself at all in the matter it was to the opposite effect. I might have said it to Mr. WALMESLEY, before the examination at the Law Institution, as I said it to many people at Croydon, but I am positive I never said it to any person after the examination."

GEORGE BINGLEY: "I reside in Norfolk-street, Strand. For forty years I lived in South America, and visited Santiago frequently. I was there in 1854, and visited the English Hotel. I was also there in 1853. I stayed nearly the whole of these two years. . . I recollect a stranger arriving at the hotel. It was notorious in the house that the gentleman was a young Englishman named TICHBORNE. He was accompanied by an attendant. He put up at the hotel, and I saw him every day. I dined with him at the same table, and saw him continually. He remained there for more than a week and less than a fortnight. . . He was remarked by the people in the house, and that fixed my attention on him more than it would otherwise have been. I frequently heard him converse. . . When at the table there was a peculiar pronunciation of some of his words."

"On the 26th of June, 1868, I had a visit from Mr. TICHBORNE. . . I talked to him for more than two hours. I recognised him within a minute. . . I was satisfied he was the individual. I have no doubt on the subject whatever."

JOSEPH MANNTON: "I am librarian to the Westminster Hospital. Formerly I was a sergeant-major in the 6th Dragoon Guards. I left the service in 1859. I recollect Mr. ROGER CHARLES TICHBORNE joining the regiment at Portobello Barracks. I was a private then. I saw him frequently. . . I was attached to the same company, and saw him frequently. In Clonmel I was with him for nearly a year, and then talked to him frequently."

[After his return.] "I saw him at Croydon for an hour. . . I saw him again in Victoria-street about the commencement of the trial. . . I believe him to be the Mr. TICHBORNE I knew in the Carabineers. . . I have no reason to modify the judgment I have formed respecting him. I believe him to be the man."

WILLIAM ANDREWS: "I was senior partner of the firm of Messrs ANDREWS & Co., helmet and accoutrement makers, 9, Pall Mall. . . I remember Mr. TICHBORNE perfectly well. I saw him from September, 1849, until he retired from the army in 1853. He had two months' leave of absence, and during that time I saw him frequently at his uncle's, 39, Upper Grosvenor-street, and in Pall Mall."

"I have seen the Claimant, and I haven't the least hesitation in declaring him to be the same person that we fitted out in 1849. . . I am perfectly ready to swear he is the man."

MICHAEL CARROLL: "I was formerly a private in the 6th Dragoon Guards. I am now a servant of Colonel SWINFORD. . . I remember Mr. ROGER C. TICHBORNE joining in 1849. I was attached to the troop which he commanded. . . I knew him well. . . I had opportunities of conversing with him."

"In December, 1867, I saw him for the first time since 1853. . . I remained in conversation with him a considerable time, and feel certain of his identity. . . I have no doubt whatever that the Claimant is the same gentleman who was an officer in the regiment."

HENRY RAINES (who wore several medals): "I was formerly in the Carabineers. In 1849 I recollect an officer named TICHBORNE joining the regiment when in Dublin. He was attached to the troop to which I belonged. . . I had frequent opportunities of seeing him. . . I went over in the same steamer with him to Herne Bay. . ."

"Since his return I have seen him several times. . . I was going down to his house to satisfy myself when I met him. . . I saluted him, when he stopped and said—'Your features I recollect, but I cannot remember your name.' I said, 'My name is RAINES.' When he said, 'Oh! Alonso!' . . . I have not the least doubt about him now."

FREDERICK MATHER: "I am by birth a Frenchman, and am in the employ of the London, Chatham and Dover Railway as an interpreter. In 1851 I enlisted in the Carabineers. . . I knew young TICHBORNE well."

"In February, 1868, I went to the Queen's Hotel, Leeds, and there saw the Claimant. . . I am positive he is the same man who was in the Carabineers in 1851 to 1853. [Pointing to the Claimant] That is the same gentleman."

ANDREW BOGLE: "I am 64 years of age. . . I have been very ill lately. I used to go out shooting and fishing with Mr. ROGER TICHBORNE. . . He used to make a good deal of noise with the French horn. . . In Sydney I used to take particular notice of every man I met from 1854 to 1866 to see if he were Sir ROGER or not."

"About the middle of August, 1866, I heard something from Captain DELVIT which caused me to go to the neighbourhood of the Metropolitan Hotel, Sydney, where I saw the Claimant. Directly I saw him I said he was Sir ROGER TICHBORNE. I knew him at the first glance."

PATRICK HOGAN: "I am now a private in the Royal Horse Guards Blue, stationed at Hyde Park Barracks. . . I entered the 6th Dragoon Guards in 1848, and remained in the regiment three years and nine months. I perfectly well remember young TICHBORNE joining. I saw him perhaps five days out of seven. I was with him sometimes for an hour and a half."

"In March, 1867, I saw the Claimant. I saw him also when coming out of Mr. HOLMES'S office. . . He is the same man who was in the regiment. I have not the slightest doubt on the subject."

Sergeant JAMES CAIRNS: "I am now a warden at Norwich Castle. I was twenty-four years in the Carabineers. . . I recollect Mr. TICHBORNE coming into the regiment in 1849. I was then drill-corporal, and drilled him a portion of drill—the foot-drill."

"I have not the slightest doubt but that the Claimant is the same man."

MARY ANN CAIRNS (the wife of the last witness): "I remember Mr. R. C. TICHBORNE joining the regiment. . . I had frequent opportunity of seeing him in the yard when drilling."

"I saw him next on the 29th of June, 1868, at the Duke Hotel, York. . . I have not any doubt whatever the Claimant is the Mr. TICHBORNE I knew in the regiment. . . I had not the slightest doubt he was the same man."

Mr. JOHN ANDREWS: "I am a son of Mr. ANDREWS, who was examined yesterday. . . I measured Mr. TICHBORNE for a helmet on the 1st September, 1849. . . I find an order entered by me on the 10th of April, 1852, for a dress pouch. . . and there are many other measurements in the book. There are two or three orders, but no alteration in the head is presented." . . The helmet fitted rather tight."

Colonel LUSHINGTON: "I am upon the record as the Defendant in this suit. I am in the capacity of tenant of Tichborne Park. Any interest I may have would be rather the other way than for the Claimant, as far as the money goes. . . I made his acquaintance on his return. Up to the time of his coming I had formed a decidedly unfavourable opinion of his claim."

"In February, 1867, I heard the Claimant was on a visit to Mr. HOPKINS, and I took the opportunity of being introduced to him. . . I walked over to Tichborne (from Alresford) with Sir ROGER.

"I have seen a good deal of him since, and have done all I could to bring him into communication with the members of his family. . ."

"I supported his wife and children during his absence when he went to Chili."

ARNOLD HAMLET: "I reside at Moss Bank, in Lancashire, and am troop sergeant-major in the Lancashire Yeomanry Cavalry. I was at one time troop-sergeant in the 6th Dragoon Guards—the Carabineers. I remember ROGER TICHBORNE joining at Portobello Barracks. I saw him nearly constantly. I saw him again in Liverpool after he had left the regiment."

"I saw the Claimant in Liverpool, at the Victoria Hotel, in 1868. . . I am of opinion that he is Mr. TICHBORNE of the Carabineers. I was an hour in conversation with him, and the more I talked with him, the more I became convinced it is he."

HENRY WOOD (of Willow Lodge, Mitcham, Surrey, Florist): "I was head-gardener at Tichborne Park from November, 1849, to the end of July, 1850, and frequently saw Mr. ROGER TICHBORNE." [After his return.] "I took an interest in the inquiry that was going on. There was a particular circumstance by which I should know Mr. TICHBORNE. I saw him at the Waterloo Hotel. Independently of his appearance, gait, and manners, I believe him to be Sir ROGER TICHBORNE. I picked him out as Sir ROGER from some gentlemen who were present."

Captain JACOB SANKEY: "I am a captain in the Royal Navy. I am upon the retired list. I am now residing at Coolmoor, in the county of Tipperary. . . I had known ROGER TICHBORNE when he was in the regiment quartered in Clonmel. I had a nephew in the regiment. He was a captain in Mr. TICHBORNE'S troop. I saw Mr. TICHBORNE frequently. I have a good recollection of his appearance." [After his return.] "I arrived at the conclusion he is the same young man I knew in the Carabineers. . . I certainly have not any doubt about his being the same man I knew in former years."

JAMES HOLMES: "I am a private in the 6th Dragoon Guards. I joined the regiment in 1849. I have served in the Crimea and India. I very well remember Mr. TICHBORNE being in the regiment. . ."

"About two years ago I heard of a person claiming the Tichborne estates. . . I looked, saw Mr. TICHBORNE, and knew him at once. . . I have not the least doubt in my mind that he is the same man."

HENRY MCELENY: "I am bandmaster of the 6th Dragoon Guards. . . At first I did not recognise Mr. TICHBORNE; but after I had conversed with him for some little time, and had got him to turn his face to the light, and then conversed with him again, I recognised him. . . I have not the slightest doubt about his being the person. . . I have not the slightest doubt now that he is the same person."

DAVID LESLIE, M.D.: "I was educated for the medical profession, though I have not followed it. I had a son, JOHN, who was in the Carabineers in 1851. . . On several occasions I dined in the mess-room at the Portobello Barracks, and when my attention was directed to Mr. TICHBORNE. . . I had on many occasions opportunities of seeing him and remarking him."

". . . . I was brought into the Court to have a look at the Claimant. I have formed the judgment that he was Sir ROGER TICHBORNE. I went into the Court with the impression that he was not Sir ROGER. I have not the slightest doubt about his being Sir ROGER TICHBORNE."

PATRICK BARRY: "I live at Mill-hill, Leeds, and carry on the business of a grocer and provision dealer. In 1831 I enlisted in the Carabineers, and in 1837 I was appointed servant to one of the majors. In 1855 I was discharged with a full pension. I remember Mr. R. C. TICHBORNE joining the regiment at Portobello Barracks. I occasionally waited upon him at mess. I remember his appearance."

"I had not seen him after he left the regiment until February, 1868. I formed the opinion he was the same ROGER TICHBORNE I knew when in the Carabineers. . . I am of opinion that the Claimant is the same person I knew in the Carabineers."

ROBERT COWEN: "I live at Dulwich, and am bandmaster of the London Irish Rifles. . . I used to see Mr. TICHBORNE in the Carabineers very often."

"My opinion is that he is the same Mr. TICHBORNE I had seen in the Carabineers. . . I still believe the same."

JAMES PLEGG LINDON: "I enlisted in the Carabineers in 1846. . . I remember Mr. TICHBORNE when lieutenant."

"About six months ago I was asked to come to London to see if I could recognise him again. . . I pointed him out directly. . . I have no doubt about his being the person."

JAMES MARKS: "I have been sergeant-major in the 4th Dragoon Guards. . . I was in the Carabineers in 1849, and I recollect TICHBORNE joining the regiment. . . I had many opportunities of seeing him daily. I left him in the regiment in 1852, when I joined the 4th Dragoon Guards. . ."

"In October, 1867, I saw him at the railway station, Alresford. . . I saw him in the waiting-room, and had a good look at him, and recognised him directly. . . I have not the slightest doubt he is the same man I knew in the Carabineers. . . The moment I had a fair look at him, I recognised him at once."

MARTIN BURKE: "In 1841 I enlisted in the 6th Dragoon Guards. . . I remember Mr. ROGER TICHBORNE coming to the Portobello Barracks in 1849. I had almost daily opportunities of seeing him and of speaking to him."

"I saw him [again] at Bolton at the end of January, 1868. . . Having seen him on those occasions, I believe he is ROGER TICHBORNE whom I knew in the Carabineers."

HENRY MILLS POWELL: "I reside at Basingstoke, and am a music-seller. I lived at Alresford, where I was a teacher of music. I taught young TICHBORNE the French horn, and he used to come to my house for that purpose."

"I do certainly believe him to be ROGER TICHBORNE."

ANN NOBLE: "I am the wife of HENRY NOBLE, of Tichborne. My husband was farm bailiff at Tichborne. I remember Mr. ROGER TICHBORNE quite well. I saw him very often before he went abroad."

"In December, 1866, I remember a strange gentleman came with Mr. ROUSE to Tichborne Farm. I saw in a moment that he was a member of the Tichborne Family. . . I went to see him at the Swan Hotel. I was quite certain the moment I saw him. I knew him directly. I have on all occasions expressed my opinion that he is Sir ROGER."

HENRY NOBLE: "I am farm-bailiff at Tichborne Park. . . I remember young TICHBORNE, and have spoken to him often."

"In February, 1867, I saw him on the platform at the railway station at Alresford. . . I knew him well the moment I saw him. . . My opinion is that he is the same TICHBORNE I saw as a youth at Tichborne. . . I believe he is the same man now."

JAMES HOWLISTON: "I am a poor-rate collector at Poole. I was in the employment, in 1851, of Mr. HOPKINS, a grocer and farmer. I saw Mr. TICHBORNE then several times."

"I went yesterday (Nov. 15) to see if I could recognise him. He is the same person."

WILLIAM BAILEY: "I am landlord of the Anchor Inn, at Ropley. . . Few people had more opportunities of seeing Sir ROGER than I had" [before he went abroad].

"I have seen the Claimant. He is the same man I knew as Sir ROGER TICHBORNE. There is not a single doubt about it."

WILLIAM COOPER: "I reside at Alresford, and am a bricklayer. I lived at Cheriton, within a mile and a half of Tichborne House. . . I knew the various members of the Tichborne family, including Roger. . . I often saw him from the beginning of 1847 till the end of 1852. . . I recollect his personal appearance very well. . . I have seen him a great many times since he came home in 1866. . . I saw him at Alresford on the last day in 1866. . . I recognised him in a minute or two. . . I have no doubt whatever that the Claimant is Sir ROGER TICHBORNE."

JEREMIAH COLE: "I was in the Carabineers twenty-five years and nine months. I was in the regiment in 1849. I recollect ROGER TICHBORNE joining in Dublin, but I was more acquainted with him when in Canterbury. . . I waited at mess regularly in my turn, and had opportunities of seeing Mr. TICHBORNE almost every day. I saw him on Friday last; the first time I had seen him since he left the regiment. I say that he is Sir ROGER TICHBORNE, whom I knew in the Carabineers. . . I am sure he is the same man. . . I am as sure he is Mr. TICHBORNE as I am that I am JEREMIAH COLE."

WILLIAM DAVIS: "I was in the 6th Dragoon Guards from 1840 to 1861, and went through the Crimean War and the Indian Mutiny. During my first year's service I was in the same company with him for about four hours and a half each day."

"I saw the Claimant yesterday. I had not seen him for eighteen years. . . He answered my questions satisfactorily."

GEORGE PIKE: "I was in the Carabineers in 1849, and remained till 1853. I knew ROGER TICHBORNE, an officer of the regiment, when we were quartered at the Portobello Barracks, Dublin. . . I had many opportunities of seeing him until he left the regiment."

"I saw the Claimant on the 21st of October, 1870, at the Waterloo Hotel, Jermyn-street. . . I believe him to be Sir ROGER TICHBORNE, the same gentleman I knew in the Carabineers."

THOMAS MARKS: "I was transferred to the 6th Dragoon Guards on the 26th of January, 1847. I remember Mr. ROGER TICHBORNE joining at Portobello Barracks in the latter part of 1849. He was the cornet of the troop to which I belonged. I used to see him daily, he being my squad officer at the time. The last time I saw him was on the 6th of April, 1850. I have a good recollection of his features and appearance. . ."

[After his return] "I saw him at the hotel, and immediately recognised him as Sir ROGER from amongst nine or twelve persons there. I had not the slightest difficulty about it. I have not the slightest doubt about his being the man, any more than I have about my own existence."

CHARLES PHILLIPS: "I am now a warder in the Kent County Prison, at Maidstone. I was in the 6th Dragoon Guards formerly, and was instructor of musketry at one time. I saw a good deal of Lieutenant TICHBORNE previous to his leaving in February, 1853, both mounted and dismounted."

"I next saw him last Friday, at the Waterloo Hotel. I saw that he was the Lieutenant TICHBORNE who was in the Carabineers. I have not the least doubt about it."

ELIZABETH INGLIS: "My first husband was in the Carabineers. I had many opportunities of seeing Mr. ROGER TICHBORNE at the time."

"I first saw the Claimant last Friday. I recollect sufficient of him to know that he is the man. I believe that he is Sir ROGER TICHBORNE."

WILLIAM ROBINSON: "I was in the Carabineers in 1849, and knew Mr. ROGER TICHBORNE when he joined the regiment at Portobello Barracks, Dublin. I left them in 1852."

"From that time I did not see Mr. TICHBORNE till 1868. I believed the Claimant to be Sir ROGER TICHBORNE. I had not any doubt at all about it. I knew the Claimant at once."

JOHN MORLEY, farmer and maltster, of Hampner, in the County of Southampton: "I have known the TICHBORNE Family for many years. For twenty-one years I lived with the two Sir HENRY'S. I knew Sir ROGER. I used to meet him, perhaps two or three times a day about the place. I used to see him in the housekeeper's room, where he would often go and talk about old times and about his forefathers."

"I saw him after his return to this country, about two years ago, at the Swan Inn, Alresford. . . I saw him twice. . . I have not the least doubt about his being Sir ROGER."

THOMAS PARKER: "I am a corndealer, and live near Alton, in Hampshire. I knew Mr. ROGER CHARLES TICHBORNE about the year 1850. He used to come riding to my house with Mr. JOHN GODWIN, one of the servants. I had dealings with him. I sold him a hunter."

"I have seen the Plaintiff in this case. I came to the conclusion that he was the same gentleman I knew in 1850. He described the horse perfectly. I have not the slightest doubt who he is."

ROBERT BROMBY: "I am commissioned out-door officer of Her Majesty's Customs, at Poole, and have held the position eighteen years. I saw Sir ROGER TICHBORNE frequently at Upton and Poole."

[After his return.] "The first time I saw him was at Poole Quay, in 1867. . . I have not the least doubt about his identity."

JOSEPH SMITH: "I am a gardener in the employ of Canon FISHER, who lives near Derings. . . I was for six years with Sir EDWARD DOUGHTY as under gardener. I knew ROGER TICHBORNE before he joined the army. I was in the habit of seeing him frequently when he was at Tichborne."

"I saw the Claimant on the 1st of February, 1870, in Jermyn-street. I recognised him by his walk, and being so like Sir HENRY TICHBORNE. I saw him afterwards at Alresford. I have not the slightest doubt he is Sir ROGER TICHBORNE."

MICHAEL ARTHUR HEALEY, a Licentiate of the College of Physicians in Dublin: "I remember seeing Mr. ROGER C. TICHBORNE at Buenos Ayres, in 1866. He came on board the 'City of Brussels' steamer, of which I was the surgeon. Two or three days after we left Rio I put him under examination. He was not in a state to undertake a long, difficult, or arduous journey. His maladies were of a serious and painful character."

WILLIAM WHITEAR BULPETT, Esq.: "I am a member of the firm of BULPETT and HALL, bankers, of Winchester. I am Justice of the Peace for the county. I know the whole of the TICHBORNE family. . . I had seen young Mr. TICHBORNE on several occasions when hunting. I recollect his features decidedly."

"I saw him in March, 1867. . . I said, 'I have great pleasure in recognising you as ROGER CHARLES TICHBORNE—as being the same gentleman I saw in the hunting-field.' I recognised him without any sort of hesitation whatever."

TERESA HUSSEY: "I am the wife of Mr. JAMES HUSSEY, of Upton. I was formerly in the service of Sir EDWARD DOUGHTY, at Tichborne. . . I saw ROGER TICHBORNE frequently. I had opportunities of seeing him for two or three years also at Upton. I think, in 1852 and 1853. I saw him every day at Tichborne. . . I danced with him at the ball."

"I have seen him once since he came from Australia, at Upton, about four years ago. I recognised him directly he came to my cottage. . . I have not the least doubt about who he is. He is ROGER TICHBORNE."

REV. ROBERT PINKNEY: "I am the Vicar of High Cliff Church, Hampshire. I knew Mr. TICHBORNE in his younger days. I saw him for two or three days at the Barracks, Dublin, and I have preserved a perfect recollection of his person since. . ."

"Yesterday was the first time I have seen him since I met him in Dublin, and as yet I have not spoken to him at all. I have a very strong and decided opinion that the present Claimant is the same man that I saw as ROGER TICHBORNE in the Carabineers. I have a very positive opinion about him."

FRANCIS LONGLAND: "I live on my own property in Northamptonshire. . . In 1854 I went from Melbourne to Sandridge. . . We all three took a boat and went on board the 'Osprey,' which was lying off Williamstown. I saw the 'Osprey,' which was a three-masted schooner. In consequence of something the two sailors told me I went on board the 'Osprey.' The sailors were Americans. I took them home, and they stopped with me two or three days, till they got a shift. I gave them board and lodging and clothes. They went off to Callao. They were not part of the 'Osprey's' crew. They were wrecked from the 'Bella.'"

HENRY CRABB: "I live at Upton, and am a gardener. I was in the employ of the late Sir EDWARD DOUGHTY for thirty-two years. I saw ROGER TICHBORNE at Upton often in 1852 or 1853. He was there about two months."

"I saw the Claimant in this action in October, 1867. I have not the slightest doubt he is the same man."

ELIZABETH STUBBS: "I am the wife of JAMES STUBBS, of West Tisted, in Hampshire. Tisted is part of the Tichborne Estate. I was born there, and knew Sir EDWARD DOUGHTY and Sir HENRY TICHBORNE well. I saw ROGER TICHBORNE often before he went away. He came there before he went away when he was sporting. He had lunch in my house."

"I have seen the Claimant in this case, the summer after he came back. I saw him at Alresford. . . I came to the conclusion that he was Sir ROGER TICHBORNE. I recognised him by the questions he asked me in October of the same year, at our house. He was there in the afternoon. . . I have not the least doubt about him."

JOHN BURDEN: "I live at Upton, and have lived there a great many years. In Sir EDWARD DOUGHTY'S time I worked on the farm. I remember Mr. ROGER TICHBORNE when there. I looked after his horses in the stable. I saw a great deal of him, almost every day."

"I have seen the Plaintiff in this case at our house at Poole, a couple of years ago. . . I thought he was the same man—ROGER TICHBORNE."

CHARLOTTE HOLDER: "I was in the service of Sir EDWARD DOUGHTY, as charwoman, for seven years. While there I saw much of ROGER TICHBORNE. I saw him enough to know him."

"I have not seen the Claimant except in the windows."

"I was at the Lady Dowager TICHBORNE'S funeral, and I recognised Mr. ROGER TICHBORNE coming out of the chapel at Tichborne. . . I have talked with him, and I have no doubt he is the right heir."

WILLIAM LILLYWHITE: "I am a shepherd in the employ of Mr. STUBBS, on the Tichborne Estate. I was a servant of Sir EDWARD DOUGHTY when he was staying at Tichborne. I used to look after the poultry. I used to see Mr. ROGER TICHBORNE there when he came on a visit to his uncle. I used to see him enough to know his personal appearance."

"I saw him at the Swan Hotel, at Alresford, on the 1st July, 1867. I thought he was Sir ROGER TICHBORNE. . . I have no doubt about it."

HENRY JACKSON: I am a gardener, living at Poole. I saw Mr. ROGER C. TICHBORNE there in 1852 and 1853. I used to see him frequently about the farm with Mr. HOPKINS, my young master."

"I saw the Claimant in 1866 or 1868 at the London Hotel at Poole, after his return to England. I recognised him as the gentleman I had seen before at Upton and Tichborne in 1852. I have not the least doubt who he is."

Sergeant BEAKEN: I am now a sergeant of police at Poole. I was employed in the stables at Upton during Sir EDWARD DOUGHTY's time, and saw Mr. ROGER TICHBORNE there in 1841 and 1842."

"I never saw him again until I met him in Poole. I saw him in October, 1867, at the London Hotel, in Poole. I recognised the Claimant as Sir ROGER TICHBORNE. . . I recognised him from the Family likeness."

Mr. FRANCIS JOSEPH BAIGENT: "I reside at Winchester, and have done so all my life. My father is the drawing-master at Winchester College. . . I am an Associate of the Archæological Association. . . I have been acquainted with the TICHBORNE Family from my childhood, and had associated with members of the Family. I knew the father of Sir ROGER and Sir EDWARD DOUGHTY well. . . I knew the mother of Sir ROGER very intimately indeed. I remember Mr. ROGER before he went abroad, perfectly well. . . I was in his company fifty or sixty times perhaps. On several occasions he and I associated alone, without company. I saw him at Winchester within two or three months of his leaving England. . . I continued on terms of intimacy with members of his Family after he left."

"On the 31st December, 1866, I saw him at the back of the Swan at Alresford. He was about thirty or forty yards off, and Mr. HOPKINS said, "There is Sir ROGER. Depend upon it he knows us both."

"I have not any doubt at all that he is the ROGER TICHBORNE I knew in former days. There is no possibility for one to have any doubt.

Mrs. JUDITH WOODMAN: "I am the wife of Mr. WOODMAN, a clerk in the employ of Messrs. HOLMES and Co., of Stroud. . . I had known ROGER TICHBORNE when the Carabineers lay at Cahir Barracks. My father and mother kept the park gates, and Mr. TICHBORNE used to pass through two or three times a day.

"I knew the Claimant the instant I looked at him. Mr. BOWKER paid my expenses. . . I have not the least doubt he is the ROGER TICHBORNE I knew in Ireland. . . I had seen no one connected with the Claimant before I saw himself."

Mrs. PEARCE: "My husband is BENJAMIN PEARCE, of Stroud. Before I was married I resided with my father and mother, who were lodge-keepers to the Earl of GLENGALL. I lived there at the time the Carabineers were quartered in Cahir, and I was in the habit of seeing the officers every day. I recollect amongst them Mr. ROGER TICHBORNE. I saw him frequently going in and out of the park. . ."

"The last day I saw the Claimant he was coming out of the Court at Westminster. I came to the conclusion he was the Mr. TICHBORNE I knew in the Carabineers. . . I said, 'That is Mr. TICHBORNE and no one else.' That night Mr. BOWKER asked us if we wished to go home, and we said we did very much, and he paid us our expenses, and we left town. Since that I have seen the Claimant coming into this Court, and I have no doubt about his being the same man."

JAMES BEAKAN, a sergeant of the 8th Hussars, who wore four medals and a number of clasps: "I was formerly in the Carabineers, and knew Mr. ROGER CHARLES TICHBORNE. We were drilled in the same class together for about twelve months."

"I have seen the Claimant at the Waterloo Hotel, on the 23rd of last month. I came to the conclusion he was the ROGER TICHBORNE I knew in the Carabineers. . . I have not the slightest doubt."

THOMAS RATCLIFF: "I am a sergeant in the First Sussex Rifle Volunteers. I was in the Carabineers for upwards of twenty-one years, and knew Mr. TICHBORNE well. I saw him drill, and he stood beside me in the ranks."

"In November, 1867, I was at Brighton, when I saw two gentlemen near the Grand Hotel, and was struck with the appearance of one of them. I thought I knew him. I looked at his countenance, and then at his walk, and was convinced it was Mr. TICHBORNE. I did not know that Sir ROGER was in Brighton at the time, and little expected to see him there. . . I have not the least doubt in the world about his being Mr. TICHBORNE."

JOHN HENRY MUNDAY: "I am assistant-warder at the convict-prison at Chatham. I was in the Carabineers for ten years, and knew Mr. TICHBORNE well. I drilled him on several occasions."

"I saw the Claimant again on the 22nd of November, coming into the Court, and I identified him as Mr. TICHBORNE . . . I have not the slightest doubt upon the matter."

THOMAS DORNEY: "I am a hair-dresser at Clonmel. I remember the Carabineers being quartered at Clonmel, as I had the honour of cutting the officers' hair. I remember an officer who I thought belonged to the Carabineers, but I was not sure. He had a mark at the back of his head, and I had to leave the hair a little longer to cover it. . . I cut his hair more than once, and I knew him well."

"I saw the Claimant, in this case, about three weeks ago at the Waterloo Hotel. I examined the back of his head, and found there a similar mark to that which was on the head of the officer whose hair I had the honour of cutting about twenty years ago. It was the same kind of mark, both in appearance and position. . . Upon my oath, no one had told me where to find the mark."

Sir W. FERGUSSON: "I was requested to see the Claimant in this suit with a view to making an examination of his person. I saw him in conjunction with Mr. CANTON, and afterwards with two other surgeons. I examined certain marks on the ankles. There were several scars, or what might be called scars, under the ankle, which were not particularly distinct, except the one under the left ankle, which was a clear mark of the kind. I should attribute those marks to wounds.—Would they be accounted for by the incision of a lancet? They might be so. I could not say positively. The one that is distinct is a decided incision. . . A thorough incision of a lancet would have made such a mark. There was a round scar on the front of the left forearm. There must have been a large boil, or some wound there at some previous time. . . I found the vaccination marks in the usual place, on the outside of the shoulder, on each arm. One was larger and more distinct than those we see in England. I found a scar in the outer edge of the right eyebrow. It must have penetrated the skin deeply. It was a scar which might have been produced by a fish-hook, or a cut to take a fish-hook out. There was a very distinct scar on the bridge of the nose, and indications that the bones in that locality had been broken. . . He looked what you would call an in-kneed man. . . There was a scar on the back of the head, about three-quarters of an inch long. . . There was a brown mark on his left side, about three or four inches long, and about three in breadth. . . It was very pale, but still distinct. . . His hands were what you might call fat hands, and in such you generally find that the knuckles appear the smallest part of the fingers. . . They were soft hands. The knuckles were not so marked as in other hands. They were supple. They could be pressed back easily. . . The left thumb is peculiarly pointed about the extremity—unusually so. The flesh part projects beyond the nail more than usual, and more than in the other hand. The photograph (taken of Sir ROGER in South America) shows an exact representation of the thumb of the Claimant.

Dr. SUTHERLAND, Dr. CANTON, and Dr. THORP were examined to the same effect.

Captain STUART WORTLEY: "I have retired from the army, and have for many years given attention to the science of photography. . . I have experience of daguerreotypes as well as photographs. . . There are marks on the daguerreotype (of ROGER TICHBORNE) that are not on the photograph. There are some smudges about the edge of the daguerreotype which could not have been there when the photographs were taken. In every other respect the photographs seem to have been taken from it. . . The daguerreotypes appear to have been rubbed with some coarse, sandy matter."

Mr. W. SAVAGE and Mr. J. TAYLOR, were examined to the same effect.

CHARLES LOCOCK WEBB, Q.C.: "I was originally retained for the Claimant when the cause first came before the Chancery Court. . . I advised the Claimant. . . I laid great stress on the recognition of the Claimant by his mother, and on the fact that his identity had not been disputed by any one who knew him and was disinterested. . . I am of opinion that Sir ROGER could not fail in establishing his identity; and Claimant had been well advised in offering to his relations every opportunity of satisfying themselves upon the point. Claimant had now done all that could be expected of him, and the conduct of his relatives was most unjustifiable, for they had at once stigmatised him as an impostor. . . I believed that the recovery of the estates was a mere matter of time."

Mr. J. F. ADAMS was examined with regard to deeds, &c.

Mrs. ROSALIND LANSDERG was examined with regard to his language.

Colonel MACKINNON: "I was formerly in the Carabineers. I left the regiment a few months before TICHBORNE joined. I met him at dinner at Colonel LUSHINGTON's, about three years ago. . . I found he remembered many things a regimental officer ought to remember. One thing in particular he remembered which occurred on the occasion of my dining with the regiment."

It may be as well to supplement this astounding body of direct evidence by a few extracts from the Plaintiff's own affidavit, as read by Mr. HAWKINS in the Common Pleas:—

23. The said Sir JAMES FRANCIS DOUGHTY TICHBORNE died on the 11th day of June, 1862, leaving his wife, the said HENRIETTE FELICITE, and myself, his eldest son and heir-at-law, and the said ALFRED JOSEPH TICHBORNE, his only issue, him surviving.

24. Upon the death of the said Sir JAMES FRANCIS DOUGHTY TICHBORNE, I succeeded to the title, and became the eleventh Baronet of TICHBORNE, and also became, and I am now, entitled, as tenant for life in possession, to the TICHBORNE estates settled by the said indenture, of the 4th day of May, 1844, under the limitations therein contained.

25. I resided with my parents at Paris from the date of my birth until the year 1845, when I was brought over to this country, and was shortly afterwards placed at Stonyhurst College, Lancashire, where I received my English education.

26. In the month of July, 1849, I was appointed cornet, and subsequently lieutenant, in Her Majesty's 6th Dragoon Guards (Carabineers). I joined that regiment in the month of October, 1849, at Dublin, where it was then quartered, and remained on duty with the regiment from the month of October, 1849, until the month of January, 1853 (except during temporary leave of absence). I retired from the regiment in the month of February, 1853.

27. During my vacation from college, and while on leave of absence from my regiment, I usually resided, from the year 1845 until I left this country to travel in foreign parts, as hereinafter mentioned, with my uncle, the said Sir EDWARD DOUGHTY, at Tichborne Park, the family seat of the TICHBORNES; and I was in the habit of shooting over the TICHBORNE Estates, and hunting in that neighbourhood, and I gave up much of my time to field sports and the management of horses.

28. I left my regiment with the object of travelling for some years in distant parts, and in the first instance I determined to proceed to South America. In the month of March, 1853, I took passage on board a ship bound for Valparaiso, where I arrived in due course, and from that time until the month of April, 1854, I travelled from place to place in various parts of South America.

29. In the month of April, 1854, the ship "Bella," of Liverpool, Captain BIRKETT, master, was at the port of Rio de Janeiro, and learning that she was bound, and shortly intended to leave that port, for New York, I took my passage in the "Bella" for that city. The "Bella" left the port of Rio on the morning of the 20th day of April, 1854, with myself on board, and proceeded on her voyage. To the best of my recollection and belief, when she left Rio the crew of the "Bella" (including the captain) consisted of about seventeen persons, I being the only passenger on board.

30. All went well until the fourth day after the "Bella" had left Rio, and was far out of sight of land, but on the morning of that day the mate reported to the captain that she had sprung a leak, and all hands were instantly set to work at the pumps, and every effort was made to save the ship, but without effect. Very shortly after the mate reported the leak, it became apparent the vessel was fast filling with water, and the captain announced that all further efforts to save the ship were useless, and that all on board must instantly take to the boats.

31. The "Bella" carried a longboat on deck, and two smaller boats, one of which was swung from the davits on each quarter.

THE OSPREY.

One of the small boats was stove in and rendered useless, but the crew succeeded in safely lowering upon the sea the longboat and the other boat, which was the larger of the two small ones, hereinafter referred to as the "second boat," and in stowing some provisions and casks of water into the boats. I and, to the best of my recollection and belief, eight of the crew got into the second boat, and the captain, and, to the best of my recollection and belief, the rest of the crew got into the longboat, and immediately pushed off from the "Bella," and the ship "Bella" soon afterwards sank.

32. The captain, who had in the longboat the ship's charts, ordered that the second boat should keep in sight of the longboat, which she did for two days, but in the night of the second day a high wind and storm came on, and the boats were soon out of sight of each other, and the longboat was not again seen by those in the second boat. The man who had the command of the second boat then determined to let her drift with the wind. On the morning of the fourth day after the "Bella" had sunk, the crew of the second boat descried a ship in the distance, and used every means to reach her and to attract notice, and for that purpose a red flannel shirt, which one of the crew of the boat wore, was attached to an oar and hoisted as a signal. Ultimately a signal was made in reply, and the crew of that boat rowed to the ship, and I and the whole of the crew on board the second boat were thus saved, after we had been three days and nights at sea in an open boat.

33. I was in a very exhausted state when I was rescued, and I was for some time seriously ill on board the ship which saved me, but I was landed at the port of Melbourne, in Australia, about the end of July, 1854.

34. I had saved nothing from the "Bella" except the clothes I wore, and when I landed at Melbourne I had no means whatever there for my support.

35. On the first day I landed, the captain of the ship which brought me to Melbourne took me to an office, which I believe was the Custom-house, and had a conversation with some person there as to what should be done for me, but nothing was arranged except that I should be allowed to sleep on board the ship that night, which I accordingly did. Before returning to the ship the captain and I together called at an office, and made inquiries for the purpose of ascertaining how I could get a passage to England, but without any useful result. I learnt that Melbourne was then in a very unsettled state in consequence of the gold mania, that the crews of the ships as they arrived very frequently deserted for the gold-diggings, and that there was consequently great difficulty in procuring a passage to England. There was a great

number of ships then in the port unable to start for want of hands.

36. On the day after I first landed at Melbourne I was strolling about the town, and went into a yard called Row's-yard, situate in Burke-street, Melbourne, where a large number of horses were being sold. I was much attracted by what was taking place, and a person, whom I afterwards discovered to be Mr. WILLIAM FOSTER, an extensive stock-keeper of Gippsland, spoke to me, and after ascertaining that I was a good rider, offered to take me with him to Gippsland, where there was good hunting and shooting.

37. I accepted such offer, and for family reasons I assumed the name of TOMAS CASTRO (after that of a friend named DON TOMAS CASTRO, whose acquaintance I had made at Melipilla, in Chili), and I continued to use, and was known in Australia by the name of TOMAS CASTRO until shortly prior to my return to England as hereinafter mentioned.

38. I immediately afterwards left Melbourne with Mr. FOSTER and his horses, and proceeded to Mr. FOSTER'S station at Boisdale, in Gippsland, on the Avon River, nearly 300 miles from Melbourne, where I remained about nineteen months. Mr. FOSTER then gave me charge of the Dargo station, in the Australian Alps, about 115 miles farther inland, where I remained for about eighteen months, and then returned to Boisdale, when after staying for about three months, I travelled about and remained at various places, as in the 38th paragraph of my said Bill mentioned.

39. On the 29th of January, 1865, I intermarried with MARY ANN BRYANT, spinster. I and my wife are both Roman Catholics, but, being then desirous of concealing my real name, which I could not have done if the marriage had been solemnised by a priest of the Church of Rome, inasmuch as I must, prior to my marriage, have attended the confessional, my said marriage was solemnised by the Rev. FREDERICK THOMAS BRENTWILL, a minister of the Wesleyan Church, at the residence of Mrs. ROBINSON, of Wagga-Wagga, I being then married under my assumed name of TOMAS CASTRO.

40. I and my wife thenceforth continued to reside at Wagga-Wagga, passing under the assumed name of CASTRO, until shortly prior to my return to England, as hereinafter mentioned.

41. I have been informed by my mother, and believe, that in or about the year 1858, a sailor, whose name is unknown to me, solicited alms at Tichborne Park, and represented that he had come from Australia; and that she had a conversation with the sailor, and made inquiries of him as to whether he had ever heard of the "Bella" or any of her crew having been saved, and that the sailor replied that he had heard, when in Australia, of some of the crew of a ship, which he thought was the "Bella," having been picked up at sea and brought to Melbourne. I have also been informed by Mr. FRANCIS JOSEPH BAIGENT, of Winchester, that he was then at Tichborne Park on a visit, and that at the request of my mother, he, the said Mr. BAIGENT, then saw the sailor and made the like inquiries of him, and that he repeated to the said Mr. BAIGENT the information he had previously given to my mother as aforesaid, but that no information as to myself, nor any further or more definite information as to the "Bella" or her crew, could be obtained from the sailor.

42. I have been informed by my mother, and believe, that my father, to whom the statement made by the sailor was communicated, expressed the opinion that it was not worth notice, and that no further notice was taken of such statement in his lifetime, save that my mother frequently referred to it, and that when the marriage between her younger son and the Hon. TERESA MARY JOSEPHINE ARUNDEL was in contemplation, she stated that she had a presentiment that I was still alive.

43. I have also been informed by my mother, and believe, that after the death of my father, and in the year 1863, she caused advertisements for me, in the English, French, and Spanish languages, to be inserted in the *Times* newspaper, and that she some time subsequently communicated with Mr. ARTHUR CUBITT, of the Missing Friends' Office, Bridge-street, Sydney, New South Wales, advertising agent, and that the said Mr. CUBITT, by her direction, caused advertisements to be inserted in various newspapers published at Melbourne, Sydney, and elsewhere, announcing the death of my father, and giving a description of me, and offering a reward for my discovery.

44. Ultimately, and towards the end of the year 1865, I for the first time learnt, by means of such advertisements, of my father's death; and in the early part of January, 1866, I wrote and sent a letter to my mother, informing her that I had at last made up my mind to face the sea once more, and requesting that money might be sent out to enable me to return to England. I had been informed by my mother, and believe, that she received such letter in course of post, and that she wrote and sent me a letter urging my immediate return, and I have been informed by my mother, and believe, that she subsequently remitted a draft for £100 to defray the expenses of the voyage.

45. As soon as practicable, in the year 1866, I made arrangements to return home with my wife and child, without waiting the receipt of the draft. I believe that such draft reached Australia after I had left for England, and I have been informed by my mother, and believe, that the same draft has since been returned to her through the post.

46. Having determined to return to England, I, on the 9th day of July, 1866, again went through the ceremony of marriage with my wife under my proper name at the Roman Catholic Church of St. Peter and St. Paul, at Goulbourne, New South Wales, according to the rites of the Church of Rome, the ceremony on that occasion being solemnised by the Rev. MICHAEL M'ALROY, a priest of that Church. There has been issue of my said marriage two children, and no more—namely, TERESA MARY AGNES, the before-mentioned child, who was born at Wagga-Wagga aforesaid, on the 18th day of March, 1866, and the above-named Defendant, ROGER JOSEPH DOUGHTY TICHBORNE, who was born at Croydon as aforesaid, on the 1st day of May, 1867.

47. While remaining at Sydney, previous to my embarkation, I accidentally met there a person named GUILFOYLE, who was for many years in the employ of my uncle, the said Sir EDWARD DOUGHTY (deceased). When I was at Sydney, GUILFOYLE was, and I believe that he is now, carrying on business there as a nurseryman. GUILFOYLE and his wife, who also saw me at Sydney, well knew me before I left England in the year 1853, and upon seeing me at Sydney they recognised me as the eldest son of the said Sir JAMES FRANCIS DOUGHTY TICHBORNE.

48. I also met at Sydney ANDREW BOGLE, who also had for many years been in the employ of my uncle, the said Sir EDWARD DOUGHTY, as valet, and to whom I was well known before I left England in the year 1853. The said ANDREW BOGLE, upon meeting me at Sydney, also recognised me as the eldest son of the said Sir JAMES FRANCIS DOUGHTY TICHBORNE, and the said ANDREW BOGLE at his own request accompanied me to England.

49. I have been informed by the said ANDREW BOGLE, and believe that he, the said ANDREW BOGLE, acting in the full belief that my relatives would be glad to hear that I was alive and had been recognised by one who knew me well, shortly before his embarkation, sent to my aunt, Dame KATHERINE DOUGHTY, a letter informing her of the fact, and that I and himself were about to embark for England. I believe that such letter was received by the said Dame KATHERINE DOUGHTY, in course of post, and in or about the month of October, 1866, and that the said Dame KATHERINE DOUGHTY at once communicated the contents of such letter to the above-named Defendants, TERESA MARY JOSEPHINE DOUGHTY TICHBORNE, WILLIAM STOURTON, and RENFRIC ARUNDELL.

50. In the month of September, 1866, I, my wife, and child embarked at the port of Sydney, on board the "Rakaia," bound for Panama, and having arrived there, proceeded across the Isthmus to Aspinwall, and from thence, by way of New York, to England, and arrived on the 25th day of December, 1866, at the Victoria Docks, Limehouse, on board the steamship "Cella."

51. Shortly afterwards, and in the same month of December, I visited Alresford, near to Tichborne, and found that Tichborne House was occupied by Colonel LUSHINGTON. Having remained at Alresford a few days, I returned to London, and subsequently stayed for a few days at the Clarendon Hotel, Gravesend. On or about the 5th of January, 1867, the Defendant VINCENT GOSFORD, accompanied by Mr. PLOWDEN, a distant relative of mine, and Mr. CULLINGTON, of the firm of Messrs. SLAUGHTER and CULLINGTON, solicitors for several of the Defendants hereto, visited Gravesend and saw me.

52. On Tuesday, the 8th day of January, 1867, the said VINCENT GOSFORD again called upon me and had a prolonged interview with me at the said hotel, and accompanied me in the train to London. During such interview I and the said VINCENT GOSFORD discussed various matters and circumstances relating to the TICHBORNE and DOUGHTY families, and the neighbourhoods of Tichborne and Upton, with which we were both familiar. The said VINCENT GOSFORD has since had another interview with me, and I then again very fully discussed with the said VINCENT GOSFORD such matters and circumstances, and recalled to the memory of the said VINCENT GOSFORD various facts which occurred previous to my leaving England in the year 1853, some of which were only known to me and the said VINCENT GOSFORD; and the said VINCENT GOSFORD admitted that some of such facts had escaped his recollection until they were recalled to his memory by me, but that he then well remembered that such facts did occur as stated by me, and I proved to the said VINCENT GOSFORD beyond a shadow of doubt that I was the eldest son of the said Sir JAMES FRANCIS DOUGHTY TICHBORNE.

53. I verily believe that no circumstance whatever has arisen to lead or to justify the said VINCENT GOSFORD in raising any doubt whatever as to my identity.

A few days after the Defendant's committal to Newgate, the following Letter appeared. It is stated to have been written by one of the Judges.

TO THE EDITOR OF THE "DAILY NEWS."

SIR,—I have frequently remarked your generous advocacy of the unfortunate and the distressed, and I now appeal to you in the name of suffering thousands, if not millions, of my fellow-countrymen. The transference of the Claimant to Newgate has only deepened our despair; for if the prophet has been hitherto an enigma, the veiled and concealed prophet has now become a torture. I can assure you, sir, that my fellow-countrymen and myself expect nothing less from the Government—a Government which has shown its paternal tendencies in Habitual Criminals Bills and the like—than a full and clear explanation of a mystery which has for months back been a burden to our lives. Naturally the most peaceful and loyal of subjects, we are driven to desperation by suspense. If the Claimant were proved to be ARTHUR

DOOLAN we should be happy. If it were demonstrated that he is ARTHUR ORTON, we should all say to our friends, "I told you so." If it turns out to be that he is Mr. MORGAN the Bushranger—a gentleman whose antecedents are buried in obscurity—we should calmly accept our fate. If, after all, he should turn out to be Sir ROGER TICHBORNE, the hearts of many would be gladdened. But in the meantime, sir, we are not all lawyers or persons of clear convictions and decisive judgments; and the necessity of being buffeted about by all the stray winds of opinion is a serious matter for a human being who values his digestion.

My own experience cannot be exceptional, unless in so far as I possess a tendency to believe in my friends. I cannot imagine that they are all unreasoning, ignorant, and prejudiced persons; and yet, when I try to give due weight to their various hints and assurances, I find that the only result is that they express doubts about my being able to comprehend the simplest argument. Many a time I have wished the Claimant at the bottom of the sea—if it were possible for so stout a person to sink. I have believed and disbelieved in him a hundred times during the course of the trial. I have considered him a martyr when the Solicitor-General was pestering him with questions; I have darkly suspected him while Mr. BAIGENT was being cross-examined. But all the perplexity of the case heretofore is as nothing to what it is now. Every man one meets has his own theory. "Don't you see what an obvious conspiracy that business of the tattoo marks was? Don't you know what the Catholics are doing?" says one. I confess I have no such knowledge. "Now, *do* you really believe this man is the young Englishman who knew French, music, chess, and a dozen other accomplishments?" inquires another. I admit that I don't. "Why," says a third, "are you not aware that the Claimant at this moment can play an excellent game at chess, and perform very passably on the piano? He was dazed during his cross-examination. Mr. So-and-so told me only yesterday that he had himself played a game at chess with him, and been considerably smashed up, that's all!" Well, I did not know the Claimant could play music and chess admirably; but I know my friend does not tell lies—as a general rule; and so the weathercock once more makes a right half-face.

It is really too bad. You ask a man whether he considers the Claimant an impostor; and at the very moment that he answers Yes, he begins to throw out mysterious hints. There is more involved in the case than meets the eye, he says. It is a strange thing that no one has come forward to swear that this man is ARTHUR ORTON. If you were to go to Australia, he remarks, and pass yourself off as somebody else, would not a hundred persons be procurable to swear you were yourself? That is a contingency you have not contemplated, and so the orator triumphs. Then he throws out other dark suggestions. What did Sir JOHN COLERIDGE mean by referring to a "fugitive likeness?" Is it not an astonishing thing that this man, whoever he may be, is acknowledged by his opponents to have given out vague stories, on his first arrival in South America and throughout his subsequent career, of his belonging to an English family of distinction who were Catholics? "Well," you say, with some natural indignation, "if you place such store by these things—if you believe that they mean anything—how do you come to have so clear a conviction that this man is an impostor?" Of course, your friend does not answer. He smiles in a mysterious and compassionate manner—conveying to you in a gentle way his impression that you are a born idiot. Sir, the sufferings which harmless and well-meaning people like myself have to bear in this way are too grievous to be borne.

Then as to that question of the likeness. At one moment I am enticed by the beautiful legends of a portrait of the Claimant having been mistaken by several members of Parliament for that of the gentleman whom he called, if I remember rightly, "Uncle ALFRED;" and no sooner have I given ear to these stories than some other friend, smiling in a curious way, as if he were guilty of a monstrous condescension in even mentioning the case, asks me to explain away the startling likeness between the Claimant and ARTHUR ORTON's sister. I can't do it. I am not anxious to do it. But I want to know who and what this man is, so that my puzzled fellow-countrymen and myself may recover their faith in the infallibility of the British jury. Only yesterday, now, a most excellent and intelligent lady told me she had been in the Westminster Sessions-house when Mr. SEYMOUR and the Claimant were both present, and that she had scarcely ever in her life seen two people more alike in facial features; but when I proceeded to ask her whether she considered the Claimant to be Sir ROGER TICHBORNE, she drew back altogether from that conclusion. No wonder. We are all in a fog; and we are becoming apprehensive that the Claimant may be spirited away before the mystery is cleared up.

Another conundrum which is being continually thrust before us unfortunate people who cannot reconcile contradictory statements, and so arrive at a judgment, is the manner of the Claimant. All the ladies who have been in court declare that his manner is most quiet, self-possessed, and courteous—in a word, gentlemanly; and I am asked to show how a butcher in Australia could have taught himself so much, even after two or three years' study. Of course I can't explain that, or anything else belonging to the case. But I should prefer that my friends who point out these things would say that they are a proof that the Claimant is ROGER TICHBORNE. They won't do that; they leave me in worse doubt than ever. They take it for granted he is not ROGER TICHBORNE; they hint that he cannot be a butcher; and who, then, is he? I am not sufficiently acquainted with the career of Mr. DOOLAN to say that such manners might be his. As for MORGAN, the bushranger, I hope there was such a person, but I should not have liked to meet him on a dark night, about fifty miles from anywhere. I do not think he is likely—or was likely, perhaps I ought to say, for careers are cut short sometimes in Australia, as the Attorney-General hinted—to have a very polished manner. Indeed, if it comes to that, for all I can read and hear about ROGER CHARLES TICHBORNE, I can scarcely avoid the conclusion that the Claimant has too much shrewdness and *savoir faire* to be a possible development of the gawky lad who escaped from the jeers of his brother-officers to console himself with the sickly sentimentality of CHATEAUBRIAND. That has been the nearest approach to an opinion I have been able to form, amid the distraction of the various bits of special information and confident assurance which have been freely tendered me. But it leaves me only where I was—in a darkness worse than the darkness of Egypt.

Now, sir, what will it cost to prosecute the Claimant? I am told—but this is only one of the opinions that have been clouding the air lately—that it will be impossible to convict him of perjury. If he be a rank impostor, I should like to see him convicted of all the crimes in the statute-book; but that may be merely one of the prejudices I am anxious to banish from myself. What I say, on behalf of thousands of my fellow-countrymen, is, that a twentieth part of the sum likely to be spent by the Government might be profitably employed as an offer to the Claimant to tell us who he is, accompanied by a guarantee that no further proceedings would be taken against him. I am afraid my proposal is horribly out of consonance with legal rule, and probably with justice; but I look upon the real question at issue as one of comparative results. If the Claimant is tried, acquitted, and allowed to return to his native wilds, and to the picturesque if disagreeable duties of a butcher's shanty, we shall have our belief in the English jury, and in the English Attorney-General, terribly shaken; while the problem as to who was the Claimant, and whence his origin, will remain to disturb the peace of many families, and break the equanimity of many an after-dinner talk. On the other hand, if the enigma weighing twenty-six stone, who is now in Newgate, be convicted of perjury, without some definite statement being made as to his antecedents, the same blind confusion and contradiction of belief will continue among us. I am sure I don't know what Mr. GLADSTONE thinks about the case. Perhaps he could prove to you in the same speech that the Claimant is and is not an impostor; but if he would kindly direct the law officers of the Crown to find out, as far as they can, the difference between ROGER TICHBORNE, ARTHUR DOOLAN, ARTHUR ORTON, TOM CASTRO, and MORGAN the Bushranger, he would confer an immense favour on a multitude of his admirers, and on yours truly, FACING-BOTH-WAYS.

March 12, 1872.

To this letter the following answer appeared, written by Mr. LABOUCHERE:—

WHO IS HE?

TO THE EDITOR OF THE "DAILY NEWS."

SIR,—The suggestion of your correspondent "Facing-Both-Ways," that some offer should be made to the "Claimant" to tell us who he is, is an exceedingly sensible one. If he is not Sir ROGER, he appears at least to have thrown the world off his scent as to his real identity. Many have made up their minds that he is an impostor, but whether he be ORTON, CASTRO, or DOOLAN, is a question which no one is able to solve to his own satisfaction.

I am myself, and have always been, a neutral. Facts came out on the trial which made it impossible for me to believe that he is Sir ROGER TICHBORNE; but then, on the other hand, facts came out which it is impossible to account for on any other theory.

I was talking the matter over with a friend of mine shortly before the collapse of the trial, when he suggested that we should call at the Waterloo Hotel, and interview the great riddle ourselves. This we determined to do. We obtained an introduction to him from a gentleman with whom he was acquainted, and at 8 p.m. we sent in our cards, and were at once admitted. The Claimant was seated at a table, smoking, in company with two of his adherents. He rose, and, welcoming us very civilly, offered each of us an excellent cigar, which we accepted. After a few preliminary observations, we soon drifted into the "trial." He talked of it with a cool quiet manner, as though it in no way personally interested him. Some one observed that the Attorney-General had used very strong language respecting him. He replied that often lawyers will use strong language, but that he thought that it was a mistaken policy, as it usually produced a counter effect to what was intended on the minds of a jury. "I do not complain," he continued, "of the Attorney-General abusing me, but I consider that he had no right to introduce my wife's name into the case, and read my private letters to my mother respecting her. Whether I am an impostor or not does not depend upon these letters." "Who is GUIDES, the priest?" I asked. "Wait," said an adherent, "till we have him in the box, the 'Serjeant' will turn him inside out." "No," observed the Claimant, "you will never get anything out of a priest by cross-examining him; he uses few words, and is too well trained in fencing to allow himself to be caught." We then asked him about the tattoo marks. He said, "I cannot understand how anyone can suppose that ROGER TICHBORNE was tattooed. For five years the 'Family' have concealed their knowledge of the fact. They say that, had they published it, I should immediately have tattooed myself; but surely when Mr. and Mrs. RADCLIFFE and Mrs. NANGLE were with me, they might have called upon me to turn up my coat-sleeve. Had I refused to do so, they would have stated it, and I never should have been able to raise the money to carry on proceedings. Now, I have four marks on my person, which are so like those that were on the person of ROGER, that they are obliged to assert that I made them myself. To do so I must have known of their existence. MOORE, BOGLE, or some one, consequently, must have told me of them. Is it probable that the person who did tell me of them, supposing this theory to be a correct one, would not equally have told me of this tattoo mark? A man who would cut open his legs, his eye, and the back of his head would not shrink from tattooing himself. Mrs. RADCLIFFE says that she saw the tattoo mark when I was catching minnows to fish in the Itchin. Now, no one does fish with minnows in any part of the Itchin, and in no part of the world does a person catch minnows with his left hand." "And where, pray, do you think ARTHUR ORTON is?" was my next question. "Somewhere about the Swan River," he answered. "I should recommend you to get hold of him," I said. "That's more easily said than done," he replied. "ORTON has committed some crime under another name, and is keeping out of the way." "It's perfect nonsense," observed an adherent, "to suppose that Sir ROGER can be ORTON. Why, where could ORTON have learnt fly-fishing, and no one denies that our friend here is an accomplished fly-fisher; to become one requires years of practice." "Not it," muttered the Claimant; "I'd teach anyone to fly-fish, and well too, in a month." "I suppose the Attorney-General's cross-examination a little confused you," I said, "although you appeared to take it so coolly." "I did not know whether I was standing on my head or my feet," he answered; "for instance, he asked me whether I knew the difference between a rook and a pawn; I said that I did not, and yet I can play a good game at chess." "Perfectly true," observed an adherent; "you beat a fair player a few evenings ago three games out of five; and what is more, although you are supposed not to know a word of French, you translated to me a day or two ago a letter in French which I happened to have in my pocket." After this we got on the subject of bush life. The Claimant told stories—and by no means bad ones—about kangaroo hunts, and different rides which he had taken, and he then diverged to South America, and the quality of South American horses. He had now run into a period when, according to his case, he was the original Sir ROGER; but he did it so naturally, that it was impossible to detect the transition.

It was now past twelve o'clock; the Claimant, swindler or no swindler, had naturally contributed to our passing a very pleasant evening. His manners are not by any means vulgar; on the contrary, they are natural and unaffected—indeed, they are a good deal better than those of the majority of Englishmen. He certainly takes great liberties with the letter "h," but his accent is not a Cockney one. He pronounces almost every word in an odd, outlandish manner, and when he becomes excited in conversation this accent becomes stronger. He speaks in that low, wheezy tone which is peculiar to those who have had much to do with horses, and generally before commencing a sentence, he pants like a seal. He wore a double chain from his button-hole, and sat most of the time with his hands—which are small and well-formed—passed between it and his waistcoat.

When we left him, my friend, who is a hard-headed man of the world, and who had always regarded him as a swindler, declared that he was convinced that he was the real, genuine Sir ROGER. "Such acting," he said, "is beyond the limits of possibility. If he be not the man, we have a greater actor among us than KEAN." For my part, I was staggered, but I still remained undecided, as I never care to risk a headache by trying to find out this sort of conundrum. Notwithstanding the collapse in Westminster-hall, I remained undecided still. The strongest point in favour of his being Sir ROGER is his thumb. At the trial a photograph was put in of the original man, with the thumb of one hand peculiarly formed, the nail being smaller than that on the other thumb. Now, I narrowly examined this thumb, and most assuredly the nail is smaller. The theory of the Attorney-General is that the Claimant, having during the trial observed this photograph, immediately tore off his nail; and in support of this suggestion he begged the jury to remember that never, when he was in the witness-box, was his left hand ungloved. It must, however, be remembered that during this time he was daily seen by persons who would not have been parties to a fraud, and that they declare that when out of the witness-box he rarely wore gloves, and that they did not observe that he had been "doctoring" his thumb. As long, therefore, as the thumb remains unexplained, and as long as no sort of attempt is made to show who—if he be not Sir ROGER—he really is, I shall remain in doubt as to whether he be a swindler. MARCO POLO, when he returned to Venice after his Eastern travels, was not recognised by his relatives, mainly because he had forgotten his native language. If it be said that anyone, after an absence of ten years, ought to be able to prove his identity without the shadow of a doubt, it may also be asserted that there ought to be no real difficulty in proving the identity of a person who admittedly has resided for many years in Australia, when those interested in doing so have had the unlimited command of time and money. The Attorney-General asserted in his speech that the Claimant had, and must have had, confederates. He never, however, ventured to say who those associates were, nor, acting as a law officer of the Crown, and no longer as an advocate of a private cause, does he venture to indict them.—Your obedient servant,

March 14. A NEUTRAL.

The next that we hear of Sir ROGER is the following, which is taken from the *Daily Telegraph* of March 23rd, 1872. It is headed

THE CLAIMANT IN NEWGATE.

The public who watched the progress of the long Trial in which the Claimant—as it has always been convenient to call the plaintiff in that celebrated suit—endeavoured to obtain possession of the broad lands of the TICHBORNE Estate, may be somewhat interested to know how he fares in his present very difficult and trying position, what he thinks about the conclusion of the Case, and what he believes are his prospects in the future. At all seasons Newgate Prison is sufficiently repulsive; but on a day when the snow covers the ground, and the bitter winds test the lungs of the strongest, it is to the last degree cheerless and melancholy. The rules of the place are always strict and sternly kept; but so many artful dodges have been practised by persons anxious to "interview" "Sir ROGER TICHBORNE so called," that the janitors are more than usually cautious about those whom they admit, and whom the Claimant desires to see. The visitor is subjected to an interrogation which could not have been excelled in minuteness by the Inquisition. I found that it was not sufficient that the prisoner himself had requested my presence. It was necessary I should satisfy his custodians that I really was the person he expected, and the process of investigation was so long and wearisome that I soon became heartily sorry the invitation was not addressed from the hotel where I last saw him, when his hospitality was free and he himself far more accessible. Probably the Lord Mayor and Sheriffs do not pretend that the "waiting-room" at their famous City prison is in any sense comfortable. Whoever the visitor may be, he shares the dubious privilege of standing in a dreary, whitewashed vault, so perfectly ventilated through the open doorway, that a voyager in the Arctic regions alone would be safe from bronchitis or neuralgia, if he were detained there for more than a few minutes. Not that the Governor or his staff subject the caller to any unnecessary inconvenience. He and his officers justly have the reputation of being most humane and considerate even to strangers. It is the villainous old building itself which, not content with being the ugliest of its kind, must needs appear the most disconsolate and inclement besides. So disheartening was the gloom of its close walls and narrow passages, and the slamming and locking of door after door as I proceeded to the cell in which the Claimant is confined, that I already expected to see him much changed through his incarceration, and with far less buoyant spirits than in the days when he was plaintiff, and not prisoner.

He was not in his cell when I was taken there by the gaoler, but he shortly after entered, and as soon as I could perceive him in the semi-darkness, I noticed that his face showed evident traces of anxiety and care. In answer to my first inquiries respecting his health, he said that, considering the circumstances in which he was placed, he was pretty well, though he found the confinement very irksome, and that it was made doubly so, he added, by the recollection of the most unfair and improper manner in which he had been treated, and upon which he commented strongly during our conversation. Referring almost immediately to the mode in which the Attorney-General had conducted the case against him, he expressed his indignation that the learned gentleman had not cross-examined him upon the tattoo marks, but had kept that part of the defence in reserve, in the hope that it would, as it certainly did, deal a successful blow against him. "If he had ventured to examine me on this matter," remarked the prisoner, "it would have given me the opportunity, which I ought to have had, of denying that I was so marked, and of bringing forward good witnesses who could have sufficiently proved it." "And what I particularly complain of is, that Mr. ALFRED SEYMOUR, M.P., who says he knew all along I was tattooed, did not at once state it. Can we consider it a proper thing if he allowed me to impose myself as Sir ROGER TICHBORNE upon his mother and sisters? Surely, if he did this, he could not regard me at that time as an impostor. Why did he not turn me out of the house at once? Then, again, there are the letters of Mrs. PITTENDREIGH. The Attorney-General tried to win his case with them, but failed, and he had to acknowledge he could not rely upon them. If I had done this, I wonder what would have been said? I should not have been surprised in that case to have found myself where I am now." In replying to a question about the general conduct of the trial, he criticised the speedy decision which the jury gave when they had only heard a few witnesses for the defence. He acknowledged that a trial which had already lasted upwards of a hundred days had imposed a great strain upon them; but he did not think it was fair they should have brought it to such an abrupt conclusion. He contended that they ought to have heard the case fairly out to the end, and then have given a verdict upon the whole of the evidence which had been adduced. "Could it be that the jury were frightened at the prospect of two hundred witnesses being placed in the box by the Attorney-General?"—and at such an awful prospect as this, the prisoner himself laughed, as if it was, indeed, an ordeal through which no mortal flesh and blood could be expected to pass. "The Attorney-

General," he said, "knew that such an idea was enough to terrify any juryman in the world." A further subject of complaint was the way in which the daguerreotype was handled—a way which was greatly calculated, he said, to injure his case. I told him that the public at large considered he had had a most patient hearing, and if there was any complaint at all, it was at the length of time it had occupied, to the serious hindrance of other important business. He readily acknowledged this, but explained that a great deal of the delay would have been saved had the case come before some of the other judges. Nor did he seem satisfied with the perfect impartiality of the judge—in fact, he expressed himself in a very opposite sense.

Up to this point he had spoken in subdued tones, as if dejected —not an extraordinary feeling either, considering the locality in which we were seated—a cell in Newgate; and a cell in Newgate seems a place many degrees worse than the most cheerless cell in any other prison I have ever visited. Rousing himself, he now spoke rapidly, and in almost angry tones, about the publication of the "MARTIN GUERRE" case in *The Month*, a periodical, he said, which was edited by the brother of the Attorney-General. I observed that I had seen such an account in some of the newspapers, but that I had not read it. He stated, in a very clear manner, what the story was, and said that, as published in the periodical mentioned, it was materially altered from the book in which it originally appeared. "Whatever might have been the object with which it was given in 'The Month,' there can be no doubt," said the Claimant, "that it did prejudice public opinion against me." "For what purpose," he continued, "was the case made so parallel to mine, and then distributed all over the kingdom? In 1868, too, anonymous notes, which were calculated to injure me, were sent to my friends." Several further remarks which he dropped showed plainly that he considered he had been subjected to a good deal of unfair and sharp practice.

What do you think really caused your case to break down, I asked?—Money, he answered quietly, and with a tone of certain conviction.

And what won the decision for the Defendant?

Money (the answer being given in an equally decided manner); and money is all that I want to free myself from this place, and prove my innocence of the charge upon which I am committed.

And win your estates?—Win my estates, certainly.

Here the Claimant passed his hand through his hair, brightened up considerably, and seemed to realise the time when he would be acknowledged as Sir ROGER TICHBORNE, and be once more recognised in the world from which he is now shut out.

Money you certainly require just at present if you desire to obtain bail,—I remarked.

"Ah! here again I want to know why I should be treated differently to other people?" he said, in a protesting voice. "Why should they require me to give them sureties in a manner which they do not require of other defendants who are placed in a like position to myself? Is it fair? Is it right? The judge asks them to submit to conditions to which very few people would submit even for their dearest friends. It is not enough that my sureties are men who are known to be of respectable position. No, that won't do; that isn't enough. They are first to be judged themselves. They must have all their accounts examined—everything must be known about them. Who would like this? If it hadn't been for such examination I could have got plenty of friends who would have been bail for me. Nor is this the worst. See what else they have done. By a most unfair proceeding I was made a bankrupt, and altogether they"—his enemies, generally speaking, as I understood—"have left me bound hand and foot." (I have preserved his own words throughout.) "They have seized everything—absolutely left me nothing. All my papers have been taken, and [this was spoken with bitter sarcasm] they have appropriated my last change of linen. All that I possess is the suit of clothes I now wear. How can it be expected that I can meet the charge against me when I am thus treated?"

Do you complain of the prison officials?—Not at all. "They do all the rules permit. I have not any complaint against them. What I say is, that it was most unfair to attack me all round like this. One Court commits me to prison, and another Court seizes everything belonging to me.

Do you think it was unjust you should have been committed, after the decision of the jury and the various circumstances of the case?

"What I contend is this," he replied—"that it was not fair my eighty-eight witnesses (I forget the exact number), who so distinctly swore in my favour, should go for nothing, and that the jury should have so readily believed the few on the other side, and particularly those who swore about the tattoo marks, none of whom agreed as to what the marks actually were. Some said one thing and some said another. Upon evidence which did not agree, and which I and my witnesses, and more still, could have denied, the defendant won. If the jury had given me the chance, I could have proved everything I said. I do not mean (he added with marked emphasis), that there were not certain discrepancies in my evidence; but was that very surprising? Consider the length of time I was under examination, and the long space over which the examination and cross-examination spread, and I say [this with considerable warmth] that they were discrepancies which might have been expected and which I could have explained. To charge me with perjury was too bad."

"With regard to your trial for perjury," I asked, "have you any confidence that the result will be in your favour?"—"Why, of course," the Claimant replied; "of what perjury have I been guilty? I have proof of everything I said. But I will not consent that the trial shall take place at Westminster. I shall demand to be tried at the Central Criminal Court. There I shall expect to get a fairer trial; not that I anticipate the case will come on yet. How can it? I have not been able to prepare my defence. They have carefully prevented me from doing so by putting me in this dilemma, and seizing all my papers."

Still you believe in an acquittal?—"Certainly I do: and, when I am tried, I think the country ought to find me a full jury."

And when you are acquitted?—"Ah!" he said—as if the very idea imparted fresh vigour—"then I shall go on with the action for the restoration of my property."

Go on with the action? (I observed, with an air of unconcealed incredulity.)—"Most assuredly I shall."

But how are you to obtain the funds? Is it not requisite you should first pay the costs incurred by the defendant in the late action, which it is said amount to something like £80,000?—"No; I shall not go on with that case; I shall prosecute the DOUGHTY case."

At this moment a warder entered to say that some one wished to see "Sir ROGER," and afterwards we did not continue this particular subject, so that I can give no explanation of how he hopes to proceed when that opportune moment arrives, except that he several times repeated, "I shall go on!" "I shall go on!"

Although the Claimant asked the warder if he would be good enough to request the gentleman who had just called to wait, I arose from the small bench, on which we could find barely sufficient room to sit face to face, and expressed the hope that he would be able to make a good defence, and that he would have every facility in giving instruction to the able counsel engaged to defend him.

"Let them restore my papers," was his answer, "which have been so improperly seized, and I shall have a better chance; but, above all, it is essential that I should be bailed, for how am I to know what is really doing when I am locked up here? I don't know what is being done, for I am not allowed to see any newspapers."

After a few further observations, in which the Claimant again repudiated with gestures of contempt the charge of perjury, positively asserted his innocence, and reasserted his determination to prosecute another action for the recovery of his title and estates, I wished him good afternoon, and withdrew.

During the brief interview which I had thus had with the Claimant, the intelligence he evinced, and the general correctness and clearness with which he expressed himself, indicated that whatever might be his character, or the issue of the charge against him, he is by no means the illiterate man sometimes represented. The statements made by him I leave without comment.

This article was followed by a letter from Mr. ALFRED SEYMOUR, the Defendant's Uncle, and his living image. It was addressed

TO THE EDITOR OF THE "DAILY TELEGRAPH."

SIR,—In an article in your paper of this day, your correspondent gives a report of a conversation which occurred in Newgate, between himself and the Claimant to the Tichborne Estates.

The words are as follows:—"And what I particularly complain of is that Mr. ALFRED SEYMOUR, M.P., who says he knew all along I was tattooed, did not state it at once. Can we consider it a proper thing if he allowed me to impose myself as Sir ROGER TICHBORNE upon his mother and sisters? Surely, if he did this he could not regard me at that time as an impostor. Why did he not turn me out of the house at once?"

Why not, indeed? For the simple reason that he never would give me the chance of doing so. He never was in my house, or that of any of my family, in his whole life. Many appointments were made, which were never kept. Of his own free will, or by legal advice, he never came to see, or made any effort to see, either my mother or sisters. Of their Christian names even, and sequence in age, he had, when under cross-examination, no correct knowledge. ROGER TICHBORNE well knew that he would at all times have been heartily welcomed by all members of my family. He would have preferred spending the Christmas of 1866 at Knoyle, to wandering about Wapping under a false name.

Now, about the tattoo marks. I never said this man was tattooed. Of course I was not likely to tell him, or his legal advisers, who always refused to allow his body to be examined, what were the actual marks, which were well known to have been indelibly ingrained upon ROGER CHARLES TICHBORNE. The reasons are obvious. No whist-player is fool enough to declare beforehand with what particular card he intends to trump his adversary's knave. But, sir, surely this interviewing the Claimant may be carried too far. Assertions are deliberately made by him, and published, which are, to speak mildly, the grossest inventions, and have already been disproved in the witness-box, and will be again. The repetition of these erroneous statements by your able correspondent is giving them a considerable weight and importance. I venture to contradict what concerns myself, but others may not trouble to do so; and then the Claimant's uncontradicted lie becomes, to some, an accepted truth.—I remain, sir, your obedient servant,

ALFRED SEYMOUR.

47, Eaton-square, March 23rd.

To this letter the following reply was sent :—

To the Editor of the "Daily Telegraph."

Sir,—Mr. Seymour has, by his letter in your paper of the 25th inst., publicly opened the tattooing, and as my client is confined within four stone walls, I feel it my duty to reply to it. The question is worth a little consideration, that the public may not be misled. Mr. Seymour and other members of the Family (with the exception of his own brother, who did not remember any tattoo marks) have laid before the Court that the real Roger was elaborately tattooed with three symbols and his own initials, and that the initials upon the wrist were so near the hand that they were discerned by Madame Chatillon as he sat at breakfast. It is obvious that nothing is so decisive of a person's identity as the recognition of tattoo marks which the original party had, or their absence, if the party representing him has them not. It is admitted on all hands that the present Claimant has not these tattoo marks; the only question remaining is, did the original possess them?

1. If he was tattooed, must not his mother have known it? If she had even forgotten it, was it not the duty of the family to remind her, and to heap up before her their own consentaneous evidence, and incite her to search for the same marks on the Claimant? The Family acknowledge they never made any attempt to deliver Lady Tichborne from one they deemed to be an Impostor by challenging him upon the tattoo marks. This excites the suspicion, *did they then believe in these marks themselves?*

2. The Claimant arrives in England at Christmas, 1866, and is acknowledged by his Mother and the Family Solicitor, so that the Family is thoroughly roused to the seriousness of his claim. Mr. Seymour's brother, Henry Seymour, meets the Claimant at the house of the Family Solicitor in February, 1867; Mr. and Mrs. Radcliffe with Mrs. Towneley have an interview with the Claimant at the beginning of March. In June, the Claimant files two Bills in Chancery, alleging himself to be Sir Roger Tichborne, and files his own and seventy other affidavits. His prayer to the Court was that a receiver might be appointed of the rental of the estate, upwards of £25,000 a year. On the 30th of July the Claimant was cross-examined at the Law Institution on behalf of the Family defendants, but no questions whatever were asked about the tattoo marks. On the 30th April, 1868, the Court of Chancery, on hearing both parties, made an order impounding the rents of the estates until the Claimant's case should have been tried at law. Anyone conversant with the proceedings in Chancery must know it was competent for the Family to have filed affidavits alleging the original Roger was tattooed, and to deposit under seal the particulars of the tattooing, not to be opened until the Claimant's person was examined, and to ask for an order that the Claimant should submit to a personal examination to ascertain if he had the same marks. This was not done, but the Family submitted to have the rents impounded, and an action at law commenced, instead of taking the short and sharp course of exposing the imposture, which they could have obviously taken, had the original Roger been tattooed.

3. The action at law is commenced, and goes to trial, involving, as the Family allege, an expense to them of something like a hundred thousand pounds. If the fact of the tattooing had been undoubted, the Family might have challenged every witness who swore to the Claimant's identity on this point; and the Claimant's Counsel and Solicitors, knowing that the Claimant was not tattooed, would soon have stopped the case, seeing the impossibility of overcoming such a fact, if it were undoubtedly proved. The Family did not, however, cross-examine to this point, nor make any assertion of the fact, and thus, in their view of the case, wilfully involved themselves in the expenses of such a trial.

4. The Claimant's case was supported by between 80 and 90 witnesses of undoubted credit. These witnesses, with two exceptions, both of whom denied that Roger Tichborne was tattooed, whenever questioned as to tattoo marks. If such marks had existed many of these witnesses must have seen them, and would necessarily abandon their opinion of identity when they found the Claimant did not possess them; but they never were so questioned. The witnesses upon this point, and those of them who had the opportunity of seeing his arms before, and which embraces a very considerable number, declare, as I am informed, that the original Roger had no such marks on his person, and on the forthcoming Trial they will be called to declare upon oath the truth of their assertions.

The questions which must arise in the public mind will be—Is it possible the Mother of the Claimant could not know of these marks, and that the Family should not inform her? Is it possible that the Family should suffer the Court of Chancery so far to recognise the Claimant as to enable him to impound all the rents, and order this expensive Trial, when, if they believed the tattoos, by bringing the fact before the Court on affidavits, and procuring an examination of his person, *his case could have been disposed of without further inquiry or expense?*

Mr. Alfred Seymour, in his letter, says, "Roger Tichborne really ell knew that he would at all times have been heartily welcomed by all the members of my family." The heartiness of such a welcome would have been best shown by the frankness of their communication. If they knew that the original Roger was tattooed, and had challenged the Claimant on this at their first interview, they would at once have brought the matter to an issue by reference to his Mother, to the domestics, and to those most intimate with him, so as to have led at once, either to the abandonment of his claim, or to the abandonment of their assertions about tattooing, which, upon the facts above cited, *bear very strongly the appearance of an afterthought.* As it stands, the conduct of the Family is perfectly incredible, upon the assumption that at that time they knew of the tattooing, and if they did not then know of it, it can scarcely be credible at the present moment.

To show how miserably weak was the tattoo evidence, I have had a short analysis of it prepared, with a few comments thereon, which I shall be glad if you will insert with this letter.

I must apologise for the length of this letter, but after giving so prominent a place in your paper to Mr. Alfred Seymour's, which may do my Client great injury if not replied to, I am sure you will insert it.—I am, Sir, your obedient servant,

Francis G. Gorton, Sir Roger Tichborne's Solicitor.

46, Bedford-row, March 27.

Analysis of the Tattoo Evidence.

1. Lord Bellew, schoolfellow of Roger Tichborne, at Stonyhurst. He stated that he tattooed Roger on the left arm with the letters "R. C. T.," and that at the time he so tattooed "R. C. T.," there were thereon the emblems "Faith, Hope, and Charity," and a heart, cross, and anchor on his arm. The letters were stated to be one half an inch, "at a guess." On cross-examination, his lordship stated, that he had made no communication to anyone until last spring, and that on the 7th of June, 1871, while the Claimant was in the box, he received what he called a letter in general terms from Mr. Bowker, which contained the following words: "I understand your lordship was at Stonyhurst with Roger Tichborne, and during that time tattooed on his arms emblems, 'Faith, Hope, and Charity.'" His lordship's reply was dated June 8th, and is to the following effect: "I was at Stonyhurst with Roger Tichborne, and remember his having heart, anchor, and cross tattooed on his arm, also 'R. C. T.' I remember assisting to tattoo his arm, but find it difficult to remember whether I tattooed heart, anchor, and cross, or 'R. C. T.' The former was on his left arm, and I am not certain whether the other, 'R. C. T.,' was not on his right arm, above the wrist. That may account for my want of accurate memory on this detail."

The difference will be observed in the statement that he tattooed "R. C. T.," and the letter of last June, stating that he assisted to tattoo his arms. His lordship states that he has an indistinct recollection of Roger Tichborne stating that the emblems were done by sailors, and that a Mr. Segar was present at the Stonyhurst tattooing, but he is not positive on either statement. Mr. Segar is dead. He recognised the Plaintiff, having written letters saying he should never have doubted his identity had he not heard of the opposition of the Family. He never asked to see the "tattoos."

2. Mr. Alfred Seymour, half-brother of the Dowager Lady Tichborne. He corroborated the tattoo marks, but admitted he had never described them to his sister, giving as a reason "that she would have told the impostor, who would have tattooed himself accordingly." Also, "that it had been agreed not to mention the subject for that reason." He could not tell why the tattoo marks were not alluded to at the examination at the Law Institution, in 1867, whilst the Dowager was alive, when, if the fact were known, by merely asking the Plaintiff to expose his arm, all the Chancery and other proceedings might have been stopped.

3. Mrs. Radcliffe was the next witness. She confirmed the tattooing, stating that she "saw the marks in the summer of '49, when Roger, at the early age of 15, pulled up his sleeve to get some flowers out of the river." Afterwards, on cross-examination, she said she had seen them "when he was gathering water-flowers, and when he pulled up his sleeve to get minnows out of the river;" adding, "He asked me to be tattooed, but I said I did not like pain." He must have been eccentric in early life to have been tattooed before he was 15 years old, and to have endeavoured to catch minnows in the clearest stream in Hampshire with his left hand, for on his left arm the tattoos were said to be.

4. Mr. Henry D. Seymour did not recollect the tattoos.

5. Lady Doughty swore to the tattoos, but had not mentioned them to her solicitors till 1870, and their proof when called for was not allowed to be produced. She contradicted Mr. Alfred Seymour by saying there was no Family arrangement for keeping the tattoos secret.

6. Mrs. Nangle, a member of the Family, stated that "Roger showed me the tattoos on the last day of his visit to Tichborne, and asked me to undergo the operation."

7. Monsieur Chatillon, the French tutor who educated Roger, had seen the tattoos for the first time on the last morning of Roger Tichborne's residence in France.

8. Madame Chatillon, his wife, corroborated in every particular, only she mistook Lady Doughty's sketch for that of her husband.

9. Jules Barraut, the servant of Roger Tichborne for five months, who sent home in 1855 what purported to be a "textual extract from his diary." Plaintiff had affirmed that this witness never sent his luggage on board the "Bella." A paragraph in the textual extract said, "I go twice on board in the course of the

day to see Mr. TICHBORNE, and hand him various things which he had forgotten."

When the original diary was produced it was found to contain no such paragraph. He could not swear to the tattoo marks.

10. Monsieur D'ARANZA, like JULES BARRAUT, had not spoken with the Plaintiff, and could not swear to the tattoo marks.

11. Mr. ROBERT MANSFIELD, a near relative of Mr. HIBBERT'S, who deposed to having a vivid recollection of having seen ROGER TICHBORNE once in the Alfred Club. He knew nothing of the tattoo marks.

12. The Abbé SALIS, who, the Plaintiff stated, was his mother's confessor, and to whom he had confessed, but who denied the latter assertion, and remembered the tattoo but could not describe it. These particulars are taken from the reports in the various papers. It will be observed that only eight witnesses swear to the tattoo marks, while I am assured that there is not one officer in the Carabineers who would swear that "the real ROGER" was tattooed, and thirty-two of them have been called by the Claimant.

All those who gave evidence for him deny that they ever heard of his being tattooed; and about two dozen different persons, five of whom were ROGER TICHBORNE'S body servants, are ready to swear that they have seen ROGER TICHBORNE'S arms bare, and never saw any tattoo marks upon them.

A day or two after Major JOCELYN rushed into print. At the Trial, Dr. KENEALY knew nothing of this correspondence, or of that which precedes. Had he done so, the witnesses would have heard of it. But in truth, from first to last, Dr. KENEALY'S "instructions" were hardly worth the paper they were written upon.

TO THE EDITOR OF THE "STANDARD."

SIR,—I request the insertion of the annexed memorandum in the *Standard*. The original manuscript is in my possession, and I vouch for the correctness of the copy and the authenticity of the signatures. There can be no doubt that Captain EDWARD M'EVOY, M.P., and MELFORT CAMPBELL, late of the Carabineers, would sign the memorandum, as they are well known to have strong convictions on the subject, but being out of England, it is impracticable to communicate with them.—I am, Sir, your obedient servant,

AUGUSTUS G. F. JOCELYN,
Major, late Captain, Carabineers.

Army and Navy Club: March 28.

"MEMORANDUM.

"The undersigned officers who served in the Carabineers with the late Mr. ROGER TICHBORNE having been deprived of any other opportunity of expressing their opinion, take this method of making public their firm and undoubted conviction that their old brother officer ROGER TICHBORNE has never been seen in England since he left this country in 1853:—

"HENRY RICHMOND JONES, Major General, late Commander, Carabineers.

"ROBERT BICKERSTAFF, Lieut. Colonel, late Major, Carabineers.

"WILLIAM T. BETTY, late Lieut. Colonel, Carabineers.

"JOHN FORSTER, Major, late Carabineers.

"THOMAS BOTT, Major, late Carabineers.

"WILLIAM S. PHILLIPS, Major, late Carabineers.

"THOMAS MANDERS, late Paymaster, Carabineers.

"FREDERICK POLHILL TURNER, late Captain, Carabineers.

"WILLIAM B. PHILLIMORE, late Lieutenant, Carabineers.

"GEORGE FRASER, late Quartermaster, Carabineers.

"AUGUSTUS G. F. JOCELYN, Major, late Captain, Carabineers."

Mr. GORTON replied to this most improper attempt to influence the public and the Grand Jury.

TO THE EDITOR OF THE "STANDARD."

SIR,—In your paper of this date appears a letter from Major JOCELYN, inclosing a document purporting to be signed by certain officers of the Carabineers, who desire to make public, to use their own words, "their firm and undoubted conviction that their old brother-officer, ROGER TICHBORNE, has never been seen in England since he left this country in 1853." The names appended were Major General JONES, Major BICKERSTAFF, Lieutenant Colonel BETTY, Major FORSTER, Major BOTT, Major PHILLIPS, Paymaster MANDERS, Captain POLHILL TURNER, Lieutenant PHILLIMORE, and Quartermaster FRASER.

Major JOCELYN adds, "there can be no doubt that the Captains E. M'EVOY and MELFORT CAMPBELL would sign the memorandum, as they are well known to have strong convictions on the subject."

It is difficult to conceive why Major JOCELYN should have evinced the partisanship which this expression indicates, and I am sure you will feel that it is only just and fair to the Claimant that the public should be informed that of the officers signing the manifesto only three have spoken to the Claimant, and they are Major PHILLIPS, Major FORSTER, and Quartermaster FRASER. It is possible some of the above officers may have seen him, but it could only have been passing in the street or when he was in the witness-box.

It is rather strange that a body of gentlemen should have desired Major JOCELYN to make public such an assertion as "their firm and undoubted conviction that their old brother-officer, ROGER TICHBORNE, has never been seen in England since he left this country in 1853;" but I presume they can only mean that he has not been seen by themselves. It would be absurd to suppose that the motive actuating them is that of a mere desire to have the fact made public. It only shows the immense amount of influence and pressure that is being brought to bear against the Claimant. Under these circumstances, I ask the favour of your making as public as Major JOCELYN'S letter my reply.

The writer of the letter was asked to have an interview with the Claimant, in order that he might judge whether he was his brother-officer, or not, and declined in the following words:—"Major JOCELYN does not consider that any evidence he could give would influence the decision in the case alluded to in such letter. He, therefore, thinks it useless to arrange an interview." This will enable the public to judge of the value of Major JOCELYN'S testimony, and I shall be happy to produce the letter to Major JOCELYN or any one who chooses to call and see it.

I will not encroach on your space by giving any particulars with regard to some of the other officers who have declined interviews, and their motives for doing so; but against the statement which has appeared in your paper I must ask to be allowed to state that the following officers have, after long interviews with the Claimant, recorded on oath their convictions of his identity. They are General CUSTANCE, C.B., Colonel SAWYER, Lieutenant-Colonel NORBURY, Major HEYWOOD, and Captain SHERSTON. These gentlemen have written stating they have no recollection of ROGER TICHBORNE ever having been tattooed. Another officer has written also to the same effect.

It has already been made public that a considerable number of persons, all of whom have identified the Claimant, and some of whom are non-commissioned officers of the Carabineers, will prove that they have seen ROGER TICHBORNE'S arms exposed and not observed any tattoo marks upon them, and of these six will swear positively there were no marks whatever. It is somewhat surprising that with the strong feeling of partisanship which must have prevailed amongst Major JOCELYN and his friends, not one word is said about these tattoo marks, but if they believed in them they would no doubt have published their "undoubted conviction" upon the point.

In conclusion, I may add that Major JOCELYN and his friends will have an opportunity of appearing against the Claimant in the Central Criminal Court, and I should have thought as officers they would have been manly enough to reserve the expression of their convictions until that time arrives, when their truthfulness can be tested by cross-examination, instead of stating them in a newspaper, which they know very well the Claimant is not permitted to see.—I am, Sir, your obedient servant,

FRANCIS G. GORTON,
Sir ROGER TICHBORNE'S Solicitor.

46, Bedford-row: April 2.

He was followed by an eminent member of the Bar in this letter.

TO THE EDITOR OF THE "STANDARD."

SIR,—I observe in the papers a memorandum from some of the officers, late of the Carabineers, stating that ROGER CHARLES TICHBORNE has not been seen in England since 1853. Now, it is an established fact that almost an equal number of officers of the same regiment have sworn that they have not only seen that gentleman but have conversed with him. I would ask those officers who have signed this memorandum whether there is anything extraordinary in their not being able to identify the features of a man who has increased in weight from 11 stone in 1865 to 26 stone in 1872, and whether more credence ought not to be placed in the sworn testimony of those officers, non-commissioned officers, and privates of the Carabineers who have not contented themselves with seeing only, but have put the Claimant to the TICHBORNE Estates to the severest test of repeated conversations during the past five years?

It is also an established fact that the Australian climate alters the features of Europeans in a manner unknown in any other. The test of conversation, therefore, would be a far better criterion to judge from than the mere sight of a man obtained by these officers when the Claimant was in court.

I trust you will kindly insert this letter for the sake of your obedient servant, FAIR PLAY.

Major JOCELYN again appeared in print:—

THE TICHBORNE CASE.

TO THE EDITOR OF THE "STANDARD."

SIR,—The letter of Mr. GORTON, in your paper of yesterday, contains such an extraordinary mistake—to use the mildest term—about me, that I must request your insertion of this statement. In the summer of 1867, on my return from the Paris Exhibition, I received a letter from the Claimant expressing a wish to see me. I replied that I would meet him here at any time he might appoint. This communication produced no result. On the 1st November, 1870, I received a letter from Messrs. BAXTER, ROSE, and NORTON, asking me to assist the Claimant in his Case, and requesting me to have an interview with them for that purpose. To this letter—having previously declined a similar request from the Solicitors for the opposite side—I returned the answer so dexterously quoted by Mr. GORTON. So much for the allegation that I "declined an interview with the Claimant." To the other parts of Mr. GORTON'S letter I shall not allude. From one, judge all.—I am, Sir, your obedient Servant,

AUGUSTUS G. F. JOCELYN, Major,
late Captain, Carabineers.

Army and Navy Club, April 4.

He was thus replied to by Mr. Gorton:—

To the Editor of the "Standard."

Sir,—Major Jocelyn, in his letter in your paper of yesterday, states that my letter of the 2nd inst. contains an extraordinary mistake: but although he makes the assertion he fails to prove it. He carefully evades the point to which my letter was directed as regards himself, and states that in 1867 he received a letter from the Claimant expressing a wish to see him, to which he replied that he would meet the Claimant at any time he might appoint, and that such communication produced no result. Whether any such offer was ever made to the Claimant personally, I do not know, and it is quite immaterial.

The communication I referred to (and of which Major Jocelyn was well aware, because he referred to it in his letter) was one from the Claimant's late solicitors, in November, 1870, in which Major Jocelyn was asked to have an interview with the Claimant, which he declined, stating that "he did not consider any evidence he could give would influence the decision in the Claimant's case," and upon such facts I left it to the public to judge of the value of Major Jocelyn's "undoubted conviction" that Roger Tichborne had never been seen in England since 1853.

When a gentleman pledges publicly his "undoubted conviction" upon a point, the public may fairly assume that he has very strong grounds for doing so; but from Major Jocelyn's own letter it is clear that he knew nothing that could influence the decision as to the Claimant's case in any way, and that being so, he was not justified in making public his "undoubted conviction" upon the subject stated in the manifesto.

Major Jocelyn concludes by saying that he will refrain from noticing the other parts of my letter. He does so for no other reason than that he knows them to be founded upon truth.—I am, Sir, your obedient Servant,

Francis G. Gorton,
Sir Roger Tichborne's Solicitor.

46, Bedford-row: April 6.

He was followed by Sergeant-Major Marks:—

To the Editor of the "Standard."

Sir,—In reply to a memorandum from Major Jocelyn which appeared in the *Standard* on the 2nd inst., I beg to state I was corporal in the Carabineers when Roger Tichborne joined, and served in the troop with him; he was the officer in charge of my squad, and during midday stable hours he was in the habit of asking me several questions respecting the men, their horses, and appointments. I have drilled with him both mounted and dismounted, and I am quite sure that the Claimant is the Roger Tichborne which I knew in the Carabineers. I saw the gallant major in town during the Trial, when I addressed him, and his reply was, "I do not know you.' I said "You do, very well; I had the honour of serving under you for nine years. I was one of your corporals." He says, "Do tell me who you are." I replied "I would rather wait and see if you could recognise me," which he failed to do. I now ask the public to judge if the major is competent to form an opinion respecting Roger Tichborne's identity, the Claimant having joined in October, 1849, and went to Cahir with head-quarters of the regiment in 1850, Major Jocelyn leaving Dublin for Limerick with his troop in March, 1850, at which time the gallant major left the service altogether. Now his acquaintance with the Claimant would be six months. How is it possible, after not knowing me, whom he saw every day for nine years, he can say that the Claimant is not the real Roger Tichborne? I will leave that for the public to judge.

Major Jocelyn asked when in town what I thought about the Claimant. I said, "He is Roger Tichborne, Sir," and his reply was, that he could not say whether he was or not; but I think the major has been converted in consequence of the Claimant's ignorance of military tactics, for he would never have made a cavalry officer. It was next to impossible to teach him his drill. I have frequently seen him placed in the ranks with the men for not knowing his place when he was a troop leader, and I have myself ridden beside him in the ranks.

Now as regards General Jones, who commanded the regiment, failing to identify the Claimant, he also did not know me, until an officer called his attention and said "That is Marks." The general then asked me when I left the regiment—was it after we came from India? I replied, "It was in 1852, before you went to India," he having signed my transfer documents to the 4th Dragoon Guards, and did not know me.—I remain, yours,

James Marks, Corporal of Carabineers,
late Sergeant-Major, 4th Dragoon Guards.

Nearly simultaneously with this appeared the following:—

To the Editor of the "Standard."

Sir,—Will you be good enough to allow me to acknowledge, through the medium of your paper, the numerous letters addressed to me, and to my solicitor, suggesting that I should appeal to the public for subscriptions for my defence, and to thank all those who have promised to subscribe for their kind feeling towards me in my present painful position?

It is with the greatest reluctance that I adopt the suggestion, sure, however, as I am that it is inspired only by a sense of justice; but as a victim of "might against right," what other course am I to adopt? True it may be that my friends, who have already assisted, will, to some extent, help me further; but it would be unreasonable for me to hope that after the assistance they have already afforded me I can fairly look to them for the large sum necessary for my defence. If a few hundreds, or even a thousand, would suffice, I might not perhaps despair; but I am charged with being a perjurer, and am also, so it is said, to be charged with being a forger, which, I suppose, means that I have used my own name of Roger Charles Doughty Tichborne. These foul and groundless charges will involve the whole question of my identity, to disprove which the Solicitor of the Government, advised by the Attorney-General (the leading counsel against me in the late trial), has retained the Attorney-General, Mr. Hawkins, Q.C., Sir George Honyman, Q.C., Serjeant Parry, Mr. Bowen, and Mr. Archibald against me. I am not surprised at six Counsel being engaged at the expense of the country; my only wonder is that the Attorney-General, who will, on the approaching Trial, have to represent the "Crown and justice," did not employ the whole of the English bar to crush me, to gratify the personal feelings he has expressed.

Fortunately for me, I have many friends who will never desert me, and who have obtained for me the best legal assistance.

But how is it possible for me, utterly penniless, to avail myself of it, and to obtain justice, against the purse of the Government of England, the strings of which will, no doubt, be freely pulled for the purpose of proving me to be a perjurer and a forger—charges which, with others, have already been made against me by the Attorney-General, without proof? However, here I am, and am likely to remain, unless I can find, not only four persons worth £1,250 each to bail me out, but four persons who will allow all their affairs to be exposed to the public for the purpose of showing that they can at any moment pay the sums for which they offer themselves.

When I have found four such friends, I am told that the advisers of Government will then, in my case, raise an objection to the sufficiency of my own recognizance for £5,000, unless I can prove that I am worth the amount. In fact, every effort will be used to keep me here.

Cruelly persecuted as I am, there is but one course that I can see, and that is, to adopt the suggestion so many have made to me, viz., to "appeal to the British public" for funds for my defence, and in doing so I appeal to every British soul who is inspired by a love of justice and fair-play, and who is willing to defend the "weak against the strong."

That I am Roger Charles Doughty Tichborne I solemnly declare, and which fact I have already proved by 86 witnesses, and will prove again by more than 200, if necessary; and that I am not Arthur Orton I will prove beyond a shadow of a doubt, by witnesses who knew both Orton and myself. As to the tattoo marks, at least 24 disinterested witnesses will prove that I, Roger Tichborne, was never tattooed; but that Arthur Orton was there will be conclusive evidence forthcoming.

Be all this as it may, true lovers of justice will, I feel satisfied, never allow me to be convicted without a fair trial, which it is impossible for me to have without counsel, solicitors, and witnesses on my behalf, and I therefore appeal to the public for subscriptions for my defence.

Caged as I am, it is impossible for me to get a single witness without the assistance of my solicitor.

Mr. William Warren Streeten, of 7, Old-square, Lincoln's-inn, barrister-at-law, has kindly consented to receive subscriptions, which I will thank all subscribers to pay to him, "in trust for the purpose of my defence only,"—otherwise the solicitors under my bankruptcy may claim it, as they did the paltry sum I had about me when I was conveyed here.

All subscriptions will be acknowledged in the daily papers in such manner as subscribers may desire.—I am, Sir, your obedient servant,

R. C. D. Tichborne.

Newgate Gaol: March 25.

This called forth an admirable letter—

To the Editor of the "Daily News."

Sir,—In response to the appeal signed "R. C. D. Tichborne," I inclose a cheque for £5, to be paid over in trust for the purpose of his defence only. Whoever the man now confined in Newgate is, be should, in common justice, have a fair opportunity either to clear himself or to demonstrate satisfactorily that he is an even greater scoundrel than he is conceived to be. He has sufficiently explained that, without the aid he seeks, that opportunity will be denied him.

In common with some of your correspondents, I think that there is a mystery in this case which ought to be cleared up, and the only legitimate form our assistance to that development can take is the one now proposed by the Claimant. I do not in the slightest degree pledge myself to any sympathy with or belief in him.

The Claimant very properly describes the overwhelming forces that are marshalled against him. The British toady, in the shape of a Member of Parliament, or any other development of modern sycophancy, may, as soon as the man has been kicked out of court by a histrionic Judge and a weary Jury, applaud the ministers who bring all the power and resources of Government to the aid of enormous wealth and opportunity, in the final attempt to crush him; but, as a taxpayer, I have a right to protest against the injustice and inconsistency of their action. Some time since a number of gentlemen of high standing were charged with offences which, had they been actually committed, were infinitely worse in their nature and effects than those charged upon this man. When they were sent for trial the evidence against them was at least as strong as that on which the Claimant has been committed. But the prosecutor was only a middle-class person of limited means. It was made plain to the Government that he was unable from his own resources to conduct the prosecution in a manner befitting the gravity of the case. In that instance property and position happened to be on the side of the defence—in the present instance it happens to be on the side of the prosecution. In the former case Government refused its aid—in the present case it spontaneously offers it. Can you, or they, or any reasonable person wonder if many persons draw the conclusion that our Government is a class Government, the friend and patron of property and position? Against such unequal sympathies it is hopeless to expect a Parliament like ours to enter a protest; but Englishmen with a conscience may at least do something, by contributing to the Claimant's defence, to neutralise an injustice and partiality of which they are ashamed.—I am, sir, your obedient servant, EDWARD JENKINS.

5, Paper-buildings, Temple, E.C.: March 27.

[We have forwarded Mr. JENKINS's cheque to Mr. W. W. STREETEN; but we cannot undertake to receive or transmit any further subscriptions for the purpose named in his letter.]

We have preserved the Editor's footnote, as it shows the bias of that gentleman and his employers.

One or two observations we may make, before we pass away from this Trial in the Common Pleas. As in the hearing before Mr. ROUPELL in Chancery-lane, the Plaintiff and his counsel were obliged to complain of the jeering, the sneering, the indecent behaviour of those who were gathered there against him, consisting of various members of the Family, and certain toadies of military men; so in the Common Pleas, the same game was practised, for the purpose of influencing the jury and disconcerting the witnesses. The Court was packed every day with partisans of the priests and the Family; a hundred incredulous eyes and mocking lips were ever turned full against the witness in the box; the Judge himself behaved all through with indecent bias; and whenever Serjeant BALLANTINE or Mr. GIFFARD were absent, the Counsel

SIR W. BOVILL, C. J.

for the Defendant was allowed to do as he pleased, to violate every rule of evidence, to use documents not before the Court, and which could not legally be brought before the Court; while the Junior Counsel for the Plaintiff, who were hardly better than sweeps, sat by, and either through ignorance did not, or through cowardice dared not, interfere. Over and over again Dr. KENEALY—then a wholly disinterested individual—strolled across from Westminster into the Sessions House, or wandered into the Queen's Bench or Common Pleas, to see what was going on; and he never did so without coming away deeply disgusted with the treachery which he beheld. BOVILL, from the first, was all on one side: the jury soon took their cue from him. COLERIDGE was allowed to do as he pleased, just as HAWKINS subsequently was permitted at the Great Trial at Bar; BALLANTINE was constantly absent upon some miserable question of fees; and a more complete, open, and scandalous betrayal of a man's rights, and violation of justice, had never been seen in England since COCHRANE's Trial before ELLENBOROUGH, and the arraignment of the infamous GURNEYS before COCKBURN. From that moment Dr. KENEALY loathed the profession to which he belonged; and there are hundreds in Westminster Hall who heard him enunciate his feelings, and who then expressed their own full concurrence in them. One of the occasions—but their name was legion—to which allusion is made, was on Tuesday, November 28th, 1871. Mr. BAIGENT was under cross-examination, and was the object of the most indecent ridicule. At last Serjeant BALLANTINE interfered thus: "I am quite sure that your lordship will feel that while it is necessary a witness should be cross-examined, a certain amount of decorum should be observed by those who are in Court."

The Chief Justice: What have you to complain of? My attention was directed to Mr. BAIGENT, and I wasn't aware of what was passing.

Serjeant BALLANTINE: I am quite aware of that, my lord; but I am sure I am doing that which every juryman feels proper to be done under the circumstances.

The Foreman of the Jury: It is exceedingly difficult for the jury to interfere. The witness is giving his evidence under material difficulties, and your lordship will feel that those difficulties are increased by the behaviour of the people in Court, and the noise and tittering which prevail. I know your lordship's attention was entirely directed to the answers given by the witness.

The Chief Justice: I am glad attention has been called to this matter. The misfortune is that there are persons interested in this question beyond the parties immediately concerned.

The Foreman of the Jury: I have been requested more than once to name the matter.

The Chief Justice: It comes to this, that at last I shall be obliged to clear the Court of everybody, except the counsel, the jury, the witnesses, and the Press.

These observations were without effect. The same course of packing the Court with the partisans of the priests continued to the end: as it did from the beginning to the end of the Great Trial at Bar, which is the subject of the following pages.

On the subject of the great quarrel between Messrs. BAXTER, ROSE, and NORTON, we do not think it necessary to say anything. It could not fail, of course, to do the Defendant the greatest injury, and it succeeded in doing so. But it is necessary to allude to the conduct of Mr. ROSE's son—one of the counsel engaged in the case. It was well known in Westminster Hall that this gentleman, while engaged for Sir ROGER, sneered at his case, and was almost churlish with his adherents. On the 14th of May, 1872, Sir ROGER, addressing his friends and tenants at Alresford, thus alluded to this conduct. We quote from the *Weekly Hampshire Independent* of May 18,—a paper, be it noted, which is sadly misnamed:—

"He said he was glad to be present to acknowledge the great kindness he had received from the people of Southampton, and after a few more general remarks, proceeded to say that he should like to explain why Mr. ROSE, one of his solicitors, had left his case. One night after going to the theatre he and some friends were at supper at EVANS's, and while in the room he heard that Mr. ROSE had told a Mr. LAWSON that the case looked very doubtful, and that it was very likely the firm of BAXTER, ROSE and NORTON would retire from it. He said nothing then, but the next morning he went to Messrs. BAXTER, ROSE, and NORTON, and had an interview with Mr. SPOFFORTH, telling him what he had heard, and that under no circumstances would he again allow Mr. ROSE to appear in his behalf. Mr. SPOFFORTH entreated him to reconsider his decision, but he adhered to it, and that was the reason why Mr. ROSE had withdrawn from the case, and that withdrawal had been followed by that of his father. He thought that explanation was due to the public, as the withdrawal referred to had somewhat prejudiced him in the eyes of the public. Although he had called 86 witnesses, the fact was to be borne in mind that he had the sworn testimony of 580 witnesses, and it was only the lack of funds that had prevented him calling the greater portion of those. He had to complain, in consequence of being unable to continue the fees to Counsel, that his case had been conducted towards the last in a very indifferent manner, more especially as regarded the cross-examination of witnesses. The jury saw that, and there was no doubt that it influenced them. The Attorney-General also noticed the fact. (Cheers.) That gentleman told the jury, on the 102nd day of the Trial, that he had 280 witnesses to examine, which was equivalent to telling them that unless they gave him a verdict they must sit for a whole year. (Cries of "Shame.") He also had to complain, and he did so bitterly, of the Judge. They would recollect that he had told him that so long as he sat on that bench the other side would need no Counsel. (Groans.) Why had not the learned Judge committed him on that occasion, for it was clear contempt of Court, except that he dared not do so? (Cheers.)"

These observations produced the following Correspondence, which we think it prudent to preserve:—

TO THE EDITOR OF THE "STANDARD."

SIR,—With reference to a statement which appears in your paper of this morning as having been made by the Claimant in the TICHBORNE Trial at a meeting of his friends at Alresford, to the effect that the late Mr. W. B. ROSE, one of the junior Counsel, was, by his desire, withdrawn from the case, I request your permission to contradict that statement, which, if correctly reported, is untrue.

I remember the Claimant, on or about the 7th of January, 1872, mentioning to me a rumour that Mr. W. B. ROSE had expressed to Mr. LAWSON an unfavourable opinion of his case, and suggesting that, if true, he might be prejudiced by Mr. W. B. ROSE representing him as Counsel; but I found, as I expected, that the Claimant had been misinformed, and that there was no justification for the rumour; and Mr. W. B. ROSE continued, with the Claimant's full knowledge and approval, to render his valuable services, until prevented by that illness which, to the deep regret of all, terminated in his death.

It is equally incorrect that the withdrawal of Mr. ROSE, senior, with that of his eldest son and partner, Mr. P. FREDERICK ROSE, from a further connection with the case, had any relation to this circumstance, Mr. ROSE having communicated to his partners the grounds for his determination in the beginning of December.

Upon the subsequent withdrawal of Mr. ROSE and his son as solicitors in the cause, and the issue of new retainers to Counsel by the other members of the firm, no fresh retainer was offered to Mr. W. B. ROSE, the illness from which he was then suffering entirely incapacitating him from attending Court.—I am, Sir, your obedient servant, M. SPOFFORTH.

6, Victoria-street, Westminster, S.W.; May 15, 1872.

TO THE EDITOR OF THE "STANDARD."

SIR,—Will you do me the favour of publishing the following reply to a letter from Mr. SPOFFORTH which appeared in your issue of Thursday, the 16th, in which that gentleman accuses me of having misstated certain facts with reference to the late Mr. ROSE?

I much regret that the subject of a conversation I supposed to be private should have by any means obtained a newspaper publicity; but, such being unfortunately the case, I am compelled in my own justification to defend myself from the imputation of falsifying a fact for my own benefit.

It was hard to be called "a thief, a liar, a perjurer, a forger, and a villain of the deepest dye" by a paid advocate specially engaged to vilify me. It is harder to find myself accused of duplicity by one to whom I owe myself deeply and gratefully indebted for many acts of kindness.

Although my opponents have not set me a very Christian example as to the respect due to the dead—(had my lamented mother been living, how differently would she have been spoken of! and how different would have been my position!)—I still, I say, regret that any public reference should have been made to the late Mr. ROSE, and simply in my own defence, I beg to inquire of Mr. SPOFFORTH whether I did not on the 5th of January, 1872, address a letter to him in which I stated I had been at EVANS's with some friends on the previous evening, where I heard, on good authority, that Mr. ROSE had (on the evening previous to that) been talking about my case, that he had asserted it "looked very fishy," and that "the firm thought about giving it up." Under these circumstances I at the same time wrote Mr. SPOFFORTH that I would not allow Mr. ROSE to appear at any future consultation on my behalf. I hereby not only authorise, but specially request, Mr. SPOFFORTH, as a matter of common justice to me, to publish that letter.

The unfortunate difference between Mr. ROSE and myself does not for a moment lessen my feeling of gratitude for the zeal, energy, and talent displayed in the conduct of my suit by the other members of that eminent firm.—I am, Sir, your obedient servant, R. C. D. TICHBORNE.

Harley Lodge, Harley-road, Brompton; May 20.

The Alresford Meeting gave rise to the following letter:—

SIR,—At your request, and knowing your desire always to furnish the public with all the information in your power, I will, by your kindness, lay before the general public some facts in connection with our visit to Alresford on Tuesday last, in order to meet the Claimant, to have a personal interview, and to assist in the demonstration, feeling that our cause was a just one. Our acting Committee consists of the following gentlemen, and are daily on the increase:—Myself, as Chairman; Mr. SHETTLE, Secretary; and Messrs. GREY, HAWKESWORTH, GODDARD, HARRIS, LLOYD, CLARKE, HARDIMAN, SPAIN, STEVENS, OXENHAM, ROOMES, JORDAN, DENHAM, BENNETT, WEBB, and BUDDEN. These gentlemen, with a few ladies, formed the deputation from the general committee, some of whom travelled by train. On arriving at Alresford we were received by the general public with enthusiastic shouts (as the friends of justice), and after some necessary delay, we proceeded to meet Sir ROGER TICHBORNE and his friends. The remainder you already know. A band of music preceded the carriage into the town, the horses were taken out, and, amid the shouts of a crowded assembly of the inhabitants of Alresford, it was drawn into the premises of the Swan Hotel, where the Claimant, with GUILDFORD ONSLOW, Esq., addressed the public. They afterwards continued their observations in the large room, where the Southampton Committee had the opportunity of a personal conference with the Claimant. Our conveyance on leaving the town received, as when we entered, the continuous shouts of an observing and expectant public so long as we continued in sight, and I may say (and speak for all the Committee then present, both ladies and gentlemen) that we left Alresford if possible more convinced than when we entered it that the Claimant was no impostor, but the veritable Sir ROGER TICHBORNE, and with a prayer on our lips that our efforts to obtain justice would not be in vain.

I should like, before closing my letter, to make one or two remarks as to the unmistakable identity of the Claimant, and which has been spoken to by nearly all the witnesses on his side in the late Trial—namely, the eye. It may be called most truly a TICHBORNE eye: and I do feel astonished when considering the verdict of the jury as one of the institutions of our country, and one on which we have been accustomed to look with so much confidence as to its justice, that they should have ignored the evidence of a Mother, backed up by the opinion of more than eighty witnesses. After the identification of a son by his mother, with the peculiarity of such an organ, I have no doubt, had the Attorney-General been engaged on the other side, but that this peculiarity would have been used as one of his strong arguments. I may say that the TICHBORNE Family were well known to me when a resident in Winchester, and when I saw the Claimant I at once recognised him as Sir ROGER, and I think I never saw two persons more alike than the Claimant and his uncle, who when I resided in Winchester, was in the possession of the estates, and resided at Tichborne—the same style of person in every respect, with that, I may say, most peculiar eye. Our prayer is, sir, that justice may be done in this case, and that one of our most glorious institutions—trial by jury—may not be disfigured by a one-sided and unjust prosecution, as proposed by the Attorney-General. I may say that our Committee has already sent out, to Members of Parliament and the general public, about 500 extracts and appeals, and in no case has one farthing been deducted from the subscriptions, but all expenses have been borne by the Committee.

I am, Sir, &c., JOSEPH KNOWLES.

Southampton, 16th May, 1872.

This gentleman was not called as a witness at the Great Trial, because those concerned never heard of him; and indeed, they were wholly uninstructed on the most material points. No wonder the Crown won an easy victory. The Claimant himself, who must have known all, never told his Counsel anything.

We think it well to preserve the names of the Jurors in this Trial. A. HAMILTON CHEKE, Esq. (foreman); Capt. DENNIS, R.N.; Capt. GUNNELL, R.N.; the Hon. W. DUDLEY RYDER; BONAMY MANSELL POWER, Esq.; EDWARD CLARK, Esq.; PAUL F. MORGAN, Esq.; Capt. J. SIMPSON, R.N.; THOMAS TAYLOR, Esq.; Colonel AIKMAN, V.C.; and ARTHUR DEEDS, Esq.

One particular and peculiar device to which the Family, or the Jesuits, resorted during this Trial in the Common Pleas, can be palliated by no man of honest mind: we mean the circulation of a printed paper calculated to prejudice its readers against TICHBORNE. We have the best reason for asserting that the one to which we are calling special attention was sedulously brought under the consideration of the jurymen, their friends, and connections. This was the story of MARTIN GUERRE, which was published five days after the first Trial began, to wit, on the 15th of May, 1871, in a periodical called *The Month*, edited by the Rev. HENRY COLERIDGE, a member of the Order of Jesuits, and a brother of the leading Counsel for the Defendant in the action. It is entitled *A Case of Personation in the Sixteenth Century*, and it is drawn up with consummate subtlety, perpetually suggesting that the (so-called) Impostor of the bygone day was but the prototype in every respect of the unhappy gentleman who was claiming, and was swindled out of, his inheritance. The Jesuitical writer in *The Month* did not hesitate to put forth MARTIN GUERRE as being a convicted and confessed Impostor: and this he did for the purpose of assimilating TICHBORNE to him in all things. But a wiser and honester man than he, the Sieur de MONTAIGNE, writing of the famous case of MARTIN GUERRE, had some doubt whether injustice had not been done in that case, as it has been in TICHBORNE'S. "I saw in my younger days," he says, "a report of a process that Coras, a counsellor of Thoulouse, put in print, of a strange accident of two men who presented themselves the one for the other. I remember (and I hardly remember anything else) that he seemed to have rendered the imposture of him whom he judged to be guilty, so wonderful, and so far exceeding both our knowledge and his who was the judge, *that I thought it a very bold sentence that condemned him to be hanged*." Our present administrators, and our learned wiseacres in the Press, do not seem to exercise the same caution as this wise old Frenchman did; but have decided irrevocably and everlastingly that TICHBORNE is ORTON, and can, and indeed ought, to be no one else.

It is evident from this that our sagacious old Essayist did not believe in the confession which the Jesuit in *The Month* pretends was made, and could not have believed that the real man appeared to convict his double; otherwise he would not have penned such a passage as that which we have cited. But the Jesuit writer did not cite MONTAIGNE; but rather relied upon a sort of mixed romance of French and German writers, who are not near so well worthy of credit as the great scholar and philosopher whom we have cited. But thus it is that, by garbling and fiction, History is written.

It is evident that the persons who resorted to this trick must have doubted the honesty of their case, or they would not have used such roguery to support it. Had the jurymen to whose notice it was brought been honourable men, or made of the stuff of which olden jurors were formed, they would have formally complained to the Court of this scandalous device: though, if they had, in all probability the Jesuits of the plot would have loudly asserted that it was done by TICHBORNE, or his friends. Indeed, there never has been any falsehood too black for them to use in the furtherance of their conspiracy; and if Mr. ONSLOW'S conjecture be right, that JEAN LUIE, the Swede converted (as appears by the prison records) from Lutheranism to Popery, was indeed a "plant" of theirs, coached up with true information about the "Osprey," which the Jesuit confraternity, through their means of getting information from all parts of the world, had obtained; —if they were capable of this, and of inventing the Tattoo, of what degrees in crime may they not be well suspected?

Another remark may be added: There was but one feeling of indignation throughout England—even among the worst opponents of the Claimant—at the vituperative language of the Attorney-General, Sir JOHN COLERIDGE. Never in human memory had such a torrent of foul abuse been poured forth. This sentiment found expression in the following verses, circulated freely during the learned gentleman's long harangue; and which we preserve as a curious memento of the day:—

ODE TO THE ATTORNEY-GENERAL.

Is it worth your while,
O'ercharged with spleen or bile,
Day after day, thus wearily to fag hard,
Simply to earn the name of dirty blackguard?
Will all your monstrous brawling,
Vituperation and name-calling,
Unmeasured and unmerited abuse,
Be to your client half the real use
Of (from which you strangely keep aloof)
One well-authenticated legal proof?
"ROGER" is not himself. Why do you smother
The truthful evidence of his own mother?
Make her (a Lady by the right of birth,
Of fame unsullied and acknowledged worth,
In the foul eloquence of your harangue,
As void of Justice as replete with slang),
"The vile accomplice"—or the idiot tool
Of one who first you stigmatised as "fool."
And then—
Subtlest of men!—
Describe "the dull and half-taught ROGER"—
More than your equal, learned legal dodger!—
"Able"—(the thing is marvellous, if true)—
"Just as he please," *to cross-examine* you,
With more ability and less abuse
Than through this Trial you've been wont to use;
And this so well, despite *your* legal knowledge
And *his* strange backwardness at school and college.
He coolly turns—no longer fool, but knave—or
Something still worse, your words in his own favour!
"Speech may be silver," as we have been told,
"But Wisdom's silence the more precious gold."
Then pray "dry up" this babbling stream of chatter;
Let's something have "more germane to the matter."
If you can fight, why not at once begin?
Produce your proofs (time's up), go in and win;
Nor thus, despite reason and common sense,
Saddle the sought estates with more expense!
Leave something for the victor, let him be
The Claimant—or your client! Don't let's see
Them *both* made bankrupt—give the world the pain
"JARNDYCE and JARNDYCE" to sigh o'er again.

About this period an extraordinary incident occurred, which makes one think that even *then*, the Family were assured of success in the Great Trial at Bar. The *Morning Advertiser* thus comments upon it.

THE TICHBORNE KNOLL.

Ottery St. Mary, in the County of Devon, has achieved celebrity. It is the chosen retreat of Sir JOHN COLERIDGE, Her Majesty's Attorney-General; and he has recently carried out, with much success, it appears, a new plantation—trees of large growth having been transplanted and grouped on a conspicuous elevation; and in commemoration of the happy conclusion of the great TICHBORNE Trial, there they may stand for generations to come, with the name and memories of the Tichborne Knoll. The *Law Times*, from which we quote this interesting event, further informs us that the trees in question lately ornamented Tichborne Park or estates in Hampshire, and that having been presented to the Attorney-General by "the ladies of the TICHBORNE family as the only expression of their appreciation of his services which the Attorney-General would receive," we are at a loss to conjecture which out of many reminiscences this famous Tichborne Knoll will carry forward to future generations.

It is not only possible, but certain, that the Attorney-General's memorable speech, thanks to the hard-handed men of England, will be replied to; and it is also not impossible that when the verdict of the British jury, not yet given on this case, shall be pronounced, it may give to this Tichborne Knoll a memory that shall not be altogether pleasant to those who have given, or to him who has planted the trees. When it is also remembered that the private civil advocate became the adviser of the Crown, and he himself being the prosecutor, took possession of the public purse for the purpose of carrying out this prosecution, and commenced by thrusting into Newgate a man who during the Trial was often almost at the point of death,—what, we ask, will be thought of the Tichborne Knoll if, after all—tattoo marks and the rest of it notwithstanding—some future inheritor of Tichborne Park should ask for his trees?

The Court of Chancery, it appears, has hastened to assume, with "the ladies of the TICHBORNE Family," that this case is at an end, and has given them at their own sweet will to deal with and dispose of the trees of Tichborne Park; and the Attorney-General, by accepting this graceful tribute, has thus made himself more than ever a party to the suit, in so far as that he has now a veritable stake in the cause which is not yet decided. Is it right that during a case yet to be tried, and for which the Government prosecution is preparing and procuring fresh evidence at any cost, a Government law officer, who directed that case, should receive a present from the parties concerned in establishing the guilt of the individual prosecuted—given as an emblem of gratitude for the services he has already rendered them—if not in the anticipation of the termination in their favour of the whole issue? Let us imagine—for it is not impossible—that a complete change of affairs should yet occur. What a memory will there be connected with these trees, should they be suffered still to grace the knoll at Ottery St. Mary. There is something ominous in such a gift. It reminds us of Birnam-wood coming to Dunsinane. When those trees stand naked and leafless in the winter on the knoll of Ottery St. Mary, they may serve to remind him who looks at them of the possible stem of an ancient family stripped of all, and blasted by the fiery-forked tongue of unjust abuse. When they are clothed again in their leafy garb, who knows but that one with whose name and ownership they are connected, may be rehabilitated himself? That such a thing will be, of course we cannot and do not say; but that it may be, we are equally unable to deny. But for the respectability of the authority cited, we should have been inclined to doubt the authenticity of the story of the gift, offered in such undeniably bad taste, and accepted with so little proper judgment and discretion. For every tree will in imagination bear one of those warnings to trespassers and other ill-conditioned persons with which our woodland landscapes are so often disfigured—the application of which still awaits decision at the hands of an impartial tribunal. In future years, if the trees are suffered to grow, the Tichborne Knoll may become as celebrated as the Tichborne Dole formerly was; the latter as an act of charity, the former as an act of triumphant right; but not perhaps exactly as intended—that remains still to be seen.—*Morning Advertiser.*

The annexed Correspondence indicates also part of the system of intimidation resorted to by the Family before the first Trial commenced.

57, Lincoln's Inn Fields: 21st April, 1870.

SIR,—As the London Solicitors for the Guardians of the Infant Sir HENRY TICHBORNE will you allow us to ask if you are the writer of a letter dated Reform Club, 11th April, 1870, and of which we inclose a copy? The letter has been printed and put into circulation.—We are, Sir, your obedient Servants,

G. H. WHALLEY, Esq., M.P. DOBINSON & GEARE.

(Copy.)

Reform Club: April 11th, 1870.

SIR,—I have delayed replying to your letter about Sir ROGER TICHBORNE until I could further satisfy myself as to the fact of the Claimant being the man he professes to be, and I now state that having examined the case thoroughly I am completely convinced that he is so. And I am further of opinion that the opposition to his claim is so entirely baseless that I can only regard it as a case of such grievous persecution and injustice, as to demand the sympathy and aid of those to whom the circumstances become known to Sir ROGER TICHBORNE in exposing and resisting it. Having no interest whatever, present or prospective, in the question, I have to-day subscribed £25 towards a fund for prosecuting the claim.—I am, yours truly, G. H. WHALLEY.

57, Lincoln's Inn Fields: 26th April, 1870.

SIR,—You have not thought proper to answer our note of inquiry of the 21st inst., but as it was addressed in conformity with your own letter to which we referred, we must assume it has reached you.

We fully admit that you or any other partisan of the person who for the last three years has chosen to call himself Sir R. TICHBORNE may possess an unquestioned right to express an opinion upon the merits of the claim he has put forth, but when in addition to promulgating such an opinion you publish a manifesto that the opposition to his claim is so entirely baseless that it can be regarded only as a case of grievous persecution and injustice,—We, as solicitors for the guardians of the Infant Sir HENRY TICHBORNE, tell you in their behalf that in so saying, without possessing the means of forming any judgment whatever on the *real* case, you are guilty not only of a great impertinence but of stating that which is wholly untrue in fact.

We may add for your information that which you appear to be ignorant of, that in subscribing to support the litigation of the person in question, you are committing a breach of the Law of Maintenance.—We are, Sir, your obedient Servants,

G. H. WHALLEY, Esq., M.P. DOBINSON & GEARE.

6, Mansfield-street, Portland-place: 26th April, 1870.

SIR,—We have had a copy of your circular dated from the Reform Club 11th April, 1870, placed in our hands stating that the opposition to the claim of the person whom you call Sir ROGER TICHBORNE "is so entirely baseless that you can only regard it as a case of such grievous persecution and injustice as to demand sympathy and aid."

We are concerned for the Trustees of the Doughty Estates and certain members of the TICHBORNE Family, and we beg to know to whom you intend the observations in your Circular to apply.

We reserve the right to make any use of this correspondence.

We are, Sir, your obedt. Servants,

G. H. WHALLEY, Esq., M.P. CULLINGTON & SLAUGHTER.

Garlant's Hotel, Suffolk-street, Pall Mall: 27th April, 1870.

Messrs. DOBINSON & GEARE.

GENTLEMEN,—Your letter of the 21st inst., addressed to my Club, I received together with your second letter of the 26th on my return to town late last evening, and I fully admit your right to an explanation of the circumstances under which I wrote the letter of which you sent me a copy.

Being somewhat connected with Hampshire, the Tichborne district, may account for my being requested to give my opinion on that case, and being so I adopted all the means available to obtain information, and you admit that I was entitled to express the opinion at which I arrived in favour of the claim, and as to this I may add, that on the day I wrote the letter in question, Messrs. BAXTER, ROSE & NORTON, by whom the case had been for some time under consideration, conveyed to me in writing their concurrence in that opinion.

With reference to your objection to the remarks accompanying such expression of opinion, I have to offer the following observations.

It is of course possible that the evidence of Sir R. TICHBORNE's identity may be the result of fraud, perjury, and conspiracy, but it seemed to me that if such was or was ever believed to be so, it was inconceivable that, for the three years to which you refer, it should have been undetected and unexposed; and I must be permitted to differ from you in the view that I or any disinterested person should be at liberty to express publicly any opinion whatever upon the question except so far as it involves a public scandal, and the belief of grievous persecution and injustice alone justified me in offering any opinion whatever on the case.

Any information you may communicate to me in justification of your observations I will adopt any means you may suggest for publishing as fully as you inform me my letter has been; and as to the illegality of the subscription noticed by you I must refer you to my Solicitors, Messrs. BLOXAM & ELLISON, 1, Lincoln's Inn Fields.—I am, Gentlemen, your very obedient Servant,

G. H. WHALLEY.

Garlant's Hotel, Suffolk-street, Pall Mall: 28th April, 1870.

GENTLEMEN,—In reply to your letter dated the 26th and received by me late yesterday evening, I beg to inform you that I know of no "circular" of mine that could have been received by you. With reference to your quotation from a letter written by me, I consider that my observations fairly apply to all persons engaged in denying the identity of Sir R. TICHBORNE unless they have reason to believe that he and those who have made affidavits of his identity are combined in a course of fraud, perjury, and conspiracy.

Having received a similar communication from Messrs. DOBINSON & GEARE, I send you a copy of my reply, and repeat that I will readily give due publicity to any information you may think fit to convey to me in justification of your suggestion that Sir R. TICHBORNE is not the person he represents himself to be.—I am, Gentlemen, your most obedient Servant,

Messrs. CULLINGTON & SLAUGHTER. G. H. WHALLEY.

57, Lincoln's Inn Fields: 28th April, 1870.

SIR,—We are in receipt of your letter of yesterday. As Messrs. BAXTER & Co. could have no better means than yourself of arriving at a judgment on the real case, we do not see that their concurrence in your view alters the matter.

The case as you describe it is not undetected, but it is unexposed for the simple reason that the Trial is still pending, and to give you now the information which you suggest would be to do that which, from the commencement of the proceedings, we have carefully abstained from doing, namely, presenting the case to the public in anticipation of its coming before a jury.—We are, Sir, your very obedient Servants,

G. H. WHALLEY, Esq., M.P. DOBINSON & GEARE.

Reform Club: April 29th, 1870.

GENTLEMEN,—I have to acknowledge the receipt of your letter stating that the Tichborne Case, as I describe it, is not undetected but that for reasons connected with some trial to take place before a jury you have carefully abstained from exposing for three years fraud, perjury, and conspiracy.

I must be allowed to add to my former remarks that those who for private reasons are content to allow a public scandal to remain so long unexposed appear to me to incur a grave responsibility, and cannot reasonably impute impertinence to any one who may infer from such delay the absence of evidence of any such offences.—I am, Gentlemen, your most obedient Servant,

Messrs. DOBINSON & GEARE. G. H. WHALLEY.

57, Lincoln's Inn Fields: April 30th, 1870.

SIR,—We are in receipt of your letter of yesterday's date. As far as we can extract a meaning from your letter, you appear to us to find fault with a Solicitor because he does not pander to public curiosity by publishing his client's case to all the world while it is yet under adjudication by the proper tribunal to decide it. As a Member of the Bar and a legislator, we should have thought you had not yet to learn that to do so is visited with heavy punishment by the Courts.

We have no wish to say more than we have already said, but you must excuse us for adding that your letters exhibit an extraordinary inaptitude for forming any opinion upon such matters, and shew that the office of legal censor is not your forte.—We are, Sir, your very obedient Servants,

G. H. WHALLEY, Esq., M.P. DOBINSON & GEARE.

Reform Club: 3rd May, 1870.

GENTLEMEN,—Our correspondence on the Tichborne Case as also that of Messrs. CULLINGTON & SLAUGHTER, it seems to me right to forward to those at whose request I expressed the views to which you object with permission to give thereto, the same publicity as to my letter of the 11th April.

Your letter of the 30th ult., received by me to-day I am happy to find requires no reply, freely excusing you as I do, under the circumstances, for concluding this correspondence, commenced by threats of legal penalties, with remarks intended to be personal and offensive.—I am, Gentlemen, your most obedient Servant,

Messrs. DOBINSON & GEARE. G. H. WHALLEY.

NARRATIVE OF PROCEEDINGS BETWEEN COMMITTAL AND TRIAL.

At the Sessions which commenced April 8th, 1872, the Deputy-Recorder, Sir T. CHAMBERS, made the following allusion to the great case when addressing the Grand Jury. His enunciation of the law of forgery is enough to make any lawyer stand aghast; but nearly all lawyers have been aghast at this Trial:—

The Deputy-Recorder said there was one name in the calendar which had unhappily been very frequently before the public—that of TOMAS CASTRO, otherwise TICHBORNE; but no depositions had been furnished to him, and he really knew nothing whatever of the case. He could only merely, therefore, say that if the charge against the Defendant should be that of perjury in falsely swearing that he was Sir ROGER TICHBORNE, all that they would have to do was to see whether a *prima facie* case was made out in support of that charge, and, if they were of opinion that such a case had been established, it would be their duty to return a true bill for that offence. The Defendant would also very probably be charged with the offence of forgery, in issuing certain bonds for the payment of money in the name of ROGER CHARLES TICHBORNE, who was alleged to have been deceased many years before. With regard to that description of charge, if it should appear that the Defendant had really issued such bonds in the name of Sir ROGER TICHBORNE, well knowing that he had no authority to do so, it was his duty *to tell them that the offence would amount to forgery.* This was all he could say to them on the subject, and he would merely observe that all that devolved upon the grand jury was to see whether a *prima facie* case had been made out. In that case they would return a true bill, and the whole of the facts would be investigated afterwards before another tribunal.

The grand jury then retired.

The Defendant was described in the calendar in the following terms:—"TOMAS CASTRO, *alias* ROGER CHARLES DOUGHTY TICHBORNE, Baronet, aged 42, of no occupation, and of imperfect education, committed by Lord Chief Justice BOVILL for wilful and corrupt perjury."

Later in the day Mr. MONTAGU WILLIAMS said he was instructed to make application in the case of a prisoner who was described in the calendar as TOMAS CASTRO, *alias* Sir ROGER CHARLES TICHBORNE, who had been committed for several weeks upon a charge of perjury by the Lord Chief Justice of the Common Pleas, to be furnished with a copy of the indictment and be made acquainted with the precise nature of the charges that would be preferred against him. He was merely informed that the law officers of the Crown intended to prefer a charge of some kind or other against the Defendant, and it appeared to him that it was only common fairness he should be made acquainted with the nature of the charges that were to be made against him. An application would probably be made for a reduction in the amount of bail, and this application might be resisted on the ground that the Defendant was not prepared to take his trial, and it was quite impossible that the Defendant should be so prepared until he was made acquainted with the nature of the charge that would be preferred against him.

The Deputy-Recorder said he was unable to assist the learned Counsel. He was quite as ignorant of the charge that would be preferred against the Defendant as the learned Counsel was, and all he knew was that it appeared by the calendar that the Defendant was committed to take his trial for perjury.

Mr. MONTAGU WILLIAMS said it appeared to him that this was a great hardship upon the Defendant. He was surely entitled to know what precise offence he was charged with.

The Deputy-Recorder said he was informed that a bill would be preferred against the Defendant to-morrow, and if it was found a true bill the Defendant would have a copy of the indictment.

Mr. MONTAGU WILLIAMS said he should renew the application on the following day, and the matter then dropped.

On April 10, at the Old Bailey, before Mr. Baron CLEASBY and Mr. Justice QUAIN, the Defendant, under the names of TOMAS CASTRO, alias ARTHUR ORTON, alias Sir ROGER DOUGHTY TICHBORNE, Bart., was placed in the dock and charged with the crimes of Perjury and Forgery in connection with the TICHBORNE Trials in the Court of Common Pleas and Chancery. His appearance had been somewhat altered by his five weeks' incarceration in Newgate. His features were less ruddy, and he looked sallow and careworn. His self-possession, however, did not fail him; he surveyed the spectators with calmness, and did not evince the slightest embarrassment at the position in which he was placed.

Mr. ARCHIBALD and Mr. POLAND (instructed by the Solicitors to the Treasury) appeared to prosecute, and Mr. MONTAGU WILLIAMS (instructed by Mr. GORTON, solicitor, of Bedford-row,) to defend the prisoner.

Mr. AVORY, the Clerk of the Court, read the various charges to be preferred against the prisoner. He said: TOMAS CASTRO, otherwise ARTHUR ORTON, otherwise Sir ROGER DOUGHTY TICHBORNE, Baronet, you are indicted for wilful and corrupt perjury, alleged to have been committed by you in an affidavit made by you and filed in the Court of Chancery, whereby you falsely swore that you were the eldest son of the late Sir JAMES TICHBORNE, the tenth baronet of Tichborne; that you resided at Paris from the date of your birth until 1845, when you were brought over to England and placed at the Jesuits' College, Stonyhurst; that afterwards you were appointed cornet and subsequently lieutenant in Her Majesty's 6th Dragoon Guards; that you joined that regiment at Dublin, and remained with it until January, 1853, except during any temporary leave of absence; that you retired from the regiment in February, 1853, and in the month of March sailed for Valparaiso, where you arrived in due course; that from that time you travelled in various parts of South America; and that in April, 1854, when at Rio, you took passage in the ship "Bella" for New York. Are you guilty or not guilty?

The Claimant, in a firm voice: Not guilty.

Mr. AVORY: By another indictment you are charged with wilful and corrupt perjury upon the trial of an issue at Nisi Prius, before Lord Chief Justice BOVILL at Westminster, and the charge alleged is that you falsely swore that you were not ARTHUR ORTON. To this charge are you guilty or not?

The Claimant: Not guilty.

Mr. AVORY: By another indictment you are charged for that you, on the 12th June, 1871, feloniously did forge a deed with intent to defraud, and by a second count you are charged with uttering and putting off that forged deed with intent to defraud, you well knowing it to be so forged. In another part of the indictment the deed is described as a mortgage debenture. Are you guilty or not?

The Claimant: Not guilty.

Mr. MONTAGU WILLIAMS: My lord, I am instructed on the part of the Defendant to mention the fact that these indictments—the two for perjury and the one for forgery—were only brought into Court yesterday. With regard to the indictment for forgery, *we had no notice until yesterday that such an indictment would be preferred.* Your lordship is aware that a question of bail has been raised in Chambers before Mr. Justice WILLES, but that the Defendant has not been released. By this indictment the circumstances have been altered altogether. We have endeavoured to obtain from the Crown some intimation as to when the Defendant may be expected to be tried, but hitherto we have failed. I think that in common fairness, we should be informed when the Crown intends to proceed.

Mr. ARCHIBALD: I am told by the Solicitors to the Treasury that no such application has been made to them, so that my friend Mr. WILLIAMS is in error on this point.

Mr. AVORY: At this moment I have received a writ of *certiorari* for the removal of these indictments to the Court of Queen's Bench, at Westminster.

Mr. MONTAGU WILLIAMS: I know the Attorney-General has a right, in his official capacity, to remove the trial by *certiorari*, and, according to that, it will stand for the sittings after Trinity Term, or some time about June. I am afraid the trial is, therefore taken out of your lordship's jurisdiction by this right of the Attorney-General.

Baron CLEASBY: It is now out of my jurisdiction entirely.

Mr. AVORY: The prisoner, I suppose, will remain in gaol until discharged in due course of law.

Baron CLEASBY: Certainly.

The Claimant was then removed to the cells below.

TICHBORNE's advisers now applied for bail. They went before a Judge at chambers—Mr. Justice BRETT. They could hardly have made a worse selection. Mr. Justice BRETT had made no secret of his opinion that the Defendant was a rank impostor. This was the phrase in fashion. The Government, of course, opposed; as they opposed this unhappy gentleman in everything. Mr. GRAY, Q.C., Solicitor to the Treasury, attended on their behalf for that purpose. Mr. GORTON moved on the following affidavit:

I am the Solicitor acting for and on behalf of a prisoner who has been committed to, and now is confined in, Her Majesty's Gaol of Newgate, in and for the City of London, under the name of TOMAS CASTRO, otherwise called ARTHUR ORTON, otherwise called Sir ROGER CHARLES DOUGHTY TICHBORNE, Bart., upon two charges of perjury and one of forgery. The said T. CASTRO, otherwise called ARTHUR ORTON, otherwise called R. C. D. TICHBORNE, Bart., has been in Newgate Gaol for five weeks and upwards, and was originally committed there on the 6th of March last, upon a warrant of commitment of the Lord Chief Justice BOVILL, there to be detained until the then next general session of Oyer and Terminer and gaol delivery to be holden for the jurisdiction of the Central Criminal Court, to the intent that he should then and there answer Our Lady the Queen concerning a charge of perjury, unless he should in the mean time enter into recognisances, himself in the sum of £5,000, with two sufficient sureties in the sum of £2,500 each, or four sureties in the sum of £1,250 each, conditioned for his personal appearance at the said then next session of the Central Criminal Court. The said T. CASTRO, otherwise A. ORTON, otherwise Sir R. C. D. TICHBORNE, Bart., was up to the 9th April last unable to obtain sureties on his behalf for so large a sum as £5,000. On the said 9th of April last two indictments for perjury and one for forgery were preferred against the said T. CASTRO, otherwise A. ORTON, otherwise Sir R. C. D. TICHBORNE, Bart., at the Central Criminal Court, and a true bill was found on each indictment, and he is now in custody at Newgate Gaol aforesaid upon such two charges of perjury and one of forgery, there to be detained until discharged in due course of law. The said three indictments have been removed by the prosecution by writ of *certiorari* to the Court of Queen's Bench, and I believe that the said T. CASTRO, otherwise A. ORTON, otherwise Sir R. C. D. TICHBORNE, Bart., cannot be tried earlier than in the month of June, and probably will not be tried until the latter end of this year. I am advised that all three charges will involve, amongst other questions, the questions of whether the said T. CASTRO, otherwise A. ORTON, otherwise Sir R. C. D. TICHBORNE, Bart., is Sir R. C. D. TICHBORNE, Bart., or not; and also whether he is or not the person called A. ORTON. For the purpose of proving that the said T. CASTRO, otherwise A. ORTON, otherwise Sir R. C. D. TICHBORNE, Bart., is Sir R. C. D. TICHBORNE, Bart., and not A. ORTON, it will be necessary for a very large number of persons to see and converse with him in order to test him as to his identity; and this, in my opinion, cannot fairly be done whilst he is a prisoner in Newgate. The papers connected with the case comprise many thousands of folios, and are of so heavy a character that I believe it would be impossible for me to master them without the daily and constant attendance of the said T. CASTRO, otherwise A. ORTON, otherwise Sir R. C. D. TICHBORNE, Bart., at my office, and I do not believe it possible that I can obtain from him all the necessary information for his defence whilst he is confined in Newgate Gaol. I am prepared with sureties who are ready to enter into recognizances for a reasonable amount for the said T. CASTRO, otherwise A. ORTON, otherwise Sir R. C. D. TICHBORNE, Bart., to appear and take his trial, and also to appear and receive sentence if called upon. I have for the last month been almost exclusively engaged upon the papers connected with this case, and from what I have learned from such papers and from persons I have seen who will be witnesses on behalf of the said T. CASTRO, otherwise A. ORTON, otherwise Sir R. C. D. TICHBORNE, Bart., I believe the said T. CASTRO, otherwise A. ORTON, otherwise Sir R. C. D. TICHBORNE, Bart., has a good defence to all the charges made against him.

Mr. GORTON, after reading the affidavit, said: The prisoner has been in custody now for five weeks, and, as the indictments have been removed to the Court of Queen's Bench, it is possible that the case will not be tried for some eight or ten months; and to keep this man in prison instead of admitting him to bail would be in point of fact to sentence him to a term of imprisonment before his trial. I think I have made out a sufficient case to show that it is almost impossible, on account of the complicated nature of the evidence—in fact, I think the Attorney-General said enough on that subject in the House of Commons the other night——

The Judge: I cannot listen to anything the Attorney-General said.

Mr. GORTON: I say it is almost impossible for the prisoner to prepare his defence unless he is admitted to bail.

The Judge: What is your position?

Mr. GORTON: I ask that he may be admitted to bail.

The Judge: On what ground? Do you put it as a matter of discretion or right?

Mr. GORTON: I put it as a matter of right that he should be admitted to bail, and a matter of discretion as to the amount.

The Judge: What authority have you to show that it is a matter of right, *a true bill having been found against the prisoner for forgery?*

Mr. GORTON: Well, I suppose it will be in your lordship's discretion. It is discretionary in all cases, I think—even murder.

The Judge: What ground do you rely upon?

Mr. GORTON: First, upon the ground that it is almost impossible to get up the defence if he is not released; and, secondly, because he may have to be kept in prison for twelve months awaiting his trial; and after that the trial will, in all probability, last two or three months.

The Judge: You have said nothing at all about twelve months in your affidavit.

Mr. GORTON read again the part of the affidavit where it was said that, probably, the case would not be tried till the end of the year; and continued: It is impossible, of course, to say exactly when the case will be tried, but it cannot be tried earlier than the sittings after term, and may stand over till November. I don't know what the learned Counsel for the Treasury has to say.

Mr. GRAY: I cannot dispute that the case may go over till November.

The Judge: What do you say?

Mr. GRAY: I say there are no grounds for admitting him to bail. I take it the Judge must consider the nature of the offence. It is necessary for anyone who is committed to take his trial to show that the offence is bailable.

The Judge: *There is no allegation here that the attorney has not had access to the prisoner in Newgate.*

Mr. GORTON: That is so. I can see him in Newgate. But in a case of this kind I want to see him constantly, and we cannot have all the papers in Newgate.

Mr. GRAY: I say that is really no legal ground as to bail. The way in which this has happened is, as your lordship knows, that the Lord Chief Justice of the Court of Common Pleas committed the prisoner on the charge of perjury, and, as far as these charges are concerned, he fixed the bail at a certain amount, viz., £5,000 for himself, with two sureties for £2,500 or four for £1,250 each. But in addition to the charge of perjury on which he was committed by the Lord Chief Justice, and for which bail has been fixed, *there is now a serious charge of forgery.* I do not mean to make use of any argument one way or another, but simply—pointing out these facts—to leave the matter to your lordship's discretion. It is for your lordship to say *whether you think he should be admitted to bail at all upon the charge of forgery,* and, if he is admitted to bail, upon what terms he should be.

The Judge: The application could be made to the Court of Queen's Bench, could it not?

Mr. GRAY: In the affidavit there is nothing as to the nature of the case, but I am not going to make any objection on that ground.

Mr. GORTON: It is whether he is TICHBORNE, or not, I take it.

Mr. GRAY: I suppose your lordship knows the nature of the case pretty well, and has, therefore, a knowledge of the circumstances which ought to affect the exercise of your lordship's discretion in dealing with the matter. I have nothing more to say. I have no desire that the man should be kept in prison.

The Judge: Very well. (To Mr. GORTON.) Do you wish to say anything more?

Mr. GORTON: I have said all I have to say. It is a case which I cannot get up properly unless he is released.

The Judge: I think it must be taken that the facts of the case are before me. That being so, it is clear to my mind that *the charge of forgery is one of a most serious kind. It is as serious a charge of forgery as could be made, and under those circumstances I think that I ought not to admit the prisoner to bail except upon very strong grounds;* and in the absence of any allegation that the attorney has not had access to the prisoner in Newgate, the grounds with regard to the necessity of interviews between him and his attorney, and with regard to the delay in the trial, are not sufficient. As to the delay, it cannot be foreseen. The trial may take place in June, and even if it does not take place till November, it appears to me there is not sufficient ground to say that the prisoner should be admitted to bail. Therefore I decline to make any order.

Mr. GORTON: I shall make an application to the Court.

The Judge: You may take what course you are advised.

The matter here dropped.

Any comment on this would be unnecessary. It is clear that it was intended to keep him in prison until he was tried.

To the Court of Queen's Bench, against this decision, an appeal was accordingly made. The following is a report of what took place on April 17th, 1872:

The Lord Chief Justice and Justices BLACKBURN, LUSH, and QUAIN being on the Bench, Mr. Serjeant BALLANTINE, with whom were Mr. GIFFARD, Q.C., and Mr. MONTAGU WILLIAMS, said—In the case of a person now in the gaol of Newgate, I am instructed to move for a rule nisi calling upon the Solicitors for the Treasury to show cause why the prisoner should not be admitted to bail. He is described in the indictments by different *aliases*, such as CASTRO, ORTON, and TICHBORNE; and, in mentioning these names, I need hardly mention any further particulars connected with the case, except so far as relates to his present position. It must be in the knowledge of your lordships that the case was tried before the Lord Chief Justice of the Common Pleas, and lasted for a considerable time; but it is unnecessary that I should call attention to the mode in which the case was terminated. Suffice it to say, that at its termination his lordship thought it his duty to commit the then Plaintiff on a charge of perjury to Newgate, at the same time calling on him to find bail himself in £5,000, and two securities in a like amount, and where he is at present confined. At the last session of the Central Criminal Court two indictments were preferred against him by the Crown for perjury, and one for forgery, and these three indictments having been found by the grand jury, they have since been removed into this court by the fiat of the Attorney-General, and in consequence I am obliged to come here to make this application, and in order for the Court to appreciate my remarks I may observe that the removal took place antagonistic to the views and wishes of the Defendant. *Primâ facie* he would have been entitled to be tried at the Old Bailey, and although there is nothing to show that he was able to oppose any motion to be made, inasmuch as it was done by the Attorney-General himself, I may venture to say that the prisoner was not consulted in the matter, and those who prosecute are the persons who by their own act have brought the indictments into this Court. I do not refer to it for the purpose of making any complaint, but to point out that by this mode of dealing with the indictments he has been placed in the present position of having to apply to your lordships, in consequence of the length of time that must necessarily elapse before he can be tried. We know, from the arrears in the Court of Queen's Bench, that the case as now put into the list for trial cannot be tried for some months, if it could at all come on within the present year. I believe, however, that on the application of the Crown—I do not know if it has the power of itself to fix an earlier day—the Court would in this case fix an early day for the trial.

The Lord Chief Justice said the Crown had not the power *proprio motu* to take it out of its turn, but the Court could, on an application, if it thought it desirable, make special arrangements for the trial.

Mr. Serjeant BALLANTINE: It is not impossible, either by such permission or by the act of the Crown, that the case might be tried at an earlier period than by the ordinary course of events it would otherwise be; but under the circumstances I do not see well how it can be done. Some of the allegations in the indictments can only be proved or disproved by witnesses who are now residing in Chili and Australia, because, although the depositions of those witnesses under a commission can be used in a civil case, they cannot be used in a criminal case, but the witnesses themselves must be called on the trial, and, therefore, this case cannot certainly be tried in the ordinary way this year, and therefore it is that I now apply to your lordships to admit the prisoner to bail. The removal of the indictments into this Court was no act of his, and although I admit the same delay would have arisen if the case had been tried at the Old Bailey as in this Court, for the production of the witnesses from Chili and Australia, the question of admission to bail rests upon the nature of the charges. In an indictment for perjury a Defendant as a matter of right is bailed, but in a case of felony it is a matter in the discretion of the Court, and therefore, under the circumstances, I submit that the two ought not to be used in this case as a substantial objection to the prisoner's admission to bail. By the rules of our Criminal Courts a prisoner has no right to a copy of an indictment preferred against him for felony, although he has in a case of misdemeanour, and it was only when he was called upon to plead that he became in any way acquainted with the nature of the charge that had been preferred against him. No doubt in one case the punishment is much more severe than in the other, and that is an element which governs the disposition of a Court in giving a prisoner an opportunity of escaping.

The Lord Chief Justice: Or rather, not to give him the opportunity.

Mr. Serjeant BALLANTINE: I must call your lordships' attention to the position in which the prisoner has been placed by the course that has been adopted by the Crown. *It is an almost unexampled thing for an indictment to be preferred for forgery without a preliminary inquiry, and if the Act under which the prisoner was committed had not been passed he would have had to have undergone a lengthened preliminary examination, and under Mr.* RUSSELL GURNEY'S *Act, the 30th and 31st of* VICTORIA, *chapter 35, a prisoner charged with a particular act is entitled to have the witnesses produced on his behalf bound over at the expense of the prosecutor or the Crown to appear on the Trial to give evidence in his favour, but by the course pursued in this case the prisoner has been deprived of the privilege which is a matter of vital importance to him.* The question being one of identity, it is of the utmost importance to the prisoner that he should not be locked up in prison for a number of months, but that he should be able to communicate freely with his solicitors and have frequent opportunities of seeing his witnesses.

Mr. Justice BLACKBURN said *it was the solicitor's duty to get up the client's case, and it could be done as well when he was in prison as when he was out of prison!!*

Mr. Serjeant BALLANTINE: The identity of the prisoner is the real issue to be tried.

The Lord Chief Justice: I should feel the force of your observations were it not known that the whole of the case on both sides, or to a very great extent, was well known to each side on the recent trial.

Mr. Serjeant BALLANTINE: That is so. But in the indictment it is broadly charged that the prisoner is ARTHUR ORTON. *Now, with regard to that question, no evidence was gone into on either side.*

The Lord Chief Justice: Without asking you what your case is, if the trial had gone on both parties were prepared with affirmative and negative evidence, and therefore it is not too much to infer that it was pretty well known to both sides what evidence was likely to be given.

Mr. Serjeant BALLANTINE: There is no doubt we were in possession of much information on the point as to the prisoner being ARTHUR ORTON, but it is of extreme importance to him that he should have an opportunity of personally conducting his defence.

The Lord Chief Justice: *I think it much better that a man's legal adviser should communicate with the witnesses than the man himself!!*

Mr. Serjeant BALLANTINE: I have endeavoured, in the observations that I have made, to refrain from saying anything with regard to the peculiarities of the inquiry, but to deal with it on general grounds. I take it that, *primâ facie*, the restraint of a prisoner until he is convicted is contrary to the law of England. The only object of restraint is to secure the presence of a prisoner when an inquiry is to take place into the charges that are to be brought against him. The charge of forgery might be used as a means for keeping the Claimant in gaol, because it is not, *per se*, a bailable offence; but I do not think that it is a charge that can ever be tried. I apprehend the reason why the case is brought into this Court is, that the case of forgery might be tried by a Special Jury; but there is no power to summon a Special Jury in a case of felony, although there is in a case of misdemeanour.

Mr. Justice BLACKBURN: Is that so?

Mr. WINING (the Master of the Crown Office): Yes.

Mr. Justice BLACKBURN: I was not aware of that. That will destroy the main reason that has hitherto been supposed to exist for removing cases into this Court.

Mr. Serjeant BALLANTINE: There is another matter which no doubt has presented itself to your lordships' mind, that if the charge of forgery is to be tried the jury will have to be locked up from day to day during the whole of the trial. This is a case of great difficulty, and I hardly know how the existing rules of law can be made to tail in with the possibilities of carrying on such a case. *All these things tend to impress one with the belief that the charge of forgery will never be tried.* I would merely further call attention to the fact that all our extradition treaties refer to cases of felony, and that, coupled with the appearance of the prisoner, his size, and other matters, will make it exceedingly difficult for him to escape (laughter). I shall have no difficulty whatever in producing the requisite amount of bail.

The Lord Chief Justice: You do not ask to have the amount of bail lowered?

Mr. Serjeant BALLANTINE: No; we do not complain of the amount of bail. There will be no difficulty about that.

The Lord Chief Justice: You may take a rule *nisi*, but you must understand that it will be open to the Court to consider whether, looking to the nature of the charges now preferred against the prisoner, *the amount of bail may not have to be raised.* You must not understand us to pledge ourselves one way or the other. All we say is that the question of whether the prisoner shall be admitted to bail is one worthy of consideration, and that therefore you may take a rule nisi.

Rule nisi granted accordingly.

On April 22nd, this rule came on to be argued; we insert the report. The bias manifested is worth recording: the more especially is it to be condemned, as the legal offence of Forgery had never been committed by the Defendant. The threat to increase the amount of bail, is worthy of consideration.

(Sittings in Banco, before the LORD CHIEF JUSTICE, and Justices BLACKBURN, LUSH, and QUAIN.)

The Attorney-General, with whom was Mr. ARCHIBALD, asked to be allowed to show cause, in the case of "The QUEEN v. CASTRO," although this was special paper day. He was unable to attend yesterday from illness.

The Lord Chief Justice said that under the circumstances he could do so, but it must not be made a precedent for interfering with the ordinary business of a special paper day.

The Attorney-General, in showing cause against the rule that had been obtained to admit the Claimant to bail, said—I shall not have to trouble your Lordships much on the subject, but there are one or two matters to which I should like to draw your attention, and then it will be for your lordships to say whether in your discretion you will grant the application. The prisoner cannot claim bail *de jure*, neither can I say that, except in the case of treason, the Court cannot in their discretion grant bail. I think your lordships should know that application was made to Mr. Justice BRETT to admit the prisoner to bail, but that the learned judge declined to accede to it. The true principle to be adopted in these cases is that security shall be taken to insure, under all the circumstances, the appearance of a prisoner for trial on the charge on which he is committed. The Crown has no right, and certainly here it has no wish, to shut the man up for nothing more than simply to secure him. It is always, and it must be, a considerable element in considering bail, first, the nature of the case, and secondly, the nature of the evidence by which it is to be supported. There is a case on the books where a man having pleaded guilty, and before he was tried was admitted to bail. The nature of the case as well as the character of the evidence are therefore elements for the consideration of the Court in acceding to or refusing bail. The public have a right to demand that the highest security shall be given, in order that justice shall be done if the person is proved guilty. The prisoner is here charged, first, with perjury, and secondly, with forgery. No doubt many of the assignments for perjury do not raise the question of identity, but there are others, and in the case of forgery, which raise the question whether or not the prisoner is the person he professes to be. He has supported his case by a number of statements excessively defamatory of other persons, and he has brought them to the bar of public opinion in a way excessively offensive and painful to their feelings, and which, if untrue, constitute a very grave—the gravest and most serious crime a man can possibly be guilty of. The forgery—*if it be forgery*—is an attempt to raise money) and a successful one, I believe—but that is not the question' on securities signed in the name of a person whom the prosecution believe to be dead—a fraud of the highest kind, if true.

The Lord Chief Justice: *I must say that in my humble opinion the perjury in this case, though not in the eye of the law, is a graver offence than the forgery. It is, morally speaking, the far more heinous of the two,* because, with regard to the bonds said to be forged, the persons who lent money on them lent it on a speculation, and in many instances no doubt they have offended against the law, which prohibits such things being done. They are entitled to no sympathy, assuming that it turns out they have been deceived, and the bonds become worthless. Whereas, the perjury involved, if proved, was *an attempt to rob an innocent person of his birthright and inheritance, and it also brought in question in a remarkable degree the honour and character of more than one person. Morally speaking, therefore, the perjury is of a more heinous character than the forgery, under the peculiar circumstances of the case*—that is, always assuming that the charge is made out. But there is another way in which the application ought to be looked at, viz., in reference to the principle laid down in the books for admitting prisoners to bail—how far a prisoner under a charge of forgery is more likely to evade his trial than he would be on a charge of perjury. In that way it becomes material. There is now added forgery to the perjury on which the prisoner was originally committed. Though that must strongly weigh with the Court in admitting the prisoner to bail, we were told the other day there was no probability of his being brought to trial for many months to come. That is a serious matter in considering the application for bail.

The Attorney-General: I ought in candour to say that so far as I am concerned, concurring in what your lordship has said on the subject of the two crimes, it will be necessary, in my view of the case, to produce witnesses from the other side of the world. By our law the evidence taken on commission in a civil case is not admissible in a criminal case.

The Lord Chief Justice: That is a serious element in the consideration of the case; and when the rule was obtained the probability of having to bring witnesses from other parts of the world was very properly brought to our notice.

The Attorney-General: I admit that at once, and that in order to make out my case it will be necessary to bring witnesses from Melipilla and Australia.

Mr. Justice BLACKBURN: That does not throw blame on those who have to postpone the trial, but it is an element of consideration whether the prisoner should be admitted to bail. If he was to be tried in a week there would be little harm if, in their discretion, the Court refused bail, but to keep a man in gaol for twelve months before his trial, and he ultimately proved himself innocent, was a very serious thing.

The Attorney-General: I am not going to dispute it, but if there is to be a trial of charges the acts to prove which took place at the other end of the world, it is hardly a matter of complaint on the part of a prisoner if any necessary delay takes place in the trial in consequence. The circumstances many witnesses will have to prove took place 14,000 miles away. It is a misfortune to a man to be so placed, but having so placed himself by his own act, he has no right to ask to be let out on bail because accidentally, and unfortunately for him, he is charged with having done certain things 14,000 miles away, and which can only be proved by the production of witnesses from that distance.

Mr. Justice LUSH: There is another element to be taken into consideration. The existence of extradition treaties renders a man's escape from justice more difficult.

The Lord Chief Justice: I do not think there is any European Power where we have not an extradition treaty.

The Attorney-General: We have none with America, but I hope we shall soon have one.

Mr. Justice BLACKBURN: Not one with America? Has it expired?

The Attorney-General: Negotiations for one are going on at this moment.

Mr. Justice BLACKBURN: We certainly had one—I was not aware that it had expired.

The Lord Chief Justice: I hope the Government will not allow such an important thing as an extradition treaty with America to fall through.

The Attorney-General: I know that negotiations are now going on between the two countries as to certain crimes.

Mr. Justice BLACKBURN: All the treaties, I believe, include forgery, but not perjury; therefore, an indictment for forgery is more favourable to the prisoner against his escape. The security is better for him than if he were only indicted for perjury.

Mr. Justice QUAIN: Can you prove a *prima facie* case against the prisoner without the foreign evidence?

The Attorney-General: Undoubtedly. I do not want to do more than to bring to your lordships' notice the great importance and the gravity of the offences charged against the prisoner. If the charges of forgery are true, I venture to think that *many a man has been hanged for far less moral guilt than appertains to this man.* If the charges are made out, it is a case of the worst possible description, and if he is found guilty he will be punished probably with the heaviest sentence that the law will allow. He must know that he runs that peril.

The Lord Chief Justice: With regard to the perjury, the bail was fixed by the learned judge who committed him, and we should not at all desire to interfere with the discretion he then exercised, but there is now a more serious charge of forgery brought against the prisoner, and although morally it might amount to a far less heinous offence than the perjury, it involves graver considerations as to punishment, rendering it more likely, if he is conscious of his guilt, of a temptation on his part to evade justice. It is not for us to assume it, but the evidence that sustains one charge will sustain the other, and, therefore, there is a greater inducement in a man who is conscious of his guilt to evade the law, and we ought to hesitate before allowing a prisoner that chance, in which case we might consider it necessary to increase the bail. Then, on the other hand, there is the argument that has been fairly used, that the period that must elapse before the case can be tried requires such a lengthened imprisonment as to make it become a very serious question whether the prisoner ought to be kept so long a time in prison if reasonably sufficient bail can be found to secure his appearance to take his trial at the proper time.

The Attorney-General: I can and I have no other wish than that the man shall be produced at the proper time.

Mr. Justice BLACKBURN: Have you any grounds to urge that the amount of bail named is not a good and reasonable security for his appearance? *The maximum punishment for perjury is seven years**, but for forgery it is transportation for life.

The Attorney-General: I know no difference, except the difference of punishment. *There are twenty assignments for perjury, but the punishment is concurrent.* The two indictments are substantially the same, and were only preferred to prevent technical objections. One assigns oral perjury, and the other perjury in the prisoner's affidavits in Chancery.

The Lord Chief Justice: When do you expect to go to trial? It is impossible, no doubt, to give a definite answer; but when do you think you really can expect to proceed to trial?

The Attorney-General: I do not think that having to send to Australia for witnesses will have much effect on the delay. As the case stands in the list, there is very little chance of it being reached this side of the long vacation. *I shall be ready beyond all doubt by the 2nd of November, if it is not tried in July.* The communication with Chili is rapid, but I do not see how we can hope to have the witnesses over from Australia by July. Practically, it would be impossible to have the witnesses from Australia before November.

The Lord Chief Justice: The probability is that the second trial will not last so long as the first, but it must occupy a very long time.

The Attorney-General: I do not see how it is possible to have the witnesses over before November.

The Lord Chief Justice: *You will then be ready to go to trial?*

The Attorney-General: *I have no reason to doubt it.* As a matter of fact, I understand there are no extradition treaties with Norway, Sweden, Switzerland, and Spain.

Mr. Serjeant BALLANTINE, with whom were Mr. GIFFARD, Q.C., and Mr. MONTAGU WILLIAMS, said: I have very little to add to the observations I made in moving the rule. I can hardly adopt the views of the learned Attorney-General, that the case can be tried at the early period he mentions. I do not think it can be tried much before December.

The Lord Chief Justice: We can make special arrangements for the trial.

Mr. Serjeant BALLANTINE: If ready, it might be tried in November; but there are a great number of witnesses spread over a considerable tract of country, that will have to be brought from Melipilla and Australia. It must occupy a considerable period of time, and there would be some difficulty in obtaining their attendance.

The Lord Chief Justice: I should think, with the knowledge you all possess of the case, that all the witnesses for the prosecution and the defence might be here by November.

Mr. Serjeant BALLANTINE: There is no certainty of it.

The Lord Chief Justice: *You must take your chance of that.*

Mr. Serjeant BALLANTINE: Assuming there is a chance of them being here by that time, it would be a very long time to keep the prisoner in custody. It is impossible to exaggerate the character of the offences with which he is charged, and in considering the legal character of the charges, that circumstance, I am sure, will not be lost sight of in fixing the amount of bail. The offence for which he will in reality be tried will be that of perjury. The Attorney-General has not intimated any serious intention of trying the charge of forgery, and the difficulty attending such a trial every one must readily realise. It would be impossible to lock up the jury, as must be done in a charge of felony, during the whole of the inquiry, without their being able to go to their homes every day at the rising of the Court.

The Lord Chief Justice: I have heard it incidentally, and with great satisfaction, that it is proposed to have legislative interference on that point.

The Attorney-General: It is not right for me to say here what I am able to state elsewhere.

The Lord Chief Justice: I should rejoice to see an alteration in the law. It is a cruel thing to keep a jury locked up for a week or ten days.

Mr. Serjeant BALLANTINE: In the present state of parties we have no right to rely on the Government being able to carry anything. (Laughter.)

The Lord Chief Justice: That might apply to some matters connected with the Government, but not to the Attorney-General's Jury Bill.

The Attorney-General: The fate of the Government is not wrapped up in the Jury Bill.

Mr. Serjeant BALLANTINE: I have a right to argue the point as the law now is, and it being as I have stated, I cannot imagine that the trial for forgery will ever take place.

The Lord Chief Justice: If we could come to that conclusion, we might consider the bail for the perjury sufficient.

Mr. Serjeant BALLANTINE: If the prisoner is tried for forgery he can only be tried by a common jury, but I should think the prosecution would rather have a special jury. It is usual in ordinary cases for bail to show cause on affidavits setting forth there is reason for believing the prisoner intends to evade his trial, but here no such affidavit has been produced, and the only reason given is the statement that has been made by the learned Attorney-General. The result of the late trial must have been anticipated before the case was stopped, and there was abundant opportunity for evasion if the prisoner had desired it. The indictment for forgery is, in fact, a stronger appeal than any the prisoner could make for bail. Looking at all the circumstances of the case, anything like evasion of the trial is impossible on his part. There are four countries with which we have no extradition treaty; but although there is none, it is made exceedingly inconvenient for a criminal to find himself in such countries, especially when there is a desire on the part of this country to obtain possession of him. They do not deliver him up, but he is made so very uncomfortable that he is obliged to seek another asylum, and in endeavouring to get away he is generally apprehended.

Mr. Justice BLACKBURN: There is the case of a special pleader who took refuge in a country where there was no extradition treaty; but the police said he was a stranger, and that they must turn him out of the country. They had previously sent notice to the English police the particular time and place where he would be turned out, and they went and apprehended him, and he was put upon his trial.

Mr. Serjeant BALLANTINE: I submit no grounds have been laid before your lordships to induce you to suppose that the prisoner will evade his trial.

Mr. GIFFARD: I have to submit that the manner in which the

* Yet he got 14 years.

case has been conducted has deprived the prisoner of the advantage he would otherwise have enjoyed in the ordinary course of law. In all cases, except where the Attorney-General intervenes, an indictment can only be removed into this Court on recognizances that in due course it shall be proceeded with and tried, and if it is not done there are two remedies—one is *procedendo* for a breach of it, and the other to bring it on by proviso, both of which are inapplicable in this case, the Attorney-General being especially excepted from them.

The Lord Chief Justice: If the case had come here in the ordinary course, there would have been nothing to prevent the Crown from applying to postpone the trial, on the ground that important witnesses had to be brought from foreign parts, in which case you are not now in a worse position.

Mr. GIFFARD: You would in that case have had an affidavit of the particular witnesses required, and the probability of their being here by a given time. It is taking it somewhat vaguely when it is only said that the witnesses may be here by November. There are no facts to guide the Court. Some of the witnesses may be reluctant to come, others may have arrangements to make before coming, and in fact they are not bound to come at all.

The Lord Chief Justice: The indictment being in this Court we have control over it, and can compel the trial to proceed if we think fit. We should not allow the indictment to remain indefinitely hanging over a man's head because the prosecution did not choose to go on with it. *It will be very unreasonable to postpone the trial longer than November.* We must assume what is reasonable; that what can be done will be done. *I shall be very much surprised if we are asked again to postpone the trial in November.**

Mr. GIFFARD: But it may so happen that the witnesses will require time to make arrangements before leaving Australia, which may have the effect of delaying the trial.

Mr. Justice BLACKBURN: Is such a difference of time worth discussing in a matter that is in our discretion?

LORD RIVERS.

The Lord Chief Justice, in delivering judgment, said—We are of opinion that the application made on the part of the prisoner should be acceded to. We cannot help drawing the inference, from all the circumstances of the case, that what Brother BALLANTINE has suggested is likely to happen—viz., *that the prisoner will in all probability be put upon his trial for perjury rather than for forgery.* Nothing that we can say on the subject can have the slightest influence on the prosecution, nor is it intended to suggest anything of the kind. What Brother BALLANTINE has said on the point is worthy of attention; and as the Attorney-General has not contradicted the statement, I cannot help thinking that the prisoner will only be tried on the original charge on which he was committed. That being so, the amount of bail fixed by the Lord Chief Justice in the Court of Common Pleas, at the time he ordered the prisoner to be committed on the charge of perjury, should be taken to be fully sufficient to insure the reasonable probability of the prisoner taking his trial when the time for trial comes. The only question is, whether an indictment for forgery having been found by the grand jury, which involves on conviction a more serious punishment than for perjury, which holds out to a prisoner an inducement and temptation to evade his trial, there is in his mind a conviction that he is running the danger of being found guilty upon such an indictment; and that being so, it would be a reason for refusing bail, or for increasing its amount. There is this to be said against it, that the prisoner will possibly be tried for perjury only; and then, again, there is this question in the application for bail, that is by no means unworthy of consideration, viz., the fact that by the admirable treaties that exist now between civilised countries for giving up criminals that have fled from justice, that the difficulty of escape and of eluding justice is now rendered much greater than in former times; so that whilst, on the one hand, an indictment for forgery having been found, which was an additional inducement for the prisoner to escape, on the other hand,

* Unreasonable as it was, it was postponed till April, six months longer, when the Plaintiff's funds were all exhausted.

the fact of the alleged criminal being within the reach of the extradition treaties renders the chance of escape from trial for forgery less likely. *Looking to the fact that the prisoner will be tried, after all, on the indictment for perjury, and not for forgery,* we have come to the conclusion that the bail which has been thought sufficient and reasonable to insure the prisoner taking his trial upon the charge for perjury, should be considered as sufficient in all probability to insure his attendance to stand his trial on that charge. Therefore, considering these circumstances, with the additional fact that ought not to be overlooked, that, from the nature and necessity of the case, the trial cannot take place for many mouths at the earliest possible period, I think we may safely admit the prisoner to bail in the same amount originally fixed, believing it to be sufficient to insure his taking his trial for perjury and forgery. The rule must be made absolute.

The Attorney-General: I suppose the usual notice will be given *in order to insure strict examination into the proposed bail.*

The Lord Chief Justice: Certainly. Forty-eight hours' notice to be given; and if any objection is raised to the proposed bail, the question can be heard and decided by a judge at chambers.

The Attorney-General: Will your lordship direct that notice shall be given to the Crown solicitor, before five o'clock in the evening, that being the time when the office closes?

The Lord Chief Justice: Certainly. There will be no necessity for the prisoner's attendance before the judge at chambers. After the bail has been accepted an alderman can attend at Newgate and take the required recognizances.

APPLICATION FOR BAIL.

A day or two after this order (April 26), Mr. Montagu Williams, his Counsel, and Mr. Gorton, of Bedford-row, his Solicitor, with the four gentlemen who had consented to become sureties for his appearance at the Trial in November on the charges of perjury and forgery in connection with his claim to the Tichborne Estates, attended before Mr. Justice Byles at the Common Pleas Chambers, when the requisite forms were gone through, and a certificate given for the release of the Defendant, Tomas Castro, *alias* Arthur Orton, *alias* Sir Roger Doughty Tichborne, from the prison of Newgate.

Mr. Archibald, Counsel, with Mr. Gray, Q.C., Solicitor to the Treasury, Mr. Pollard, and other gentlemen, were present on behalf of the Crown.

Mr. Montagu Williams (addressing his lordship) said: In the matter of Tomas Castro, otherwise Arthur Orton, otherwise Sir Roger Tichborne, Bart., now a prisoner in Newgate, I am instructed to attend here and offer the bail which has been fixed by the Court of Common Pleas for his release.

Mr. Justice Byles: I understood from the newspapers that bail would have to be justified before an alderman.

Mr. Montagu Williams: No, my lord; it is to be justified before your lordship, in order that the Defendant shall not be brought through the public streets. The Lord Chief Justice of the Queen's Bench said that the recognizances might be taken in Newgate, but that the bail must be justified in Chambers: and, my lord, the four gentlemen are now present.

Mr. Justice Byles (to Mr. Archibald): Do you object to this?

Mr. Archibald: *I merely wish to ask each of them a few questions, my lord.*

Mr. Montagu Williams: Then I shall proceed to deal with them in the ordinary way.

Mr. Justice Byles: Is there any rule?

Mr. Gorton: Yes, my lord. I produce the original rule of the Court.

Mr. Justice Byles: I see the Defendant is to enter into his own security of £5,000, and there are to be four others of £1,250 each, or two in £2,500 each.

Mr. Montagu Williams: We propose to offer four sureties in £1,250 each.

Mr. Justice Byles (to Mr. Archibald): *Are you content?*

Mr. Archibald: *I do not wish to offer any more objections than I can help, but I feel that I must ask the sureties a few questions as to their means.*

Mr. Justice Byles: But are you content with that division of the bail?

Mr. Archibald: That is a matter which I cannot help, as it is the order of the Court.

Mr. Montagu Williams: I will now proceed to examine my bail in the ordinary way.

Horace Pitt Rivers, Lord Rivers, of Rushmore Lodge, Shaftesbury, Wilts, then advanced to the table, and was examined as follows:

Mr. Montagu Williams: Are you, my lord, after payment of all your just debts, worth the sum of £1,250?—Oh, certainly.

Are you willing to become one of the sureties for the Defendant in this case?—I am.

To surrender and take his trial when called upon?—Yes.

Mr. Justice Byles: On all these charges?—Yes, my lord.

Cross-examined by Mr. Archibald: *Are you bail in any other case?*—No.

At whose request do you become bail here?—At nobody's. I volunteer to do so.

I will just ask you this question, Lord Rivers: *Have you been indemnified in any way?*—Not in the least.

You have received no promise, or anything of the kind?—None whatever.

Not from any one?—No.

I do not want to go into matters of detail unnecessarily: but, after payment of all your debts and liabilities, are you worth the sum of £1,250?—Yes, certainly.

Have you any liabilities which are not specified in this paper?—None whatever.

Mr. Guildford Onslow, M.P., of The Grove, Ropley, Hampshire, was next examined.

Mr. Montagu Williams: Are you worth, after payment of all your just debts, the sum of £1,250?—I am.

Are you willing to become one of the bail for the Defendant to surrender and take his trial when called on in reference to this charge?—I am.

Cross-examined by Mr. Archibald: Are you bail in any other case?—No.

Do you receive any indemnity for coming here?—No.

Any promise of indemnity?—No.

You have furnished me with the particulars of your property, in which I see there are certain life premiums payable annually. Can you tell me from what source such payments are provided?—From the returns of my property, out of my landed estate in Yorkshire.

Mr. Justice Byles: Does that provide fully for the premiums?—Certainly.

Mr. Archibald: Then I understand that the rental more than covers your life premium?—It does.

Is there any balance left, after providing for the payment of those premiums, that would be equal to the sum for which you are now willing to become bail?—It does not come immediately out of my estates, as I have property in the Funds quite independent of them.

But does the return leave a balance equal to £1,250?—It does.

What have you in the Funds?—I have money in the Three per Cents.

Then you have to recur to that as well as to the rental from your estates to provide for your life premiums?

Mr. Justice Byles: I understand the gentleman to say that the rent from his estates more than covers the life premiums, and that there is a balance left of above £1,250.

Mr. G. Onslow: That is so, my lord. I have the Three per Cents. in addition to my landed property.

Mr. Archibald: *Have you any liabilities not included in these particulars?*—None whatever.

Dr. William Alban Atwood, 129, Ladbroke-terrace, Notting-hill, was similarly examined by Mr. Montagu Williams.

Cross-examined by Mr. Archibald: *Do you receive any indemnity in this case, or any promise of any kind?*—No.

You have given us particulars of your property, which I need not refer to in detail. I only want to ask you *where are the two pieces of land referred to?*—There are two pieces of land in The Grove, with houses upon each. On one piece there are four freehold houses, and on the other six houses, with stables and coach-houses unfinished.

When did you purchase this freehold land?—About a year and a half ago. I gave for one of the pieces £1,000, and I have advanced £5,000 to builders. The houses are now mortgaged to me for that amount.

Mr. Archibald: And since then you have advanced money to builders?—Yes; I have also advanced money upon the six houses which are unfinished. I am entitled to receive interest for the land which I have conveyed to the builders. For the second piece of land I paid £1,985.

Mr. M. Williams: The value of the whole property is given at £6,000.

Mr. Archibald: *Have you any debts or liabilities in addition to those which are given here?*—Not a penny.

Did you borrow any money to enable you to purchase the ground?—Not a penny.

It was all your own money?—Yes; I had £11,000, which I have invested in that way.

Mr. Justice Byles: I must say you have not succeeded in impoverishing Dr. Atwood. (Laughter.)

Mr. Archibald: I am only performing a duty, which is certainly a disagreeable one.

Mr. Justice Byles: Just so. You have cross-examined the doctor very accurately.

Mr. James Lamont, 16, Bolton-street, Piccadilly, the fourth surety, deposed that he was worth the sum of £1,250 after all his debts were paid.

Mr. Archibald: Is your property in England or Scotland?—Scotland.

Are you a housekeeper in England?—I am renting a furnished house for the season.

You have not a house of your own?—Yes; I have recently purchased one in Queen-street, Mayfair.

The lease or the freehold?—The freehold.

Mr. M. Williams: These, my lord, are the sureties.

Mr. Justice Byles: Is the Crown satisfied with them?

Mr. Archibald: I don't know that I can urge, after this cross-examination, any objection. I assume each gentleman to be worth £1,250, and I have no proof to the contrary. I must say that I am satisfied.

Mr. Justice Byles: You may now safely leave it in my hands.

You say you are satisfied with the parties, and I think you are quite right, for I myself am fully satisfied as to their stability.

Mr. M. WILLIAMS: It is necessary for your lordship to make an order for the attendance of an alderman at Newgate, in order that he may take the recognizances of the prisoner.

Mr. Justice BYLES: That can be done. The Court of Queen's Bench have said so, and it must be right.

Mr. M. WILLIAMS: An appointment has been made with one of the aldermen to attend at the prison at half-past one.

Mr. Justice BYLES: As Mr. GRAY is here, I wish to ask him if the recognizances are quite right.

Mr. GRAY: Oh yes, my lord, in every way.

Mr. Justice BYLES then gave his certificate, adding that on the prisoner entering into his recognizances of £5,000 before an alderman of the City, he should be delivered out of the custody of the gaoler forthwith.

THE CLAIMANT'S RELEASE FROM NEWGATE.

Many thousands of persons assembled in front of the prison, and waited anxiously to catch a glimpse of "Sir ROGER" on his release. At half-past one the thoroughfare was completely filled with men, women, and boys, who cheered loudly when a couple of cabs, conveying Mr. Alderman OWDEN and the officials from the Guildhall Police-court reached the private entrance to the gaol. A body of police did their best to keep the crowd in order, but the dense mass swayed backwards and forwards, and the scene, as one of the warders observed, was worse than at an execution. Mr. M. WILLIAMS and Mr. GORTON, bearing the judge's certificate, were present when the Alderman arrived, and as soon as Mr. POLLARD, for the Treasury, reached the gaol, the legal gentlemen proceeded to a room where the Claimant was awaiting their presence. By the desire of the Alderman, as was understood, the reporters were not allowed beyond the inner office, so that no report of what actually took place in the presence of the prisoner can be given, except the fact that the documents were read over, and the Claimant, without being questioned, entered into his recognizances, and was then for some time left in the company of his Solicitor. The question then had to be solved how the Claimant was to leave the prison so as to avoid the public demonstration which might be made for or against him by the thousands outside. Three of the bail, Mr. ONSLOW, Mr. LAMONT, and Dr. ATWOOD, reached the gaol about two o'clock, and were cheered, though it was doubtful whether a single person knew who they were or what their business was within the gloomy portals. The belief that they were in some way or other connected with the Claimant was sufficient to evoke a cheer. Dr. ATWOOD, who is a tall, portly gentleman, was by many mistaken for a relation of "Sir ROGER," and he received an especial ovation as he left his carriage. Following the advice of Mr. JONAS, the Claimant consented to remain in his quarters for upwards of half an hour longer, till the crowd began to disperse, the idea having gained ground amongst those outside that the longer they waited the more unlikely was the Claimant to appear. The legal gentlemen and the bail left one by one, and at half-past two there was a visible thinning of the crowd, but still upwards of a couple of thousand men and boys remained. It was now decided to follow out a plan which had been originally devised—namely, to allow the Claimant to leave the prison by means of the underground passage between it and the dock of the Old Bailey, and thence into the street through the main entrance to the Courts. At twenty-five minutes to three a close carriage, drawn by a pair of handsome greys, stopped at the Sessions House, and at the same time the Claimant, accompanied by Dr. ATWOOD, descended the stairs, and entering the carriage, was driven rapidly away towards Ludgate-hill (*en route* to his residence, Harley Lodge, Brompton) amid the cheers of some hundred persons, who, owing to their swiftness of foot, had managed to reach the spot in time to see him. "Sir ROGER" looked remarkably well, and was evidently highly pleased with his release from custody.

A gentleman living at Southampton offered, it is said, to send up a carriage and four greys, to convey Sir ROGER from Newgate; but the offer was declined with thanks, the preference being given to a brougham and pair.

The following letter was addressed to, and published by,

THE EDITOR OF THE "DAILY TELEGRAPH."

SIR,—In spite of the persistent opposition of the legal advisers of the Crown, and notwithstanding Mr. Justice BRETT refused to release me from gaol, I have now obtained my release by order of the full Court of Queen's Bench, and that upon precisely the same evidence as the Judge—a member of the Court over which the Lord Chief Justice BOVILL presides—refused my application, stating that the fact of detaining me in gaol till November, and perhaps longer, was no sufficient reason for admitting me to bail.

That I shall appear and take my trial none need doubt. I am ready for it, and without delay. But to whom am I indebted for my release? To the British public! to whom I must ask you to allow me to tender my most sincere and heartfelt thanks for the support afforded me. With that support I have been enabled to appeal from the decision of a single Judge, and, with the assistance of three of the most able men at the English bar, I have obtained my release.

When I penned my appeal to the public (although confident of my own innocence), I was too much crushed in spirits, and felt too strongly the tremendous power brought against me, to hope that I should ever have the chance of proving myself to be Sir ROGER CHARLES DOUGHTY TICHBORNE. That fear is now dispelled.

One word more. My attention has been called to a letter in the *Daily Telegraph* of the 18th instant, in which the following question was asked—"Will any officer (whether friendly or adverse to the Claimant) who was in the Carabineers with ROGER TICHBORNE assert that his old comrade was tattooed?" Such letter was written by no one in any way connected with me, nor could it have been written by any one connected with the Defendants on the late trial; they would not have asked such a question. The author of it must, therefore, have been some neutral person. Eight days have elapsed since it appeared in print, and, although at least some of the persons to whom the question was put must have known of the tattoo marks had they in fact existed, none of them have ventured to suggest any knowledge of them. What, then, is the inference to be drawn? I leave the public to judge.

—I am, Sir, your obedient servant, R. C. D. TICHBORNE.

Brompton: April 26.

THE GREAT TICHBORNE CASE.

Before we pass from this subject, we think it well to insert an article from an American paper, of large circulation, which was widely diffused through England about this period:—

(*New York Herald*, March 7, 1872.)

The abrupt and extraordinary termination of the famous TICHBORNE Case will not surprise our readers, as the despatches received from the *Herald* correspondent in London a day or two since, announcing that the Jury had expressed themselves satisfied with the evidence so far as it had progressed, and ready to declare a verdict, indicated that the Claimant's case had virtually broken down. Upon this declaration the Court adjourned until yesterday morning, to enable the TICHBORNE Claimant and his Counsel to agree upon a line of action. Their conclusion was announced yesterday, the Counsel for the Claimant saying that their client had resolved to withdraw his claim. The Attorney-General, who represented the defendants, immediately made an application to the Court for an order to arrest the Claimant upon the charge of perjury, and to hold him in bail in the sum of five thousand pounds. The order was granted, and the "baronet," and assumed heir to one of the oldest and proudest names in the English baronetcy, was arrested yesterday and locked up in Newgate prison.

So ends, for the present, one of the most extraordinary trials in the history of English jurisprudence. . . . The leaders of the English Bar were arrayed against each other—the Attorney-General, Sir JOHN COLERIDGE, leading the case for the defence; Mr. BALLANTINE for the Claimant. The Trial has been going on, with a few intervals, since May. During the proceedings, the Claimant went upon the stand and told his own story. For several weeks he was cross-examined by the Attorney-General in what certainly was the most extraordinary examination known in any trial. All the resources of legal skill, handled by the leader of the English Bar, were exhausted in this controversy. When this was concluded, it was felt that, while Sir JOHN COLERIDGE might have shaken the case, he had not destroyed it. If TICHBORNE was an impostor, he was certainly a most remarkable impostor, for he had submitted to an ordeal that would have tried the most profound and accomplished intellect. He held to his story; and the Trial went on until the defence presented its case, and advanced a part of the evidence. The result of the evidence has been to convince the Jury that the Claimant is an impostor, to throw him out of Court, and to send him to Newgate as an alleged perjurer, awaiting bail in five thousand pounds.

This is a sudden and dramatic close of the Case, if it really ends here. We do not see that it is the end. The Claimant was sustained by extraordinary evidence, and there is no doubt that there is a large party in England who regard him as the real baronet, as a man deprived of his rights by an aristocracy which does not care to admit a butcher, a vagabond, and a horse-thief to share precedence with noblemen and baronets. But the common English mind has heard of the Marquis of HASTINGS and the Duke of NEWCASTLE, and even of his Gracious Majesty GEORGE IV., and it sees in this stolid, ungainly, ignorant TICHBORNE quite as much nobility as in any of them. The severity of the Court's action—his committal to Newgate under bail which makes his release impossible—will excite sympathy. Somehow there is an impression that the Court has been unfair towards him, and that in no event has he had abundant and even-handed justice. What the details of the last few days' proceedings will develop we do not know; but it would not surprise us to find the Newgate prisoner the cause of as much excitement as was known in the days of the MONMOUTH who was believed to have been the legitimate son of CHARLES II., and who, but for his own foolish, feeble vanity, might have risen by the credulity of the common people to the English throne.

We insert also a letter from Mr. GORTON, which ought to have appeared as part of the correspondence at page 87, but which was accidentally omitted there:—

MAJOR JOCELYN.

TO THE EDITOR OF THE "DAILY TELEGRAPH."

SIR,—In the *Times* of the 1st instant appeared a letter from Major JOCELYN, inclosing a document purporting to be signed by certain officers of the Carabineers, who desire to make public, to use their own words, "their firm and undoubted conviction that their old brother-officer, ROGER TICHBORNE, has never been seen in England since he left the country in 1853." The names appended were Major-General JONES, Major BICKERSTAFF, Lieutenant-Col. BETTY, Major FOSTER, Major HOTT, Major PHILLIPS, Paymaster MANDERS, Capt. POLHILL TURNER, Lieutenant PHILLIMORE and Quartermaster FRASER. Major JOCELYN adds, "There can be no doubt that Captains E. M'EVOY and MELFORT CAMPBELL would sign the memorandum, as they are well known to have strong convictions on the subject."

It is difficult to conceive why Major JOCELYN should have evinced the partisanship which this expression indicates, and I am sure you will feel that it is only just and fair to the Claimant that the public should be informed that, of the officers signing the manifesto, only three have spoken to the Claimant, and they are, Major PHILLIPS, Major FISHER, and Quartermaster FRASER. It is possible many of the above officers may have seen him, but it would only have been when passing in the street, or when he was in the witness-box. It is rather strange that a party of gentlemen should have desired Major JOCELYN to make public such an assertion as "their firm and undoubted belief that their old brother-officer, ROGER TICHBORNE, has never been seen in England since he left this country in 1853"; but I presume they can only mean he has not been seen by themselves.

Under these circumstances, I ask the favour of your making public my reply to Major JOCELYN's letter. The writer of the letter was asked to have an interview with the Claimant, in order that he might judge whether he was his brother-officer or not, but he declined, in the following words:—"Major JOCELYN does not consider any evidence he could give would influence the decision in the case alluded to in such letter; he therefore thinks it useless to arrange an interview." This will enable the public to judge of the value of Major JOCELYN's evidence, and I shall be happy to produce the letter to any one who chooses to call and see it. I will not encroach on your space by giving any particulars with regard to some of the other officers who have declined interviews, and their motives for doing so, but against the statement that appears in the *Times*, I must ask to be allowed to state that the following officers have, after long interviews with the Claimant, recorded on oath their convictions of his identity:—They are, General CUSTANCE, C.B., Colonel SAWYER, Lieutenant-Colonel NORBURY, Major HEYWOOD, and Capt. SHERSTONE. These gentlemen have written, stating they have no recollection of ROGER TICHBORNE having been tattooed: another officer has also written to the same effect. It has already been made public that a considerable number of persons, all of whom have identified the Claimant, and some of whom are non-commissioned officers of the Carabineers, will prove that they have seen ROGER TICHBORNE's arms exposed, and not observed any tattoo marks upon them, and of these, six will swear positively that there were no marks whatever. It is somewhat surprising that, with the strong feeling of partisanship which must have prevailed amongst Major JOCELYN and his friends, not one word is said about these tattoo marks; but if they believed in them they would, no doubt, have published "their undoubted conviction" upon the point. In conclusion, I may add that Major JOCELYN and his friends will have an opportunity of appearing against the Claimant at the Central Criminal Court, and I should have thought, as officers, that they would have reserved the expression of their convictions until that time arrives, when their statements can be tested by cross-examination, instead of publishing them in a newspaper, which they know very well the Claimant is not permitted to see.—I am, Sir, your obedient servant,

FRANCIS G. GORTON,
Sir ROGER TICHBORNE's Solicitor.

46, Bedford Row: April 3.

LORD RIVERS AND MR. HAWKINS.

The reader will not fail to have noticed the style of opposition to which Counsel resorted in cross-examining the four gentlemen who presented themselves for bail, or the insulting tone adopted towards Lord RIVERS—a nobleman of at least £12,000 a year, wholly unencumbered—and Dr. ATWOOD. From the following it appears that unworthy attempts had been made to prevent Lord RIVERS becoming bail for Sir ROGER.

TO THE EDITOR OF THE "STANDARD."

SIR,—In the *Standard* of Saturday I observed a letter from Mr. ONSLOW in reply to an article (which I have not seen), stating that in your opinion the Claimant to the Tichborne Estates "is unworthy of the intimacy or countenance of honourable or right-minded gentlemen." As I have advocated the cause of the Claimant by being one of his bail through a firm belief in the justness of his claim, I cannot allow remarks to pass unnoticed which are as applicable to me as to those gentlemen named in the article alluded to, and I am by no means ashamed of the assistance I have afforded, nor of the intimacy which that assistance has occasioned. *No one can be in the company of the Claimant without seeing that, both in manners and demeanour, he is a gentleman, and therefore I have always believed the theory of the Wapping butcher to be a mistake.* I have, from the outset, only wished to see the truth arrived at by means of a fair trial; and that an impartial judge and intelligent jury should prove beyond all doubt whether the Claimant deserves punishment as an impostor, or the possession of those estates to which he lays claim: and it was with this view that I declined to accede to the request of Mr. HAWKINS (addressed to me through a mutual friend) that I should cease in my endeavours to procure his liberation.—I remain, Sir, your obedient servant,

Rushmore, Shaftesbury: Sept. 22, 1873. RIVERS.

In commenting upon this letter, the *Standard* said at the time:—"We have been awaiting with no little interest the answer of Mr. HAWKINS to the letter of Lord RIVERS, in which that nobleman states the learned gentleman, who is Counsel for the prosecution in the TICHBORNE Trial, to have requested him, Lord RIVERS, through a mutual friend, to cease in his endeavours to procure the liberation of the Claimant on bail. We offer no comment upon this allegation of Lord RIVERS, further than to say that, in our opinion, it is one requiring an explanation or an answer. Can it be possible that a Counsel at the English Bar, whose great talents were employed on a trial which resulted in sending a man to gaol on the charges of felony and perjury, should think it right or expedient to take what we may term private steps to prevent the accused from benefiting by the efforts of those who could possibly have no sinister motive to procure a fair and complete trial of the case? To us it simply seems an impossibility, and therefore we have awaited an answer to the letter of Lord RIVERS published in the *Standard* before even giving additional publicity to that letter in our columns. We trust that even now Mr. HAWKINS will reply to Lord RIVERS, and remove the unpleasant impression which this statement may make upon unsophisticated minds. We never remember to have heard before of a Counsel for a prosecution going out of his way to take such a step as this."

Mr. HAWKINS did not reply, because he could not deny the fact openly; though he did so in a covert way to certain of his acquaintances. For this unprofessional conduct he ought to have been called to account by the Benchers of the Middle Temple; but in place of punishment or censure being inflicted upon him, Lord Chancellor CAIRNS actually offered him a seat on the Bench—a sop thrown to that three-headed Cerberus—the Jesuits, the Family, and the Snobocracy of the day—who all arrayed themselves against this unfortunate gentleman.

POVERTY OF THE CLAIMANT.

The Claimant was now in a most lamentable state of poverty. The death of his Mother, and the opposition offered by the Family to his obtaining probate of her will, had deprived him of all pecuniary resources. He was actually living on public charity. It was suggested, therefore, that in order to evoke more general sympathy through all parts of the kingdom, he should attend public meetings, to explain his wrongs, to challenge examination, to demand scrutiny. It is obvious that no Impostor would dare to go about in this open manner. If he were ORTON, as his enemies pretended, he never could know in what place witnesses to that fact would not start up against him, and put him to public shame. But so far from evidence arising to show that he was a Wapping butcher or sailor, at many of the places to which he went on his tour, witnesses existed who came forward voluntarily to own their recognition of the old lieutenant of Carabineers, whose peculiarities had impressed themselves so deeply on their recollection.

The first place to which the Claimant went, after his release from Newgate, was to Alresford. We extract the following report of his visit, from the *Morning Advertiser*. It is headed—

THE "CLAIMANT" AND THE TICHBORNE TENANTS.

When it became known to his old friends, the tenantry on the Tichborne Estates, in Hampshire, that the "Claimant" was on a visit to Mr. GUILDFORD ONSLOW, M.P., at his charming residence, The Grove, Ropley, they eagerly availed themselves of the opportune moment to invite his presence once more amongst them, and in that request they were joined by the townspeople of Alresford, who, ever since "Sir ROGER" commenced proceedings to establish what he believes to be his rights, have accorded him the full measure of their sympathy and support. Yesterday afternoon was fixed upon, and May 14, 1872, will long be remembered by the Tichborne tenantry. From all parts of the estates they flocked into Alresford to congratulate him whom they pronounce to be the rightful owner of the property on his release from unmerited incarceration, and they signalised his reappearance by a demonstration which certainly forms not the least remarkable and interesting feature in the romantic episode of the Claimant's struggle to defeat those who, with powerful influence, are contesting his right to the honours of the Tichborne titles, and to any participation in the ownership of the property. From early morning Alresford assumed holiday attire. In the leading streets the houses were gaily decorated; flags, banners, and bunting floated at prominent points; the Union Jack and other national emblems were suspended across the main thoroughfare, right away in front of that comfortable old hostelry, the Swan, so capitally conducted by the comparatively new host, Mr. NEWMAN, and now so well-known throughout the world by the frequent references made to its pleasant inner life during the progress of the TICHBORNE Trial.

It is only an act of simple justice towards those who took the most active part in yesterday's great TICHBORNE demonstration at Alresford, to state that everything they undertook was carried out in the most complete and successful manner. As neat a waggonette as ever attracted attention in Hyde Park, with four spanking bays, decorated with rosettes of TICHBORNE colours, and postillioned with adepts to the road in scarlet satin-cloth jackets, despatched from the Swan by its proprietor, reached The Grove about three o'clock, and in less than the twinkling of an eye the Claimant, surrounded by a group of staunch and stedfast friends, took his seat. From Mr. ONSLOW's residence at Ropley to Alresford is just three miles, through an extremely picturesque bit of landscape. Every inch of the route was crowded, and the windows of all the gentlemen farmers' residences were filled with lovers of fair-play, young and old, male and female, who enthusiastically cheered as the waggonette conveying the Claimant, Mr. ONSLOW, Mr. BAIGENT, sen., Mr. BLOXAM, and five or six other gentlemen, rattled merrily along. There were groups of ladies immediately outside The Grove gate, and at various other points, not the least noticeable being the entrance to the Master of the Hampshire Hounds' abode, where at least one very lovely young sympathiser stood waving her snow-white handkerchief in welcome of Sir ROGER's return to the scene of early associations. The huntsmen and whips, too, were "mounted" on the adjoining fence, and they cheered lustily, first for the Claimant and then for the local member, who throughout the day came in for an adequate share of the popular greeting. "Glory to you, Sir ROGER—GOD bless and spare you, Sir ROGER," issued from hundreds of voices close by Bishop's Sutton, when Mr. BAILEY, of the Anchor Hotel, who was the first to recognise Sir ROGER when he returned from Australia to the district, cordially greeted the Claimant. Mr. YATES's racing establishment seemed frantic with delight when the *cortége* passed, the trainers and jockey-boys rushing in absolute ecstasy from the stables to the roadside. A little further on, the Tichborne tenantry mustered in greater strength, and from there up to the outskirts of Alresford were to be found groups of those who claim Sir ROGER as their landlord. They came from Tichborne village, Cheriton, Hockley, Bramden, West Tisted, and Old Alton. Southampton, twenty miles distant, sent a deputation from the TICHBORNE Defence Fund Committee, consisting of Mr. JOSEPH KEMBES, Chairman, Mr. THOMAS LITTLE, Mr. G. E. GRAY, Mr. JAMES WEBB, Mr. DODMAN, Mr. G. GODDARD, Mr. J. STEPHENS, and Mr. S. DENTON. Their admirably-appointed waggonette, with four spanking bays, and a stunning good "whip," took up with the cavalcade near Bishop's Sutton. Here, too, there was an accession of the Alresford fifers and drummers and the Cheriton band, who, immediately upon espying "The Grove" party, struck up, first, "Should auld acquaintance be forgot," weaving in "Auld lang Syne," and completing the compliment with "Home, sweet Home." The cheering at this point became still greater and more enthusiastic than it was at any preceding part of the route. Nearing the outskirts of Alresford, where the road was completely blocked, another large body of Tichborne tenants, all most respectable, well-to-do-looking men, wearing blue silk rosettes, appeared upon the gay and exciting scene. They, as if by magic, took the horses from the waggonette, and, amidst the most enthusiastic cheering, the heartiest acclamation, and shaking of hands with the Claimant, the vehicle was drawn up a steep hill into the town, thence to the spacious courtyard of the Swan Hotel, where the people assembled, to the number of about three thousand, and constituted a meeting. The old folks especially flocked around the Claimant, recognising him over and over again, and repeatedly crying out, "GOD bless you, Sir ROGER!" "Bravo, Sir ROGER!" In fact nothing could have been more hearty, genuine, and enthusiastic than the reception which the Claimant received from all who constituted the gathering. When the enthusiasm somewhat subsided, the occupants of the waggonette asked for silence, and two or three speeches were delivered in an earnest and impressive manner.

Mr. GUILDFORD ONSLOW, M.P., who was received with enthusiastic cheers, said: "As we are all here among the old friends and tenants of Sir ROGER TICHBORNE, I take the opportunity of congratulating him on being again restored to liberty from the dismal gaol of Newgate, where he was incarcerated certainly without being convicted. (Cheers.) I think we have a right to thank the British public for the part they have already taken, and for the handsome manner in which they have come forward to assist the Defence Fund, thereby enabling us to resist the Government prosecution. Had it not been for the working classes, in all probability Sir ROGER TICHBORNE——(cheers for Sir ROGER)—would be still in prison, and be perfectly defenceless. We have received pressing invitations from different parts of the country—from Birmingham, Bristol, Southampton, Nottingham, and from Bradford and several smaller towns, which it is proposed we should visit, or rather, which it is intended we should visit. We shall visit them on their invitation for the sole purpose of engaging the public voice in the cause of fair-play, with a view of getting Sir ROGER—(cheers for Sir ROGER)—that fair-play which has hitherto been denied him. (Loud cheers.) But I am happy now to see Sir ROGER down here amongst his tenants, his old friends, and his servants—(great cheering)—who have better opportunities of knowing him than anybody else. I am glad to see that his first visit since his liberation from unjust imprisonment—(hear, hear)—is amongst his old acquaintances; and the spontaneous manner in which he has been received, and the very flattering manner in which he has been greeted to-day in Alresford show, I think, what the feelings of the public are about him. (Cheers.) There may be a few exceptions, but the general public in the neighbourhood—I mean in this neighbourhood—is decidedly in favour of our friend Sir ROGER TICHBORNE—(enthusiastic cheers)—for no other reason than that they are satisfied as to his identity. (Renewed cheers.) The general public look upon his case as one in which fair-play should be secured—(hear, hear)—but here, in his own neighbourhood, we know him before he went away, and therefore with you it is a case of actual identity. (Great cheering.) I am, my friends, very happy to say that the Defence Fund already reaches a good round sum; but this will be a very expensive lawsuit, and it is very necessary that Sir ROGER TICHBORNE—(cheers for Sir ROGER)—should have the best advice and counsel—(A voice: "So he shall!")—and therefore I hope the public will not stop in their efforts to supply that fund, and to meet the expenses of a prosecution for which we have no precedent. (Hear, hear.) Sir ROGER is being prosecuted by the Government at an enormous cost to the country—(cries of "Shame! shame!")—for of course it must involve the expenditure of a large sum of money, though in this case the Family could well afford to pay it—(cheers)—and I believe there will be a very great objection taken in the House of Commons when that vote which will be put upon the estimates for this prosecution comes before it. If the Government are sincere and really desirous to see fair-play on both sides, it is very necessary—absolutely necessary—they should bring from Australia GEORGE ORTON, the brother of ARTHUR ORTON, whom they say Sir ROGER TICHBORNE is. (Great laughter.) Let us have him over from Australia, and hear what he has to say. (Cheers.) We are preparing a petition to the Treasury for that purpose, and if it is refused, that, I think, will show that they are not sincere. It certainly is a strong point in our friend's favour, and it must have its effect with all thinking and sensible men, that Sir ROGER TICHBORNE, immediately after arriving in this country, and also after the death of his mother, made Alresford for nearly two years his home. If he was an impostor, that was coming into the very mouth of the lion. (Cheers.) Bear in mind too, my friends, that the first time he visited this place he came disguised; but you will recollect his disguise was of no use to him, as he was immediately recognised. (Cheers.) Then again, the moment he comes out of prison he first visits Alresford, and visits it on the invitation of his old friends, tenants, and servants, who have asked him to come down here. (Cheers.) We hope next week to visit Bristol, as it was from there we received the first invitation, and there I hope to enter more minutely into the details of this great Case, which I maintain up to the present moment has never been allowed to be explained by any reply to the Attorney-General's speech. Many people were led away by the long-winded speech of the Attorney-General, though I have every reason to believe they would have been led the other way if they had the opportunity of listening to the reply which Serjeant BALLANTINE would have made. (Loud cheers.) I am sure Sir ROGER feels the deepest gratitude to the British public for the efforts they have made in subscribing towards his defence, and I can assure them, in his name, that we mean to fight out his case to the very end. (Loud and prolonged cheers.)

The CLAIMANT then presented himself, and was received with loud cheers. He said: My friends, tenants, and neighbours, I have not very much to say, but to thank you kindly for the invitation which has brought me once more amongst you; for it gives me great gratification to come here amongst those who knew me in former days, and who know that I am not the impostor, the villain, the scoundrel, as branded by the Attorney-General—(great cheering)—and which he has certainly not yet proved that I am. (Cheers.) I hope that my days here will be many more than they have been; for I look forward with every hope and with full confidence to regaining my estates, and living once more amongst you. (Loud cheers.) If, as the Attorney-General stated, I am an impostor, surely I have given you every opportunity of finding me out; for I have lived among you with my family for nearly twelve months. You have seen me on two or three hundred occasions. I have been continually with you—you who knew me in former days—(enthusiastic cheering)—and yet no one here has ventured to call me an impostor except the connections of my family, who are interested in so doing. I also hope you will remember that when I first returned to England I was invited to come down here by my former solicitor, Mr. HOPKINS, who is well known to, and very much respected by, you all. (Hear, hear.) It is not necessary, therefore, to say anything more of Mr. HOPKINS, because you know him almost better than I do myself. Now, if I had been an impostor, he had in his possession during all that time documents which would have convicted me at once. He would have found out if I was an impostor, and no one could have lived in his house for a fortnight, as I did, without being detected. (Hear, hear.) I wish to ask why should my Mother's evidence be ignored? Is Mr. HOPKINS, who did all my business before I left England—is he to be ignored? Are all those who lived in this neighbourhood, and knew me before I left England—are they all to be ignored because a lord—(ironical cheers)—comes forward and swears he tattooed me? (Cheers, and cries of "All humbug.") Then, again, there was the military evidence—the evidence of my brother-officers—men who were above bribery—(hear)—and the evidence of the tenants and the workmen on the estates—they are men, and honourable men, although they work for their living—why should not their evidence be as good as Lord BELLEW's? (Great cheering.) I distinctly tell you, gentlemen, that the tattooing business was neither more nor less than a conspiracy, concocted at a moment's notice when they found they could not beat me in any other way. (Cheers, and "Shame.") It is true I was sent to Newgate, but that was by the direction of a biassed Judge—a man unfitted to sit on the Bench—backed up, though he was, by one of the most learned men of the day, as he showed throughout the trial—the present Attorney-General. (Groans.) However, I thank you kindly for the great interest you have taken in me and on my behalf, and for the fair-play which you insist I shall have, and which is all I ask. Again thanking you for your kind invitation down here, I will conclude by saying I hope the time will shortly come when I shall come and live among you again. (Loud cheers. I will then prove to you I am not the impostor, the forger, the villain, and the vagabond that I have been branded by the Attorney-General. (Great cheering.)

Mr. G. ONSLOW, M.P., again came forward and said: As I have before said, it is a source of deep gratification to me to be present here and see this great assembly to meet Sir ROGER to-day in this, as it were, his cradle and his home (cheers)—for it is here, above all other places, where he is better known than any place in the world. (Great cheering.) No man but the right man could have stood that twenty-eight days' cross-examination when the Attorney-General stated he had met his match, and that Sir ROGER was the cleverest man he ever had to deal with. If Sir ROGER is an impostor, he is the cleverest man that ever lived since the days of ADAM, to have stood such a cross-examination; but on the other hand, as he is Sir ROGER, there is nothing extraordinary in it. He has stood up like a man, and the public have come forward to support him to enable him to resist the prosecution of the Government, and they are going to stand by him to the last. (Cheers.) It is true he was committed to Newgate, but without being convicted; and I am convinced he never will be convicted, because the voice of the public is in his favour, and I have never known the public voice to be wrong. It is right on every great occasion, and it is right on this occasion, believing as it does Sir ROGER TICHBORNE to be the right man. The voice of the public is with him, and it is a righteous voice; and how much more honourable it is to him, and how much more detestable to those who opposed him, to see that meeting in the midst of his tenants, servants, and friends. (Cheers.) Sir ROGER was unfairly dealt with both before and at his trial. The evidence of seventeen interested witnesses was received by the Court, but his Mother's evidence was ignored, as well as that of eighty-six witnesses who were disinterested from the first. I have seen that poor Mother with her pale face, and I know that she died of a broken heart from the way in which her son was treated. Gentlemen, I have supported Sir ROGER from the commencement, and I will continue to do so to the end. (Loud cheers.) As a parting word, let me say that I am indeed pleased to see around me to-day so many ladies and gentlemen whom I have known from their childhood, and I will add that a more honourable or truthful class of people never existed in any part of the world. (Cheers.)

An adjournment then took place to the assembly-room of the Swan, where the Claimant received a deputation from Southampton of the Local Defence Fund.

Mr. GUILDFORD ONSLOW, M.P., with a few words of welcome, introduced the deputation to the Claimant, who was received with the warmth that had characterised the previous proceedings.

The Claimant then observed that he was glad to be present to acknowledge the great kindness he had received from the people of Southampton. After a few more remarks of a general character, he said he should like to explain. Although he had called 86 witnesses, the fact was to be borne in mind that he had the testimony of 580 witnesses, and it was only the lack of funds that had prevented him from calling the greater portion of them. He had to complain, in consequence of being unable to continue the fees to Counsel, that his case had been conducted by them towards the last in a very indifferent manner—more especially as regarded the cross-examination of witnesses. The jury saw that, and there was no doubt whatever that it influenced them. The Attorney-General also noticed the fact—(cheers)—and when, towards the last, he told the jury on the 102nd day of the Trial that he had 280 witnesses to examine, that was equivalent to telling them that unless they gave him a verdict they must sit for a whole year. (Cries of "Shame.") He also had to complain, and he did so most bitterly, of the Judge. They would recollect that he had told him that so long as he sat on the bench the other side would need no Counsel. (Groans.) Why had not the learned Judge committed him on that occasion, for it was clear contempt of Court, except that he dared not do so. (Cheers.) Allusion had been made during the Trial by the Attorney-General to the fact that he had given 200 guineas for a horse. That was intended to prejudice him in the minds of the public for extravagance, but he would tell them that he had bought the horse on the condition that it was not to be paid for until he obtained his estates, and he would only say further that a capital horse she—for it was a mare—turned out. Referring to the fact that he used to come to the court in a carriage, while Lady DOUGHTY used to come in a cab, he said he would inform the Attorney-General that the carriage had been provided by his friends, and that Lady DOUGHTY no doubt might have come in a carriage had she been so disposed. The tattoo-marks matter he again denounced as a vile conspiracy, and asked why it was that, during his three days' examination at the Law Institution, no reference whatever had been made to those marks. Adverting next to the testimony of Mr. ALFRED SEYMOUR, he asked why that gentleman had allowed him to remain in the house with his sister (Claimant's mother), when in one moment he could have said, "This man is an impostor; he has not the tattoo marks which your son had." (Cheers.) Referring next to his cousin's evidence, who declared she saw him catching minnows with his left hand, he said that those present knew that the Hampshire streams were clear as a looking-glass, and that if a man waited until he could catch a minnow in that way, he would have to wait a long time for his dinner. (Laughter.) As to the evidence of the servant who had robbed him of his clothes at Rio, who stated he had never seen any tattoo marks, they would judge of the value of his evidence; but the whole story of the tattoo marks was concocted at the last hour to crush him. He then thanked the deputation from Southampton, and especially Mr. GRAY, who had supplied means to his wife and children while he was in prison. (Cheers.)

In the evening Mr. ONSLOW, M.P., entertained the Claimant and a number of other friends to dinner—a very capital dinner, by the bye—at the Swan Hotel. Towards nine o'clock there were several flights of rockets, and then a grand display of fireworks, the bands continuing to promenade th town until midnight, and the inhabitants appearing thoroughly to enjoy every incident connected with Sir ROGER'S visit.

The following comments upon this Meeting, by the most able and honest Editor of the *Morning Advertiser*, appeared in that journal on May 16th, 1872:—

SIR R. TICHBORNE AT ALRESFORD, AND HIS CONTEMPLATED TOUR.

The reception by the Claimant at Alresford, which we duly chronicled yesterday, was an event most suggestive in its bearings upon the case and the identity of the man who, if he be not the impostor painted by his foes and opponents, is one of the most foully and cruelly treated martyrs to oppression ever known. It cannot be denied that this recognition and acceptance of him who has just been extracted with such difficulty from the jaws of Newgate and of Death, on the part of hundreds of the tenantry of the contested estate, servants, neighbours, and old people, who knew the young Sir ROGER, is a remarkable and pregnant fact. These honest folks have not been shaken in their belief and conviction that the penniless adventurer, the bankrupt litigant, the man upon whose devoted head the foulest abuse has been heaped, and who has been held up as a bloated monster to whom it is an iniquity to accord a grain of justice or fair-play, is really the lost heir to the TICHBORNE Estates. Solicitors and Counsel may fall off, legal agents may pass over to the enemy's camp with the plunder of the papers and documents intrusted to their care; but the faith of the simple villager and cottier, of the Hampshire farmer and the grey-headed servitor and tenant, remains unshaken. Nay, what is still more, men of intelligence and position remain true to the opinions they have formed, and say that they are determined to fight to the last the monster combination of State and Law, of influence and wealth, of "Society" and "Respectability," of the real Jabber-wock that has eaten at least its share of the "infant's" estate, and talked a jury's brain into pulp and mash, till they apparently did not know upon what they had made up their minds—the tattoo evidence so wonderfully kept back to the last, or the whole case, of which they had chiefly heard only one side, with one colouring, one advocacy, one bias, and one leaning all throughout. Down in Hampshire on Tuesday the cry was, marvellous to relate, "God bless you, Sir ROGER!" "From all parts of the estate the Tichborne tenantry flocked into Alresford to congratulate him whom they pronounce to be the rightful heir of the property on his release from unmerited incarceration." Strange to say, not only was the Claimant received with demonstrations of holiday delight, with flags, and garlands, and festoons of flowers, with music and waving of kerchiefs, and clapping of hands: but the persons who were abused on that day were the Attorney-General and the Chief Justice of the Common Pleas. The huntsmen and whips, and gentlemen farmers, trainers, and jockey-boys, the lovers of sport and fair-play, groups of ladies, aged grandams and young girls, hundreds of respectable men, from the landlord of the Anchor Hotel to the local member of Parliament—there they were, reversing, at least morally, the judgment by which the Claimant stands, if not indeed convicted, yet so far condemned, that, but for the irregular interference of the public, he was a doomed and lost man. Let the utterances of the unfortunate man speak for themselves. Strange to say, the writer, in a contemporary, of a flippant attack upon the "Waggawock among his Borrogroves," which is the title of his description, contradicts all else that he has stated in the following words, which seem almost unconsciously given. He says that Sir ROGER "spoke with ease and evident feeling, in a low but clear voice, and with the accents and speech of a gentleman. Assuredly in his utterances or appearance were no traces of Wapping butcherdom."

If so, we presume the fair inference is that he is not, and never was, a Wapping butcher. What, then, becomes of three parts of the Billingsgate that has been heaped upon him by those who have prejudged the case? What becomes of the sting and *raison d'etre* of the *facetiæ* of the *Daily News* correspondent who signs himself, in the nonsensical slang of the day, "An Uflish Non-Chortler"? With what effect does he call the Claimant "a colossal heap of flesh"? He might quote his master in coarse personality correctly, if he does not aim at rivalling him in bad taste. With what truth does he recur to the charge in the matter of grammar, in the repetition of the word "howsomdever," and the illiterate spelling attributed to the Claimant? If that individual spoke "with ease and evident feeling, and with the accents and speech of a gentleman," what must all the rest be but sheer malignant invention, thoughtlessly it may be, but no less cruelly, repeated to prejudice the case of a man against whom so much is arrayed—the money of an unwilling country, the mighty engine of the Law, the Government, and, we regret to say, hitherto the majority of the Press? . . . Here let us point out the telling nature of the latter part of the second speech of the Claimant about the tattoo marks, and the statement of Mr. GUILDFORD ONSLOW, somewhat more touching, we fancy, than the tearful allusions of the Attorney-General to Mrs. RADCLIFFE and the infant heir, that he had seen "that poor Mother [Lady TICHBORNE] with her pale face, and knew that she died of a broken heart from the way in which her son was treated." We beg the facetious gentlemen who display their wit and humorous fancy at the Claimant's expense, to remember that he, too, has four children, whose interests are involved, and who are at least postulants for justice and fair-play, as much as the little boy with the long minority whose interests are so stoutly, and, in some respects, so singularly, maintained and defended.

About this time was published the following letter, which contains some curious particulars:—

Mr. ROGER TICHBORNE was very fond of natural history, and the Claimant is an enthusiastical naturalist. I don't think ORTON ever displayed any turn that way. I had the pleasure of seeing the Claimant one evening for an hour or two with some friends, among whom was a well-known naturalist, and it was remarkable how he turned from all other points of conversation and went into natural history with my friend, telling us many of his adventures in South America, in the course of which he spoke of "the lion and tiger," and when I remarked that there were no lions nor tigers in South America, he at once corrected the mistake by stating that the puma and panther are there called the lion and tiger, which is a well-known fact, and, being aware of it, I wanted to test his familiarity with the natural history of South America. His sketches of scenery and hunting scenes were wonderfully graphic and life-like, and from the energy and interest he displayed in talking of them, there could not be a doubt that he was speaking from an experience which he rejoiced to remember. As a fisherman of much experience, I tried him on that topic, and I soon found that he was an old and practised brother piscator, and knew well what he was talking about, and that he had not hastily picked up his knowledge of it merely to personate TICHBORNE. Had this been the case, I am perfectly sure that I should have found him out in three minutes. In connection with this, a curious circumstance occurred to me. When first the TICHBORNE Case was talked about, I was down at Winchester, and I asked JOHN HAMMOND, the well-known tacklemaker there, what he thought of the Case. His answer was "He is the man, Mr. FRANCIS, without a doubt." "Why do you think so?" I asked. "Well, sir, before he went away he used to have his flies of me, and sent me orders for various flies from time to time. As soon as he came back he sent to me just the same kind of letter he used to send, ordering some flies, and the very same kinds of flies he used to send for before he went away. Now, there are a great many flies used in our rivers, and, as you know, we are frequently using new ones. He, however, sent for the same old sorts he used to use twelve or fifteen years ago." These may be thought trifles; but many trifles put together make big things in time. I may be "a fanatic," and I may be "a fool;" but I do not reject the evidence of my senses.—I am, &c.,

FRANCIS FRANCIS.

Several false representations of what occurred at the Alresford Meeting having been disseminated by the friends and agents of the Family, the following was published:—

SIR ROGER TICHBORNE AND HIS FRIENDS.

A number of the tenants on the Tichborne Estates in Hampshire have published a letter in which they express a desire that there should be no misunderstanding as to what has occurred between them and Sir ROGER TICHBORNE. They say they "were delighted to receive Sir ROGER TICHBORNE at Alresford on the 14th of May last," and that they were "proud and happy to find that he had responded to their invitation to come among them again." They add that they "were present on that memorable occasion to welcome him back after his unjust, unfair, and cruel incarceration of fifty-two days in Newgate Gaol." The tenants signing the letter are:—JAMES STUBBS, Manor Farm, West Tisted; JAS. HOLMES, farmer, Cheriton; FREDK. MOULD, Cheriton; STEPHEN STRATTEN, Cheriton; HENRY HARFIELD, Cheriton; THOMAS MARINER, Cheriton; WILLIAM BULDING, West Tisted; ROBT. CROCKFORD, Cheriton; STEPHEN HOPGOOD, Tichborne; WM. MARINER, Tichborne; HY. WEBB, Tichborne; JAS. ADAMS, Tichborne; HY. WHITEAR, Tichborne; WM. GUY, Tichborne; ROBERT MANSBRIDGE, Tichborne; JOHN MANSBRIDGE, Tichborne; CHARLES GATES, Tichborne; WM. SIMPSON, Tichborne; JAMES NORGATE, Tichborne; and HY. NOBLE, bailiff, Home Farm, Tichborne.

The verses that follow—said to be written by Mr. SHIRLEY BROOKS—allude to Sir JOHN COLERIDGE's copious tears for the workhouse infant who claimed the title and estates of Earl WICKLOW; and to those which he shed for the very butcher-like young gentleman whose likeness appears in page 57 of this volume. There are many curious speculations down in Hampshire as to whose production this youth really is. This song was sung with great applause at many of the Claimant's festive banquets:—

BRANDY TEARS! BRANDY TEARS!!

A New Comic Song, respectfully dedicated, without permission, to Judge and Jury—with the earnest wish that their "ears may never be less."

Gem'men, you axe the reason why
I groans in spirit and pipes me eye?
And how it comes this look I vears?
Why, it's all along of them brandy tears.
CHORUS: Brandy tears, brandy tears;
Hic, hic, hic! them brandy tears!

What brought me into this woful state
'Ud take a long time to relate;
But this I says, no matter who sneers,
It's all along of them brandy tears.
CHORUS: Brandy, &c.

There's nothing goes down among the "ton,"
Like "orange tipple" to weep upon;
If I follers suit, and liquors and beers,
I'm only in fashion with brandy tears.
CHORUS: Brandy tears, brandy tears;
Very *re-hic-freshing* them brandy tears!

A crafty 'ooman as had a son,
(Liverpool vorkhus was his "run,")
Says she, "I'll pitch him among the peers,
By 'high falutin' and brandy tears."
CHORUS: Brandy, &c.

"I'll seek a Counsel who'll take a drop,
Dear man, from 'Wicklow' sheebeen shop;
And if for the 'baby' he but appears,
He'll carry the Lords—by brandy tears."
CHORUS: Brandy, &c.

"There he talked tall, with no end of cheek,
For the 'innocent baby' as 'cannot speak;'
Drops bedewing the robes he vears,
By reason of (hic!) them brandy tears."
CHORUS: Brandy, &c.

But the Lords, as swoller'd the Yankee's tale,
And settled the Aberdeen peerage "entail,"
Though well the Wicklow "flam," he steers,
Soon threw it out, 'mid brandy tears.
CHORUS: Brandy, &c.

Then he goes in for a hundred days;
A most pathetic part he plays;
For another "infant" he now appears,
With more "falutin" and brandy tears.
CHORUS: Brandy, &c.

Buckets of water flowed apace,
As touching-lie he put the case.
Photos. and truths he both besmears,
While blubb'ring out—the brandy tears.
CHORUS: Brandy tears, brandy tears,
How they rolled down, them brandy tears.

Well, the end of all this is fearful to write;
The world's gone mad on the subject, quite,
For that "wrong is right," as many now sweers,
When looked at through—them brandy tears.
CHORUS: Brandy tears, brandy tears;
Perverting justice, them brandy tears.

My wife half-crazed, when scolded says,
She's been reading the speech of a hundred days;
And all as I gits, when she wickedly leers,
Is, "Oh, give me two penn'orth of brandy tears."
CHORUS: Brandy, &c.

If I scolds my boy, he "pokes his fun,"
And says, "'Dad,' Sir ROGER is BUBBLE's son."
And wherever one goes it rings in the ears—
"Bill, let's have a go of brandy tears."
CHORUS: Brandy tears, brandy tears;
Nothing goes down like brandy tears.

I'm sick of life, and soon will be
Conveyed to Highgate Cemetree;
My days cut short, my dust in "biers,"
With the epitaph—"*Killed by brandy tears!*"
CHORUS: Brandy tears, brandy tears,
Killed off by the orange-brandy tears.

While the motto of him as caused this doo
Will be "*Lachrymo ex spiritu.*"
Translated, just this meaning bears:
"*From orange-brandy I draws my tears.*"
CHORUS: Brandy tears, brandy tears;
"*Ex spiritu—I draws my tears!*"

As we have again mentioned Alresford, we add in this place, the affidavit of a gentleman which was accidentally omitted:—

AFFIDAVIT OF MR. JOHN HUGGINS, OF NEW ALRESFORD, HANTS.

I, JOHN HUGGINS, of New Alresford, Hants, chemist, make oath and say as follows:—

1. I have just completed my 53rd year. I came to Alresford in 1836, as an assistant to Mr. RENNIE, then a surgeon at Alresford. I remained as assistant to Mr. RENNIE until his death in 1838. Immediately on Mr. RENNIE's death, the business was sold to Mr. JOHN KERSLEY LIPSCOMB, now practising as a surgeon at Alresford. I continued with Mr. LIPSCOMB as assistant for above seven years, and then started in business as a chemist in Alresford, and have remained in such business ever since.

2. During the whole time I have been in business the TICHBORNE Family have been customers of mine—first, Sir HENRY JOSEPH TICHBORNE, until his death; then Sir EDWARD DOUGHTY, until his death. During the time that Sir EDWARD DOUGHTY lived at Tichborne Park, Mr. ROGER CHARLES TICHBORNE, the eldest son of the late Sir JAMES FRANCIS TICHBORNE, was in the

habit of coming very frequently to my shop for cigars and other purposes. His home in England was at Tichborne Park, and he was generally there during his holidays. During such visits to my shop, the said Mr. ROGER C. TICHBORNE often conversed with me, and I had very frequent opportunities of judging of, and I well remember his personal appearance and habits. I had such opportunities up to the time of his going abroad, in the year 1853, but less frequently during the time he was in the army. I saw him very shortly before he left for abroad, when he was on horseback before my shop door, and remained some time selecting cigars.

3. I also knew his father, the late Sir JAMES FRANCIS TICHBORNE, and also his brother, the late ALFRED TICHBORNE, whom I knew intimately from a child. ALFRED very frequently came to me. He was more frolicsome and talkative than the said ROGER C. TICHBORNE, who was naturally taciturn and shy.

4. I have frequently seen and conversed with the above-named Plaintiff during the present year (1867), and I am perfectly certain that he is the same person whom I formerly knew as Mr. ROGER CHARLES TICHBORNE. *He is altered in size, but I distinctly recognise in him the same general expression of countenance, person, and peculiarities as the said* ROGER CHARLES TICHBORNE *had when I formerly knew him, and more particularly the formation of his head and a peculiar twitch of the eyebrows. I also recognise in the Plaintiff some peculiar characteristics of the* TICHBORNE *Family.*

5. The several statements hereinbefore contained are within my own knowledge.

JOHN HIGGINS.

Sworn at New Alresford, in the County of Southampton, this 1st day of July, 1867,—Before me,
JNO. FRAS. ADAMS,
A Commissioner to Administer Oaths in Chancery in England.

From Alresford the Claimant proceeded to Southampton. We append a report of the public meeting held there:—

THE TICHBORNE CLAIMANT IN SOUTHAMPTON.

In Wednesday's impression we announced the arrival of the TICHBORNE Claimant at Southampton, and gave a report of the meeting which was held on his behalf at Messrs. PERKINS and Sons' spacious repository at the rear of the York Hotel. We also, in an article on the subject, published a statement which had appeared in the *Manchester Courier*, affirming that Dr. WHEELER, who was said to have identified the Claimant as TOMAS CASTRO, was not in a position to identify the Claimant as the TOMAS CASTRO he knew at Wagga-Wagga. In consequence of this the Southampton Defence Fund circulated handbills containing an extract from the *Hampshire Advertiser*, and also giving a copy of Dr. WHEELER's affidavit, which is dated the 4th of June, 1872, and winds up:—"I can swear, to the best of my belief, that Sir ROGER TICHBORNE is TOM CASTRO, but I can swear most positively that he is not ARTHUR ORTON." During Wednesday the Claimant was visited at his quarters (the Castle Hotel, High-street) by many friends and sympathisers, and it was announced privately by some of the Committee that his visit had had the effect of converting many who were previously great opponents of him. Soon after six o'clock in the evening a brass band paraded the High-street with a banner, on which was, "Welcome, Sir ROGER TICHBORNE, the rightful heir to the Tichborne Estates," and they afterwards proceeded to Messrs. PERKINS' repository, where the adjourned meeting was held. While the audience was assembling the band played several airs, and, on the arrival of the Claimant, "Auld Lang Syne." The banner was placed at the back of the platform, and here also was painted up the words, "Thou shalt not bear false witness against thy neighbour." The attendance at first was not quite so large as on the previous evening, but there must have been considerably more than 2,000 persons present at the commencement of the proceedings, and towards the close the hall was quite filled, many having evidently gained admittance without payment. On the platform with Sir ROGER were Mr. G. ONSLOW, M.P., Mr. WHALLEY, M.P., Mr. BLOXAM, Alderman TUCKER, Councillors S. S. PEARCE and PURKIS, Messrs. SHETTLE, KNOWLES, ELLIS, FASHAM, HARDIMAN, W. BAIGENT, DAVIS, and other members of the Southampton Defence Fund, while BOGLE, the coloured servant, was also in attendance. We noticed there were quite as many ladies present as on the previous evening, and who joined in giving the Claimant a hearty reception on his arrival.

On the motion of Mr. KNOWLES, seconded by Mr. SHETTLE, Alderman TUCKER was unanimously voted to the chair.

The Chairman commenced by saying he hardly knew how to express his thanks to them for the distinguished honour they had conferred upon him for the second time, and announced that since the previous evening the many congratulations he had received on the position he had taken in the cause had more than compensated him for any little trouble, if it might be called such, he had been put to. He was pleased to find such a large attendance that night, as it showed the sympathy felt for the gentleman on his right (the Claimant), and that sympathy had been evoked entirely in consequence of the unfair treatment he had met with. (Cheers.) A gentleman stopped him in the street that day, and told him that the Lord Chief Justice interposed extra-judicially no less than 2,000 times in the course of the 103 days which the Trial lasted, but on no one occasion in favour of the Claimant. ("Shame.") This was to say nothing of the extra-judicial remarks the Attorney-General made with regard to him. He could tell them if this had been said of any gentleman of a less amiable disposition than his friend on his right he would have horsewhipped the Attorney-General when he came out of Court, and he knew that everyone in that company would say "It served him right." ("Hear," and cheers.) Then they put the bail for the Claimant at £5,000 in order to keep him in gaol, thinking that he would not be able to procure it, while the threat held out by the Attorney-General, to the effect that it would be a matter of consideration what they should do with Sir ROGER's witnesses, was only made to prevent others coming forward in his favour. Some resolutions would be proposed, but previous to that a presentation would be made to the honourable baronet by a gentleman who had written an acrostic which he was sure would please them all. (Cheers.)

Mr. ELLIS then proceeded to read the acrostic he had written, but not being heard at the other end of the hall, there were cries of "Let TUCKER read it," "Speak out," "No, no," and "Order." Mr. ELLIS read the acrostic, and then handed it to the Chairman, who presented it to Sir ROGER.

The Claimant accepted it, and said he should keep it until the end of his life—that was, providing his enemies did not take it from him. (Laughter.) He should always keep it as a memento of the kind reception he had met with at Southampton. (Cheers.)

Mr. GUILFORD ONSLOW, M.P., after expressing the pleasure it gave him to meet such a large number again that evening in the town of Southampton—a town which he had known for many years as always ready to come forward to give aid to those who were in distress, or to welcome among them those who had been trampled on with a desire to crush them—said he believed that in this case their sympathy had not been misplaced, and had it not been for that sympathy the Claimant would probably have been crushed. They had many enemies around them. He was personally persecuted in all quarters for the position he had taken, but he thanked God that he had broad shoulders which could bear it. He hoped the time would come when they would be proved in the right. He believed they had the support of two classes out of three, and that the time was fast approaching when they would have all classes around them. At the present moment they had only one member of Parliament beside himself supporting them on the platform; but he held that this great cause must be heard on the hustings at the next dissolution of Parliament. In reading a newspaper of that town that morning, he found a communication made of a most important nature to them, and it had reference to the evidence of Dr. WHEELER. In consequence of that it had been deemed necessary to publish his sworn affidavit. Dr. WHEELER had never been examined as a witness, but he was now subpœnaed, and if his evidence was true—and they had every reason to believe it was—then the gentleman who was sitting by the side of him could not by any possible means be ARTHUR ORTON. (Cheers.) Up to the present, when a witness had come from among the working-classes, he had been pooh-poohed at and all that sort of thing; but the moment they got a gentleman like Dr. WHEELER, a gentleman who was known to many members of Parliament, the first thing the other side did was to give a flat contradiction to his affidavit. He (Mr. ONSLOW) might tell them that he was present when Dr. WHEELER made that affidavit; he heard him swear to it, and he only hoped he would live to say in Court what he had sworn to in it, and then there would be an end to the fable that this gentleman (the Claimant) was ARTHUR ORTON. (Cheers.) Mr. ONSLOW then entered into the reasons why the Claimant should have forgotten his French, remarking that he was as savage when he came out of the bush as he was gentlemanly and mild before he went into it—(loud laughter)—and proceeded to clear up the mystery surrounding the picking up of the Claimant from the wreck of the "Bella" and his being landed at Melbourne by the "Osprey," telling the audience that the moment questions were asked in the Court of Common Pleas on this subject of the five witnesses who came forward and swore that they went on board the "Osprey," and were told that she had shipwrecked men who had been picked up off the coast of South America from the "Bella," they were at once objected to. Although they could not get the captain of the "Osprey" to come forward and confirm this, still he contended it was positive evidence that the "Osprey" did exist, and that it was not a myth, as the Attorney-General had put it. Then it was clear that ROGER TICHBORNE was put on board the "Bella" while he was drunk, and when he landed in Australia he went into the interior of the country, taking a menial situation. It had been said that he had a large sum of money at his bankers' (GLYNS'), and why did he not draw on them? That was all very well, but even if it had been the great ROTHSCHILD himself who had landed in the way ROGER TICHBORNE did, and had wished to draw on a bank, he would have received a movement of a peculiar nature. (Laughter.) It was quite true that ROGER might have waited at Melbourne, and said "Take my cheque, send it home, and I'll wait here until its return." But just at that time the "gold fever" had set in; ships were lying at their anchors, deserted by the sailors, who, with the rest of the people, had gone to the diggings, and he might have waited there until all eternity without having his cheque returned to him. He went into the bush, and not wishing his real name to be known, he took the name of TOMAS CASTRO. When he married and had a child he said, "Well, this life is all very well, but I must leave it now, for I have a wife and child, and while it would do for me, it will not for them." (Cheers.) If he was an impostor he was an unwilling one, because he was found out by Mr. GIBBES, and it was said in the Court of Common Pleas that he was "found out by Mr. GIBBES to be Sir ROGER TICHBORNE to his huge disgust." (Cheers.) Then much had been said about the will he had signed in Australia: that he signed it in a wrong name, that he called his mother the wrong name, and that there were certain things which went against him. Sir ROGER's impression was that he was bound to make this will as a security for the payment of some money, and when he signed this will he did it with a view to deceive, in order that they might not know who he really was. He (Mr. ONSLOW) did not take his part for doing this, but he looked upon it as an act of folly, and not one of fraud, because no money passed between them. It was a foolish thing—an act of folly—but it proved him to be Sir ROGER TICHBORNE, and he would tell them why. He spoke in the will about his property called the Hermitage, and the Attorney-General said he meant the Hermitage Wharf at Wapping. "This was the only property," said ROGER TICHBORNE in his will, "that I inherited from my father." The Hermitage was a farm by that name, and was situated near to where he (Mr. ONSLOW) lived at Ropley, in Hampshire, and was the only property he inherited from his father; and why, if he was afterwards coached with regard to the names of his mother, was it that he could recollect the Hermitage? This went to prove he was not the impostor some people wished them to believe. (Loud cheers.) Then Mrs. RADCLIFFE recognised the Claimant as her cousin; she could not declare he was not ROGER, but on the second occasion when she was to meet him she missed the train, and she had never spoken to him since. ("Shame.") These were things they had not heard, and there being no chance of a reply after the long-winded speech of the Attorney-General it had left them in the dark as regarded the case. If people could have heard a reply after that speech, he was sure they would have all thought the other way. Mr. ONSLOW next referred to ROGER TICHBORNE's career at Stonyhurst, and said if he were to be cross-examined as to what he did twenty-

M. SPOFFORTH, ESQ., SOLICITOR FOR CLAIMANT.

five years ago, he should be terribly at fault. It was said he was an impostor because of the things he had said about Stonyhurst, but forgetfulness did not prove that a man was not what he represented himself to be. (Cheers.) He mentioned these facts in order to show that they had led him to divest his mind of the belief that this man was not the true Sir ROGER TICHBORNE. (Loud cheers.) Dr. WHEELER's would be very strong corroborative evidence, and the other side knew it. They had other evidence, but they did not feel inclined to say what it was, as they had told their opponents too much before. Then, again, there was Mr. ROUS, of the Swan at Alresford, who was almost their private secretary. He received all the private correspondence of Sir ROGER when he went away to South America, and was allowed to open both his and his wife's letters. Nothing was hid from him; he knew everything, and had it not been for ROUS, as the Attorney-General admitted, there would have been no material on which to cross-examine the eighty-seven witnesses. If they had been supporting an impostor, if they had been doing things under the rose, they would have been found out in consequence of the manner in which Mr. ROUS acted. (Hear hear.) With regard to Mr. BAIGENT, he was the most deserving and truthful man he ever knew. He stood the cross-examination nobly, and never broke down. That he was speaking honestly and truthfully was proved by the traitorship of the flabby-minded gentleman, Mr. ROUS. (Cheers.) Then respecting the peculiarity in the thumb of ROGER TICHBORNE. False evidence could be brought, and the Attorney-General could make black appear white, but the sun of Heaven never flattered, and fortunately they were enabled to produce that peculiarity of thumb, and that alone proved this man to be the real Sir ROGER TICHBORNE. (Cheers.) But the opposite party had smudged out the thumb, and this was as disgraceful and dishonourable as the attempt to prove that he was tattooed, if they proved that he was never tattooed. (Hear, hear, and loud cheers.) The issue mark was on his arm; it was known to MOORE (the valet) and to Lady TICHBORNE, and when she told MOORE to look on his arm for the issue mark, why did she not tell him to look for the tattoo as well? Sir ROGER stood alone with his Mother. If the Family knew he was tattooed, why did they not challenge him there and then to take off his coat—(cheers)—tuck up his sleeves, and exhibit the tattoo marks? What would have been the consequence? If he had refused to comply, he would have been stopped in his career: £100,000 would have been saved, a child would not have been cheated by an impostor, and the estate would have been saved over £150,000. He would ask them, "Have the Family acted honourably in this case?" (No, no.) He said they had not. (Cheers.) They allowed MCCANN to get into the witness-box—the man who held his arms while he was bled when he had fits—they allowed that man to get into the witness-box when he was at the point of death—for he was now dead, and gone to a purer tribunal than the Court of Common Pleas—but they did not dare ask him the question whether he saw any tattoo marks on his arm. This was the way in which the case was conducted. They allowed the Attorney-General to speak until everybody was tired of hearing him, and when Sir ROGER TICHBORNE elected to take a nonsuit—the only means by which he could get another trial—he was sent to Newgate—committed without being convicted. ("Shame.") If those tattoo marks proved to be untrue, he pitied those ladies and gentlemen who said they were there. (Cheers.) Mr. ONSLOW then referred to the discrepancies in certain parts of the evidence, and to the numerous persons whom the other side said the Claimant was telling the audience that he supposed they would say next that he was an illegitimate child of the Attorney-General. (Loud laughter and cheers, and the Claimant shook his head.) In conclusion, Mr. ONSLOW thanked the public of Southampton for the reception they had given him, and trusted that their efforts might eventually be crowned with success; resuming his seat amidst loud cheers.

Mr. KNOWLES then conversed with the Chairman and others, which led to a little noise in the hall, but order was very quickly restored, and Mr. WHALLEY, M.P., rose and addressed the meeting. He announced that he had decided to return to London, but he felt it his duty to remain and give such support as he could to Mr. ONSLOW in the difficult and heroic task he had undertaken, and he never felt more rewarded than in listening to the statement of the hon. gentleman that night. It seemed to him almost providential that his hon. friend should have given himself up to the cause. He never heard any statement more ably rendered or more thorough justice done to a case than that night, without the artificial skill of the barrister—he had never in his life heard a more able, pointed, and admirable statement than Mr. ONSLOW had made. (Cheers.) He begged to give a confirmation, as far as he could, to every fact and every suggestion which Mr. ONSLOW had made, as being within his own knowledge, in the moderate and far from exaggerated statement he had brought before them. (Cheers.) Referring to the tattoo marks, Mr. WHALLEY asked what would be done with the parties who swore to them if they failed in the matter? Would not justice be done in the case of those gentlemen who have persecuted the Claimant? Mr. WHALLEY alluded to the statement published with regard to Dr. WHEELER, and remarked that the line of procedure the Press had taken in this matter would be a disgrace to the journalism of this country, which was received with loud cheers.

When Mr. WHALLEY had finished his speech, Mr. ONSLOW gave an account of the interview between Dr. WHEELER and the Claimant, saying it was some time before they recognised each other; but as soon as they did so they began talking about old friendships, and it left on his mind the impression that Dr. WHEELER was speaking nothing but the truth, and because it corroborated the statement of GEORGE ORTON, the brother of ARTHUR ORTON.

The Chairman thanked the hon. member for Guildford for the information he had given them, and introduced the Claimant to the meeting.

The Claimant, who was received with loud cheers, said he asked them to accept his sincere thanks for the reception they had given him at Southampton, and which he should never forget as long as he lived. Had he been a prince, or anyone else in a high station of life, they could not have given him a more hearty reception. He would again tell them that he was not come there to ask them to believe that he was Sir ROGER TICHBORNE. He had come there to ask them to insist upon his having a fair trial—(cheers)—and not allow him to be crushed by the Attorney-General and all his associates who might be working with him. (Renewed cheers.) He was now going to explain a few points in his case. In the first place, many of them would remember that the Attorney-General held up some letters to him, and asked him if they were in his handwriting. He replied that they were. The Attorney-General then read those letters, and after that he was convinced they were not his. He asked him to let him look at them. He did so, and he was then convinced that they were not in his writing, and that they had never been in his hand before. ("Shame.") The moment he (the Claimant) stated this there were roars of laughter on the other side, for he might tell them where he had one friend in Court the other side had a hundred. The Judge would only allow him tickets for two friends during the whole of the 103 days. When the Attorney-General sat down, after bullying him as much as he liked about the letters, he was heard to say "I knew two of them were not his, but I thought the third was." ("Shame," and "Forged letters.") Again, in his speech the Attorney-General admitted that they were forgeries, and he would ask them what would have been the case with him if he had forged any documents? He would have been sent to Newgate, and very properly so, and they could not have said one word about it. (Hear, hear.) Now, respecting the rubbing out of the thumb. Mr. BOWKER, of Winchester, had copies of the daguerreotype taken and sent out with the Chili Commission, and while he was in the Court he happened to lean his thumb over the railing of the box. By some means the other side got possession of the original daguerreotype, and when it was called for again the thumb was gone. ("Shame.") But Mr. BOWKER forgot that they had copies of it, which were taken before the thumb was rubbed out. (Cheers.) Then there was JULES BARRATT, his servant, who said he (the Claimant) was taken on board the "Bella" at night. He was very sorry to admit it, but he must speak the truth, and tell them that in his earlier days he was addicted to hard drinking, and that when he went on board the "Bella" he was the worse for liquor. (Cheers.) The "Bella" had to remain some forty-eight hours while Mr. HOLLICOMBE was looking about Buenos Ayres for him. When he went on board the "Bella" he believed his luggage, was there, as BARRATT told him he had taken it on board. He would tell them that JULES BARRATT stole his luggage, and he would tell them why he said so. He produced in the Court of Common Pleas a part and parcel of his luggage—he produced the bill of lading of the things which he sent to Mr. GOSFORD. He was quite sure on that point, because the "Bella" went down and he saved nothing from her, and as he (Claimant) did not get his luggage, where did BARRATT get these things from? But his Counsel was too tired at the time, and did not put these questions. ("You are hard on BALLANTINE.") The Claimant then referred to his interview with Mr. and Mrs. RADCLIFFE, Mrs. TOWNLEY, and Mrs NANGLE, stating that his Mother was pushed out of the room at Croydon and the door shut in her face, and it was excitement and a little temper that caused him to act as he did. (Cheers.) The Claimant gave an account of his interview on the second occasion with Mr. RADCLIFFE and others, and pointed out how Mr. RADCLIFFE deceived him, while the ladies there told Mrs. HOLMES, at whose house the interview took place, that he had ears as long as—he would not say what—but a female pig. (Laughter.) While the interview lasted Mrs. HOLMES was bundled out of the room, and he asked why Mrs. RADCLIFFE did not attend then? It was because she had recognized him, and had not turned round up to that moment (Cheers.) That was why Mr. RADCLIFFE did not bring her. In consequence of the way in which he was treated he went out of the room, and would have nothing more to do with them. After that Mr. RADCLIFFE came again, but he had with him one of his (the Claimant's) deadliest enemies. He was now going to say something about the Attorney-General. ("Give it to him hot.") He spoke for thirty days. He was in the Case for 103 days, and yet he had the impudence to tell the Premier the other day that he could prove him to be ARTHUR ORTON in twenty minutes. (Laughter.) In addition to that he had actually threatened Members of Parliament, and he sent a most insulting letter to Mr. WHALLEY, which he handed to him (the Claimant). Was this proper conduct for the chief law-officer of the Crown? ("No, no," and Mr. PURKIS: "He's the Lord Chief's Scoundrel.") There was no doubt that Sir JOHN COLERIDGE would be made the Lord Chief Justice of England or the Lord Chancellor, and all he could say to them was—"Don't have such a blackguard." The whole country ought to rise up and protest and say they would have a gentleman, and not such a blackguard as he was. (Cheers.) He would remind them that the Attorney-General abused him for thirty days, and they must not say that he showed malice if he now had his turn. (Hear, hear.) He could not answer him in Court, but here he could give a reply and to every British subject. ("You gave it to him pretty hot sometimes.") He would ask them—"Did I give it him as hot as he gave it to me?" ("No, no.") He did not throw the Attorney-General into Newgate, and let him remain there for 52 days—(Mr. PURKIS: "I wish you had")—if he had the power he did not know that he should do it, because he was a humane man. (Cheers.) He wished to correct an observation that fell from Mr. ONSLOW. He said that he (the Claimant) gave Mr. ROUS permission to open his wife's letters. This was not so, as he did not allow him to open his wife's letters. He opened his (the Claimant's) letters when he was absent, and frequently in his presence, when he was too lazy to do it. (Laughter.) ROUS copied the letters, and then sent them to the other side. ("Shame.") He thanked them for the kind reception they had given him that night, and it would be ever borne in his mind—till the day of his death. (The Claimant sat down amidst much cheering.)

Mr. HARROLD, of Winchester, proposed: "That this meeting is of opinion that the taxpayers are entitled to every explanation and information relative to this gigantic Government prosecution now being carried on at such an enormous cost, and deprecates the conduct of the Chancellor of the Exchequer and the other members of the Government in refusing to answer questions put them by hon. members, as representatives of the people as regards this Case, and considers such conduct neither honourable nor just."

Seconded by Mr. G. DAVIS, saddler and harness-maker, Orchard-street, Southampton, and carried unanimously.

Mr. S. S. PEARCE moved the next resolution, which was seconded by Mr. FASHAM, an ex-Royal Engineer, who, on rising to second the motion, said he appeared before them as a man in three shapes

—first, he was a working man; second, he was an old soldier; and third, he was an old Australian bushman, and was able to give some particulars of the state of Australia at the time the Claimant was stated to have arrived there. There were two things just then happening, which made the place in such a state that it would be an impossibility to form any idea of what the state of affairs was at the time. The gold fever might then be stated to be at its height, and matters in such a state at Melbourne as to baffle description; and just at this time the convicts in Norfolk Island and at Hobart Town, who had been set at large, naturally made their way there. Ships from all nations were daily arriving. As many immigrants as 15,000 had been known to arrive in one week. London, Liverpool, Glasgow, and every place in England, Scotland, and Ireland, were sending their thousands. Singapore, China, New York, California, besides all the other colonies, were sending crowds off to the land of gold. Clerks, police, sailors, mechanics, and everybody else were all flocking to the diggings. He mentioned a case, which he knew personally, of a vessel which sailed from Freemantle, in Western Australia, to Melbourne, and returned, without having come into contact with either pilot, harbour authorities, or Custom House officers, the captain not knowing whether such authorities existed or not; and stated that it was his decided opinion that it was not only possible, but highly probable, that Sir ROGER did arrive at Melbourne as stated, for many ships must have done so in the then state of affairs. The speaker next alluded to the tattoo marks, which he characterised as a most miserable affair, and spoke in the strongest manner as to the way the military evidence had been treated, and, after alluding to the high character of the officers of the British army, said it was the greatest insult that could possibly be offered to the profession generally, and he would hurl it back to the parties implicated with all the contempt he knew how to do so, both as regards the discharged soldiers and those now serving; and that officers and men were no conspirators or perjurers, and not used to such dirty work. The speaker here stated that as time was late, he would not speak any more; but being most loudly cheered, and cries of "Go on; we will wait an hour," coming from all parts of the hall, he continued to talk of the tattoo marks, asking whether Sir ROGER was ever examined by any military medical authority, previous to obtaining his commission, and where was the record of it? (Cheers.) "Ah!" said he, "why, if those who invented that affair were to go into the stables of the Carabineers, the very horses would kick their brains out." (Laughter, deafening cheers, and clapping of hands.) The speaker then stated that he could inform them of a plan by which to obtain excellent evidence from Australia, and at a much cheaper rate than was said to be proposed by the Attorney-General; and to spend £16,000 there was no need of, for there were lots of old lags who would be only too glad to accept the offer of a free passage to England, would require but little coaching, and would appear on the boards at Westminster as first-class witnesses, and make a much better job than the tattoo affair. The speaker then referred to a capital case of convict evidence occurring in one of the colonies, where thirteen witnesses all told the same tale about some timber being carted away; but on finding the weight of the load, they had sworn to a horse drawing nearly four tons seven or eight miles over an unmade road, through loose sand and over rocks and loose stones, and then the case broke down. Alluding to the case of Sir ROGER growing so stout, he mentioned the case of a comrade who had, in ten years' residence in the country, grown from about nine stone to about sixteen or seventeen stone; and, joking Sir ROGER, said that kangaroo-tail soup, 'possums, and other Australian dainties, which, owing to the absence of the game laws—(loud cheers)—were easily comeatable, would certainly assist in making him so stout. Concluding from what he had seen in Australia personally, he had every reason to believe all be heard about the Claimant there. He had no doubt of the truth of the statement, and hoped soon to see the right man in the right place. The speaker then resumed his seat by the side of Mr. WHALLEY, who cordially took him by the hand, and complimented him on the excellence of his speech.

Mr. Councillor PURKIS thanked the reporters of the weekly papers for the scurrilous way they had spoken of him on the opening of the Wednesday proceedings.

Mr. KNOWLES rose and moved: "That it is the opinion of this meeting that the whole of the proceedings against Sir ROGER TICHBORNE, from its first commencement in Australia, before the arrival of Sir ROGER in England, and up to the present time, forms one of the grandest conspiracies against a private gentleman, to swear away his name, to rob him of his inheritance, his fame, his title, and respectability, ever attempted in this country, and that his case is worthy of the confidence and support of every British subject."

Mr. Councillor PURKIS seconded the resolution, amid shouts of "BOGLE," when the worthy councillor announced that BOGLE was poorly, and could not say anything. He was of a nervous temperament.

Mr. BOGLE then came to the front of the platform, and announced that he was poorly—suffering from rheumatic gout.

Mr. LUMBY supported the proposition, which was agreed to unanimously.

The Chairman proposed a vote of thanks to Messrs. PURKIS for their great kindness in having placed that large building at their disposal for the purpose of their meetings. They were entitled to the thanks of the whole community. (Cheers.)

Mr. KNOWLES seconded the motion, and it was carried with acclamation.

On the motion of the Claimant, seconded by Mr. G. ONSLOW, M.P., a vote of thanks was given to the Chairman for presiding, and the Committee for making the arrangements connected with the visit, and the Chairman having replied, the audience quickly left the hall, many of them remaining in the Above Bar-street, and cheering the Claimant as he was driven down in a closed waggonette to the Castle Hotel.

Sir ROGER remained at Southampton on Wednesday night, and on Thursday morning paid a visit to Messrs. RIDER and BARRETT's photographic establishment in Prospect-place, where several negatives were taken. In the afternoon he left the Castle Hotel for Mr. ONSLOW's residence at Ropley.

Two matters were alluded to at this meeting, to which we think it well to call attention. The first was the interview between the Claimant and the RADCLIFFES. In the *Hampshire Advertiser* of March 30th, 1867, appears the following narrative. It bears internal evidence of having been written by HOLMES, who afterwards became so much the enemy of his Client:—

SIR ROGER AND MRS. RADCLIFFE.

In the performance of our promise recently made, we are, being in a position so to do, about to place before our readers new and reliable facts in connection with the above deeply interesting topic, and also to give them an authentic account of the recent interviews between Sir ROGER CHARLES TICHBORNE, Bart., and certain members of the Family, versions of which have been put in circulation industriously by those adverse to the interests of, and anxious for the failure of, the baronet's claims to the ancient honours and estates of his house. The particulars we are about to give will show how little reliance is to be placed on such rumours, whether written or oral, as also on the strenuous efforts made to damage the Claimant's cause by endeavouring to prejudge it by aspersions on his character, which are utterly unfounded. In the first week of the present month Mr. and Mrs. RADCLIFFE (formerly Miss DOUGHTY) paid a visit to Mrs. GREENWOOD's at Brookwood. On the 1st and 2nd of March Mr. and Mrs. RADCLIFFE and Mrs. GREENWOOD made excursions to Ropley, for the sake of travelling thence by railway to Alresford, in the expectation that Sir ROGER might by chance be travelling in the same train, and so as to appear to meet him accidentally on his alighting at Alresford; but Sir ROGER being at this time laid up with a severe sore throat, their contrivance bore no fruit. Mr. HOLMES, the solicitor to Sir ROGER, came to Alresford by the mid-day train on the second day, and the above party went to Mr. ADAM's office (Sir ROGER's local solicitor) for the purpose of having an interview with Mr. HOLMES. They were together for about four hours. At its commencement Mr. RADCLIFFE, in a dictatorial, off-hand manner, and in a haughty tone, spoke to Mr. HOLMES, but that gentleman at once checked such conduct by a severe reproof, which had its effect in producing a more conciliatory demeanour. The result of this interview was that he begged to be allowed an interview with Sir ROGER, he promising, on the part of himself and the ladies, to treat the baronet with every courtesy and respect, and to take no unfair advantage of the interview or consent. On March 8th Mrs. TOWNLEY (Mrs. GREENWOOD's sister) and Mrs. RADCLIFFE suddenly made their appearance at Essex Lodge, Croydon, the residence of Sir ROGER and Lady TICHBORNE, and of his mother the Dowager Lady JAMES TICHBORNE. Their entrance into the house was somewhat abrupt, and the ladies exchanged names and tried to pass themselves off under this *ruse*, but Sir ROGER fortunately at once detected and corrected their names. The Dowager was at this time sitting in a room separated by folding doors (open at the time). Sir ROGER said to the ladies, "Here is my mother," whereupon Mr. RADCLIFFE closed the doors upon the Dowager Lady TICHBORNE. This placed Sir ROGER in a very awkward position, and his first impulse was to ring the bell and direct them to be shown out of the house, but upon second thoughts he felt it would be more agreeable to his solicitor if he kept up a conversation with them. After an hour's converse they left, shaking Sir ROGER warmly by the hand, expressing moreover the pleasure they would have in again seeing him. On the same day Mr. RADCLIFFE wrote a note to Mr. HOLMES, saying, "Mrs. TOWNLEY, Mrs. RADCLIFFE, and myself went down yesterday afternoon to see your Client. We regret to say that we do not feel satisfied with our interview; we should require some further conversation before we can be quite certain he is the ROGER TICHBORNE we formerly knew." They asked for another interview. Mr. HOLMES wrote back to say that "he was glad they had been to Essex Lodge, as he felt the more the baronet saw of his relatives the sooner a satisfactory settlement would be arrived at of the doubts and uncertainties; but that Sir ROGER had said it was most painful to him, their declining to see his Mother." He promised to see Sir ROGER, so as to arrange another interview. On the next day Mr. HOLMES wrote to say that the doctor deemed it inexpedient for Sir ROGER (he being then ill) to go out in the then inclement weather, and Mr. HOLMES assured them that Sir ROGER was placed in a most painful position by their declining to see the Dowager, through whose solicitations and exertions it was he had heard of his father's death, and was now back in England. They might well imagine what a pang it gave him then to find her so rudely treated, although she was in the house ready to receive Mr. RADCLIFFE and his party. His Mother was naturally angry that her son did not resent such conduct. Mr. HOLMES added that he hoped that whatever family differences existed they might be reconciled and the plain truth brought out,—and with that view Mr. HOLMES proposed that Lady DOUGHTY, Sir ROGER's aunt, and his cousins (Mrs. TOWNLEY and Mrs. RADCLIFFE) should meet him at Mr. HOLMES's house, 3, Sydenham-road, Croydon, which he would freely place at their disposal whenever Mr. RADCLIFFE pleased to appoint, and intimated that he (Mr. H.) would not be present at such an interview. This message was sent by THOMAS CARTER, Sir ROGER's groom, during the last fifteen months he was in England; and that Mr. RADCLIFFE was at perfect liberty to ask CARTER any questions he might think proper. Mr. RADCLIFFE sent back, in writing, word that he would see the ladies so as to arrange a meeting as Mr. HOLMES proposed. Next day Mr. RADCLIFFE wrote to say that he had seen the ladies respecting the next proposed meeting with Mr. HOLMES's Client, and that they agreed with him in the propriety of another interview in company of their aunt (Lady DOUGHTY); but only in consideration of their wish to clear this matter up as soon as possible, would they consent again to go down to Croydon, more particularly when they remembered the age of one of the ladies (Lady DOUGHTY, 73). They, therefore proposed to come to Croydon by the two o'clock train. Mr. HOLMES wrote back to say that Sir ROGER would be glad to see his aunt (Lady DOUGHTY) and cousins at Mr. HOLMES's house to-morrow at three o'clock, as proposed. Mr. RADCLIFFE sent word back that there was some mistake, as the day named was Wednesday, not Tuesday; and that the appointment must stand for the former day, as the ladies had engagements for Tuesday. Mr. HOLMES replied that Mr. RADCLIFFE had named no day for the meeting, but only asked him to give the bearer a reply. He inclosed Mr. RADCLIFFE a copy of his letter in proof of the same, and promised to let him know whether Wednesday would suit. Notwithstanding this, on Tuesday, March 12th, Mr. RADCLIFFE and three ladies suddenly made their appearance at Mr. HOLMES's house, demanding to see Sir ROGER, who of course was not there. Mrs. HOLMES offered to send for the baronet, but Mr. RADCLIFFE preferred going for him himself. During his absence on this errand the ladies remained with Mrs. HOLMES in conversation. One was Mrs. TOWNLEY, the others were strange women, and their remarks were anything but complimentary. They told Mrs. HOLMES that Sir ROGER was "an impostor," an "Australian navvy," and freely indulged in similar aspersions on one they had not even seen—thus showing the spirit which animated them. Sir ROGER accompanied Mr. RADCLIFFE in a cab, and was told he was going to see his aunt Lady DOUGHTY, Mr. RADCLIFFE assuring him that she was at Mr. HOLMES's with his cousins, Mrs. TOWNLEY and Mrs. RADCLIFFE. On entering the dining-room, Mr. RADCLIFFE, in an excited manner, ordered Mrs. HOLMES out of her own room. Then turning round to Sir ROGER, he demanded of him who the lady sitting in the chair was. Sir ROGER, having been rendered wary by the former ruse of exchanging names, seeing the lady was thickly veiled and sitting down, desired her to remove it and stand up. On her doing so Sir ROGER said he did not know her. He was then asked if he knew the other stranger. He looked at her, replied that he did not think he did, and if he had she could only have been a girl about twelve years of age when he left England. On this the party commenced a tirade of uncomplimentary language. Sir ROGER, from the trick and falsehoods played on him (unsuccessfully), was most indignant. Turning to RADCLIFFE, he denounced his conduct, saying that he was anything but a gentleman, and then to his cousin, Mrs. TOWNLEY, added, "Lucy, you will be sorry for this," and at once he left the room. The whole interview certainly lasted less than five minutes. Mr. RADCLIFFE then shouted for Mrs. HOLMES, who, on making her appearance, was informed that her husband's client was a "rank impostor," &c. Mr. HOLMES, as soon as he heard of this, wrote to Mr. RADCLIFFE next day as follows:—"The way in which you and three ladies who were with you yesterday behaved for the very few moments Sir ROGER TICHBORNE condescended to see you, was an entire breach of the arrangement we made at Alresford, and could only result in his withdrawing himself. I regret it very much, because, after what Mr. GOSFORD told me on Saturday, it is certain that if Sir ROGER had been treated by you and your party with common civility, the litigation which must ensue would have been entirely avoided; however, neither myself nor my client can now be blamed. You did wrong in going to my house without a previous appointment, or in taking any one there respecting whom we had not arranged. My wife was surprised that neither of the three ladies favoured her with their names. Their remarks whilst Mr. RADCLIFFE was gone to fetch Sir ROGER were altogether unjustifiable, for they had not then seen him. I am very sorry indeed to find that your attempted surprise on Sir ROGER and manner of treating him were as unfair as the conduct pursued towards him by his Family since his arrival in England, but the same spirit evidently animates all those whose interest it is he should not succeed. It is, however, a great satisfaction for Sir ROGER to know that the Court will disapprove the conduct complained of, and in the end his rights, which are founded in truth, must prevail." On the same day Mr. HOLMES wrote a letter to Messrs. SLAUGHTER and CULLINGTON, Solicitors of the Hon. Lady DOUGHTY, and Mr. and Mrs. RADCLIFFE, Mr. GOSFORD, and others, stating "that the result of a long discussion which took place between Mr. and Mrs. RADCLIFFE and Mrs. GREENWOOD and myself, at Alresford, was that it was agreed that my client should be treated with every consideration by them, and they should meet him at Tichborne. Sir ROGER's health prevented him from going there, and Mr. and Mrs. RADCLIFFE and Mrs. TOWNLEY called and spent an hour with him on March 8th, at Essex Lodge, Croydon, where he was living with his mother, the Dowager Lady JAMES TICHBORNE. Unfortunately for my efforts with a view to peace, Mr. and Mrs. RADCLIFFE and Mrs. TOWNLEY refused to see her ladyship, and Sir ROGER was placed in consequence in a most painful position. The next day Mr. RADCLIFFE wrote to me a letter, in which, so far from denying, he tacitly admits that my client is Sir ROGER TICHBORNE, and asked for another interview for himself and the two ladies, in order that they might be 'be quite certain.' Mr. GOSFORD, who went to Croydon with them, but did not go to the house, called on me on the 9th instant, and told me that Mrs. RADCLIFFE recognized Sir ROGER by his eyes, his eyebrows, and shape of his forehead, &c., and that certainly none of the party could declare it was not him. I promised Mr. GOSFORD to bring about an interview between himself and Sir ROGER as soon as possible. I replied to Mr. RADCLIFFE's note, stating that Sir ROGER would be happy to see his aunt, Lady DOUGHTY, as well as the other two ladies, and I placed my house at their disposal so as to avoid the unpleasantness of their refusing to see the Dowager, and intimated that I should not be present. Mr. RADCLIFFE wrote to me on the 11th, saying the ladies would go again to Croydon in company with Lady DOUGHTY, and asked me for an appointment. I answered, fixing the next day at three o'clock. On that day Mr. RADCLIFFE sent another letter, stating that the ladies would not go until Wednesday (the 13th). I therefore sent a telegram to Sir ROGER, and postponed the appointment. To my great surprise, on arriving home on Tuesday, I found that Mr. RADCLIFFE and three ladies went to my house on the afternoon of that day." The result of the interview we have given above. Mrs. RADCLIFFE called after the party had left Croydon. Mr. HOLMES then wrote a letter to Mr. RADCLIFFE, complaining of the breach of faith, adding that he need not say how sincerely he regretted, for the sake of all parties, that such unfair conduct had been used towards his client, but he was sure the Court would condemn it. Every disinterested witness who had seen and conversed with him (and they were now very numerous) was perfectly convinced that his client was Sir ROGER TICHBORNE. He had no hesitation whatever in permitting interviews with Mr. and Mrs. RADCLIFFE, and Lady DOUGHTY and Mrs. TOWNLEY, but certainly did not expect any trick would be attempted or his confidence abused. Mrs. and Colonel WILLIAMS and Colonel GEORGE GREENWOOD have had invitations to meet Sir ROGER, but have not responded to them." Such were Mr. HOLMES's communications to the solicitors on the opposite side. On March 19th, in consequence of rumours, adverse rumours, prevalent at that time, Mr. W. W. BULPETT, a country magistrate, and the well-known banker of Winchester, Alresford, and Alton, called on Mr. HOLMES, who very soon disabused his mind by showing him the correspondence. They continued in conversation some time, although Mr. HOLMES had more than once intimated his desire to fulfil an engagement. During the talk a gentleman walked into the room, and went straight up to Mr. BULPETT saying, "How do you do, Mr. BULPETT, I am very pleased to see you." Mr. B. was taken aback by this sudden and unprecedetend recognition, and, looking at his interrogator, exclaimed at once "Why, it is Sir ROGER TICHBORNE." Being asked by Mr. HOLMES how he knew it was Sir ROGER, he said, "By the upper part of his face," adding, with an exclamation, "that there was no mistake about it. What can your relations mean by asserting you are not the man?" Mr. HOLMES desired them to sit down and have a quiet chat, placing, moreover, Sir ROGER in such a position that the light should fall on his face. The banker and the baronet chatted about adventures in former days in the hunting-field, and which interested both, and Mr. BULPETT, on leaving, assured Mr. HOLMES that Sir ROGER was the gentleman he had, as Mr. R. C. TICHBORNE, met frequently in the hunting-field. Any further remarks on the above are needless. It is the singular feature in the case that those who have *not seen* the gentleman have no hesitation in denouncing him as an impostor and adventurer, and other expressions of the most uncomplimentary character, refusing communication with him, and neglecting the common politeness of answering his letters, and those of persons who have seen him and have recognized him without doubt. Such blindness and obstinacy it is difficult to explain, as among those who are ready to declare and attest that he is Sir ROGER CHARLES TICHBORNE, Bart., may be mentioned, first, his own Mother, second, his old and intimate friend, Mr. F. J. BAIGENT, of Winchester; third, Mr. HOPKINS, the Family and his own old solicitor; fourth, the Family doctor (Mr. LIPSCOMBE) who on several occasions attended Mr. R. C. TICHBORNE professionally, and even sat up with him all night a short period before Sir ROGER left England in 1853; fifth, the Family banker, Mr. W. W. BULPETT; sixth, the Rev. A. BISHOP, rector of Bramdean, and incumbent of Tichborne from 1840 to 1853; seventh, Mr. Superintendent EVERITT, of the County Constabulary. We, adds our correspondent, could mention other witnesses equally reliable and equally honourable; indeed, there is a "cloud of witnesses," and abundance of documentary evidence, such as the most strenuous doubter could not hope to overthrow. Our space, however, forbids us from further detail, otherwise we could cite the names of many of the local gentry. In conclusion, we venture to assert that the return of Sir ROGER will be beneficial to the neighbourhood and estates, and his administration of them honourable to himself.

The second was the affidavit of Dr. WHEELER, which we print with the following preface:—

DR. WHEELER.

This gentleman made an affidavit on the 11th of June, 1872, which, if true, disposes of the ORTON verdict. The Defendant had no means of keeping him in England, and it is said that he received an appointment of £800 a year from the late Ministry, which appointment necessitated his absence from this country. We know not how this was; but he was thousands of miles away when the TICHBORNE Trial was on. The Editor of *Reynolds's Newspaper* thus introduces Dr. WHEELER's affidavit:—

THE LATE GOVERNMENT AND THE TICHBORNE PROSECUTION.

As our readers are aware, we espoused the cause of the Claimant, believing that he was not given fair-play. Every day we receive fresh proofs, tending to confirm our suspicions. We now lay before our readers an affidavit that has come into our possession, made by an eminent surgeon, who could not, however, afford to remain at home for the sole purpose of giving evidence in the Claimant's behalf. The Government refused to act in this case as it had done in that of Captain OATES, who was induced to abandon his professional avocations for a time, in order that he might appear as a witness for the prosecution, being handsomely remunerated by the Government for so doing. This fact confirms what we have already written as to the impossibility of the Claimant, with very narrow and precarious resources at his command, contending on even terms with the prosecution, having an unlimited command of money at its disposal. Here is the affidavit:—

I, WILLIAM MASSEY WHEELER, of 18, Luxor-street, Camberwell, in the County of Surrey, doctor of medicine, do solemnly and sincerely declare that I am forty-three years of age. I went to Adelaide, South Australia, in 1852. I stayed there twelve months, then went to Melbourne. I stayed there and in Victoria five or six years. Was there in 1853 and 1854; and some years about the bush and the diggings. I met a man named ARTHUR ORTON in 1859, at Castlemaine. (I was at Bendigo, twenty miles from Castlemaine, in that year, and until 1860 and 1861, when I went out on the exploring party, called HOWITT's party, of which I was the officially-appointed surgeon. My appointment was from the Victoria Government.) ARTHUR ORTON was about 5ft. 11in. or 5ft. 11½in. in height, dark complexion, wore an American goatee, or Yankee beard, straight legs, big hands and feet, marked or pitted with small-pox, and wore earrings. I thought he was a foreigner. He was thoroughly sunburnt, and like a weather-beaten, drunken sailor. He was carrying a swag, which means tramping. There was with him a man named TOM, whom I afterwards heard called CASTRO. Both ORTON and TOM were thin. I met with them at a public-house or shanty. I think it was the Bush Inn. The next time I saw either of them was when I met ARTHUR ORTON at Wagga-Wagga in 1865. He said he was engaged as a stock-rider at a station. I was passing through Wagga-Wagga on my way from the Darling River to Melbourne. I camped outside the town. Passing over the bridge at Wagga-Wagga I saw a number of men, and on the ground was ARTHUR ORTON, who told me he had had a fall from his horse. He was taken into a shanty with several men. He said the horse had been buck-jumping and threw him. He had a slight concussion of the brain. I told him what to do, and started next day for Melbourne. This would be in 1865. TOM CASTRO was there, and asked me questions as to ORTON's state. There was a man named MACKIE there (of this I was reminded in my interview with Sir ROGER TICHBORNE on the 4th June instant). I told him ORTON was to be kept quiet, and not to drink. They were the same two men I met in Castlemaine in 1859. I went to New Zealand in 1865. I stayed in New Zealand about twelve months, and practised in Dunedin, Otago. I stayed there over twelve months, and then went to Queensland as surgeon to a barque called the "Panamá." I went up to the Peak Down Diggings, 300 miles north-west of Rockhampton, where I practised. I remained there five or six months, till taken ill with fever and ague. I then took steamer from Brisbane to Sydney, and from Sydney to New Zealand again. I then took another ship to Queensland, and practised at Bonner's Nob and Taroom, till January or February, 1869. Got to Brisbane in March, 1869, and there saw ARTHUR ORTON again at a public-house (DEACON's). He had just arrived from the Gympie Diggings. We talked of old times. He told me he had been up at the diggings near Brisbane. He looked awfully bad, as if he were consumptive, and said he had had hard times. I saw him several times, and had nobblers with him. I had never heard anything about the TICHBORNE Case there. He had no wife or child. Had on digger's costume, moleskin trousers and Crimean shirt. He had a South American sash round his waist. I slept in the same room with him at Brisbane for three weeks, and saw him stripped to the waist. He was tattooed on both arms, and on the breast over the region of the heart with the figure of a woman. The tattoo on the right arm was the flags of all nations, as they are called, and a full-rigged ship on the left arm. I did not see any initials. I saw his earrings. I never saw him without them. I asked him why he wore them, and he said he was recommended to wear them for his sight. He was three weeks in Brisbane, and then went back to the diggings. He was then going by the name of MORGAN. I called him ORTON, and he said, significantly, "My name is MORGAN." He said he was a ticket-of-leave man, and had been "lagged" for horse-soldiering. I asked him if it was for that affair of Castlemaine. He said, No, it was not; he never stole the horse; it was a false charge. Horse-soldiering or stealing is by meeting with a horse in the bush, putting your swag upon him, and leaving him at the next station. I had seen ORTON and TOM (his mate) at Castlemaine in 1859, and ORTON told me they had got into a row about soldiering a horse, and they expected to be charged with horse-stealing. There was a man named O'HARA BURKE, Inspector of police at that time. He is dead. He died on the Victoria exploring expedition at Cooper's Creek, where I found his remains. I was surgeon to HOWITT's exploring party. We found KING, who told us about BURKE, on September 15, 1861. I have seen TOM CASTRO's arms stripped: he was not tattooed. He looked like a man of gentle birth. His hands and feet were small. He never swore as ORTON did. ORTON was a very foul-mouthed man. CASTRO was a man who did not care much about talking. I did not speak much to him. I left Queensland in April, 1869—up to that time I had heard nothing about the TICHBORNE Case or ORTON. I first read it in the papers when the Trial was going on, and saw the Attorney-General had asked the Claimant whether he was ARTHUR ORTON. I immediately said to my friends that he could not be ARTHUR ORTON, whom I had seen at Brisbane in 1869. I did not write, because I was engaged in a sailing ship, the "Wymmera," as surgeon. I am still in that line, and expect to go in one of GREEN's ships in about two months. After the above statement was taken down I attended with Mr. GUILDFORD ONSLOW, M.P., at the residence of Sir ROGER TICHBORNE, Harley Lodge, Brompton. I there saw Sir ROGER, talked with him, and identified him as the TOMAS CASTRO whom I had seen in company with ARTHUR ORTON at Castlemaine and Wagga-Wagga. I can swear to the best of my belief that Sir ROGER TICHBORNE is TOM CASTRO, but I can swear most positively he is not ARTHUR ORTON. I shall be leaving England for Australia in about two months, but expect to return in December or January next, when I shall be prepared to give in evidence on the trial of the case of REGINA *v.* CASTRO the facts above stated.

And I make this solemn declaration conscientiously believing the same to be true, and by virtue of the provisions of an Act made and passed in the sixth year of the reign of his late Majesty King WILLIAM the Fourth, entitled "An Act for the more effectual abolition of oaths and affirmations taken and made in various department of the State, and to substitute declarations in lieu thereof, and for the more entire suppression of voluntary and extra judicial oaths and affidavits, and to make other provisions for the abolition of unnecessary oaths."

WILLIAM MASSEY WHEELER.

Declared at No. 48, Bedford-row, in the County of Middlesex, the 11th day of June, 1872—Before me,

GEO. C. PARKER,

A London Commissioner to administer Oaths in Chancery.

Mr. FASHAM, one of the speakers at this meeting, published the annexed letter, which we think interesting:—

SIR,—The remarks I made at the Southampton meeting on some of the proceedings of Sir ROGER TICHBORNE, respecting what might have occurred in Australia, have had the effect of doing something to throw a little light on that hitherto dark phase of the matter. Had it not been for the lateness of the hour at which I spoke, and myself somewhat fatigued with a hard day's work, and had I been allowed time to collect my thoughts and refresh my memory, I might have performed that task better than I did.

At the time I spoke, I had not seen, nor did I know of, the existence of Sir ROGER's affidavit published in your last number; and I am glad I did not know a word of its contents, or it might have been said I had had a little coaching-up. If you look at paragraphs 35 to 38 of that document and then at my speech reported in your columns, I think you must admit that Sir ROGER's statement bears every appearance of being quite true. Knowing Australia and the bush well, as I do, I have no doubt but his story is as true and as faithful an account of what really did occur as it is possible for a man to give.

I will, with your permission, deal with some of the points at the late Trial in a plain, homely, matter-of-fact way, leaving the public to form their own estimate of the value of my remarks.

He lost his French! Did he ever properly know that language?

This I reply to as follows:—Dr. LIVINGSTONE—and I need mention no more worthy name—some years ago entered the continent of Africa. Travelling through that country, amongst various different tribes and nations of that little known land, he held no intercourse with any Englishman during the five years he was pursuing his lonely travels. Month after month, year after year, he plodded on, and at the last found himself at the side of the continent opposite to that which he entered. Finding a vessel bound for Port Louis, in the Island of the Mauritius, he embarked on board her, and on landing, he says in the narrative he gives of his travels, "*I had forgot my mother-tongue. Nor could I hold conversation in the English language until I had been some time in English Society.*" Dr. LIVINGSTONE is a highly educated man, has received a high education, and holds high University honours, and is certainly one of the most popular men of the world; and if he in *five* years had in the deserts of Africa forgotten his mother-tongue, why not allow it to be possible for Sir ROGER TICHBORNE in ten or *twelve* years, in the Australian bush, to forget his French, which was never properly taught him? What Dr. LIVINGSTONE's company might have been, I can only conjecture from his own writings of himself. What Sir ROGER TICHBORNE's was I can tell by many years' experience.

On a horse-run of 300 miles in the bush he might see a white man or two perhaps once in a few months, and these speaking a broken language, partly English and partly the language of the aboriginal natives of the bush—a style of speaking used in all parts of that wonderful, almost unknown land. The most frequent sounds he would hear would be the abominable howling of the wild dogs, the squeaking of the various kinds of parrots and cockatoos, the jabbering of the Widla, naked savages—a race lower in the scale of humanity than any hitherto-found specimen of the human race—and this for many years, shut out entirely from civilized society in the wild grandeur of the Australian bush. His rifle and kangaroo-dogs and his horse (every stockman on a run is always splendidly mounted on as fine a charger as need grace a cavalry regiment) are his only companions, and being "lord of all he surveys," either with or without a chum, his is a life hundreds of young fellows, thoroughly enjoy. In all this he forgets his French, which, at best, those best capable of judging say he never knew. He is then to be robbed and branded as an impostor, while the man who in less than half that time forgets his mother-tongue is made a hero, and deservedly so. Had Sir ROGER gone to France and mixed up with *entirely* French society, is there any reason why he should not have had what French he ever did know return to him again? I will not trespass further on your columns this week, but in my next letter I will reply to the question why he did not get money from the balance due to him on arriving penniless in Melbourne.—I am, &c.,

JOHN FASHAM.

We next find the Claimant in Bristol. We copy the narrative of his visit from the *Western Telegraph*:—

THE ARRIVAL.

At no period probably since the arrival of GARABALDI in Bristol has the terminus presented such a spectacle as yesterday, when the Claimant was expected to arrive from London to attend the evening meeting at the Broadmead Rooms. It had been anticipated that Sir ROGER would arrive by the 2.21 train, and the consequence was that long before the hour came thousands of persons wended their way in the direction of the station, hoping to catch a glimpse of the person who has created so much interest during several months past. The Committee who had the arrangement of the meeting kept the time a profound secret, from the simple fact that, as it happened, they were themselves in ignorance of it, although professing to know by which train he was coming. The event, however, showed that they, as well as the public generally, were "sold." The approach to the station was lined with spectators, and as the time for the arrival of the train grew nearer, the station was crowded with spectators, who burst into the place on all sides, and the excitement was intense. At 4.21 those who had patience to wait were rewarded by seeing the Claimant, who, having been staying at Alresford, came by the train at the time mentioned from Salisbury. There were probably 1,100 or 1,200 persons present in and near the station on his arrival. The Committee formed a circle round Sir ROGER to keep the crowd off, but it need scarcely be said that the ring was speedily broken up by the eager spectators who crowded round the hero of the hour. So great was the rush, that the door of the brougham was forced off, and almost before the Claimant had time to seat himself, and even leaving Mr. ONSLOW behind, the vehicle was driven off, in order to prevent the people taking the horses out of the carriage and dragging it to its destination. The Committee at length got together in their break, and followed the brougham to St. Vincent's Rocks Hotel, followed by an immense crowd, who were, of course, soon out-distanced. On arriving at the hotel, the Committee were ushered into the rooms set apart for the Claimant, and were individually introduced to him. Sir ROGER shook hands heartily with them, and thanked them for the cordial support they had given to him and his cause. After which, the Committee retired, and three cheers were given for the Claimant, welcoming him to Bristol. We should state that the Claimant apologised to Mr. CROSS, the Chairman of the Committee, for not having telegraphed the time of his arrival, admitting that he was to blame in the matter. The reception throughout, at the station, along the streets, and at the hotel, was of the most enthusiastic character.

THE MEETING AT THE BROADMEAD ROOMS

Commenced at eight o'clock, and the Claimant, on making his appearance on the platform with his friends, was very heartily cheered by the audience, which, however, was not a full one. The chair was taken by Mr. H. CROSS, the Treasurer of the Tichborne Defence Fund, and was supported by the members of the Committee.

The CHAIRMAN, who was received with loud cheers, remarked, in opening the proceedings, that he occupied that position with some diffidence, but it was the unanimous wish of the Committee that he should take the chair, and he had acceded to that wish. (Applause.) They were met together that evening not to inquire into the various opinions on the question—they were assembled there to demand, as Englishmen, justice to a fellow man. (Applause.) He asked them as Englishmen—whatever opinions they might entertain—to stop till the Claimant had had a fair trial—which as an Englishman he was entitled to—before expressing any decided opinion on the case. (Cheers.) It was all very well for the Attorney-General, Mr. COLERIDGE, who had had one fortune out of this case, to now put himself forward in order to pick out another plum. (Loud applause.) He thought it hard that Sir ROGER should be prosecuted at the expense of the country, when villains stained with every crime were allowed to escape. (Applause.) Because Mr. COLERIDGE wanted to make himself a popular man—(a voice: "He is a muff," and laughter)—he had taken up this case, and was filling his pocket with enormous fees, such as he had never earned before. He asked them simply to accord a fair trial to a fellow Englishman, and he could not but express his surprise that certain of the public papers should be so far forgetful of decency as to call them, the promoters of the meeting, idiots and lunatics. (Groans.) He begged to tell the *Times and Mirror*, and every other paper which had condescended to apply these epithets to them, that all they wanted was fair-play. (Applause.) They had respect for every one's opinion: but why should opponents wish to see the Claimant deprived of every shilling, and on the other hand to have six eminent Counsel to pull at the public purse-strings to the tune, perhaps, of hundreds of thousands? (Applause.) He asked them whether seventy odd witnesses of respectability and position, including Colonel LUSHINGTON, who, if the Claimant were to be the owner of the estates, would be a loser of about £25,000, the uncle of the lad in possession, and the Defendant in the suit, but who, notwithstanding the possibility of his losing all this money, swore positively that the Claimant was the man. (Loud cheers.) He would ask the gentlemen present whether it was possible for a revered parent seeing her child—however much altered he might be, and they all altered in the course of years—(hear, hear, and laughter)—to be so grossly mistaken? or whether it was just to her memory to say, "Oh, she was an imbecile when she swore to her son." (Hear, hear, and "Shame.") Was it, he asked, Christian-like or manly? (Loud cries of "No.") Why did they not tackle that lady when she was alive, and swear that she was an imbecile? (Hear, hear.) With her last dying oath the Mother swore that the Claimant was her legitimate son. (Hear, hear.) Referring to the tattoo question, the Chairman said he would ask any gentleman—even the bitterest opponents of the Claimant—whether they ever heard a single word said about the tattoo marks until near the termination of the last case, when Lord BELLEW was brought forward? They had heard nothing about the tattoo question till then, and he asked them whether they believed this man—this lord—had sworn to that which he did not believe? (Voices: "Yes," and cheers.)

Mr. EWENS was called upon to move the first resolution, as follows:—"That this meeting is of opinion that the recent TICHBORNE Trial was not conducted in the spirit of fair-play which Englishmen have a right to expect, and that the language of the Attorney-General was utterly unworthy of the British Bar." He denounced the scurrilous language applied by the *Times and Mirror* to the supporters of the TICHBORNE Defence Fund, remarking that it must have been picked up in a fish-market, and that it was a disgrace that any paper should condescend to reduce itself to that low fishmonger's standard. (Hear, hear.) He briefly commented on the conduct of the Attorney-General, asked for justice for the Claimant, and concluded by moving the resolution.

Mr. C. SNACKELL seconded the resolution, and said it contained two serious charges: for it first said, in unmistakable language, that the gentleman who appeared before them to give some account of his proceedings had not been fairly treated; and secondly, that the Attorney-General quite forgot himself. (Hear, hear.) Now as the gentleman who was personally interested in the matter was present that night with other gentlemen, it would be unwise in him to touch upon that very delicate question; but as regarded the Attorney-General, he was a public servant, and therefore public property. He asked them whether the language used by the Attorney-General to the gentleman now before them was proper language? (Loud cries of "No.") In using it he was descending below the level he had been educated to, and such language would be looked upon with contempt by the British public. (Hear, hear.)

The resolution was then put to the meeting, and carried unanimously.

Mr. TAYLOR, corn merchant, West-street, proposed the second resolution, which was as follows:—"That this meeting cons[illegible]s the engaging of six Counsel in the present prosecution as an atte[illegible]pt to crush a defenceless man, and hereby protests against the [illegible]mous waste of public means." He said that amongst all the extraordinary things in connection with the recent extraordinary Trial, was the fact that a Government which had reduced the number of quill pens, and been noted for cheeseparing economy, should be willing to spend a hundred or a hundred and fifty thousand pounds to prosecute the Claimant. If those who were present, who had given to the Defence Fund, had also to pay towards the prosecution, they ought to exercise their privilege as Englishmen, and "grumble." (Hear, hear.) He had accepted the office of secretary to the Local Committee in the interest of fair-play. He asked them to contemplate the spectacle of the Claimant in Newgate. Here was a gentleman incarcerated in gaol, without a penny in the world, and yet the Government were employing six Counsel to prosecute him. ("Shame.") He asked them if it did not look as if the Government were trying to crush a defenceless man.

Mr. J. F COLLINS, licensed victualler, seconded the motion. He said they were there to consider a serious question. To him there was no fun in it, and he considered it behoved them to consider it seriously as Englishmen always did serious subjects. He took the side of the Claimant simply on the principle of fair-play, and he would tell the papers, and the *Times and Mirror* especially, that they made a mistake when they said that all the members of the Committee believe the Claimant to be the right man. (Hear, hear.) He contended that engaging six Counsel to prosecute the Claimant was carrying the thing too far. He did not like crushing a man, especially after the Claimant stood up as he did for so many days without having his evidence materially shaken. (Applause.) After all the cross-examination the Plaintiff said: I am the Sir ROGER TICHBORNE. If the Claimant had been an impostor—he was speaking according to the dictates of his own conscience—he could not have stood out once he was within the walls of Newgate, but he would have said to himself, Now you are done; retribution has come upon you. But it was not so. When in Newgate, and even Fate was against him, the Claimant said, "I am the rightful heir; I am ROGER TICHBORNE." (Applause.) There was bound to be a fair trial now. This meeting in Bristol would do good, for England knew what Bristol was. (Applause.) He would say, "God speed the right," whatever might come to the Claimant. (Cheers.) He knew that they were the weak against the strong, but he hoped the country would take the cause in hand. All they asked for the Claimant was fair-play.

The motion was carried with only one dissentient.

Mr. GUILDFORD ONSLOW, M.P., who was received with the most enthusiastic and prolonged cheers, then addressed the meeting. Before he ventured, he said, to enter into details of this great Case he would avail himself of the earliest opportunity of thanking them most kindly for the flattering reception which not only Sir ROGER TICHBORNE had received, but which they had been kind enough to greet him with that evening. (Cheers.) That meeting was, as had already been said, a most important one. It was indeed a most important meeting, because Bristol was the first great place where they had enlisted public sympathy on behalf of Sir ROGER TICHBORNE, and he trusted and hoped that the cheers which they had heard that evening might, through the pilgrimage they were about to take, be an augury of future prosperity and success in the undertaking they had adopted, and which they believed to be the right one. (Applause.) He was well aware that it was a very great privilege indeed to address an audience of the great city of Bristol; and it was very deep gratification to him to see in that vast assemblage so many good Bristol men. (Cheers.) He was satisfied by their appearance there that evening, that they were imbued by those great principles of honesty, fair-play and justice, which were the characteristics of the English race. (Cheers.) There were two gentlemen in the House of Commons who were his great friends. One, alas! was no more. He had gone to that country from whose bourne no traveller ever returns. He alluded to a favourite of theirs in this borough—Mr. HENRY BERKELEY. (Cheers.) They came before the Bristol public that day upon the ground of enlisting their sympathy for fair-play, and Mr. H. BERKELEY, he confidently believed, if he had been alive, would have been on that platform. The other gentleman he referred to was Mr. BERKELEY's colleague, and his (the speaker's) intimate friend, Mr. GORE LANGTON. (Applause.) He had in his pocket a letter from that gentleman, saying how deeply he regretted his inability to be present there that evening. (Hear, hear.) Mr. GORE LANGTON, he was sorry to say, was now suffering from illness, and the excitement of a public meeting would have a dangerous tendency, but otherwise he was satisfied Mr. LANGTON would have been with them. (Cheers.) It was on the grounds of fair-play that he wished he could have that poor, dear gentleman, Mr. BERKELEY, present, and Mr. GORE LANGTON in perfect health, in order that they might have had the pleasure of seeing those two honourable gentlemen on the platform. (Hear, hear.) They were all aware that the Case in question was one which had occupied the attention of the world for more than a year. It commenced in the spring of last year by that great Trial in the Court of Common Pleas. The greater part of that great Case was occupied in the examination and cross-examination of witnesses, but it was suddenly brought to a stand-still most unexpectedly by the jury saying that they had heard sufficient evidence, and by doing that forced Sir ROGER TICHBORNE, very much against his will, to accept a nonsuit. Now that jury ignored by their conduct the evidence of eighty-six honourable, respectable, and disinterested witnesses, not one of whom, including the Claimant himself, ever broke down; but the jury accepted the evidence of seventeen witnesses who, with the exception of the two Mr. SEYMOURS, were all Jesuits—(laughter, and a Voice: "Shame")—and every one of them more or less interested in the Case almost as much as the Defendant himself. Who were these seventeen witnesses? The seventeen witnesses were composed of ladies and gentlemen who, with the exception, he believed, of Mr. ALFRED SEYMOUR and Mrs. RADCLIFFE, never took the opportunity of examining Sir ROGER TICHBORNE for the purpose of ascertaining by word of mouth whether he was Sir ROGER TICHBORNE or not. Therefore their evidence simply did not recognize him as a man they had known in former days. The jury accepted their evidence, which was negative evidence, and they refused the affirmative evidence of eighty-six, who were highly respectable, honourable, and disinterested men. (Shame.) Now he repeated that, with the exception perhaps of Mr. SEYMOUR and Mrs. RADCLIFFE, not one of them exchanged a word with Sir ROGER TICHBORNE since his return to this country. But, in the case of Mrs. RADCLIFFE, he did not wish the facts to be misunderstood, for it had never yet appeared in this Trial—the suit just collapsed—and before the public, that she, Mrs. RADCLIFFE, had actually acknowledged the Claimant as her cousin; that was to say, if the words of Mr. VINCENT GOSFORD were to be believed. Mr. ONSLOW then proceeded to read an extract from the sworn evidence of Mr. JOHN HOLMES, the first Solicitor in this Case, wherein he "distinctly and positively swore" that the said VINCENT GOSFORD called on him at his office on the 8th March, 1867, and stated that Mrs. RADCLIFFE went to see the Plaintiff (the Claimant) on that day at Croydon, accompanied by her husband and Mr. TOWNLEY. Subsequently, a few days later, Mr. GOSFORD again called on Mr. HOLMES and stated that Mrs. RADCLIFFE had recognized the Plaintiff by his "eyes and eyebrows, and that none of the party could declare that it was not him." Now Mrs. RADCLIFFE and that party, satisfied with that meeting, acknowledged to Mr. GOSFORD, according to his account, that Sir ROGER TICHBORNE was her (Mrs. RADCLIFFE's) cousin, and absolutely fixed another meeting with him. His friend Sir ROGER TICHBORNE—(loud applause)—appealed to the British public for fair-play—(a voice: "He shall have it," followed by loud cheers)—and it was, as a friend of his had said just now, a case of most serious and important moment. He was about to be tried for perjury and forgery, and the result of that Trial would either send him into penal servitude or send him into the possession of his title and his estates. (Hear, hear.) It had been said that he (Mr. ONSLOW), in urging the Case for Sir ROGER TICHBORNE, had attempted to set class against class—(a Voice: "No; I don't believe it," and cheers)—but they would allow him to say this—that they were, with very few exceptions, completely deserted by the upper classes. (Shame.) In this country the upper classes did not like one coming forward to claim estates from the hands of one who was in possession. Their minds were so blinded in this Case, that they, the friends of Sir ROGER TICHBORNE, had appealed to the British public, and boldly had the British public responded to their appeal. (Cheers.) The working classes were the classes who, with their hardly-earned wages, came forward with their sixpences—aye, and even pennies—to give support to Sir ROGER TICHBORNE; and he (the speaker) thought it was extremely honourable to the working classes that they did so. (Applause.) Sir ROGER TICHBORNE did not belong to their class, yet they supported him—they would not see any man, high or low, crushed or trampled upon. (Cheers.) It was a paltry cry, that he wished to set class against class. He said the working classes of this country gave their support to Sir ROGER TICHBORNE, and he said, moreover, that Sir ROGER was honoured in receiving their support. (Loud applause.) The British public were in his favour, and he had never known the British public to be wrong. (Hear, hear.) If they went back to the days of the agitation about the Corn Laws, the British public were right then; if they went back to the emancipation of the Roman Catholics, the public were right then; and in later days, in the matter of the party conflict in America, the public were right then. (Hear, hear.) The British public were right in the Prussian and French war, but in the American war the upper classes were wrong, and the House of Commons was wrong. (Cheers.) There were not six men in the House of Commons who stood for the Northerners on that occasion, and he felt happy and proud to say that he was one of them. (Applause.) He repeated, the British public was not wrong in taking the part of Sir ROGER, and he was sorry to say that the Case was comparatively unknown to the public. (Laughter.) He could tell them things that would startle them. The Attorney-General spoke for days and weeks, but he was never replied to. They knew nothing of the TICHBORNE Case. Serjeant BALLANTINE never replied, nor was there any opportunity given to him to reply, and it required a certain amount of moral courage to reply to it. He wouldn't say that Mr. Serjeant BALLANTINE quailed under it, but like most Englishmen, he didn't fight so well as he would have done if he had a full belly. (Laughter.) He wished he could have veiled it, but the fact was their misfortune, as had been said that evening, was that they had to starve that trial. They starved the Counsel on that Trial. They had no money. The little they had was used to the best of purposes—(hear, hear)—and Sir ROGER TICHBORNE, at this moment, would have been in Newgate, and his beautiful children and his wife in the workhouse, if it had not been for the working classes—that noble part of the British public. (Loud cheers.) Sir ROGER TICHBORNE had been five years in this country, and during those five years he had never been proved an impostor; and he (the speaker) said if he was an impostor it was a disgrace to the laws of this country that he had not been found out before. (Hear, hear, and applause.) He did not hesitate to say, and he said it with a certain amount of grief, for he was the last man in the world to use abusive language to anybody—that after deep consideration, and after having made this Case his study for years, that the speech of the Attorney-General was a gross misrepresentation of facts, and was a foul assumption—backed up by abusive language. The speech was unworthy of a lawyer and unworthy of a gentleman. (Loud applause.) The Attorney-General's bad blood was up, his bad feelings were aroused—he had been baffled and beaten by Sir ROGER—hence all the temper and his venomous abuse. He (the Attorney-General) had said that he had never met with a cleverer man, and he admitted himself that he never could break him down. (Cheers.) Picture to themselves ARTHUR ORTON, the butcher of Wapping, standing twenty-eight days of the longest and the most severe cross-examination that ever happened to a British subject, and not breaking down! How was it possible? He asked them, and put it to their common-sense—how could a man who was an impostor have stood before the cross-examination of those critical cross-examiners, the Attorney-General and Mr. HAWKINS, and come out of the box unscathed? (Applause.) The Attorney-General said it was against common-sense to believe him anything but an impostor; but he (Mr. ONSLOW) said it was against common-sense to have any doubt about this man. (Loud cheers.) He had to make a charge against the Attorney-General. (Hear, hear, and a Voice: "Give it him," followed by loud laughter.) When Serjeant BALLANTINE and Mr. GIFFARD stated that they were working that Case, and acting without fees, and the Lord Chief Justice said that it did them infinite credit, up jumped the Attorney-General and said "That will also apply to our side." When the Attorney-General knew on that very day he had touched a crisp £50 note, when the Attorney-General knew that he had drawn £6,000 out of the estate, and was being paid at the rate of 6s. 4d. a minute—he said that when the Attorney-General made that assertion that it would apply to him, he allowed it to go forth to the Press and the public, and it was distributed throughout the country, and it was not until the evening of the day after it had gone forth that he made an apology, and said that he did not know what was meant by it. Well, that was not the great thing he had to charge him with. If the Attorney-General chose to cloak himself under a wig and gown and his privileges, he supposed he might be as abusive as he liked. (Hear, hear.) He would say nothing, for he did not charge him with that; but he did charge him with this—that the Attorney-General, as a lawyer and a public man, paid by the country, had no right to abuse, vilify, and libel the character of a honest man. (Hear, hear.) Of Dr. LIPSCOMBE, of Alresford, he said that he was the sort of man who would take up the case of an impostor. (Shame.) He did not use the word impostor, but he implied as much. He said he was the sort of man to take up a case, and that he should like to know what offer was made to Dr. LIPSCOMBE for his services. Now, Dr. LIPSCOMBE had been his (the speaker's) medical attendant for many years, and a more upright, a more honest, and a more scrupulously truthful man he never met with in the whole course of his life; and he distinctly stated before that meeting and before the world that Dr. LIPSCOMBE would be the last man in the world to take the part of an impostor. Dr. LIPSCOMBE was very cautious in acknowledging Sir ROGER TICHBORNE. Two or three times he visited him before he would say whether he was the subject whom he had attended for illnesses in former years. He at last arrived at the conclusion that the Claimant was Sir ROGER, and he had ever since remained of that opinion. (Applause.) Their witnesses had abusive language applied to them. Well, it was bad enough to abuse the living, but it was far worse to abuse the dead. (Hear, hear.) The Attorney-General abused poor Lady TICHBORNE, the Mother of Sir ROGER TICHBORNE, and called her a poor, foolish, imbecile woman, willing to take anybody, whether he was an impostor or not, as her son. (Shame.) He (the speaker) had the honour of knowing Lady TICHBORNE intimately, and she was an honourable and honest woman. (Applause.) If she had one fault it was that she was suspicious of everybody and everything, and he could assert that she was the last lady in the world that would be imposed upon by anybody who came forward to establish himself as her son. (Hear, hear.) She said to Mr. CUBITT—and it could be verified by looking back to the report of the Trial—she said, "Be careful what you do, and don't put an impostor in my house." She felt her way inch by inch, and was by no means an imbecile old woman, who would be likely to take up with an impostor. (Hear, hear.) Referring to a very painful scene—the burial service of Lady TICHBORNE—Mr. ONSLOW said he was in the chapel and saw the Mother's coffin. It was a Roman Catholic chapel, with all the paraphernalia of the Roman Church, with lighted candles, burning incense, and so forth. Sitting at the head of the coffin was his friend Sir ROGER TICHBORNE, and if he (the speaker) lived for a thousand years he could never forget his face at that moment. No one saw his face but him, because he (Sir ROGER) was fronting him, all the rest being behind him. That face was deeply imprinted on his memory. He was broken down with grief and with tears. Those tears rolled down his face and spoke of the grief of Sir ROGER'S mind. Those tears were not like the tears of the Solicitor-General, who, with £6,000 in his pocket, pretended to cry. (Ironical laughter.) The tears of Sir ROGER came from the grief of his heart, as he beheld the best friend he had seen on earth lying dead before him. From the position in which he was, he was the only one who saw the expression on Sir ROGER'S countenance, and should never forget. When the funeral was over, he saw a female standing about, and asked who it was. He was told it was the lover of ARTHUR ORTON. After this he was coming through the park, when he saw WHICHER, the detective. (A laugh.) Sir ROGER came along, and he did not think that Sir ROGER had exactly the figure to cause a lady to faint away. However, as Sir ROGER came to the oak-tree in the park, Miss LODER, ARTHUR ORTON'S sweetheart, fainted in the arms of Mr. WHICHER, the detective. (Laughter.) And this Miss LODER was a "wopper," he could tell them. (A laugh.) After this he left them to judge the kind of witnesses which the prosecution were going to rely upon. The prosecution might make a fool of him, but they could not make fools of the public. (Cheers.) He now came to a serious charge against the Attorney-General, who had tried to brow-beat and trample on Sir ROGER. Sir JOHN COLERIDGE produced forged letters, written by Mrs. PITTENDREIGH. This was the charge which he had to make against the Attorney-General. Sir JOHN would say that he knew nothing about the forgeries; that the letters were put in his hands by the solicitor, but the lie, like the father of lies—it was "gross as a mountain, open, palpable." (Applause.) They knew how the Claimant was sent to Newgate without a conviction, and how he was kept there for fifty-two days. (Cries of "Shame!") When a guilty man entered into Newgate he felt that he deserved his fate; but when an innocent man was taken there they could understand the man's feelings. (Applause.) He visited Sir ROGER the first time when he was in Newgate. (Great cheering.) It was a difficult thing to sympathize with a man in that position, but he asked Sir ROGER: What do you most suffer from? Sir ROGER replied: That a TICHBORNE should ever be in this horrible place. Was that the language of an impostor? (Cries of "No.") An impostor would have immediately begged him to go and get bail—(hear, hear)—but Sir ROGER felt for his family. What did the Court before which the Trial took place consist of? It was almost a packed Court. (Hear, hear.) The public was admitted by ticket. The Court was filled by the aristocracy, and it was impossible for a working man to obtain admission. The jurymen sat until they were exhausted, and he would say that they retreated. (Cries of "Yes, they did.") There was an aristocratic Court. Having given the names of the numerous persons whom it had been alleged the Claimant was, the speaker gave a history of ROGER TICHBORNE'S life, and showed that the Claimant had many things—such as marks on his person—which were admitted to have belonged to the original Sir ROGER. He said he was as confident of Sir ROGER'S identity as he was of his own existence, and he concluded by comparing the Claimant to the prodigal son who had sown his wild oats, and now deeply regretted the past. Like the prodigal son, Sir ROGER "was dead, and is alive again; was lost, and is found." (Great cheering.)

The CLAIMANT rose amid deafening cheers, which were again and again repeated. He said he was not a good speaker, and did not intend saying much. Indeed his friend Mr. ONSLOW, had almost exhausted what he had to say, for Mr. ONSLOW knew the Case as well as he did. He would thank them for coming forward to assist him, and for the invitation which they had given him to come amongst them. Without the assistance of the public he would never have a fair trial. (Applause.) There was one subject on which he ought to say a word. ALFRED SEYMOUR, his uncle, said that when he was examined at the Law Institute, he (SEYMOUR) knew that he was an impostor, because of the absence of the tattoo marks. Was ALFRED SEYMOUR an honourable man to allow him to live with his (SEYMOUR'S) sister if he was an impostor? (Cheers.) If SEYMOUR knew that he was the villain and vagabond which he had been said to be by the Attorney-General, why did SEYMOUR not kick him out of the sister's house? (Great cheering.) Would they not have done it, and the more so if they thought the sister was not in her right mind? Did SEYMOUR do so? No; he laid down like a cur. Had ALFRED SEYMOUR acted right by the British public in allowing him to obtain thousands upon thousands of pounds from the British public, when SEYMOUR had the means of proving that he was an impostor? (Applause.) The tattoo business was a conspiracy from beginning to end—(cheers)—and it was got up to prevent GOSFORD being put into the box. He asked the public to insist upon GOSFORD being examined at the forthcoming Trial. He denied that he locked himself in when GOSFORD came to see him at Gravesend. He wished GOSFORD to produce the letter which he wrote to him (GOSFORD) at that time. Mr. ROBERTSON GLADSTONE had furnished some documents which his attorneys had seen, and upon which he wished GOSFORD to be questioned. They would then see whether he was TICHBORNE or not, and whether he spoke the truth or not as to the sealed packet. (Cheers.) GOSFORD was one of his advisers in his earlier days, and he left some documents with GOSFORD when he left England. He concluded by thanking them for the assistance they had rendered him, without which he would never have a fair trial. (Cheers.) If it had not been for the public he would have been in Newgate ten or eleven months waiting for his trial, just to give the Attorney-General an opportunity of boasting what he could do as the head of the law.

Mr. GUILDFORD ONSLOW has also published the following letter upon this question of the Sealed Packet:—

AN EPISODE IN THE TICHBORNE CASE.

Sir,—One afternoon in the year 1871, on my arrival in London, I thought I would walk down to Westminster and see how the TICHBORNE Case was going on. At that time the case was being tried at the Sessions House there. On my arrival, I saw the Claimant coming out of the Court, supported by two policemen, one on each side. He was as pale as ashes, to all appearance dead, except the movement of his legs. One of the policemen begged I would call his brougham as he was very ill. I did so, and with difficulty we got him into the carriage. I ordered the coachman to drive to the Waterloo Hotel, Jermyn-street. I then jumped into the brougham after him and said, "For God's sake, TICHBORNE, tell me what is the matter;" he tried to speak but could not. Thinking he was in a fit, I said no more. Putting my head out of the window, I urged the coachman to drive as fast as he could. All was silent until we got opposite the Horse Guards, when he said, "Put your hand into the side-pocket and give me my flask." I did so and handed him a silver flask, the contents of which he finished at a draught. I again said, "What on earth is the matter? Are you ill?" He replied, "I am a miserable man. I have done a thing I shall never cease to re-

ret." I begged him to explain; when he said, "I have divulged he contents of the Sealed Packet I gave to GOSFORD." Not nowing what had occurred in Court, I said, "Never mind, tell he truth and shame the Devil."

"Ah," he said, "that's all very well for you to say; but I ave taken away the fair fame of my cousin, with a large family f children. Oh, what will people say of me? But I had no lternative. Both my Counsel threatened, unless I replied and old the truth when asked, they would get up and leave the 'ourt, and I should then be sent to Newgate, and my wife and hildren starving in the streets."

I said, "The responsibility is on your Counsel, not on you; hey ought to have advised you to stand out to the last, and ather go to Newgate for contempt of Court. Then the whole vorld would have stood by you."

He added, "I told the Judge the responsibility must be on his shoulders, not on mine. I was forced to answer. But it is a dreadful thing: I can never, never get over it, even if I get a verdict."

I took him to his hotel, where he threw himself on his bed, and cried like a child.

I did all I could to comfort and soothe him, but in vain; and as I walked to my club I said to myself: "And is this the man they dare to call ARTHUR ORTON?"—I am your obedient servant,

"HIS CONFIDANT."

We insert also the following narrative of the "smudged thumb," from the *Englishman* for October 3, 1874, being Number 26.

TICHBORNE'S THUMB.

We think it well to bring before our readers a Correspondence that has hitherto been confined to a very narrow circle; and in

Photographs of my thumb
also from Photo with
thumb. Thumb enlarged.
and the Photo — you
gave me for Copying —

which there will be found a remarkable proof of the Claimant's identity with ROGER TICHBORNE. This Correspondence was for the first time alluded to by Dr. KENEALY in his Lecture at Leicester: he was unable, of course, by what are called "the rules of law," to make any reference to it at that mockery, the Trial; though even if he had been allowed, we do not suppose he would have prevailed very much with "the TICHBORNE Jury."

One of the peculiarities of ROGER TICHBORNE was a formation of the thumb-nail such as is not often seen. This was shown in the Chili daguerreotype, which he sent home to Lady DOUGHTY. Before this daguerreotype was forwarded back to Chili, in 1867, for the purposes of the Commission, it was photographed by order of Mr. BOWKER, the Solicitor to the Family; and the peculiar thumb is shown, both in the glass negative and in the photographic copy. When the daguerreotype was brought back to BOWKER from Chili, the thumb and hand were smudged out, so that the peculiarity was no longer visible. Fortunately, however, it remains as we said in the glass negative, and in the copies taken from it. These were deposited in Court; and though Dr. KENEALY repeatedly pointed out the peculiarity to both the Court and the Jury, they would not see it; the Chief Justice taking it upon himself to say it was not there at all—in this, giving evidence, as it was his wont—and several of the jurymen positively averring that *they* could not see what was perfectly visible to a disinterested eye. Dr. KENEALY was more disgusted with this wilful blindness than with perhaps any portion of the jurymen's conduct; for the defect in the photograph portrait is so plain and manifest that no honest man can truly say he cannot see it. This will be demonstrated when we examine young ROGER TICHBORNE's portrait* (ante page 17), which is a most accurate copy of Mr. BOWKER's photograph; and it would be rendered still more apparent if we had the glass negative, where, when held up to the light, it is visible as the sun itself. Dr. KENEALY exhibited the Claimant's thumb to the jury; and asked him to get photographic copies taken of his thumb, so that he might put them before the jurors, and they could, with magnifying glasses, compare the thumb of ROGER with the thumb of the Claimant; thus providing that they should not have a shadow of an excuse for their professed blindness. The Claimant, however, with his usual carelessness and almost indifference to his case, did not get these photos done until after Dr. KENEALY had finished his evidence, when it was impossible for him to get them before the Court. They were inclosed in an envelope with the foregoing inscription. The *fac-simile* being a good representation of the Claimant's writing.

The Family, of course, distinctly swore that ROGER had no such peculiarity; but the following correspondence, we think, disposes of that. We print it, and it speaks for itself:—

"11th July, 1871.

"SIR,—We are informed by Mr. W. PEET, of Waterford, that you were well acquainted with Mr. ROGER TICHBORNE when he was quartered with the Carabineers at Cahir: that you met him at your father's dinner-table, and remarked certain peculiarities, which Mr. PEET alluded to.

"Will you kindly inform us if this is the fact, and also whether you think, if you were to have an interview, your recollection is sufficiently strong to enable you to identify him?—We remain, Sir, your obedient servants, BAXTER, ROSE, NORTON, & Co.

"AUGUSTUS GRUBB, Esq., J.P., Rugby."

"Hillmorton-road, Rugby: 25th July, 1871.

"GENTLEMEN,—In answer to yours of the 11th inst., I fear I cannot be of any assistance to Mr. R. C. TICHBORNE, as my acquaintance with him was very slight; and twenty years having elapsed since I had the pleasure of seeing him, it is very doubtful whether I should be able to recognize him or not. It is true he dined with me at my father's, Cahir Abbey, and I observed a slight malformation of one of his thumb-nails, but I forget on which hand. This is the only peculiarity I remember, and which I remarked to Mr. PEET only in a casual way, and did not intend it to go further. From the tenor of this letter you will be able to judge whether my having an interview with Mr. TICHBORNE would be of any service to him or not.—Gentlemen, I remain, your obedient servant, AUGUSTUS GRUBB.

"Messrs. BAXTER, ROSE, NORTON & Co., London."

"Hillmorton-road, Rugby; December 5th, 1871."

"DEAR SIR,—In answer to yours of the 4th inst., I am thankful to say that my husband is a shade better. Indeed, he has frequently said to me that, if he felt equal, he and I would put ourselves in the train, and go up to London, without any prearrangement, and he would call at your office. This he may still be able to do in a few days; but, if you would prefer to make the thing more certain, Mr. GRUBB and myself will be most happy to see Sir ROGER TICHBORNE and yourself, Mr Serjeant BALLANTINE, Mr. GIFFARD, or any other friend you would like to bring with you, and offer you what hospitality our humble abode can afford—only give us what notice you can. Have you not a

holiday on Saturday? I must confess my ignorance; I do not understand exactly the nature of the "Commission" to which you allude. *I inclose two sketches of the thumb-nail, done to the best of* Mr. GRUBB's *recollection*. If he identifies the Plaintiff as Sir ROGER TICHBORNE, would not an affidavit taken in either London or Rugby be sufficient? as I may tell you at once my husband could not possibly go through the ordeal poor Mr. BAIGENT has done! In fact, it is only the last year or so he has been able to attend church regularly. I have often known him to be obliged to leave soon after going in.—I remain, dear Sir, yours truly, M. E. GRUBB."

"M. SPOFFORTH, Esq.

Mr. GRUBB (says Mr. ONSLOW) died before the second Trial. He had an interview with the Claimant, and although he could not identify him as the ROGER TICHBORNE he knew in former days, he instantly recognized the malformation of his thumb.

In connection with this subject we insert also an

EXTRACT FROM DR. KENEALY'S LECTURE.

When the photographs of ROGER TICHBORNE were produced at the Trial, I put them into GOSFORD's hands, saying, "You must have seen his thumb, of course, very frequently?"

GOSFORD answered, "Very frequently."

I asked him: Are these photographs of ROGER beyond all doubt?

Yes; no question. (The witness looked at them.) I see what I presume you allude to in the thumb most distinctly in this one (pointing to the red case of photographs).

Will you look at the small one, and say whether you will not find it equally distinct?

You mean, I presume, a large protuberance of flesh on the thumb?"

Let the Defendant show his thumb. (The Defendant did so.) I am curious to see; I have heard so much about it. (The witness looked at the Defendant's thumb.) I see distinctly.

Do you see that in these photographs?

Yes; it is perfectly distinct in all three.

Perfectly distinct in each of them?—Yes.

Do you mean to say that ROGER had not that little peculiarity?

I am sure he had not. It never appeared in his thumb as it appears in that photograph-book. This is very peculiar. Nobody could have a man's thumb before him, and not notice it. Nobody could look at that, and not notice it.

It appears the Sun noticed it!

ROGER TICHBORNE had been gone a year before the photographs were taken. *He might have had his thumb-nail knocked off.*

GOSFORD, therefore, as you see, did not deny, but readily admits that in the photograph the peculiarity of the thumb there represented, was identical with the peculiarity which the Claimant showed him in open Court.

How did it get into the daguerreotype if ROGER had it not? Why was it smudged out but because the Claimant had it?

How could GOSFORD see what the Judge said was not there at all, and what some jurors protested they could not see? Nice questions these!

SOUTHSEA MEETING.

We next find the Claimant at Southsea. We insert the report of a Special Correspondent:—

The railway-station at Portsmouth was besieged all Monday afternoon, 24th June, with vast crowds of people who were expecting the arrival of "the Claimant," but it was not till about a quarter-past six that their curiosity was gratified. The station-master had some time before this, however, received a telegram stating by what train the Claimant would arrive, and had wisely taken the precaution to clear the arrival platform of the hundreds and thousands who had previously taken possession of it; and there were, when the train steamed into the station, only the Local Defence Fund Committee and a few of the chief supporters of the Claimant and their friends on the platform. On alighting at the station Sir ROGER and Mr. GUILDFORD ONSLOW, M.P., were introduced to the local Committee, and a carriage and four greys being in readiness, they were at once driven to the "Royal Oak" Hotel, Queen-street, Portsea, followed by vehicles containing the members of the Committee. Outside the railway station there were immense crowds of persons, whose frantic efforts to get a sight of the occupants of the leading carriage nearly resulted in its overturn. The cheering as the unostentatious procession passed along the streets was very hearty. The most direct line to the hotel was not taken, the object being to avoid accident in consequence of the pressure. When the hotel was reached the whole party had great difficulty in alighting, although a *posse* of police did their utmost to keep the people back. A large banner was suspended across the street, on which was inscribed in coloured letters, "Welcome, Sir ROGER." After a brief stay at the hotel, the Claimant, Mr. ONSLOW, and the local Committee drove to the East Hants Grounds at Southsea, a distance of about two miles, and were heartily cheered the whole of the distance, the crowds being so dense in some places that it was necessary to proceed with great caution to prevent accident. These grounds are ordinarily used for cricketing purposes, and are occupied at the entrance by a club-house, from the balcony of which on this occasion the speakers addressed the spectators, who were standing on the green below. A few reserved seats, however, were provided for those who preferred comfort and could afford to pay for it. Altogether there could not have been less than from 1,500 to 2,000 persons present, and they evinced the greatest interest in the proceedings, which were throughout of a most enthusiastic character. After the balcony had been taken possession of by the leaders of the company, and accommodation found for the reporters,—

* Note, that although in the likeness it appears in the right thumb, this is an optical delusion, which all acquainted with photography will understand. The apparent right hand in the photograph from the daguerreotype, is in reality the left. Chief Justice Cockburn was at first (or pretended to be) of the contrary opinion at the trial; but Dr. KENEALY, in a few words, explained the delusion.

Mr. J. R. Van Den Bergh, Consul at Portsmouth to several different countries, took the chair, and, addressing the compact assembly, said that as Chairman of the Local Defence Fund Committee he had the honour to introduce to them the real Sir Roger. (Cheers.) Of this, however, they could judge for themselves. They had read the Case, and now they saw the man before them; and his only object in being there was to ask the people of Portsmouth to see that he had a fair trial. (Hear, hear.) Mr. Guildford Onslow, who accompanied Sir Roger, knew more about the Case than he (the Chairman) did, and would address them in vindication of the cause which he had espoused, and then they would have the pleasure of hearing the Claimant himself, and he had no doubt at all that the people of Portsmouth would do their best to secure him fair-play as an Englishman, and not allow him to be crushed by a large number of Counsel being arrayed against him at the public expense. (Cheers.)

Mr. Guildford Onslow, M.P., who was received with reiterated cheering, said he might truly say that their sole object in attending these meetings throughout the country was to endeavour to the best of their ability to enlist the sympathy of the British public on behalf of a man who, they believed, had been unfairly treated in the late Trial in the Court of Common Pleas. They knew very well that if they looked back during the past century the English people had never been wrong on any public question they had taken up. They had only to look back to the early part of the century, to the days of a celebrated naval hero well known in Portsmouth—Lord Cochrane—to see that when a man was wrongly persecuted the public would take his case up, and, as time proved in the case of Lord Cochrane, they were invariably right. (Hear, hear.) They were always right on the great political questions of the day. They were right on the repeal of the Corn Laws, they were right in the part they took in the American War, and he believed that the part they were now taking in the case of Sir Roger Tichborne would prove itself right in the long run. (Cheers.) The great Case that they had met that evening to relate, and endeavour to explain, was one that was attracting attention not only in England, but throughout all parts of the world. The great characteristic of Englishmen was to stand by a man if they saw he was not having fair-play; and he maintained that Sir Roger Tichborne, by the decision of the jury, had not had fair-play. He ought to have had an explanation before the public in reply to the long-winded speech of the Attorney-General. (Hear.) The jury were composed of men of education, honour, and uprightness, but they came too prematurely to a decision, without waiting to hear the reply of Mr. Serjeant Ballantine, which would doubtless have turned them as much in favour of Sir Roger as the speech of the Attorney-General turned them against him. (Hear, hear.) At that Trial there were eighty-six witnesses of unblemished reputation, and amongst them were the Mother of Sir Roger Tichborne, whose affidavit was read in Court; ladies of respectability, honest men, many of them wearing the medal for good conduct on their breasts—disinterested men, who had well weighed and considered whether the Plaintiff was the right man or not, who had visited him and tried him time after time during the last five years—they one and all swore affirmatively to his identity as Sir Roger Tichborne. (Hear, hear.) And what was the upshot of it? The seventeen interested negative witnesses went into the witness-box, and at the close of their examination the jury said they were satisfied. (Shame.) He (Mr. Onslow) was abused in every direction for the part he was taking in this matter: but he was only fulfilling the engagement he made to Lady Tichborne that he would never abandon her son. (Cheers.) His constituents were backing him up in this case, and they knew that he was not the man to flinch when he was in the right path, and knowing he was in the right path he supported his friend, and he gloried in doing it. (Applause.) Their object in attending these meetings was not to show themselves, for there was no great beauty in them—(laughter)—but to explain to the best of their ability the ins and outs of this great Case, and to lay it before them in a manner it had not yet been laid before the public. If Sir Roger was an impostor, would he not, after having been bailed out, have taken the first steamer from Portsmouth and gone to Spain, where he could live unmolested, because there was no extradition treaty there? (Hear, hear.) The very circumstance of his being before them now showed that he was not an Impostor. He had never bolted, but stood the test of years. There was one who stood by him during her lifetime, and that was his Mother; and was it likely she should not know her own son? (Hear, hear.) Lady Tichborne exhibited a great amount of religion in the Roman Catholic faith, and it was doubtful whether she did not die owing to the strict observance of her religion; and was it likely she would have died and gone to her Maker with a lie upon her lips? (Hear, hear.) When she first saw her son after his return to Europe she rushed to his arms, and she had two years' experience of him afterwards, living in the same house with him, and she died acknowledging him as her son. (Cheers.) Referring to the scars and marks upon the original Sir Roger Tichborne, Mr. Onslow went on to say that the gentleman before them had every one of them. M. Chatillon, when called to identify Sir Roger, spoke of the scar on the back of his head, caused by a fall from his pony in Brittany; but when placed in the witness-box he harked back, and said the scar was not on the back of his head, but on the forehead. (Laughter.) Every one of the marks he ought to have he had got. But the Attorney-General had said he manufactured them. (Laughter.) He must be a very wonderful manufacturer to arrange all those marks and scars to fit in every way those which were known to exist on the body of the original Sir Roger Tichborne; and at all events he must have thoroughly known of their existence to have been able to have done it. (Hear, hear.) Then, how came it that he did not have the tattoo marks? Why did he not manufacture them too? When the first meeting took place in Chancery-lane, Lady Doughty, his aunt, sent Moore, the valet, to see whether he could recognize him, telling him to see if he had an issue pea-mark upon his arm, but there was not a word said about tattoo marks. (Hear, hear.) They therefore had a right to assume that Sir Roger never was tattooed, and that the whole of that evidence was false. (Hear, hear.) Sir Roger stood the test of twenty-eight days' cross-examination before one of the most critical audiences in the world, and if he had been Arthur Orton or an impostor, he would have broken down as a moral certainty. (Hear, hear.) It was true he forgot many things, but who amongst them did not forget things which took place in his early life? He never said things that did not happen. What he said was true, and what he forgot was only the result of the infirmity of human nature. (Hear, hear.) Mr. Onslow then read a letter he had received from a solicitor in Staffordshire, speaking in the highest terms of the Case in favour of the Plaintiff, and proceeding to say that if there was one thing more than another that the public found fault with Sir Roger Tichborne for, it was for divulging what he knew of the contents of the sealed packet. He (Mr. Onslow) could tell them something about that. When Sir Roger had an interview with Mr. Gosford at the Grosvenor Hotel, Mr. Gosford said to him, "If you are Sir Roger Tichborne you can tell me what is in that sealed packet." Sir Roger fenced and tried to get rid of the question, and did everything a man of honour could possibly do to avoid answering it, till at last Mr. Gosford said "If you do not tell us what is in that packet, we will throw over your case." What would they have done under the circumstances? [A voice: Spoken the truth.] (Cheers.) People might say they would rather die than have divulged that secret; but under the pressure that was put upon him, Sir Roger, having a wife and four beautiful children to look to, had no other course to pursue. He stated it at first by writing it on a piece of paper, and handing it to the Judge, appealing to his lordship to know whether he ought to reply. It was then handed to the Attorney-General, who took it to Mr. Hawkins, and he was literally forced to say what he did. (Hear, hear.) He (Mr. Onslow) saw Sir Roger on the afternoon of the day he had given that evidence, and he was so agitated and overcome that he could scarcely speak a word. On being questioned as to his condition, he said that he had told the contents of the sealed packet, and had taken away the character of a lady, whereupon he (Mr. Onslow) remarked that he should "tell the truth and shame the devil." (Cheers.) With regard to the tattoo mark, M. Chatillon stated that it consisted of a crucifix so long (measuring by his arm); Lord Bellew stated that it was about as long as a cable; Lady Doughty said it was about an inch long—(laughter)—and some of the witnesses said they saw it when Sir Roger was at breakfast drinking a cup of coffee; others saw it on his left arm when he was picking flowers; and then, again, it was seen when he was catching minnows—(laughter)—but, strange to say, none of the officers of his regiment saw it when he was taking a glass of wine in the mess-room; none of his servants ever saw it; and as for catching minnows with his left hand, why he might as well attempt to harpoon whales in the British Channel. (Laughter, and hear.) He (Mr. Onslow) pitied the parties who gave this evidence, if it should turn out, as he believed it would, that Sir Roger never was tattooed. (Hear, hear.) But he was said to be an impostor of the blackest dye. When he came over to this country, five years ago, what did his opponents say of him? They first started the idea that he was a man of the name of John Moore, until they found him living in Scotland. Next, that he was a servant at Tichborne to Sir Edward Doughty; then that he was a man named Smith, son of an old servant; and it was stated by a Mrs. Greenwood that they all knew it was him. (Laughter.) Then he was an old servant of Mr. James Tichborne's in Paris; then a man who was Sir Roger's servant in the Carabineers; next an old Carabineer soldier; then a sailor from Poole; then he was positively John Case, a native of Poole, whose mother was taken up to London in July, 1867, to identify him as her son—(laughter); then an illegitimate son of James Tichborne; next an illegitimate son of Sir James Doughty; then an illegitimate son of Mr. Robert Tichborne; again, an illegitimate son of Sir Henry Tichborne—pretty good morals they must have had in that family—(great laughter)—then the son of a woman in Australia who was coming over to identify him; an Australian navvy; an Australian prize-fighter; an Australian native whose father and mother were on their way to England to swear against him; then Edmund Orton, next Henry Orton, then Arthur Orton; then an illegitimate son of Dowager Lady Tichborne before marriage; then George Jarvis, a man who sailed from Liverpool, and many other persons besides; and he (Mr. Onslow) should not be a bit surprised if at last they made him out to be the illegitimate son of Lord Chief Justice Bovill himself. (Roars of laughter.) One of the great reasons why Sir Roger was called an impostor was, because he had forgotten his French. But did he ever know his French? He was always a bad French and English scholar. He (Mr. Onslow) had several letters in his possession written by the original Sir ROGER, both in French and English, and he sent these letters to Mr. LOTTH, who was, perhaps, the first French scholar at the Foreign Office, and he had received from him this letter :—"The French and English letters from ROGER TICHBORNE to his father and mother in 1854, and for some years previously, show, in my opinion, that his education must have been very much neglected. They are but illiterate productions. The French are worse than the English, containing more glaring faults in grammar—in fact, they are all, of both languages, so full of faults of grammar, construction, and spelling, that they suggest the idea that the writer had never learnt any grammar." Was it likely that a man whose education was so imperfect was likely to improve it by a long career in the bush? If he had come back to this country a perfect Frenchman he (Mr. ONSLOW) should at once have said that he was not Sir ROGER TICHBORNE. (Hear, hear.) But the gentleman before them could not help occasionally cropping up with the French in all directions. Would ARTHUR ORTON ever put in a word of French? There were many English words which Sir ROGER would still persist in calling by their original French names. When he came to this country, if he had been an impostor, he would have waited for his mother to have come and acknowledged him, but instead of that he went to his mother in Paris. He also went down to TICHBORNE, fourteen miles from Portsmouth "as the crow flies," and he went there in disguise, and if he had been an impostor he would have gone away without anyone knowing anything about him; but, in spite of his disguise, he was recognized as Sir ROGER. They asked him what his name was, and he replied, "TAYLOR," and they said, "No, you are not TAYLOR, but Sir ROGER TICHBORNE." (Cheers, and hear.) What did Mr. ROUS say in his affidavit? "On the 28th December, 1866, the Plaintiff arrived at my hotel by the train from London which reached Alresford at ten minutes past seven, and about nine o'clock the same evening he sent for me to his private room. Upon entering he accosted me as Mr. ROUS, and said he supposed I did not recollect him; that he was some years since on a visit in the neighbourhood, and had been to Alresford before. The Plaintiff told me that Sir ROGER TICHBORNE had arrived in England on Christmas-day, having landed at Gravesend on the evening of that day, and that he had come over with Sir ROGER from Australia, and represented to me that he was himself connected with the press, and had come down to take notes relative to the Tichborne Estate. But I formed my own opinion from the great resemblance of the Plaintiff to a Mr. ROGER CHARLES TICHBORNE, and from his conversation relative to the TICHBORNE Family and Estates, that my visitor was no other than Sir ROGER TICHBORNE himself, and I consequently particularly scrutinized his features and appearance generally, and I discovered a great resemblance to his late brother, and also to his late uncle, Sir HENRY TICHBORNE." The Plaintiff and Mr. ROUS subsequently went for a drive in the neighbourhood, and on this Mr. ROUS in his affidavit went on to say, "Frequently, whilst talking of the late Sir JAMES TICHBORNE and the Dowager Lady TICHBORNE and the late Sir ALFRED TICHBORNE, the Plaintiff spoke of them unconsciously as his father and mother and his brother, but always checked himself immediately he found he had slipped out those words. His knowledge of different places we passed, and the result of his conversation during our drive, confirmed my opinion that he was Sir ROGER TICHBORNE." Mr. ROUS said he now believed the Plaintiff was an impostor, because he had read the opinion-evidence; but if Dr. WHEELER'S account was true, then the whole of that evidence was false. (Hear, hear.) It was a very extraordinary circumstance that between 300 and 400 persons had recognized Sir ROGER as the right man since he had been in this country. Not only had these people recognized him, but it was an undoubted fact that he was recognized by Mrs. RADCLIFFE herself. The fifth clause in the affidavit of Mr. JOHN HOLMES, Solicitor to Sir ROGER when he first came over, proved this. It was sworn on the 9th March, 1867, and was as follows:—"VINCENT GOSFORD called at my office and informed me that Mr. and Mrs. RADCLIFFE and Mrs. TOWNELEY had had an interview with the Plaintiff on the previous day at his then residence at Croydon, and that Mrs. RADCLIFFE recognized the Plaintiff as her cousin by his eyes, eyebrows, and the shape of his forehead, and that certainly none of the party would declare it was not Sir ROGER." The great question was one of identity, and he (Mr. ONSLOW) had no doubt whatever that at the forthcoming Trial in November he would have an honourable acquittal. (Loud cheers.)

The Claimant then rose, in deference to repeated cries of "Sir ROGER," and after the cheering which greeted him had subsided, he thanked them for their attendance there that evening, and said that by the kind assistance they were rendering him he should be able to be represented at the coming Trial by at least a junior Counsel, but there would be arrayed against him six of the most eminent men at the bar. (Shame.) The Attorney-General had written a letter to the papers to say that he did not intend to be present at the Trial himself, and it was probably a good job for him (the Attorney-General) that he did not, inasmuch as the unfair way in which he had treated him (the speaker) had been taken up by the British public, and it was more than he was worth to attempt again to go into the Court at Westminster to prosecute him. (Hear, hear.) The Attorney-General, however, was the man who ought to do it, and he (the Claimant) would like to see him there doing it. But what did he do? Why, he had engaged Mr. Serjeant PARRY—an infinitely better man—to prosecute him. However, considering the British public had taken up his case, he had some chance now of having a fair Trial. But for the kindness of the public he should probably have lain in the cell in Newgate for the next ten or twelve months to come. [A voice: Don't go there any more.] (Laughter.) With regard to what Mr. ONSLOW had said about his running away, he could tell them that if he were now a thousand miles away he would hasten back again. (Cheers.) In 1868 he went out on the South America Commission, and he then had in his possession £800, and left in England £2,400, so that if he had been an impostor he could have stopped abroad. (Hear, hear.) But he was fighting for his children, and not for himself, and although they might incarcerate him in a place like Newgate it would not damp his ardour nor discourage him. (Cheers.) He knew he was Sir ROGER and the son of his father—(Laughter)—and when he died his children would be the natural and lawful inheritors of his estates. The Claimant then gave an interesting narrative of his visit to South America in 1868, and proceeded to say that when his poor Mother died all he had in the world died with her, and what he had got since that time had been by his own exertions and the exertions of a few noble friends like Mr. GUILDFORD ONSLOW. (Cheers.) He promised that the funds which were subscribed for his defence should be used in a proper manner. He wished that the press would speak the truth regarding him. Mr. OSBORNE, secretary to the Defence Fund, had been discharged by three of the trustees; and Mr. STREETEN, one of the other trustees, took offence at it, and declined to act any longer; and out of this some of the papers had tried to make capital against him. Then the newspapers were continually saying that he was at different places—the Derby, Ascot, and so on—whereas he had not visited one of those places, but was busily engaged at home, day after day, answering letters and attending to other business. (Hear, hear.) Before he concluded he would ask them to draw up petitions to Government praying that his Trial might come on within a short period; for it was a great shame that he should have to lie under the imputations which had been cast upon him for such a length of time. (The Claimant then resumed his seat amid general applause.)

Mr. LAW briefly addressed the meeting, and concluded by moving the following resolution:—"That this meeting is of opinion that the recent TICHBORNE Trial was not conducted in the spirit of fair-play which Englishmen have a right to expect, and that the language of the Attorney-General was utterly unworthy of the British bar.

Mr. W. LUCIUS CURTIS seconded the motion, which was carried unanimously.

Another resolution, proposed by Mr. CURTIS in an appropriate speech, was then passed. It condemned the conduct of the Government in attempting to crush a defenceless man, and protested against the enormous waste of public money in engaging six Counsel for the prosecution.

On the motion of Mr. ONSLOW, a vote of thanks was presented to the Chairman, and the meeting gradually dispersed, not, however, before the Claimant had received a cordial shake of the hand by a gentleman who said he recognized him as Sir ROGER, whom he had known intimately in his youth.

Singularly enough, yesterday (Tuesday) a Mr. PETER CHICK, jeweller, of Bognor, wished to see the Claimant, and his desire having been gratified, he said he had no hesitation in pronouncing him to be the Sir ROGER TICHBORNE whom he had known in early life, and as a proof of his faith he gave a gratifying subscription to the Defence Fund.

So much has been said about "forgetfulness of language," that we think it well to print an extract from Dr. LIVINGSTONE'S Book of Travels in South Africa, published by MURRAY, Albemarle Street, 1857; at page 682 he thus writes:—

"On going on board a fine large brig of 16 guns, with a crew of 130, I received so hearty a welcome from Captain PEYTON and all on board, that I felt myself at once at home in everything except my own mother tongue. I seemed to know the language perfectly, but the words I wanted would not come at my call. When I left England I had no intention of returning, and directed my attention earnestly to the language of Africa, paying none to English composition; with the exception of a short interval in Angola, I had been three and a half years without speaking English, and this, with thirteen years of previous disuse of my native tongue, made me feel sadly at a loss on board the "Frolic."

The Claimant's next appearance was at Swansea. We print the following report:—

THE CLAIMANT AT SWANSEA.

The Claimant to the Tichborne Estates arrived at Swansea on Wednesday night, accompanied by Mr. GUILDFORD ONSLOW, M.P., and Mr. G. F. BLOXAM. With the view of keeping his arrival as private as possible, a large assemblage being anticipated at the railway-station, the Committee arranged for him to be met at Neath, and to be brought thence to Swansea. At half-past two o'clock a brougham and four greys, with two postilions, started from the Mackworth Hotel, at Swansea. Accompanying were Mr. H. CUTTING, Chairman of the Committee, and Messrs. CROOK and BURGE, two members of the Committee. A large crowd assembled in the vicinity of the hotel, it being the prevailing opinion that the Claimant had actually arrived and that the equipage in waiting was that by which he had been brought. On the whole line of route—up High-street, Greenhill, Landore, Morriston, Llansamlet, Skewen, and Neath Abbey, numbers of people, anticipating the bject of the passing equipage, througed forth and watched its progress with considerable interest. The Claimant and his friends left London by the down express, which arrives at Neath at five o'clock. By that hour it had got wind that he was coming, and hundreds flocked to the station to get a glimpse of him. By the timely promptitude of Mr. Superintendent PHILLIPS, who placed a detachment of the borough force on duty at the station, no inconvenience was felt from the unusual crowd. A few minutes after the advertised time the train dashed up to the station, and the Claimant and his friends alighted. He was met by the Chairman of the committee, and other members of the Committee who accompanied him, each wearing rosettes of scarlet and white ribbon. The introduction being over, there was a general rush to see the Claimant, who passed on rapidly, followed by the crowd, the large assemblage cheering him as he emerged from the station. He and his friends then got into the brougham, which drove off, arriving in Swansea at a quarter past six. There was a large concourse of people assembled in front of the Mackworth Hotel, who cheered the Claimant lustily as he alighted, and walked quickly into the building. He was here met by a deputation of the Committee, who had been told off to receive him, and who gave him a hearty welcome to Swansea. He seemed in excellent health and spirits, and was evidently gratified at the enthusiasm with which he had been received on all hands.

The first meeting was held in the Music Hall on Thursday evening. There were about 20 persons only in the reserved seats; the other parts of the hall were well filled, it being calculated that altogether 2,000 were present. There were a few ladies, and a considerable number of the working classes. The feeling of the audience generally was strongly in favour of the Claimant, and violently adverse to the Attorney-General and the other persons who were supposed to be among his chief persecutors.

The Claimant, attended by Mr. WHALLEY, M.P., Mr. ONSLOW, M.P., Mr. CUTTING, Chairman of the Local Defence Committee, Mr. CROOK, and other prominent members of the same, entered the hall shortly after eight o'clock. His appearance was the signal for a burst of cheering, which he acknowledged by bowing to them from the platform.

Mr. CUTTING, as Chairman of the Committee, first came forward, and said he thought it his duty, on behalf of the gentlemen who were associated with him in the movement which had resulted in bringing the Claimant down, to assure the meeting that every farthing which would be received by them after the payment of the expenses—which would be kept down to the lowest possible point—would go entirely towards the TICHBORNE Defence Fund. These remarks had been suggested, and appeared to the Committee to be called for, by the fact that certain statements had been made to the effect that the bringing of the Claimant down was a "spec." on the part of the Committee. He begged to assure the audience that no statement could be more untrue, that no insinuation could be more unjust (cheers); every farthing over and above the expenses would go to the benefit of the Claimant in the gigantic cause which he would have to defend. (A voice: "Call him Sir ROGER.") He thanked them for the correction, but really his delicate nature (laughter) had prevented him from saying too much in favour of an opinion in which his own feelings were so strongly engaged. He need hardly tell them, that after most carefully looking into the matter, he was thoroughly satisfied that the Claimant was no other than Sir ROGER TICHBORNE. (Loud cheers.) He did not, however, ask any lady or gentleman present to pin their faith to his sleeve. He simply asked, "Had the Claimant had fair-play, or not?" (Loud cries of "No, no.") He did not ask them to say that he was or was not Sir ROGER. (Cries of "He is.") All he said was, that he had not yet had what every true Briton had a right to demand—fair-play—and that they would agitate till he got it. (Loud cheers.) He was glad, in conclusion, to announce that the chair would be taken that evening by Mr. WOOLLEY, who, he was sure, would perform his duties most satisfactorily.

Mr. WOOLLEY, commercial traveller, then took the chair, and briefly opened the proceedings by asking the audience to give all the speakers a fair hearing.

Mr. HORNE, of the Telegraph Office, Swansea, moved the first resolution:—"That it is the opinion of this meeting that the Claimant here present has not had a fair trial; and that, having regard to the enormous power brought against him, the unlimited supply of money by the Government, the character of high officials already pledged against him, with not a shilling of his own, and that, but for the generous interposition of Lord RIVERS and others, he would be still in Newgate, it is a public duty to give him such sympathy and support as shall secure for him a fair trial."

Mr. CUTTING supported the resolution. He said that every Briton boasted of his freedom—he would not give much for the Briton who did not; but what was the use of advancing a theory if they did not carry it out in practice? It was little use talking about their rights and privileges, if they stood calmly by and suffered a man whom they believed to be innocent to be crushed and deprived of his rights by the influence of wealth and power. His own firm conviction was that the Claimant was Sir ROGER CHARLES DOUGHTY TICHBORNE, and no other. (Loud cheers.) It was very gratifying to hear those bursts of sympathy which had been met with in every meeting at which Sir ROGER had spoken; there was continually arising some new proof that, thanks to the sympathy and support of Englishmen, the Claimant would at last have fair-play. He had great pleasure in seconding the resolution.

Mr. WHALLEY, M.P., supported the resolution. He was proud to meet his fellow-countrymen in the metropolis of Wales on such an occasion, believing as he did that he was engaged in a cause than which none more worthy of the support of Welshmen—indeed, more obligatory upon them as true men, loving fair-play and hating oppression—had ever been laid before them. He strongly commented upon the suspicious circumstance that the evidence as to the tattoo marks, in reliance upon which principally the jury had nonsuited the Claimant, had only been produced at the eleventh hour; if true, surely it would have been forthcoming at once, as it would have conclusively settled the question, and prevented the vast expenditure of money which had taken place. Surely, if the evidence given as to this point were true, the other side would have said to the Claimant, as soon as he put forward his claim, "Turn up your shirt-sleeve, and let us see your arm; the true Sir ROGER has marks on his arm; if you have not, you cannot be he." But no; not a whisper of anything of the sort took place till the end of the case, and it was impossible to resist the belief that it was made up. The people of Hampshire—where his property was situated—had almost to a man recognized him, and they sent to other parts of the kingdom this message: That the vilification and slander and abominable utterances of the Attorney-General, in the first place, and of the press following him—all the abuse of the Claimant, in every shape and form—only proved that they had nothing to rely upon except abuse (cheers), and only rendered him more deserving of the sympathy and support of all true Englishmen and Welshmen. He would only say in conclusion, that he was never more convinced of anything in his life than that the Claimant was the man he professed to be. New proofs of this were continually arising, and would be produced at the proper time.

The Claimant, who was received with loud cheers, then came forward and spoke as follows: Ladies and Gentlemen—in the first place allow me to return you my sincere thanks for your attendance here this evening. It is very gratifying to me to see assembled here so many lovers of fair-play, for I am quite certain there is nobody here but what is a lover of fair-play; and, had it not been for your kind labours, there is no doubt I should have been left in the cells of Newgate to be crushed by a man who is in great power in England. (Cheers.) Allow me to say I am not come here to ask you to believe I am Sir ROGER TICHBORNE. ("You are.") That we will leave to be decided by the Courts of law. But what I do ask is, to say and insist upon my having a fair trial like any other Englishman. (Cheers.) I shall now pass a few remarks upon my late trial. I have no doubt many of you remember the Attorney-General saying that I was a "mass of flesh." (Cheers and laughter.) Probably it is so. But still I have no power over nature. I am as nature formed me, and I am very well satisfied with what I am. (Cheers and laughter.) But I think you will all agree with me that it was not an expression which the chief law officer of England—a man we ought to look upon as being a gentleman, in every sense of the word—ought to have used. I will now make a few remarks on several matters in the late Trial. It happened once in the course of my cross-examination by the Attorney-General—I believe it was the last day—that I saw a great many people coming on the bench and sitting by the side of the Judge. Several other Judges came in their wigs and gowns who had not time to change them. I suppose the word had been passed that I was going to be crushed, and they came in to see the operation. The Attorney-General held out three letters to me and asked if they were in my handwriting. I answered "Yes" to each letter. I then set to to read the letters. When I had read the first it appeared quite strange to me. When I had read the second I began to have my suspicions that they were not written by me. When I read the third I was confident I had never written it, because it represented that I had offered a woman a large sum of money in order to induce her to give a certain evidence—a thing I had never done, and which I knew to be a falsehood. I then asked to see the letters again, and, having looked over them attentively, I declared them to be forgeries. ("Shame.") This caused a laugh in Court, which was filled principally with the friends of the other party. However, the Attorney-General afterwards admitted that they were forgeries. ("Shame.") Now I ask you, How should I have stood if I had put in a forged letter? Why, I should have been sent to Newgate there and then, and very properly too. But what did they send me to Newgate for? That has remained a mystery to the present day. In the course of last autumn a clause was put into an Act of Parliament, giving a Judge the power to send any witness to Newgate for trial. Who put the clause in? That remains to be seen; but I have no doubt in my own mind that it was put in for the purpose of putting me into Newgate—nothing else. Therefore you see they had made up what to do six months ago. Then there was the case of the Daguerreotype. A daguerreotype of me was put in, and my left thumb was visible. It was produced again and the thumb was gone. (Cries of "Shame.") It had been rubbed out by the other side. But they had forgotten that when the Chili Commission went out they had to supply us with copies, and in those copies the thumb was perfectly visible: and when this was brought to their notice they were obliged to excuse themselves by saying that the thumb had been rubbed out by accident. But this could not be the case either, for the Daguerreotypes were carefully framed, and had glass over the face, so that rubbing out would be impossible. Again I say, What would be said, and what would be done, if I had tampered with the evidence in this matter? (Cheers.) I have always been taught from my childhood that justice in England was fairly balanced, but it was not so in my case. But, after all, I don't know that I can much blame them, because the Judge had to make acquaintance with the nobility, and he could only do it through me. He had to keep in with them. He knew very well that if he did not send me to Newgate he would offend almost all the aristocracy of England, and no doubt that ruled him very much in his conduct: and I have no doubt many of you who have heard the evidence will agree with me that a more partial Judge never sat on the bench. (A voice: "He's a disgrace to the bench!" Another voice: "Send him to Newgate!" and laughter.) I am going to address you on another subject. I have long borne imputations on my character, and will bear them no longer. One paper remarked the other day that I had voluntarily gone into the witness-box, and voluntarily and without cause defamed the fair name of my cousin, and that hanging was too good for such a man as me. I have made up my mind that I will bear these imputations no longer. I will place the facts before you and you shall judge for yourselves. You shall have the whole truth about that affair, though I am afraid it will weary you; if I bore you you must let me know. The Claimant then went into a long and detailed statement of the mode in which the contents of the "sealed packet" came to be made public. He made the first mention of it at a meeting at the Grosvenor Hotel, London, but declined to mention its contents. Shortly afterwards he was advised by his Counsel, Mr. Serjeant Ballantine, that it was necessary that he should state the contents, in order that the cross-examination of Mr. Gosford should be conducted properly: but he declined most positively to state it, knowing how it would affect his poor cousin. He was told by his Counsel that if he refused to state the contents they would have nothing more to do with the Case, and at the same time pledging their word, through his attorney, that if he could write down the statement no eyes but theirs should see it. When he thought of his wife and children, he thought he had a right—and, indeed, under the circumstances was bound—to supply the information which his Counsel required to cross-examine Gosford, and he did so; but the very same evening he discovered that the document which his solicitor, Mr. Holmes, had promised should be kept under lock and key, had been shown by him to three different gentlemen. They would not wonder that he was never friends with his solicitor afterwards. How could he be with a man who had thus broken his solemn word of honour? Of course it caused Mrs. Radcliffe great pain and annoyance, but it was not through him. He was innocent of it. He was afterwards cross-examined on the subject by the Attorney-General. He baffled him all the day, nearly at the cost of his life, and at four o'clock had the best of him, because he had not answered his questions. But on the following day he attended a consultation of Counsel, at which, besides Mr. Ballantine, Mr. Giffard—whom many of them knew, and who would tell them if he was speaking falsely—was present. When he entered the room, Mr. Ballantine addressed these words to him: "It is evident to Mr. Giffard and myself, and the rest of the Counsel, that you were evading the questions put to you by the Attorney-General yesterday. We have consulted together on the subject, and I am empowered to tell you that if you do not answer these questions in a straightforward way next Monday morning, Mr. Giffard and myself will get up and leave the Court." His (the Claimant's) answer was, "Then you may do it. She is my cousin, and the mother of nine children, and I would rather lose my estate than do it." (Cheers.) Mr. Ballantine then asked if I had any objections to again write the contents of the packet; and when the Attorney-General asked the question, to say, "There is my answer in writing." He thought he had a perfect right to do it, and he did so; and this was how it came to pass that the statement was fairly drawn out of him. The Claimant then said he had often been asked why, when he had money in his name in the Bank of England, he had not written for it. He would answer this question. Almost immediately upon his arriving in Australia he had a situation offered him, which he accepted, and which took him far into the interior of the country. It never occurred to him to write home: he was living nineteen miles from the nearest post-house, and he always intended some time or other to go back without writing, and surprise them. He did not want money. He received 30s. a week as salary for the first two years, and afterwards £2. 2s. a week, and had no means of spending it unless he went to Melbourne; consequently, the money accumulated on his hands. There was no necessity for him to write home for money, because he had more than he could possibly spend as it was. Besides, he was never sure of staying three months in one place, so that he did not know where to tell them to send the money to. He thought this was a very fair explanation of why he had not written. (Hear, hear.) He might also say—though, perhaps, it did not say very much in favour of his own character—that he had on several occasions saved enough to pay his passage to England, and had actually gone to Melbourne with the intention of returning, but unfortunately he spent the money, and returned to the bush. (Laughter.) He again thanked them for their kind attention, and on the following afternoon and Saturday evening would give some account of his journey through life in different foreign parts, endeavouring to amuse them, but at the same time saying nothing which was not strictly true. (Loud cheers.)

Mr. Onslow, M.P., then addressed the meeting. In the course of his remarks he combated the argument that the Claimant could not be Sir Roger Tichborne because he (the Claimant) was uneducated, whereas Sir Roger had received an excellent classical education. He replied that this was altogether a fallacy. Sir Roger Tichborne had never received a good education. In proof of this he would read a letter which he had recently received, which he considered to be evidence of great value as bearing on this point:—

"My Dear Onslow,—The French and English letters from Roger Tichborne to his father and mother in 1854, and for some years previously, show, in my opinion, that his education must have been very much neglected: they are but illiterate productions. The French are worse than the English, containing more glaring faults in grammar; in fact, they are all, of both languages, so full of faults of grammar, construction, and spelling, that they suggest the idea that the writer had never learned any grammar.

"I return you the letters forthwith.—Yours sincerely,

"Blandford: March 23rd." "George Lotth."

The hon. gentleman concluded an animated and argumentative speech on behalf of the Claimant by an eloquent appeal to the People of England to stand by him and see that justice was done.

The motion was then put to the meeting, when the great majority of persons present held up their hands in its favour. The contrary was not put.

The Claimant came forward and stated that at any of the meetings, if any of his friends and supporters wished to have an explanation of any particular point, he should be very pleased to give it to them. He again cordially thanked them for the reception he had met with.

The proceedings ended with a vote of thanks to the Chairman, moved by Mr. Onslow, and seconded by Mr. Whalley.

On Friday the Claimant attended another meeting at the Music-hall, at which there was a large audience. The meeting was presided over by Captain Prust, and was afterwards ably addressed by Mr. Whalley, M.P., Mr. Onslow, M.P., the Claimant, and other gentlemen. In the evening about 40 gentlemen dined together at the Mackworth Hotel, under the presidency of Mr. Woolley. The Claimant and his friends were present, and a very pleasant social evening was spent.

The following appeared in a Swansea paper next day.

Saturday.—A Hoax!

This day, says our daily contemporary, a new surprise awaited everybody, and the postman handed it round to a variety of people of all classes and conditions in the good old town of Swansea, in the shape of the following missive neatly printed on rose-pink paper:—

"Sir Roger Chas. D. Tichborne being anxious to meet his Committee and principal sympathisers, to express his gratitude for his warm reception at Swansea, begs to inclose an invitation to a luncheon at his hotel, on Saturday next, at 11.30 a.m., and trusts ——— Esq., will be present.—Mackworth Arms, June 28, 1872."

Together with the foregoing missive came a handsome card, nicely printed, the whole enwrapped in the finest of superfine envelopes, the inscription on the card being as follows:—

Mackworth Arms Hotel.
To Sir Chas. D. Tichborne's Luncheon,
On Saturday, June 29th, 1872,
11.30 a.m.

Now the excitement commences! Those who heretofore thought the Claimant an impostor, and said so, softened down wonderfully in the light of that rose-pink circular, that nicely printed card, enwrapped in the finest of superfine envelopes, addressed to themselves in the most modern of clerkly hands, with the delightful affix of "Esquire;" and "the poor illused Sir Roger," as they now termed him, became all at once the jolliest of jolly good fellows, who ought never to be allowed to be crushed and trodden under foot of men like this. Bah! A rush was made to M'Caskie's for kid gloves and neck-ties; Challicombe's pomatum all ran out from the run upon its resources; nurserymen and floral friends were at once looked up for bouquets and cut flowers, the one from Bellevue-street carrying off the palm; cabs were ordered three deep for 11.30 a.m. sharp; and the whole aspect of anti-Tichbornedom changed as if by magic. The "impostor" became a gentleman, and the "Australian bushranger" a worthy scion of true nobility. The newspaper organ which young Radicalism swears by, and whose advertisements are edited with such signal ability, is said to have sent a "special" to represent it, on receipt of the rose-pink missive, with power from the editor of the advertisements to say that all hard words against Sir Roger Charles Doughty Tichborne should be at once withdrawn, recalled, corrected, and apologised for in our next, and a leading article or two written as much in his favour as he chose himself to indite; while the organ which nobody swears by, having no representative to represent it, and therefore no card to go with, sent to the office of a wee contemporary to borrow one, and was refused the favour, our wee but plucky contemporary remarking that he "intended to lunch wi' Sir Roger hisself;" that it was "owre pleasant to dinner wi' a laird, and e'en better than a' to sympathize wi' a poor doon-trooden body, wi' nae han' to help him in his sair need but his ain. Oot mon!"

The front of the Mackworth at 11.30. a.m. was all commotion.

The prize bouquet was there, and the air was thick with Challicombe's pomatum. Everybody looked at everybody else, and all at the bar toasted Sir Roger and themselves at the same time. Then whisperings went round, blank faces ensued, long countenances followed. "It's my opinion, gentlemen, that we've been sold," said the prize bouquet. And sure enough it was true. Sold they were. It was a hoax, at which no one laughed more heartily than the Claimant himself, when he came to hear of it, though deprecating, at the same time, the inconvenience to which not less than fifty of his sympathizers, and others whose sympathies only commenced with the receipt of the invitation, had been put by the folly of some inconsiderate practical joker.

SWANSEA.

Enthusiastic Meeting on Saturday.

On Saturday night the Claimant and his sympathizers held their meeting at the Music Hall. There was a good attendance, and the proceedings throughout were of a most enthusiastic character.

Mr. Woolley, the local agent to Allsopp and Co., was voted to the chair. The Chairman having offered a few remarks,

Mr. Cutting, Chairman of the Swansea Defence Fund Committee, read the resolutions passed at the previous meetings.

Mr. Whalley, M.P., was received with applause. He said that the object of the meeting was to express sympathy with, and secure a fair trial for, the Claimant. He denied that he was a party to any conspiracy. (Cheers.) The question was, whether the members of the Family who for six years had been spending an infant's estate knew that the Claimant was not an impostor. Did or did not these persons from the first know the Claimant to be Roger Tichborne, and had they known it all the time during the past six years? If they did, there had been one of the vilest conspiracies that this country had ever known—(cheers)—a conspiracy to deprive the Claimant of his rights, to deny his identity, and to deprive him of his estate. (Applause.) As to affirming that the Claimant was Roger Tichborne, that meeting would not be asked to express an opinion on that point. He proposed to show, in the first place, that the knowledge that the Claimant was Roger Tichborne was present to the mind of the adviser of the Family, a gentleman who was the executor to Sir Roger's will—Mr. Vincent Gosford. At the time when Sir Roger returned to this country Mr. Gosford happened to be in this very neighbourhood, being at Carmarthen engaged for Mr. Plowden in some business there. When the Claimant appeared, Mr. Gosford was suddenly telegraphed for, no doubt by some member of the Family, to interview the man. Mr. Gosford proceeded at once to Gravesend, where Sir Roger was at that time staying with his family. What took place there was no necessity to detail. It was enough to say that Mr. Gosford did not behave courteously towards Sir Roger's wife. After the visit Mr. Gosford saw Mr. John Lewis, of Carmarthen, and the first words Gosford said were "Why, Jack, he is the man!" adding: "This is rather an awkward job this." They had had this information from a Mr. Taplin of the Vine Inn, Carmarthen. If this evidence was true, Gosford was one of those who had been engaged in the conspiracy—(hear, hear)—to crush the Claimant. They got into the conspiracy some of the highest members of the Roman Catholic Church. He respected many Roman Catholics—Jesuit Fathers, men like Father Methick and Father Cooper, with others who did not go against the Claimant. But Roman Catholic influence was at work in every village, in every town, in the press and elsewhere, joining the bell-hounds. (Cheers and hisses.) He would ask them, on the best evidence which he had, to make an appeal to the Government as to the evidence respecting Gosford. Now, he had to bring forward another piece of evidence. The principal agent of the Defendant, the man who went to Australia, was a man who had been living in this neighbourhood. Being in these parts, this gentleman waited upon their fellow-townsman, Mr. Crook, and deliberately proposed that Mr. Crook should receive £50 to withhold the evidence which he gave at the meeting the previous day. (Cries of "Shame.") Luckily Mr. Crook not only acted as an honest man, but he made the solicitor believe that he would withhold the evidence, and he actually received £10 on account. (Applause.) Mr. Crook put this blood-money in his pocket. Where did this £10 come from, he would ask? Mr. Whalley, at the close of his speech, stated the nature of the resolution which would be proposed.

Addressing Mr. Crook, Mr. Whalley said: You have heard the statement which has been made: is it the truth?

Mr. Crook replied: It is.

Mr. Crook added a few words, after which

Mr Horace Cutting proposed a resolution affirming the truth of the statement made by the speaker, and declaring it to be the duty of the Government to afford every aid to the Claimant to inquire into and punish the authors of the conspiracy.

Mr. Daniel Jones (coal merchant) formally seconded the resolution, which was put to the meeting and carried amidst great cheering, there only being two or three hands held up against it.

The Chairman then said: I have very great pleasure in calling upon Sir Roger Tichborne to address the meeting.

The Claimant was received with vociferous cheers, which were again and again repeated. He wished, in the first place, to thank those present for their attendance that evening, and for the support which they had given him. Although he did not have many opponents there, judging by the two hands held up against the resolution, he would say a word by way of explanation. He was not there to ask them to believe that he was Sir Roger Tichborne, but he wanted them to demand fair-play—that fair-play which every Englishman was entitled to. (Cheers.) He was willing to let the law decide whether he was himself or not. (Laughter.) He asked them that the unfairness with which he had been treated, and the hundreds of pounds which had been wasted, might not happen again. The gentleman who had come forward on the previous evening (cries of "Briggs"—"Bryant Briggs") had said that he was Arthur Orton. (A Voice: "He was not in the bush at all.") He gave the gentleman an interview on Friday to enable him to see whether he (the Claimant) was Orton or not. The gentleman wrote these lines: "I knew A. Orton in Avoca as a digger in the end of 1856 or the beginning of '57." On the other hand, they would read in the evidence taken before the Australian Commission that Orton was in Van Diemen's Land from 1853 to 1856, and that Orton afterward went to Castlemaine. What he would do was this—If the meeting appointed two or three gentlemen from the audience, he would give them the book on the table (the evidence of the Australian Commission)—it was sworn evidence, and the three gentlemen, whoever they might be, should say whether he was Arthur Orton or not. After this statement he need say nothing as to Mr. Briggs. (Applause.) Then a word as to Mr. Vincent Gosford. Mr. Gosford was one of the executors of the will; he left Mr. Gosford £500 in the will. After he had returned to England he was coming up by train from Gravesend in company with Mr. Gosford and Mr. Holmes, who was his solicitor at the time. He asked Mr. Gosford who had proved his will. Mr. Gosford replied that he did not know. Mr. Holmes was present at the time, and hearing about the will, went on the following day to Doctors' Commons, when he found the will had been sworn by Mr. Gosford. (Cries of "Shame.") Mr. Gosford said, when he (the Claimant) came home, that it was a very "awkward job," and it might be an "awkward job" for Mr. Gosford—(applause)—when he got that gentleman into the witness-box. As to the tattoo marks, he did not hear a word about them until he had been examined by the Judge, the Jury, and the Counsel on both sides. If the other side knew of the tattoo marks on his arrival in England, why did they not come forward and say, "If you are Roger Tichborne, show us your tattoo marks"? (Cheers.) When for three days he was under examination at the Law Institute, in 1867, why was he not asked to show his arm. (Applause.) It was strange that with the exception of the tattoo marks he had all the marks which were known to be on Sir Roger Tichborne, and his explanation of the reticence on the other side was that they had not heard anything about tattoo marks until nearly the close of the Trial. The Attorney-General had said that he was clever, and he must be very clever if all Mr. Coleridge said about him was correct. (Cheers.) In the first place, he must have made his features very much like the features of his family. He must have manufactured eighteen or twenty marks in such a way as to deceive Dr. Fergusson and other able medical gentlemen. If he was able to do this, he was very clever indeed: that was all he could say. The Attorney-General had made his boast to the Premier that he would prove him (the Claimant) to be Arthur Orton in twenty minutes. If so, what necessity was there to extend the Trial over 103 days? There was no necessity for the Attorney-General to make a long-winded speech of thirty days—(hear, hear)—and there was no necessity for Mr. Coleridge to say, at the end of that speech, that he did not say the Claimant was Arthur Orton, but he would say that the Claimant was not Roger Tichborne. (Applause.) If the Attorney-General could prove he was Orton in twenty minutes, what right had Mr. Coleridge to allow the Trial to occupy 103 days? (A Voice: "It is a swindle.") They knew that he had no money except what he had from his friends, and it was nothing better than robbery to put him to such an enormous expense. He was now about to relate something concerning his cousin, Mrs. Radcliffe. He was sitting in his drawing-room with his mother, when a lady and a gentleman drove into the grounds past the window. They were shown into the back room, and were announced as Mr. and Mrs. Radcliffe. He opened the door to escort his mother into the room, when Mr. Radcliffe thrust his mother back, and said, "We don't want you here." (A Voice: "You ought to have knocked him down.") They might easily understand that any son would be annoyed at such conduct as that. (Applause.) He was confused, but as he knew it was stated out of doors that he would not see some members of the Tichborne Family, he thought it was best to go into the room. When he did so a lady came forward and said, "How are you, Roger?" He said, "I am well, thank you," and sat down. In a minute he saw that the lady was not his cousin, and he said, "You are not Mrs. Radcliffe; you are Mrs. Townsend." She said, "Yes, Mrs. Radcliffe is outside." Afterwards Mrs. Radcliffe came in, and shook him warmly by the hand when she left. This, however, she denied in Court, but they should hear what he had to say, and then judge whether it was true or not. He was asked to give Mr. and Mrs. Radcliffe another interview. He said, "Yes, but this is my mother's house, and as you have insulted her you shall not come here again." His solicitor consented to allow the interview to take place in his office. When the day arrived a messenger came to say that persons were waiting for him at the solicitor's office. He said he had just received a telegram to say that the ladies could not be present. However he went, being given to understand that he was to meet his aunt Lady DOUGHTY. He went into the room, and in one corner saw a lady very closely veiled. Mr. RADCLIFFE said, "Is that your aunt?" and he replied, "Well, considering that at present I cannot see her face, how I can be expected to know who she is." (Laughter.) The person then took up her veil, and he at once said:—"That is not my aunt, Lady DOUGHTY. What right, Mr. RADCLIFFE, have you to attempt to impose upon me in this way?" He then left the room. (Applause.) As to Mrs. RADCLIFFE shaking hands with him on the first occasion, he would ask them to listen to the sworn testimony of Mr. JOHN HOLMES. (One portion was to the effect that on the 9th of March, 1867, VINCENT GOSFORD called on Mr. HOLMES and told him that Mr. and Mrs. RADCLIFFE and two female cousins had had an interview with the Claimant on the previous day; that Mrs. RADCLIFFE had recognized the Claimant by his eyebrows, and that none of the party could deny that the Claimant was Sir Roger.) There had been an imputation cast upon his character with respect to Mrs. RADCLIFFE. One paper had stated that he went voluntarily into the box to defile the fair name of his cousin. He would distinctly deny that. His Counsel had told him that unless he showed that he knew the contents of the sealed packet, they would throw up the Case. At the same time they pledged him their words of honour that they would not divulge the secret. When the Attorney-General questioned him as to the packet he baffled Mr. COLERIDGE all day long until four o'clock came. In the evening Serjeant BALLANTINE said to him: "Mr. GIFFARD, myself, and the other Counsel are satisfied that you were evading the Attorney-General's question as to the sealed packet. Now, unless you answer the question in the morning, I will get up and leave the Court." His reply was: "Serjeant BALLANTINE, you can get up and leave the Court if you like, but I shall not defile the fair name of my cousin—(loud cheers)—who is the mother of six children." Subsequently, however, he consented to write the contents of the packet on a piece of paper, on being distinctly told that only the Judge, his own Counsel, and the Attorney-General were to see it. This he had no objection to do, for of course he was fighting for his children. On the following morning the Attorney-General questioned him several times as to the packet, and he declined to state the contents. At last he appealed to the Judge as to whether he was obliged to answer the question. Judge BOVILL—the unfeeling person that he was, because he could call him nothing else—said he was obliged to answer the question. (Groans.) Many of those present had no doubt read his evidence, and they would say that a more partial Judge never sat on the bench. ("Shame.") He fought his case as long as he could fight it, and he had only £74, which was in his pocket when he was taken to Newgate. His wife and little ones were at home without any money, and because he had no more money Judge BOVILL thought proper to send him to the dismal cells of Newgate. When he commenced his action he did so in the name of ROGER CHARLES DOUGHTY TICHBORNE, but at the same time acknowledged that he had gone by the name of TOMAS CASTRO. The Judge re-christened him, for when he was sent to prison it was in the name of TOMAS CASTRO, not of R. C. D. TICHBORNE. (A Voice: "He had no right to do so.") He would not detain them longer, but begged again to thank them for their attendance. He could only say that as long as he had the people of England with him, so long would he fight like a tiger. (Prolonged cheering.)

The Chairman then gave an "open invite" to anyone in the room to come on the platform and put a question to Sir ROGER.

A person who sat in the reserved seats, and who had continually interrupted the proceedings during Mr. WHALLEY's speech, here stepped on to the platform. It is fair to state that this gentleman, who was respectably dressed, was not only rather sunburnt, but seemed to have been "in the sun" during the day. He gave his name to the Chairman as Captain CUTHBERT. He made his *début* before the audience amidst cries of "Send him to Bridgend Asylum," &c.

Captain CUTHBERT said he supposed he was addressing Welshmen, Englishmen, Irishmen, and Scotchmen. He was a cosmopolitan of the world. He had been in Avoca diggings, in Wagga-Wagga, &c., &c., as a digger, and he was at Swansea as the master of a ship. (Confusion, followed by cries of "Let him speak.") The only question which he wished to put to the Claimant, and he was sure they would like to have it answered was, How did he (the Claimant) arrive in Australia? (Cries of "Nonsense." "How did you get there?" "He walked there, to be sure," and "Turn him out.") As a master of a ship, as a nautical man, as a digger, and as a pioneer of the continent of America, he wished to have an answer to this question, which could be put in a cocoa-nut, or in a nutshell, as the saying was. (Uproar.)

The Chairman said he must request the speaker to put a question, and give Sir ROGER an opportunity of replying to it.

Captain CUTHBERT said the question he had to put to the Claimant was this:—After the "Bella" went down, how did you get to Australia? (A Voice: "Everybody knows that." Voice No 2: "He swam ashore.")

The Claimant rose amidst applause.

Some individual in the body of the hall here caught the eye of the Chairman, who said: I will thank you to behave, or I will have you turned out.

The Claimant said that Captain CUTHBERT had asked a question and he had great pleasure in answering it. After the sinking of the "Bella" he was picked up—that was to say, the boat which he was in was picked up—by a vessel named the "Osprey," which took him into Melbourne. When in Melbourne he went ashore with the captain, and called at two offices. He went next day down to a horse-yard, and fell in with FOSTER, with whom he went to Gippsland, where he remained until 1859.

Captain CUTHBERT again came forward, and was received with cries of "Turn him out."

The Claimant came to the front of the platform, and said: May I ask you to oblige me by giving this gentleman a fair hearing? (Applause.)

Captain CUTHBERT then proceeded to say that he arrived in Australia in 1851 as chief officer of a large vessel. *He knew the "Osprey"—that was a three-masted vessel—in 1853 or 1854.* If there were only two "Ospreys," one a small boat and the other this three-masted schooner, the Claimant could not have been picked up by the "Osprey" which he knew was going from Melbourne to Sydney in 1852. No seaman belonging to the "Osprey" had ever come forward to say that they picked up a shipwrecked crew. He presumed the Claimant's agents had referred to the register, but they had not been able to prove that there was an "Osprey" in Melbourne at the time in question. (Cries of "No speech.") If the captain and seamen were all dead, what had become of the owners? (Here there was great uproar, and the voice of the speaker was completely drowned.) Captain CUTHBERT became very much excited, and clapped his hands frantically for about two minutes. He then retired amidst cries of "What did you have for coming?"

Mr. WHALLEY, M.P., asked to be allowed to call attention to Captain CUTHBERT's speech. (A Voice: "He is not worth notice.") Instead of going to the point and proving that the Claimant was not TICHBORNE, the previous speaker tried to trip the Claimant by asking a question. This was an old trick; and they had at Southampton a man named LAWRANCE who, without giving grounds for his assertion, kept saying, "I know the Claimant as ARTHUR ORTON." He would conclude by moving a vote of thanks to the Chairman.

Mr. ATKIN seconded. He remarked that those present knew he was an old sailor. He would take Captain CUTHBERT on his own words. That gentleman spoke of two "Ospreys." The Attorney-General was going to show that there was only one "Osprey." (Applause). So that after all Captain CUTHBERT's statement was favourable to the Claimant rather than otherwise. He begged to second the vote of thanks.

The motion was carried amidst loud applause, and the meeting terminated.

The BIGGS here alluded to was evidently one of those numerous "plants," or spies, whom the Family were in the habit of sending to the Claimant. We republish from the *Hampshire Chronicle* of August 3, 1872, letters relating to this person. Captain CUTHBERT was, no doubt, a person of the same class and calling.

THE TICHBORNE CLAIMANT.

TO THE EDITOR OF THE "HAMPSHIRE CHRONICLE."

SIR,—I have, to-day, seen in your paper a letter signed "BRYANT BIGGS," giving an account of his proceedings at Swansea, and in which he also speaks of Mr. ONSLOW and myself.

I request you will allow me to state that all that occurred between this person and Sir ROGER TICHBORNE, as also with myself, was committed by me to writing at the time, and in the presence of several witnesses, including two persons whom he brought with him to these interviews, was read over by me to him, and subsequently recounted to the public meeting held in that town, at which he either was, or was invited to be, present.

The result was that every one, to the best of my belief, was convinced that Mr. BIGGS was employed, or instigated, by Sir ROGER's opponents to check or control the enthusiasm which at Swansea, as elsewhere, he has met with.—I am, &c., G. H. WHALLEY. August 1, 1872.

TO THE EDITOR OF THE "HAMPSHIRE CHRONICLE."

SIR,—In your paper of last week I notice a letter signed by "BRYANT BIGGS," in which he has made such gross misstatements that I feel compelled to correct the same through the medium of your columns, in which they obtained publicity.

In the first place Mr. BIGGS states, "There was a mutual recognition between the Claimant and himself." This is false. On Mr. BIGGS being introduced to the Claimant at the "Mackworth Hotel," he said, "Do you know me?" The Claimant's reply was "I never saw you before in my life." "What? you don't know me! Do you not remember me at the Avoca diggings, in 1851? You are ARTHUR ORTON." The Claimant's reply was, "I was never at any time at the Avoca diggings, and if you saw me and knew me there, in 1851 or 1855, you quite upset the evidence the Attorney-General has taken so much trouble to find as to ORTON's whereabouts in those years."

BIGGS then asked him, "Did you sell me a double-barrelled gun on the road to the Avoca diggings?" The reply was, "I certainly never sold you a gun, and was never at the Avoca, or on my road to it." BIGGS replied, "I could *almost* have sworn you were the ARTHUR ORTON I knew." Mr. BIGGS propounded several questions to the Claimant, but, never having seen him, he could not reply to matters of which he was totally ignorant. Mr. BIGGS was requested to sign a declaration before a Commissioner as to the truth of his statements. This he agreed to do on the following morning if Mr. WHALLEY would embody the gist of the conversation on paper. But the next morning, on being asked if he was prepared to make his statement before a Commissioner or magistrate, he declined to do so.

During the conversation, he stated that he had been in communication with the Attorney-General, and that he had received from him copies of the photographs from Alresford, and that he had recognized the Claimant as ARTHUR ORTON by them; but he also managed to so far forget himself as to mention the fact that the Attorney-General told him that he must be more particular in his *dates*, as those he had given did not by any means tally with other evidence. [*Par parenthese*—this was rather suggestive].

Mr. BIGGS also says, I addressed him thus, "Now, BIGGS, we don't want to be unfriendly to you. We are old Australian friends, and ought to pull together." This I most emphatically deny, for I had never seen him, and consequently, could not class him in the circle of my friends. Instead of the interview lasting six hours, it did not occupy more than three-quarters of an hour.

Mr. BIGGS evidently attempts to be sarcastic in his pretended ignorance as to who "GUILDFORD ONSLOW" is. It would be quite preposterous to occupy your columns by giving him, as an individual, the information, as I presume it would be very uninteresting to your readers to inform them of facts of which they are well aware.

As my name has been introduced by Mr. BIGGS in his correspondence, perhaps you will allow me to state that I knew both TOMAS CASTRO and ARTHUR ORTON individually and at the same time. The latter I have every *reason* to remember, as I bear a mark of his playful disposition in the shape of a bullet wound through the fleshy part of my left arm, and am also the owner of the weapon, a five-barrelled revolver, with which it was inflicted. This was given to me afterwards by ARTHUR ORTON, and his initials are engraved on the trigger-guard. I may say it is now

GUILDFORD ONSLOW, Esq.

and has been for many months past in the hands of Mr. SPOFFORTH of the firm of BAXTER, ROSE, and NORTON, and, strange to relate, the very time the Attorney-General so pathetically lamented his inability to trace either ORTON or CASTRO, was the exact time I was acquainted with them, and which I can prove by documents in my possession, emanating through the Government offices, and officially signed, and which I *shall* produce.—I am &c.,

WM. CROOK

Swansea, July 30, 1872.

We follow this Correspondence up by the following, which corroborates powerfully the foregoing statements, and indicates also how the stream of public feeling ran at this period.

Copy of a letter to the Editor of the *Birmingham Daily Post.*

Ingleby Arms, Ingleby Street, Birmingham: June 17.

SIR,—As regards your remarks in Monday's *Post*, I can substantiate Dr. WHEELER's information respecting the TICHBORNE Claimant. I knew ARTHUR ORTON well. I also knew TOMAS CASTRO personally well, living with CASTRO at the Australian Hotel, Wagga-Wagga, under Mr. HIGGINS, for upwards of three years. I saw ORTON and CASTRO together frequently. I will swear that they are two distinct persons. By inserting this you will oblige, yours,

(Signed) JOHN DYKE.

The following is a copy of a letter that was written by Dr. M. WHEELER to the *Hampshire Chronicle.*

I have seen the Claimant, and am persuaded he is the same person I knew in Australia as TOMAS CASTRO; the other individual, "ORTON," I left in Brisbane early in March, 1869. Knowing such to be the case, I have communicated to the Solicitors to the Treasury. Having been in the Government service, I deemed it my duty to give the Government here first information.

By inserting this in your valuable paper, you will greatly oblige, yours faithfully,

W. M. WHEELER, M.D.

[Copy.] Wagga-Wagga, N. S. Wales, 20th Dec., 1873.

To Baxter, Norton, and Co.

Dear Sir,—I have seen Mackie, the late toll-keeper, several times lately. He remembers distinctly an accident happening to a man whom he knew to be a companion of Castro, Osborne, and others. He says the man had been drinking, and was riding his horse furiously over the bridge. It became unmanageable, and rushed at one of the fenced approaches to the bridge; the rider was thrown over the fence violently, and was stunned, and the horse was left on the opposite side. Mackie cannot describe the man minutely; he merely remembers he was rather a large, slovenly-looking fellow, with reddish face. He had no recollection of features, feet, hands, or any other particulars. His wife and daughter remembered the accident, and the man too—that is, his general appearance. Mackie says a few people gathered round after the accident, but he cannot call to mind any individuals. He cannot fix the date either; but, from other circumstances he mentioned, I believe the year must have been 1864 or 1865. He thinks it was in the summer time. A gentleman who resides here, and from whose house there is a view of the bridge, tells me he has a vivid recollection of an accident of that kind. He was in his garden, and heard the gallop, and then the crash. He said it was on a Sunday, and that one of his sons soon after came in and told him about the affair; and that a doctor who was passing over the bridge at that time had given directions about the wounded man. This gentleman's statement, I feel sure, can be relied upon; his son is away, but I will try and get his recollection of what passed on the occasion. It seems very probable that these incidents are referable to the identical accident at which Dr. Wheeler was present. Mackie says the man who was hurt was not long in the district; that he is sure he was a "mate" of Castro and Osborne, as he has often seen them passing over the bridge together; that they were a "larky set of fellows," and he has often watched their antics. (Signed) W. A. Cottee.

This is copy of a letter from Mr. Charles Ballanger, Queensland:—

Pioneer Plantation, Mooloolah; March 20, 1873.

To Guildford Onslow, Esq., M.P.

Dear Sir,—I saw in one of the English papers Dr. Wheeler giving evidence about one Arthur Orton, at Deacon's Hotel, Edward-street, Brisbane. About the time the Gympie gold fever broke out, I was living at a place called Burngary Sugar Plantation, about twenty-eight miles to the north of Brisbane, and half a mile eastward of the Gympie road. There was a man came to me and asked me for a job; and I wanted an extra man for a fortnight, and so I put him on. He told me he came from Victoria, and he had spent all his money at Gympie, and so he had to take the first job he could get. I put him on, and did not ask him his name for a day or two. Two men came down and asked me for a job, and they saw him and said, "Why, here is Arthur Orton." After then I asked him his name. He gave me a name, but it was not Arthur Orton. I said to him, "The men that were here yesterday called you Arthur Orton," and he said, "That is my name; but I do not want everyone to know it."

I entered that name in a book. He stopped with me two weeks, and I gave him fifteen shillings per week and rations. I thought, as the Trial comes off next month, I should have given evidence before the Commissioner of the Supreme Court, but I found that would be of no use unless there was a Counsel appointed by the opposite side to cross-examine me. I have just written these few lines as I thought the information I know might be of some value to the Claimant. I wish I had written before; but still I was persuaded by some of my friends to write and let you know, and I have done so.—I remain, yours truly, C. Ballanger.

P.S. I swear that this man answered the description Dr. Wheeler gave of Arthur Orton.

As the statement of the Claimant at Swansea alludes to the Sealed Packet, we think this a convenient place to insert an extract from the Englishman for May 16, 1874, being No. 6. It should be read in conjunction with Mr. Onslow's letter, printed *ante* page 112.

TICHBORNE.

Mr. Guildford Onslow has printed a volume entitled Tichborne, from which we make the following extracts. It is a work of great value and interest, and will be for ever referred to as containing indubitable records, under the hand of a gentleman of the highest and purest honour, who has studied this question more than any living man, and whose opinions, supported as they are by the documents herein given, *must* carry conviction to the minds of all who have not prejudged, but who read with honest minds, anxious to learn only truth. This, however, we fear the majority of the anti-Tichborne faction are too indolent to do. We, ourselves, know that when Tichborne, in a fatal moment, and after the strongest importunities, and even threats, that ever were brought to bear upon a man, consented to write the substance of the Sealed Packet, the instant he had completed the copy, and handed it to his lawyer, he laid his head down upon the table, and bursting into tears, exclaimed—"*Now I am disgraced for ever: I shall never be able to hold my head up again in Hampshire.*" His sensitiveness on this matter was curiously illustrated at the first consultation which he had with his Counsel in the presence of Lord Rivers, Mr. Onslow, Mr. MacMahon, and Mr. Hendricks (at that time his Solicitor). The question of Lady R. was discussed, and his leading Counsel having used an observation not highly complimentary to that lady, Tichborne, quite unconsciously, as it would seem, half rose from the chair, as if with the design of striking Dr. Kenealy, but immediately, by a most violent effort, restrained, and threw himself back—the whole thing being the gesture of a rapid moment, and so evidently the impulse of the fiery Tichborne blood, which could not brook an irreverent allusion to one of the Family, that it produced a most powerful influence on the mind of Dr. Kenealy that the man before him was indeed the cousin; and that his almost irrepressible movement against his Counsel was one of offended rage and pride, which he checked only by the most powerful self-effort. The recollection of this vivid incident never can be removed: and it was one of the reasons why Dr. Kenealy never, during the whole Trial, said a word against Lady Radcliffe in the presence of the man who had thus manifested such violent emotion.

THE HISTORY OF THE SEALED PACKET.

Shortly after the meeting between Gosford and the Claimant, the former spoke about a sealed packet, given him by Mr. Roger Tichborne, and said that if he was that person he must know the contents; the conversation was reported to Counsel, they immediately had an interview with the Claimant, and told him *he must* write down the contents of the said secret packet. Not with a view to publicity, but that the Counsel for the Claimant might challenge Gosford to place in a sealed letter the contents of the sealed packet, and on comparing it with the written statement of the Claimant, if correct, they would secure a verdict for him. The Claimant, under the solemn pledge of secrecy, wrote his version of it. His solicitor, who was present at the meeting, took this document home. Very shortly after, Mr. B. happened to call, and the solicitor asked Mr. B. to put his initials to it, which he refused to do until he had read it. In a few days the whole was divulged by some one in the hunting field in Hampshire, much to the Claimant's horror and disgust, and he stated at the time that he never would trust any one after that; the consequence was the test which had been proposed fell to the ground.

Time went on, and when the Claimant was cross-examined, his Counsel told him if he did not reply when asked the contents of the packet they would get up and leave the Court. He replied, then, "Get up and leave the Court, for I will never divulge the secret I hold most sacred." But pressed for a reply by Judge Bovill, he said, "Let the responsibility then fall on your shoulders, *not mine.*"

How I Knew Him.

In the month of September, 1867, I met the Claimant at the house of a gentleman in Hampshire, on the occasion of a shooting party. I had about one hour's conversation with him before we started; the first word I said was, "Your face is very familiar to me, and although much stouter, I recognize you." Upon which he said, "I don't remember you. I knew your brother very well; he had a peculiar nickname which I have forgotten, and I have often thought of him." I mentioned five or six nick-names, and he picked out the right, rather a peculiar one. He described my brother's personal appearance and peculiarities exactly; but he said, "When did I meet *you*?" I said "In France, and once at Tichborne." "France—France!" he said, "then I remember. It was at Boulogne." I said it was. He then said, "It was when I was stopping at my cousin's, Lady Dormer's, in 1847." This was correct. The second time I met him, I said, was at Tichborne Park. This he did not remember, until I told him the circumstances under which I *then* spoke to him, and he said he remembered it, adding, "Your father was driving a pair of ponies," which was a fact. We proceeded on our shooting excursion. Feeling much interested in the man, I began to think of some former incident by which I could test him. One occurred to me. Knowing the propensity his father, Sir James Tichborne, had of swearing, especially when out shooting, and there was a dispute about who killed, I formed the following plan to see if he recognized it. The party, consisting of four, walked in line down a turnip field, a bird rose, the Claimant killed it, upon which I ran up and said, "Oh, this is Roger's bird!" using the exact oaths Sir James used to do, mimicking his manner; on which he burst out laughing, and said, "Oh! I see what you are at; you are taking off my poor father; *but you ought to say, Really, really.*" The party, who knew Sir James well, immediately exclaimed, "Ah! that's just what he used to say."

This anecdote I mentioned to one of the Tichborne Family, who exclaimed, throwing up his hands, "Why he must be the real man, for that is perfectly true." Since that day I have been most intimate with the Claimant—he in my house, I in his, talking of bygone days, and bygone scenes—anecdotes of his Family, *their oddities and peculiarities.* Over a cigar in my smoking-room we have passed many an hour, full of anecdote—full of fun. I always found him exhibit a perfect knowledge of his Family and their ways; and a most amusing companion have I ever found him.

He often used to shoot with me. I found him perfectly up to all the rules of the field, and a fair game shot, although above the average at the pigeon trap. Whilst shooting together he used to relate sporting anecdotes; and places where they occurred, at or near Tichborne. He told me he found more hares *in the "Crawl,"* for instance, than any other place; the spot where the snipe laid in the Tichborne meadows; the places at Colmore where he shot in the coverts; how he rolled over the hares in crossing, from certain points; who used to shoot with him, &c., &c., all of which was correct. His knowledge about *Savernake Forest* was correct and extraordinary. One day whilst at luncheon under a hedge on the top of Burgnor-hill, which commands a perfect panorama of Hampshire, I questioned him as to all the points of view, purposely pretending I did not know the names, when in reality I knew every gate and hedge-row in the country. I first pointed to a fine avenue of yew-trees, and asked him what place it was. He said immediately it was a meet of the H. H.—which it was—called "the Old House." I asked him what old house. He said he had forgotten the name; but it once belonged to a family connected with the BARINGS; and immediately said "*Chilton Old House.*" He said the owner was a nobleman some hundred years ago. Here he was wrong as to its belonging to the BARINGS, *but right as to the nobleman*, and right as to its being the meet of the H. H. It is *now* a property of the BARINGS. I asked him, "When you found a fox there, where did he run to?" He said, "We never found a fox *there*, but had to go over the hill to Chilton-wood, which lies some couple of miles off." In this he was perfectly correct. He pointed out every headland correctly. His knowledge of Hampshire in 1867 was nearly as accurate as my own. Since that day we have shot together in Surrey and Hampshire, and many startling incidents have occurred, all proving his unmistakable identity with ROGER TICHBORNE. He has given me most accurate descriptions of men long since dead, *whom we both knew*, especially about my father, whom he knew well, and who died in 1861. He and I were once shown a caricature of a Hampshire gentleman, done by D'ORSAY, *very like in features to my father*. The Claimant on seeing it said, "That is your poor father, ONSLOW!" and I thought it was at the first glance; but it was not. Upon which the Claimant immediately said, "Oh no, *that's* LONG, *of Preshaw*," and so it was. Now, my father never had a picture taken of him, and had been dead since 1861. I was much struck with the ability with which the Claimant threw his fly out fishing. I followed him often down the river, and was astonished at the way he knew every spot of it where to find a trout. Every nook and corner and hole he pointed out to me, and showed me spots I had forgotten where he used to put his landing net in and take out trout. But he said the best place for that was a place called the *Tichborne Jar*. Now, this Tichborne Jar was in the meadows at the back of Borough Bridge, destroyed by the railroad. No one, I believe, but JOHN DOREY, waterman, and myself living, knew of that place. The Claimant described it exactly. It was a hole bricked all over, used for the purposes of irrigation. There are few men who can beat me in fly-fishing in the Itchen; and I call the Claimant one of the best I have met with. He knew every Hampshire fly, calling them by their proper names; for instance, *the dark, the light hare's ear*, the red spinner, the orange dun, and the coachman. I asked him where he got his flies from when in England. He said, "I bought my flies of a man in Winchester." On one occasion I asked him if he belonged to any of the London Clubs. He said "Yes—the Army and Navy." I said, "Who proposed you?" He said, "I think I was proposed by CUSTANCE, and seconded by either FOSTER or a Colonel HARVEY." "And when you went abroad, who paid your subscriptions?" He said, "Old HUBBARD's son-in-law, by desire of my father." Some time after this, I went to the Army and Navy Club with the late Sir JOHN SIMEON, M.P., and we looked over books of the Club, and found Mr. ROGER TICHBORNE a member in 1852 (I think), presumably drowned in 1854; proposed by Captain CUSTANCE and seconded by Captain FOSTER. On another occasion, at a large dinner-party at a club, the conversation turned upon the opinion as to which was the best club in London. Some said one; some another; the Claimant, when "WHITE'S" was mentioned, said, "Ah, that was my father's Club, and he was very proud of belonging to it." I said, "No; your father was not a member of WHITE'S, was he?" He said, "Yes; it is on the right hand side as you walk up St. James's-street." I said no more at the time; but the next day I walked up St. James's-street, and asked him to point out to me his father's Club. Upon which he immediately pointed to BOODLE'S Club, and said, "That was my father's;" and so, in fact, it was; and he added, "I used to live *in that street opposite*." I have since found this also correct. I have frequently taken him to the House of Commons, and have introduced him to members; and, on one occasion, Captain GOSSETT invited him into his private rooms for smoking. On all occasions my friends in the House have said, "I don't know who your friend is, *but he is a gentleman*." And my experience of him, after seven years' close intimacy, is, that he is not only a gentleman in manner, *but in mind also*. He can converse on every topic; is at home on all occasions; and I have heard him make a speech on Colonial Government that lasted over one hour, at Swansea, that would not disgrace a Cabinet Minister. His kind, engaging manner in the drawing-room with ladies is most remarkable, and his voice and manner is strikingly like the TICHBORNES.

He is wonderfully like the late Sir ALFRED TICHBORNE and the late Sir HENRY TICHBORNE in face and manners. I find him a capital chess-player. He perfectly understands the gambits of chess. A remarkably good ecarté player. His ear for music is good; he can hear a tune in the street, and then pick it off on the piano; a very good and scientific painter, he is an excellent judge of pictures. I introduced him to Lady BURRARD, who is an excellent artist, and paints well; she showed him her paintings, upon which he immediately entered into all the particulars of the art; *the mixing of colours*, and his opinions on colour, &c., &c., much to the amusement and delight of the lady.

He is an excellent rider, and when he first came to this country I lent him a horse, up to his weight, then 18 stone *only*, and I am told he astonished the natives in a good thing across the stiffest part of the old Surrey country, and a well-known London horse-dealer offered him £300 for the horse he was riding. His knowledge of the immediate neighbourhood of Tichborne is remarkable. He has taken me *to out-of-the-way trees* to show me where he carved his name years ago, and there it was, R.C.T., thus showing to my mind that it was not only in Australia where he was in the habit of carving and cutting his name. I remember well one evening, after a day's shooting in 1870, whilst at dinner in my house at Ropley, Mrs. ONSLOW asking him what wine he would drink. He said *not any*. We pressed him to have some champagne, but he declined; so I said, "TICHBORNE, now what wine do you like best?" upon which he replied, "Well, I confess I have a weakness for Madeira." I was delighted, for I had some 53 years old. I immediately ordered a bottle, and I said, "What do you think of that?" He replied, "*capital!* but I think I have tasted this before." I said, "*Never.*" He said, "Well, I think I have tasted it at Tichborne; it is very like the wine that HOPKINS sent some of to my father.' Upon which I immediately said, "*I bought that wine of Mr.* HOPKINS, *at his sale.*"

During the seven years of my acquaintance with the Claimant I have never heard an oath or coarse word pass his lips, except *once*, when he denounced JEAN LUIE as a plant put upon him; I have never heard an angry word against his family; he has always spoken of them in the kindest manner, and, as I flatter myself I know what a gentleman is, *I say I never met a kinder, more amiable, gentlemanlike, agreeable man in society in the whole course of my life.* He is extremely proud and tenacious, and easily put out by imagined slights and coldness of manner, but always behaves like a gentleman under these circumstances, and I have seen him tried pretty severely, more than I could have stood, by those who have shown him they suspected he was an impostor. He takes the lead in conversation at dinner-parties, discussing freely politics, religion, foreign travel, *often quoting in good French.* He will talk of BYRON, and SHELLEY, and SHAKESPEARE; and he is remarkably clever in pointing out how things are manufactured and made. I remember on one occasion, whilst standing on the steps of the Travellers' Club, having called on a friend in the club, the Claimant passed by; he said, "ONSLOW, what club is that you have just come out of?" I said, "Why? what do you know of this club?" He said, "I think I belong to it." I said, "How is that?" He said, "If it is the club I think it is, there is a rule in that club that a candidate must travel a certain distance, which distance I had not accomplished till I got to South America, when I wrote to my uncle, DANDY SEYMOUR, to put my name down." I said, "Do you remember the name of the club?" He said, "No." I said, "It is the Traveller's Club;" upon which he said, "Oh yes! it was," and added, "*I think I must have been a member.*" In a letter produced in Court, this story of the Claimant was proved to be correct.

We next find the Claimant at Sunderland, which he visited on Monday, July 15.

SIR ROGER'S VISIT TO SUNDERLAND.

At the Monkwearmouth Terminus of the North-Eastern Railway, on Monday last, several thousands of persons, of both sexes, assembled early in the morning, in anticipation of the Claimant's arrival. The arrangements made for his reception were very praiseworthy to all concerned, the public being carefully kept without the outer gates. A few minutes before the time at which the train was due, a carriage and pair was driven up to the porch for the convenience of the Claimant and his friends, followed by a break, containing the members of the Sunderland Defence Committee; the latter were greeted with cheers. Precisely at 12.35 the train entered the station, and the Claimant and Mr. GUILDFORD ONSLOW, M.P., were received by the Committee. On entering the conveyances provided for them, they were tremendously cheered. Arriving at the Committee Rooms, Mr. MORRIS's, Crown Inn, High-street West, many thousands were there assembled. With little trouble the Claimant and his friends were speedily enabled to gain an entrance. The loud cheers of the public were such that in a few minutes the Claimant was compelled to emerge from the window on to the leads, where he was greeted with a hearty reception.

After thanking the crowd very sincerely for this very warm welcome and reception, Sir ROGER assured them that he felt highly gratified at being supported by the many thousands of those by whom he was surrounded. It would encourage him to defend his rights to the very utmost for the sake of his wife and family of children, whom he loved. (Cheers.)

Mr. GUILDFORD ONSLOW, M.P., stepped forward, and said it gave the greatest pleasure and gratification to himself and to Sir ROGER C. D. TICHBORNE to see so many thousands around him. (Cheers.) It showed him the intellectual mind of the people of the North. (Loud cheers.) He had every confidence in the British public, and without the sympathy of the British public, how many others would not be crushed in like manner with the Claimant?

After some remarks from Mr. ALLEN and Mr. ROBINSON, the party retired.

Mr. WILLIAM WILLIAMS then read an address of welcome to the Claimant from the Committee of the Sunderland Defence Fund.

The CLAIMANT wished to return them his very sincere thanks for the trouble they had taken on his behalf. (Applause.) When he addressed himself to the British public he was lying in the dismal cells of Newgate. He had too much confidence in the

British public to think that they would allow him to lie there. (Cheers.) The speech of the Attorney-General, he said, entirely led away the jury, when, without waiting for the evidence of the witnesses, or the reply of Serjeant BALLANTINE and Mr. GIFFARD, he made some remarks as to the tattoo marks, which had never been mentioned until after the conclusion of his examination. (Cheers.) There was no justification for the Judge in sending him to Newgate. (Shame.) He was sent to gaol under power of a clause inserted in an Act of Parliament late one night last autumn, when no doubt they knew what they had arranged to do with him. The Attorney-General was night after night going down to dine with his (the Claimant's) relations. Was that a proper thing? Was it right for a Judge trying a case to dine day after day with the friends of the Defendants, while he was trying the case between them and the Plaintiff? He again thanked them for the trouble and loss of time they had experienced in taking up his case, and he could assure them that they would never regret having done anything in his behalf. (Immense applause.)

Mr. WILLIAMS then at some length proposed the thanks of the Sunderland Defence Committee to Mr. GUILDFORD ONSLOW, who had taken so great an interest in the affairs of the Claimant.

Mr. GUILDFORD ONSLOW, M.P., was sincerely thankful for the honour they had done him in mentioning his name in connection with that of Sir ROGER C. D. TICHBORNE. (Cheers.) He was amply repaid for all his labours by the kind words that had fallen from the gentleman who had just spoken. It was true they had been left in the cold by the aristocracy, with the exception of Lord RIVERS, Lord STAMFORD, and one or two others; but they had been supported by the middle and lower classes, whom he had never known to be wrong. (Loud cheers.)

Mr. HENSHALL, Vice-Chairman, then presented the Claimant with a coloured photograph of the Committee of the Sunderland Defence Fund.

The Claimant, in accepting the handsome present, said he would assure them when he was placed in possession of his paternal estates, he would only be too happy to place it under the great Dole picture at Tichborne. (Cheers.)

The meeting then separated, and the Claimant and Committee returned to the Royal Hotel, at which place he resided during his stay in Sunderland.

At four o'clock the Claimant, the Committee, and friends sat down to an excellent repast, provided by the worthy host (Mr. CAWTHORNE), Mr. JAMES FRAZER being in the chair. After the dinner was over, the company adjourned to the Victoria Hall, Toward-road, Bishopwearmouth, where nearly 3,000 persons were assembled. On the appearance of Sir ROGER and his friends the hall re-echoed with the repeated plaudits of those assembled.

Mr. J. C. MCINTOSH (Newcastle) was appointed Chairman, and after a brief address called upon Mr. RENWICK (brewer), who in a warm speech proposed the following resolution:—"That this meeting, believing that the Claimant has had an unfair trial, expresses strongly its disapprobation of his being thrust into gaol before he was proved to be guilty."

Mr. HENSHALL seconded the resolution, which was carried with but one dissentient.

Mr. GUILDFORD ONSLOW, who was received with immense cheering, spoke at great length in support of the Claimant's case.

Mr. W. WILLIAMS then moved, "That this meeting is of opinion that it is a great injustice to the people of England that money should be taken from the taxes of the country to prosecute a defenceless man—the Claimant to the Tichborne Estates."

Mr. POTTS briefly seconded the motion.

The Claimant then came forward, and in an exhaustive speech, similar to those delivered at Newcastle, supported the resolution, which was received with applause.

Mr. ONSLOW proposed a vote of thanks to the Chairman, which was carried by acclamation, and briefly acknowledged; after which the meeting separated amid great enthusiasm.

SECOND PUBLIC MEETING.

On Tuesday night a meeting was held in the Victoria Hall, Toward-road, Bishopwearmouth. Mr. J. C. MCINTOSH, of Newcastle, again presided. The hall, as on the previous night, was filled to overflowing by a sympathizing audience.

The Chairman, in opening the meeting, referring to the Claimant's forgetfulness of the French language, stated that when he was young he was taught Pitman's phonetic shorthand, and now to save his life, he could not make out a single sentence. (Cheers.)

Mr. T. G. RENWICK, who moved, "That this meeting strongly censures that highly-paid member of the Government—the Attorney-General, for undertaking for pecuniary gain private cases, which require so much of the time that should be devoted to the duties of his office," said it behoved them to unite firmly and endeavour to obtain for this man, be he whom he might, a fair and honest trial. (Cheers.)

Mr. JAMES FRAZER, contractor, briefly seconded the resolution.

The Chairman then called upon Mr. G. ONSLOW, M.P., who was received with deafening cheers, which were continued for some time. His only object in addressing them was to see that justice was done to his friend Sir ROGER CHARLES D. TICHBORNE. (Cheers.) In doing this he had sacrificed almost everything excepting the good opinion of his constituents of the borough of Guildford. (Hear, hear.) So long, however, as he retained that goodwill, and the satisfaction of his own conscience, he cared for little else. (Cheers.) He commented at some length upon some of the evidence given at the Trial, remarking that the Attorney-General was paid at the rate of three shillings and fourpence per minute for talking. (Shame.) It had been asserted by some of the Press that he held TICHBORNE bonds, and was thus interested in the Case. This he denied. (Cheers.) He had never in his life seen a TICHBORNE bond, and would willingly give a shilling to any man who would gratify him with the sight of one. (Cheers.) The speaker continued to relate numerous anecdotes connected with the Case, which were received with great enthusiasm.

Dr. DONKIN said that he was a sympathizer with the Claimant until one morning he found in the newspapers that the Claimant had said that JULIUS CÆSAR was a Greek, VIRGIL was a Greek, and EUCLID had nothing to do with mathematics. He wanted an explanation of these terrible mistakes on the part of a man who had been sent into a college to be educated among educated men. (Cheers.)

The Claimant, who was loudly cheered, said it was very easy for hundreds of persons to look over the evidence given in 103 days, and pick out certain points to ask him to explain. (Cheers.) While in the box his brain was completely turned and muddled. (Cheers.)

Mr. ONSLOW then said that if Sir ROGER had, when in the box, answered those questions by saying "I know nothing about it," he would have done right—(cheers)—but he had been so badgered by the Attorney-General that he became indignant, and did not care what he said.

The Claimant then rose, and after the prolonged cheering with which he was greeted had subsided, he at considerable length reviewed the evidence given against him, as on previous occasions.

The Chairman proposed a vote of thanks to Mr. ONSLOW, who had taken so much trouble in placing this case before the public, and who was now compelled to leave them.

Mr. ONSLOW replied, and moved a vote of thanks to the Chairman and to the local Committee, who had done their work so well.

This was carried by acclamation, and the meeting separated.

THE CLAIMANT AT LEEDS.

On the 22nd, of July, the Claimant visited Leeds; we append extracts from the papers, as to his movements at this period:—

Sir ROGER arrived in Leeds on Monday afternoon. From noon until midnight excited crowds congregated, first in the vicinity of the Queen's Hotel, and then in the neighbourhood of the Town Hall. Indeed, the hotel in question was surrounded by large crowds anxious to award him a hearty welcome. Several hundreds among the crowd appeared to be satisfied that the Claimant is in very truth Sir ROGER TICHBORNE, and the enthusiasm of this section of the public was overflowing.

At half-past seven a dense crowd had gathered around the Queen's Hotel, the horses were removed from the coach standing at the door for the conveyance of the TICHBORNE party to the Town Hall, and the Claimant, Mr. ONSLOW, M.P., and Mr. WHALLEY, M.P., having taken their seats in it, the vehicle was dragged along Boar-lane, up Briggate, up Upperhead-row, and down Park-lane to the Calverley-street entrance of the hall. All along the route an excited multitude accompanied the procession, which was preceded by a brass band. Cheer after cheer rose from the surging masses of people. At the Town Hall thousands had gathered to witness the arrival of the party; and it was with the utmost difficulty a passage could be forced to the middle of Calverley-street, and when that was effected, only by great exertions did the party succeed in making their way from the coach to the hall-door.

In the Victoria Hall about 1,500 persons had assembled, and when, a few minutes after eight, Sir ROGER, Mr. ONSLOW, M.P., Mr. WHALLEY, M.P., and the Leeds TICHBORNE Defence Committee came into the hall, they were accorded a most demonstrative welcome. Mr. J. R. JOY occupied the chair; and he was supported, in addition to the Committee, by the following gentlemen:—Councillor BLAKELY, Mr. A. K. DOBSON, Mr. F. A. PILLING, Mr. J. GREENWOOD, Sergeant-Major JAMES MARKS, Sergeant-Major TIMOTHY MARKS, Mr. J. T. DODGSON, Mr. WILLIAM MORLEY, Mr. R. WALKER, Mr. A. HOLBROOK, Mr. JOHN RIPLEY, Mr. PETER LAYCOCK, Mr. W. WILKINSON, Mr. J. K. ROWBOTHAM.

The Chairman opened the proceedings in a speech delivered with great energy of manner. He remarked that he felt very proud to see so many Yorkshire ladies and gentlemen present, and he felt personally, after seeing such enormous crowds through the streets, that it spoke well for the success of Sir ROGER TICHBORNE. He fiercely denounced the articles which had appeared in the *Leeds Mercury* and *Yorkshire Post* against Sir ROGER. (Loud groans for the *Mercury* and *Post*.) The conductors of the *Mercury* believed that its power was so great that none were "sufficiently strong enough" and daring enough to stand against it. They believed that the Leeds people had all become "mercurialized" through its effect and influence; but he would say that they were not to be so blinded and led by the nose. (Cheers.) They believed that all Englishmen had a power and a right to think for themselves, in spite of all the threats of the officials of the Government, and in spite of the emissaries they had thought proper to throw broadcast through the land, to stab in the dark like other dark assassins. Mr. JOY went on further to condemn the "scurrilous remarks which had been introduced in that infamous paper, the *Leeds Mercury*," and charged the "upper ten of the country" with "arraying themselves as a mighty army against Sir ROGER TICHBORNE and his supporters," without having read or considered the facts of the case. He closed by declaring that all the Leeds TICHBORNE Defence Committee wished to see was fair play. They wished to join with the poet, who said:—

" 'Tis not the voice of vain applause
That we would court: a holier cause—
The cause of Freedom, Justice, Truth,
Shall crown our age, or drain our youth."

—(Loud cheering.)

Mr. E. FOSTER moved the following resolution:—"That this meeting views with disgust and indignation the conduct of the Attorney-General, and of a large section of the press of the country, and especially of this town, in denouncing the Claimant as an impostor, perjurer, forger, &c., without proof, and in assuming his guilt before trial, as not only unjust but indecent, and contrary to the spirit of the British law, which always assumes a man to be innocent before he is proved to be guilty." He also denounced the *Mercury* and *Post* in yet more unmeasured terms than the Chairman, declaring the latter to be in its dotage, and referring to the editor as "an old Tory idiot," while he said that the editor of the *Mercury*, being unable to argue, had tried to sneer. ("Hear, hear," and cheers.) A man must have brains to argue, but any fool could sneer. (Applause.) The editor of the *Mercury* had complained that the Claimant was going about exhibiting himself for money; but that editor wrote unfair and scurrilous articles, not fit to read, for money. ("Hear, hear," and loud cheers.) He finished by expressing his regret that the two papers had become the feeble, contemptible, degraded things they saw them to be. (Vehement cheering.)

Mr. W. J. DIXON, a newspaper compositor, seconded the resolution, stating that he did so for two reasons. One was that he believed the cause was just, and the other was that he was a fellow-countryman and almost a fellow-townsman of the Claimant, and therefore thought it was his duty to stand by him.

Mr. WHALLEY, M.P., next addressed the meeting, and declared that the *Mercury* was endangering the cause of the Bible by its sickening, maudlin, miserable pretence of morality, combined with its treatment of the question. The whole fabric of morality and Christianity, he repeated, was endangered by Mr. BAINES and the *Mercury* in their attempts to divert the mind of Leeds from this simple question—ought the Claimant to have a fair trial or not? Mr. WHALLEY proceeded to avow his determination to ask his good friend Mr. BAINES in the House of Commons—which could not be better occupied than in listening to the reply—how he dared to use the great power given to him to pervert that simple question. He was able to declare, on the most positive evidence that any man ever received, or that could be conceived of, that the Claimant was the man he claimed to be. He would further say that in the House of Commons, where he had brought the matter forward, he believed there was now scarcely to be found one man who would venture to say he was not the man, or would question the fact that he was the man. Mr. WHALLEY went on to assert that never had there been for generations in the Hall of Tichborne a man more worthy of its occupation, in every relation of life—barring accidents and incidents respecting which none of them would throw the first stone—than the Claimant; not one in the memory of living man or in tradition had been more heartily welcomed in Hampshire. He proceeded to describe how the Claimant had descended from the higher circles of society to the "refreshing cold" of the lowest depths, and had come thence braced and invigorated to assert a right as sacred for Englishmen as that which JOHN HAMPDEN, his (Mr. WHALLEY's) ancestor, had asserted. But what had the Claimant done in those lowest depths? What had he done in Australia? Mr. WHALLEY had made it his business to inquire, and he was able to declare "that there never went forth from England to the wild parts of the Empire a man who did more good, promoted more happiness, prevented more misery, or carried into the darkest parts of the Empire the powers of civilisation in a more benevolent and beneficent system of action then the man before them." In a still higher flight of oratory, Mr. WHALLEY described the Claimant as having been a good angel among the people of the Australian wilds. The language which the Attorney-General had used during his twenty-six days' speech at the Trial had degraded and sullied the English bar, and—he was sorry to say it—had sullied the ermine of the Judge who tried the Case. But all this abuse was the necessity of the Attorney-General's case. He had no case except to abuse the Claimant. The tattoo evidence, according to his (Mr. WHALLEY's) information, had been given up, and without the abuse the whole conspiracy—a gigantic conspiracy, extending more widely and deeply than their imaginations could yet realise—could not have existed. The speaker next alluded to a remark made by Sir ANDREW FAIRBAIRN, to the effect that Lord RIVERS had withdrawn a statement he had made favourable to the Claimant. Mr. WHALLEY proceeded to offer a solemn warning to Sir ANDREW FAIRBAIRN, and the class to which he belongs, that they were making a great mistake in not joining the movement for securing a fair trial to the Claimant. They were trifling with "this great question of the TICHBORNE Claimant," respecting which there was a strong feeling amongst the working classes,—a "God-inspired movement." Mr. WHALLEY closed by adverting to his Parliamentary effort on behalf of the Claimant, and declared that the language of Mr. LOWE when applied to for the costs of conducting the defence had compelled Mr. ONSLOW and himself to join in the appeal that was now being made to the country.

Mr. G. ONSLOW, M.P., addressed the meeting at great length, devoting his remarks entirely to the circumstances of the Trial, and the facts of the Case. He was very emphatic in his condemnation of the jury for having accepted the testimony of half a dozen witnesses with handles to their names in preference to that of eighty-six witnesses for the Plaintiff. If they could have got two or three lords, a couple of dukes, and half a dozen bishops to speak for them, they would have carried the day. The Attorney-General, he remarked, took a fee of £6,000 out of the Tichborne estate, and then attempted to make his hearers believe that he was shedding tears. Counsel, after they had received £6,000, did not shed tears. (Laughter.) Mr. ONSLOW commented on the facts of the Case, citing various circumstances in which evidence was given during the Trial, and others that had since been discovered, as proofs that the Claimant must be Sir ROGER TICHBORNE. He referred to various marks about his body; the difference between his legs; his recognition by his Mother, whom he described as having been of a most suspicious turn of mind; his recognition by his Solicitor; and by a large number of persons who had been in constant intercourse with him before he left this country. He also showed, from the bad grammar of a letter of Sir ROGER before he left Europe, that he never either learnt French or English properly. He also stated that he himself had once gone upon the Continent for 17 years, and when he came back scarcely anyone knew him. In reference to the Claimant's evidence regarding his cousin, Mrs. RADCLIFFE, Mr. ONSLOW said the Claimant had refused to reveal the contents of the sealed packet till his Counsel threatened to throw up the cause, and then, having to choose between penal servitude, with starvation for his children on the one hand, and telling the truth on the other, he took the latter alternative. He denied that Sir ROGER had had anything to do with the pocket-book containing the famous remark that "some people had brains and no money, and others money and no brains," &c.

The Claimant, whom the audience by this time (10.30) had become impatient to hear, was next called upon to speak, and his rising was the signal for long and protracted cheers. Having repeated some of the remarks he had made at the banquet, he said that there were two charges of perjury and two of forgery against him, and he would have to meet them. He had fourteen or fifteen marks on his body which proved his identity. The Judge who heard his case declared some ten or twelve days after the Trial had commenced, at a Lord Mayor's banquet, that he (the Claimant) was the greatest impostor that had ever come to England. How could he expect to get justice from such a Judge? ("Hear, hear," and cheers.) Then, Lord Chief Justice COCKBURN, who had said four years before that he was a rank impostor, was frequently seen on the Bench talking to Chief Justice BOVILL—no doubt to his (the Claimant's) detriment. When he had said to the latter, "My Lord, it seems to me the other side don't require counsel while they have got you," he hoped to be sent to prison at once, in order that his case might be taken up by the public. He concluded by asking how he could possibly defend himself against the persecution levelled at him, unless assisted by his countrymen. (Loud cheers.)

Serjeant-Major MARKS, evidently a shrewd, straightforward, and honest man, next described his first meeting with the Claimant. He knew him in a moment to be Sir ROGER TICHBORNE, who was for three years attached to the same corps of the Carabineers as himself, and with whom during the three years he had close intercourse for an hour or two every day.

The resolution was subsequently adopted, and the proceedings terminated about half-past eleven. Crowds still surrounded the Town Hall and the Queen's Hotel, and not until after midnight did they clear away from the latter place.

On Wednesday night there was another meeting, equally crowded and enthusiastic. Speeches were delivered by Mr. ONSLOW, Mr. WHALLEY, and the Claimant, supported by many persons of local influence.

BANQUET TO SIR ROGER.

On Tuesday, Sir ROGER was entertained by the Leeds Defence Committee to a banquet at the Queen's Hotel. About sixty or seventy persons sat down to an excellent and admirably-served repast. Mr. J. R. JOY occupied the chair, and Mr. H. R. PULING the vice-chair. After the toast of the Queen had been heartily honoured, the Chairman proposed "Health and success to Sir ROGER TICHBORNE." (Vehement and prolonged applause.) He (the Chairman) stoutly contended that the Claimant was the victim of a foul conspiracy, and that on the part of the aristocracy, from whom better things might have been expected. The opposition to the Claimant was founded solely on two things—ignorance and prejudice. (Cheers.) He had not a particle of doubt but the gentleman on his left hand was Sir ROGER TICHBORNE. (Loud applause.) The Vice-Chairman having expressed the opinion that the Claimant had not had fair-play, and declared that he was satisfied that he was the veritable Sir ROGER, asked, "If he be not Sir ROGER, who is he?" (Loud cheers.) The toast was then drunk amid much acclamation, followed by musical honours. The Claimant then rose to respond, and after the applause with which he was greeted had somewhat subsided, he expressed his deep appreciation of the warm reception his Leeds friends had accorded him. He had not come to prove his identity; he would leave that to the process of the law. He had come to ask them as Englishmen to help him to secure that fair-play to which every Englishman was entitled. (Cheers.) He thought an impostor would have hesitated before attempting the task he had attempted with such small means. (Cheers.) He had said he had not come to prove his identity, but if he had he did not think a better place than that could be found, for he saw before him some who had been his comrades in the army. He would say, too, that he entertained a different opinion of the British soldier to that expressed by the Attorney-General, who had said that a soldier could be bought for a pot of beer. He thought that if the Attorney General were right in his opinion, then England was trusting to a reed in her defence. He concluded by saying that he should feel it his bounden duty to endeavour to answer any question which might be put to him, either that evening or the next day in the Town Hall.

A gentleman who endeavoured to make some remarks was ruled out of order.

Mr. FOSTER then proposed the healths of Mr. ONSLOW, M.P., and Mr. WHALLEY, M.P., and these gentlemen having responded, the proceedings shortly afterwards terminated.

We insert in this place (it being in the order of time) a powerful letter, addressed to Mr. GLADSTONE by Mr. WILLIAM COBBETT.

A LETTER TO THE PRIME MINISTER ON THE ADMINISTRATION OF THE LAW AS EXHIBITED IN THE TICHBORNE CASE.

SIR,—The great meeting at Millwall, held on July 6, passed by acclamation the resolution moved by Messrs. J. BOWLEY and G. COOK, "That this meeting is unanimous that the Claimant is Sir ROGER CHARLES DOUGHTY TICHBORNE, Bart.; and is also of opinion that the gentlemen of the bar in connection with the late Trial have not done their duty."

That resolution was nothing more than the universal verdict of the country at large, which has been guided by the safe principle that the Mother ought to know her own child; which principle had been so incontestibly confirmed by the evidences which had satisfied the Mother—viz., the brown mark on the side, and the Brighton card-case, and for the unanswerable reason, that if these were not proofs, they would have been disproofs of the identity which was the object of the Claimant to establish. The Mother naturally was satisfied with the reference to the brown mark, because, though she confessed she did not recollect it, yet the referring to it must have been as convincing as if she did. Then what passed on both sides as to the card-case, of course obliged the absolute faith of the public: because when the son only names the card-case without any word to indicate the circumstances, the Mother could not have replied as she did, indicating her knowledge of the circumstances, if those circumstances did not belong to a transaction in which the two had participated. Consequently the Attorney-General's argument, drawn from the fact (if it be a fact) that there was no record of the Dowager having drawn or raised the money which she must have required for the purpose, does not touch the point: besides which, the sort of argument has no basis, because the Dowager may have had means to raise the sum required without a record; and, indeed, her own remark and caution prove she would have chosen to resort to such unknown means.

Therefore, for such incontrovertible proofs to be met by such objections as that lately taken by Dr. DONKIN at Sunderland (on July 16), that on the cross-examination the Claimant confounded Latin with Greek, is altogether unreasonable, and of itself only proves that the Doctor himself is not learned in the superlative degree, as he is opposing that which is inconclusive and only matter of opinion, to what is conclusive and not matter of opinion. The very same objection was offered to me by the lad serving in a stationer's shop, no doubt a sharpish lad, and who had not forgotten the rudiments he had been taught; and I would suggest the same answer to the Doctor that I did to the shop-boy—that the not knowing the difference between the Roman letters and the Greek characters was only a good proof that the ORTON charge was unfounded, seeing that no butcher's boy in London would make that mistake, as they invariably ride up to the play-bills and monuments and study the announcements and inscriptions; but Mr. ONSLOW gave the Doctor the best answer—that Sir R. ought to have said he knew nothing about either.

Such having been the proofs which decided the Mother and the Public, the Family and the Government have met them by something of an equally decisive character—IF TRUE. The IF therefore, involves the grand secret—a secret that has to be divulged one way or the other, whichever way the reality is, and whatever squeezing and racking the possessors of it may have to undergo before the truth is got out, and the whole truth, too. At present the most we outsiders can do is to trace up the *tattoo story* to its incipiency or ante-birth; even to its ante-embryo state; or to paraphrase DEAN SWIFT in his theological history of snuffling at the nose, where he speaks of the period up to where, as he expresses it "As yet snuffling was not," so we may emphatically predicate as to any known existence of tattoo marks up to, and inclusive of the 11th day of February, 1867, which was within six weeks after the arrival of the Claimant in England, and when Mr. HENRY SEYMOUR, M.P. for Salisbury, journeyed to Alresford, taking the known ROGER's valet, WM. BURDON, with him (first-class), for the express purpose of applying the then known best possible test to the claim of identity made by the then supposed personating ROGER. For with the known real man's late valet in the room, the supposed unreal man is not invited to show his wrists, nor are tattoo marks a subject of, or hinted at in, the conversation, which, as related by Mr. SEYMOUR, was of the coldest and most reserved kind on his part, and ended by his drily observing to the Claimant that he was "very sorry he could not recognize him." But there was a little spice in this gentleman's evidence, for he says that Claimant being questioned to ascertain if he knew who his former valet (aged 36) was? he answered, "My uncle Nangle" (an octogenarian). Thus a mistake utterly incompatible with knowledge of the relationship would be apparent, except that (so unfortunately for the appearance) the omission to have previously greeted the supposed uncle as such would be quite inconsistent with the mistake. Mr. HOPKINS, at whose house the mistake is alleged to have been made, was, at the giving of the evidence, dead; and serious warnings abound in this case against the imprudence of risking an oath which is not corroborated by what cannot be doubted. Indeed, spiciness and present effect has been the essence and aim of the cross-examination and commentaries; and, as the Attorney-General very candidly admitted, his excessively-ingenious and extraordinarily-learned friend and right hand, Mr. HAWKINS, propounded the questions, the pertinence of which was not intended to be seen but rather to be hidden, as traps to propagate topics for speech; and it was rather there, I apprehend, where the functions of a Judge should act, to quash questioning the tendency of which is not apparent; otherwise the function of a jury is to be persuaded, and not informed. However, a moral to be drawn is that such a game is a game played with edge-tools, and with two-edge tools, too.

At any rate, now must date, from and after the 11th February, 1867, the responsibility of the legal profession; because at that time the Defendant's Family acts through one of themselves with their general concurrence, and, if the tattooing were a fact, they suppress the fact, of course on the advice and in the interest of the profession, and in no other interest, but against their own interest, and on the contrary at its peril.

Now, it is too much to affect to believe it possible that parties in possession of property will conspire to be plucked of that property. Therefore, over goes the whole groundwork of the nonsuit, and of the Chancellor of the Exchequer's calling it the "verdict of a jury," as his justification for appropriating public money to prosecute an indictment for perjury, one count for which is for making oath that deponent was not tattooed, and the whole of which is charged on his falsely deposing that he is Sir ROGER CHARLES DOUGHTY TICHBORNE, Baronet, and of which alleged perjury it is intended to convict him by the oaths of witnesses that the rightful person he claims to be, and wrongfully deposes he is, was tattooed.

Having, Sir, devoted this much of pen and ink to resting the main and previous question of the identity as claimed on the incontrovertible grounds, I now proceed to examine the law-proceedings in and connected with this Case in regard to their various irregularities, and to the various remedies open to the Claimant.

Before proceeding to recount the irregularities, there is a preliminary stage which is of the most undoubted necessity—namely, to elucidate the final part acted by the jury. This is necessary, in order to deprive the Judge, the Attorney-General, the Chancellor of the Exchequer, and all others on whose conduct I have to animadvert, of the excuses and pretences for which they seek to creep under the gabardine of the Jury, and with such effrontery and falsehood to charge the Jury with having pronounced or implied a verdict for the Defendant, and therefore against the Plaintiff, and thereby involving his perjury.

To show at once how hollow these pretences are, and how well the Chancellor of the Exchequer knows that a conviction for perjury of the Plaintiff is not probable under the present law, and also to refer to the most hideous feature in the whole case, the Attorney-General, well knowing that there would be no chance of his managing any jury to his mind, has lost no time for bringing in a Bill to revolutionize the law of ALFRED, which was a law to insure justice so far as the jury is concerned. This Bill must have been brought in very sharply after the charge made against the Plaintiff and his imprisonment, which were on the 6th of March; because it was ordered to be printed on the 15th of April. The Bill is intituled, "*A Bill to Amend the Law Relating to Juries.*" It contains one hundred and ten clauses, the last of which, with its marginal note, are—"Act when to come into operation. 110. This Act shall come into operation on the day of 1872"!!!

So that you see, Sir, that "TOM CASTRO," *alias* "ARTHUR ORTON," as he is nicknamed in the indictments, is to be made sure of as a perjurer, &c., &c., by means of a spick and span new jury-law, thus manufactured for the nonce, actually between the making and trying of the charges. And first see, Sir, the adaptability of the manufacture for the purpose; there is to be a mixture of special with common jurors, and all juries, except for trial of murder (the number for which is to continue), are to consist of an uneven number, to wit, seven. One clause is poked in, that verdicts in all cases shall be "unanimous;" but, if so, why is this unnecessary provision *inserted?* It is that it may be struck out, or else why is the uneven number invented for petty juries, and copied from grand juries, in which the purpose of the uneven number is expressly to decide by majority. So that, the intended operation is that when an Attorney-General is in the case, his superior influence shall insure the verdict.

How this particularly daring man, who now fills this

office, got into the office, is a chapter of itself, to which I shall attempt to do justice towards the sequel of this letter; but I must at present attend to what most naturally comes into this place, as it has been made the foundation for all the rest—I mean the conduct of the Jury. That conduct was very unsatisfactory sometimes during the Trial, by the coquettings and impertinent questions on the part of some of the individual jurors, but which improprieties were the fault of the Judge, and of the Counsel on both sides, as jurors have no right whatever to put questions, or to speak at all except to the Judge.

However, coming to the point, a most unwarrantable assumption is founded on their answer to Serjeant BALLANTINE's appeal to them, adopted and recapitulated by the Judge, on the 6th March. Their answer was—"I am authorised to state, my lord, that the views the Jury expressed in their communication to the Court the day before yesterday were based upon the entire evidence, as well as that relating to the tattooing." What could a jury say or do less, after about fourteen witnesses swearing positively and circumstantially to the tattooing, and after the Plaintiff had been personally inspected by them and the Judge in the presence of the Counsel, and finding that he had not and never had had any marks of tattooing, and when his Counsel offered no objection on the tattooing evidence, or any of the other evidence adduced by the Defendant, but to disbelieve the whole of the evidence he had adduced for the Plaintiff?

The thing does not admit of two opinions, so far; but, then, what is the opinion that is due to that omission and acquiescence of the Plaintiff's Counsel being converted into and nicknamed the Verdict of the Jury, by the heads of the law and the great executive officers of the Government?

Having adverted to the evident impertinences of some of the Jury and their probable predilections at earlier stages, I should be doing palpable injustice by omitting to refer to the equally evident hesitation of some others of them when (on the 6th) they required to retire to consider of their answer to BALLANTINE and the Judge. On the 4th, after the evidence of the father confessor, the Abbé SALIS, it would have been strange, indeed, if they had required anything more to settle their minds that the evidence could not be true on both sides. That was a self-evident proposition, and consequently they unanimously did what was erroneously and falsely called "stopping" the case, and was so represented in large letters in the *Evening Standard* of the same evening, thus: "THE JURY STOP THE CASE," and which was re-echoed through the country the next morning. I think their communication, which was so converted and perverted on the Defendant's side, could not be excelled for propriety in substance and manner. They simply said—"We have now heard the evidence regarding the tattoo marks, and, subject to your Lordship's directions and to the hearing of any further evidence that the learned Counsel may desire to place before us, I am authorized to state that the Jury do not require further evidence." No! but that was very different from saying that they were ready to deliver a verdict without hearing what rebutting evidence there might be, or what Serjeant BALLANTINE had to submit to them upon the gross improbabilities of this evidence which had been so heard!

Therefore, I pray you, Sir, do not lay the flattering unction to your soul, that yourself, or any of your subordinates, receive any iota of a ray of countenance from the Jury, in any of the extraordinary proceedings in which you are implicated, and to which you are committed, arising out of the TICHBORNE Case.

What is a "non-suit," and what is a "commitment?" Neither of these incidents have occurred in this case: on the contrary, for want of either of them occurring, the number of officials and professionals who would have been liable for murder if the Plaintiff had died in Newgate, is what would take too much room for me here to set forth; but this I may say, that the incidents, such as they were, coming as they did after the plot, cannot be done justice to at all in this prosaic way, or without the assistance of the drama; and that, as I cannot dramatise, I hereby announce to you my readiness to assist any one who will prepare the whole scene for the stage, by my supplying the raw materials, verging on the tragic, and abounding in the comic, throughout this deadly primogenial scramble for an aristocratic estate. Some of the best efforts in the dramatic way have been partnership works, such as those of Beaumont and Fletcher, analogous to the ordinary callings in business, where the opposite talents of buying and selling show distributing those talents between different persons to be frequently very expedient; and therefore, as by the mercy of Providence, there has not happened the ingredient for tragedy, yet for a comedy of governmental and forensic errors this case affords a profusion, as I am now going to show as to the non-suit, copying from the report of what was said and done on the 6th March:—

"The Lord Chief Justice (to Serjeant BALLANTINE): Is the Plaintiff in Court?—Mr. Serjeant BALLANTINE: No, my lord.—The Lord Chief Justice: Is he in the building?—Mr. Serjeant BALLANTINE: I believe not, my lord. I am told not.—Mr. SPOFFORTH: He is not.—The Lord Chief Justice: You ask to be non-suited upon that statement made by the jury?—Mr. Serjeant BALLANTINE: Yes, my lord.—The Lord Chief Justice: Then let the Plaintiff be called.—The Clerk of the Court (Mr. TURNER) then called three successive times, "Sir ROGER CHARLES DOUGHTY TICHBORNE, Baronet, come forth to hear you are to be non-suited;" but the Plaintiff did not appear."

Does not this seem to chime in, Sir, with that scene from SHAKESPEARE, where a gaoler calls upon a certain convict named BARDOLPH to "come and be hanged?" However, would anybody understand that the party so-called was a free man, untainted and at liberty, and exercising his liberty of electing to be non-suited, and well entitled to the choice between a non-suit and a verdict, and in case of the verdict being against him, equally well entitled to move to set aside that verdict, as against the weight of evidence, and for a new trial, with or without payment of costs; and on which motion there would be the fullest range to discuss the evidence, and weigh that of the tattoo swearers, against the overwhelming weight of their own contradictions and improbabilities, not to say also against that of his own eighty-six unimpeachable witnesses?

Indeed, I strongly surmise that that form of "calling" was new, if not peculiar, if not concocted, for "that turn only," as the sheriff said to his man, when employed for a particular execution. The calling forth *to hear* something or anything is in the most express contradiction to the theory of the form, which is that he purposely absents himself to avoid a verdict against him in consequence of a material defect in his evidence, such as the non-attendance of a necessary witness, and which defect he may possibly cure on another trial. All the non-suits at trials that I have ever heard were in this form: "A.B., come forth, or you lose your *Nisi Prius*," which, if the ancient meaning only were enforced, would be that he would lose that trial, but under the modern practice means that he would lose his present action altogether; and the whole theory is founded on this: that anciently the personal presence of both parties in Court was indispensable for the delivery of the verdict.

Premising this little as to the form, what the Judge was thinking about when so troubling himself to know if the Plaintiff was in Court or in the building, cannot be reconciled with any known ordinary course of proceeding, because it does not matter at all whether the Plaintiff be really in Court or not. The Plaintiff does not go through the personal performance of leaving the Court at all, but he is non-suited, so to say, before his face, and in his own hearing; and it is totally out of the question, and has been obsolete for hundreds of years, to think of his so going actually out of Court in order to exercise his right of being non-suited.

Now, as to the occasion and propriety of the non-suit: referring to the second part of this letter, if the Plaintiff's Counsel could not, even after an adjournment, produce evidence to rebut the tattoo evidence, and if he preferred and determined nevertheless to proceed that way in another action, in place of now commenting on the improbabilities and impossibilities of that evidence which were palpable and needed no rebutting to destroy it, then his advising the Plaintiff to elect for non-suit would be intelligible, but there is no such intelligibility in it. The most usual case where the plaintiff elects to be non-suited is where the Judge would otherwise direct the verdict against him on a point of law, and of course there it is of no use to address the jury; but now see, Sir, how what was done, or left undone, is reconcilable with law, even the Statute Law, made and provided, as it would almost seem to be, for the very case. I refer to the 18th section of the Common Law Procedure Act, 1854, viz.:—

"Upon the trial of any cause the addresses to the jury *shall* be regulated as follows: The party who begins, or his Counsel, *shall* be allowed, in the event of his opponent not announcing at the close of the case of the party who begins, his attention to adduce evidence, to address the jury a second time at the close of such case, for the purpose of summing up the evidence; and the party on the other side, or his Counsel, *shall* be allowed to open the case and also to sum up the evidence (if any), and the right to reply *shall* be the same as at present."

The wise policy of this was to alter the practice theretofore existing, under which the defendant could, by not adducing evidence, prevent the plaintiff from replying. But here, in this horribly-managed case, what does the Plaintiff's Counsel do to avail himself of his improved position? Why, he abandons not only his new right—that is, of summing up his own evidence—but also even his old one of reply, whether to the speech or to the evidence for the Defendant!

I commend to your very serious consideration, Sir, the word "shall," which occurs no less than four times in this provision, and request you to observe how it is applied to the several duties of regulating and allowing, and of performing, respectively belonging to the offices of Judge on both sides, and of Counsel on each side. Of "Counsel," indeed, ranked always with the party himself, and thereby identifying the said Counsel with the interests of such party. And, Sir, now let me ask you if there can be a more grotesque absurdity than to imagine Sir ROGER, after voluntarily going down to the back-parlour of the Court for his arms to be examined by those who were to judge of the tattooing evidence, then, that sort of evidence being given, quietly referring to the jury as to what they thought of it altogether, without offering any word of reply, either in support of his own evidence, or in answer to the speech or the evidence against him! That which would have been possible only for "the man without guile" acting in *propria persona*, what was it in the Counsel? And, bearing in mind, now, the forerunners of this scene, which have been at last related to the world by the party himself (at Nottingham, on the 17th July)—namely, that he had been compelled by his Counsel—with the only alternative of throwing up their briefs—to write and intrust them with the contents of the Sealed Packet, which they then, in violation of their trust, made notorious, and of which notoriety his opponents have made such use against him; and seeing that he had, even during his imprisonment, been under the same sinister influence to such an extent as to employ the same Counsel about his bail when they named him only in the same terms in which he was imprisoned; and, since his liberation, to have ever signed public letters speaking of the same Counsel in terms of respect and praise. Seeing all this train of unparalleled circumstances, we can liken the administration of the law, I mean the management of this so-called "non-suit," so far as the "party" was concerned or acted personally, to nothing else but the calf "that licks the hand which sheds its blood."

I have spoken of them as "unparalleled" circumstances, but meaning only in the sense of their *scale:* for it is out of the question to believe that such like are not of fearful occurrence in the lower regions of practice, if impunity can have been calculated on by the actors in the higher. And, though adverting to *remedies* is here rather anticipating what I shall offer you in detail under that head, this place is too tempting for me to omit the observation that if the old practice had been restored, of independent gentlemen being allowed to patronise and speak for their friends in civil cases, so that Mr. ONSLOW, for instance, might have interfered at this pretended "non-suit," and he had only made to the jury of the eleven any one of the clear and pithy speeches he has lately made to the jury of the million, that Jury would have been as unanimous. About three weeks ago I sent a middle-aged lady, of great attainments, two or three numbers of the *Tichborne News* containing some of those speeches, for which she thanked me by a letter, observing—"I must think this is Sir ROGER TICHBORNE, but how can it ever be settled?" *Like drawing on an old glove,* I say! But I will not anticipate any more, and it is more immediately pressing to go on with the awful narrative of Sir ROGER at Nottingham, the reporter of which thinks he is "not a very effective speaker;" albeit, reporting at the same time that the ladies present appeared "*idolatrously fond of him,*" and that many of them kept crying "*poor thing!*" He was standing before a phalanx of the female sex, and clearing himself of "the greatest crime between heaven and hell," a rocky navigation to steer through for the prize of their verdict; but that is a prize which the most successful of orators would be very well pleased to reach, and therefore I think he can be rated an effective speaker, if that be of any importance. But I think the most important reflection arising out of the occasion is the affecting scene of the female sex sitting in justice and humanity, and protecting one of the other when he is the victim of one of their own, through concoction of the charge of falsely insinuating he had done against her something akin to what, under the old law, he might have been hanged for if true. The female mind appears to me to shine resplendent in comparison with the male for penetration and soundness, equally with heart for humanity; and of course you know I allude to those high dignitaries in various departments of State, even the highest of the high, who have committed themselves to such ludicrous ideas on this subject, and which have only excited the mirth of all women when not their indignation. And as for the examinations and pretended cross-examinations, and the judicial queries and dicta on the particular point, they must ever be matter for jocularity, and will greatly enliven my theatrical piece when it appears, especially for the pit and shilling galleries. One of the cross questions of Serjeant BALLANTINE, or of Corporal GIFFARD, I forget which, forced me, in spite of myself, to fancy a steward of a household going into a fishmonger's shop and asking if his fish were fresh! Consequently, all that part of the business and the particular witnesses ought to have been kept a hundred miles off and never have been brought on the stage. I say this impertinently to my own argument; and it is only what some person with common-sense in his or her head should have admonished the persons who were at the bottom of the plots: for the ever-unfortunate Sealed Packet and the tattooing *coup-de-grace* are the two Jonahs of the Defendant's ship: without them he had a fair voyage before him, but with them on board he founders; and the worst of it is, they are inseparable—they are twins, like the two Siamese—and if he attempts throwing out one, that kills the other! GOD is just, and severe too, for here is retributive justice with a vengeance; also, whom He means to destroy He first makes foolish; and here has been folly past all compare.

All this, Sir, belongs to the question of the so-called "non-suit," which I have now touched on as regards both its form and its substance, and shown it to be irregular in the one and defective in the other, or, speaking more adequately and accurately, null and void in both.

Jewry-st., Aldgate: Aug. 4. WM. CORBETT.

This visit to Swansea called forth the following letter, descriptive of Australian life:—

REMARKS ON THE TICHBORNE CASE.

BY A WANDERING "COLONIAL."

SIR,—A very great experience of life, and its many vicissitudes in the colonies, induces me to crave a space in your valuable paper for a few remarks on colonial life generally, and more especially in its bearings on the life of Sir ROGER CHARLES TICHBORNE. I will pass over as an undisputed fact that the Claimant embarked in the "Bella," and that the "Bella" was wrecked. From that time we must rely mainly on the *ipse dixit* of the Claimant, whose description of the loss, the leaving in the boats, the parting company during the night, &c., is perfectly natural. We will assume—for there is no reason to doubt—the probability that he was picked up, and landed in Melbourne; and also not forget the fact that he landed penniless. It is stated that he had letters of credit on bankers in England when he left Rio, and it is pretty generally asked why he did not make use of them to place him in funds. Well, considering the admitted fact that the "Bella" was lost, and the crew and the passengers took to the boats, it would be very surprising to me if the letters of credit were not lost with her.

There may be some confiding bankers in the world who would advance their cash to any one who entered their house of business, say my Lord SO-AND-SO, the Duke of NOWHERE, or Sir R. C. TICHBORNE, without their producing any document by which they were to be identified, but I can only say I have never found such bankers. In fact, the simple idea is preposterous. As I have previously remarked, there was a probability of the Claimant arriving in Melbourne; and this at a time when the great rush was made from all parts of the colonies to the Gold Diggings. I may say, *en passant*, that I have known ships to bring up inside the light ship, at that time, and captain, officers, and all hands make a clean bolt, and leave the ship to the tender mercies of whoever chose to take care of her. What was more natural than that a man who had made up his mind to lead a wandering devil-may-care sort of life, should at once sink the gentleman, and accommodate himself to circumstances? To his mind there would be something attractive and compatible with his tastes in the life and freedom of a stock-keeper, and not particularly wishing to kill himself with hard-work in digging for dross, that he could command by writing to his friends for, he would probably decide on trying a life in the bush. A new "chum," particularly after such a sea-voyage as had befallen the Claimant, would naturally be delighted with the idea of riding about all day in pursuit of countless herds of wild cattle, driving them to kraals for branding, &c., and leading a life of absolute freedom. It very seldom occurs at the time to the minds of adventurous young men the privations they may have to endure, and the menial services to perform for themselves. We will assume our new "chum," the Claimant, meets with a stock owner and enters his services (for remember, he must either live, starve, or become that most contemptible of all men, in colonial parlance—a "loafer"), he goes some hundreds of miles up the country, and on his arrival is located with a fellow-stockman. Everything is new to him, but through seeing his chum doing everything for himself he naturally falls into the same groove, and learns to help himself. He finds he has to fetch the water (perhaps a couple of miles) before he can make his tea, make his damper before he can eat it, and kill, skin, and cook his mutton before it can be consumed. This, certainly, is rather unexpected work for our new chum, but there being no one to criticise his actions, and to twit him with his apparent fall in the social scale, he suits himself to circumstances, and from its being at first a hardship, in a short time it ceases to be so. This is the first fall in the social scale. His chum is a man, we will suppose, not possessed of two ideas beyond his actual occupation as stockman; conversation is limited to the work each performs, and consequently there is little intellectual progress.

This continues some time, then there is a desire for change, and by-and-by some fellow on the tramp espies the hut and makes towards it. Society is by far too scarce for the "chums" not to hail with pleasurable feelings the advent of a fresh face, and to offer unbounded hospitality in the shape of tea, damper, mutton, and "baccy." The visitor perhaps, too, is on his way to a distant station farther up the country, and gives a gloomy description of the place and its surroundings. Our new chum—the Claimant, for instance—being infatuated with the sound of a new voice, and having a prospect of further adventures, shoulders his blanket, tin-pot and haversack, and starts for fresh fields and pastures new. They travel on foot for some days, and then come across some fellow, who hails them "Hollo mate! D'ye want a job?" "Don't care. What is it?" "Oh, to split posts and rails, and do some fencing."

They agree; thus another phase from stock-keeper to wood-splitter. Remember, our new chum is some hundreds of miles up country, and must live. There were no railroads, or any other roads scarcely then. This job concluded; the same thing occurs, and our new chum soon becomes an old chum, and is able to turn his hand to anything and everything. I have known two sons of titled families driving tandem passenger carts between Port Adelaide and Adelaide; the son of a noble Earl a sawyer; a son of the inventor of the steam printing-press keeping school for children, for his "grub." University men who have carried off high honours at Cambridge and Oxford, one boots at an inn, others bullock-drivers, masons, labourers, &c. I well knew the son of a Captain in the Navy who left his ship, and to save himself from starving, assisted a butcher in slaughtering, and occupied his spare time in cleaning pig pens and stables. Nay more, I well remember in 1853 taking out to Australia a young lady of the name of SEYMOUR, the daughter of a solicitor, in——, in Wiltshire, who, by the bye, was said to have been fitted-out and her passage paid by the Dowager Lady SEYMOUR. That young lady obtained a situation as domestic servant. I wonder if Lady DOROTHY and the Misses SEYMOUR would also disown this distant member of the Family. I cannot, of course, but admit that the Claimant in his transactions with Messrs.

GIBBES, CUBITT, and Co., acted most absurdly to all appearances, but I should imagine those circumstances are open to explanation; and doubtless, if the Australian Commission was printed, many things now inexplicable would be perfectly comprehensible. I will now endeavour to follow the Claimant through his erratic life in Australia, but I will refer to the conduct of his Family from the first period they were aware that Sir ROGER was, as it were, and to their "inconvenience," resuscitated. Now, what was their course of procedure? They did not wait an opportunity to identify him, or brand him as an impostor after an interview, but they were so eager to throw every discredit on his claim, that long prior to his leaving Australia he was stigmatized by them as an impostor. This shows in a most unmistakable manner, that there was no intention or wish to recognize their lost kinsman; but unfortunately they over-reached themselves in the eyes of the public by denouncing the man unseen and unheard.—I am, Sir, yours, &c.,

SWANSEA TRADESMAN.

The visit to Swansea also caused the discovery of a witness who could never after be found. This man was MORGAN HARRIS. He is thus mentioned in the subjoined newspaper cuttings:—

THE DISCOVERY OF ONE OF THE "BELLA'S" CREW.

We have been favoured by Mr. GUILDFORD ONSLOW with copies of the declaration of the father of the alleged MORGAN HARRIS, one of the crew of the "Bella"; of Mrs. BENSON, the landlady of Mr. HARRIS, sen.; of GEORGE JONES, of Swansea, an acquaintance of MORGAN HARRIS, jun.; and four others. We append three of these declarations:—

DECLARATION OF MRS. BENSON, LANDLADY OF MORGAN HARRIS'S FATHER.

I, ELIZABETH BENSON, of Gower-court, Park-street, Swansea,

GEORGE HAMMOND WHALLEY, Esq., M.P.

Widow, do solemnly and sincerely declare that I have kept a lodging-house for about eight years past, and MORGAN HARRIS has lodged in my house for about three years. I know his son, MORGAN HARRIS, the sailor, who has been in the habit of calling here to see his father, and have often heard his father speak of his son being wrecked in the "Bella," and have also heard him talking with his father about it. MORGAN HARRIS, the sailor, called here to see his father on Monday last, and after some talk, I said, "Are you going up to London about this TICHBORNE Case?" He said, "No, I will have nothing to say about it." Before MORGAN HARRIS, the son, came home, I told his father that Mr. CROOK had called twice to see him, and I asked him why he did not go down to Mr. CROOK, and he replied, "I will have nothing to do with it until MORGAN comes home."

He was not home on Friday night, but when he came in on Saturday morning (August 3), I asked him if his son had gone to sea again, and he said, "Yes; he is gone for seven months." I then told him I believed they had both been bribed, to which he made no reply.

And I make this solemn declaration, conscientiously believing the same to be true, and by virtue of the provisions of an Act made and passed in the sixth year of the reign of his late Majesty King WILLIAM the Fourth, entitled an Act for the more effectual abolition of oaths and affirmations taken and made in various departments of the State, and to substitute declarations in lieu thereof—and for the more entire suppression of voluntary and extra judicial oaths and affidavits, and to make other provisions for the abolition of unnecessary oaths.

Declared at Swansea, in the County of Glamorgan, the day of August, 1872.

DECLARATION OF MORGAN HARRIS, SENIOR.

I, MORGAN HARRIS, of Gower-court, Park-street, Swansea, do solemnly and sincerely declare that I am sixty-eight years of age, and have lived all my life in Swansea. I have had twenty children, of whom eleven are now living, of whom MORGAN is the eldest, and will be forty-two years old on the 2nd December next. He is a sailor, and has been to sea ever since he was fifteen years of age; he has told me that he was in the "Bella" some time in 1851, and also that he was wrecked in that ship, and that having been picked up at sea, he was landed at Australia; he also told me the name of the ship that had picked him up, and I think the name was the "Osprey;" he first told me of this after his return to England, after being absent about ten to twelve years, and this was about 1866; the way he mentioned it was, that in talking together, he said, "Well, father, I have been wrecked twice—I was wrecked in the 'Bella,' and the 'Thetis,' of London; in the 'Bella' in 1851, and in the 'Thetis' in 1856." I have often spoken of his having been wrecked in the "Bella," as he told me, and it is well known to my family and others. He came to Swansea last Saturday, the 27th of July, and he went off again in the "Corsyra" steamship on Friday evening last. During his stay here I said to him, "Why don't you go down and tell Mr. CROOK all you know about the 'Bella?'" and he replied, "I'll be d——d if I do until I come back." In talking with him about his being saved from the wreck of the "Bella," he has told me that one of the men saved with him was Mr. TICHBORNE, who afterwards in Australia went by the name of CASTRO.

And I make this solemn declaration, &c.

Declared at Swansea, in the county of Glamorgan, the day of August, 1872, before me, &c.

DECLARATION OF GEORGE JONES.

I, GEORGE JONES, of No. 14, Croft-street, Swansea, do solemnly and sincerely declare that I am well acquainted with MORGAN HARRIS, the son of MORGAN HARRIS, of Swansea, shoemaker. I have known him since he was a boy, and when he comes to Swansea he makes his sister's (Mrs. EVANS), in Croft-street, near to where I live, his home; he left Swansea in a ship on Friday evening last. On that day I had a talk with him in the "Lamb" public-house in High-street, having heard that he was a sailor on board the "Bella," and was saved from the wreck of that ship many years ago. I asked him the question whether it was true that he was saved from the wreck of that ship; he said yes—it was true; he had been shipwrecked twice—once in the "Bella," and afterwards in another; but he did not tell me the name of the other ship; he told me that the time he was wrecked in the "Bella" was either in 1854 or 1855, but was not quite sure as to which year it was. I then said to him, "Why don't you go to Mr. CROOK and tell him all about it, if you were cast away with the man?" He then said, "I have shipped, and am going away this afternoon." He also told me he had seen Mr. CROOK, but he wasn't sober at the time. Just before I went into the "Lamb" public-house, I saw him talking with two gentlemen, and the conversation they had with him was about this TICHBORNE Case. I did not hear all the conversation they had with him, but at the end of it HARRIS said, "I will do nothing of the sort."

And I make this solemn declaration, &c.

The other depositions are by Mr. WM. CROOK, tobacconist, Wind-street, Swansea; Mr. SIMPKINS, gentleman, Swansea; and the two sisters of MORGAN HARRIS; all of which corroborate the foregoing statements. It is also stated by a young gentleman in Swansea, now on his death-bed, that a person with whom he is acquainted received the sum of £10 for the purpose of getting MORGAN HARRIS out of the way. A reward of £15 has also been offered by Mr. WHALLEY and other friends of the Claimant, to any person who will give information of the party, with his address, who met MORGAN HARRIS in Gloucester, and continued constantly in his company until the sailing of the "Corsyra" at Swansea, on Friday last.

(FROM THE "FERRET.")

Mr. WHALLEY, M.P., one of the most active friends of the Claimant, came to Swansea on Saturday last, to make inquiries respecting a man named MORGAN HARRIS, a sailor, who had, to several parties in the town, given himself out as having been wrecked in the far-famed "Bella," and remembered that one of the passengers saved with him was a person named TICHBORNE. It is known, we understand, for a fact that HARRIS was paid off from the "Susquehannah," a vessel which was frequently named in connection with the recent trial of the claims of Sir ROGER. This, together with other statements made by him, caused the friends of the Claimant to keep a sharp look-out as to his whereabouts. Accordingly, as it became known that on Monday week HARRIS was expected to arrive with his vessel at Gloucester, Mr. CROOK, of Swansea, repaired thither, and waited for some time for the arrival of the ship. As it did not, however, enter that port so soon as looked for, the Claimant's friends at Swansea did not see him until his visit to that place. During the interview, he appears to have been extremely taciturn, and continually under the influence of a mysterious stranger, who permitted him only to answer such questions as he thought proper. Mr. WHALLEY, however, has procured the depositions of the various parties—HARRIS's father and landlady amongst the number—to whom he had previously made important statements, which, it is believed, must have the greatest possible influence on the forthcoming Trial. Having seen these depositions, we can vouch for the great majority of the facts deposed to being perfectly consistent with dates, and a number of other important particulars referred to in the history of the Case. On Thursday, to the great surprise of HARRIS's father and relatives, he announced his intention of immediately going to sea, and on the same afternoon, about four o'clock, he went on board the screw-steamer "Corsyra," lying at the Swansea Docks, for Valencia. "He was," says a contemporary, "in a state of intoxication when he came to Swansea on Monday—continued in that state all the time he was in that town, and was intoxicated when he left the port." Mr. WHALLEY, though telegraphed for, unfortunately arrived too late to see MORGAN HARRIS. The honourable gentleman contented himself with procuring a copy of the depositions, as we have stated, which he intended reading on Monday night to a public meeting; but as there was some difficulty in obtaining a hall, the resolution was abandoned.

On first consideration of the above extraordinary facts, we were disposed to put down the statements of MORGAN HARRIS as the ravings of a drunken braggart; subsequent events, however, have come to light to alter this opinion; and we think there can be now no doubt that what he has stated is almost, in every particular, correct; nor does the care which was taken of him by the mysterious stranger tend to lessen this impression. We believe, if the truth were known, emissaries by persons interested are at the present moment scattered all over the kingdom with the view, at any cost, of subverting the ends of justice. If this be not the case, why should MORGAN HARRIS be taken so much care of, and spirited out of the way, never probably again—like ORTON and his sisters—to be more heard of? There certainly is something throughout the entire proceedings most unsatisfactory; and not the least so, the fact that the Claimant was magniloquently, by Attorney-General COLERIDGE, talked out of Court, in a speech of some twenty-one days' duration.

We are now firmly convinced that the Case of TICHBORNE, CASTRO, or whatever else the Claimant, for the nonce, may be called, is one the public of England ought to look sharply after. It has every appearance of being a case of Jesuitical and aristocratical conspiracy; and though we have throughout expressed ourselves as not being perfectly satisfied with the clearness of the Case of the Claimant, this, to our mind, is only an additional reason why the claims should have further trial. It is impossible to believe that an impostor is capable of undergoing the long and trying ordeal of examination he has passed through. As yet the country has only had the advantage of the one side stated; and all in any way acquainted with the "privilege" which the law affords a barrister to distort and pervert evidence, must admit that the breakdown of a trial under such circumstances, and with such stupendous results pending, ought not to satisfy the intelligent and justice-loving people of England. Wales, we hope, will do her duty, and see justice done; and the sooner that the "sinews of war" raised on behalf of the Claimant in Swansea are forwarded to the proper quarter the better.

THE CLAIMANT AT LEICESTER AND LOUGHBOROUGH.

On Sunday evening the Claimant arrived in Leicester from London. He was met by a deputation from Loughborough, and on entering the station-yard was received with immense cheering by a large concourse of people. He drove off with his friends in a waggonette drawn by greys, with postilions, to the White Hart Hotel. The Claimant afterwards started for Loughborough, and a crowd of about 10,000 persons assembled to see him depart, and cheered him lustily to the outskirts of the town. Similar demonstrations took place at various points on the route; and at Loughborough almost the entire populace turned out.

At an amalgamated meeting of Foresters at Loughborough on Monday evening, which was attended by the Claimant to the Tichborne Estates (who also spoke and addressed an assembly of about 12,000 persons), Mr. GUILDFORD ONSLOW, M.P., said it was only within the last few hours that he had heard of one of the crew of the "Bella" turning up at Swansea. He had read an account of it in a Welsh paper, showing beyond doubt that the individual was saved in 1854 from the wreck of the "Bella," and carried into Melbourne, and that Mr. TICHBORNE, whom this man knew, lived there under the name of CASTRO. Two individuals, however, got hold of this man MORGAN HARRIS, and put him on board a steamer on Thursday and carried him off to Spain. At the Trial they would produce his family and father with his grey hairs, who would testify to his son being saved from the wreck of the "Bella," and carried into Melbourne harbour. He had often applied to the Government as to GEORGE MOORE, of the "Rodney." That man died at Falmouth the other day, and they had proved that he was saved from the "Bella," while the other man WILLIAM EVANS died next to him when he lay in the hospital at Rio. So they accounted for three out of the five of the crew of the "Bella."

We next find, and transcribe, a newspaper report of

THE CLAIMANT IN EAST LONDON.

Last Saturday's demonstration in East London, says the writer, eclipsed all the provincial pronouncements which since the "Claimant's" release from Newgate have taken place, with the avowed object of protesting against his oppression, and of raising funds to secure for him in the future a fair trial on those alleged criminal charges which Sir JOHN COLERIDGE, acting in the two-fold capacity of leading Crown Counsel and professional advocate for the TICHBORNE infant, determined some time since to prefer.

Mr. G. ONSLOW, M.P., was received with oft-renewed bursts of applause on presenting himself. He went at considerable detail into the history of the TICHBORNE Case, and taking up point by point those portions of the Attorney-General's opening speech for the defence, which on the surface at least told most against the Claimant, answered them in a manner that elicited assuring and sympathizing cheers from his audience. He expressed his full and firm conviction in the righteousness of his friend Sir ROGER's claim to the estates and title, and declared his determination, no matter how ungentlemanlike some might consider the occupation, of standing by him under all circumstances until full and ample justice placed Sir ROGER in the position to which he was entitled. (Loud cheers.)

The Chairman said that Sir ROGER would next have the pleasure and satisfaction of addressing his East-end London friends and staunch supporters. (Cheers.)

The Claimant, who was received with long and continued cheers, to which he bowed acknowledgment several times, commenced by thanking the audience for their attendance, and for the support in his arduous undertaking which their presence on that occasion so conclusively manifested. (Cries of "You're welcome to the East-end;" "You must have justice from the West-enders also.") He had not come down to that great demonstration to ask them to believe he was Sir ROGER TICHBORNE. (Cries of "It's not necessary," and loud cheers.) That he would leave to the course of the law; but he appealed to them as Englishmen to see that that fair-play was shown him to which every Englishman was entitled. ("You must have it," and cheers.) He was quite willing to stand his trial on the twofold criminal charges of perjury and forgery. For that ordeal, though the prosecution would be conducted with all the weight and power which the Attorney-General—(groans)—could bring to bear against him, he was perfectly prepared, being satisfied that even at that moment he had quite sufficient evidence to upset the accusations which were manufactured in the vain hope of crushing him, and thus placing that property to which he was entitled beyond his reach. (Cries of "Shame," and "It won't be done.") He wished to impress upon all those whom it was that day his privilege to address the responsibility which the Attorney-General—(groans)—had taken upon himself. (Cries of "He has cheek and neck enough for anything."—Laughter and cheers.) The character and ability of the Attorney-General were at stake in crushing him. That learned law officer had made no end of charges against him. In the course of his examination and of his long-winded address to the jury—(Cries of "At the rate of 3s. 4d. a minute,")—he had applied to him every vile and offensive epithet that he could think of, or that was to be found in the English language. ("He was well paid for doing so by Mrs. RADCLIFFE.") That language, disgusting and debasing, was not fit to be used by any man, and he would not repeat it. (Hear, hear.) More especially was it unfit for the lips of the chief law officer of England, as Sir JOHN COLERIDGE was so fond of styling himself. (Cheers.) Let them bear in mind the continued and unmitigated hostility and virulent animus which this supposed impartial public prosecutor had brought, and was hourly bringing, to the front in furtherance of his own views and the interests of those who retained him. In every place he had got his agents. Here, there, and everywhere his parasites were at work against him (the Claimant). (Cries of "Shame," and groans for "GLADSTONE's law officers.") Now, why was this so? The fact was the Attorney-General felt that, failing to prosecute and transport him, he would instantly become a fallen man, and would cease to be looked upon with respect. (Several Voices: "That has happened already."—Laughter and cheers.) It was everything to him and his reputation to succeed, and therefore he had recourse to a line of conduct the most dishonourable, and from which every right-minded man would shrink; but in defiance of all that, he (the Claimant) felt that the truth was on his side—(hear, hear,)—and so long as the British public stood by and supported him, he did not care one pin's point for Sir JOHN COLERIDGE—(bravo)—or for one hundred and fifty Attorney-Generals. (A Voice: "If you stick to that, Sir ROGER, you will do.") All the evidence adduced in sustainment of his claim to the title and property was genuine, *bonâ fide*, straightforward, and unimpeachable. (Hear, hear.) He had never condescended to employ a detective or to sneak about as others had done, eavesdropping and spyholing. Was that so with the other side, who, it was notorious, had expended several thousands of pounds alone in the preparation—he would not use a more expressive phrase—of evidence? (Cheers.) To the great annoyance of his friends, they were followed wherever they went by detectives in the pay of the defendants. (Cries of "Shame.") His own letters were even watched to post—(Cries of "Sir JAMES GRAHAM again")—and altogether the system of espionage to which he and his supporters were subjected was most intolerable. Now if the Attorney-General and the compact crowd of barristers and solicitors and law agents of one kind or another associated with him had the genuine Case they represented they had, surely they would not require to have this small army of detectives. For the reasons already stated, he (the Claimant) felt that he had no occasion for such services, and therefore they were not enlisted in his favour. (Hear.) But this was not the extent of the foul and unfair play practised by the other side. The Attorney-General, he understood, had even gone the length of directing retaining fees to be sent and offered to all Counsel most experienced and most eminent at the criminal bar, so as to prevent him (the Claimant) being able to take advantage of their ability and legal acumen against the array of Crown lawyers who at the earliest moment were banded together for the purposes of his criminal prosecution. (Cries of "Shame, shame.") Was this English justice, or English fair-play? (Cries of "No, no.") Was this the manner in which an English law officer, himself the private Counsel of Defendants in a civil suit, should be allowed to expend the public money towards securing the conviction of the Plaintiff in that selfsame civil suit which was only part heard, and which must be fought to the end? (Tremendous cheering, and cries of "No, no.") Now let him say a few words upon one point of the Case which was not the least remarkable, as it certainly was not the most creditable. He alluded to the tattoo marks. (Hear, hear.) Until after the examination of his person by the Judge, the jury, and the Counsel on the other side, there was not a word said about these marks. (Hear, hear.) Let it be remembered that this examination did not take place until months and months of preliminary skirmishing was over and the trial had far advanced. When they had satisfied themselves that he had not got those marks, they then, and only then, said that he ought to have them. (Laughter, and cries of "Just like COLERIDGE.") On the first occasion of the examination there was one man in the room to whom he objected. That person was DONALDSON,* the solicitor for his opponents. He (the Claimant) called Judge BOVILL to remove him. The Judge asked why there was an objection to his presence. He (the Claimant) replied, because DONALDSON had never offered any satisfactory explanation about certain forged letters which were permitted to be put in evidence. Judge BOVILL, however, overruled the objection raised, allowed DONALDSON to remain, and he (the Claimant) was then and there compelled to tell that in consequence of this decision he considered that he would not have a fair trial. (A Voice: "And you were right: your trial was a sham from beginning to end.") The Attorney-General boasted in the early stage of the proceedings that in the short space of twenty minutes he would prove him (the Claimant) to be ARTHUR ORTON. (Great laughter, and cries of "Why does he not come down to Wapping?") Well, if that was so, the Attorney-General was no better than a robber, for he continued the Case for 103 days, and at the end of that period he turned round and said it was no part of his duty to prove him (the Claimant) ARTHUR ORTON; that it was sufficient for his purpose to say that the Claimant was not ROGER DOUGHTY TICHBORNE, the heir to the estates. (A Voice: "And that is English justice and fair-play.") They might hear perhaps with some surprise that his was the first instance in which, through Parliamentary sanction, a man was sent to Newgate without having any trial. (Hear.) Simply and for no reason than because his funds were exhausted he was compelled, however reluctantly, to stop his case; and it was his opinion that, if the money originally at his command had been twice as great, the Attorney-General would have continued wasting time until the money was run out. (Cries of "Shame.") That great legal oracle made it his boast that he would win the Case on his speech to the jury; and he did so because of the knowledge that the witnesses for the defence could not be trusted. (Hear, hear, and laughter). No doubt the Attorney-General made an impression on the jury when he burst out crying in the Court—(a Voice: "Crocodile's tears")—tears, he said, which flowed from him in consequence of the imputations on Mrs. RADCLIFFE's character. There were no doubt many present who remembered something of the WICKLOW Peerage case. (Hear, hear.) The Attorney-General was engaged in that remarkable contest. He represented the infant claiming through its illegal mother the WICKLOW title and estates. For many days the inquiry went on in the House of Peers. Sir JOHN sobbed and cried in depicting the injustice that would be done to his client—who could not, as he pathetically observed, speak for itself—if the claim were not recognized; but it turned out that the Attorney-General's tears were shed on behalf of an infant that was brought out of the workhouse at Liverpool—(great laughter)—and who had no more right to the WICKLOW estate and titles than another infant in more recent times, with the advantage of the Attorney General's advocacy and eloquence, had to the Tichborne Estates and title. (Tremendous cheers, and cries of "Bravo, Sir ROGER.") But to revert to his imprisonment in Newgate. It was only last autumn that a clause was put into an Act of Parliament empowering a Judge to send a witness to Newgate on a charge of perjury alleged to have been committed during the trial of a case before him, and there could be very little doubt that the Legislature—or, rather he should say, the Government—had him (the Claimant) in its mind when the insertion of that clause was sanctioned. (Cheers.) After alluding to an act alleged to have been committed by Judge BOVILL when off the Bench, and to conversations which two of Judge BOVILL's brothers were represented to have had with his cousin in connection with the result of the Trial, the Claimant proceeded to remark that in the "WICKLOW Peerage" case the Attorney-General made precisely the same defence for the impostor infant there as he had done for the TICHBORNE infant, pledging himself in the most solemn and sacred manner that his youthful client was the rightful heir to the estate. (Hear, hear.) That was what he did in more recent cases, taking upon himself the functions and powers of Judge, jury, and Counsel, and deciding the issue, at least for the present, his own way. (Hear.) (A Voice: "He frightened the jury into what they stupidly did.") Now, having made this simple statement, he thought they would agree with him that he had great odds to fight against. Before

* The Claimant, no doubt, meant DOBINSON; but ROGER TICHBORNE was hardly ever accurate about names.

he arrived in this country, even when he was on his return journey in New York, he was assailed with abusive paragraphs in the public Press, proclaiming how an Australian butcher claimed to be an English baronet. (A Voice: "Never mind, you will have the laugh at them by-and-by.") (Cheers.) All this took place before he reached his poor dear mother in Paris, when he found that solicitors had even then been engaged by the Family to try and prove him an impostor. (Hear, hear.) Well, if he were the impostor it was attempted to make him appear, would he have gone direct to his mother? and if they had faith in their pretended convictions as to his imposture, why did they not show their courage by taking the bold course of at once, then and there, sending him off to a police office? (Cheers.) It would not have been a difficult, though it might have turned out to those who initiated it, an expensive proceeding, for when he arrived in this country he had only £3 in his pocket, and that sum they might rest assured was not over long in being expended. Well, then, looking at all the difficulties with which he had to contend, they would agree with him that if he were an impostor he could not have lasted so long. (Cheers.) Again thanking the people of the district for the magnificent reception they had given him, and for the sympathy they had manifested in his cause, he respectfully asked them to believe that he was deeply grateful to them in common with other lovers of fair-play and justice, who so abounded from one end of Great Britain to the other; and he felt morally convinced that with such assistance, no matter how desperate or continuous were the attempts made to crush him, he would in the end prove successful. (The Claimant resumed his seat amid loud and long-continued cheering for "Sir ROGER TICHBORNE," and vehement groaning for the Attorney-General.)

Mr. WHALLEY, M.P., who was very cordially greeted, next addressed the meeting. After thanking them for the kind reception he had experienced, he proceeded to say—The Claimant whom you recognize here to-day as Sir ROGER TICHBORNE has told you that he does not ask you to make any other declaration or decision than this, that he shall have a fair trial—(hear, hear)—and I am here to-day for the purpose of declaring, on my own part, that this is all I aim at, taking part in this agitation, prepared as I am to prove that without such help as you and the public generally may thus be induced to afford, he cannot have a fair trial. (Cheers.) I look upon it as a serious matter that any man holding the public position of a member of Parliament should feel justified in turning his back upon Westminster Hall and the courts of justice, and appealing to the people for a fair trial to a man under the heavy charges of perjury and forgery. (Hear, hear.) For what is it but to say that justice is not to be had there in spite of all the millions a year we pay for the due administration of our laws, and the confidence and pride which we ought to feel that no gigantic wrong, such as we complain of in this Case, can there be committed? And still more do I regard it as a painful position to turn my back upon the House of Commons, and appeal to you for a hearing not granted to me there or by the Government, after doing all in my power to prevent the necessity for this agitation, so far as regards the raising of money for the Claimant's defence, by urging them to provide at the very least for the necessary expenses of the witnesses to be called on his behalf. (Cheers.) And yet such is my position and such my excuse for joining in this appeal to you to-day. (Hear, hear.) It is to me, however, a day of extraordinary pride and exultation as an Englishman; for never did I feel so strongly that our country is true to all its traditions of public spirit, and as ready as ever to maintain the laws, constitution, and liberties which our ancestors have handed down to us, as in the long and perilous journey we had to make before reaching this platform. For above three miles the streets have been too small to hold the masses who have crowded round to show their sympathy with the Claimant's demand for justice; and I could not but think of those past events, when, in the very front of our battles for civil and religious liberty, London has ever been found the prompt and resolute champion; and I tell the Government plainly that I for one will do all in my power, if we have to visit for that purpose every parish of the metropolis, to give to London the opportunity of thus asserting its grandest title to be the capital of the British Empire. (Loud cheers.) Give me your best attention while I refer to the paper in my hand, which contains the answer by the officer in charge of the prosecution to my appeal to him for such help in investigating the evidence, and providing for the attendance of witnesses upon the Trial as might enable the Claimant to dispense with this appeal for public sympathy and support, and to await, like others, the ordinary course of justice. (Loud cheers.) Being told by the Attorney-General that he would not reply to any question, or give any information in the House of Commons, I wrote on the 2nd of this month to the Solicitor of the Treasury, stating that having been present at public meetings at Southampton and Swansea, much evidence had come to my knowledge, and after specifying it, I asked that he would, on the part of the Government, investigate that evidence, and if he deemed it material either for the prosecution or the defence, he would provide the means for bringing it forward on the Trial—(hear, hear)—and not receiving from him a prompt reply, I gave notice of addressing to the Government the like request during the sitting of the House of Commons last night. Having given such notice, on my return last night to the nine o'clock sitting of the House I there found this letter, and as the correspondence will be published in the newspapers, I need only now refer to such parts as are material to the business of this meeting. (Hear, hear.) The Solicitor of the Treasury begins by stating that it is not his intention to enter into any such investigation of evidence as proposed by me, but he subsequently seems to leave it open to him to do so, for he uses these words:—"Before I would think of investigating such matters as you bring forward in your letter, I should require some explanations on the following points, which I invite you to give me:" and he proceeds to specify five separate points, which he considers call for explanation on the part of the Claimant. Now, I think you will agree with me that this letter of the Solicitor of the Treasury, thus pointing out what is the real ground for this prosecution, is a very important document; and if it can be made to appear that the points thus specified either are utterly immaterial and frivolous, or that they can be, or have been, already fully answered, then I think the public will have a very definite reason for demanding, either within the House of Commons or without, some explanation as to the enormous outlay threatened by the Attorney-General against the Claimant—(hear, hear)—and that the evidence in his favour should be fairly investigated and brought forward. (Cheers.) The five points on which, and on which alone, as it would appear, the Government rely, are as follows:—First: The Claimant's having sent to ARTHUR ORTON's sisters portraits of himself and of his own wife and child, pretending that they were ARTHUR ORTON's. Second: That sixteen Chili witnesses swore that they had never known nor heard of anyone of the name of TICHBORNE, but that they did know ARTHUR ORTON in 1849 and 1850. Third: That the Claimant, if his account be true, must have acquired a knowledge of the Spanish language in ten or twelve days. Fourth: That when he made his will in Wagga he did not know his own mother's name. Fifth: How it happens that not one of the eight sailors said to have been rescued from the "Bella" had appeared, nor any of their relations or friends, whom he reckons must have numbered up to at least 104 individuals. Now this may fairly be taken to be a complete statement of the case as it stands against the Claimant, thus formally and officially set forth by the Solicitor of the Treasury, Mr. JOHN GRAY, who is a gentleman very well known to me as an honourable and honest man, who for a long period has been recognized as one of the best lawyers in the legal profession; and I take it upon myself to say that there is not one of these points that cannot be shown to be either utterly immaterial to the question as to whether the Claimant is or is not the man he claims to be, or that cannot be fully and completely answered. Why, every one knows that it was not upon any one or all of these points that the jury stopped the Case, and that he was sent forthwith to Newgate, but upon the tattoo marks. (Hear, hear.) Now that was really material, and yet you see this is not mentioned by Mr. GRAY, and for the very good reason that everyone, including, it may be presumed, the Attorney-General, has given up all faith in that evidence, as being not only—as was admitted—a complete surprise, but also as being, when carefully read, so badly got up as to be contradictory in itself—the French witnesses giving one account, and the relatives another, as to the circumstances under which the tattooing was done, and as to what the tattoo marks were. (Hear, hear.) Well, this is given up by the Solicitor to the Treasury, and he asks how about the portraits sent to ARTHUR ORTON's sisters. The explanation to this and to all the other Wapping incidents is that the Claimant desired to gratify and become friendly with the relatives of ARTHUR ORTON; and though it must appear to everyone that he took odd methods of doing so, yet no one will be surprised at this when it shall be proved, as I understand it will be, that a detective, who was sent out by the Claimant's relatives to meet him at New York on his return home, actually contrived to get into his confidence and to take upon himself the chief part of all these communications with the ORTON family. (Hear, hear.) *The Attorney-General seemed to have admitted that some of the letters put in as the Claimant's were deliberate forgeries, and I think the Solicitor to the Treasury would be better employed in investigating the evidence that I offered to him showing beyond the possibility of a doubt that the Claimant is not* ARTHUR ORTON, *than in running after such will-o'-the-wisps as the Claimant's motives and conduct in respect of* ORTON'S *sisters, all of whom have sworn that he is not their brother,* ARTHUR ORTON. (Cheers.) Then as to the sixteen Chili witnesses, who swear that they knew an ARTHUR ORTON in 1849 and 1850, but never knew TICHBORNE. I wonder whether the £16,000 which, as stated in the newspapers, the Attorney-General required for bringing over these intelligent foreigners, was estimated at the cost per head. However this may be, I believe that I am fully justified in stating that the only advantage of bringing such persons before a British jury will be to exhibit the best mode of obtaining useful evidence from such countries as Chili, and that, like the detective sent to New York, it will be shown that a Chili lawyer was employed for 18 months in drilling these witnesses into the very words of the evidence which they ultimately gave. And again I say, why will not the solicitor investigate the evidence offered to him that the Claimant is not ARTHUR ORTON? and thus settle the question, in spite of anything that all the inhabitants of the Chilian Empire or Republic were to swear, as possibly under skilful treatment they might do, to the contrary. (Hear, and cheers.) As to the acquisition of the Spanish language in 10 or 12 days, I am really surprised that the Solicitor to the Treasury should have overlooked the fact, that before the Claimant went, as he alleges, to Melipilla he had been in Spanish America for nearly a year, and had made the language a special and favourite study. (Hear, hear.) Then we have the Will Case, and the wrong spelling of his mother's

Christian names. My friend Mr. ONSLOW, who has made himself master of these details, insists upon it that the will is of itself excellent evidence that the Claimant is ROGER TICHBORNE; for although being written out and dictated, as is proved, between the bush lawyer Mr. GIBBS and ARTHUR ORTON, and against the wishes of the Claimant, and therefore having no pretence to accuracy, it does mention a fact that would be known only to ROGER TICHBORNE—namely, that his father had become possessed by recent purchase of a farm called "The Hermitage," and which the Attorney-General, you will remember, supposed to be identical with one of your Wapping wharves which goes by the same name. (Hear, hear.) As to the sailors of the "Bella," I think the Solicitor to the Treasury is not quite fair in making the Claimant responsible for not producing any of these men, when, in the same letter, he refuses to afford any assistance in tracing out one of them, who, I believe, may by due efforts be yet brought before the Court. (Cheers.) It was at Swansea that we heard of this man, and when the Solicitor to the Treasury expresses his opinion that if not one of these sailors, at any rate some one of 104 relatives or acquaintances whom he ingeniously reckons up, would have come forward, he will perhaps be surprised to learn that in less than one hour's inquiry at Swansea I saw and conversed with at least thirty people who have long since known that the sailor we were in search of had repeatedly talked about his escape from the "Bella," and yet had never thought it worth their while to convey their information beyond the maritime gossip of the courts and alleys in which they live. (Hear, hear.) Not much to be wondered at, after all; for they might reckon with certainty upon being charged with some degree of perjury, like the 86 witnesses who gave evidence for the Claimant in the late Trial. The Solicitor of the Treasury says in this letter that if I can find a sailor from the "Bella" he "will find one from the Osprey to cat him." He may have been reading about the Fiji Islands when he used this threat; but there is no doubt that every witness for the Claimant has very good reason to fear that he may possibly be sent to Newgate, like the Claimant, upon the mere suspicion of having stated what was untrue. (Cheers.) Now I have gone through all these points on which, as I stated before the Solicitor to the Treasury—by far the best lawyer who has been connected with the Case—rests the Claimant's conviction for perjury and forgery, and I ask you—assuming I have done it fairly—whether he ought still to refuse to investigate the evidence which at every step we take is springing up, as it were, under our feet, as here, in this honest old soldier of the Carabineers, who recognized him to-day on this platform. I speak with deliberation, and a full sense of responsibility for my words; and although the Solicitor to the Treasury says he attaches no importance to the opinions expressed by public meetings, I repeat what I stated to him, that we have, in fact, no other Court to appeal to, and that unless you will give sympathy and support by money, the Claimant must inevitably be crushed and sent back to prison, there no doubt to die, as I believe, an innocent man, and his children to the workhouse. (Loud applause.) I will not detain you longer, but ask you to join with me in declaring with one voice that, not forgetting in whose hands are the issues of all contests where right and justice is concerned, we will so far as in us lies—every one of us in his own position and in his sense of duty as an Englishman—see to it, that this man shall have a fair trial.

Captain HUNT, Honorary Treasurer of the TICHBORNE Defence Fund, having referred to various points which went to establish the Claimant's identity, went on to state that money, of course, was needed to obtain that which they all as Englishmen so much desired, a fair and searching trial. Their organization for that purpose was good, and it needed only an earnest response on the part of the English people to obtain for Sir ROGER his just rights. (Hear, hear.) They might rely upon it whatever was subscribed would be expended in a right, proper, honest, and careful manner. (Hear, hear.) He looked without any apprehension to the result, and he anticipated that the day was not far distant when that wonderful knoll of trees which the Attorney-General, at the request of certain ladies, had planted in his demesne would be, in a spirit of honest restitution, sent back to their original growing place in Tichborne Park. (Cheers and laughter.)

Mr. G. ONSLOW, M.P.—There is present on this platform a gentleman who many years ago was one of the sergeants in Sir ROGER TICHBORNE'S regiment, the 6th Carabineers. He has recognized Sir ROGER—(cheers)—and he desires to say so in the face of this great mass meeting.

ALEXANDER KENNEDY, who was loudly cheered, said—That gentleman (the Claimant) I have not seen until to-day since the occasion when, with his troop in the 6th Carabineers, he left Canterbury. (Cheers.) Sir ROGER joined in Dublin, and I was then sergeant. The Claimant, I have no hesitation in stating, is Sir ROGER TICHBORNE, and I am quite prepared to swear that he is the man and no other. (Cheers.)

The Treasurer of the Committee then presented Captain HUNT with a large and liberal contribution towards the TICHBORNE Defence Fund.

Mr. G. ONSLOW, M.P., in highly complimentary terms, moved, and the Claimant seconded, a vote of thanks to the Chairman for his conduct in presiding, and to the Committee for the really admirable manner in which they had carried out to so satisfactory a conclusion all details of this great East-end demonstration.

The Chairman returned thanks, and the meeting separated, cheering vociferously for Sir ROGER TICHBORNE, and wishing every success to his cause.

MACKENZIE.

The libels alluded to by the Claimant at this meeting were published under the auspices of MACKENZIE, a so-called lawyer who was sent to Australia in the interests of the Family, and who spared no pains—like JACOB OMNIUM HIGGINS in England—to poison the public mind against the Claimant. The following extracts will, we think, satisfy our readers of the infamous arts to which they resorted.

Transcript from the Australian Commission, July 13th, 1869, page 184.

DAVID GRIFFITH JONES, examined by Mr. WYATT, Counsel for Plaintiff (Sir R. TICHBORNE), upon his oath saith: I am a newspaper proprietor, and surgeon by profession; I am the proprietor of the *Deniliquin Pastoral Times*, and I was so at the date August 3rd, 1867. (*Pastoral Times of Aug. 3, 1867, shown to witness.*) This is a copy of the paper published by me on that date. I see a paragraph in the fourth column of the second page, headed "SIR ROGER TICHBORNE." I am the writer of that. Just previous to the publication of this, Mr. JOHN MACKENZIE called on me; he was introduced to me by bringing a letter of introduction from Wagga-Wagga. I mean Mr. JOHN MACKENZIE from London, agent for the Defendants. He brought a letter of introduction to me from Mr. COTTER, manager of the Joint Stock Bank, Wagga-Wagga. He called several times. The information conveyed in this paragraph was chiefly ratified by Mr. MACKENZIE. I may mention I had read the chief part of it in other journals. Two points in particular he did not confirm thoroughly. The information came from different journals. These points were—the one, in regard to the Dowager Lady TICHBORNE, the other in regard to the advance made by LEVI of £1,000. I got that about the Dowager Lady TICHBORNE, I think, from a Goulburn paper; he admitted she was weak in intellect, but not to the extent stated in this paragraph. I think I got some original information. To the best of my knowledge it is the passage about BURDON I got from Mr. MACKENZIE originally; and the passage beginning, "None but the weak-minded," and ending at "France." If you take out the words "weak-minded" they would be almost Mr. MACKENZIE'S words. The passage beginning "The trustees of the deceased Baronet," down to the words "To the friends of his youth," is from Mr. MACKENZIE; and the passage from "He has written to Mr. TURVILLE," down to "declined," was also obtained from Mr. MACKENZIE; and I think the whole of the remainder from there downward, to the best of my belief, is from Mr. MACKENZIE. Mr. MACKENZIE expressed a wish to take evidence for and against the present Claimant, but would not wish to take evidence only against him, *but would take it in his favour.*

From the Pastoral Times, Deniliquin, August 3rd, 1867.

SIR ROGER TICHBORNE.

A solicitor, Mr. JOHN MACKENZIE, of Glasgow, has been at Deniliquin in the week specially to make inquiries respecting our old friend TOM DE CASTRO, the Claimant of the Baronetcy of TICHBORNE. Young ROGER TICHBORNE, the second son of the late Baronet, sailed in 1853 from England to South America, and was not afterwards heard of, the vessel having been lost at sea, until lately, when the man known here in Deniliquin as DE CASTRO set up his claim as the missing heir. He followed menial occupations here; was a journeyman butcher, a horse-breaker, and carter; from hence he went to Wagga-Wagga, where he married a girl of very low habits and character, a common servant of a certain class, who, previous to marrying DE CASTRO, had succumbed to the attentions of several men, by one of whom she had a child. DE CASTRO, while here at Deniliquin, spoke at times, oracularly, that he was a high-born man in disguise, and that one day he would turn up titled. He was a very inferior looking man, about five feet eleven inches high (the lost heir was about five feet seven inches), low in his habits and customs, and had not apparently the most latent appearance of a gentleman, much less did he look or act as belonging to one of the high-bred English families. He was in those parts very desirous of getting married, and had made several offers to servant-girls, all of whom rejected DE CASTRO. He had to all appearances been in South America, as he used the lasso with ease, and could talk a little Spanish. His career at Goulburn, Tumut, Wagga-Wagga, and Deniliquin, has been well traced, and the evidence of his being the lost heir is overwhelmingly against his pretensions. The manner in which he got the start in search of the prize is very easily explained. He was talking in a mysterious way at Wagga-Wagga of his future prospects, when a lady (Mrs. GIBBES) the wife of a solicitor of that name, seeing TICHBORNE advertised for, pronounced DE CASTRO, after he had made certain admissions, the lost heir of the TICHBORNES. Mr. GIBBES took DE CASTRO to Sydney in order to inquire further into the matter, and he was partially, but too indiscreetly, recognized by Mr. TURVILLE, the private secretary of the Governor, to be, if not a TICHBORNE, very much like the father of the missing heir. This was enough for DE CASTRO, a man of low cunning, a master of deception of this kind, so on he went raising money at an exorbitant interest on the strength of his future prospects. Messrs. LEVI and DE LISSA, Solicitors, of Sydney, advanced £600 on his bond of £1,000, and several others were let in for smaller sums. The lost heir, as a matter of speculation, was advertized for by Mr. CUBITT, the advertising agent of that city, and DE CASTRO turned up as stated, for which he had been preparing for years, even when in Deniliquin. Of this we are assured by Mr. MACKENZIE there is ample evidence. DE CASTRO was always searching the London papers for evidence as to the TICHBORNE Family, and there is sufficient to justify the idea he knows something of that Family. It is alleged that he is possibly an illegitimate child of the late Baronet (grandfather to the infant heir). Since DE CASTRO's arrival in England he has never been once recognized by any one of the Family as the missing man, excepting the Dowager Lady TICHBORNE, who had previously adopted three men in succession as her lost son, and has given other indications of insanity on this head. Mr. DANBY SEYMOUR, M.P. (the Dowager Lady TICHBORNE's brother), has seen DE CASTRO, and told him to his face that he was an impostor. A respectable person of the name of BURDON, who was military servant to young TICHBORNE for two or three years while the latter was in the Carabineers, and who followed TICHBORNE into the army, has also seen DE CASTRO, and the latter never recognized BURDON, and BURDON immediately told DE CASTRO that he was an usurper. None but the weak-minded Dowager, who has lived, and still lives, on the idea that her lost son would some day turn up, countenances DE CASTRO in England or France. The trustees of the deceased Baronet, the missing heir's younger brother, have offered to recognize DE CASTRO forthwith if he will show himself to some of the companions of his youth (if he be Sir ROGER), and those who have been imposed upon in England and France have now "dropped him." He has written to Mr. TURVILLE, asking him to be God-father of the newly-born infant, but the honour has been declined. The father of the first child of the *soi-disant* Lady TICHBORNE, the maid-of-all-work of Wagga-Wagga, is also missing. It is well-established at the latter town that DE CASTRO was physically incapable of being a father. The trustees of the heir in possession, therefore, are seeking for evidence as to who this DE CASTRO really is. In those parts he said he had served his time in London as a butcher, and had given all kinds of versions of his previous life. We are assured by Mr. MACKENZIE (who had only landed in England a few weeks from a visit to Australia, when he was specially sent back again to prosecute inquiries as to DE CASTRO's life), that there is no desire on the part of the trustees in the Tichborne Estates to throw any obstacle in the way of the missing heir (if he be living) taking his legitimate inheritance. It is to provide against DE CASTRO's recognized children being put in a position to litigate with the children (if any there should be) of the infant heir, that the trustees are taking steps to discover DE CASTRO's antecedents. They represent that there is no fear of present but future proceedings. They are, of course, for the sake of the living members of the Family, also anxious to set at rest DE CASTRO's pretensions, who has exchanged his position as a butcher's assistant to that of the lost heir. The difficulty seems to be, not to defeat DE CASTRO's claims, but in discovering the genus to which he belongs. Time may reveal the mystery, but so long as he keeps his own counsel the TICHBORNES are not likely to succeed in tracing the mystery to its origin.

Manuscript Note by Sir ROGER *on this extract.*

The paragraph accused my mother of having adopted as her son three persons in succession, which is altogether false.

Transcript from the Australian Commission, May 13, 1869.

THOMAS COOK JUST, examined by Mr. WYATT, Counsel for the Plaintiff (Sir ROGER): I am sub-editor of the *Hobart Town Mercury*. I was, in February, 1868, head of the reporting staff of the same journal. (*Hobart Town Mercury shown to witness.*) On the second page, column four, the lower half of the column is a paragraph headed "TICHBORNE Baronetcy," &c.

Q. Who furnished you with that?

A. I can't swear that any one furnished me with this, because I am not in a position to swear I wrote the paragraph. At the time the paragraph was written, or shortly before, the Mr. JOHN MACKENZIE mentioned in the paragraph visited this place. Both myself and Mr. BARRY—another member of the reporting staff—were instructed to see him, and ascertain from him what information we could, as there was a good deal of public interest in the Case. I met Mr. MACKENZIE several times at Mrs. NEWMAN's, Union Club Hotel, and other places, and derived from him all the information contained in the paragraph. I also saw a likeness he had of the alleged ARTHUR ORTON; whether I or Mr. BARRY put it into this shape I do not know. The photo shown to me now (p. 2) is evidently from the same negative as the picture shown to me. It was shown to me as a picture of the Australian Claimant of the TICHBORNE Baronetcy. The Australian Claimant is, in my mind, identified with ARTHUR ORTON.* In the course of my conversations with Mr. MACKENZIE, he told me that he was acting under authority from England, from the Court of Chancery. I understood him to say so. Authority to collect evidence. He said he had collected a great deal and sent it to England. He did not say to whom he had sent it, but he said he had sent home a great deal of evidence to England which would very much surprise the people in England, and confirm the justice of the Case he was engaged in; I can't say whether he said he was acting under an order of the Court, or anything of that sort.

Q. Does the paragraph assume through Mr. MACKENZIE that ARTHUR ORTON and TOM CASTRO are identical?

A. It does so through Mr. MACKENZIE.

TICHBORNE BARONETCY, ETC.

From *Hobart Town Mercury.* 18th February, 1868.

Mr. JOHN MACKENZIE, a gentleman of the legal profession, who has been in these Colonies for some months past, prosecuting inquiries in the above cause, under an order from the Court of Chancery, has again paid our town a visit. We understand Mr. MACKENZIE has ascertained as the result of his investigation that the Australian Claimant, who was known in New South Wales as TOM CASTRO, is identical with a young man named ARTHUR ORTON, who, early in the year 1853, arrived in Hobart Town from London in the ship "Middleton," Captain STOUT, now of the "Harrowby" in this port, in charge of two Shetland ponies imported by Mr. T. D. CHAPMAN. ORTON signed ship's articles as a butcher, and was afterwards in the employment of various butchers in this town, and ultimately was engaged here by Mr. JOHN JACKSON to proceed to his station of Mewburn Park, Gippsland, to act as stockman and general servant. We also understand that the photographs of TOM CASTRO, who is now in England as Sir ROGER CHARLES DOUGHTY TICHBORNE, Bart., have been recognized by his former employers and other parties here as correct likenesses of the above-mentioned ARTHUR ORTON.

Manuscript Note by Sir ROGER *on this extract.*

From this it is apparent that MACKENZIE, the Defendants' agent, furnishes the information for this most abominable paragraph, containing amongst other things an assertion that I was no other than ARTHUR ORTON.

It is evident that MACKENZIE must be held to be responsible for *all* that appeared in the Australian papers, against the just pretensions of the Claimant. We cite only one more.

LADY TICHBORNE.

TICHBORNE's wife, whose portrait appears at page 137, thus shamefully dragged before the public, with the most utter disregard of her feelings, or those of her husband, has favourably impressed all who came in contact with her: and these are persons of rank and position—ladies as well as gentlemen. Like all connected with the unhappy Claimant, she has been made the subject of unmitigated slander. Mr. HAWKINS, at both Trials, made it his constant practice to jest and jeer at every allusion to her—wholly heedless of the presence of her husband; while the writers of the horrid paragraphs which appeared in the daily and weekly Papers, all had their pot-house joke upon this unhappy woman. There are few persons who could have borne better than Lady TICHBORNE the wrongs and sufferings which she has had to endure. The Family, hating or insolently despising her for her humble parentage and occupation, have done what they could to make her life unhappy. That old and true friend of the Claimant, Mr. BLOXAM, regards her with respect and friendship, and never has deserted her. Mr. SKIPWORTH knows her well, and has always spoken of her in high terms. Sir TALBOT CONSTABLE and Mr. BIDDULPH would hardly have become godfathers to her children if she were the objectionable person whom these hired scribblers and slanderers describe. Miss BRAINE, a lady of the purest and most religious character, lived in the same house with her for many months. The two Misses ONSLOW and Mr. GUILDFORD ONSLOW never have deserted her; and at the present moment they allow her an annuity. Mr. and Mrs. HELSBY, of Lymington, evince and continue the most ardent interest in her welfare; and no more honourable or praiseworthy man than Mr. HELSBY can be found. All these things tend to show that she cannot be the person whom she is described to be. We ourselves have no knowledge of her, never having had the advantage of seeing her for more than about half an hour; but during that time, Lady TICHBORNE in no way failed to realize what we had heard from others to her disadvantage. We are sorry to say that, though Mr. BIDDULPH and a few others allow her the annuity which they have promised, it is wholly inadequate to support herself and her four lovely children: that it is utterly inadequate to bestowing on them anything like education; and we must add that in the thousand benevolent hearts that throb in England with the most sublime emotions of heaven-like charity, none could be moved to a better bestowal of the good things which Fortune has given them than in alloting a mite to this unfortunate Lady and her children. In no case could it be more blessed for him, or her, that gave; and in no case, certainly, that we know of could bounty thus dispensed be a greater boon to the recipient.

THE DOUGHTY TICHBORNE BOWLED OUT.

From the *Hobart Town Mercury, March 13th*, 1868.

When, many months ago, we exposed this impudent attempt on the part of TOM DE CASTRO, otherwise "Tom the Cutter," once of Deniliquin, to secure for himself and his heirs the Baronetcy and broad lands of the TICHBORNE Family, we were accused of prejudice against DE CASTRO. Knowing but little of him, not having the honour of his acquaintance while he belonged to the butchering trade in this town, it could not be supposed that we had any *animus* against the *quasi* "DOUGHTY TICHBORNE." DE CASTRO never came within the range of probability as the lost heir, and, as we wrote from accumulated facts for and against him, collected with great care, we felt satisfied—the age of miracles having long since passed away—that DE CASTRO could not possibly be the long-lost ROGER CHARLES DOUGHTY TICHBORNE. DE CASTRO was, when here, a butcher's assistant, and held other occupations which do not prejudice us in the least, as "Doughtyer" men than CASTRO have, in this strange land of ours, felt it necessary to fill menial avocations. About the time that DE CASTRO published to the world that he was the heir of the TICHBORNE title and estates, Mr. O'GRADY, the heir to an

* This witness never saw ARTHUR ORTON.

Irish Peerage and property, was discovered in our inland districts engaged as bullock-driver, so that DE CASTRO's sphere of life in Deniliquin had no influence with us in deciding against his claims. Young ROGER TICHBORNE was upwards of twenty-one years of age when he left England, his education was of the first-class, he had been an officer in the Carabineer Guards, and we need hardly say that he was a gentleman. He was, we believe, about the medium height, and, when he left England, was in possession of a circular letter of credit. He could draw on the family bankers from any part of the world. He sailed for South America some sixteen years ago; the ship was lost with all hands, as it was supposed and believed. Nothing was heard of the lost heir. The younger brother, who was then heir to the title and estates, died in the meantime, leaving an infant son; and the Dowager Lady TICHBORNE, having been thus deprived of both her sons—one by drowning and the other from natural causes—gave way to passionate grief. She felt an inward conviction (as many persons before her have had, when struck down by like misfortune) that ROGER TICHBORNE was still alive. The sailor-man, we hear, called at her mansion, and supported the Dowager's hopes in regard to young ROGER. He informed her (very likely at the instigation of DE CASTRO) that the missing heir was alive, which she believed—on the principle, it is fair to presume, that "the wish was father to the thought"—sustaining herself by hope that her son ROGER had escaped from a wreck wherein all the other persons on board were drowned. It was this fond feeling that induced this lady to accept, before seeing DE CASTRO, no less than three persons in succession as her lost son. Buoyed up by the sailor's strange story that her son lived and would return to her, and having, as stated, been disappointed in the three instances referred to, DE CASTRO made his appearance: he evidently had been prepared for the trespass on Lady TICHBORNE's credulity. Having succeeded in getting the start in the race for the brilliant prize of a Baronetcy and £15,000 a year by gaining support in Sydney, and the ex-Governor's private secretary, who once knew well the TICHBORNE Family, having declared that DE CASTRO was like the TICHBORNES, the latter raised means and boldly made for London and Paris. What did "Sir ROGER" do when he reached the latter gay city? Did he call upon any of his relatives, friends, and acquaintances after an absence and silence of thirteen years or more? He did not. Overcome by mental anguish, and fearing the shock would be too great for him, TOM DE CASTRO, who had, as stated, been butchering in Australia—he, a man of iron nerve, strengthened by the roughing he passed through at the Antipodes—turned into bed, sent for the Dowager Lady TICHBORNE, and there (his body had grown from five feet eight inches to five feet eleven inches) he saw his mother! The Old Man of the Sea never stuck more closely to Sinbad than did DE CASTRO stick to the credulous Dowager, who immediately recognized in TOM her long-lost son. "I am as satisfied," said the Dowager, in her affidavit on the subject, "that he (DE CASTRO) is my long-lost son, ROGER CHARLES DOUGHTY TICHBORNE, as I am of my existence." A Major, who served with young TICHBORNE in the Carabineers, swears, to the best of his belief, that DE CASTRO is ROGER TICHBORNE; the Drill Sergeant swears this is Mr. TICHBORNE whom he drilled. The Father Confessor (the Family being Roman Catholic) affirms that TOM is the "Doughty" Tichborne. But here ends the proof in his favour. The Court of Chancery is not so easily imposed upon; so they dispatched a Glasgow legal gentleman to Australia to make inquiries as to the truth of TOM's allegations, and this gentleman has followed on the track of the *quasi* heir with the vigilance of a first-class detective.

The following letter from DOBINSON and GEARE, the Family attorneys, shows the manner in which they proceeded to secure evidence against Sir ROGER, and connects them also with MACKENZIE:—

57, Lincoln's Inn Fields: April 1st, 1869.

Dear Sir,—We have just received your letter of January 31st last, and for which we are greatly obliged to you. The nature of WILLIAM HOPWOOD's evidence is that which we particularly desire to obtain; that is, the evidence of several reliable persons who can prove that THOMAS CASTRO, the butcher of Wagga-Wagga, is the same identical person as ARTHUR ORTON whom you and others knew in Boisdale, and we shall esteem it a great obligation if you will aid Mr. MACKENZIE's exertions by getting as many persons as you can, who will be able, clearly and distinctly to prove the above fact. To assist in doing this we inclose portrait of ARTHUR ORTON, which was taken for him in his assumed character of Sir ROGER TICHBORNE. For this portrait allowance must be made for the lapse of time, for his increase in size,—he is now enormously stout—for superior dress, and the effects of superior living. Previous to the receipt of your letter we had seen Mr. PITT and obtained from him all he knew of the ORTONS. ARTHUR ORTON was for several years in South America, and we have traced him there by his real name, ARTHUR ORTON. All who knew him concur that he knows some Spanish and can throw the lasso, whilst it is certain that Mr ROGER could not speak Spanish. By this mail we shall write a line to Mr. MACKENZIE to tell him we have inclosed you a photograph.—We are, dear Sir, yours truly,

DOBINSON & GEARE.

Mr. G. S. GRAY, Bairnsdale, North Gippsland, Australia.

57, Lincoln's Inn Fields, London: May 23, 1869.

Dear Sir,—Accept our best thanks for your letter of February 28th last, and the statements inclosed made by WILLIAM HOPWOOD and JAMES THORPE, and also for your communicating the statements to Mr. MACKENZIE. Both these persons will be very useful witnesses, especially HOPWOOD, from his being enabled to identify TOMAS CASTRO of Wagga-Wagga as ARTHUR ORTON of Dargo and Boisdale. It is very desirable, if it can be done, that we should in like manner find witnesses who knew the impostor by the names of THOMAS CASTRO and ARTHUR ORTON, to prove that the persons bearing those names at different times and places was one and the same identical person. From the great kindness and interest you have taken in this most atrocious case, we are sure you will help us to evidence of the above kind, if in your power.

We see both from the Australian papers and from Mr. MACKENZIE's dispatches to us, that the enemy is apparently pursuing the desperate measure of setting up another ORTON who is stated to have been a convict. If he does pursue that course he will certainly help to destroy himself.

Our evidence is so plain, clear, and distinct, that ARTHUR ORTON of Hobart Town, then of Mewburn Park—then in Mr. FOSTER's employ, and then of Sale, is one and the same person as not to leave the smallest room for doubt on the subject. There is besides one fact which the impostor can never get over: he has sworn more than once that he was engaged by Mr. FOSTER and continued the whole time in his employ under the name of TOMAS CASTRO, whilst the books of the station, and the persons employed there, will prove that there never has been any person employed at Mr. FOSTER's station under the name of CASTRO. That circumstance is enough to defeat all the bluster of the enemy; but as we have to deal with persons who will stick at nothing, it behoves us to get the best and strongest evidence possible to defeat the conspiracy raised against the infant Baronet.—We are, dear Sir, very truly yours,

DOBINSON & GEARE.

GEO. H. S. GRAY, Esq., Bairnsdale, Gippsland, Australia.

As we have alluded to MACKENZIE in this place, we think it well to insert some of the evidence given on behalf of Sir ROGER in Australia: given in the face of bribery, cajolery, terror, misrepresentation, falsehood, and all the influence of Jesuit force, cunning, or corruption. When it is remembered that the Claimant was poor, and the forces arrayed against him were clothed, as it were, and covered with gold, little doubt can remain in any honest mind that the very highest credence ought to be reposed in witnesses who voluntarily came forward under such trying circumstances.

PLAINTIFF'S EVIDENCE.

At the office of Messieurs KLINGENDER, CHARSLEY, and LIDDLE, Bank Place, Melbourne, the second day of December, 1869.

Examined by Mr. WYATT, Counsel for the Plaintiff.

JOHN JOSEPH SHILLINGLAW, being sworn and examined upon his oath, saith:—

My name is JOHN JOSEPH SHILLINGLAW; I am proprietor of the *Colonial Monthly Magazine*; I have been in this colony from October, 1852; I was in 1852 Clerk of the Bench at Williamstown, the port of Melbourne; in January, 1854, I was appointed inspector of water police, succeeding Captain PASCO; I remained in that position till February, 1856, when I was appointed Government Shipping Master; I held that office for thirteen years, when I was relieved on general reduction of the Civil Service on motives of public economy, and compensated; I, in part of 1854, as inspector of water police, was the head of the whole Victoria water police force, consisting of about ten or twelve boats' crews of five men each; the arrivals of over-sea shipping were larger then than before or since.

I have taken from Custom House returns the numbers from 1852 to 1857.

1852	1657 vessels arrived.
1853	2594 arrivals.
1854	2596 arrivals.
1855	1876 arrivals.
1856	1920 arrivals.
1857	2190 arrivals.

I know of my own knowledge, without reference to return, that in the year 1854 there was more shipping in Hobson's Bay than any year before or since; I took the census of the population afloat in June, 1854; in 1854 there were great difficulties in manning a ship outward bound; almost universal desertion to the diggings prevailed; it was the duty of the police to board every ship entering the bay; to the best of my knowledge that duty was performed; it is also the duty of the immigration officer to board ships; in 1854 I boarded many hundreds myself; I found the desertion applied to officers as well as men—captains as well as others; I have known masters of ships to form a party out of their own crew to go to the diggings; the police arrested many thousand deserters; there were over 3,000 men a year reported as deserters during 1854 and 1855; we have brought up as many as 80 men in a morning to the police-court. There were very many ships laid up, with perhaps only one or two men left on board; on one ship we found only a boy and a cat, who had been three or four days there; a ship called the "Duke of Bedford" was converted into a lodging-house; it was a common thing to find lightermen's boats adrift. Once we found a man swimming ashore, pushing a plank before him, and his clothes lashed in the middle; another time a man getting ashore by a carpenter's bench.

In one case a party of 30 escaping from the "Great Tasmania" were shot at, and one was wounded in the back.

Before the Merchant Shipping Act came into force in May, 1855, it was the practice under the law here to levy a poll tax of 5s. per head on every male statute adult.

There was not to my knowledge any practice of rewarding masters for bringing shipwrecked persons to the port before May, 1855; there was no inducement to masters to bring such persons; if a master had any such persons, there was no pecuniary inducement for him to publish the fact; in the case of the "Waterwitch," I believe you will find that was a special case, and a vote in the estimate for it; I think a master bringing shipwrecked persons to this port before the passing of the Act would let them go ashore as soon as possible; he might inquire at the Custom House to see if there was any reward; but I am pretty sure he would find there was none; I do not remember any shipwrecked persons being brought here; now you mention them, I remember the "Waterwitch" case; I remember also that of Mr. LAZAR, who was wrecked at the Cape, and if I hunted up the duty-books I might find others.

Cross-examined by Mr. MARTIN.

On referring to the Local Act, 18 Victoria, No. 5, I find that the poll tax of 5s. per head imposed by that Act did not come into force till 1855; there were regular liners left this port in 1854. R. and I. HENDERSON's ships left; I have seen £50, £60, and as much as £70 paid to an able seaman for the run home.

I did not take the census in 1857.

The master of a vessel was bound by law to give a return of all passengers to the Immigration Office in 1854.

Q. Was there any difficulty in a man's getting home as a passenger in 1854?

A. There was no insuperable difficulty. Ships did get away somehow.

To the Defendants' Commissioner:

Q. Was there any difficulty?

A. Yes, there was a difficulty.

The difficulty was simply delay; ships did go at that time; any man who could do anything on a ship could get home; there was no difficulty in a sailor getting employment; a man might have got away easily if he would work his passage home.

Re-examined by Mr. WYATT.

I imagine the word "passenger" did not include shipwrecked persons.

To the Commissioner for Plaintiff:

Mr. CASSELL, who was Collector of Customs in 1854, is dead.

At WEBB's Hotel, Hobart Town, on Thursday, the 13th May, 1869.

Examined by Mr. WYATT, Counsel for the Plaintiff.

JAMES ANDREWS, being sworn and examined, upon his oath saith:—

My name is JAMES ANDREWS; I am a sawyer by trade; I have have been in this colony since February, 1844; I went in 1855 from this colony to Port Albert; I engaged with Mr. GUESDON here to go to Mr. JOHNSON's, of Mewburn Park, in Gippsland; I arrived in Port Albert about September of 1855; I went by the "Eclipse" schooner; there was one other man on board known as JACK, under a similar engagement to Mr. JOHNSON; I only knew him as Bristol JACK; my engagement was as a sawyer; I went to Mewburn Park; I got there in the same year, 1855; I got there in about a week from Hobart Town; I was engaged for six months; in three months I and JOHNSON had some words, and I left; my work was that of a sawyer for the three months; during that three months I knew a man named ALECK NIELSEN; I believe NIELSEN came from here, because he told me so; I do not know whether he was there before me or after me; I am almost certain he was there when I got there; NIELSEN was carpentering there; he used the sawn stuff that I supplied; there was an old man at work there with him filling up the place; NIELSEN was under him like; I daresay there were 30 or 40 men squandered about on the station; there was a man there they called ARTHUR the Butcher; I do not know his surname; it was very seldom I saw him at all; he used to be knocking about the stockyard, killing a beast when it was wanted, feeding pigs; I know this because I have seen him doing it; that was the work of a station butcher up there.

Q. Describe ARTHUR the Butcher's appearance.

A. He was rather a fair complexioned cove, 5ft. 8in. or thereabout; he was a rather raw-boned sort of a man; he was a man of three or four and thirty to the best of my belief; I could not say; I cannot say whether he had whiskers or moustache, or that, about his face; I think he had whiskers but I cannot be positive, a little whiskers; his hair was a lightish colour; he wore it generally combed at the back of his ears; I noticed nothing particular about his legs; to the best of my opinion he was a little bow-legged about his walk; his nose, I believe, was a little crooked, it looked as if it had been like that since he was born; he was slightly pock-marked; only slightly; but that you could see it plainly enough; not deep; nothing about his eyes or eyebrows; he was rather round-shouldered; I never recollect seeing him again after I left Mewburn Park; during the three months I was at Mewburn Park, my wife was with me; I never returned to Mewburn Park; I have seen ARTHUR the Butcher stripped up to his arms, while killing a bullock; in fact he always had his sleeves up when I saw him; there were tattoo marks across his arm about here (pointing half way between his arm and wrist) pricked with ink, I suppose; a dark-blue colour; I cannot swear they were pricked with ink. (Sydney photograph put in by Plaintiff and shown to witness.) That is not like ARTHUR the Butcher to my recollection. (Exhibit D. 5 shown to witness.) That is not like him. (Exhibits D. 6, 7, 8, 9, and 10 shown to witness.) None of them are like the butcher according to my recollection; I do not know any of them as him; the butcher turned his hair back, and that is the only resemblance to the butcher; he had a fashion with his hand of putting his hair back; I was at JOHNSON's about three months; when I left there, I went to Flooding Creek; I left JOHNSON's before Christmas, 1855; I think I was at Flooding Creek about two months; ultimately, I think about April, 1856, I got to Melbourne; I stayed there, I think, rather better than seven months; then back again to Port Albert, and then to the Omeo diggings: before I left JOHNSON's there was TOM TOKE there; he was a stockrider; there was another stockrider there named DUNCEY; another named BARNEY WOODS, a splitter; I do not recollect a man named CHAPMAN there; I got to Omeo in the beginning of January, 1857; my wife went with me; I went up there to dig; when I got there I found sawing was good, and I went to the saw; I was sawing about four or five weeks; my camp was on the Leveson Creek; while I was camped there NIELSEN came up and TOKE; there were two men with them; one they called CHAPMAN, and the other BILLY the Groom; I cannot say there was any one else with them; I cannot say how long these men worked together; there was another man came about the same time, a constable named HINES, and a foreigner; the foreigner was working with HINES; I believe he afterwards worked a fortnight with me; the man I had in the pit left; so I took the foreigner and learnt him.

Q. Describe the foreigner.

A. Fair complexion, light hair, hair round the chin; I could not say for certainty, but, I think, blue eyes; I should take him to be 5ft. 9in. or 10in.; I am 5ft. 7in. and he was two or three inches taller than me, if not more.

Q. Anything peculiar about his features, or as to his eyes or eyebrows?

A. Nothing more than that he had a little twitching of the eyebrows when he was speaking to you; if he was not talking to you for any length of time you would not notice it; when in the pit we used to strip; I have seen him stripped to his arms; to the best of my belief I never noticed anything on his arms; he spoke as if of foreign descent, but spoke as good English as I do; I should take him for a foreigner; I was seven months at the Omeo diggings; I should take the foreigner to be about seven or eight and twenty; when I left he was still there; I have seen him several times over at NIELSEN's, CHAPMAN's, and TOKE's; there was no distance between the places; NIELSEN's and TOKE's party had two horses with them; one was a black horse, the other an iron grey; the foreigner was of a very gentlemanly appearance; a very quiet man, with little to say to anybody; I believe he come to the Leveson's Creek either from a place called the Nicholson or else the Mitchell; I think it was the Nicholson; he told me that himself; I have no other means of knowledge; I asked him; he told me many things I can't remember now; he said he had been helping to put up a house there.

Q. Did he mention any name in connection with putting up that house?

A. I think the name was MARSH.

ARTHUR the Butcher and this foreigner were nothing like one another at all; they were both tall, but the foreigner was taller than him; they were both fair; the foreigner combed his hair back behind his ears; they both wore their hair in the same way.

(Exhibits P. 1 and P. 2 shown to witness.)

P. 2 resembles the foreigner, but looks older and bigger; I don't think P. 1 resembles him at all, except in the hair being put back, but it looks too dark.

(Exhibits D. 6, 7, 8, 9, and 10 shown to witness.)

Q. Do you see any resemblance in any of those to any person you have ever seen before?

A. No, they are neither like the foreigner nor the butcher at the time I knew them; but a few years make a deal of difference.

(D. 11 shown to witness.)

Q. What do you think of that one?

A. That looks something like the foreigner; but I would not swear it is him. I cannot see the butcher in it.

(D. 5 shown to witness.)

I see no resemblance in that to any one.

Cross-examined by Mr. Attorney-General.

The butcher promised to be a big man—no taller but stouter; I should take him to be two or three and thirty; I will swear that he was more than three and twenty; I could not swear he was more than thirty; I only go by guess as to his age.

Q. Allowing for fourteen years, and his growing stouter, look at D. 8, and see if he could have grown into that?

A. No, not to my recollection; he might, but I should not know him by that.

Q. Look at P. 2 and D. 8; are those the same man?

A. I don't think they are; they might be.

I was a sawyer at JOHNSON's; I camped about a mile and a half from the homestead; I and my wife lived alone in our tent; there was one other tent near us—my mate and his wife; ARTHUR lived in a hut on the station; I think he did not live alone; I was not there of a night; that hut was a mile and a half from my tent; it was very seldom that I saw ARTHUR at all; I used to go on the station for rations and milk, or anything I wanted, sometimes twice a day, morning and evening; I used to go about eight or nine o'clock in the morning, and on Sundays I have been there; I could not say how many beasts I have seen ARTHUR kill; there was another man used to kill—this DUNCHY, as they used to call him—at least, he used to help; ARTHUR was the head butcher; there was not much butchering—only killing meat for the station; I always saw him with his shirt-sleeves up; I could see there were marks on his arm; but I could not tell what it was; I never took particular notice whether it was a ship, or house, or what; I will undertake to swear that the mark I saw was not on the muscle of the arm above the elbow, but he might have it on both for all I know; I will not undertake to swear he was not marked on both arms below the elbow; when DUNCHY assisted him he turned up his sleeves; I can't swear whether he had any marks or not; to the best of my opinion he had, about the same place as the butcher.

Q. The same colour?

A. Well, I would not swear that he had any at all, but to the best of my belief he had, and about the same colour and place as the butcher; there was nothing to call my attention more particularly to the arms of one of these men than to those of the other; I could not swear the mark was tattooed with a needle—it was tattooed with something.

Q. Will you undertake to swear the mark was blue?

Witness: Blue? Well, it was dark blue.

Q. Will you undertake to swear it was blue?

A. I would not swear it was blue.

Q. When did you first tell anyone that you recollected the mark on the arm.

A. I will not swear that I told anybody about it, and I will not swear that I did not tell anybody about it; NIELSEN came to me about the beginning of last week, I think, and asked me if I recollected the name of a digger that he could not recollect, that

MARY ANNE, WIFE OF SIR ROGER TICHBORNE, BART.

lost gold; I mentioned the name BENNETT; he asked me if I recollected ARTHUR the Butcher at Mewburn Park; and I said, Yes; that is all he asked me about him, and all I said; that I swear was all that passed between us about ARTHUR; my wife was present; I do not know whether she was in the bar or not; I keep a public-house; I have had a conversation with Plaintiff's agent's clerk about him; NIELSEN came with him at the same time; he asked me, Did I know such a man. I told him what I knew of him, and when I had seen him; NIELSEN was present; my wife was out at the time; I will not swear that I did not speak of the mark in NIELSEN's presence; it might have been mentioned, we spoke of the pock-marks; I said the likeness could not be like ARTHUR, because he was pock-marked; I first spoke of the pock-marks; I swear I was the first person that mentioned it; I said so directly I saw the likeness; I have been a publican twelve months; before that I was in Sydney for four years; before that I worked as sawyer for Mr. RISBY, of this place; the pock-marks were slight, to the best of my belief; I know he was pock-marked. (P. 1 and P. 2 shown to witness.) These are the photographs shown me in NIELSEN's presence.

Q. Will you undertake to swear, looking at No. 2, that that person is not slightly pock-marked?

A. I don't think it is, but I would not swear to a photograph at all.

I would not on that photograph swear whether the person, from whom that photograph was taken, was pock-marked or not.

I said on seeing this it was not ARTHUR, because he was pock-marked; I don't think this is pock-marked now; I never saw ARTHUR after leaving Mewburn Park. I do not know what became of him; the foreigner had nothing the matter with his nose, not then, to my knowledge; the foreigner was a good hand with the pick and shovel; he helped me sawing, that is all I know of him; I would not swear he had nothing on his arm, but I never noticed it; I will swear he was not marked with the small-pox; I never, to my knowledge, heard of Ballarat HARRY; I did not know a Ballarat HARRY, a mate of TOKE's; they lived higher up the river than me; I think the foreigner used to smoke, but I will not be certain; I never heard from him where he came from; he never talked of South America; he talked of plenty of things I can't remember; I think he said that he had been passenger aboard some ship; he told me about the ship he came in, I don't recollect the name of the ship or captain; he never told me he was shipwrecked; he might have told me that too; I don't recollect; he mentioned something about a ship; he spoke as good English as I do, I never heard him speak a foreign language; I have seen him reading a book; I can't say I ever saw him write.

Re-examined.

Q. What did you mean when you said you would not swear the mark was blue?

A. I could not swear it was black or blue—it was dark; I think it was a dark blue; it was not red or yellow; Mewburn Park is a cattle station; my tent was about one and a half miles from the homestead; I cannot say it was north, south, east, or west; I was nearer the port way; the butcher's hut was close to the homestead.

Q. (Exhibit P. 2 shown to witness.) When you look at this and say there is no likeness between this and the butcher, is it the pock-mark alone that decides you?

A. No, it is not that alone.

Examined by Mr. WYATT, Counsel for the Plaintiff.

ALEXANDER NIELSEN, being sworn and examined, upon his oath saith:—

My name is ALEXANDER NIELSEN. I am messenger at the Public Works Office, Hobart Town; I can't exactly say when I came to Tasmania; it is a good many years ago; I was here in 1853 and 1854; my occupation then was a house carpenter; I knew WILSON and LORING, the butchers; I did not know any of their men or their names; I did not know an ARTHUR ORTON in Hobart Town; I left here for Port Albert, in Victoria; I left to go into the employ of Mr. JOHNSON, of Mewburn Park; I partly engaged here; but signed the agreement at Port Albert, on board the schooner "Eclipse;" I partly engaged here with Mr. JOHNSON; he was here himself, and went over in the "Eclipse" to Port Albert with me; Captain BURGESS commanded the "Eclipse;" I engaged for eighteen months as carpenter, and to make myself otherwise useful, on the station at Mewburn Park, near Sale, then commonly called Flodden Creek; I got there about the month of June, 1854; I served for the eighteen months; after that I remained with him about four or five months longer; while I was there I saw a man named ANDREWS; he came from Hobart Town to saw for Mr. JOHNSON; I did not know him here; he sawed there—he sawed timber for the building and fencing; I have been to his place, and have seen him in the saw-pit; there were others I remember at Mewburn Park—JOHN LUCKMAN, COLIN MACLAREN, DONALD MACINTOSH, who was overseer, HIGGINS, and the butcher, who went by the name of ARTHUR ORTON, and a large number of others; I lived in the men's hut, about 300 yards from Mr. JOHNSON's house; those men I have named lived in the hut with me and several others; ORTON lived there; I slept in the hut all the while I was on the station, that was about two years; ORTON lived in the hut six months to my knowledge; I believe he was there longer; I was there first, and I went away first; when I went away on the first occasion I went to the Nicholson; THOMAS TOKE was stockrider at Mewburn Park before I went, not when I left; he left about two months before me; I remember WILLIAM ROBERTSON, a groom on the station, two months before I left; he was called BILLY the Groom; he came from Hobart Town in one of Mr. JOHNSON's vessels; ROBERTSON told me so.

Q. Describe ORTON.

A. He was a man about 23 years of age, as near as I could judge, from 5ft. 8in. to 5ft. 10in., fair complexion, hair light, brushed back behind his ears, between 10 and 11 stone in weight; he came to JOHNSON's as stockrider and butcher; I have seen him act as butcher several times; he used to kill once or twice a week; that is, when he was on the station; sometimes he was off, driving cattle.

When I left for the Nicholson, ORTON was still there; he was the last person I saw; I went to the races, and in returning had an accident with one of the horses, Mr. JOHNSON's, named the "Buck-jumper"; he was hipped; I was riding him; he threw me off, and got hipped; ORTON met me, took the horse from me, and put it in the stable; I then ran away to the Nicholson; ORTON and I had a conservation before I left about the horse; I told him I thought I had better run away; Mr. JOHNSON seemed in such a way; he wished me good-bye; I asked him to take care of what few things I had, and give them to JOHN LUCKMAN for me; the Nicholson is sixty or seventy miles from Mewburn Park; that is the place where I went; it lies north of Mewburn Park; the Nicholson is from thirty to sixty miles from the Dargo Station; the Dargo Station is to the westward of the Nicholson; the Mitchell is eight miles further north of the Nicholson; I stayed at the Nicholson one night, at MARSHALL's accommodation house; while at the Mewburn Park Station, a party came consisting of two viz., THOMAS CHAPMAN and a young man who went by the name of the foreigner; the foreigner came twice, the first time by himself; he came on horseback the first time he came an iron-grey horse.

He told me he came from the Mitchell; I know because I heard him say so; he stayed one afternoon the first time; that was about three or four months before I left; the second time he came he came with one THOMAS CHAPMAN; THOMAS CHAPMAN had been employed at MARSHALL's, at the Nicholson, but was then out of employ; no others came with them; they both came on horseback; the foreigner came on his own horse, the iron-grey.

To Mr. DOBSON:

I know it was his own because he sold it afterwards; my partner bought it; I knew the iron-grey, and have often ridden it about; CHAPMAN borrowed a horse from MARSHALL's and returned it; I knew that because they said so—it was a bay; they stayed a day or so; maybe, two or three; when they left two station hands went with them, named THOMAS TOKE and WILLIAM ROBERTSON; ORTON did not go with them; they went towards the Nicholson diggings; I saw them go that way; they went along the main road from the station to Stratford; that is the way to the Nicholson; that was about two months before I left; when I left, I left ARTHUR ORTON on the station; that is the last I saw of him; I saw the other four again at the Omeo diggings, Leveson Creek; ANDREWS left Mewburn Park between the first and second visits of the foreigner; I went from the Nicholson to the Omeo diggings; I was about four or five days on the journey; I fell in at the Mitchell with a man of the name of HINES; he was formerly a policeman at the Tara Township, Port Albert; we kept company all the way; I was ill on the way; I have made a mistake; the Mitchell is eight miles on the Mewburn Park side of the Nicholson, not the other side; I missed my road and went about four or five miles in the wrong direction, I turned back to where the roads parted; I then met HAINES; I was thirsty and weak, and HAINES offered me a glass of brandy, I asked him if he had got it with him, he gave me a glass; we both went on to the Nicholson and stayed at MARSHALL's accommodation house; the next day we proceeded to the Omeo on Leveson Creek; the first persons I saw after I got to Leveson's Creek were THOMAS TOKE, THOMAS CHAPMAN, WILLIAM ROBERTSON, and the foreigner; I was at those diggings eleven months; during that time I worked several claims with different parties; I worked with TOKE, CHAPMAN, and ROBERTSON; I worked with them about six weeks, perhaps; after that CHAPMAN went away and joined RYAN; RYAN's party it was called; TOKE was my mate; the foreigner never joined me; he was a partner with TOKE, CHAPMAN and ROBERTSON; when I arrived I arrived in the evening, and they asked me to stay with them. In the morning the foreigner had some words with TOKE, and said he would not work with them any more; he gave me what interest he had in the party; they were shallow sinking from eight to ten feet; the foreigner then joined HAINES or HINES, who came up with me; Mr. and Mrs. ANDREWS were there. He was working another claim with a man named GEORGE the Swede, a river claim; there was a horse named Charcoal; that was the iron-grey belonging to the foreigner, and a black horse called Prince, belonging to THOMAS TOKE; the foreigner sold the iron-grey to Mr. TOKE; when I left the Omeo diggings I left the foreigner there; I then returned to Mewburn Park and saw JOHNSON, and again entered his service; ORTON was not there when I went back; I never saw him again.

Q. Describe the foreigner.

A. He was a well-built man, about 5ft. 10in., fair complexion, lightish eyes, light hair; he wore his hair pushed back over his forehead behind his ears; he had a little whiskers of light colour; no moustache; eyebrows, lightish, but heavy; he knitted his brows when he was offended; nothing about his skin—it was fine like, not pock-marked; he had a foreign accent, but spoke good English; you could clearly understand every word he said, but he had a foreign accent.

(Exhibits P. 1, P. 2, and D. 5 shown to witness.)

Q. Are any of these like any one you ever saw?

A. Yes; D. 5 and P. 2 are the foreigner.

(P. 1 again shown.)

Yes, the eyes of that are like; this would be not so bad a likeness if it were fair; it looks too dark.

In D. 5 and P. 2 he looks rather stouter.

(Exhibits D. 6, 7, 8, 9, and 10 shown to witness.)

Q. Making allowance for stoutness and lapse of years, what do you think of all or any of those?

A. D. 6 and D. 9 are something like him, only he is more dressed here.

Q. Suppose the foreigner two or three years before you saw him, is D. 11 like him?

A. It is like him in the eyes and the mouth.

Q. Making the same allowance, would ORTON have grown into any of them?

(Exhibits D. 5, 6, 7, 8, 9, 10, and 11, and P. 1 and P. 2 shown.)

A. No, I don't see ARTHUR ORTON in any of them; I see D. 8 is a very good likeness of the foreigner, but he seems to have increased in size; ORTON was generally plainly dressed; he never had many clothes, he was a loosely-made sort of young man; ORTON was reserved, but I cannot say there was anything gentlemanly about him; the other one was very particular in his dress; the foreigner did not wear butcher's things; I can't recollect about his things; he was tidier on a week day than any of us, and had the appearance of being a respectable person.

Q. Did the foreigner come from Mr. FOSTER's station?

A. He had been previously in his employ.

Q. How do you know that?

A I have heard him say so.

Q. Where—at Mr. FOSTER's?

A. About Boisdale and Dargo stations, I have heard him say so.

Cross-examined.

I saw Exhibit P. 2 about four or five days ago; I saw that at Mr. ANDREWS' public-house; I have spoken to ANDREWS about ARTHUR ORTON on the evening when the likeness was shown to me; that is the first time I ever spoke to him about him; he gave an account of the foreigner in my presence; his wife was not present; he mentioned ARTHUR ORTON then; he said he knew him; I can't recollect what else; on the same occasion I asked him about a man named BENNETT; the wife was not present; it might have been three-quarters of an hour we were conversing, not altogether on that topic; we found we both knew the parties; I went to ANDREWS to show Plaintiff's agent I had been to Omeo, and knew the foreigner; I never heard the foreigner or anyone else mention his name; I have been to ANDREWS' within the last fortnight; I think only twice, to the best of my belief; from my own recollection I cannot say whether ORTON was pock-marked or not; I am not positive; exercising my recollection, I do not remember seeing any pock-marks on him, nor do I recollect seeing any marks on his arms; I seldom saw his arms; I occupied part of the same hut with him; I believe his sleeves were not constantly tucked up; I lived at the homestead, ANDREWS about a mile away; I had better opportunities than ANDREWS of seeing him with his sleeves tucked up; I was nearer him.

Q. Did you ever hear the foreigner called DU MOULIN?

A. No; I knew DU MOULIN; he took Mr. MACKINTOSH's place at Mr. JOHNSON's as overseer; he was with me when the horse was hurt; I never heard him (the foreigner) called DE CASTRO or CASTRO.

The foreigner came twice to JOHNSON's; TOKE, ROBERTSON, a man named "'Possum JACK," the old milkman, and myself saw him the first time he came; they only stayed an afternoon the first time; the second time all I have named were there, and may have seen him; Mr. DU MOULIN was overseer then; I can't say whether he saw them; they stayed at the men's hut; they stayed on the station two or three days; I think the foreigner slept in the barn; GEORGE the Swede, at the Omeo, was a very tall man; very big—over six feet; he had lightish hair; he was in ANDREWS' claim; he may have been called Dutch GEORGE; the foreigner did not work with ANDREWS, that I recollect, at Omeo; I think he cut some boards with him in the saw-pit; there were not many foreigners about at the time; there was a Frenchman at Mewburn Park called MICHAEL; we called him "MICKEY, the Frenchman"; I never lived with the foreigner for any time; I arrived at Mewburn Park in or about June, 1854; it might have been May or the beginning of June; I was under an engagement for eighteen months, and remained four or five months after that time; ORTON came across in one of Mr. JOHNSON's vessels; the foreigner was about twelve stone when at Omeo; ORTON was about ten or eleven stone at JOHNSON's; he had not large ears; I could not give a description of his nose; I can say it was not turned up. (Exhibit D. 8 shown to witness.)

Q. Would you undertake to say ORTON would never grow into such a man as that?

A. I do so, sir; he never would; he was not a big, hulking fellow; he was a raw-boned fellow; he was large boned, but he was thin.

Q. Is No. D. 11 either the foreigner or ARTHUR ORTON?

A. It is like the foreigner in the eyes and mouth; not like ORTON at all; I never would believe it was ORTON, that is, ARTHUR ORTON the butcher.

I went from JOHNSON's to the Omeo in about six or seven days; the foreigner was then at the Omeo; it might have been two or three months between my seeing him at JOHNSON's, and again at the Omeo; I left the Omeo first after I had been there about eleven months.

Re-examined by Mr. WYATT.

When we addressed the foreigner we called him "Bon."

At WEBB's Hotel, Hobart Town, Friday, May 14th, 1869.

Examined by Mr. WYATT, of Counsel for the Plaintiff. MARY ANDREWS, being sworn and examined, upon her oath saith:—

My name is MARY ANDREWS. I am the wife of JOHN ANDREWS, of the Neptune Hotel, Hobart Town; I accompanied my husband to Gippsland in the "Eclipse" in 1854 or 1855; we went to Mewburn Park, Mr. JOHNSON's; I was not under an engagement; my husband remained about three months; I lived down at the saw-pits in a tent about two miles from the homestead; there may have been a shorter way; I used to go to the homestead for milk every day; when there I used to see a man named ORTON the Butcher; he was the station butcher; there was no other butcher I am aware of.

Q. Describe him.

A. I can't say how tall he was; he was taller than my husband, fair complexion, and hair; I can't say I remember his eyes; I could not exactly say whether he had whiskers or moustache; he wore his hair straight up, combed back with his fingers; he was there before I went and after; I, afterwards, not so much as a couple of years I think, accompanied my husband to the Omeo diggings on Leveson's Creek; we were to the best of my knowledge on Leveson's Creek five or six months; we lived in a tent; after we had been there some time, one or two came who had been at Mewburn Park; NIELSON came first, then there was BILLY the Groom; there were two more, one was TOKE, I can't tell the other name. I never saw ORTON in the diggings; I remember while my husband was sawing in the pit for some time there were several sawed with him, but there was the foreigner sawed with him, too. The foreigner was with my husband a fortnight or ten days in the pit; they then both went digging, but in different claims; the foreigner was one of the men that came up with BILLY the Groom, and a man named TOKE, and another whose name I can't remember; four came up together; the foreigner's name I did not know. After the foreigner came there I had opportunities of seeing him the whole time I remained on the diggings.

Q. Describe him.

A. The foreigner was a tall man—taller than the butcher; fair complexion, fair hair; I can't say I remember his eyes; he had a little hair on his face—a little whiskers; they were fair ones; he wore his hair brushed back; the foreigner was taller than the butcher, but I could not say which was biggest in size; I can't describe the butcher's clothes; sometimes he had a blue jumper and sometimes a coloured shirt; the foreigner used to wear Crimean shirt and cord trousers; I remember the foreigner's clothes because I washed for him all the while we were there together. [Exhibits P. 1, P. 2, D. 5 to 10, both inclusive, shown to witness.]

Take those in your hands and tell if you can see in any of those any person you have ever seen before.

A. Yes; P. 2 is the foreigner, D. 5 is something of the set of the foreigner, the way he used to sit with his hands. If he had a Crimean shirt on I should know him better; but P. 2 is the foreigner's appearance.

Q. Looking at P. 2, have you any doubt about it or certainty?

A. No, there is no doubt about it.

Q. Allowing for fourteen years, he is the same age as when you knew him?

A. By the appearance he is of about the same age as when I knew him; I took him to be about seven or eight and twenty years of age when I knew him.

(Exhibits again shown to witness.)

Q. Can you see ARTHUR ORTON in any of those?

A. No, I cannot; they are all bigger than ARTHUR ORTON.

(Exhibit D. 11 shown.)

I do not recognize that.

When I left Omeo I went to the Port Albert on my way to Tasmania; I went with my husband; we went in the "Helen S. Page," Captain SPRING; we were at the Port about a week; while there my husband sold a horse.

Q. Describe the selling of the horse, and what happened.

A. When we came from the diggings he sold a horse for six pounds; a horse I rode from the diggings; It was a draught horse, but we did not know it when we sold it; after we sold it the man we sold it to put it in harness, and went for a load of gin; ORTON the Butcher stood against a fence, at the stockyard hotel, looking at it; he said,—Mrs. ANDREWS, the master has sold the horse; I said, Yes, for six pounds; he said I think your husband was a fool, if he had left it a day or two longer he would have got more for it; ORTON spoke first, I did not see him till he spoke, I did not know he was there; this must have been about ten days since I left the foreigner on Omeo; I had no further conversation with ORTON, except he asked me if we were going to Hobart Town; I am sure it was ARTHUR ORTON spoke to me at the Port; ORTON spoke good English, no foreign accent; he was an Englishman; the foreigner spoke English well, considering he was a foreigner, but you would know he was a foreigner; I never called him anything but the foreigner; he had a name, but I have forgotten it; I have heard it at Omeo, I have got it on the end of my tongue, it sounded like CASSITTER, or CASS, or something of a CASS.

Cross-examined by Mr. DOBSON.

I have not heard him called Bon, to my recollection; I won't swear he was not, I can't exactly tell you what people called him; if I went to his hut and he wasn't in, I used to say, was the foreigner in; I have never to his face addressed him by any name, behind his back I called him the foreigner.

I saw a likeness like P. 2 one night before to-day; I saw it in my parlour; Plaintiff's agent's clerk, my husband, and another gentleman, whose name I do not recollect, were present; I know NIELSEN, he was with my husband at the Omeo; he was there too; I know young LUCKMAN, he was there too; I do not know LUCKMAN's name; there was no one else; I was out when they came, and came in just before they went away; when I saw the photograph in my parlour, I saw the Plaintiff's agent's clerk, my husband, NIELSEN, Mr. LUCKMAN, and another person; I walked into the parlour and walked out; my husband told me to come in; I think NIELSEN asked me first what was the man's name that lost the gold; then I think one of the gentlemen asked me, did I ever see the likeness; I said No, but I have seen some one like it; no one in my presence mentioned either the foreigner or ARTHUR ORTON, not while I was present; did not know then what they showed it me for; they afterwards asked me if I had any objection to give evidence; I have seen NIELSEN twice within the last fortnight at our public-house; this night was the second time NIELSEN came by himself; the first time I can't say whether he had any conversation; the master and he were talking, but about what I can't say; I think he asked me if I knew Mr. HINES, who had been a trooper; I said I knew one at the diggings; the foreigner and ORTON were not then mentioned; I and my husband have not talked together about the Omeo since we first saw

NIELSEN, nothing whatever; not even mentioned the name; we are on good terms, of course; he knew I was summoned to give evidence, and I still swear that I and my husband have never spoken a single word about what occurred at the Omeo, nor about what I was coming here to-day for; it was no business of ours; I have spoken of it, but not to my husband; I gave a statement the night I was shown P. 2 in the presence of Plaintiff's agent's clerk, Mr. LUCKMAN, Mr. NIELSEN, not in my husband's presence; he had walked out before I began my statement, and took charge of the bar during it; LUCKMAN and NIELSEN were both present; I can't say what LUCKMAN and NIELSEN were talking about; they had their own affairs; they neither of them made a statement in my presence, or that I am aware of, none of the three men, in my presence, made any remark as to P. 2; I washed for the foreigner; there were no marks on his clothing; he had no collars; I never saw the foreigner ride; I know he had a horse that he lost; I could not tell you whether he kept dogs; there were dogs, but I can't say who they belonged to; I have been in Tasmania 28 years; I came in the "Emma Eugene" the first; she has made three voyages; that was the first voyage; Crimean shirts and cord trousers were common articles of dress on the diggings.

Re examined by Mr. WYATT.

Q. Were you asked not to communicate with your husband on this subject?

A. No; I was not asked.

Q. Did not Plaintiff's agent's clerk request you not to do so?

A. I knew myself I ought not, but Plaintiff's agent's clerk might have done so, but I did not notice it. NIELSEN came and asked me about a man named BENNETT that lost some gold; BENNETT had shifted his claim and built a new hut, and the gold he had in a jar was left in the old hut; and he gave the hut to another man, and the gold was planted in a jar in the fireplace; BENNETT told me so; the man who took the old hut found the gold and stuck to it; there was a great quantity of it; they called a meeting on him and found the gold on him; when they found the gold, they blindfolded him first, and were going to hang him; then they were going to cut his ears off; afterwards gave him half an hour start to leave the diggings, and put the dogs on him; BENNETT had a nephew, or there was a person who called himself his nephew; of all the people on the diggings the foreigner was most intimate with BENNETT's nephew, or the man that called himself so.

To Mr. DOBSON:

I have been married more than once; my former husband's name was TODD; my maiden name was COGEN; I came from Liverpool: I cannot write.

At the Metropolitan Hotel, Sydney, the 25th day of June, 1869.

Examined by Mr. WYATT, of Counsel for the Plaintiff.

MATTHEW AARON WORMS, being sworn and examined, upon his oath states as follows:—

My name is MATTHEW AARON WORMS. I am a merchant at 21, Wynyard-lane, Sydney; I know Mr. MICHAEL GUILFOYLE, florist, of Double Bay, Sydney; I have known him eight or ten years; I have bought plants of him occasionally; I have been to his gardens at Double Bay; I have had business relations with Sir ROGER TICHBORNE in this colony, whom I believe to be the Plaintiff in a suit for the recovery of the Tichborne Estates, the same person whom I have read in the papers passed by the name of DE CASTRO in this colony; I had conversation with GUILFOYLE about TICHBORNE; I had money transactions with TICHBORNE; before the loan there were negotiations for it.

In course of these negotiations TICHBORNE referred me to GUILFOYLE as to his identity.

In consequence of that I applied to GUILFOYLE; I had four or five interviews with GUILFOYLE, first and last, about this matter, that is, before and after the loan; the first interview was before TICHBORNE left, in July or August; I think I went up to GUILFOYLE at his place at Double Bay in a cab, at TICHBORNE's request; I saw GUILFOYLE in one of his greenhouses; he was unwell at the time, and I first saw his son, I think, who referred me to him in the greenhouse. I told Mr. GUILFOYLE, senior, when I found him, my object. I said, "TICHBORNE has referred me to you as regards his identity." He said, "Yes; I expected it was for that you came." I said, "I have known you so many years I feel certain you would not deceive me; it is a large amount he has applied to me for." He said, "I am positive that he is the party he represents himself to be: I could swear to him as I could to my own child;" and he said also, "I nursed him when a child; I wish I had the money to lend him, and he should have it." That was all that occurred at the interview.

In consequence of that I lent the money.

Q. Would you have lent the money if GUILFOYLE had not said as much as he did?

A. Most decidedly not. I think I told him the amount TICHBORNE had applied for.

Q. Did anything pass as to the possibility of being mistaken?

A. Yes, it did; the words he made use of were, "It is impossible I can be mistaken; I nursed him as a child."

Q. Did you know that GUILFOYLE had been in England?

A. I understood from GUILFOYLE that he had been either TICHBORNE's father's or his uncle's gardener.

Q. Did anything pass in which the word pocket was used, and the safety of the investment?

A. Yes, GUILFOYLE said, "You are perfectly safe in lending the money; it is as safe as if it were in your pocket."

The next interviews were after the loan, and after the Plaintiff had left the colony for England; I met him in the street; I think we spoke of this matter of TICHBORNE's, and said it was all right. I expressed a wish to know if he thought it was all right, and whether he was still of the same opinion. "Oh, yes," he said, "it is all right." I do not remember what the words I said to him were as well as his; I was more interested in what he said; I do not think we had any further conversation about the matter till after a Mr. MACKENZIE arrived some months after. I think after I had heard of the arrival of TICHBORNE in England, to the best of my belief, after I had received advice of the dishonour of the bill in England; the amount of the loan was £600; I have now the third of exchange. I am ready to produce it if desired by either party; I met Mr. GUILFOYLE in George-street; in consequence of something I had heard I said to Mr. GUILFOYLE, "I am given to understand, GUILFOYLE, that you have latterly expressed a doubt about Sir ROGER TICHBORNE being the Simon Pure;" and he said, "I am now convinced he is not the man; I have talked the matter over with a Mr. MACKENZIE, who has come out from England, and my opinion is very much strengthened that he is not who he represents to be; in fact, now I feel certain he is not the party;" those are the very words he made use of; I was very much annoyed, and said, "I think it neither honourable nor to your credit to have given me the assurance you did, and I fancy there must be some undercurrent at work;" he said, "No, nothing of the sort; I have altered my mind; I think it very possible I shall have to go to England to give evidence in this matter;" I said, "I think it is very strange that you should have so far deceived me;" he said, "I was myself deceived." I do not remember the word "impostor" being used at any time.

Cross-examined by Mr. ISAACS.

I some time since made an affidavit in this matter, but I do not remember the date; I should think about twelve months since; the words used in the conversations between me and Mr. GUILFOYLE were at least as fresh in my mind then as now; I had the first interview with GUILFOYLE about August, 1866; I cannot give the exact date, it was some two or three days after the first interview that I lent the money; £600 was the amount I gave Plaintiff; the amount of the bill is £1,100. I think the words GUILFOYLE used when I told him at the first interview what I had come for, were, "I expected it was for that." I made the affidavit of March, 1868, at the instance of LEVY and DE LISSA, solicitors, Sydney; LEVY is partly interested in the loan, not DE LISSA; Mr. DE LISSA came to me about it; he did not bring an affidavit ready drawn, but took the words from my lips I was to swear to, requesting me to give the words as accurately as I could recollect, and I did so, as passage read from affidavit sworn in Sydney by witnesses, on 27th March, 1868, before COLIN MACKENZIE, read to witness, and last sentence but one of paragraph 2. Witness: Yes, GUILFOYLE used those words; I do not recollect his using any words as to Sir ROGER TICHBORNE having altered in appearance; I distinctly recollect the words, "nursed him as a child." I only had two or three interviews with GUILFOYLE about this matter, only three altogether; it was once only, so far as my memory serves me, he repeated the assurance as to TICHBORNE's identity; I do not recollect the term impostor being used at the third interview, he almost implied as much; the bill has not been paid; I expected it would extend over several years; the charge I made was in accordance; it would depend on his establishing his identity; I never was at BUTT's Hotel in Pitt-street; it has been pulled down. The third interview was a casual one, in George-street; when I met him I knew of MACKENZIE's arrival; I did not see GUILFOYLE. I met him casually. I still hope the bill will be paid. If it is not I shall not break my heart.

Re-examined by Mr. WYATT.

I have never seen the affidavit I made in March, 1868, since I made it. Now that you read to me the passage in Paragraph 2 "that Sir ROGER TICHBORNE had slightly altered, having become much stouter," I recollect those words were used. I recollect those words perfectly. In all our interviews, both GUILFOYLE and I spoke of the Plaintiff as Sir ROGER TICHBORNE; he never spoke to me of DE CASTRO; I had great faith in GUILFOYLE; it was entirely on what he said I advanced the money.

At the Metropolitan Hotel, aforesaid, the 28th day of June, 1869.

Examined by Mr. WYATT, Counsel for the Plaintiff.

STEPHEN BUTTS, being sworn and examined, upon his oath states as follows:—

My name is STEPHEN BUTTS. I am an hotel-keeper in Sydney. In 1866 I kept the Metropolitan Hotel in Pitt-street; in that year I knew a person who passed in my hotel by the name of Sir ROGER TICHBORNE, and who had previously passed in this colony by the name of CASTRO; he stayed at my hotel; he came in the beginning of June, 1866; he came by himself. I know Mr. GUILFOYLE, florist, of Double Bay; I saw him at my hotel when Plaintiff was there; I saw them together once; that was not very long after Plaintiff came to my place; I should say it was about the beginning of July; it might be earlier or later; Mrs. GUILFOYLE was with him; it was on a Sunday morning; I did not hear anything, but I saw Mr. and Mrs. GUILFOYLE and Sir ROGER at the end of the verandah of the hotel, at the entrance of the coffee-room, downstairs, at the back of the hotel; they had not then been in the house; I saw them go in; Plaintiff and Mr. GUILFOYLE had their hats on.

I saw Mr. and Mrs. GUILFOYLE look at him as if they recognized him; they smiled.

I went to Mr. GUILFOYLE's place at Double Bay the night before Plaintiff left. I called upon him and asked him to endorse a bill for Sir ROGER. He said, "I am only a poor man, I will not do it; I will not place myself in that position for any man." My son was present; Mrs. GUILFOYLE was also present; this took place in his parlour. My son's name is TRUTH WILLIAM PALMER BUTTS. He said, "If he wants money, he can send to his mother or friends at home, and he can get it directly." He appeared particularly sulky and I was very much disgusted with him; nothing had passed between GUILFOYLE and myself to lead me to expect he would endorse the bill.

Mrs. GUILFOYLE said to me, in Mr. GUILFOYLE's presence, "We were much disappointed in Sir ROGER not coming to dinner; we had invited several friends to meet him—and I think she added, a priest or priests—and put ourselves very much out of the way." I am sure Mrs. GUILFOYLE called him Sir ROGER. When I asked GUILFOYLE to endorse the bill, I spoke of the Plaintiff as Sir ROGER.

Nothing in the slightest degree occurred on the part of Mr. or Mrs. GUILFOYLE, to deny or question Plaintiff being Sir ROGER.

Q. In the course of the conversation between you and Mr. and Mrs. GUILFOYLE, did they give any designation to the Plaintiff?

A. Both of them did; Mr. GUILFOYLE used the words, "If Sir ROGER wants money he can send to his mother or friends and get it."

I was there nearly half an hour; not many sentences passed on this subject; Mr. GUILFOYLE in this interview never used the word "impostor," or anything equivalent to it; he gave no other reason for not lending the money than saying he was a poor man, and would not do it for any man. I did not ask him for money, but GUILFOYLE said he would not endorse the bill for any man. I have seen a Mr. LONG at my hotel; I believe his name is JERVIS MORANT LONG; he nearly always stops with me; he left me his address when he went to England; I have heard him and Plaintiff holding conversations together.

Cross-examined by Mr. ISAACS.

I first saw Sir ROGER and Mr. and Mrs GUILFOYLE standing in the verandah, at the side of the entrance from the archway, which leads into the street; I am deeply impressed I then heard the church bells ringing for eleven o'clock service. Where they were is some distance from the front-door; they may have met in the street, or the archway from the street, I could not say; I made an affidavit in March, 1868.

I think my recollection of the facts was as vivid then as it is now, most likely more so; I may not have given the exact words either then or now; the purport is the same.

To the Commissioner for the Defendants:

I am quite certain GUILFOYLE used the words, "I am a poor man, and would not do it for any man;" at the time I made the affidavit I knew he had said so; I do not recollect whether I gave that reason in my affidavit.

Re-examined.

If I had been asked the question then, I should have recollected it then as now.

To the Commissioner:

Contingently the Plaintiff is liable to me in a sum of money; mine and his names are on some bills which are due and unpaid; they are his acceptances.

Examined by Mr. WYATT, Counsel for the Plaintiff.

TRUTH WILLIAM PALMER BUTTS, being sworn and examined, upon his oath saith:—

My name is TRUTH WILLIAM PALMER BUTTS; I live with my father, STEPHEN BUTTS, of the Metropolitan Hotel, Castlereagh-street, Sydney; the hotel he now keeps is not the same as the one he kept in 1866 in Pitt-street. In 1866 I knew Mr. GUILFOYLE, of Double Bay, Sydney, florist, and in that year I knew a person in the town whom I understood to be Sir ROGER TICHBORNE. I have seen Mr. GUILFOYLE in Sir ROGER TICHBORNE's presence upon three different occasions, twice at Mr. GUILFOYLE's residence, and once at my father's hotel in Pitt-street; the first time was at Mr. GUILFOYLE's; I think that was at the end of July, or commencement of August, 1866; Sir ROGER and I went to Mr. GUILFOYLE's, I am not sure whether on horseback or in a conveyance; we arrived at GUILFOYLE's in the afternoon; we went into the drawing-room; Mr. GUILFOYLE let us in at the gate. He said at the gate, "How do you do, Sir ROGER?" and shook hands. We went into the drawing-room. Mrs. GUILFOYLE was present. Sir ROGER was walking round the room examining the pictures, and saw either a photograph or painting of Upton, or Tichborne, I am not sure which, and said, "Oh, you have got a painting of Upton or Tichborne," a painting or photograph, I am not sure which. Sir ROGER said to Mrs. GUILFOYLE, "The beds have been altered since I last saw them." Mrs. GUILFOYLE said, "Yes, they have. When I last saw you, you were a thin little fellow, you have now grown stout; but I should know you anywhere."

Q. Anything more about any reason for knowing him anywhere?

A. No, nothing more.

Sir ROGER then referred to a fishery at Upton. I can't remember what he said; something about a fishery at Upton. Nothing further was said on that occasion; we went simply to pay a call of courtesy, and came away; we were there about half an hour in the room and on the verandah: we did not go about the garden. It is possible something else may have passed in that half-hour which I do not now recollect. This was within about five weeks after Sir ROGER came to the hotel. The next interview of Sir ROGER and myself was at Mr. GUILFOYLE's house about a week after the first. We rode down on horseback. Sir ROGER had a black horse, and I had a cream-coloured one; the black one belonged to Sir ROGER, and the cream-coloured to myself. We called at Mr. GUILFOYLE's house at Double Bay. Mr. GUILFOYLE was in the garden; I saw him there. He came to the gate, and shook hands over the gate with Sir ROGER. He said, "How do you do, SIR ROGER?" We hung the horses up and went into the house—into the same room as before. I was looking at pictures while they were conversing, and did not hear what they said; that lasted about ten minutes. Sir ROGER had a little brandy-and-water; I am not sure whether any one was present on that occasion. The next interview was at my father's hotel in Pitt-street. I saw a son of Mr. GUILFOYLE's on the last occasion at the gate with his father, but he did not speak. I was present at an interview between Plaintiff and GUILFOYLE at my father's hotel; Mr. GUILFOYLE showed Sir ROGER a likeness, and asked, "Do you know this likeness?" Sir ROGER said, "Yes, it is a likeness of my uncle." It was one of the said old-fashioned black profile likenesses. I know old BOGLE; BOGLE brought one—a small likeness. I can't say whether the one Mr. GUILFOYLE brought was the same picture; they were pictures of the same person. I took one bottle to Mr. GUILFOYLE; I am not sure whether I took two; it was brandy on that occasion. I saw Mrs. GUILFOYLE. Mrs. GUILFOYLE said, "I am sure he is the man." Mr. GUILFOYLE was there too, and said, "I can swear that he is the man; he resembles his uncle;" those were the words he used.

Cross-examined by Mr. ISAACS.

I knew GUILFOYLE by sight only before I went out with Sir ROGER; there is no circumstance by which I can fix the date of the first interview, as stated by me to be in July or August; I do not remember how we went the first time; whether we rode or walked on the first occasion; Mr. GUILFOYLE came and opened the gate; there was no bell to ring; we went down a steep place to Mr. GUILFOYLE's from where the omnibus stops; we turned to the left; Mr. GUILFOYLE's is pretty close to the sea; Mrs. GUILFOYLE was present on the first occasion, to the best of my recollection; Sir ROGER said, when examining the pictures, "Oh, you've got a picture of Upton [or Tichborne]; the beds have been altered since I last saw them." GUILFOYLE said, "Yes, they have." GUILFOYLE's house is one storey; there are two entrances; we went in at the entrance at the side facing the hill, and the street we went down; there is a little garden in front of the house, and a little gate opening from that into the grassy part of the road; we went in at that gate: Mr. GUILFOYLE opened the door leading into the room, which I have called the drawing-room; there is no passage; the room is a square room to the best of my knowledge; it has two doors, with the same aspect, I believe, facing his large garden opening into the verandah; the windows are at right angles to the road; the room was carpeted; there were a few pictures round the wall; I cannot be mistaken about our having gone there; it was a call of courtesy; we did not go about the garden; I speak of the first time we went; I believe I wrote some letters for Plaintiff; I cannot remember whether I ever wrote one for him to Mr. GUILFOYLE; I only saw Mr. and Mrs. GUILFOYLE the first time; there is no circumstance by which I can fix, with anything like certainty, how long elapsed between the first interview and Plaintiff's arrival at my father's hotel; the second interview between these parties was also at Mr. GUILFOYLE's, I think about a week after the first, and before I took the bottle of brandy; the second interview was somewhere about the beginning of August; we went on horseback to GUILFOYLE's by the same road; I saw Mr. GUILFOYLE before we got to the gate; he was in the garden at the side of the house, close to the gate which opens on the road; when I first saw him we were about 200 yards from the gate; one of his sons was at the gate with him; I only know his sons by sight; the son I refer to, I should fancy, was about nineteen; he was somewhat shorter than I; I should think he was about 5ft. 8in.

To the Commissioners:

I stand 6ft. 1in.

In other respects he was about my size; the son did not accompany us into the room; I believe Mrs. GUILFOYLE was not there at all the second occasion; on this occasion I was looking at pictures, and did not hear what was said; on this occasion we had some refreshment and left; we had some brandy in the same room.

Q. Do you know how the brandy came in?

A. I believe it was on the table; I do not remember any one bringing it in; I did not see any one.

I think the third interview was a few days after the second, it was subsequent to the other two.

D. 17 shown to witness.

I believe this is a photograph of a likeness shown to Sir ROGER by Mr GUILFOYLE, and also by Mr. BOGLE; I was present when Mr. GUILFOYLE produced it; GUILFOYLE asked Sir ROGER if he knew who it was, and Sir ROGER said, "It is my uncle;" I am not positive whether he said anything else, but I believe he said DOUGHTY; Plaintiff stopped at my father's house a little over three months; I think he came on the 16th June, he remained at my father's up to his leaving; he left on the 1st September; I went on another occasion to GUILFOYLE's with a bottle of brandy; I saw Mr. and Mrs. GUILFOYLE. Mrs. GUILFOYLE said,

"I am sure he is the man;" and Mr. GUILFOYLE said, "I will swear he is the man, he resembles his uncle;" I distinctly remember those words; I am not aware that my father has any interest in Sir ROGER gaining this suit; I myself have none further than my salary as secretary to Sir ROGER TICHBORNE for two years at £500 a year; there was not that I am aware of an action of BUTTS against TICHBORNE, or anything else; I do not know; I never heard from my father whether Sir ROGER owes him any money. I have had correspondence with Plaintiff since he went to England; I have his letters at home.

Re-examined by Mr. WYATT.

I went to England in 1866, and have returned only within the last three months.

Examined by Mr. WYATT, Counsel for the Plaintiff.

ANDREW BOGLE, junr., being sworn and examined, upon his oath states:—

My name is ANDREW BOGLE; I am a hairdresser at Darling-street, Balmain, near Sydney; I am a son of ANDREW BOGLE, who was valet of Sir EDWARD DOUGHTY; I was born at Upton, in Dorsetshire; I know Mr. and Mrs. GUILFOYLE; I knew them at Tichborne; I never saw ROGER CHARLES TICHBORNE, the youth, in England; I knew Sir ROGER TICHBORNE in this colony; I had a conversation with GUILFOYLE in his nursery about Sir ROGER. He said, "Well, ANDREW, my boy, how are you? What do you think about ROGER TICHBORNE? He is the man right enough; wherever he has been to since he left England, he is the man right enough." No mention of money that time; that visit was while Sir ROGER was in Sydney.

I went again after Sir ROGER left—about six months after. I saw him in his nursery. He said, "Have you heard from Sir ROGER?" I said, "I have not heard from him;" he said, "He is no more Sir ROGER TICHBORNE than you are. Why did not he come out here to dinner as he promised? Because the scoundrel was afraid I should detect he was an impostor." I went out a third time to GUILFOYLE'S; I took my wife with me; at the second interview GUILFOYLE said, "If I had as much money as would fill this room I would not lend it to him;" at the third interview, as I was going away, GUILFOYLE said, "You'll be all right: you will get your money right enough." I had told him on the second occasion I had lent Sir ROGER money.

Cross-examined.

I have not been repaid the money I lent Sir ROGER; it was a considerable sum for me; my father had two paintings or lithographs, which purported to be pictures of Upton House; I remember them being in my father's, ANDREW BOGLE'S, possession for about fourteen years, and before we left England. D. 17 shown to witness; I have seen a picture like this before my father had one like it; I remember it in his possession about fourteen years.

At the Metropolitan Hotel aforesaid, the 29th day of June, 1869.

Further cross-examined by Mr. ISAACS, of Counsel for the Defendants.

TEETH WILLIAM PALMER BUTTS, being recalled and examined, upon his oath states:—

I stated in my evidence that on the second occasion of Sir ROGER going to Mr. GUILFOYLE'S place, that one of his sons was present; I cannot now identify any one of those three gentlemen now before me as the person I described as the son of Mr. GUILFOYLE, who was present at the gate with his father on the occasion of the second visit of Sir ROGER to Double Bay; I recognize the eldest son as corresponding in bulk to the person I said I saw at the gate.

Two pictures shown to witness. These are the pictures of Upton I said in my evidence Sir ROGER looked at, and said something about the flower beds being altered; I do not know which he referred to.

MICHAEL GOLDEN, being sworn and examined by Mr. WYATT, on behalf of the Plaintiff:—

My name is MICHAEL GOLDEN; I am an officer in H.M. Gaol, Wagga-Wagga; I am warden, and have been there seven years the 17th June last; I was soldier in the 99th Regiment for 13 years and 169 days; I got my discharge in Perth, Swan River; I then went into the mounted police, King George's Sound, for eighteen months; I left there by mail steamer for Sydney, and was in the police for six years; I was appointed here in Sydney; I knew TOM CASTRO here very well; he was a butcher most of the time; the first time I saw him he was killing a pig for BYRNES the butcher; he was close to the road; I knew nothing about the man then; he spoke to me first, and said, "I think by your walk you are an old soldier;" I got crabbed, and said it was nothing to him whether I was or not; he said, "I know you are, for I have been a soldier myself part of the time." I said, "You might belong to the Failbacks, or some other corps that's no account." The next time we had a conversation was at Mr. HIGGINS', for whom he was working; he was brought up for something at the court, and came over, and was out of temper, and said "I have seen the day when Mr. BAYLIS would put his hand to his hat for me." I laughed, and said, "A magistrate will look well putting his hand to his hat for a butcher." He said, "Yes; and he might do it now if he knew what I was, or who I am." We had another conversation. He said, "If I let my parents know where I was I could have plenty of money; but they do not know whether I am dead or alive." I said, "If I could get money that way, I'd soon have it." He said, "I wouldn't; I am different; but I may have plenty by-and-by." This last conversation was about six years ago; it might be more; it is more than four or five years ago; I was not twelve months in the town when it happened; we had another conversation before he got married; he told me he was going to get married; he told me to MARY ANN BRYANT, his lady now. I asked him where he was going to get married; he told me he was going to get married in the Catholic Chapel; I am a Catholic. I said, "You're no Catholic;" then he said, "Yes, I am, and all belonging to me, and one of the oldest Catholic families ever stood in England;" afterwards he told me the priest would not marry him for not attending to his duty—I mean his religious duties—for not attending the confession. I am a married man.

Q. Were you required to attend confession before you were married?

A. Yes; I was required by my clergy; I was married in Swan River by Bishop BRADY.

Q. Did he ever say he was in the service?

A. I knew he had been a soldier through his conversation with me; he has told me he could go through the broadsword exercise as well as any man in the country; they do not learn it in the foot.

He mentioned other Catholics in the service; he said there were only two other Catholics in the regiment with him altogether, I could not say officers or men.

Did he ever say anything about his trade of butchering?

Nothing more than he said he learnt it in the colonies; he knew nothing about it till he came to the colonies; I have heard him speak some foreign language; I do not know what it was.

Q. Was any reference ever made to hunting cattle?

A. "Yes, I heard something about lassooing cattle."

When I first knew CASTRO he was about 5ft. 10in., or 5ft. 11in. and about 11 or 12 stone weight, not a quarter the size of when he left; when he left he was far bigger; he was as straight as an arrow when he first came to the town; I should say he was about 13 or 14 stone when he left; he got bloated up like to what he was when he came into town first.

At the Commercial Hotel, Wagga-Wagga, the 10th day of July, 1869.

Examined by Mr. WYATT, of Counsel for the Plaintiff.

ROBERT CLARK ROBINSON:—I am a physician and surgeon; I have been resident in Wagga-Wagga five years since 17th March last; I knew TOMAS CASTRO in Wagga-Wagga; he was butchering for HIGGINS, making sausages, &c.; he was managing man for HIGGINS; I once attended him professionally in a surgical case; this was 23rd December, 1864; he had a fall from his horse, and broke his nose and cut it; I did not see the accident; he rode up to my door; his face was still bleeding; he was not tipsy nor drunk, certainly not; I saw him frequently, but never saw him tipsy; one nasal bone was broken and loose, and projecting so far I thought it best to take it away, and did so; there was so slight an attachment of muscle to it I took it away; I think it was the left nasal bone; I took away not quite half an inch long, about a fifth of an inch broad; it healed up quickly and so well, he gave me two guineas on the 18th of January, 1865, while I was only charging him one; the wound left very little mark indeed; I think the nose got a little more prominent in the centre, and larger; I am certain of it; I do not think that the nose had previously been injured, but I could not say for certain; I believe the nose was not ever broken before.

Examined by Mr. WYATT, of Counsel for the Plaintiff.

JAMES FEGAN, being sworn and examined, upon his oath saith:—

My name is JAMES FEGAN; I am a foot constable; I have been in the force eleven years; I am now stationed at Narrandera, sixty miles from Wagga-Wagga, down the Murrumbidgee, north of the river where I have been about eight months; I was stationed at Urana for five or six years; I knew CASTRO in Wagga-Wagga; he was in HIGGINS' butcher's shop; this is about three years ago; I first knew him about 1856 or the beginning of 1857, at Myer's Flat, a diggings near Bendigo in Victoria; I was digging there; he stopped at the same hotel as I did—MOORHEAD'S Hotel, on Myer's Flat; he was passing through and stopped there; he was selling some horses; I can't say whose; a man of the name of PEARCE or PEARSON was with him; I do not know where he came from. I heard from himself where he came from.

Myer's Flat is about 200 miles from the Jordan Diggings, which are in the Gippsland district. Myers Flat is about forty miles from Moamaton, on the New South Wales side of the Murray, opposite Etrusca, in Victoria; I think I saw him on the Myers Flat in the spring of the year, about August or September; I next saw him in Castlemaine; about three weeks after I saw him knocking about at MOORHEAD'S hotel; I was three weeks boarding at the same table with him at Castlemaine; I only spoke to him, and we had a drink together; I next saw him at Deniliquin; I had then joined the police force at Deniliquin; he came to Deniliquin with FRED. BURROWS, a friend of mine, from Victoria; FRED. BURROWS and his brother JOHN were horse-dealers and butchers at Deniliquin; CASTRO was with them butchering in the shop; JOHN BURROWS was the butcher, FRED. the horse-dealer; CASTRO came with FRED. to Deniliquin, and was with JOHN in the butchering business; I was at Deniliquin four or five years in the force; I joined the force in about 1858, thence I went to Urana for five or six years, thence to Wagga for nine or ten months; from Wagga to Narrandera; I knew CASTRO about two years at Deniliquin; I believe I left first; the BURROWS were at Deniliquin all the time I was there; JOHN is alive still and at Deniliquin.

Q. Do you know the sword exercise?

A. I went through it, but not properly; I know the sword exercise; CASTRO knew it; I have seen him handle the sword.

I know by the way he handled it he was a drilled man.

One day I was going to Mr. KELLY's and was taking out an old sword to him; CASTRO took up the sword and began to make game of the force, and showed me some passes and cuts.

Q. Did he ever state he had been in the army?

A. Yes; at the time he was using the sword he said he had been an officer in the army.

Mr. KELLY's place was then about a mile outside Deniliquin; that was about 1862, or a little earlier or later, while he was with Mr. BURROWS the butcher. I told him on several occasions he was a foreigner, he said he was an Englishman; he mentioned he was heir to a property, and would be able to help us all.

I took him to be a foreigner from his appearance, his action, and the way he spoke: sometimes I heard him speak some foreign language to several people.

At the time of his saying he was heir to a property, I told him to come into Deniliquin, and see Mr. SHAW, the solicitor, and I would lend him the funds to make inquiries about it. I understood him to say he thought his father was dead; at the time I think he was in doubt about it.

He has spoken about America; he talked to a man named KNOX about it; I do not remember which America. KNOX had been a sailor; they spoke of it as a place they had been in; I believe KNOX is alive; I saw him last four or five years ago at Moama; I believe he is now on the Victoria side in the Swan Hill country. When I saw CASTRO at Deniliquin he was about ten or eleven stone; when I next saw him about four years after in Wagga-Wagga he seemed to be three or four stone heavier; I did not know him again, and passed him several times in the streets of Wagga without knowing him; he changed so much, and got so rough and bush-like. I did not know him again till he was pointed out to me by BLEWITT, who knew us both, and knew that I knew him in Deniliquin; I never knew PEARCE or PEARSON since I saw him on Myer's Flat.

Cross-examined by Mr. ISAACS.

I last made this statement the day before yesterday in Mr. GIBBES', the solicitor's office, to Plaintiff's attorney's agent. I just gave a regular account of him. There was an affidavit of my own read to me. I never expect to get anything from Plaintiff if he succeeds in this matter; I am wholly disinterested; I was at Myer's Flat about 1857, not more than six months either way; it could not be as late ago as 1861.

By the Commissioner for the Plaintiff.

Q. Did you state just now that, in consequence of your having lost your papers, you could not be certain as to dates, but the circumstances you have mentioned might have happened a little earlier or later than you have mentioned?

A. Yes, I did; the barracks were burnt down, and I lost all my papers.

NOTE.—This question is objected to by Mr. ISAACS, Defendants' Counsel.

WILLIAM ALFRED COTTEE, being sworn and examined, upon his oath saith:—

Examined by Mr. WYATT, of Counsel for the Plaintiff.

My name is WILLIAM ALFRED COTTEE; I am manager of the Australian Joint Stock Bank, Wagga-Wagga; I have been so for about eight years and a half. I know Mr. WILLANS, the solicitor, and Mr. GIBBES; those two gentlemen were present when a document was read. Mr. MACKENZIE was present; I can't call to mind the date.

Q. Was this in 1866, 1867, or 1868?

A. I think it was in 1867; there was a conversation between them; they all came together. Mr. GIBBES asked me for TICHBORNE's will; I produced it and gave it to Mr. GIBBES. I believe Mr. GIBBES read it aloud in my office; I produced it on the authority of Mr. GIBBES, solicitor for a person known here as THOMAS CASTRO. GIBBES had previously deposited it with me. On that occasion no portion of what was read out was taken down in writing, that I am aware of. Mr. WILLANS may have taken some down, but I did not see him. WILLANS and GIBBES came a second time. I knew Mr. WILLANS to be acting as solicitor with Mr. MACKENZIE in this Case. Mr. GIBBES asked me for the will, and I believe he read it again to Mr. WILLANS. I am not certain whether Mr. WILLANS read it. Mr. WILLANS and Mr. GIBBES stood near each other, possibly near enough for the latter to read it himself. I think Mr. WILLANS took some memoranda on a piece of paper; no permission was asked of me to do that; I could not help it. I believe they left together; I believe Mr. WILLANS did not stay after Mr. GIBBES left.

Q. If Mr. WILLANS stated he stayed after Mr. GIBBES left, and you allowed him to copy down some key words, is it correct?

A. It is not accurate. Mr. WILLANS came in a third time, and asked me to show him the will. I told him the document was left with me by Mr. GIBBES in a sealed packet for safe custody, and I could not show it without Mr. GIBBES' authority; I do not know whether Mr. GIBBES was in town or not.

Q. Did Mr. WILLANS or Mr. MACKENZIE ever offer any inducement for a copy of that will?

A. Not to me.

I first saw Mr. MACKENZIE, I think, in 1867, at my office; on that occasion we had some conversation about the TICHBORNE matter.

Q. Did Mr. MACKENZIE ever tell you in what capacity he was acting?

A. He told me once, "I am collecting evidence for both sides, and with the authority of the Lord Chancellor." He showed me a letter then, and said, "Here is a letter of authority." I do not think it was signed by the Lord Chancellor; I think I should have noticed the signature. To the best of my belief, Lord Chancellor were the words used; I am quite sure the words "Collecting evidence on both sides," were used.

Cross-examined by Mr. ISAACS.

Q. Is your recollection of the words used by Mr. MACKENZIE quite clear?

A. It was either under the authority of the "Lord Chancellor" or the "Court of Chancery."

Q. Might not Mr. MACKENZIE have used the words, "I am collecting evidence in a Chancery suit, under the authority of the Lord Chancellor, or the Court of Chancery.

A. I am quite clear it was not that. It was either under the authority of the Lord Chancellor or the Court of Chancery. I do not remember whether the words Vice-Chancellor were used; I glanced at the letter or note produced by Mr. MACKENZIE; I believe it was headed Whitehall; it had not the great Seal attached; I do not know what has become of the document; it has left the bank; I know it is not there; it was given up while I was away, and Mr. GIBBES has signed for it in the security book. I know Mr. GIBBES's signature. I do not think GIBBES had told me he got it; he may have done so; Mr. GIBBES one day made a copy of it, and I compared it with him; Mr. GIBBES read from the original or copy, I do not know which; I followed with the other. I remember a name or two in it but not any sentence; I remember the names "ANGELL" and "BIRD," and either "Lady HANNAH" or "Lady HARRIET TICHBORNE;" I do not remember the word "Paris" occurring; I do not remember "Cowes;" I remember "the Isle of Wight;" I said before the will was signed by "ROGER CHARLES TICHBORNE;" I think I said that before; it was signed ROGER CHARLES TICHBORNE; I think there was no description after his name; I do not recollect the name "JERVIS" occurring; I have never had any letters from CUBITT, nor written to him, nor from Lady TICHBORNE; I have had some correspondence with Claimant about some bills; I have some letters written to me from Sydney by Claimant; I may have some he wrote from England.

I produce the following documents:—

A cheque signed TOMAS CASTRO, dated June 13th, 1865, for £6, on the Australian Joint Stock Bank, Wagga-Wagga.

A promissory note signed "ROGER CHARLES TICHBORNE," in favour of JAMES WARBY, dated 4th July, 1866, for £367 10s., payable six months after date.

Another promissory note, dated 11th July, 1866, signed ROGER CHARLES TICHBORNE, in favour of JAMES WARBY, payable six months after date, for £152 13s., indorsed WILLIAM GIBBES, JAMES WARBY; second and third of exchange for £500 drawn by WILLIAM GIBBES, on Sir ROGER CHARLES TICHBORNE, Tichborne Hall, Hampshire, payable to drawer's order, "accepted payable at the Consolidated Bank, London, ROGER CHARLES TICHBORNE," and dishonoured and duly protested for dishonour.

A letter, dated Sydney, 5th July, from ROGER CHARLES TICHBORNE, Bart., to myself.

A letter undated, from Metropolitan Hotel, Pitt-street, from R. C. TICHBORNE to me.

A letter dated 21-3-7, from R. C. D. TICHBORNE to myself.

A letter dated July 24th, from R. C. TICHBORNE to myself.

A letter dated Wagga-Wagga, May 10th, 1866, from TOMAS CASTRO to Mr. MCINTOSH.

Part of letter, undated, signed "R. C. T." on one side, and R. C. TICHBORNE on the other, with the DOUGHTY and TICHBORNE crest, being part of a letter from him to me.

WILLIAM ALFRED COTTEE, being recalled, saith:—

I produce D. 33 Ex. in the handwriting of TICHBORNE, already produced on this examination.

Exhibits D. 36, 37, 38, 39, 40, and 41 shown to witness.

These are photographic copies of letters from TICHBORNE to me in his handwriting, already produced by me in my examination, and one to Mr. MCINTOSH.

At the Commercial Hotel, Wagga-Wagga, aforesaid, the 14th July, 1869.

Examined by Mr. WYATT, Counsel for the Plaintiff.

WILLIAM FEARNE, being sworn and examined, upon his oath saith:—

My name is WILLIAM FEARNE; I am a photographic artist. In the course of my avocations I make a circuit of the various towns in New South Wales, carrying my apparatus and portrait rooms in caravans; during the last few years I knew THOMAS CASTRO; I first knew him at MCLAREN's Yarra-Yarra Station on the Billabong River, about forty-five miles from Albury, about north, and between fifty and sixty miles eastward of Wagga-Wagga; CASTRO was engaged on the station, but I do not know how; stopping on the station taking portraits, I lost a horse; I spoke to Mr. MCLAREN: he said he would send his man to look for it; during the day the horse was brought to me by CASTRO, whose name I did not then know; I tendered him five shillings for his services, which he refused; then I offered to take his portrait as an acknowledgment. He said, "I will see you in the evening." He came in the evening; he stated he wanted one card portrait for his own use, and could I finish it while he remained? I said no; he then said he would not have it done, as he did not want any chance of his portrait being about the country; after being there some time he said "Mr. FEARNE, I will give you a reason why; my family at home hold position, and they believe that I am dead, and I have no wish for them to think otherwise;" he remarked that very likely a number of the family's friends and connections were in the country, and my travelling with a portrait of his, it might be recognized by them; I advised him to have a glass picture taken; he had one taken the following day in a case which he took with him; when he came down the evening before we were in conversation for a couple of hours. He said, "Well, Mr. FEARNE, I was not bred on a station—I have not been on a station all my life." This was in the first week of November, 1863; I left Albury on the 23rd October, 1863. I met him again in Wagga-Wagga in July, 1864, in the bar of the Australian Hotel. CASTRO spoke first, and said, "I suppose you don't recollect me, Mr. FEARNE?" Looking at him, I said, "Oh, yes, you are the man that got my horse on MCLAREN'S Station. I stayed here a little over four months; I saw him nearly every day; we met mostly at the butcher's shop, HIGGINS', where he was employed, or at the Australian Hotel bar; one evening at HIGGINS' there were seven or eight of us present in the back room talking of MORGAN the bushranger, whose exploits were a matter of general talk; I understood from the conversation there that MORGAN was a Roman Catholic; I made a remark concerning it that made them all angry, which I can't remember; at that time it was a dangerous thing to make any remark in the southern part of the colony at the expense of MORGAN; I have been cautioned in my travels scores of times; CASTRO came behind me, pulled my coat, and walked out, I followed him, he said,—Mr. FEARNE, excuse me for giving you advice about the remark that you made; there are men in there that would not mind knocking your brains out for what you have said; as far as I am concerned, I don't care anything about the allusion you made to the Catholic faith; little though you may expect it, I am a Catholic. He remarked.—My family is about one of the most ancient Catholic families there is in England. That must have been about September or the beginning of October, 1864; I left Wagga that year in December for Albury; I met him by appointment one evening, I can't fix the date, about November, 1864, the subject of conversation was MORGAN again; that was what he wanted to see me about; just at this time a reward of £1,000 had been offered for the capture of MORGAN after the Round Hill murder; I think two or three murders had been committed at that time; he told me he had made up his mind to attempt to take MORGAN; he said he had no hesitation in saying he could go direct to him, and he believed MORGAN would have no suspicion of him, in consequence of having met him so many times camped on the Yarra Station; he said there was a little matter to consider before he went; he said,—I want to place some confidence in you; he said,—I think I can do so; my name is not CASTRO; my family, as I told you before, hold high position at home, and they think I am dead, and I don't wish them to know I am alive, but I wish for it to be known in case of my death who I am. I always carry that on me whereby I should be recognized in case of my death; he said,—If I die by MORGAN'S hands what I have about me will be destroyed or made away with or never come to light, or words to that effect. He said, "If you will swear to return a packet to me in the same state as I gave it to you, if I return I will carry out my idea; if by accident I should get killed, you can open the packet, and get your instructions what to do." The subject was a matter of further conversation with us for a fortnight; after the preparation of his horse, and other matters, he said, that for his own protection he should speak to Mr. BAYLIS before he left, as otherwise, if the police met him armed, he might get into a mess himself; he said he intended to start about the end of November, as I was to start in December. His horse became lame; I saw that myself. He then said he should have to postpone it for a time. I left in December, and did not see him again until I returned to Wagga-Wagga, in August, 1865. CASTRO was much stouter when I last saw him than when I saw him at MCLAREN'S.

Cross-examined by Mr. ISAACS.

I know that the police make great use of the photographic portraits in the hands of photographers, in fact, that occurred to me when he objected at MCLAREN'S Station to having his likeness being taken about the country. He objected to my carrying his portrait about the country. I produce photographic copies made by me of the original letters now produced. They are *fac-similes*, except slightly reduced in size.

Exhibits marked D. 36, 37, 38, 39, 40, and 41, put in by Defendants.

At the office of Messieurs KLINGENDER, CHARSLEY, and LIDDLE, Bank-place, Melbourne, aforesaid, the 22nd day of November, 1869.

Examined by Mr. WYATT, of Counsel for the Plaintiff.

JAMES HENRY KEMMIS, being sworn and examined, upon his oath saith:—

My name is JAMES HENRY KEMMIS. I am a native of the colony of New South Wales. I am now a prisoner of the Crown, at the Police Barracks, Richmond. I was in Gippsland in 1850. I took the management of a station at the latter end of that year—the Strathfieldsaye Station, belonging to my uncle, WILLIAM ODELL RAYMOND. Strathfieldsaye Station is about thirty or twenty-eight miles from Boisdale, which then belonged to JOHN FOSTER. I knew WILLIAM FOSTER, nephew of JOHN FOSTER. I was several times upon the Boisdale Station, generally assisting to muster stock; sometimes as a visitor. I think I remained a year or eighteen months at Straithfieldsaye. The first time I was there I went to Maneroo for about thirteen months; I returned then to Strathfieldsaye. I also had an interest in Dighton Station, now Mr. DESAILLY'S Station. JOHN LOVEL was my partner; he was originally manager for Mr. FOSTER. In about 1856 I again became a permanent resident at Strathfieldsaye, in charge of the stock for Mr. LEMUEL BOLDEN. I think I left Strathfieldsaye, and got to Maneroo the first time in the Spring. I think that was about 1852; between 1852 and 1856. I was several times in the neighbourhood of Boisdale. To the best of my belief I was on Boisdale in 1854. At any time I was on Boisdale, I knew all the station hands. I think I would know them all if I saw them.

Exhibit P. 1 shown to witness.

To the best of my belief this is the portrait of a man I saw there.

Q. Tell me the circumstances under which you saw him.

A. I had just ridden to Boisdale Station. Upon my taking my horse to the stable, I met Mr. FOSTER, Mr. WILLIAM FOSTER.

Q. Did anything Mr. FOSTER said attract your attention to this individual?

A. Yes.

In consequence of that I afterwards spoke to that person. This person had no peculiarity of accent or speech, that I noticed. I should not have taken him for a foreigner. I certainly would not have taken him for a Spaniard or Mexican. This person's name was TOM CASTRO.

His ability to throw the lasso struck me. I can throw the lasso. To the best of my belief I afterwards saw CASTRO at Dargo. NORMAN NICHOLSON was at Dargo with him. I am certain he was one party with him. I am certain NORMAN NICHOLSON was at Dargo; I mean that at the time I saw CASTRO, as I suppose, I saw NICHOLSON, I am certain, at Dargo.

The next time I saw CASTRO was at Deniliquin. I spoke to him, and am certain it was the same man I saw at Boisdale.

CASTRO was more particularly conversant with horses, and was a good rider.

He was a big-framed man; I should say a heavily-framed man; darkish hair, not dark; I should call it brown hair and lightish whiskers, both in quantity and colour. The whiskers were, to the best of my belief, lighter than his hair. It is so long ago that I cannot speak with certainty to the actual colour and quantity of his hair and whiskers. I do not remember the colour of his eyes. I remember a peculiarity in one of his eyes; a sort of nervous twitching when he spoke to you. There was a peculiarity about one of his legs very noticeable; it was very much bowed. I think it was the left leg. When he stood upon it it bowed outwards; and when he walked it gave him a little halt, as if that leg were shorter than the other.

Cross-examined by Mr. IRELAND, Q.C., of Counsel for the Defendants.

I was in Gippsland and Maneroo between 1852 and 1856, and then frequently went to Boisdale. I said I thought I was there in 1854, but I am not sure of the dates. I know Boisdale station.

Exhibit P. 1 shown to witness.

When I saw the man I suppose this represents he was not so full as in this; a considerable difference in the lower part of the face; I know him best by the features above the mouth; I should know all the station hands in Boisdale if I saw them. I can name some dates I cannot fix. My memory is defective as to dates. I say I believe I was at Boisdale in 1854. I only remained one or two days there on that occasion. At that time WILLIAM FOSTER, I believe, was manager at Boisdale. I believe this was in 1854. I remember a Mr. MORRISON there at that time; he was a sort of overseer. I remember a Mr. DURHAM in about the same position. I remember an old hand on the station; he was called the Highland man. It was, as I believe, in 1854, on the occasion I have spoken of, that I spoke to CASTRO in consequence of something that fell from Mr. FOSTER. DAVID CAMPBELL was on the station then.

I spoke to TOM CASTRO several times during the time I was there; I did not hear any one else but Mr. FOSTER address him as TOM CASTRO; he was called TOM by the others; Mr. FOSTER was speaking to me, and on addressing him called him TOM CASTRO; I never heard him addressed by Mr. FOSTER, or any of the men, by any other name than CASTRO, or TOM; I am not positive as to the year 1854; I undertake to say positively it was not in 1856; I think not in 1853; I think I am right in saying 1854; most certainly I undertake to swear WILLIAM FOSTER was living at Boisdale before 1856; I could not positively undertake to say that Mr. FOSTER was resident manager; he had the management of that muster, at all events; I do not think there was anyone specially living there as manager. Mr. FOSTER was backwards and forwards between Boisdale and the Heart Station at this time. I am not certain where his residence was; at one time he was resident at Merriman's Creek; I am not sure whether he resided at Merriman's Creek before or after he went to reside at Boisdale. I should say Dargo was forty or fifty miles from Boisdale, but I am not certain. I know NORMAN NICHOLSON. I did not see him at Boisdale in 1854. I saw him after that at

Dargo; I could not say how long after. I believe I saw TOM CASTRO at Dargo, but am not sure. On that occasion I was there one night; NORMAN NICHOLSON was the only one I am sure was there. There was a boy there who had killed a horse shortly before; I can't recollect his name. I think there were four hands at Dargo at that time; they were then tailing weaners at that time. I was only there one night, and did not stop in the hut; I camped out. I believe I saw CASTRO there, but am not sure. Besides these occasions at Boisdale, I did not hear him addressed as CASTRO anywhere else. I saw him more than once at Boisdale; I saw him immediately after the first occasion in 1854; I think a week would be the longest time I ever stayed there.

I cannot say whether Mr. WILLIAM FOSTER was resident manager at Boisdale any time I was there; Mrs. FOSTER was there once; I did not know any resident manager there; I never heard at any time any one but FOSTER call him CASTRO; he went by the name of TOM; I never saw NORMAN NICHOLSON at Boisdale; I saw him either at Dargo or Bushy Park; I was at Dargo Hut only once; I went there between three or four in the afternoon, and was away from there at daylight next morning; I never saw NORMAN NICHOLSON, CASTRO, and myself in actual contact at any time; the man I thought was CASTRO was at some distance from me, he was some 300 yards away, leading his horse after the heifers or weaners; I last saw the man I call CASTRO in the beginning of 1859; I think it was at Deniliquin, in the township: he was walking through the town by himself; I recognized him, and he recognized me; we spoke to one another; I was in his company about ten minutes.

I never heard the rumour of the murder of BALLARAT HARRY; I left Gippsland in the beginning of 1857 or late in the end of 1856; I know a man of the name of McCOLL, a blacksmith in Gippsland; I did not know a man named PETER McCOLL at Dargo; I remember blacks being at Dargo; but not their names; I remember a man named MILLER, he was pound-keeper in Gippsland at the time I knew him; I do not remember him at Dargo; I first heard of this claim being put forward just before I got into the trouble I am in now; I got into trouble on August 15th, 1868, just a few nights prior to that I heard of this claim; I was applied to in the gaol to give evidence in this cause; I do not know how I was traced there; on several occasions I heard FOSTER call him TOM CASTRO, but none of the other men; I never knew a man named ARTHUR ORTON at Boisdale; I said I knew all the permanent station hands on Boisdale; during the time I speak of there was no such person; I do not remember a pock-marked man named ARTHUR ORTON; I know a man called the butcher on Mr. SMITH's station, at Lindenow, but never on Boisdale; I knew him from 1850 to 1851; he was principal stock-keeper at Lindenow; I never saw him employed anywhere else.

PORTRAIT OF SIR EDWARD DOUGHTY.

I do not remember a short stout man pitted with small-pox, named ARTHUR ORTON, at Boisdale; the butcher at Lindenow would not correspond with that description of ARTHUR ORTON; I am not sure there was not a person named ARTHUR ORTON in Boisdale in 1851 as a permanent hand; I fancy I knew all the hands; but I am not sure; I was not shown any documents in the gaol prior to my stating what evidence I could give; I should decidedly say Mr. NORMAN NICHOLSON would know the names of the men employed on Dargo better than I; the only document I have seen is my evidence taken at the first time the gaol; I think there must have been other persons present than Mr. FOSTER; when he called him CASTRO I never knew there was any secret in his name; I think Mr. DURHAM must have been present some time when they called him CASTRO; I do not know where LEONARD MASON is; I am not certain either of them was present when they called him CASTRO.

I have not heard of Mr. DURHAM's death. I have heard of Mr. WILLIAM FOSTER's death. I never understood there was any secret about CASTRO's name; I have frequently heard him called CASTRO by Mr. FOSTER, both speaking of him and addressing him; and I think there must have been some person present when so addressed or spoken to, yet I never heard any of these people call him CASTRO.

Re-examined by Mr. WYATT.

By all the others he was called TOM. I should take CASTRO to be a Hispano-American name; I know one, and have been intimate with several Spaniards. I was intimate at Sydney with the whole of the officers of the Spanish ship "Ferrolana." Immediately before I went to Gippsland, I said in cross-examination that I could not say with certainty who was the resident manager at Boisdale, because there were several persons who might have been taken as managers; there were Mr. WM. FOSTER, Mr. DURHAM, and Mr. MORRISON. At the time I saw CASTRO at Boisdale it is possible Mr. FOSTER may not have removed there from Merriman's Creek at that time. Mr. MONTGOMERY lived at the Heart Station at the time I saw CASTRO. The Heart Station, Merriman's Creek, Boisdale, and Dargo were all properties of Mr. JOHN FOSTER; Mr. WILLIAM FOSTER was his nephew, and afterwards became manager of Boisdale. I do not know whether Mr. DURHAM is now alive at the police barracks, Hobart Town: I have heard nothing of him since I left Gippsland.

By Mr. IRELAND.

I cannot say positively whether I ever heard him called CASTRO by anyone but FOSTER.

Examined by Mr. WYATT, Counsel for the Plaintiff.

BERNARD CONMEE MCGAWRAN, being sworn and examined, upon his oath saith:—

My name is BERNARD CONMEE MCGAWRAN, residing at Carlton, Melbourne. From 1854 to 1858 I was in business at Myer's Flat. I was a licensed victualler, and wholesale wine and spirit merchant. I built the Junction Hotel there in 1854. I gave up my wholesale business in 1856, but kept on the retail business up to 1st February, 1858. I knew a Mr. PEARSON very well; he had a small block of land near Myer's Creek, and dealt in horses; he frequently came to my hotel; I have not seen him for the last seven or eight years.

Exhibit P. I shown to witness.

I have seen the original of this picture in the company of PEARSON at the Junction Hotel, in Myer's Flat; he then went by the name of CASTRO; I heard all others call him by that name. Nothing particular fixes the name of CASTRO in my mind. I do not think I knew anyone else of that name. I think I saw PEARSON and CASTRO together at the end of 1856 or beginning of 1857; I could not be positive as to the month.

PEARSON went frequently to the Gippsland side, and to the Murray side, to buy horses.

I could not recognize the body of the photograph, Exhibit P. 1, but the face I do.

Cross-examined by Mr. IRELAND, Q.C.

I saw him, I think, about the beginning of 1857; I do not think it was quite the end; I do not think it could be later than the middle of 1857; I do not think there is any difference between him in this photograph and when I saw him in 1857; I do not think there is much change in his face or figure.

Re-examined by Mr. WYATT.

Q. Should you think he was as stout as that?

A. He seems a little more bloated; I think he was as stout then, but his face seems more bloated; Myer's Flat is about four miles north of Bendigo, as it was then called; now called Sandhurst.

BRIEF SUMMARY OF THE AUSTRALIAN COMMISSION.

The evidence given on this Commission on behalf of the Claimant goes in a great measure to prove that he is the man he represents himself to be. We give a short summary, so as to make it more intelligible to the general reader, who has not studied the Case carefully. We see that Mr. MACKENZIE, the agent for Messrs. DOBINSON and GEARE (as admitted by their own letter to Mr. GRAY), went throughout the country, holding him up in the Australian papers, and doing his cause the greatest injury in his power. It is quite evident that no money was spared; but, notwithstanding all his efforts, and the detectives employed by him, various most respectable persons gave their testimony in favour of the Claimant, and proved to the satisfaction of any unprejudiced mind that TOMAS CASTRO and ARTHUR ORTON were two separate persons, and that they were seen with each other in various places and at different times. Even the Claimant's greatest enemies readily admit *that if he is not* ARTHUR ORTON *he must be* TICHBORNE, and this evidence utterly destroys the theory of his being the Wapping sailor, butcher, and vagabond.

1. JOHN JOSEPH SHILLINGLAW, who was the Inspector of Water Police at Melbourne, in the year 1854 (when the "Osprey" arrived) proved by Custom House Returns that in that year there were more ships in Hobson's Bay than ever anchored there from 1852 to 1857; that the police arrested many thousand deserters, including captains, officers, and men; and that the greatest excitement existed there in consequence of the gold-diggings, to which thousands of emigrants were flocking every week, as will be seen by the following letter and extracts, which illustrate strongly the value of the evidence of SHILLINGLAW on this point, and throw a strange light upon the astounding and extraordinary testimony given at the Great Trial by one of Mr. GLADSTONE'S Cabinet, Mr. HUGH EARDLEY CHILDERS—a very plausible, smooth-tongued gentleman. The letter was addressed to Mr. GUILDFORD ONSLOW:—

SHIP DESERTION IN 1854.

21, Russell-street, Leek, Staffordshire: Jan. 2, 1875.

DEAR SIR,—Being a subscriber to the ENGLISHMAN newspaper, and seeing a letter from you in that paper of last week (viz., Dec. 26), headed, "Insinuations of the Lord Chief Justice," I beg you will excuse me taking the liberty of writing to you, my object being to confirm one thing in particular mentioned therein, and in which letter you refer the readers of the ENGLISHMAN to pay particular attention to clause 13 of a letter written by Mr. J. E. LIARDET on the same subject, and published in the ENGLISHMAN of last week.

Now, there were several witnesses for the Crown, and one a Cabinet minister, at the late trial of Sir ROGER TICHBORNE, who swore most emphatically, that in the year 1854 Melbourne was not in a confused state, and that there were no desertions of ships' crews.

Since reading those letters, I have, for the satisfaction of myself and others, perused the volume of the *Illustrated London News* for the year 1854, and I now inclose extracts, which I have copied from it, respecting two vessels which sailed from the port of Melbourne in that year, viz. 1854.

I think the inclosed extracts of the two ships, "Asia," and "Marco Polo," are positive proofs that such was the case.

The evidence, therefore, given by the witnesses for Sir ROGER was most undoubtedly true and honest.

You can make what use you think proper of this letter and the inclosed extracts.—Yours most respectfully,

C. K. HYDE.

THE SHIP "ASIA."

[*Extract from the Illustrated London News of April 22, 1854.*]

A waterspout at sea is a most destructive phenomenon; for no ship could escape if it were carried entirely within the vortex. In the instance here illustrated, the vessel was only partially caught by the spout, and providentially escaped. The ship "Asia" is one of the HALL and Brothers' Australian line of packets. She left London last year, on the 23rd of March, and Plymouth on the 8th of April, with nearly 200 passengers on board, for Port Phillip. She arrived there in safety, *but was detained by the desertion of the crew, which has become so general in that land of gold.* Accordingly she did not leave Port Phillip until the 27th of November for Bombay. While on her passage, and in lat. 0 deg. 57 min. 47 sec. south, and long. 82 deg. 15 min. 15 sec. east, she was unhappily caught by a waterspout upon the 22nd of Jan. last, and almost totally dismasted. The weather, but a few hours before, was as follows:—Jan. 21st, midnight, light breeze from northward with mizzling rain and heavy lightning at south-west. About 1.15 a.m., light breeze with rain from the westward, steering north by west, going two or three knots per hour. At about 1.30 a.m., the second officer, in charge of the midnight watch, remarked that it looked very black ahead; almost at the same moment a tremendous roar was heard ahead, and a gust of wind, taking the ship flat aback, laid the masts prostrate on the decks. So instantaneous was the wind after the roar, although halyards and sheets were let fly, it was of no avail. The wind was succeeded by a torrent of rain, which lasted about five minutes, and then left all calm and quiet, but water ankle-deep on the deck. The ship was a wreck, her decks stove, launch and bulwarks smashed by the fall of the foremast, and the first cutter crushed by the main topsail-yard. At four a.m. the weather was calm and sultry, with rain.

THE SHIP "MARCO POLO."

[*Extract from the Illustrated London News of May 20, 1854.*]

The celebrated clipper ship "Marco Polo" arrived at Liverpool on Saturday last, after a very quick run of eighty-three days, having left Melbourne on the 10th February. The present voyage may be classed as one of the best ever made by this vessel, *when it is considered that she had scarcely half her complement of crew, owing to desertions.* She passed everything before her; amongst other ships the celebrated "Boomerang," which sailed four days prior to the "Marco Polo," for Callao. The "Marco Polo" was at the River Plato thirty-five days after leaving Port Phillip Head. The screw steamer "Australian" sailed from Port Phillip Head on the 10th of February for London with several passengers, and 78,907 ounces of gold. She was to call at the Cape of Good Hope, for which she had £1,000 in specie.

The news by the "Marco Polo," though late, does not possess much interest to an English reader. Adelaide papers state that the Government measure of having two Chambers, one composed of nominees of the Crown, was very unpopular, and a memorial against its adoption largely signed. A letter from Forest Creek, Mount Alexander, dated Feb. 10th, says:—"Hundreds of persons are daily passing through here on their way to the Tarrengower diggings, and the number of teams loaded with stores of all kinds for the same place is almost incredible. The reports of these diggings are very favourable, but the great scarcity of water is a serious impediment to the operations of the diggers. There is another new rush about four miles from Castlemaine, and the same distance from Campbell's station, in a parallel line with the river Loddon, and leading into the Tarrengower diggings at Bryant's Creek. There are some thousands at work there, doing well, and with every prospect of the gold field being extensive.

Dry Creek, Red Jacket P.O., via Woodspoint, Victoria, Australia.

We should like to hear from Mr. CHILDERS on this subject, and shall be glad to publish his explanation.

The next point which Mr. SHILLINGLAW proves is this—that the Merchant Shipping Act, which provides that a recompense should be given to the owners and masters of vessels which pick up shipwrecked crews at sea, and that a sum of money should be paid for their keep while on board the ship that saved them, did not come into force until May, 1855; consequently, the Captain of the "Osprey" would have no inducement to go to the Custom House at Melbourne to report the rescue of the "Bella's" crew.

2. Mr. JAMES ANDREWS was acquainted with ARTHUR the Butcher at Mewburn Park. His' description of him tallies very well with the testimony of the Wapping witnesses in the Court of Queen's Bench, who knew ARTHUR ORTON, and it is evident that they are the same persons. When shown a photograph of the Claimant, taken in Sydney, he says it is not like ARTHUR. He also knew a foreigner, of a gentlemanly appearance; and, when a photo. of the Claimant was handed to him, admitted that there was a resemblance, but candidly owned that it was too long ago for him to positively swear to him. He also remembered that ARTHUR the Butcher *was marked with the small-pox.*

3. ALEXANDER NIELSEN remembered ARTHUR ORTON at Mewburn Park, and lived in the same hut for six months with him; gave the same description of him as last-named witness; also knew a foreigner who knitted his brows when offended. When shown the photo. of the Claimant, he immediately recognized it as that of the foreigner. Had heard from the foreigner that he was employed at Mr. FOSTER'S, at Dargo. The Claimant, when cross-examined in the Common Pleas, swore that he was a stockrider on Mr. FOSTER'S station. In the Trial at Bar, FOSTER'S books were produced to show that TOMAS CASTRO never worked for him; but on examination they were found to be mutilated, and several leaves torn out—a very suspicious circumstance, and calculated to throw a grave doubt on the genuineness and truth of the witnesses who brought such fragments from Australia.

4. The evidence of the next witness, MARY ANDREWS, is most important. She also knew ARTHUR ORTON, the butcher at Mewburn Park, and the foreigner, whose name she could not recollect, but knew that it sounded like Cass or Cassetoo (evidently CASTRO). When shown a photo. of the Claimant she also said that it was the foreigner; she washed for the foreigner during his stay at Dargo, and had many opportunities of seeing and conversing with him.

5. MATTHEW A. WORMS, merchant, of Sydney, advanced money to the Claimant in consequence of what GUILFOYLE (the gardener of Sir EDWARD DOUGHTY, who knew ROGER TICHBORNE well when he was a youth) said. This GUILFOYLE identified the Claimant as the young ROGER TICHBORNE whom he had often nursed in his arms at Upton, and persuaded this witness to advance money to him. GUILFOYLE often saw the Claimant, and was as positive as he was of his own existence that he was the rightful heir of the Tichborne property, until the Claimant offended him by not keeping an appointment to dine at his house; afterwards the breach widened, and some months after, being visited by the detective, MACKENZIE, he declared that he was an impostor, and that he was afraid to meet him.

6. STEPHEN BUTTS, proprietor of the Metropolitan Hotel, Pitt-street, Sydney, proved that the Claimant and GUILFOYLE were *on intimate terms* until the unlucky day when he disappointed him by not keeping his appointment to dinner.

7. The evidence of the son of the above witness, TRUTH WILLIAM PALMER BUTTS, is very important. He testifies to going with the Claimant to GUILFOYLE'S house; that the Claimant walked round the room, and, seeing a painting or photograph hanging to the wall, immediately exclaimed, "That is Upton!" or Tichborne, the witness did not remember which; but the Claimant also remarked that the flower-beds had been altered since he was there, which GUILFOYLE at once admitted was a fact. On the next occasion that GUILFOYLE met the Claimant, he produced a profile or silhouette likeness of Sir EDWARD DOUGHTY, which appears in page 145,* and said, "Do you recognize this?" "Oh, yes," said the Claimant; "it is a likeness of my uncle." These are most wonderful facts, and totally destructive of the ORTON theory, which, it would seem, originated with MACKENZIE.

8. ANDREW BOGLE, son of the faithful valet of Sir EDWARD DOUGHTY, was called to prove that GUILFOYLE was satisfied of the identity of the Claimant until interviewed by his enemies.

9. MICHAEL GOLDEN testified to some remarkable conversations which he had with the Claimant, in the course of which the Claimant told him that he had been in the army, and that his family was one of the oldest Catholic families in England; that he was going to be married in a Catholic chapel, but subsequently that the priest would not marry him there because he refused to confess. He had heard him speak in a foreign language, and knew that he was able to lasso cattle.

10. JAMES FEGAN, a constable, proved that CASTRO was well acquainted with the sword exercise; that he said he had been an officer in the army; that he was heir to a property, and would be able to help all his friends.

11. Notwithstanding the importance of the above evidence, it is far exceeded in value by the testimony of WILLIAM FEARNE. It appears that the Claimant had some intention, in the year 1861, of endeavouring to capture the notorious bushranger, MORGAN, but before going on his perilous journey he had some thought of entrusting his secret, in a Sealed Packet, to this witness, so that, in case he was killed by MORGAN, it might be known that he was ROGER TICHBORNE. He communicated this idea to the witness, and also mentioned that he belonged to one of the most ancient Catholic families in England, and gave him, altogether, to understand that he was a person of high position in his native country.

The evidence of the two witnesses who follow is important, as it goes to prove that the Claimant was employed on FOSTER'S station, and was known by the name of THOMAS CASTRO. We close this summary with a letter which bears strongly on the case, and an affidavit of Mr. HENRY MILFORD.

D. 21. (COPY.)

City Coroner's Office, Sydney: 24th December, 1867.

SIR,—I am in receipt of yours of the 28th October last, having reference to the recent claim preferred to the Tichborne Baronetcy by TOM CASTRO, formerly of New South Wales.

I lived at two of the places mentioned in your letter, viz., Deniliquin from 9th March, 1854, to the 6th May, 1859, and Hay from the 7th May, 1859, to 9th May, 1866, and I cannot recall to memory "TOM CASTRO'S" residence at either of those towns, nor the receipt of any letter of the tenor referred to in yours. I have a perfect recollection, however, of a large-framed tall man of prepossessing appearance, who, whilst employed in the capacity of bricklayer's assistant during the erection of the Electric Telegraph Station at Hay, more than once told me that he was heir to a baronetcy, but I do not now remember his name, or whether I ever heard it, in fact I paid little or no attention to the statement, which was generally made when under the influence of drink. He was a man of education and appeared a gentleman, altho' in reduced circumstances.—I am, Sir, yours truly.

HENRY SHIELL, City Coroner.

JOHN HOLMES, Esq., London.

I, HENRY MILFORD, of East-street, Rockhampton, in the colony of Queensland, attorney and solicitor, make oath and say as follows:—

1. I was practising in Sydney, in the colony of New South Wales, as an attorney and solicitor, in the month of August, 1866.

2. In or about the said month of August, application was made to me by a person who, as I was informed and believed, had recently been living at Wagga-Wagga, in the said colony, under the name of DE CASTRO, and who represented himself to be Sir ROGER CHARLES TICHBORNE, Baronet, and who I am informed and believe is the Plaintiff in this suit, to procure him a loan to enable him to proceed to Europe, and I applied to several persons for the purpose, and interested myself in procuring some evidence of his identity.

3. The said Plaintiff having referred me for information respecting his identity to Mr. MICHAEL GUILFOYLE, of Double Bay, near Sydney, aforesaid, florist and market gardener, I saw the said MICHAEL GUILFOYLE on several occasions upon the subject, when he expressed to me his perfect confidence that the Plaintiff was the rightful heir to the Tichborne Estates; especially on one evening when I called at his house, and went fully into the matter with him. In pursuance of the conversation I then had with the said MICHAEL GUILFOYLE, and the information he then gave me, I prepared the declaration marked with the letter "A," produced and shown to me at the time of my swearing to this affidavit (which is in the handwriting of a clerk formerly in my employ), and a copy whereof is hereunto annexed, to be made by the said MICHAEL GUILFOYLE.

4. I was shortly afterwards informed and believe that the said Plaintiff had procured a loan from or through some other person or persons, and the matter was taken out of my hands.

HENRY MILFORD.

Sworn at Rockhampton, in the colony of Queensland, the 9th day of April, in the year of our Lord, 1868, before me,

FRANK U. BEDDIT,
A Commissioner for Affidavits, lawfully authorized to administer Oaths in the colony of Queensland.

FALSEHOODS IN ENGLAND.

Every species of lie now beset the Claimant, his cause, and its friends or supporters. It would not be saying too much if we averred that from 1866 down to the present moment—very nearly an interval of ten years—there has been no cessation of falsehood in this most hapless Case. It was perpetually stated that no one could interfere for the Claimant, except from the most selfish motives. Even the gentlemen who were bail were assailed. One of them thought it necessary about this time to publish the following letter:—

THE CLAIMANT'S BAIL.

TO THE EDITOR OF THE "DAILY TELEGRAPH."

SIR,—Many acrimonious remarks have been made in my hearing about the conduct of myself and other gentlemen in becoming bail for the Claimant to the Tichborne Estates and I daresay many thousands more, still more acrimonious, have been made out of my hearing. I should like to say a very few words in explanation.

* The reader is requested to compare the nose, chin, forehead, and eyebrows of this shadow-likeness with those of the Claimant, as represented on page 25, bearing in mind that the first represents a man of sixty; the second, that of one twenty years younger.

First—I have not a penny of interest in the matter one way or another.

Second—I disclaim, for the present, even giving my opinion as to the identity or non-identity of the Claimant.

Third—I assisted in finding bail for the Claimant simply and solely from a desire to see fair-play—that fair-play to which I have always hitherto understood that the meanest criminal was entitled.

Fourth—I hold it to be anything but fair-play that a man should be imprisoned like a condemned murderer, in Newgate, for an indefinite period, until it pleases his accusers to say that they have ransacked the uttermost corners of the earth for evidence to convict him.—I am, Sir, &c. J. LAMONT.

16, Bolton Street: April 26, 1872.

About this period, the *Times* in like fashion thought it expedient to publish an elaborate article condemnatory of the Claimant (for it was felt by those in power that his cause was steadily advancing in the public mind) which drew forth from Mr. WHALLEY, M.P. for Peterborough, the following admirable letter:—

THE TICHBORNE CASE.

To the Editor of the "Times."

SIR,—The evidence for the prosecution in this TICHBORNE Case of which you give so able a summary in this day's paper, is fairly divisible into three classes:—

First—The evidence given by persons professsing the Roman Catholic faith.

Secondly—Other persons of known character and position, such as officers, soldiers, &c., and,

Thirdly—A class which may, without offence, be termed miscellaneous, and whose evidence, so far as it is material, the defendant may reasonably allege, even with more force than to the other witnesses, he is entitled to favourable consideration, owing to his knowing nothing of such witnesses or their evidence before they appeared in Court, and being without means of procuring information.

No one who read your analysis of the evidence could retain much doubt that the defendant is guilty, unless some extraordinary influence can be proved to have been in operation to bring about a concurrence of testimony altogether unparalleled in support of so simple a question as personal identity; and it is evident that the strength of the Case as presented by you against the defendant, constitutes a claim to state on the other side any possible means of escape.

As to the Roman Catholic witnesses, if it be shown that the Church of Rome in this country has recognized the duty to its own interests of retaining the Tichborne property in its present possession, it is no disparagement to Catholic witnesses, whose evidence has promoted the views of their Church, to suggest that their evidence must be tested by those rules which recognize all other obligations as nugatory that conflict with absolute submission to the authorities charged with declaring what those interests require.

As to officers, and other persons of known character and position, who have spoken to identity or non-identity, it must have struck the most casual reader that the information on which they relied was, in almost every instance, less than it was in their power to obtain as to the Defendant's identity. If, for example, a man says he knows he is not TICHBORNE from the sight of him as he sits in Court, or from seeing or hearing him on the late trial, or other circumstances affording only a partial or prejudiced impression, it is obvious that this is of the nature of secondary evidence, and by the ordinary rules of criminal jurisprudence may be regarded as suspicious, suggesting that better evidence resulting from further intercourse would have been provided if truth were the object.

As to the "miscellaneous" class of witnesses, whether brought from Australia, Chili, or Wapping, it can hardly be said they are of more weight than those who gave evidence in the Common Pleas—86 in number—being as many as he had then the means of producing out of above 300 who had made depositions on oath to the Defendant's identity as ROGER TICHBORNE.

The Defendant has not one shilling even for his daily subsistence, beyond what is contributed by the public; and, therefore, in so far as your mode of presenting the Case against him carries conviction to the public mind that he is an impostor, you effectually prevent his defence.

The Court has declared and enforced the law of "contempt" to such an extent as to prohibit any effectual exposition of the Defendant's Case, and the mode in which you have presented that of his opponents completes his isolation from all public sympathy and support, so far as human ingenuity can accomplish that object.

As one of those who retain unabated confidence in his innocence, I am engaged, under the special permission of the Home Secretary, in soliciting subscriptions to enable him to bring up his witnesses, and I trust that you will deem it but fair and just, having regard to these circumstances, to give insertion to this letter, written as it is without communication with the Defendant or any of his friends and advisers.—I am, Sir, your obedient servant,

Plas Madoc, June 28. G. H. WHALLEY.

The same abominable course is still pursued even by the *Times*, which boasts to be "the leading journal of the world." Only the other day it published an elaborate, false, and fulsome review of the most garbled volume ever known. (Sir A. COCKBURN's version of his summing-up at the Trial), and when Mr. GUILDFORD ONSLOW sent the Editor a reply, it refused it publication. Our readers will not be sorry to see it here; we take it from the ENGLISHMAN for February 27, 1875.

To the Editor of the "Englishman."

SIR,—You will oblige me by inserting the inclosed letter to the *Times*, which the Editor refused to publish. The Press is indeed gagged, as you so truly say, in regard to the TICHBORNE Case.—Your obedient Servant, GUILDFORD ONSLOW.

To the Editor of the "Times."

SIR,—As I take it for granted you are imbued with the principle of fair-play, I trust you will kindly give insertion to this letter in your next edition, in reply to the remarks that appeared in your journal on the 12th of February, on the TICHBORNE Case. On the assumption that you never knew Mr. ROGER TICHBORNE, or his mother, and as I have had the pleasure of knowing both, I may be permitted to give my opinion with some ground for authority. You impute to Lady TICHBORNE the fearful and unheard-of crime of acknowledging an impostor, knowingly, as her son, to the detriment of her own grandson and daughter-in-law, for the mere gratification of a whim, or to substantiate (as you say) an acknowledgment before she saw him. Is it possible that the Editor of the first Journal in the world can impute a crime of this magnitude to a lady who was eminent for her piety and virtue, and whose word was unchallenged during her lifetime?—whose perfect sanity was admitted in forcible language by the Lord Chief Justice of England, in spite of the vain attempts that were made to prove her mad? Are you aware that her daughter-in-law, Lady TICHBORNE, the mother of the Infant, wrote a letter to her mother-in-law, in Paris, to ask if she had acknowledged the Claimant—which letter, and the reply, I venture to give as they were produced in Court?

"Hyde End House, Brimpton, Reading: January 19th, 1867.

"MY DEAR MAMA,—As I have not heard from you lately, I hope that you are not ill with this cold weather. There are so many reports, and so different, that I am going to ask you to let me have a line, to say whether you recognized ROGER, as soon as you can, as I feel so anxious to know. Hoping to hear from you soon, I remain, always your most affectionate daughter,"

"TISSIE TICHBORNE."

"Paris: 21st January, 1867.

"MY DEAREST TISSIE,—Many thanks for your kind letter, which I received yesterday. I have not written to you lately because my time was taken up with attending on my dear son ROGER. I have fully recognized him, as it is really him, and I cannot conceive those who knew him very well not knowing him now. I told ROGER yesterday that I was in hopes, one day, to hold my dearest little grandson in one hand and my dear little grand-daughter in the other: he said "I hope so." As soon as I can, I will come back to London. You do not mention whether my dearest little HENRY's hair begins to grow. I shall be so glad to see him when I come back to England. Ever believe me, your affectionate and devoted Mother. "H. F. TICHBORNE."

Are we to believe, after reading these letters, breathing devotion to her family, that there can be such a monster in human form, such a JEZEBEL, such a BORGIA amongst our country women, that can be guilty of such an atrocious crime as you charge her with? As her advocate, her friend, and her defender, I repudiate it. Lady TICHBORNE, like Lady ABERDEEN, did certainly acknowledge her son by the identification of his handwriting before she saw him, as did also the clerks in Doctors' Commons to the Claimant's Solicitor, when they acknowledged his signature to be identical with the signature of ROGER TICHBORNE's Will; and as also the Partners in GLYN, MILLS, and Co., who admitted his signature was the facsimile of the one in the books of the Bank. I hold a large correspondence of Mr. ROGER TICHBORNE's before 1854, both in French and English, and of the Claimant's since his arrival in this country, and every honest and impartial person who has seen these letters declare they are identical.

Mons. CHABOT was paid handsomely for his evidence, whilst the unfortunate Claimant was unable to produce his expert, Mr. BROWN, for want of funds, who could have proved the similarity of the handwriting perhaps in a rather more satisfactory way than Mons. CHABOT, when we remember that Lord COLERIDGE, in a recent trial, said he put no confidence whatever in Mons. CHABOT's opinion.

If the Lord Chief Justice of England acted in an impartial manner, how do you account for his never mentioning to the Jury the fact of ARTHUR ORTON's sailor's registered ticket, at 18 years in a growing state, proving him 5ft. 9½in., whilst the Claimant measured, in the precincts of the Court, but 5ft. 9in., by the Horse Guards' standard. Was it *impartiality* that prevented the presiding Judge informing the Jury that some eighteen or twenty witnesses for the Crown swore Mr. ROGER TICHBORNE had a remarkably narrow chest: "as narrow as it could be," and one gallant captain swore he had "no chest at all," and yet the books of the regimental tailor proved ROGER TICHBORNE's chest was 37 inches—broader than the average of the whole British army; and on his address to the jury, the Judge stated that the Claimant, could not be ROGER TICHBORNE with a congenital mark unknown to his mother, but he might be ARTHUR ORTON, having the congenital mark, without its being known? Is that impartial? if so, by the same hypothesis, I would ask, could ROGER be tattooed without his mother knowing it?

The question yet undecided is—Is he ROGER TICHBORNE, or is he not? Is he ARTHUR ORTON, or is he not? If he is ROGER TICHBORNE, all Dr. KENEALY has said is right, and all the Lord Chief Justice has said is wrong; and, as I infinitely prefer my powers of identification to any living man's, I unhesitatingly swear the man in Dartmoor Prison is the Mr. TICHBORNE I knew in former days; and I feel confident that Mr. HAZELTINE SHARPEN, the brother of the Mayor of Scarborough, spoke truthfully when he swore at the Trial, that he recognized in the Claimant the identical passenger that he saw amongst *the saved crew of the "Bella,"* in Melbourne Harbour, on board the "Osprey," in July, 1854. I remain, Sir, your obedient servant, GUILDFORD ONSLOW.

Ropley: February 16th, 1875.

P.S.—The Editor of the *Times*, NOT being imbued with the principle of fair-play, refused to insert this letter in reply to his remarks on the TICHBORNE Case.

But we should never have done, if we were to notice every horrid slander, mis-statement, or villanous lie with which almost every daily and weekly paper teemed, against this most unhappy, most persecuted man. We shall advert to only one more at present, which was made the subject of observation by Mr. WHALLEY, M.P., at the public meeting held in East London (as reported in page 132).

STRANGE CONDUCT OF THE MINISTRY.

The following Parliamentary Return, being No. 297, ordered by the House of Commons to be printed, 11th July, 1873, contains the Correspondence alluded to by Mr. WHALLEY, in his speech at the foregoing meeting.

We call attention to the fac-simile of handwriting: a more deliberate fraud upon the public has seldom been effected. The letter headed "ARTHUR ORTON to his sister" was taken or lent, out of the archives of the Court, to the Family or their agents for the purpose of creating a false impression on the public mind. It was scattered widely all over London, and exhibited for sale in every news-shop, as being a fac-simile of the handwriting of ORTON; whereas the Treasury who gave it out, the Crown who lent it, and the Family who paid for its diffusion, *knew* that it was the writing of the Claimant himself, who wrote it, or was induced to write it, under one of these unaccountable freaks of folly, drunkenness, or half-lunacy, which led him into so many scrapes and difficulties. Nothing, however, could justify its publication, and Mr. WHALLEY, in his letter to the Solicitor of the Treasury, dated 14th September, 1872, has well characterised it as "a false and malicious libel intended to prejudice the Claimant." It is another proof of the lengths to which parties in power proceeded, for the purpose of destroying the Defendant with the public. Of the same kind of villany, was the publication by the Family or their agents of the photo-portraits of old ORTON, the butcher, and his wife. There were deposited in Court by order of BOVILL, when he committed the Claimant, amongother things, two miniatures of those persons. These miniatures bear evident proof of having been tampered with by somebody who had an interest in making them bear a resemblance to Sir ROGER. Dr. KENEALY, in his address to the jury, pointed out how in many places they were overlaid with new and fresh-coloured paint. The eyebrows were enlarged and darkened so as to be like those of the Claimant. The lower part of the face was rounded; the chin was marked with shadows; the eyes, the lips, the ears were all perceptibly altered. It seemed, indeed, as if a new face had been painted over the old one. Never was a greater imposition. Strange it is however, but true, that the more they dabbled with the miniatures of the old ORTONS, the more they unwittingly caused them to resemble the features of the Wapping-like youth, whose likeness is given in page 37 of this volume. By whom, or when, these things were done, Dr. KENEALY never learned. But photos of those false faces were sold everywhere in London and the country, and in many places they were put in close juxta-position with some of the photos of the Claimant, which they had been painted up to resemble. If this was done after they were deposited in Court, there must have been treachery somewhere; if it was done before, then the Family who produced them were in this proceeding also as wicked and unscrupulous as in the PITTENDREIGH Forgery, and a score of similar deeds.

No. 1.

The Secretary to the Treasury to the Honourable A. F. O. LIDDELL.

Treasury Chambers: 14 May, 1873.

SIR,—I am desired by the Lords Commissioners of Her Majesty's Treasury to transmit herewith, to be laid before Mr. Secretary BRUCE, a memorial addressed to the Chancellor of the Exchequer by certain inhabitants of Southampton, for a grant of money from public funds to the Claimant of the Tichborne Estates to enable him to bring up witnesses and provide Counsel.—I am, &c. (Signed) CHARLES W. STRONGE, pro Secretary.

The Hon. A. F. O. LIDDELL, &c., &c., &c.

To the Right Honourable ROBERT LOWE, Chancellor of the Exchequer.

RIGHT HONOURABLE SIR,—The petition of the undersigned inhabitants of the Town and County of Southampton and Woolston, in the parish of St. Mary's Extra, in the county of Hants—Humbly showeth,

That in the county of Hampshire, and a few miles from the above-named parishes, is the Tichborne Estate, formerly the property of Sir JAMES TICHBORNE, bart., and now claimed by Sir ROGER CHARLES DOUGHTY TICHBORNE, recently consigned a prisoner to Newgate on a charge of perjury and forgery, but now liberated on bail.

That your Petitioners are apprehensive that as the Claimant has not sufficient means at his command either to employ Counsel or to bring up his witnesses, the true facts of the Case at the forthcoming trial may not and cannot be fully elicited.

Your Petitioners, therefore, humbly pray that you will kindly grant from the public purse to the Claimant a sum of money, a like advantage he would receive as if a pauper prisoner to be tried at the Central Criminal Court, to enable him to bring up the whole of his witnesses and provide Counsel, in order that equal justice may be secured for him as in the case of the prosecution, that during the excitement of the trial and at its close the people of England may be satisfied that the Government of a free, enlightened, and patriotic nation did accord to the Claimant that pecuniary aid which, as an Englishman, your humble Petitioners feel he has a right to claim, and pray he may receive at your hands.—And your Petitioners will ever pray.

ROBERT JACKSON, 29, Cook-street, Southampton.
FREDERICK JACKSON, 29, Cook-street, Southampton.
And 184 others.

No. 2.

Mr. WHEELHOUSE, M.P., to the Lords Commissioners of the Treasury.

House of Commons, 10 June, 1873.

MY LORDS,—The accompanying Petition has been forwarded to me from Leeds, along with a request that I should present it to your Lordships; I therefore do so, and I am, &c.

(Signed) W. St. J. WHEELHOUSE.

The Lords Commissioners of Her Majesty's Treasury.

To the Right Honourable the Lords of the Treasury.

To MY LORDS—The Petition of the undersigned inhabitants of Leeds, in the County of York, Humbly showeth—

That your Petitioners are apprehensive that as the Claimant to the Tichborne Estates, now being tried for perjury, has not sufficient means at his command either to employ Counsel or to bring up his witnesses, the true facts in the present trial may not and cannot be fully elicited.

Your Petitioners, therefore, humbly pray your Lordships that your Lordships will kindly grant to the Claimant means that will enable him to bring up the whole of his witnesses, and provide requisite Counsel, in order that justice may be secured for him, equal to that afforded to the prosecution, so that during the trial and at its close the people of England may be satisfied that the defence of the Claimant has not suffered for the want of sufficient pecuniary aid.

And your Petitioners will ever pray.

(Signed) GEORGE AMBLER, HENRY BARKER, and others.

No. 3.

Mr. W. LAW to Mr. WHEELHOUSE, M.P.

Treasury Chambers, 17 June, 1873.

SIR,—I am desired by the Lords Commissioners of Her Majesty's Treasury to acknowledge the receipt of your letter of the 10th instant, and inclosed memorial from certain inhabitants of Leeds, praying that means may be granted to the Claimant to the Tichborne Estates to enable him to bring up witnesses and provide Counsel, and I am to state that my Lords have forwarded the said memorial to the Home Office, which is the department of State having cognizance of matters of that nature.—I am, &c.

(Signed) WILLIAM LAW.

W. ST. J. WHEELHOUSE, Esq., M.P., House of Commons.

No. 4.

Mr. W. LAW to the Honourable A. F. O. LIDDELL.

Treasury Chambers, 17 June, 1873.

SIR,—I am desired by the Lords Commissioners of Her Majesty's Treasury to transmit herewith, to be laid before Mr. Secretary BRUCE, the enclosed memorial of certain inhabitants of Leeds, praying that means may be granted to the Claimant to the Tichborne Estates to enable him to bring up witnesses and provide Counsel, which has been forwarded by Mr. WHEELHOUSE, M.P., with a letter, which is also inclosed.—I am, &c.,

(Signed) WILLIAM LAW.

The Hon. A. F. O. LIDDELL.

No. 5.

The Honourable A. F. O. LIDDELL to the Secretary to the Treasury.

Whitehall, 25 June, 1873.

SIR,—I am directed by Mr. Secretary BRUCE to return herewith the memorial of certain inhabitants of Leeds, praying that means may be granted to the Claimant to the Tichborne Estates to enable him to bring up witnesses and provide Counsel, and I am to acquaint you, for the information of the Lords Commissioners of Her Majesty's Treasury, that in Mr. BRUCE's opinion, an acknowledgment of the receipt of the petition (as in the case of a similar memorial from inhabitants of Southampton, forwarded in your letter of the 14th ultimo), will be sufficient.—I am, &c.

(Signed) A. F. O. LIDDELL.

The Secretary to the Treasury.

Acknowledged by Letter No. 6.

II.

Copy of the Correspondence between Mr. WHALLEY, M.P., and the Solicitor to the Treasury, on the subject of the prosecution, QUEEN *v.* CASTRO *alias* TICHBORNE.

No. 1.

Mr. WHALLEY, M.P., to the Solicitor to the Treasury.

Reform Club, 2 July, 1872.

MY DEAR SIR,—Large public meetings were held in the town of Swansea on the 27th, 28th, and 29th of June, for the purpose of raising money for the Claimant (TICHBORNE v. LUSHINGTON), and a unanimous opinion was expressed that he is truly ROGER CHARLES TICHBORNE. Similar meetings, followed by the like expression of opinion, have been held at Southampton (at which I was also present), and elsewhere, and I have been requested to attend at Newcastle, and other large towns and centres of population.

You will, I feel assured, agree with me that such meetings are to be regretted, tending, as is obvious they do, to impair public confidence in the fair and impartial administration of justice; and I consider that the Government should be informed of any facts, that, being duly investigated, may satisfy them that this prosecution is a mistake.

Such is the view of the public meetings at Swansea, and I was requested to bring to your notice some evidence not before known, and which appears to be entitled to your attention.

At the meeting on the 28th, Mr. WILLIAM CROOK, a respectable tradesman in Swansea, stated that he well knew the Claimant in Australia, and also ARTHUR ORTON, the person designated by the Attorney-General as identical with him, and that he is not ARTHUR ORTON, thus confirming the evidence of Dr. WHEELER and others to the same effect.

Mr. CROOK also stated that Mr. MACKENZIE, an agent or solicitor of the Defendants, by whom the Australian evidence was collected, did offer to and agree to pay him £50, on the condition that he would not give evidence on the part of the Claimant.

It was also made known to the meeting at Swansea, that Mr. VINCENT GOSFORD, another agent of the Defendants, stated to Mr. LEWIS, now residing at Carmarthen, that the Claimant is actually ROGER CHARLES TICHBORNE; such statement having been made in January, 1867, shortly after Mr. GOSFORD'S visit to the Claimant at Gravesend, thus confirming evidence given to this effect in the cause.

WILLIAM HEWITT, now living at Llanelly, and for fourteen years a servant in the SEYMOUR family, also voluntarily came forward, and stated to the meeting that, having seen and conversed with the Claimant, he fully recognized and was absolutely certain that he is ROGER CHARLES TICHBORNE; and the like testimony was given by RICHARD HILLS, formerly colour-sergeant in the Rifle Brigade, who well knew Mr. TICHBORNE when with his regiment at Canterbury in 1851.

I have reason to believe that one of the sailors saved with the Claimant from the wreck of the "Bella" is well known in Swansea, and will shortly return to England.

I have to request that you will, as Solicitor of the Treasury in charge of the prosecution, investigate these facts, and any further information you may require for that purpose will be readily afforded.

Acting as I am in discharge of a public duty, you will not object to my making known this communication, and any reply which I may receive thereto.—I am, &c.

(Signed) G. H. WHALLEY.

JOHN GRAY, Esq., &c., &c.

No. 2.

The Solicitor to the Treasury to Mr. WHALLEY, M.P.

Treasury, 4 July, 1872.

DEAR SIR,—I received your letter of the 2nd instant, wherein you request me to investigate certain statements, which you call facts, and as I do not mean to enter upon any such investigation, I for certain reasons think it right to set forth in my reply to your communication the grounds of my determination; and you may, if you please, give me any reasons you can to convince me I have taken an erroneous view of the case. You know that in private I have often, when you spoke to me about the case, tried to get from you your idea of any answer to the difficulties involved in it, which I am about to mention; but I could never get you even to attend to me when proposing them, nor could I discover that you had ever taken the trouble to read or understand a word of the evidence on such points, and certainly I could not discover in you any consciousness that there were any such points in the case, and my conviction has been and is, that you are acting in the case, as it is now notorious you are, without having taken the trouble to make the least effort to understand it; but now that I have the opportunity of putting to you in writing what I have often tried to put to you by word of mouth, I give you the opportunity of removing my objections to the investigation to which you invite me, and also the opportunity of trying to understand the case, in order that you may do so.

First, you tell me of large public meetings at which an unanimous opinion was expressed that the person whom you call TICHBORNE, and whom I call by the names of CASTRO and ORTON, is truly ROGER CHARLES TICHBORNE. If you place any value on the opinions of such meetings, you and I differ very much in that respect; but I see you say that such meetings are to be regretted as (in effect) mischievous, and yet you are one of the chief promoters and supporters of them; I cannot see what it is relating to these meetings that you require me to investigate.

Now, with regard to the evidence which you speak of as not before known, I will first refer to WILLIAM CROOK, and I perhaps know more of WILLIAM CROOK than you do, having had occasion to send to Swansea to inquire into his antecedents when he was offered as bail for Mr. TOMAS CASTRO shortly after he was sent to Newgate, and also to inquire elsewhere; and after these inquiries had been made his name was withdrawn, and he was not offered as bail again. I require no further investigation as to him. As to Dr. WHEELER, he wrote to offer information to the Government, and I wrote and asked him to meet me and give the information; instead of meeting me, he wrote to me declining to do so, and saying he did not intend any further to interfere in the case, and so, I suppose, there is an end of any investigation as to him. As to Mr. CROOK'S statement that Mr. MACKENZIE offered him a bribe of £50, let it go for what it is worth; Mr. MACKENZIE denies it, and I believe Mr. MACKENZIE. As to the statement that Mr. VINCENT GOSFORD said that the Claimant is ROGER CHARLES TICHBORNE, I have formed my own opinion as to the truth of that allegation, and I have no desire to see the person who makes it. I have not had the case in my hands for months without forming a very clear opinion as to what Mr. VINCENT GOSFORD said, and did, and thought, in regard to TOMAS CASTRO. As to WILLIAM HEWITT and RICHARD HILLS, they may be two more witnesses added to those of a similar kind called on the trial of ejectment; but they require no investigation on my part. As to the sailor saved with the Claimant from the wreck of the "Bella," when he returns to England, I will undertake to find one of the crew of the "Osprey" to eat him.

But before I would think of investigating such matters as you bring forward in your letter, I should require some explanation on the following points, which I invite you to give me: When ARTHUR ORTON'S sisters asked the Claimant, after his expedition to Wapping, for a portrait of their brother ARTHUR'S wife and child, why did he send them a portrait of his own wife and child as those of their brother ARTHUR, as, on his oath, he admitted he did? Why, when the sisters asked him for a portrait of their brother ARTHUR, did he say he had only one, and that he would send them copies when he had got them made, and then on his oath swore and confessed that the one portrait he referred to was his own portrait, and that he had no portrait of any other ARTHUR ORTON? If he be not ARTHUR ORTON, why did he not, when they pressed for portraits of their brother, and his wife and child, say, "Your brother has no wife and has no child, and was never married," for he swore that that was so when asked the question?

How was it that the sixteen Chili witnesses (and amongst the rest those whom the Claimant said, with undoubted truth, that he had made the acquaintance of), one and all swore that they had never known nor heard of anyone of the name of TICHBORNE, but that they did know ARTHUR ORTON, and no other young Englishman whatever, and that their acquaintance with him was in 1849 and 1850, which was when ROGER TICHBORNE was in Ireland with his regiment; and is it not true that his own counsel, after he came from Chili, said he believed all these witnesses to be truth-telling people?

How was it that ROGER TICHBORNE, who, on his arrival in Chili, knew no Spanish, should in a week or two make the intimate acquaintance of a number of the inhabitants of Melipilla, who were strangers to him, and knew no French or English, and that this could be accomplished in the space of 10 days or a fortnight, as he swore it was?

How is it, if the Claimant were ROGER TICHBORNE, that when he made his will in Wagga-Wagga he did not know his own mother's name, but called her HANNAH FRANCES, her real name being HENRIETTE FELICITE?

He said eight British sailors were saved with him from the "Bella;" now I think I may assume that, on the average, each of those sailors must have had five relations, and seven friends or acquaintances not relations: this, including the sailors themselves, makes 104 individuals; how does it happen that not one of those 104 individuals has been heard of or come forward to say any one was saved from the "Bella"?—and the argument is much strengthened when it is considered that the same observation applies to all the persons who were on board the supposed "Osprey." As to your sailor who is supposed to be known in Swansea, I should think he is an invention palmed off upon you with a view to take off the pressure of the above argument while the meetings are going on.

I observe you intimate an intention to publish your letter and my reply, and suppose that I will not object to your doing so. I have never published or thought of publishing anything about the case; my intention has been to wait quietly for the trial, but as your intention evidently was to prejudice the case for the prosecution, if I had answered your letter, as you perhaps wished or expected, and, as I think, to draw me into a trap, I have written a reply which I have no objection to your publishing if you please, and with your answers to it, if you please; if you drop it altogether and make no similar attempt, I shall drop it too, but if you publish your own letter and only refer to mine, without giving it at length, I shall myself, if I think it necessary, publish it, to show what was the exact reply to your communication.—I am, &c.

(Signed) JOHN GRAY.

—. WHALLEY, Esq., M.P., House of Commons.

P. S.—Since writing the above I have received your letter of this day, in which you refer to a letter from Dr. WHEELER'S brother-in-law, Mr. HORNBY, and signed by him and Dr. WHEELER; that was a letter desiring to withdraw the letter of

Dr. WHEELER offering the information to the Government, and you tell me that Dr. WHEELER is now willing to come to me if I will send for him, which you ask me to do; Dr. WHEELER being now offered to me by you, I might merely say, "*Timeo Danaos, &c.,*" but I own to a curiosity to see Dr. WHEELER, yet, as his last letter tells me he will not come, I cannot comply with your request that I will write to him; if he wishes, as I understand you to say he does, to retract his retractation, and to give information as offered in his original letter, let him take the initiative.

No. 3.

Mr. WHALLEY, M.P., to the Solicitor to the Treasury.

The Reform Club, 4 July, 1872.

MY DEAR SIR,—Dr. WHEELER has called on me and requested that I would explain to you in reference to a letter written by Mr. HORNBY and signed by that person, and also by Dr. WHEELER, that it was so written under the feeling of alarm at the difficulty and risk he would be exposed to in giving evidence in the TICHBORNE Case, including the probable loss of his appointment in GREEN'S mercantile navy; and further, that in so far as it spoke of his statement having been exaggerated, &c., he referred solely to what had appeared in the *Morning Advertiser*, and which, differing as it did from his statutory declaration, was, in fact, an exaggerated statement.

He informs me further that he adheres strictly to the terms of his statutory declaration, and by my advice he will present himself to you, in compliance with your note to him, to give you all the information he possesses.—Yours, &c.

(Signed) G. H. WHALLEY.

JOHN GRAY, Esq., &c. &c.

Dr. WHEELER awaits a note from you, fixing a time for him to call.

No. 4.

Mr. WHALLEY, M.P., to the Solicitor to the Treasury.

House of Commons, 11 July, 1872.

DEAR SIR,—The five points which you specify as requiring explanation in the case of the TICHBORNE prosecution, are all matters of inference and of opinion, and it is needless to discuss them either verbally or in writing, if it can be proved by direct and reliable evidence that the Claimant is not ARTHUR ORTON, and that he is ROGER CHARLES TICHBORNE.

I submit to you also that it is no part of the duties of a public prosecutor to decide the question of guilty or not guilty; at the public meetings which I have attended since the receipt of your letter, I have endeavoured to do full justice to the case you present against the Claimant, and have given such explanation as appears to me, and has been fully accepted by large masses of people, as satisfactory, and if you could overcome your indifference to such expressions of opinion, and would read the report of my observations at Millwall, in the *Morning Advertiser* of the 6th inst., you would learn my views thereon.—I am, &c.

JOHN GRAY, Esq., &c., &c. (Signed) G. H. WHALLEY.

P.S.—I shall send the correspondence to the trustees of the TICHBORNE Defence Fund, who will do as they please as to publishing it.—G. H. W.

No. 5.

Mr. WHALLEY, M.P., to the Solicitor to the Treasury.

The Reform Club, 27 July, 1872.

DEAR SIR,—Having been again prevented from formally calling the attention of the Home Secretary, in the House of Commons, to the question of which a copy is inclosed, I spoke to him privately on the subject, and am induced to believe that you may perhaps consider yourself authorized to reply thereto.

With reference to your letter to me, I did not deem it necessary to trouble you with any reply thereto; the points on which you required explanation having no other bearing on the case than by way of inference and opinion, on which I could not expect that you would be influenced by my views or suggestions, but if you are desirous of ascertaining on what grounds it is that I believe the Claimant to be ROGER CHARLES TICHBORNE, I am now better prepared even than when I last wrote to you to submit for your investigation conclusive evidence to that effect.

I understand that you have taken down the evidence of Dr. WHEELER, and I inclose you an extract from a newspaper received by me to-day, and suggest that you should investigate in like manner the evidence of Mr. HOFLAND.

In the course of my attendance at the public meetings recently held, many persons of competent knowledge and good character have, in my presence, and under circumstances free from suspicion of collusion or error, fully and conclusively recognized the Claimant as ROGER CHARLES TICHBORNE.—I am, &c.

(Signed) G. H. WHALLEY.

JOHN GRAY, Esq., &c., &c.

No. 6.

The Solicitor to the Treasury to Mr. WHALLEY, M.P.

R. v. CASTRO.

Treasury, 29 July, 1872.

SIR,—I have no desire to ascertain on what grounds you believe the Claimant to be ROGER CHARLES TICHBORNE.

I do not now desire you to take the trouble to give any reply to the points I suggested to you in a former letter. You referred me to your Millwall speech as reported in the *Morning Advertiser*, and I there saw the use you made of my letter. I also saw that one of the points I put to you, was answered not by an argument but by a pure falsehood,* possibly not invented by you, but suggested to you by some one else; but you seem to me to be in this dilemma, that either you knew your allegation to be false, or you were ignorant of the A B C of the case you seem to have taken up. I refer to your allegation that before July, 1853, the time at which the Claimant alleged he had spent a fortnight at Melipilla, and made the acquaintance of his numerous Chilian friends there, the real ROGER CHARLES TICHBORNE had spent a year in Chili studying or learning the language.

In performing my duty in the conduct of this prosecution, I shall be ready to attend to, and treat with respect, all proper communications from the Defendant's accredited representative, his attorney; but you have no recognized position with respect to the Defendant that I am aware of, and therefore I decline in future to have any correspondence with you on the subject of the case.—I am, &c. (Signed) JOHN GRAY.

G. H. WHALLEY, Esq., M.P., Reform Club, Pall Mall.

No. 7.

Mr. WHALLEY, M.P., to the Solicitor to the Treasury.

House of Commons Library, 31 July, 1872.

The TICHBORNE Prosecution.

SIR,—The contents and the tone of your letter of the 29th instant manifest the intention to withhold from the Defendant reasonable and customary information and assistance for his defence, and as a Member of the House of Commons, considering it to be my duty to do what may be within my power to secure for him a fair trial, I shall adopt for that purpose such means as are best calculated to promote that object; whether by further correspondence with you or otherwise.

You appear to have forgotten that in your previous letter to me you complain that I declined to discuss with you certain "points" in the case, and that you invited me to do so; as also, that the Chancellor of the Exchequer stated in the House of Commons, as a reason for not replying to questions addressed to him by me, that you, as the officer in charge of the prosecution, were the person to whom such questions should be addressed.

With reference to your expression "a pure falsehood," I beg to state that you have not correctly quoted the statement to which you think fit to apply those terms; and when, as in your previous letter, you also impute to me that "I have laid a trap for you," and so forth, I consider that you go far beyond either the duties or the privileges of your official position.—I am, &c.

JOHN GRAY, Esq. (Signed) G. H. WHALLEY.

No. 8.

The Solicitor to the Treasury to Mr. WHALLEY, M.P.

4, Gloucester-crescent, Regent's Park,

2 August, 1872.

DEAR SIR,—I shall not attempt to interfere with anything you may think fit to do with the Claimant, so long as you do not attempt to interfere with me.

I have not forgotten what I said about the points I put to you, but having failed, apparently, to draw your *bona fide* and deliberate attention to any of them, I no longer desire to trouble your mind with them.

Let me say that I did not intend to impute falsehood to you. I never supposed the falsehood I spoke of was yours; my explanation was that some one else had told you that which you said at the meting, and that you adopted it without examination. I have known you for a very long time, and I never had any reason for supposing that falsehood formed a part of your character, and I should be very sorry that you should think I was seriously imputing it to you now. I should be glad that this correspondence should close without anything acrimonious, at least on my side. —I am, &c. (Signed) JOHN GRAY.

G. H. WHALLEY, Esq., M.P.

No. 9.

Mr. WHALLEY, M.P., to the Solicitor to the Treasury.

House of Commons, 7 August, 1872.

SIR,—I consider it right to inform you, in further reply to your letter of the 27th July, of facts which have come to my knowledge since I wrote to you, and which I invite you to investigate for yourself.

In your letter of the 4th of July, in reply to my statement that Mr. MACKENZIE, the recognized agent or solicitor of the Defendants in the late trial, had offered to Mr. W. CROOK, of Swansea, a bribe of £50 not to give evidence on behalf of the Claimant, you say that "Mr. MACKENZIE denies this, and that you believe Mr. MACKENZIE;" stating also, as to Mr. CROOK, that you "probably know more of W. CROOK than I do, having had occasion to send to Swansea to inquire into his antecedents when he was offered as bail for Mr. TOMAS CASTRO."

It was due to Mr. CROOK to make further inquiry into this matter, and I am now prepared to submit to you, if you will again send to Swansea for the purpose, the evidence of two persons who will corroborate the statement of Mr. CROOK, one of them having seen the delivery to Mr. CROOK by Mr. MACKENZIE of 10 sovereigns, as part payment of the proposed bribe.

* The following words are extracted from the speech of Mr. WHALLEY, referred to by him, as reported in the *Morning Advertiser*, of the 6th July, (really the 8th), and are the words here referred to:—"As to the acquisition of the Spanish language in 10 or 12 days, I am really surprised that the Solicitor to the Treasury should have overlooked the fact, that before the Claimant went, as he alleges, to Melipilla, he had been in Spanish America for nearly a year, and had made the language a special and favourite study."

In the same letter of the 4th of July you also reply to my statement that I "had reason to believe that one of the sailors of the 'Bella' saved with the Claimant was well known in Swansea;" and you say, "as to the sailor saved with the Claimant from the wreck of the 'Bella,' when he returns to England, I will undertake to find one of the crew of the 'Osprey' to eat him."

As on this question, I call your attention to the inclosed extract from the *Western Mail* of the 6th instant, a local paper of large circulation, by which the public are informed "that MORGAN HARRIS had made statements which lead to the conviction that he was on board the ship 'Bella' at the time Sir ROGER TICHBORNE was there; that he was accompanied from Gloucester by a person who appeared to have conspicuous control over him, and who never left his side from first to last; that on Thursday" (it should be Friday), "to the astonishment of his father and other relations, he intimated his intention of going to sea, and that at four o'clock in the afternoon, accompanied by his mysterious companion, he went aboard the screw steamer 'Corcyra,' bound for Valencia, parting with his mysterious friend at the docks, who was the last person he spoke to and shook hands with."

Having in this case also made personal inquiry, and taken the depositions of several persons as to the facts so referred to by this newspaper, I have no doubt whatever that MORGAN HARRIS was a sailor in the "Bella," and was rescued with ROGER TICHBORNE; and that on his recent visit to Swansea he has been by some means influenced to withhold the information on that subject which years ago, and before the TICHBORNE Case arose, he freely communicated to his relations and friends.

I am not prepared to say whether MORGAN HARRIS has been bribed, as was attempted in the case of Mr. CROOK, or whether, becoming informed of your views of the case, he may have desired to avoid exposure to such risks as your zeal suggests; but that MORGAN HARRIS was one of the sailors of the "Bella" can be established by the best evidence the circumstances of the case admit of, and of this I can afford you the means of satisfying yourself.—I am, &c.

JOHN GRAY, Esq. (Signed) G. H. WHALLEY.

Inclosure in No. 9.

THE TICHBORNE CLAIMANT AND THE CREW OF THE "BELLA." MYSTERIOUS PROCEEDINGS AT SWANSEA.

It has already been notified that a man named MORGAN HARRIS, whose father and friends reside at Swansea, has made certain statements which lead to the conviction that he was on board the ship "Bella," at the time Sir ROGER TICHBORNE was there. It is, however, certain that, as he himself avers, he was paid off from the ship "Susquehannah," which vessel, it will be remembered, was named prominently in connection with the late TICHBORNE Trial. This being the presumption, it was natural that the arrival of MORGAN HARRIS at Swansea, on Monday, from Gloucester, at which port he arrived off voyage, should have put the local friends of the Claimant on the alert. HARRIS was "interviewed," but to no purpose. To all the questions put to him about the "Bella" he was mute, and could not be got to enter into the matter at all. He was accompanied from Gloucester by a person who appeared to have conspicuous control over him, and who never left his side from first to last. On Thursday, to the astonishment of his father and other relations, he intimated his intention of going to sea. At four o'clock in the afternoon, accompanied by his mysterious companion, he went aboard the screw-steamer "Corcyra," bound for Valencia, in which vessel he went to sea, ostensibly on her intended voyage, parting with his mysterious friend at the docks, who was the last person he spoke to and shook hands with. He was in a state of intoxication when he came to Swansea on Monday, continued in that state all the time he was in the town, and was intoxicated when he left the port. In the meantime the Claimant's friends were telegraphed to in London, and Mr. WHALLEY, M.P., lost no time in coming to Swansea, where he arrived the day after the "Corcyra" sailed with the man HARRIS on board. HARRIS's friends were at once communicated with, and from what has transpired, we believe in all probability a public meeting will be held to fully consider the matter, which abounds in mystery in reference to this most mysterious case.

No. 10.

Mr. WHALLEY, M.P., to the Solicitor of the Treasury.

The Reform Club, 8 August, 1872.

DEAR SIR,—If there is one man whom I have ever known for whom I felt greater respect than another, for all that belongs to the profession of the bar, I can very truly say it is yourself, and I have never referred to your own correspondence, either in the House of Commons or elsewhere, without doing this justice to my feelings. You may suppose, therefore, with what pleasure I receive your note of the 7th (though only to hand this morning, having been sent to Wales).

As to the case, having the most thorough convictions on the subject, and a sense of duty to act them out, I sincerely wish the Government would put an end to the excuse for these public discussions, by providing reasonable funds for the defence.

Again thanking you and reciprocating your friendly expressions,—I am, &c. (Signed) G. H. WHALLEY.

JOHN GRAY, Esq., &c., &c.

I consider this and your note private. I think of moving for copies of the correspondence with you and Mr. BRUCE.

No. 11.

Mr. WHALLEY, M.P., to the Solicitor to the Treasury.

The TICHBORNE Prosecution.

Plas Madoc, Ruabon: 14 September, 1872.

SIR,—On the 18th and 19th instant at Liverpool, and on the 20th at Manchester, I am invited to attend public meetings, and it is my intention to bring before them the following facts:—

The paper which I inclose is publicly sold in the shops of London, and in so far as it purports to be a fac-simile of the handwriting of ARTHUR ORTON, is undoubtedly a false and malicious libel intended to prejudice the Claimant.

In the course of an inquiry as to the authorship of a false telegram lately sent in my name to Mr. W. CROOK, the publication of this fac-simile paper has been traced to Mr. E. ROUS, lately the landlord of the "Swan," at Alresford, by whom the private correspondence was furnished for use in the late trial in the Common Pleas, and there is reason to believe that he has acted in this matter in concert with Mr. MACKENZIE, known to you as the person charged with tampering with this Mr. W. CROOK.

You have already informed me that Mr. MACKENZIE is a person on whom you rely in the conduct of this prosecution, and I think you should know that in addition to the evidence of two witnesses who confirm the statement of Mr. CROOK, that he was offered, and in part paid, £50; the proceedings of Mr. MACKENZIE, in reference to the Australian evidence, have been spoken of by Messrs. SEDGFIELD and ALLPORT, Solicitors of high standing, in the following terms:—

"MACKENZIE, the agent of the Defendants, returns to England by this mail, and we beg most emphatically to caution you against him. He has done great injury to the Plaintiff's case by his unscrupulous statements and tampering with witnesses, and we believe it is his intention to see all the Plaintiff's witnesses in England, and give them a garbled version of the Australian evidence."

It is no part of my duty to carry further the inquiry into what has so much the appearance of a deliberate conspiracy against the Claimant, but I submit that it is of the utmost public importance, and at the present stage of the proceedings, that some explanation should be given how it has happened that letters in the custody of the Court have come into the hands of Mr. ROUS, and also whether the services of that person are recognized in the conduct of this prosecution.

In reference to your previous inquiry as to the interest taken by me in this affair, I repeat that I am acting in the discharge of what I deem to be my duty as a Member of the House of Commons, and in accordance, as I have reason to believe, with the views of my constituents.

Any reply to this letter will be read at the meetings I have referred to.—I am, &c. (Signed) G. H. WHALLEY.

JOHN GRAY, Esq.

No. 12.

The Solicitor to the Treasury to Mr. WHALLEY, M. P.

Treasury, 16 September, 1872.

SIR,—I beg to acknowledge the receipt of your letter of Saturday last.

I deny your assertion that I informed you that Mr. MACKENZIE is a person on whom I rely in the conduct of this prosecution; that must be an imagination of your own, for I have not, nor said that I have, in any way employed either Mr. MACKENZIE or Mr. ROUS, or received or recognized any services from either of them.

I find nothing else in your letter which I am called upon to notice.—I am, &c., (Signed) JOHN GRAY.

G. H. WHALLEY, Esq., M.P., Plas Madoc, Ruabon, Denbighshire.

No. 13.

Mr. WHALLEY, M.P., to the Solicitor to the Treasury.

TICHBORNE Prosecution.

Plas Madoc, Ruabon: 17 September, 1872.

SIR,—In reply to your letter "denying my assertion that you informed me that Mr. MACKENZIE is a person on whom you rely in the conduct of this prosecution," I beg to remind you that having apprised you of Mr. CROOK's statement that he had been tampered with by Mr. MACKENZIE, you expressed your disbelief of Mr. W. CROOK, giving as a reason the denial of Mr. MACKENZIE, and inferring from this that Mr. MACKENZIE is a person on whom you rely, I expected that you would accept the confirmation of the statement of Mr. CROOK, which I was enabled to afford, as worthy of your notice in the interests of the public service.

In reference to the reason you give for imputing to me "imagination" in this matter, namely—

"For I have not, nor said that I have, in any way employed either Mr. MACKENZIE or Mr. ROUS, or received or recognized any services from either of them"—

I beg leave to point out that as I only asked you the question "whether the services of Mr. ROUS are recognised by you in this prosecution," your reply would have been complete without connecting it with "an imagination of my own."

As you do not feel called upon to notice the evidence of conspiracy against the Claimant which I submitted to you, I should not again trouble you on such topics, but that as to the fraudulent use of the Telegraph, the aid of the Government seems to be essential.

In a letter received this morning from Captain HUNT, R.A., the Secretary of the TICHBORNE Defence Fund, he states, "I have had a visit from the detective officer at Bow-street; he wants the original telegram, that you and I may inspect it, and see if we know the handwriting."

I have myself seen Mr. SCUDAMORE, who with the utmost courtesy promised to aid in detecting the fraud, but not having received the original manuscript, or other information, I presume he requires such authority for that purpose as you, on the part of the Government, can of course exercise.—I am, &c.

JOHN GRAY, Esq. (Signed) G. H. WHALLEY.

No. 14.

The Solicitor to the Treasury to Mr. WHALLEY, M.P.

Treasury, 19 September, 1872.

SIR,—I should very much regret your thinking that I meant anything offensive by the use of the expression "you imagined." I thought it likely, from what passed about Mr. MACKENZIE before, that from an inaccurate recollection of what I had written, you supposed that I had been availing myself of the assistance of Mr. MACKENZIE, and had told you so, and therefore I really meant nothing more than that you were mistaken.

I have a sufficiently heavy burthen cast upon me by having to get up the prosecution, and I desire not to take upon myself the labour of inquiring into alleged conspiracies against the Claimant, in which I have a profound disbelief, and which is not within the scope of my duty, and I shall be glad if you will relieve me from corresponding with you on such subjects. I shall always be ready to attend to anything that does fall within my duty.—I am, &c., (Signed) JOHN GRAY.

G. H. WHALLEY, Esq., M.P., Plas Madoc, Ruabon, Denbighshire.

OBSERVATIONS ON THE WRITING.

The reader is requested to notice the *fac-simile* of the Claimant's letter to his Mother as given here, most minutely. It is, with the exception of two or three short notes to GIBBES, perhaps the first attempt at writing a letter that he made during his twelve years in Australia. He is supposed to have had no practice whatever, beyond that of signing a few scanty bills. Examine carefully each word, and note how free and flowing many of the words appear. Note the easy flow of the united vowels, as if written by a hand once practised and easy, and after that, look below at the signature of the undoubted ROGER, and the same appearances will be recognized. Note in particular the vowels in the word "*January*," and the word "*France*," above it, written by the Claimant—also the flourish over the *F*, and the *T* in TICHBORNE. Supposing for one moment that an uneducated man, such as ARTHUR ORTON, had to write words in French, a language he never could have seen written: would he have scrawled off the French address with the ease he wrote this? In fact the elements of a foreign hand break out in every line, and the word "*Maria*" seems like a reminiscence of his youthful life. It is curious to note the letter *y* at the end of the word "*mercy*;" at one time ROGER TICHBORNE always dotted every final *y* he made; this was in the middle part of his life; after which he entirely left off the habit, when in the first letter to his mother he resumes it unconsciously. The friends of this unfortunate man are nearly united in concluding that the whole of the letters said to be written by ARTHUR ORTON are simply FORGERIES, based on an imitation of the Claimant's letters from Australia and elsewhere which passed into the possession of the Family or their agents.

In the first line of the Letter to Lady TICHBORNE, "*recered*," is a recollection of the French verb "*recevoir*;" the entire line is a gentleman's writing; the fourth line deserves the same remark. In the word "*mama*," the French again breaks out, as the word in English is always written with double *m*. Note also how well it and the *Mama* in the address are penned. "*You have cause*" is a reminiscence of French. In the tenth line "*no wish*" is beautifully written.

In line 13, "EDWARD" is the penmanship of a gentleman; in line 15, "*been living*;" in line 16, "*you must*;" in line 18, "*the Garden at*;" in line 19, "*was staying*;" in line 20 "*knew me*;" in line 21, "*see me*;" in lines 21 and 22, "*wife was with him*," and "*look*;" in line 23, "*and yet she has*;" in line 26, "*I have made*;" in line 27, "*not find him*;" in line 29, "*I have seen him, and had*;" in line 30, "*with him*;"—all these, and others which the reader can easily discover himself, indicate the hand of a gentleman by education; and never could have been accomplished by a person brought up in Wapping as ORTON is known to have been, under the worst and lowest auspices; and with that particular style of penmanship which is known to belong to all time, to such as are taught in common schools. But no one who has thoroughly examined this subject now believes that any genuine writing of ORTON exists, or perhaps ever existed.

With reference to the mis-spellings, we insert the following:—

TRANSCRIPT OF LETTER WRITTEN BY ROGER CHARLES TICHBORNE IN JULY, 1845, ON HIS ARRIVAL AT STONYHURST COLLEGE.

[Put in Evidence, July 6th, 1871. See page 1805 of Shorthand-Writer's Notes.]

The errors are in italics.

No. of Line in Original.

1. Ma chere Maman,—
2. Je suis entré au collège
3. *Staune haust* hier premier *Juillete*.

No. of Line in Original.

4. Nous sommes *arriver* a midi et demi de
5. *Prestone* quand nous sommes *arrivé* nous avons
6. été voir le supérieur qui est *une* homme très
7. aimable et qui nous a très bien *recu* il nous
8. a montré *l'etablisement* avec beaucoup de
9. complaisance L'*Etablisement* est *magniffique*
10. le *pave* est très *etandu* et une chose qui est
11. *tres* belle *s'est l'avenu* par *l'aqu'elle* on
12. arrive au college qui a pres de deux milles
13. de *longues* et qui est très large, l'aspect
14. de la maison est *magniffique* il y a une
15. très belle Église *autre* plusieurs chapelles.
16. Je serai très bien ou je suis je serai dans
17. la *clase* de *philosophe* j'ai une chambre,
18. je *travairai* dans ma chambre et je suivrai
19. les cours qu'on *suis* dans le collège, je serai
20. sous la direction du père *waitersone* que vous
21. avez connu autrefois et qui sera mon
22. *superieur*.
23. Je me plairai très bien ou je suis et ma
24. santé loin d'en etre altéré s'y fortifira
25. beaucoup, je prendrai beaucoup de force et
26. de santé. Adieu chère Maman je *vou*
27. *embrase* de *tous* mon cœur. Et soyez toujours
28. sure de mon *obéisance* sans bornes.
29. Votre très affectioné fils,
30. ROGER C. TICHBORNE.
31. Je vous prie *chere* Maman de ne pas vous *inquiété*
32. du *partie* que papa *à pri parce* ma santé
33. ne s'en trouvera que mieux.
34. Madame TICHBORNE.

MISTAKES IN THE FOREGOING LETTER.

3rd line. "Staune haust" should be Stonyhurst.
"Juillete" should be Juillet.
4th line. "arriver" should be arrivés.
5th line. "Prestone" should be Preston.
"arrivé" should be arrivés.
6th line. "une" should be un.
7th line. "recu" should be reçu, with a cedilla under the c.
8th line. "etablisement" should be etablissement.
9th line. "Etablisement" should be Etablissement.
"maguiffique" should be magnifique.
10th line. "pave" should be pavé, with an accent on the e.
"étandu" should be étendu.
11th line. "tres" should be très, with an accent on the e.
"s'est" should be c'est.
"avenu" should be avenue.
"l'aqu'elle" should be written laquelle, without division or apostrophe.
13th line. "longues" should be longueur.
14th line. "magniffique" should be magnifique.
15th line. "autre" should be outre.
17th line. "clase" should be classe.
"philosophe" should be philosophie.
18th line. "travairai" should be travaillerai.
19th line. "suis" should be suit.
20th line. "waitersone" should be Waterton.
22nd line. "superieur" should have an accent—supérieur.
26th line. "vou" should be vous.
27th line. "embrase" should be embrasse.
"tous" should be tout.
28th line. "obéisance" should be obéissance.
31st line. "chere" requires the accent—chère.
"inquiété" should be inquieter.
32nd line. "partie" should be parti.
"à" should be a, simply, without accent.
"pri" should be pris.
"parce" should be parceque.

Thirty-three mistakes.

Probably the reader will not require any better proof that ROGER TICHBORNE, though brought up in Paris till his seventeenth year, never knew French, and was famous for bad spelling; and will regard but lightly the jokes of the summary writers in the penny papers upon this subject, of which they have always made so much.

Upon this subject of the handwriting we insert here a letter from Mr. GURNELL, which appeared in the ENGLISHMAN for January 30th, 1875, being Number 43:—

THE HANDWRITING OF THE CLAIMANT DOES NOT PROVE HIM TO BE ARTHUR ORTON.

TO THE EDITOR OF THE "ENGLISHMAN."

SIR,—The great point upon which the Prosecution relied for the conviction of the Claimant was the theory that the mental emanations of a man, *i.e.*, his letters and sayings, give a truer portrait of his identity than his physical appearance does. Their strongest argument—the very keystone which, if displaced, would tumble their edifice upon their own heads—is this:—"There is not," say they, "a much surer test of a man's identity than that of his writing. We don't mean the mere formation of the letters of the alphabet, but of his general style and mode of expressing his ideas, and also his grammatical idioms. When, however, the original compositions are had and compared with each other, there will be, of course, certain peculiarities in the writings themselves to be seen, such as particular marks and forms of letters, and the method of correcting omissions and mistakes. There were before the Court three series of letters—namely, the genuine letters of TICHBORNE, those of the Claimant, and those of ORTON to Miss LODER. In the first series are found many words misspelt: more in the second series: and some in the third series, which consisted of a much smaller number of letters. In the first and second series there were *only a few words misspelt in common between them*, all the rest being *differently* misspelt." Such is virtually the citadel of strength of all who defend the course taken by the Prosecution, and is by them deemed impregnable. This was the very heart and centre of all Chief Justice COCKBURN's summing-up.

In a former letter I asked: If the letters and sayings of a man invariably give a true and unmistakable photograph of his identity, how is it that no one would be able to recognize the parentage of MARLBOROUGH's utterances in his dotage, conjointly with that of his meridian intellect? Who would know, by any power of their own perception merely, the drivellings of SWIFT to be embers of the same genius which could once scathe and scorch like the flame of a furnace? Who could have imagined that the gorgeousness of BURKE's language would be reserved for his old age, and the matter-of-fact for his youth—thus reversing the usual order of the human mind? Nor is it senility merely which produces this astonishing difference in the human mind. Who would recognize in the youthful works of Miss BURNEY, so easy and artless, the same talents that penned the stilted productions of her maturer years?—changed by commingling with fashionable society. We have plenty of the correspondence remaining of the Reverend Mr. HACKMAN, who was executed in the last century for the murder of Miss REAY; and most interesting and striking productions they are, so much so that when once read they can scarcely ever be forgotten. Yet if he were alive now who would dare to swear to his identity merely from his epistles? And if the outcomings of the mind of a man always give an unmistakable photograph of his identity, then the authorship of JUNIUS would have been settled long ago, and upon a much more undisputed basis than Sir A. COCKBURN has endeavoured to settle the TICHBORNE Trial. But so far from either JUNIUS's composition or handwriting affording any clue to his identity, no less than ten persons, at least, have been suspected as the authors of those letters, and the question is not settled even now. Mr. POTTER, Lady CHATHAM, Mr. HENRY SEYMOUR (brother to the Duke of SOMERSET), Colonel BROMWELL, CLAUDIUS AMIENS, Lord CARYSFORT, DE LOLME, Mr. BOYD, General LEE, and Lord GEORGE SACKVILLE,—all of these have had learned debaters seriously maintaining each one to be the real and veritable JUNIUS. By the simple fact of handwriting and composition all the talent of the whole world has never been able to decide who JUNIUS was. A masterly poem was published many years ago, entitled the "Devil's Walk," but so far from the composition or style proving the authorship, it is not known to this day whether SOUTHEY, COLERIDGE, or Professor PORSON wrote it: and, finally, it is not a decade since that a poem was found in the British Museum and supposed to be both the composition and handwriting of MILTON;—all the newspapers were teeming with discussions on the subject from connoisseurs and critics, and yet the matter still remains in the utmost doubt. It is, then, to say the least, rather a dangerous precedent to send a man into penal servitude by so uncertain and deceptive a test as the mere question of his chirography and his style, as though these could prove his identity with the same certainty that a mathematical problem can be demonstrated. Such a criterion is, as I have shown—beyond all dispute, from numerous examples—vague, unreliable, and frequently utterly false, even under the best circumstances, and where no inducements of any kind come in the way as temptations to dishonesty; but what shall we say when in all respects the reverse of this is the case? Can we then rely upon the test of composition and style being an infallible criterion of personal identity?

In the first place, it is all very well for the supporters of the Prosecution to say that there were three series of letters from which to draw sure conclusions by comparing them, and that the work was intrusted into the hands of a clever expert, who would not be at all likely to make a mistake in the matter. I do not impugn the honour, the veracity, or the skill of Mr. CHABOT in the slightest degree, but what I do impugn is that unfairness in the Trial which granted the assistance of an expert to the Prosecution, and denied it to the Claimant, because he was too poor to pay for it. This was no less than marshalling great professional acuteness and experience together on purpose to crush a defenceless man without giving him a chance of escape. It was an act no less cowardly than if a celebrated Pugilist were to enter the ring on purpose to fight a citizen who never learnt the art of self-defence; no less cowardly than if a soldier were to draw his sword and cut down an unarmed civilian. Now, the supporters of the Prosecution assume that all those three series of letters were *bonâ fide*; but I am going to produce instances in which the opposite was the case. We know that the Attorney-General substituted the word "*swindled*" in the reading of one of the Claimant's letters, which in the sense it was used, if it had been there, would have proved the Claimant a rogue; and Sir JOHN COLERIDGE badgered and browbeat him over this word, which, when read by Master COCKBURN in the Court of Queen's Bench, was simply "*overhauled*," which the most honest person might have justly used. We know that the Attorney-General produced the PITTENDREIGH forgeries in Court as evidence against the Claimant. We know that the Claimant was asked to recognize a view of Cahir Barracks so misleading that Major CAMPBELL himself, a brother officer, had said of it, "I should never have known it." We know that the Claimant was shown a picture of Knoyle, a place he used to visit, and he did not recognize it, and for this very good reason, that the Prosecution preferred to take a side view, and one which he might never have noticed. "Yes," added the Lord Chief Justice, "And that had all the more effect in confusing him, because, as I understand it, *the part of the building shown had been added since he saw it*." We know that a witness of the name of DAVIES, who was cross-examined by Mr. HAWKINS in the Court of Queen's Bench, had a letter handed to him, *the postscript to which he indignantly repudiated, declaring that a child could see it was not his handwriting.*

Are the friends of the Prosecution going gravely to ask us to believe that the series of letters scrutinised by M. CHABOT were all genuine, and that no one connected with the Prosecution had tampered with them? As far as M. CHABOT himself is concerned, I believe there is nothing on his part but what is proper, just, and right; but, unfortunately, there was a host connected with them besides the gentleman who was employed as expert. The friends of the Prosecution will first have to explain how garbled correspondence, forged documents, and false photographs were put forward in the two Courts of Common Pleas and of Queen's Bench, and how it was that no persons who had perpetrated those crimes were made to answer for their guilt, or were even so much as rebuked by either of the Chief Justices or their assistant Judges. The supporters of the Prosecution will also have to show me, before they advance the question of the series of letters in Court being *bonâ fide*, that the Claimant had the same opportunity for testing them as the other side had; but what will they say when I remind them that the whole of the funds of the Treasury could be drawn upon by the Prosecution, but that the accused man was absolutely a pauper, depending upon the charity of his friends for support; that those who spoke in his favour were either fined or imprisoned, and some of them had to endure both punishments; and that the only means by which he could obtain money for his defence were forbidden him; and that he was held down by the iron hand of the Judges from even so much as daring to attend a public meeting of his own friends in his own behalf? Nor is this all by a long way. He had three Judges, five Counsel, and a celebrated Expert, together with a hostile Press, and adverse Jurymen, all sitting as critics upon him, and who made no allowance for a single inadvertency that might naturally fall to his lot in common with all human beings. If there were—as I have already proved—some garbled documents, some false photographs, some forged letters advanced against him by learned Counsel in behalf of his enemies in the two Courts, is it unreasonable to suppose, I ask, if he had had the advantage of an expert on *his* side, that more of those documents against him would have been found surreptitious or tampered with? I believe that half of them at least were either forged or garbled by the Prosecution. If some should say, "Oh! that notion is most extravagant and wild," I shall ask them to account for the villanies I have stated; and if they fail to do this, every impartial person will say that the wildness and extravagance are on their side, and not on mine.

It has been said by some that the uniform mode of correcting omissions in the TICHBORNE series of letters were by putting a mark *over* the space where the word was left out, and supplying the omission in the marginal space of the letter with a similar mark and the omitted word; but, say they, in the Claimant series, the way to supply the omission was by writing the word *under* the omitted space, and this was the uniform practice. I have an answer to give to this by producing an authentic statement, to which I think our friends on the side of the Prosecution will find it hard to return a rejoinder. The *Daily Telegraph*, May 20th, 1873, speaking of the PITTENDREIGH forgeries, says: "When shown one of these letters in the Common Pleas, the Claimant was himself deceived, and admitted that the signature was his! but when the contents were read over—containing an offer of £200 to Mrs. PITTENDREIGH for certain information, he at once repudiated it, for the plain reason that at the time it professed to be written, he possessed no such means as to make an offer of the kind. Mr. HAWKINS now admitted that this letter was undoubtedly fabricated. It was CURIOUS that *in another epistle of Mrs.* PITTENDREIGH's, *the Jury had pointed out certain lawyer-like abbreviations, on which the Lord Chief Justice suggested that it had been* COPIED FROM A LAWYER'S BRIEF, *and both bench and jury appeared to agree that it disclosed a* TRAP *which the defendant on a former occasion declared had been too successfully laid for him*." Before the friends of the Prosecution press upon us the *peculiar* way of TICHBORNE and ORTON supplying omissions, and making corrections in their letters, they will have to prove to us beyond dispute that it is improbable that any more of these *lawyer-like abbreviations* occurred in any other of the letters brought by the Prosecution against the Claimant, except in the PITTENDREIGH forgeries. For my part, I believe these "lawyer-like abbreviations" were a part of the dodge adopted by the Prosecution throughout all the series of letters, whenever it suited their purpose to garble them in that manner. No one has any right to question this reasonable suspicion until he can satisfactorily answer me respecting the aforenamed statement from the *Daily Telegraph*. This observation equally applies to the peculiarity which, some say, is in a letter of the Claimant to Mrs. JURY, in which he is alleged to have signed the name of "STEPHENS," and put a mark after the signature described as two capital C's back to back—divided with dots between them. In the TICHBORNE series it is alleged that no such mark occurs, but that a similar mark does occur in some of the LODER series. I am still thinking of the "lawyer-like abbreviations" introduced into other letters against the Claimant. Will our friends for the Prosecution kindly explain them to me before they presume to talk about handwriting being any test in the case of the Claimant's identity?

Though the Claimant during the Trial had no expert, he had Dr. KENEALY to act as an expert for him. Now, the Doctor is well known as being one of the most accomplished scholars and linguists in Europe. No man in the world, whether M. CHABOT or anybody else, is a greater connoisseur of handwriting; no one better able to point out all those nicetics and peculiar features by which it may be characterized. For *three* whole days did the learned barrister undertake this task in the Court of Queen's Bench. I myself was there an entire day while he was pointing out with the greatest minuteness every remarkable up and down stroke, every conspicuous straight and curved line, every singularly united and disunited hook, every peculiar dot to the *i*'s, crossing of the *t*'s, and loop to the *f*'s. What mention did the Lord Chief Justice, in his summing-up, make of all this arduous and skilful three days' work by Dr. KENEALY on behalf of his client? None at all; and Why? Now, mark the subterfuge—a subterfuge which showed Sir A. COCKBURN's total inability to deal with the case according to his own inclinations, except by sophisms. The reason no notice was taken of what the Doctor had said was because he was not a mere official expert, but a Counsel, and therefore his proofs, amounting to demonstration, were not evidence—though the Judges themselves had illegally given evidence from the Bench whenever it suited their purpose to do so, knowing that they were sheltered from any examination or cross-examination. No one can put more than one meaning on all this, namely, that the Prosecution could get a conviction when they wanted, because they had money, and that the Claimant could not get justice because he had no money—a very fine state of things in a Christian country, certainly!

The blunders of M. CHABOT:—He said that TICHBORNE always joined to his "*c*" the letter that follows it. Dr. KENEALY, in photograph 85, in the word "college" pointed out that he did not join on the vowel; and in the signature "CHARLES" the "*h*" was not joined to the "*c*." A further peculiarity pointed out by CHABOT was that ROGER made his insertions *above* the line, and he considered that a remarkable thing. "Really," said Dr. KENEALY, "he did not seem to have examined the matter so carefully as he might have done, for I find here, in line 26, an insertion *below* the lines. Again, in photograph 22, you will see there is another insertion *below* the line, in the words 'West Indies.' Here we have CHABOT again very much in fault. In one of ROGER's French letters the insertion, instead of being made *above* the line, is at the *side* of the letter, and in the draft instruction which he gave to Mr. SLAUGHTER you will see that the word 'property' is below the line."

These are a few, and but a very few instances, indeed, in which the learned Doctor proved M. CHABOT's theory to be mere moonshine. If anyone doubt this, I bid him turn to any of the Daily Papers for August 20th, 21st, 22nd, 1873, and they will there find what I say to be beyond all contradiction. I challenge any one, no matter who he may be, to disprove a single statement I have made. The secret of the whole matter was simply this, that Dr. KENEALY was not an expert, and therefore Judges and Jury brought the Claimant in as ARTHUR ORTON, which it would have been impossible for them to do if the Doctor had been allowed to give evidence. He stated his case clearly and unanswerably enough; but the law allowed them to be conveniently deaf to all that; and having eyes they would not see, and possessing ears they were determined to be deaf, and by that process alone was it possible for any Judges or Jury on the face of the earth to be able to bring the Claimant in by his handwriting as ARTHUR ORTON.
—I remain, Sir, yours faithfully, R. M. GURNELL.
108, Turner's-road, Burdett-road, Mile End, E.: Jan. 22, 1875.

Chief Justice COCKBURN, in the pretended version of his Summing-up, which he has recently published, has a part devoted to a comparison of Sir ROGER's and ORTON's handwriting. These he has borrowed from a publication that was issued by the Treasury. *No man in England ought to know better than he that the whole of the letters produced at the Trial, which purported to be written by* ORTON, *were forgeries.* The Agents of the Family, having TICHBORNE's letters in their possession, *forged* letters in imitation of them, which they put forth as being in ORTON's writing. The PITTENDREIGH plotters were quite equal to this.

Our readers cannot have failed to notice the remarkable phrase used by Mr. JOHN GRAY, in his letter to Mr WHALLEY, dated 4th July, 1872, and which is as follows:—"*As to the sailor saved with the Claimant from the wreck of the 'Bella,' when he returns to England, I will undertake to find one of the crew of the 'Osprey' to eat him.*" From so cautious a man as Mr. GRAY, this is remarkable: it shows how prejudiced *his* mind had become. We think it expedient therefore to preserve in these pages the evidence upon that question which was given in the Common Pleas. When it is compared with the facts subsequently proved at the Trial at Bar, and is contrasted with the wicked and persistent testimony by which the Prosecutors sought to negative the appearance of an "Osprey" at Melbourne in 1854, the whole constitutes such a body of proof as cannot be resisted, without letting conviction enter the mind. It will be remembered that TICHBORNE, in the Common Pleas, swore that he pledged or sold his ring when he arrived at Melbourne, being then wholly destitute. This very ring is now in the possession of a gentleman at Melbourne; but the Defendant had no money to pay his passage to and from Australia to this country, so as to have the ring produced by the buyer of it; and without his personal attendance, the ring was not legally evidence. Its mere production in Court here would not suffice: its history should have been explained by both the seller and its present owner. And thus TICHBORNE always failed, for want of funds.

TICHBORNE IN AUSTRALIA.—The *Melbourne Herald* of the 14th February, 1872, contains the following:—"In one of the Government offices, Melbourne, is a clerk, who has in his possession a ring, bearing the TICHBORNE coat of arms, and on the inside the name of ROGER TICHBORNE's mother engraved. This ring was purchased for a trifle from a pawnbroker, who disposed of it at a low figure on account of a difficulty being experienced in selling it, owing to the crest. This ring was seen by our informant in the possession of the individual referred to.

OSPREY EVIDENCE IN THE COMMON PLEAS.

WILBRAHAM FREDERICK EVELYN LIARDET, examined by Mr. Serjeant BALLANTINE: I now reside in the Walham-green, Fulham. From 1839 to 1856 I lived at Sandridge, Hobson's Bay, and there carried on the business of a *ship-mail contractor with my sons.* It was our *duty to take the mails to and from vessels in the harbour.* I was the founder of Sandridge, and built the first jetty there. I recollect a number of vessels arriving in the harbour during the gold-field mania.

Have you any recollection of a particular vessel arriving in the harbour in 1854?—There was a great *furore* at the time, and a great number of vessels arrived from all parts of the world.

Do you recollect an American vessel?—I remembered the "Osprey" from the fact that she was a large three-masted schooner with peculiar rigging.

Did you recollect exactly at what time she arrrived?—No; there were two vessels of that name in the harbour nearly at the same time—one a sloop and the other a schooner, both being American vessels.

Did you go on board the "Osprey" at all?—Yes; it was my duty or my son's to board every vessel immediately on its arrival, but sometimes the duty was performed by our men. As there were no mails, I remained but a few minutes.

Were there any persons on board except the crew?—I did not observe any, but I was told that there were some wrecked men on board.

The Chief Justice: Then you saw nobody except the crew?—Nobody but what I imagined were the crew.

Cross-examined by the Attorney-General: When did you come back to this country?—Last February.

Have you come back to stay in England?—Yes; for a time, at any rate.

When did you first communicate this matter about the "Osprey"?—A gentleman called upon me about a fortnight ago.

Who was he?—I do not know him exactly. He was no acquaintance of mine.

What was his name?—He mentioned it to me, but really I have forgotten it. He did not leave his card.

Did he come to you unsolicited?—Yes. I was well known in the colonies, and he thought, I suppose, that I could give him some information.

Did he ask you if you recollected the "Osprey?"—Yes.

And did he ask you if it was an American vessel?—No. I told him it was an American.

Did he inquire the year when she came?—Yes.

Did you ever, from the time you saw the vessel in 1854 until the time the gentleman called upon you, do any act to cause you to remember the vessel?—No. I was a sportsman, and so I remember the name.

Was the "Osprey" a common name in Hobson's Bay for ships?—I have known three of that name. There is a small sea-going schooner now trading, I believe, between Melbourne and New Zealand. The ship I boarded I have never seen since.

Did you make any note or memorandum of the "Osprey"?—None particularly.

And you had no book to refer to?—No; but that I remember.

And you remember the name of the vessel and the date from having shot birds of that name in the harbour? Have you tested your memory as to the ship?—Yes, I recollect her perfectly well.

Do you remember her tonnage?—I believe she was of a *size between* 400 *and* 500 *tons.* I was impressed with her size for a schooner.

Have you busied yourself, like other people, with reading the account of the TICHBORNE Trial?—Yes; I have frequently read the reports, and I think there is scarcely any person who has not.

Then you saw an account of the "Osprey" in the TICHBORNE papers?—Yes; that fixed it in my memory the more.

Do you recollect the dates when both of the vessels, each named the "Osprey," entered the harbour?—No; but I think it must have been somewhere about the same time.

Were they both American vessels?—Yes, decidedly.

Was there an American Consul in Melbourne?—Yes.

Did you have dealings with him?—Yes; occasionally I waited upon him.

Were you told where the vessels came from?—Yes, from some of the South American ports.

How do you recollect the time?—From the *furore* there was, and the name of the bird.

Have you any doubt as to the name of the "Osprey"?—No; I remember the name of the "Osprey" perfectly well.

How much rent do you pay for your home at Walham?—£40 a-year.

By the Foreman of the Jury: How was the "Osprey" manned?—She was what is called a Yankee vessel.

How many men would she have?—About a dozen, I should say.

Did they speak English?—I can't tell; but I believe so.

Did the officers speak English?—Certainly.

Were you the first to board her?—I was amongst the first. We always boarded vessels the first thing coming into port.

Did you interchange news with the captain on his arrival?—I might have done.

How long were you on board?—About five minutes.

If a wrecked crew had been on board it would have been notorious to the entire crew, would it not?—I suppose so.

Was there any institution in Melbourne for shipwrecked sailors?—One has been established since I left.

What kind of provision was there when you were at Melbourne?—Well, it is a kind, hospitable country, and the agents of vessels generally provided for contingencies of that sort. If it was a foreign vessel the sailors would go to their Consul.

Then, an American coming in with a shipwrecked crew would, as a matter of course, report it to the proper quarter?—Yes; to the Consul of his own country, I should say.

Your observations relate to the schooner, not to the large ship?—Yes; to the schooner only.

Then there was no institution in Melbourne at that time for castaway seamen?—None whatever. The newspaper reporters were generally very vigilant, and boarded vessels in order to pick up any information they possibly could.

Had there been a shipwrecked crew on board, then, it would have been reported?—I should say so.

Then, if eight men had come into harbour in the "Osprey," you think the fact would have been made notorious in the local papers?—Yes; it ought to have been so; but there was a great excitement at the time, *and such a matter might have been overlooked, certainly.*

Did you yourself hear any talk of the shipwrecked crew?—Well, we did not go into those matters much, because it was our duty to get the mails and leave as quickly as possible. We were under a heavy penalty if there was any delay.

Can you say whether the crew were white or black men?—I cannot say. The crews of American vessels, generally speaking, are of mixed men.

There was a LLOYD's agent, I suppose?—Yes.

And was it not part of his duty to report shipping intelligence?—Yes.

Would it not be your duty, as a Government officer, to make some mention of such a circumstance?—Well, I had to look after the mails only, but I frequently gave information to the Press. The arrival of a shipwrecked crew was a sort of thing to be taken notice of, but in *the excitement that prevailed just at that time it might have been overlooked.* Pressure of business might have prevented the reporters from making any inquiries.

JOHN EVELYN LIARDET, examined by Mr. Serjeant BALLANTINE: I am the son of the last witness, and reside at No. 1, Munster-road, Fulham. I resided in the colony of Victoria in 1854, and at that time assisted my father.

Have you any recollection of the vessel of which your father speaks?—Yes; the very day that I arrived in Melbourne the vessel was pointed out to me. I remember the circumstance well, because Sir CHARLES FITZROY was giving up the Government of New South Wales, and was sailing out of the harbour of Port Jackson. I was going into Melbourne at the same time. I know from that that it was in 1854. I arrived at night, and saw the vessel the next morning. She was pointed out to me *by my brother's boat's crew as having saved the lives of a shipwrecked crew*, and I, seeing that she was a finely-built vessel, told the men to pull round her.

What was your brother?—He was an emigration officer and gold commissioner in New Zealand.

Did you board the vessel?—Yes, but I can't say who I saw there. I went on board for curiosity's sake. There were two persons on board, but I can't say whether they were officers or crew. I spoke to one of the men. She was a large three-masted schooner of *between 400 and 500 tons*, I dare say. She was a remarkably large vessel for her peculiar rig, and a very handsome one too.

Then there was a statement made to you by one of the persons on board?—Yes.

Mr. Serjeant BALLANTINE: *Which we cannot have.*

Cross-examined by the Attorney-General: You are living, you say, at Fulham?—In the Munster-road.

Are you residing there permanently?—Yes, for the present.

What particular occupation have you?—I am assisting my father. He is in this country on important business—making large claims against the Government. (Laughter.)

And you are assisting him?—Yes, in matters connected with the Deptford Dockyard.

Oh, I see, the Deptford Dockyard. What were you at Sydney?—I was Clerk in Petty Sessions, a Commissioner of Crown Lands, a Commissioner of the Supreme Court, and Clerk of the Peace.

Then you must have been a lawyer?—What is your age?—Very nearly forty.

What is it that has called your attention to the "Osprey?"—I have frequently spoken of her amongst my family and friends, and as recently as yesterday.

When did you first begin to speak about it in this country?—That is a difficult thing to say. I am constantly talking about it.

Had you time enough to read the TICHBORNE Trial?—No, I have not read it.

Then you are much to be envied. (Laughter.)

Did you see anything in the papers about the "Osprey"?—No; but I spoke about it to a kinsman about three months ago.

Who first applied to you about it?—A gentleman from Messrs. BAXTER, ROSE, and NORTON's came to me about a month ago, and I referred him to my father.

Had you thought of the "Osprey" between 1854 and the time you say you spoke of it to your kinsman?—Yes, I frequently spoke of it to their honours the Judges.

To their honours the Judges?—Yes; I frequently spoke of it to the Chief Commissioner in Sydney.

Had you heard of the TICHBORNE Trial then?—Yes; it was the common topic of conversation in Sydney, and I used to joke with my friend Mr. FORBES, the Commissioner, about it.

Was there anything to draw your attention to any particular vessel?—Yes; there had been a conversation as to the vessel the Claimant came in, and, by putting different things together, I remembered the "Osprey," and thought it was the one in which he arrived.

Do you know Messrs. SEDGEFIELD and ALLPORT, of Sydney?—I only know Mr. ALLPORT by name.

You saw no more than this one ship then?—Not at that time. I have seen the little trader spoken of which runs between Melbourne and New Zealand, but it is a totally different ship to the "Osprey."

How long were you on board?—Only a few minutes, I believe.

Were the persons on board officers or crew?—I think they were part of the crew.

You did not see the captain?—No, I am sure of that.

Re-examined by Mr. Serjeant BALLANTINE: Did your hear of the shipwrecked crew before you went on board?—Yes; my brother's boatman pointed out the *vessel as having saved a portion of the crew.*

Have you mentioned the name of the "Osprey" yourself, or has anyone told you about it?—It was the frequent topic of conversation when coming home from Australia, and I told the captain that I perfectly recollected the vessel coming into Hobson's Bay.

NINIAN TERTIUS LOCKHART, examined by Mr. Serjeant BALLANTINE: I am a flax-spinner, living at Kirkcaldy. I went to Melbourne in 1853, and entered the firm of LUMSDEN and LOCKHART as shipowners. It was our duty also to board all vessels on their arrival. I lived at Williamstown, and used to come up every day.

Do you recollect going to Melbourne in the "Comet" steamer?—Yes, with Captain CARDER, who is dead.

Do you remember the year when you made that trip?—Yes, in May, June, or July, 1854. It was some months previous to October, and when it was very hot indeed.

Did Captain CARDER make any communication to you?—Yes.

Did he point out any persons on board his vessel?—Yes.

And was the communication in reference to those persons?—Yes.

Mr. Serjeant BALLANTINE: I propose to ask the witness what the communication was.

The Attorney-General: I object, my lord, on the ground that the captain is not present, and that it was made behind the back of the Defendant.

Mr. Serjeant BALLANTINE: But it is explanatory of an act done. I cannot put it on any higher ground.

The Chief Justice: What was the act done? The question is certainly not admissible if it is put for the purpose of pointing out the act of a particular person.

Mr. Serjeant BALLANTINE (to witness): At all events, he pointed them out to you, and made an observation?—Yes.

Did you see those persons?—Yes.

How many men were there?—Ten or twelve, I should say.

What did they appear like?—Sailors.

Could you tell whether they were part of the crew?—They were passengers, the same as myself, from Williamstown to Melbourne, a distance of about ten miles.

Were they gentlemen or common sailors, or what did they appear to be?—They were like sailors coming off a ship.

What language did they speak?—Some of them spoke English. There were foreigners amongst them. I talked to them a little time.

Did you learn from them where they came from?

The Attorney-General objected to the question, and it was not allowed.

Mr. Serjeant BALLANTINE: Had they any sea boxes or chests with them?—Not that I saw.

How were they dressed?—As sailors usually are.

Were their clothes in good preservation?—I can't say.

How long were you in their company?—About an hour and a half or two hours.

Did you ever see any of them again?—No.

Was there any person with them whom you noticed in particular?—Yes, a ship captain.

Did you know him personally?—I did not.

Had you any conversation with him?—I conversed with him mostly.

What kind of countryman was he?—I thought he was a Welshman.

Was any vessel pointed out to you?—Yes, the captain pointed to one lying a long way out. She was a three-masted vessel.

Did you hear the name of any vessel mentioned at the time?—Yes.

What sort of a vessel was she?—A black painted ship with an elliptic stern.

Were there many vessels arriving at that time?—Yes; and the crews deserted generally as soon as they got in.

How long did you reside in Melbourne?—From 1853 to the middle of 1855, I think.

Did you then go to New Zealand?—Yes.

And then you came over to this country?—Yes, in September, 1870.

When was your attention first called to the TICHBORNE Case?—About four years ago in New Zealand. I saw there a large placard and said that if I was in England I was sure I could tell them something about it.

What became of the "Comet"?—She was lost subsequently. She went down with all hands in 1864.

What practice was adopted as to reporting crews that were picked up?—The captains were supposed to report them.

Do you know anything of the practice at the time?—No. It was a captain's duty, but he was not bound to report it.

Cross-examined by Mr. HAWKINS: There was an emigration office in 1854?—Yes.

Where they keep lists?—Yes.

According to your experience, then, it was the duty and practice of the captain to report shipwrecked crews?—Yes.

Was it during the summer time or not that you were on board the "Comet"?—I know it was previously to October, because I went up the country then. I have no documents to refresh my memory, but my impression is that it might have been during June, July, or even August.

Do you call October summer?—No, it is spring.

What made you say it was summer time?—I was speaking of October. I know it was very hot weather. The seasons in that country are nearly the reverse of our own.

Could it not have been in September?—No; but I have no documents to refer to. It must have been earlier than that time.

Tell me one reason that makes you think it must have been earlier than September?—Well, the bay was not at all crowded in that month. I believed it was in June, July, or August, and I am on my oath. My impression always has been that it was May, June, or July. I can give you the names of several vessels that were in the bay at that time, but not in September.

The Chief Justice: Can you swear positively it was not in September?—Well, I am not going to swear it.

Mr. HAWKINS: Was it in October?—No, I should say not.

Then give me a reason why you say so.—It was not in October.

Give me a reason if you can.—Because I know it was months before that.

You say there were ten or twelve persons on board the "Comet" dressed like sailors?—Yes, they appeared to be ordinary sailors, but very hard-up.

Was the captain there in addition to the men?—THE CAPTAIN WAS THE MAN WHO PICKED THEM UP.

But there was an extra captain with them?—Yes, my impression is that there were ten or twelve men altogether.

Where did they land?—I can't tell. I jumped ashore as soon as the boat touched, and never saw any of them afterwards.

Re-examined by Serjeant BALLANTINE: Have you any interest in this Case, either on the one side or the other?—No, none whatever.

Have you any doubt whether it was before September that you saw this crew?—None. I have always thought so.

Was the captain part of the crew?—He came up in the same vessel with the men. I knew nothing except what he told me.

JOHN STEER, ship's carpenter, examined by Mr. HARDINGE GIFFARD: Did you go in 1853 from Greenock to Melbourne?—Yes, and reached the Heads in April, 1854. I remained there about a fortnight, then sailed to Launceston, and on the 10th June returned to Melbourne, where I remained till August.

Was your attention called to a vessel?—Yes.

What sort of a vessel was it?—The "Bella."

Just explain what you mean.—I met a shipmate of mine, and he said "There's the 'Bella's' crew picked up."

Did you see the vessel?—No.

Nor any other vessel?—No, sir. (Laughter.)

Did you afterwards have your attention called to an American vessel?—No; but the same party told me that an American vessel had brought the crew in.

Did you know who the shipmate was?—Yes.

What was his name?—HEWEN.

Did you ever see the American vessel?—No, never.

The Attorney-General: Then good day to you, sir. (Laughter.)

Mr. Serjeant BALLANTINE: I have another witness in England bearing upon this portion of the case, and others whom we expect; but we do not intend going into this subject further at present, and shall recall a witness who has been partially examined, in order that he may speak to different matters altogether.

FRANCIS LONGMAN, examined by Mr. GIFFARD: I live on my own property in Northamptonshire. In the year 1853 I was in New York, and sailed from there to Melbourne. In 1854 I went from Melbourne to Sandridge. My journey had reference to a loan of money to a person named TAYLOR on mortgage. Whilst on the journey I met a sailor who had come with me in the same vessel from New York. He was in company with two other sailors whom I had not seen before. The other sailors were Americans. We all went to Sandbridge pier, took a boat, and went on board the "Gipsy," which was lying off Williamstown.

Did you see a vessel called the "Osprey"?—Yes.

What sort of vessel was she?—A three-masted schooner.

Did you go on board the "Osprey"?—I did.

Was it in consequence of something which the two sailors had said to you?—It was.

After you had been on board did you take the two sailors anywhere?—Yes; I took them home.

Did you supply them with anything?—Yes, they stopped with me two or three days until they got a ship.

Did you give them anything besides board and lodging?—Yes; clothes.

Do you know what became of them ultimately?—They went off to Callao.

Are you able to fix the date of your visit to Sandridge?—I am.

By what means?—I went to meet my man, to whom I was about to lend some money on mortgage. I gave him a cheque, and I can prove it by my cheque-book. I was at Sandridge about ten days before I paid the money. It was on the 3rd of August that I met the sailors.

Just look at your pass-book and refresh your memory.—(Witnessed referred to his book.)

Cross-examined by Mr. HAWKINS: You have not looked at the book before?—I had not seen it for twelve years till the day before yesterday.

When first did you give your account to anybody?—A week last Friday or Saturday.

Were you then in Northamptonshire?—Yes.

Where in Northamptonshire?—Yardley Hastings.

What is your property there?—Leasehold cottages.

What is the amount of rental?—About £100 a year.

Where is your property?—Part of it is in Yardley Hastings and part of it in Lavendon, Buckingham. I have twenty in the former and four in the latter place.

Do you live in one of these cottages?—No, in a house adjoining them.

How long have you been there?—Fourteen years. I was bred and born in the parish.

To whom did you first communicate your story?—To BAXTER, ROSE, and NORTON.

Did you write to them?—Yes.

Had you read a good deal of the great TICHBORNE Trial?—I had read a portion of it. I did not read the Claimant's evidence, but I read part of LIARDET's about his living at Melbourne, and so forth. Certainly I could have read the whole if I had thought proper.

Did you know LIARDET in Australia?—Not to my knowledge.

What portion of his evidence attracted your attention most?—That about his going on board the "Opera."

On what?—I mean the "Osprey."

The Chief Justice: Did you say "Opera," or "Osprey"?—I said the "Osprey."

What part of LIARDET's evidence did you read?—About his being postmaster, and his living at Melbourne a good number of years—about his boarding the vessel as postmaster.

Did what you read interest you?—Yes.

And you read about his boarding the "Osprey"?—Yes; I don't recollect any more.

That he boarded the "Osprey"—is that all you read?—Yes; I don't remember any more.

Did you read that part of the evidence which would have given you a notion when the date was?—No; I did not.

That you swear?—I could not say. I did not read that he gave any date at all.

Did you read anything about what he did?—No.

Or what he saw when on board the "Osprey"?—I read that he did not see any of the crew.

In what paper did you read it?—In the *Daily News*, I think.

Did you read any more?—Not that I can remember.

Did you read any more than what you have told us?—No.

You say you could have read the whole if you thought proper?—Yes.

But you were not interested enough to read on?—I was not.

Did you keep the *Daily News*?—No, I did not. I had an opportunity of looking at it occasionally.

When was it you read this?—Some time during the week before last.

Was it after LIARDET had given his evidence here?—No, I don't think it was. It was on the Friday or Saturday the week before last.

Was it the evidence of the elder LIARDET or his son?—The elder one.

Did you read anything of young LIARDET's evidence?—No.

Or any part of the Trial?—No.

Did you know LIARDET?—No; but I had heard of him hundreds of times.

Did you yourself communicate with anybody?—Yes, with BAXTER and NORTON.

How soon after you had read this portion of LIARDET's evidence?—The same evening.

Did anybody call upon you from BAXTER, ROSE, and NORTON's?—No: nobody came.

Did you receive a communication from them?—Yes, and I came to town yesterday.

I suppose you had not, as I understand, looked at your pass-book before you communicated with BAXTER, ROSE, and NORTON?—No.

Were you in London when you looked at the pass-book?—No, I looked at it at home.

Did you keep any journal or diary at the time you were in Melbourne?—No, only my bank-book. I have only that, as I know of.

Was there only one letter passed between you and BAXTER, ROSE, and NORTON?—No: they wrote to a solicitor in Northampton to ask me to come up.

And when did you come up?—Yesterday.

Have you since read the whole of LIARDET's evidence?—I have not.

Or any part of LOCKHART's?—No.

Do you remember the date of your voyage from New York to Melbourne?—Yes. I left New York January 1, 1853, and arrived at Melbourne on the 3rd June.

What was your occupation in 1853?—That of a brickmaker.

Master or journeyman?—I went as a journeyman first. I was a journeyman at New York.

Why did you go to Australia?—With the intention of gold digging.

Did you mix with the sailors on board?—Yes, certainly. I was a steerage passenger. I think there were nearly 200 souls on board, all told. The name of the vessel was the "Bothany."

B-o-n-t-h-a? (Laughter.)—Well, they called it the "Bothany."

Did you talk much to "the sailor" on the voyage?—I was obliged to be in his company every day, and I talked to him a good deal at times.

What was his name?—They called him New York. I have never heard a sailor's name.

Didn't they call him "Yorkey"?—No, New York.

What did you do in Melbourne?—The first six months I was employed as a journeyman brickmaker. Afterwards I traded backwards and forwards to the diggings.

You say you saw this sailor with two others—where did you meet them at first?—At Melbourne; they were standing at the docks.

What were their names?—I only knew what they were called.

What was that?—Boston and Savannah.

These two men were perfect strangers to you?—Perfect strangers.

Did you see them after then?—Yes, for two or three days.

They stayed with you at your house?—Yes, at Brunswick, two miles out of Melbourne.

When did they leave you?—On the 3rd of August.

They had been with you two or three days?—Yes.

You are sure about the 3rd of August?—Yes.

Will you swear it?—I will.

What makes you fix it as the 3rd of August?—Because I know the date from the business I went on. I know it by my bank-book and the cheque.

On the 3rd of August you say you paid the money?—I paid the money on the 2nd. I know they went away the next day.

How many days before you paid the money had you seen them? I can't say whether they were with me three or four days.

I understood you to say that the first time you saw the American sailor with New York was three or four days before the 3rd of August?—Yes.

Let me see your pass-book. (Handed to the learned Counsel.) Did you see where the two men went afterwards?—I saw them ship to Callao.

What was the name of the ship?—I don't know. It was an American vessel, but I did not see her. I merely went to the American shipping office with them.

Did you ever inquire the name of the vessel?—No. So long as they got a ship I didn't care.

Where did you part with them?—On the dock in about half-an-hour. They went on a tender to the vessel.

Did the gentleman in the shipping office mention the name of the vessel?—I did not go in.

Where was the vessel?—Lying in the harbour about eight miles off. Only small vessels came up to the docks.

You never made an inquiry as to the real name of the sailors?—No; but I knew they were Americans.

You provided them with what they required?—Yes, and gave them a box of clothes to leave with. You only know them by their nicknames?—Yes. And you never knew where their homes were?—I only know that one belongs to Boston and the other to Savannah.

And from that time to the present you have never seen them?—I have not.

Nor had any communication with them of any sort or kind?—No.

The Jury: Did they pay you for what you provided?—No; they had no money. I bought a sailor's chest by auction, and I gave them the clothes that were in it.

Mr. Hawkins: What did the chest cost?—Six or seven shillings. I did not know what was in the box. I bought four boxes.

You did not know what was in the box when you bought it?—No; they were sold locked.

Was there anything else that you gave them?—Nothing but clothes and victuals.

Did you ever hear whether they got to Callao, or evaporated elsewhere?—No; but sailors are a good sort of people.

Was the name "Osprey" painted on the vessel you boarded?—Yes, or else I should not have known of it. I never saw a vessel without a name. When I have been on board a vessel I can tell her name, if it is ten or fifteen years afterwards.

Have you been on board many vessels?—Yes; I have sailed in twenty, I should think.

Can you recollect their names?—Yes, those in which I went long voyages, I can.

I suppose, if you went in a penny steamer from London Bridge to Westminster, you would not remember the name?—No, I should say not.

Then you read the name "Osprey"?—Yes, before I went alongside of her. I was after the man TAYLOR, who was going in the "Gipsy."

You made no memorandum of this at the time?—No, not at all.

What was the amount of your loan to TAYLOR?—Three hundred pounds.

Did you make him any other loans?—Yes; I believe there was £400 afterwards.

I see there are in this book entries of a good many loans to TAYLOR?—Yes; but that was a different man, and they are of smaller amounts.

Was it in the summer or winter when you saw the two sailors? It was in the spring of that country.

I see the last entry in your book is "March 16, TAYLOR and Co."? No, there is no "Co." I lent the money on mortgage. It is the same man who had the first £300.

There is TAYLOR and something, certainly.—Well, it does look like "Co," but it refers to the same man who borrowed the £300.

Re-examined by Mr. GIFFARD: Did you expect to find TAYLOR in the "Gipsy"?—Yes.

Was there anything to call your particular attention to the "Osprey"?—*Only what the sailors told me.*

I must not ask you that. How came you to have the two sailors in your house without payment?—Because they had got nothing. The things which I gave them were no use to me. I took them out of charity.

Did you go on board the "Osprey" at once?—Yes, after I had been on the "Gipsy."

Did the sailors go on board the "Osprey"?—Yes.

Could you tell how long the "Osprey" had been in the harbour?—I could not; but I know the hatches were not open.

So she had but newly arrived?—Yes.

The Foreman of the Jury: You seem to have combined other occupations with that of brickmaking in Melbourne?—Yes: but I had no other occupation until I had done brickmaking.

Mr. GIFFARD: Were you a lodging-house keeper?—No.

And you kept the three seamen out of pure charity?—Yes.

At the shipping office was no advance paid to the men?—No; they were sent on board. If there had been any advance, they might not have gone again.

Did you get repaid for what you had provided out of the money to be advanced?—No, it was only a matter of a few shillings. I did not give them the box, but only the clothes that were in it.

Why did you do that?—Well, I had been in America, and found the people very hospitable; and, of course, I thought it was my duty to help any of them when I could.

You went on board the "Osprey" merely because of those two men?—Well, I wanted to go to the "Gipsy," and then to the "Osprey," to see if any of their mates were on board.

The "Osprey's" hatches had not been removed, you say?—No.

Then she had not discharged her cargo?—No.

WHERE HAD SHE COME FROM?—FROM SOME PORT IN SOUTH AMERICA.

Was there any other vessel called the "Osprey" in the harbour at the time?—I did not see any. I merely pulled to her in an open boat. I had been in a boat before I arrived in the colony.

Then the men were destitute?—Yes; they told me they had lost everything.

Had they no means of getting anything?—Of course, they could have shipped, as there were plenty of ships wanting sailors at that time.

Were your cheques paid the same day they were drawn?—I can't say, but I think the £300 was paid in the next day.

Then that marked the period in your mind when you saw the sailors?—Yes; TAYLOR was going to Hobart Town in the "Gipsy," and I wanted to see him first.

That was two or three days after you met the men?—I saw him that day, and went on board the "Gipsy."

How many days was it before you drew the cheque that you went on board the "Osprey"?—It was three days afterwards.

After you drew the cheque?—No; I think I drew the cheque three days previously to going on board.

Was the "Osprey" the sailors' last ship?—I don't know.

When a seaman ships he has to state the last vessel in which he served, does he not?—I don't know. I never saw a sailor ship.

They have to sign articles?—Of course.

WERE THOSE SAILORS PART OF THE "OSPREY'S" CREW?—NO, THEY WERE WRECKED FROM THE "BELLA."

The following is the deposition of Mrs. LONGLANDS, wife of the above witness. Her evidence was not tendered in Court, as it was considered that Mr. LONGLAND'S evidence being supported by his respectable position and character, and by documentary evidence, which he put in to prove his statements and dates, that Mrs. LONGLAND'S evidence was unnecessary.

CATHERINE JANE LONGLANDS, wife of FRANCIS LONGLANDS, of Yardley Hastings, Northamptonshire, will prove:—

I went to Melbourne with my husband from New York, in the ship "Bothna," as steerage passengers. We arrived at Melbourne in muddy weather. I cannot recollect the year, as my memory is very bad as to dates. We went to reside at a place called Brunswick. I RECOLLECT MY HUSBAND BRINGING HOME THREE SAILORS, WHO SAID THEY WERE SHIPWRECKED. I SPOKE TO THEM AND ASKED THEM WHAT SHIP. THEY SAID, "THE BELLA." They said they were badly off and hadn't got anything, and were hard drove; they also said THERE WERE SEVEN OR EIGHT OF THEM SAVED AND ONE PASSENGER. They were roughly dressed in sailors' clothes; one was a tall young man and good-looking.

I did not learn their names, except one who was called *New York*. Two of them were Americans, which was the reason my husband took such an interest in them, he having received kindness from Americans. My husband is of a charitable disposition, and would bring any one home who was in need. I have often told him not to do so.

They stayed two or three days, and slept in a place outside the house, which we used to call the shed, and where straw and wood were kept. They used to come into the house to dinner, and went about in the daytime looking for employment.

I recollect my husband bringing home a box of sailors' clothing. I saw him open the box and take out the clothes. There were underclothes, boots, and hats, and serge jackets and jumpers, which served for waistcoats.

I looked at all the things, and gave some to the men, and my husband gave others. We have the box now.

My husband had a great deal of talk with them. They used to come in and talk at night. I think the day after the clothes were given to the men they went off, and I have never heard of or seen them since.

I do not remember my husband ever bringing home any other shipwrecked sailors.

We take in the newspaper at our house at Yardley Hastings. It comes at 4 o'clock, and is fetched away at 6.20.

If my husband is at home he reads it. If not, it goes away unread, as I cannot read. Therefore, I have not read the Plaintiff's evidence, nor heard it read; nor Mr. LIARDET'S evidence, nor Mr. SHARPEN'S evidence, and not even my husband's evidence.

HASELDINE SHARPEN, examined by Mr. Serjeant BALLANTINE: Are you an architect and building surveyor, of York?—Yes.

The late Mayor of Scarborough was your brother?—Yes.

And he is magistrate now?—Yes.

Did you practise for some years as an architect at Ripon?—Yes.

And acted for the committee of the Diocesan Training Schools?—Yes.

In the year 1853 did you go out in the "Crœsus" to Australia?—Yes, to Melbourne. I was bound to Sydney, but as I did not think the vessel was safe, I landed at Melbourne.

When did you reach there?—April, 1854.

How long did you remain?—About a month. Then I went to Sydney, and returned to Melbourne about July.

Did you land at Sandridge Pier at Melbourne?—Yes; it was originally called Liardet's landing-place. I was in Melbourne also in 1849 and 1850.

Do you remember being, in July, 1854, on board the "Comet"?—Yes.

What sort of a steamer was she?—About 200 tons; she used to run from Hobson's Bay to Melbourne.

How came you to be on board the vessel?—I was going from Williamstown to Sandridge.

Did the "Comet" take any person off a vessel in the bay?—Yes.

Was your attention called to the vessel?—Yes; she was a rakish-looking three-masted vessel, low in the water, fore and aft rigged—schooner-rigged, in fact, and with a round stern.

And you saw the "Comet" take some persons off?—I was down below when she stopped alongside the vessel, and I went on deck to see what was the matter. I then saw some persons, evidently sailors, coming down the paddle-boxes. Some of them went aft, and others stood near to the chimney.

Did you notice two of the persons whom you saw come down the paddle-boxes?—Yes, I saw that one was a well-dressed man. There was a young gentleman with him, evidently not a sailor. Though he was dressed like a sailor, he had not the bearing of one.

Had you any conversation with the young gentleman who you said was dressed like the sailor, but had not the bearing of one?—I was talking to another party, and he turned round and made an observation.

Did you notice anything in his accent when he made the observation?—Yes; it was decidedly French. So much so that I took him for a Frenchman.

While you were talking to him did you observe anything peculiar in his countenance?—I saw him lift his eyebrows.

Was that in a way to be quite noticeable?—Yes; I particularly remember it.

Were you at the last meeting of the York races?—Yes; in August last.

Did you see there a person whom you now know to be the Claimant?—Yes.

Were you any distance from him?—When I was nearest to him he had his back to me.

Were you some distance off when you saw his face?—He was sitting in the balcony of the grand stand. When I was nearest to him his back was towards me, and when he was further off on the grand stand, I used my opera-glass to see him, and I had a good look at him then.

Had you any belief that you had seen him before?—Not at that time.

Since then have you seen the Claimant and conversed with him?—Yes.

Will you tell the Court whether or not he is the same person you saw at Melbourne in 1854?—Yes; I have come to that conclusion, and I believe him to be the same person.

Before you came to that conclusion had you seen a portrait of him?—Yes. I bought one in London on Saturday, similar to one I had seen at York. It was the portrait of the person I saw on board the "Comet." (A carte of ROGER TICHBORNE as he appeared in 1854 was handed in by the witness.)

Was it shortly after the York meeting you saw the portrait in a shop window of that city?—Yes; but I did not particularly notice it until the 9th or 10th of this month.

And then you thought you recognised the young man you had seen in 1854?—Yes.

You saw in a shop window at York a photograph similar to the one you bought on Saturday?—Yes.

When did you see it at York?—At the fore part of this month.

Did you recognise the person represented?—Yes, as the young gentleman I saw on board the "Comet."

Did you know Mr. LIARDET?—Yes, in 1849 and 1850. I dined with him. In January, 1850, I left Melbourne. I saw his son in 1854.

What was the name of the vessel from which these sailors disembarked?—The "Osprey."

When you saw the Claimant on Saturday morning, had you a long conversation with him?—Perhaps three-quarters of an hour.

Did you ask him any questions in relation to the circumstances you have detailed to us?—Yes; but I cannot recollect the exact words.

Did you ask him any questions about the person who accompanied him?—No; but he told me it was the Captain of the "Osprey."

Have you a good memory of faces?—Yes, generally.

Just give us the impression in your own words. What is your belief about him now?—That he is the same person I saw on board the "Comet."

The Chief Justice: I see that the carte which the witness has produced is not a copy of either of the two daguerreotypes which have been produced as portraits of Sir ROGER when in Chili. The carte must have been taken from some photograph. If the jury will look at it they will see the difference instantly. In the small picture the coat is drawn close in front, and such is not the case in either of the two daguerreotypes. Therefore it cannot be a copy of either of them.

Mr. Serjeant BALLANTINE (to the witness): Where did you buy this carte?—In Regent-street.

Mr. GIFFARD: Photographers are able to dress up any face they please, and in any form they please.

The Chief Justice: Are they? Then that may account for some of the other photographs which we have seen in the course of this case.

Mr. GIFFARD: It is a common form of libel in Paris. There photographers put the face of some important personage on to a figure of a grotesque kind.

The Foreman of the Jury: In MOORE'S evidence he stated that there were only three daguerreotypes of the Claimant taken.

The Chief Justice: One of which was lost?

The Attorney-General: That in both of the daguerreotypes there is a strong light, but there is none in the carte.

The Foreman: Probably the photograph of the Claimant which the witness bought has been recopied from a former copy, and which might previously have been touched up and improved by the artist.

The Chief Justice: In the carte I don't see the waistcoat which appears in the other.

Mr. Serjeant BALLANTINE (to the witness): Was it your opinion, after seeing the photograph, that the Claimant was the man?—Yes.

Are you still of the same opinion?—Yes.

The Chief Justice: There is no material difference in the faces, which appear to be much the same in the three.

Cross-examined by the Attorney-General: Do you think those three are all equally alike?—No: there is a little alteration in the dress.

I mean as regards the face?—In my judgment they are portraits of the same party.

Do they all three, then, resemble the person you remember?—Yes, one more particularly (the oval daguerreotype in the case).

You have been living lately at Ripon?—No; the last eight or nine months I have resided at York.

How long have you returned?—I left Australia in 1855, and have been in this country ever since.

Has Mr. SHARPEN, the late Mayor of Scarborough, anything to do with this case?—Not that I know of.

What has been your occupation lately?—I have made plans for the York and Ripon Diocesan Training Schools.

Is that the amount of your practice now?—Yes.

What did you do when at Ripon?—There was a school attached to one of the churches, and I built an additional classroom. A little over a year ago I made plans again for a further enlargement, but it came to nothing.

What is your general practice?—Building surveyor.

Do you mean taking out quantities for builders, more particularly valuing property for mortgagees?—I am asked to value property for solicitors.

Is that how you make your fortune?—I make my living in that way.

What property had you at Ripon?—A house worth about £20 a year, which I sold when I went to York.

What were you doing in Australia?—I shipped goods out there. I shipped a lot of brandy from London to New Zealand.

What else?—Some ironmongery. I bought it in Melbourne, and shipped it to New Zealand.

What took you to Melbourne the first time?—My health. I was advised to take a sea voyage.

Did you ship anything at that time?—No.

Then you went there for the benefit of your health?—Yes.

And you came back when?—I landed in Liverpool in 1850.

What were you doing in 1851?—I kept the Minerva Hotel till 1853.

Did the hotel answer?—Yes; but I did not like the life. I had some brandy in stock in bond in London and Hull, and I shipped it to New Zealand.

The Chief Justice: What quantity or value?—Six or eight hogsheads.

The Attorney-General: Did you go with your brandies to New Zealand?—It was there some months before me. I went from Melbourne to Sandridge on the day that the railway was opened. I went to Australia by the screw-steamer "Crœsus," and landed in Melbourne. I stayed there a month, and then went to Sydney.

What were you doing in Melbourne?—I stayed with my friends and old shipmates.

And there you bought the ironmongery?—Yes; and took it to New Zealand.

The Chief Justice: To what value?—Under a hundred pounds, perhaps.

The Attorney-General: And you sold it in New Zealand?—Well, I almost gave it away.

Then you came back to Melbourne?—No; to Sydney.

What were you doing at Sydney?—Nothing; I stayed with my friends.

Then you went back to Melbourne?—Yes.

In July, 1854, you were there?—Yes.

How long did you stay there?—Until September; until the Sandridge Railway was opened.

What were you doing there?—I was visiting some of my old shipmates. I was frequently on board the "Comet"—perhaps once or twice a week. I think I was crossing from Williamstown to Sandridge when the "Comet" took the people off the "Osprey."

How soon, after you got to Melbourne the second time, was this passage in the "Comet"?—It was about the end of July. I cannot say the exact day, or the time of day, or the hour.

Were there a good many ships at Port Phillip at that time?—Yes; perhaps 200 or 300. A great many were abandoned in the Salt Water Creek. They were laid up there fast with nobody on board.

Were there a good many lying out in the Bay?—Yes; there were between 200 and 300, I should think, in Hobson's Bay.

Was the "Comet" a steamer that went about shipping lying in the Bay, and took passengers from them up the river to Melbourne?—Yes. She used to run from Geelong occasionally, about forty miles distant.

Who was with you on board the "Comet"?—My son, a lad between ten and eleven years old.

You mention having seen a vessel which you described, but the name of which you did not know. Now, when did you discover that it was the "Osprey"?—The next day, I believe.

The Chief Justice: You never saw her name?—I can't say that I did. When we rounded the ship I was below.

The Attorney-General: Did you see the sailors come down a ladder or the paddle-box?—They came down the paddle-box, to the best of my recollection.

Did you see them?—Yes: some of them were down when I came up from below, and others were coming down.

How many did you see on board the vessel altogether?—I cannot say; but there were four or five, and there might have been one or two more. I saw two on board the "Comet," and three came down on to the paddle-box.

The Chief Justice: How many altogether came on board the "Comet"?—About half a dozen, I should say; but I cannot speak for certain.

Did you see what became of them when you came to Sandridge?—I did not. I was about the first to land.

Did any of them land with you?—I can't say: they might have gone up the river to Melbourne. I landed, and walked about two miles. I remember that I was chilly, and that I walked quickly, and my little boy ran by my side. My impression is that they landed. I had seen all the passengers of the boat land at Sandridge on previous occasions.

Did you see any of the sailors afterwards at Melbourne?—No. I saw two of them at Cole's Wharf the next day, and spoke to them. They were comparing the narrowness of the river at Yarra with the breadth of the river at Rio. They spoke of its being ridiculously narrow, and said it was a mere drain to the one at Rio.

Is that the last you saw of any of them until you were at York races?—Yes.

You never saw the young man again till the York races of this year?—No.

How long were you in his company on board the "Comet?"—I was standing near to him, I should say, for five or ten minutes.

Had you been fortunate enough to avoid hearing about the TICHBORNE Case until you were at York races?—I had read part of the evidence in the papers.

Did it interest you?—Not particularly.

Did you read the Claimant's cross-examination?—Yes, part of it.

The Melbourne part?—Yes.

Did that interest you?—Rather; it brought back recollections.

Had you heard between the year 1866 and the York races of 1871 anything about the TICHBORNE Case?—I don't remember.

Don't they talk about it in the North then, as much as they do in the South?—Well, they did not before the Case came on.

Did you not hear the account which the Claimant gave that he was picked up by a vessel and taken to Melbourne?—I think I remember something about it.

When did you first hear of that? Was it as far back as 1867?—No, I think not, but I heard something about it, certainly.

Had you heard so far back as 1867?—No.

When did you first hear of his being lost in the "Bella"?—Since the Case commenced.

Not this year?—No.

There was an examination in Chancery.

Mr. Serjeant BALLANTINE: But that was not published.

The Attorney-General: Did you hear of it in 1867?—I might; but I did not feel interested about it.

When did you see the "Osprey" mentioned?—In the Claimant's statement. That was the first time I particularly remembered the name, and it came to my mind then.

Do you mean to state that you never heard of the "Osprey" being mentioned before the present year?—Yes, certainly.

You mean to swear that?—Yes; I have no recollection of hearing the "Osprey" named until the Case was opened.

Will you swear you did not?—I could almost swear I did not. I had forgotten it if I had.

Did you know some years ago that his story was that he had been picked up in 1854?—No, I did not feel interested in the case before it was opened.

Did you know the fact that the Claimant had been in Australia? Did you know the general outline of the story—that he had been in Australia for years working as a common man?—Well, I can't say.

What was it you heard—that there was a case of the kind coming on?—I heard of a gentleman being "wanted" who had been in Australia. It was a common thing for people to be lost in Australia. I have been interrogated many times as to missing friends.

All your friends were aware that you had been in Australia in 1854?—Of course.

Do I understand you to say you never had your attention awakened until you saw the "Osprey" mentioned in the Claimant's statement?—I never saw the "Osprey" mentioned until I saw it in his statement.

Did you ever have your attention called to this Case so as to take an interest in it before you read about the "Osprey"?—Not before I heard the Claimant's statement in court. My attention was not awakened until I saw the statement he had made two or three years ago.

But did you know the fact that ROGER TICHBORNE had been supposed to be lost at sea?—Well, I might have done; but I had forgotten it until the Case was brought up in June or July of this year.

Then, you saw the Claimant on York race-course—off the Grand Stand?—I saw him in the ring at first, but he had his back towards me.

I suppose that did not remind you of your old friend?—No.

The Chief Justice: Where were you when you saw him in the ring?—Some sixty or seventy yards outside.

The Attorney-General: And then you looked at him through your opera-glass, and were struck with the likeness?—No, not until I saw the photograph.

And you believed that to be a photograph of the Claimant?—Yes.

Was the photograph you saw at York an exact copy of this one? I believe so.

How was your attention attracted to it? Was there an inscription of this sort: "Photograph of the Claimant in the TICHBORNE Case"?—I think there were the words, "Previous to being lost in the 'Bella,'" or something of that sort.

The Chief Justice: Do you recognize in this one any likeness of the Claimant, and do you say that it is the likeness of the person you saw on board the "Comet"?—There is a decided likeness of the Claimant.

The Attorney-General: Then you mean that it recalled the Claimant to you? I thought you said he did not recall to your memory the young man you had seen in Melbourne.

The Chief Justice: I understood that he did not recognise the Claimant until he saw this photograph at York.

Mr. Serjeant BALLANTINE: What he said was that it did recall to him the young man he had seen at Melbourne. It brought his mind back also to the appearance of the person he had seen at York races.

The Attorney-General: Then at York races you saw his back and face?—Yes.

Then neither of those recalled your young friend?

Mr. Serjeant BALLANTINE: He never said his young friend. It is sneering at the evidence.

The Attorney-General: However, wherever you saw him, did any sight of him recall to mind the gentleman you saw on board the "Comet"?—No; I did not get a good look at his face.

Then you saw a photograph at York, and came to the conclusion that it was like the person you saw on board the "Comet"?—Yes.

Then you knew that the person you saw at York was a man

PORTRAIT OF MR. SERJEANT BALLANTINE.

who had said he had been saved on board the "Osprey"?—Yes.

How came you to town?—I wrote to Sir ROGER TICHBORNE on the 10th or 11th of November.

Then you heard from BAXTER, ROSE, and NORTON, and came up?—Yes.

Where did you go to?—To their office.

When?—On Friday last.

Whom did you see there?—Mr. SPOFFORTH, Mr. LIARDET, and some of the clerks.

Did you see any other of the gentlemen who are present here?—Yes; Mr. BAIGENT was there when I went next morning.

Had you much talk with Mr. SPOFFORTH?—About half an hour over night.

Then the next morning you spoke to Mr. SPOFFORTH, Mr. LIARDET, and Mr. BAIGENT?—Yes.

Where did you go then?—To the Waterloo Hotel to see the Claimant.

How long were you with him?—Not exceeding three-quarters of an hour.

Who went with you?—Mr. SPOFFORTH and Mr. BAIGENT were there.

Do you know Mr. LIARDET?—Yes; I remember dining with him when in Australia in 1849; and although I had not seen him for twenty-one years, I recognized him directly I met him in Mr. SPOFFORTH's office.

Have you got a copy of the letter you wrote to the Claimant?—No.

The letter was handed in by Mr. Serjeant BALLANTINE.

Mr. Serjeant BALLANTINE: I apprehend, my lord, now that the letter is in the possession of the Court, it must be read?

The Attorney-General: I beg your pardon.

The Chief Justice: First of all, what is the letter?

Mr. Serjeant BALLANTINE: It is a letter written by this gentleman to the Claimant, called for and produced by us. I say that I have a right to have it read openly in Court.

The Attorney-General: I must say that this appears to be done merely for the purpose of interruption. I called for the letter in the course of my cross-examination of this witness, and I have a right to read it myself first.

The Chief Justice: You can't refuse to read it now that it has been called for.

The Attorney-General: My learned friend is not entitled to have it read at this moment. I must read it myself first. I must protest against the interruption.

Mr. Serjeant BALLANTINE: You looked very much as if you intended to have it read.

The Attorney-General: That may be a smart observation, but it is not regular.

The Chief Justice: I understand it will be put in, so that I need not take a note of it.

The Attorney-General: Certainly, my lord.

The Chief Justice: What is the date of the letter?

The Attorney-General: The 11th of November, 1871. (To witness.) You had had no communication with him at all?—No.

How did you know his address?—I saw it in the paper. I think it was in BOGLE's evidence I got it.

Had you read the evidence of Mr. LIARDET?—Certainly.

And of Mr. LOCKER?—Yes.

This is the letter—

"SIR,—I beg to say that I was on board the 'Comet steamer, from the bay to Melbourne, on the very occasion of her carrying up the crew of the 'Bella,' and I feel sure I spoke to you respecting the narrowness of the Yarra, and I think I told you the pelicans had left the bay in consequence of so much shipping, but that they could be shot sometimes up the Salt-water river. I remember asking some of the crew of the 'Bella' if you were a Frenchman, on account of your slight accent, and were told you were an Englishman and a passenger. I yesterday saw for the first time a photograph of you when you were not so stout as when I saw you on the Grand Stand at York, on the first day of the races, in August last. I only saw you standing at a distance. I feel confident I should know you as the person I met in the small steamer 'Comet'—I think in June, '54: and if I can be of any use, I shall be at your command. I inclose my passage ticket to show you I was there. I booked for Sydney, but left the 'Crœsus' in Melbourne, she being in a bad state, and me not liking to go in her. I also inclose you a few testimonials, to show you I am not an unknown stranger, but can speak with some hope of being believed. "H. S."

From having heard the evidence of LIARDET and LOCKER you heard about the "Osprey"?—Yes.

And that is how you came to write the letter?—Yes. I was satisfied in my own mind.

When you came to meet the Claimant, did you talk to him about this former meeting of yours on board the "Comet"?—Yes.

Did he recollect the circumstance?—He recollected being with a well-dressed gentleman on board. He said that the person was more of a gentleman than a captain.

Did he tell you his name?—No.

Did you ask him?—Not that I recollect.

Well, you know, that was on Saturday, and this is Monday. Can't you recollect?—No. We were talking about pelicans, and he said he had shot a great many on the Murrumbijee River, in the interior of Australia.

Did he remember your having mentioned the pelicans on board the "Comet"?—He didn't say.

The Chief Justice: You reminded him of talking of pelicans on board the steamer?

Witness: Yes.

The Attorney-General: Did he recollect the remark about the narrowness of the Yarra?—No.

You mentioned that to him, did you?—I think we talked about it on Saturday. He said his recollection was not very good.

Did you ask him what became of the captain, or if he knew anything about him?—No.

Or any of the crew?—No.

Were you the chief talker, or was he?—He said very little—something about the pelicans being easily shot at.

I am speaking about what he said on Saturday?—We were talking about pelicans, and he said he had shot a good deal in the country.

I mean, was he the chief talker on Saturday?—It was first one and then the other.

Did he seem to remember the people you mentioned?—No. I asked him if he remembered BUTTS, who kept the Commercial Hotel in Burke-street. He said he did not; but that he remembered the Limerick Castle Hotel.

What else did you talk about except BUTTS, the Yarra, and the pelicans? We talked about LIARDET and about Liardet Beach at Sandridge, but he didn't seem to know anything about it.

Did he say anything about the jetty or landing-place?—No; he said his recollection was not very good.

But his being on board the "Comet," and being with the well-dressed gentleman, he perfectly recollected? Yes.

Did he say he landed at the jetty, or went on to Melbourne?—He thought they landed at the jetty, but didn't well remember.

Didn't he give you an account of the shipwreck?—No.

Did he say anything about the course of the "Osprey," or where they had been to?—I don't think he mentioned the subject at all.

You were three-quarters of an hour with him, but you have given us very little of what you were talking about.—I wasn't talking to him the whole time. Mr. SPOFFORTH and he were talking about matters that did not concern me.

You were satisfied by the letter that he was the right man?—Yes.

You didn't go to satisfy any doubts?—I have no doubts in the matter.

Did you put any questions to him at all?—I can't say I did—at least, any questions of consequence.

What did you talk to Mr. SPOFFORTH, Mr. LIARDET and Mr. BAIGENT about at BAXTER, ROSE, and NORTON's office?—We talked about the early days in Melbourne—I mean about 1849.

Had you any conversation with him about the TICHBORNE Case?—We didn't speak about the matter.

Do you mean to say you were all this time with LIARDET, and didn't mention the TICHBORNE Case?—We talked of a man named BUCKLEY, who was found amongst the natives of Australia.

Did that resemble this case, you mean?—Yes, as regards its being quite possible that a man could forget his mother-tongue.

Had BUCKLEY forgotten it?—He couldn't speak a word; at least, so it is said.

Did it come back to him?—Yes, I suppose so. LIARDET told me he had either seen him or known him.

Then do you mean there was a question about the Claimant having forgotten his French?—I don't think that was mentioned.

How came the case of BUCKLEY to come round?—I asked him if he remembered it, and he said he did.

Was that without any reference to the TICHBORNE Case?—Yes; I said it was quite possible for a man to forget his native tongue.

Had you been talking about the Claimant's case?—It is quite possible; but I can't tell.

Just look at your letter (produced). What did you write it from?—I wrote it right off.

Have you any old diary or memoranda of your life up to '54?—I had a chart of my course, but I lent it, and I haven't received it back.

When you wrote the letter you relied on your memory?—Yes.

You have had no memoranda since?—Yes; I saw by a letter that I was in Sydney in July, '54.

But you say in your note to the Claimant, "I feel I should recognize you as the person I met on board the small steamer 'Comet'—I think in June, '54?"—After I posted the letter I found it was July.

What answer did you get to that letter to the Claimant?—I received a note from his solicitors.

The following was produced and read by the Attorney-General:—

"MY DEAR SIR,—Serjeant BALLANTINE has handed us your letter of the 11th, and we write to ask you to be kind enough to come to town by first train to-morrow, in order that we may confer with you on the subject of your letter. We inclose you a Post-office order for £2. 10s. for your travelling expenses.

"Yours, &c.,

"BAXTER, ROSE, and NORTON."

Was there any such conference upon the subject of your letter?—I gave them an outline of all I knew.

Was there anything said about the date?—I said it would be after the 3rd of July, because I was in Sydney on that day.

How came you to say it would be after the 3rd of July?—Because I found the letter after writing that which you have read, and I remembered that I had mentioned June.

Did you say it in answer to anything?—No; I volunteered it because I found it wasn't right with regard to the month. My letter was read over to me, and I corrected it, and said July was the month.

Do you mean to say your attention was not called to the fact that June was an incorrect date?—Certainly not.

That was not suggested by Mr. SPOFFORTH?—Not at all.

When did you find the letter?—A day or two after I wrote.

Did you immediately communicate the fact?—No.

In the view of LIARDET's and LOCKER's evidence, didn't it appear to be material?—It did.

And didn't you say anything about the matter?—I didn't expect to hear any more about it.

Do you really mean to say that?—Yes. When a week had elapsed I thought I should hear no more about it.

Then you never corrected the mistake about the date until you came to town?—Not until I went to the solicitor's office.

Does the Claimant remind you of the young gentleman you met in '45?—Yes.

Do you think him like?—Yes, in the expression of his eyes and eyebrows, coupled with his French accent—I mean at the time. I didn't detect it the other day.

What is there in the eyes and eyebrows?—When I spoke about the pelicans, he turned round and lifted his eyebrows, as if he were interested.

Do you mean on Saturday?—No; on board the "Comet."

Well, what did you see on Saturday?—I saw the same expression.

Did he lift his eyebrows?—He did.

About what?—We were talking about the pelicans.

Oh! then, when you were talking about the pelicans, up went the eyebrows?—Yes.

What about the French?—I can't detect it at all.

Is the voice the same?—I can't say anything about that.

"Nothing about the eyebrows?—He lifted his eyebrows now and then when he was speaking.

The size is different?—Yes.

What about the height?—He was a thin, tallish young man from what I saw, above the middle height—or, say, about an inch or two taller than I.

How tall are you?—Five feet seven inches.

Were his general manners the same?—I really can't say. I noticed particularly that he hadn't the bearing of a sailor on board the "Comet."

And the expression?—There is something in the expression of his face which I can't describe, but it is not easily mistaken.

Then, except the natural alteration caused by time and his being stouter, is he the same person?—Well, I had only a short opportunity of observing him, but I have no doubt in my own mind. I don't know how to explain myself, but that is my impression.

Do you really mean to say that, except being older and stouter, he looks the same man as in '51?—He has the same expression in his eyes that he had then. To my mind, he has the same face and expression.

Re-examined by Serjeant BALLANTINE: I have resided in York since the 1st of March.

And I suppose everybody in the neighbourhood knows where to find you and who you are?—Oh, yes.

You say that on the occasion of your being on board the "Comet" your son was with you?—Yes.

I believe he is dead now?—He is.

Until you heard the name of the "Osprey" mentioned, you were not aware your evidence could have any relation to the matter?—No.

Did Mr. SPOFFORTH, or Mr. BAIGENT, or any person at Mr. SPOFFORTH's office suggest any evidence to you, or any alteration of evidence?—Certainly not.

Did Mr. BAIGENT take any part in the matter?—He didn't interfere at all.

Had you communication with LOCKER, or any person connected with the Case, until you wrote the letter which found its way to my chambers?—No.

You say that as soon as you sent the letter you found another in which the correct date was given?—Yes. I wasn't satisfied that June was the month, and I hunted up my letters and found this.

Are these (produced) the shipping receipts and testimonics forwarded with your letter?—Yes.

The Foreman of the Jury: You have told the jury that you made more than one voyage to Australia?—Yes.

And to New Zealand and back?—Yes.

You have also told us that you detected that the mien and bearing of this young man whom you saw with somebody in the "Comet" were not those of a sailor. Then it is fair to assume that you are conversant with the appearance and habits of seamen?—Yes.

Now, you have told us that you saw a party of seamen disembark from the "Osprey" over the paddlebox to the "Comet," and so embark. Tell me, in noticing this party of seamen, did you observe that they brought with them their sea-kit, their sea-chests, their hammocks, and what not?—I didn't see them.

Did they take anything with them in leaving the "Osprey?"—No; the articles belonging to them were sent by the lighter.

But seamen do not generally send them by lighter?—It was only a small one, and they would take my luggage.

These men, as I understand you, were not going ashore for a day, but permanently going. When going into the "Comet" had they anything with them?—They might have had a bundle but I didn't take any particular notice.

Did you read in the newspapers of those days an account of the occurrence?—I don't think I did.

How was the young man dressed?—He had a pea or "monkey" jacket on. I remember that perfectly well, but nothing else.

Not widely different from the seamen?—No; he went to the upper part of the "Comet."

That would be the decks?—Yes; but the other seamen were about the funnel.

Then it was more from where he stood than his mien or gait that struck you?—All the appearance was different. He didn't look like a seaman.

How far was the "Osprey" from the landing-stage at Sandridge Pier?—I can't say just now; it might be half a mile.

Was the person with whom you saw him conversing dressed as a civilian or as a seafaring man?—As a civilian. I think he had a black coat on.

Where would a destitute set of seamen naturally go to at Melbourne?—I don't know.

It wouldn't be notorious?—I don't know; there is no Sailors' Home in Melbourne that I know of. I fancy they would go to LLOYD's agency.

Mr. LIARDET, the son, whose evidence we have set forth above, gave valuable testimony at the Great Trial. The following letter from Mr. ONSLOW is in allusion, and it covered a valuable communication from Mr. LIARDET, which was published with it in the ENGLISHMAN for December 26, 1874, being No. 38. The letter of Mr. ONSLOW was headed—

INSINUATIONS OF THE LORD CHIEF JUSTICE.

TO THE EDITOR OF THE "ENGLISHMAN."

SIR,—In reading over the admitted partial and unfair summing-up of the Lord Chief Justice of England, Sir ALEXANDER COCKBURN, I observe, on the 5th day of his address to the jury, he makes the following remarks:—

"Another witness, Mr. LIARDET, tells us he came to Melbourne in July, 1854, and when he arrived he saw an 'Osprey' there. He says that, on the following morning, being out in a boat belonging to his brother-in-law, who was the principal Emigration Commissioner in Melbourne, his attention was directed to a particular vessel, which turned out afterwards to be the 'Osprey,' a very fine-looking craft. He went on board, when he saw only one or two persons, and, somehow or other, they told him she came from South America; the men looked like sailors. No doubt this gentleman did go on board the vessel which he was told was the 'Osprey,' and had come from South America; but, with respect to the date, it turns out to be a deep misapprehension. It was not until the ensuing year that he could have been in Melbourne at all; because he fixes the date, with respect to a particular circumstance. He says he knows when it was because it was contemporaneous with the departure of Sir CHARLES FITZROY from Sydney. Having about that time obtained a month's leave of absence from Sir CHARLES FITZROY, who was Governor of New South Wales, he went to Melbourne; but we have Mr. and Mrs. MARSH, who left Sydney in the same vessel as Sir CHARLES FITZROY, proving a very different thing. Mr. MARSH came over as a Commissioner from Sydney to the Paris Exhibition of 1855; and not only is the fact fixed in that way, but Mr. MARSH keeps a diary, which he produces, and shows that they left Sydney on the 27th of January, 1855. It is thus proved to demonstration, that Mr. LIARDET could not have been in Melbourne, and gone on board the 'Osprey,' in 1854."

Such, Sir, is the summing-up of the Lord Chief Justice of this country. Now, as I think your readers ought to have Mr. LIARDET's version also of what really occurred, I beg to inclose you his statement, which he was kind enough to forward to me in 1872, after the first trial, in which he clearly explains the difference of dates; and having done so, his evidence is of the utmost value to the unfortunate man, who, I believe, is unjustly convicted. Mr. EVELYN LIARDET is the gentleman who was a candidate for Greenwich in the Conservative interest at the last election, in opposition to the ex-Premier. In reading over Mr. EVELYN LIARDET's statement, I beg to call the attention of your readers especially to his 13th clause, and then refer to the evidence of that Cabinet Minister, and remember what he swore to in reference to the gold excitement in that year.

I may add, in conclusion, that Mr. EVELYN LIARDET is a gentleman of the highest position and honour, both in this country and Australia, and is a very near relative of WILLIAM EVELYN, Esq., of Wootton, in Surrey, late M.P. for the Western Division, and one of the oldest families in the county, whom I have had the honour of knowing for many years; and when I consider with disgust and indignation the scandalously untrue insinuations of the Lord Chief Justice regarding myself, and the photograph of the grotto, I must say that I infinitely prefer the following manly and straightforward statement of Mr. EVELYN LIARDET to the one-sided and partial assumption of a prejudiced Judge.—I beg to remain, Sir, your obedient servant, GUILDFORD ONSLOW.

The Grove, Ropley, near Alresford, Hants:
November 27th, 1874.

TO GUILDFORD ONSLOW, ESQ.—THE TICHBORNE TRIAL.

SIR,—The Attorney-General having mis-stated, and misrepresented my evidence, and that of my father, in the above Case, and full publicity having been given to such statements in the reports of the proceedings; and I am informed that were I to address Mr. Serjeant BALLANTINE on the subject, much time would elapse before notice could be taken of my objections, and corrections of the Attorney-General, I beg to forward you this statement, seeing that the highly improper inference of the Attorney-General has been heralded before the world.

1st. I have not my evidence before me, but I have a perfect recollection of what I stated, namely—In July, 1854, Sir CHARLES FITZROY, Governor-General of New South Wales, gave me a month's leave of absence to visit Melbourne, and my relatives there, whom I had not seen for nine years. I left New South Wales in the "City of Sydney" steamer, Captain MOODY. On the morning after my arrival in Hobson's Bay, as I was proceeding from Williamstown to Sandridge, in my brother-in-law's boat, the coxswain pointed out to me the "Osprey," a large three-masted schooner, a very fine model. The boat's crew pulled me round her. I went on board and saw two people. My brother-in-law, Mr. CHARLES BROAD, was senior Emigration Officer, stationed at Williamstown, and it was his duty to board every vessel visiting the port. *The boat's crew told me she had arrived from South America*, and had brought some part of a ship-wrecked crew to Melbourne. *One of the men on board told me a similar story.* I stopped a minute or two on board, and then left the vessel.

2nd. I was asked how I fixed the date. I answered that Sir CHARLES FITZROY was giving up his government of New South Wales, and proceeding to England, and I was proceeding to Melbourne.

3rd. I never said Sir CHARLES FITZROY and I together left in the same ship, which is untrue.

4th. I said Sir WILLIAM DENISON succeeded Sir CHARLES FITZROY.

5th. I cannot believe I said "*immediately*," because I believe the senior military officer on the Australian station performed the duties of Governor during the interim, which would account for the discrepancy of the interval in which Sir CHARLES left, and Sir WILLIAM's arrival in January, 1855.

6th. From the end of July, 1854, to the 27th of January, 1855, is *six, and not twelve months*, as stated by the Attorney-General.

7th. I was asked if I knew of any other "Ospreys." I said "Yes, I knew a small 'Osprey,' an ordinary schooner of 60 or 70 tons, trading between New Zealand and Melbourne."

8th. My father described three, *a barque* and two schooners.

9th. My father is a gentleman, and went to reside at Melbourne in 1831, *and was there over 30 years*, where he is well known and respected. I know Melbourne, Sandridge, and Geelong *thoroughly*, therefore I think it presumptuous of the Attorney-General, *who has never been there*, to attempt to interpose his opinion to over-rule our evidence in this Case. I have no interest in this Case whatever. I was called upon by Messrs. BAXTER, ROSE, and NORTON, to give evidence, as I have so recently arrived from Sydney.

10th. I was not called to support my father's evidence. *I was applied to by the Solicitors*, and I asked my father to join me in stating *that which we both knew*, which I then considered was only an act of justice; *and I have had no communication whatever with the Claimant.*

11th. I asked Messrs. BAXTER and Co. to apply to the Secretary of State for the Colonies to ascertain the date of the appointment of Sir W. DENISON, and Sir CHARLES FITZROY relinquishing the Government, as the date on which I visited Melbourne. I still think it was. *Nevertheless, I am sure I went to Melbourne at the close of July*, 1854, *and saw the "Osprey" at her moorings, as I have stated.* And it may be that Sir CHARLES FITZROY *left so shortly after my return, that I marked the date by his Excellency's departure*; and surely a few months' discrepancy, on being asked in a witness-box to fix a date of a circumstance I never anticipated being referred to, and after the lapse of nearly eighteen years, is no serious crime.

12th. I did not say the "Osprey" arrived the day after I arrived in Melbourne. I said she was pointed out to me the morning after my arrival, and that I must have boarded her after my father. She may have been some time in port before I saw her; and having only two men on board would lead to that conclusion. *I positively adhere to having seen the "Osprey," as I described.* I feel the Attorney-General, in his attempts to upset, has strengthened the Plaintiff's case. What has he to say to his first statement, that the story of the "Osprey" has gone into thin air, when he now states to the public that he knew of no less than four "Ospreys"?

13th. *As to the excitement having ceased in reference to the gold-producing mania at Melbourne, in* 1854, *any person to make such a statement must be grossly ignorant of the Colony.* People may have become more used to its favourable reports, but certainly the influx of population continued to increase to a great extent, and thus the large inland towns were formed, such as Ballarat, Bendigo, &c. *Anyone making statements to the contrary must either be lamentably ignorant or biassed to do so.*

14th.—I consider it ungentlemanly and impertinent of the Attorney-General to remark on the anticipated evidence of Mr. and Mrs. MARSH, who, if I am not in error, resided at Wellington, in New South Wales, a long way up the country, and were not likely to afford evidence so faithful as that of persons on the spot.

15th. I repeat, I have no interest in the matter beyond correcting the unfaithful statements of the Attorney-General—which, if not corrected, might lead the public to believe I accepted them; and I cannot consent to be misrepresented by any one.

16th. The Attorney-General appears to me to twist the various "Ospreys" to suit his own course. I do not hesitate to say that American ships are not so particular as to rules as the Attorney-General would make appear. They go where they choose for and with freight, and claim protection under the American flag.

17th. I now call attention to another "Osprey," reported in the Shipping News as having returned to Milford. This makes six "Osprey's," and yet, when the Attorney-General is presumed to have known four "Ospreys," he stated the "Osprey" was like the "Flying Dutchman." *I feel the Attorney-General has jumbled up truth and falsehood together, so as to confuse the jury; and not at all careful as to whose honour he may attack.*—I am, Sir, yours faithfully,
J. EVELYN LIARDET.

1, Munster-road, Fulham, S.W.:
February, 1872.

TO THE EDITOR OF THE "ENGLISHMAN."

SIR,—Towards the close of the defence in the great TICHBORNE Trial, I was in daily expectation of being called as a witness, after the correspondence between CHAS. HARCOURT, Esq., and myself. You might here ask the question, What do you know about the matter? Well, guided by a true and upright conscience, I hereafter explain, viz.: I have spent upwards of a quarter of a century in the Australian Colonies, most part of the time in Port Phillip, now Victoria; and while acting in the capacity of a digger, on the so-called Nine-Mile Creek or diggings, situated at the head of the Yaccahdandah Creek, and nine miles from the town of Beechworth, I then purchased a *Herald* newspaper to read, for pastime in my tent. The snow was laying on the ground at the time (rather a rare occurrence), and the storm not over. The newspaper, for which I paid one shilling, I read over again and again, as we could not go out to work. The said paper contained a paragraph, giving an account of the arrival of a vessel called the "Osprey," an American schooner, bringing with her a picked-up shipwrecked crew and one or two passengers from the "Bella," which had foundered at sea. The time of my reading that account was about the latter end of July or the beginning of August, 1854. There was a second "Osprey" (which was much commented upon by ———), but smaller, which traded to the westward of Port Phillip, that picked up a crew *at* Lowitt Bay, and brought them into Melbourne or Geelong, I could not say which. On my leaving the diggings, I went to reside at "Oxley Plain Station," in the year 1855. I then saw CASTRO and spoke to him. If the photographs are correct—I believe the prosecution admits that they are—then the Chili one *is that of* Sir R. C. D. TICHBORNE. He *then* bore the same *identical face*, as *that* represented in the Chili daguerreotype, and is most undoubtedly the same individual. I afterwards, in 1856, about the month of March, saw ARTHUR ORTON, and spoke to him, who is a pock-marked man, and the marks were most seen on the left cheek, and from the lower part of the left ear, down to the mouth; the marks appeared to run into each other, as if caused by a scratch from the nails of his own hand, while lingering under his complaint. There was another man in his company when I saw and spoke to him; the other man told me they were going over to Gippsland, and were then on their way. They intended to cross the Snowy Mountains (Australian Alps). According to my colonial experience during my sojourn there, I can clearly state to have known and witnessed men who came there *thin* and *bony*, who afterwards became fat and stout, and others who were fat and stout, became thin, like that of ARTHUR ORTON, when I last saw him. I saw CASTRO about two or three years afterwards at a distance, while riding along the road between Billybong and Albury, on the Murray River. He was then beginning to get stout, and was much stouter then than what ARTHUR ORTON was when I saw him last. ARTHUR ORTON had as much of the slubberdegullion about him, in appearance and every way, as CASTRO had that of a clean, respectable, and perfect gentleman.—I am truly yours, &c.,
ISAAC B. BEEBY.

Glasgow: 8th October, 1874.

LETTER FROM THE OWNER OF THE "OSPREY."

Boisdale, Gippsland, Victoria: August 2nd, 1874.

To GUILDFORD ONSLOW, Esq.

SIR,—Perhaps the following information may be of use in the TICHBORNE Case:—

In 1854, I purchased from Messrs. OGILVIE and ROBINSON the three-masted schooner "Osprey;" she lying in the Yarra-Yarra River. She had just arrived off a voyage.

While I was inspecting the schooner, the Captain, named LEWIS HODGE, remarked that if I purchased the "Osprey" I should be certain to have luck with her, as she had picked up a wrecked boat's men *off the South American Coast her last voyage.* While we were remarking upon this circumstance, Captain HODGE pointed to a man on the wharf, saying: "That man was a passenger in the boat of wrecked men." This was afterwards corroborated by one of the sailors.

Captain HODGE afterwards had command of the schooner "Martha," which was wrecked off Port Albert, and *both captain and crew were lost.*

I gave this information to a Mr. JEUNE, who I understood was over here collecting evidence for the Claimant. I presume he thought it valueless, as I heard nothing of it afterwards. I have been advised to send it to you, as it might assist in the release of an innocent man.—I remain, Sir, your obedient Servant,
R. C. MORRISON, Justice of the Peace.

EVIDENCE NOT PRODUCED AT THE TRIAL.

A correspondent sends us the following printed extract from a newspaper:—

A WITNESS FOR THE TICHBORNE CLAIMANT.—The discovery of a document in connection with this celebrated Case has been quite the topic of conversation in this town. According to the *Halstead Times*, it appears that Mr. A. E. CLARKE, bill-poster of this town, whilst in conversation with Mr. ISAAC DAVEY, a resident in New-street, casually elicited the fact that the latter had in his possession several letters from a brother JAMES (who is now residing in New Zealand), who had formerly been ship's steward on board a vessel called the "Bella." CLARKE requested permission to look over the letters, and on examination found that, in this correspondence with his friend in Halstead, JAMES DAVEY told the story of the wreck of the "Bella," and his subsequent rescue by the "Hosprey" ("Osprey"), in which, he wrote, he was conveyed to Melbourne. The importance of the correspondence to the Claimant was evident; and ultimately, with Mr. DAVEY's consent, it was taken to London, and placed in the hands of Mr. HENDRICK, the Secretary of the TICHBORNE Defence Fund. It is stated that the letters will play an important part in the pending Trial, and that both Mr. ISAAC DAVEY and Mrs. JAMES DAVEY, the wife of the steward, will be called as witnesses for the defence. These letters would not have been admissible in evidence; and TICH-

BORNE had no money to bring the writer of them from New Zealand.

The following is another important link in the chain of proof:—

THE "OSPREY."

Mr. WILLIAM BARTLETT, painter, plumber, &c., of 24, New Vauxhall-terrace, Duddeston Mill, Birmingham, writes to the *Birmingham Post* as follows:—

I was at the diggings in Australia for several years before 1854. In August, 1854, I was in Hobson's Bay, when I saw the "Osprey." I was passing on board the "New Comet," steamer, to the "Lightning," in which I engaged a passage. I wanted to go to Melbourne, to do some business, and I got aboard from off Kay's Wharf. My attention was attracted to the "Osprey" by her remarkable build and the remarks passed on her. She was a three-masted schooner, and her foremost mast was the highest, the hinder ones being shorter. She was rigged, too, very peculiar, and had a foresail, with a "clear" deck. She was painted green, and on the side in gold letters was her name, "Osprey." She had no figure-head. There was a friend of mine steering her, a man named SCUDAMORE, who came from Birmingham, but whom I have not heard of since. Seeing him there, I went on board, and took a turn for him at the wheel, out of friendship, so to say. Some of those on board were dressed rather peculiar, and they had these worsted caps on. I got talking to my friend, and he told me there were five or six people on board which had been taken off the "Bella" out at sea, and I saw them. I noticed one man in particular, from his curious make. He was about 5ft. 8in. or 9in. in height, and he had a downcast look. He seemed to me like a gentleman who had been in some trouble. He looked like a gentleman (emphatically). He was very thin—in fact, I might say a stripling. I have never seen the TICHBORNE Claimant, but I have seen a portrait. From that I recognize him to be the man I saw. I firmly believe he is the same man. I wrote to Messrs. BAXTER, ROSE, and NORTON in November last about this, and received an acknowledgment thanking me for the information. I don't know whether I am to be called as a witness. I went on to Melbourne by the "Lightning" after seeing the "Osprey," but I did not return by it to this country, as I could not get my business done in time. I came back by the "Ocean Chief," commanded by Captain TOBIN; first mate, BROWN. We were becalmed twenty-eight days on the line, and in consequence were in great distress. We brought an action against Messrs. BAINES and Co., Liverpool, and it was referred to arbitration. I was an intermediate passenger, and we got £600 between us. Both the "Ocean" and the "Lightning" have been burnt since, the former at Otago. I tell you all this to show it is the truth, and if you want to verify it you can write to BAINES and Co. I was in Australia three or four years, and knew MORGAN; I could swear that he isn't. I remember when MORGAN was shot. I was in England at the time, but it caused a great deal of talk. When I was at the Ballarat diggings in 1853, I knew a man named TOM CASTRO, who kept a butcher's shop on the Red Hill flat, near Goldpoint. CASTRO was rather short—that is to say, about 5ft. 6in.—but very stout. I could swear the Claimant is the same man that I saw in the "Osprey" in Hobson's Bay.

Copy of a letter from HENRY E. MICHELL, Esq., the brother of General Sir JOHN MICHELL, C.B., of Ringwood, Hants, to GUILDFORD ONSLOW, Esq., with the inclosed Declaration of the Melbourne Pilot, Captain ROCHETTS, who boarded the vessel that saved Mr. ROGER TICHBORNE and the wrecked sailors of the "Bella," in 1854, in Melbourne Harbour, and who conducted the shipwrecked crew of the "Bella" on board the steam-tug "Comet," from the vessel that saved them, up the river to Melbourne.

Melbourne, Sept. 7th, 1874.

MY DEAR ONSLOW,—I am writing this at two in the morning, to save the post, in time to register for the home-going mail. I have found Captain ROCHETTS, who was good enough to come up here by *train to make his statement on oath*, which I inclose. He says Mr. JEUNE, the barrister (who was sent out here by BAXTER, ROSE, and Co., to get evidence regarding the horse-stealing case at Castlemaine, when TOMAS CASTRO and ARTHUR ORTON were acquitted, and to get information respecting the saving of the "Bella's" crew), that Mr. JEUNE *was nearly taking him home, but could not raise the money to do so.* Now I want to know how it is that if "JEUNE" knew all these things, these facts have never been laid before the world. You may publish this letter, and the following statement, taken from Captain ROCHETT's own lips, by myself, as follows:—

Sworn to at Melbourne, Sept. 6th, 1874.

I am brother to Mr. ROCHETT, the Manager of the York City and County Bank, at Goole, Yorkshire. I have been a Pilot for upwards of twenty years at the Port of Melbourne. *I went on board the vessel which brought in the wrecked men of the "Bella."* The vessel which brought these men in, in my belief, had no pilot on board, pilots being then very scarce for the number of ships arriving. It was not unusual for one ship to follow in the wake of another, for want of pilots.

One of the shipwrecked men of the "Bella" was a Freemason, *and the Captain of the little steamer, the "Comet,"* was also a Mason, Captain CARDEN (since dead). Finding this out, he asked me, I being then a W. M. in Masonry, to look after this man, and so it came to pass that I saw and spoke to them all. *My attention was particularly directed to a young man who was a passenger with them in the "Bella;"* he was thin, and looked ill, but the sailors told me *it was brought on by hard drinking.* He was very silent and reserved. The name of the *mate of the "Comet"* was WILLOUGHBY; he is now alive, and at Sandridge, *and he will tell the same facts:* he is now Captain WILLOUGHBY. He bought from one of the *wrecked men of the "Bella"* a sort of rug, or poncho, as it is called in South America, *which belonged to this saved young gentleman*, as a curiosity, and Captain WILLOUGHBY either still has it, or at least had it in his possession very lately.

I took my shipwrecked sailors of the "Bella," and the Captain of the vessel that picked them up, and the gentleman, all in the "Comet," up the river to see Melbourne. I took them to the Royal Highlander hotel, and stood treat for them; they then went out to see the town, the *Captain and the young gentleman going by themselves, not with the sailors.* In the evening I again met the Captain and the young gentleman.

For several days after *I saw the shipwrecked sailors of the "Bella,"* and once spoke to the young gentleman, who told me he was going up the country.

There were *three different* "Ospreys" in Melbourne Harbour at that time *that I remember.* One was a regular trader, belonging to the Eagle Line of Messrs. GIBBS, BRIGHT, and Co., Liverpool; another was a three-masted schooner, from Glasgow; and then there was the barque-rigged vessel (three masts) *from South America*, with some dark men on board.

Mr. JEUNE, the barrister, sent out by the Claimant from London to take evidence, saw me and Mr. ALPORT, the solicitor, in Melbourne, *and they both took my affidavit of all these facts.* Mr. JEUNE produced several photographs, *which he showed to me and* Captain WILLOUGHBY; these were photographs of the Claimant, *and I picked out* the photograph of Mr. ROGER TICHBORNE as being that of the young gentleman I saw, *saved from the "Bella," on board of the "Comet."* I immediately distinguished the likeness.

The captain of the vessel that picked up the crew and passenger of the "Bella," being a stranger at this port, *and the place being all in confusion,* he asked me what he had better do with these shipwrecked men he had picked up, and whether he ought to go before the water-police magistrate? I advised him to let them go, and not trouble himself more about them. Some short time after this, *I saw the carpenter of the "Bella"* on board the "Wyvern," which brought Lord ALFRED CHURCHILL out. The "Wyvern" was afterwards lost, with all hands, of course including *the carpenter of the "Bella."*

All these facts I am prepared to swear to, by statutory declaration, or to come to England, as I may be required.

(Signed) ROCHETT, Pilot, Melbourne, Australia.

The following is a statement, made by Captain WILLOUGHBY, late the mate of the "Comet," on oath, before HENRY E. MICHELL, Esq. (brother to Gen. Sir JOHN MICHEL, C.B., of Ringwood, Hants,) at Melbourne, October 6th, 1874:—

I am now the storekeeper at Deane's Floating Dock, Williamstown, Melbourne.

At the time in question, July, 1854, I was chief mate of the "Comet" steamer, which plied about the harbour of Melbourne, Australia, and up the River Yarra. I remember well taking on board the "Comet" steamer, a number of shipwrecked men; there might have been half a dozen, but I cannot swear positively.

There was a young gentleman with them, who had also been wrecked. Captain ROCHETT *was on board of the "Comet" that trip*, for he spoke to me about these men. I bought from one of these shipwrecked men a chequered quilted counterpane, which I had for many years afterwards, which makes me recollect the circumstance well.

The ship was a three-masted one, but I am quite unable to swear to her name, as at the time it made no impression on me, but I was told at the time that *she came from South America.*

I saw Mr. JEUNE, the barrister, to whom I told all this, and he produced some photographs, and I picked out one as representing the young gentleman in question.

(Signed) Capt. WILLOUGHBY.

Late Mate of the "Comet" Steamer, Melbourne.

The following is the sworn declaration of Mr. CLAY, who now lives in Condall-street, Fitzroy, Australia, taken before HENRY MICHELL, Esq., October 6th, 1874:—

I am by profession a seafaring man, and have, all my early life, been brought up in sea affairs; I *distinctly* recollect the arrival of a three-masted vessel in Hobson's Bay, with a number of men on board, who had been picked up, about the time in question, July, 1854.

I distinctly recollect inquiring where she came from, and to the best of my recollection I was told from Pernambuco, and on her way to Melbourne had called in at Rio de Janeiro.

(Signed) JOHN CLAY, Melbourne.

The following letter, from Mrs. ALEXANDER, the sister of the Rev. COMPER GRAY, and niece of the Banker of Chichester, Messrs. COMPER, appears in the *Gippsland Mercury*, July 30th, 1874:—

SIR,—I beg to acknowledge yours of the 16th, and in reply, must inform you that ROGER TICHBORNE and myself had several conversations in 1853, respecting his family and friends, and he greatly blamed Lady DOUGHTY for opposing the marriage of himself and the present Lady RADCLIFFE, and he told me that he intended to see life in Victoria, *and let his friends think him dead.*

I remonstrated, but I might as well speak to the wind as ROGER TICHBORNE *when his mind was made up* on any subject. He felt a great animus against his family in 1855. He told me that he was shipwrecked in the "Bella." (I remember the word Bella, through having a friend whom we always called BELLA, and I thought of her when he named the vessel.) I am not certain of the name of the vessel which saved him; *it might have been the "Osprey,"* but I fancy it was a longer name. I had no doubt, when the Trial commenced, but that he would get his estates, and I had not the slightest desire to mix myself up in the affair; but when I found he was committed to Newgate, in 1871, because they swore he was tattooed, I wrote to Mr. ONSLOW, and told him that I knew TICHBORNE was not tattooed upon the arms, for I had seen him wash them many times. I also told Mr. ONSLOW all particulars of my acquaintance with ROGER TICHBORNE, *both in England and in Australia*, and I forwarded a statutory declaration to a certain effect, but I also requested Mr. ONSLOW not to call me as a witness nor to make the affair public, unless it was absolutely necessary to save him. I have written to say that I will come to England, *and do so without fee or reward*, but simply for the expense of travelling and hotel charges; more than this I cannot do, and it will be a great sacrifice on my part, and give me a notoriety for which I have not the slightest ambition; still, for the sake of truth and justice, it shall be done.—Yours truly,

A. M. ALEXANDER.

Dry Creek, Red Jacket, Australia:
July 24th, 1874.

The following is the statutory declaration of Mrs. ALEXANDER, forwarded to Mr. GLADSTONE, M.P., and placed by him in the hands of the Treasury:—

[COPY.]

I, ANNA MARIA ALEXANDER, wife of CHARLES BOOTH ALEXANDER, of Dry Creek, in the Colony of Victoria, do solemnly and sincerely declare, that in the years 1847 and 1848, *I was well acquainted with* ROGER CHARLES TICHBORNE *in England.* That in the year 1855 I met in the said Colony of Victoria, a man named TOMAS CASTRO, *the identical person I had known as* ROGER CHARLES TICHBORNE, *in England.* That I told the man called THOMAS CASTRO, otherwise ROGER CHARLES TICHBORNE, that I knew the name of CASTRO to be an assumed or false name; and then the said TOMAS CASTRO owned that his right name was ROGER CHARLES TICHBORNE; that for family reasons he intended to be known in Australia as CASTRO; *that the said* CASTRO *had been wrecked in the "Bella."* And I know from observation that in the year 1855 the said TOMAS CASTRO *was not tattooed.*

And I make this solemn declaration, conscientiously believing the same to be true, and by virtue of the provisions of an Act of Parliament of VICTORIA, rendering persons making a false declaration punishable for wilful and corrupt perjury.

ANNA MARIA ALEXANDER.

Declared before me, at Wood's Point, in the Colony aforesaid, this seventh day of July, in the year one thousand eight hundred and seventy-three.

ANDREW J. NASH, J.P.

I, ROBERT BROOKS PETERS, Town Clerk and Custodian of the Seal of the Borough of Wood's Point, in the Colony of Victoria, do hereby certify, that I did see the within-named ANNA MARIA ALEXANDER, and ANDREW NASH, a Justice of the Peace in and for the said colony, severally sign the within statement or declaration on oath, in my presence, and that their signatures are of their own and proper handwriting of the said ANNA MARIA ALEXANDER and ANDREW NASH. In witness thereof I have hereunto set my hand and affixed my seal of office, on the seventh day of July, A.D. 1873, at Wood's Point.

(Signed) R. BROOKS PETERS,
Town Clerk and Custodian of Seal
of the Borough of Wood's Point.

We insert another letter which Mr. ONSLOW has received from Mrs. ALEXANDER, after sending her his volume entitled "TICHBORNE," together with two of MAULL and POLYBLANK's photographs of the Claimant, that lady having already given Mr. ONSLOW the full particulars as to how and when she first became acquainted with Mr. ROGER TICHBORNE, in the years 1847, 1848, and 1849, in England, and how she met him again whilst travelling in Australia, in the summer of 1855 (the year after the shipwreck of the "Bella"), when he was living under the assumed name of CASTRO.

LETTERS FROM MRS. ALEXANDER.

SIR,—I beg to thank you for the volume of "TICHBORNE," and I am very glad of its publication, for I think the impartial reader will admit, after perusing the straightforward documents which it contains, that the late so-called Trial has been but a farce and mockery of Justice, and I cannot but rejoice that I for one have quitted a country in which there is obviously one law for the poor and another for the rich. I wonder sometimes when the working man will cease to be a machine, and learn to be a man; and, as a man, claim his legitimate position in our best empire; then we may hope for the impartial administration of Justice, and that the pure ermine of the Bench be not sullied by unscrupulous or venal Judges. I write warmly, for I feel warmly upon the subject. I who know, and well know, that the true ROGER TICHBORNE was living in Australia in 1855, refuse to agree with the Jury that he is lying at the bottom of the sea, an inhabitant of "old ocean's coral caves and cells," because it is a LIE.

Did I know where to find a publisher, I should be sorely tempted to try my poor abilities in composing a novel, the subject of which should be ROGER TICHBORNE, and the main incidents I would pledge my honour as an Englishwoman to be true; but locked in, in the mountains of Gippsland, and with the daily cares of a large family, I give my sympathy to the Case, but am unable to do more; still, if need be, you know where to find me.

I see by the volume that you have kept sacred that which I trusted to your honour. I felt certain such would be the case, and am glad to find myself correct. You will have a large packet from Mr. SHANKLIN this mail.—Hoping it will serve you, I am your obedient servant,

A. M. ALEXANDER.

Dry Creek, Red Jacket: August 3, 1874.

To GUILDFORD ONSLOW, Esq.

Dry Creek, Victoria, Australia: Sept. 1, 1874.

To GUILDFORD ONSLOW, Esq.

SIR,—I beg to acknowledge your letter of June, inclosing photographs. I should have been well pleased if they had been the likeness of a man who was a stranger to me—well pleased if I could have written to you and said, "Mr. ONSLOW, *the photographs you have sent me are the likenesses of an impostor, this man was never* ROGER CHARLES TICHBORNE." In that case I should have felt free from all responsibility, *instead of which, truth compels me to say that the photographs are the photographs of* ROGER TICHBORNE, *and of no other man.* It is the likeness of the same ROGER who used to write to me, long years ago, when he was at Stonyhurst College, and when I afterwards met him *out here in* 1855, when he was calling himself CASTRO, and who is now, under the name of ORTON, incarcerated in Millbank gaol: the true heir of TICHBORNE herded amongst felons and convicts. Now I, who felt little or no compassion for him when he was driving in his brougham in London, yet, from such an unmerited and shameful fate, to save this man who is, notwithstanding all his faults and follies, the true ROGER TICHBORNE, I here avow myself willing to come to England, and give my evidence, without fee or reward. I regret exceedingly that I am living at such a distance from England, as the production of witnesses costs so much money. Of course, before quitting Victoria, it will be necessary to obtain affidavits in confirmation of my evidence, so that the truth of it cannot be doubted.—I am yours faithfully,

A. M. ALEXANDER.

Mr. HARRIS, of Walhalla, who seems to take a special interest in the affairs of the Claimant, has sent us the following letter for publication:—

Dry Creek, Red Jacket: 11th Sept., 1874.

To MR. HARRIS,—Sir, It is a very easy thing to call people fools and fanatics who differ from the verdict arrived at by the jury in the TICHBORNE Case, as some celebrated personages are in the habit of doing; but perhaps they are more to be pitied than blamed. Might I remind these well-informed persons that to make good the assertion before referred to is another thing. I know this, that twenty verdicts could not make me believe that ROGER TICHBORNE was at the bottom of the sea in 1854, when I conversed with him for days together in 1855. This is no case of mistaken identity; for allowing for the sake of argument that the two men are alike (which *I* deny), in 1855 ROGER must have been at least 26 years of age, and ORTON about 20, a mere boy; and ORTON must not only have seized ROGER TICHBORNE's face and limbs, but also his mind, since he conversed with me respecting his family, and their treatment of him. Especially did he tell me about Lady DOUGHTY. How could ORTON do this? Now, ROGER would not have talked like this had he not been drinking; but ORTON could not have talked upon these subjects, either drunk or sober, because he knew nothing about it in 1855. If my examination ever takes place, it will form the sensation part of the most sensational Case that has ever been known. I can easily believe, that to stand in the witness-box, with Judges as well as Counsel against one, would be anything but enviable; still, the frightful fate of this unhappy man urges me on in the endeavour to save him. Let us hope in the end that the justice of our cause will triumph, though baulked at present.—I am, Sir, yours respectfully,

A. M. ALEXANDER.

MR. GLADSTONE.

The following correspondence between Mr. ONSLOW and Mr. GLADSTONE shows two things very plainly; first, that those who prosecuted the Claimant are determined to close their ears to all inquiry into the grave question as to whether or not an innocent man is unjustly condemned; and, secondly, shows how true it is that courtesy and civility to an old and faithful political supporter does not exist in the minds of the late Ministry, the want of which drove away so many adherents to the Liberal party, and eventually caused its disruption.

MY DEAR MR. GLADSTONE,—I feel most anxious to see you, and shall esteem it the greatest favour if you will kindly grant me an interview at Hawarden Castle, on a day and hour most convenient to yourself, and allow me to introduce the Rev. Mr. —— ——, the brother of the lady whose letters and statutory declaration I had the pleasure of forwarding to you some months ago, in reference to the TICHBORNE Case. Mr. —— is well known to Mr. SAMUEL MORLEY, the Member for Bristol, and Mr. STANSFELD, M.P., and was the gentleman appointed to move the vote of confidence in Sir CHARLES WOOD and Mr. STANSFELD at Halifax, and was the intimate friend of the late Sir FRANCIS CROSSLEY, also the author of the Commentary on the New Testament, in five volumes, specially recommended by several of the Bishops and the organs of the Church of England. I feel sure the importance of the communication we wish to impart will be sufficient excuse for the

liberty I have taken, and for the request I have ventured to urge. —I remain, yours faithfully, GUILDFORD ONSLOW.
The Grove, Ropley, Alresford, Hants: Sept. 5, 1874.
To the Right Hon. WILLIAM EWART GLADSTONE, M.P., Hawarden Castle.

DEAR MR. ONSLOW,—I found on the 26th your letter of the 7th, which had remained here during my absence in Germany.

I regret that, had I received it at the proper time, it would not have been in my power to enter orally on the consideration of the TICHBORNE Case.

Indeed, my private and personal engagements, long neglected to fulfil my public obligations, are in such arrear, that I must at present endeavour to devote my time to disposing of them.—I remain, very faithfully yours, W. E. GLADSTONE.
Hawarden Castle, Chester: September 28th, 1874.

MY DEAR MR. GLADSTONE,—I beg to thank you for your letter of the 28th of September, and to express my deep regret to find by it that you refuse to grant me an interview at Hawarden Castle. Truth and Justice demanded it, independent of that act of courtesy I had a right to expect at your hands after the correspondence that has passed between us.—I beg to remain, yours faithfully, GUILDFORD ONSLOW.
The Grove, Ropley, Alresford, Hants: October 2nd, 1874.
To the Right Hon. WILLIAM EWART GLADSTONE, M.P.: Hawarden Castle, Flintshire.

31, Charles-street, Fitzroy, near Melbourne, Australia, June 15th, 1874.

SIR,—I have the honour to acknowledge the receipt of your letter of 19th March last, informing me of Sir ROGER TICHBORNE being convicted as being "ARTHUR ORTON," and sentenced to fourteen years' penal servitude. I have been unable to see or hear from Mr. DEAKIN up to this date, but have read my declaration as appears in full in *Reynolds's Newspaper*, Sunday, 5th April, 1874, page 2, and am prepared to substantiate on oath all herein contained. With regard to there being no records able to be produced relative to the Case alluded to in my declaration, I, at one time being an officer stationed there (Castlemaine), can easily explain.

I saw Mr. JEUNE, the barrister, who came from England, at Mr. ALPORT's office, and stated what I knew of him, but he, in my opinion, overlooked my evidence, especially when I offered to accompany him to Castlemaine and Sale, in order to corroborate what I stated. I gave him all particulars, and, apparently, when here or elsewhere, he made no use whatever of it.

Mr. ALPORT showed me the photograph of Sir ROGER TICHBORNE as forwarded from England, and *I am confident* that it is *not one* of "ARTHUR ORTON," the party alluded to by me, *but is that of* "TOMAS CASTRO."

I have personally seen Mr. MICHELL, whom I believe you have communicated with, and consulted with him on the matter, and he is using every endeavour to find out ARTHUR ORTON if possible. Mr. DEAKIN, when he called at my house the last time, informed me "that he was present in court at Castlemaine, when CASTRO and ORTON were charged with horse stealing," and that he had made a similar declaration as myself on the subject. As to the amount I shall require to come to England, not that I require the means for that purpose, but taking into consideration having to leave my business and family for such a lengthy period, I could not do so under £500.

I am confident were some one appointed here to receive funds for any movement in the matter, it would be a success, as numbers are yet of opinion that the Claimant is wrongly convicted. I myself would willingly give £5 5s. towards it, believing him innocent.

I forward you a photograph of myself, should you feel disposed to accept it, which may hereafter be of use in this terrible Case.

Judge NOEL, who certified to me and my declarations, is now in England, on leave, and reference that may be required I submit to him. In conclusion, as to printing this, or any portion of it, I would most willingly leave it to your own judgment, and still further be only too glad to do anything in my power to assist you. —I have the honour to be, Sir, your most obedient servant, W. H. LOCK.
To GUILDFORD ONSLOW, Esq., M.P., Ropley, Alresford, Hants.

THE REV. WILLIAM BUCKINGHAM TO THE RIGHT HON. JOHN BRIGHT, M.P.

SIR,—I must apologize, as a perfect stranger, for troubling you with another letter. I am not, as you have been, a minister of our most gracious Majesty, but I am a humble minister of the King of kings, and to the best of my ability I preach His gospel. I read in the Birmingham newspaper a correspondence between Mr. MEREDITH and yourself, on the TICHBORNE Case, and as I am a lover of truth and justice, and from your life I believe you are, I think it my duty to inform you that that poor man in prison, condemned to fourteen years' penal servitude as ARTHUR ORTON, and from whom you withhold your sympathy, is not, nor can be by any possibility be, that person.

I was well acquainted with ARTHUR ORTON for many years at Wapping; and in my letter I informed you I pierced his ears with my own hands, and put in his earrings.

I was also present with Mr. INGRAM, my co-missionary, the person before named, when I saw a woman of the town, in a street brawl, cut off the top of ARTHUR ORTON's little finger. I have seen and spoken to the prisoner in Millbank; he has no holes in his ears, and the tips of his fingers are perfect; all the sophistry and argument in the world cannot make him ARTHUR ORTON.

I say there is no resemblance to him; be he who he may, he is not ARTHUR ORTON, which I solemnly declare before my Heavenly Father, and before the world—before the tribunal we are all hastening to. I would venture to ask you whether sympathy, therefore, is not due to the unfortunate person now unjustly suffering in the prison in Millbank?—I remain truly yours,
The Limes, Plaistow, Essex. W. BUCKINGHAM.

THE "OSPREY."

Illustrated Australian News, Feb. 25th, 1874.

The following addition to the already voluminous pages of Tichborniana, which only comes to light at the eleventh hour, will be read with interest. It is furnished by the *Ballarat Courier*:—"An old resident of Ballarat has been called upon to supply some information in the interminable TICHBORNE Case. By the last mail from England Mr. WILLIAM BARDWELL, photographer, of Sturt-street, received a letter from Mr. ONSLOW, M.P., asking for an accurate account of the now famous three-masted schooner "Osprey," which arrived in Melbourne in July, 1854, and on board of which the Claimant asserts he reached this colony, after being shipwrecked. During the evidence of EDWARD GODRICH, taken at the trial on 22nd October of last year, that witness deposed to having been asked by Mr. BARDWELL, in Melbourne, in 1854, to subscribe to a fund which he (Mr. BARDWELL) was then raising for the relief of some ten or twelve men, who had been rescued at sea by the "Osprey," and brought on by that vessel to Hobson's Bay. Accordingly, Mr. ONSLOW is anxious to learn all that Mr. BARDWELL knows of this matter. What Mr. BARDWELL does know of it is the following:—In 1853, 1854, and 1855, he was manager for Messrs. THROCKMORTON and Co., shipping agents, of Melbourne. The "Osprey" arrived in 1854, with a number of persons on board who had been picked up at sea by that vessel. Messrs. THROCKMORTON and Co. purchased the "Osprey," and cut her down to a lighter. In the meantime they suggested to Mr. BARDWELL the desirability of raising a subscription for the shipwrecked persons, and he did so. At that time GODRICH, the witness mentioned above, was a clerk in the same establishment. He was also a shipmate of Mr. BARDWELL's, the two having arrived in Melbourne the previous year from New York, on board of the "Lady Arabella." Mr. BARDWELL cannot distinguish one of the shipwrecked men from the other, but he is quite clear as to the three-masted schooner "Osprey" having reached Melbourne in 1854, having a number of such men on board. Mr. BARDWELL will supply Mr. ONSLOW, M.P., with the above facts by the outgoing mail steamer, as also inform him that Mr. THROCKMORTON is now settled in Sydney, and can furnish him with all details. Documentary evidence in support of the above facts can also be obtained from the books of the late firm, which are now in possession of a Melbourne official assignee, if they have not been destroyed. This evidence will reach London too late to be of any use to the Claimant in the Trial now pending, as in all human probability it will then have closed. But perhaps other proceedings are contemplated when that part of the TICHBORNE Case has been brought to a termination."

The following is from Mr. BARDWELL to GUILDFORD ONSLOW, Esq.

Short-street, Ballarat, Australia: Feb., 1874.

SIR,—In 1853, 1854, and 1855, I was manager for Messrs. THROCKMORTON and Co., shipping agents, of Melbourne. The "Osprey" arrived in 1854 with a number of persons on board, who had been picked up at sea by that vessel. Messrs. THROCKMORTON and Co. purchased the "Osprey," and cut her down to a lighter, and they suggested to me the desirability of raising a subscription for the shipwrecked persons, and I did so. At that time GODRICH, the witness mentioned in your letter, was a clerk in the same establishment, and was a shipmate of mine, he and I having arrived in Melbourne the previous year from New York, on board the "Lady Arabella."—Your obedient servant,
WILLIAM BARDWELL, Photographer.

Finally, so that no present proof may be absent of the strength of evidence on this matter of the "Osprey," we reprint from the ENGLISHMAN of October 24, the following:—

LETTERS FROM AUSTRALIA ON THE TICHBORNE CASE.

FROM MR. JAMES SMITH.

DEAR SIR,—I received yours of July 15th, 1874, relative to the "Osprey" and TICHBORNE Case, and in reply I beg leave to forward you what I know about them, and if called upon I shall speak the truth. In the first place, I know nothing at all about either TICHBORNE or ORTON; I have never seen either them or their likeness to my knowledge; but with regard to the vessel "Osprey," I may perhaps be able to give you some information that may be useful. In the year 1854, I arrived from New Zealand in a barque named the "Bellacreo"; we anchored in Hobson's Bay, and remained on board for three days; on the third day we were paid off on board by Captain HEFFERMAN. On the second morning after our arrival in Hobson's Bay, at 8 a.m., there was anchored alongside of us a three-masted schooner painted black, her name painted in gilt letters on her stern, which was a round one—"Osprey;" clean scraped masts, very rakish, about 400 or 500 tons; what her cargo consisted of I do not know, or if she discharged it in Melbourne; or how long she remained in Hobson's Bay, I am not in a position to state, as I did not visit Hobson's Bay for some time afterwards; at 8 a.m. she hoisted the American flag at the peak. On the third day, having received our wages, our ship's boat put myself and three more ashore at Williamstown. I waited there for the steamer from Melbourne, and during that time a boat came ashore from the schooner "Osprey" with a number of men on board; I distinctly saw the name "Osprey" on the boat's stern. Upon the arrival at Williamstown of the steamer from Melbourne (I think the "Comet"), I went on board, and at the same time six or seven of the men who came on shore in the "Osprey's" boat, went on board the steamer to go to Melbourne; during our passage up the river Jarra Jarra, I had a long conversation with some of the men from the "Osprey's" boat. They distinctly told me that they had been shipwrecked, that their vessel had sunk, that they had to take to their boats with what they stood up in, and after a great deal of suffering and hardships, they had been picked up by the schooner "Osprey" and brought to Melbourne. Upon our arrival at the wharf, Melbourne, we parted company, and I have neither seen nor heard of any of the said men since. I forgot to mention that on board the "Osprey" there was a black dog. Such a length of time having elapsed, I cannot speak accurately as to dates, but I can positively swear that the said "Osprey" arrived in Melbourne in the year 1854, about two months previous to the Ballarat riot.

I believe evidence has been given that no vessel entered Hobson's Bay without a police or Customs boat boarding her. I know that to be false; for when we arrived in the "Ballaereo," carrying mail from Wellington, New Zealand, we had a flag hoisted at the fore for two days before they came for our mail, and neither police, health, or any boat except the butcher's, boarded us. I may, perhaps, be able to remember other events that happened when I tax my memory; if so I shall forward it to you, let it be ever so trivial, for trifles might turn the scales of Justice in the prisoner's favour.—Allow me, dear sir, to remain yours truly,

James Smith,
Shaving Point, July 29th, 1874.

To Mr. Robert Shanklin, Sale.

STATUTORY DECLARATION OF MR. CLARKE.

I, John James Clarke, at present residing at Bernly-street, Richmond, Melbourne, in the colony of Victoria, Australia, herewith make oath and do solemnly swear to the following facts:—That I personally knew and worked with one, Arthur Orton, butcher, groom, &c., during the many months he was on my late father's (Mr. Duncan Clarke, of the Royal Exchange, Raymond-street, Sale, North Gippsland) employ, then as a groom and breaker-in of horses; that I have frequently seen the waxwork figures of the Claimant in Bourke-street, Melbourne; have seen the profile in Dr. Kenealy's publication called the Englishman, and moreover have likewise been shown in Mr. Robert Shanklin's surgery, Sale, the illustrated and pictorial record of the Tichborne family, and do most positively assert and swear that, according to my knowledge and the best of my belief, there is not the *slightest* trace or likeness between the late Claimant to the Tichborne Estates, and the groom, &c., known as Arthur Orton, who was in my late father's employ.—Witness my hand this

John James Clarke.

Declared before me, at Sale, this 29th day of July, 1874,
George Ross, J.P., Sale, Gippsland.

STATEMENT OF W. CRUICKSHANK, Esq.

I, William Cruickshank, of Sandridge, make the following statement, which Mr. Michel has taken down. At the time in question, during the winter, about July or August, for I remember well it was a white frost in the morning, I kept a large outfitting store for sailors at Sandridge, and, amongst other things, sold large numbers of sailors' oil-skin suits. A person of the name of John Leitchfield kept a sailors' boarding-house three doors from my store, and I recollect well the arrival of six persons, sailors, and one gentleman, the wrecked men of the "Bella." For these men a subscription was got up. They remained in Sandridge for upwards of a fortnight waiting for a fresh ship. During this period I saw them and spoke to them repeatedly, and also to the gentleman, whom they treated with great respect, and who was undoubtedly Sir Roger. In those days much liquor was knocking about, and I always gave some to my customers. Sir Roger, as I shall call him, lodged at the same house as the sailors, and had little money. He used often at night to come and sit by my fire, and talk about England and other matters. He was a perfect gentleman in manners, and I recollect well he told me he came from Hampshire, or the West of England. He was rather reserved, but was fond of his glass, and would then inveigh against the hollowness of society. I at first doubted some of his assertions, but the sailors told me he was a very rich gentleman of England, so then I believed him. I saw the ship that picked these men up. She was a vessel with very rakish masts, but I have no recollection of her name. I also saw her captain in my place talking to Sir Roger. About this time three more sailors of the "Bella" also arrived; that is to say, the cook and two others. They were brought by another ship, who picked them up, and, I imagine, landed them at Melbourne Wharf, up the river Yarra. The vessel which saved these three men went somewhere else, I imagine to Hobart Town, and they came over in some small craft. These might be the men mentioned by Longland, in page 89 of Mr. Onslow's book. However, hearing that their mates had got a ship, they applied, and were accepted as men in the same ship. Thus eight men shipped, leaving only Sir Roger and the cook. Previous to their departure, they were all fitted out with oil-skin coats at my shop, and Sir Roger himself gave each man an order on his friends in England £20 a man, as a remembrance for saving his life. He wrote the orders in my shop, at my desk. Not one of these men ever reached home, as the ship with all hands was lost. I am in a position to prove the shipping of these men, and the name of the ship they sailed in, and that the ship was lost, but do not choose to do so at present, as I consider my secret valuable. The shipping registry will, of course, give the names of the crew. The story of the wreck as told by the sailors and Sir Roger was, that the vessel being on the point of foundering, the six with Sir Roger got into the long boat, which would hold no more, and one of the sailors jumped into the sea and seized hold of the boat to be taken in, upon which one of those in the boat cut off his fingers to make him let go, and he sank and was drowned. They then pulled away, abandoning the others. Their sufferings were frightful, till at last it was decided to cast lots who should be killed and eaten, but finally it was agreed that the casting of lots should be postponed for two days, and the next day they were picked up in a frightful state. The rest remained on board some short time longer, and got in then into the little boat called the captain's gig. They remained near till they saw the "Bella" go down. I cannot swear it, but I think they said the captain was drowned. Some bad feeling existed amongst the new arrivals and their mates, in consequence of cutting off the fingers of their mate and drowning him, which ended, one night when they were drunk, in a fight in which knives were drawn. I interfered, and one of the men stabbed at me, only, however, piercing my clothes, for which I knocked him down and beat him till I nearly killed him. The cook was the only man who did not ship, and he and Sir Roger left my place together to proceed, as he said, up the country. Therefore that cook is the only man in the world who can tell what happened to Sir Roger. I have frequently spoken about this matter to several persons for some years past, and I was much surprised and annoyed at Mr. Jeune taking so little notice of what I had to say, and referring me to Mr. Allport, the Attorney.

The cook was a stout-built man, and had an animosity against Sir Roger, in my opinion, because they had saved him, and drowned the sailor. At least that was my impression.

Sir Roger, when I saw him, was in his perfect senses, in spite of his previous sufferings. Unfortunately, all my shop books and entries were burnt by a fire two years afterwards, else the ledger would prove these sales.

The evidence given at the Trial at Bar on this question of the "Osprey" may be said to have conclusively established Tichborne's narrative. The following may be read with the present, and with that evidence, as testimony which was ready, but which Mr. MacMahon, for some reason, dissuaded the Attorney from calling. Dr. Kenealy recently learned that the witness whose proof follows was ready in Court; but he did not know of it then or he would have called him:—

Evidence of William Brougham Penny, 11, Bradley's-terrace, Wandsworth-road.

Was in Melbourne in the year 1854. Remembers a vessel called the "Osprey" arriving at Melbourne in July, 1854. Saw some of the crew of the "Osprey," and conversed with them. They told Penny they had picked up a boat belonging to the "Bella," the other side of Cape Horn, and that they had brought this boat's crew into Melbourne.

He does not remember how many the boat's crew consisted of. Some of the crew of the "Osprey" went to the Diggings, and Penny thinks all the boat's crew of the "Bella" went.

It was a very common thing for people on going to the diggings or bush to change their names. Penny did it himself when he went to the diggings, and no one there knew his name.

Penny, during the time he was there, lost both his writing and spelling to a great degree. Has resided in Bradley's-terrace, in business as a draper, nine years; was abroad nearly seven years.

TICHBORNE IN AUSTRALIA.

The following letter was received by Mr. Onslow, on the 6th September, from Mr. George Ross, the Mayor of Sale, Gippsland, Australia, and Justice of the Peace:—

My Recollections of Matters affecting Tichborne and Orton.

I came to Sale, Gippsland, in April, 1858; have been engaged as storekeeper there continuously since. I entered into partnership with another, who was resident there some three or four years before me, who died in 1860; the name of Castro was there common as that of a man who had been stock-keeping on the Dargo Station. I several times spoke to my partner regarding him, especially in 1859, when this individual (Castro) made a tour through the district. I have a distinct recollection of his telling me he was a Baronet's son, and was passing under an assumed name; that his mother was either a Spanish or a French lady, and that he took the name of his friends. This same Castro left Sale about 1856 or 1857.

I knew A. Orton personally; he came to Sale about 1859, and was ostler at the Royal Exchange Hotel. He came to Sale, either from Boisdale Station or Mewburn Park Station, and either was engaged as a butcher, or was known as the "Butcher"; he may have remained in Sale eighteen months or two years. I do not know what became of him afterwards; *I am positive the two men were here, and engaged as I say.* Notwithstanding all that has been said or written, I always maintained the above; and, although I cannot follow either of them past the time of their leaving here, I firmly believe TICHBORNE is CASTRO.

Sale was known then as Flodding Creek, and it is a notorious fact that on the day a large portion of the township was put up to auction in Melbourne, there were purchasers in the room waiting till the Flodding Creek lots should come on for sale while the Sale lots were put up and purchased before them, without their knowing it; they being sold as Sale lots, while expecting them to be called Flodding Creek lots.

My partner's name was ALEXANDRA DAVIES; he came to Sale to manage the new store business for CROMBIE, CLAPPERTON & Co.

This is my principal point. I have a distinct recollection of my partner coming in one day, I think in 1859, and mentioning to me that he had just been across the way, having a nobbler with CASTRO, and his then repeating that he was a Baronet's son from England. TICHBORNE's statement in his defence that he made a tour through the district is thus borne out.

When one of the Commissions, taking evidence in Sale, showed their photographs to Mr. JOHN JAMES ENGLISH, of Sale, he recognized TICHBORNE's likeness as that of one he had a conversation of about an hour's duration with, the subject being South America; *this* Mr. ENGLISH mentioned to me *at the time.*

I had no recollection of his tour through the district, and insisted it must have been a mistake, as CASTRO must have left here, I said, in 1856 or 1857, whereas Mr. ENGLISH did not come to Sale until 1858. He was positive then, however, of the identity. When I saw the evidence from England, and that the Claimant said he made a tour through the district, I reminded Mr. ENGLISH of our previous conversation, and any objection to my mind was thus more than coincided.

The Claimant's answers as to the SADDLERS, SAYER, and BRAY

PORTRAIT OF JAMES CARTER.

and others, were correct. SAYER and BRAY came to Sale in 1858, consequently he could have no acquaintance then with such a question; however, it would be a trap for ORTON, as they were together.

From sheer curiosity I examined the books kept on the Boisdale Station, as I knew the names of the servants, and would be likely to spot out any payment made to CASTRO. I scrutinised every line, and could not find a single entry of the kind. I considered this against my theory; but, on consideration, a few days after, I made a second scrutiny, the object being to discover whether payments to the servants at Dargo were entered in the books, going over them every item as before. *I then found there is not a single payment to the servants on the Dargo Station entered in those books;* consequently believe *they are no records of the Dargo Station at all;* and the evidence has not the advantage of being so much as of a negative character. Only one or two lines refer to the Dargo Station, and that is in the examination of stock: so many head at Dargo, and so many on each of three or four other stations.

If ROGER was drowned in the "Bella," where did ORTON get his information? Some say BOGLE; if so, BOGLE must have gone to him in the first instance. Believe this who can.—Yours truly,

Sale: 8th July, 1871. GEORGE ROSS, Justice of the Peace.

P.S.—I have no interest in this matter; my mind is biassed in favour of the Claimant for the reasons given. If I can be of any service I shall be very glad.

GEORGE ROSS, J.P., Sale, Gippsland.

Surely the information conveyed to the Public in these pages, by so many disinterested witnesses, demands inquiry.

The Lord Chief Justice, Sir A. COCKBURN, admitted that he had once condemned an innocent man to penal servitude; may he not have committed a similar error in the case of the Claimant?

We supplement the whole of this important episode with a

letter from one of TICHBORNE's former Counsel. We have reason to think that his opinion is still unchanged.

The writer, Mr. KARSLAKE, Q.C., is an eminent member of the Chancery Bar, and brother of the late Attorney-General:—

Lincoln's Inn: Oct. 18th, 1872.

TICHBORNE V. LUSHINGTON.

DEAR SIRS,—I noticed in the *Times* last week a letter written by you, from which it appears that this case will be fixed in the course of next month.

I have been Counsel for the Claimant in Chancery since the case was first launched there, but as it has now left Equity for ever, except, perhaps, on some little formal matters, I have no delicacy in expressing my opinion upon the merits, as I have no bias, not even that of a Counsel (if a Counsel ever has any in the matter), up to a certain point, at least. I have studied the evidence so carefully that I may almost say I know it by heart, and I have no hesitation in saying that *I am as firmly and clearly convinced that the Claimant is the real man as I am that the person writing these lines is the person who signs them.*

The Case (one of the most extraordinary and most romantic ever brought before an English Court) is so full of difficulties that justice may possibly make default. This is the extreme improbability of the Claimant's case. But even if he fails, my opinion will remain the same.

I write you these lines because I know you will have plenty of difficulties to encounter in getting up your Case, and it may not be wholly unimportant to some of those with whom you come in contact to know that a Q.C. who has been in large practice for more than twenty years, having not a particle of interest in the result, entertains not the slightest doubt as to the justice of your client's Case.

You can, of course, show this letter to anyone. Believe me yours truly, (Signed) E. K. KARSLAKE.

Messrs. BAXTER and Co.

A more powerful accumulation of evidence upon any matter than this upon the subject of the "Osprey" was probably never known: but the jury on the First as well as the Second Trial, treated it with scorn.

Before we pass from it, and Mr. GRAY's remarkable expression of incredulity, we think it well to insert from the ENGLISHMAN for January 30, 1875, the following notice of the death of Mr. GRAY, which occurred about the middle of that month.

MR. JOHN GRAY, Q.C.

We read with regret of the death of Mr. JOHN GRAY, Q.C., Solicitor to the Treasury. Under him the TICHBORNE prosecution was conducted; but we believe he was too honest to acquiesce in, or to approve of many of the things that were done in that Trial. When he entered upon it, he was a hale and hearty man: day by day, as fraud accumulated upon fraud, he grew paler and thinner: and he was evidently disgusted at the work that he was compelled to witness and to go through. When Dr. KENEALY once asked him, as an old friend, to let him have a copy of an Index to the Cross-examination of the Claimant, which had been compiled at the public expense, and which, being an Index, and only that, would have greatly lightened the Doctor's labours, while it would in no way have injured the Prosecution, both he and Serjeant PARRY at once promised; but, subsequently, under the advice of HAWKINS, the promise was broken. Dr. KENEALY remonstrated with Mr. GRAY, pointing out how greatly it would help him, in his unparalleled difficulties, explaining at the same time how much he needed it, as he had no Brief, and had not had time to read over one-tenth of the Papers and printed Volumes, which had been thrust upon him in a mass, a few weeks only before the Trial. He offered also to pay for a copy of the Index. Mr. GRAY, who had been always on the most friendly terms with the Doctor, sighed, and said pathetically: "Ah! KENEALY, *you wouldn't press me, if you knew what I had to contend with.*" We have no doubt he had awful difficulties to contend with. We believe the Case killed him, as it killed BOVILL. It destroyed the first, because his natural honesty rebelled against what he was forced to assent to; it broke down the second, because the little remnant of conscience that he had, perpetually reminded him of his guilt.

We resume our narrative of the Claimant's further progress through the nation, and of the various Meetings which he attended. In August we find

SIR ROGER AT LEEDS.

The meeting in support of the Claimant to the Tichborne Estates and Baronetage took place in the Victoria Hall, Town Hall, on Thursday night, and was attended by about 2,000 persons. The Claimant and his friends were driven to the hall in an open carriage, with four greys and outriders. As on previous evenings, large and enthusiastic crowds had assembled to witness the progress of the party through the streets. Mr. JOY, Chairman of the local Defence Committee, again presided in the Victoria Hall.

The Chairman wished to tell the large and respectable audience before him that one great object of the Committee was to afford the public of Leeds an opportunity of hearing the Claimant for themselves. (Hear, hear.) He acknowledged the services of the *Express* in giving publicity to the proceedings of the Claimant in Leeds. (Cheers.) For the Claimant they only asked justice. (Cheers.) He condemned the conduct of Chief Justice BOVILL and the Attorney-General, and argued that the law officers of the Crown ought not to be permitted to undertake private cases. He then asked the audience whether they approved of the Government finding money for the prosecution of Sir ROGER. (Loud cries of "No, no.") He hoped the People would exercise the influence they possessed in this matter wisely and justly, and that the right would prevail. (Loud applause.)

Mr. E. FOSTER said it gave him unfeigned pleasure to see such a large assembly before him. He would not take up much of their time, but he had a resolution to move, namely: "That this meeting desires to tender its best thanks to Lord RIVERS, GUILDFORD ONSLOW, Esq., M.P., W. STREETON, Esq., and Dr. ATTWOOD, for becoming responsible to the Government for Sir ROGER TICHBORNE's appearance at the forthcoming Trial. Further, this meeting desires to express its strongest objection to any of the public money being spent in the prosecution of Sir ROGER TICHBORNE." Mr. FOSTER then proceeded to criticise the treatment the Claimant was receiving at the hands of the Press. He pronounced strong censure upon the *Leeds Mercury* and *Yorkshire Post*, and spoke in most eulogistic terms of the *Express*, pointing out that but for the *Express* the proceedings and enthusiasm of the enormous gatherings they were holding would have passed almost unrecorded. (Applause.) He also acknowledged the reports of the meeting of Monday and Tuesday which had appeared in the *Bradford Observer*. He then affirmed that the man whom infamous prints had so cruelly wronged was Sir ROGER TICHBORNE. (Loud cheers.) In asking for the Tichborne Estates he was simply asking for his own. (Applause.) Sir ROGER had, however, married a lady who did not belong to the aristocracy, and thus, they said, had brought discredit upon his order. ("Oh, oh," and "That's it.") That was the simple reason why he was being robbed of his property. (Applause.) Our laws were made to protect our rights and liberties, but in this instance they had been prostituted to deprive that man [pointing to the Claimant] of his rights and his liberties. (Loud applause.) CROMWELL used to say, "Trust in GOD and keep your powder dry." (Hear, hear.) He (Mr. FOSTER) would say to Sir ROGER TICHBORNE, "Trust in GOD and the People, and if your cause is just it shall prevail, and all shall yet be well with you." (Loud applause.)

Mr. GREENWOOD, master tailor in the regiment to which Sir ROGER TICHBORNE belonged, seconded the motion. He described the circumstances under which he had identified the Claimant as the self-same gentleman he had known as Mr. ROGER TICHBORNE. When he had gone to "interview" him, he provided himself with an old order-book, which he had previously looked over to see what work he had done for Sir ROGER. He was convinced that the Claimant was that gentleman before he had been in his company more than a few minutes; yet after he was satisfied he tested him severely with questions. He asked him nothing about regimental dress, but got him to tell him of certain specialities he had made for him. Without hesitation, he told the speaker that he had made him a pea jacket, and that was right. (Cheers.) He also, unprompted, told him of a scarlet hunting coat he had made for him, with H. H. (Hampshire Hunt) on the buttons; and that was right. (Cheers.) He then told Sir ROGER that there was another garment he had made for him: could he tell him what it was? and after a little consideration, he said, "GREENWOOD, didn't you make that drab driving coat which I wore when I was driving a tandem?" He (GREENWOOD) said, "You are right." (Loud cheers.) He then gave to the audience a number of particulars as to the identification of the Claimant as Sir ROGER by Sir ROGER TICHBORNE's servants. He also said that he never saw any tattoo marks about Mr. ROGER TICHBORNE, although he considered that few persons were so likely to have done so if he had any.

The Claimant then rose to address the meeting, and was greeted with rounds of cheers. He said that as he had entered the hall he had heard some one hiss. He would ask that man, if he thought that to hiss a man who was only seeking fair-play was English? (Hear, hear.) He had not come to Leeds to prove his identity, but to ask for fair-play, and he hoped there was no Englishman unwilling to help him to secure that. (Cheers.) He then read a number of extracts from letters which had appeared in the *Yorkshire Post*, which elicited from the audience cries of "Shame."

In regard to one statement in the *Post*, that in speaking he put the letter "h" to words with which it had no connection, which was "Cockneyism," he affirmed that it was a fault of Hampshire people, whilst "Cockneys" were well known to be mostly in the habit of dropping the "h" so that if using the "h" too frequently proved anything, it proved that he was not a "Cockney," but a Hampshire man. (Applause.)

Having condemned the Attorney-General for his want of courtesy, he charged him with intimidating the jury, for he had said to them, after the Case had been going on for 100 days, "I have 260 more witnesses to call yet if this Case goes on." The jury took alarm; in fact, they showed themselves to be cowards, and thereby threw £120,000 of his (Claimant's) money away. (Cheers, and "Shame.") The Attorney-General had said, "I don't say he is ARTHUR ORTON. Oh, no. But he is not Sir ROGER TICHBORNE." Yet a fortnight after the Trial, that gentleman told the Prime Minister that he could prove him to be ARTHUR ORTON in twenty minutes. ("Shame.") He then stated that his opponents had, at various times, held him to be all the following different persons: —1, JOHN MOORE; 2, a man who was servant at Tichborne to Sir E. DOUGHTY; 3, a man named SMITH, son of an old servant; 4, an old servant of Mr. JAMES TICHBORNE in Paris; 5, an old servant named COLES; 6, a man who was Sir ROGER CHARLES TICHBORNE's servant in the Carabineers; 7, an old Carabineer soldier; 8, a sailor from Poole; 9, JOHN CASE, a native of Poole; 10, an illegitimate son of a former TICHBORNE; 11, an illegitimate son of Sir EDWARD DOUGHTY; 12, an illegitimate son of Mr. ROBERT TICHBORNE; 13, an illegitimate son of Sir HENRY TICHBORNE; 14, the son of a woman in Australia, who was coming to identify him; 15, an Australian navvy; 16, an Australian prize fighter; 17, an Australian native; 18, EDWARD ORTON; 19, HENRY ORTON; 20, ARTHUR ORTON; 21, an illegitimate son of Dowager Lady TICHBORNE before marriage; 22, GEORGE JARVIS, a man who had sailed from Liverpool; and many other persons. He gave a humorous account of the attempts made to induce Mrs. CASE to believe that the Claimant was her son, but the old lady, after gazing at him through her spectacles for an hour, declared that he bore no resemblance whatever to her son DAVID.

He alluded to existing testimony in his favour, and said he had faced 500 people who had known him thirteen years before, and either they had gone mad, or he must be superhuman. (Applause.) Before concluding, he stated that Mr. ONSLOW, M.P., had already advanced to him the sum of £3,000, and he could not expect him to advance more. He was, however, working most strenuously in his behalf. (Cheers.)

In reply to a question, the Claimant stated that he and Mr. BAIGENT were as good friends as ever, but the latter had been completely broken down in health and spirits since the Trial.

Sergt.-Major MARKS and Mr. P. BARRY, both of whom served under Mr. ROGER TICHBORNE, testified that the gentleman on the platform was the same ROGER CHARLES TICHBORNE they had known in the army.

The resolution was then carried unanimously, and the proceedings terminated with cheers for the *Express* and the Chairman.

Yorkshire did not rest here. It sent a copy of the following letter to every Member of the House of Commons:—

Leeds, August 6th, 1872.

SIR,—We have the honour to call your attention to the agitation now going on with respect to the Claimant to the Tichborne Estates. Public meetings have been held in the Victoria Hall, Leeds, on four consecutive nights; and, although a charge was made for admission, on each occasion the hall was crowded, and the Claimant and his friends received a most enthusiastic welcome. The number of people present could not have been fewer than ten or twelve thousand; and, on each night, resolutions expressing a firm conviction in the Claimant's identity with Sir ROGER TICHBORNE, condemning the conduct of the Attorney-General, and calling upon the Government not to spend the public money in this prosecution, were unanimously passed.

The reception given to the Claimant outside was of the most enthusiastic description. The streets and squares, and every available space where a glimpse of the persecuted man could be had, were densely packed with people connected with almost all classes of society, who, by waving of handkerchiefs, cheers, and almost by every conceivable method, showed their sympathy with him, and their abhorrence of the methods which are being adopted in order to crush him. Such enormous gatherings, such enthusiasm, such unanimity, were never before witnessed in Leeds. Now Leeds is the capital of the West Riding of Yorkshire, and, we believe, represents the views and feelings of a vast majority of the entire County on this question. The minds of the people are agitated and gloomy, and we would entreat you, as one of the representatives of the people, to watch this TICHBORNE question, and to take heed to the mutterings of the approaching storm.

The British people will not allow one of their number to be sent to gaol without cause, to have his character slandered and vilified, and his estates withheld from him at the instigation of any official, however high or unscrupulous he may be. They will insist that the decisions of their Judges and juries shall be based upon fact and evidence, and not upon falsehood and assumption, nor on the speeches of Counsel paid and retained in order to bewilder and mislead. The results of the late Trial have alarmed most thoughtful Englishmen, and have made this nation the laughing-stock of the world. A firm conviction has taken hold of the public mind, that the Claimant has been the victim of a foul conspiracy, and has not had a fair Trial. A movement is now on foot which it would be dangerous to ignore. It is daily, and we may say hourly, acquiring fresh force, and will never cease until the chief actors in this conspiracy are discovered and punished, and restitution be made to the man who has been so cruelly robbed both of his honour and his inheritance.

We have entered on a crusade, and we shall never lay down our arms until justice is done, and the honour of the nation satisfied.

Trusting you will give this important question your most serious consideration, we have the honour, on behalf of the Leeds TICHBORNE Defence Committee, to remain, your obedient servants,

J. R. JOY, Chairman;
EDWARD FOSTER, Secretary;
RICHARD WALKER, Treasurer;
W. J. DIXON, Member of Committee.

The House of Commons treated this manly and dignified remonstrance with contempt. Everyone in that honourable assembly seemed mad or blind.

SIR ROGER AT BIRMINGHAM.

Sir ROGER's reception by the people of justice-loving Birmingham surpassed all others given him in the provinces. Notwithstanding that the press almost unanimously cried down him and his cause, and laid themselves open to several libel suits, his reception at the station will never be forgotten by him or those present. It was by sheer manœuvring, and great presence of mind, that his supporters were able to get him to his hotel without his being dragged there in the carriage awaiting him. We are glad to see that the men of Birmingham, ever ready to fight in a just cause, used their own discretion, and were not led "by the nose" by the "Liberal" Press of their time-honoured borough.

THE DINNER.

A public dinner was held at the Royal Hotel. The company numbered about 110. Among those present were CAPTAIN HUNT, R.A., in the chair; Dr. GOFF (Darlaston) in the vice-chair; Mr. GUILDFORD ONSLOW, M.P., Dr. MASSEY WHEELER, Sergeant-Major BRITTLEBANK (late of the Carabineers) Mr. MATTHEW GALL (ditto); Messrs. LOVEGROVE, J. J. POWELL, CHAPLIN, INSHAW, MACARTIE, ONIONS, HAMMOND, MCKENZIE, SAUNDERS (secretary), and Sir ROGER.

The Chairman, in proposing the health of the Queen, said it afforded him the greater pleasure to do so, because he knew from the undoubted authority of a noble Lord, a peer of this realm, that Her Majesty had taken for some time past, and still took, a deep interest in the affairs of the Claimant. (Cheers).

The Vice-Chairman proposed the toast of the evening—the health of "Sir ROGER CHARLES DOUGHTY TICHBORNE, Baronet." (Loud and continued cheers.) He said he should not go into the question of Sir ROGER's career, as he hoped to meet thousands of people at night in the Town Hall—(cheers)—they were met there simply as a social gathering, and he hoped they should meet Sir ROGER as they would meet any other gentleman, and propose his health according to the rules of polite society. (Hear, hear.) He had known Sir ROGER for six years. He had the pleasure of coming across the Atlantic with him in 1866 in the good steamship "Cella." Sir ROGER was a passenger, and he (the speaker) happened to be the doctor on board. He conversed often with Sir ROGER, and could assure them most heartily that he was proud to meet him, and he gladly associated Sir ROGER's name with himself, as one of his dearest friends on earth. Sir ROGER's wife and little child were with him on board, and a kinder husband and a more affectionate father he should not wish to see, and he never met with a man more worthy the name of a gentleman in the fullest acceptation of the word. (Cheers.) The glorious bard of Avon, WILLIAM SHAKSPERE of old, in one part of his works, said, "A man that keeps a gig is a gentleman." He begged to differ with WILLIAM SHAKSPERE in that respect. He cared not whether a man wore on his back a suit of hempen hodden gray or the finest broadcloth that the mills of old England could produce, if that man did to others what he would that others should do to him, he was a gentleman in the fullest acceptation of the word. (Cheers.) He had spoken of his own knowledge of Sir ROGER CHARLES DOUGHTY TICHBORNE, baronet of England. He had not seen him for six years, but he recognized him in a moment from his own recollection of him on the passage, and he was fully justified in saying that he was entitled to the name of an English gentleman. (Cheers). In conclusion, he asked them not to be misled, but to study the subject from the beginning, and they would all come to the same conclusion as himself, that Sir ROGER was the right man in the wrong place. (Cheers.)

The Claimant rose amid great cheering, and said he could not find words to express his gratification at the very warm reception which he had received, and which he certainly had not deserved; it was more fit for a prince than an humble individual like himself. Of one thing let them rest assured, that during his career he would never do that which would cause them to regret having given him that reception. (Cheers). At the same time he would ask them to thoroughly inquire into anything they might hear of him before they believed it, and he was in duty bound to ask them to do this, inasmuch as he had been most falsely represented to them in the past. He was very pleased to say there was one party there that evening that knew the tale the Attorney-General told them was utterly false and untrue, as regarded his Australian career. He would tell them that he had held a station in Wagga-Wagga second to none; as a proof of that, he was intrusted with thousands and thousands of pounds passing through his hands every month, without any overlooking, for the space of about four years. That was in itself a proof that he could not be exactly the villain as painted by the Attorney-General. That gentleman was Mr. DYKE. He (the Claimant) arrived in this country in 1866, and Dr. CROPP* was very well aware that when he arrived on England's shore he had to borrow £13 of a fellow-passenger. He believed Dr. CROPP* was witness to his borrowing that sum of money. When he came to England to claim this large baronetcy and estates, he came without any money in his pocket. Certainly he expected to find, as he did, his poor mother alive, and he relied on her kindness and generosity to enable him to recover his estates. He was not aware at that time that there was going to be any litigation, as he naturally thought there could not be any further dispute when his mother acknowledged him as her son. He had to thank the British public for taking up his cause in the manner they had done, and he thought it would teach those in authority in future that they must not play with even one of the humblest of Her Majesty's subjects. (Loud and repeated cheers.)

Mr. INSHAW proposed the health of Mr. ONSLOW.

Mr. ONSLOW, who on rising was loudly cheered, expressed his satisfaction at the reception which had been given to the Claimant in Birmingham, and said he meant to continue to "stump" the country in behalf of the Claimant, who had not had justice done him,

* The Claimant, in his usual way, blundered about names. He meant Dr. GOFF.

and that he did not care for all the obloquy and opprobrious terms that were used about him. (Applause.) He declared that he knew the whole of the Claimant's Case, and that he was prepared to argue it with anyone who would come forward. (Hear, hear.) He was glad to speak in behalf of Sir ROGER in the very atmosphere in which his friend JOHN BRIGHT had addressed the people of Birmingham. He mentioned Mr. BRIGHT's name, because Mr. BRIGHT was adverse to the Claimant. He said he did not know the whole Case, but he could not believe the Claimant, and he believed him to be an Impostor. That was the word of an honest man; but it was equally the part of an honest man to say, as he (Mr. ONSLOW) did, that he knew everything about it, that he believed the Claimant, and that he knew him to be Sir ROGER TICHBORNE. (Cheers.)

The toast of "The Ladies" closed the proceedings.

THE MEETINGS AT THE TOWN HALL.

On Monday night, in accordance with the announcement of the TICHBORNE Invitation Committee, a meeting was held in the Town Hall in support of the Claimant's Defence Fund. Long before eight o'clock a large crowd assembled at the Congreve-street entrance, and on the arrival of the Claimant there was a long and continued cheering. The great gallery of the Hall (1s.) was well filled, but the floor (2s.), the side galleries (3s.) and the orchestra (5s.) were only half occupied. Upon the Claimant making his appearance on the platform, the audience rose, cheered, and waved their hats and handkerchiefs, and he acknowledged his reception by bowing. The Claimant was accompanied by his Invitation Committee, Mr. ONSLOW, M.P., and Captain HUNT, and several prominent townsmen.

Mr. POWELL, of Knapp's Hotel, presided, and in opening the proceedings he said Mr. ONSLOW had requested him to take the chair that evening. He should not go into details for want of time; but they were familiar with the important Trial which had so long occupied the attention of the public. They were also aware of the present position of the Case. The Government, persuaded by their law officers, had decided to prosecute Sir ROGER CHARLES DOUGHTY TICHBORNE at the expense of the country. (Shame, shame.) It would be an enormous expense to the country. Sir R. C. D. TICHBORNE was an Englishman, who they all knew, from the expense he had been put to, was without means of defending himself, except those means which were provided by the British public. In addressing them on behalf of the committee, he wished to say that they did not ask them to assert, nor did they themselves assert, that the gentleman upon his right hand (the Claimant) was Sir R. TICHBORNE, though the vast majority of the English public believed he was. (Cheers.) There were many gentlemen, out of 500 witnesses, who were willing to state upon their solemn honour, that their present guest was who he stated himself to be. There were present that evening gentlemen who would address them, and show them most convincingly that their guest was Sir R. C. D. TICHBORNE. The public press of Birmingham had not acted with fairness and justice in this case. (Cheers, hooting, and hissing). The doctrine taught by one of the local "divine" newspaper philosophers was this—that, because a man was a sinner, he must be excommunicated and debarred from all justice. ("Name," and "shame.") He said, let that man who was without sin cast the first stone. (Cheers.) The Chairman then called upon.

The Claimant, who was received with loud cheers, many times renewed and said, that, in the first place he wished them to clearly understand that he had not come there to press upon them his identity. That could only now be decided by the process of the law. (Cheers.) He had come there as one of themselves, as an Englishman, calling on his fellow-countrymen to aid and assist him in having fair-play in his forthcoming Trial. (Cheers.) There need be no dispute about that, for he thought no thinking man would say that in his late Trial that impartiality was shown to him that ought to be shown to every person tried. (Cheers.) There might be people present who differed in opinion as regarded his identity; but surely they could not disagree with what he asked of his countrymen—and it was all he asked—that he might have fair-play shown him. (Cheers.) It was now his duty to explain several things which had happened and which he did not consider fair. In the first place Government had granted £100,000 for his prosecution. (Cries of "Shame!") In the second place, before doing so, it must be remembered that he was deprived by the Court of Bankruptcy of every shilling's worth of property he had. (Shame.) For the Attorney-General—(groans, hisses, and cries of "Turn him out," "I wish he was here to-night")—in connection with some of his colleagues, caused an Act, or rather a clause to be put in an Act last autumn, which enabled the Judge to send a prisoner direct from the Court to Newgate. (Shame.) Well, he had suffered very severe losses by that clause being put in the Act, and for this very reason. Had that not have been done, he would have been able to have brought his witnesses up before the magistrate in the usual way, and they then would have been bound over at the Government expense to appear at his forthcoming Trial to give evidence; but by that clause being put in the Act, he was deprived of that privilege. (Shame.) Therefore, it had caused him to "stump" the country, as they said in the House of Commons, and ask his fellow-countrymen to aid and assist him by putting their hands in their pockets to enable him to produce his witnesses at his forthcoming trial. (Cheers.) The Attorney-General shed tears in his (the Claimant's) Case—(laughter and hisses)—and he had no doubt they had a great effect upon the jury. He said it was on behalf of his (the Claimant's) cousin that he shed those tears. (Laughter.) Don't be at all deceived; he shed those tears because he could not break him down. (Shame.) There was nothing black but what he called him; he certainly did paint his Australian life very black. He (the Claimant) had very great pleasure in telling them that there was a gentleman on that stage who knew him for several years in Australia, and was a townsman of theirs—Mr. DYKE—(cheers)—and if any of them wished to know the office he held in Australia he would refer them to Mr. DYKE, who would tell them that he held a very different one to that represented by the Attorney-General. (Cheers.) During the time Mr. DYKE knew him £4,000 or £5,000 a quarter passed through his hands from the business in which he was employed; and therefore, if he was as black as the Attorney-General painted him, he did not think that he would have held the situation for four years. (Cheers.) He might also mention that at the end of four years, when he declined to conduct the business any longer, although his employer was offered £2,000 for it, the moment he left it was shut up, and had not been opened since. (Cheers.) Now, a word about Lord Chief Justice BOVILL. (Groans and hisses.) Before saying a word about the Lord Chief Justice, he would just remind them that if he uttered an untruth, it would be taken down by the gentlemen of the press, and be produced against him at the forthcoming Trial. When he was under cross-examination, the Lord Chief Justice had his wife sitting by his side, and that lady amused herself during a greater part of the time by continually holding up an opera-glass at him. He had no doubt that lady could tell how many wrinkles and pimples he had on his face. (Laughter.) He did not, however, so much object to her staring him in the face with her opera-glass, as he did to her handling private notes put in to the Judge. (Shame.) It annoyed him exceedingly to see that lady handling papers which never ought to have been seen by her. Therefore, *he could expect very little help from the Lord Chief Justice, for he publicly denounced him as an Impostor at the Lord Mayor's dinner during the Trial.* (Shame.)

Sir ROGER then went at great length into his Trial, and also complained of the great injustice of the Birmingham press, and especially of the *Birmingham Morning News*. ("Oh," and loud groans, hisses, and a Voice: "DAWSON.") It was dated 23rd Aug., and contained a scurrilous article. (Groans.) If the writer—(a Voice: "DAWSON")—was in the room he was sure he would feel utterly ashamed of himself before he left it. (Loud cheers.) He could only compare the man who wrote an article of that description to an assassin—(cheers and a voice; "G. DAWSON")—because he did not give a person an opportunity of knowing who he was. He was a cur and nothing but a cur. (Loud and continued cheering.) He was not going to read the article; and no doubt most of them had read it. (Voices: "Oh dear, no," Other Voices: "Read it, read it.") The Claimant, who appeared fatigued, then sat down.

The Chairman said that in order to give Sir ROGER time to rest, Captain HUNT would read the article.

Captain HUNT then read from the *Birmingham Morning News* as follows:—"Our enterprising local showmen, who are to favour us with a view of the lion recently freed from his legal den—(Capt. HUNT: 'There's language,' and hisses)—are about to continue a custom common in travelling menageries. Not content to offer to the public two nights' roaring at the Town Hall, they will give, for 10s. 6d. extra, an opportunity of seeing the noble creature and his parliamentary keepers fed. (Hisses, and a Voice: 'Put him in the pillory.') At first they appeared to think men only would have the curiosity and the courage to see the show; but, on second thoughts, they have decided to admit ladies at the reduced figure of 7s. 6d. (Hisses, and cries of 'GEORGE DAWSON,' 'He wants hanging.') Touching gallantry! Considerate half-crown! What can these men mean by ladies? Do you think that any woman who respects herself and her sex will countenance a man who said—nay, swore—that he had seduced his cousin, and succeeded only in persuading those who heard him that he had perjured himself? (Capt. HUNT: 'Most unfair; this rascally article,' and hisses.) He may be Sir ROGER TICHBORNE, but that is doubtful; but that he is not a gentleman is clear. We hold that nothing can justify a man in betraying to the world what love passages have been between him and a woman. If he has sinned, let him repent. If he is a Roman Catholic, let him confess to his priest—('Ho! ho!' 'GEORGE DAWSON.' 'Assassin,' and hisses and uproar)—his secret will be safe; if he is a Protestant, let him confess to his GOD, and his secret will be even safer; but his confession should be secret and silent. Not to the world does he owe confession, but to the woman he owes silence, however brazenness or cowardice may incline him to publish his own shame. But to try to blast a woman with a lie! the ink with which we write is not so black as that. The woman who will go to this banquet we must regard as a traitress to her sex. ('Shame.') Now, then, 'ladies,' walk up, for the low charge of seven and six! Again we say that this amazing person's conduct cannot determine his claim, and must not interfere with his legal rights or wrongs. We give no opinion on what is his real name, but we do protest against the unseemly honours that have been paid to him, and are sought to be paid to him here. We are happy to say that the Committee do not intend to invite the public to illuminate in honour of the Claimant, and we have not yet been informed that the publicans intend to do so." (Hisses and groans.)

The Claimant, resuming his speech, amid cheers, said it was unnecessary for him to pass any comments upon the article. It was like the Attorney-General's speech, and recoiled in the teeth of the writer. He would, however, give an explanation with regard to one passage. It was that which deprecated the conduct of the man who betrayed what love passages had been between him and a woman. Upon this point he quite agreed with the writer. He said that any man who would do such a thing ought to be spurned from society, even from the society of scavengers who swept their streets. But in his case it was very different. His cousin "disacknowledged" him, though he had it upon oath that she knew him. Mr. GOSFORD, after his first meeting, said that Mrs. RADCLIFFE had recognized him by his eyebrows and the upper part of his face. For about half an hour, Sir ROGER continued speaking respecting the sealed packet, and proved, beyond a doubt, how nobly he had endeavoured to shield his cousin. He said he had made this explanation ten times, and the writer of the article must have seen his explanations. (Hear, hear, and "Groans for the writer.")

The Chairman then intimated that they would be willing to hear what anyone had to say on "the other side."

Mr. GUILDFORD ONSLOW, who received quite an ovation, then addressed the meeting at considerable length.

Sergeant-Major BRITTLEBANK and Sergeant-Major MARKS also addressed the meeting, giving the history of their connection with Mr. TICHBORNE in the Carabineers, and of their recognition of the Claimant as the same gentleman.

THIRD MEETING IN THE TOWN HALL.—A third Meeting at the Town Hall of this great centre of intelligence and industry followed. It was held August 28th, 1872.

On his way to the hall in the street the Claimant was loudly cheered by a number of persons who had assembled there, as on previous evenings, to witness his arrival. When he made his appearance, a few minutes afterwards, on the platform inside the hall, he was also met with an enthusiastic reception. The chair was occupied by Mr. J. C. MEREDITH, and amongst these present were CAPTAIN HUNT and some members of the Local Committee.

The CHAIRMAN briefly introduced the Claimant, describing him as "This large-souled man—our friend ROGER TICHBORNE." (Cheers.)

The CLAIMANT, who was received with loud cheering, said: I want you to clearly understand that I am not here for the purpose of proving my identity, or trying to make you believe that I am ROGER CHARLES TICHBORNE. I stand here as an Englishman, as one of yourselves, asking you my fellow-countrymen, to aid and assist me in having fair-play in the forthcoming Trial. According to the *Daily Post*—I have no doubt a great many of you have read it—this morning, it seems rather too much fair-play has been meted out to me. Therefore, I shall quote a line or two:—"In the evening the Town Hall was only about half filled. Last night the prices of admission had to be woefully cut down to get an audience, and altogether it may be safely affirmed that the speculation has proved a failure—(laughter)—so far as the town is concerned, it is in no way responsible for this unwelcome visit. Birmingham couldn't help it—the thing was thrust upon us, and we had to endure it. Everybody is acquainted with that most troublesome of characters, 'the man who will know you.'" (A Voice: "That is a falsehood.") Now, ladies and gentlemen, I beg to say that I did not force myself upon you—(hear, hear)—and although I was asked on several occasions to visit this town I declined doing so till I received an invitation sent by a committee of the inhabitants of this town. (Hear, hear, and cheers.) Even after that I declined to visit the town, because I had heard there had been persons here representing themselves as my agents, and I knew not what these men might have done or said, and for a long time I declined to come to Birmingham. I beg to say I never had an agent in Birmingham. I sent no agent. The invitation came spontaneously from this town to me without either my asking for it or expecting it. (Hear, hear.) In another part the writer says, "His agents or persons professing to represent him have been here for weeks, trying to get an invitation for their patron or Claimant, whichever may be his relation to them." Now, I don't think it is necessary for me to quote more of this article, for really it speaks for itself. (Hear, hear.) It is an article written by a bitter, malicious-minded man—(hear, hear)—and when you take into consideration that I have to appear before two tribunals of this country to answer three charges—two for perjury and one for forgery—I don't think it is altogether English for the public press of England to abuse and vilify a man who has to meet three such charges as these. (Hear, hear.) This is not the only paper that has taken that course. The other two papers have taken, to a certain degree, the same line of conduct, and I should like to caution the editor of one of these papers that if he don't leave me alone—and I beg him to know that people who live in glass houses should not throw stones—I caution him that if he writes another article about me I will come to this hall and expose his character—(cheers, and Hear, hear); and you will find it is not the first time he has been mistaken in an impostor. (Cheers, Hear, hear, and cries of "Bravo," and "Polish lady.") I distinctly wish you to understand I am not abusing the Press by passing these remarks. I have no wish to abuse anyone. If it comes to my part to have to tell you facts that have occurred, I hope you will not take them as abuses. You must also bear in mind that if I utter a falsehood to you, it will be recorded by these gentlemen of the Press, and it will be brought against me at my forthcoming Trial. Therefore, you may depend what I tell you are facts, and facts only. The speaker here referred to the number of witnesses that were called in support of his Case, and the number called against him, and complained of the jury and Judge believing the twelve witnesses called against him in preference to his 86 witnesses. They did not, he said, succeed in breaking down any one of the 86 witnesses that I placed in the box; therefore there is no accounting for why the jury believed twelve witnesses, and disbelieved those 86 disinterested witnesses that gave true evidence. (Hear, hear.) You will hear some of those witnesses to-night, and you will be able to judge whether they are such witnesses as were described by the Attorney-General. (Hisses.) That learned gentleman gave you to understand that private soldiers could be bought at any time for a pot of beer. (Hisses.) Well, it would be a bad job for Englishmen in England if that was the case, and the only wonder to me is that every man in the British army did not throw down his arms on hearing the chief law-officer making remarks of that description. There is no doubt that it was only the love they had for the country and for the Queen that prevented them doing so. The Claimant then proceeded to remark upon various points involved in the late Trial, saying that it was not until after he had been examined by the medical gentlemen and they found he had no tattoo marks upon him, that the question of the tattoo marks was brought up. They would remember that JAMES MCCANN, who was a regimental servant of his, was examined at that Trial, and he asked if that witness was not a more fit person than any one else to have been asked that question as to the tattoo marks when he was examined, if the opposite side knew anything about it at that time. (Cheers.) He again alluded to the speech of the Attorney-General, and remarked that his strong language showed that he had a weak case. If it had come from Mr. HAWKINS, who had been accustomed to practice at the Old Bailey, they should not have thought anything about it, but to come from the pious Sir JOHN DUKE COLERIDGE was certainly something rather startling. (Cheers.) The papers had alluded to him "abusing" the Counsel, but he did not hesitate to say nobody had ever heard him use a word against any Counsel excepting Sir JOHN DUKE COLERIDGE, who, they would bear in mind, for thirty long days vilified him when he had not the opportunity to answer him. He contended he had a perfect right, therefore, to answer that long-winded speech. (Cheers.) Before going into the Case, he would show them how far prejudice had been carried against him. General JACKSON, who was in the Carabineers when he (Claimant) was, was walking along Pall Mall with Major BICKERSTAFF, another Carabineer, when they were met by Major NORBURY. The latter gentleman saluted General JACKSON by "How do you do, General?" "Don't know you; you were never in the Carabineers," said the General. "Oh! yes," Major BICKERSTAFF said, "you are making a mistake. This is Major NORBURY." "NORBURY, my dear fellow, how are you? I thought you were that —— fellow, TICHBORNE," replied the General. (Loud laughter and cheers.) *He now had to draw attention to the conduct of the two brothers of the Judge during the Trial. They asked his cousin, ANTHONY BIDDULPH, if he would bet on the Case.* His cousin said he certainly should not, and if he did bet he should not bet with them, because they were brothers to the Judge. (Cheers.) They afterwards promised to go and revoke all bets that they had made. Now he asked them what case could be carried out impartially when a brother of the Judge was acting in such a disgraceful manner, and if this one thing was found out, how many other such things might there have been found out? He then described his meeting with his alleged cousin at Croydon, and the meeting at the office of Mr. HOLMES, and read the affidavit of Mr. HOLMES, to the effect that there was not one of his relatives at the office, who could deny that he was Sir ROGER. (Cheers.) He likewise read the affidavits of a general in the Carabineers, and referred to the affidavit of Dowager Lady TICHBORNE, and asked whether it was at all likely that in the face of this, and of the evidence of 86 witnesses, the Case should be upset by 12? ("No, no," and cheers.) In conclusion he said: I ask you, is there anything in the world that would have upset the evidence of my 86 witnesses? If those witnesses had belonged to the Attorney-General, he would have described them thus: Here are men who have fought and bled for their country, and men who stake their lives, and stake it every day—can you disbelieve such evidence as that?" That is the way in which he would have spoken if a man's life depended upon it. But why should there be any difference between life and property? If that evidence would have been strong enough to deprive a human being of his life, why should it not be strong enough to return to me my property? (Loud cheers.)

On the proposition of the Claimant, seconded by Captain HUNT, a vote of thanks was passed to the authorities of the town for the use of the hall, and the proceedings terminated.

Nearly simultaneous with this visit, was published a letter written by poor CARTER on his death-bed: we publish it, with an account of his death; his letter and his death both appearing in the same paper. He died in August, 1872.

TO THE EDITOR OF THE "TICHBORNE GAZETTE."

SIR,—As you have been kind enough to insert several letters from the various witnesses connected with the great TICHBORNE Case, I should feel greatly obliged by your inserting the following from me (THOMAS CARTER), another witness in the Claimant's behalf, designated by the Attorney-General as a thorough rascal, and the Claimant's chief prompter. I have seen a little of the world, and mixed with various grades of society, and amongst the many who know me, I don't think there is one who would address me in the same terms as Sir JOHN COLERIDGE, or think I deserve the invectives with which he has endowed me.

I am but a poor man, depending entirely upon my own industry for the means of subsistence, and yet I hold my oath as sacred as Lords and M.P.'s do theirs, or even as the Attorney-General himself, and hope it is to be relied on as much as theirs.

There is not a man living that knew more about Sir ROGER TICHBORNE than I did, both previous to his leaving England and since his return, and I will affirm before GOD and man, that he is the same man—son of the Dowager Lady TICHBORNE—for whom I worked before leaving England for foreign parts. So far from my being the Claimant's prompter in everything, I can say without fear of contradiction, that at our first interview, things which had entirely slipped my memory were brought so vividly to my mind by him, that had there been a doubt existing, it would have been instantly dispelled.

As regards the tattooing of Sir ROGER, I will solemnly swear that I never saw any such marks as the witnesses for the defence described in the late Trial, although no man had more opportunities of observing them, had they existed, than I had. But after mentioning a few facts, I will leave it to the public to judge whether they (the tattoo marks) could have escaped my notice.

I saw him entirely stripped at his apartments at Canterbury, and was likewise present with him when bathing at Herne Bay. I have also seen him at Upton House with his sleeves rolled up above the elbow, busily employed in a favourite pastime of his, namely, preparing the carcases of birds and small animals ready for the stuffing process.

But I will mention something still more convincing than the former facts, and that occurred during Sir ROGER's illness at Upton. He was laid up there with a severe cold, and was ordered by the doctor to have a mustard plaister fastened on so as to effectually cover his chest. This was placed on by my own hands. After removing it, his chest was swollen to such an extent, that for a minute or two I was alarmed. I then dressed it with lard. The next morning, he being too ill to do it, I washed his hands, arms, and face. I ask again, could the tattoo have been there without my observing them?

With this remark, I will close my somewhat lengthy letter.—I beg to remain, Sir, your obedient servant, THOMAS CARTER.

THOMAS CARTER, a witness in the TICHBORNE Case, died on Monday in the infirmary of Kensington Workhouse. He was for some time an inmate of the imbecile ward, but died from bodily illness in the new infirmary. He was a most important witness, and was, it may be remembered, most severely handled in cross-examination by Mr. HAWKINS. His evidence was regarded as one of the main points of that part of the Case affecting the alleged life of the Claimant in the army.

We supplement this with a most important affidavit of CHARLES HINGSTON, Spanish Shipping Broker, of 13, Crutched Friars, London.

I first became acquainted with Sir ROGER C. D. TICHBORNE, the Plaintiff, in the spring of 1867, whilst he was living at Croydon.

I was present at the interview between him and Mr. GOSFORD at the Grosvenor Hotel, Victoria Station, on the 6th of June, 1867. The interview lasted from eight to twelve. Mr. BULPETT and Mr. WHITE were also present. The Plaintiff and Mr. GOSFORD continued to converse the whole time, and I observed their treatment of each other—it was that of two persons who knew each other well; and I was quite satisfied that Mr. GOSFORD knew him quite well, and that he also knew GOSFORD, both from the questions asked and answered, and their demeanour one to another. They smoked and took their wine together in a friendly manner. In the autumn of 1867 I became acquainted with the late Dowager Lady TICHBORNE, the Plaintiff's mother, and from that time till the night preceding her death I often saw her and was in her company; I knew her well. It was at Wellesley Villas, Croydon, I used to meet her—the Plaintiff's residence—and used to converse with her in the most friendly terms. I was struck with and observed the close and affectionate relation which used to exist between her and the Plaintiff; it was that of mother to a son, and they mutually understood each other. I had never witnessed such affectionate behaviour before. She always manifested the greatest anxiety for his welfare and that of his wife and family, and I never saw her manifest greater affection and anxiety for him than she did on the 11th of March, 1868, when she was at his house at Croydon expecting his return home. She waited till the last train that night, anxiously expecting him, being unwilling to return to London without seeing him. The next evening I saw her lying dead at Howlett's Hotel, and the Plaintiff overwhelmed with grief. In August, 1867, the Plaintiff wrote a letter in English to Don TOMAS CASTRO, of Melipilla, Chili, and wished it to be translated into Spanish. It was rather difficult to do so, as the Plaintiff had not expressed himself very clearly or knew the proper spelling of the names. I saw the Plaintiff on the subject at Wellesley Villas one evening, and took with me a little Frenchman named HENRIQUE MYALL, who is since dead (he was a clerk of the Spanish Naval Commission), to translate it into Spanish, and to make the best we could of it. The Plaintiff and myself smoked our cigars whilst it was being done, and a great deal of talking took place before it was completed. The draft has not the word godfather in it, nor was that word used or alluded to. The words "my old companion" occur in the original draft, and MYALL used the Spanish equivalent for companion or friend, *Compadre*, in translating the letter into Spanish. I have lived some years in Spain, and can speak Spanish well, and am accustomed, almost daily, in the course of my business, to speak Spanish to Spanish captains, sailors, and others. I could not otherwise carry on my business. *Compadre* is a familiar expression of friendship. When people are very friendly, it is very usual for persons to come up and pat them on the back, and say, "*Hola compadre*," which is on a par with our "*Hollo, old fellow!*" *Compadre* is a sort of endearing expression between men who are very thick or intimate; they call one another *compadres*.

From this place the Claimant went over to Wolverhampton; he did not meet with the reception which he anticipated. We append the report—evidently the composition of an enemy.

THE CLAIMANT AT WOLVERHAMPTON.

Mr. O. S. WALSH, being voted to the chair, said he should merely ask them to be attentive to the speakers, and to keep order. He had much pleasure in calling on the worthy baronet to address them. (Cheers.)

The Claimant, on stepping forward to the front railing, was cheered. He said the public press had thought proper to say he was going about the country abusing Judge, Counsel, and others connected with the Case. ("No, no.") Such was not his intention. (Applause.) He hoped any remark he made would not be taken as such. He was in duty bound to relate such things, and to make such remarks as would show them that he had not had such fair-play as ought to have been shown to an Englishman. (Cheers.) He would refer, in the first place, to the remarks made on his person. There were no remarks made about the tattooing until he had been examined by the jury, by the Counsel, and by four medical gentlemen, at the very end of the Case. They had read the evidence of Lord BELLEW, who swore that he tattooed ROGER TICHBORNE at Stonyhurst. When Lord BELLEW was asked who was present, he replied, "Mr. SEAGER," a personal friend of his, who was now dead and gone; and they all knew that no question could be asked of the dead. Lord BELLEW was not aware that he was staying at Mr. SEAGER's house, as his guest, shortly after his arrival in England. (Cheers, and "You never was tattooed, Sir ROGER.") He read to them a list of witnesses who were examined on his behalf, and after that he thought it was not a conspiracy; indeed, a conspiracy was impossible under the circumstances. He had yet to learn upon what authority the jury thought proper to stop the Case after hearing the evidence of eighty-six witnesses. (A voice: "They never ought.") They must also remember that during the Trial the Attorney-General tried to break him down—("Shame")—and won his Case by means of forged documents. (Cries of "Shame, shame.") If he (the Claimant) had produced forged documents of any description, there would have been an end to the Case there and then. He could not understand how the Judge, after the Attorney-General had produced those forged documents, allowed the matter to pass. There were no remarks made about these documents. (A Voice: "He had an interest in it.") Some time afterwards the Attorney-General himself acknowledged those letters to be forgeries. ("Shame.") Then as regarded the daguerreotype produced in Court, the thumb of his left hand was shown—they would perceive the nail was deformed. During the time he was in the witness-box they got that daguerreotype somehow or other, though it was in the possession of the Court, and actually rubbed that thumb out—(cries of "Shame")—but they forgot, when doing so, that they had supplied him with photographic copies of that same daguerreotype. (Cheers.) Therefore, when they denied that the thumb was shown, he produced the copies of the daguerreotype they had given him, and there was the thumb. (Cheers and laughter.) He thought they would agree with him when he said that if he had done such a thing there would have been an end to the case. (A Voice: "No doubt of it.") They would have sent him to Newgate, and properly too. There was a person named MACKENZIE employed on the other side to go out to Australia, to get up evidence against him. He heard from time to time of MACKENZIE's whereabouts; and he heard from his agents in Melbourne that he was tampering with the witnesses, and bribing them. In fact, they had it on sworn testimony that he (MACKENZIE) said he had been sent out there by the Lord Chancellor to gather evidence *pro* and *con*. MACKENZIE was sent out there simply as a detective, to gather what evidence he could. He was not saying anything that he could not substantiate by documents. (Hear, hear.) Messrs. SEDGFIELD and ALLPONT, his agents at Melbourne, wrote to him saying that Mr. MACKENZIE, the agent of the Defendants, returned to England by that mail, and they begged most emphatically to caution him against that person. He did not think that Messrs. SEDGFIELD and ALLPONT would write such a letter if they were not able to substantiate it. No doubt the prominent part which the Attorney-General had taken in the Case was well-known to many of them; he had taken such a prominent part that his character was actually at stake. (Hear, hear.) Even the character of the Government was at stake by the part which they had taken. The Attorney-General had either to crush or transport him, or otherwise he (the Attorney-General) would never be looked on again as long as he lived. (Hear, hear.) The language the Attorney-General made use of towards him, they all knew how disgusting it was. (Cries of "Shame on him; he must get some waste to wipe his tears next time.") It was well known that when a Counsel made an opening speech he ought to be in a position to prove all he said. The Attorney-General's opening speech lasted for thirty days. There was no doubt that when a man was paid at the rate of 3s. 4d. a minute, he could go on speaking for a very long time. (Laughter.) For thirty days the Attorney-General continued his speech in the Court; and he asked them, out of all the material he (the Attorney-General) spoke of, how much did he prove by substantial witnesses? (A Voice: "Nothing." Laughter.) They must remember that he (the Attorney-General) never said anything about the tattoo marks until the end of the speech, and then he put his witnesses in the box to swear to the tattoo marks and nothing else. If the Attorney-General had known of the tattoo marks, and if he could have proved that he (the Claimant) was tattooed before he left England, what occasion was there, he asked, for that thirty days' speech? (Cheers.) The Attorney-General might have said at the commencement of his Trial, "Gentlemen of the Jury, I am not going to bore you with a speech. I can prove that ROGER TICHBORNE was tattooed before he left England; this man is not tattooed." But that would not have filled the Attorney-General's pocket so well as it had been filled by the course he had adopted. The Attorney-General had thought proper to make a boast before he (the Claimant) went into the witness-box that he would have him from the witness-box to Newgate within twenty-four hours. He did not hesitate to say that *the Attorney-General made a bet on the subject of some few bottles of wine.* (Oh, oh, and laughter.) He mentioned that to show how positive the Attorney-General was that he could do as he said he would. For twenty-three days he stood under a severe cross-examination, and during that twenty-three days the Attorney-General never succeeded in breaking him down. (Cheers.) He assured them that it was not for the want of material at the disposal of the Attorney-General, for there were over 100 of his relatives and connections who had given him (the Attorney-General) all the possible information they could muster and get together. That information the Attorney-General placed before the rest of his colleagues in order that he might be cross-examined on their statements. The Attorney-General had at his disposal the remembrances of 100 different people to cross-examine him on, and to tax one brain. Some of them might wonder how it was that he was so stupid as to make some of the remarks he did: but he would only ask them to try twenty-three days' cross-examination of the Attorney-General, to inform them how he felt in the box. When he was sent to Newgate, he was hardly within the walls before the Court of Bankruptcy left an order that all the property found on his person should be taken possession of, and on no condition was that property to be appropriated towards his maintenance. The Solicitor of the Treasury also sent an order to Messrs. BAXTER, ROSE, and NORTON (his solicitors), ordering them not to part with any of the documents. He asked them, having been deprived of every shilling he possessed in the world, with his papers impounded, how was it possible that he could have a fair Trial? In addition to that, the Government had voted £100,000 for his prosecution. ("Shame." A voice: "There will be a row about that yet.") He was about to ask them a simple question: Supposing he had committed a murder some twenty years ago, and he had bolted from this country. Supposing, also, that he returned, and eighty-six witnesses had given evidence as to his identity, including his mother. Would that have been sufficient to have hanged him? (Hear, hear.) Why, nothing would have saved him. He therefore argued, that if the evidence was sufficient to deprive a human being of his life, why should it not be sufficient to restore to him his estates? (Cheers.) But human life was one thing, and property was another. When property was at stake, especially estates worth £25,000 a year—this year it would be more than that—that was a very different matter; they had hundreds engaged against them who had interest in the result. Money, to a certain extent, worked and ruled the law in this country. He said it was scandalous that because he had been a few years away, and had neglected his property, that he should lose it. He had already spent £120,000 to regain it. He complained of the jury who, when they came to a certain part, said that they had come to a conclusion before they had heard one-third of the evidence that was to be put before them. Was it not, he asked, scandalous that the jury should leave the box without hearing the whole of the evidence? (A voice: "It was un-English.") They had entirely lost him the large amount of money expended on a trial during 103 days. It was a scandal that a man could not recover his rights without expending such a large amount of money. What they wanted in the House of Commons was a thorough Law Reform Bill, so that they might no longer be obliged to pay £1,000 on the delivery of a brief, and 50 guineas a-day during the Trial. He thanked them for the kind and attentive manner in which they had listened to him, and resumed his seat amidst loud cheers.

Sergeant-Major MARKS, who had served with Sir ROGER CHAS. D. TICHBORNE in the army, prior to his voyage to Australia, identified the Claimant as the man he knew years ago, and he stated his reasons, asserting that he could not be mistaken, for he knew the Claimant as soon as he saw him.

Mr. GALE, who also served with Sir ROGER TICHBORNE in the Carabineers, also identified the Claimant.

Sergeant-Major CHEER, of the Yeomanry Cavalry, also spoke.

Captain HUNT proposed a vote of thanks to the Chairman, which was seconded by the Claimant, and carried amidst cheers.

The Chairman acknowledged the compliment, and the public business terminated.

The Committee and Claimant partook of luncheon.

THE CLAIMANT AT DEWSBURY.

Sergeant-Major MARKS, in supporting a resolution, spoke of his knowledge of Sir ROGER TICHBORNE whilst he was a subaltern officer in the Carabineers, from 1849 to 1853. Sir ROGER was posted to the troop in which he (the speaker) was serving as corporal, and it was his duty to initiate the Claimant into his several duties. Having volunteered into a heavy cavalry regiment, he never saw Sir ROGER from 1852 to October, 1867, when an old comrade came to him at Aldershot, and asked him if he remembered Mr. TICHBORNE, who was a member of his troop? He replied that he did very well, and offered to go and see if he could swear to him. He then alluded to the means taken by him to identify the Claimant. He severely condemned the remark made by the Attorney-General, that a soldier could be bought for a pot of beer, and said he would tremble for the honour of England if such were the case. He would swear that Sir ROGER never was tattooed four inches from the wrist, or he (the speaker) would have seen the marks, and such a thing was never mooted until his opponents found their Case had broken down.

The Claimant was received with loud cheers. He said: I stand here as one of yourselves—as an Englishman, asking you to assist me in having justice done. (Hear, hear.) I have been now nearly six years in England. During that period I have been watched by a staff of detectives in such a manner as no other man has ever been watched. I don't mean police detectives, but a set of scamps set on by my relatives—as to the detectives of the police force, we cannot exist without them—but I am alluding to those men who have been allowed to do these mean and dirty things; therefore I hope, when I say detectives, you will not think I am alluding to the police detectives. My every act was made known to my opponents, and surely, if I was an impostor, six years are sufficient to find it out. They have had me in the witness-box for twenty-eight days—longer than any man living has been in a witness-box—and I have been examined by one of the most learned men that ever lived, Sir J. D. COLERIDGE, and he was backed up by five as equally clever lawyers as himself, and they had the brains of one hundred different people to help them. Place such material in the hands of such men as England can produce—and no country can produce cleverer men—with such material as one hundred different brains, and the information they have received from those scamps who have watched me about, being handled by those clever men—I say, if I was an impostor, with such clever material to act upon, the Attorney-General ought not to have allowed me to remain in that box five hours. (Cheers.) But no matter how clever a man may be, it's hard to make a man into another person. (Laughter.) The Attorney-General did succeed in turning black into white as none else could do, but at the conclusion of his examination he said I was the cleverest man in existence. If I was an impostor, to stand against such material and such men, I should be a very clever man indeed; but inasmuch as I am not another man, and inasmuch as I am not very clever, I don't think there is anything very clever about it. You know there is a great power of oppression brought against me. Detectives followed me wherever I went, and they told the tradesmen in the towns which I visited to be careful, for I never paid my way. ("Shame.") Such petty annoyances I have been subjected to for the last five years. There has been a great stir about my friends being connected with the aristocracy of England. No doubt, had my parents been poor people, I should have had a fair trial; but inasmuch as my aunt is Lady DOUGHTY, and as I have very high connections, they did not like me to bring to England my wife, who was a humble servant; but I have four very pretty children—(applause)—and if I lose my estates I shall not regret it if they are lost through that. (Cheers.) *The Judge denounced me as an Impostor at the Lord Mayor's dinner.* You may imagine I have not had much faith in that Judge. When I was compelled to insult him as I did, I think you will think I have more common-sense than to insult a Judge, on whom depended my Case, without cause. This is what I said to him: "My Lord, it appears to me the other side don't require Counsel when they have you for a Judge." (Laughter.) You may imagine, I was in hopes the Judge would have sent me to prison for contempt of Court, because I knew what I had said to him would be taken notice of by the British public. I am thankful to the public of Dewsbury, and I hope it will not be the last time I shall have the pleasure of meeting you. If ever I should be so fortunate as to regain my estates, and I have confidence in so doing—("hear, hear," and cheers)—I will come to this town and thank you for your assistance rendered to me on this occasion. (Loud cheers.)

The CLAIMANT then proposed three cheers for the Chairman, which were duly responded to.

The gathering then separated.

THE CLAIMANT AT THE EAST END.

On Saturday, August 17, 1872, the Claimant to the Tichborne Estates accepted an invitation from an active East-end Defence Fund Committee, and attended a meeting of his supporters, held in the Cambridge Music Hall, Commercial-street, Bishopsgate-street. Crowds of people flocked from the most remote districts of Spitalfields, Bethnal-green, Bishopsgate, Cambridge-heath, Hackney, Shoreditch, and Kingsland; and when the Claimant, accompanied by some friends, drove through Commercial-street to the appointed rendezvous, he was welcomed by the East-enders with an enthusiasm which has not been surpassed at any of his provincial demonstrations. There were the same hearty cries from the assembled populace, of "Welcome, Sir ROGER," "Bravo,

Claimant." "Fair play,'" and the same eager anxiety to catch even a glimpse of the man who for the last two years has held such fore-front rank in the judicial proceedings of the country. The charges for admission to the hall were rather high: "private boxes, 21s.; reserved seats, 3s.; stalls, 2s.; balcony, 1s." But when the doors were thrown open, nearly an hour before the time fixed for the Claimant's arrival, the building, more especially the stalls and balcony, rapidly filled, and the reserved seats, though not crowded, had many occupants of the fair sex, who seemed to take the warmest possible interest in the proceedings.

Shortly after half-past eight o'clock, the Claimant entered the hall, preceded by the Spitalfields Defence Fund Committee. He was accompanied by Sergeant-Major MARKS, formerly of the 6th Carabineers, Mr. POWELL, of Basingstoke, and some tenants on the Tichborne Estates, who reside in Alresford. There was much cheering of an unmistakably hearty character the instant the audience recognized Sir ROGER's now well-known features; and as he walked across the stage to the seat assigned him, the applause became, if possible, more vehement and sustained.

Mr. SOMERSET J. HYAM, vestry clerk of Christ Church, Spitalfields, took the chair, and immediately proceeded to say that it afforded him the utmost possible pleasure to introduce to the meeting Sir ROGER CHARLES DOUGHTY TICHBORNE, the Claimant to the estates in Hampshire: an announcement which was the signal for renewed cheering. He felt confident that the very mention of their distinguished but most ill-used and badly-treated friend's name would arouse enthusiasm, and he was gratified that they had accorded that gentleman on this, his first appearance among them, so hearty a reception. (Cheers.) It was unnecessary for him to refer to the details of the ever-memorable TICHBORNE Trial, which had lasted from the 18th May, 1871, until nearly the end of March, 1872, but he desired to call attention to the peculiar circumstances which surrounded Sir ROGER. The Attorney-General aided in every way, and backed up by four of the most celebrated advocates of the day, tried his best and his worst, by means of an unprecedented prolonged cross-examination, to confound the Claimant, but most ignobly had he failed in the attempt. ("Three groans for COLERIDGE" were here demanded by one of the balcony occupants, and the company not only responded *con amore*, on this occasion, to the request, but, without invitation, repeated the compliment at five-minute intervals during the remainder of the evening.) Well, Sir ROGER TICHBORNE having baffled Sir JOHN COLERIDGE—the great law-officer having failed in his mission—what comes to pass? Why, the Government takes up a private dispute between Sir ROGER TICHBORNE and his relatives, and whilst the senior member for this borough (groans for "AYRTON"), one of the GLADSTONE Administration, sets to work quarrelling with the most distinguished scientific man of the day, the members of that Government determine to spend thousands of pounds on the prosecution of the Claimant, and thereby drive him, however repugnant the course may be to the feelings of himself and his sympathizers, to appeal to his fellow-countrymen for the means to resist such rank injustice, and unparalleled usurpation of power.

The Claimant then presented himself, and had quite an ovation. In the course of an address, which occupied more than half an hour, he reproduced all those points in the history of his Case which at previous meetings, both in the provinces and at the great Millwall demonstration, were brought out in great detail.

Mr. W. SAUNDERS, a working man, rose from his seat in the gallery, and greatly interested the audience by a most effective and telling speech. He well expressed his views, which obviously were views of the audience, as to the treatment Sir ROGER TICHBORNE had met with from the law-courts, and dwelt upon the patriotic spirit of Mr. GUILDFORD ONSLOW, M.P., and Mr. WHALLEY, M.P., in their noble advocacy of the Claimant's cause. Mr. SAUNDERS' observations were loudly applauded.

Mr. KARSLAKE, Q.C., of Lincoln's Inn, or Mr. LOCOCK WEBB, we forget which, about this time received and published an extract of importance from a Hobart Town letter, dated June 14:—

"Permit me to mention that some short time since a gentleman was sent out here to collect evidence for the Defendant (in the late Trial of TICHBORNE *v.* LUSHINGTON). One of the witnesses was a gentleman who lived next door to the butcher's shop, and who knew ARTHUR ORTON well. In the course of his examination he was shown a photograph of the Claimant, and was asked whether that was ARTHUR ORTON. His reply to the question was, 'Not in the slightest degree.'"

Soon after appeared the following correspondence:—

THE CLAIMANT AND HIS FRIENDS.

The Grove, Ropley, Hants: July 29, 1872.

MY DEAR MR. BAINES,—As I understand you are the proprietor or manager of a newspaper called the *Leeds Mercury*, I venture to take the liberty of inclosing you a paragraph contained in that journal of the 27th inst., and to state of my own knowledge that a more impudent falsehood and scandulous publication was never written. I am proud to say I was one of the associates of Sir ROGER TICHBORNE on his late visit to Leeds, and our reception was a regal one, never to be forgotten. I appeal to you, as a gentleman of morality and a lover of justice, to insert this letter in the next edition of the *Leeds Mercury*. And I leave it to your judgment whether it would not be advisable to give instructions to those who wrote that article to adhere more to truth in their reports in the future, and not mislead the public in the manner they have done.—I remain, my dear Mr. BAINES, yours faithfully,

GUILDFORD ONSLOW.

To EDWARD BAINES, Esq., M.P., House of Commons, London.

House of Commons: July 30, 1872.

MY DEAR MR. ONSLOW,—I am one of the "proprietors" of the *Leeds Mercury*, but after seeing me so many years a constant attendant in the House of Commons, you cannot suppose it possible that I should be "the manager." I can, therefore, only be the medium of transmitting your letter to the editors, and must leave it to their discretion how to deal with it.

For some months I myself was a believer in the Claimant, but the evidence at the Trial led me, as well as the Judge and the jury, to conclude that he was a clever impostor, who by marvellous tact and impudence had succeeded in persuading many honourable men—you among the number—of the truth of his pretensions. And if an impostor, no words can well be too strong to describe his character, and to denounce his attempt to obtain the Tichborne property, and to gull the public.

But I do not remember that I have ever conversed or corresponded with the editors of the *Leeds Mercury* on the subject.

When you told me in the Lobby of the House, with your wonted frankness, that you were going to Leeds with "Sir ROGER," I told you that the *Mercury* was strongly opposed to his pretensions; but I took no further thought about the matter, and have not heard a word about the Claimant, except what I read in the paper.

As to the editors, I know them to be men of honour, incapable of wilful misrepresentation. I believe the same of you. One of you is desperately mistaken; but I am not the person to decide whether it is you or they. It is for the people of Leeds to judge. I regret that you seem to be included among the shameless persons denounced, and therein they have certainly confounded the deceived with the deceiver. But, as far as I can judge, the educated classes of the country are nearly unanimous in believing your protégé to be a fraudulent pretender,—I am, dear Mr. ONSLOW, yours faithfully,

EDWARD BAINES.

The Grove, Ropley: July 31.

MY DEAR SIR,—I thank you for your letter, and all I will say is, that you, with many of the upper classes, are grossly misled in believing the Claimant an impostor. I live within one mile of Tichborne, and have known the Family all my life, and the Claimant for six years; and repeat to you what I wrote to Mr. GLADSTONE, that from information I possess, and from what I learnt from the mother, to whom I promised faithfully I would never abandon her son, I stake my honour as a gentleman, and my reputation as a Member of Parliament, that the Claimant is Sir ROGER C. D. TICHBORNE. The jury unanimously agreed that he was ARTHUR ORTON, but had not sufficient evidence to prove him so; and they also agreed, if proof could be given he was *not* ARTHUR, that he was ROGER TICHBORNE. We have now got that proof beyond contradiction; and we also hold positive proofs of his being ROGER TICHBORNE. At all our great and glorious meetings, surrounded by millions of the British public—a public that was never wrong on any great question—we challenge anyone to come on those platforms, and give us one solid reason why he is an impostor, whilst we are ready to give 1,000 reasons why he is the right man; and we carry all before us. That he had a fair trial no one can admit. He shall have one now, and assuredly Not Guilty will be his verdict.—I am, yours truly,

GUILDFORD ONSLOW.

EDWARD BAINES, Esq., M.P.

The following letter from Mr. GUILDFORD ONSLOW, M.P., is believed by that gentleman to be a verbatim copy of the one addressed by him to the Editor of the *Leeds Mercury*, and which has not appeared in that journal. We challenge the Editor to produce the original letter.

TO THE EDITOR OF THE "LEEDS MERCURY."

SIR,—In reply to Mr. BAINES' statement that no educated people believed in the identity of the Claimant, I will give the following list:—

Sir GEORGE GIFFARD.
Sir JOHN HOLT.
Judge SELWYN.
Judge HANNEN.
Sir JOHN KARSLAKE.
Mr. GIFFARD, Q.C.
Mr. KARSLAKE, Q.C.
Mr. LOCOCK WEBB, Q.C.
Dr. TRISTRAM.
Serjeant BALLANTINE.
W. HOPKINS, Esq.
— HOLMES, Esq.
Messrs. MORGAN and Co.
Messrs. BAXTER, ROSE, and NORTON.
Messrs. GORTON and Co.
Sir TALBOT CONSTABLE.
General CUSTANCE, J.P.
Lady TICHBORNE.
Lady RODNEY.
Colonel SAWYER.
Colonel SHERSTONE.
Rev. CÆSAR BISHOP.
F. J. P. MAUX, Esq., J.P.
J. W. SCOTT, Esq., J.P.
— BULPETT, Esq., J.P.
Major PINKNEY.
The Misses ONSLOW.
Major HEYWOOD.
Major STILLMAN.
Mr. ANTHONY W. BIDDULPH, J.P.
Colonel LUSHINGTON, K.C.B.

All of whom either swore to his identity or believed he was the person he represented himself to be.—I am, Sir, your obedient servant,

GUILDFORD ONSLOW.

SIR ROGER TICHBORNE, BART., IN BRADFORD.

MEETING IN ST. GEORGE'S HALL.

The Claimant to the Tichborne Estates, who arrived in Bradford on Monday afternoon, and took up his quarters in the Victoria Hotel, addressed a meeting in St. George's Hall on Tuesday, Oct. 15. Charges for admission of 2s., 1s., and 6d. were made, and the gallery and area were nearly filled, while the stalls had a fair sprinkling of occupants. It is believed that about 3,000 persons were present. Amongst the audience was a considerable number of ladies. The Claimant, on making his appearance on the platform, accompanied by the Committee, was received with loud and prolonged cheering, to which he bowed his acknowledgments.

Mr. WALKER, of Leeds, occupied the chair, and in a few words opened the proceedings.

Sir ROGER, who was enthusiastically cheered, said that before he proceeded to address the meeting he would read the following letter, which he had received that afternoon:—

"This is to warn Thee if tha tells ony moor foul and blaggardly lyes abaht honest folk there'll be them in that hall to-morn't ncet as will mak thee wish thee sen back at Wagga Wagga. Soa moind what tha ses. A WIBSEY CHAP."

He hoped that the silly-minded individual who wrote the letter did not imagine for one moment that taking his life would injure him, for it would be one of the greatest blessings which could be conferred upon him, after the trouble he had had during the last few years. He was quite sure they would agree with him that his life was hardly worth having under the circumstances, although he had too much courage to take by his own hands that life which God had given him. (Applause.) At the same time there was no man so willing to part with his life as he was; nevertheless, the man who threatened to take his life must remember that he could not injure him (the Claimant) in the sight of God, but he would send his own soul to eternal damnation. (Applause.) With regard to his identity with ROGER TICHBORNE he contended that had already been proved. It had been proved

G. B. SKIPWORTH, ESQ.

to the British public by eighty-three witnesses, and it had been disputed by twelve. (Cries of "Shame.") They must remember that not one of his witnesses broke down when under cross-examination, although subjected to one of the most severe cross-examinations that witnesses ever went through. There were twelve witnesses examined against him. Five of these witnesses were his own relatives, two uncles, two aunts, and a cousin; and yet the jury thought proper to stop a case that had continued for 103 days, upon the evidence of twelve witnesses. (Cries of "Shame.") He won his case in Chancery quite easily. In fact, it was hardly opposed. Probably many of them were not aware that when the Court of Chancery held an estate for an infant, they had no power of ejecting any tenant without getting the permission of the Vice-Chancellor. They had to obtain the requisite permission by producing affidavits, and he produced 280. The Case was disputed by the Judge for one day, and on the Saturday Vice-Chancellor STUART ordered that the Case should be argued on the following Monday, although his opponents had not defended it. He was put to an expense of £60 for Counsel, and on the following Monday his lordship decided that he should have permission to eject. He then took his Case into the Court of Common Pleas, and it was tried before Lord Chief Justice BOVILL, and lasted 103 days, when it was resulted in his electing to be nonsuited, for the best of all reasons—he had no money to carry the Case further. The Claimant then described the class of witnesses who were examined in support of his Case, and remarked that the evidence against him was principally the tattoo marks. He also described the nature of the alleged tattoo marks, as severally represented by Lord BELLEW, Mons. and Madame CHATILLON, Lady DOUGHTY, and Mrs. RADCLIFFE, and pointed out the discrepancies in their evidence on this point. He also criticised the evidence of Mr. DANBY SEYMOUR and Mr. ALFRED SEYMOUR respecting the tattoo marks. He remarked that two of the Carabineers would address the meeting that evening, and they could judge for themselves whether they were the kind of persons described by the Attorney-General, who ought to have vindicated the British soldiers, instead of saying they were to be bought for a pot of beer. The Attorney-General made a speech of thirty days' duration, and he painted him very black. Well, he supposed it was not the first time that he had been painted black by a lawyer, and he could stand it very well without changing colour. (Laughter and applause.) It was a great consolation to him to know that all the Attorney-General had said about him was false, and that some day it would be proved to be false. (Hear, hear.) No doubt, after the jury were told by the Attorney-General that if they did not come to a conclusion they would have to sit and hear 260 more witnesses, and that being kept from their business, they after hearing the evidence about the tattoo marks, were glad to stop the Case. But he asked them whether that jury showed the moral courage which Englishmen ought to show. (Cries of "No, no.") After putting him to an expense of £120,000, they had not the moral courage to hear the Case to a conclusion. (Applause.) It was not only the loss to him of that large sum of money, but the question was, what would it cost him to put the Case in the same stage again. (Cheers.) In addition to this, through their misconduct he had been incarcerated within the stone walls of Newgate for fifty-two days. (Cries of "Shame.") Not satisfied with this, the Attorney-General actually brought a charge of forgery against him, knowing that forgery was not a bailable offence. The Claimant complained strongly of the treatment which he had received in respect to his incarceration, and went on to say that the Case had gone on so far that the character of the Attorney-General depended entirely on the issue of the Case. There was no doubt that the Attorney-General had committed himself to a very great extent, and the Government had equally committed itself in coming to his rescue. (Cheers.) Why, he asked, should the Government intervene in a civil action between himself and his relatives? The Government refused to interfere in OVEREND and GURNEY's affair, and in several cases where they might have done some good to the British public. It was strange that before the Case was finished, the Judge came into Court with all his documents ready prepared to send him to Newgate, and the Attorney-General had instructions from his Government to prosecute. (Cries of "Shame.") It showed that not only did the Judge prejudge the Case, but the Attorney-General had instructions to prosecute him before the Case was concluded. The Claimant then referred to the remark he made to the Judge, that he had taken upon himself the position of Judge and Counsel, and he asked them if they thought it possible that he would have insulted his lordship in that manner if he had seen the slightest prospect of having a fair trial. (Hear, hear.) He did so in the hope that the Judge would have committed him there and then for contempt of Court, that the public might see the unfair manner in which the Trial was conducted. Then, they never heard of him putting in any forged letters. They never heard of him tampering with evidence in any way. But what did the other side do? The Attorney-General placed before him three forged letters, and afterwards admitted that *he knew* two of them were forged, but that he did not think the third was. Then there was the thumb in the daguerreotype. Although the daguerreotype was in possession of the Court, and by right there ought to have been no access to it, it so happened that it was taken home by Mr. BOWKER, of Winchester. When it was shown to Mr. BAIGENT, the thumb had been rubbed out. His lordship said, "Oh, impossible: it never was there." Mr. BAIGENT said it had been, and the Lord Chief Justice said it had never been out of the possession of the Court. But he produced a photograph of the daguerreotype in which the thumb was visible. His lordship then said the thumb had been rubbed out by handling, but his lordship forgot that it was in a glass case. (Laughter.) The Attorney-General menaced the jury by saying that if they did not come to a conclusion then, the Case would in all probability last three or four years. He asked them whether there was any fairness in addressing a jury like that. Why, it was neither more nor less than intimidating the jury. (Cheers.) The speaker then read from the affidavits of Lady TICHBORNE, as to his identity; and also from those of Mr. HOPKINS as to the tests that gentleman had adopted to settle the same point. As to the scars on his body, he said he had twelve or thirteen of them, which the Attorney-General declared had been fabricated. Now he asked them if it were possible that Sir WILLIAM FERGUSSON, Dr. CRAMPTON, and some of the most eminent physicians in London, could not detect those scars as having been recently made? (Hear, hear.) Another matter to which he wished to direct their attention was this, that two brothers of the Judge went about the country making a £100 bet against his winning the Case. They had gone to his cousin, Mr. BIDDULPH, and asked him to bet, but he declined to do so, saying that they had already a tout in the stable—meaning the Lord Chief Justice. He asked them whether such conduct was not shameful? (Hear, hear.) He also complained that all his papers had been taken from him whilst he was in Newgate, so that he was deprived of the proper means of defence in the forthcoming Trial, and he exposed the conduct of a detective named MCKENZIE, who had attempted to bribe a witness at Swansea named CROOK. He condemned the conduct of ROUS, who, he said, had been taking copies of the evidence in his favour and sending it to the other side. Why was all this necessary, if he could be proved to be an impostor? He also related the circumstances under which he had interviews with Mr. and Mrs. RADCLIFFE, and other of his relatives, for the purpose of identification, and complained that they had told him lies in order to entrap him into making a mistake. He mentioned that the other day, when he was at Birmingham, he saw in a copy of the *Sydney Morning Herald* an advertisement offering £1,000 reward to any person who would prove the relationship to the Claimant otherwise than TICHBORNE; so they saw his opponents were not yet quite certain that he was ARTHUR ORTON. He would, in conclusion, tell them the different persons he had been made out to be since he had been in England. First, he was JOHN MOORE, but JOHN MOORE turned up, and gave evidence in his favour; second, he was WILLIAM, a servant with Sir EDWARD DOUGHTY TICHBORNE; third, he was SMITH, son of the old butler, but SMITH turned up, so that he could not be him; fourth, he was an old servant of Mr. JAMES TICHBORNE, his father; fifth, he was an old servant named COLES, but COLES came to life, and came to see him; sixth, he was his own servant in the Carabineers; seventh, he was an old Carabineer; eighth, he was a sailor from Poole; ninth, he was DAVID CASE, a native of Poole; tenth, he was an illegitimate son of his father; eleventh, he was an illegitimate son of Sir EDWARD DOUGHTY, his uncle; twelfth, he was an illegitimate son of Mr. ROBERT TICHBORNE; thirteenth, he was an illegitimate son of Sir HENRY TICHBORNE; fourteenth, he was the son of a man in Australia who was coming to England to identify him; fifteenth, he was an Australian prize-fighter; sixteenth, he was an Australian navvy; seventeenth, he was an Australian native, whose father and mother were on their way to England to identify him; eighteenth, he was EDWARD ORTON; nineteenth, he was HENRY ORTON; twentieth, he was ARTHUR ORTON; twenty-first (and the most cruel of all), he was an illegitimate son of his mother, the Dowager Lady TICHBORNE, before marriage; twenty-second, he was GEORGE JARVIS, who sailed from Liverpool; and many other persons. The Claimant then intimated that to-night he would treat of the sealed packet and Mrs. RADCLIFFE, and resumed his seat amidst loud cheers.

Sergeant-Major MARKS and Private BARRY, both of whom had served in the Carabineers with Sir ROGER TICHBORNE, both addressed the meeting, and stated that they were ready to swear positively to the identity of the Claimant. They had both instantly recognized him without him being pointed out to them.

On the motion of the Claimant, a vote of thanks was awarded to the Chairman for presiding, and the assembly dispersed.

SECOND MEETING IN ST. GEORGE'S HALL.

The Claimant to the Tichborne Estates addressed a second meeting in St. George's Hall last night, and, as on the previous evening, was most enthusiastically received. The attendance was not so large as on the previous night; but probably there would be about 2,000 persons present. He was accompanied on the platform by several members of the local Committee of the "TICHBORNE Defence Fund," and also some ladies.

Mr. WALKER (of Leeds) again occupied the chair, and in a few remarks introduced

Sir ROGER, who, at the outset of his speech, said he had received another threatening letter which had been sent to him, and which he would scarcely have noticed, unless to intimate to the writer—whoever he might be—that it would take something more than the silly endeavours of a scurrilous writer to frighten him. (Hear, hear, and cheers.) He received the letter about twenty-five minutes before coming to that hall, and opened and read it in the presence of three or four gentlemen, who were then on the platform. The letter ran as follows:—

"This is to warn you that if you appear in the hall to-night, you must beware of me and a few more, who are already with daggers in their hands—(laughter and cheers)—and if they fail there are others to take their place, you coward. So mind your life if you value it, trying to take other people's money out of their pockets, and don't tell any more of them lies, you big-bellied thief. (Cheers and laughter.) So beware of me you have wronged. (Renewed laughter.)

"October 16."

Well, he could only say that if a man was such a coward as to require *five* or *six* to help him to attack one defenceless person, he was sure he did not care for fifty like him. (Applause.) Presuming that a large portion of the audience had not heard his previous night's speech, he proceeded to recapitulate the principal portions of it, and followed this up by reading several extracts in his favour which had recently appeared in some of the leading London and provincial newspapers. He complained of the course the Government had adopted—on the authority of a newspaper paragraph (which he read)—of indicting for perjury only, so that *they* could have the benefit of a Special jury, instead of a Common jury, thereby being able to secure a verdict in *their* favour. He characterised this as a most monstrous proceeding, inasmuch as were the indictment laid the other way, he could prove to all the world that he was ROGER TICHBORNE, and nobody else. (Loud cheers.) After reviewing at some length the nature of the proceedings at the Sessions House, Westminster, he passed on—in fulfilment of his promise made on the previous evening—to give some explanation as to the history of the "sealed packet," about which so much had been said. He repeated what he had said on so many previous occasions, that the statement had been extorted from him in Court, first by threats—which he defied—and next by persuasion, it being clearly understood that nobody but the Judge, the jury, and the Counsel in the case should know the contents of the packet, a copy of which he furnished them. He trusted to the honour of his friend, Mr. HOLMES, who solemnly declared that the document should be kept carefully locked up in his safe until asked for by the Court, and yet only a few days afterwards Mr. CHARLES HINGSTON called upon him and told him that he and several others had seen it. He contended that he was blameless in the matter, and at the Trial he had told the Attorney-General that the responsibility must fall on that gentleman and not on him (the Claimant). He would ask them to consider that he was suing for property worth half a million of money, not for himself, as he did not care so much about it, but for his children; and he, as their father, felt bound to fight, and fight he would, until the day he died. (Loud and prolonged applause.)

Sergeant-Major MARKS and Private BARRY, both of whom had served with ROGER TICHBORNE in the Carabineers, each addressed the meeting, and asseverated their belief that the gentleman who had just addressed the meeting was Sir ROGER and no other.

Sir ROGER then proposed a vote of thanks to the Chairman, and in doing so expressed his thanks for the support accorded to him in Bradford, and stated that he should count the two or three days he had spent there as some of the pleasantest of his life.

The vote of thanks being duly carried, and briefly acknowledged, the meeting broke up.

We cite the following, which was published the next day, from the *Bradford Chronicle*:—

When the mountain would not come to MAHOMET, MAHOMET had the good sense to go to the mountain; and as it was obviously impossible that the entire country could go to the metropolis to see Sir ROGER, that gentleman has very properly gone to the country, like other great men, to give the provincial British public an opportunity of seeing him. The announcement that Bradford was to be one of the favoured places was no sooner made public than my wife, who is a strong friend, not to say partisan, of the Claimant, because she has, as she says, "a strong sense of justice," insisted that I should at once procure a couple of tickets for the Hall, in order that, under the escort of myself, she might have an opportunity of seeing and hearing him. My wife, let me say in passing, is one of the best of women—superb, inestimable—with the most delightful of domestic tempers. I have invariably found, however, that when she insists upon having anything done, it is folly on my part to hang back. I have to yield at last, and I find it best policy to yield at once, and with a good grace. I have my own opinion about Sir ROGER, and on several occasions I have ventured to express it, but on each I was regularly "floored"—in an argumentative sense, I mean—by my better half. She has a ready answer to all the weak points in his Case. She makes nothing of the "Baronet's" self-contradictions, nor of the contradictions of others on his side; and she is never weary of parading the array of respectable witnesses—the colonels, the majors, the captains, and others—whose testimony could not have been bought, who swore to his identity before the eyes of gainsayers. It is long since I have expressed an opinion of my own on the subject in her presence, and as I had a sneaking desire to see the great man myself, I got a glimpse of a portion of his back once in London, as he was entering that little crib at Westminster which will henceforth be associated with his name. I secured the necessary pasteboard, at a cost of 4s., and proceeded to St. George's Hall, on Tuesday night, in time to secure a good seat. This would have been a difficult matter, so far as the area and gallery were concerned, as they were packed soon after the doors were thrown open, but the two-shilling sympathizers with Sir ROGER in Bradford were less numerous. The stalls were comparatively empty, the attendance there being a mere fringe round the front seats, broken here and there by gaps of empty space. The "local Committee" did not turn out to be a strong one. Less than a dozen persons accompanied "Sir ROGER" to the platform. Tremendous was the cheering when the great man arrived, one gentleman in the front row of the patron's gallery being specially conspicuous in the manifestation of his feelings, but whether they were in favour of or against the hero, I am not prepared to say. My first thought, after I had got a good view of the "Sir ROGER" was, "What a magnificent FALSTAFF he would make!" "A plague of sighing and grief!" Can it be that his vast obesity came of "the law's delay," of which he has been the victim? "Poor fellow," whispered my wife, "don't you think he looks sad and melancholy?" "No, my dear," I replied; "I think he looks uncommonly jolly. 'A goodly, portly man, i' faith, and a corpulent; of a cheerful look, and a pleasing eye, and'"—— "He's got beautiful eyes," she interrupted, "and any one can see at a glance that he belongs to the aristocracy. Why, he looks exactly like—you remember, my dear, that Lord—what's his name?" "He looks just like ROGER," I said, without prompting her memory, as to the name of the nobleman that had escaped it, and at this point the Chairman rose to commence the proceedings of the evening. His speech was brief, and when "Sir ROGER" came forward to the rails to speak, the applause was tremendous. I am bound to say that my wife was the most demonstrative among the stall people, at which I confess I was somewhat ashamed. At last the great man was permitted to proceed. Of his speech I need say nothing, as the ample report you gave of it in the *Chronicle* is quite sufficient: but I may say a few words as to the impression the speech produced upon me. In the first place—if the composition is his own, it shows a much higher degree of culture than might be expected from a Wapping butcher, who had spent the greatest portion of his life under conditions calculated to root up any degree of mental culture he may have learned in his boyhood. On the other hand, the composition of such a speech was quite within range of the capacity of a man who had the same educational advantages as were enjoyed by ROGER CHARLES TICHBORNE in his youth, but who had spent many years in a semi-barbarous state of society. The grammatical errors were those of a badly-educated, but not of a wholly uneducated man. They were such, indeed, as are made every day by speakers who have not been regularly trained in the art. His eccentricities of pronunciation were of the same character. He was not perfect in his "h's," and the addition of the letter "r" to "law," and other words ending in "w," though undoubtedly savouring of Wapping, are not special to that region, nor to the class to which ARTHUR ORTON belongs. It was a clever speech, and it was well spoken. Some of the points were specially telling, and I shall not be surprised, judging from the manner in which these were received by the audience, should the Government find out that the stumping tour of the Claimant has resulted in a considerable decrease of their popularity. The tattoo marks were exceedingly well managed, and the assertion of the Attorney-General, that the evidence of British soldiers can be purchased for a pot of beer, was used in such a manner as brought down the house. In short, the speech bristled with points, and there can be no doubt that had it rested with the Tuesday night meeting to declare that the speaker was the rightful heir to the Tichborne Estates, a resolution to that effect would have been carried *nem. con.* "Are you not convinced now?" said my better-half, when we had got seated in the cab that was to take us home. "I am very hungry, my dear," was my reply, and my meaning was quite well understood. I must say, however, that the man does not look like an impostor, and that Sergeant-Major MARKS looks the impersonation of honesty and truthfulness.

We insert some clever verses, published at this time:—

UNSOLICITED QUESTIONS,

Asked by a Solicitor-General of an unwelcome visitor from that [Tich]borne from which some travellers (who are least wanted or expected) do return.

Would it surprise you to hear,
 Though now big, you are really small?
Would it surprise you to hear
 That you never were born at all?

Would it surprise you to hear
 The fact—which is sure as a gun—
No matter what you may think,
 You were never your father's son?

Would it surprise you to hear—
 (I am going to draw it mild)—
Would it surprise you to hear
 You're the original "Nobody's Child"?

Would it surprise you to hear
 The letters of your inditing,
Although *you* held the pen,
 Are somebody else's writing?

Would it surprise you to hear,
 When wrecked and nearly dead,
You were not in the bed of the ocean,
 But asleep on a feather bed?

Would it surprise you to hear
 That somebody else is you,
And that you are somebody else?—
 A fact clear, simple, and true.

Would it surprise you to hear—
 A thing plain to every fool—
You learnt all you happen to know
 At a place where you ne'er went to school?

Would it surprise you to hear
 Your mouth's not your own, nor your eyes?
Would it surprise you to hear
 You never were half your own size?

Would it surprise you to hear—
 A rather smart thing for a dunce—
Though you think you are standing here,
 You are now in two places at once?

Would it surprise you to hear,
 Though married, you haven't a wife?
Would it surprise you to hear
 For years you've departed this life?

Would it surprise you to hear
 (Though ne'er in that part of the town)
You were born in the Wapping back slums,
 And your father as ORTON was known?

Would it surprise you to hear,
 While badgered in Westminster Hall,
That, not only you are not yourself,
 But decidedly no one at all?

If you don't want to be thus surprised,
 And go through six months' awful bother,
At once own you've never been born,
 And never had father or mother.

(*Badgered Party turns suddenly on Badgerer.*)

Would it surprise you to hear,
 Like "DOGBERRY" sage, alas!
In spite of your horsehair wig,
 You *may* be "written down an ass"?

Those that follow are not less pungent:—

THE MYSTERIOUS TATTOO.

Whence came the tattoo hullabaloo?
Were the marks jet black, or were they blue?
Who assisted to make them, my Lord BELLEW?
This surely must be the Devil's tattoo.

A sailor, perhaps, from a phantom crew,
Tattooed the first marks on *you know who*;
For *if not Sir* ROGER, my Lord BELLEW,
He's the Devil! said one, who the real ROGER knew.

You put it upon us, my Lord BELLEW,
The friend of Sir ROGER—Sir ROGER the true,
That you were afraid of giving a clue
To *that other*, lest he should himself tattoo.

We may take it, perhaps, then, my Lord BELLEW,
That your marvellous reticence may have been due
To the fear of awaking a hullabaloo,
Suggestive at least of the Devil's tattoo.

The Claimant was in Lincolnshire on Monday, 2nd September, 1872. We give the report:—

THE CLAIMANT AT GRIMSBY.

Sir ROGER CHARLES DOUGHTY TICHBORNE addressed a crowded meeting at the Town Hall, Grimsby, on Monday evening last. The reception accorded him here was as hearty as elsewhere, and, whether in the streets or otherwise, was most gratifying to him and his supporters. He has been well supported by some of the most influential gentlemen of Grimsby and district. Councillor CAMPBELL presided.

The Chairman, in opening the proceedings, said he felt glad to see such a large number of persons present. They had met to hear and see one whose name was familiar to all. The name of that person had been circulated throughout the length and breadth of the land; nay, he might say throughout the length and breadth of the world. The name of that gentleman to whom he alluded was none other than Sir ROGER CHARLES DOUGHTY TICHBORNE, Bart. (Cheers.) He (the Chairman) would not make any further remarks, but leave the speaking to be done by others.

G. B. SKIPWORTH, Esq., of Moortown, Caistor, moved the first resolution, as follows:—"That this meeting, believing the Claimant to be Sir ROGER TICHBORNE, the rightful owner of the Tichborne Estates, according to evidence produced at the Trial, will use every lawful endeavour to procure a fair and impartial trial in order to restore possession of his estates, and trusts that the country will never cease its agitation until justice is done to him, and the honour of the nation satisfied." In moving the resolution, he observed that as he placed himself in that conspicuous position, he should like to give some account of the reasons why he unhesitatingly believed the Claimant to be no impostor, but the veritable Sir ROGER TICHBORNE, Bart. To make a starting-point in the evidence, he should say, first, in familiar language, does not a fond mother know her sucking child? The recognition by Lady TICHBORNE was from the Claimant mentioning certain facts which could only be known between mother and son. Would a stranger, or any but an own mother, or someone equal to her, give a person £1,000 a year? They were asked to believe the unheard-of inhumanity that the £1,000 a year was given to an unknown stranger, who might be the vilest monster out of the wilds of Australia—and to supplant whom? Why, one of her own flesh and blood, a mere infant, and that the child of another dead son. (Applause.) They said she was eccentric. Her eccentricity was in acting the part of a fond and affectionate mother. Did she not sign a solemn declaration, and who should gainsay it, that he was in truth her son? and did she not look on him to the day of her death as her long-absent, but restored son? (Applause.) Put the most honest men in Sir ROGER's position of being examined on the principle of his being an impostor, credited with nothing appertaining to truth or honesty of purpose, but at the same time being expected to answer any question that a Counsel thus attacking chose to put. Would not nature revolt at questions put under such views and circumstances? Would not they, in spite of themselves, be moved with a scorn and contempt that would make even truth look dark against them? Would not their mind, instead of being fixed on the subject brought to their notice, almost waver between giving a direct reply and none at all? And though a lie might be pardonable under such an awful system of cross-fire as was practised—if he had been so situated he thought he should have given a lot of lies—he did not believe that Plaintiff intentionally told an untruth. If they believed, as he did, the Claimant to be Sir ROGER TICHBORNE, the true and rightful heir, and to be robbed of his inheritance, they must not give sleep to their eyelids till they, as English men and women, had made their sympathies known and felt. (Applause.) But how much more conclusive the evidence of the mother when that was thoroughly substantiated by thousands of other incidents, all tallying so minutely, and bearing so unmistakeably the mark of truth, that however they came to be distorted into lies was a mystery which no reasonable mind could fathom. (Hear, hear.) They could do so on the principle of its being the most unreasonable, the unfairest, and most partial Trial that ever disgraced the records of a Court of Law. Here was a Case where eighty-six truthful and impartial witnesses, backed by the dying declaration of the mother and the family solicitor, were so thoroughly ignored that if they had never uttered a voice, as far as that Trial was concerned, they would have done more for the Cause than all the testimony which was brought forward by them; and more than this, they would have saved themselves from the vile epithets and coarse insinuations of the Attorney-General, from which no character, however unsullied, no mind, however pure and refined, could shield them. (Applause.) And whilst upon that, he would ask, was it to be endured by the People that a member of the English Bar, whether the head or not, should take advantage of that position to insult, browbeat, and stultify, if possible, every witness that came forward with the intention of speaking the honest truth? (Hear, hear.) Because in that position, was he to escape the same law that would visit any individual in the land who, with no other cause but to satisfy his own selfish ends, chose to slander wilfully or injure the character, honour, or reputation of any man, however humble, whose only motive in coming forward was to honestly, faithfully, and truthfully say what he knew for his fellow-man? Such a system, whilst it placed nearly every witness at the mercy of a Counsel, gave him a license so unbridled that neither justice nor fair-play could attach to a Trial conducted on so mean and dastardly a principle, and such a Trial, he did not hesitate to say, was that in which the Claimant was concerned. (Applause.) Where was the justice if, on a mere notion or fancy, the Plaintiff was to be branded with all that was vile and infamous, and to have a charge of conspiracy brought against him? By implication, others besides the Claimant were stamped as being liars, perjurers, and conspirators. Had evidence been brought to prove the Claimant another person, that would have settled the question. (Applause.) They had said he was some score of people, the final upshot being that he was ORTON, and the Attorney-General was barefaced enough to tell the Prime Minister he could prove him ORTON in twenty minutes. He would tell the Attorney-General to his face that if he said the Claimant was ORTON he was a liar. (Applause.) The conspirators laid their heads together, and then came the statement about the tattooing. Plaintiff's witnesses, who had equal, if not better, opportunities of knowing whether he was tattooed, declared with positive certainty that he was not. (Applause.) If it was true about the marks, why not have asked the Claimant to unbare his arm immediately upon his arrival in this country? He believed the matter, like many others, was exploded, and that the Defendants had not one leg to stand upon, barring the rotten and shivering timbers of the Attorney-General and Justice BOVILL. (Applause.) But fortunately the Case on the other side was so full of evidence confirmatory of the Plaintiff's rights, and he did not hesitate to say that nothing but the vilest piece of iniquity, amounting to the grossest conspiracy, kept him out of possession of his just and lawful rights. (Applause.) Three of the crew of the "Bella" had also been heard of, but one, named HARRIS, had been kept in a drunken state, and went to sea shortly after his arrival in England, and GOD only knew where he was at the present time. There seemed to be some secret agency which was ever ready to pounce upon any mortal thing or body that might be of advantage to the Claimant, and remove them from his reach. (Applause.) In conclusion, Mr. SKIPWORTH said the evidence for the Claimant was so complete, that if he failed to get his rights upon it, it was good-bye to justice in England.

Sergeant-Major MARKS, formerly of the regiment of Carabineers to which Sir ROGER TICHBORNE belonged, seconded the motion. He said he had opportunities of seeing Sir ROGER whilst in the army, drilling with him constantly. He had not the slightest hesitation in saying that the Claimant was Sir ROGER TICHBORNE. (Cheers.)

Sir ROGER, who was received with loud and renewed cheering, then addressed the meeting. He observed that he was a very large landed proprietor in Lincolnshire, having a very large property within a few miles of Lincoln. He had never had an opportunity of knowing his tenants. He was in Hampshire in his younger days, and had ample opportunities of knowing well his tenants there. Those tenants had had ample opportunities of knowing him well, and it was a source of delight to him that not one who knew him in his younger days would say he was not Sir ROGER TICHBORNE, but, on the contrary, came and swore positively that he was the heir to the Tichborne Estates. (Applause.) The press had never ceased to abuse him since the day he went to Newgate. ("Shame.") He had never ceased to be clear of detectives since the day he landed in England. At every place he was watched and followed. *The addresses of letters he had sent to the post had been taken, and people hearing his house had been offered 2s. 6d. for the blotting-paper on which he had dried his writing.* No doubt the intention was if the blotting-paper had been obtained to hold it before a looking-glass to ascertain what he had written. He could stand all this unfairness, because he had got truth on his side. (Applause.) As to the witnesses examined on his behalf, they went through such a cross-examination as no witnesses had ever gone through before. They went through that severe cross-examination, and not one of them broke down. Then they must remember that he himself was in the witness-box for twenty-eight days, and although he might get confused under such a cross-examination, he came out of the box without breaking down. (Applause.) The Attorney-General had the remembrances of one hundred brains with which to confuse his (the Claimant's) one, and he very much doubted whether the Attorney-General could have come out of the witness-box in such a manner. (Applause.) He could not understand why, after depriving him of the benefits of a law which had stood for hundreds of years, and preventing him bringing up his witnesses at the Government expense, £100,000 should be voted, with which to bring witnesses from Australia to prosecute him. (A Voice: We won't pay it.) He could not tell why they should send to Australia, unless it was to get witnesses at a cheaper rate, as there were plenty of people there desirous of securing a return passage to England. The Attorney-General had acted on the authority he possessed, and had the Case removed from one Court to another. Not satisfied with the charges made against him, his friends who were desirous of bailing him were put to every possible annoyance, and had to make statements as to their property. Mr. LOWE had stated in Parliament, in reply to Mr. WHALLEY, that the Attorney-General had nothing to do with the matter, as it was now in the hands of Mr. BRUCE. Why should the Attorney-General have been at so much trouble in shifting the Case from one court to another, and in making a faithful promise to prosecute? Had he retired because he was ashamed? or was it because the voice of England was unmistakeably heard in the matter? (Applause.) A friend of his had taken singular note as the Trial proceeded, and it showed *There were 9,080 interruptions against the Claimant by the Judge*, and only one for him. That friend was one of the Town Council of Southampton, and made the statement at a recent meeting. He (the Claimant) remarked to the Judge during the Trial that it did not appear the other side wanted any Counsel when they had him. On other occasions when passing the Judge near the Court, he touched his hat to him, but there was no response, and he was passed by his lordship as though he was a dog. He assured the meeting that he ceased touching his hat. If he (the Claimant) was an impostor, Mr. SEYMOUR must be 10,000 times worse. He was in duty bound to unmask at once an impostor, if he knew of one. It was worse. What had they to say to a man and a brother who allowed him (the Claimant) to remain in Lady TICHBORNE's house two years, and to enjoy half her income, if she was, as represented, an imbecile? There were not words too bad to describe such a man. He asked any of the audience if they knew an impostor to be dwelling in the house of an imbecile sister if they would not go and kick him out? (Applause.) Another strange thing was, how, if she was an imbecile, did she herself conduct her banking account so well up to the last days of her life? And what had Mr. SEYMOUR repeated to a member of Parliament, a friend of his (the Claimant's)? Mr. ALFRED SEYMOUR said, "What about your friend the impostor?" The friend replied, "Well, you forget your Sister acknowledged him." Mr. SEYMOUR then observed, "Well, she is grilling in hell for it at the present moment." (Cries of "Shame.") He (the Claimant) asked if a man who would revile his dead sister's name in such a manner was to be believed. Sir ROGER, on resuming his seat, was loudly cheered.

Mr. R. SMITH then moved "That this meeting strongly condemns the action of the Government in the matter of the prosecution of the Claimant, and using the public money for that purpose, and that their excuse for doing so on the order of a Judge who showed himself thoroughly biassed throughout the late Trial, backed by the Attorney-General as the opposing Counsel, is not such as to satisfy the people of this country, and it calls upon members in their places in Parliament to stand up and protest against such an iniquitous application of the nation's money." He observed that the Plaintiff's witnesses were in the proportion of five to one at the late Trial.

Mr. S. SMETHURST seconded the motion, observing that the evidence of the Frenchmen convinced him that it was a diabolical conspiracy on their part.

Sergeant GALL, formerly of the 6th Dragoons, briefly addressed the meeting, stating that he would swear most positively that the Claimant, who was present, was the real Sir ROGER TICHBORNE. (Applause.)

Votes of thanks to the Mayor, for the use of the Town Hall, and to Councillor CAMPBELL, for presiding, closed the proceedings.

As the Claimant left the building, he shook hands with the people, who crowded around him on all sides, and he was loudly cheered as he proceeded to the Royal Hotel.

On Tuesday afternoon there was a dinner to the Claimant.

Sir ROGER attended a second meeting, of which we give the report:

THE CLAIMANT AT GRIMSBY.

Sir ROGER TICHBORNE attended a public meeting in the Oddfellows' Hall, Grimsby, last week. The attendance was very large and enthusiastic. Mr. Councillor CAMPBELL presided, and called upon

Mr. WILLIAM COLLEY PARKER to move the following resolution:—"That this meeting strongly condemns the action of the Government in the prosecution of the Claimant, and using the public money for that purpose, and that their excuse for doing so, on the order of a Judge who showed himself thoroughly biassed throughout the late Trial, backed by the Attorney-General, his opposing Counsel, is not such as to satisfy the people of this country. And it calls upon members in their places in Parliament to stand up and protest against such an iniquitous application of the nation's money."

Mr. OSMOND said: Mr. Chairman, Ladies and gentlemen,—It is with great pleasure I rise to second the resolution. This arises from a two-fold source. First, because as a Committee we are actuated by that spirit which characterizes every true Englishman —a desire for justice and fair-play. Second, because we believe, from evidence produced at the Trial, that we have in our presence the real Sir ROGER TICHBORNE. The institutions of our country are noble and glorious, they exalt her in the scale of nations, and make her the glory of the earth, and the admiration of all around her. As Englishmen we boast of her freedom, liberty, privileges, the security of our homes, the sacredness with which we regard human life, and on the whole, the code of laws which regulate and govern us as a nation. For these our fathers shed their blood and nobly maintained them, and through their death we now enjoy them; and in our generation, what we say to nations we say to thrones, parliaments, societies, and individuals. Directly you infringe on these in any shape or form, you touch our very existence, and we in our turn will fight to the bitter end to uphold them, and hand them down to our children if possible safer, purer, and in a more healthy condition. The heart of our country ever beats and throbs when appealed to by want or calamity. It does not ask the question whether friend or foe. The expiring negro, with his lacerated back, dying beneath the oppressor's lash, stretched out his hand to the British nation for justice; nobly and bravely she came forward, fought his battles, burst asunder the shackles that bound him, emancipated the slave; and now, tens of thousands rejoice in British rule, and are taking shelter beneath the English flag. Our country is ready with her mighty arm to cover and protect the defenceless, and throw princely wealth into the lap of the unfortunate. Now, shall we as a nation, possessing these sterling qualities, calmly and quietly look on, and see one of the noblest political institutions of our land—I mean, trial by jury—stained by miscarriage of justice, and make no effort to redress the wrong? Shall it ever be said that a man was placed at an English bar whose cause suffered damage on account of the Judge being biassed, backed by the vile assumptions of the Attorney-General, his opposing Counsel, and as a country that we remained unmoved? No, sir; public opinion, which seldom goes wrong, has lifted up its voice—that opinion which dictates to empires, kingdoms, and senate houses—and that governs the world—has proclaimed itself throughout the length and breadth of the land in tones that cannot be mistaken. Whether the Claimant be Sir ROGER TICHBORNE or ARTHUR ORTON, this man or that man—he will, he must, he shall have a fair and impartial trial. It is not always the first question with an Englishman, whether a man is innocent or guilty; this at times must remain in abeyance. Another one stands out more prominently towering above the rest? Has justice been done? As a nation, we do not believe in the expression, "When a man is down, kick him for falling." And we say on the present occasion, let the Government at the next trial arraign their six Counsel, headed by the Attorney-General, supported by £100,000 from the public purse. We, on our part, will place the Claimant on an equal platform, and he shall meet his antagonists face to face, and the battle shall be fought fairly, openly, and honestly, let the extent and issue be what it may. This Trial at its commencement aroused little interest or feeling in our breasts—we cared not about its extent or issue; but now, almost every man has an opinion, from the QUEEN to the peasant. Opinions on this question have been derived chiefly from three sources. Many have disbelieved because others have done the same. Now we have no faith in any man who pins his opinion to the sleeve of another, and in point of fact says, "Because thou believest, I believe also." We adhere to the admonition: "Prove all things, hold fast that which is good." Men have gathered their ideas in respect to the identity of Sir ROGER from reading a portion of the Press, and it has so transpired that it presented a difficulty unfavourable to his cause. For instance, the *Grimsby Observer and Humber News*, dated Aug. 7 and 28, each contains assertions unwarrantable, untrue, and unjust. They are gross and unmitigated falsehoods, and any man having common-sense and good English feeling would never have written them. And any editor possessing those sterling qualities which fit him to represent the cause of truth and justice would never have inserted it. Any paper that the public cannot rely upon its accuracy, and which invites discussion in misrepresentation, the sooner that light is extinguished the better. On the other hand, there are men who have waded their way through all the mass of evidence produced, not excepting the Attorney-General's speech, and, after weighing it in all its parts, carefully analyzing each portion according to the best of their judgment and discretion, have arrived at the conclusion that the identity of the Claimant has been clearly established. Let us glance for a moment at a few of the witnesses. There is the mother's evidence. We say, can a mother forget her boy? We appeal to the maternal love. What a tremendous weight is a mother's testimony; if that is to be ignored, to whom can we look? it is worth a host of other witnesses. They say Lady TICHBORNE was weak in her intellect, yet, strange to say, she kept her banking account to the very last; and although Sir ROGER had been with her since his return for a long time, up to her dying, acknowledged him as her son: in proof of this she left her affidavit, which was never questioned. There is BOGLE, the good faithful old servant of the Family, who for his devotion and services rendered to that Family, received an annuity of £50; this he enjoys for twelve years, he goes abroad and meets with a man who calls himself Sir ROGER. Now, we ask any honest impartial man if it is likely that BOGLE, in whom they had reposed so much confidence—who, no doubt, was acquainted with family matters—and who would at any time, during his services, have laid down his life willingly and freely to maintain the interests and honour of the Family—I repeat, Is it at all likely or reasonable that BOGLE would seek to deprive the Family whom he had served so faithfully of their estates, and place them in the hands of a man whom he knew to be an impostor? If any man in the world knew Sir ROGER, it must have been BOGLE. Honesty, truth, and justice answer, No. There were officers and soldiers, many of whom were intimately acquainted with Sir ROGER. Some drilled him, others taught him stable duties; his private servant, MOORE, who went with him abroad, acknowledged him. The evidence of Sir TALBOT CONSTABLE respecting the hedges, and the sentry, in reference to the donkey, was most conclusive. These, and many more, swore positively and distinctly, without sustaining any damage in cross-examination, as to the identity of Sir ROGER. We know the result. He was incarcerated, his money taken from him, deprived of the documents that were necessary to prove his identity, left in his prison cell destitute, but not friendless, with his case to all appearance hopeless. To crush him in his hopeless condition, a heavy amount was required for bail, to quench the last ray of hope, and bring it to a climax; to extinguish this man once and for ever, Judge BOVILL ordered that Sir ROGER's bondsmen should produce their books, and their accounts be thoroughly investigated. This iniquitous ordeal was overruled by a superior Court, bail produced, and Sir ROGER released. On the Defendants' side we find they intercepted and opened Sir ROGER's letters, which he had to acknowledge were forged; witnesses were bribed; detectives were watching him continually; they went to an hotel where Sir ROGER was staying, and stated that he was an impostor, consequently he was obliged to leave. They attempted, but failed, to prove that Sir ROGER was ARTHUR ORTON; in fact, we understand that this piece of evidence, which was so important, and could be proved in twenty minutes, but by the way occupied the Attorney-General for three weeks, and then as we stated, a failure, has been altogether abandoned. Just one word on the tattoo. I believe there never was a greater falsehood produced in Court than this. Take, for instance, the evidence of Lord BELLEW: when cross-examined, he said he tattooed him, but could not tell if anyone was there; he thought some one was, but that person was dead; he did not know whether it was pre-arranged; could not tell if the marks were the emblems of Faith, Hope, and Charity, or the initials of Sir ROGER. Such evidence is worthless and useless. The memory of Lord BELLEW is a perfect blank upon this subject. No one, excepting the Family, those who were interested in the Case, could be brought to support the tattoo. We say, could a youth be tattooed in a school of 140 boys without some of them knowing it. It is a libel on our reason and judgment to say so. In addition to this no soldier or officer has ever come forward and stated that Sir ROGER was tattooed. To crush this infamous falsehood there is the evidence of Sir ROGER's mother, who distinctly denies the tattooing of her son. On the Claimant's side everything has been straightforward and above board. On the other side there has been trickery, bribery, and undercurrent at work. What faith can any man have in a cause that is supported by such a course of action? We answer, none. The very great majority believe the Claimant is either ORTON or Sir ROGER TICHBORNE. If they fail altogether to prove that he is ARTHUR ORTON, he must be Sir ROGER TICHBORNE. They have thrown down the gauntlet, and the public has taken it up, and it says, let the Government bring talent, power, might, influence, backed by £100,000 of public money, it accepts the challenge in the name of justice and truth: and the battle shall be fought openly and fairly. Our motto shall be, Right and not Might, and may God defend the Right.

The Claimant addressed the meeting, and was followed by G. B. SKIPWORTH, Esq., Mr. R. SMITH, Sergeant-Major MARKS, Sergeant GALL, and others.

A vote of thanks to the Chairman concluded the proceedings.

EVIDENCE OF JOHN MOORE.

JOHN MOORE, who was servant to ROGER TICHBORNE, and who accompanied him to South America, fully recognized the Claimant as his old master, and gave the following evidence at the first Trial in the Common Pleas. It is almost conclusive in his favour. MOORE could not be got to repeat it at the Great Trial—why, we cannot tell:—

Examined by Mr. GIFFARD.

What is your age?—51.

Do you remember being at Upton House, near Poole, when you were young?—I do.

Your father was servant, I believe, for a great many years in the DOUGHTY family?—He was.

For how many years?—25 or more, from the year 1823 to 1851, I think.

You yourself, I believe, went to Upton House when you were young?—When I was fourteen years of age.

I believe you were in one or two places; you were with a Mr. JONES, and remained with him until his death?—Yes, I went from Upton House to Mr. JONES; I left him on one occasion and then returned to him.

You remained with him until his death, and I believe he left you a legacy?—He did so.

I believe you had a letter shortly after that bringing you back to Tichborne, saying Mr. ROGER TICHBORNE wanted a servant?—Not bringing me back to Tichborne; I had a letter announcing that Mr. ROGER did want a certificate.

And in consequence of that letter you went?—Not to Tichborne.

Where?—Stapehill, near Wimborne.

I believe you have no memorandum to tell you exactly when the engagement took place, but somehow about 1852 you did engage in his service?—I did.

I believe you are able to fix the year by the Duke of WELLINGTON's funeral as being somewhere about the close of 1852?—Yes, I think the Duke of WELLINGTON's funeral took place about the 24th of November of that year, and I was at Upton at that time.

After you had been in the service did you go about the estates with Mr. ROGER TICHBORNE?—I did.

Shooting, I mean?—Exactly.

Do you remember his stocking the island with rabbits at Canford?—Perfectly well.

Do you recollect being with him near Poole with a person named GOULD?—Not at Poole, but GOULD used to come to Upton.

Used GOULD to be a good deal with young Mr. TICHBORNE about the bay?—They used to make appointments, and GOULD used to meet him with the boat, bringing his own boat from Poole, and then going about on the water.

Do you remember a somewhat curious pair of boots that GOULD bought from Mr. TICHBORNE?—Yes, he bought two pairs, or more than two pairs, of large fishing-boots, and Mr. TICHBORNE bought the smallest pair, and they were too large for him.

Do you remember Mr. TICHBORNE complaining of the boots being too large for him?—Yes.

Do you remember an incident that happened when there was no water in the bay?—Perfectly well.

What happened on that occasion?—He wanted to prove if there was water in the bay, and I asserted there was not. He said he was sure there was; he said he would go down and try, and we both went down together, and when he reached the water's edge, or rather the edge of the mud, I said, "Now what do you think of it?" and so he stepped on the mud, and got stuck fast.

What got stuck fast?—Mr. TICHBORNE and his boots.

Did he get out of the mud again?—He found himself stuck fast, and the boots being so large, he pulled his feet out of the boots, and remained in the mud.

Leaving them in the mud?—Yes, he was going to leave them, but I advised him to throw them out.

Do you remember an incident happened about that—a boy named WILLY CRABBE?—Yes, I do.

What was WILLY CRABBE doing?—He was sent up to the garden-house to get the oars of the boat, and the boots had been thrown out previously to the arrival of WILLY CRABBE, and Mr. TICHBORNE said, "Boy! go back and fetch those damned boots." And the boy said to me, "What does the silly man say?" I beg your pardon—no, that was not the word, "What does he say?" And I said, "Go back and fetch those boots." "What boots," said the boy. "Why those boots, don't you see?" And looking at Mr. TICHBORNE, whose legs were black as though he had boots on, he said, "What in the world has the silly man got on now?"

The black mud on his legs looked as if they were boots to the boy?—Yes, precisely so.

And Mr. TICHBORNE was at that time, I understand, walking without boots?—He was.

Where was he walking?—Towards the island, so as to get from the main land to the island where there was sufficient water to get across by means of a boat generally placed there.

Do you recollect on one occasion being asked by Mr. TICHBORNE to go into a boat to chase some poachers?—Yes, I do.

Did you object to go or agree to go?—I objected to go.

The Lord Chief Justice: I take it for granted that these matters will be made material in some way, but if this sort of evidence is to be given, I do not see how the Case is to end under five years. Of course, I cannot tell how far this particular matter is material or not, but I must interpose to say, I suppose you mean to make it material?

Mr. GIFFARD: Yes.

The Lord Chief Justice: Otherwise you see what I mean?

Mr. GIFFARD: I quite see what your lordship means.

The Lord Chief Justice: If everything that occurred during the life of a gentleman, who was twenty-five years of age when he went away, is to be gone into, the Case will never end; and at present, unless by your undertaking to make it so, it is not evidence.

Mr. GIFFARD: It is evidence on the principle which we discussed very early in the case, and I think the importance of it can hardly be exaggerated, when your lordship hears the mode in which we propose to prove this matter.

The Lord Chief Justice: So long as you state that you intend to make it material, I accept the statement.

Mr. GIFFARD: Yes, but I think your lordship should know how it is, because it seems absurd detail.

The Lord Chief Justice: It is quite sufficient when you say you undertake to make it material. I am only desirous of stating at the present moment that the evidence is clearly irrelevant to the issue, except on your undertaking to make it material.

Mr. GIFFARD: I quite understand.

Mr. Serjeant BALLANTINE: The discussion we had early in this matter.

The Lord Chief Justice: That is a different matter. The matter that was discussed before was as to the facts that were stated to or by the Claimant.

Mr. GIFFARD: That is laying the foundation for it.

The Lord Chief Justice: Yes, exactly; but then there is the difficulty that arises from the Claimant not being called. It may or may not become material.

Mr. GIFFARD: Yes; because what I propose to prove by this person is that he cross-examined Sir ROGER TICHBORNE himself about these details, which we shall argue that no one but he and the witness could know.

The Lord Chief Justice: In that way you make it material. I did not wish you to state it, but to call attention to this to guard against our getting into a sea of evidence, of which no one can see the end, and I asked you whether you undertook to make it material, and the moment you did, my question was answered, and you may proceed.

Mr. GIFFARD: There is another mode of doing it.

The Lord Chief Justice: You need not say a word more. I receive it upon your assurance. I am only desirous, gentlemen (*turning to the jury*), to put it within right limits. Unless I kept some hold, we might be here for a year.

The Solicitor-General: Of course my learned friend will take his own course about it, but I understand what my learned friend says is this: "I am going to prove that certain incidents happened in fact. I am then going to show that witness had conversations with the Claimant," which, of course, according to your lordship's ruling, is no evidence in this cause, "and that in these conversations he confirms these facts, or some of them." That is what he means to say. I apprehend that that does not make this in this shape evidence, and the proper way to make it evidence in the Case is to say, subject to your lordship's ruling, "Did you meet the Claimant? did you ask him questions. And what passed between you?" because the result is, he gives the facts; and then will be asked whether the man alluded to him and stated them correctly?

The Lord Chief Justice: You are quite justified in your observation. The legitimate course would be to make it evidence. At this moment it is not evidence, and could not be received. It would only be evidence on the principle I ruled the other day, adversely to the Solicitor-General's contention, and that is saying the Claimant had knowledge of circumstances which went to prove his identity mentally.

The Solicitor-General: Just so.

The Lord Chief Justice: This evidence, some time or other, may be material or not. I cannot tell whether it will; but I am obliged to act on the assertions of Mr. GIFFARD, that he will make it so; but his now having stated the mode in which he proposes to make it material, shows there can be no objection, if the Solicitor-General wishes, to putting the evidence in the regular form—put the conversation with the Claimant first, and then it legitimately is evidence; but it is not evidence strictly, without the previous evidence having been given. In many instances we are obliged to trust to the assurance of Counsel; for instance, various communications take place with agents, servants, and others, and the conversation is proposed to be given in evidence, when it is agreed it would be admissible, but is only received for convenience on the assurance of Counsel that he will show the agency afterwards, and, in many cases, it is a convenient course.

The Solicitor-General: I do not want at all to embarrass my friend, but it is an objection in substance.

The Lord Chief Justice: I quite see the reason, and you have satisfied my mind. It is like as if a question arises in an ordinary case as to the conversation, and the question is put in this form—"Did you have an interview with A. B., and did you communicate that to C. D.?" And in that form it sometimes is received and at other times you must prove the conversation with C. D., and if the fact is material you prove the fact as stated.

The Solicitor-General: I mean here so much bears on the words and the expression that it makes it extremely different, according to the one form or other in which it happens to be done. My learned friend will not suppose I am doing it for the purpose of obstruction, if I submit that the proper course in this Case is the one my friend should follow.

The Lord Chief Justice: It is not only the strictly correct course, but it has this great merit and advantage, that then I can see whether the evidence proposed to be given of the fact is or is not material. It is made material by introducing the conversation first.

Mr. GIFFARD: I need hardly say that any suggestion from your lordship—whatever my strict rights, I should waive them instantly and follow any suggestion you made. I should have thought that this was following the ruling which we are bound to assume now is correct, to proceed which way I pleased, for this reason: it is a compound fact; you cannot prove everything at once, and whether a compound fact exists, the relevancy of which arises from the combination of the two facts, there is no rule of law, I take it, which compels you to begin at one end rather than the other. The relevancy must be ascertained by the combination of both.

The Lord Chief Justice: Quite so, but I must then be satisfied of the relevancy. At present, it appears entirely irrelevant. It is proposed to be made relevant, as it sometimes is, upon the assurance of the Counsel; therefore I put the question to you and you gave me that assurance, but if any objection be taken at the present moment, you must make it relevant first; then you must resort to the other evidence.

Mr. GIFFARD: It seems to me, if I may venture to say so, there is a fallacy in that; because if we begin at the other end, that is not relevant evidence until the other fact also is proved, that these things in truth occurred; the same observation arises.

The Lord Chief Justice: Not at all, the conversation being introduced, becomes a relevant fact in the case. The conversation takes place, and then also the existence or non-existence of the facts; whereas if you take it the other way, you might prove everything that occurred on any day and any minute of the day during the existence of the person who disappeared in 1854. You might prove, from circumstances and the whole of it, or nearly all, might be perfectly irrelevant or perfectly material.

Mr. GIFFARD: It might be so.

The Lord Chief Justice: Then you do give a point to the matter by introducing a conversation, and then it does limit the facts that would have to be proved during the last twenty-five years.

Mr. GIFFARD: As I have said, I would much rather follow any suggestion of your lordship's than argue the question, whether I am entitled or not. The only objection I should have upon it is one of the most mechanical description, that my proof has been arranged chronologically, which is that we thought most convenient; and therefore it is very likely a little out of order, but there is no other objection.

The Lord Chief Justice: There is no pressure of time upon you.

Mr. GIFFARD: I dare say I can do it if your lordship wishes. After what your lordship has said, I daresay that you will not feel that I am not following the suggestion, if I am going a little out of the order I was going.

The Lord Chief Justice: Certainly, as far as we have gone into this matter, and got into the mud, it may be well to conclude it.

Mr. GIFFARD: I think your lordship has got out of the mud, boots and all, by this time.

The Solicitor-General: I did not interfere, thinking we had better get on to something else.

Mr. GIFFARD: Now, in 1866 where were you living?—Hastings, I think, in that year.

And where when you heard, as I daresay you did, that Sir ROGER returned?—I was at Edinburgh.

When did you first hear of the fact of his return?—I heard of his reported return when I was in the Highlands of Scotland, in Argyleshire, from a letter from my brother.

You were staying with your brother?—No, I was living with Mr. FLETCHER.

Who is your brother?—Mr. ROBERT MOORE, keeping an hotel in Edinburgh.

What are you yourself now?—I am a butler by profession, but have recently left my situation.

How long have you been a butler?—Since my return, or in my last situation. I was eight months in my last situation.

With whom were you butler?—Mr. ROSKELL.

Of Messrs HUNT and ROSKELL?—That firm.

Before that where were you?—I was living with Mr. REGINALD TALBOT, of Road Hill, Lyme Regis.

How long had you lived with him?—Nearly two years and a half.

Is that Mr. TALBOT a gentleman who is the nephew of Lady DOUGHTY?—Exactly.

Were you in communication with Mr. BOWKER or Messrs. DOBINSON and GEARE in the early part of 1867?—I never had any communication with either.

I think there were other gentlemen employed; were you in communication with Messrs. CULLINGTON and SLAUGHTER?—With Mr. CULLINGTON.

Then may I ask you here, have you kept a diary for some years?—When I was on board ship.

And when you went out, as we shall presently hear, with Mr. ROGER TICHBORNE?—Yes.

Did you give the diary to Mr. CULLINGTON to make what use he thought proper of?—I put it in his possession. I did not give it to him.

You handed it over to him?—Yes.

When did you first have an interview with this gentleman, ROGER TICHBORNE?—The first interview I had with him was the 24th of January last.

The Lord Chief Justice: The 24th of January, 1871, do you mean?—Exactly.

Mr. GIFFARD: The first interview with him?—The first interview to speak to him.

But you had seen him since his return to this country before that?—Yes.

Where?—I saw him at Croydon pass from a cab to Mr. HOLMES'S; that is, fifteen yards, more or less. Then I saw him at what I undertood to be the Law Courts, Chancery-lane.

The Law Institution?—The Law Institution.

The Lord Chief Justice: What was the date you saw him at Croydon?—I cannot say.

About the year?—The year he returned.

Mr. GIFFARD: 1867 it would turn out to be?—Soon after his return; it might have been the month of May or the month of June.

Mr. GIFFARD: Your lordship will take July 30th, 1867, as the date of the examination at the Law Institution.

How came you to go to Croydon?—I first went to Croydon, in order to see him with Mr. WHICHER.

That is the detective?—Yes, but I did not see him upon that occasion.

With whom did you go upon the next occasion?—With a friend of mine.

What was his name?—He has a great objection to my mentioning his name in Court, unless I am obliged to. If it is suppressed in the newspapers, I will mention it.

My learned friend will ask you if he deems it important. I do not think it is.

The Solicitor-General: We know who it was.

Mr. GIFFARD: My learned friend says he knows who it was; and therefore I will not press you. Upon the next occasion when you went to the Law Institution who were there then?—I went from Mr. CULLINGTON's house with, I believe it was, young Mr. SLAUGHTER. I understood it to be.

Did you hear this gentleman examined by Counsel?—I did.

Did you yourself supply any of the materials to Counsel for the cross-examination?—Mr. CULLINGTON having my journal. had every information, not only the journal, but other information besides.

That is what I want to know; not only the journal, but other information besides?—Yes.

Do you know whether that information was taken down in writing?—I gave it in writing to a Mr. FITZGERALD.

Mr. FITZGERALD is a gentleman apparently interested in this Case, on the side of the Defendants?—Exactly.

You gave him your statement in writing?—I did.

Without going into the contents of it, did you give all the information you could upon the subject?—All that occurred to my mind.

Let me ask you before you went to the Law Institution, and heard this gentleman examined, what was the state of your mind as to whether he was an impostor, or the real man?—That it was impossible for ROGER TICHBORNE to come back, for I fully believed he was drowned, according to the evidence that had been brought forward with respect to the loss of the ship.

Now having seen the Claimant, and having heard him cross-examined, what conclusion did you arrive at yourself?—On the first day I arrived at no conclusion; I was very careful about coming to any conclusion.

I do not know whether you were able to see him as well the first day as the next day?—Certainly not.

What was the difficulty of seeing him upon the first day?—I was advised by Mr. CULLINGTON not to go too far in advance, for I might be ordered back the same as Lady ALFRED TICHBORNE had been the previous day.

But you had a good opportunity of seeing him, and did you arrive at any conclusion?—Certainly.

What conclusion did you arrive at?—On the second day when I went, I had a better opportunity of seeing him, as he rose from his chair and went to the further end of the room, and there was more light on his face, and I saw his face fully and distinctly, I saw him laugh, and saw him almost fit to cry. I may say his features changed very much and I was astonished. I then retired away for a bit, and pondered over in my own mind,—"Really it must be Mr. ROGER TICHBORNE, but I will not say yet." I pondered and looked at him again an hour after that. I do not think it could be so much as an hour, because it would be the time they rose for refreshments, but it was half-past two, I think, when I came to a conclusion. I do not know the time that they rose, perhaps a little after one.

Did you arrive ultimately at any conclusion?—I did.

What conclusion was that?—A decided conclusion that it was Mr. ROGER TICHBORNE.

As soon as you had arrived at that conclusion, did you write a note to Lady DOUGHTY?—I did not.

Did you at any time write a note to Lady DOUGHTY?—Not on that subject. I went to see her.

Did you see her?—I must explain I went to a house, expecting to see her in South-street, Brompton, understanding she was likely to call there. Her ladyship had been and gone, and then left my impression that I had a conversation I may say with Mrs. LAWSON.

How do you mean; in writing, or you said something?—Verbally.

Then we need not go into it. The next day, I think it was, did you see Lady DOUGHTY herself?—I did.

Was it on the next day?—The next morning.

On that occasion, did you tell Lady DOUGHTY what your impression was?—I did.

What did you say to her as well as you remember?—I had seen her and I could not tell her—

The Solicitor-General: You cannot go into this.

Mr. GIFFARD: I was under the impression at the moment that Lady DOUGHTY was one of the Defendants in interest, although not on the Record.

The Lord Chief Justice: She is not either a party to this Record or the proceedings in Chancery.

The Solicitor-General: And has not a sixpennyworth of interest in either.

Mr. GIFFARD: I will not go further into that. At all events you made a statement at that time to Lady DOUGHTY?—Yes, I did.

And you had gone there the day before to make the statement?—No, not the day before. The first day of her attendance I was there at the sitting of the Court.

I think you say you went there the day before to see her, and she was gone?—She had gone from South-street, where she was likely to make a call. She lived at Kensington.

The next day you went and saw her?—I did.

Now, I think you say the first time you communicated with Sir ROGER TICHBORNE himself was in January this year?—The first interview to speak to him.

Did you ask him a variety of questions about things that were known to you before, and known to him?—I did.

Before I go into the particulars, have you seen him on several occasions?—Since then?

Yes—had interviews with him for the purpose of satisfying yourself and asking him questions?—Yes, in the presence of Mr. SPOFFORTH, and never alone.

The Lord Chief Justice: He is one of the solicitors for the Claimant, gentlemen.

Mr. GIFFARD: Did you, as far as you could, select matters to examine him upon that no one but you two would be likely to know?—I did.

What is your judgment and conviction upon the subject now?—The same as I had three years ago.

That there may be no doubt about it, what do you mean by that?—That I feel perfectly confident, and from the questions I have put he has convinced me, I could take a solemn oath from what he says, because they are convincing things, and other things that he is no one else than Mr. ROGER TICHBORNE, or it is the devil himself.

Now, I will ask you to tell me what things they were, before I come to the particulars you asked him, and which he told you, that were so convincing to your mind. Just tell me generally the history of your service with him, to see what opportunities you had.

The Solicitor-General: That leads to the same objection.

Mr. GIFFARD: I am not going into the particulars.

The Lord Chief Justice: I understand that is, in what capacity he was his servant, and where he went.

Mr. GIFFARD: Yes, the voyage, and so on, without the particulars.

The Lord Chief Justice: The dates when he entered the service, and so on.

Mr. GIFFARD: Yes.

The Lord Chief Justice: If you will put the question pointedly, so as to keep it within limits.

Mr. GIFFARD: I will.

You were telling me when I first examined you, that you were with Mr. ROGER TICHBORNE about the year 1852, the latter end of the year 1852; and did you go abroad with him?—I did.

In what capacity?—As his one servant.

Do you remember embarking with him?—Perfectly well.

Was that from Havre?—It was so.

Do you remember about the date of the embarkation from Havre?—The 1st of March, 1853.

Where did you go to?—It was destined for Valparaiso.

The Solicitor-General: I apprehend, if all my learned friend is going to get is what I understood him to say, of course it would not be worth while objecting, and if it were, probably I should be wrong, therefore I will not take up time. The general outline—he went from Europe to America, and so forth, and so many weeks or months, and then parted from him and never saw him again, of course I cannot object to. But if it is to be anything like detail of the movements of this gentleman from place to place, I must——

The Lord Chief Justice: I don't understand that it is so.

Mr. Serjeant BALLANTINE: We have been put to considerable inconvenience in consequence of yielding, I think unnecessarily, to the objections raised by my learned friend. What I propose to do now is to give by the mouth of this witness the history of his career, with such minuteness as we think necessary for the purposes of this Case, from the time he embarked on board the "Pauline" until he separated from him in South America; and having given that, we then propose to call his attention to those details which came out in conversation, and upon which he has founded his judgment, among other matters, that he is the real person. And I think your lordship will feel how difficult it would be to conduct this Case in any other way. It is quite clear that all the transactions between him and young TICHBORNE up to the time of their separation in South America is material evidence in this Case.

The Lord Chief Justice: But what I understand is that at present you are merely going to prove that on a certain day he started, and that he arrived on a certain other day?

Mr. Serjeant BALLANTINE: No. I propose to give the incidents of the voyage, the incidents of their travelling, not at greater length than I am absolutely obliged to, down to the time of their ultimate separation in South America.

The Lord Chief Justice: Then, as I said before, I do not see how those matters, incidents of the voyage, are material at present, until they are made so.

Mr. Serjeant BALLANTINE: They will be made material when we call Sir ROGER TICHBORNE.

The Lord Chief Justice: That is exactly the point. The other side have always a right, in a matter of this sort, to insist on the giving of the evidence which makes it material before giving the other evidence. In many cases the assurance of Counsel is accepted, but always subject to this, that the other side have a right to insist you shall give the evidence first. Take, for instance, a matter which is extremely familiar—that of election petitions. Under the old rule, in giving evidence of acts of bribery, or other matters of that kind, sometimes parties were allowed to do it, undertaking to prove the agency of a particular individual; but if objected to, you were bound to prove agency first, and it required a special Act of Parliament to render proof of agency in the first instance not necessary. But the rule is that you must, in the first instance, give evidence which makes it relevant before the evidence can be taken, if they object to its being taken.

Mr. Serjeant BALLANTINE: There is no doubt we should not be in a position in an election petition, except by the provisions of a recent Act of Parliament.

The Lord Chief Justice: I give that as an illustration.

Mr. Serjeant BALLANTINE: If an illustration, no doubt it is entirely correct, but I apprehend this is part of the transaction. We have the admittedly genuine ROGER TICHBORNE, and every incident that took place in his career undoubtedly, I should submit, is material evidence in this Case. With regard to conversations between the gentleman who proves to be Sir ROGER and this witness, it is rendered relevant by asking some other questions. I quite admit that there may be a difficulty, but, with regard to the facts, I apprehend that every part of the actual history is relevant.

The Lord Chief Justice: Just apply it in this way. You propose to give this kind of evidence, that they were going from Havre to Valparaiso, and while he was shaving he cut his face. How is that fact material unless it is made so?

Mr. Serjeant BALLANTINE: I apprehend I can prove that, and then make it material by calling another witness.

The Lord Chief Justice: According to that you may prove everything during his voyage from Havre to Valparaiso—what time he got up in the morning, whether he wore a blue coat or a black coat or a dressing-gown, whether he lay down upon a bed or upon a sofa, what he had for breakfast, dinner, and the whole matter would be endless.

Mr. Serjeant BALLANTINE: I have not the least doubt in the world, according to my view, that that would be evidence; not that in arguing the matter I intend to intimate that I shall do anything of the kind, but I shall maintain that it was perfectly good evidence, and that I am entitled to prove at the present point of the Case every incident from the time of embarking in the "Pauline" until this witness left him in South America, and

SIR JOHN COLERIDGE, SOLICITOR-GENERAL.

I must press the matter on your lordship because it would so thoroughly interfere with the conduct of this cause if the contrary is held. We feel it really to be of almost essential importance, and we should not withdraw upon the question except upon your lordship taking a note on the subject, and my learned friend insisting upon that course.

The Solicitor-General: If my learned friend had called the Plaintiff, and had proposed to put this to him, it would not have been relevant in the first instance; but of course I should have made the whole of this relevant by cross-examining the Claimant to it, and I might have cross-examined the Claimant from information at my disposal, and then my learned friend, if he had thought fit, might have called persons other than the Claimant to corroborate what he had said in answer to me in cross-examination. Then I could not have objected. I should myself have rendered it material by the course I had taken. At present, I apprehend that my friend is merely attempting to give that evidence which, if relevant at all, is only relevant when I put it to the Claimant; that is, endeavouring to give that confirmation to the Claimant in his hearing before the Claimant is called; and the reason I object is, that it makes the cross-examination of the Plaintiff on these matters useless, because he hears the whole story. As a mere matter of convenience to my learned friends, I need not say I would waive it at once, so far as that goes, but I feel it to be my duty to object.

The Lord Chief Justice: I have not any doubt about this. That the usual and the ordinary course in such cases is to put the Claimant forward and let him be examined and cross-examined. For reasons which I do not find fault with, the Counsel for the Plaintiff have not thought fit to adopt that course. I make no observation upon that, because they are at perfect liberty to conduct their Case in whichever way they please; but, at the same time, when a Case is taken out of the ordinary course, the Solicitor-General, representing the Defendants, has a perfect right to interpose objections which, as he says, arise in consequence of the course that has been taken. The matter now proposed to be given in evidence probably will become material some time or other, and it may be made material by the Solicitor-General's cross-examination of the Claimant: may be made material by showing that some statements were made by or in the presence of the Claimant or to him, and that such statements were known and could be known only to him, or might be known to him, and so testing his identity in the manner described the other day. But then it is a very difficult matter where it is proposed to give evidence of every little incident that occurs in the life of ROGER TICHBORNE, say from the time he arrived at years of discretion until the "Bella" went down in 1854. It strikes me, I must say, that those circumstances ought to be made material and relevant before evidence of them is given. I express that opinion, and the Solicitor-General says, as you on the one side, on the part of the Plaintiff, do not choose to defer to that opinion, rather than have any objection recorded on the note, he will not persist in the objection, as I understand; but at the same time I think it right to intimate very strongly my opinion as to the course which ought to be adopted where the Claimant is not put into the box, and where the evidence has not been previously given to make these circumstances material.

The Solicitor-General: I shall, certainly, representing the parties I do—and I need say no more than that, with the Case I have—I shall not persist in the objection.

Mr. Serjeant BALLANTINE: I think it is quite impossible that your lordship, or any other human being, could form an accurate judgment as to what should be the conduct of this cause for the purpose of furthering the ends of Justice. I am not going into the question of what Case my friend may have got; that I do not propose to anticipate. We considered that the most convenient course to adopt would be the one we are now pursuing. I should be sorry if your lordship intimated, until the conclusion of the proceedings, any opinion as to the fairness or unfairness of the course we have taken. If we have proceeded unfairly, that will, of course, prejudice us hereafter; but I think no one can tell, until they have heard the whole Case, whether the course we have been pursuing is fair or not. I do not propose to ask any questions except those which I presume to be strictly relevant: and my friend will either object or not, and the matter must be dealt with.

The Solicitor-General: I have already said that I shall not persist in my objection under the circumstances.

The Lord Chief Justice: I have already intimated my opinion. Not that the course you have pursued is unfair, but that it is an unusual one.

Mr. Serjeant BALLANTINE: There is present to my mind a Case in which your lordship took a very distinguished part; and, as far as my recollection serves me, the course pursued on that occasion was almost identical with the one we are pursuing now.

The Lord Chief Justice: You have used expressions which imply that I thought you had adopted an unfair course. I did not express that; nor did I intend that my words should convey that meaning; but it does occur to me that it is an unusual course. If it were put to me to decide, I should decide in favour of the objection of the Solicitor-General; but he thinks of the serious consequences that might result if the matter were in doubt, and rather than have the objection recorded, on which there might be an opportunity to take the opinion of the Court, he says, I will not persist in the objection. You have my ruling upon it, and you will do what you think best.

Mr. Serjeant BALLANTINE: We have not had your lordship's ruling upon it, and if you had thought it was an illegal question, I should have taken the means of raising the question hereafter.

The Solicitor-General: I have already said, under all the circumstances of the Case, I would not persist in the objection.

Mr. Serjeant BALLANTINE: I cannot accept any favour from my friend, but I must stand on my rights.

The Lord Chief Justice: There had better be an end of the discussion. I have expressed my opinion, and under all the circumstances of the Case, the Solicitor-General says he does not persist in his objection.

Mr. Serjeant BALLANTINE: I will consult with my friend for a moment, and see if we can in any way whatever meet your lordship's views. *(The learned Counsel consulted for a short period.)* I do not know whether we shall be successful, but will endeavour to meet your lordship's views as far as possible.

Mr. GIFFARD: You say you saw Mr. ROGER TICHBORNE in order to have some conversation with him in January last?—Yes.

Tell us as nearly as you can what questions you asked him, and what answers he gave?—Having received a note to meet him, I answered the note, a copy of which I think I have here.

Where was it you saw him?—At the Waterloo Hotel, Jermyn-street.

In the presence of Mr. SPOFFORTH?—Just so.

Tell us what questions you put to him at that interview, and what were his answers—I will ask you presently what they referred to?—I said, "I have come to see you, and put some questions to you as to what you and I only possibly can know." I said, "Can you tell me anything you took with you to South America?" Yes, he said, I can tell you something; did I not take a large box? I half nodded assent without saying anything. Did I not take some tools?" I again half nodded assent. "Amongst those tools did you take any peculiar instrument?" That was my question. He stood for an instant, and he said, "What, do you mean the tomahawk?" I said, I do.

I would pause here for a moment. Can you suggest any means by which this gentleman, if he is not the real man, could have known of the "tomahawk"?

The Solicitor-General: I object to this witness answering such a question as that. That is for me to ask, not for my friend—how can it be relevant?

Mr. GIFFARD: I will waive the question. Will you go to anything else that you asked him?—He then pointed to a skin or rug, that was lying on a chair, and he said, Do you recollect that, or an animal like that (pointing to the skin), which I left with you?

Who is the person now asking the question?—Sir ROGER. He pointed to a skin or rug, which was lying on the chair, and he said, Do you remember anything like that, or an animal like that? I said, Yes; what is the name of it? He said, The guanaco. The Plaintiff said, did I not leave an animal like that with you? He then gave me the name. I said, Was it alive or dead? He said, I believe it was alive. I said, Where did you get it? He said, I am sure I do not know.

Who said that?—I asked the question, Where did you get it? and he said, I am sure I do not know. Then he afterwards recollected where he did get it: that he had got it from a Mr. HELSBY, who was out at Santiago.

He mentioned shortly after where he did get it—was that at the same interview?—Not at the same interview.

What more did you ask him?—Then, I believe, I commenced asking him about a fishing-hook.

Tell me what you asked him, and what he answered?—I am not quite positive as to the way in which I commenced it. I brought up something about a fish-hook, if he recollected it. He thought for a time, and said something about his eye. He seemed to forget all about it: by-and-by he seemed to think more, and ultimately he said there was something about a fish-hook, and that he ought to have a mark on his eye.

After a time he seemed to remember it?—He seemed to recollect something about a fish-hook, and he seemed to remember that he ought to have a mark on the eye.

When you say he seemed to remember, did you help him at all?—No, I did not try to assist him. I tried all I could to the contrary, not to lead him on to any question; my object was to convince myself that he was not an impostor, but the real man.

He did not answer at once about the fish-hook?—No, he had to think.

After he had thought, what did he say?—I do not know what he said. I asked him again how did it happen, and he seemed not to have any distinct recollection of how it happened. Then I asked him how it was taken out? He said it went through the eyelid, and it was dragged right through. I said, More than that, how was it got out?—He said, With pincers, I think. I said, No. He did not know whether it was or not—he could not be certain. I then said it was filed off. Then he professed to have a recollection of seeing the pincers before his eyes; he had a positive recollection of that; he said he had seen the pincers, which, I think, was correct; they tried to pinch it out and could not, then it was ultimately filed. He said he had a perfect recollection of seeing the pincers before his eyes while the operation was being performed. It was a strong hook; I have got a similar hook in my possession, as near the size as I could judge.

When he mentioned the pincers, had you recollected the fact of the pincers being used at all?—No, it escaped from my memory until he reminded me of it.

Was anything more said about it at the time?—I asked him if he recollected where it was that it happened; he did not seem to have a recollection of where it happened.

Do you mean where on board the vessel?—He could not say in what part of the vessel it happened.

What more passed, if anything?—I believe he said he remembered being laid on his back to have it cut out.

Do you remember anything more being said about the fish-hook and the cutting it out?—He got up to the window for me to see if I could see any mark.

A Juror: Was it the eye or the eyelid?—It was not the eye, the eyelid. I looked at the eye and I saw what I thought was a speck or mark,—very slight.

Mr. GIFFARD: Was this all that passed as to that particular incident?

The Lord Chief Justice: Let him tell us what he saw a little more minutely, and where.

Mr. GIFFARD: I thought that might come into the narrative of what took place.

The Lord Chief Justice: What he saw involves where he saw it; was it on the eye or the eyelid?—I thought I saw a speck about the middle of the eyelid, that was my impression.

On which of them?—On the right.

The upper or lower eyelid?—The upper one. I said I would leave the doctor to decide on its being a mark or not.

What was the size of the speck or mark which you saw?—It was as small as a very large pin's head.

Can you make a mark like it on a piece of paper?—I can hardly describe the mark, or whether it was round or long.

Mr. Serjeant BALLANTINE: The mark has been seen by Sir WILLIAM FERGUSSON, who will speak to it.

You say it was as large as a pin's head?—I mean an ordinary pin, such as a woman may wear in her dress—a common pin.

Mr. GIFFARD: Have you finished all he said about the fish-hook?—I think I have. I remember the exact occurrence, and how it happened, which he did not recollect.

Will you now describe the incident to which this matter related?—I remember perfectly well that it happened on a Whit-Sunday. I have the date down. I remember the circumstance well, because the Plaintiff invited the captain to go with him to teach him how to skin birds, I having refused to go myself, it being Sunday.

What was it that happened?—He said, "Well, you will put all the things in readiness." I said, "Certainly." I went to the place where they were in the habit of skinning numerous birds, which was the W.C. I placed all the various implements that he had there, and suspended a fish-hook from the beam of the ship by a string of this length (*describing it*). He had not been there long before he met with the accident. It was a poop ship. I was walking on the poop, and we had to descend a ladder down to the W.C., looking out from the stern of the vessel. The hook being suspended from the beam in the W.C., would naturally move to and fro, by the motion of the ship; and, I presume, it was when he was stooping to pick up something in a quick way that it cut his eye, and the hook passed through the eyelid.

Was the place you have described on deck?—No, below; on a level with the cabin floor. Being a poop ship, it was on a level with the deck of the ship; we passed on to a cabin at the end; we had to descend a ladder outside, and then passed on to the cabin, and then there were bedroom cabins on each side.

The Lord Chief Justice: What was the length of the string attached to the hook? Was it two feet, or a foot and a half?—No, not so much. As near as I can guess, the height of the cabin would be some six inches higher than I am. The string would be sufficiently long to hook a bird on, and sufficiently long for the hook to catch his eye. We used to string them there the same as you see butchers' meat suspended from a hook.

Mr. GIFFARD: Was there any bird there?—They had got a bird; it was not suspended. There were lots of birds to be skinned; perhaps half a dozen various sorts of birds.

Do you know the names of any of them?—The sailors gave them the French names. I have no idea what their names were in English.

You were in a French ship?—Yes.

Do you know whether this incident is in your diary?—No, it is not, for certain reasons.

Is it in the written statement which you gave to Mr. FITZGERALD?—I have no doubt it is.

You say you do not know the English names of any of the birds which were there?—No, I do not.

You do not know them at all?—No.

Cannot you describe their appearance?—The birds they used to catch were speckled birds like pigeons; the sailors used to call them damios, but I have looked in the dictionary, and could not find such a word.

Were they sea-birds?—Yes.

Were you actually present at this place when the accident happened?—I was not.

You do not exactly know how it happened?—No, not the exact mode. I was not in the room at the time. I was in the room before the hook was taken down from the beam.

You put out the tools for him to skin the birds with?—Exactly so.

Was this the same hook you had taken down there?—I had suspended the hook; he had not been there long before an alarm was given, and there was a great outcry on account of this accident. I ran from the poop of the ship down the ladder into the cabin, and I went into the water-closet and found the hook suspended to the beam through the eyelid. I took it off the beam immediately.

The Lord Chief Justice: You found the hook suspended as you had left it?—I found the hook suspended precisely as I had left it. I untied it from the nail to which it was attached. He walked into the cabin, and was laid on the cabin table, and then the hook was found so large at the end to which the string was attached, that it was obliged to be filed off, but the Claimant said it was pinched off. I said I believed they did bring the pincers to pinch it, but that ultimately it was filed off.

Mr. GIFFARD: This is what in fact happened as to the accident to the eye?—Yes.

Can you tell me anything else you asked him on this occasion in January of this year, when you saw him at the Waterloo Hotel?—For the moment I do not recollect. Am I allowed to refer to the notes which I made?

Did you make them at the time?—No, only from recollection.

When did you make them?—Only four or five days ago.

You must try and do without them as well as you can; take time and consider. You had many interviews with him?—I believe I asked him about Santiago; he did not seem to have a recollection of the correct description of the places there.

You mentioned your diary just now. Do you remember whether you asked him anything about that?—I do not remember whether I asked him on that occasion, or whether it was on a subsequent occasion when I asked him that question.

I wish to keep the interviews distinct. Tell me what you do remember.—He asked me if I remembered the death of a person at the time he was there—some young woman who was found dead on a seat in a place which the Spaniards call the Alameda, which, I think, they there call the Cannida, a walk planted with trees. I said I did not recollect it, but that the fact might have occurred.

Did you ultimately remember it or not?—No, I did not remember it.

Do you remember anything being said about the spot where the skinning of these birds used to take place?—Yes, I asked him about that.

Tell us what you asked him, and what he answered to you?—He could not give any very correct description of the exact position; he said it was in the water-closet, he believed, was it not? I said I must not say—I did not try to give him any information whatever—or words to that effect—perhaps a shake of the head.

What more happened?—That was correct, that was our place for operating.

That is all that passed about that?—I believe it was.

Was there anything else that you remember?—I daresay there are a good many things that I cannot remember. I was with him for about an hour. Perhaps if you ask me any questions you may bring it to my mind.

Do you remember at any time having a conversation with him about some pistols?—Yes, I brought that up about his guns and pistols. He mentioned something about his gun having been bought at Dublin. I said no, I did not think it was. He said, "I have forgotten all about them now. I should never have thought of those." I said, "Where did you get them?" He said, "I must have got them at BLISSETT's." I said, "No." He said, "I think it was." I said, "I think the name was REILLY." I remembered the position of the shop perfectly well. I did not ask him for that. I thought the name was REILLY; he said it was BLISSETT. I could not contradict him, because I was not certain myself whether it was REILLY or not.

Did you afterwards go and see the shop?—I did.

And whose shop is it?—BLISSETT's.

At any time, whether upon this occasion or not, did you ask any question about the diary which you have mentioned to us?—Yes. I asked him did he remember saying anything to me about the diary? I forgot whether I alluded to my own or to his, because he kept one himself. There was something in the question in reference to both; which do you allude to?

I allude to your diary?—I asked him if he recollected anything about the diary; that when he saw me writing he told me not to jot down anything there about him.

Did you bring this book to his recollection when you had this conversation with him?—I asked him if he recollected saying anything to me about it. Perhaps the word might have been "put" instead of "jot."

Was that the fact, that ROGER TICHBORNE had said this to you?—It was the fact.

Whereabouts was it that this happened when you were with ROGER TICHBORNE?—In my bedroom—my cabin.

Where did all this happen to you? On the voyage?—On the voyage, certainly. I never kept a diary at any other time.

He said that to you during the voyage, in your cabin?—Yes.

It is not an unimportant matter, and I may as well ask you: you say this happened on the voyage?—Yes.

Was this before or after the matter which had happened about the hook and the birds?—That I do not recollect. At all events, I remember perfectly well his saying that I was not to put that down about the hook; I was not to tell Lady DOUGHTY about that.

Did you act upon that direction of his, or not?—I certainly did. There is very little in the diary concerning him.

Was it in consequence of that direction of his?—Yes.

Do you remember anything passing about some spinning machine?—Yes, perfectly well.

Will you describe what you asked him first, and what he answered to you?—After speaking of various things that had happened on board, he said, "I recollect very little about what did happen on board; I remember perfectly well the spinning machine for spinning tar-cord."

He said that himself?—Yes.

And was there a spinning machine on board for spinning tar-cord?—I had to think some considerable time before I remembered it.

Do you remember whether ROGER TICHBORNE did anything upon that?—I cannot swear on my oath that he did; I think I did it myself.

In order to bring it to your recollection, did he do anything? Did he draw it on a piece of paper?—Yes, he did; I think I have got it with me, should you wish to see it.

Certainly, if you have got it. If you cannot find it now let us have it some other time; he did draw it?—Yes, he did.

You had to think some time before you recollected it?—Yes.

You did ultimately recollect it?—Perfectly well.

Did ROGER TICHBORNE show you how it was done?—Yes, I got him to describe the motion. He seemed to know it better than I did. I remembered it perfectly well when he brought it to my recollection; he described it perfectly, and brought it very vividly to my mind.

Had you ever seen such a thing before or since?—No; I had not.

Have you been a good deal on board ships?—Only on my voyage out to Valparaiso and back again.

You did not, in fact, remember it until he brought it to your recollection?—I did not; I should never have thought of such a thing.

Was there anything else about the deck of the "Pauline" which he mentioned to you?—He mentioned the pigs running about the deck, which he remembered perfectly well. I had to think for a moment whether that was correct, and I said, yes it was.

Is there anything else you remember about the vessel, or which happened on board, that is in your mind now?—Yes, I recollect the rudder getting out of order.

What was said about that?—I asked him if he had any recollection about the repairs of the rudder, or anything connected with it.

What did he say?—After thinking a great deal, he seemed to have a recollection of some gearing for steering, but did not seem to recollect much about the rudder. I asked him whether the repairs were in wood or iron, and he said he believed in both—he could not say.

What more did he say about it?—Nothing more concerning it.

Do you remember anything being said about what he wore at Santiago?—Yes, I remember the clothes he wore.

Tell us what passed?—I forget whether I asked the question or not. I rather think he brought it up himself. He said, "You know very well I wore breeches and boots when I was there."

What did you say to that?—I think I nodded assent.

Did you ask what sort of breeches they were?—I asked what they were. He said they were leather—dirty brown or ochre colour.

Was that the fact?—Yes.

Was anything said as to your own occupation there?—He could not remember that, to my astonishment. He said something about keeping a store: he could not very well define where the store was.

Was it the fact that you did keep a store?—It was the fact.

Had you mentioned that you had kept a store until he said it?—No.

Do you remember questioning him upon the subject of a dog?—Perfectly well.

Did you call it a dog when you questioned him?—No, I did not. I took care not to do so. After alluding to the other animal he had left with me, I asked him whether he had left anything else with me when he went from Santiago to Chili?

Was he able to remember that?—Not for a long time.

Did he afterwards remember it?—Yes, he did.

What did he say?—He had left Mr. SPOFFORTH's office, and soon after Mr. SPOFFORTH received a note stating what animal it was.

How long after he left the office did he send the note?—I can hardly tell, it might be a quarter of an hour.

Just see if that is the note?—I have never seen it before.

Had you told Mr. SPOFFORTH what the animal was?—I had not.

Nor ROGER TICHBORNE?—No; Mr. SPOFFORTH was surprised when it turned out to be a dog.

You had not told it to anyone?—No, it was a perfect secret.

You say he was a long time thinking about it?—A very long time.

Mr. GIFFARD: I tender the letter. I understand my friend objects to it.

The Solicitor-General: I cannot understand how a letter from the Plaintiff to his attorney can be evidence for him in this cause.

Mr. GIFFARD: There is no difference between written words and spoken words. If he had written down all these answers instead of speaking them, the same objection might have applied. That written paper discloses the knowledge that is common only to these two persons.

The Witness: I said I had never seen the note before. I was present when Mr. SPOFFORTH received the note.

The Lord Chief Justice: Will you look at the letter, Mr. Solicitor, read it through, and see whether you object to it.

The Solicitor-General: I do not think it is worth while to object to it.

The Lord Chief Justice: When was it written?—Perhaps a fortnight ago. "Wednesday, May 3rd, 1.40. Dear Mr. SPOFFORTH,—The animal MOORE spoke of was a dog, dark colour, almost without hair. It occurred to me just after I left. It was rather an Eliphant-skined dog. Please communicate this to MOORE.—Yours truly, R. C. D. TICHBORNE. M. SPOFFORTH, Esq., 6, Victoria-street."

The Solicitor-General: The word "elephant" is spelt with an *i*, and "skinned" with one *n*.

Mr. Serjeant BALLANTINE: It leads to but one conclusion, that no thoroughly-educated person could have written it. If it conveys the idea of an elephant, that is all we are putting it in for at the present moment.

Mr. GIFFARD: The question which I understood you put to him was, what sort of an animal it was that he had left in your care on this occasion—then the receipt of the note which has just been read it appears to have been what he calls an elephant-skinned dog, almost without hair. Is that a correct description of the dog?—I do not fully understand the meaning of an Elephant-skinned dog.

Is that a proper description of the dog?—What is an elephant-skinned dog?

Perhaps you will be good enough to describe the dog which you had in your care at this time?—It was a large, smooth-skinned dog.

Was it a dark colour?—It was the colour of that table where those gentlemen are writing, or of the desk behind. It was an oak colour.

Was there anything peculiar about the skin of the dog itself as distinct from the hair?—It might be a little mottled, or striped or shaded, and it had a rather smooth, bright, shiny skin.

You mean the skin below the hair?—I mean the hair itself which was very short.

The Lord Chief Justice: You mean that the hair was shiny?—Yes.

Mr. GIFFARD: After he had written this note to say what the animal was, did you see him again to see whether he could tell you the name of the dog?—I did.

How soon was this after the day when you had seen him on the former examination; when you had seen him on some day in May?—Do you mean with regard to the date?

How soon after was it that you pressed him for the name of the dog?—I think I pressed him for the name there and then, but he could not recollect it.

I want to know what you said to him on this occasion?—I do not think I pressed him much for the name then. I could not tell what animal it was then. I did not ask him the name then, or perhaps I did. I cannot recollect at this moment; most likely I did press him for the name; I said it was an animal to which he had given a name, and that he ought to recollect it.

And you have said that he could not recollect it at the time?—No, he could not.

Neither could he recollect the animal itself at the moment?—No.

Was it the next day, or more than the next day, or how soon after that, that you saw him again to see whether he could tell or not?—I do not know what time elapsed, or how many days elapsed—I cannot say, but I still pressed for the name.

Was he able to remember the name?—No.

When you found he could not remember the name, did you say anything to him?—I suggested whether it would be proper to get a list of names—whether that was a fair thing to do him. I was told it was, and the list was fairly made out, with the name in the midst of them.

Did you write out the list?—I did.

Have you got it?—I have.

Just produce it.

The witness produced it.

Did you show the list to the Plaintiff?—I did.

Did you ask him whether he could point out the name of the dog?—Yes.

When he saw the list did he point out the name or not?—Immediately.

What was the name?—"Tearcoat."

I think there were fourteen or fifteen names that you mentioned?—I have a paper to convince you that was the right name—from the bill for the keep of the dog.

That list you made out of all events?—Yes.

The Lord Chief Justice: A bill for the keep of the dog?—Yes, my lord, I have a bill, because I had to place the dog in other hands to be kept; I had no convenience to keep it myself.

The Solicitor-General: A bill?—An account for the keep of the dog, showing the name that is written in the bill; it shows that that is the correct name given according to the bill.

The Solicitor-General: Have you got the bill?—Yes (*producing it*).

Mr. GIFFARD: Your lordship had better see that. There are sixteen names of dogs. I said fourteen just now (*handing a paper to his lordship*).

The Lord Chief Justice: Where was it that you had to pay for the keep of the dog?—I paid it to a man of the name of CAMPBELL, at Santiago, in Chili.

Mr. GIFFARD: Had you found that before you were examined on the subject?—No, I had not; I did not know that I could find it, but I thought I had it in my possession, and I might have had it in London or not, I was not sure.

But you have since looked for it and found it?—Yes.

Mr. GIFFARD: My lord, this is the bill:—"Mr. MOORE to COLIN CAMPBELL, debtor to 108 days for the dog "Tearcoat;" paid the cook for going to market for beef; to woman-doctor to set his leg; to tearing dresses belonging to servant-girls. Santiago, May 8th, 1854.—COLIN CAMPBELL."

Had you mentioned the name—you told me you did not—to Sir ROGER or Mr. SPOFFORTH? Had you mentioned the name before to anybody?—I kept it quite a secret.

Now, do you remember anything being said by you to test the Plaintiff, as to a meeting between you and Sir ROGER after he had gone over the mountains?—Yes, I asked him if he recollected my meeting him when he came to Santiago the second time, and he recollected the meeting.

Just describe what questions you put, and what answers he gave?—I cannot recollect about the exact meeting. I went on to say, where did we go, and he said—"went to take a bath, did not we?" I said where did we go?—"Went to take a bath?"—I did not answer him yes, or no. "We went out, did we not?" and I said "yes." "Down the street, I think;" he described it; "went out, down the street somewhere, I do not know the name of it." He described that we did not take the bath in the hotel, but went out down the street to take it, which was the fact.

The question you say to which that was an answer was, "Do you remember what we did"?—Will you repeat the question again?

The Lord Chief Justice: What was the question to which that was an answer?—I said, "What did you do," "What did we do," when I met him. I did not ask him under what circumstances we met, but said, when I had met him what did you do." He said, "Took a bath, I believe." "Where was I?"

Mr. GIFFARD: That is what I wanted to know. I may as well ask you about the fact. Will you just describe how that matter happened?—Why, he had occasion to take a bath.

Never mind about the occasion, tell me when you saw him; first of all, what were the circumstances? How long had he been away?—He had been away four or five months, from July to December; the latter end of December, I think, he arrived back again at Santiago, after having been to Peru and other places.

I only want the circumstance of your meeting. I do not want to take his journey?—My store was situated exactly opposite, or nearly exactly opposite the entrance to the hotel door, and sitting before the counter, or behind the counter, I could see anyone going up the steps or stairs of the hotel, and on one occasion, I saw a pair of legs and boots, and these boots struck me as being the boots of Mr. TICHBORNE, and the thought crossed my mind, "I declare somebody has got boots in Chili besides Mr. TICHBORNE," and presently——

What was his appearance at that time?—I was coming to that.

Just describe it at once?—I could only see his legs up to this moment. I should never have gone to look after him unless a boy had not come down to inform me that he had arrived.

I do not want you to go into those minute particulars; they are not what we want. When you ultimately saw him what was his appearance?—When I ultimately saw him he was covered with dust from head to foot, a broken nose, or rather a scarred nose, and really wanted a bath.

Was he the same as when he left, or did he appear very much altered?—Very much altered.

Had you any difficulty, in the first instance, in recognizing him?—Not in the least.

You recognized his boots at once?—I did not recognize his boots at once until I was sent for. The thought struck me, not that they were his boots, but that somebody else had boots like them.

Did you ask him anything about the boat at Poole—what I was beginning to ask you about?—About GOULD and the boat?

Yes?—Do you mean in connection with GOULD, or when he was after the poachers?

What I want you to do is to tell me all you asked him, to which he gave answers to show you he was the man?—I asked him if he recollected anything about chasing poachers: I asked him if he recollected anything about people being on the island, and he would be naturally afraid of his rabbits; and did he recollect going after them?—and he seemed to recollect it.

He seemed to recollect it?—Yes.

What I want you to do is to give us, as near as you can, what questions you asked, and what answers he gave, that showed he recollected it.—He seemed to recollect it, and I asked him what he recollected about it.

What did he recollect about it?—He seemed as if he knew he had chased them across the bay, and ultimately into the harbour. He did not mention Poole Harbour, but he mentioned the harbour.

He said across the harbour?—He said, "to the harbour," I believe. I did not answer, or say yes or no.

Now, just tell me what the matter was to which he was referring. You began to tell us, a long time ago, that story, and we interrupted you. I meant you to tell us what the story was that he seemed to recollect, when he said he chased them across the harbour?—The story was this: He saw people on the island, and he wanted me to go with him.

Was that the island on which it took place?—Yes; to which I objected, making some excuse, and said I had something else to do.

You say, people on the island: poachers, I suppose?—It was common enough for people to come from Poole, and rest themselves on the island; and if there were any rabbits, I have no doubt they would take them, if they could.

On the occasions on which you say you were asking him, did he seem to remember he had chased them across the bay? I want to know what that refers to, we do not know yet.—He wished me to go into the boat, which I objected to. I am stating the fact. He could not give a very accurate description. I could describe the thing accurately, but he could not describe it accurately; he said about the harbour.

You say it produced an impression on your mind that he seemed to remember it?—Yes.

I want to know what he said to you, which produced that impression?—He seemed to recollect the fact that he followed them into the harbour; his own words.

His own words were, that he followed them into the harbour?—Yes; then I questioned him what further ——

Before we go any further than that, had he followed those persons into the harbour?—Most decidedly; if not direct into the harbour, to the side near the harbour.

What more did he say about that; do you remember anything?—I asked him what further he did then? and he did not recollect what more happened.

As I understand you, all the matter that he remembered was chasing them into the harbour—across the harbour?—Yes.

Had you said anything to show him what you were inquiring into, what the chasing was, or what he had done? Had you told him?—No; I put the thing in such a way. I think if I was putting it in an improper way, Mr. SPOFFORTH would have prevented me.

Let us hear what it was?—I forget how the subject began.

I want to know what the question was to which he made that answer?—I really forget how I began the subject; to refer to it, I daresay I asked him, "Do you recollect anything about chasing poachers?" I dare say that was the question I asked, as far as I recollect.

Chasing poachers?—From the island.

Do you recollect anything about gathering ivy?—I do.

Just tell us what that was.

The Lord Chief Justice: What was said, you mean.

Mr. GIFFARD: I mean what was said. I ought to have put it more distinctly. I am asking, first, what you said to him, and what he said to you, before I ask what the fact was. You understand me, do you not?—Yes.

I want to know what passed between you about gathering ivy?—I remember gathering ivy for a certain purpose; but I do not recollect what the facts were that passed between him and me.

Do you remember your asking him any questions on the subject?—No; I do not.

Do you remember the Plaintiff asking you if you knew why he left England?—I do. Not exactly why he left England.

Give me the exact words, as nearly as you can. Give me the words that passed between you and him on the subject.—Put the question again. I do not know that he asked me.

The Lord Chief Justice: What did he say was the reason why he left England?—I do not recollect that he told me anything as to why he left England.

You may think of it presently; but were there other matters that you asked him about?—I can say certain things that may apply to the question, perhaps.

I do not want to go more into particulars at present; perhaps I shall hereafter; after I hear what questions are asked on the other side. What I ask you now is, did you ask him a variety of other things besides those now mentioned?—Do you mean the Plaintiff? That I asked him since his return?

Yes; since his return. Have you given me all you asked him?—I daresay there are many things, if you remind me of them.

That is exactly what I ask.—I was thinking that you were actually referring to facts which occurred on board the ship.

Will you attend to me for a moment? Are there more things that you asked him about than you have told us of to-day?—There is one pointed fact, which I could refer to, which is fully on my mind.

The Lord Chief Justice: Something you asked him, is the question?—Yes, my Lord; that convinces me more than all that transpired.

The question is, whether you asked him anything more than you have told us, that you remember?—I can remember a distinct thing that I told him.

That is what the gentleman is asking you.—I asked him what he did with the tomahawk. He did not know what he had done with it.

Mr. GIFFARD: He said so?—Yes; I said, "What made you take it out with you?" "I do not know." "I thought you were going to give it to some Indian chief."

That is what you said?—Yes. "Do not you recollect what you have done with it? What did you take it out with you for?" "I thought it would do to chop something with." I thought it was a very remarkable reply.

Why?—Because he told me the very same thing before he started away with it.

Is there any other matter that you remember?—Not without referring to my paper, I believe.

You cannot refer to your paper, because you have only written it recently; but were there other matters, though you do not remember them at this moment?—I think we referred to the mules, and about the photographs.

To the photographs?—Yes; and the supper.

The photographs and the supper? I meant to hear what was said about those things; have you got it in your mind now?—Which subject would you begin with, the photographs or the supper?

Either; whichever is first in your mind, the photographs or the supper.—With regard to the supper; he had invited a number of friends to take supper with him the night previous to his leaving.

Now, you are telling us what the fact is?—Yes.

What my lord wishes you to do is to tell us first what you said to him about it, and then what he said to you; and then tell us afterwards what the fact was.—I asked him if he recollected anything about it?

About what?—The supper, and who he had invited.

Where?—At Santiago de Chili, the Hotel Inglese.

Well?—He seemed to have first little or no recollection about it; and then he mentioned the name of APPLEBY, a person well known to me.

Then he mentioned the name of APPLEBY?—Yes, and asked me if he was there.

He asked you if APPLEBY was there?—Yes; I thought it was not fair to answer the question, yes or no, and pressed him for others; but he was hard upon APPLEBY.

Well?—I doubted very much whether he would be present for he was an old gentleman, and he said he thought he must be there, "for I was out at his place;" and I said, "Well, I cannot tell whether he was or not; I did not see him." Then he did not seem to recollect anything more about it. Then, I think a day or two afterwards, he had a brighter recollection of it—a fuller recollection of it.

What was the recollection he had then?—He remembered he was on the bed, fast asleep, and that he got no supper.

Now, then, was that the fact?—That was the fact.

Had you mentioned to anybody, between the first day, when he had not much recollection of it, and the day or two afterwards, what the facts were?—No, unless I had mentioned them to Mr. SPOFFORTH; and that I cannot say, because I was very careful to keep the facts to myself; I think I should not have done so; no one outside Mr. SPOFFORTH's office, that is quite certain.

Mr. GIFFARD: I do not know whether I should go on with the photographs now my Lord, or wait.

The Lord Chief Justice: You have not generally taken the photographs to the other witnesses.

Mr. GIFFARD: No, my lord, I am talking of an incident about photographs.

The Lord Chief Justice: I think it would be better.

Mr. GIFFARD: It is an incident about photographs of the same character as the evidence which I am now giving.

The Lord Chief Justice: Is that all you have to ask him?

Mr. GIFFARD: I have a great deal more to ask him.

The Witness: There is a great connection between the photographs and the supper.

(*The Court adjourned for a short time.*)

Mr. GIFFARD: Just before we adjourned I was asking you about the photographs. You said the photographs were connected with the supper. I want you to tell me as nearly as you can what it was you said to the Plaintiff about the photographs, and how far you tested him about that. Tell us what you said to him, and what he said to you; and then, presently, what the facts were?

I forget whether I asked him any questions about the photographs, or whether he commenced by speaking of them; he said he did not recollect anything about them, or how they were taken.

He said he did not recollect anything about them, or how they were taken?—No.

Do you recollect anything more that passed between you on the subject?—No; I took care not to inform him how they were taken. I was not surprised at that. He did not know how they were taken, and I was not surprised at it.

As I understand you, Sir ROGER, the Plaintiff, did not at all recollect how the daguerreotypes, or photographs were taken?—No.

Nor did he, I think, at all recollect, at any time?—No.

Now tell us how the fact was?—They were taken on the morning that he started from Santiago to Chili, across the Cordilleras. You speak of the photographs I sent home from South America, I presume. The photographs in question, I suppose, are the photographs, or daguerreotypes, which I sent home from South America?

These gentlemen do not hear what you say. The photographs which you sent home from South America?—The photographs in question.

You were going to tell us under what circumstances they were taken, which leads you to say you are not surprised that he did not remember anything about it?—I speak of the Plaintiff. He had had the supper previous to his departure the following morning; or, rather, he went without his supper, and other people ate it; but he recollects pretty well what was left. He mentioned there was a salad left for him, and a bit of goat. I do not know what was left beside the salad; but he particularly mentioned about the salad being left.

That is a thing you have not mentioned before. He distinctly mentioned about the salad being left?—He was not in bed the whole of the night, nor I neither. I was anxious to get the photographs or daguerreotypes of him, and I did it by a stratagem. I was living in the house of the daguerreotyper, Mr. THOMAS HELSBY. He was a very good-natured man, and the person who attended me when I was sick; and that reminds me of another occurrence that Mr. TICHBORNE spoke of fetching the doctor for me. I went and called Mr. THOMAS HELSBY up, and told him I would bring Mr. TICHBORNE round on the plea of wishing him good-bye, but my object was to get the daguerreotype taken of him. I told him to get the things prepared. I do a little of it myself, as I have been employed by Mr. HELSBY. The plates were to be prepared in readiness, and I was to bring him in, and encourage him to sit down before the camera, because if I had asked him to do it, I do not believe he would have done it. So I said, "Mr. TICHBORNE has come to wish you good-bye, sir." So they mutually spoke to each other, and by degrees he said, just sit down in the chair, and let me have a look at you through my camera, or glass. He sat down just as he was attired for starting across the Cordilleras, without any further change of clothing, to the best of my belief, and two, if not three, daguerreotypes were taken of him; I thought at one time that there were three. I sent one to Lady TICHBORNE—the late Lady TICHBORNE—and had an idea that I sent one to Lady DOUGHTY, but Lady DOUGHTY never received it, if I sent it; the other one I kept myself, so I cannot be positive whether I had the three, and whether I sent one to Lady DOUGHTY or not, but I was under that impression.

The Solicitor-General: You sent one to Lady TICHBORNE and one to Lady DOUGHTY?—I thought I had done so, and when I came to England I found she had not received it.

The Lord Chief Justice: You kept one yourself?—Yes.

The Solicitor-General: You say, one you sent to Lady TICHBORNE, kept one yourself, and you believe you sent one to Lady DOUGHTY?—I was under that impression, but Lady DOUGHTY said she never received it.

You were under the impression that you had three?—Yes.

Mr. GIFFARD: You kept one yourself? There is no doubt about that?—Yes, I did.

You sent one to Lady TICHBORNE?—Yes, I sent one to Lady TICHBORNE, or Sir JAMES, I forget which.

You did send one home?—Yes.

And you did believe you sent one to Lady DOUGHTY?—I had that impression on my mind.

And until you found out that she had not received it you were under the impression that you did?—I was.

You will not positively say that you did?—I will not positively say that I did.

Have you got the one that you say that you kept in your own possession?—The one I brought home myself I ultimately gave to Lady DOUGHTY. I handed it to her myself before there was any talk of the Claimant's return.

Would you be able to know it again if you were to see it?—Positively; I should know it again by its frame.

That is to say, if it is contained in the same frame?

Mr. HAWKINS: That is the one in a wooden frame which has been produced.

The Lord Chief Justice: Just ask him.

Mr. GIFFARD: Is that the one? (*Handing a daguerreotype to the witness.*)—If it is not the identical one, it is a copy of it. I presume it is the same. At all events the position of the man is just the same, and all things.

The Lord Chief Justice: Have you any reason to doubt that it is the same?—I have no reason to doubt it, unless it is to try whether I do recollect the original or not. I have every reason to believe that is the original. It is a daguerreotype.

Mr. GIFFARD: So far as you can see, that is the identical one?—Yes.

It may be a *fac-simile*, but to your mind, is that the same?—Yes.

Mr. HAWKINS: It may be convenient for your lordship to know that that is the one exhibited in Chili. It is the identical one.

The Lord Chief Justice: Marked AA?

Mr. GIFFARD: Yes, my lord; marked AA.

The Witness: That has been to Chili. There is a name put upon it that I know in Chili. EASEMAN, whom I know in Chili.

Mr. HAWKINS: It is marked.

The Lord Chief Justice: Just hand that to me. (*The daguerreotype was handed to his lordship.*) It is one that has been produced.

Mr. GIFFARD: It is the only one that has been produced in a wooden frame.

The Lord Chief Justice: That is all.

Mr. GIFFARD: Is the frame the same?—Yes.

The Lord Chief Justice: Would you like to see it again, gentlemen, now we know what this is?

Mr. GIFFARD: I think my last question was what state of mind or body was Mr. TICHBORNE in at the time that was taken?—His state of mind, I suppose, was *compos mentis*.

How had he spent the night before?—He had only been laying in his bed. He had not actually been to bed; and he had had a good portion of sleep, most decidedly. The photograph may not be a good one of the man, because it makes him look so very sleepy.

The Lord Chief Justice: Do you say he did not have any sleep, or a good portion?—He had a good portion; because they had eaten the supper while he was asleep. He had not actually undressed or gone to bed. I suppose he was walking about from three o'clock in the morning to half-past five or six, the hour he started away.

Mr. GIFFARD: Now, when you were telling us about the photographs, you appear to remember something that was said to you by Sir ROGER about having been to the doctor?—I do remember that.

Just tell me what it was—what the Plaintiff said to you and what you said to the Plaintiff—before we inquire what the fact was?—Was it not true that he went to fetch the doctor for me when I was ill.

He asked you that?—Yes.

Had you mentioned that circumstance to him?—No.

Or to anyone?—No.

Was that the fact?—It was the fact.

Do you remember anything else now? Do you remember asking something about what went home in a box?—I think I did ask him whether he remembered about sending anything home—about the linen.

Tell me what the question was, and what the answer was?—I really do not remember what I asked him. I never thought I should be questioned about that.

I daresay not. What I want to know is whether you gave him an opportunity of knowing what you were questioning him about when you put the question?—I always endeavoured to do the contrary.

Can you bring back your memory to what the question was that you put to him, and what his answer was?—I think I asked him if he sent any skins of birds home, and he said, Yes; that he had seen them at Tichborne, and pictures that he had bought in Peru; and he had told me, when in Chili, that he had sent off some pictures from Peru.

What I want to bring your mind to is this: Was any question asked about dirty clothes; how the question was asked; and how the answer was given?—Upon my word I cannot remember.

Do you remember anything being said about shirts?—I do not remember asking him anything at all about it. I remember the fact about shirts on board the ship. I do not remember asking him.

Do you remember whether he told you anything?—I do not remember whether we conversed on the subject or not.

Now, then, tell me what is your own deliberate conviction as to this gentleman who has been sitting here?—He is not here at the present moment.

You have seen him here this morning?—My sincere and deliberate conviction with regard to speaking the solemn truth?

Yes; whether he is the same ROGER TICHBORNE you were servant to or not?—Taking into consideration the answers he has given me so pointedly, on so many points, which I may even forget now, convinces me, beyond measure, he can be nobody else. Putting his looks and so forth aside, he is ROGER TICHBORNE as sure as I am JOHN MOORE.

Mr. GIFFARD: Now, my lord, I have brought the examination to that point which appears to me to exhaust that portion of the evidence which, according to your lordship's view, it seemed fair to give. I should say that I have a large quantity of evidence which my learned friend, Mr. Serjeant BALLANTINE, and we all, think of great importance to give. We think, subject to what may appear hereafter, that after what your lordship has said, we ought not to give it now, but that we should be at liberty to give it after the Claimant himself has been examined.

The Lord Chief Justice: That is the correct course. It may be material after the Claimant has been examined. I think you adopt the right course.

Mr. GIFFARD: That is what we are desirous of doing, to meet your lordship's views. I do not know what course your lordship thinks it is reasonable now to take with reference to the evidence the witness has given; whether it would or would not be right to call on my learned friend the Solicitor-General to cross-examine on these matters now.

The Lord Chief Justice: At present he would be bound to cross-examine.

The Solicitor-General: I hope your lordship will not say that without hearing me.

The Lord Chief Justice: I beg your pardon. I did not express any opinion absolutely, but only upon the Case as it is presented to me.

The Solicitor-General: I was afraid that your lordship might assume I was not going to say something on the matter.

The Lord Chief Justice: No. As far as this present matter was concerned you have acted in accordance with what I think is the correct rule, Mr. GIFFARD. That is to say, you are not at liberty to go into evidence as to matters that may or may not be relevant to the extent that you proposed; whether they will or will not depends in a great degree upon the cross-examination of the Claimant.

Mr. Serjeant BALLANTINE: We all feel that your lordship is most desirous the matter should be conducted in a way most conducive to the ends of justice. On receiving intimation from your lordship, my learned friends and myself determined that we would adapt ourselves to it in every possible way.

The Lord Chief Justice: I think you adopt the right course. Supposing I had ruled, without asking you first, that must be the course adopted, then the Solicitor-General would, of course, be entitled to cross-examine upon the evidence that was given; but simply because the witness might be able to give some further evidence, that would not, as a matter of course, entitle him to postpone the cross-examination.

The Solicitor-General: Certainly not.

Mr. Serjeant BALLANTINE: There will be so much of the further evidence similar to the evidence already given, that if my learned friend, the Solicitor-General desires to postpone his cross-examination, I shall be bound, in common fairness, to consent to that course being taken.

The Solicitor-General: My friend does not like my saying I speak from my heart; but I say that is a most candid and considerate offer, and, certainly, I should prefer to do so. I did not make the application, although I told my learned friend I should; but, if my learned friend yields without the application, it is more pleasant to me.

The Lord Chief Justice: I quite understand that is the course the Solicitor-General would prefer to take, and I think it is a very graceful concession on the part of Brother BALLANTINE.

The Solicitor-General: Perhaps I may say it will, in the end, save both of us time; if he is to be recalled, and there is to be a second cross-examination, it is inevitable.

The Lord Chief Justice: I do not know what course you may be going to take, but it strikes me, with reference to the class of evidence—such as the military evidence, and other friends' evidence from Hampshire, persons that recognized him, and that class of evidence—that it would be more important after the Claimant has been examined, and the witnesses have had an opportunity of seeing him after examination and cross-examination.

Mr. Serjeant BALLANTINE: We are governed by the fact that several gentlemen are living at a distance, and we have been obliged to arrange for the days when they could come up. To-morrow two or three gentlemen are coming who travel with difficulty, and whom we must call on that point. I shall be able to communicate to-morrow morning to your lordship the course we shall take throughout the remainder of the evidence.

The Lord Chief Justice: If you call witnesses of that class before the Claimant has been examined, it will be open to some observation afterwards; but if they are called after the Claimant has been examined, the observation would not occur. Just consider that.

Mr. Serjeant BALLANTINE: We have considered it, my lord, and I remember considering the same question when your lordship was at the Bar in a very important Case which I had the honour to be in with your lordship, in Surrey. I think my friend Mr. JAMES remembers it very well; and your lordship will see the reason why we have pursued the course on the present occasion.

The Lord Chief Justice: I quite remember the Case.

TICHBORNE IN SOUTH AMERICA.

Of the Claimant's life in South America, some of the evidence of MOORE gives a few strange features. The following letter appears to complete the picture:—

TRUTH STRANGER THAN FICTION,

To the Editor.

SIR,—Sir ROGER CHAS. DOUGHTY TICHBORNE, Bart., the gentleman now in Dartmoor Prison, answering to the name of THOMAS CASTRO, having been my intimate friend during and before the late Trial, I had special opportunities for proving the fallacies of the arguments used against him by the prosecution, as well as the utter unreliability of many things accepted as facts by the Court. I may also here remark that having been frequently in his company during many months of the most trying part of the late Trial, I never once heard a blasphemous word pass his lips, nor the expression of one bitter sentence, even against his most deadly enemies. His moderation, also, at the dinner-table was the admiration of all who met him. So much for my observation of his personal character; and, as for what has transpired since the Trial, it strongly suggests CICERO's definition of the orator—"*Clarescit urendo*"—"He brightens as he burns." The conduct, since the Trial, of some of the witnesses who were brought to swear against him, gives an idea of the means used to crush him—*coûte qui coûte*.

The great importance attached by the Lord Chief Justice to the non-production of a living witness from the "Osprey," as telling against the Claimant, is shown at page 74 of the summing-up:—"Now, let us ask ourselves whether there is any reasonable probability of the 'Osprey' having picked up and brought into Melbourne the shipwrecked crew of the 'Bella,' &c. Yet from that hour to the present no person has come forward." Your readers must remember the "Osprey" was a schooner hailing from an American port, sailing from America to Australia, and never known to have been in Europe. Now, is it not far more extraordinary that not a living soul except MOORE, who swore to the Claimant's identity, belonging to the "Pauline," ever appeared upon the scene. The "Pauline" was also a schooner sailing from Havre de Grace, a port within ten hours of London, to South America, yet no surprise or comment is expressed at the non-production of a member of her crew; certainly this is far more remarkable. The subjoined extract from the summing-up produced in an unexpected manner, and when too late, a veritable member of the crew of the "Pauline," in the historical voyage, March, 1853, ROGER TICHBORNE, passenger, and to the production of this man and its results I wish to call the special attention of your readers.

On the fourth day of the summing-up I read:—"You will remember that he (ROGER TICHBORNE) left MOORE behind, and that the Defendant has told us that having left MOORE behind, the captain of the 'Pauline' allowed him to take one of the people of the 'Pauline'—the second mate, I think—as his servant. Is that statement consistent with what ROGER writes to his brother at that time? He says that at Valparaiso he engaged as valet a Frenchman who had an eighteen years' certificate. Does that apply to a servant with eighteen years' character, or does it refer to a man who was one of the crew of the 'Pauline'? If you think that the term 'Frenchman with eighteen years' character' means a servant, it is inconsistent with the statement the Defendant has made."

Now, on the 9th of February, 1874, I received from Sir ROGER TICHBORNE the following note:—

"The Court, Feb. 9, 1874.

"DEAR MR. EAST,—Many thanks for your cheque this morning. It is very kind of you, and enables me to send £1 to my wife. My friends do not know I am so hard pressed, and I do not like to tell them, as the end is so close. I do so hope this week will finish it; but I fear not. He is getting on worse than ever today, perverting truth and facts into ridicule and lies by the score. The other day he told the jury that I must have been mistaken when I stated that the second mate of the 'Pauline' left that vessel in Arica, and travelled with me as my servant, saying had such a thing occurred I would be sure to have mentioned it in one of my letters; thus putting a fact as a lie before the jury.

"Now, strange to say, this man, PIERRE FERON, has just written to me from Havre. The last time I saw him was at Lima, where unfortunately I had to leave him, after I had remained nearly two months waiting for him to recover. Hearing from his medical attendant that he was not likely to recover, I engaged JULES BARBACT, who had been manager at the 'Globe d'Or,' in Lima, in his stead. He is now living at 44, Rue Beauverger, Havre. I have not the least doubt he is the man, for he mentions circumstances in his letter that no one else could possibly know. I have sent the letters to the Doctor, who promises to see about it. I fear I am somewhat boring you.

"With kind regards, yours sincerely,

"R. C. D. TICHBORNE."

The following is the letter from PIERRE FERON referred to in the above letter from Sir ROGER:—

"Havre, 6 Fevri, 1874.

"Sir ROGER TICHBORNE.—En vous reportant à 20 ans en arrière nous devons trouver, l'un et l'autre dans nos souvenirs plus d'un rapprochement. En maître d'equipage à bord de la 'Pauline' j'ai assisté à votre embarquement. Nous avons l'un et l'autre voyagé ensemble dans l'intérieur près d'une année. J'ai en ma possession divers objets et plusieurs confidences que je serai heureux de mettre au service de votre cause, certain de l'éclairer. E'crivez-moi, donnez-moi les moyens pécuniaires d'aller à Londres, et je partirai de suite. Moi seul ferai à triompher votre cause,

"PIERRE FERON, ex-Maitre d'Equipage de la 'Pauline.'

"Havre, Rue Beauverger, 4."

(Translation.)

"Havre, 6th February, 1874.

"Sir ROGER TICHBORNE,—In speaking of twenty years since, we should have mutual remembrance. As second mate of the 'Pauline,' I assisted at your embarking. We travelled together for the best part of a year in the interior. I have in my possession several objects of confidence presented to me, which I shall be pleased to place at the service of your cause, and which are certain to throw light on the matter. Give me the pecuniary means, and I will start at once for London, as I alone can make your cause triumphant.

"PIERRE FERON, Boatswain of the 'Pauline.'

"Havre, Rue Beauverger."

On my receipt of the above letter from Sir ROGER TICHBORNE, I at once wrote to PIERRE FERON, requesting his attendance in London, and at the same time I requested an agent in Havre to furnish him with funds. Also to procure certificates from the Department of the Minister of Marine for the Seine Inferieure, and a guarantee from the British Consul of his identity with the second mate of the "Pauline," in March, 1853.

PIERRE FERON arrived at my house on the 12th February with the above-named certificates. I found him a strong-built, powerful man, of about 60 years of age, not understanding any English—not being, I believe, able to write nor read.

I produced Sir ROGER's letter, and read to him in French the part of it referring to himself. Thrice during my reading he replied, "*Tiens, c'est vrai*" (It's true, it's true). I also ascertained from him that ROGER TICHBORNE was in the habit of getting very drunk in Lima, and leading in other respects a very wild and loose life; that PIERRE FERON never entertained any feeling of respect for his young master, and that he had ultimately shammed illness at Lima to get clear of him. I arranged a meeting for that evening at a West-end Hotel, at which were present Sir ROGER TICHBORNE, PIERRE FERON, Mr. HARCOURT, Solicitor, Mr. HENRY CRAWLEY, Mr. BIGGS, Mr. DAVIS, a friend, and myself, all residents in London. Mr. DAVIS, of Regent-street, and his friend, I had never had the pleasure of seeing, nor have I seen either of them nor communicated with them since. I had written Sir ROGER at the Court desiring him to meet me at the hotel. Upon his arrival I observed, "Well, Sir ROGER, I have your old servant FERON here; can you recollect his appearance?" He replied, "Well, after 20 years it is difficult to say; but this I can clearly remember— he was as tall as myself and weighed sixteen or seventeen stone." Such proved to be the case. I then went down stairs to fetch FERON, and as we ascended the stairs I said, "FERON, was ROGER TICHBORNE tattooed?" He replied, "No, certainly not."

Having desired Sir ROGER on no account to appear to recognize FERON when he should enter the room, I so managed as to have him opposite to Sir ROGER, but at a distance of seven or eight feet. After a few minutes' general conversation by the whole party in English, I asked FERON if there was anyone in the room he recognized. He took quite a minute to consider, and then said "No." Upon which I said, "Sir ROGER, he does not remember you." Sir ROGER answered "No; but I remember him, and will see if I cannot revive his memory."

Sir ROGER then said to the company, "Gentlemen, I am in this difficulty. It will be a waste of time to ask any questions of this man which have been put in either Trial, as you may justly say he has been coached. Hence my difficulty; as although many matters which I can refer to are, from their small importance, likely to have become forgotten by him after the lapse of 20 years. However, we shall see."

Sir ROGER then said to me, who acted as interpreter on the occasion, "Mr. EAST, ask him if he recollects ROGER TICHBORNE being robbed in the neighbourhood of Callao of his watch, chain, tobacco-box, and about £3 in money."

Answer: "Yes, he was robbed of his watch, chain, tobacco-box, and about 36 francs. It was his own fault, for going into so low a neighbourhood by himself."

Sir ROGER: "Ask him if he recollects going up a river in South America with ROGER TICHBORNE in a canoe with two black men to paddle."

Answer: "Yes, but not with two black men; they were copper-coloured."

Sir ROGER: "Ask him if he recollects going to a cock-fight in Chili with me one Sunday morning, and that one cock killed five others."

Answer: "Yes, but I think it killed more than five."

Sir ROGER: "Ask him if he recollects frequently going with ROGER TICHBORNE to a sailmaker's shop just through the turnpike on the left-hand side of Valparaiso, and drinking freely."

Answer: "I recollect."

Sir ROGER: "Ask if he recollects going with ROGER TICHBORNE to the suburbs at Valparaiso to see the barracks."

Answer: "I do; but I want to know the names of those suburbs."

Sir ROGER—after a few seconds' consideration—first named them in Spanish, and in the same breath in English—"the fore, main, and mizzentop."

Answer: "That is correct."

It is not, Sir, necessary that I occupy your space by reporting all which was said in an hour's conversation of this nature, but I will at once come to the question that so forcibly impressed me.

Sir ROGER: "Ask him if he recollects ROGER TICHBORNE being ill at Viakiel."

Answer: "Yes."

Sir ROGER: "Ask him if brandy was not the cause of his illness."

Answer: "No, certainly not."

Sir ROGER then observed: "Well, God knows I used to take enough of it. I do not know what he can mean," and then added to himself, though loud enough for me to hear him, "I used to take a great quantity of arsenic; but there, he would know nothing of that."

This having been said in an indifferent manner, I took little notice of it, and it would have passed without an observation but for a lull in the conversation, during which I said to PIERRE FERON, "Was it a white powder which caused his illness?"

To which he answered: "Justement." (Just so.)

Mr. EAST: "Was it arsenic?"

Answer: "Yes, it was, and I stole it from him."

Sir ROGER then observed: "Well, I was not aware anyone knew I took arsenic. I used to carry it ostensibly for preparing the skins of birds, but as I had suffered from spasms since 16 years of age, I found relief from arsenic. But one night at Viakiel, having previously been drinking freely, I had an attack of spasms at the heart, and being also half tipsy, I took an overdose; and PIERRE FERON, finding me in my room in an insensible state, sent for a doctor, who, with the ordinary appliances of warm baths, emetics, &c., unfortunately for me, saved my life. Yet I was not aware that he knew the cause of my illness. Please ask him why he stole the arsenic."

Answer: "Because I did not wish it to be said I poisoned him, nor did I wish to leave his bones at Viakiel."

Question: "But why did you steal the arsenic?"

Answer: "Well, one night I went into his room at Viakiel, and found him raving and foaming at the mouth like a mad dog, and insensible. I sent for a doctor, who informed me it was the result of arsenical poisoning."

In the above statement I have, Sir, adhered strictly to the facts, and the original letters are still in my possession, and I leave your readers to discern for themselves.

It is a matter for deep reflection, and perhaps for strong expressions; but I refrain from using strong terms with reference to either Judges, or jury, or witnesses. Impartial history will surely place the main actors in this drama in their true light.

Individually, it will always afford me pleasure in feeling I have been of some slight practical assistance to a sorely-tried man.

And "that voice whose approval makes us walk by day serene, and makes our pillow smooth by night," enjoins me not to desert the cause of a fallen friend, although it may be unpopular, ridiculed, or not deemed even respectable.—I remain, Sir, yours, &c.,

W. QUARTERMAINE EAST.

Queen's Hotel, St. Martin's-le-Grand.

GUILDFORD ONSLOW, ESQ., M.P., ON THE CLAIMANT AND LAW REFORM.

At Guildford, on the occasion of the great demonstration of his constituents in the Public Hall, Mr. ONSLOW said:—

We must have reform in the law. (Loud cheers.) Hitherto law and justice have been only for those who can afford to pay for them. (Cheers.) And in no country in the world do we find the want of reform more than in our own. It is impossible not to arrive at the conclusion that on the subject of Law Reform the Government, as a Liberal Government, is bound to carry out its traditions. The great Liberal party cannot permit the question law reform to cease to belong to our political programme, and if law officers do not reform, they must let us reformers reform m. (Loud cheers.) Lovers of justice in this country can no ger see the justice and fair-play we expect the subject to receive. are the laughing-stock of the foreigner, who infinitely prefers own system. (Hear, hear.) There never was such a burlesque British justice as the late great Trial of the TICHBORNE Case, en might prevailed over right—(cheers)—and influence, money, d power over reason, justice, and fair-play. (Loud cheers.) here ought to be a law to exempt jurymen from sitting on these otracted Trials, when their physical powers fail them, and prent their sitting to hear the whole of a Case, so as to enable them meet the ends of justice in their ultimate decision. The system ts in a manner prejudicial to truth and justice, and thus renders o verdict unsatisfactory to all parties concerned. (Hear, hear.) allude more particularly on this occasion to the Case in which I have taken so prominent a part, in giving my support to a man no, I am confident, was cruelly and unfairly committed, without conviction, to that most detestable of English dungeons, Newgate prison, for fifty-three days—(cheers)—and after having introduced him whom I consider SIR ROGER CHARLES TICHBORNE to several of my constituents, and having also introduced him to a public meeting in Guildford, I am in duty bound to you to state the reasons why I have supported him, and I gladly avail myself of this public opportunity of placing the whole matter before you. (Loud cheers.) I gladly take this opportunity to contradict a report which has gained currency—that I have given my support to SIR ROGER TICHBORNE from mere pecuniary motives. On the contrary, I may tell you that in defence of that man I have spent £3,000, and that is the only claim I have upon him. If he pays me, well and good; if he does not, thank God! I have bread and cheese to live upon. (Loud and continued cheering, and cries of "Bravo!") There are those who say I hold TICHBORNE bonds; really I never saw a TICHBORNE bond in the whole course of my life, and I will gladly give half-a-crown to anybody who will show me one. I have been drawn through the mud, taken to

A. BIDDULPH, ESQ., COUSIN TO SIR ROGER.

Bow-street, and received abuse in the House of Commons and elsewhere for my adherence to his cause. (Cries of "Shame.") I have risked that kind support you have given me. (A Voice: "You shall have it again.") I knew I was in the right path. (Hear, hear.) I supported a man who was crushed. (Cheers.) I condescended more than that, I was obliged to go to Bow-street with a man I never spoke to further than to say, "Get out, you brute." (Hear, hear, and cries of "He ought to have it.") I became, gentlemen, the trustee of public money, and because I would not allow this blood-sucker to touch the children's mite and the widow's penny, I suffered wrong, and I ask you to suffer with me. (Cheers, and Voices: "We will.") I trust to you, gentlemen, to support me in the course I am taking. (Renewed cheering, and cries of "Stick to him.") The path I have taken I have chosen from the purest motives. I knew SIR ROGER TICHBORNE's father and mother; I was indebted to his father for much kindness, and when his poor mother died of a broken heart, she thanked me for the part I had taken in support of her boy, and she begged and entreated me to stand by him, and I will stand by him till I see that man gain his rights. ("Bravo" and cheers.) I maintain, gentlemen, that he has not had a fair Trial, and it is upon that great issue I stand. (Cheers.) And I say more: supposing he is an impostor, he is an Englishman, and as such is he not entitled to a fair and honest Trial? (Applause.) I am happy to say I am backed up in the position I occupy by the bulk of the working classes, the bone and sinew of the country, who never did a more honourable thing than they have in espousing the cause of the Claimant to the Tichborne Estates. (Cheers.) Here is a man who belongs to the upper ten thousand, and yet it is to the working portion of the community that he owes his success so far as it has gone. (Hear, hear.) It makes me blush to think that the labouring classes alone come forward to assist a man who has been oppressed. How many, like the old Levite, turn the other way? But true to the old Samaritan instinct, I have determined to do unto him as I should wish to be done by. (Loud cheers.) During the Pilgrimage I have made with SIR ROGER, I know that he has found many a staunch friend in large towns like Birmingham and Manchester. (Applause.) I will not enter into details, but simple facts, which I am prepared to prove. What I find fault with is, that he should undergo a Trial of 103 days, and at the eleventh hour, when they thought it was going against them, his opponents should bring a charge against him which they did not utter in Chancery Court in 1866. I refer to the tattoo marks. (Hear, hear.) Common-sense tells us that if they knew of the tattoo marks in 1866 that they would too willingly have advanced that point then. They would then have saved the infant whom they profess to care so much a deal of money, and the country would not have been robbed of £200,000. But this was not heard of when he was examined. He had twenty-seven different marks on his body, and the Attorney-General said every one of them was fabricated. How was it then that the tattoo marks considered were not also fabricated? (Hear, hear, and cheers.) How was it that the Claimant, after twenty-eight days in the witness-box, subjected to the fire of the most eminent Counsel in Europe, was acknowledged by him to be a better man than he was? If you make this case your study, gentlemen, as I have for the past six years I am quite confident that you will agree with me that if we had had the opportunity of replying to the Attorney-General's speech we should have turned the scale. (Hear, hear.) But no, we were brought to a standstill for the want of money. Watch the Case for yourselves, and I believe at the coming Trial you will see Sir ROGER CHARLES DOUGHTY TICHBORNE receive an honourable and triumphant acquittal. (Loud cheers.) I am about to ask you to do me a personal favour, and that is to allow a gentleman who knows the Claimant well, in short no other than Mr. BIDDULPH, SIR ROGER TICHBORNE's cousin, to address a few words to you on this subject. (Loud cheering, amid which the honourable gentleman resumed his seat.)

Mr. BIDDULPH said: I have always been averse to obtrude myself unnecessarily on the public; but when a great principle is involved, when the character of a friend is at stake, it is one of those occasions on which I hope I shall be the last to allow private feelings to interfere with public duty. (Loud cheers.) In pursuance of such a principle, I have come before you to-night, and as my esteemed friend, your honourable member, has introduced me to you as the cousin of Sir ROGER TICHBORNE, I am proud to say, I stand before you as his supporter during his late Trial, and to tell you that at the forthcoming Trial I shall again stand by him, with my confidence unabated in his claims to his title and estates. (Loud cheers.) I still tell you that I believe him to be my cousin, and believing his cause to be righteous, I shall not desert it. (Cheers.) I have heard it said, that these so-called TICHBORNE Demonstrations are illegal, or if not illegal, something very like it; if they are so, I remind the present assembly that a gentleman whose name has been already mentioned on this platform was the first to give the example of discussing in public the last Trial; I refer to the Lord Chief Justice BOVILL, who, under the soothing influence of turtle and milk punch, made comments on the trial when in progress. (Laughter.) How, then, can a public, less legally wise, be expected not to make their comments on that same Trial, when an affair of the past? (Cheers.) Your honourable member has referred to the want of legal reform as exemplified in the present Trial. I can only endorse his opinion on this subject, and say, with such a requirement of proper legal direction, patent to all, it was the duty of any high-minded legislator, irrespective of any sympathy for the [illegible] Claimant, to stand forth, as Mr. ONSLOW has done, to demand that justice be done. (Loud cheers.) I am not going to enter into details as to the reasons for my believing in the identity of my cousin, Sir R. TICHBORNE: they have been already given in Court; and Mr. ONSLOW has dwelt so ably on the Case, that it is superfluous for me to say more; but this I will say, that many of these discrepancies which, to some minds, appeared in the evidence, could have been reconciled if the Case had been heard out; while concerning the loss of memory of the Claimant in certain things, which was so much insisted on, hundreds of precedents may be cited of [illegible] of forgetfulness much more glaring. (Hear, hear.) Of men, for example, who, after a few years of colonial life, have forgotten, not only the country, but the town or the village in which they were born and spent their life. (Cheers.) I will not now say more than that I wish I could see in the House of Commons more men with the fearless courage, the love of justice, and independent spirit, of my friend Mr. ONSLOW. (Loud cheers.) Such qualities as these, I may safely say, would inspire the confidence of not only Guildford, but every borough in the length and breadth of England, and no constituency would hesitate to trust its interests to such keeping. (Loud cheers.)

MR. WHALLEY'S SPEECH AT LIVERPOOL.

The following is a report of Mr. WHALLEY's speech at the [illegible] Tuesday, Sept. 19, copied from the *[illegible]*.

My friend Mr. O[illegible] said to hold a brief in this Case from the [illegible] ROGER TICHBORNE, and I join heartily in the applause with which you recognize the way he discharges the duty. I speak not for my personal interests, but on behalf of the law and constitution of the country, outraged and discredited in this Case. The Claimant has at length reached Liverpool, the most important of all the great centres of public opinion to which he has submitted his claims on public sympathy and support, and it is due to you, that those who have shared with him this toilsome and hazardous pilgrimage should here present you with a review of the great work which we have taken in hand. When I failed in my appeal to the Government and the House of Commons to afford to the Claimant the same aid in insuring a fair Trial which any ordinary criminal charged with such offences would be entitled to demand, and when the Government, or the Court of Common Pleas, surrendered to the Attorney-General, and dealt with him as guilty of those offences, without evidence or trial, I, for one, knowing as I firmly do, that he is ROGER CHARLES TICHBORNE, demanded a fair Trial, and this being refused, I have since taken my share in making this appeal to the country. And now let us consider what is the result. I was not at Birmingham or Wolverhampton, and many large towns have been visited by the Claimant alone, without either Mr. ONSLOW or myself being present, and therefore I can speak of the results of the campaign thus far without any suspicion of being biassed by my own share in the work, and no one can contradict me when I say that whether at such meetings as I have attended, or whether the Claimant has stood alone, fairly among the Tens of Thousands of Englishmen who have everywhere crowded around him, *there has never been anything short of the most complete success—nothing but entire unanimity, [illegible] him, that he is truly* Sir ROGER CHARLES TICHBORNE. Every town he has visited may be said to have given that verdict with entire unanimity; the more striking, because it has so happened that in every place he has visited the local newspapers have, with scarcely an exception, written against him, sometimes bringing forward merely the leading points in the Attorney-General's speech; at others, adding thereto most virulent and scandalous abuse and deliberate falsehoods that have ever disgraced the Press: and this, too, not by obscure and uninfluential papers, but such as the *Leeds Mercury* and the *Yorkshire Post*, which last, however, has had the manliness and courage to fall in, as some others have also done, with the torrent of public feeling and judgment in his favour. It has been, however, the most remarkable feature of this Case, that while the public opinion thus fully tested and expressed has throughout been favourable to the Claimant, notwithstanding the continuous hostility of the Press, the sentiments of what may be called the upper classes have been almost as unanimous against him, and I recommend this most singular fact for the examination and discussion of some of our social science philosophers. While leaving it to them to settle it in some of their congresses, I can inform them of another feature not less striking in its exhibition of the moral condition of "the upper classes of the period." Almost to a man I now find in those who, in the clubs, at the dinner-table, or wherever the "upper ten" condescend to discuss this question, a marked change in the tone of their conversation. They are, if possible, more angry than ever with the Claimant for being Sir ROGER TICHBORNE; they ring the changes of the Attorney-General's epithets about Mrs. RADCLIFFE and his horse-stealing adventures, and every other scrap of scandal they can recall; and they openly and avowedly declare that, be he the man or not, it is disgraceful on the part of Mr. ONSLOW, myself, or other of the genteel classes, to support such a man, and that he ought to be left to the fate which Judge BOVILL, and the Attorney-General, and the Government have, whether he is TICHBORNE or ORTON, consigned, and tried to keep him within the walls of Newgate. Let those, then, who are concerned with our social science problems, accept this challenge from me, that any man who shall deliberately say that the character of the Claimant, be it what it may, justifies any man in standing by and seeing him punished as an impostor, without a fair Trial, is acting a part that, if successful, will brand with infamy the social morality and the character of the upper classes of society of this generation and period; and when our children shall hereafter read of the conduct of the Courts of Law, the House of Commons, and the Government, supported by the "moral" sentiment of the "educated" classes in regard to this TICHBORNE Case, they will wish to trace their descent to some working man such as I now see before me, and to free themselves as far as possible from the taint of such falsehood, injustice, and hypocrisy as will for ever attach to those, whether as individuals or classes, who, under the specious pretence of Sir ROGER TICHBORNE being a bad man, have lent the aid of the law and of Parliament to deprive him of his name and his inheritance. I was lately engaged with Captain HUNT in tracing out the threads of what is beyond all doubt a conspiracy to injure the Claimant. I refer to what has been brought before the Bow-street Police Court and in conversation with a simple-minded wife of one of the parties. She innocently said, "*We are afraid he is the man after all,*" just as Mr. GOSFORD after his first interview with him in 1867, said to his servant; [illegible] good woman being asked why she was afraid, replied, "Because he is such a bad man;" and [illegible] the best services that Mr. ONSLOW and myself can render to those who tell us we ought not to give our [illegible] Claimant "because he is a bad man," is [illegible] his character, conduct, and antecedents [illegible] we are prepared to establish, [illegible] claim to be recognized as a gentleman, [illegible] and able in the future to discharge honourably and [illegible] fully every duty of the position to which he lays claim; and I propose to submit to you in a few words the grounds on which I make this statement. He has been in England now near seven years, residing for the first two years with his Mother, then at Alresford, a small town in Hampshire, where every eye was upon him and every ear open to the last whisper in scandal there, and now at Brompton, and living also n some sort a public life at the Waterloo Hotel, with a view to he work he had on hand, and all this time, except while his mother's allowance of £1,000 a year lasted, living entirely on money lent or given to him by those who had faith in him and his cause; and I should think it is within the mark that his creditors are out of pocket above £100,000. Now I ask whether it is possible for any man to be exposed to more severe criticism as to every act of his life since his return to England than Sir ROGER TICHBORNE has been, to which is to be added that night and day for the greater part of that period no ticket-of-leave man was ever under such constant watch as he has been by detective police employed by his opponents; and I ask with confidence whether one single act has been brought home to him, so far as I know imputed to him, that is unbecoming, or inconsistent with the position or conduct of a gentleman. The Attorney-General, as we know, calls him a villain, a liar, a perjurer, a scoundrel, and other epithets, but he at the same time was fair enough to say that he would prove all this; and as he never did anything of the sort, it of course, on his own showing, goes for nothing. He said he traduced the character of Mrs. RADCLIFFE, but the butcher ORTON could have no object in fixing a scandal on Mrs. RADCLIFFE, and if a TICHBORNE, it was not he, but the Attorney-General who brought that evidence out, in spite of everything it was possible for TICHBORNE to do to prevent it. Then he charged him with horse-stealing, but it turns out that *he no more stole a horse than the Attorney-General, nor ever was charged with doing so*, for according to the evidence of Professor ANDERSON and others, all he was required to do was to produce the receipt for the purchase of a horse, which being in his possession was claimed by some one who had lost that horse, and nothing short of a deliberate design to impute to him some unknown offences could justify the Attorney-General in Court, or Mr. HENRY JAMES in the House of Commons, from construing his refusal to reply to certain questions, on the ground that he might criminate himself, into anything else than a desire not to injure other persons, such as ORTON, or those whom he may have been connected with in Australia; and as to this point, too—his career in Australia—we have received during our campaign the most striking and conclusive evidence that his conduct in Australia gained for him, to an extraordinary degree, the confidence and regard of every class of persons with whom he had dealings. We have besides Dr. WHEELER, Mr. DYKE, Professor ANDERSON, and others, who have come on to the platforms, and shown a great variety of testimonials, showing that he was generous, kind, hospitable, very brave, and very gentle, and that no man who was sick or in trouble of any sort ever appealed to him in vain to render him all the comfort in his power; and I can assure you that I have heard such tales of his generosity, bravery, and self-sacrifice in Australia as would draw tears, if I could do him justice, from your eyes, the more so as he himself never says one word in his own praise or justification. And there is another point on which great stress is laid, namely, the hardship of depriving people of property, after being left so long by him, in the belief that he was dead; and as to this, I can tell you that his brother, ALFRED TICHBORNE, never had such belief, but on the contrary, repeatedly stated that he knew he was alive, and it was an excuse that he made for spending so freely that ROGER might return any day; and his mother wrote to that effect to LORD ARUNDELL's family, before his daughter was married to this son ALFRED; and in this Trial between him and his relatives, assuming him to be the man, and also, as beyond all doubt you may, that they knew it from the first, which of the two is most entitled to your sympathy—the man who comes by the passionate entreaty of his mother, to be a comfort to her in her age, and, his brother being dead, to resume his position, with every desire to do justice to any whom his absence may have injured or disappointed. Look at that picture on the one side, and on the other a family conclave resolved to defy the laws of England, and, under the name of the infant child of his brother, to maintain the wrongful possession of these great estates. Assuming him, I say, to be TICHBORNE, it is not possible to doubt that his family have known it, or have wilfully and deliberately refused to take the ordinary means of finding out the fact, from his first appearance in England to this hour; and the laws of England will not be worthy of our confidence if they do not stamp such conduct with the stigma of a conspiracy, justly demanding signal exposure and punishment. This challenge of mine is one that I published in the Hampshire newspapers in 1870—within a few weeks of my looking into the merits of the Case, and being threatened with legal penalties by the solicitors for subscribing £25 for his relief, I distinctly charged them with knowing he was TICHBORNE unless they did at once prosecute him as an impostor. And if there be still some mystery hanging over this extraordinary Case, in which it would appear that a family conclave have, under the plea of protecting the estate of an infant child from the assault of an Australian butcher, spent probably £200,000 without having yet convicted this impostor, and are now pensioners on the public purse for another £100,000 with as little prospect of success, I believe that an answer can be given to that question also, and it is this that the High Catholic party have set their eyes on this inheritance, and decided that it will be for the interests of the Catholic Church that it should remain in the hands of this infant than be intrusted to those of a man who, though a Catholic, as all his forefathers were, is like many of them in times past disposed not to say I am a Catholic, if you please, but I am, first and before all, an Englishman. Will LORD ARUNDELL say for himself—for his daughter and he infant son—I am an Englishman first; or will he not say with LORD DENBIGH, I am a Catholic first?—and is not this difference sufficient to account for all the efforts that have been made to deprive this man of his name and inheritance—to deprave and blacken to the uttermost his personal character; and is it not consistent with the conduct of Mr. GLADSTONE in every act of his official life to render freely the aid of the Government to that which, on this theory, is neither more nor less than a gigantic Jesuit conspiracy? If anyone called this folly and fanaticism, or any of the other ill names to which I have grown familiar, let him suggest some better explanation, and tell us why, amongst the gentry, the Marquis of BUTE and others of his way of thinking are the most prominent opponents of the Claimant. How far this feature of the Case may confirm and explain my charge against the Government, that they are lending the purse and the power of the State to crush this man, I leave for the present to others—but am prepared at any fit time to justify by such evidence as I believe will, in the end, be accepted by the country that such is the fact. (Great cheering.)

At this time a Leicester gentleman, of great literary abilities, published the following excellent letter:—

WHO IS THE CLAIMANT, *IF NOT* SIR ROGER C. TICHBORNE?

MR. EDITOR,—I believe this question has been truly answered by scores of honest witnesses. But as I am not a member of the inner circle of the Claimant's friends, but have my stand amongst the thousands of his sympathizers, I raise the question, that I may in a few words express the general surprise that those who deny that the Claimant is Sir ROGER C. TICHBORNE, *have not before now found out who he really is*. If my recognition of a man be challenged by another, I rejoin, "If he is not so-and-so, why, you tell me who he is!" That is the common-sense way of settling such a dispute. If the man is found to be somebody else, why, then he cannot be the man I took him for. The Attorney-General and Aristocratic sympathizers say the Claimant *is not* Sir ROGER. The English people very sensibly rejoin—"Who, then, is he?"

The great efforts and signal failures which go to make the history of the Defendant's proceedings, in striving to answer this question, have contributed, I believe, more than anything else, to enlist public opinion on the side of the Claimant, and to lull the unreasonable hostility of the newspaper press. It is thought to be more than probable that at the ensuing Trial the prosecution will fail to produce such an answer to the query, as months ago they believed they should be able to produce. Permit me to glance at the history of the attempt to get a favourable answer to my question. It was asked nearly *four years* before the late Trial. For months it echoed round the world, wherever on the face of the earth the Claimant had been, or was supposed to have been. *Lawyers, spies*, and *informers*, with golden arguments, flitted about, to catch the faintest response, until at length they swarmed at Westminster, and laid the information they had collected at the Attorney-General's feet. Then came on the great Trial, TICHBORNE v. LUSHINGTON. This four years' mystery will now surely be cleared up, and the impostor unmasked. When lo! the great leader of the English bar deemed it prudent to shirk the question, and assured the jury, "*That it was not necessary for his purpose to show who the Claimant was!*" What is the inference? Why, as proving the Claimant to be an ORTON, or some other man, would have been the shortest and most effectual way of serving his clients, that he did not do so, is conclusive evidence that he could not, and in fact was an admission that four years' search in Australia, with America and Wapping, to discover the Claimant to be somebody other than Sir ROGER TICHBORNE, had signally failed.

Who is the Claimant? resounded through the ancient halls of English Justice for 103 days, and the acutest intellects were all the time prying into evidence to find the solution. The unshaken evidence of 86 *witnesses* testified that he was none other than the man he said he was, viz.—Sir R. C. TICHBORNE. Whilst disputing this testimony with all the skill and art of his profession, the Attorney-General conducted the Trial to an abrupt conclusion, left the great question unanswered, and threw the Claimant into prison, *that it might never have an answer*.

Sir, throughout this wonderful inquiry, to my mind no proceeding showed more palpably the weakness of the Attorney-General's case than this, and disclosed the little faith he had in it at the time he was making such vigorous protestations, and staking his reputation; for if he believed the Claimant to be some other person, then the shortest way to finish the Case in his client's favour was to get at who he was. What more could he wish, than that the Claimant should be free to roam up and down the country, visit all the large centres of population, be seen by hundreds of thousands of English men and women? For the chances were that if he was not the man 86 witnesses swore he was, some old father might recognize him to be a scapegrace son who years ago left his home; or a neighbour might possibly point him out as one of old JONES's family, who emigrated. For as it was settled that the Claimant was an Englishman, it surely was as well worth trying to find out if any of his family were living in the densely-inhabited districts of the country, as it was to send out agents to Chili and Australia; and no better means of doing so could his enemies have devised, *than letting the Claimant go himself to see*.

The Attorney-General, however, preferred to *lock him up out of sight*—a proceeding altogether inconsistent with the hypothesis which he set up that the Claimant was not Sir ROGER TICHBORNE.

If, however, the prosecution believed him to be the *real* Sir ROGER, why, then, *lock him up* in Newgate, and keep him there, if possible, that he may have neither friends nor money to aid him?

On the other hand, I call attention to the course the Claimant pursued when his true friends obtained his liberation—a course which, if he were not Sir ROGER, would have been the most likely to show who he was—play into the hands of his foes, and seal his fate.

No sooner free, than he shows himself in every large town in the kingdom. His brave champion, Mr. ONSLOW, challenges his opponents to say who the Claimant is, if not Sir ROGER. Before hundreds and thousands the challenge has been thrown down; and *none but new witnesses to his identity have come forth.* And now the campaign is well nigh over, the question is unanswered; and therefore will not die. It is now asked, not by the interested few, but by the great body of the people, and they demand an answer.

By what right? I reply, "By a better right than the Government has to spend the nation's money in crushing a man who claims his birthright."

To cover the rash vow of a colleague in office, the Cabinet has consented to prostitute the public money. But to vindicate the proverbial reputation which Englishmen have for right and fair-play, the people will know *who the Claimant is, if not* Sir ROGER.

Upon the approaching Trial, in no figurative sense, the eyes of the nation will rest. The Upper Ten, and those who servilely follow in their train, have plainly shown their bias, and the eye-glass fraternity would transport the "*vulgar feller.*" But the strong sense of the nation, which has been thoroughly aroused, will, at his Trial, have no *forensic bamboozling, windy harangues,* or *getting weary,* in the discharge of a solemn public duty; but Judge, jury, and Counsel will be expected to address themselves to the business of the Trial with a manifest *earnest, impartial,* and *honest* endeavour to supply a true answer to the question, *If the Claimant is not* Sir R. C. TICHBORNE, *then who is he?*—Yours truly, G. R. SEARSON.

Leicester, October 26, 1872.

At this time rumours were afloat that Sir J. COLERIDGE was likely to succeed Lord PENZANCE. These rumours called forth the following letter:—

LORD PENZANCE'S SUCCESSOR.

TO THE EDITOR OF THE "MORNING ADVERTISER."

SIR,—I notice a report in the *Observer* and other papers of this date, that the Attorney-General is about to succeed Lord PENZANCE in the Probate Court. If this report is true, another great injustice will have been done me, inasmuch as Lord Chief Justice BOVILL has ordered me to pay £46,000 before I can proceed again with my Trial in the Court of Common Pleas; and not having the slightest chance of being able to pay so large a sum of money, the Probate Court is the only one left me in which I can proceed—namely, to prove the probate to my mother's estate, and thereby proving my identity as her son, and then asking the Court of Probate to return to me my will, and revoke the same, which was proved by Messrs. SLAUGHTER and GOSFORD in 1853. These two gentlemen received £500 each, which I had bequeathed to them in my will, and although one of them is still alive, he was not produced by the Defendants at my late Trial.

Upon this will the whole of the Doughty and Tichborne Estates are now held.

Should the Attorney-General be made Judge of the Court of Probate, I think, sir, you will agree with me, after his violent and unjustifiable language about me during my late Trial—not one word of which he ever proved—that I should stand no chance of receiving justice at that Court with him as Judge. I found it hard enough at my late Trial to fight against rich relatives and a partisan like the Attorney-General with the Government at his back; for he stated when I elected to be non-suited, that he had received instructions from his Government to prosecute me. Therefore he must have received those instructions from the Government before it was known what determination the jury would arrive at. I leave you, sir, and the public, to judge what chance I shall have with the Attorney-General as Judge in this, the only Court left open to me.—I am, Sir, yours, &c.,

R. C. D. TICHBORNE.

Harley Lodge, November 3, 1872.

SIR ROGER TICHBORNE AT SOUTHAMPTON.

At the special request of his many and heartily-sympathizing friends at Southampton, Sir ROGER paid them a visit on his way from Jersey, where he had been staying a few days.

He arrived at Southampton on Wednesday evening. His reception was characterized by the same enthusiasm which marked his visit in June last.

Two meetings were held at the Victoria Rooms to do him honour and to express sympathy with his cause. The first took place in the afternoon; and the other in the evening.

Sir ROGER was attended on the occasion by Mr. GUILDFORD ONSLOW, M.P., G. B. SKIPWORTH, Esq., and several other gentlemen of distinction, as well as by the members of the Committee and other gentlemen of influence in the town.

At the meeting in the afternoon, Mr. C. F. SAUNDERS was voted to the chair, at the proposition of Mr. Councillor PURKIS.

After some preliminary remarks, the chairman called upon Mr. Councillor PURKIS to address the meeting.

Mr. Councillor PURKIS proposed the following resolution:—"That this meeting views the course determined upon by the law officers of Her Majesty's Government as to the criminal charges to be arraigned against the Claimant of the Tichborne Estates, as contrary to the usual legal procedure, and most cruel and unjust, to debar him of the privilege of being tried as a common prisoner at the Criminal Court, before a common Judge and jury, which method we assert he has a right, as a British subject, to claim, and will best harmonize with the liberties of our country, the spirit of the age, and the progress of society. Against any other course we lift a warning and a protesting voice, and, heard or unheeded, successful or foiled, acquit ourselves of the debt and duty we owe to our free institutions and our British freedom of action as to main bulwarks of our country's liberty, and, therefore, of our country's all." This was seconded by Mr. SHETTLE, and carried unanimously.

Sir ROGER next addressed the meeting. He urged that he ought to be tried for forgery, and that the Attorney-General ought to prosecute him, for as he had not proved one iota of the slander he had uttered against him, one and all the country ought to call upon him to prosecute him, and to prove what he had said was true, and not be allowed to sneak out of the Case in the way he had. Then, again, on the last day of the Trial, the Judge appeared in Court with the documents *ready* signed for his committal to Newgate. How was that? His Lordship could not have known then that he was about to be nonsuited; and why, then, should he have shown such partisanship? The Trial has been removed from the Old Bailey to the Queen's Bench, but he contended that was not fair, because he lost considerably by not having a common jury, for there were thousands of persons knocking about England who were very glad to act on special juries, and the Attorney-General would have more influence over them than he would over a common jury. Sir ROGER then went on to refer to other features of his Case, saying that the Attorney-General told tens of thousands of lies about him in that long-winded speech of his, and added that he saw from the first he had not the slightest chance of winning his Case before *that Judge, whose two brothers were* at that very time going round the country *making a bet of £900 against his winning his Case.*

A Voice: They're corn merchants.

The Claimant: How could he expect, then, to have a fair trial, when the Judge's relatives were acting in that way, and when, too, the same Judge at the Lord Mayor's dinner got up and said that at that time he was trying one of the greatest *impostors* who ever came to this country? Sir ROGER proceeded in a like strain for several minutes, and next said that the meeting would remember the Hampshire papers took a great deal of trouble to state that he had had agents down here to incite the people to cause a riot. (A laugh.) This was only another of the falsehoods which were generally read in the Hampshire papers. (More laughter.) He had no agents here: and, what was more, he did not know that Colonel LUSHINGTON had sold his lease until he saw the paragraph. He supposed they looked upon everything as Gospel which they read in the papers of this town. The hon. baronet resumed his seat amidst loud applause.

Mr. GUILDFORD ONSLOW, M.P., who was most heartily cheered, next spoke, and said that he was very glad to pay a second visit to Southampton, when he remembered the very enthusiastic reception which was given to Sir ROGER TICHBORNE earlier in the year. He himself attended at some inconvenience; indeed, he might say that he had risen from a bed of sickness to come there, risking his life in so doing, but he was willing to risk even that for Sir ROGER TICHBORNE. Dealing with "the Case," he referred to the great meetings which had been held in the provinces, and said that the enthusiasm which had been displayed showed that the country at last believed that the gentleman who had first spoken was an Englishman, and should be treated as such. He was the only man who had been sent to prison without being convicted.

Mr. ONSLOW then proceeded to refer to some leading features of the evidence, and said they were acting the part of gentlemen, of Christians, and of men of honour in taking the part they had. They were compelled to appeal to the public of England, for even the press of this country was against them. Only last Wednesday he addressed his constituents at Guildford, and the speeches which he delivered might at least have then appeared in the London papers, but they were studiously kept out, and even the fact that Mr. ANTHONY BIDDULPH, J.P., of Burton Park, Sussex, had come forward last week and sworn that the Claimant was Sir ROGER TICHBORNE, his cousin, and was prepared to swear it still, had not even been reported.

Sergeant-Major MARKS, with whom Sir ROGER TICHBORNE served in the Carabiniers, next addressed the meeting, recapitulating the evidence he gave, and taking up what he termed the disgraceful remark of the Attorney-General that a soldier was to be bought for a pot of beer, said that all the pots of beer in Europe would not buy him. He was offered a number of pots of beer, and something else, too, by a gentleman—he would not call him that, though, but a miscreant—who said that if he would be guided by him he might be a gentleman for the rest of his days, and that he would be a fool if he did not look after himself. He told him he had come to the wrong man—(bravo)—and that the sooner he got out of his company the better, and that he would not perjure himself for all the money in England. He then slunk off out of the room. (Cheers.) He had lost over this Case. He had been discharged from his situation for doing what he had done; but if he was on his dying bed, and had but one gasp left, he would still swear that that gentleman (pointing to the Claimant) was his old captain, Sir ROGER TICHBORNE.

The Claimant then proposed a vote of thanks to the Chairman, which was carried, and after a brief reply from Mr. SAUNDERS the meeting closed.

MEETING IN THE EVENING.

In the evening there was a larger attendance, the room being crowded. The Claimant was loudly cheered on entering, and was accompanied by the same gentlemen who were with him in the afternoon, as well as Alderman TUCKER and Councillor S. S. PEARCE, the latter of whom, upon the proposition of the Alderman, seconded by Councillor PURKIS, was voted to the chair, and having briefly opened the meeting,

Mr. GUILDFORD ONSLOW was the first speaker, and took much the same line of argument as he did in the afternoon. Sir ROGER TICHBORNE had been to Jersey, and might, had he so chosen, have sent his bail to the winds, but here he was, and they had no fear that when he went away from the country he would not come again. Apart from the question whether he was Sir ROGER TICHBORNE or not, he (Mr. ONSLOW) had taken the part he had from a desire to see justice done to one who he believed had not had a fair Trial, and that this feeling was largely shared in was shown by the popular sympathy which had been evinced towards him throughout the length and breadth of the land, and surely these numerous brains were better able to judge of the Case than the upper ten thousand. (Cheers.) Commenting upon the removal of the Case from the Old Bailey to the Queen's Bench, he said that finding what a fearful thing they had done in having had him committed to Newgate for forgery, the opponents of Sir ROGER TICHBORNE said:—"We won't allow this man to slip through our clutches, but will drop the forgery, and have him removed into the Queen's Bench to be tried by a special jury," and more than that, continued Mr. ONSLOW, to be tried by a Judge who, more than any other man in England, was likely to convict him. What Judge was that? Why, none other than Lord Chief Justice COCKBURN, who once represented that borough. A certain noble lord who now held an appointment in India had told him that at the beginning of the late Trial that same Lord Chief Justice told him that Sir ROGER TICHBORNE was an impostor. He said so before the Case came into Court; and during the Trial he sat on the Bench on several occasions, and papers were handed from him to Mr. HAWKINS, the Counsel to the Plaintiff, and the Defendant and his friends thought such conduct was a great scandal. He characterized the conduct of the Attorney-General as being unworthy of a lawyer, a barrister, or a gentleman, and the Trial from first to last had been one great gigantic fraud. He did not blame the jury who tried it, he indeed rather pitied them, but he hoped that now he would obtain Counsel, and that a fair trial would be afforded him. It they could not get a Serjeant BALLANTINE, they should, if it was allowed, have a Serjeant ONSLOW; for although he did not pretend to be a lawyer, he was ready to put a wig and gown on, and to go into Court and defend him. (Hear, and cheers.) The jury were tired of the Case, and towards the end forgot all the first of it; they had only the remembrance in their minds of what the four or five witnesses who were called for the Plaintiff had said; and they went, he supposed, upon the principle that a lord and lady could not tell a lie. So far from the tattooing being evidence against him, they would find that that really would win his Case, because they would be able to prove that Sir ROGER TICHBORNE never was tattooed. Once get rid of that part of the Case, and his cause was won; and the very witnesses who had sworn he was tattooed should win that cause for him. (Cheers.)

Councillor PURKIS then submitted the resolution which was proposed in the afternoon, and which Alderman TUCKER seconded, saying he had watched the Case all the way through, and he certainly never knew a Case which was conducted with less fairness in his life. He, however, was rather sorry to hear his honourable friend, Mr. GUILDFORD ONSLOW doubt the fair-play and sincerity of Sir ALEXANDER COCKBURN—(hear, hear,)—because that gentleman was a plant of his watering. (Laughter.) Sir ALEXANDER never came to Southampton without asking, "Where's TUCKER"—(cheers)—and once when he was engaged upon a very long trial his father came down to canvass for him, and he, too, said, "Where's TUCKER? I shan't go out without him." (Laughter and cheers.) Sir ALEXANDER COCKBURN had a character to lose—(hear)—and no doubt he would bear that in mind; and although he would, perhaps, sum up and give the sentence to the jury, he would remember that the outside world would look at the evidence as well as Sir ALEXANDER COCKBURN. (Hear.) His lordship stood in need of great caution; and no doubt if he heard him (Alderman TUCKER) speak, he would exercise it. (Loud laughter.)

The motion having been carried unanimously, a man came from the body of the hall, and mounted the platform. Having given the name of WILSON, he said he knew nothing of Sir ROGER TICHBORNE, but his wife could say he wasn't ARTHUR ORTON.

Sir ROGER TICHBORNE spoke next, and during the first quarter of an hour occupied himself with stating that his identity was already proved.

Sir ROGER next referred to the tattoo evidence, and then called the attention of the audience to the fact that in addressing the jury, the Attorney-General burst out crying, and of course tears had their effect upon the jury, who threw up the Case because they had not the moral courage to do their duty. If, however, they had referred to the *Times* newspaper of about eighteen months ago, they would have seen that the Attorney-General was engaged in the Wicklow case, and that he said then, as he said now, that he was speaking for a child who could not speak for himself, and that he burst into tears on that occasion also. (Hear, hear.) In conclusion he said he had much to thank the people of Southampton for. Southampton was his county town, and the Committee here which had been formed to assist him had done wonders.

Mr. G. B. SKIPWORTH, of Moortown House, Caistor, Lincolnshire, next addressed the meeting, and said that long before he saw Sir ROGER TICHBORNE, he was convinced that he was the person he represented himself to be. Sir ROGER would have been in possession of his estates long ago if it had not been for the great power on the other side, but that power, great as it was, would be cut down by truth and justice. He contended that it was nothing but a foul conspiracy which kept him out of his estates, and they had never endeavoured to prove it was anything else. In the course of his able speech he said that Serjeant BALLANTINE dined with the jury after the case was over, and sooner should he have been undefended than he taken in by Counsel as he had been. He added that although many did not want to believe the Claimant was Sir ROGER TICHBORNE, they would have to believe it yet. (Loud cheering.)

Sergeant-Major MARKS entered into a justification of the course he had pursued in the Case, and was followed by Mr. BAILEY, of Ropley. Both of these gentlemen were very warmly applauded.

Sir ROGER then proposed a vote of thanks to the Chairman, which being seconded by Alderman TUCKER, was carried by acclamation. The Chairman thanked the company, and the meeting closed with "three cheers for Sir ROGER," and "one for Mr. GUILDFORD ONSLOW."

PRESTON.

The Claimant was present at a Great Meeting at Preston, where the following questions were asked through the Chairman:—

1. Will you give the name of the colonel of the regiment you first joined? ("Bosh," and applause.)

The Claimant: With great pleasure. Colonel JACKSON, and he was succeeded by Colonel JONES. (Hear, hear.)

2. Was the colonel referred to tall or short?

The Claimant: As we used to call him "Big JIM," I will leave you to say. (Laughter.)

3. Did anyone succeed him as colonel, and if so, who?

The Claimant: I have already answered that; but I should have said that it was Colonel HAY who succeeded Colonel JACKSON, and Colonel JONES succeeded Colonel HAY at Keogh. ("Oh, oh.")

4. What place was your regiment stationed at prior to being sent to Dublin?

The Claimant: I can't tell, as I joined the regiment at Dublin

5. Had the removal of your regiment to Dublin anything to do with your horses, and if so, what?

The Claimant explained that it was some time after the removal to Dublin that some of the horses were picked out and sold on STEPHEN'S Green, and others were transported to other regiments; and, in fact, the Carabineers were changed from heavy dragoons to light dragoons, but they refused to give up their helmets, and on that account they were the only regiment of light dragoons that wore helmets at the present day. They sailed for Dublin on their way to India, but on their way orders were countermanded while they were on the English coast, and they marched to Canterbury —12 miles—which he was not likely to forget. (Laughter.)

6. Why do you refuse to give up the name of the Stonyhurst priest who wrote the letter you read?

The Claimant said he was one of his witnesses, and they might judge from that, but he thought he might have some objection to reading his name. He would show it to the Chairman, which would guarantee its genuineness.

7. Why should you have a worse memory than all the other sane people in the world? (Great laughter, and cries of "Bosh.")

The Claimant: The question is so ridiculous that I will leave the questioner to answer it himself. (Laughter.)

8. Do you know any instance in the world except your own of a person learning a language and afterwards forgetting it?

The Claimant said it was a well-known fact—and many in the room knew it—that a person could learn a language and forget it. The thing was common. Dr. LIVINGSTONE forgot his mother tongue. Look at MORELL among the aborigines. He forgot English; and there was also the case of JOHN BUCKLEY. Then there was his (the Claimant's) excitement after the wreck of the "Bella"—as it was nothing else but excitement for the first ten years—but during that 10 years he learnt four aboriginal dialects, and yet never uttered a word of French. (Hear, hear.)

9. In your regiment you seem to have been associated with one person more than with any other. Can you give us the name of that particular officer?

The Claimant said it was hard to understand what was meant. Gen. JONES, then Capt. JONES, was one of his captains; but his most intimate friend in the Carabineers, and the man who took the most intimate interest in him, was Capt. MORTON in G troop, and after gaining his lieutenancy Capt. MORTON got him attached to that troop, and went to Clonmel, and remained in that troop until he retired.

10. Have you been in communication this afternoon with any one connected with your regiment, and if so, did he recognize you?

The Claimant said he had had a conversation with a person who was in his troop, this afternoon, for half an hour, at his hotel. He (the Claimant) joined the F troop, and was afterwards attached to B troop, which was detached from G troop. He would ask that man what his impression was?

LAWRENCE RICHMOND, formerly a private, said he was the man alluded to, and that he honestly and fairly believed he was the Mr. TICHBORNE he knew at Portobello Barracks. (Applause.)

A working man, in the audience, stood up to ask a question, but he was informed he must come to the platform. Amid a noisy demonstration, he asked: I wish to ask "Sir ROGER TICHBORNE" how he accounts for so long an absence without corresponding with his family? (Loud yells, and cries of "He's drunk," &c.)

The Claimant: I have very great pleasure in answering the question. I believe I led a life there that no other person ever lived. I never knew what home was—I never knew what a true home was except for a few days when I stopped with my uncle at Tichborne. I was glad to get out of the clutches of my friends, who were continually quarrelling one with another, and so I spent my life being continually worried with one relative and another. And it was a great relief to get into a country where nobody knew me, that I was determined not to make myself known to anybody on earth. I would refer you to a letter read by the Attorney-General—because he knew if he did not read it, it would be read for him—stating that I wished my brother to take my place, as I did not think I was fit to fulfil the position of a baronet in England. I said I was going away, that he might take my title, and that it would be years before I came back to England. It was in 1853 that it was written to Lady DOUGHTY. (Applause, and the questioner retired amid many marks of opprobrium.)

The proceedings then terminated.

In our judgment, that the Claimant should have thus visited a place so near Stonyhurst, and the priestly influence, and so evidently unprepared to give him a welcome, is a strong indication of his identity. We call attention to the Questions and Answers, which strike us as interesting.

THE TICHBORNE CLAIMANT IN DUNDEE.

Last night, November 15, the Claimant to the Tichborne Estates addressed a meeting in the Kinnaird Hall. The audience was most respectable, and included a number of ladies. A few minutes after eight o'clock, Sir ROGER appeared on the platform, accompanied by Sergeant-Major MARKS, of the 6th Dragoons (Carabineers), both of whom were received with great applause.

On the motion of Sir R. TICHBORNE, Sergeant-Major MARKS took the chair. The Chairman, in a vigorous speech, appealed to the audience for their sympathy towards the Claimant, stating his firm belief that he was the officer, the Mr. TICHBORNE, under whom he had served in the Carabineers. He gave a summary of the evidence of others connected with the regiment to the same effect, which he held was conclusive. He had refused to be bribed to swear to the contrary, even although he had been told that for doing so he would be made "a gentleman for life." He had said in reply to such offers that he would not be bribed by all the gold in London. And if he were to die the next moment, and had but a gasp of breath left, he would with it swear that the gentleman before him was his old officer and Sir ROGER TICHBORNE. (Applause.)

Sir ROGER TICHBORNE, on rising, was received with great applause. He was dressed in a plain black suit, with no ornament but a gold guard watch-chain. His appearance is well known to all our readers from the photographs to be seen in the windows, and it may simply be added that his manners are prepossessing and gentlemanly. He spoke with ease, coolness, and effect. He was listened to with attention; the interest of the audience never flagged, for he skilfully selected the points of the evidence which told in his favour, and put them in a very clear and telling way, so much so, that he evidently carried his audience with him, and towards the close of his address the applause was general and hearty. Sir ROGER TICHBORNE proceeded to criticize the evidence which had been led in this case, and the speech and general conduct of the Attorney-General on the occasion. If what the Attorney-General said about him were true, he would admit that he (the Claimant) was such a villain that he was not fit to be in any society; but, on the other hand, if what the Attorney-General said was false, God and his conscience told him that he was one of the basest lawyers that ever stood at the British bar. Sir ROGER TICHBORNE went on to criticize severely the proceedings at the Trial, to defend himself against the reflections which he said had been unwarrantably made against his character, and to condemn the procedure to which he had been subjected in connection with his imprisonment in Newgate. As to the forthcoming Trial, he thought they were trying to shirk out of it, but they never would if he could help it. (Applause.)

An opportunity was then given to any one to put questions, but none were put.

A vote of thanks was then passed to the Chairman, on the motion of Sir ROGER TICHBORNE, and the meeting dispersed.

SIR ROGER TICHBORNE AT GREENOCK

The Claimant to the Tichborne titles and estates addressed the public at Greenock last night in the Townhall. Two thousand persons, including influential citizens, were present, and the speaker was greeted with great enthusiasm. Captain CAMPBELL occupied the chair.

Sir ROGER held that his identity had been proved, when they took into consideration that his mother had sworn to him being her son, and this being corroborated by 85 independent witnesses, not one of whom broke down. He challenged the evidence brought against him, and contended that the tattoo mark argument was a conspiracy. He referred to the daguerreotype statement, and held that his condemnation was a foregone conclusion, as evidenced by the fact that his Judge, at a dinner with the Lord Mayor of London, in answer to a toast, said he was trying a case of the greatest imposture that ever came before the British law courts, while his two brothers were going about the country betting against his winning. He deprecated the conduct of the Government in interfering in this civil action between his relatives and himself, but the people of England were determined that justice should be done him. He had requested his Counsel to make application this week, as there was a necessity for the Case being brought on at once, and he said no doubt the nation at large would assist him in insisting on the Case being heard without delay.

Sergeant-Major MARKS addressed the meeting, and amid great applause solemnly declared that the gentleman now before them was his old officer, Sir ROGER TICHBORNE.

Votes of thanks closed the proceedings, which were throughout of the most orderly and enthusiastic character.

On leaving the hall Sir ROGER received an ovation.

THE CLAIMANT IN AUSTRALIA.

The following is from the *Mount Perry Mail*—an Australian paper—of April 25, 1872:—

"In the face of the extinguishing force of the Attorney-General's speech in the TICHBORNE Case, the following must excite some wonder:—Mr. DAN MURRAY, the tailor in this town, used, with his father, to lead a travelling company of theatricals over the colonies. He tells us that before the long-lost baronet was talked of they had a musician in their troupe called PADDY BYRNES, who, when they were in Wagga-Wagga, recognized TOM CASTRO as an officer in the regiment to which PADDY had been field-bugler and clarionet player in the band. PADDY had his old knapsack with him, on which was painted '6th Carabineers.' CASTRO also recognized PADDY, and the two hob-nobbed together for a day or two. The old bugler often afterwards reverted to the circumstance, remarking that he could not have believed that an officer such as CASTRO had been could have fallen so low as he had."

AFFIDAVIT OF MR. HERRIOTT.

I, WILLIAM HERRIOTT, late of the township of Deniliquin, in the colony of New South Wales, Australia, proprietor of the Sportsman's Arms Hotel, now residing at Falkirk, in the county of Stirling, in the kingdom of Scotland, make oath and say as follows:—

1. I am 37 years of age. I went to Australia in July, 1852, and in or about the year 1857 I settled at Deniliquin, where I continued until the month of December, 1867. In or about the year 1861 I became acquainted with TOMAS CASTRO, who about that time came to reside at Deniliquin. He was then in the employ of Mr. JOHN BURROWS, breaking in horses and acting as general manager. Previous to this he was in partnership with FREDERICK BURROWS, brother to the said JOHN BURROWS in Gippsland. The said FREDERICK BURROWS told me of the circumstance of his being in partnership, and was known to him only by the name of TOM CASTRO. During the time he resided in Deniliquin, extending over a twelvemonth, I knew him intimately. I used to see and converse with him three or four times daily, and he was frequently in my house and in my company. He was at that time about 11 stone in weight, and extremely active in his habits, and a first-class rider. He used to dress with some care, and was much given to kangaroo hunting and very fond of horses, and generally had some for sale on his own account.

2. In 1866 I heard that the said TOM CASTRO had gone to England, and was in reality Sir R. C. D. TICHBORNE, and had as such claimed the family estates.

3. In January, 1868, I left Australia for England; and, whilst staying on a visit with my father, I wrote to Sir R. C. T. to come and see me as an old acquaintance. He replied by saying that he was so engaged with his Case he could not come to me, but invited me to come to Alresford to see him. Accordingly, on the 2nd of July I went to Alresford, when I saw him. I was greatly surprised at the enormous increase in size of his person, so much so that I did not recognize him for full ten minutes. I knew his voice when he spoke, but it was some time before I could recall his features, and form them to my mind as I knew him in Deniliquin. I am quite sure and certain that he is the same man whom I knew in Deniliquin as TOMAS CASTRO. I particularly noticed the same twitching of his eyes; but his nose is considerably altered, and quite different in shape to what it was when I knew him, owing to an accident, the marks of which are plainly visible.

About the month of November, 1867, a Mr. JOHN MACKENZIE called upon me, and was anxious to learn from me what I knew of TOMAS CASTRO during his stay at Deniliquin. I asked the said Mr. MACKENZIE whether he was gathering information in favour of or against the Plaintiff; he, in reply, told me he was sent out by the High Court of Chancery in England to find out what information he could both for and against the said TOM CASTRO. He showed me several photos, and I at once picked out from amongst them one which I recognized immediately as the said TOMAS CASTRO. MACKENZIE *subsequently gave me his address in England.*

We have republished these accounts of the various Meetings, at, we fear, too great a length, but we think them important, as signs of the times, not only for the present but for the future, when perhaps it may be impossible to preserve any record of them. We conclude our account of this remarkable tour, by simply stating that we ourselves have not found in any of the great centres thus visited and addressed by the Claimant, a single person whose faith was shaken by the result of the Trial at Bar.

The following appeared at this time:—

ON THE DEATH OF LADY TICHBORNE.

Hushed is the voice whose greetings fond
  Welcomed the long-lost Son;
Closed are the eyes that would have beamed
  To know his victory won;
His victory! though a host may fight
Against him—God defends the right!

The Mother's voice is hushed in death,
  And yet her death (who knows?)
May help him, in God's Providence,
  To triumph o'er his foes:
Propelling on the Trial fair,
Where Justice shall his rights declare.

No British Jury shall be found
  To do such grievous wrong,
As put a veto on the rights
  That lineally belong
To him, whose claim the Mother's heart
Accepted without legal art.

What Mother's Son could e'er believe
  A Mother's eyes could fail
To recognize her first-born son?
  What foes in triple mail
Successfully may hope to fight
Against a sacred filial right?

If friends might fail (though few have failed)
  To recognize the face
Long lost to sight—familiar ways,
  Gestures and tricks to trace—
When once the Mother claimed her Son,
His victory virtually was won! H. H.

At one of these meetings Mr. ONSLOW produced an immense effect by reading and commenting on the following paper, which had been drawn up for Counsel by Messrs. BAXTER, ROSE, and NORTON, from information in a great measure imparted to them by the Claimant.

DATES AND OCCURRENCES RELATING TO SIR ROGER CHARLES DOUGHTY TICHBORNE.

DATE.		PARTICULARS AND AUTHORITIES.
1827.	August 1.	Marriage of his Father and Mother at St. George's, Hanover-square.
1829.	January 5.	Born at Paris.
1829.	January 6.	Registered and Baptized.
1845.	June 10.	Present at the funeral of his uncle Sir HENRY JOSEPH TICHBORNE, at Tichborne, and thence went to Upton.
1845.	July 1.	Arrived at Stonyhurst College.
1846.	April 1.	Rev. W. H. WALMESLEY, Rector of Stonyhurst, writes to Plaintiff's Mother, an answer to her letter complaining of her son not writing home, and desiring him to inculcate in him the principles of filial duty.
1848.		Visits Burton Constable for four or six weeks, spending the vacation there.
1848.		Left Stonyhurst at Midsummer or Michaelmas.
1848.	Sunday, Nov. 26.	Left Knoyle for Wardour Castle, to stay there the week.—*Letter of his maternal Grandfather,* HENRY SEYMOUR, *dated November 29, 1848.*
1849.	June 27.	At Tichborne.—*Letter to* Mr. HOPKINS.
1849.	July 2.	Passed his examination at Sandhurst. —*Certificates of examination and height.*
1849.	July 13.	Gazetted as a Cornet in the Carabineers. —*See Gazette and Army List.*
1849.	August 18, 19, and 21.	In London at Mr. SEYMOUR'S.—*Letter to Mr.* HOPKINS; *Letter of* H. SEYMOUR; *Letter to Mr.* HOPKINS.
1849.	August 29.	Signed his name in Messrs. Cox's books. (Army Agents, London.)—*Messrs.* Cox's *books.*
1849.	October.	At Tichborne.
1849.	October 25.	Reached Ireland.—*Letter to his Mother, dated Oct. 30, 1849.*
1849.	October 26.	At Kingstown.—*Letter to Mr.* HOPKINS.
1849.	October 27.	Joined his regiment at Portobello Barracks, Dublin.—*Letter to Mr.* HOPKINS, *and letter to his Mother.*
1849.	October 28.	Military duties began.—*Letter to* Mr. HOPKINS *and Letter to his Mother.*
1849.	October 29.	His drilling began. — *Letter to* Mr. HOPKINS *and Letter to his Mother.*
1849.	December 25.	At Portobello Barracks.—*Letter to his Mother.*
1849.	December 30 or 31.	Left Dublin for Tichborne, to celebrate his majority there.—*Trumpet Major* LESSWARE'S *Letter Delivery Book.*
1850.	January 5.	Came of age.
1850.	January 6.	At Tichborne.—*Letter to Mr.* HOPKINS.
1850.	January 8.	At Portobello Barracks, Dublin. — *Trumpet Major* LESSWARE'S *Book.*
1850.	February 21.	At Portobello Barracks, Dublin.—*Letter to Mr.* HOPKINS.
1850.	April.	Left Dublin and went to Cahir with the head-quarters of Carabineers.—*Horse Guards Return.*
1850.	April 14.	At Cahir.—*Letter to Mr.* HOPKINS.
1850.	May.	Mr. HOPKINS visits him at Cahir, and procures his signature to the Deeds of Settlement.—*Letter to Mr.* HOPKINS.
1850.	June 7 to 10.	At Cahir.—*Letter to Mr.* HOPKINS.
1850.	November 19.	At Cahir.—*Letter to Mr.* HOPKINS.
1850.	November 22.	Gazetted a Lieutenant. — *Gazette and Army List.*
1851.	Jan. 13 or 14 to Jan. 29 or 30.	Absent from his regiment, and address left, Alresford, Hampshire.—*Trumpet Major* LESSWARE'S *Book.*
1851.	February 1.	Cahir.—*Letter to Mr.* SLAUGHTER.
1851.	March 12.	Cahir.—*Letter to his Mother.*
1851.	March 21.	Cahir. —*Letter to Mr.* SLAUGHTER.
1851.	April 9.	Proceeded with a troop of the regiment from Cahir to Clonmel. — *Horse Guards Return.*
1851.	April 27.	Artillery Barracks, Clonmel.—*Letter to Mr.* HOPKINS.
1851.	July 17.	The troop he was attached to marched to Waterford, but he remained at Clonmel with the troop that arrived from Cahir.—*Horse Guards Return.*
1851.	July 17.	39, Upper Grosvenor-street, London. Had several interviews with Mr. SLAUGHTER in London about this time.—*Letter to Mr.* SLAUGHTER, *and marginal note on copy.*
1851.	October.	Rejoined his former troop at Waterford, (and stayed there till Dec. 15.)—*Horse Guards Return.*
1851.	December 15.	Had leave of absence till February 14, 1852.—*Horse Guards Return.*
1851.	December.	Came to London from Ireland, and saw Mr. SLAUGHTER. — *Correspondence about making will.*
1852.	January 5.	At Tichborne Park, and gives instructions in writing for his will.—*Letter to Mr.* SLAUGHTER.
1852.	January 13.	Had a long interview with Mr. SLAUGHTER in London. — *Mr.* SLAUGHTER'S *Note on Will correspondence.*
1852.	Tuesday Jan. 13.	Wrote to his Father to say he should be in Paris on Thursday or Friday. — *Letter to his Father.*
1852.	Jan. 15 or 16.	Date of his arrival in Paris.
1852.	January 23.	Gave Bill to CALLAGHAN and Co., in Paris.—Cox's *Ledger.*
1852.	January 28.	At Paris, and his Mother cuts off a lock of his hair. — *Endorsement, in his Mother's handwriting, of packet containing the hair.*
1852.	Feb. 3—10.	At Tichborne. — *Dr.* LIPSCOMB'S *Books.*
1852.	February 9.	At Tichborne, and will try to be in London by Wednesday, Feb. 11—*Letter to Mr.* SLAUGHTER.
1852.	February 11.	In London, had a long interview with Mr. SLAUGHTER, and conference with Mr. BURROWS about his Will. — *Memorandum by Mr.* SLAUGHTER.
1852.	February 14.	Returned from leave of absence and rejoined the troop stationed at Clonmel. —*Horse Guards Returns.*
1852.	March 13.	Marched with troop from Clonmel to Dublin, where the whole regiment assembled.—*Horse Guards Returns.*
1852.	March 19.	Marched into Dublin. — *Letter to Mr.* SLAUGHTER *dated 10 April.*

Date.		Particulars and Authorities.
1852.	April 10.	At Portobello Barracks, Dublin.—*Letter to Mr.* Slaughter.
1852.	April 15.	At Portobello Barracks, Dublin.
1852.	April 18, or 19.	The regiment appeared on parade for the first time in their blue clothing as Light Dragoons. — *Letters to Mr.* Slaughter.
1852.	May 23.	At Portobello Barracks, Dublin.—*Letter to Mr.* Slaughter.
1852.	May 30.	At Portobello Barracks, Dublin.—*Letter to Mr.* Slaughter.
1852.	June 1.	The Regiment embarked at Dublin on board the "Duke of Clarence" steamer.—*Horse Guards Return.*
1852.	June 4.	Disembarked at Herne Bay and marched to Canterbury.—*Horse Guards Return.*
1852.	July 27 to August 6.	Goodwood and Brighton races.
1852.	October 27.	At Canterbury.—*Letter to Mr.* Hopkins.
1852.	October 28.	Leave of absence from this day till December 30.—*Horse Guards Return.*
1852.	October 30.	At Upton House, which his Uncle had placed at his disposal, and met Gosford there.—*Letter to Mr.* Hopkins.
1852.	December 30.	Leave of absence expired.—*Horse Guards Return.*
1853.	January 4.	Cavalry Barracks, Canterbury.—*Letter to Mr.* Slaughter.
1853.	January 24.	Had leave of absence till his retirement from the service.—*Horse Guards Return.*
1853.	January 25.	In London and signs his name in Messrs. Glyn and Co.'s Book. — *Messrs.* Glyn's *Signature Book.*
1853.	February 4.	Retired from the Service. Went to Paris from Dover, and stayed there two days. Went to Tichborne for a day.—*Army List Gazette.*
1853.	February 22.	In London. Had letter of credit from Messrs. Glyn for £2,000 payable at Valparaiso, Buenos Ayres, &c.—Glyn's *books.*
1853.	March 2.	Left London (34, St. James's-square) for Southampton to embark for Havre. Slept at Winchester.—Thomas Carter's *Evidence.*
1853.	March 2 or 3.	Left Southampton for Havre. Left Havre in "La Pauline."
1853.	March 12.	Sailed from Falmouth.—*Letter dated Valparaiso.*
1853.	April 10.	Passed the Line.—*Letter dated Valparaiso.*
1853.	June 19.	Arrived at Valparaiso.—*Letter dated Valparaiso.*
1853.	June 20.	Went on shore. There was another passenger on board "La Pauline," who was sick the whole time, more or less. *Letter dated Valparaiso.*
1853.	June 20.	Received letter from Lady Doughty conveying the intelligence of Sir Edward Doughty's death.—*Letter dated Valparaiso.*
1853.	June 20.	Wrote to his Father. — *Letter dated Valparaiso.*
1853.	June 30.	Went to Santiago (95 miles from Valparaiso), stopped and slept half-way.
1853.	July 2.	Arrived at Santiago about 6 p.m.
1853.	July 4.	John Moore, his servant, taken ill in the middle of the night, and the third attack he had had in less than a month. The doctor pronounced him not fit to travel, but must stay at Santiago for some time and then go back to England. He then settled with Moore and left him there. — *Letter dated Valparaiso.*
1853.	July 5.	Left Santiago for Valparaiso to sail in "La Pauline." When he got there found she was not to sail so soon.—*Letter dated Valparaiso.*
1853.	July.	On leaving Santiago he went by way of Melipilla, and when there, sent a letter to inquire of the Captain, the day fixed for the departure of "La Pauline," and received a reply as to her not leaving till the latter part of the month. He stayed in the neighbourhood of Melipilla during the intervening time.—*See Statement, page* 18.
1853.	July 27.	Left Valparaiso in "La Pauline" for Arica. At Valparaiso engaged a Frenchman with 18 years' good character, and took him with him as his valet.—*Letter to his Mother, dated Lima, August* 25, 1853.
1853.	August 11.	Arrived at Arica.—*Letter to his Mother, dated Lima, August* 25, 1853.
1853.	August 20.	Left Arica on board the "Pacific" Steamer for Callao and Lima.—*Letter to his Mother, dated Lima, August* 25, 1853.
1853.	August 23.	Arrived at Lima.—*Letter to his Mother, dated Lima, August* 25, 1853.
1853.	August 25.	Still at Lima. Going to start in a few days for Quito, but only to stay there a few days, and then to go again to Valparaiso, or Santiago, and thence to Buenos Ayres and Montevideo by land.—*Letter to his Mother, dated Lima, August* 25, 1853.
1853.	About middle of Sept.	Makes a longer stay at Lima than he intended. When he had seen every thing at Lima, he went on board a schooner for Guayaquil, a voyage of about seven days—*Letter to his Mother, dated December* 31, 1853. After staying a few days at Guayaquil, he went up the river about 300 miles in a canoe with two blacks, and made several excursions up and down.—*Letter to his Mother, dated December* 31, 1853. Embarked on board the "Pacific" steamer and returned to Lima. He stays a short time at Lima. His servant being ill, was obliged to leave him there.—*Letter to his Mother, dated December* 31, 1853.
1853.	November 25.	Engaged Jules Barraut, as his servant at Lima.—Jules Barraut's *Statement &c., and Letter to his Mother March* 1, 1854.
1853.	December 3.	Left Lima on board the "Bogota," commanded by Captain Strachan. — *Evidence of* Henry Watson, *Chilian Commission, page* 105 *and* 106.
1853.	December 15.	Reached Valparaiso.
1853.	December 31.	At Santiago.—*Letter to his Mother of this date.*
1854.	January 11.	Left Santiago to cross the Cordilleras. *Letter to his Mother, dated Buenos Ayres, March* 1.
1854.	January 19.	Arrived at Mendoza. — *Letter to his Mother, dated Buenos Ayres, March* 1.
1854.	January 27.	Left Mendoza with the Post for Buenos Ayres.—*Letter to his Mother, dated Buenos Ayres, March* 1.
1854.	February 13.	Reached Buenos Ayres.—*Letter to his Mother, dated Buenos Ayres, March* 1.
1854.	March 1.	Still at Buenos Ayres, but going to leave in a few days for Montevideo.—*Letter to his Mother, dated Buenos Ayres, March* 1.
1854.	April 4.	Left Buenos Ayres on board the English boat "La Camilla," at 6 p.m.—*Statement of* Jules Barraut.
1854.	April 5.	Reached Montevideo at 8 a.m.—*Statement of* Jules Barraut.
1854.	April 12.	Arrived at Rio at 2 p.m. and put up at the Hotel de la Bourse.—*Statement of* Jules Barraut.
1854.	April 20.	Left Rio on board the "Bella." The "Bella" had on board 4,350 bags of coffee, and 900 bags of rosewood.—*Statement to Messrs.* Stockmeyer.
1854.	April 23.	The "Bella" wrecked. — *Plaintiff's Affidavit.*
1854.	April 26.	The American ship "Kent" picks up the longboat of the "Bella."—*Shipping News, &c.*
1854.	April 26.	Crew of 2nd Boat rescued with Mr. Tichborne on board. — *Plaintiff's Affidavit.*
1854.	About end of July.	Landed at Melbourne. — *Plaintiff's Affidavit and Bill filed in Chancery.*
1854.	July.	Accompanied Mr. Foster into Gippsland, to the Boisdale Station, and stayed there till about February, 1856.

DATE.	PARTICULARS AND AUTHORITIES.	DATE.	PARTICULARS AND AUTHORITIES.
	"*About nineteen months.*"—*Plaintiff's Affidavit and Bill filed in Chancery.*	1858. about May.	Went to NORMAN MCLEOD'S on Mitchel River, and joined FREDERICK BURROWS. Stayed there until about September, 1858. "*About four months.*"—*Plaintiff's Affidavit and Bill filed in Chancery.*
1856. about Feby.	Went to the Dargo Station, and stayed there till about August, 1857. "*About eighteen months.*"—*Plaintiff's Affidavit and Bill filed in Chancery.*	1858. about Sept.	Went to the Omeo Diggings, and stayed there until about January or February 1859. "*About four months.*"—*Plaintiff's Affidavit and Bill filed in Chancery.*
1857. abt. August.	Went back to Boisdale, and stayed there till about November, 1857. "*About three months.*"—*Plaintiff's Affidavit and Bill filed in Chancery.*	1859. abt. August.	Went to Deniliquin and entered LUCAS' employed for nine months.—*Plaintiff's Affidavit and Bill filed in Chancery,*
1857. about Nov.	Went to Sale on Flodden Creek, and stayed till about May, 1858. "*About six months.*" *Plaintiff's Affidavit and Bill filed in Chancery.*		

OMEO DIGGINGS.

1859. abt. August.	*and Note Statement in Australian Commission.*	1863. about June.	To Tumut till about January, 1864.—*Statement in Chancery Bill* "*about seven months.*" MR. COOKE *swears he knew him at Tumut about* 1863.
1860. June 4.	Entered JOHN BURROWS' employ and continued with him till Dec. 3, 1861. —*Evidence of Mr.* BURROWS, *Australian Commission.*	1863. September 21	Gives Bill to ROBERT COOKE at Tumut. —*See original Bill belonging to* COOKE.
1861. December.	Went to Hay and stayed there until about September, 1862.—(*About nine months*), *Statement in Chancery Bill.*	1864. about Jan.	To Gundagai for about a month.—*Statement in Chancery Bill.*
1862. about Sept.	To Wagga-Wagga, Doree and Narandra till about January, 1863. "*About four months.*"—*Statement in Chancery Bill.*	1864. about Feb.	To Wagga-Wagga, where he remained till June, 1866.—*Statement in Chancery Bill.*
1863. about Jan.	To Nangus till about April, 1863. "*About four months.*"—*Statement in Chancery Bill.*	1865. January 29.	Married at Wagga-Wagga.—*Certificate.*
1863. about April.	To Melbourne and thence to Bendigo till about June, 1863. "*About two months.*"—*Statement in Chancery Bill.*	1865. April.	Writes "R. C. T. Hampshire, England" in Ready Reckoner (Exhibit P. 6) REARDON'S *Evidence, pages* 79 *and* 80, *Australian Commission.*
		1865. May 19.	His Mother, the DOWAGER Lady TICHBORNE, writes to Mr. ARTHUR CUBITT,

DATE.		PARTICULARS AND AUTHORITIES.
1865.	May 19.	for him to insert advertisement.—*See Correspondence with* CUBITT.
1865.	August 4.	Mr. CUBITT inserts advertisement in various Australian Newspapers.—CUBITT's *Correspondence and Advertisements.*
1865.	September.	Sees his Mother's advertisement in the Australian Newspaper, brought to him by a man named SLATE.—*Claimant's Statement.*
1866.	January 17.	Writes to his Mother for the first time from Australia.—*See Letter.*
1866.	January 18.	GIBBES writes his first letter to the DOWAGER Lady TICHBORNE, to which Plaintiff puts his initials.
1866.	January 26.	Writes a letter to Mr. CUBITT from Wagga-Wagga.—*See copy of letter,* CUBITT's *Correspondence.*
1866.	February 22.	His Brother, ALFRED TICHBORNE, died suddenly and unexpectedly at Fencote, in Yorkshire.
1866.	February 25.	His Mother writes to him, having received his letter, and sent it inclosed in a letter to Mr. CUBITT, who received it about April 18.—*See copy of letter, Australian Com., p. 218.*
1866.	March 18.	Birth of his first child, TERESA MARY AGNES TICHBORNE.
1866.	April 2.	Writes letter to Mr. CATOR and gives it to him on condition that he does not open it until at sea.—*See copy.*
1866.	abt. April 18.	CUBITT receives letter from the Dowager Lady TICHBORNE, dated February 25, 1866, with inclosure for her son.—CUBITT's *Correspondence.*
1866.	May 2.	CUBITT sends letter to GIBBES at Wagga-Wagga for delivery.—*Correspondence.*
1866.	May 21.	Writes his second letter to his Mother.
1866.	June 2.	Left Wagga-Wagga en route for Sydney, stopping at Goulburn on his road.—*Statement.*
		Arrived at Sydney.
1866.	abt. June 15.	Sees Mr. CUBITT.—*Sir* ROGER's *letter, dated Sydney, June 23, proves he had seen* CUBITT, *and made arrangements with him, and* CUBITT's *letter of 22nd June, 1866, says he has had several interviews with him.*
1866.	June 23.	Writes third letter to his Mother.
1866.	July.	Returns to Goulburn.
1866.	July 9.	Re-married at Goulburn.—*Certificate.*
1866.	July 9.	Returns to Sydney with his wife and child. Sees GUILFOYLE.
1866.	after July 24.	Sees BOGLE.—*Sir* ROGER's *letter of July 24 says he had not been able to find* BOGLE.
		Leaves Sydney on board the "Rakaia" for Panama.
1866.	September 2.	Vessel calls at Wellington, New Zealand, where he writes to Mr. FREDERICK WELD, Ex-Prime Minister of that Colony.—*See* Mr. WELD's *reply.*
		Arrives at Panama.
		Leaves Panama for Aspinwall, and embarks on board the "Henry Chauncy" for New York.
1866.	before Oct. 9.	Stays at New York a month at the Clarendon Hotel, and sends a telegram to his Mother.—*Statement, affidavit, &c.*
		Leaves in the Steam Ship "Cella" for London.—*Statement, affidavit, &c.*
1866.	December 25.	Arrives at the Victoria Docks and left the Ship between 3 and 4 o'clock and proceeded to Ford's Hotel, Manchester-street, accompanied by wife and child, nurse, BOGLE and his son, and BUTTS.—*Statement, affidavit, &c.*
1866.	December 26.	Went to the Clarendon Hotel, Gravesend, with wife, child, and nurse.—*Statement, affidavit, &c.*
1866.	December 28.	Left Waterloo Terminus by 5 o'clock train for Alresford, and due there at 7.10. Went to the Swan Hotel (seen by WILLIAM BAILEY at the Ropley Station)—*Statement, affidavit, &c.* WILLIAM BAILEY *swears to him: the first person that recognizes him in England.*
1866.	December 29.	Went to Tichborne with RORS (landlord of the Swan Hotel).—RORS *recognizes and swears to him.*
1866.	December 30.	Walked over to Tichborne.—*Statement, affidavit, &c.*
1866.	December 31.	BOGLE arrived at Alresford in the evening by the 7.10 train from London.—*Statement, affidavit, &c.*
1867.	January 1.	BOGLE went to Tichborne Chapel to Mass, and saw and conversed with Mrs. GREENWOOD, FREDERICK BOWKER, and has interview with Sir ROGER.—*Statement, affidavit, &c.* Mr. BOWKER *offers his services to the Claimant. Claimant's statement.* Returned to London by 7.20 p.m. train.
1867.	January 1.	Saw Mr. LEETE at the International Hotel, London Bridge, who gave him Mr. HOLMES' name and address.—*Statement, affidavit, &c.*
1867.	January 3.	Calls upon Mr. HOLMES and introduces himself.—*Mr.* HOLMES' *Declaration, p. 76, book of printed affidavits.*
1867.	January 5.	Calls again upon Mr. HOLMES, and shows letter he had received from his Mother. On his return to Gravesend finds GOSFORD, PLOWDEN, and CULLINGTON at the Hotel, refused to see them, but wrote GOSFORD a note and sent it to him by PEACOCK the waiter. Landlord afterwards demands payment of his bill.—Mr. HOLMES' *Declaration. Refer to* PEACOCK's *statement.*
1867.	January 6.	
1867.	January 7.	Mr. HOLMES receives his letter giving an account of the treatment he had experienced. Mr. HOLMES and Mr. LEETE go down to see him in the evening, and arrange to accompany him to Paris in order that no further obstacles should be thrown in the way of his seeing his Mother.—Mr. HOLMES' *Declaration, p. 77.*
1867.	January 8.	Mr. HOLMES visits Gravesend to bring the Plaintiff and his family to London. Mr. GOSFORD is announced, and has a long interview with him in the presence of Mr. HOLMES, and accompanies them to London. Sleeps at the International Hotel, London Bridge.—Mr. HOLMES' *Declaration, p. 77.*
1867.	January 9.	Goes to Mr. HOLMES' house at Croydon. GOSFORD writes to Mr. HOPKINS.
1867.	January 10.	Starts for Paris accompanied by Messrs. HOLMES and LEETE.—Mr. HOLMES' *Declaration, p. 77.*
1867.	January 11.	Sees his Mother, who identifies him and acknowledges him to be her son in the presence of Sir JOSEPH OLLIFFE and Dr. SHRIMPTON.—Mr. HOLMES' *Declaration, p. 77.*
1867.	January 12.	BOGLE proceeded to Paris in consequence of a telegram received from Mr. HOLMES.—BOGLE's *Affidavit.*
1867.	January 19.	Lady TICHBORNE makes a declaration at the British Embassy that the Plaintiff was her son.—Messrs. HOLMES and LEETE, and Sir JOSEPH OLLIFFE, and Dr. SHRIMPTON also make declarations.—*See Declaration, p. 79.*
1867.	January 21.	Left Paris and arrived at Croydon at 9 o'clock p.m.
1867.	January 23.	Mr. HOLMES' letter appeared in the *Times* Newspaper, stating that the Dowager Lady TICHBORNE had recognized the Plaintiff as her son.
1867.	February 2.	Mr. HOLMES went to Alresford and saw Mr. HOPKINS, the Plaintiff came by the next train, and dined with Mr. HOPKINS.
1867.	February 3.	Mr. HOPKINS sent the Plaintiff an invitation to come and stay at his house as a guest and wrote to Lord ARUNDELL and Mr. HENRY DANBY SEYMOUR, informing them that the Plaintiff was indeed his former client, ROGER CHARLES TICHBORNE. The Plaintiff wrote a note to his cousin Mrs.

DATE.	PARTICULARS AND AUTHORITIES.
	GREENWOOD, afterwards called again upon Mr. HOPKINS and had a walk with him. The Plaintiff and Mr. HOLMES returned to London by train from Alton.
1867. February 8.	Went to Alresford on a visit to Mr. HOPKINS.
1867. February 9.	GOSFORD came to Alresford. Mr. HOPKINS refused to see him. He then went to Winchester, and saw Mr. BOWKER and Mr. BULPETT.
1867. February 11.	GOSFORD left for London by the 9.15 train.
1867. February 13.	Mr. HENRY DANBY SEYMOUR (accompanied by WILLIAM BURDEN, has an interview at Mr. HOPKINS' house. Plaintiff returned to London by the 7.20 train. Farmer NOBLE saw him at the station and identified him.
1867. February 15.	The Dowager Lady TICHBORNE arrived from France, and took up her residence with her son, at Essex Lodge, Croydon.
1867. Feb. 22—23.	Went to Alresford with Mr. HOLMES. Left Alresford by the last train for Croydon.
1867. March 2.	Mr. HOLMES at Alresford, and had an interview with Mr. and Mrs. RADCLIFFE and Mrs. GREENWOOD.
1867. March 8.	Mr. GOSFORD calls on Mr. HOLMES. Mr. RADCLIFFE, Mrs. TOWNLEY, and Mrs. RADCLIFFE called at Essex Lodge and saw Plaintiff.
1867. March 9.	Mr. GOSFORD calls again on Mr. HOLMES, and informed him that Mrs. RADCLIFFE *had recognized the Plaintiff.*
1867. March 12.	Mr. RADCLIFFE, Mrs. TOWNLEY, and two other ladies see Sir ROGER at Mr. HOLMES' house, Croydon.
1867. March 14.	Unpacked his military accoutrements.
1867. March 22.	At Alresford with Mr. HOLMES.
1867. March 23.	At Alresford.
1867. March 29.	The Dowager Lady TICHBORNE went to Winchester to find letters, &c.
1867. March 30.	Found that her boxes had been opened, and all letters and papers abstracted, as well as watches and other articles. On inquiry found that they were *opened by order of* GOSFORD.
1867. April 1.	The Dowager Lady TICHBORNE returned to Croydon.
1867. April 10.	Majors BETTY and BOTT seen by Mr. HOLMES, at Essex Lodge.
1867. April 12.	Mr. BULPETT and GOSFORD dined with Mr. HOLMES at the New City Club.
1867. April 25.	The Dowager Lady TICHBORNE left Essex Lodge for London, on account of her health.
1867. May 18.	His cousin, Mr. BIDDULPH, calls on him at Croydon, and identifies him.
1867. May 20.	His eldest son (ROGER JOSEPH DOUGHTY TICHBORNE) born at Croydon.—*His cousin,* ANTHONY BIDDULPH, *Esq., was godfather.*
1867. June 6.	An interview with GOSFORD at the Grosvenor Hotel, which lasted four hours (from 8 p.m. till 12), Messrs. BULPETT, HINGSTON, and WHITE being present.
1867. June 27.	The two Bills, TICHBORNE v. TICHBORNE and TICHBORNE v. MOSTYN, filed in Chancery.
1867. June 29.	Went to Sandhurst with Mr. HOLMES and thence to Alresford.
1867. July 1—2.	Thirty-three affidavits taken at Alresford.
1867. July 3.	Thirty-seven affidavits filed in support of identity.
1867. July 10—13.	At Alresford.
1867. July 15—16.	At Malvern with Major NORBURY.
1867. July 17.	Eight more affidavits filed.
1867. July 18.	Proceedings against newspapers in the Court of Chancery.
1867. July 30, 31, and Aug. 1.	Cross-examined at the Law Institution upon his affidavit.
1867. August 1.	Mr. GOSFORD examined at Law Institution.
1867. Sept. 18—25.	At Alresford.
1867. Sept. 30 to Oct. 5.	At Alresford.
1867. October 8.	At Alresford.
1867. October 9.	Left Alresford for Romsey.
1867. October 10.	At Bath, and saw ALLEN.
1867. October 12.	At Salisbury, and saw General CUSTANCE and Captain PINCKNEY.
1867. October 12.	At Alresford.
1867. October 11.	Went from Alresford to Poole, and saw GOULD and others, who recognized and swore to his identity.
1867. October 16.	Left Poole for Alresford.
1867. October 17.	Returned to Croydon.
1867. November 9.	At Brighton.
1867. November 10.	At Brighton, and saw Colonel SAWYER, who recognized him.
1867. November 15.	At Romsey, and saw Captain SHERSTON, who also recognized him.
1867. Nov. 26—27.	Romsey again, and saw Captain and Mrs. SHERSTON, who also recognized him.
1867. November 28.	At Bath, and saw TOOWELL.
1867. November 29.	At Alresford.
1867. November 30.	Returned to Croydon.
1868. January 28.	Went to Colchester.
1868. January 29.	At Yarmouth.
1868. January 31.	At Leeds.
1868. Feb. 1—2.	At Bolton.
1868. February 3.	At Preston.
1868. February 4.	At Liverpool.
1868. February 5.	Returned to Croydon.
1868. Feb. 11—12.	VINCENT GOSFORD at Winchester.
1868. March 7.	Left Croydon for Boulogne.
1868. March 11.	Returned to Croydon about midnight.
1868. March 12.	The Dowager Lady TICHBORNE died.
1868. March 14.	Inquest held.
1868. March 19.	The Dowager Lady TICHBORNE buried at Tichborne.
1868. March 31.	Went to Liverpool.
1868. April 4.	Returned to Croydon.
1868. April 9.	Went to Alresford.
1868. April 11.	Returned to Croydon.
1868. April 27.	Left Croydon for Alresford.
1868. April 28.	Resided at Alresford from this date till 12th March, 1869.
1868. June 24.	Went to London in company with Colonel LUSHINGTON, who induced Colonel GEORGE GREENWOOD to travel with them from Guildford.
1868. June 30.	His second son (JAMES FRANCIS TICHBORNE) born at Alresford.—*Sir* TALBOT CONSTABLE, *Bart., was godfather.*
1868. September 9.	Sailed for Rio Janeiro in the "Oneida."
1869. January 27.	Arrives at Falmouth from South America.
1869. January 29.	Reached Alresford.

We insert next the evidence of Sir TALBOT CONSTABLE given at the Trial in the Common Pleas. We call the attention of our readers to the remarkable facts it contains in favour of the Claimant.

SIR FREDERICK AUGUSTUS TALBOT CLIFFORD CONSTABLE, sworn. Examined by Mr. GIFFARD.

Are you a Deputy-Lieutenant of the East Riding of Yorkshire —Yes.

What is your age?—42.

Used you, when you were a boy, to go to Paris frequently with your parents?—Yes.

About what age were you when you first went?—I could not tell exactly; perhaps six or seven.

While you were in Paris used you to be constantly associated with young ROGER TICHBORNE?—Yes.

Do you also remember ROGER TICHBORNE coming on a visit to Burton Constable?—Yes.

I believe that was in the year 1848?—I think it was.

Did he spend his vacation with you then?—Yes.

At that time were you constantly together as companions?—Yes.

Was that the last occasion when you saw him before he left for South America?—Yes.

How long would that be? How long was he there altogether during that time when he was spending his vacation?—I do not remember whether it was three weeks or six weeks.

When did you next see him: I do not mean the day, but the year?—I cannot tell you exactly; three years ago, perhaps, three or four years, somewhere about that.

That is near enough. May 1, 1868, I think, will turn out to be the date. Where did you see him then?—In Hull.

Was that the Royal Station Hotel?—Yes.

And from there did you take him with you to Burton Constable?—Yes.

Was he from that time for three or four or five days in your company?—Yes.

Did you or did you not recognise him as the same person that you had known when you were a boy?—Not personally, not exactly personally.

What conclusion did you ultimately arrive at?—That he was Sir Roger.

Now, will you tell us what were the circumstances which brought you to that conclusion?—He reminded me of cutting down the hedge in the engine field.

Just describe the circumstances of his reminding you, how did it happen, how did he remind you? What did he say of the circumstance by which he reminded you?—He asked me if I would mind walking over to the field where I cut the hedge down.

He said that to you?—Yes.

What did you say?—I said, Not in the least.

What happened upon that?—He walked to the direct spot where he cut the hedge down, and asked what had become of the stump.

Did you then remember the fact that he had cut a hedge down?—Perfectly.

Did he go to the place where he had cut it down?—Yes.

Did you know as a fact what had become of the stumps?—No.

What happened upon that; did you take any means to ascertain what had become of the stumps?—We made inquiries and it could not be proved what had become of them.

Did you remember the fact that there were stumps there?—Perfectly.

Do you remember anything else that passed between you? He asked what had become of a square hedge near the building where we used to go and smoke. He said there was no necessity he thought for removing that, since they had put up iron palisading in the same place.

Was he accurate in his recollection of the circumstances to which it referred?—Perfectly.

Did you remember that yourself in the first instance?—The square hedge.

You did remember it in the first instance?—As soon as he told me, I remembered it.

Before I ask you any more, let me ask you this: generally, did you, in your conversation with him, suggest things to him, or were you careful to see whether he knew without your suggestions?—I never suggested anything.

Do you remember anything being said about his putting some wine on the table?—Yes.

First of all, tell me what he said?—He said during that time, I got up, because the butler did not bring the wine round, and did it for him.

Did you remember the circumstance to which that referred?—Perfectly.

Did he accurately represent the circumstance that had occurred?—Yes.

Do you remember anything being said about a black mare of a Mr. LAMBERT?—Yes.

Just tell us what he said about that?—He said he went over at my request to buy a black mare from Mr. LAMBERT.

What circumstance did he remind you of first, and then I will ask you what the circumstances were?—That he led it home himself after purchasing it.

Was there anything more that he mentioned about the circumstance of the purchase, anything about LAMBERT himself?—He said he believed he had got it at a reduced price, because LAMBERT had taken rather too freely.

Now the circumstances that he mentioned; were they accurately mentioned such as they occurred?—I believe so; I was not present.

I mean were they represented by the real ROGER TICHBORNE, and had they taken place?—Yes.

Do you remember taking him through several of the bedrooms at Burton Constable?—Yes.

Did he exhibit any knowledge of them?—Not the first evening, with the exception of mine.

Did he recognize that the first evening?—He thought he knew something about it very well.

Do you remember anything about a window of a bedroom?—Yes.

What was it he said about that?—He did not say anything on that occasion. Oh yes, he said he had not seen his room yet.

He had not seen his room yet?—Yes, because it had a peculiar window that came on the garden.

Did he remind you of any peculiarity that used to be done at that window?—Yes, we used to go out and smoke.

Did he remind you of that?—Yes.

Before you mentioned it?—Yes.

Do you remember taking him into the library to show him the theatre?—Yes.

Do you remember a conversation amounting to a dispute between you?—Yes.

Just tell us how that was.—I said the theatricals were in the theatre; he said no, they were in one of the recesses of the library.

Did that dispute continue for any time?—That evening, I believe; I cannot tell how much longer.

Did he repeat that they were in one of the recesses of the library?—Always.

Did you ultimately find out that he was right and you were wrong?—Yes.

Do you remember when ROGER TICHBORNE was staying with you in early times, in 1848, your going to a Mr. WHITE or being with a Mr. WHITE?—I never went with him there.

But there was a man named WHITE in the neighbourhood?—There was.

When he was staying with you in Hull in 1868 did you have occasion to call at Mr. WHITE's shop?—Yes.

And was Sir ROGER with you?—Yes.

Did you either tell Mr. WHITE or Sir ROGER who the other was when you went into the shop?—No.

Did you see whether they recognized each other or not?—I believe Mr. WHITE did so at once.

The Lord Chief Justice: What did he do?—I believe he recognized Sir ROGER at once.

Mr. GIFFARD: Do you remember being together with the Plaintiff and Mr. WHITE, that same evening going along the road together somewhere?—I remember going to Burton Constable, but whether it was the same evening or not I could not say.

At all events, you remember going with Mr. WHITE and the Claimant along the road to Burton Constable?—Yes.

I had better ask you at once—Mr. WHITE is dead, I believe, now?—Yes.

While you were on your road did the Plaintiff point out to Mr. WHITE any alterations that had taken place?—I believe he did.

In your hearing?—Yes.

Was he accurate or not in what he pointed out?—Mr. WHITE said perfectly accurate.

Do you remember, at all events, coming near a place called Bilton, and anything passing about a public-house?—I do not know of a public-house there; there is no public-house about there before you get to Bilton.

I want to know whether you remember any conversation between Mr. WHITE, and yourself, and the Plaintiff about a public-house being there of the Bishop, the Soldier, and the Sailor?—Yes.

Just tell us how that conversation was?—He said that he remembered that place, and I do not remember anything further than that.

What did he say? Did he give any description of what used to be there?—I believe he did; but I forget. I did not pay much attention to it.

Mr. GIFFARD: Your lordship has the affidavit of Mr. WHITE on your note; it has never been read yet I see. I wanted to see whether it had.

Do you remember coming past a place called Whiton House?—Yes.

Do you remember anything passing between you when you came there?—I think he said RIBY NICHOLSON lived there.

I do not know whether you heard the whole of the conversation with Mr. WHITE at that time or not?—I did not; I was driving.

Were they behind you?—Yes.

You had ample opportunity, at all events, of examining his features, and the expression of his face, during those four or five days?—Yes.

Did you notice anything at all about his personal appearance that you recognized?—Merely a twitching of the eyes.

Anything in the expression of the face?—I cannot say that I did.

Anything with respect to the voice?—When reading, yes.

When reading?—Not otherwise.

Putting together all you observed, and the questions you heard him answer, what is now your deliberate judgment and conviction as to whether he is the same man or not?—I have not a doubt of it—the same ROGER I used to play with years ago as a boy.

Cross-examined by the Solicitor-General.

You heard of his coming home, I suppose, Sir TALBOT?—Yes.

The time when you first saw him was nearly eighteen months after he came home?—Perhaps it would be. I do not know the exact date.

You had heard of his being in England many months before you saw him?—Not so very long.

Did you not hear of his being home in 1866, at the end of 1866 or the beginning of 1867?—I cannot remember.

Cannot you remember when you first heard? I think the families are connected, are they not?—Is there not some connection between your family and the TICHBORNES?—I did not know of it.

I beg your pardon. I thought there was. There had been friendship between you?—Between me and TICHBORNE?

Yes?—Formerly, yes.

Do I understand you to say that you cannot recollect when you first heard of the supposed return of the ROGER TICHBORNE who had been your playmate?—The first time that I paid any attention to it at all was when his mother wrote to me.

When was that?—It was previous to his visit—his visit to me, I mean.

Have you that letter?—No.

Mr. GIFFARD: Mr. SPOFFORTH has.

The Solicitor-General: I meant that. It is in existence?—Yes.

(The Court adjourned for a short time.)

The Lord Chief Justice: I have sent for the Bank Holidays Bill. I believe there is some clause introduced affecting the sitting of the Court. The Bank Holidays Bill, I believe, contains some clauses making a particular day a general holiday. I have sent for a copy of it. It has not yet been printed by the QUEEN's printers, I believe. We should know what our powers are of sitting on Monday.

The Solicitor-General: Yes.

The Lord Chief Justice: I was going to ask Mr. MATTHEWS if he would mind going to the House of Lords and see the copy. It has been amended several times. We can get a copy of the Bill, but not of the amendments. If anyone could see it at the proper office, in the House of Lords, that would do.

Mr. MATTHEWS: I will go, my lord.

Mr. DENMAN: There is no doubt Whit-Monday is one of the days. The very object of passing the Act so rapidly was to save Whit-Monday.

The Lord Chief Justice: We must take care that all our proceedings are regular.

Mr. DENMAN: It applies to all transactions of business, I believe.

The Lord Chief Justice: I mentioned it to you, Mr. MATTHEWS, because, being in Parliament, you might have an opportunity of seeing it. We can easily get a copy of the Bill; but what is necessary, is to see how far any of the amendments alter the Bill, so far as it bears on this point.

Mr. DENMAN: It received the Royal Assent last night.

The Lord Chief Justice: If you can get a copy of the Bill as it went to the House of Lords, and see how far it is altered, that will do.

Mr. MATTHEWS: I will go presently.

The Lord Chief Justice: I shall be much obliged to you if you will.

The Solicitor-General: I should think we might leave it to your lordship and the jury to interpret it in the absence of anything.

The Lord Chief Justice: If the law says it is to be so, I shall not prevent it. I do not wish to adjourn.

The Foreman: As regards Monday, the majority of the jury would wish the Case went on.

The Lord Chief Justice: Yes, we are all agreed about that. At the same time, we must not go against the authority of the Act of Parliament.

The Foreman: It is a Commercial Act, I think, and one which refers to Bills of Exchange, I think.

The Lord Chief Justice: I think the lawyers did put in a clause. I am under the impression that they did.

The Solicitor-General (*to the witness*): Now you were saying when we broke off, the first intimation that you had was from his mother, and that has been handed to me. That was early in the year 1867, I think?—Probably.

Had you repeated communications from the Dowager during the year 1867?—It may be two or three; they are all there.

I merely want to know in a general way whether you had repeated communications from her?—Perhaps two or three.

At various intervals?—Yes.

Were you yourself in or near London during the year 1867?—can you recollect?—I may have passed through. I cannot say.

Is your recollection that you did?—I went to the Exhibition at Paris. I forget what year that was.

That was in 1867, I am told?—That was the time I went. I passed through London in going.

Were you a few days in town?—I am wrong; I did not go by London, at all.

Can you recollect whether you were in London a few days during any time of the year 1867?—Not at all.

About May—do you know whether you were in or near London about the Derby-day, in May, 1867?—I think not.

It was the 22nd of May, I think, in that year?—No.

Did you write to the Claimant yourself. Were you in correspondence with the Claimant?—After his mother's letter, I think I wrote to him twice or three times.

Did you get any letters from him?—Yes.

Have you got them?—You will find them all there.

I had better read this—"My dear TALBOT. With great pleasure."—It does not seem to be dated. It is 9. 3. '67. That would be March. "With great pleasure I received your kind letter last night. I am very sorry to hear that you have been ill. I have not been very well myself for this last ten days. I had RADCLIFFE and KATTY and LUCY TANNDY here to see me yesterday, the meeting was not so agreeable as I should have wished it, because they could not see Mamma. You must know how I must have felt but what could I do. If i had not seen them they would have gone and said I was frighten to show myself and it was my solr. wish for me not to deny myself. I wish my dear TALBOT you would come and spend a few days with me my House is not very large but we will find plenty of room for you. I expect to be able to go to Upton before long. Col. LUSHINGTON who lives at Tichborne has been so kind to me that I really cannot turn him out he offered to give up the house to me the first time I went to Alresford when every one seemed against me. But since my brother officers have been to see me. every body seems to change. How they all want to be my friends. But I say no I dont want them what right had they to write such things about me as they did. they reply that they ware told it was not me. but then they had no right to judge before they see me they all say they are sorry for what been done. But that does not alter the expressions that those scandalious paragraph have made on the minds of the public against me. I have already entered actions against some of them, and they donot seem to like it. I hope, my dear TALBOT, to have many a good hunt with you yet. I hope you will remember me to your father, who I hope to have the pleasure of seeing before long. Of course I have seen a great many things since I have been away, that we can talk of when we meet. Mamma tells me that you are now married, so we shall both have the pleasure of introducing one others wifes. I must now conclude, for you know I am not very fond of writing. Mamma is very thankful for your kind letter. I am sorry to hear that you have given up smoking, for my part I have given up buying retail, for I have to buy wholesale now, but the Dr. have put me on short allowance, they only allow me twenty a-day now. But I take care to get the largest cigars I can. This is the Longest letter I have wrote this two years, so I shall now say good bye for the present.—I remain, Dear TALBOT, truly yours, R. C. D. TICHBORNE, 9/3/67. J. C. CONSTABLE, Esq., 106, Coltman St., Hull." This is a letter in answer to one of yours apparently?—Just so.

Mr. GIFFARD: The one you ask for was Lady TICHBORNE'S. Sooner or later they must be read. The first one you asked for has not been read. They ought to be read in their order.

The Solicitor-General: At present I do not put in Lady TICHBORNE'S letter.

Mr. GIFFARD: I beg your pardon, Mr. Solicitor. Having asked for it, it is put in.

The Solicitor-General: That is not so.

Mr. GIFFARD: Then I shall take my lord's opinion upon it.

The Lord Chief Justice: If the Solicitor-General calls for a document in your custody he must put it in, if he asks for a document, that he may look at it himself and not put it in—that is it. The solicitor, as I understand it, asked the witness where the documents were. Somebody below produced them to you. They really belong to the witness, because they are his documents. The Solicitor-General, in my hearing, did not call upon you, as representing the Plaintiff, to produce the documents. They were produced by somebody. No doubt they have been handed to him by the witness on your side. These are documents that might properly be in possession of the witness. If they were placed in the hands of your client, it was only for convenience.

Mr. GIFFARD: What I submit is, that they ought to be read in order.

The Solicitor-General: I do not say that I am not going to put them in, but I am not going to put them in at this moment.

Mr. GIFFARD: My point is about the time. If there is any doubt about its being in, I shall reserve it till it arises. I handed it to the Solicitor, and that displaces me from any right which I should otherwise possess.

The Lord Chief Justice: Certainly not. The Solicitor-General would not think that for a moment. The impression on my mind when it was produced was that it was a document that was in the possession or control of the witness, and intrusted by the witness to your client, which is a very common thing.

The Solicitor-General: Those documents were in the possession of my learned friend representing Sir ROGER TICHBORNE. A letter to the witness would not naturally belong to Sir ROGER.

Mr. GIFFARD: I do not know that.

The Lord Chief Justice: It is quite consistent: a gentleman like the witness coming here and seeing the solicitor, he hands the documents to him, and says, these are the documents I have got. Those documents are his; he has the right to have them back again.

The Solicitor-General: On our side, if my learned friend will allow me to say so, his courtesy cannot displace him from any right; neither, on the other side can his courtesy displace me from any right I have, or it ceases to be courtesy. I do not say I will not put it in, but at this moment I will not put it in.

Mr. GIFFARD: My present objection is, that those letters have to be put in sooner or later. I was saying, if they do so, the proper course was that they should be read in order. I protest against my friend's right to read a letter which is not written by the witness, and as to which there is no particular reason why it should be read now. He may make it part of his case, because it is a part of my client's writing. As against him it is evidence I quite admit. I submit at present that there is no reason why those letters should be read. If they are to be read, it ought to be a matter of condition that they should be read in order.

The Lord Chief Justice: When a document is produced by the witness, it is a letter written to him. In that case the inquiry takes a very wide range, not only as to the facts, but as to his knowledge, and not as to particular things. Knowledge or representations made to the witness become very material in many respects. If the witness says, I have certain letters, and they are handed to the Counsel who is examining, he may look at them, and may then cross-examine with reference to anything he finds in them, or that he may possibly have inferred from them, and he may use them in any order of date that he pleases. Eventually, either he or you would claim a right to use those letters; therefore the Solicitor-General at present is perfectly in order. Having possession of the letters, he may look at them and read them, and examine or cross-examine upon them, in any order he pleases. He may, if he can, contradict the witness, after he has made a statement, by something he finds in a letter. In this particular case, I do not suppose it will be necessary to contradict the witness, but I only allude to it as a general principle. The question is this: whether the Solicitor-General is to put them in, or whether they are admissible.

Mr. GIFFARD: Having said that I have, I do not wish to keep up the discussion. I should have thought my friend was bound by the letter I gave him. I do not know how he has got the others. I only gave him one.

The Solicitor-General: I called for them.

Mr. GIFFARD: I was not here, or I should not have allowed them to have been given.

The Lord Chief Justice (*to the witness*): Are those letters under your control in this sense, that you can have these letters back whenever you choose to ask for them?—I should hope so.

The Lord Chief Justice: That is what I understood—that, in reality, they are letters of the witness.

The Solicitor-General: I do not at all say I will not put this in. My friend does not propose, nor has ever pointed out to your lordship's attention, that the letter I now read is a letter from a party in the cause. The letter which my learned friend wishes to read is a letter from no party in the cause. The Dowager Lady TICHBORNE cannot be cross-examined upon it. It is put into my hands.

Mr. GIFFARD: I must say this, if we are to go on with the discussion, the way in which it arose was this. The witness was asked whether this was the first communication he received from Sir ROGER TICHBORNE, and his answer was, he received first a letter from Lady TICHBORNE. Upon which the Solicitor-General asks, where is this letter. He says, I have not got it. It is in the custody of Mr. SPOFFORTH, who instructs me, and it was handed to my learned friend, who reads what he likes of that letter. Then, I say, if the letters are to be read in the order in which they are asked for, that is one thing. It is written by my client, and it may be hereafter evidence, and may be valid evidence, for all I know to the contrary. It is a question of the order of procedure. My friend has read this. It was obviously done simply for the purpose of pointing out the bad spelling.

The Solicitor-General: I beg your pardon. If you had not have interfered I should have asked questions long ago, and I shall do so immediately you stop.

The Lord Chief Justice: It is a simple question now as to the convenience of reading the documents at one time, and, generally speaking, as to who shall read them. If there be a question as to the matters contained in the letters upon which the Solicitor-General cross-examined, it will be rather more convenient to read the letters through before or after the examination. Generally speaking, it is after the examination.

Mr. GIFFARD: Having appealed to your lordship, and pointed out my view, I shall say no more. Let me put this to your lordship—supposing some question should arise about the bad spelling in Sir ROGER TICHBORNE's letters. That might be a question put to the witness. I will put it by way of hypothesis. Do you think that it would be fair to read it to the witness when *you find that the gentleman's own mother actually made use of the same bad spelling, and putting small letters where there ought to be large capitals.*

The Lord Chief Justice: It does not strike me so.

The Solicitor-General: Does my friend mean to say that?

Mr. GIFFARD: I certainly do mean to say it.

The Lord Chief Justice: As I understand the matter, the mother of ROGER TICHBORNE was a Frenchwoman, FELICITE was her name; so, I suppose, she was a French lady.

Mr. GIFFARD: She was a daughter of Mr. SEYMOUR; she was not actually a Frenchwoman.

The Solicitor-General: Her mother was.

Mr. GIFFARD: She was not.

The Lord Chief Justice: She had a French name?

Mr. GIFFARD: Yes; but she herself was not a Frenchwoman.

The Lord Chief Justice: She was born of a French mother.

The Solicitor-General: And her last letter, my learned friend knows, was to her son in France.

The Lord Chief Justice: As regards the reading of the letter at a particular moment, whenever the question arises as to whether the Solicitor-General is entitled to read it, or ought to read it, if the letter is handed to me, I should be able to form an opinion about it. The truth is, from the commencement of the Case, your case has been broken in upon. In the first instance a serious interruption was made, but it was in consequence of your side requiring a document to be read. I refer more particularly to the examination and affidavit of the Claimant himself, and which necessarily involved the reading of the cross-examination. That was interposed at a very early period of the Case, when your case was going on. At the same time, Brother BALLANTINE having said that if the questions were pressed, and extracts read from the affidavit, that the affidavit must be put in: the Solicitor-General said, "I will put it in." The consequence of that was, he got in the cross-examination of the Plaintiff.

Mr. GIFFARD: Your Lordship has not forgotten how that arose. We wanted to prove a letter from Mr. BOWKER, and it was not admitted, and that rendered it necessary for me to call Mr. [illegible].

The Lord Chief Justice: As regards the conduct of the Case, I see nothing against it. It was an unfortunate thing you having pressed it.

Mr. GIFFARD: We did not regard it so.

The Lord Chief Justice: When you got the letter in, it seemed it was not worth pressing.

Mr. GIFFARD: That is getting to a wide discussion. We were desirous of shewing that the first witness had been informed by Mr. BOWKER before he had pronounced any judgment at all upon the Claimant, that the person who said he was Sir ROGER TICHBORNE was nothing but a mere impostor.

The Lord Chief Justice: The fact is that your Case has been broken in upon by evidence on the part of the Defendant from time to time.

Mr. GIFFARD: I am not complaining of that. I may submit to your lordship that these letters should be read in their order. If your lordship thinks they ought not to be, I have no more to say.

The Lord Chief Justice: The letters are handed to the Solicitor-General. He must make what use he thinks of them. He may use them in what way he thinks fit. Sometimes I have known it important to use a subsequent letter before an earlier one. I cannot say as a positive rule.

Mr. GIFFARD: I must leave it entirely in your lordship's hands. I appeal to your lordship simply as a question of form.

The Lord Chief Justice: Let me look at the letters, and I will form the best judgment I can.

The Solicitor-General: If my learned friend objects, I presume I may just say, it is put by my learned friend upon two grounds—first of all, it is put as a matter of law, and then as a matter of conduct. As far as regards the law, I have stated I have called for no letter from him for the purpose of putting it in. I apprehended, unless I have done something to make it evidence, I am not bound to put it in. My friend says I ought not to displace him from any legal right, because, as a matter of courtesy he handed it to me. My reply to that is, courtesy is to be courtesy. If it is insisted on as a matter of legal right, though I perfectly agree that I cannot displace my friend from any legal right by courtesy, yet neither can he, by what he is pleased to call courtesy, displace me from any legal right. It was merely handed to me when I might have got it in some other way.

Mr. GIFFARD: At present I am submitting it to my lord.

The Lord Chief Justice: The first letter has been read.

Mr. GIFFARD: No, my lord; the second letter.

The Solicitor-General: I do not say I shall not do so hereafter, but at present I will not put it in, nor have I used the Dowager Lady TICHBORNE's letter.

The Lord Chief Justice: Let me see the letter. (*It is handed to his lordship.*) I have read through the letter. I do not think it is worth discussion on either side. I do not suppose, when the Solicitor-General considers that he will care whether it is put in before or after: it is immaterial.

The Solicitor-General: I only object, because I do not like to be put out. I am not bound to put it in now; therefore, I say I will not put it in now. I do not say I will not put it in by-and-by.

The Lord Chief Justice: I cannot conceive that the Solicitor-General will object to put it in. It is a mere point between you: because you object, he says I will not put it in now.

The Solicitor-General: That is exactly why I will not put it in; because Mr. GIFFARD insists I shall.

Mr. GIFFARD: I do not understand your lordship to have decided it either way.

The Lord Chief Justice: It is not worth a discussion; it really is not.

The Solicitor-General: I do object to be interrupted.

The Lord Chief Justice: The Solicitor-General will not put it in at this moment, because, he says, I will conduct my case in the way I like, and you persist you will object because he says he will not conduct it as you like.

Mr. GIFFARD: I object to my friend saying I interrupted him. I waited until he had read the whole letter.

The Lord Chief Justice: I am perfectly certain of this, that the moment the Solicitor-General proposes to put in that letter you will not object and the moment you propose to put it in, he will not object. It is a mere discussion on the conduct of the case.

Mr. Serjeant BALLANTINE: We need not ask your lordship to take a note.

The Lord Chief Justice: I will take a note of any objection you please, and you may have the benefit of it on either side; at present I have not, because, I do not consider the objection a serious one; it is a mere matter of punctiliousness.

The Solicitor-General (*to the witness*): I observe that in this letter he speaks of having received a kind letter from you, so that you must have written to him at that time?—I answered his letter.

The 9th March, 1867? I answered his letter.

"With great pleasure I received your kind letter"; that is how this letter begins, so that it is plain there must have been a letter from you?—It was in answer to his.

In answer to his? Then this is not the first?—I fancy not.

I was going to ask you upon this point, whether you yourself had been in or near London about the Derby-day in 1867?—No.

Do you recollect writing a letter to him?—this letter that has been given to me appeared to be dated in March. Do you recollect writing that letter to him on, about, or towards the end of May, and apparently—I am not sure—I put it to you whether you did mention in it that you were coming up to London to see him?—I did.

About that time, in 1867?—I did.

Did you come?—No.

Do you recollect who replied to your letter of May, 1867, in which you mentioned your intention of coming to town?—No.

Do you recollect whether you had an answer to that from the Claimant, or from the Dowager?—I do not remember.

Had you had any applications made to you about that time from anyone—any communications of any sort made to you from anyone except the Claimant and the Dowager Lady TICHBORNE?—I think not.

Are you certain?—Pretty nearly.

I may take it you are tolerably certain that it was so?—Yes.

Was there any question, at that time, of your being godfather to one of his children?—There was.

Were you?—Yes.

Did you come up to the christening?—No.

You had not seen him at that time?—No.

Your father was alive, I suppose, at that time?—Yes.

Did you never see him before he came down to Hull?—Never.

You say you had?—Except before he went abroad.

I mean the Claimant. I mean between the time. (You understand, when I say that, it is for shortness.) I mean you had not seen him between the time of his return and the time of his coming to Hull?—Exactly.

And you say you had letters from him, and you had letters from the Dowager. Had you letters from any one else? From Mr. HOLMES, or from any legal person?—Not from Mr. HOLMES, certainly.

Had you from Mr. BAIGENT?—No; I did not know him.

Had you from anyone on behalf of the Claimant, besides himself, and ——

Mr. Serjeant BALLANTINE: Mr. HOLMES.

The Solicitor-General:—No; he said not Mr. HOLMES.

Had you any from anyone besides the Plaintiff and the Dowager?—I think Mr. NORRIS wrote to me.

Mr. NORRIS?—Yes.

He was the Dowager's attorney?—I did not know what he was.

You did not know that, but, however, we know that he was. Did he send you copies of affidavits, or any papers of any kind besides the letter?—No.

When did you hear from Mr. NORRIS?—I believe the day Sir ROGER arrived.

At Hull?—Yes.

But immediately between the time of this letter early in 1867, and the time when he arrived at Hull in May, 1868, had you had any letters from any person on his behalf except himself and the Dowager?—No.

Are you certain of that?—I believe I am.

No one?—No one.

Had you when he came to Hull and Burton Constable in May, 1868; had you seen any copies of the affidavits that had been filed in the preceding year?—I do not know that I did.

But do you know that you did not?—I think not.

Did you see them at any time?—I have seen them latterly—some time ago.

Do you mean in the last five or six months or ——?—Yes, perhaps more than that—eight months.

Eight months ago. Well, then, you can tell me, I dare say, whether you had ever seen them before?—I believe I did not.

You believe you had?—I did not.

I beg your pardon. You believe you had not. I do not suppose you very often give yourself the trouble to look at affidavits, Sir TALBOT. You can tell me whether you had a lot of affidavits sent you before that?—Well, to tell you the truth, I believe I have only read three out of the lot.

Do you mean that you only read three out of the lot eight months ago?—No, I have only read three out of all the lot.

Well, unless one is obliged to do it that is another matter; but had you them sent to you so that you might read them if you had been inclined before that?—No.

Are you sure?—Positive.

When did you succeed to the title?—Somewhere about December—in December, I think.

In December, when?—Last December.

Last December?—I think so.

Was Sir CLIFFORD CONSTABLE alive?—Of course he was.

Was he at Burton Constable when the Claimant was there with you?—Yes.

I think he did not make an affidavit?—No, I never saw him.

Was he at Burton Constable at the time—in the house?—Yes.

And how long was Sir ROGER, the Claimant, there?—Perhaps two hours the first time.

And how much the second? He was there two or three days, was not he?—No, he only called there twice.

Oh, went there twice; and how long was he there the second time?—Perhaps the same, perhaps a little more.

Was Sir CLIFFORD aware of his being there?—Yes.

But did not see him?—No.

Sir CLIFFORD, I presume, was at Burton Constable at the time when ROGER CHARLES TICHBORNE was there in 1848?—Yes.

The house was full? I mean there was a party at the house?—Yes.

And Sir CLIFFORD knew ROGER CHARLES TICHBORNE very well?—Oh, yes.

I think you say, when you swore your affidavit, Sir TALBOT—it was in 1868—you say that you were 40. You are just 43 now, then?—Yes, about that.

Just so. Now, are there any servants now, or were there any servants at Burton Constable in 1867 and 1848 who had been servants when Sir ROGER TICHBORNE was there in 1848?—Had you any of the old servants still there?—Yes.

Several?—Two that I remember at present.

Who were they?—The coachman, and my valet.

The coachman and your valet?—I believe my valet. I am not quite certain about him.

Those two, at any rate were there.

Mr. Serjeant BALLANTINE: No, he says he believes it.

The Solicitor-General: You believe the valet was, and you are not sure about the coachman?—Yes.

Were there any others, to the best of your recollection?—Perhaps the huntsman; the huntsman would be there.

Was there anyone else—any of the women servants?—I think most of them were gone.

I do not ask you. I can hardly expect you to be very certain about it?—I think they are all gone.

You think they are all gone that were there at that time? In 1848—they are all gone.

Oh, they were all gone in 1867 and 1868?—I think they are all gone now.

Ah, but I am speaking of 1867 and 1868, if you can recollect?—Most of them I should say.

Well, but were there any left?—I cannot answer that.

Was there a servant, do you recollect, in 1848, of the name of CHRISTOPHER PRESTON?—We had such a man, but when he lived there I could not say.

You do not know whether he was there in 1848?—I could not say.

You say that you had had these communications—these various communications with the Claimant and with the Dowager—was there much discussion, was it a matter, after you had had those communications, that was much discussed in the neighbourhood of Hull among the people that you saw about whether this gentleman was the right man or not?—I do not think anybody spoke to me without it was Mr. WHITE, on the subject.

Mr. WHITE?—Yes.

He had spoken to you on it?—Yes.

Were there any other persons that you had talked to?—I should say not.

I mean now, any of the servants—any of the old servants, who might have remembered him?—I do not remember.

You probably had not at first. Tell me—perhaps I have no right to ask that—but I would ask you whether at first you had at all made up your mind, one way or the other, upon the subject?—I had not, when I first saw him.

I say, before that? I am coming to when you first saw him, but I am speaking of the time when you first had communications opened with you, you know, by the Dowager and him. Up to the time you saw him—that would be nearly twelve months. One letter I have got as far back as March, 1867, and one was before that. Therefore, it was as far back as March, 1867, that you first had communications. What I am asking is, whether you had made up your mind, when you first had those communications, as to whether he was the right man or not? Upon his mother writing me I had no doubt.

Upon his mother writing?—Yes.

The Lord Chief Justice: I think it would be the convenient course to read the mother's letter out. Do you object?

The Solicitor-General: No, my lord, I should not have read it at this moment, but I know my duty too well, my lord, to object.

The Lord Chief Justice: He says: "Upon receiving the mother's letter, I had no doubt he was the man." It is convenient to have the mother's letter read.

The Solicitor-General: This is dated 4th March, 1867: "Though many years have elapsed since I have had the pleasure of seeing you, I have not forgotten your intimacy with my son, Sir ROGER TICHBORNE."

Mr. GIFFARD: "Sir ROGER" is spelt with a little "r," and TICHBORNE with a little "t." You have remarked upon the others. I thought it only fair to say that.

The Solicitor-General: Well, the jury shall see the letters and judge. As far as that goes, the "TICHBORNE" is spelt with a big "T" in the mother's letter.

Mr. GIFFARD: In "my Dear Son," dear is spelt with a big "D," my lord.

The Lord Chief Justice: The object for which I suggested that this letter should be read was this. The gentleman said that upon receiving the mother's letter he had no doubt that the Claimant was the man. The first point, therefore, is to see what the mother stated to Sir TALBOT CONSTABLE. Very well, then after that has been done, you can call attention to any peculiarity that there is in the letter, as to the way it is spelt. You may say that the same observation applies to the other letters, but you cannot suggest that the Solicitor-General reads it for the purpose of showing the spelling, therefore it is not the same thing. This letter is read for the purpose of showing what induced this gentleman to come to the conclusion that the Claimant was the son. After it has been read, and the effect of it in that respect is known, then call attention to any peculiarity in the spelling. That is the best way. We want to see what it was that induced this gentleman to come to that conclusion.

The Solicitor-General: Well this letter has been effectually interrupted very successfully and effectually.

The Lord Chief Justice: Perhaps, Mr. Solicitor, you don't mind beginning it again.

The Solicitor-General: No, my lord (*reading*): "4 March, 1867. My dear Mr. TALBOT CONSTABLE, though many years have elapsed since I have had the pleasure of seeing you I have not forgotten you intimacy with my son Sir ROGER TICHBORNE, I have often thought that both him and myself would be happy to see you again, and as he is returned from his long absence I cannot help writing to you to ask you when it will be possible for him to meet you, he is anxious to see his old friend and I told him I would write to you to let you know of his return home if you come to London with Mrs. TALBOT CONSTABLE, I shall also be happy to see her, as I have known you so very young that I can never be indifferent to your happiness. I knew your dear mother and aunts so well also, that I am sure you will understand my joy at seeing My Dear Son again after 14, years absence, of course he meets with many difficulties to recover his properties but all's well that ends well; and in a short time everything will be happily settled if you go to London ROGER will be happy to meet you there, we are come to Croydon to spend two months and we hope that after that time we may be allowed to go into the country. With kind regard to Sir CLIFFORD CONSTABLE and kind remembrance to yourself from your early friend Sir ROGER TICHBORNE I remain my dear Mr. TALBOT CONSTABLE, sincerely your's H. F. TICHBORNE—this is my address Lady H. F. TICHBORNE essex Lodge Lady H. F. TICHBORNE essex Lodge thornton heath Croydon Surrey"—Then it is in some other hand apparently outside. I think it is a different hand there.

The Lord Chief Justice: Now, Mr. GIFFARD, you can call attention to any peculiarities about this.

Mr. GIFFARD: I think the better way, after what your lordship has said, is that I should wait till after the Solicitor-General has done.

The Lord Chief Justice: I did not mean that, Mr. GIFFARD.

Mr. GIFFARD: Then I will do it now with great pleasure. The first, my lord, is what I have already called attention to—"Sir ROGER TICHBORNE," a little "r" and a little "t," as I read it. The "t" appears to be more doubtful. The jury will see that for themselves. Then there is "him and myself would be happy to see." Then there is "Mrs. TALBOT CONSTABLE," TALBOT spelt with a little "t." Then there is "My Dear Son," spelt with a capital "D" in the "dear." Then it is signed "H. F. TICHBORNE," "H. F." both being small letters. Then "My address Lady H. F. TICHBORNE"—"H" capital letter, and "f" small letter. "essex Lodge" with a small "e." Then repeated "Lady H. F. TICHBORNE," "f" and "t" both small letters. "essex Lodge" with a small "e" in Essex; "thornton heath" small "t" and small "h."

Mr. Serjeant BALLANTINE: And there is "recover his properties."

The Lord Chief Justice: Perhaps there is a little peculiarity as the writing of a French Lady.

Mr. Serjeant BALLANTINE: Yes, it is a matter for remark.

Mr. GIFFARD: The education would be the same in respect to the Plaintiff.

The Lord Chief Justice: Do you suggest the same amount of education in these two letters.

Mr. GIFFARD: No, my lord; only the peculiarity as to great and small letters.

The Solicitor-General: When we see his early letters we shall see what weight there is to be attached to that observation.

Mr. Serjeant BALLANTINE: I hope the jury will live long enough to have those before them.

The Lord Chief Justice: Just hand those letters to the jury.

(Two letters were passed to the jury.)

Mr. GIFFARD: You suggested, my lord, that the jury should see one letter—two have been passed to them. I do not object to their seeing the other letter.

The Lord Chief Justice: Do you wish them not to see both?

Mr. GIFFARD: No, my lord, I do not object, indeed. I am sorry that I should always be misunderstood. Your lordship suggested that the jury should have one letter, and some person, without your lordship's intervention, handed another letter.

The Foreman of the Jury: There are two letters placed in my hand, my lord.

The Lord Chief Justice: They were passed to you without my sanction, both of them. In looking through it, with the plaintiff's letter, I saw the same "i" only once—the small "i" with a dot over it. Will you hand me the long letter for a moment, gentlemen.

(The letter was passed to his lordship.)

The Solicitor-General: Now then I call for the letter of Sir TALBOT CONSTABLE, to which the letter of the Claimant is an answer.

Mr. GIFFARD: The letter to him?

The Solicitor-General: The letter to the Claimant. It begins, "I received your kind letter"—and I call for that kind letter. We have given notice; we have given notice to produce it, and it is in Court. Is it produced or not. If not——

Mr. Serjeant BALLANTINE: The Solicitor-General should hardly say that it is in Court.

The Solicitor-General: Well, I withdraw that observation. We have given notice to produce it.

Mr. Serjeant BALLANTINE: We do not produce it; you must put yourselves in a condition to call for it.

The Solicitor-General: Well, we are not likely to have secondary evidence of a letter of Sir TALBOT CONSTABLE to the Plaintiff.

Mr. Serjeant BALLANTINE: Well, at present that is your difficulty. I am only saying we do not produce it?

The Solicitor-General: You do not produce it?

Mr. Serjeant BALLANTINE: You do not put yourself in a position to ask for it?

The Solicitor-General: Oh, yes I do. Here is the notice to produce.

The Lord Chief Justice (*to Mr. Serjeant* BALLANTINE): The letter from your client, as I understand, refers to a letter from Mr. TALBOT CONSTABLE. Well, there is evidence that there is such a letter, and it is in your client's possession, and then that being so, there is notice given.

Mr. Serjeant BALLANTINE: Well, that is the point, my lord.

The Lord Chief Justice: What, whether notice has been given?

Mr. Serjeant BALLANTINE: Yes, I have asked for documents from time to time, and this is not produced to me. I should think it is one among so many that it is totally immaterial.

The Lord Chief Justice: Perhaps it would be as well to go on and try and finish this witness.

The Solicitor-General: Here is the notice, my lord.

The Lord Chief Justice: Before you came into Court, the jury said they were very anxious to be released at four o'clock to-day.

The Solicitor-General: Well, this is the purest technicality as to whether we have given the right notice.

The Lord Chief Justice: However, you can give it here to-day. You can give them the notice here for to-morrow.

The Solicitor-General: Well, we will give a fresh notice.

Well, Sir TALBOT, you say that you cannot tell me about the servants, and you cannot say that you had any conversation with any one except Mr. WHITE. Were you aware of any persons being down at Burton Constable making inquiries?—Never.

Were you yourself resident at Burton Constable in Sir CLIFFORD'S lifetime, or did you reside at some other house?—At Hull principally—latterly.

At Hull principally?—Latterly.

I see that you were married as far back as 1867, so you had a separate establishment I suppose after that?—I lived in Hull latterly.

Then you would not know from day to day, though I dare say you were there often, you would not know from day to day what was going on at Burton Constable?—No.

And what may have gone on at Burton Constable in 1867 and 1868 in the way of inquiries you cannot of your own knowledge tell me?—I never heard of anything of the kind.

Now, when the Claimant came down to Hull, had you notice that he was coming? Did you know that he was coming?—I might have heard that morning, but certainly not before?—I think not.

Not before the morning he arrived?—I think not.

Are you sure about that one way or the other?—As near as possible.

I may take it that from the receipt of the letters of Lady TICHBORNE and from what you knew of the Dowager's impression of the Claimant, you had made up your mind that he was the man?—I thought when she said it was her son there could be no doubt about it.

Just so, and you had acted upon that in becoming godfather to his child, and so on?—Yes.

Well, who came with him? Whom did you see at Hull?—Mr. NORRIS in particular.

Mr. NORRIS in particular, and who besides was there?—Mr. BAIGENT, I think.

Mr. NORRIS and Mr. BAIGENT, any one else?—No one that I know of.

Had he got a servant with him, did you see?—I never saw one.

You did not see a servant?—I believe not.

There were those three. Was anybody else with him, did you see?—Certainly not

Mr. NORRIS, Mr. BAIGENT, and himself. How long were they in Hull?—Three or four days—perhaps the better part of a week—nearly a week, I should think.

And did you see him the first day he came?—Yes.

The first day he came. Now had you a lively recollection of your companion of twenty years before?—Not the slightest in the world.

You did not remember him at all?—Not the least.

Then you could not tell whether this man was like him or not to the outward eye?—I could not say anything at all about him.

I beg your pardon. I asked whether you remembered your old friend of 1848—whether you had a recollection of him?—When I saw him I did not——

I mean had you sufficient recollection of your friend of 1848 to be able to say whether your friend of 1848 was like him?—Yes.

And he was not a bit like him?—No.

Was his manner like him?—I could not say it was at first.

Was his voice like him?—I could not say that it was.

In 1848 had the young ROGER CHARLES TICHBORNE a strong French accent?—Partially.

I do not quite understand you. I ask you whether he had a strong French accent?—Well, he had a little French accent.

You would accept the word "strong" probably? No, a little.

Only a little?

The Lord Chief Justice: You were brought up in France, I think?—I beg your pardon, my lord.

You spent a great portion of your time in France?—Yes.

The Lord Chief Justice: The appreciation by an Englishman of French accent, and the appreciation by an Englishman brought up in France, would be different.

The Solicitor-General: It may be quite different.

But did he talk French or English by preference in 1848? I suppose you being brought up in France spoke French perfectly well?—Yes.

As easily as English?—I could make myself understood.

I do not say anything about the accent, but you had a perfect command over the language?—Yes.

Did the ROGER CHARLES TICHBORNE of 1848 talk French or English by preference when he had got a person to whom he could talk French?—As much one as the other.

As much one as the other—half and half?—Yes.

You say he talked with a ——, I forget your expression, but not a strong accent?—To explain it better, he spoke broken English—what I call broken English.

You were brought up in France, though you are pleased to say you do not put your own French high. Now, was his a good command of French—a good accent?—When I first knew him?

Yes?—No, nothing particular.

In 1848?—No, nothing particular.

Do you know whether he wrote at that time in French or English?—That I could not answer.

Now, the house was full. This was the only time at which he was at Burton Constable was not it?—In 1848?

In 1848?—Yes, the only time.

But I will ask you, before we get there, upon this matter of the French. Were you in France—in Paris, during the time, from time to time, when he was brought up by the Frenchman—when he was under different tutors? We have heard of M. CHATILLON and others?

Mr. Serjeant BALLANTINE: We have not had that.

The Solicitor-General: Yes, it is mentioned in his affidavit. I say CHATILLON. That is the only one I mentioned.

RIGHT HON. R. LOWE, Chancellor of the Exchequer in the GLADSTONE Cabinet.

Mr. Serjeant BALLANTINE: You said, "and others."

The Solicitor-General: Well, we will drop the others. I will not have any dispute.

Mr. Serjeant BALLANTINE: But as a matter of accuracy, I think he is the only one mentioned in the affidavit.

The Solicitor-General (*to the witness*): Do you recollect that?—I might have been there, but I do not recollect his tutors.

You do not recollect his tutors at all?—No.

Very well then, we will come back. Now, when he came back there, you say the house was full. At that time, was Mr. RADCLIFFE staying there?—I do not remember.

You know whom I mean?—Oh yes, perfectly.

He is some connection of yours?—Distant perhaps.

Well "distant, perhaps." That is a matter—well, I will not press it. I am sure if——?—I am not aware.

What?—I do not know.

You do not know whether Mr. RADCLIFFE is connected with you? However, he was there?—I do not know whether he was or not.

Do not you remember whether Mr. RADCLIFFE was there?—I could not say whether he was there or not.

The time that you have spoken of the theatricals, you know?—Yes.

Cannot you recollect whether Mr. RADCLIFFE was there?—I cannot.

Or whether he took part in the theatricals?—I have not the slightest recollection.

And do you say that the Claimant would have it that the theatricals, as I understand you, were in a bow window or recess of the library?—Yes.

You thought they were not?—I did.

And you say you inquired, and you found out afterwards that he was right?—Yes.

From whom?—From Major CHICHESTER, for one.

Major CHICHESTER?—Yes.

Who is Major CHICHESTER?—A cousin of mine.

Was he in the house at the time?—He said so.

He said so?—Yes.

Anyone else?—Well, the valet fancies so.

The valet fancies so. That is, the valet you have spoken of; your valet?—Yes.

What is his name, your valet?—JAMES WATSON.

Anyone else?—The carpenter.

The carpenter who was about the place at time?—Yes.

He was about the place also in 1848, was he?—Yes, he must have been.

Anyone else?—I think not.

You think not. Well, now, from the inquiries you have made of these persons, you were satisfied that he was right and you were wrong?—Yes.

Well, Sir TALBOT, but have you any independent recollection yourself now of where these theatricals were?—I believe he is right. I could not swear to that.

You could not swear to that. And how far can you undertake to say that at that time the theatricals were not in a separate room altogether from the library?—I should say decidedly not without they were in the theatre as I imagined.

Was that your impression at the time?—My impression at the time was that they were in the theatre.

And the theatre is—?—A separate room.

Entirely separate from the library?—Yes.

And your impression was that they were in the theatre. Well now, the house, I never had the pleasure of seeing it, the house is a large one I suppose?—Yes.

And I suppose at a time of this kind the house was pretty full?—Yes, I believe it was.

Was there an audience? Were there the gentry of the neighbourhood. Were they invited to it, or was it a thing amongst yourselves only?—Well I should think there was an audience. I should say so.

Of invited people?—Some invited, and what people we had with us.

What people you had with you and some invited. Well, I suppose a good number of persons?—That I could not tell, it is so long ago.

Did the performances last more than one night, or were there several nights of them?—I think two or three, but I won't be certain.

Well, now, he came to you, as I understand, or rather you met him at Hull and drove him over to Burton Constable?—Yes.

And was the first thing he asked you when you got to Burton Constable about the cutting down of the hedge, whether you remembered the cutting down the hedge?—I believe it was the first thing the second time, but not the first time.

It was the first thing he asked on the second occasion?—Yes

He went and asked whether he might go to the field where the hedge was cut down?—Before he went to the house.

Then you say he asked what had become of the stumps?—Yes.

Well, I suppose the hedges of Burton Constable, like other hedges, have stumps in them?—I believe it is the proper way to cut them up and not down. He did not do it properly, you know.

But I mean all hedges that I am acquainted with. I do not know how it may be in Burton Constable, but all hedges have stumps in them, as far as my experience goes?—Yes.

And, if a hedge is to be cut down and got rid of, I suppose the stumps have to go somehow?—They are left a certain length.

But if the hedge has to be taken down, sooner or later the stumps have to go?—Yes.

This was twenty years ago?—Yes.

Then I do not suppose that you would expect much remaining of the stumps?—He was surprised to see them gone, and so was I.

He was surprised and so were you?—Yes.

Had they been left then, or what?—Well, they were thought so unsightly that I believe they were dug up afterwards.

That I suppose is not a thing wholly foreign to your experience in cutting down hedges: they grub up the stumps afterwards because they look ugly. I mean that you have seen that done hundreds of times?—I have not noticed.

Well, you have not noticed it; perhaps it is not your business to notice what becomes of your hedges, but I should have thought you might have seen that. Well, now, was this near the house, this field where the hedge and the stumps were?—Two fields from the stables.

Two fields from the stables, which were close to the house?—Yes.

And was it a throwing of two fields together?—They were separated by a hedge.

And I say, throwing down the hedge threw the two fields together?—No, there was a clump in the middle of the field, and this hedge was round the clump.

Oh, then it left the clump standing out?—Yes.

And do you know when the stumps had disappeared?—No.

You had not, perhaps, paid much attention to it since the time?—Some little time after that I left altogether. I had nothing more to do with the field. I knew nothing about it.

The Lord Chief Justice: Who was it you got the information from about it?—About what, my lord?

About the fence and the stumps?—From Sir ROGER at first.

But afterwards?—Afterwards I inquired of the bailiff, and he said he thought they were removed; but he could not answer. He believed they were removed.

The Solicitor-General: They were gone; undoubtedly they were?—They were gone: he fancied they had been dug up.

Well, now, he also remembered handing round the wine when the butler was away?—Yes.

Do you remember what butler it was?—No.

Was it Preston—Priston or Preston?—He never was the butler.

Was he the footman or under-butler?—He might have been under-butler. I believe he was footman, but I am not certain.

Now, was this during this Christmas party. Was it during this time?—At the time he was staying there.

And what was it—was it at luncheon, or dinner, or what?—Oh, at dinner.

At dinner. The butler was out, was he?—Yes.

And ROGER CHARLES TICHBORNE handed round the wine?—Yes.

And you had forgotten all about that, I dare say?—No, I had not.

Did you remember it perfectly?—Yes.

Did you ever mention it to anyone at all?—I might have done to my father, perhaps.

Your father was there, I suppose?—When he handed round the wine?

Yes.—Oh yes.

You might, in talking over the matter with your father, have mentioned that?—Yes, afterwards.

And did the butler come in before ROGER TICHBORNE had quite done?—I cannot answer, but perhaps he did.

You cannot answer for a certainty but perhaps he did. Very well now, you say that he went to buy a black mare for you?—Yes.

Of a man called CLAMBER?—Yes.

And did he buy it?—Yes.

Of CLAMBER?—Yes.

You are quite sure that it was of CLAMBER?—Quite.

Did you ever buy any other horse of CLAMBER?—I did not.

You did not?—I did not myself.

You did not?—Not myself.

I meant you. You did not yourself?—Yes, I believe I did. I bought another several years afterwards.

Several years afterwards—of the same man?—Yes.

And was he in the habit, do you know whether your father, Sir CLIFFORD, bought horses of him?—He might or might not.

That you cannot tell?

You are quite sure that it was CLAMBER, and no one else, that you bought this black mare of?—Yes, quite certain.

Who brought it over?—Sir ROGER brought it.

He brought it himself, did he?—Yes.

And when did you pay CLAMBER—how did you pay CLAMBER? Did you go or send it by post or how?—I do not remember anything about paying.

Is CLAMBER alive?—Yes.

Does he live near—near Burton Constable I mean?—I do not know exactly how far it is—18 or 20 miles.

Is he a breeder of horses, or rather a large breeder of horses?—A large farmer, and breeds horses.

Well now, did the Claimant introduce these things chiefly, or did you?—He did entirely.

He did entirely?—Yes.

You then, I understand, heard different things he had to say, and you found that those things had really happened—you ascertained, or people told you, or you remembered that those things had really happened when ROGER CHARLES TICHBORNE was there in 1848?—Yes.

And from that you concluded that he was ROGER CHARLES TICHBORNE?

The Lord Chief Justice: No, no; from the mother's letter.

The Solicitor-General: And from the mother's letter?

The Witness: But it was these facts principally that led to my decision.

The Lord Chief Justice: I understood you to say it was the mother's letter?—That was the first thing that led me to think about it.

The Solicitor-General: You said you had been godfather to his child, and that you acted upon the feeling that he was the real man?—Yes, I had acted.

Now, about his room. Did he volunteer that—the room where he slept?—He had to come over the second day to find his room, as he could not find it the first day.

That he also volunteered? Then I may take it you did not put any questions to him at all?—Not any.

Such things as he recollected he told you, and as I say you either remembered them or ascertained by other means that they happened in the real ROGER CHARLES TICHBORNE's time?—Exactly.

You say he could not find his room the first day. Was he long about it—was he some time over it the first day?—Well, it was very dark when we arrived. It was in the evening—perhaps about 8 o'clock—as far as I can remember. Everything was shut up and he could not make it out at all, and I took him first into one room, and then into another, to show him which was his own, and he did not recognize any till he came to my room, and he said he remembered something about that, but he could not say distinctly what he remembered about it. He remembered that most of any of the rooms.

Just so. And then next day he walked pretty confidently into the room where he had been—did he?—He did so.

Did he walk straight into the room where he had been?—Well, I showed him one room after another.

Yes.—As I did the previous day.

And when he came to this room——?—He said, "That is mine."

A Juror: Had he seen that room the night before?—Yes.

The Solicitor-General: The jury asked you whether he had seen that room the night before?—Yes, the evening before.

And had not recognized it?—And had not recognized it.

He told you, you say, every one of the things; he volunteered, you asked him no questions?—No.

Would it make any difference to you if he were to be cross-examined and could not answer questions?—I should be astonished.

I do not know how deeply rooted your judgment is, but do you think it would aid your judgment to hear him cross-examined?—I could not be persuaded to the contrary after what he has told me.

It might aid your judgment to hear him cross-examined?—I think it would make a very little difference.

But showing an ignorance altogether of things he ought to know?—Well, I could not account for his remembering them before.

Well, I won't repeat that; but what would you think if he recollected things that he might have been told, and could not recollect things he could not have been told; how then?—These things he could not have been told, I am satisfied of that.

You are satisfied?—Yes.

But supposing he was not able to say things that he certainly could not have been told?—It did not so happen in my instance, at any rate.

Would it alter your judgment at all?—I cannot say.

Now, let me ask you a question or two. I won't press you upon that, but you say the first appearance of the man was not a bit like?—Just so.

That you recognized him, I think I understand you to say, by the twitching of his eyes?—Yes.

Was that a very marked feature with ROGER CHARLES TICHBORNE?—Yes.

A marked characteristic, was it?—Yes.

And when did you see this man twitch his eyes—the Claimant?—Oh, every now and then.

Did he do it at first?—Not the first few minutes; after a little time.

Was it an easy sort of twitch?—Oh, yes.

Quite?—Oh, yes.

Did he twitch his mouth at all?—I did not notice that.

The side of his face?—I did not notice that either.

That is, you won't call that a marked characteristic?—Nothing but the eye.

Nothing but the eyes? The eyebrows, did they twitch?—Yes, certainly; there was a general twitch in them.

The forehead—did the forehead twitch?—No, I do not remember anything particular about the forehead—principally the eyes.

The eyes and the eyebrows?—Yes.

Was it in both eyes, or only in one?—Both.

Both eyes twitched, and all the time that you were with him at intervals—did they?—Yes, decidedly.

Decidedly?—Yes.

And that you recognized him by, and then you recognized him?—I think not at first, by the voice, but afterwards, when he got reading.

What did he read?—Well, I really do not know. I think it was something in the newspaper, as far as I can remember.

How was it? Had the ROGER TICHBORNE of 1848—had he read? What did he read?—I beg your pardon.

What did ROGER TICHBORNE, in 1848, read? Did he read anything to you?—On this particular occasion, when I last saw him, he read, I think, something out of a newspaper.

I mean the ROGER TICHBORNE of 1848—what did he read? Anything?—I do not know that he read at all.

What was it, then, that in reading made you recognize the voice?—Because he had the same voice that he had when speaking to me formerly. I did not perceive it so much at any other time, except in reading.

May I take it that in speaking you would not have been struck by the likeness to the voice?—Certainly not so much as in the reading.

Should you at all in speaking?—Well, no. I should think not.

But when he came to read, then it was the same voice?—I knew him directly.

It is difficult, perhaps, but what sort of a voice should you have described it as being?—Well, a voice with an accent, as I described before. That is what I call broken English.

Then you speak rather of the accent than of the tone of voice?—Yes.

Just so. I did not appreciate that. Then do I understand you that in reading, when he came to read the newspaper, he read it with a foreign accent?—Yes.

But in talking the foreign accent was gone?—Yes, not the same.

Well, that was the accent. Now, can you tell me, or can you not tell me anything about the voice—the sound of the voice apart from the accent? What was ROGER TICHBORNE's voice in 1848, when he played in the theatricals?

The Lord Chief Justice: I have got it down already that he could not say what it was.

The Witness: I could not say. I could not answer as to that.

The Solicitor-General: You cannot tell me whether it was gruff or not?—No.

The Solicitor-General: Well, we gave notice to produce upon the 23rd May, 1871. "Take notice that you are required to produce on the trial of the cause a letter of THOMAS CARTER, and all the letters written by the said THOMAS CARTER," &c. (*Read notice to produce.*) Now then, perhaps you will produce the letter I want.

Mr. Serjeant BALLANTINE: I have no right to say more than that I do not produce it.

The Solicitor-General: Very well.

Now, just before I finish, Sir TALBOT, I ask you again, can you recollect whether, about the 22nd May—you say you know that you did write about that time—can you recollect whether, towards the end of May, 1867, the Dowager answered your letter, or himself?—I cannot recollect that.

The Solicitor-General: If your lordship pleases, we will put in that notice. It applies to other documents, my lord.

Now, had you at that time written at all coldly or doubtfully to the Plaintiff?—I do not think I did.

About the 22nd May, you know, in 1867—the letter that is not produced—I ask whether you had written?—You have all the letters I have got.

Oh, as far as you are concerned, Sir TALBOT, I make no complaint of you, please to understand. Well, had you given any reason to the Plaintiff at that time, as far as you can judge, to think that the parties on the other side had been holding communications with you?—No.

You are sure of that. Had you given him any reason to say that he did not like the way you wrote?—I never heard of that before.

That his mother had better answer the letter instead of himself, for that he did not like the way you wrote, and he thought you had been tampered with by the other party?—I never heard of it before.

You had not written at that time anything to justify this, to the best of your recollection?—No.

The Solicitor-General: Very well, then, my friends won't produce the letter.

Mr. Serjeant BALLANTINE: Do not say that, Mr. Solicitor, please.

The Solicitor-General: Well, you do not produce it.

Mr Serjeant BALLANTINE: You say we *won't*. We do not say we have got it.

The Solicitor-General: Well, I will read the Plaintiff's account of the letter: "22nd May, 1867.—My dear Mama—I spoke to Mr. HOLMES about you a-going to call on him to-day, and he says he will not be at home. This is the Derby-day and they have all gone to the races. It was very kind of you to send me the oranges and sparrowgrass. MARY and the baby pass a very good night and are quite well as also little AGNES. AGNES seems to be very fond of the baby, as she cries to go and see it every time she goes upstairs. I receved a letter from TALBOT CONSTABLE yestrday. I hope he does not come until I am well, it make me so ill to be talking so much. I am not very well to-day, so I am keeping my bed and I do not intend to get up to-day to see anybody, the Dr. as not been to day yet, he told me yesterday morning to go to bed and put a poltice on. But I did put it on until last night when I went to bed, so I think that made me worse to-day; but I will soon be all right Mama dear, it only a little inflemed and will so go away if I keep quite. Will you my dear Mama answer TALBOT letter for me. I don't lick the way he writes. I think he has been tampered with by the other parties. We must be very careful my dear Mama, now my case is so strong. If he was to come up to be Godfather to my son and then say he did not know me, it would ingure my case very much. I will leave all to you my dear Mama only be careful. MARY and little AGNES joins me my dear Mama in kind love to you. Your affectionate Son, R. C. D. TICHBORNE." Well, now, that is the account, you see, of your letter, Sir TALBOT. Can you recollect anything about a letter that he should not "lik"?—No.

Well, now, there is another letter which I will read in which he gives an account of your letter to him. That is the 31st May, 1867.

Mr. Serjeant BALLANTINE: Let us see the original.

The Solicitor-General: Yes, certainly, 31st May, 1867. But I will take one of the 23rd first. "May 23rd, 1867. AGNES sends you a kiss. My dear Mama,—I receved your kind letter last night. I am very sorry I forgot TALBOT letter, but I was so unwell I could not think of nothink. I am a great better to-day thank God, as I hope this letter will find you the same. I receved a letter from you Mama dear and it had a black seal, and I thought it was from TALBOT, so I oppen it. I did not read it when I look at the signature. I expect Mr. BULPETT here to-night with Mr. HOLMES. I hope my dear Mama that I shall see you on Saturday if it a fine day, but if it not, do not come out in the wet. MARY and the little boy are doing quite well, and poor little AGNES as been playing with me all day; she misses her Mama very much. Let me know Mama dear if you have heard from Mr. TUCKER and when he coming here, and I would likewise like to know what Mr. NORRIS says about it. I think my dear Mama I would not bother with them any more as I can get the money on those terms much quicker. Hoping soon to see you my dear Mama, I remain Your affectionate Son, R. C. D. TICHBORNE."

Well, do you recollect a letter? Did you write a letter about that time to ROGER TICHBORNE?—I cannot say what time.

Now, this is a letter of the 31st May, 1867: "My dear Mama,—You will think it very strange that I did not write to you yesterday, But I gave BOGLE and CARTER leave to go and see the races, and several persons called, that the day passed away before I knew it was gone. My dear Mama, Mr. TUCKER called to see me last night, but did not stay long. He was saying that he was coming down on Saturday with you to have baby christened. You must remember, my dear Mama, that Mr. TUCKER is a Protestant, and cannot be a sponsor. Besides, my dear Mama, I find he is not so respectable as I should wish, and a nother think, my dear Mama, it would be wrong to make TALBOT Godfather until I see him suppose when he came he did not remember me, and I know RADCLIFFE has been continually writing to him about me."

Had you told him that that Mr. RADCLIFFE had been continually writing to you about him?—No.

"It would be very serious, and injure my case very much. My dear Mama, the COOK case is settled, so do not worrat yourself about that. I hope, Mama dear, you will come on Saturday to see me, although I should like to leave the christening for some time yet. There is nothing to fear, as they are both so healthy. Mr. BAIGENT is here, and I am so glad, as I was so lonely before, he beg to be remembered to you, my dear Mama. Do not forget to let me know who that Captain BARSTOW was. MARY and Baby and little AGNES are quite well, and joins me in love to you, my dear Mama, I have not said anything to MARY about the christening, but I have very strong reasons for not having it done on Saturday, which I cannot commit to paper, But which I will tell you all about when we are alone. GOD bless you, my dear Mama, from your affectionate Son, R. C. D. TICHBORNE. Dear little AGNES as just gave me a kiss to send to you."

Re-examined by Mr. GIFFARD.

The Lord Chief Justice: Have you much to ask him?

Mr. GIFFARD: Not very much, my lord, but I am afraid I should go over ten minutes.

The Lord Chief Justice: What do you say, gentlemen?

The Foreman of the Jury: Oh, ten minutes will not be material to us, my lord.

Mr. GIFFARD: Just tell me, had you, in fact, written to Mr. RADCLIFFE at all, or Mr. RADCLIFFE to you?—I had not corresponded with him for years.

Had he written to you at all?—No.

"Corresponded." I mean, had you received any letters from Mr. RADCLIFFE, that you remember?—No.

Had you seen him?—I saw him yesterday for the first time.

I mean, between the year 1866 and the present time. Had he been down to you?—I think not.

You think not?—I am certain of it.

Now, just tell me. When the Plaintiff came down to Hull, did you go with him from Hull to Burton Constable? What time did he get down, do you know—down to Hull? What train did he come by?—I do not know. I saw him in the morning. I do not remember when he came.

Did he come to you at once?—No, I went to see him.

Where was he? At the hotel?—At the hotel.

How far is that from Burton Constable?—Ten miles—between ten and eleven.

Well, then, you and he drove over there in the evening?—Yes.

I think you said it was late when you got there. Did you have anything to eat before you went over the house, or did you go over the house at once?—I think we had some sherry and biscuit. I cannot say whether it was before going over.

At all events, when you did go over the rooms it was dark?—It was, quite; we went with candles.

How many rooms are there at Burton Constable?—I cannot tell—a great many.

Well, thirty or forty?—Oh, more than that.

Well, you see, we do not know it, Sir TALBOT, as well as you do. More than thirty or forty rooms. And did you take him over a great number?—Yes.

Were they all lighted?—The only one that has that particular window is——

At that time it was dark. Had you no artificial light with you?—We went in with candles.

With ordinary candles?—Bed candles.

Into all the rooms?—Yes.

And then, as I understand you, the only room he recognized was the room that had been your room.—Yes.

When he was there staying in the year 1848, had he been in the habit of going into your room?—Oh, yes.

And he did seem to remember that one?—Yes.

Well, now, the next day, when you went over the rooms again, was it day or night?—Daytime.

It was daylight? Then, of course, you required no artificial light to see the rooms?—No.

And when he saw his own room by daylight, did he seem at once to recognize it, or not?—At once.

Did he point out anything particular about it?—The door where he used to go out and smoke.

Yes, I think you mentioned that originally in chief, and that was the fact, I think you said—that you used to go out there?—Yes.

Now about this hedge. There seems to have been something that you remember that was peculiar about leaving these stumps which made an impression upon you, which you have not quite explained to us all. What was there about the stumps that was peculiar?—Well, they were very unsightly. They did not look nice.

He himself, as I understand you, had cut down the hedge?—Yes.

And he had done it in some way or another so that he left these stumps in an unsightly way. Tell me this: was the hedge being entirely grubbed up or destroyed, or was it only cutting the hedge?—Only cutting.

Only cutting the hedge?—The top part.

The top part of the hedge. Then it was not, as my friend seemed to suggest, that the hedge was being grubbed up, or anything of that sort?—No, that was done afterwards.

But he had cut it in some clumsy or unskilful manner, and left these unsightly stumps?—Yes.

That you remember?—Certainly.

Do you know how many years after he left it was that these stumps were entirely removed?—I could not say.

Now then, about the theatricals: as I understand, although you won't positively swear, your own impression now is that he was right about where the theatricals were?—From what I have been told.

But I want to know whether you have any impression of your own. Apart from what you have been told, do you now think yourself that he is right?—I think he is.

Well, you have been about persons who may have been there; do you remember anybody at all who could have told him of the things he told you?—Not a soul.

You would know better than any of us whether there would be likely to be anybody there who could have informed him of these different things he mentioned?—I am certain there was no one.

PROCEEDINGS IN PARLIAMENT.

The friends of TICHBORNE were not idle in the political world, though there was this important and observable difference between their exertions and those of the Family—that the former never gained anything, but the latter were always successful. Several questions were asked in the House of Commons, but the Jesuits and Family were too powerful for the Ministers, in their then condition, to act with independence; and nothing came accordingly from these proceedings. We insert some examples here, as a specimen of the way in which Mr. GLADSTONE'S Cabinet thought it decent to behave, and with a comment, from one of the newspapers, leave the matter to our readers to form their own opinion.

THE TICHBORNE CLAIMANT.

Mr. G. ONSLOW presented a petition from 891 persons, resident in Tichborne, Alresford, Cheriton, and other places in Hampshire, which, on the motion of the hon. gentleman, was ordered to be read by the Clerk at the table. The petitioners stated that, it being the intention of the Government to prosecute the Claimant to the Tichborne Estates for perjury, at the public expense, and believing in the credibility of the said Claimant, which belief was, in their opinion, shared in by the great bulk of the public at large, and knowing him to be without pecuniary means for his defence, they submitted that if public money was supplied for his prosecution, it also should be provided for the defence: because the petitioners were informed that the case was one in which widely different opinions prevailed as to his right to the estates.

Mr. A. GUEST presented a petition from Poole on the same subject, which was also read by the Clerk at the table. The petition set forth that immediately adjoining the town of Poole was Upton, formerly the property of Sir EDWARD DOUGHTY; that ROGER C. TICHBORNE resided at Upton during the lifetime of Sir EDWARD DOUGHTY, and was known to a large number of persons living in Poole, including the petitioners, some of whom had already recognized the Claimant as the said ROGER CHARLES TICHBORNE, while others were prepared to swear to his identity; that the petitioners, from these and other facts within their knowledge, were apprehensive that, as the prisoner had no means of defence, the true facts of the case could not be known, and they therefore prayed that the House would take precaution that no advantage was afforded to the prosecution which was not in like manner afforded to the prisoner, in order that no public suspicion should exist that the said prisoner was liable to be crushed, at the public expense, by inveterate enemies.

Mr. GLADSTONE appears to have bound himself, body and soul, to the Jesuit Party, and to the Family; he was well aided by his satellites, Mr. BRUCE at first, and Mr. LOWE afterwards: the latter succeeding the former as Home Secretary; and each rivalling the other in rampant insolence to all friends of the Claimant. Lord RIPON, President of the Council, had become covertly a convert to Romanism, and no doubt instigated Mr. CHICHESTER FORTESCUE and Mr. CHILDERS to the parts which they subsequently played in this most horrible drama.

The following is the text of the Petition:—

COPY OF PETITION PRESENTED BY A. GUEST, ESQ., M.P. FOR POOLE.

To the Honourable the Knights, Citizens, and Burgesses of the United Kingdom of Great Britain and Ireland, in Parliament assembled.

The Petition of the undersigned, the inhabitants of the town and county of Poole and its neighbourhood, HUMBLY SHOWETH—

I. That immediately adjacent to the town and county of Poole, is the estate of Upton, formerly the property of Sir EDWARD DOUGHTY, Baronet, and now claimed by Sir ROGER CHARLES DOUGHTY TICHBORNE, recently consigned a prisoner to Newgate, and now confined therein.

II. That ROGER CHARLES DOUGHTY TICHBORNE resided at Upton during the lifetime of Sir EDWARD DOUGHTY, and was well known to many of the inhabitants of the town and county of Poole, and to some of your petitioners. That the prisoner now in Newgate has been recognized by numerous persons who were so acquainted with him at Poole, some of whom have sworn, whilst others are prepared to testify to his identity; and that such deponents are credible and respectable persons, in whom your petitioners have every confidence.

III. That the testimony of their fellow-residents, and other concurring and striking circumstances, lead your petitioners to the conclusion that the prisoner now in Newgate is identical with the ROGER CHARLES DOUGHTY TICHBORNE formerly resident in this locality.

IV. That your petitioners are informed and believe that the prisoner now in Newgate is about to be prosecuted for wilful and corrupt perjury, for swearing that he is the aforesaid ROGER CHARLES DOUGHTY TICHBORNE who formerly resided at Upton, near Poole. That they are informed and believe that such prosecution is to be conducted at the national cost, by Her Majesty's Attorney-General and other Counsel, who were opposed to the Claimant at the Trial. That your petitioners, from these and other facts within their knowledge, are apprehensive that, as the prisoner now in Newgate has no means at his command, the true facts of the Case may not be fully elicited.

Your petitioners therefore humbly pray that your honourable House will take due and proper precaution that no advantage shall be afforded to the Crown prosecutors in this Case which is not in like manner afforded to the prisoner now in Newgate, in order that no public suspicion may exist that the said prisoner, claiming to be and recognized as Sir ROGER CHARLES DOUGHTY TICHBORNE, is liable to be crushed, by the use of public means, at the instance of inveterate enemies or relatives, seeking to possess themselves of his inheritance.

And your petitioners will ever pray.

But Mr. GUEST appears to have been immediately frightened by what he did, for he at once published the letter that follows:—

PETITIONS IN THE TICHBORNE CASE.

TO THE EDITOR OF THE "STANDARD."

SIR,—As in the leading article of your publication of this evening, referring to the presentation of certain petitions in the House of Commons, relative to the Claimant to the Tichborne Estates, these words appear: "As the Claimant is not without friends who can write M.P. after their names, we may expect to hear more of the matter," permit me distinctly to state, that it was in the exercise of my duty to my constituents alone, that I presented the petition to which your article alludes.

I positively refused to move "that the petition be read by the Clerk at the table of the House," as by so doing I should have implied an agreement with its allegations and prayers.

I have no acquaintance of any kind whatever with the Claimant, and am not desirous of venturing an opinion as to whether he is or is not the person he represents himself to be.

The insertion of this in your next publication will oblige, Sir, your obedient servant, ARTHUR E. GUEST.

House of Commons, April 11.

The Southampton Committee sent the following petition, which was signed by 3,771 inhabitants, and presented by WILLIAM COWPER TEMPLE, M.P. for South Hants, on the 1st of August, and was *read* at the *table of the House*.

To the Honourable the Commons of the United Kingdom of Great Britain and Ireland, in Parliament assembled.

The humble Petition of the undersigned inhabitants of the town and county of Southampton, SHOWETH,

That your Petitioners are informed, and believe that the *prisoner now on bail*, under the names of TOMAS CASTRO, otherwise ARTHUR ORTON, otherwise Sir ROGER CHARLES DOUGHTY TICHBORNE, Bart., has been indicted, and is about to be tried and prosecuted for forgery, and also for wilful and corrupt perjury, for swearing that he is the ROGER CHARLES DOUGHTY TICHBORNE who formerly resided at Upton, near Poole. That they are informed, and it is well known, that such prosecution is to be conducted at the national cost, by Her Majesty's Attorney-General, and other Counsel, who were specially retained against and opposed to the said prisoner on bail, commonly known as the Claimant, at the recent trial of ejectment in the Court of Common Pleas; and that no fewer than six eminent Counsel have been retained to conduct the prosecution on the part of the *Crown*, also that witnesses are to be brought from distant countries, regardless, it is believed, of expense. That your petitioners, from these and other facts within their knowledge, are apprehensive and believe that, as the prisoner now on bail has not sufficient means at his command commensurate with those of the prosecution, the *true facts* of the Case may not, *and cannot be* fully elicited.

Your petitioners therefore humbly pray that your honourable House will take due and proper precaution that no advantage shall be afforded to the Crown prosecutors in this Case, which is not in like manner accorded to the prisoner now on bail, in order that no public suspicion may exist that the said prisoner, claiming to be and *recognized* as Sir ROGER CHARLES DOUGHTY TICHBORNE, is liable to be crushed by the use of the *public purse*, without having means at his own disposal properly to defend himself.

And your petitioners deeply deplore the exhibition of so much animosity, rancour, and personal feeling on the *part of Her Majesty's Attorney-General* against the Claimant, especially in having personally opposed his admission to bail, believing such conduct calculated to excite the gravest suspicions, and a tendency to swerve the scales of Justice; therefore humbly trust and pray that your honourable House will, in its wisdom, see the propriety of enacting that the *Law Officers* of the *Crown* be henceforth disqualified from private practice whilst in office.

And your petitioners will ever pray, &c.

But every Petition was laughed at or despised.

We print a report of what took place on the 8th of April, 1872:—

THE PROSECUTION OF THE CLAIMANT.

Mr. NEVILLE-GRENVILLE asked the Attorney-General whether it was a fact that *six* learned Counsel were retained to prosecute a prisoner now in Newgate charged with perjury; if so, whether it was necessary or usual to employ so many lawyers in a Criminal Case; and, further, whether it was the intention of the Government to maintain the system of disallowing the expenses of prosecution in the provinces.

The Attorney-General: With regard to this somewhat complicated question, it is true that the number of Counsel to the extent indicated in my hon. friend's question have been retained and will be employed in the prosecution of the various cases that will arise out of the several indictments preferred against the person who has lately laid claim to the estates of the TICHBORNE Family, if the bills containing these indictments should be found to be true bills by the grand jury at the Old Bailey in the course of the present week. My hon. friend has not mentioned the name of the person, but I assume that is what is meant by the question. If it is not, I am unable to answer the question, and I have no means of procuring the information he desires. On the assumption that this is the question, he goes on to ask me whether it is necessary or usual to employ so many lawyers in a criminal case. But as I am not raising a question, but only answering one, I will not say anything about the language in which it is couched, except that in coming from him to me it might be improved. In reply to him, I may say, that I should have thought that the slightest reflection would have shown my hon. friend that the proper answer is dependent on the nature of the case, for what might be proper in one might be extremely improper in another. When he asks me whether it is necessary and usual to take a particular course in such a criminal case, I have to say that I cannot tell him, because I do not know from my reading, and have no experience, after 25 years' practice at the bar, of any case resembling this, or one which could be deemed a fair precedent to it. It is not the difficulty of the case, because, as I have always said, it is extremely simple, *because it is an insult on the common sense of mankind*. (Oh, oh.) From the enormous mass of the case there is an amount of papers and details of which no one who has not the misfortune to be engaged in it can have the slightest notion. I suppose my hon. friend has not the slightest idea of the subject-matter himself, from the manner in which he has put the question; but I can say for myself, that without the incalculable invaluable assistance I have received from my colleagues, it would have been perfectly impossible for persons even superior to myself to put the case in an intelligible manner before the jury. I do think that it is necessary that the Counsel should be retained and employed as they have been retained and will be employed. They have been retained on my responsibility and under my directions. I was accepted, with the sanction of the Government, to perform the duty cast upon me by the Lord Chief Justice of the Common Pleas of prosecuting, and that duty I shall endeavour to discharge to the best of my ability so long as I hold my office; and I shall take the steps I think proper for discharging it with success, because I believe it to be a duty in the proper discharge of which the whole of society are deeply interested. (Cries of "Order.") With regard to the latter part of the question, I can only say that there has been a debate already on the subject, and the matter is under the consideration of the Government, but it is a matter with which the Attorney-General has nothing more to do than my hon. friend himself.

Nearly the same conduct was repeated a day or two after:—

PROSECUTION OF THE TICHBORNE CLAIMANT.

Mr. ONSLOW asked the Chancellor of the Exchequer whether he would state to the House the reason why the Government intended to use the public money for the purpose of prosecuting the Claimant to the Tichborne Estates, and why in the case of OVEREND and GURNEY they refused to prosecute, on the ground of its being a private matter. (Hear, hear.)

The Chancellor of the Exchequer (Mr. LOWE):—Mr. Speaker, I will answer the last part of the question of the hon. gentleman first, for a reason that will appear presently. It appears that the First Lord of the Treasury and the Attorney-General in 1869 defended the conduct of the Government with regard to the refusal to prosecute Messrs. OVEREND and GURNEY with reference to three principles or tests which they applied. The first of the tests was this, Was there likely to be a conviction? The second was, What was the moral turpitude of the offence charged? And third, Was or was it not likely that if the Government did not prosecute private persons would come forward and prosecute? They argued in that case that Messrs. OVEREND and GURNEY had not been guilty of any great degree of moral turpitude. (Oh, oh, and laughter.) They argued that such offences were unhappily very common in the commercial world—(laughter, loud cries of "Oh, oh," and "Order")—the difference being that in this case these practices—which of course no one can defend—had been productive of very widespread ruin. (Hear, hear.) They argued also that these were offences on the confines of civil and criminal law, where private and public crime were hardly distinguishable from each other, and that it was scarcely likely under the circumstances that a conviction would be obtained, and that if they did not prosecute there were plenty of persons possessed of sufficient means to institute a prosecution of their own. And they were so far borne out in the result that a prosecution did take place, and the Defendants were acquitted. Now I propose to answer the question of the hon. gentleman with regard to the prosecution of the Claimant in the TICHBORNE Case with reference to these three principles. But I must state, in the first place, that there is one thing which entirely distinguishes this case from the OVEREND and GURNEY and most other public prosecutions, and it is that this prosecution was not instituted or suggested originally by the Government, but was directed, under the powers given him by Act of Parliament, by the Lord Chief Justice of the Common Pleas. (Hear, hear.) That is a very different thing from saying that we should commence the prosecution or refuse to give assistance out of the public funds. I will go a little further into the matter. In the first place, I may say, without prejudicing the case, that there is every reason to expect the conviction of the Claimant, for this reason—that the Claimant was the principal witness himself, and that the jury stopped the Case, mentioning as one ground that they did not believe a particular fact, implying in effect that they did not believe what had been sworn to by the Claimant—namely, the absence of the tattoo marks. There is, moreover, the finding of a true bill by the grand jury. Then comes the question of moral guilt. If it should turn out that this person is guilty of what is charged against him, it is difficult to imagine a greater degree of moral turpitude. If the Claimant be guilty, he is guilty of seeking, not by misrepresentation, such as was charged in the case of OVEREND and GURNEY, but by wilful and corrupt perjury on the most gigantic scale, to deprive the helpless infant of his inheritance—(cheers)—and of seeking to take away by false statements the character of a most respectable and honourable lady. (General cheering.) Lastly, if he be guilty, in the prosecution of these guilty ends, he has caused a great amount of inconvenience and disturbance to the public service—(laughter)—and therefore I think that, having regard to the magnitude of the offence, there can be no doubt that the Government are perfectly justified in coming forward to prosecute in this Case. (Hear, hear.) I am not over anxious to embark the public money in that prosecution, but I can only say I give my hearty assent to the prosecution. (Cheers.) If we did not prosecute the Case, the very complexity of the machinations of the Claimant would turn out to be his defence, for by the enormous expense he has caused to the Family, it might put it out of their power to incur further expense in bringing him to justice. It is hardly to be supposed that a family which has suffered so much should come forward for the sake of the public, to bring the Claimant to justice. (Hear, hear.) These are the reasons why I think the assistance of the Government should be given to the prosecution, and I hope it will be understood, that I entirely concur with the Attorney-General in the propriety of the course he has followed. (Cheers.)

Mr. HERMON said: In consequence of the answer given by the Chancellor of the Exchequer, I give notice that on a future day I will ask him for the names of those firms which have been guilty of commercial dishonesty to which he made allusion. (Oh, oh.)

The Chancellor of the Exchequer: I stated what was the purport of the defence made by the Government in 1869. I stated no opinion of my own. If the hon. gentleman will refer to the speech of the Attorney-General in 1869, he will see the words to which he seems to object. I entirely decline to be drawn into a controversy on the subject, as I did not use the words on my own responsibility. When I spoke of the Attorney-General, of course I alluded to the Attorney-General of that day. (Cheers and laughter.)

The following, which occurred May 2, 1872, is another instance of Mr. LOWE's conduct and insolence:—

PROSECUTION OF THE CLAIMANT.

Mr. MELLOR asked the Chancellor of the Exchequer whether the Government intend to prosecute at the public expense the person calling himself TICHBORNE for perjury? and if so, whether he is prepared to lay before the House an estimate of the probable cost of such prosecution, and to take a previous vote of the House upon it. (Hear, hear.)

The Chancellor of the Exchequer: It is the intention of the Government to prosecute, at the public expense, a person calling himself TICHBORNE, for perjury, he also having been committed for forgery. The hon. gentleman asks me to lay an estimate on the table of the expense. I should be glad to do so; but as I am informed, it is impossible to make one, I must decline to do so, under the circumstances. I can only refer hon. gentlemen to their own experience, if they have been engaged in law. (A laugh.)

Mr. MELLOR: The right honourable gentleman has not answered the last part of my question as to whether he will take a previous vote of the House on the question.

The Chancellor of the Exchequer: If I spend the money first, how can I take a previous vote? (Laughter.)

THE TICHBORNE CASE.

Mr. WHALLEY gave notice that on the reassembling of the House he would ask the Attorney-General, with reference to the TICHBORNE Case, to afford some explanation of the grounds on which—assuming the evidence as to the tattoo marks is reliable—it is necessary to incur the delay and the great expenditure involved in the course of proceeding adopted by the Government; also, whether in advising the Government to provide the funds for this prosecution due consideration was given to the circumstance that the tattoo marks were well known, as now appears, to members of the Family when the offence of perjury was first committed, many years since, and that no satisfactory explanation has been given why the Claimant was not then prosecuted.

THE TICHBORNE CASE.

Mr. WHALLEY rose to call attention to the TICHBORNE Prosecution, and to ask the Chancellor of the Exchequer whether he would instruct the Solicitor of the Treasury to investigate such evidence as might be brought to his notice, with a view to providing the means of bringing forward the same on the trial, in the event of its appearing to him to be material either on the part of the prosecution or of the defence. There had been very large meetings at Millwall, Newcastle-upon-Tyne, and other places on this subject, and there were many other places which had desired to hold meetings. He held that the Claimant was an injured, and a persecuted man. It was impossible for him to be heard unless adequate means were provided. He was convinced, from circumstances within his knowledge, that this man was not an impostor, but that he was the man he professed to be. He said this, although he had been warned from mixing himself up with the Claimant. Still, there must be a large proportion of the House who would feel that the conclusion should not be come to that the Claimant was guilty until he had been tried. That was the opinion expressed by multitudes who were earnest in their views, and had formed them deliberately. The people of this country would not be doing their duty if they should allow the Claimant to be prosecuted at the expense of the public, when he had no means of defence. He should like to know whether the charge about the tattoo marks had been abandoned. He admitted the power of the speech of the Attorney-General on this question, but there were some portions of it which it was not very easy to understand. He had received a letter from the Solicitor of the Treasury, declining to make the investigation asked, and he had now to put the question of which he had given notice to the Chancellor of the Exchequer.

The Chancellor of the Exchequer, in reply, said that if it came to pass that this House should set itself up as a Court of Appeal against the judgment of a Court and the verdict of a jury, the effect would be a great scandal to public justice, and as the hon. gentleman had admitted that the Claimant was in possession of sufficient funds to conduct his own defence, the hon. gentleman should not have made any such application. No such direction would be given to the Solicitor of the Treasury as the question of the hon. gentleman pointed at.

The House then went into committee of supply, and immediately resumed.

These discussions drew forth the following observations from a paper of great power and ability, and which has always adhered most consistently to the Claimant's cause:—

Reynolds's Newspaper.

Mr. LOWE, the Chancellor of the Exchequer, prides himself, we believe, on being a logician as well as a humourist. He is prepared to give what appears to himself, but, perhaps, not to others, a valid reason for everything he does. He never would admit that his famous Match-Box imposition was a mistake; but attributed its compulsory withdrawal to the ignorance, the perversity, the mental obliquity, and the financial ignorance of the masses of the people. On Tuesday night he was fairly brought to bay by Mr. GUILDFORD ONSLOW, who asked him some very ugly questions respecting the prosecution by Government of the TICHBORNE Claimant.

In the first place, Mr. LOWE argues that the Government should not prosecute unless it *feels* pretty certain of a conviction. How happened it, then, that in the BOULTON and PARK business the Government vigorously prosecuted at first, then relaxed in its energies, and ultimately let the Defendants slip through their hands? And this after thousands of public money had been expended on the case! Surely the law officers must have been very obtuse, or the Government gave way under the pressure of influences that we know not of. There was never a stronger *primâ facie* case of fraud made out than that brought against Messrs. OVEREND and GURNEY, and up to the last moment it was very doubtful whether they would be found innocent or guilty. And yet here the Government refused to prosecute, although Mr. LOWE admits that the practices of which the accused had been guilty, and which *ruined* thousands and tens of thousands of people, were indefensible.

In the second place, Mr. LOWE, like the Attorney-General, assumes the positive guilt of the Claimant, and that, because he is *not* tattooed, as the original ROGER is said to have been. *That* is the precise point we want to arrive at, and most assuredly the evidence on the subject is as yet far from conclusive or satisfactory. Nevertheless, had not the public come forward with funds to assist him, the Claimant's case was clearly hopeless, simply because he was utterly destitute of the means of prosecuting it. The TICHBORNE Family which, as Mr. LOWE alleges, has already "incurred such enormous expenses," had a fine property, producing something like Twenty-three Thousand per annum, as a resource to fall back upon for its defence. They were allowed by Vice-Chancellor STEWART to draw at will upon the revenues of the estate, so as to enable the infant baronet to protect what he alleges are his rights thereto. If, therefore, the Tattooing question is to be considered as settling the question of identity, and as that matter has certainly not been fully elucidated, why, if either party had a claim upon the Government for pecuniary aid in prosecuting it to a satisfactory solution, it was the *penniless* Plaintiff, not the wealthy Defendant.

"But," says the Chancellor of the Exchequer, "if it should turn out that this person is guilty of what is charged against him, it is difficult to imagine a greater degree of moral turpitude. If he is guilty, he is guilty of seeking, not by misrepresentation such as was charged in the case of OVEREND and GURNEY, but by wilful and corrupt perjury on a most gigantic scale, to deprive a helpless infant of its inheritance, and of seeking to take away, by false swearing, the honour and character of a most respectable and honourable lady. Lastly, if he be guilty, he has, in the prosecution of these guilty ends, produced an amount of inconvenience and disturbance to the public service."

Has Mr. LOWE already forgotten, or does he choose to ignore the fact, that the suspicious smash did not only ruin one "helpless infant," but hundreds—caused several persons to commit suicide—probably drove many women to prostitution, and most unquestionably beggared thousands who had previously enjoyed comfort, if not affluence? The failure of this firm was a great National calamity—it inflicted a severe blow on our Commercial credit—and, by causing the suspension of many other banks and business houses, created a far greater amount of "inconvenience and disturbance" to the public than the prosecution of the Claimant's suit can have done to the "public service." The latter is merely a private matter, which Justice BOVILL, at the instigation of Sir J. COLERIDGE, has converted into a public prosecution. The lawyers, like hungry vultures, sniffing the scent of blood, smell heavy costs on both sides; and thousands of the public money are to be expended in investigating a matter in which they have no material interest. Mr. LOWE's explanation was as illogical as it must be, to all thinking persons, unsatisfactory. To the question why public funds are expended on a private family affair, he only vouchsafed a homily on commercial rascality in general, and the Claimant's presumed iniquity in particular.

The dissatisfaction thus expressed was not confined to England, it passed to the Antipodes; and we find it thus embodied in an Australian newspaper, the *Geelong Advertiser*:—

THE CLAIMANT'S CASE.

There can be no doubt that in the minds of a very large proportion of the public, British Justice is under a cloud, owing to the manner in which the Counsel to one of the parties in the great TICHBORNE Trial has mixed up his public and official duties as one of the law advisers of the Crown, with the pecuniary interests of one of his private clients. It is very widely felt, that but for the fact of the present Attorney-General having been so deeply committed to the theory of the Claimant's imposture, the Treasury would never have adopted the unparalleled course of employing *six* eminent Counsel, four of them silk gownsmen, to prosecute a prisoner charged with the comparatively unimportant offence of perjury.

Some slight retrospect of the manner in which this case has hitherto been conducted, certainly seems to point to one of two conclusions—either that Sir J. COLERIDGE, or, at all events, those who instructed him, believed in the genuineness of the claim set up by the man that was in Newgate, or else that he and they had determined to make of the imposture a harvest for themselves at the expense of the estate. Of course, it would be doing so eminently pious and conscientious a lawyer as Sir J. COLERIDGE an injustice to adopt either hypothesis; yet it is not to be wondered at, that they are accepted by many people, when we remember that to reject them lands us in the difficulty of believing that the Attorney-General of England could not conduct an ordinary suit with anything approaching common-sense. For thus stands the case: Sir J. D. COLERIDGE knew the genuine Sir ROGER was tattooed, and yet, although he might have had the Claimant examined in the Court of Chancery years ago, he preferred to conceal his knowledge, while he allowed this infamous impostor to raise money from a credulous public, and the infant, for whom he appeals so pathetically, to be robbed of a quarter of a million of money, on a Trial which was altogether unnecessary.

On this point there can be no doubt. If Mrs. RADCLIFFE, Mrs. NANGLE, Mr. DANBY SEYMOUR, Madame CHATILLON, and the rest, really knew of the tattoo marks at the time they swore to them, they must equally have known of them at the time the claim was first raised, and the examination of the prisoner's arm could have been made quite as satisfactorily in the Court of Chancery as in the Westminster Sessions House. It is therefore most astounding, that this secret, known to so many people, was so well kept; although, perhaps, it is even more wonderful, that a knowledge of the facts was confined to so few. Most assuredly, if any writer of fiction had dared to trace a plot in which a dozen persons, some of them mere casual acquaintances, not only knew that one of the characters in his story was tattooed, but knew also, from internal consciousness, that the mother, the valet, and the regimental servant of the individual were ignorant of the seemingly notorious fact, he would have been accused of outraging probabilities. For here, again, among all the quicksands of the Case, we are on firm ground.

If this claim be an imposture, it *must* also be a conspiracy, and among the parties to the conspiracy must be numbered BOGLE, MOORE, and CARTER; while the Dowager Lady TICHBORNE, if not an absolute conspirator, was at least a ready tool in the hands of the others. Yet we are now asked to believe that the real ROGER walked about, pulling up his coat-sleeve, to exhibit his tattoo marks, on the most *unlikely* occasions, and yet carefully concealed their existence from his Mother, and from the men whose duty it was for years to assist him to dress. For, presuming MOORE and CARTER to be conspirators, it is certain if they had known of the tattoo marks on the arm of ROGER TICHBORNE, the same marks might easily have been forthcoming on the arm of the Claimant; yet not only were they ignorant of their existence, but the other side all along confidently assumed their ignorance.

It is unnecessary for us at this moment to point out the discrepancies in this tattoo evidence. How one witness swore to the emblems of Faith, Hope, and Charity; another to the letters "R. C. T.;" how one swore they were executed by Lord BELLEW, another that they were the work of a sailor in Brittany, and yet another that they were done at sea; how one witness swore he saw them when he pulled up his sleeve to gather water-lilies, although common-sense suggests this sleeve would be the right one, while the marks were on the left arm; or how another remarked them through ROGER's anxiety to conceal them. This will be Mr. MONTAGU WILLIAMS's task at the coming Trial; for us, it is sufficient to say, there is evidently perjury and conspiracy somewhere; that the public mind is divided as to which is the guilty side, and that, therefore, if the Government is to interfere at all, in a purely private suit, it should be solely with a view to see that justice is done.

Can it be said by anyone that the course pursued by the Attorney-General has been actuated by any such motive? Has he not, on the contrary, strained his official powers to the utmost, to treat the Claimant with unfairness? Has he not even abused his position as a representative of the people, by making partisan speeches in the House of Commons, in which he has so far forgotten the spirit of English law as to describe the necessary defence of a man awaiting his trial for a criminal offence, but as yet unconvicted, as "an insult to common-sense?" Then, too, how is it possible, on any ground of fairness or justice, to understand the proceedings with reference to bail? The Lord Chief Justice, when he committed the Claimant for perjury, could only have done so on the ground that he was not Sir ROGER TICHBORNE, yet he fixed the bail at an amount reasonable enough for a wealthy and high-born baronet, but out of all reason for the son of a Wapping butcher. Then the bail, instead of having to swear to their sufficient solvency according to the universal practice in such cases, were required to submit to a perfectly inquisitorial inspection of all their affairs. Even this being insufficient to damp the enthusiasm of his friends, a second count was added to the indictment, without notice, and then the Judge refused to accept bail at all.

Now, be it understood, we are by no means expressing any opinion as to the truth or falsehood of the Claimant's case, but we do say, that the conduct pursued by the Bench, and by many members of the Press, is a disgrace to the country. All we have to do is to see justice done, and to protest against the national funds being misappropriated for the benefit of the Attorney-General's private clients. On these grounds, then, we cordially hope the public will respond liberally to the Claimant's appeal for a defence fund; and if he be, as many of those who should know best believe, the real Sir ROGER TICHBORNE, we trust he will yet prove his title to name, rank, and estates. In this latter event, by the way, we fancy that not a few people will be ready to exclaim, that the conduct of Sir J. D. COLERIDGE has been the real "insult to common-sense."

Nor was this the only animadversion on the Case which this widely-circulating paper published. We transcribe in their order of date, June 28, July 2, and July 16, the following comments:—

The Geelong Advertiser, Friday, June 28, 1872.

ANOTHER LINK IN THE TICHBORNE-CUM-ORTON CASE.

The articles which appeared in *The Mercury*, copied from the London *Standard*, in which the career of ARTHUR ORTON was traced, having come under the notice of Mr. KNIGHT, of this city (Hobart Town), he has furnished us with the following particulars of his knowledge of ORTON whilst in this colony. Mr. KNIGHT, who carried on business in Murray-street, is the butcher referred to in the *Standard* article with whom ORTON found employment on his arrival in Hobart Town. Mr. KNIGHT, who carried on business for nearly twenty years in this city, states that ORTON was in his employ either in 1854 or '55, and remained with him up to the time of his leaving the colony to proceed to the service of Mr. FORSTER, of Gippsland, Victoria. The statement as to his having taken a butcher's shop in the New Market is, Mr. KNIGHT thinks, erroneous, as he left for Gippsland immediately on quitting his employment at Mr. KNIGHT's. During ORTON's period of service with Mr. KNIGHT, the latter had many conversations with him regarding his birth, and the course of life which he had led. In these conversations, ORTON told Mr. KNIGHT that he had first come to this colony with a consignment of Shetland ponies for Mr. T. D. CHAPMAN, of Tasmania. His brother in London imported these ponies from the Shetland Islands. His father was, he said, a butcher in Wapping, and it was by this means that he became acquainted with the butchering business. ORTON stated that he had been at Valparaiso, in South America, and knew the use of the lasso, it having been employed there by him in catching buffaloes and wild cattle. He told Mr. KNIGHT that he arrived by the ship "Middleton." Mr. KNIGHT, who is a retired pedestrian, and has been a very fair specimen of what is known as a "sporting butcher," says that when ORTON was in his service, he matched him to fight for £10 a-side, with a man known as "BOB BELL, the Cabman." Mr. KNIGHT was a connoisseur in the selection of likely pedestrians and promising aspirants for the distinctions of the prize-ring, and his close study of the physique of ORTON, when judging of his chances of success with his cab-driving adversary, would, he says, enable him to identify him anywhere. This prize-fight, however, did not come off, the "articles" not being completed; the first deposit of £5 a-side was eventually withdrawn. The money was staked with a Mr. MATTHEW WILKES, publican, of the White Conduit House, Murray-street. Mr. KNIGHT had, he says, many opportunities of observing closely the person of ORTON, as he often saw him stripped when using the dumb-bells and boxing-gloves, in both of which exercises he was very proficient. He was not a good butcher, and could not be trusted with "slaughtering work," only inferior jobs at butchering being given to him. In fact, according to our informant, he was more reliable as a "bruiser" than a butcher. As bearing upon ORTON's weight, when in Mr. KNIGHT's employ, one of the conditions of the fight, as arranged, was, that he was not to exceed 12 stone on the day fixed for the encounter. Mr. KNIGHT says he could identify ORTON by his mouth, which was much shattered and out of shape, a circumstance which ORTON accounted for by stating that he had frequent falls from horses. Although a young man at the time spoken of, ORTON had not a sound tooth in his head. Mr. KNIGHT says he could recognize ORTON from among a thousand others, by the peculiar disfigurement of his mouth.—*Mercury.*

The Geelong Advertiser, July 2, 1872.

Respecting the TICHBORNE Claimant, the *Hay Standard* says that "JOE MADDEN, the horse-trainer, who is now in this town, rode the mail between Hay and Wagga, along with TOM CASTRO for some two years. MADDEN's opinion of him is, that he is TICHBORNE. They used to meet and sleep in the same hut one night a week. At that time CASTRO had a silver drinking-flask, with the initials or name of R. C. D. TICHBORNE engraved on it, and a crest, which MADDEN had drunk out of. Once a man, shorter than CASTRO, came to the hut, and inquired for CASTRO, and they recognized each other, and CASTRO told MADDEN that the man was called ARTHUR ORTON. The hair of the two was within a shade of the same colour. MADDEN was seen by MACKENZIE, the agent for the defence, while in Australia, whom he told that CASTRO and ORTON were different individuals. We understand that afterwards Mr. MACKENZIE abandoned the theory that CASTRO and ORTON were identical; if ever he did so, the theory must have been re-adopted, as the averment that CASTRO is ORTON seems the most crushing point against the Claimant.

"CORNELIUS M'CLINCHY" writes as follows to the editor of the *Geelong Guardian*:—

SIR,—Observing in your issue of Wednesday a paragraph relative to ARTHUR ORTON and his whereabouts, will you please to allow me, through your columns, to state I was steward on board the ship "Middleton," Captain STORIE, Commander, on her voyage in 1853, leaving Torbay 10th January, and arriving in Hobart Town on the 1st day of May. On board of this vessel was the said ARTHUR ORTON, in charge of two Shetland ponies. In all there were but five passengers. Upon the ship's arrival at Hobart Town I obtained my discharge, and crossed to Victoria. ORTON at the time was about 21 or 22 years old, 5 feet 9 or 10 inches high, light brown hair, and blue eyes. Having been 105 days in his company, I feel certain, under any circumstances, I could identify him again. If I can render any service by information, I shall be happy to give the same.

The Geelong Advertiser, July 16, 1872.

COMMENTS ON THE TICHBORNE CLAIMANT.

The English journals, received by the last mail, teem with adverse comments on the TICHBORNE Claimant, who was at the time awaiting his trial for perjury. Looking at it from this distance, and away from the excitement caused by the late Trial, it seems an outrage on British justice, that a man should be so universally condemned, while his case in the criminal court is *sub judice*. He is branded with every epithet short of absolute obscenity, to be found in the vocabulary of abuse; and yet up to that time, he was merely a "nonsuited" Plaintiff. The law had actually left him power to commence his action again. In New South Wales, whatever shortcomings may be ours, the Press, as a rule, abstain from all comments on either civil or criminal cases until a decision has been arrived at. The Judges of our courts have always enforced this golden rule on the consideration of the Press, and invariably with success. It seems to us, therefore, the more atrocious—and we offer no opinion as to whether the Claimant is a perjurer or not—that the "whole ear" of England should be prejudiced in this way. According to the strict rules on which juries are empanelled, it seems an impossibility that one sufficiently impartial to try the case should be obtained in England.

There was at this period, however, a party in Parliament so rampantly the followers of the GLADSTONE policy with respect to the TICHBORNE Case, that it required the very highest moral courage to face them. They were fierce, furious—almost bloodthirsty. They did not hesitate at any falsehood or corruption in the interests of the Jesuits and the Family. A specimen may be seen in the following report, which we preserve as a curious record of insolence, intolerance, and servility to the Powerful. Taken with what has preceded it, it carries us back to the very worst spirit of the very worst times.

THE PROSECUTION OF THE CLAIMANT.

In the House of Commons, on August 9, Mr. WHALLEY presented a petition from the inhabitants of Nottingham, praying that steps should be taken to secure a fair trial for the Claimant. The petition, on Mr. WHALLEY's motion, was read by the Clerk at the table.

At a later period of the same sitting, Mr. WHALLEY rose to move for a copy of all applications made to the Secretary of State for the Home Department or to the Solicitor of the Treasury as to providing the means for the Defendant in the case of "The QUEEN v. CASTRO," *alias* TICHBORNE, to bring forward witnesses in his defence, and for such information as to the evidence that would be brought forward in support of the prosecution as the Defendant would have been entitled to receive if he had been committed for trial by any other process than that of the order of a Judge at Nisi Prius; together with the replies that have been made to such applications.

The hon. member was interrupted in his preliminary explanations by

Mr. R. GURNEY, who said he desired to protest against the return being made, and described it as scandalous, and as intended to prejudice the case with the public, and forward the efforts made to obtain pecuniary assistance to enable the Claimant to defend himself in the pending prosecution.

Mr. WHALLEY, referring to this interruption, said he had stumped the country on behalf of the Claimant, and would beg from door to door to obtain funds for him to insure his obtaining a fair trial, being as satisfied as he was of his own existence that the Claimant was rightfully entitled to the Tichborne Estates. He then proceeded to state that the correspondence to which his motion referred, and which he desired should be brought to the knowledge of the House, consisted of three or four letters that had passed between himself and the Solicitor to the Treasury, at the suggestion, he might say, so far as he was concerned, of the Government. Speaking in that House, the Chancellor of the Exchequer, it would be remembered, commented with his customary grace on the questions which he addressed to him, terming them absurd and ridiculous, and referred him to the officer in charge of the prosecution; and on one occasion called upon him to read a letter he had received from that officer; and it was the object of his motion that not only one letter, but the entire correspondence should be made public. His motion also included memorials from several large towns which had been received by the Home Secretary, supporting the application which he had thus made to the Solicitor to the Treasury. The question raised in the correspondence and memorials was whether the defendant was to have a fair trial or not, and the reply which had been given was to the effect that he must depend for that upon the liberality of the public in providing the requisite funds for bringing forward his witnesses and conducting his Case in the forthcoming Trial; the Chancellor of the Exchequer expressly stating that the contributions of the public might be expected to provide such means. Now, it was not his intention to reargue the question. The public had been invited at public meetings and otherwise to comply with this requirement, and he trusted the appeal would be successful. He again declared, and did so with regret, that he thought the Government had given their sanction to an agitation which might lead to results which they did not anticipate. Their decision, he presumed, was irrevocable; but what he did ask was that the grounds of that decision should be placed fully before the public, in order that justice might be done in this respect as well as otherwise: that the public might know on what grounds it was formed, and what was the justification on the part of the defendant for this exceptional appeal to public sympathy and support. He was fully conscious that the feeling of the House was averse from hearing anything about this Case until it again came before a court of law, and, though quite ready to place at the service of the Attorney-General any amount of money he might demand for his Counsel and his witnesses, it was declined to make any inquiry or to listen to any arguments about the Case itself, treating it, in fact—as the Chancellor of the Exchequer insisted it ought to be treated—as an ordinary trial, with which alone the courts of justice had to deal. But he ventured to point out and to insist it was not an ordinary case, inasmuch as the prosecution itself was originated, and the management of it and the expenditure of the public money upon it were intrusted to the Attorney-General. He had no interest in the matter, but having some property in the neighbourhood, and not having a shadow of doubt that the Claimant was the man he represented himself to be, he had taken up his cause. The serious question before the House was whether it ought to give money to prosecute this man on the information before the country, and on the authority solely of a month's speech from the Attorney-General.

Mr. Mundella here rose to order, and addressing the Speaker, asked whether he thought the time of the House should be occupied in the discussion of such a subject.

Mr. Whalley continued. He submitted that he had a perfect right, as a member of that House, to discuss the question in an assembly called on to vote money for the purposes of a prosecution, the more so as the Attorney-General's strongly prejudiced view had influenced the Government.

Mr. Bruce rose to order. The conduct of the hon. gentleman was, in his opinion, to say the least of it, most indecorous. Over and over again he had stated what was not the fact, that the House of Commons was called on to spend money at the bidding of the Attorney-General. The fact was his hon. and learned friend had nothing whatever to do with it. The prosecution was ordered by the learned Judge who presided at the trial of the cause. It was not right that these misstatements should be made; and as to the guilt or innocence of the party, that was a mere question of argument, and would have to be decided hereafter by an impartial tribunal.

The Speaker could not say exactly the hon. gentleman was out of order, but in his opinion it was more a question of propriety. (Hear, hear.)

Mr. R. N. Fowler here moved that the House be counted, and 40 members being found present on a second counting of the House,

Mr. Whalley resumed. He contended that he was interrupted by the right hon. gentleman the Secretary of State for the Home Department in a most unprecedented manner. He said he made no misstatements, but he had no hesitation in saying that in this particular Case the Attorney-General acted in a manner not worthy his personal character. (Order, order.) He repeated that charge against the hon. and learned gentleman. Although a public officer, bound to exercise his office solely with a view to the public interests involved, it was impossible but to regard him as having

RIGHT HON. H. A. BRUCE, M.P., now Lord Aberdare, Home Secretary under Mr. Gladstone.

also his own personal feelings, and, to no slight degree, his professional position and conduct, involved in the result of this prosecution. It would, he submitted, be no answer to their constituents, who might demand the reason for the expenditure of this money, to say that they took no heed of the merits of the question, having left all such considerations to the Attorney-General; because the Attorney-General, by the unusual—indeed, the unprecedented—course he adopted, had made himself to a great degree personally responsible for the conviction of the Defendant for the offences with which he charged him during the recent Trial in the Court of Common Pleas. As he, for one, considered that he was doing his duty in watching over the public expenditure in this Case, he did not hesitate to repeat, with the same confidence with which the Attorney-General spoke elsewhere, that the Defendant was innocent of the charges made against him, and he pledged his character for a due regard to the public interests as freely as the Attorney-General, entirely impartial as he was in the matter, to this declaration, that the Defendant was the man he claimed to be, and was not therefore guilty of the charges which, at so vast an outlay, were being pressed against him. The correspondence he moved for would to some extent show the ground for that opinion, and also the means by which the fact itself could be established by evidence of the most conclusive character. He said that in refusing to discuss this Case the House incurred the risk of wasting the public money in the prosecution, and sanctioning a course of agitation from which no other result could arise than a want of confidence in the just administration of the law. To suppose that the public had before them the materials for a safe opinion in the month's speech of the Attorney-General, with not a word of reply, was, indeed, to use the language of the Chancellor of the Exchequer, absurd and ridiculous, and as this correspondence would also show, he believed, that the Tattoo evidence which closed that speech was not now relied upon, and therefore was itself, like a false *alibi*, conclusive evidence against those who brought it forward. He submitted that the Government would do well to consent to its being published, and if not that the House itself should to this extent relieve itself from the responsibility of these proceedings by giving its assent to his motion. (Cheers.)

Mr. STACPOOLE seconded the motion.

Mr. H. JAMES did not rise to say one word with regard to the guilt or innocence of the person chiefly concerned in this matter. He considered that it was most unbecoming for any member of that House to declare he believed that any person awaiting his trial was either guilty or innocent. (Hear, hear.) Whilst the Government had to deal with this matter in the manner they thought best, there was a view of the question which ought to be taken by the independent members. If it was deemed right by certain members to wander all over the country in carriages of their own providing, as a matter of money speculation; to stand by the side of a man, who had himself admitted he could not answer questions because they would tend to criminate him: to stand by him whilst he used indecent epithets towards the Attorney-General, and took part in charging the jury with having been bribed, the House could do no more than regret that such proceedings occurred; but when the House was sought to be made the means and the arena for continuing them, when they were asked to listen to opinions of a prisoner's guilt or innocence, which had never or never could have been done by the English House of Commons—simply because the man in question had personal friends in the House—then he thought the time had come when the House should protest against their being made parties to such a transaction. They could not prevent the member for Peterborough by the rules of the House, or the rules which were more binding on some men, namely, those of taste and propriety, from introducing such matters, yet they could by their silence or even by their words show the public that they at least took no part in what out of doors was a mountebank performance and in-doors was an insult to the House and the country generally. (Hear, hear.)

Mr. BRUCE said the documents which the hon. member asked for consisted of two memorials, one from Southampton and the other from West Hartlepool, asking the Government to comply with his recommendations. He was much mistaken if he did not recognize in these memorials the Roman—(Laughter)—hand of hon. member for Peterborough. They emanated from the hon. gentleman, and he did not see how they could serve the interests of justice. With respect to his (Mr. BRUCE's) interruption, he agreed with his hon. and learned friend the member for Taunton, that the conduct of the hon. member for Peterborough in discussing this question, and stating his views as to the innocence or guilt of persons about to be placed on trial, was not only unusual, but highly reprehensible. He begged to remind the hon. gentleman that this prosecution was ordered by the learned Judge who heard the Case, and that it was clearly the duty of the Government to undertake it. (Hear, hear.) In some cases the Government had recourse to the advice of the law officers of the Crown, but the vast majority of cases were conducted without any regard to such a resource, and in this instance the responsibility rested jointly with the Home Office and the Treasury. The Claimant would be in no better or worse position than if he had been committed in the ordinary way. With regard to the hon. gentleman's proposal that the defence should be conducted at the expense of the Government, he begged to say that such a course was entirely unusual, and that there was nothing in the Case to warrant the Government in creating a precedent. (Hear, hear.)

Mr. WHALLEY, replying, said that his connection with the county of Hants first led to his taking an interest in the Case, and his opinion was that it had not been fairly tried. (Oh, oh.) The hon. and learned member for Taunton had left the House after attacking him in the manner he had done. It would have been more becoming had he remained to hear his reply. He assured the hon. and learned member who had charged him by implication with being a mountebank, that he was only a mountebank in the sense of going to certain parts of the country; but he must remind him that while mountebanks went about the country for money for their own purposes, he was driven to the course he was pursuing by the refusal of the Government to give the assistance which was absolutely necessary in order that this man should have a fair trial. He had never before witnessed such a degree of anxiety, earnestness, and even enthusiasm as was shown by the public in this respect.

The motion was then negatived without a division, the House refusing to sanction its withdrawal.

At the sitting of the House on August 10, Mr. WHALLEY asked the Under-Secretary for the Home Department, with respect to the statement made on the previous evening by his chief, that the person calling himself TICHBORNE, about to be tried for perjury, would have the same advantages in regard to his defence as were afforded to other persons similarly situated, whether he was aware of the Act 30 and 31 Vic., cap. 35, sec. 3, which provided that when any person was charged with an offence he was entitled to demand from the committing Magistrate such *pecuniary* assistance as might be necessary to enable him to bring forward material witnesses, and whether the accused in this instance, having been committed by a Judge of one of the superior courts, was deprived of an advantage which every person committed by an ordinary Magistrate enjoyed?

Mr. WINTERBOTHAM replied that the person in question would be tried in the ordinary way, and it was not the duty of Government to defend him.

Mr. WHALLEY wished an answer to his question whether the Claimant, owing to the fact of his having been committed by a Judge sitting in Nisi Prius, did not now stand in a worse position than a man committed by an ordinary magistrate.

Mr. WINTERBOTHAM answered that that was a question of law which he was not competent to determine.

From the *Morning Advertiser*.

Mr. JAMES is a very promising performer in the grand Ministerial orchestra, and may naturally look forward, with his undoubted talent, to place and patronage himself at no very distant period. Some of these days we shall see the tadpole transformation of this lively supporter of the Administration take place, and he will become, in all probability, a Solicitor or an Attorney-General, if his party remain in. Under such circumstances it is but natural that he should rush into a well-assumed rage at the attack which is undoubtedly made upon high official legal personages by the mere effort to promote the interests, so far as anything like fairness and impartiality are concerned, of the individual called the Claimant. But surely the possession of that legal education and training which, *teste* Mr. AYRTON, places a barrister or attorney far above the *status* of such petty men as the leaders of science and pioneers of philosophical research, should teach Mr. JAMES a few simple doctrines of ethics, and the maxim of impartiality, which we used to suppose when fresh from the study of BLACKSTONE, and ignorant of the practice of modern law, was inherent to the administration as well as the precepts of judicial economy. There are, for instance, two sides to a case. No man is pronounced guilty until he is proved to be so; much less dealt with as a criminal. It is supposed also, by a beautiful fiction much prized by the ancients, that the humblest and poorest citizen is entitled to justice equally with the richest and the most powerful; and that in this consists the chief strength and well-being of a State. Therefore, when Mr. JAMES indignantly rebuked Mr. WHALLEY for his Quixotism in expressing his conviction of the innocence of the Claimant of the charges brought against him, pressed too as he is—perhaps somewhat unduly—by the whole legal machinery at the disposal of the Government, it was hardly candid of that gentleman to ignore the fact that members of the House, including Her Majesty's Attorney-General, had expressed themselves in that House most positively, and in the strongest terms, as to the guilt and fraudulent personation of the man whom Mr. WHALLEY sought to defend. Nor was it decent, "nor according to the rules of good conduct and propriety," to characterize the proceedings outside the House in which some of its members had taken part, and in which thousands of the people of England assisted, by the term "mountebank performances." Nor, to the best of our knowledge, has Mr. WHALLEY ever been party to a suggestion that "a jury of his country had been bribed" in this case. Nor has such a charge ever been made by the Claimant himself. As for going about the country "in carriages provided as a money speculation," we should like to know what hired carriages for any purpose do not partake in some sort of the nature of a money speculation. It is all very well to talk of these proceedings as "an insult to the House and to the country;" but we should be sorry to think that the House deems itself insulted by an extraneous and even informal effort to procure justice to an individual; and as for the country, it is pretty clear, from the receptions accorded to the Claimant, and the feeling with which he is universally received, that if the country is insulted it is insulting itself.

No one can doubt the purity of Mr. WHALLEY's motives. He has been made the butt of ridicule for years by the Jesuit and Ultramontane party; but they would do the same to Prince BISMARCK if they could, and the march and development of events have only shown Mr. WHALLEY to have been a little in advance of his time. As Englishmen, we must express our admiration of the moral courage and persistent determination he has shown. He believes the Claimant to be Sir ROGER TICHBORNE. What then? He has thought him in any case to have been unfairly dealt with. Millions of Englishmen think the same. We consider that the interruptions to Mr. WHALLEY on Friday were most unseemly and uncalled-for. We now learn from Mr. BRUCE that the Attorney-General has had nothing to do with directing the prosecution of the Claimant. This is not in accordance with the declaration of that great legal functionary himself. He spoke of the assistance to himself of the *six* able Counsel retained. True, we were lately informed that he had withdrawn as Counsel from the case. If that case is only one-tenth as strong as he would have led us to suppose, surely the Government need not fear to produce any papers demanded by Mr. WHALLEY. Even the chief Sunday organ of the Government is candid enough to say that Mr. BRUCE (Mr. JAMES?) had no business to "assure the hon. member for Peterborough that it is indecent even for a member of Parliament speaking from his place to state his views as to the innocence or the guilt of a person whose innocence or guilt is about to be submitted to a legal tribunal. For unless we mistake (and this is meant to be a severe hit at the Claimant) persons fully as entitled to their opinion as Mr. WHALLEY have not hesitated in the House of Commons to denounce the Claimant as a *perjurer*." Just so; then mark the ruthless injustice of burking and abusing Mr. WHALLEY. "It is too much, however," continues the organ, with its usual flippancy, to "expect Mr. BRUCE to bestow any of his spare 'consideration' upon Mr. WHALLEY's questions. The Claimant is to be tried, and he will be tried fairly. *Had Sir* JOHN COLERIDGE *been less bitter*, public sympathy would never have veered towards the Claimant." Just so! It is of that "bitterness" which the public complains.

It was that "bitterness" which poisoned and prejudiced vulgar and unreflecting minds against the Claimant. It was that "bitterness" which led other men to doubt of the fairness of a trial so conducted. The beautiful principle of "hanging a man and trying him after" is not exactly that which Englishmen admire. Every citizen is interested deeply in every case into which the element of "bitterness" is introduced by a great law officer of the Crown. The people have to contribute towards the enormous cost of this prosecution, into which the element of fresh witnesses procured from the ends of the earth is to be introduced in order to prove the guilt of a man already imprisoned and treated as guilty. Mr. WHALLEY, on the part of those who choose to subscribe their money against the money forced from them by the Government to carry on this immense undertaking, which ought to be so plain, easy, straightforward, and to require no fresh witnesses, if the Claimant has received his deserts and been fairly dealt with, desires to have such "information as to the evidence that will be brought forward in the prosecution of the Defendant as he would be entitled to have had he been committed for trial by any other process than that of the order of a judge at Nisi Prius"—in short, just as he has been dealt with, to wit, committed, gagged, and bound without the means of any defence whatever. This is the plain English of the request. Is it a monstrous demand? But for the labour and agitation of his friends, the Claimant would in all probability have died in prison ere now. Why should the Government fear to meet the country in its just demand? Are we to suppose that they would deny anything in the shape of justice, because they are so far committed to this prosecution, through the "bitterness" of their Attorney-General? It is a hard case when the Government organs are driven to make fresh capital against the Claimant out of the trumpery episode of Mr. ANIDJAR's extraordinary little freak. Any man may "get into police-courts," as Mr. WHALLEY got into one the other day. The question is, what brings him there, and how he gets out of them? Mr. BRUCE's "consideration" sometimes extends too far in the opinion of many unprejudiced observers. It may well be extended even to the Claimant and his friends, at least so far as strict justice and impartiality are concerned. The public ask to have the matter which has unhappily engaged so much of their attention thoroughly and honestly investigated. Mr. WHALLEY has asked for the simple means at the disposal of the Government to attain this desirable end. It has been refused by taunts, insults, and an attempted count-out, and we are in addition told that the Attorney-General has had nothing to do with the direction of this prosecution. It stands on record that he has had; and he is still the chief law officer of the Crown. One thing is certain, which is, that the public mind has been disabused of one-half of the allegations made against the Claimant during the Trial. Thousands and tens of thousands have seen him and heard him, and know that he is not the vulgar, brutal, very illiterate personage painted by the Attorney-General. On the contrary, they have beheld in him a man of singularly gentlemanly and prepossessing manners; a man who, if he is not what he represents himself to be, is certainly not what he was represented on the Trial. When part of a thing is discovered to be utterly incorrect, is it not suggestive that the whole may be devoid of truth?

To THE EDITOR OF THE "MORNING ADVERTISER."

SIR,—Mr. H. JAMES, in answer to Mr. WHALLEY last night, in the House of Commons, stated that I took part in charging the jury at my late Trial of "TICHBORNE v. LUSHINGTON" with having been bribed. I beg to state that I did not take any part in the accusation named. It would be well for the hon. member for Taunton to ascertain facts before making statements to the House, the more so when attacking a man who has to meet three such charges as are brought against me. What I stated was that the jury showed cowardice in stopping the Case before hearing all the evidence. By so doing they lost me the whole of the money expended in that long litigation of 103 days.—I am, Sir, yours, &c., R. C. D. TICHBORNE.

Harley Lodge, West Brompton, August 10, 1872.

About this time the following letters appeared:—

TO THE EDITOR OF THE "HAMPSHIRE CHRONICLE."

SIR,—Having read your leading article on the TICHBORNE Case, I would say that at Bristol and Southampton I endeavoured to reply to all the accusations you have made against the Claimant, many of which replies you do not report in my speech delivered at the latter place. Perhaps, therefore, you will be kind enough to insert in your next edition the following remarks on the Case, which are facts, and cannot be controverted:—First of all, the Claimant's defective education, as proved by his French and English letters, and Mr. LOCTH's report thereon, read by me at the meetings; the constant quarrels that existed between himself and father, and his father and mother, making his home, as Serjeant BALLANTINE expressed it, "a hell upon earth;" the well-known dislike both himself and brother had of mixing with their equals in society; his leaving England, threatening never to return during his father's lifetime; the wreck of the "Bella," and saving of certain of the crew, as spoken to by Messrs. SHARPEN, LOCKHART, LANGLAND, and LIARDET; the existence of the "Osprey" proved; and Dr. WHEELER's statement as to ARTHUR ORTON and TOMAS CASTRO being two distinct persons.

His life in Australia was natural to a roving disposition like his, and his consorting with low company would certainly cause him to lose what little education he possessed. His intention to write home was not carried out for want of the opportunity, and delayed until circumstances rendered it impossible to return. As to his life in the bush (stock-driving, butchering, &c.), is it not constantly the life led in that country by men of position and education?

Would anyone but a son have ventured to mention in the letter to his mother the circumstance of the body-mark (of course, considering that she was fully aware of it), which, if untrue, would have satisfied Lady TICHBORNE at once that her correspondent was an impostor? Lady TICHBORNE, being a Frenchwoman, was not in the habit of nursing her children, and, doubtless, was not cognizant of the mark on the side, but the nurse to ROGER TICHBORNE has been found, and identifies *the mark on the Claimant as the one on his body when born.*

His being for a month in New York on his way home, and seeing the papers continually denouncing him as an impostor, naturally made him shy as to seeing his relatives on his return to England, not knowing on whom to rely except his mother; and when he did obtain an interview with certain of the Family, it seems there was an attempt to deceive him, though Mrs. RADCLIFFE, according to a statement made by GOSFORD, *recognized him at the first interview* by his eyes and eyebrows, and the upper part of his face; but neither Mrs. RADCLIFFE, nor any of the persons opposed to him, asked either himself or his mother whether he had the tattoo marks or not. The tattoo marks were never mentioned in any letters, either directly or indirectly, to any of his friends. Lady ALFRED's letter to Lady TICHBORNE, and Lady DOUGHTY's letter, say,—"From all we hear, he must be ROGER." Could the Family solicitor, Mr. HOPKINS, be deceived after the test letter, and in possession of the secret between himself and ROGER TICHBORNE as to Miss BELLEW? On his recognition of the officers of the regiments, Drill-Sergeants MCCANN, CARTER, and Troopers, none of them referred to the tattoo marks (which one would imagine some of them ought to have seen and remembered, when we are told by the witnesses for the defence that the marks were visible below the *wristband*, when the Claimant had been seen carpentering, catching minnows, and at the breakfast-table); but MCCANN *did* mention the ankle marks, and, on an examination of the Claimant being made immediately after by Dr. LIPSCOMBE, the marks were found. The old scars—the scars from the cut on the back of the head, mentioned by CHATILLON—and other marks of identity, are still visible on the Claimant. The Attorney-General suggested that these marks were all manufactured. Why, then, were not the tattoo marks also manufactured? Surely, those who knew of these cuts and scars would also have known of the tattoo marks, if they were so prominent as stated.

The seton-mark, the issue pea-mark, and the French vaccination mark, were all sworn to, and Lady DOUGHTY asked MOORE about these marks when he went to the Law Institution to identify the Claimant, by her own orders, but not one word was said about the tattoo marks. The twitching of the eyebrows, turning in of the left knee, small hands and feet, and enlargement of the instep, sworn to by the witnesses who knew ROGER TICHBORNE, are still apparent on the Claimant. Also the malformation of the left thumb—*smeared out in the daguerreotype*, as proved by Colonel STUART WORTLEY and others, the destruction of which was rather suspicious, yet little or no remark was made on it. Why was not an affidavit made in 1867 by the Family that ROGER TICHBORNE was tattooed, and an order obtained to have the Claimant's body examined? It would then have stopped all further litigation, if it had been undoubtedly proved the original ROGER TICHBORNE had been tattooed. But there is the fact that Lady DOUGHTY and Mrs. RADCLIFFE had never mentioned the subject to their lawyer until 1871, when they state that what they then said on the matter was taken down in writing, and, on such depositions being called for, the defendants could not produce them. The Claimant has challenged his brother-officers to come forward and state that he was known by them to have been tattooed, but not one has ventured to do so. Major PHILLIPS, Captain TURNER, and Captain PHILLIMORE have all said that *he was not* tattooed.

The scandalous imputations against witnesses whose only motive was to speak the truth (and many of whom had rather the Claimant was not the man he represented himself to be), the abuse by the Attorney-General, levied at Mr. BAIGENT, Miss BRAINE, BOGLE, Dr. LIPSCOMB, Mr. HOPKINS, the poor mother, attorneys, and Counsel, and almost all concerned for the Plaintiff, the lengthened cross-examination and speech of the Attorney-General, all appear to have been done for the purpose of prolonging time, and to to defeat the Plaintiff by breaking down his finances, and to weary the jury (certainly the last object appears to have been obtained), and yet it is said the Plaintiff has had fair-play.

The Attorney-General, it may be remembered, once admitted the resemblance of the Plaintiff to the original ROGER TICHBORNE, and afterwards said he had forgotten the first sixteen years of his life. I would ask—how many of the jury could have stated so many details of their boyhood as the Plaintiff did? The Attorney-General said ROGER TICHBORNE was a high-minded, chivalrous gentleman, *developed* into "the rascal, and the enormous man of flesh we have had before us for so many days," and the "low ruffian, and associate of low ruffians, which his cross-examination shows him to have been." The Attorney-General also stated that at the first interview of the Plaintiff with his mother he was covered up in bed, in a darkened room, whereas HOLMES and LEETE both said he was merely lying on a sofa-bed.

The Attorney-General denied that ROGER TICHBORNE ever used

the word "Papa" in his letters, but quoted one with the expression in it on the very first day of his speech; and also stated that the Plaintiff had said on his examination that he never wrote a letter to Lady DOUGHTY, whereas he stated he had written so many it was impossible to recollect them. In the Wagga-Wagga will the Attorney-General said that Hermitage Farm was suggested by the "Hermitage Wharf" at Wapping; but it was the *Hermitage Farm at Colmore* which the Plaintiff referred to in the will, it being the only property he inherited from his father. Again, let us not forget the admissions that the PITTENDREIGH letters were forgeries, they having been used on an occasion when distinguished persons were invited to attend the Court and see the Plaintiff collapse under the cross-examination of the letters. Did not the Attorney-General afterwards admit they were forgeries?

I observe in your article of the 15th instant you quote a passage from Mr. SCOTT's letter, but you neglect the important part where he said he was convinced of the Claimant's identity. I wish also to quote part of a letter from Mr. SCOTT to myself on the Case, as follows:—

"I quite agree with you that this is a detestable and most iniquitous attempt to rob the head of an ancient house of his titles and estates. Nothing has occurred during my long life which has so much lowered my estimate of human nature. That a low, unscrupulous attorney should leave no stone unturned to put more money into his pocket, is natural enough—it is his practice; but that noblemen and gentlemen of position should allow themselves to be led by the nose through so much dirt (and that is the most charitable construction that can be put upon their conduct), is incredible."

Now, this is the opinion of one of the first gentlemen in Hampshire on the TICHBORNE Case.

In conclusion, Sir, I must say that I agree with many persons who assert that the Trial was one of the greatest miscarriages of justice ever known in this country; and apologizing, as I do, for the length of this letter, I trust, for the sake of Truth, Justice, and fair-play, you will kindly allow it to appear in your next edition.—I remain, &c., GUILDFORD ONSLOW.

The Grove, Ropley, Hants: June 18, 1872.

THE CLERGY AND THE TICHBORNE CASE.

TO THE EDITOR OF THE "TICHBORNE NEWS."

SIR,—Clergymen do not usually travel far out of their own sphere, yet there are occasions when it may be both righteous and necessary for them to do so. It seems to me that if the very general feeling of the clergy in respect to the TICHBORNE Case were known, there would not have been such boldness on the part of the Press as one meets with in almost every newspaper.

No doubt the *moral* aspect of the Trial, so far as it went on, has had its effect in inducing clergymen to be silent about it. Yet that very silence amounts to negative evidence of their private conviction that the truth has not yet been elicited—for had this been clearly done, I am sure that the London clergy at least would ere this have made use of the Claimant's tale to point the moral of many a pulpit discourse. It seems to me that the question at issue is not at all one of moral character, but altogether one of personal identity. This appears to have been greatly lost sight of in the cloud of argument so ingeniously raised by the Attorney-General at the First Trial, and imitated by the Lord Chief Justice at the Second. What the jury had to decide upon was not whether the Claimant was good, bad, or indifferent, but whether or not he is Sir ROGER TICHBORNE; and I do think that that question has not been satisfactorily determined by the course of action at the recent Trial, or at the first.

I cannot help adding, that I knew something of COLERIDGE's practice on the Western Circuit, and I particularly noticed that when his case was strong he made it a point not only to abstain from the use of epithets, but to state his deliberate purpose to do so, in order that the evidence might go to the jury without any *ex parte* colouring. I waited anxiously for his opening of the Case for the defence in the First Trial, in order to satisfy myself as to his own private conviction, so far as I might judge from his antecedents as an advocate, and when I found that he commenced with an outburst of vituperation, I felt tolerably assured that his conviction lay in one direction, and his advocacy in another.—Your obedient servant, M. A.

A STRANGE CONTRAST.

TO THE EDITOR OF THE "TICHBORNE NEWS."

SIR,—Any person who will take the trouble to look into the *Daily Telegraph* of May 11th, 1872, will find at page 3 a forcible commentary on the vagaries of law, and the manner in which evidence is accepted. On that same page 3 we see the Plaintiff, "TICHBORNE *v.* MOSTYN," put summarily out of court, his claim repudiated, on question of identity, although his identity as "TICHBORNE" had been testified to by his mother and upwards of eighty credible witnesses—officers of all ranks, and men who had served with him, magistrates, clergymen, schoolfellows, and old family servants; while in a parallel column we have the decision on the "GORDON Peerage," in which case we are told that a refined and highly-educated young nobleman left—1866—his estates, and the enjoyments of civilized life, to become a companion of common sailors, on board a small American coasting sloop, and there of necessity to fraternize with men as low as any Australian squatter. There, under the name of GEORGE OSBORNE, we find he was washed overboard, and drowned, 1870—*i.e.* to say, a Yankee sailor named PRATT made affidavit that he is "*morally certain* that the man (GEORGE OSBORNE) was lost." Well, on this and some other affidavits, and a statement from the Dowager Countess, the title and estates are handed over to a younger brother.

Here the testimony, on affidavit, of a Yankee sailor—no highly-feed Attorney-General or ingenious Chief Justice being present to twist and distort evidence—mainly settles a property and title, such faith has our D. T., like his patron in anything American, while another Plaintiff is shunted out of court as an impostor, although his own mother, and upwards of 200 witnesses who saw and *conversed with him*, are not only "morally certain," but have sworn that they have no more doubt of the Claimant being Sir ROGER C. TICHBORNE than they have of their own existence; and yet the public are called on by highly-paid officials to believe one of two things, that the Claimant has either befooled all the witnesses, or, worse still, has persuaded them to combine and perjure themselves to serve the purposes of an impostor.

FAIRPLAY.

The conduct of Parliament and the Ministry called forth the following letter from Mr. SKIPWORTH, a gentleman of fortune and a member of the bar.

TO THE PEOPLE OF ENGLAND.

And this might and perhaps ought to have been the cry lon[g] since in the TICHBORNE Case. But it does not bear that impression less because not raised before, but rather has its monste[r] form increased, whilst the very atmosphere is tainted with th[e] vices that it brings in its train, and its foul proportions have well nigh, if not quite, out-reached the palace itself.

The QUEEN has been appealed to in temperate, but exhortin[g] language, to make her gracious influence felt in a matter whic[h] addresses itself solely to the heart, and should, therefore, over ride any attempt to pervert justice by misapplying or misem ploying the laws of the country, and where kind and Christia[n] advice must have been disregarded at the peril of those to who[m] it might be given. For if the Crown shall be supported by i[n] justice, where will that Crown soon be? And the ministers w[ho] counsel acts of injustice are traitors to their QUEEN and uproote[rs] of that constitution which they have sworn to uphold. And [as] traitors to their QUEEN, so would they be to their country, havi[ng] sworn her their allegiance. To the appeal I have received t[he] following reply:—

"Whitehall, November 2, 1872.

"SIR,—I am directed by Mr. Secretary BRUCE to acknowledg[e] the receipt of your letter of the 23rd ult., transmitting a letter [to] Her MAJESTY on the subject of the TICHBORNE Baronetcy, and [to] acquaint you that the same has been laid before the QUEEN, b[ut] that Her MAJESTY cannot be advised to interfere in the case.—[I] am, Sir, your obedient servant,

"HENRY WINTERBOTHAM.

"G. B. SKIPWORTH, Esq., Moortown House,
"Caistor, Lincoln."

The Government, it is almost needless now to say, has ignor[ed] all sense of justice in the Case; and after a Judge had unjustly se[nt] Sir ROGER TICHBORNE to prison, and every device been resorted [to] without avail to keep him there, they, by the advice of their l[aw] officer, who had been engaged as Counsel against him—and [in] such capacity had not only sacrificed truth, but even tried to w[in] his client's case by producing Forged Letters, and which he aft[er]wards acknowledged he *knew* to be forgeries—still branded [as] he was by that public disgrace, by his very advice ordered t[he] prosecution of Sir ROGER TICHBORNE, at the nation's cost, [for] alleged perjury, and even forgery, in signing his own name, [not] one atom of which have they been able to, nor can they, pr[ove] against him. When may a man be considered himself, and [not] another? Sir ROGER has been more than six years before t[he] eyes of the public, and by that public, as well as by his relati[ons] and former acquaintance (except those leagued in conspira[cy] against him), he is acknowledged to be, what he undoubtedly [is,] Sir ROGER TICHBORNE. Those who assert the contrary, must [be] devoid of reason and common-sense. To suppose for a mom[ent] that a man could go through the country, addressing the milli[ons] who greet him by his own name and title, as he has done, a[nd] yet not be the man he represents himself to be, is to supp[ose] an impossibility. It would be an insult to the powers of d[is]cernment, and the members of a Government would be more [fit] for a place of confinement than to have in hand the affairs [of] this country, if, after all their opportunities of discovery; [the] evidence of the late trial; public discussion since; the aid [of] eminent leading Counsel; every assistance money can furni[sh] and the power to search into every nook and corner of [the] universe, and make evidence where there is none to be had,—[if] we attributed to them any want of that knowledge we oursel[ves] possess. What, then, can be their plea? A Judge's order, t[hat] sent a man to prison avowedly for speaking the truth? And that Judge to treat the members of the Government, who sho[uld] be his masters, like so many schoolboys, and threaten them w[ith] the rod if they did not do his bidding? Depend upon it, t[hey] would not be so ruled if it did not suit their purpose. But if t[hey] are so ready to shelter themselves under an order which t[hey] know to be unjust, what better are you—the people of Engl[and] —than slaves, if you have to abide by it? The charact[er,] reputation, or property of any one of you, however dear the o[ne] or however much you may value the possession of the other, is [no] longer safe, but subject to the freak or fancy of some one in of[fice] r power who chooses to doubt your integrity or dispute the title to your estates.

Such pusillanimity in our rulers we may despise, and cannot excuse. Sad it is to think of, but there is a foul conspiracy somewhere, and the name of those engaged in it is almost legion. To say the least, they are conniving at, if not actually aiding in, that conspiracy— are using the public money for an illegal purpose, and the Counsel and all parties engaged in the prosecution are guilty of unlawfully receiving the same, if they have no evidence on their side, nothing to justify them in undertaking a prosecution at the public cost. We may well conceive that the six eminent or leading (so-called) Counsel engaged may be in some kind of perturbation at receiving the public money (we know not how much), and find that the only one case they can make is one bolstered up by perjury. If they wish to save their character and reputation, they must either throw up the case, or, regardless of consequences, back up the Government, their employers, and their "General" leader, and play the desperate neck-or-nothing game of going in for a conviction at all hazards. That not only one, but a body of men, could be found prepared not merely to risk, but to sacrifice a professional name for money, or (so-called) honours, however great, is a picture we do not wish to contemplate. We know it would be done to save the credit of a Government, but which would only in that way suffer a further stain. If, however, we are to judge by the unseemly display on the part of Counsel, we can hardly free ourselves from the conclusion that honour and justice are not, as they were not in the former Trial, to be the guide in any forthcoming proceedings. As an instance, it was only a short time since, that Mr. HAWKINS, Q.C., boasted to a nobleman and friend of the cause that he would send Sir ROGER TICHBORNE (the Claimant he would say, I suppose,) to penal servitude within two days of his coming into Court, as easily as he would go through a dinner. In his zeal for his former, and perhaps he considers *present*, clients (though, as a matter of *delicacy*, one would have thought that the Government would have left him out), he no doubt forgot all sense of duty to the public, whose money he is receiving, to see justice and fair-play. Unless he has secret instructions as well, which we fear is the case, from his employers, to "fight us to the knife," as *kindly* intimated not long since—our persecuted friend having actually escaped by a miracle from that *pretty murderous weapon*, when he went out on that memorable Chili Commission. And thus some of his supporters have come to the conclusion that by the production of false evidence, and using other unfair means, he will be sacrificed to design and treachery, unless a considerable sum is found for his defence. I am unwilling to think that, in spite of the violent collapse of the late Trial, any such catastrophe could happen now, seeing that the public mind is so additionally informed. True, there is the Government influence, powerful even in the cause of wrong; an array of Counsel, pledged, we will take it, horrible as is the idea, against all right and reason, and evidence or no evidence, to make a clean swoop of the unfortunate Sir ROGER, and send him into penal servitude, "as easily as go through a dinner"—a second edition, it *might* be, of a Common Pleas Special Jury.

And, worse, perhaps, than this, it is said that his avowed enemy, Lord Chief Justice COCKBURN, is to be the Judge. This gentleman, when on the Bench at the late Trial, is said to have passed down written observations to Mr. HAWKINS, and even declared how soon he and Mr. HAWKINS would have sent Sir ROGER to prison had they been associated as advocates. He is also said to have, both publicly and privately, denounced him as an impostor, even very lately. So that if the Government were desirous of placing Sir ROGER under every possible disadvantage, they have done it most successfully. To crown all, it is hinted, we hope with no truth, that the Attorney-General may be appointed Judge of the Probate Court, where Sir ROGER could have proved his Mother's will, and so have recovered possession of his estates, before being compelled to pay the £46,000 which Chief Justice BOVILL ruled should be done before he could proceed again in the Common Pleas.

I think you will allow that I have already said enough to take ordinary thinking persons aback, but a vast deal more remains to be said. It is for you to say whether you will bear this infliction on the public mind longer—diverting, as it does, the attention from regular avocations and pursuits—because justice is perverted, reason and common-sense outraged, and the rights and liberties of the people set at nought. Private and selfish views have preponderated over duty in the councils of the nation; we have witnessed our courts become the scenes of corruption and vice, and are promised a still further exhibition of prostituted justice and outraged order and decency such as were never practised in any age or country. Laws so administered, or attempted to be administered, are only a subterfuge for wrong and robbery, and that which should be a protection becomes a curse.

As you value, then, the safety of your homes and families, endure not the existence of this foul stain longer. You, as Englishmen, are responsible for its removal. At once, then, I say, assemble yourselves together from all parts to London, as the centre. There let the subject be fully and freely discussed as to the measures to be taken to bring the Government to task and stay this constant and feverish agitation throughout the country. It is announced that the Solicitor to the Treasury has given notice of trial. Be not misled by that. He will never try such a rotten Case as he has if he can help it; so you may expect it put off from day to day, dragging its wearisome and fiend-like form along to the waste of public time and public resources, making matters worse every day and even hour it continues. It is for you, then, at once to step forward, and demand that this mockery shall cease, and restitution be made personally by the Government, not only for the wrongs inflicted on the people by a misappropriation of the funds of the public treasury, but on Sir ROGER TICHBORNE in his private capacity as an Englishman and one of ourselves, by unlawfully using their influence and power in depriving him of possession of his title and estates.

That the Government of this country, in the course they have taken, have rendered themselves liable to an impeachment for treason, if not high treason, in the strongest sense of the word, I have little hesitation in asserting; and it is for you, after calm and deliberate discussion, to decide upon adopting steps such as the justice and emergency of the Case demand.

For that purpose, then, let us have a day named—say, for the present, Monday, the 25th, for a mass meeting in the Agricultural Hall. I have not named it to Sir ROGER TICHBORNE, but feel sure he will attend. For want of a better champion, my humble services shall be at your command; and, trusting that you will show by your numerous presence the vast importance of the subject,—I remain, fellow-countrymen, yours faithfully,

G. B. SKIPWORTH.

Moortown House, Caistor, Lincolnshire: November 6, 1872.

MR. MADDEN.

The following important communication was at this time made to Sir ROGER, by Messrs. NOLAN and JORDAN, Solicitors:—

53, Bourke-street West, Melbourne: 16th July, 1872.

SIR,—Mr. JOSEPH HENRY MADDEN, of Hay, New South Wales (for whom we have, on several occasions, acted as solicitors here), has requested us to forward you the inclosed letter, which contains his likeness, and a statement relative to some circumstances connected with your acquaintance with him in New South Wales, in order to assist you, which, if it should be of any service on your impending Trial, he is prepared to verify on oath.

We may mention that Mr. MADDEN has been known to us for many years (having come to this country in the same ship with us—the "Mendoro"). He is a most truthful and trustworthy person, and although—like many young men who have come to this country—he has led a wild bush life, he belongs to a respectable family in the county of Galway, in Ireland, and is known to many persons holding high positions there, and amongst them Sir THOMAS BURKE, of Marble Hill, and Mr. WILLIAM HENRY GREGORY, members for the county of Galway, to whom he has authorized us to refer you.

Should you think Mr. MADDEN's evidence material in your case, by communicating with us his attendance can be procured on very short notice. His business often compels him to travel about, but he always keeps us informed of his address.

We may state, in conclusion, that some time ago we, on behalf of Mr. MADDEN, laid before Mr. ALLPORT, of this city, the solicitor acting in this colony for your London solicitors, a statement similar to the one we now inclose, which he stated he would forward to your solicitors; but he informs us that, as yet, he has not heard from them on the subject.

Awaiting the favour of a reply,—We are, Sir, your obedient servants,

NOLAN & JORDAN.

Sir ROGER C. TICHBORNE, Bart.

[COPY]

Yattersall's Hotel, Hay: 8th July, 1872.

In 1863, the Claimant, Sir ROGER C. TICHBORNE, *alias* TOM CASTRO, and myself drove the mail on this river (the Murrumbidgee) for Mr. JAMES GORMLY. I drove from Hay to Boree twice a week, and he took the mail on from there once a week to MCNEIL's and once to Narandera. We both stayed at Boree, being the principal depot on the line. We lived in a tent on the bank of the river, and when in that neighbourhood he generally led us to believe he was a native of Windsor, in this country. His reason for so saying was, I think, that he tried to get a mob of colts to break in, at Groongal, the station upon which we had our changing depot; and he fancied by saying he was an Australian native he would get them more readily, as the natives are supposed to be the best rough horsebreakers. Well, one day in particular, we were both together in this tent: the Claimant lay on a bunk reading a book, and I was mending a green hide halter, made fast to the doorpost, when suddenly we commenced an argument about countries. He asked me what part of the old country I was from. I answered the county Galway. He said he had known some respectable people in Ireland. I said to him, "I don't think, TOM, you are a native of this country," and he laid the book out of his hand on the bunk, and answered me, "No; but I am of an English family, and brought up in my early days in France." He asked me if I ever heard of Sir JAMES TICHBORNE, whose son he said he was; that he had got into a little mess in Hay, contracting a small debt, and having formed rather a close intimacy with a bootmaker's daughter the name of ANDERSON, and that, after a little, if he could make himself all right at Hay, and get some money together, he would go home, as he *was entitled to large property in Hampshire, and his father's titles*. To all this conversation I only replied he was foolish; he should try and get home. We talked about long voyages at sea. I told him a tale I experienced myself, coming to this country on board the "Mendoro," and he told me, in reply, about being at Rio Janeiro, and boarding the ship "Bella," and getting wrecked, and only a few saved. He then told me about creating some disturbances with his father, and being in the Army, and leaving home. He talked about the TICHBORNE Family being Roman Catholics, and mentioned about a charitable bequest that was inheritant in the Family.

The brandy-flask that was used between us was his property. It was a german-silver, flat-sided flask, and upon this he wrote his proper name, ROGER C. TICHBORNE, on one side, with his assumed name, TOM CASTRO, on the other. This flask I carried alternately with him. Some time after we had this conversation, I was having dinner at the station, and told them that TOM CASTRO was telling me he is the son of a baronet, when old BUCKLEY, the overseer, had a good laugh. BUCKLEY nicknamed him Neck-or-Nothing, from a narrative of CASTRO's own, too long to write.

Just about that time he had a passenger on the Mail, an old man now dead, a hut-keeper of BUCKLEY's, and to this man he told he had large properties in England, and that he had now wasted some years of his life badly. I have heard him speak of ARTHUR ORTON, who, I believe was at BOREE, and the man that I saw at the time, and supposed him to be ORTON, he is not at all like the Claimant.

The above is a correct statement.

JOSEPH HENRY MADDEN.

[COPY.]

Yattersall's Hotel, Hay, Murrumbidgee: 8th July, 1872.

Sir ROGER C. TICHBORNE.

DEAR SIR,—So little familiar is my writing to you now, I scarcely think you will recognize it; but then, assuming that you are, like myself, fully sensible of the wandering and unsettled life some young men are prone to lead in this country, you will, no doubt, arrive at the conclusion it is not from a want of friendly or sympathetic feeling a person so much evades communication to the old country, but simply that one gets on a path of negligence, and each successive year passes on, and the greater in number still greater is your disinclination to write.

I thought before now you would be settled at the head of your estates in England. You have certainly undergone a frightful ordeal, and severe cross-examination, during intervals of the Trial: however, it is to be hoped you will ere long overcome your difficulties, and show your oppressors you are not the person they have in a cowardly way endeavoured to prove you to be. I have not read much of your lawsuit, being at many different places, where it was difficult to procure a paper. I am getting Mr. NOLAN, a solicitor in Melbourne, to write to you and send you a written statement of a conversation that took place between you and myself one day at Boree, when we were driving the Mail for GORMLY. It was the day I was trying to tail the green hide halter, and you went to show me; but neither of us could do it neatly. When you read the statement, and think of our Boree life, you will find it correct; but I fear it is too late now to be of any particular service to you.

I inclose my likeness in this letter to you, knowing you will be glad, after an absence of some years, to once again look on the features of an old mate. It has been taken in Hay, and, as you see, in our old style of strapped trousers; consequently, you can't expect it to be up to the style of London finish. There are many changes in this part of the country since you left: a great deal of the runs are taken up by free selectors, and nearly all new squatters on this river. Poor old BUCKLEY lost all his money by the failure of HARVEY, COCKBURN, and ALLEYNE. He is still at Groongal, nearly blind for some years past. The FLOODS are all broke up. Hay has grown to be a big town: it is now corporated. JAMES WARBY is in business here, and now commencing to do well again; but when he first opened here he lost £5,000. He is likely to be proclaimed mayor. Wagga-Wagga—poor old place! where you and I also had many an encounter—has been going ahead too. HARRY MONHAM has bought the Australian from HIGGINS for £8,000, and HIGGINS gone clean smashed. GORMLY and BEVERIDGE have joined in partners in the many lines of mail they now hold, but they have not had the down-river mail for years. The HALBISH Brothers took it from GORMLY. MITCHELL, the sporting saddler, is also burst up. I have had numerous twists and turns myself since you left, and am, as usual, still fond of the racing. Sometimes I have made a few pretty good touches; but then, again, it goes. I made £100 over Nimblefoot winning the Melbourne Cup, but at Ballarat, a few weeks later, got up in the morning as free from money as from feathers.

I have been over in Sale, in Gippsland, for a season. Of course you know that part of the country well. I like Gippsland very well if it were not so dreadfully cold, through which I was compelled *to leave*. I frequently lost my temper over there, men saying they knew you that I am sure never saw you or yet were in Gippsland at the time you were there. I was very lucky at this last meeting here; every horse I had was a winner. I had three of Mr. H. B. WELSHE's. CHARLIE COX is expected to return in August. I don't think he had much to say on your Case after going home. I don't think it will terminate in a very judicious trip for him, as he is rather a fast chap when out, and those London boys are just the men to make an Australian bleed. When he lands he will find the Caledonian hotel burned down, and two large actions to be brought against him.

I will now conclude, trusting your wife and little ones are well, and that before long you will be able to get over all your difficulties. I should be so pleased to get a letter from you with your likeness inclosed.—My dear Sir ROGER, I remain, yours very truly,

JOSEPH HENRY MADDEN,
Hay, Murrumbidgee, New South Wales.

Mr. MADDEN wrote a second letter, addressed to Mr. GUILDFORD ONSLOW, under the date of Dec. 13, 1873, from Melbourne, as follows, inclosing a photograph of himself, which was identified by the Claimant. That letter was as follows:—

"In 1863, TOM CASTRO (the present Claimant) and myself drove the mail on the Murrumbidgee for Mr. JAMES GORMLY, the mail proprietor. I took the mail from Hay to Boree twice a week, and he (TOM CASTRO) took it on to Narandera township once a week, and to MCNEIL Brothers' Station twice a week. During that time, one day in particular, as I was tailing—in other words, platting—a new piece on to a green hide halter, at the door, TOM lay on a bank, reading a book. We suddenly started an argument about countries and horses, when I said to him, I did not think he was a native of this country, as he sometimes told us about there he was; his reason for so doing, I think, was (and he may tell you so himself) that there was a mob of colts to be broken in at Groongal station, upon which run we had the mail depot, and as old BUCKLEY, the overseer, was partial to natives as breakers, he thought he would procure them more easily. Then, to my question, he said he was not a native of this country, but of England, and brought up in France in his young days; and he asked me if I had ever heard of Sir JAMES TICHBORNE? I said, No; and he said he was his son, and entitled to the title and estates in Hampshire, and other places. When I answered he was a fool not to go home; he said he had got into a little mess in Hay, with a bootmaker's daughter, ANDERSON's, and contracted a few small debts; and if he could square off matters there, and could get a little money together, he would return home. *He also told me about the 'Bella,'* and being in South America, and a long tale about a charitable bequest, inheritant to the TICHBORNE Family, and as to their being great Catholics. On telling him I belonged to Galway, in the West of Ireland, he said he knew some respectable people there. We carried a small brandy flask, which was his property; it was a small flat-sided pewter one; no doubt he recollects it well; and on it he wrote, with an old pocket-knife, ROGER C. TICHBORNE, on one side, and TOM CASTRO on the other. I am positive he is not ARTHUR ORTON, as he was up there at the time; and I also say, conscientiously, and will take the same opinion with me to the grave, that he is the person he represents himself to be, Sir ROGER TICHBORNE. I know him and his feelings so thoroughly well, and being a man who can be surpassed by few as to the knowledge of the nature and habits of Australian life, both rough and smooth, and that I am connected with some of the most respectable families in the West of Ireland, I should be an important witness for him. If there is anything I can do in his behalf, I should be most happy, and without incurring any unnecessary expense. It is only within the last twelve months that my parents in Galway knew that I was alive myself, as I was here for twelve years and never communicated with any one in the old country, or any one in this that would be likely to do so; so when I wrote to my father, after a protracted silence, I said I might go home and give evidence on the TICHBORNE Case; in his reply he cautioned me from having anything to do with it—to come home, and not mind it. However, that has no particular weight with me, after my open wanderings in the Southern hemisphere, so long. Mr. W. H. GREGORY, late Governor of Ceylon, and Member for Galway, knows our family well. I inclose a likeness of mine, to my old friend TICHBORNE, with whom I have spent many a hard wet night, and at whose service I am at any time, to render him any possible good."

A few months after we read of an act of persecution by the Family, to one of their tenants.

THE TICHBORNE TENANTRY.

To THE EDITOR OF THE "TICHBORNE GAZETTE."

SIR,—I venture to ask the favour that you will kindly insert in your journal the inclosed letter from the Bailiff at Tichborne Park, one of the witnesses for the Claimant in the late Trial of TICHBORNE *v.* LUSHINGTON.

The letter speaks for itself.

I have been informed that all *the Tenants and Cottagers on the estate, who swore to the identity of* Sir ROGER TICHBORNE, *have received orders to quit.* This act of injustice ought to be known throughout the length and breadth of the land. Let us contrast the conduct of the Claimant, who refused a character to his own servant, CARTER, because, after repeated warnings, he had been found drunk in his service. Rather than impose on the public, he risked the *ill-will* of this servant; who, according to the speech of the Attorney-General, had coached the Claimant to all he knew. This poor man CARTER, in consequence of his inability to procure a character for sobriety from his master, became a pauper on the streets of London, and eventually died in the hospital at Brompton, and, with his last breath, swore to the identity of his master!

Look on *this*—then on *that*.

I am, Sir, your obedient servant,
October 8, 1872. GUILDFORD ONSLOW.

[COPY.]

Tichborne Park: Saturday, Sept. 30, 1872.

DEAR SIR,—Owing to having given evidence at the late Trial, on behalf of Sir ROGER TICHBORNE (knowing full well as I do that I have spoke the truth), I have received notice to leave my situation as Bailiff. Mr. STUBBS, my employer, told me that Mr. BOWKER, of Winchester (Solicitor to the Defendants), said unless I was discharged, Mr. STUBBS would have to leave his farm in six ths. This I think a very great hardship, after having been y present situation twenty-five years. I was six years with Edward Doughty Tichborne; nine years with Sir James hborne, and ten years with my present master, Mr. Budd nbs, who rents the home farm and park at Tichborne. Mr. ker (the solicitor) told my employer that Lady Alfred Tichne had bought the lease of Tichborne Park of Colonel Lushton, and that she would not come to live there until I had n discharged.

rusting you will excuse the liberty I am taking,—I remain, rs respectfully,

Henry Noble.

Ve insert here the affidavits of poor Noble and his wife. Both se witnesses were examined at the Great Trial, on the 3rd of tember, 1873.

Henry Noble, of Tichborne, in the county of Hants, Farm liff, make oath, and say as follows, viz.:—

1. I am in the 57th year of my age. I formerly lived in Suf-, and about the year 1847, at the recommendation of Mr. cent Gosford, I came to Tichborne, as farm-bailiff to the Sir Edward Doughty, and continued in his service until he l; and I was also in the service of the late Sir James Francis ghty Tichborne, when he came into the possession of the ghty estates, and remained in his service as farm-bailiff until death.

. I well knew the Plaintiff, then Mr. Roger Charles Tichne, who was frequently at Tichborne during the lifetime of his le, Sir Edward Doughty, and I often saw and conversed with , before he left England in the year 1853.

. On the 13th of February, 1867, I saw the Plaintiff on the tform of the railway-station at Alresford, and immediately ognized him, and the Plaintiff also recognized me, and came and shook hands with me, and spoke to me.

. I am perfectly sure that the Plaintiff is the Mr. Roger arles Tichborne whom I formerly knew, the eldest son of late Sir James Francis Doughty Tichborne. There cannot any doubt about his being the same person.

. I have heard read the affidavit of my wife, Ann Noble, rn in this cause on the 1st day of July, 1867, and speaking itively, as far as I am personally concerned, and to the best of knowledge and belief, as to the several other matters therein ntioned, I say that the several statements contained in such davit are true in all respects.

. I have again seen and conversed with the Plaintiff to-day, l am certain of his identity.

. The several statements hereinbefore contained are within my n knowledge, save as hereinbefore appears, and in such lastntioned cases, are believed by me to be true, on the grounds ein appearing,

The Mark of × Henry Noble.

tness to the mark of } John Holmes.
he said Henry Noble, } 25, Poultry, London.

Sworn at New Alresford, in the County of Southampton, this 1st of July, 1867, the witness to the mark of the deponent having n first sworn that he had truly, and distinctly, and audibly d over the contents of the above affidavit to the said deponent, l that he saw him make his mark thereto, before me,

John Francis Adams,
A Commissioner to administer Oaths in Chancery, in England.

Ann Noble, wife of Henry Noble, of Tichborne, Hants, farmliff, make oath and say as follows, viz.:—

. I am in my 51st year. My husband and myself formerly ed in Suffolk, and about the year 1847, at the recommendation the above-named Defendant, Vincent Gosford, we came to hborne, my husband as bailiff to Sir Edward Doughty, and self to attend to the dairy. We continued in those positions ing the life of Sir Edward, and also during the life of Sir es. Sir Edward died in 1853, Sir James Francis Doughty hborne in 1862. I knew both Sir Edward and Sir James y well. During the time they were in possession of the Estates y constantly resided at Tichborne Park.

. During Sir Edward Doughty's lifetime, Tichborne was the ne of the Plaintiff, then Mr. Roger Charles Tichborne. en we came to Tichborne, the Plaintiff was constantly about re, and I well knew him, and have often seen him going to meet hounds, and look after his dogs. I quite recollect his peral appearance.

. I remember the Plaintiff leaving Tichborne to go abroad in year 1853.

. About the end of December, 1866, a gentleman came to hborne Farm with Mr. Rous, the landlord of the Swan Hotel, esford. Mr. Rous comes very often for butter. Mr. Rous ocked at the back door, and I went to him, and gave him what wanted. After I had waited upon Mr. Rous, I saw a gentlen in a gig; he seemed to me like a foreigner. I saw only the er part of his face, and I fancied I knew him, for it struck he had a Tichborne face.

. When my husband came home to dinner, about noon, I asked if he had seen a strange gentleman, and told him of the tleman coming with Mr. Rous, and that I could not help aking he was a Tichborne. My husband said he had seen a tleman with Rous. He looked like a foreign gentleman ning from abroad. We could not make out who he could be. I said why it can scarcely be Sir Roger, for we had not heard his arrival. At tea-time my husband came in again, and said he had seen the same gentleman walking about the farm, and my husband said to me that the gentleman walked very much like the late Sir James Tichborne. We kept talking about it, and wondering who he could be if he was not Sir Roger.

5a. On the following day I heard that the Plaintiff had been in our neighbourhood, and on Monday, the 11th of February, 1867, I was in New Alresford, and saw a gentleman walking with Mr. Hopkins and Colonel Lushington. I only saw his back. I was in Mr. Baker's, the linen-draper's shop. Mr. Baker was coming in at the time, and I remarked to Mr. Baker, "That is Sir James's walk," referring to the Plaintiff's walk. They were going down Broad-street, towards the Weir.

6. On Saturday, the 23rd day of February, 1867, I went to Mr. Rous's, at the Swan Hotel, Alresford, and was there introduced to the Plaintiff, and I immediately recognized him as the Mr. Roger Charles Tichborne I formerly knew, the eldest son of Sir James Francis Doughty Tichborne. He was the same person I had seen with Rous, Mr. Hopkins, and Colonel Lushington, as before mentioned.

7. I well remember, in particular, the upper part of his face, his walk, and voice. I am sure that the Plaintiff is the Mr. Roger Charles Tichborne I formerly knew.

8. I have again seen and talked with the Plaintiff to-day, and am quite certain of his identity.

9. The several statements hereinbefore contained are within my own knowledge. Ann Noble.

Sworn at New Alresford, in the County of Southampton, this 1st day of July, 1867, before me, John Adams,
A Commissioner to administer Oaths in Chancery, in England.

The virulence thus manifested by certain powerful persons induced the Claimant's friends to counsel him to recommence his Meetings; it became necessary to do so, likewise, for the purpose of procuring funds, as the Defendant had no money for his defence. What had been raised had been, to a great extent, embezzled by persons, who wormed themselves into his confidence, with the most dishonest purposes. Accordingly, in November we find

SIR ROGER TICHBORNE, BART., IN LEICESTER.

Sir Roger Tichborne, as the Claimant to the Tichborne Estates, arrived in Leicester Nov. 22. In the evening a crowd of persons assembled near the George Hotel, awaiting his departure to the Temperance hall. Long before the time of meeting a great number had paid for admission to the hall, and at about a quarter to eight the barrier between the shilling and two-shilling seats was broken through, and the body of the hall, as well as the galleries, were soon filled. Hundreds were unable to gain an entrance, who, however, employed themselves in heartily cheering Sir Roger and his friends on their arrival. A few minutes after eight the Claimant came on the platform, preceded by T. M. Evans, Esq., the High Bailiff of Leicester, and his appearance was the signal for loud and long repeated cheers. On the platform were also Guildford Onslow, Esq., M.P., G. B. Skipworth, Esq., Messrs. Robert Warner, H. T. Porter, Brown, Dunbury, Colton, Searson, Nutman, Sergeant-Major Marks, and others.

The Chairman, who was received with great applause, said, at the request of the meeting he took the chair. He was pleased to see so large an assembly present. Many in that room were aware that he was a firm believer in the Claimant being Sir Roger Tichborne. (Hear, hear, and applause.) He was not only a firm believer in the Claimant, but he was a warm sympathizer in his cause. (Hear.) Indeed, he considered him a deeply wronged man. (Hear, hear, and applause.) He was, however, there that evening himself to tell them of the injury that had been done him. (Applause.) He, the Chairman, then went on to say that they must excuse him if he did not prolong his remarks, inasmuch as that was the first time he had been called upon to take the chair in that hall, and nothing could have induced him to have done so even then had it not been that he had such confidence in the identity of the Claimant with Sir Roger Tichborne. He hoped, therefore, they would give that gentleman a fair, impartial, and calm hearing. He had only one other remark to make, and that was that he was pleased to be able to announce that they had that evening present on the platform another gentleman whom he was sure they would be all glad to hear, and that was Guildford Onslow, Esq., M.P. (Applause.) They had also another most able advocate of their friend Sir Roger Tichborne, namely, Mr. Skipworth; and last, but not least, they had their great and noble friend, Sergeant-Major Marks. As all those gentlemen would address the meeting that night, he, the Chairman, said he would at once have the honour to introduce to the meeting Sir Roger Charles Doughty Tichborne, Baronet, of England. (Loud applause.)

Sir Roger, on rising, was received with loud and continued applause. He said, before proceeding to address them he would return his sincere thanks to some lady, who had been kind enough to send him a purse containing twenty guineas—(loud cheers)—as a Christmas-box for his little children, and that lady had also sent him a guinea for his old and faithful servant Bogle. He could assure that lady that the twenty guineas should all go to his children and no one else; and, as regarded Bogle, he did not think there was anyone in the world more in need of the guinea than he was, as he was a poor old man, afflicted with rheumatism, and who had been deprived of £50 a year because he told the truth, and recognized him (the speaker) as Roger Tichborne.

Lord BELLEW was the first witness produced by the Attorney-General, and he told a falsehood. He swore that he made a mark similar to that Sir ROGER here held up a piece of paper on which was the alleged sketch on his arm at Stonyhurst. He was asked by his Sir ROGER's Counsel when he first remembered the tattoo marks. He had received a letter from Mr. BOWKER asking him as to the tattoo marks, which he answered, stating that he believed the marks were the emblems of Faith, Hope, and Charity, but the sketch he held in his hand did not look like those emblems. Mr. BOWKER answered the letter stating that he thought his lordship must be mistaken, as they had a sailor coming from Normandy to say that he did that when Sir ROGER was a child. Lord BELLEW reconsidered the question, and came to the conclusion that the marks were the crown, anchor, and heart. Madame CHATILLON swore positively that she saw the mark of an anchor on his arm up his shirt-sleeve, as he was at breakfast one morning when in Paris. (Laughter.) Lady DOUGHTY also said she saw the mark, and took the trouble to paint one and took it into court. When the French witness was shown the sketch she said that was not like the mark she saw. It was twenty years ago that she saw the mark, but she could distinctly recollect it. It was plain enough to anyone to see that one of the parties had been shown the wrong sketch at the office. JULES BARRATT, a servant-man whom he engaged at Chili, and discharged at Rio Janeiro for stealing his luggage, was also called, and said he was not Sir ROGER. He did not blame him for that, because if he had sworn anything else he would have lost the commission he now held in the Brazils. He was asked if he ever saw any tattoo marks on his master's arm, and he said "No," and that there were no marks on them. (Laughter.) They had forgot to put that witness up to the tattoo marks, and that was a serious slip on the side of the defendants. BARRATT could not speak English, so that they would have some difficulty in making him understand tattoo marks. During the whole of the thirty days the Attorney-General was speaking, he was vilifying and scandalizing him. (Shame.) Mind, he did not grumble at that. If he was what the Attorney-General said he was, he had a perfect right to make the nation aware of it. But what he did grumble at was, that a law-officer, because he happened to be Attorney-General of this country, should go into a court of justice, above all other places, and vilify him in such a manner, well knowing that he dare not interrupt him in any shape or way, and then to leave that Case without proving one iota of what he had stated. What he said and what he maintained was, that the nation ought to call upon the Attorney-General to prove what he had said about him—(cheers)—because it remained that either he (the speaker) was one of the greatest villains that ever trod on earth, or that the Attorney-General was one of the basest, wickedest men that ever lived. (Cheers.) He said it was the duty of the nation to inquire into the matter, to see which was right; and nothing satisfactory could be done until that question was decided. What was it they were determined to do, then? They were going to try him upon an indictment for which he had already been incarcerated fifty-two days in the cells of Newgate—(shame)—but of three indictments they had arranged forty-three counts, and their intention was to try him upon one or two of the minor ones, so that he might not be able to call many witnesses. But he should protest against that. He was sent to Newgate for perjury—for saying that he was Sir ROGER TICHBORNE. Upon that point he should demand to be tried, and he asked them as fellow-countrymen, to demand it with him. (Cheers.) He had lost, through he might say the want of moral courage on that jury, over £200,000. In the first place, it took him £120,000 to get the case to that point it was when the Judge, that kind, impartial Judge—(hisses)—had ordered him to pay £46,000 to his opponents before he could proceed again, and that would bring it to about £200,000. It would cost him to get the Case to the same point again another £120,000, and therefore it had been a loss to him of nearly £300,000. Leaving that out of the question, he said that if they tried upon the indictment of perjury for saying he was ROGER TICHBORNE, he could prove to the world that he was Sir ROGER TICHBORNE, and that would be a great stepping-stone towards gaining his own. And that was why he should demand a trial upon that indictment. One of the indictments for which he was sent to Newgate was perjury, for saying that he was ROGER TICHBORNE, and that he was not ARTHUR ORTON, and he was confined there until bail could be found for him in £10,000. Liberal bail! But they saw that he had still friends left who did not care about £10,000—(cheers)—who came forward and bailed him out of the dismal cells. In not being taken before a magistrate, he had not the advantage of having his witnesses examined, and bound over at the expense of the Government to give evidence at the forthcoming trial. When they got him there they brought another indictment against him for forgery, and it was then clearly the intention to have kept him in Newgate till the present moment—he should not have been there now, but in a much happier place, he hoped. There was not the slightest doubt that it was their intention to have kept him in Newgate till his death should have put an end to the TICHBORNE Trial. (Shame.) He saw by the papers that Sir JOHN DUKE COLERIDGE had received from the TICHBORNE Family a number of trees out of Tichborne Park to place in his own. He should like to know upon whose authority he received that stolen property. He did not hesitate to call it stolen property. Supposing that the estates were not his property, but the property of his nephew, who was a minor, the estates were in the Court of Chancery, and what right had the Court of Chancery to make presents any more than the ladies of the TICHBORNE Family? If he had possession of his estates to-morrow he would not ask to have them returned, but would leave them with the Attorney-General to keep in his park, and to look upon them, but probably with different feelings to what he thought he should. In cross-examining him (the speaker) the Attorney-General had all the letters that Sir ROGER had written in his life placed before him by some of the most eminent lawyers in England. For twenty-three days he tried to prove that black was white with that material, and then failed—and this on the part of a gentleman who boasted to the premier of England that he could prove him to be ARTHUR ORTON in twenty minutes. He had not done that yet but if what he then said was true, it did not say much for his ability as a lawyer. On the seventy-sixth day of the Trial, the Attorney-General said, "I do not pretend to be a clever cross-examiner, for I have had very little experience in that. But I ask you, has he not got a great deal more out of me than I got out of him." (Cheers.) He asked them how he could do that if he was not ROGER TICHBORNE. (Cheers.) During his cross-examination, the Attorney-General said "Do you know what a troubadour is?" He said "Yes, I do. He's a wandering minstrel playing on the guitar." What did they think he asked him those questions for? During the time he was stationed in Ireland his brother wrote to him saying that he had bought a guitar, and was going to learn to play on it. In answering that letter, instead of saying "My dear brother," he wrote "My dear troubadour." Was not that sufficient proof of what he was? He never expected during the whole Trial that justice would be done him. On the nineteenth day of the Trial he could see that, and he said to the Judge "You are determined I shall not have a fair Trial, for since I have been in the witness-box you have been both Judge and Counsel too." He thought they would give him credit for having a little common-sense, and he would not have insulted the Judge if he thought he was going to have fair-play. (Cheers, and a voice: "He's a vagabond.") A few months after Judge BOVILL went to a Lord Mayor's dinner, and in responding to a toast said "He was at that time trying a case of the greatest imposture that ever came before a British Law Court." That was before the whole of his witnesses had been examined. One of the twelve witnesses called for the Defendant at the Trial was his uncle, Mr. ALFRED SEYMOUR, the Member of Parliament for Salisbury. No doubt his constituents were very proud of him. He said that he was not Sir ROGER TICHBORNE, because he remembered seeing the emblems of "Faith, Hope, and Charity," on the arm of the real Sir ROGER; but in the Law Institution in Chancery-lane, in 1867, he said he was not tattooed. Well, what do they think was his excuse? He said at the time he stated that, he (the speaker) was standing before him, and he did not mention it because he thought he might go and tattoo himself. (Laughter.) If they remembered at the latter part of the speech of the Attorney-General, he referred to the case of MARTIN GUERRE, the French impostor. It was not the case of MARTIN GUERRE as reported in the French books, but altered. It was published in a periodical called the *Month*, and a copy of that book was kindly forwarded by some one to his witnesses for the purpose of prejudicing them against him. And who did they think the writer was? Why the Rev. HENRY J. COLERIDGE, the Attorney-General's brother. (Oh, oh.) Mr. BALLANTINE said he did not mention that book because it was so cleverly written that if he had said anything about it everybody in court would have bought a copy, and the writer would have reaped a little fortune. (Laughter.) They would also remember that towards the close of his speech the Attorney-General wept in court like a child. (A voice: Crocodile's tears.) Well, there was no doubt but that that had great effect upon the jury. Eighteen months ago, Sir JOHN DUKE COLERIDGE was leading Counsel in the Wicklow case, which was tried in the House of Lords. He then represented an infant, as in the present Case, and when he pleaded in behalf of that child who, he said, could not speak for itself, he cried like a child. (Laughter.) It was proved that the infant he represented on that occasion was brought out of the Liverpool Union Workhouse for the purpose of depriving the young Earl of Wicklow of his property. (Renewed laughter, and cries of "Shame.") So that they would see they must not rely much on his tears and weeping. He had heard that a relative of his, Mr. WASHINGTON HIBBERT, had given a grand dinner-party a few days ago, at which Lord Chief Justice COCKBURN and the Attorney-General were present. (Shame.) He should not say one word about them going there under ordinary circumstances, but for them to go there while that Trial was pending he did think was hardly decent. (Hear, hear.) He begged to thank them sincerely for the kind manner in which they had heard him, and the hearty way they had received him that night, and would now give way to his friend, Mr. GUILDFORD ONSLOW. (Sir ROGER resumed his seat amidst loud cheering.)

Mr. ONSLOW next addressed the meeting. He assured them it was always a source of pleasure to him to advocate the cause of his friend Sir ROGER TICHBORNE wherever he chanced to be. He felt most competent to speak on the question of Sir ROGER's identity because he was living on the borders of Tichborne Park, where he had been for the past fifty-two years of his life. There had been an intimate acquaintance between his family and the TICHBORNE Family. Sir ROGER's father and mother were both friends of his, and to the latter he was indebted for many kindnesses. As Sir ROGER said the other day, he was either one of the most despicable of villains, or one of the worst men that was ever born of women. The question lay in a nutshell. Was the man, or was he not? (Cries of "He is.") If he was the [m]an, he (the speaker) was proud of the part he was taking, and he [def]ied anyone to prove that the gentleman before them was any[bo]dy else than ROGER CHARLES TICHBORNE. But whether he [wa]s so, or was not, he was an Englishman, and as such was at [lea]st entitled to fair-play. Now, he had not had that fair-play and [ju]stice which he was entitled to. He had had a trial which lasted [a h]undred and odd days, without its being proved whether he [wa]s Sir ROGER TICHBORNE or not, and he had been condemned to [N]ewgate without a conviction. They were told that the Attorney-[Ge]neral had stated to the Prime Minister that he would prove [hi]m to be ARTHUR ORTON in twenty minutes. But Mr. HAWKINS [ha]d said that ninety days would probably not see the end of the [Tri]al. They appealed to the British public, and he thought that [Si]r ROGER had already to thank the British public, and especially [th]e working classes for their support, for they had provided a [fu]nd, which he was glad to say was increasing, to endeavour to [do] him justice and fair-play. The speaker then went on to relate how he first came to take an interest in the Case. He had stated that he was a resident near Tichborne Park, and he first took up the Case from a promise he had made to Lady TICHBORNE, that he would never abandon the case of her son. He had tested the gentleman before them in every way, and put questions to him of which no human being could have any notion but himself. He had referred to certain documents in his possession, and they had only tended to confirm what the Claimant had stated. He repeated that he had tried him in every way, and was fully satisfied that he was ROGER TICHBORNE. The speaker then related several anecdotes of little things that had occurred with respect to the locality where they lived, which went to prove his identity. The speaker, in his concluding remarks, said they should be able to produce the policeman who apprehended Sir ROGER and ARTHUR ORTON in Australia, at the ensuing Trial, and he had no doubt they should be able to pull him (Sir ROGER) through, and place him in a proper position. (Applause.)

Mr. G. B. SKIPWORTH said he had never attended a meeting

RIGHT HON. W. E. GLADSTONE, M.P.

where the people were so heartily in the cause of the Claimant. It would seem they were all in one mind to say a great injustice had been done, and therefore they were determined to see justice done in the future. (Hear, hear, and a Voice: "Have a penny subscription.") He hoped that a penny subscription would not be wanted to place Sir ROGER TICHBORNE in possession of his estates. It was a disgrace to this country that a man who had the right to estates the Claimant had, should have been for six years unable to obtain possession of them. In a country like England this ought not to be submitted to. They were all Englishmen, and if one man could not obtain his rights another might not be able to do so. It had been said that the Trial in this case would commence about two months hence, and during that time Sir ROGER TICHBORNE would go to different towns and places to deliver addresses, in the hope that he might become possessed of his rights and property. (Applause.) The speaker concluded by proposing, "That more than six years having elapsed since Sir ROGER TICHBORNE came to England to claim his title and estates, during which time his opponents have, to his great cost and damage, disputed his right thereto, but without being able to prove him other than what he is; this meeting is of opinion that it is due to him as an Englishman, that he should be acknowledged by that title, and that the attempt to withhold the same from him is an injustice which ought not to be longer endured; and this meeting further considers that the Government in undertaking and carrying on the prosecution against him, and standing in the way of his recovering his lawful rights, lay themselves open to very grave charges from the people, not only by misapplying the public funds, but being responsible for an incessant and groundless agitation, and acting adversely to the well-being and the best interests of the country."

Mr. R. WALKER said he had great pleasure in seconding the resolution, because he believed everyone in that hall to be in the same position as himself with regard to the Claimant. They did not know whether he was Sir ROGER TICHBORNE or not, but before the Government had acted as they had done, he thought they ought to have let them know who he was. He had taken an interest in this Case, which had occupied the attention of the country so long. He had had an opportunity of conversing on the subject with many friends, and some had said the Claimant was the greatest impostor in the world. He did not believe that. (Hear, hear.) So far as the Government prosecution was concerned, he held that the public had no right to pay towards it, especially if they believed it was an injustice. (Hear, hear.) He was pleased to see on the platform a gentleman whom he believed to be Sir ROGER CHARLES DOUGHTY TICHBORNE. (Hear, hear, and applause.) After hearing the speech of Mr. GUILDFORD ONSLOW, who lived in the neighbourhood of the TICHBORNE family, he was more than ever inclined to believe that the Claimant was the real Sir ROGER TICHBORNE. The speaker then condemned the Attorney-General for having spoken in such disparaging terms of the Claimant, and remarked that justice had not been done to him, and said he ought to have a fair and impartial trial. (Applause.)

Sergeant-Major MARKS said he had great pleasure in having the opportunity of addressing that meeting as to the much-injured and oppressed Claimant. He recollected serving under Sir ROGER TICHBORNE, as corporal in the Carabineers, and he was certain that the Claimant was that gentleman. He gave several reasons why he had arrived at this conclusion. He said that he delivered a speech in favour of the Claimant at Oldham, and being sergeant-major in a yeomanry regiment at the time in a town not 1,000 miles from Leicester, had it read over to him afterwards by an officer in the face of a number of other members of the regiment. When it was being read he (the speaker) said "hear, hear," to almost every sentence, and at its conclusion said the report was perfectly correct, and that he was not the least sorry for having delivered the speech. The officer asked him what he meant by going about with that man, and he inquired whether he alluded to Sir ROGER TICHBORNE. (Hear, hear.) He (the speaker) however, was informed that if he left the town without leave he would be dismissed, although he had never previously neglected his duties, but he replied that he should please himself. The officer next said the uniform should not be disgraced, and he told him he was wearing plain clothes, and although he told the officer he had served in one of the most distinguished regiments of Her Majesty's service, he was eventually dismissed, and the next day he joined Sir ROGER TICHBORNE. In conclusion, he wished to say that if he was on his death-bed that minute, he would swear that the Claimant was his old officer, Sir ROGER TICHBORNE. (Applause.)

Mr. H. G. PORTER proposed, "That this meeting, having heard the Claimant of the Tichborne Estates, is of opinion that justice was not done to him at the late Trial, and whilst it insists that the charge of perjury preferred against him should at once be proved or abandoned, emphatically protests against Government interfering in the Case; and that the appropriation of public money for the purposes of the prosecution will be a great wrong done to the taxpayers of this country." He said, if he had had a shadow of a doubt as to whether the Claimant was Sir ROGER TICHBORNE, he should have been convinced after hearing the speeches of Mr. ONSLOW and Major MARKS, the last named of whom had spoken out with the fearlessness of a British soldier. He (the speaker) believed the Claimant was the man he represented himself to be, and considered no man had ever had a more unjust or unfair Trial. Whether the Claimant was Sir ROGER TICHBORNE or not, he was an Englishman, and as such, had a right to claim a just, fair, and impartial Trial. (Applause.)

Mr. NEIMAN seconded the resolution, which was carried unanimously.

Mr. ONSLOW, M. P., moved a vote of thanks to the Chairman for presiding.

Sir ROGER, in seconding the vote, said the Chairman had been a strong supporter of his cause, not only by his influence, but his pocket. Therefore it was a double pleasure to him to ask them to record a vote of thanks to their worthy Chairman.

The vote was carried unanimously.

The Chairman having briefly acknowledged the vote, three cheers were given for Sir ROGER TICHBORNE, and three groans for the Attorney-General.

The meeting then terminated.

Sir ROGER, on leaving the hall, was loudly cheered.

SERGEANT-MAJOR MARKS AND MAJOR JOCELYN.

The following is taken from a speech of Sergeant-Major MARKS at Nottingham, at a meeting for the purpose of raising funds for the Claimant. Sergeant-Major MARKS said he was corporal in the regiment when ROGER TICHBORNE joined, and served in the troop with him. He was the officer in charge of his squad, and during mid-day stable hours he was in the habit of asking questions respecting the men, their horses and appointments. He had drilled with him both mounted and dismounted, and was quite sure that the Claimant was ROGER TICHBORNE whom he knew in the Carabineers. Referring to a letter from Major JOCELYN in the *Standard*, MARKS said he saw the Major in town, during the Trial, when he addressed him, and his answer was, "I do not know you." He said, "You do very well; I had the honour of serving with you for nine years. I was one of your corporals." He said, "Do tell me who you are." He replied, "I would rather wait and see if you could recognize me," which he failed to do. He (MARKS) now asked the public to judge if the Major was competent to form an opinion respecting ROGER TICHBORNE's identity, the Claimant having joined in October, 1849, and gone to Cahir with the head-quarters of his regiment in 1850. Major JOCELYN leaving Dublin for Limerick with his troop in 1850, at which place the gallant Major left the service altogether. Now his acquaintance with the Claimant would be six months. Was it possible, after not knowing him (MARKS), whom he saw every day for nine years, that he could say that the Claimant was not the real ROGER TICHBORNE? He left that for the public to judge. Major JOCELYN asked, when in town, what he thought of the Claimant. He said, "He is ROGER TICHBORNE, Sir;" and his reply was that he could not say whether he was or not; but he thought the Major had been converted owing to the Claimant's ignorance of military tactics, for he would never have made a cavalry officer. It was next to impossible to teach him his drill. He (MARKS) had frequently seen him placed in the ranks for not knowing his place when he was troop leader, and he had ridden beside him in the ranks. As to General JONES, who commanded the regiment, failing to identify the Claimant, he also did not know him until an officer called his attention and said, "That is MARKS." The General then asked him when he left the regiment—was it after they came from India? He replied, "It was in 1852, before you went to India." He had signed his (MARKS) transfer documents to the 4th Dragoon Guards, and did not know him.

MR. GLADSTONE.

It has often been a matter of mystery to us how or why it was that Mr. GLADSTONE could possibly connect himself in the violent way he did with the proceedings against TICHBORNE. One theory, suggested by a most intimate friend of his own, was, that being an eminent Greek scholar, he came to the conclusion that no man could ever forget his Greek; and the Claimant, like a vain coxcomb, having been silly enough to tell Sir J. COLERIDGE that he learned Greek at Stonyhurst (just as he said that he learned Hebrew, which was never taught there)—he, in point of fact, never having learned even the Greek alphabet—Mr. GLADSTONE became convinced that his forgetfulness of even the letters proved him to be a Butcher—an Impostor: in a word, ARTHUR ORTON; and, having formed this conclusion, he troubled himself no longer about the matter, but surrendered his own judgment, like that of a child, to the tricksters and schemers by whom he was surrounded; so that he continued, during the whole Trial, almost wilfully blind to the horrible measures that were brought into play against the Claimant.

SIR ROGER TICHBORNE AT ST. JAMES'S HALL.

The second of the "Demonstrations" in aid of the Defence Fund held, as was announced in the placards, during the Cattle-show week, took place in St. James's Hall. Sir ROGER and his friends, upon making their appearance on the platform, were received with great applause.

On the motion of Mr. IRELAND, Mr. G. B. SKIPWORTH, of Moortown Hall, Caistor, Lincolnshire, was called to the chair. He said: For himself, he would not appear in any cause which he did not sincerely believe to be genuine; and from all he knew, and all he could ascertain, there was no doubt on his mind that the gentleman who sat at his right was the real Sir ROGER TICHBORNE. Mr. SKIPWORTH then proceeded, at great length, to give a narrative of the Case, from the time it was supposed that Mr. ROGER TICHBORNE was lost in the "Bella;" the advertisements inserted by Lady TICHBORNE, in the belief that her son had been saved; and the efforts made by GIBBES and others to discover the lost heir. They had sought him, not he them. On the other hand, he charged the opposition with having organised a conspiracy from the very commencement to deny Sir ROGER's claims, and make him out somebody else—called ARTHUR ORTON. A detective, named FORSTER, came over in the same ship with the Baronet, who recommended him to destroy a letter he had in his possession, and to write another, signed "ARTHUR ORTON." In an evil moment he consented to do so, and from that moment complications of all kinds arose. For himself, he saw no difference in the letter of ROGER TICHBORNE of 1852 and that of ORTON in 1866, and he handed the letters to the gentlemen around him to compare and judge for themselves. He complained, also, of the manner in which the affidavit of the Mother who had recognized her son was shut out of Court. Why did they do that? Why, because they did not want the truth. Why did the Attorney-General vilify and try to make out the 85 witnesses in favour of the Claimant to be liars? Because they did not want the truth. Why did they send the Claimant to Chili? Only to get rid of him, as thirteen or fourteen were killed in the diligence by which he should have gone, but fortunately did not. He did not know why the Government should pursue this course of persecution, except that Mr. GLADSTONE's Government had lost their senses. (Cheers.) All he could say was, that if they had lost their senses, that did not excuse their conduct. (Cheers.)

The Chairman then announced that the gentleman about to address them was Mr. WHALLEY, the Member of Parliament for Peterborough. (Cheers.)

Mr. WHALLEY said he could easily understand that the President of the evening, a country gentleman of the highest standing, not a professional advocate, should have felt an intellectual pleasure in entering upon a narrative of this Case. Of course, he and and his friend Mr. GUILDFORD ONSLOW, who were non-professional, had done their best to direct public opinion to the real questions at issue, and he (Mr. WHALLEY) had in fact come to that meeting from a sick-bed, the result of an accident, to address the meeting, as a duty, having presided at the meeting on the previous night. There were in this case two questions—1. Was this man truly Roger Tichborne? 2. Is that fact, if fact it be, known to the Attorney-General, to Her Majesty's Government, or to Mr. Gladstone? And knowing that, have they given £100,000 to prosecute that man, without having taken the trouble to ascertain —which they could easily have done—whether his claims were valid or not? It had been said there was a conspiracy. He had no doubt there was, and he had also a strong opinion as to which side the conspiracy was on. Mr. Whalley explained the circumstances under which, with personal inquiry of the most minute character, he had come to the conclusion that the Claimant was the real Sir Roger Tichborne. He had gone as a Member of Parliament with the Claimant to all the large towns of the kingdom. There had sprung up, as it were under his feet, witnesses from the Carabineers, and others, all of whom met Sir Roger as an old friend, and their talk of dogs, horses, old friends, and old associations, was such as could only have happened between persons who had long known each other. He felt that his character as a Member of Parliament was not less at stake in this affair than that of the Claimant. For his own part, he had never hesitated to say that the Tichbornes, the Doughtys, the Radcliffes, the whole lot of them, had combined to deny the claims and the rights of the real heir. They met in a drawing-room, six years ago, and came to the conclusion they were strong enough to defy the law and the justice of England. He was not now in a position to prove that conspiracy, but he hoped to live long enough to prove what he said; and further, that the Attorney-General and the Government were attempting to prosecute under a penal Act a man whom they knew was innocent of the charges made against him. The object was to keep the large Tichborne Estates in the hands of the Arundel family—a family which they all knew was very influential in certain sections of English society. He had no hesitation in saying that the Plaintiff had been committed to prison under most unusual and tyrannical circumstances. (Cries of "Time," "Turn him out," and confusion.) How could their time be better employed, than in inquiring into the motives and conduct of the Attorney-General introducing a measure of law-reform which had the effect of sending this man to prison without the opportunity of hearing the charges made against him, without hearing witnesses, and without the opportunity of asking the magistrate that his own witnesses' expenses should be paid? He was as assiduous an attendant to his duties in Parliament as most men, but he knew nothing of the passing of such a measure by that very young law-reformer, Sir J. Coleridge. Well, now, they had hitherto "stumped the country," as it was called, but now they appealed to the metropolis to step forward to help a man who had been beaten by a wealthy combination and a hostile Government. The hon. member proceeded to refer to the evidence on the tattooing, the incarceration of the Defendant in Newgate, and various other well-known incidents connected with the Case, and said that three months ago he had said that he would be there to reply to anyone who denied that the Attorney-General knew, or had the means of knowing, that this man was Roger Tichborne. He had two documents in his hands. They had been sold throughout the streets at 6d., but were not to be had now, as they had been suppressed. Those documents gave two letters, signed Arthur Orton and Roger Tichborne. They were unquestionably in the same handwriting, and if they were to be accepted as genuine, the inference was obvious. But this document was issued by the agent of the defence to the action of the Claimant. (Cheers.)

Mr. G. Onslow, M.P., said he only wished to say a few words before Sir Roger rose to address them. He had received, since he arrived there, a short time before that meeting was commenced, a letter, dated 172, Strand, Dec. 10, in which the writer stated that, having met with two of the crew of the "Bella," while in the United States ship, "Lancaster," he had no objection to state what they had told him, as to the wreck of the "Bella." The letter was signed "J. Perceval." He had sent to 172, Strand, to ask the writer to come at once, and his messenger brought back for answer, that the writer had gone to the hall, and was in it at that moment. If so, he (Mr. Onslow) most earnestly trusted that he would come forward, and make his statement.

The Chairman said he hoped Mr. Perceval would answer the appeal of Mr. Onslow.

A little further delay took place, but no one put in an appearance; and

Sir Roger then rose amidst cheers. When order was restored, he said that he must beg of the meeting to excuse him if he could not speak very loud. He was suffering from a cold, and had been in a cloudy Court all day, which had not improved his power of making himself heard in so large a building. He would ask them to look at the materials he, the Attorney-General, had to go upon at the Trial. He had all his letters, written either in French or in English, while he was in England or abroad, and yet if with all that material, after a Trial which lasted 103 days, and in which he (Sir Roger) was 23 days under cross-examination, the Attorney-General left off without being able to prove that he (Sir Roger) was anybody else than himself, he must be a very great bungler indeed. (Cheers and laughter.) They all knew that he was not a bungler, but, on the contrary, very clever; and yet, with all his cleverness, he had not the power to change Sir Roger Tichborne into anything else than what he really was, and, therefore, he supposed he should be Sir Roger Tichborne as long as he lived. That was the net result of a Trial which lasted 103 days, in the course of which the Attorney-General occupied 30 days by a speech which was filled with language only fit to be used by fishwomen in Billingsgate. If at the end of 103 days he found that he had no more money to pay Counsel to go on, and allowed himself to be nonsuited, was that any reason why he should be called an impostor? (Hear, hear.) In a recent case in a Vice-Chancellor's Court, the Vice-Chancellor took exception to the description of him in an official paper as Sir Roger Tichborne; but he thought that he had done very well in carrying on the Case so long as he did at so enormous a cost, and leaving at all events the question an open one. (Cheers.) But the Attorney-General knew very well what he was about. He prolonged the Case as long as he could, day after day, and night after night; he threatened the jury with the 200 or more witnesses he was prepared to call, and gave them to understand that they might have to serve on the jury for two years more. Well, when the Case was at last closed, under those circumstances they sent him at once to Newgate. (A female voice at the lower end of the hall—"Where he ought to be."—Laughter, cheers, and cries of "Turn him out.") What was the object of the Attorney-General in removing this Trial from the Old Bailey into the Court of Queen's Bench? Why, common juries did not suit the Attorney-General; he preferred a special jury of half-bred swells—(Hear, hear, and Oh, oh!)—and he changed the Court especially when he found that the Chancellor of the Exchequer declined to sanction the expenditure of £100,000 on the Trial on which he had calculated. He soon found somebody else to undertake the duty. If he had got the £100,000 he would not have done that. As to the 206 witnesses with whom he had threatened the jury, he (Sir Roger) believed that when he produced the last of his twelve witnesses he had not twelve more left to put into the box. He did not complain of what the Attorney-General had said of him, but what he did complain of was that his fellow-countrymen should have allowed the first law officer of the Crown to retire from his position as prosecutor without having either proved what he had said of him (Sir Roger), or being compelled to withdraw his aspersions and calumnies. Mr. Bruce, the Home Secretary, said he had retired from the Case. He contended that the Attorney-General had no right to retire from the Case. What recompense could be given to him (Sir Roger) for the days he had been confined in the stone cells of Newgate Gaol on the action of the Attorney-General? What money would measure his sufferings and that of his family during his incarceration? What compensation would equal the torture and the loss inflicted upon him by the delay in bringing the questions at issue to a close? It was now eight months since he was committed on two charges, one of which had since been abandoned. It would be April before the Trial could come on upon the other. Was that not contrary to Magna Charta, which declared that no man could be tried for any offence after the expiration of a year and a day? He said to that meeting, and to the country, that he had a right to be tried; and that was what he demanded, without delay. Was it intended to force him to remain in this country, and probably to leave his children orphans before securing for them their rights to his title and estates. They would in that case be paupers for life. But he did not believe a combination of rich and clever people would be able to prevent justice from being done. But for that purpose such meetings as these he addressed were necessary. Sir Roger, who seemed very much exhausted, sat down amidst general applause, and was followed by

Mr. Onslow, who said that the system of public meetings had been forced upon them when justice had been refused in the House of Commons. It was strange that, in spite of repeated invitations, no one would come forward at any of the meetings to offer any reasons why they considered the Claimant an impostor. He (Mr. Onslow) complained that his friend had not had that fair-play in the late trial to which, as an Englishman, he was entitled. The delay and procrastination in the criminal trials he believed was intentional, and if the Attorney-General had been sincere in recently demanding a Trial at Bar, why had he not taken that course last April? The hon. member declared that the Claimant was one of the best chess-players, ecarte-players, musicians and riders, and that he would challenge the Attorney-General to compete with him for £1,000 in a four-mile ride across the country, weight for weight. (Cheers.) Many remarkable statements were made by the hon. member, which, if true, make it impossible that the Claimant could be any other than the real Roger Tichborne. A complete answer given to twelve questions in writing which were handed up to him from some bitter unbeliever in the Claimant, was given offhand in a way that evoked a storm of applause. Under the influence of the good feeling thus created, a vote of thanks was given to the gentleman who occupied the chair, and the proceedings came to a close amidst loud applause.

LEGAL PROCEEDINGS.

We now resume our narrative of the legal proceedings.

The numerous Meetings at which the Claimant attended produced an influence on public opinion which the Family and their adherents felt. It was deemed incredible that an Impostor should show himself thus publicly before the whole Nation; accordingly they applied for a postponement of the Trial of Sir Roger Tichborne.

At the sitting of the Court of Queen's Bench Nov. 14, before the Lord Chief Justice Cockburn, Mr. Justice Blackburn, and Mr. Justice Quain, the case of the prosecution of the Claimant to the Tichborne Estates was mentioned by Mr. HAWKINS, Q.C., who was the leading Counsel for the Crown.

Mr. HAWKINS said—I am about to mention to your lordship a case that I am not quite sure I ought not to mention to the Lord Chief Justice in Chambers, as Judge at Nisi Prius, rather than to the full Court. In the Case of "The QUEEN v. CASTRO," as your lordships know, the Defendant stands charged on three indictments involving perjury of a very serious character, and I am bound to tell your lordships that the Case which will be tried must of necessity, from the nature of the charges, occupy a very considerable time. My present application is this—I understand the Case now stands 30 on the list.

The Lord Chief Justice: I think there are thirty special jury remanets, and this Case stands first of the new causes.

Mr. HAWKINS: All the parties concerned are desirous of having a Case of this character tried and disposed of as speedily as consistent with the practice of the Court and the justice of the Case; and my application now is simply to know whether, in the present state of the list, the Lord Chief Justice will be disposed to appoint a special day for the trial of this Case in advance of the other causes.

The Lord Chief Justice: I am in this difficulty, that I don't see how I can displace the other suitors in the Court. Besides that two of our number are going immediately on the winter circuit, there are sittings in error after Term, and other business to dispose of; so that I think it impossible to make arrangements for the trial of the Case at these sittings. I don't see how you can ask for the postponement of special jury cases now standing over simply to facilitate the trial of this Case.

Mr. HAWKINS: As we have received notice from the Defendant that it is intended to apply on his behalf to the Court to fix a day for the Trial, I thought it was only right on the part of the Crown to apply to the Court to know what could be done.

The Lord Chief Justice: You say the Case must take a considerable time to try?

Mr. HAWKINS: Yes. I believe it must extend over many weeks.

The Lord Chief Justice: But what power have we to sit for so long a time? We are limited by the Act of Parliament to twenty-four working days. I have very much doubt, in the first place, whether the Common Law Procedure Act applies at all in criminal cases; but if it does, I doubt if we can go beyond the twenty-four days. It is a very doubtful case, and I fear there are no means of getting over the difficulty.

Mr. HAWKINS: If the case were to be commenced now, it must extend over the period fixed for the sittings, and in that case a difficulty would arise as to the adjournment.

The Lord Chief Justice: There is but one way that I see at present of getting over the difficulty, and that is to commence the Trial on the first day of next Term, and devote the whole of the Term and the after-sittings to it. If that is agreed to by both sides, will it give sufficient time to satisfactorily dispose of the Case?

Mr. HAWKINS: I cannot say that it will. I must candidly state that the difficulty mentioned by your lordship has occurred to me, Mr. Serjeant PARRY, and Sir GEORGE HONYMAN, who are with me. We have seriously considered it, and we are still gravely considering what is the best course to adopt, so that when the Trial commences it shall be continued to its termination.

The Lord Chief Justice: All we can say now is, that we cannot sacrifice the interests of other suitors by taking it at the present sittings. We might make arrangements for taking it at the commencement of next Term, and continuing it till the end of the sittings. At present it is vain to ask us to appoint a day that must have the effect of displacing the other cases; and if it is done it will be useless, because from what you state it will be impossible to bring the Trial within the period allotted for the sittings.

Mr. HAWKINS: It is the opinion of myself, Mr. Serjeant PARRY, and Sir GEORGE HONYMAN, that it impossible to hope that it can be concluded at these sittings; and, therefore, we thought it right to mention it to the Court, that all parties might know at once that there is no prospect of its being tried at these sittings.

The Lord Chief Justice: The Judges of this Court have to attend chambers, two Judges will have to go the winter circuit, and others to attend the Court of Error, and without sacrificing all the other suitors, which we ought not to do, it is impossible to make arrangements for commencing the Trial now.

Mr. Serjeant SLEIGH, with whom was Mr. HORACE BROWNE, said—My learned friend has forgotten to state that a notice was served by the Defendant on the Solicitor to the Treasury that an application would be made by me this morning to the Court, to fix, if possible, a day for the Trial of the Case. I mention that fact because the Defendant, like all persons under a criminal charge who assert their innocence, is anxious to be tried. I shall feel grateful on the part of the Defendant if Mr. HAWKINS can point out any way by which the difficulty that presents itself can be got over.

The Lord Chief Justice: I understand Mr. HAWKINS to say that the learned Counsel who are acting with him are considering the best course to adopt, and I dare say he will communicate with you; and, if you can all agree, I have no doubt the Court will be ready to facilitate your views if we can consistently do so.

Mr. Serjeant SLEIGH: I quite concur with my learned friend Mr. HAWKINS that if the Case were to be taken on the first day of Term it would be impossible to conclude it within the time then allotted to the sittings.

Mr. HAWKINS: If my learned friend Mr. Serjeant SLEIGH will give me credit for an earnest desire to consider the matter, and to suit his convenience, to make such arrangements, with the assent of the Court, as will insure the Trial at the earliest moment and without interruption, I will communicate with him the moment I intend to mention the Case again to the Court, and before final arrangements are made.

The Lord Chief Justice: If you mention the Case again before the end of the sittings, we will consider in the interval the best course to pursue.

Mr. HAWKINS: Quite so. I will inform my learned friend when I intend to mention it again, and if he can make any suggestion I shall be happy to facilitate it.

The Lord Chief Justice: I have no doubt the prosecution will feel bound to do everything that is right and fair towards the Defendant.

Mr. HAWKINS: Everything in accordance with fairness and justice shall be done.

The Lord Chief Justice: Before you make your final arrangements you can mention the Case again to the Court.

These repeated postponements were so unfair that the Claimant's friends deemed it proper that something definite should be arrived at. We transcribe the next step in the proceedings.

Court of Queen's Bench, November 18th.

(Sittings in Banco, at Westminster, before Lord Chief Justice COCKBURN, Mr. Justice BLACKBURN, and Mr. Justice MELLOR.)

It will be recollected that a few days ago Mr. HAWKINS, Q.C., leading Counsel for the Crown in the contemplated prosecution of the Claimant to the Tichborne Estates, made application to the Court of Queen's Bench to fix a day for the Trial, and that by direction of the Court, the learned gentleman undertook to communicate with the Counsel for the defence to see whether an arrangement might not be come to between them in reference to a time when the Trial might come on, with a prospect to its continuance to the close without interruption, and without inconvenience to the interests of other legal business.

Mr. Serjeant SLEIGH, with whom was Mr. HORACE BROWN, said—In this case I have to move the Court for a rule nisi calling upon the Attorney-General to show cause why in this Case, which has been brought into this Court by writ of certiorari, a writ of procedendo should not issue, or in the alternative why the Defendant should not have a Trial at Bar. I feel it is unnecessary that I should enter into anything like details as regards the importance of the Case both to the Defendant and the public.

The Lord Chief Justice: Certainly not. Have you mentioned your application to the other side?

Mr. Serjeant SLEIGH: I have not, and I have acted advisedly in not communicating to the other side my intention of making this application; but if your lordships wish me to justify my conduct, I will do so.

The Lord Chief Justice: I don't know that it is necessary. I only asked because the other day it was presumed some arrangement might be come to.

Mr. Serjeant SLEIGH: What happened then has caused me to exercise my discretion, and not do so. On the former occasion I gave notice of my intention to apply to the Court, and then Mr. HAWKINS, who is my senior, came down to the Court and anticipated my motion. It is an axiom of law that the Crown can do no wrong, and cannot be guilty of any laches; but the only instance in which writs of procedendo have been granted has been when private parties have been at fault.

Mr. Justice BLACKBURN: Upon what ground do you ask for a writ of procedendo?

Mr. Serjeant SLEIGH: The main ground is that, according to the existing state of the law, and having reference to the amount of business already upon the paper of the Court, there is no probability whatever of the Trial taking place for a considerable time, unless extraordinary powers be had recourse to.

The Lord Chief Justice: You are entitled to exercise your discretion in conducting the Case.

Mr. Serjeant SLEIGH: I am well aware that in order to induce the Court to issue a writ of procedendo on the part of the Defendant very good reasons must be shown for its being done. I am also well aware that, according to almost universal practice, whether the Court deals with a writ of procedendo, or, what is analogous to it, bring down a trial by proviso where the certiorari has been moved for and obtained by the Crown, that strong reasons must be shown to the Court before granting such writ of procedendo. In this case it is impossible that the Defendant can be tried within any proximate period. A very large number of witnesses will have to be examined on both sides; and it must be obvious to your lordships that, unless I can have this remedy a very long time must elapse before the Trial can come off.

The Lord Chief Justice: I think a Trial at Bar takes place under the 11th Geo. IV. and the 1st Will. IV.; and, if I remember right, in such a trial the Court is not tied down to the duration of Term, but that the Court can then make its own arrangements for continuing the Trial after it has once commenced.

Mr. Serjeant SLEIGH: Just so.

The Lord Chief Justice: The Court has then absolute power to make any arrangements for continuing the Trial.

Mr. Serjeant SLEIGH: I feel bound to state a matter that has occurred to my mind in connection with the Trial at Bar, namely, that it will have to be presided over by four Judges.

The Lord Chief Justice: I don't think it must absolutely be before four judges, but such a number as would satisfy the exigencies of a Court in Banco, and as there are now six Judges of the Court, three can very well preside at a Trial at Bar.

Mr. Justice BLACKBURN: Considerable difficulty must arise from it in a trial that it is stated is likely to occupy 90 days.

The Lord Chief Justice: There is one advantage in a Trial at Bar, that the proceedings are final points of law and evidence. There is no appeal from one Court in Banco to another Court in Banco. It is a matter deserving consideration, and the defendant is entitled to bring it forward. We will give you a rule.

Mr. Justice BLACKBURN: Sufficient time must be given to the Crown to show cause against this rule this term.

Mr. Serjeant SLEIGH: I have waited from Thursday until today, expecting to hear from the prosecution.

The Lord Chief Justice: It is time something was done.

Mr. Serjeant SLEIGH: PALMER's Act does not apply to this Case. To remove a case under that Act into the Old Bailey, the offence must have been committed out of the jurisdiction of the Old Bailey.

The Lord Chief Justice: Take your rule, and make it returnable on Thursday if possible; and if not, let it be returnable on Friday.

Rule granted accordingly.

The following powerful comment on this appeared in the *Morning Advertiser*:—

THE RULE NISI.

The TICHBORNE Claimant has obtained a rule *nisi* calling upon the Attorney-General to show cause why a writ of procedendo should not be issued to compel his Trial at Bar. In such case there will be three Judges instead of one. Let the foes and detractors of the Claimant say what they will; let those who feel compromised by their hasty condemnation of this oppressed individual stick to their opinions as they may; it cannot be denied that an immense reaction has taken place throughout the country with regard to the merits of this extraordinary Case. The indomitable courage and the wonderful talent—we might almost say genius—displayed by the Claimant in addressing vast assemblies has told upon the English people. His clearness and straightforward style, the precision and tact with which he has stated his case, have made a deep and wide impression wherever he has gone; and the circle of his friends, and the believers in the justice of his claim, have increased, and are increasing to a vast extent daily. In proportion as he has advanced in estimation the Law has suffered. It would seem, indeed, as if the mighty engine set in motion against this one penniless individual, this single reputed and branded impostor, perjurer, and forger, had got thoroughly jammed and blocked, and that its wheels refuse to move and grind him to powder, as was so loudly menaced. Let us reconsider a little the state of things. Let us recall the monster Trial when Sir JOHN COLERIDGE talked against the limited monetary means of the other side by the day and by the week, until they were exhausted. Let us recur to the famous tattoo evidence, when the jury gave in, and the Claimant was committed to a dungeon on charges, one at least of which we understand is abandoned, and that the graver of the two. There, in that prison, he would probably have died ere this, had he not been rescued by generous and devoted friends. We were told then that the Attorney-General could convict him with overwhelming evidence in a day; nay, in three-quarters of an hour. Was not that the boast? And, we venture to observe that, if he could not, the consignment of the Claimant to Newgate at all was an act of the highest injustice. Then, after his liberation on bail, we began to hear of new evidence and new Commissioners. Where are they? The Bench seems to apprehend a longer trial than ever. What! to prove this impostor already treated as a felon guilty, is there so much still needed, that the pick of the most learned Counsel at the Bar cannot see their way to the end of it? Where is the ARTHUR ORTON proof? Let no one be deceived. The Claimant—whoever he is—is no Wapping butcher. There are tens and hundreds of thousands now throughout England and Scotland convinced of this. We give elsewhere a report from the *Dundee Courier*, which shows what is being done by this extraordinary man, who makes friends, and even converts, wherever he goes; and this not only amongst the "rabble," as his enemies would call them—that is, the honest working men and artisans of Great Britain, but in intellectual and educated coteries as well. We have pronounced no opinion in this paper as to whether the Claimant is Sir ROGER TICHBORNE or not; but we have stated our firm belief as to his not being ORTON. We are also of opinion that the evidence has hitherto failed to establish that he is not Sir ROGER TICHBORNE. If the Government is ready with overwhelming proof, why are they so dilatory in their action? Why are they the postponers of the trial? It is true that the delay is advantageous to the accused—at least so it seems to us; but that surely is not the object of the accusers and denouncers of the Claimant, who is daily winning the sympathies of more and more of Her Majesty's lieges, and who, if he continues much longer what he is now doing, will undoubtedly walk into Westminster Hall to deliver himself up to trial with the hearty good wishes of a vast majority of the English people at his back.

TRIAL AT BAR OF SIR ROGER TICHBORNE.

Court of Queen's Bench, November 22.

(Sittings in Banco, at Westminster, before Lord Chief Justice COCKBURN, Mr. Justice BLACKBURN, and Mr. Justice MELLOR.)

Some days ago, Mr. HAWKINS, Q.C., made application to the Court to fix a time when the contemplated Trial of the Claimant to the Tichborne Baronetcy and Estates, on charges of perjury and forgery, would come on, and the Court suggested that Counsel for the Crown and the Defence might come to some arrangement between them, and mention the matter again.

Mr. Serjeant SLEIGH, Counsel for the Defence, came into Court since then, and, taking the Crown by surprise, moved for a rule calling on the Attorney-General to show cause why the Defendant should not have a Trial at Bar, before the full Court, comprising four Judges and a jury, instead of by the ordinary tribunal of one Judge and a jury.

The Court granted the rule, and it was expected that the Attorney-General or Mr. HAWKINS would appear to-day to show cause against it. The prosecution for the Crown, however, determined upon another course, and at the sitting of the Court this morning,

The Attorney-General (with whom was Mr. HAWKINS), addressing their lordships, said: I appear before your lordships today, not exactly to move in this Case, but to make a statement to your lordships, and to ask, as I have a right to ask as HER MAJESTY'S Attorney-General, for a Trial at Bar in the case of the "QUEEN *v.* CASTRO." I have from an early period of the Case handed over its conduct to Mr. HAWKINS, Q.C., Mr. Serjeant PARRY, and Sir GEORGE HONYMAN, Q.C., and as the Crown is represented by them, it would be to the last degree unbecoming in me to interfere directly or indirectly, with the conduct of the Case. I do not, therefore, appear as taking part in the conduct of the Case, but as it appears from the authorities that a Trial at Bar must be demanded by the Attorney-General, I do so now in that capacity. My learned friends who have the conduct of the Case have from the first been in anxious consultation how best it can be disposed of with the least inconvenience, and how any inconvenience that must arise can be best met. No doubt there is extreme inconvenience in a Trial at Bar. There is the employment of more than one Judge belonging to a Court already overworked, and many grave and weighty reasons why, if possible, in any case a Trial at Bar should be avoided. They have been, I hope, duly weighed and considered by us. There is, on the other hand, the extreme importance that a case of this kind, when once begun, should be tried to its end, and that any time occupied on it should not by any accident be thrown away. Besides this inconvenience there is another, upon which I do not presume to pronounce an opinion now—whether the present state of the law is sufficient for the purpose of the Trial; but I find, from the best consideration I can give to it, and the opinions also of men far more able than myself, that it is open to grave doubt indeed, and therefore it would not be right, in a case of this kind, to have the Trial begun when it is doubtful if it can be brought to a conclusion. It has further been suggested, by persons whose opinions are entitled to great weight and attention at my hands, to remedy the matter by passing an Act of Parliament, but that is open to the objection of *ex post facto* legislation. Besides that, it is not for me to say, and I have no right to assume, that the Legislature, simply on the representation of the Government, would pass such an Act—an Act affecting a person actually on his trial before a Court, by altering the state of the law under which he was brought before the Court. I think it would be presumption in me, and taking a liberty which I have no right to take, to think that they would pass such a law. Under these circumstances, weighing the inconveniences and conveniences on both sides, and there being two rules pending before your lordships, in one of which the Defendant asks for a Trial at Bar, I, taking no part in the conduct of the Case, respectfully, in my official capacity as Attorney-General, apply to your lordships to demand a Trial at Bar, and that a day shall be fixed for the Trial. With regard to the rules I have referred to, Mr. HAWKINS and his learned friends have been instructed to show cause against them, and they will take such a course in reference to them as they think best.

The Lord Chief Justice: A claim for a Trial at Bar is the right of the Attorney-General. It is quite beyond my province to express any opinion on the reasons you have urged for a Trial at Bar. They are entirely for the guidance of your own conduct, and you have a right to declare them in public. You are entitled to what you ask.

Mr. Justice BLACKBURN: I think the difficulties attending a Trial at Bar are considerably greater than a trial at Nisi Prius. But if you have well considered them, and demand a Trial at Bar, you have a right to it.

The Lord Chief Justice: Is there any occasion to show cause in the rules pending? Mr. Serjeant SLEIGH has asked in the alternative for a writ of *procedendo*, but, as the Trial at Bar has been conceded, I see no reason for dealing further with them.

Mr. Serjeant SLEIGH, with whom was Mr. HORACE BROWNE, said: After the course that has been taken by the learned Attorney-General, with the permission of the Court, I will abandon the rules. My object is attained.

Mr. HAWKINS: The only reason for showing cause would have been that the application by the other side was an evasion of what might be considered the rights and privileges of the Crown.

The Lord Chief Justice. It is not necessary for you to show that. The next thing is for the Court to make what seems to it the best arrangements for the Trial. For reasons which I stated the other day, it cannot take place before next Term, and then not before the fifth or sixth day of Term.

Mr. HAWKINS: It is entirely in the discretion of the Court to fix the day.

The Lord Chief Justice: That is so; but at the same time any suggestion from either side would have due weight with the Court. The difficulty which now presents itself is the Spring Assizes.

Mr. HAWKINS: I can do no more than state, on the part of the Crown, that whatever day is fixed for the commencement of the Trial, we shall be ready.

Mr. Serjeant SLEIGH: If I might make a suggestion, in order that the constitution of the Court might not be disturbed in Banco during Term, I would suggest that the Trial should commence on the first day of Hilary after Term sittings.

The Lord Chief Justice: Are you sure it is all right with regard to the adjournment over to the next Term after the after-Term sittings are exhausted? Besides that, I have doubts if the Court can adjourn over the Spring Circuit. It is not for the interests of justice, or for either side to adjourn over for a month after once the Trial has begun. When once commenced, it will be far better to go through without adjournment.

Mr. Serjeant SLEIGH: Yes.

The Lord Chief Justice: We will think about it in the meantime. As there are two indictments for perjury, the QUEEN's Coroner reminds me there must be two juries. It would certainly be very inconvenient to keep the second jury in suspense; therefore it is very desirable, before the Case comes on, the Crown should communicate to the Defendant on which indictment the defendant is to be tried.

Mr. HAWKINS: Certainly.

The Lord Chief Justice: The same officer informed me that in a Trial at Bar, fifteen days' notice of trial must be given.

Mr. HAWKINS: Yes; I understood so. In O'CONNELL's case—and the words of the English and Irish Acts are the same—the days they appointed for the trial were in Term?

Mr. Justice BLACKBURN: Were they all in Term?

Mr. HAWKINS: No. The trial extended over the Term. It commenced in Term, and extended over to the middle of the next vacation, and that was one of the grounds of error in O'CONNELL's case.

The Court and the passages were crowded by persons curious to hear the expected arguments against and in support of Mr. Serjeant SLEIGH's rule.

The day of Trial was at length finally fixed by the Court of Queen's Bench, on Saturday, Nov. 23rd.

The Lord Chief Justice, seeing the Attorney-General in Court, said: Mr. Attorney-General, we have been considering what should be done in the case of "The QUEEN v. CASTRO," which you mentioned yesterday. In the first place, however desirable it is that the Case should be taken at the earliest possible moment, we find, as I have already intimated, it is out of the question to hope that it can be taken this Term. That being so, we have had to consider whether it can be taken in Hilary Term. A serious obstacle presents itself to that, because there is reason to doubt whether, if we begin the Trial in that Term, we can go on with it to the end, and yet make provision for the Spring Circuits. If we have three Judges sitting, trying the Case, great inconvenience would necessarily arise in making arrangements for the Circuits. Under all the circumstances it seemed to us that as the Case had stood over for so long, the best way will be to postpone it until next Easter Term. Four days of that will be required in hearing motions for new Trials; but on the fifth day we can commence the Trial, and proceed with it to the end without interfering with the Summer Circuits.

The Attorney-General: I am much obliged to your lordship for the information. I will let my learned friend, Mr. HAWKINS, know of your determination.

The Lord Chief Justice: I have made the statement because I thought it for the convenience of all parties that they should know as early as possible what day we have fixed for the Trial of the Case.

Mr. Justice BLACKBURN. Of course the Defendant must have information of the day appointed for the Trial

The Attorney-General: I will let Mr. GRAY, the Solicitor to the Treasury, know your lordships' decision, and he will at once communicate it to the attorney at the other side.

The Lord Chief Justice: We can draw up the necessary rule next Term.

Day of Trial fixed accordingly.

DR. KENEALY.

This we believe was the last occasion when Mr. Serjeant SLEIGH appeared as Counsel for the Claimant. Dr. KENEALY was engaged to represent him in the following April.

SERJEANT BALLANTINE.

It will be noted, likewise, in the above report that Mr. Serjeant BALLANTINE no longer appears as Counsel for the Claimant. The circumstances under which he ceased to be so, are thus narrated by Mr. GUILDFORD ONSLOW in a letter :—

To THE EDITOR OF THE "ENGLISHMAN."

SIR,—I have heard so many strange rumours as to the reason why Serjeant BALLANTINE was not engaged as Counsel for the Claimant to the Tichborne Estates in the late Trial, that I venture to relate what I know of the circumstances.

One night previous to the Trial Serjeant BALLANTINE wrote a note to me at the Reform Club, asking me to call upon him, which I immediately did, at the Union Club. Upon which the Serjeant begged to know if he was to be engaged in the Case, as the uncertainty was damaging to him.

I said I could not possibly say, as it was not my affair: upon which Serjeant BALLANTINE said: "Will you see Sir ROGER TICHBORNE, and tell him I will take his case for a fee of 1,000 guineas, without any extra expenses?" I promised I would mention his offer to Sir ROGER, which I did; and his laconic reply was "Tell Serjeant BALLANTINE I will see him d——d first."

I am, Sir, your obedient servant,

GUILDFORD ONSLOW.

Ropley, April 2, 1875.

The Family were not inactive, any more than the Claimant. For the purpose of tying up the Plaintiff's hands, and preventing the trial of another action then pending, they made an application in the Court of Common Pleas, before Chief Justice BOVILL, and Justices BYLES, KEATING, and BRETT to stop an action under the title of "TICHBORNE, Bart. v. MOSTYN, Bart. and another," until the costs of the Great TICHBORNE Trial had been paid by the plaintiff. The action was brought by Sir P. MOSTYN, Bart., and Mr. MOSTYN, the trustees of the Doughty Estates, to recover a house in Gray's Inn-road, which was upon that Estate.

Mr. HAWKINS, Q.C. (with him Mr. H. MATTHEWS, Q.C., and Mr. PURCELL), applied for a rule, calling upon the Plaintiff to show cause why all further proceedings in this case should not be stayed until he had paid to the defendant costs in "TICHBORNE v. LUSHINGTON," and also given security for the payment of the defendant's costs in the present action. It was stated upon the affidavits that the previous action was tried before the Lord Chief Justice, and on the 6th of March last the jury stopped the Case and the Plaintiff was non-suited. It was true that the defendants' costs in the previous action had not yet been taxed, but when taxed they would amount to at least £40,000, and there was great reason to believe that they would be nearer £60,000 than £40,000. These sums referred to costs as between party and party, but the costs to be paid out of the Estate would be much nearer £100,000. The action of "TICHBORNE v. LUSHINGTON," was commenced upon the 29th June, 1868, and it was brought to recover the Tichborne Estates, whilst the present action was to recover the Doughty Estates. The Plaintiff claimed the Tichborne Estates as eldest son of Sir JAMES TICHBORNE under two settlements executed in May, 1844, and May, 1850. The first settlement gave the Estates to Sir JAMES for life, with remainder to his two sons and their issue in tail male. Under that settlement, ROGER would, upon the death of Sir JAMES, have become entitled to that property. In the first action the only question was whether the Claimant was or was not the eldest son and heir-at-law of Sir JAMES. The second action was also commenced upon the 29th June, 1868, and the plaintiff pretended to derive title under the will of ROGER CHARLES TICHBORNE, whom the defendants said had been lost at sea. There were no such settlements affecting the Doughty Estates as there were affecting the Tichborne Estates in reference to remainders; but upon the death of Sir JAMES, ROGER, if living, would have been entitled under settlement to the Doughty Estates in fee. ROGER made a will, and under that will the defendants held the Doughty Estates in trust. The sole question, therefore, to be raised in the present case, as in the last, was whether the Claimant was ROGER CHARLES TICHBORNE. No question would be raised in the second case which had not been raised in the first one. In the correspondence which had taken place between Mr. GORTON, the Plaintiff's attorney, and Messrs. CULLINGTON and SLAUGHTER for the Defendants, the first-named gentleman wrote: "We are perfectly well aware that the issue in this case is similar to that in 'TICHBORNE v. LUSHINGTON.'" On the 29th June, 1870, the present Claimant became bankrupt, and from that time no further proceedings were taken in the present action until after the Plaintiff had been nonsuited in the first Case.

The Lord Chief Justice: For the purpose of this application, and for most purposes, a nonsuit under the circumstances was equal to a verdict for the Defendants.

Mr. HAWKINS: On the 11th March the Defendants gave twenty days' notice to the Plaintiff to proceed to trial, and this notice was given under the 202nd section in the Common Law Procedure Act 1852, which said that if, after notice, the Plaintiff did not give notice of trial, the Defendants might sign judgment and recover the costs of the defence.

The Lord Chief Justice: And the Plaintiff acted on that by giving notice of trial and proceeding with the action.

Mr. HAWKINS: Yes. And then Mr. Justice WILLES, without prejudice to either side, made the Case a special jury case. He submitted that, to warrant the Court in acceding to the present application, it is not necessary that there should be in the two actions the same Plaintiff and Defendant. It was sufficient that there should be the same title in dispute. It was, however, the same Plaintiff and substantially the same Defendant in both cases, and it was absolutely the same issue raised.

Mr. Justice BYLES: Then there was substantially the same

Plaintiff, the same Defendants, the same title, and the same issue.

Mr. HAWKINS: Just so. There was a question as to what most affects the notice under the Common Law Procedure Act.

The Lord Chief Justice: The Plaintiff himself was most anxious to stay proceedings.

Mr. HAWKINS: Yes, to suit his own convenience; but the Defendants did not want such a suit hanging over their heads. The Defendants need have no objection whatever to the Plaintiff proceeding if they were safe as to the £80,000 costs. It must be apparent to anybody that they would be glad to have the money paid; it was apparent even to "them who has no brains." (Laughter.) If the defendants' costs were paid, the Plaintiff might proceed to trial in this Case to-morrow morning if he pleased.

Mr. Justice BRETT: Could you maintain your notice to proceed to trial within twenty days, and also that you should have security for costs?

Mr. HAWKINS: No. He would ask now simply that these proceedings should be stayed until the costs in the old action were paid. What effect a rule in these terms would have upon the notice to proceed he could not now say. It might be that by obtaining the rule he should lose any advantage to be obtained under the notice. If that were so he must submit to it; but he asked for the rule whatever its effect might be.

Mr. Justice BRETT: It might be said that the rule should not be granted until the notice were withdrawn or modified.

Mr. HAWKINS: It was not probable that the costs would ever be paid.

Mr. GIFFARD (for the Plaintiff): That was not stated upon the affidavits, and he was going to call attention to the absence of any such statement.

Mr. HAWKINS: But it was sworn that the Plaintiff was a bankrupt; and a bankrupt with £80,000 to spare was a lucky bankrupt. (Laughter.)

The Lord Chief Justice asked precisely what rule the learned counsel now asked for.

Mr. HAWKINS: For a rule staying all proceedings in the present action until the Plaintiff had paid the Defendants' costs in the previous action.

The Lord Chief Justice said that that rule would be granted.

Mr. GIFFARD, Q.C., showed cause in the first instance against the rule being made absolute, and said that his first observation was that the parties to the two suits were not the same within the meaning of the rule that entitled the Defendants to security for costs in cases of ejectment.

The Lord Chief Justice said that he did not agree that the rule was that the parties must be the same.

Mr. GIFFARD: Substantially the same parties, which was not the fact in these cases. The Defendants did not say that they had any interest in the costs of the prior suit. The costs in the second case would not fall upon ALFRED TICHBORNE alone, but upon all the persons for whom the Defendants were trustees. He should call attention to the fact that this motion was not made under the Common Law Procedure Act, but under the general jurisdiction of the Court. Bankruptcy would be no ground for asking for security for costs unless the assignees had adopted the action.

The Lord Chief Justice: The rule which we have granted is simply to stay proceedings until the costs of the former action are paid.

Mr. GIFFARD: If that were so, he submitted that his learned friends were out of court, because by their notice to proceed they had distinctly reserved any such right which they might have had. The Defendants' application now was to stay proceedings in a suit in which they themselves had forced Plaintiff on. The old rule was that actions of ejectment should not be brought a number of times for the same property, because the Court would not allow its process to be used vexatiously. Apart from this the Court would not interfere. Now in the last case tried, so far from the process of the Court being used vexatiously, he submitted that there would have been good grounds for an application for a new trial because the Plaintiff was taken by surprise by the evidence as to the tattoo marks.

The Lord Chief Justice said that he should be sorry to say anything that might affect further proceedings, but he might say that it struck him from an early period in the Trial that marks upon the body would form an important part of the inquiry.

Mr. GIFFARD observed that what he had said referred to particular marks, not to marks in general.

The Lord Chief justice did not wish to express any opinion as to whether the Plaintiff had sufficient intimation as to what would be said about the marks.

Mr. GIFFARD did not refer so much to notice to them as to notice to the witnesses who were called by the Plaintiff. The point should have been put to every witness who could know anything of the circumstances, but he found that 80 witnesses had been called for the Plaintiff, and not one of them was ever asked whether he had seen the Plaintiff's bare arm, and whether he was tattooed. Yet, according to the Defendants' case, ROGER's arm was so tattooed that the marks came down to the wrist. One witness said that he saw them as ROGER sat at breakfast with his clothes on. Neither MOORE nor BOGLE was ever asked whether ROGER was tattooed. No doubt the Plaintiff was himself asked and he said that he was never tattooed at all, but the circumstances which were alleged to have taken place in reference to the alleged tattooing were never put to him.

Mr. Justice BRETT: Should these circumstances have been put after the Plaintiff had said that he was never tattooed?

Mr. GIFFARD: Yes; for this reason. I suppose there was a tattooing at Stonyhurst, though upon another boy, and not upon him. The Plaintiff, if asked, might have said that Lord BELLEW tattooed another boy when he, the Plaintiff, was present. It was alleged that the Claimant was ARTHUR ORTON and that ORTON had a tattoo mark upon his arm in the same situation as it was said that ROGER had a tattoo mark.

Mr. HAWKINS: Oh dear, no,

The Lord Chief Justice: In one sense, in the same position.

Mr. HAWKINS: It was not said that ROGER was tattooed down to the wrist.

Mr. GIFFARD: Four inches from the wrist, I believe; and the mark upon the Claimant's wrist was suggested to be erased tattoo. The questions put to the Plaintiff were supposed to have reference to the suggestion that he was ARTHUR ORTON, so that the Plaintiff had no notice that it would be said that ROGER had certain marks upon his arm.

The Lord Chief Justice: The Plaintiff was not only asked whether he was tattooed, but his person was examined by the jury, and there was no tattoo. There was a mark upon the wrist, but that could not possibly have been an obliteration of the mark the Defendants' witnesses spoke to.

Mr. Justice GROVE: Did you apply for leave to recall your witnesses?

Mr. GIFFARD said he had not; and even if there were the right to recall them the Plaintiff could not then have got his witnesses again. What they complained of was that this important matter of the tattoo was kept from their knowledge until the last. The jury in the end gave an intimation in which the tattoo marks were prominently mentioned.

Mr. Justice BRETT: But you elected to be non-suited.

The Lord Chief Justice said that Mr. Serjeant BALLANTINE gave a sort of instructions that he would answer the suggestion as to the tattoo; but when the jury said that they proceeded, not upon that only, but upon the general facts of the Case, then the learned Serjeant elected to be nonsuited. He (the Lord Chief Justice) did not like to say anything upon these matters, because they heard that the Plaintiff was to be tried in a criminal court.

Mr. GIFFARD: Yes, at some time or other.

Mr. HAWKINS: He will be tried, you may be assured of that.

Mr. Justice BRETT: Mr. Serjeant BALLANTINE said that if the only thing the jury went upon was the tattoo marks he could have answered it; but now it was said he could not have got the witnesses.

Mr. GIFFARD urged upon the Court that the circumstances which he had stated were sufficient to show that the second action could not be called a vexatious proceeding, or that it should be stayed until the previous costs were paid.

Mr. HAWKINS, in supporting the rule, read at length from the evidence, and especially from that of Dr. LIPSCOMBE, to show that the Plaintiff had ample notice that the tattoo marks would be in question.

Mr. Justice BRETT did not see why the defendants should have asked the Plaintiff whether he was tattooed, when their case was that it was ROGER who was tattooed, and that Plaintiff was not ROGER.

Mr. HAWKINS: Just so; but the Plaintiff himself was, in fact, asked whether he was tattooed. It was absurd to say that there was any hardship or any "surprise" arising out of the course which had been pursued. The statements of his learned friend also upon the point were a long way from the question that was now before the Court, and these statements were, in truth, made in aid of the money-boxes. (Laughter.)

Mr. GIFFARD retorted that he had dealt with the merits of the Case simply, though possibly his learned friend had an eye to the newspapers in making some of his statements. (A laugh.)

Mr. HAWKINS at all events wished it to be known that the defendants in the first Case, having been put to £100,000 expense, had some little share of merit in this matter. The learned Counsel then commented upon the fact that no single affidavit was now produced from any witness who stated that ROGER was not tattooed. In conclusion, he combated the argument that the defendants, by giving their notice to force the plaintiff on, had deprived themselves of the right to ask the Court to make the present rule absolute.

Mr. MATTHEWS followed upon the same side.

The Lord Chief Justice said that the application which was made in the present action was that all proceedings in the cause should be stayed until the costs in the Case in which Plaintiff had been nonsuited were paid. Mr. HAWKINS had at first asked for security for the payment of the costs of the present Case, but eventually this did not form part of the application. The question, therefore, was simply whether the Court would stay proceedings in this Case until the costs of the former Case were paid. It was perfectly plain that the questions at issue in both cases were precisely the same. He did not mean that there were not some differences in the form of title, but the Plaintiff was the same in both cases, and so was the question to be tried; that question being whether the Plaintiff in each case was or not Sir ROGER CHARLES DOUGHTY TICHBORNE, Bart. It was true that the defendants in the two cases were not precisely the same; but it generally happened in cases of ejectment that they were not, because the action was generally brought against the tenant of a particular portion of the property in question. The two actions now under consideration were brought against tenants; and it was true that the parties defending as landlords were not the same in both cases. In one case it was the guardians of the infant son ALFRED that defended, whilst in the present Case it was the trustees of the DOUGHTY property; but in both cases the real defendant was the infant. In the former case the trial occupied 103 days; and when the jury expressed their opinion an adjournment took place, to enable Mr. Serjeant BALLANTINE to consider the statement of the jury. The foreman of the jury distinctly stated their opinion was formed subject to hearing any evidence that the Judge or the Counsel might desire them to listen to. After the adjournment the Plaintiff's Counsel referred to the tattoo marks, and said that that evidence had taken them by surprise, and, supposing that the opinion of the jury were founded upon that evidence only, and not upon the whole facts of the Case, he should not feel it his duty to withdraw from the Case, because he had evidence upon the point. The jury, having retired, came back and said that their opinion was based upon the whole evidence in the Case. Mr. Serjeant BALLANTINE thereupon said that he should advise his client to submit to a nonsuit. The learned serjeant, therefore, considered that the case of the Plaintiff was utterly hopeless, even though he might have called witnesses upon the subject of tattooing, and he thought it better to elect to be nonsuited rather than risk having a verdict against him. After this the Plaintiff now proposed to try over again precisely the same question he had raised before, and this without paying one shilling of the expenses of the former inquiry. It had been the law for many years that a plaintiff should not be permitted to do this, and there were no circumstances in the present case to take it out of the general rule. It was laid down in "TIDD'S Practice," and the cases of "KEAN on the demise of ANGELL v. ANGELL and another," and "DOE dem. BATHER v. BRAIN," supported it. Mr. GIFFARD had contended that the defendants had waived their right to make this application because of their notice requiring the Plaintiff to proceed to trial. The Case had stood over for years, the defendants desired to have it disposed of, and giving that notice was the only step that they could take in the direction of bringing the litigation to an end, and they hoped in taking it that the Plaintiff would consent to have judgment entered against him. The Plaintiff complied with the notice by setting down the Case for trial. Was what the defendants had done a giving up of their rights? He thought not, and that it was impossible after the rule that had so long prevailed to say that there had been any waiver in the right of the defendants to ask for a stay of proceedings. Mr. GIFFARD contended that they had been taken by surprise by the evidence that was given upon one part of the Case. He (the Lord Chief Justice) did not desire to express his opinion upon the subject; but, even assuming what Mr. GIFFARD said to be perfectly correct, that no information was conveyed to him by the cross-examination that it was intended to set up that ROGER had tattoo marks, this would not amount to surprise. The Plaintiff's Counsel could not, at all events, have been taken by surprise when the Counsel for the Defendants had opened the evidence as to the tattoo marks. There was no doubt that the opinion of the jury was founded upon the general facts of the Case, and not upon any particular set of facts, and the Plaintiff's Counsel acquiesced upon that when he elected to be nonsuited. It could not be said that there had not been a fair trial, for the jury said more than once that they were prepared to hear further evidence, and that their opinion was founded not upon the tattoo-marks only. There was, in his opinion, no ground for resisting this application upon the plea of surprise, or that there was no opportunity of having a complete trial. No doubt the amount that the Plaintiff was called upon to pay was large, but from the first, so far as the proceedings had been before him, it was stated that the Plaintiff was a bankrupt, and that this cause was carried on with the money of other people. There were persons behind who were speculating in this matter. It struck him that the right course to pursue would be that the rule should be made absolute to stay proceedings in the present Trial unless the Plaintiff should within six months pay the defendant's costs in the case of "TICHBORNE v. LUSHINGTON." If the money were paid, then the Plaintiff could proceed to try at the sittings after Michaelmas Term.

Rule absolute.

The Family, however, resolved to crush the Claimant and his friends by a new, another, and notable device, by which they hoped to stop public meetings altogether. They brought into action the old Star Chamber Law of Contempt of Court. They first attacked Mr. GUILDFORD ONSLOW in conjunction with Mr. WHALLEY, and the Queen's Bench fined those gentlemen in large sums, exacting at the same time a pledge that they would attend no more meetings. Well do we remember that scene: it brought back the scenes and days of JEFFREYS.

The following is a report of what occurred, copied from the *Daily Telegraph* of Jan. 13, 1873. We subjoin the comment made by that paper.

APPLICATION AGAINST MR. WHALLEY, M.P., AND MR. GUILDFORD ONSLOW, M.P.

Mr. HAWKINS, Q.C., said: In the Case my lords, of the "QUEEN v. THOMAS CASTRO, otherwise called TICHBORNE," I have to move for a rule calling upon Mr. GEO. HAMMOND WHALLEY, M.P., and Mr. GUILDFORD ONSLOW, M.P., to attend in this Court on a day and at an hour to be named by your lordships, and answer for uttering contemptuous words in speeches delivered by them on the 11th and 12th of December last, in St. James's Hall, Piccadilly, such words tending to prejudice the fair and impartial trial of indictments now pending against the Defendant.

The Lord Chief Justice: Your application is technically for an attachment for contempt.

Mr. HAWKINS: I ask for the order in one of two forms, or I might have it, I think, in the alternative. I find in "HAWKINS'S Pleas of the Crown," that a defendant might be ordered to appear in Court on a particular day for having uttered contemptuous words reflecting upon the administration of justice, or tending to prejudice a trial pending before the Court, or in the alternative to show cause why an attachment should not issue, and why he should not be punished for his contempt by fine and imprisonment. It is in the alternative.

The Lord Chief Justice: I thought the ordinary course is by attachment. You say there are precedents both ways.

Mr. HAWKINS: There are, my lord. As your lordships may be aware, the defendant, TOMAS CASTRO, was the Claimant in the ejectment trial "TICHBORNE v. LUSHINGTON," which occupied the attention of the Court of Common Pleas a great many weeks.

The Lord Chief Justice: Months. (A laugh.)

Mr. HAWKINS: Yes, my lord. I think it extended from May, 1871, to March, 1872—103 days altogether in trial. Your lordships may know also that in the spring of 1872 the proceedings terminated by the defendant electing to be nonsuited. He was thereupon committed for trial by the Lord Chief Justice of the Common Pleas on a charge of perjury, committed at the Trial. Three indictments were subsequently preferred against the defendant, one for forgery, and the other two for perjury, committed in the course of the Trial, and in the swearing of an affidavit in a suit in Chancery touching the same title. I need not refer to the indictment for felony, because it will be sufficient to allude to the other two indictments.

The Lord Chief Justice: My brother ARCHIBALD informs me that he was Counsel in the Case. He does not, therefore, wish to take part in the decision of this motion.

Mr. Justice ARCHIBALD then retired from the Bench.

Mr. HAWKINS proceeded: The three indictments were removed into this Court for trial, at the instance of the Attorney-General; and your lordships may remember that in the course of last Term, on the motion of the Attorney-General, it was ordered that the three indictments should be tried at Bar in this Court. Your lordships did not actually fix a day for the commencement of the trial, but intimated that it was probable a day would be fixed early in the ensuing—that is the present—Term. There were, therefore, at the time to which I am about to call attention, indictments for the most serious offences pending against the defendant CASTRO, and for trial before your lordships and a jury, and after the cause had been removed, and after a Trial at Bar had been ordered, the proceedings to which I will now refer took place in St. James's Hall—almost, I may say, in the very centre of the district from which, in all probability, the jurors will be empanelled to try the Case. It would be idle for me to conceal from your lordships the fact that during a considerable portion of last year, meetings were held in various parts of the country—in almost all the great towns—for the purpose of raising money for the defence of the Defendant. And *nobody could desire more than I do that the Defendant should have a perfectly fair and impartial trial. As far as in me lies—and my learned friend the Attorney-General has intrusted to me the conduct of the prosecution—he shall have the fullest and the fairest opportunity of defending himself against the serious charge made against him.* I do not, my lords, in making this application, in the least degree desire to enter into matters which might in any manner prejudice any defence which the Defendant may have to make; and the sole object of my application to your lordships is this—to prevent that which seems to me to tend directly to the destruction of all chance of that fair and impartial trial in which the public and the defendant are equally interested. For that reason it is that I have felt it to be my imperative duty to bring the matter under the serious notice of your lordships. Now, my lords, on the 11th of December, the first of two meetings was called by notice to be held in St. James's Hall, for the purpose of raising funds for conducting the defence. On that occasion Mr. WHALLEY, who is Member of Parliament for the borough of Peterborough, occupied the chair; and Mr. GUILDFORD ONSLOW, another Member of Parliament, also attended the meeting. The defendant CASTRO was in attendance and spoke; but I do not propose to call attention to his speech, because considerable allowance may fairly enough be made in favour of a man who is made a defendant in a criminal indictment. I therefore propose to take no notice of his words, but rather to confine myself to the language uttered by gentlemen whose words, from their position, were calculated to have considerable weight and influence with those to whom they were addressed. Mr. WHALLEY, on taking the chair, stated that his object was to obtain a fair trial for the Defendant. "We cannot," he added, "have such fair trial except by the support of the public; and, further, I think I may say without fear of contradiction, that there has been a unanimous declaration of opinion at all those great public meetings which have been held that he is truly and in fact Sir ROGER TICHBORNE. And it seems a proper observation to make to you, that you could not have been brought here this evening unless you believed that there was something in this Case far beyond the question whether this man, otherwise unknown to the public, had or had not committed perjury. There must be in the minds of the people the firm conviction and belief that there is a much greater question than whether he is Sir ROGER TICHBORNE to be tried—namely, whether there is not a great conspiracy—the greatest, I believe, which was ever known to the law—(cheers)—and further, that you do believe that the law of England is unequal to cope duly with and expose that conspiracy except by the aid and support of the watchful eye of the public." I shall show, further, by this speech, and by Mr. WHALLEY's speech on the following day, that that conspiracy is directly charged not only upon the witnesses who gave their testimony at the late Trial, and whose evidence is essential in the coming Trial, and whose character ought not, at all events, to be blackened by assertions of this sort pending the Trial, but also against those who have to take the part of the prosecution. Mr. WHALLEY goes on: "The question is, whether there is a great conspiracy involved in this Case on the one side or the other, and you are a jury fairly and properly impanelled to decide on which side that conspiracy lies." I will now allude to the speech of Mr. GUILDFORD ONSLOW.

Mr. Justice MELLOR: Did Mr. WHALLEY say more on that occasion?—Mr. HAWKINS: He spoke at length on the second day, and I shall allude to his second speech if your lordships think it more convenient.

Mr. Justice MELLOR: Perhaps it would be better to deal with the first meeting before alluding to the second.

Mr. HAWKINS: Mr. WHALLEY having concluded, Mr. GUILDFORD ONSLOW addressed the meeting in language which I think your lordship will hold to be intolerable in a country in which a fair trial is so much valued on all hands. Mr. ONSLOW said that the reason they addressed the British public was that they had been refused a hearing in the House of Commons when they put questions to the Ministry. Their mouths were shut in that House;

SIR JOHN KARSLAKE, M.P., Q.C.

but knowing, as they did, that they were supporting the right man in a good and honest complaint, they had nothing left but to appeal to public opinion. Then he went on to say that the Claimant had been confined in the most loathsome dungeon on a charge which when it came to trial, would be met with a verdict of "Not Guilty." He then proceeded to comment upon evidence given at the late Trial, and which must be adduced in support of the present charge. I say nothing as to the fairness or unfairness of those comments, but I think your lordships will agree with me when I say that they were comments which ought never to have been made pending the Trial, and which, being made, subjects the utterer of them to penalties for contempt of Court. What would be said, Mr. ONSLOW argues, as to the value of the evidence of Lady DOUGHTY? And he argues upon the evidence of handwriting, and upon a variety of matters, to show that CASTRO is not guilty. What, I ask, would be the penalty attaching to any person who took the opposite course, and thought fit to call a public meeting during the pending of this indictment, and publicly and openly declared the Defendant to be guilty of the crimes of which he is charged, and, moreover, proceeded to comment upon the evidence given, and to be given, on the part of the prosecution? There is not a single person who possesses any sense of justice who would not pronounce such conduct to be scandalous and disgraceful, and calculated to prejudice the trial of the Defendant.

The Lord Chief Justice: If it could be done in a case of perjury, you could do it in a case of murder.

Mr. HAWKINS: No doubt, my lord. You cannot, I submit, conceive anything which is calculated more to sap the foundation of justice, or prevent a fair and impartial trial, than to permit—while a matter is pending before a Court where both sides will be heard—the discussion of evidence to be given, and the taking of the evidence of an irregular jury of the populace prejudiced by exciting speeches. When I call your lordships' attention to the proceedings of the second meeting, I think you will say that it was our bounden duty to bring the matter before the Court. I will not comment upon Mr. GUILDFORD ONSLOW's remarks upon the evidence given, or to be given, but will content myself by reading one passage only. In the course of the investigation before the Chief Justice of the Common Pleas, a very serious question was raised as to the contents of a Sealed Packet. The Defendant alleged upon oath—and this is one of the matters assigned against him as perjury—that he had seduced his cousin, the daughter of Lady Doughty, and wife of Mr. Radcliffe. Mr. Guildford Onslow said that the moment the Defendant was asked the question, he had to weigh at the time the fact that he had a wife and four children of his own, and that the lady in question was a lover of former years "who, as he says and believes, turned traitor to him." That is Mr. Guildford Onslow's commentary upon the evidence of a lady whose testimony is of the greatest moment on the question about to be tried, and that is alleged against a witness who is again to be heard before a jury. I do not propose to investigate the falsehood or the truth of the charges made. If I made any comment whatever upon the evidence of the witnesses who are to be produced, either for the prosecution or for the defence, I would be falling into the very error for which I am here to blame those gentlemen. I will, therefore only call attention to what took place, and submit that it was calculated to prejudice the Trial, and to interfere with the due course of justice. He then went on to give a statement as to the Defendant's character, and discuss the question whether he is or is not Arthur Orton, and concluded his speech by as scandalously calumnious an attack upon my learned friend the Attorney-General as it is possible to conceive. I will call attention to this passage of the speech to show its inflammable nature, and how it was calculated to prejudice the minds of those who heard it against the prosecution and in favour of the Defendant. The hon. gentleman then said he was going to bring a serious charge against the other side, but he went on to say that he had been invited into the lobby of the House of Commons to see how the Case was about to collapse. "How do you think it was to collapse? Why, four letters were put into the hands of Sir Roger Tichborne, and the Attorney-General said, 'Are they in your handwriting?' He read them and said, 'They are forgeries.' Whereupon the Attorney-General said, 'I knew two of them to be forgeries, but I did not know that the other two were.' Now, who wrote these forged letters? The wife of Messrs. Dobinson's head clerk, a woman who had been tried for forgery before." Mr. Onslow then commented with severity against what he called the attempt then made to entrap the Claimant, and said that the Attorney-General was not reprimanded by the Chief Justice for making such use of the forged letters. He then commented upon the fact of the Attorney-General being allowed to use forged letters, and on the other side being permitted to smudge out features from a daguerreotype which had been used against the Defendant. Now my lords, a more foul charge than that could not possibly be made.

Mr. Justice Mellor: The question here is not the truth or falsehood of the charge, but the effect of making it.

Mr. Hawkins: True, my lord, and I am not about, for a moment, to utter a syllable as to the evidence adduced or to be adduced by one side or the other. But having sat beside my learned friend, the Attorney-General, for over 100 days on the Trial, I cannot refrain from saying that the charge in question is of the foulest character. So much for what took place on the 11th of December. On the following day, the 12th, another meeting was held, and a Mr. Skipworth, from Lincolnshire, took the chair. Mr. Whalley addressed the meeting, and in the course of his observations, stated that in every large town in the kingdom there was a unanimity of opinion and the unanimous verdict was that the man to be tried was Sir Roger Tichborne, "and, secondly, there was a conspiracy in the Case, a conspiracy which you, gentlemen, in the front row—you gentlemen accustomed to mix up in public affairs—are utterly unable to conceive or believe—a conspiracy, so widespread, so black, so utterly incomprehensible, and extending its roots throughout so many institutions of our country. That is the point I am here to advocate and to present my views upon. (Cheers.) Ladies and gentlemen, I ask your particular attention to this matter. I venture respectfully to speak as a man acquainted with public affairs in the House of Commons for twenty years. I do very respectfully and most earnestly ask you to consider this point. If they succeed at Sir Roger Tichborne, if they exercised their ingenuity to back up opinion by picking out from the Attorney-General's speech of twenty-three or twenty-four days some passages which are not easy to be answered, to show that the man is an impostor, the alternative being that the Attorney-General is engaged in lending himself to a great conspiracy—let these gentlemen consider this, which is a fact why such people say, 'Oh, that is all nonsense; the man is an impostor'; the common-sense of England, the common people of England, the working men of England, were never more unanimous upon any question ever presented to them from the platform, than upon this: that he is Sir Roger Tichborne, and that there is a conspiracy against him. I ask my lords and colleagues, and my lords in Parliament, to say when, in the history of England, was there such unanimity connected with untruth and falsehood? There are, gentlemen, two questions. In the first place, is this man Sir Roger Tichborne? (Cries of 'Yes, yes.') In the next place, is the fact known? Now, mark and observe this, because these are words which I speak with a due sense of responsibility to those I meet in social life. Is that fact known to the Attorney-General? Was it known to him throughout this prosecution? Is it known to her Majesty's Government and to Mr. Gladstone, who have given £100,000 out of your pockets to prosecute this man?" Then he goes into an elaborate argument to show that the defendant is Sir Roger Tichborne, and proceeds to say, "I have charged the Tichborne family"—witnesses for the prosecution—"I have charged the Doughtys, the Radcliffes, and the whole lot of them, with knowing that he is the man and combining in a conspiracy against him. What is the nature of that conspiracy—"

The Lord Chief Justice: You have said quite enough, Mr. Hawkins—take a rule. The only question is, in what form you will take it.

Mr. Hawkins: I shall only read one further passage to show the imperative necessity for this motion. He went on: "What is the nature of this conspiracy? What are the grounds on which six years ago, people met in a drawing-room in London, and said, 'We will defy the laws of England. He is the man, but we have the estates, and it is not expedient that he should have them. We will keep them. We are strong enough in Parliament—we are strong enough on the judicial bench—we are strong enough in society to defy the laws of England.'"

The Lord Chief Justice: That is quite enough, Mr. Hawkins.

Mr. Hawkins: I have only further to ask your lordships to name a day and hour for the attendance of those gentlemen.

The Lord Chief Justice: Yes. They were both parties to the meetings, and are jointly answerable. *The object was to discuss the merits of an indictment pending in this Court, and whether the one or the other used the language complained of, both are equally responsible to the Court for contempt of its jurisdiction.* Take the rule in any form you please, directing those parties to appear and answer for contempt of Court. Let them attend here on Monday week.

Mr. Hawkins: At the sitting of the Court?

The Lord Chief Justice: Yes.

Mr. Hawkins: One word as to another matter, my lord. I understand, when the Case was before the Court last term, it was stated that a day would be fixed for the Trial this Term. It was intimated that probably it would commence about the fifth day of Easter Term; but, as that day is a Saturday, perhaps it would not be convenient to commence it then.

The Lord Chief Justice: We have been talking about that this morning: and we think it would be more convenient to fix it for Monday, the 21st of April. Probably, as my brother Sleigh is here, he will take notice of that fact.

The Master here made some communication to the Lord Chief Justice, who said that, inasmuch as the new Trial motions might not be disposed of by the 21st, they thought it better that the Trial should be fixed to commence on Wednesday, the 23rd of April. They would, therefore, finally settle that day for the commencement of the Trial.

Mr. Serjeant Sleigh: I am informed it will be necessary to have a rule fixing the day. I do not know which side should move for it.

Mr. Hawkins: It is the Attorney-General's rule.

Mr. Serjeant Sleigh: It is convenient, however, meanwhile, that both sides should know that the day has been fixed by your lordship. There is no need to mention the matter again.

The Lord Chief Justice: No; the Master will take care to have the rule properly drawn up.

The Trial will therefore commence on the morning of Wednesday, the 23rd of April next.

COMMENT OF THE "DAILY TELEGRAPH."

Mr. Whalley and Mr. Guildford Onslow, both Members of Parliament, have, at their own risk and peril, moved up and down the country as champions of the Claimant. Every one has a right to form his own opinion in a free State, but the privilege does not cover assaults on the character of others, more especially upon witnesses who have appeared, and have yet to appear, in a court of justice. The language of the two gentlemen has been so forcible, that Mr. Hawkins has felt obliged to ask the Court of Queen's Bench for a rule calling on them to answer a charge of contempt. He cited passages from the speeches delivered by the accused framed in most libellous terms. According to Mr. Onslow, the Claimant is the victim of "the greatest conspiracy which has ever been known to the laws." This Member of Parliament has further gone out of his way to fling a charge of perjury at a lady who will be one of the most important witnesses at the Trial of the Claimant; for, in the face of what she said in Court he asserts that she was a lover of "Sir Roger Tichborne" in former years, "who had turned traitor"—a disgraceful imputation. In equally violent language Mr. Onslow deals with the Attorney-General, whom he accuses of having used forged letters to draw the Claimant into a trap. Mr. Whalley has almost achieved the difficult feat of surpassing his honourable colleague in the race to win the prize for extravagant impropriety. He distinctly says that the Doughtys, the Radcliffes, "and the whole lot," know that the Claimant is the man, and that they have deliberately conspired to defraud him of his rights. Lest we should not distinctly see what he means, Mr. Whalley adds that, "six years ago people met in a drawing-room and said 'We will defy the law of England; we have valuable estates, and here is the man; but it is not expedient he should get them. We will keep them. We are strong enough in Parliament, on the judicial bench, and in society, to defy the law of England.'" Even Mr. Whalley is not at liberty to libel witnesses and raise a prejudice against them. Mr. Hawkins brought up such an array of extracts from speeches at public meetings that the Court was constrained to grant a rule or rules. We can only say that clearer cases of contempt have rarely come under the notice of experienced lawyers. The application to the Court has been made on the earliest occasion, and nothing remains for Mr. Whalley and Mr. Onslow but to purge themselves of the charge in the most complete and satisfactory manner possible, or submit to such an alternative as the Judges may deem adequate to the offence.

THE PUNISHMENT AWARDED.

In obedience to the above rule, Mr. Onslow and Mr. Whalley attended the Court on the 20th of January, 1873. We copy the following account from the papers. It need not be added how well calculated all these proceedings were to prejudice and even damn the Claimant's cause, which was so soon to follow.

THE TICHBORNE CASE

In the Court of Queen's Bench yesterday, the rule for the appearance of Mr. Guildford Onslow, M.P., and Mr. Whalley, M.P., with a view to their showing cause why they should not be punished for contempt of Court, came on for argument before the Lord Chief Justice and Justices Blackburn, Mellor, and Lush. Before the proceedings commenced the Court was crowded to excess in every part, and some hundreds of persons, notwithstanding that they were early in attendance and importunate in their demand for admission, had to content themselves with learning the result of the proceedings at second hand. Mr. Guildford Onslow and Mr. Whalley occupied seats immediately in front of their leading Counsel.

Mr. Hawkins, Q.C., and Mr. C. Bowen appeared for the Crown; Sir John Karslake, Q.C., and Mr. A. L. Smith appeared for Mr. Guildford Onslow, instructed by Mr. E. Bromley; Mr. Digby Seymour, Q.C., Mr. Morgan Lloyd, and Mr. Macrae Moir were Counsel for Mr. Whalley, instructed by Messrs. Walter Morgen and Son.

When their Lordships had taken their seats on the bench,

The Lord Chief Justice said: Are the two gentlemen, Mr. Guildford Onslow and Mr. Whalley, who were directed to be here to-day, in attendance?

Sir John Karslake: I appear for Mr. Guildford Onslow, my lord, who is present.

The Lord Chief Justice: Is Mr. Whalley here?

Mr. Digby Seymour: He is, my lord; I appear for him.

The Lord Chief Justice: Do you wish the affidavit on which the rule was granted to be read?

Sir John Karslake: No; I will not trouble your lordship to read it.

The Lord Chief Justice: Then we will hear you.

Sir John Karslake: The rule was obtained, my lord, upon the affidavits of Mr. Grey, Mr. MacKenzie, and Mr. Duggey, and the exhibits attached thereto; and it directs those two gentlemen —Mr. Guildford Onslow and Mr. Whalley— to appear to-day to answer for a contempt of Court committed on the 11th and 12th of December last, by taking part in meetings and uttering the words alleged in the exhibits, and show cause why they should not be punished by the Court for such contempt. My lord, I appear on behalf of Mr. Guildford Onslow—I will not say to show cause against this motion, but for the purpose of placing before your lordship an affidavit which has been filed by Mr. Guildford Onslow in answer to the charge thus made against him. My lord, I have read the passages in the speeches which have been relied on here, and it is not necessary that I should read them again, and by so doing, give further publicity to what was stated. Your lordships are aware that the charges against Mr. Guildford Onslow are that he made certain speeches on the 11th and 12th of December last at meetings held in St. James's Hall, and that, in the course of his observations, he made remarks in reference to witnesses who had been examined on a Trial which had taken place, and with regard to matters connected with that former Trial. But it was suggested that those comments were in contempt of this Court, inasmuch as they tended necessarily to prejudice, or might prejudice, the fair and impartial Trial of an indictment which has been removed into this Court. My lord, so far as I have been able, in the short time which has elapsed since I have been consulted in this matter, to look into the authorities, I certainly find that where matters are pending in a Court it has been deemed improper to comment upon evidence given in respect of them, and that if the effect of those comments is to reflect upon the administration of justice or to prevent a fair trial being had, this is technically contempt of Court. My lord, in this Case, as I understand, the proceedings are so far pending that indictments have been preferred by bills found against a person whom I will call the Claimant, and those indictments are in this Court, and although the Trial has not commenced in one sense, it is to commence, I believe, in April next; and, so far as I can form an opinion from the authorities—although I have found, I am bound to say, no express authority upon the point —I think I am entitled to submit the question of the pending of the Trial within the meaning of the authorities. But, my lord, if I am wrong, and it is held that the Trial is pending, I am sure it will not prejudice the case of Mr. Guildford Onslow, and I shall state in his words the circumstances under which he made use of the words complained of. I need refer but very briefly to matters of notoriety. Your lordships are aware that some years ago the Claimant came to this country determined to prosecute a suit for the purpose of establishing his right to the title and estates of the Tichbornes; and, first of all, proceedings were taken in Chancery, and afterwards, in the course of last year, a Trial at Nisi Prius took place which lasted a very long time. The case of the Claimant having closed, the Attorney-General opened the case which he intended to prove in a speech of great length, in which facts were stated that, from the course which was taken, remained—many of them—unproved, and there can be no doubt that when the jury, upon the evidence given, pronounced against the Claimant, they did so while a great many of the facts which the Attorney-General said he was in a position to prove had not been made the subject of evidence. And without reading the speeches complained of here, which I am sure your lordships sufficiently remember, I may be allowed to say that the comments made by Mr. Guildford Onslow were made with reference to circumstances which, he believed, might have turned out differently had evidence been given and a reply been made. He believed that in that case a very different impression would have been produced to that which was made by the opening statement of the Attorney-General. Having said so much, I am bound to admit that, in the course of Mr. Guildford Onslow's observations references are made to the coming Trial; and even if no reference had been made to it all, I also feel bound to admit that—there being a pending Trial—observations were made which would be held to be technically in contempt of Court, and that the observations—whatever the motive and intention in delivering them— were such as might prejudice the prosecution, although your lordships will see from the affidavit I am about to submit to you that such was very far from being the feeling or desire of Mr. Guildford Onslow when he made the speeches complained of. Mr. Onslow states in his affidavit the circumstances under which he had, if I may use the expression, espoused the Claimant's cause, from the first time he came to England to establish what he considers his rights. He says in his affidavit:

"For many years of my life I lived on terms of intimacy and friendship with the late Sir James Tichborne and Lady Tichborne, his wife; and upon the death of the latter I attended her funeral at Tichborne Park. Sir James Tichborne and I were natives of the same county, and we saw a good deal of each other at different times. After the arrival of the Claimant in this country in 1866, I became acquainted with him, and was in communication with Lady Tichborne on the subject of his identity, and I knew from her that she identified him as her first-born son, the issue of her marriage with Sir James Tichborne: and, as far as I could judge, I believe she had no doubt whatever on the subject. I was earnestly entreated by her ladyship, before her death, not to abandon or desert her son, the said Claimant, and I faithfully promised that I would never do so, and honestly believing, as I have always done, and still do, that the person identified by her is her son, I have endeavoured, to the best of my ability and power, during all the proceedings in the Court of Chancery and in the Common Pleas, to assist him in establishing his claim to the title and estates. It is matter of notoriety that ever since the claim was first made by the Claimant to the present moment his identity has been made the topic of conversation and discussion among all classes—in the House of Commons, in the clubs, in society, and in almost every part of the kingdom. Such discussions continued up to and during the Trial in last year, on which occasion, after a speech for the defence, which occupied more than three weeks, and after the examination of only a few witnesses for the defence, the jury expressed an opinion adverse to the Claimant, and thereupon, by the advice of his Counsel, he elected to be nonsuited. He was then ordered into custody by the learned judge, and was for a long time in Newgate until he was released upon finding bail in May of last year, true bills having in the meantime been found against him for perjury and forgery. It is a matter of notoriety that the question as to the Claimant's identity still continued to be discussed freely after the termination of the Trial, and while the Claimant was in prison and after his release on bail; and finding that the result of the Trial had the not unnatural effect of creating a very strong prejudice against the Claimant, the greater because many statements which had been made, but not proved by witnesses, were assumed to be true, I did attempt to counteract the feeling of prejudice, with the view and object, so far as I could attain them, of preventing the result of the Trial from operating unjustly against the Claimant in the criminal proceedings taken against him. After the release of the Claimant from prison (Lady Tichborne, from whom during her life he received £1,000 a year since his return, having died), the Claimant was wholly without funds to meet the expenses of his defence. He attended meetings in parts of the country with the object of obtaining funds for the purpose of defraying the expenses of his Trial; and I have, as I admit, attended several such meetings with the said Claimant. I say that the meetings of the 11th and 12th December, 1872, mentioned in the affidavits filed upon obtaining the rule in this Case, were meetings called for such purpose as aforesaid. I say that, in the observations which I made, my desire, intention, and object were to counteract the feeling of prejudice existing against the Claimant, so that he might, if possible, go into Court to meet his trial for the criminal offences alleged against him unprejudiced by the result of the trial at Nisi Prius, and the comments which had been made upon him in the course thereof. I say that although now it is obvious to me that such observations, made with the sole object and purpose aforesaid, may be considered to have the effect of reflecting upon the character of witnesses and the conduct of the prosecution, it did not occur to me that such was or might be their effect. I have not the slightest intention of prejudging or interfering with or perverting the course of justice, and it is with great regret that I find that I have taken a course unwittingly which can be looked upon as indicative of having ever entertained any such intention. The opinion I entertain still of the righteousness of the Claimant's cause induced me perhaps to close my eyes to the natural effect of my actions, and to the consequences which my speeches were calculated to produce. I admit that I was aware that Mr. WHALLEY was expected to attend the meetings of the 11th and 12th December, but I say that I did not, on either of these occasions, know what observations he intended to make, and that our several speeches were made without the least concert, combination, or arrangement, so far as the precise topics touched upon or language used by either of us were concerned. On the 12th of December there were friends of mine, ladies and gentlemen, attending the meeting and during Mr. WHALLEY's speech I was in conversation with them, and did not pay attention to, nor was aware of, what he said. It certainly did not occur to me that I could be responsible in any way for the language used by him or any other person or persons present who addressed this or any other meeting, and I humbly submit that I am not, and ought not to be held to be, responsible for it. In conclusion, I repeat that at the time I made the observations complained of I had no intention whatever of interfering with the course of justice in the Trials which are now pending. I made such observations under the circumstances and with the objects only above stated by me. As soon as I read the report in the public papers of the motion to this honourable Court, I saw that I had been betrayed into taking a course which laid me open to the imputation of having, in trying to remove prejudice operating against the Claimant, created prejudice against the prosecution, and thereby, pending a trial, improperly commented upon matters connected with it; and I desire to express my unfeigned regret at having taken such a course, and to apologize in all sincerity to this honourable Court for the conduct for which I am arraigned."

I submit, my lords, that, even if you hold that there was, under the circumstances, a Trial pending—

The Lord Chief Justice: Upon that point we don't entertain the slightest doubt.

Sir JOHN KARSLAKE: So be it, my lord. I do not wish to press the point unduly, but, that being so, I have taken a course which, strangely enough, was adopted in this very matter at another stage of it, when, observations having been made in several of the public papers, the editors and writers of the articles were summoned to appear in the Court of Chancery for having, pending the Trial, made certain comments upon the proceedings. I am here, my lord, on behalf of Mr. ONSLOW, to express his regret for what he has done which you may think worthy of blame, and I trust you will believe that he is sincere in his expression of regret for having been betrayed into doing anything which could in any way prejudice the course of justice.

The Lord Chief Justice: It has been suggested to me by one of my learned brethren to ask you a very pertinent question, and one that must have been asked sooner or later. It is this: Are we to understand that Mr. ONSLOW, in expressing regret—which has been so happily expressed in the affidavit and by you—intimates to the Court his clear resolve and intention not again to take part in any similar proceedings?

Sir JOHN KARSLAKE: Most undoubtedly, my lord; and I make that statement by direction of Mr. ONSLOW.

Mr. DIGBY SEYMOUR: I appear, my lord, for Mr. WHALLEY, and I cannot express myself better or more happily than by adopting the terms which have just fallen from my distinguished friend, Sir JOHN KARSLAKE, in representing Mr. GUILDFORD ONSLOW. I was not aware, until I came into Court to-day, of the course that he proposed to take. It has been taken entirely on his own responsibility, and without communication with me. I fully agree with my learned friend in the point he submitted for your lordship, but as the Court has intimated its opinion that this must be treated as an indictment pending for trial in this Court, I shall not further refer to the question. I think, however, that there is some difference between this Case and the cases which have been decided both at law and in equity.

The Lord Chief Justice: You do not mean to urge that the Case is not pending for trial.

Mr. DIGBY SEYMOUR: No, my lord; but as to the nature of the offence with which Mr. WHALLEY is charged. I find, too, that there is a distinction between the case of Mr. WHALLEY and Mr. ONSLOW. So far as the second meeting was concerned, Mr. WHALLEY was only present in the room while he made his own speech. He was ill, and left the room, and cannot, therefore, be held responsible for observations which he did not hear. The line of argument taken by Mr. WHALLEY had reference to the course pursued by the Government in prosecuting the Claimant out of the public funds, and his sole object was to endeavour to assist him in obtaining funds for his defence. His observations had reference to the past Trial. The tendency of his remarks may be summed up in this way: "Here is a person I assume and believe to be the rightful heir. At great cost he has endeavoured to secure his rights in civil proceedings. The Trial is over, and he is now indicted and to be prosecuted at the expense of the public. He is destitute, and justice will suffer unless he is assisted. It is all the more necessary that he should be, because in the civil cause there was a powerful combination and array against him." That appears to be the tone of the speech. He does not appear to have commented upon the evidence.

The Lord Chief Justice: Are you not wrong? Are there not comments upon the evidence of witnesses examined at the former, and to be examined at the forthcoming, Trial.

Mr. DIGBY SEYMOUR: Inferentially, that may be said to be so, my lord.

Mr. Justice BLACKBURN: Not inferentially, but really. He says, "There must be in your minds, whether you fully recognize that he is Sir ROGER TICHBORNE or not; there must be in your minds a firm conviction and belief that there is a much greater question than that to be tried"—to be tried—"namely, whether there is not a great conspiracy, the greatest, I believe, which has ever been known to the law; and, further, that you do believe that the law of England is unequal to cope duly with, and to expose and punish that conspiracy, except by the aid and support of the watchful eye of the public." Is not that equivalent to saying that he went there for a purpose which he considered necessary to influence the question to be tried.

The Lord Chief Justice: He says that witnesses—I am not sure whether he does not name them—but, certainly, he speaks of a certain family as being leagued together to get a verdict of "Guilty" against a man whom they know to be innocent. Not in these words, but that is the purport. Has not that reference to a coming trial?

Mr. DIGBY SEYMOUR: I submit, my lord, that the object of his observations was not to influence the Trial, but to influence subscriptions to the Defence Fund.

The Lord Chief Justice: That may have been the purpose for which he made them, but they none the less had reference to a pending trial.

Mr. DIGBY SEYMOUR: In all the cases I have found the comments complained of have been made concerning particular witnesses.

The Lord Chief Justice: And that is the case, as I understand it, on this affidavit. If I am wrong, let me be corrected; but my impression is that direct and specific attacks are made on particular witnesses who have been called, and who may be called again.

Mr. DIGBY SEYMOUR: I certainly understand the observations to refer to evidence already given, and, no doubt, inferentially to evidence that may or may not be given again.

The Lord Chief Justice: There is, for instance, one passage directly referring to Mrs. RADCLIFFE.

Mr. HAWKINS: He says, "I have charged the TICHBORNE Family—I have charged them directly and in print—the DOUGHTYS, the RADCLIFFES, and the whole lot of them together—with knowing that he is the man, and with combining in a conspiracy against him.

Mr. DIGBY SEYMOUR: That is explained by the following passage in Mr. WHALLEY's affidavit: "I was first induced to take a personal interest in the TICHBORNE question by receiving a requisition signed by many persons of respectability, residing at or near Winchester, requesting to be informed whether, in my opinion, the Claimant was or was not the person he represented himself to be," and then he set out the correspondence which ensued, and the manner in which he made the charge in writing. It was to a charge long since made that he spoke at the meeting. The charge was made before the Case came before the Court of Common Pleas.

Mr. Justice BLACKBURN: And no doubt the Court of Common Pleas could deal, and we could not, with a contempt committed against it. But we are considering a contempt of the Court of Queen's Bench. Were the observations intended or calculated to influence the case which was then, and is now, pending in this Court? Were they obviously intended or calculated to influence the event of that criminal trial? That is the question before us.

Mr. DIGBY SEYMOUR: Mr. WHALLEY explains that the charge had no reference to the pending Trial, but had been made long before, as the result of the inquiries he made after receiving the Hampshire Requisition.

The Lord Chief Justice: The whole thing appears to be this. Those witnesses had been examined, and were likely to be examined again, and adversely to the Claimant, on the Criminal Trial. This meeting was called to collect funds—an object by no means reprehensible; but, speaking of the approaching Trial, those people who had been called, and as was believed would be called again, are denounced by the speaker as conspirators intending to give false evidence. What is this but a charge made at a public meeting against witnesses to be examined at an approaching trial?

Mr. DIGBY SEYMOUR: The explanation given by Mr. WHALLEY is that he "had charged"—referring to the matters which took place when no Trial was pending. It is undoubtedly ambiguous. "I have charged," not "I still charge."

The Lord Chief Justice: *Would not the test be this? Suppose that one person was at that meeting who afterwards became a Juryman. Would not that man, having heard a gentleman of position publicly charge witnesses with being guilty of a foul conspiracy, and as having committed perjury, be under the impression that those witnesses, when they came to give their evidence, were not worthy of credit?*

Mr. DIGBY SEYMOUR: Of course, my lord, if language tantamount to that had been used.

Mr. Justice BLACKBURN: Does he state in his affidavit that he did not intend to prejudice the Trial.

Mr. Digby Seymour: He says that the only way in which he sired to influence the Trial was by the collection of funds for the fence in the interest of justice.

Mr. Justice Blackburn: I should be glad to hear the passage ad.

Mr. Digby Seymour: He says "I was returned to Parliament to present the city of Peterborough." (Laughter.)

The Lord Chief Justice: What possible bearing has that fact the case? (Renewed laughter.)

Mr. Digby Seymour: It is only introductory, my lord. Laughter.) There is this other allusion to Peterborough: "Previous to my attending any public meeting for the purpose aforesaid, I stated my views freely to my constituents—(laughter)—at public meeting held at the city of Peterborough, and received from them a unanimous expression of their approval of the course proposed to be taken in this matter." (Much laughter.)

The Lord Chief Justice: Do you really mean to say that that occurs in the affidavit?

Mr. Digby Seymour: It does, my lord.

The Lord Chief Justice: Then he tells us, in effect, that in committing a contempt of this Court, he acted at the desire of his constituents. (Laughter.)

Mr. Digby Seymour: Oh, no, my lord; he acted altogether from a good motive, and from a sense—it may be a mistaken sense—of public duty. He identified himself with the Claimant, believing him to be an injured man, and his sole motive was to secure that at the approaching Trial, justice should be done. The public funds were, as he stated, to be used for the prosecution. His object was to secure funds for the defence, in order that a fair and impartial trial might be had. He says that he was connected with Hampshire, and particularly with the district in which the Tichborne Estates are situate, and had for years past been in the habit of visiting that district. Then he alludes to the Requisition, and that in consequence of receiving it, he examined into the Case thoroughly, and was of opinion that the opposition to the claim was so thoroughly baseless, that he could only regard it as oppression and injustice. He added that he had no interest whatever in the matter, and had subscribed £25 to the Defence Fund. Mr. Whalley then set forth questions he had asked in his place in Parliament of the Chancellor of the Exchequer, and of the Attorney-General, and a motion which he had submitted. He goes on to say:

"That in all that I did or said in public meetings, as well as at the meetings at St. James's Hall, as on all other occasions, I have had no other purpose whatever than to carry out the object of securing the Claimant a fair trial, and that, having no personal interest directly or indirectly, pecuniary or otherwise, in the result, I have been actuated by no other motive.

"That in the performance of what I so, as aforesaid, deemed to be a public duty, I have never said or done intentially anything to bring into contempt this honourable Court, nor to prevent in any way the due administration of justice; but, on the contrary, it has been my sole object, whether in the House of Commons or at public meetings, to promote and insure the due administrations of justice, believing that the defendant could not bring into Court the witnesses necessary for his defence without funds for that purpose.

"And I further say that the meetings held at St. James's Hall on the 11th and 12th of December last were convened for the purpose of raising money towards the defence of the Claimant, as appear by the advertisements and placards announcing the same, and for the purpose of discussing the public question involved in the course pursued by the Government and the Attorney-General in recommending the House of Commons to sanction the expenditure of public money to prosecute the said Claimant as aforesaid. And that such was the object of such meetings will more clearly appear by reference to the resolution passed at the last of the said meetings.

"I further say that I did not, at the said meetings held at St. James's Hall on the 11th and 12th of December last, nor at any other meeting, or on any other occasion, charge or impute to any one or more persons engaged in resisting the claims of Sir Roger Tichborne conspiracy, otherwise or in any other sense, or to any other extent, than I had long previously made known to the Solicitor engaged in the case of 'Tichborne v. Lushington.'"

I submit to your Lordships that there is this distinction between the present case and those which are on the books, namely, that even if the observations made at the meetings referred inferentially to a pending case, yet, as the speaker had no such intention, as such an idea was altogether absent from his mind, and as his sole motive was a perfectly legitimate one—to collect funds for the defence of a man whom he believed to be unjustly accused—he is not guilty of a contempt of Court.

Mr. Justice Lush: If I recollect aright, the observations assume that the witnesses referred to would be called at the approaching Trial.

Mr. Digby Seymour: Oh, no, my lord.

Mr. Justice Blackburn: I have been reading the speeches; and I confess the statement of Mr. Whalley, that he did not think they could influence the future Trial, startles me. He says that he was perfectly convinced that there was a foul conspiracy between the inheritors of the estates and others to send to penal servitude a man whom they knew to be innocent. Now, if he says he thinks such a statement could not prejudice a forthcoming trial, he must take a different view of the effect of words from what I do. If you argue that the observations were not used for the purpose of prejudicing the Trial, that is a question of fact as to which different views may be entertained; but do you, as Mr. Whalley's Counsel, mean to urge that they were not calculated to do so?

Mr. Digby Seymour: That may have been their indirect effect.

Mr. Justice Blackburn: Do you mean to argue that it must not have been their direct effect?

Mr. Digby Seymour: What I argue, my lord, is this: that the motive of Mr. Whalley was a legitimate one; that he had not before his mind in furthering that legitimate object any idea that he was committing any offence against the law; and that, being engaged in a legitimate pursuit, he ought not to be held guilty of contempt for the effect of words, which effect he never contemplated. That is the distinction I desire to draw between the present case, and those which are reported. The sole object in view was to obtain funds in the boná-fide belief that there was a combination against the Claimant, who was to be prosecuted at the cost of the public Exchequer.

Mr. Justice Blackburn: Suppose a newspaper editor published observations calculated to prejudice a pending trial, surely it would not be an answer to say that he did so for the legitimate purpose of selling his newspaper? The motive does not excuse a wrongful act. What we are to consider is whether there has not been a contempt of this Court. It is no answer to say that the party has committed a crime for which he might be punished elsewhere.

Mr. Justice Mellor: If he had made no reference to the witnesses, I should be the last to desire to close his mouth; but the gist of the charge is that he has charged persons, who are to be again examined, of having committed perjury to keep a man out of his estates.

Mr. Digby Seymour: That may have been the indirect effect, but it was one which was never intended or contemplated, and the direct and only purpose in view was a perfectly legitimate one.

Mr. Justice Blackburn: Have you any case to show that a man is not liable for the effect of his words upon a pending trial because there may have been some by-purpose?

Mr. Digby Seymour: No, my lord; the case is a novel one.

Mr. Justice Blackburn: Suppose a trial was pending for sedition, in which a number of persons were involved—can it be said that public meetings might be held, and exciting speeches made on the one side or the other before the trial?

Mr. Digby Seymour submitted that, at the worst, the contempt here was constructive.

Mr. Justice Blackburn: The question is—Is it not real, and not constructive?

Mr. Digby Seymour: It refers to a past charge.

The Lord Chief Justice: But he reproduces the charge.

Mr. Justice Lush: And refers to witnesses to be examined at the pending Trial.

Mr. Digby Seymour: They might be called, or they might not.

Mr. Justice Blackburn: It is laid down by Lord Cottenham that every letter written, and every observation made, having for its object to prevent the course of justice is a contempt of Court.

Mr. Digby Seymour: Quite so, my lord.

Mr. Justice Blackburn: Do you contend that the statement that there was a conspiracy to have the Defendant sent to penal servitude, does not come within that definition?

Mr. Digby Seymour said that in his opinion it did not in this sense—that the speaker had not that for his object, or, indeed, had not such an effect in his mind. His object was a legitimate one—one which the Court had already intimated was not a reprehensible one—namely, to secure funds for the defence. If Mr. Whalley had mistaken the law, no one more deeply lamented it than he did.

Mr. Morgan Lloyd: I desire, my lords, following on the same side as my learned friend, Mr. Digby Seymour, to show that Mr. Whalley, as he has said in his affidavit, has acted boná-fide in the belief that he was not exceeding the privilege to which he is entitled. There is a great distinction between this case and others which have been decided, since the observations which were made at those meetings, though they may possibly have a bearing on the Trial now pending, were observations made in respect to a past Trial, on which a person speaking had a perfect right to make any comment he pleased. I am not aware that there has ever been any case of this description, as nearly all the cases, I believe, both in Chancery and the Court of Common Pleas, have been cases either of application for a criminal information, or of a rule to show cause why judgment should not be pronounced against persons for publishing comments on cases in the Court itself, or, in other cases, giving or professing to give certain information to the public that the public were not in possession of before. I submit to your lordships that is the distinction between such cases as I have referred to and the present one.

Mr. Justice Blackburn: If you have any authority to show that, because there was a trial in the Common Pleas, statements affecting a trial in the Queen's Bench are privileged, I should like to hear it, for I certainly shall require authority for that.

Mr. Morgan Lloyd: I have not been able to find any such authority. My argument only goes to show that in the cases where persons have been punished for contempt of Court in respect to observations on a pending Trial there had been no past Trial to which such observations might apply.

The Lord Chief Justice: My definition is that these meetings were called with reference to a coming Trial, the purpose and object of the meetings being to do something with reference to that Trial, and the course and argument in these speeches amounting to this, that at the past Trial, and with the view of the coming Trial, some people have been guilty of entering into a foul conspiracy for the purpose of perverting the course of justice. Now, various members of the TICHBORNE Family were witnesses at the past Trial, and the meetings must have understood that the same evidence would be adduced in the coming Trial; and therefore, when you say you have charged those persons with being in this conspiracy, it seems it is a continued conspiracy for the continuance and furtherance of which they will give their evidence before this Court. Can there be any other construction put upon these speeches? I assume, for the purposes of argument, that the main object of the meeting was to raise funds for the coming Trial; but, if many of the observations applied to the past Trial, it is obvious they must equally apply to the Trial which is pending.

Mr. MORGAN LLOYD: I respectfully submit that, so far as Mr. WHALLEY is concerned, the peculiar objects of the meetings were legitimate, and it being also legitimate to make comments on the past Trial, there is a difficulty created by the pendency of the present Trial; and it was, no doubt, very difficult for the speaker to draw a line between comments fairly legitimate for the object in view, and those which would prejudice the coming Trial.

Mr. Justice BLACKBURN: If they thought they could not attend a public meeting without committing contempt of this Court, they ought to have abstained from attending it.

The Lord Chief Justice: Or at all events have abstained from using that sort of language.

Mr. MORGAN LLOYD: When the expressions are read, you will see that there is a great deal of rhetorical language, and all that it amounts to is this—that we are right and the other side is wrong. And what makes this Case rather peculiar is that it has been so much discussed before the public, that it is scarcely possible to say anything new about it, and it is therefore doubtful whether the observations of Mr. WHALLEY or Mr. ONSLOW would have the slightest effect in convincing anyone, all being convinced before. I hope your lordships will take that view of it—that all the observations made were harmless, and therefore no substantial injury was done in the shape of affecting the forthcoming Trial. I wish to add that Mr. WHALLEY, though he felt bound, in moral justification of himself, to lay these matters before your lordships, wishes, if you are of opinion that he has in any way exceeded that which he had a right to do, to express his humble regret.

The Lord Chief Justice: I did not hear that so emphatically expressed by Mr. DIGBY SEYMOUR, but I supposed it was his intention to do so.

Mr. DIGBY SEYMOUR: I thought I began, my lord, by saying that I fully adopted, in spirit, the course which had been taken by my learned friend, Sir JOHN KARSLAKE.

The Lord Chief Justice: I did not quite understand that, especially as you argued that Mr. WHALLEY had been justified in the course he had pursued, so that, in fact, his offer is a species of hypothetical apology. "If you insist on an apology, we make it; but if you don't, we would rather not."

Mr. DIGBY SEYMOUR: I would prefer, my lord, to put it in this way. "We hope to show the Court we have not broken the law, but if we have broken the law, it was under circumstances that would lead our minds to the belief that it was not a breach of the law."

Mr. Justice BLACKBURN: Mr. ONSLOW has stated distinctly, through his Counsel, that he will not pursue a similar course in the future; but I have not heard a similar statement on the part of Mr. WHALLEY.

The Lord Chief Justice: I was about to put that point.

Mr. DIGBY SEYMOUR: Oh, most undoubtedly. Mr. WHALLEY will pledge himself to that. If your lordships are of opinion he has done that which at the time was not before his mind, he will, if he can, endeavour to set an example of respect and submission to your lordships' high authority, and will not attend any future meetings pending the Trial.

The Lord Chief Justice: That is perfectly satisfactory.

Mr. MACRAE MOIR, who followed on the same side, said he only wished to refer for a moment to a statement of Mr. Justice BLACKBURN, that the only difference between this and the other cases in the books was, that the name of his client was WHALLEY. That gentleman had formed a very strong opinion on the subject of the Claimant; he had expressed that opinion in the House of Commons and before the country, and he adhered to that opinion. That, no doubt, would be an excuse to their lordships' minds if in this case Mr. WHALLEY had conducted himself in a somewhat unusual manner.

Mr. HAWKINS, on the other side, said: I hoped I should be spared occupying your lordships' attention at all on these affidavits, but I think it my duty to call attention to the matter as it stood on the 11th of December. If these proceedings had been confined simply to a discussion of what had taken place at the late Trial, even though that discussion might have amounted technically and legally to a contempt of Court, I should have felt it expedient to forbear bringing the matter before your lordships and probably I should have taken that course. But that is impossible—considering the proceedings and speeches of both these gentlemen, and more particularly that of Mr. WHALLEY on the 12th of December. I should, in fact, have deserted my duty to the public and to the Crown if I had abstained for a single moment in bringing before your lordships these matters, in order that your lordships might mark your sense of these proceedings, and that your view of such proceedings might go forth to the public. I shall have occasion to call your lordships' attention to Mr. WHALLEY's speech on the second occasion, with the view of pointing out that it does justify what is set forth in his affidavit before the Court. I do not find in the affidavits of either of these gentlemen that they complain of the inaccuracy of the reports of their speeches, or that either of them did not say every syllable imputed to him. Mr. ONSLOW states that the objects of these meetings were to raise funds and to remove the prejudice which has been created against the Claimant. I am not aware that any prejudice has been raised, or existed, against the Claimant. Certainly none has been raised against him on the part of the prosecution, from the moment proceedings were instituted against him. Whatever prejudice was raised, if any, was by the proceedings in the late Trial.

The Lord Chief Justice: That is what I understand it is intended to say. The Claimant labours necessarily under a degree of prejudice which might operate against him on the coming Trial by reason of the jury having interposed, and decided against him. The Case, they say, was not heard out, and therefore he has to sustain and labour against a weight of prejudice resulting from the former Trial; we think that operates unfairly against him, and therefore we desire to set him right with the public. If the persons attending those meetings had been asked to suspend their judgment until the Case had been fully heard, I think no one would have complained.

Mr. HAWKINS: Your lordships, in that case, would never have been troubled with this motion. I propose now to call attention shortly to what Mr. ONSLOW had stated on the occasion of the first meeting. The learned Counsel then read at length from the notes of the first night's meeting at St. James's Hall all the points from Mr. ONSLOW's speech which were brought forward on the application for the rule, and which have already been published in *The Daily Telegraph*; and, after a few comments on the speech of the chairman of the evening on the 12th of December (a Mr. SKIPWORTH, of Lincolnshire), he similarly reproduced the speech of Mr. WHALLEY on the second day, in which, in the most plain and direct terms, that hon. gentleman charged the Attorney-General and the Government with being in the conspiracy of the TICHBORNE Family to keep the Claimant out of his title and estates. He then showed how impossible it was that these charges could have, as Mr. WHALLEY had set forth in his affidavit, reference to a correspondence he had with the TICHBORNE Family in 1870, before the prosecution was instituted, and in conclusion he said: With these observations I shall leave the matter in your lordships' hands, offering only for your notice the resolution which was proposed to the meeting, which was as follows: "That the prosecution of the Claimant at the public cost was uncalled for, and in the absence of the explanations, which had been refused, wholly unjustifiable and demands reprobation, and that the support and sympathy of the British public is justly due to the Claimant."

Their lordships having consulted for eight or nine minutes, the two Defendants were ordered to stand forward on the floor of the Court; and, in delivering judgment, the Lord Chief Justice said:

Mr. GUILDFORD ONSLOW and Mr. GEORGE HAMMOND WHALLEY, I express the unanimous opinion of this Court of Queen's Bench, that in the proceedings set forth in the affidavits upon which you have been called into this Court to answer, you have been guilty of a gross and aggravated contempt of the authority of this Court. We are far from saying that where persons believe that a man who is under a charge or prosecution is innocent, they may not legitimately unite for the purpose of providing him with the means of making a full and effectual defence. It is unnecessary to say that the expression of that belief, even in public, when it is intended as the foundation of an appeal to others to unite also to furnish means for the defence, is a matter which, though perhaps not strictly regular, should not be made matter of complaint and punishment. We quite agree that it would be a very harsh and unnecessary proceeding to interfere with the expression of opinion honestly entertained and bonâ fide expressed for a legitimate purpose; but it is no excuse to say that where at a meeting, held it may be only to provide funds, language is used which amounts to an offence against the law and contempt of this Court, that the motive or purpose for which the meeting was held was good. That affords no excuse whatever, and still less no justification of the improper language used. But admitting this, when we find that a man against whom, in consequence of the jury before whom he gave evidence as a witness on a trial declaring their disbelief in the evidence which he gave, the learned judge who presided at the trial has directed a prosecution for perjury; when a grand jury, the proper and constitutional tribunal in that behalf, have found a true bill of indictment for the serious crimes of perjury and forgery; that that man shall be paraded through the country and exhibited as a species of show in public assemblies for money as a victim of injustice and oppression; that at these meetings, in violent and inflammatory language, the witnesses who appeared adversely to him in a former trial shall be held up to public odium and reprobation: when we find that not only the prosecution, but the judge and jury who sat upon the Trial, are reviled in terms of contumely and opprobrium, and what is still more immediately to the present purpose, that the merits of the pending prosecution are at such meetings canvassed and discussed, and the evidence which may be adduced at the coming Trial made matter of public observation and discussion: when not only does this take place in the provinces, but the matter is brought, as it were, within the precincts of this Court, within the district from which the jurors are to come who will pass in judgment between the Crown and the accused at the coming Trial—one cannot shut one's eyes to the fact that there is here an outrage upon public decency and a great public scandal committed, and that even the ordinary course of justice is here unwarrantably interfered with. This Court, therefore, cannot hesitate, under such circumstances, to exercise the authority which it undoubtedly possesses to prevent public discussion upon a trial pending in this Court. It has been attempted to contend to-day on your behalf that the meetings in question were convened solely for the purpose of obtaining money in order to enable the accused to carry on his defence, with the additional purpose of removing any prejudice which the result of the former Trial may have produced against him; but that affords no excuse for the language used, which on these two occasions has been such as to cause an unwarrantable interference with the course of justice with reference to the coming Trial. When we find that gentlemen of your station and position—gentlemen of education and members of the Legislature—condescend to lend themselves to proceedings of this character, and to hold the language which it is quite clear you have held on these occasions, one can only contemplate it with astonishment and regret; and when it is said all this was done without a consciousness that it was an offence against public justice and an offence against this Court, and that it might have the effect of creating prejudice with reference to the approaching Trial, I can only accept the apology at the expense of the understanding of those who make it. *There cannot be, I apprehend, the slightest doubt in the mind of any right-thinking man, that a course of proceeding of this kind, if it were allowed to take place, must be calculated to interfere seriously with the course of public justice. If it is open to those who take the part of the accused to discuss in public meetings the merits of the prosecution in the interests of the accused, it is obviously equally open to those who believe in the guilt of the party accused, in the propriety of the prosecution, and who believe that his conviction is necessary to the ends of justice, to hold similar meetings and to hold language of an opposite tendency: and we might then—as has been pointed out by my brother* BLACKBURN—*have in political Trials, or in any Trial in which the public felt much excited, an organized agitation carried on throughout the country, sensational meetings held, and the merits of the accusation and the defence openly canvassed by appeals such as you have not hesitated to make to popular prejudice and passion; and thus the course of justice would be interfered with and disturbed by discussions out of the walls of the court of justice, and which might in the end influence the proceedings themselves. It is quite clear that this Court has always held that comments made upon a criminal Trial or proceeding when pending was an offence against the administration of justice and a contempt of the authority of the Court. It cannot make any difference in principle whether these comments or observations publicly made are made in writing or in speeches taking place at public assemblies: nor whether they are made with reference to a trial actually commenced and going on, or with reference to a trial about to take place; and this Court can have no hesitation in applying to one the same rule that we should apply to the other.* We think, therefore, that the Counsel for the Crown have done no more than discharge their duty in bringing this case to our attention, and the case having been brought to our attention we must deal with it in such a manner as shall repress and prevent the possibility of such indecent proceedings in future. We are glad to find that on this occasion, though attempts have been made to distinguish this from other cases in which the Court has interfered with its summary authority, that both parties have, through their Counsel, submitted themselves to the Court, and have given clear, distinct, and unmistakable pledges that they will take no part in objectionable proceedings of this kind in the future. Had there been any hesitation in giving that pledge, or the slightest appearance of contumacy—if there had not been this submissive attitude and tone of apology which both gentlemen, I am glad to think, have adopted, the Court would have thought it necessary to use the full power and authority which it possesses, to impose a substantial fine, with imprisoment in addition thereto. However, we are happily spared the necessity of the latter course by the wise, prudent, and proper line of conduct which you have, under the advice of Counsel, adopted; but it must be distinctly understood that the fine or pecuniary penalty which we are about to impose must be looked upon as one of extreme moderation, and that if, on any future occasion, proceedings of this kind shall be repeated, the full power of the Court, which it undoubtedly possesses to restrain and prevent such proceedings by adequate and commensurate punishment, will be inflicted with a stern, an unhesitating, and an unflinching hand. The thanks of the public are due to the metropolitan press for its admirable conduct in its forbearance in giving the publicity which you desired to these offensive and objectionable proceedings; but your intention was not the less reprehensible and your conduct not the less open to censure. However, looking at all the circumstances of the case, we think that, considering the position which you have taken up to-day, and the apology which you have given, that a pecuniary penalty of moderate amount—I say moderate with reference to the circumstances of the case, the contempt having been, in our opinion, a very gross one—will satisfy the exigencies of public justice. But let it be understood leniency will be appealed to in vain if any other party is brought before the Court charged with and proved to have been guilty of the same offence. The sentence of the Court is that, for the contempt of which you have been guilty, you be each of you adjudged to pay a fine of £100 to the QUEEN, and be imprisoned until the fine be paid.

Mr. Justice BLACKBURN having briefly whispered to the Lord Chief Justice, his Lordship continued: My learned brother has, very properly, remarked that it is not necessary in imposing a fine on gentlemen in your position, to add that you be imprisoned till the fine be paid. Of course, we are perfectly certain there will be no difficulty about payment in the case of either of you, and, therefore, the sentence will be one of fine simply. *I beg again that it may be understood that, if anybody is brought before the Court guilty of the same contempt of public justice on any future occasion, the fine which we have now imposed will be a fine of a most moderate character indeed compared with that which we shall impose, and we shall certainly give, in addition, a long term of imprisonment for any future contempt.*

We have marked in italics some of the observations of the Lord Chief Justice. The reader will see that when on a subsequent occasion in his complaint against ROUTLEDGE the publisher, Dr. KENEALY hoped that they would be applied in the Claimant's favour, as they had been directed against Messrs. ONSLOW and WHALLEY, he was utterly disappointed.

On the following day, the Chief Justice made certain observations upon what had occurred at the passing of the sentence.

Standard, Wednesday, Jan. 22.

COURT OF QUEEN'S BENCH, JAN. 21, 1873.

(Sittings in Banco, before the Lord Chief Justice and Justices BLACKBURN, MELLOR, and LUSH.)

THE CASE OF MESSRS. ONSLOW AND WHALLEY.

The Lord Chief Justice, in reference to this case which was heard yesterday, said he was desirous of saying a word, because he found that an impression had gone forth that in remitting that part of the judgment which provided that until the amount of the fine was paid the parties guilty of the contempt should stand committed, he was supposed to have done it in consequence of his anticipating some difficulty with reference to the imprisonment of members of Parliament, from some privilege they might possess as members of the Legislature. It was an entire mistake to suppose so. Imprisonment was only pronounced in these cases as a means of insuring the payment of the fine, and he was reminded at the time by his learned brother, Mr. Justice BLACKBURN, that the payment of a fine might be enforced without having recourse to imprisonment, and it occurred to him at once that unless it was necessary, as part of the judgment, that the defendants should be imprisoned till the fine was paid, it was useless to impose the condition, as, looking to the position in society of the defendants, their ability to pay, and the means that existed for enforcing the fines, there was no necessity for having recourse to that alternative. It was on that ground alone that that part of the judgment was recalled or removed. He intended to intimate at the time, and he thought he had done it in the judgment that was pronounced, with the full concurrence of the other members of the Bench, that if there had not been perfect submission by the defendants to the Court, and the fullest and most positive assurance that there would be no renewal of the offence in question, the Court would have thought it their duty to have added the punishment of imprisonment to that of the pecuniary fine imposed. The possibility of coming into collision with the House of Commons did not appear to them to be a thing that they could possibly believe would ever occur, because in the case of Mr. LECHMERE CHARLTON, who was committed by the Court of Chancery for contempt of Court, the House of Commons declined to interfere in his behalf on the score of privilege, so he was quite sure the House of Commons of the present day would not desire to interpose the privilege of its members in the way of preventing punishment by imprisonment, if necessary, for contempt in the administration of justice in that Court. He was anxious that no misunderstanding in a case so important as this should arise, and to correct the misapprehension that appeared to prevail as to the grounds on which they proceeded in the latter part of their judgment.

MR. SKIPWORTH'S CASE.

Mr. SKIPWORTH happened to be present in Court when Messrs. ONSLOW and WHALLEY were thus punished for contempt. Fired by a spirit worthy of JOHN HAMPDEN, he resolved to protest against the proceeding. He went straight down to Brighton, we believe that very day, and took the chair at a large public meeting of Sir ROGER's friends and supporters. He made no allusion to the witnesses, but arraigned the course taken by the Court as being arbitrary and unconstitutional, and proceeded also to impeach the fitness of the Lord Chief Justice for the trial of the Case, by reason, as he suggested, of supposed preconceived opinions on the Case. These observations were not reported in any of the London papers, but some account of them appeared in the Brighton papers, and the Lord Chief Justice appealed to the Attorney-General to take such steps as he might think proper.

We copy the report of what took place:—

COURT OF QUEEN'S BENCH.—JAN. 22.

(Sittings in Banco before the Lord Chief Justice and Justices BLACKBURN, MELLOR, and QUAIN.)

THE TICHBORNE CASE AGAIN.—MORE CONTEMPT.

On their Lordships taking their seats this morning,

The Lord Chief Justice, addressing the Attorney-General, said: Seeing you in your place, Mr. Attorney-General, I desire, on the part of my learned brothers and myself, to place in your hands, as the representative of the profession, and the head of it, certain newspapers which I have received this morning, and which contain an account of a public meeting held in the matter of the TICHBORNE Trial in the public Assembly Rooms at Brighton, with reference to the course the Court took, and the sentence pronounced on Monday last. If the report of the proceedings is correct, and it seems to be the same in the different newspapers I hold in my hand, the authority of this Court has been set at utter defiance, and reflections made on the conduct of the Judges who constitute it, which, if true, cannot be looked upon in any other light than a gross aggravation of the contempt of this Court, in commenting on matters to come under our consideration on the approaching Trial. We cannot, on mere newspaper reports, take any step in the matter, but we think we have a right to claim from you, as the head of the profession, that you shall cause steps to be taken to ascertain whether the reports so contained in these newspapers are correct reports of what took place at the meeting in question, and, if so, that you should take the proper steps to bring the matter before the Court.

The Attorney-General: Your lordships may depend upon it that the matter shall receive my most careful attention.

In consequence of this Mr. HAWKINS applied for an order that Mr. SKIPWORTH should attend this Court to answer for his observations.

The Lord Chief Justice did not attend the Court, and Mr. Justice BLACKBURN, who, as the Senior Puisne Judge, presided, suggested that the Claimant ought also to be ordered to attend; and, although the Counsel for the Prosecution did not desire it, such was the order made.

The affidavits were read at length by the Master. The first were the verbatim reports of the speeches of the Claimant and Mr. SKIPWORTH at the Brighton meeting, upon which this application was particularly made, and which was as follows:—"Mr. SKIPWORTH proceeded to address the meeting as follows: Ladies and Gentlemen,—It is encouraging to find your reception after the degrading spectacle I may say I have witnessed at the Queen's Bench to-day in London. Nothing less than this, that two honourable members of Parliament have been brought up, I may say as criminals, for advocating truth and justice throughout the country. (Hear hear, and applause.) Yes, gentlemen, I say a sad spectacle it is for England that we have come to this—no less than a great infringement upon our rights and liberties—(hear, hear)—and if they had a just cause upon the other side, you may depend upon it it would never have been done. (Hear, hear, and a cry of 'Never.') And what do they mean when they rob a man of everything he possesses, and he has to go about the country for a living? They would even rob him of every friend he possesses. (Applause.) The Lord Chief Justice of England particularly stated in his judgment how mild and moderate he was to these gentlemen, inasmuch as they had apologized, but it was only an example, and that if anyone else should similarly offend, or be brought up under similar circumstances, they would be visited with the full rigour of the law—not only a fine would be inflicted, but imprisonment. (Cries of 'Shame,' and hisses.) Gentlemen, I hurl his intimidation back with the contempt that he has treated these members of Parliament with. (Loud applause.) I care not for his intimidation. I will stand here when my duty calls me in defiance of his—ay, I will call them—vulgar threats. (Renewed applause.) I am not going to be intimidated when I consider that a duty to my country calls me forth." The remainder of the speech was to a similar effect.

The report of what was said by the Claimant at the meeting was then read, and it contained these passages:—"Four years ago the Lord Chief Justice of England publicly denounced me as a rank Impostor at his club. I know of others (occasions), but cannot prove them, so will not. But I can prove that he subsequently, within these last two months, at a party where a lady friend of mine was, distinctly turned round in a very angry manner to those ladies, and said it was a disgrace to mention my name in decent society. ('Oh, oh.') I think I have a right to call on him to answer for contempt of Court. I do not suppose they would grant the rule, but rest assured I will apply for it. And I maintain, ladies and gentlemen, that he had no right to sit on that bench (to-day). At St. James's Hall, my friend, Mr. ONSLOW, stated that the Lord Chief Justice was not a fit Justice to sit on my forthcoming Trial. He gave as his reasons those I have mentioned; and that he had also, during the late Trial, while sitting by the side of Judge BOVILL, written on a piece of paper, 'Had I been Judge and you leading Counsel, we would have had this fellow in Newgate long ago.' He was a party concerned, and if he had had the slightest delicacy for his honour he would never have sat on the bench (to-day). So much have I heard that I intend to petition Parliament against his sitting on my forthcoming Trial. No doubt I shall be able to prevent him. If I do not, I will go into that Court without counsel, attorney, or witnesses, and let him crush me as he thinks proper. (No, no.) If the Lord Chief Justice has got to sit and adjudicate on my Case, I will offer no evidence, but throw myself on the country. (Applause.)" Various other matters were then read, not directly bearing on the present application, chiefly the speeches of the Claimant and Mr. SKIPWORTH at the meeting in December.

Pursuant to an order for the attendance of TICHBORNE and SKIPWORTH, they accordingly presented themselves in the Court of Queen's Bench, on Wednesday, January 29. We append the report of what took place, omitting the Summary of the Proceedings, which appeared in one of the penny papers, and which we can assert, from actual knowledge, was coloured, and even false, to an extreme degree.

The Judges—Justices BLACKBURN, MELLOR, LUSH, and QUAIN—took their seats on the Bench at twenty-five minutes past ten o'clock.

Mr. HAWKINS, Q.C., and Mr. BOWEN appeared for the Crown.

Mr. SKIPWORTH, who wore his forensic robes, and held a brief-like document, and the Claimant, sat in front of the Queen's Counsel, on the seats recently occupied by Mr. GUILDFORD ONSLOW, M.P., and Mr. WHALLEY, M.P.

Mr. MACRAE MOIR held a watching brief on behalf of Mr. WHALLEY.

Mr. Justice BLACKBURN said: Are the two gentlemen who were directed to be in attendance to-day present?

Mr. SKIPWORTH: Yes, my lord.

Mr. Justice BLACKBURN: Do you, Mr. SKIPWORTH, appear by yourself or by Counsel?

Mr. SKIPWORTH: By myself.

Mr. Justice BLACKBURN: And you, sir (addressing the Claimant), do you appear by yourself or by Counsel?

The Claimant: By myself, my lord.

Mr. Justice BLACKBURN: You may both sit down. The order has, as you are doubtless aware, been obtained upon affidavit, and it is necessary, therefore, that the affidavit should be now read, in order that you may understand what you are charged with. We will then hear you.

Mr. FREDERICK COCKBURN, Master of the Crown Office, then read an affidavit verifying the speeches delivered by Mr. G. B. SKIPWORTH and the Claimant at Brighton, of which reports have already been published.

Mr. HAWKINS: As against Mr. SKIPWORTH the rule was obtained upon reading also the speech he delivered at St. James's Hall, on the 12th of December.

Mr. Justice BLACKBURN: The material matter is what took place at Brighton on the Monday referred to. I do not know whether Mr. SKIPWORTH desires the other speeches to be read.

Mr. SKIPWORTH: The Court is quite at liberty to read anything I ever said.

Mr. Justice BLACKBURN: You can have it read if you think proper.

Mr. SKIPWORTH: Oh, I shall leave it entirely to your lordship.

Mr. Justice BLACKBURN: Well, then, we had better have it read.

Mr. HAWKINS: There are two speeches.

Mr. Justice BLACKBURN: We must have everything read on which the rule was obtained.

Mr. HAWKINS: I desire merely to say that there were two speeches of the Claimant referred to—one delivered in September, and the other in December.

The affidavits of Messrs. BEASLEY and CONNOR, reporters, of Liverpool, were then read, verifying the transcript of speeches delivered by Mr. SKIPWORTH and the Claimant at a meeting held at the Royal Amphitheatre, Liverpool, on the 19th of September last.

Mr. Justice BLACKBURN directed that the exhibit referred to in the affidavit, so far as it related to Mr. SKIPWORTH, should be read. Either of the defendants was entitled to have the whole read if he so desired. Probably they would think Mr. SKIPWORTH's speech sufficient.

Mr. SKIPWORTH: That is all I require.

The exhibit was then read of a speech of Mr. SKIPWORTH at Liverpool, in the course of which he observed that he was a purely disinterested stranger, and a country gentleman from the great county of Lincoln. The world was now sure that the Claimant was Sir ROGER, and no more proof of it was needed; they were sick now of the very word "identity." He would say that the Attorney-General himself was what he had described the Claimant to be. He, not Sir ROGER, was the liar, perjurer, and robber. He was an abomination on the face of the earth. [Some confusion was, it appears, occasioned by this, and the speaker was ultimately "reluctantly" induced to resume his seat.] The Claimant also spoke on the occasion, but said nothing of any importance.

Mr. Justice BLACKBURN: Is there any other meeting?

Mr. HAWKINS: Only the one at St. James's Hall, my lord.

Mr. Justice BLACKBURN: The affidavit must be read.

The speech of Mr. SKIPWORTH at St. James's Hall, on the 12th December, 1872, was then read:

"After some preliminary remarks, he complained of the reports of the press of the previous evening's meeting. He took up the *Standard* and the *Daily News* of that morning, and the accounts which they gave were a disgrace to the country. The *Daily Telegraph* was a little milder. Then there was the *Times*, with its contemptuous silence. If the matter was important enough for a Government prosecution, why didn't the *Times* take it up? If it was not important enough, why was a Government prosecution ordered? Then there was the *Echo*, and a pretty echo of public opinion it was. Then the *Pall Mall Gazette* had taken them to task for wearing evening dress, and for empty benches. He supposed that if they had not worn evening dress the *Pall Mall* would have been down on them for that. And were they responsible for empty benches? They talked about gagging the press. Why, he said that the sooner such a paltry and contemptible press was gagged the better. He believed this man to be Sir ROGER TICHBORNE. He believed this was a truthful case, and he defied Mr. GLADSTONE or anyone else to prove the contrary. Reference was then made to the steps taken by the Dowager Lady TICHBORNE to find out her son, and to the description which she gave by which the Claimant was identified. The other side knew that he had been found, and they were prepared to deny his identity before he came home. He went on to say that there appeared to be no intention on the part of the Crown to do what was right, and he should like to know what reason there was for it. Putting a charitable construction upon the matter, he would suppose that Mr. GLADSTONE and all Her Majesty's Ministers had lost their senses.

Mr. Justice MELLOR: If there is anything there which has been said by the Claimant it had better be read.

Mr. HAWKINS: There is a statement made by the Claimant, but I do not know that it varies much from what has already been read.

Mr. Justice MELLOR: If it is in the exhibit it must be read.

The speech of the Claimant was accordingly read:

"In the course of his speech the Claimant said that he was no hypocrite; and that although the Attorney-General occupied twenty-three days in cross-examining him, and the Trial lasted 103 days, he had left the Court without proving him an Impostor. The Attorney-General was not a bungler of a lawyer. Everybody knew that he was a clever gentleman, but he had not been able to change him (the Claimant) into somebody else. True, he had elected to be non-suited, but that was no reason why he was an Impostor. They well knew that they could not carry on a lawsuit without money, and he thought he had managed well in carrying it on so long as he did. But the Attorney-General only succeeded in stopping the Case by frightening the jury, and telling them that he had 260 witnesses more to examine. This was equivalent to saying that they would have to sit there for two years longer. The Case was then stopped, and he (the Claimant) was sent to a cell in Newgate. He (the Claimant) had applied for a Trial at Bar, because he believed that the other side intended to postpone the Case perpetually till he was dead. The Attorney-General had thought proper to remove the Case from the Old Bailey to the Court of Queen's Bench. With what object? And why had he been accused of forgery? Simply in order that he might be kept in prison, forgery not being a bailable offence. If the Judges had liberated him, it was because of the interest the People of England had taken in the matter. The object of removing the Case to a special jury was to suit the Attorney-General, who did not like a common jury. No, he preferred a special one, composed of a set of half-bred swells, whom he could nod and wink at. (A laugh.) That was the reason of the change to the Court of Queen's Bench. He maintained that the Attorney-General ought to be compelled to come forward to prosecute him at the forthcoming Trial, instead of being allowed to retire from the prosecution, as Mr. BRUCE said he had done. The Attorney-General ought to be compelled to come forward and prove what he had said against him. Referring to his incarceration in Newgate, he asked what could recompense him for the fifty-two days he was imprisoned there? No amount of money could compensate him for that. He charged the Government with taking twelve months to get up a case against him. The Government had withdrawn the charge of forgery, because they knew that they would have as much trouble in proving him not to be Sir ROGER TICHBORNE as he had experienced in endeavouring to prove that he was. He then adverted to the appearance of the publication attributed to the Rev.

MR. JUSTICE BLACKBURN.

HENRY COLERIDGE, the Attorney-General's brother. When he was in Birmingham about twelve months ago, a kind friend sent him a copy of the *Sydney Morning Herald*, in which he found an article offering £1,000 to anyone who would bring the necessary evidence in this Case. It seemed that they were not yet quite sure that he was ARTHUR ORTON. They had made a multitude of endeavours to prove his identity with other persons, and when he was examined at the Law Institution, an old lady was placed in a very favourable position that she might see and identify him as her son; but this she could not do. Then they tried to make him out to be the illegitimate son of three of his uncles. They then tried to make him out an Australian prizefighter, then an Australian navvy, then EDWARD ORTON, then HENRY ORTON, then ARTHUR ORTON, then GEORGE JARVIS, and then the illegitimate son of his own mother. He then went on to say, 'The laws of England are of very little avail; for if I am an impostor, I have been before the country for six years, and after all this trial, all they can say is that I am not ROGER TICHBORNE. How long is such a state of things to continue? They might send the Case back to the Old Bailey and have it tried out. If they wanted to try the Case, why was it not tried at once? Do you believe they ever intended to try it?' After saying that it was quite time an end was put to the existing state of things, he asked his audience to look at the partiality of his Judge in ordering him to pay £00,000 before he would allow him to commence a suit in his Court again. He asked anyone who was in that Court whether they could not see the partiality shown by the Judge who tried him. He then proceeded with a detailed account of the evidence which had been advanced against him, upon which he commented at length."

Mr. Justice BLACKBURN: Now, Mr. SKIPWORTH, if you wish to say anything, or bring any other facts before the Court, you can do so.

Mr. SKIPWORTH: Does your lordship wish me to state——

Mr. Justice BLACKBURN: Anything you may wish to say, either to alter the facts as they appear in the affidavits, or anything in your defence. You are now called on to speak, and to show cause why you should not be committed for what you have done—for contempt of Court. Now, say anything you please. If you wish to alter the facts by any affidavits you may have, you can do so, and hand them in; you can either do so, or accept the facts as stated, whichever you may please. If you have an affidavit it must be read by the officers of the Court, or you can read it, if you intend it as part of your speech.

Mr. SKIPWORTH: It is an affidavit, my lord.

Mr. Justice BLACKBURN: Very well; then you must hand it in.

The affidavit was then read by the officer of the Court as follows:—

I say: 1. That I have been informed and believe that the party styling himself Sir ROGER TICHBORNE arrived in England at Christmas, 1866. That in June, 1867, he filed two Bills in Chancery, alleging himself to be Sir ROGER TICHBORNE, and asking for a receiver to be appointed of the rental of the estate. That on the 30th of July, 1867, he was cross-examined at the Law Institution, and on the 30th of April, 1868, the Court of Chancery, on hearing both parties, made an order impounding the rents of the estates until his Case should have been tried at law. That being after his own and seventy other affidavits were filed in support that the action at law was commenced, and after a time went to trial. The Plaintiff's Case being supported by eighty-six witnesses, including the affidavit of his Mother, and on the part of the defence twelve were examined, whose evidence since the Trial, as well as the unproved assertions of the Attorney-General and the partial conduct of the Judge, have been matters of strong public comment, but upon which evidence the jury stopped the Case; and that the Plaintiff subsequently, by advice of Counsel, submitted to a non-suit, and the Judge ordered his committal to Newgate on a charge of perjury. That an indictment for forgery was afterwards framed, and upon some evidence furnished to a grand jury at the Old Bailey, they returned a true bill against him, the Case being afterwards removed to the Court of Queen's Bench to be tried by a special jury. However, as I have understood and believe, a case of forgery, being a felony, could only be tried before a common jury, and therefore it was abandoned, and it was decided to proceed on a charge of misdemeanour only, for perjury; and I have been informed and believe that the serious charge of perjury was at one time abandoned, and the Defendant was to be tried on some minor counts only.

2. That of all those 85 witnesses, not mentioning the Mother's affidavit, except, I believe, one or two, their testimony remains unchallenged, and in spite of their cross-examination during the Trial, and the time they have had for reflection since, they remain staunch as the day they went into the box; not only so, but have aided and assisted the Plaintiff, showing that they did not give their evidence without being thoroughly convinced of the truth of what they stated. That nevertheless, every encouragement has been given, both in public and in private, if not openly, by tacit countenance, to scandalize him; still more, the press of the country has followed in the same track, and every license has been allowed them unrestrained, and therefore virtually encouraged to write down that persecuted, and, I am justified in calling him, innocent man.

3. That the meetings which are complained of as held throughout the country were, as I have understood, occasionally given out to be for the purpose of raising defence funds for what is called the approaching Trial; but I did not attend them with that object in view, having no faith in that ever coming off, but with the object of openly and fairly enlisting sympathy, pecuniary or otherwise, for the cause that was advocated thereat, and impressing on the minds of the people its truth and honesty, and the injustice of the case on the part of the prosecution.

4. That in the appeals that were made to the people as aforesaid, no excitable, frantic, or inflammatory language was used, unless, as sometimes occurred, there arose interruption by enemies of the cause, if they made themselves known, and did not avail themselves of the offer always afforded them to come on the platform and a patient hearing would be given them, when they had to desist from disturbance or leave the room; and often parties attended those meetings as detectives or spies of the opposite party. That the several meetings, besides being held for pecuniary reasons, also took place through the enormous anxiety and interest that have been and are taken in the Case throughout the country—often through the invitation, always by the wish, of the people where they were held. That the whole of the said meetings were all but unanimous in declaring their belief in the identity of Sir ROGER TICHBORNE, and that, when there were exceptions, it was for the most part from parties for the mere sake of opposition, and that, when asked to give any reason for the same, either refused, or were unable to do so. That I have attended those meetings myself with a full conviction of his being the man he represented himself to be. That it was upon that ground I first took up his cause, and, hearing that the people of Grimsby, in my native county, had invited him to go and hold a meeting there, I immediately not only informed them of my intention to support him, but wrote and asked him to my house on his way. That I afterwards attended the meeting at Grimsby on the 2nd of September, 1872, and delivered the speech in the words, or to the effect, stated in the exhibit marked B. That I wrote and addressed, through Her Majesty's Secretary of State, a letter to Her Most Gracious Majesty the QUEEN, dated the 23rd of December, 1872, being the exhibit marked C. And that I received the reply thereto, in the words and figures stated in the exhibit marked D. That I have also written and published the several letters on, and in reference to, the TICHBORNE Case, being the exhibits marked respectively E, F, and G. That I have also written, and sent by post, to the Right Hon. WILLIAM EWART GLADSTONE, as Prime Minister of England (and which I believed were received by him in due course) the respective letters marked as the exhibits H and I. And I submit the said exhibits to show the animus which has actuated me from the first of my taking up the cause, which has done throughout, and up to the time of making this, my affidavit.

5. That I have had no other object either in what I have stated at the said meetings or otherwise, than to proclaim truth and justice, and if I made any misstatement at any of these meetings, of which I am not aware, it has been by inadvertence, and not from intention. That any remarks or observations I have made upon any of the judges or law officers of the Crown, the members of the Government, or any one having had to do with the proceedings or matters aforesaid, were used as fair, honest, and just comments, criticism, or censure, as the case might be, and as rightly and justly called for under all the facts and circumstances that have taken place, particularly on the principle that, Her Majesty's Attorney-General having failed to prove one word of his accusations against the Plaintiff in the said action, his (the Plaintiff's) claim must be considered genuine and deserving the support of the public. And that, in anything I have said and done in or out of these meetings, I had not the slightest intention of bringing the laws and institutions of this country into contempt; but, on the contrary, my sole object and intention has been, and is, to uphold the same in their dignity, majesty, and integrity. And it is only that I have seen that dignity, majesty, and integrity in jeopardy; that one grand principle of the English law—that a man shall be assumed to be innocent before he is proved to be guilty—has been disregarded and set at nought; and that the whole law and judicature of the country has been brought into reprehension and contempt by such an unheard-of proceeding as trying to convict an innocent man, of which at present there is no proof to the contrary: that I have come forth, urged by a solemn and conscientious duty, to declaim against the wrongs that have been done him, are in course of being done, and threatened to be further committed, unless the arm of the law is vindicated. But I have done so without having any personal or pecuniary motive or interest in any of the matters or questions aforesaid, or in reference thereto. That I have no TICHBORNE Bonds, nor ever saw one. That my action is not only entirely free from any selfish or interested views, but I have sacrificed time and money, home, domestic ties, interests, and enjoyments, in the one great aim to see justice done, and a due and righteous administration of the laws of the land executed and fulfilled.

6. That though I was in Court and heard the judgment passed upon Messrs. ONSLOW and WHALLEY for alleged contempt of Court, I could not but look upon it under the circumstances I have herein mentioned, but in the light of a degradation, a dishonour, and disgrace to the land in which we live, and it resolved itself into this—whether I was to be called upon to regard man's judgment which I was bound to consider unjust, or do my duty to my God, my conscience, and my country. I had little hesitation in deciding. And I submit that I should be unworthy of the name

of an Englishman, unworthy of the name of a Christian, or one who valued his honour or reputation, if I allowed the threats or intimidation, from whatever quarter they might come, to deter me from that sacred and solemn duty, and thus, whilst escaping the unmerited punishment of man, I should bring upon me the well-merited wrath of God.

7. The meeting at Brighton was of a very enthusiastic character, with very slight interruption. That the remarks I made as to Lord Chief Justice COCKBURN not being a proper judge to preside where the TICHBORNE Case at all came in question or discussion, were based on the well-known fact that that Judge had so thoroughly denounced the Claimant to the Tichborne estates as an impostor, that it would be improper and unbecoming that he should preside on any such occasion. I put it to the meeting as an abstract proposition—one called forth by the justice and exigencies of the Case, and in no way as a matter of offence or contempt of Court. My remarks on that subject were received with approbation. But upon two or three hisses being given, not, I feel sure, by friends, I was betrayed through, and in consequence of, that interruption, to use the expression, "I hiss the Lord Chief Justice!" meaning that I disapproved of his adjudicating upon the Case that day, and in reference to the Case generally, not only on account of his denunciations of the one side, but his predilections to the other—that I used that expression involuntarily, and because a more suitable one did not, on the spur of the moment, occur to me. But I admit that it was not a happy one, or such as I would have preferred to use with more consideration, whatever might be the motive for making it. And so far as the words themselves go, I unhesitatingly withdraw them. But I cannot forego my perfect right to criticise, or even censure, where the circumstances justify it, the conduct of a judge when his fairness and impartiality are reasonably in question, and the remarks I made on that occasion were with that motive and intent, and I do most positively swear, to the best of my knowledge, that, except the said expression or slip of the tongue, I said nothing at that meeting which could, under the circumstances I have herein mentioned, or at all, be construed into a contempt of Court. And I solemnly and sincerely swear that the statement reported to be made by Mr. HAWKINS, on the application for a rule in the Court of Queen's Bench, that on the occasion of the meeting at Brighton I used atrociously contemptuous language respecting the Court, is utterly false, and without the slightest foundation.

8. I also say that the said meeting was not for the purpose of procuring money for the TICHBORNE Defence Fund, but as I believe for the subsistence of Sir ROGER TICHBORNE and his family, he in fact, having no other means of support at the present time; and that if he were deprived of that, he and his family would be absolute paupers. So far as the act itself goes of attending that meeting, though I was in no way bound by the admissions or submissions of Messrs. ONSLOW and WHALLEY, I do not hesitate to admit that I did it in utter defiance of the threat that was held out on the occasion of Messrs. ONSLOW and WHALLEY's appearance at Westminster Hall; nay, further, that it was with the full intention of setting that threat at defiance, because I considered such a threat ought never to have been uttered from the Bench; and it was to prevent a stigma that might come upon us for being a nation of cowards, to show that there was one spark of true British pluck where a man would face fine and imprisonment rather than see the law courts made the instruments of extorting obedience at the sacrifice of a man's conscience and honour—rather than see the fair fame of his country sullied by unrighteousness and oppression, and the rod held over a man who shall dare to resist what he thinks unlawful, and who shall be bold enough to do his duty to his GOD and his country. If such a man for conscience sake is to be visited as a martyr, for GOD's sake what is to become of the criminal?—the real offender against the laws of the country—where the prison cells are once more to become the receptacles of men whose offence is that they have opened their mouths to proclaim the truth; whose only object and expressed desire has been, and is, that justice and mercy shall actuate those who have to administer the laws of the land, and that the whole order of the realm, beginning with the QUEEN upon her throne, shall be guided and influenced by that unanimous principle and sentiment. I submit that the action against me is cruel, oppressive, and unjust.

Mr. Justice BLACKBURN: Do you wish the exhibits to be read?

Mr. SKIPWORTH: Yes, my lord, I wish them all read.

The first exhibit was a letter from Mr. SKIPWORTH to the inhabitants of Caistor, in which he stated that numerous petitions had been sent to Parliament on behalf of the Claimant, and protesting against his being prosecuted by the Government. Eighty-six persons, including his mother, had sworn to his identity, and hundreds of others could have done so. The speech of the Attorney-General was founded on assumptions, and there was the fear of his putting 260 witnesses in the box. The next exhibit was the report of a speech made by the Claimant at Grimsby in September last, at which Mr. SKIPWORTH moved the first resolution, to the effect that the Claimant was the rightful heir to the Tichborne estates, and pledging the meeting to support him to the end. Mr. SKIPWORTH, in his speech, said that "Sir ROGER's" supporters would not cease their agitation until justice had been done and the honour of the nation satisfied. Personally speaking, he believed in the identity of the Claimant, and who could not be ARTHUR ORTON, as the Attorney-General would have them believe. The next exhibit was a long printed letter which Mr. SKIPWORTH had addressed to her gracious Majesty the QUEEN.

It was, he said, with feelings of deep emotion he ventured to address her Majesty on a subject which was then absorbing so much of the attention of the country, namely the great TICHBORNE Case. The cause of the representative of that family name and estate—vulgarly called the Claimant, but by right Sir ROGER TICHBORNE—had then for six years been before the British public, and, marvellous to relate, his title to that name still hung, in fact, in abeyance, because it was not duly accorded him by the QUEEN of the nation. The cause had assumed proportions calling up all the best attributes of human nature—had sent a thrill through the heart of every sober-minded Englishman, who would sacrifice almost all he held dear rather than see the institutions of his country jeopardized, or a blot on its reputation or honour, by a denial of justice to his countryman. Her Majesty, in her exalted position, had not the opportunity her subjects possessed of becoming so familiarized with their private views and sentiments on this, the great and important subject of the day, or he felt that Her Majesty could not but share with them those feelings which, emanating from a devotion and love to their country, in an equal and even enhanced force, were extended to a fellow-countryman whose only object had been to obtain his lawful rights. How that a just cause had remained unsettled before the public so long was a mystery. Had it been that gigantic imposition which it had been represented to be, instead of six years he ventured with confidence to affirm that it could hardly have stood the test of a British public for a single day. He did not claim relationship or even friendship with "Sir ROGER"—beyond that of a purely disinterested stranger—whom he had only seen a few weeks ago, when he came into his native county. But with the opportunity of a more intimate acquaintance, long-desired, he (SKIPWORTH) left the quiet retreat of a country life for the arena of large towns, such as Manchester, Liverpool, and other places. He raised his voice in his behalf, which was nothing as compared with the millions who flocked to espouse his cause. The unmistaken unanimity of the great mass of the people had been shown and proclaimed in countless numbers. The word "justice" had gone forth from a people deeply impressed with injuries long inflicted, long endured, which, if not speedily redressed, would bring such a dishonour on the name, the laws, and reputation of the country as even time would not serve to repair. It was felt that a blow was struck at the rights and liberties of Englishmen, and that there was no longer that safeguard in the glorious British constitution which had for ages past been a pride and honour to Englishmen, and the envy of the rest of the civilized world. In proof of such estimation he would quote the words of that great and enlightened statesman, Prince BISMARCK—(a laugh)—who, in reply to an address delivered by Mr. KINNAIRD, on behalf of the English Protestant notabilities, said: "The value of this address is enhanced by the fact that it comes from a country which Europe has learnt to esteem during the last two centuries as the bulwark of political and religious freedom." The nation had been appealed to most unmistakeably, and unhesitatingly had pronounced its verdict that the order of the judge who sent "Sir ROGER TICHBORNE" to prison, and ordered his prosecution, was founded on injustice; and over and over again had the people in vain challenged any opposition to the verdict. The public mind was becoming more and more agitated that, in spite of the country's conviction, the prosecution should continue, or even hang for one moment longer over the head of him against whom every accusation that had been made had been proved to be false and unfounded. England could not then afford to be held up as a mockery in the eyes of the civilized world—to have pointed at her the finger of scorn for pursuing a course against which all nature rebelled. The letter concluded thus: "On you must rest the responsibility, whatever any of your judges or law officers may assert, if you allow a man's honour, reputation, or property to become as a thing of nought and mere idle sport for the reckless in the land. I beg, therefore humbly to implore your Majesty by all the sacred ties that unite you to a loving and affectionate people, by everything that is Christianlike and GOD-like, to see that the nation's will be done.

Another exhibit, which had been forwarded to the Secretary of the Society for the Promotion of Christian Knowledge, in reply to an application for a subscription in aid of the funds of the institution, was next read. It stated that the writer forwarded copies of the letters which he had written, referring to the TICHBORNE Case, as his subscription to the Society, because he thought that the present state of the Case was a proof of greater heathenism than any that could be found either abroad or at home.

The following letter which Mr. SKIPWORTH addressed to the Premier was also read:

SIR,—To a recent appeal for aid from the Secretary of the Christian Knowledge Society, I gave the following reply:

"SIR,—I send the inclosed letters (being mine to the QUEEN, and three others since, on the TICHBORNE Baronetcy Case) as my subscription to the Society for Promoting Christian Knowledge, and do not think it speaks much for the Christian or any other knowledge (but ignorance) of the country, that such a disgraceful affair as the TICHBORNE prosecution has now been going on for years, and the very QUEEN, Lords, and Commons have become parties to it—the Lords numbering the bishops, the heads and supporters of your boasted Christian knowledge. Talk about heathenism! I think it is the worst form. There is no excuse now; it is an undoubted fact, of which the bishops and dignitaries of the Church are perfectly cognizant, that it is simply an attempt of might to overcome right. As to Christian knowledge, then, in this country, so far as the heads of the Church are concerned, I don't believe in it. And it may well be urged that those who talk about instructing others should first set about reforming themselves. At present there can be but the mere outward form or shell, destitute altogether of the weightier matter of the law—justice, mercy, and truth.

"Now, I see the bishops are calling upon the clergy within their respective dioceses to keep the 20th of the present month as a day of intercession for the Church missions. Yes, so I would, when there is such gross ignorance at home.

"Is it nothing that in England, boasting of its Christianity and civilization, a man's rights are to be set at nought, instead of being as sacred, we may say, as the laws of GOD? That what are called some of the 'upper classes' of this country should sacrifice what is exalting in human nature and dare to weigh a man's title to his property and inheritance by some selfish ideas of their own, some doctrine or judgment of 'I am more righteous or better than thou,' is what would not be tolerated in a heathen land. Is it, then, that the country has become excessively civilized, assumed a polish that will not bear scrutiny within, but only belonging to an artificial world?

"If these are the fruits of high-class education, for GOD's sake let us be without this exterior gilding, and cultivate plain, sober, honest truth, which alone can adorn the inner man."

A further exhibit read was a letter from the secretary of Mr. BRUCE stating that Mr. SKIPWORTH's communication to the QUEEN had been laid before Her Majesty, but that Her Majesty could not be advised to interfere in the Case.

The next exhibit was a letter addressed "To the People of England, or such of them as had hearts to feel for the oppressed." It mentioned that the writer had addressed a letter to the QUEEN and to Mr. GLADSTONE; that, on one occasion, Mr. GLADSTONE had been overheard saying to the Attorney-General, "For GOD's sake, do not deceive me with respect to this TICHBORNE Case." (Laughter.) To which the Attorney-General replied that he could prove the Claimant to be ORTON in twenty minutes; but, continued the writer, "he is no more ORTON than he is Mr. GLADSTONE himself." (Laughter.) The writer mentioned in the "address" as an incident in the Trial that, on the day Mrs. RADCLIFFE was to be examined, the Claimant was in Mr. Serjeant BALLANTINE's consulting-room alone. The door was open, and he saw the Attorney-General pass by with his arm round Serjeant BALLANTINE's neck. (Roars of Laughter, in which the learned serjeant heartily joined.) They were speaking, and they must have been honeyed words the serjeant heard. (Laughter.) In reference to the comments of the press, the writer said that he had heard when great trials were pending it was a usual thing for editors of newspapers to receive cheques for £500. (Laughter.)

When the exhibits had been read,

Mr. Justice BLACKBURN said: Mr. SKIPWORTH, do you desire to add anything further.

Mr. SKIPWORTH: Nothing more than this, my lord; that if, after due consideration of all you have heard, you think proper to bring me in guilty of contempt of Court, I shall think it right, my lord, not to place myself in your hands, but in the laws of my GOD for protection.

Mr. Justice BLACKBURN (addressing the Claimant): Have you anything to say in reference to the rule. If so we are ready to hear you now.

The Claimant: I am not aware, my lord, that I have committed any contempt of Court in any shape or way. If I have done so it was certainly not done intentionally, and I submit that the Case ought to be tried by a jury, for the simple reason that I could then prove that what I have stated is true. I have no opportunity of producing witnesses now. It is not because I have not faith in your lordships that I ask for the Case to be tried, but it is because it would enable me to show that what I have stated is true. If, however, your lordships intend to try me, I must ask you to allow me to read this document.

Mr. Justice BLACKBURN: What is it?

The Claimant: My defence, my lord.

Mr. Justice BLACKBURN: If you wish to read a written paper, instead of addressing us verbally, you may do so. Generally, it is more effective to speak without reading?

The Claimant: I would rather read it, my lord; but am I to understand that you decide upon trying me yourselves, and not to allow me to have a jury?

Mr. Justice BLACKBURN: Certainly. I may inform you that, according to the laws in relation to contempt, the question is to be decided in a summary way by the Court, and not by a jury.

The Claimant: If I have committed contempt it is with reference to the Lord Chief Justice, and, inasmuch as you are his colleagues, I submit that it would not be fair for you to try me.

Mr. Justice BLACKBURN: You may use that as an argument, but it has been the law for centuries that it is the duty of the Court to decide questions of contempt.

The Claimant: If that is the contempt I am accused of, then I say that if I were tried before a jury I would have an opportunity of showing that what I stated of the Lord Chief Justice is true.

Mr. Justice BLACKBURN: You are not here for contempt in insulting any individual member of the Court. The contempt of which you are accused is an attempt made by you to obstruct the ordinary course of a pending trial by using undue means to prevent the course of justice. That may be false or it may be true, but it is the nature of the contempt with which you are charged. If you have anything to say in reference to that charge we are prepared to listen to you.

The Claimant: Simply that I have not taken undue means to prejudice the forthcoming Trial. What I have said had reference to the late Trial, and I argued that after what the Attorney-General said in this Court, I should have an opportunity of defending myself against such disgraceful language used by the chief law officer of the Crown. I am afraid I must trouble you, my lord, by reading my defence.

Mr. Justice BLACKBURN: By all means.

The Claimant then read as follows:—

My Lords—I am here in obedience to your commands. I have not employed Counsel to defend me, because I am in ignorance of having committed any contempt of this honourable Court. If the language that I have made use of is considered a contempt of Court, I consider, in justice to me, that I should be tried by a jury upon the question of contempt, because if I have committed a contempt it is your lordships who are the parties that are offended, and therefore for your lordships to act as judges would be similar to my meeting a man and knocking him down and that man being put up as a judge to decide whether I was guilty or not. Therefore, if you lordships consider that I have committed a contempt of this Court, it must have been in reference to circumstances connected with one of your lordships now sitting on the bench. And now, my lords, if you decide on trying me, I propose to read my defence to the charges made against me. I am afraid I must trouble your lordships with a great many details of facts which I think it necessary to lay before this honourable Court. In the first place, your lordships will bear in mind that I was committed to Newgate on certain charges on the 6th of March without any preliminary examination before the magistrates. The facts will be before your lordships that the Lord Chief Justice committed me without any previous notice to me that such a course would be taken, and actually the warrants for my committal were prepared and brought into Court before the decision was arrived at in the action which I had brought to recover possession of the Tichborne estates. I was confined in Newgate for fifty-two days, and except through the kindness of my friends, should have still remained a prisoner incarcerated in Newgate. I complain to your lordships that great injustice has been done me in this prosecution. By the action of the Judge who presided at the Trial in the Court of Common Pleas, the ordinary proceeding which is conceded to a prisoner for the commonest offence—namely, a preliminary examination before a magistrate—was denied me, and thus I lost the opportunity of having my witnesses bound over to appear at the forthcoming Trial at the public expense. The Government then took upon itself the prosecution of me, an individual, for certain charges not in any way affecting the community at large, but merely the members of my family; and a sum of £100,000 was asked for by the Attorney-General in the House of Commons for the purpose of prosecuting me. The Attorney-General took upon himself the engagement of five of the most eminent men at the English Bar to assist him in prosecuting me, although the Government did not think it advisable in the case of "OVEREND and GURNEY" to prosecute, because it was a matter affecting private persons and not the public at large. I need not comment upon this fact to your lordships, or enter further into the details of it. I have before me extracts from different newspapers, which form the only report, as far as I know, of the matters mentioned in them. I ask your lordships to hear the language which was applied to me by the Attorney-General in his speech, which, up to the present time, remains uncorroborated by the least testimony. I was called by the Attorney-General a conspirator, a perjurer, a forger, an impostor, a villain, and an Australian thief, and he also characterized me as a loathsome reptile, who had left my noisome slime upon everybody with whom and everything with which I had come in contact. The Attorney-General admitted that, although these were strong words, he would follow them by stronger if he could find them in the English language. I need not trouble your lordships with the numerous instances of grossly improper and ungentlemanly language which was applied to me by the Attorney-General; but the whole of these statements, as I have before stated, remaining up to the present day in no way corroborated, I appeal to your lordships whether such statements should remain uncontradicted by me. I also must appeal to your lordships in reference to the tone and attitude taken by the whole of the various newspapers against my Case. Your lordships will say that I have the power in my own hands of bringing the publishers of these papers before this most honourable Court; but I ask your lordships to remember that I am entirely without the means of doing so. I would call your lordships' attention to certain paragraphs, and I would ask your lordships whether it is not highly improper that such statements should be published before I am tried by your lordships for the offences with which I am now charged? I would further impress upon your lordships attention to other extracts from different newspapers published since the above, and your lordships will then see the sort of language which was applied to me by the Attorney-General. In a speech, which up to the present time remains uncorroborated by the least testimony, I was called a conspirator, a perjurer, a forger, an impostor, a villain, and an Australian thief. The Attorney-General admitted that these were strong words, but he said he would follow them by stronger if he could find them in the English language. I need not trouble your lordships with the numerous instances of grossly improper and ungentlemanly language which was applied to me by the Attorney-General throughout the whole of his speech, which, as I have before stated, remains uncorroborated up to the present day. I appeal to your lordships whether such a statement ought to go uncontradicted by me. I have to appeal to your lordships also with reference to the tone and attitude which has been taken up against me by various newspapers. In case your lordships should say that I have the power in my hands to bring the publishers before this Court, I must ask you to remember that I am entirely without the means of doing so. First of all, then, I will call your lordships' attention to the paragraph which has appeared in the *Saturday Review*, which was not even satisfied to allow your lordships to try me, but actually wished to try me itself. I will read a paragraph from that paper:

"Let him be satisfied with showing that the then slight, shy, gentle ROGER, who spoke French better than he did English, has turned up in the big, burly, and, by no means shy, CASTRO, who cannot speak a syllable of French, who cannot even pronounce the French name of the mother he claims, and who, from the moment of his landing in England, shunned his relations as if they were the plague."

Now, I ask your lordships whether that is fair?

Mr. Justice LUSH: Was that published last Saturday?

The Claimant: Yes, my lord.

Mr. Justice BLACKBURN: I agree with you entirely that it is a most improper article to write, and I hope that no one will write such another article in future. We cannot do anything to the writers who are not now before us, but I think it would be wrong if we did not say that it was really a most improper article to write.

The Claimant: Then, on the 12th April, six days after my incarceration in Newgate, there was an article in an evening paper which, when I read it to your lordships, you will, I think, say that I was justified in going from one part of the country to another contradicting statements such as it contained, especially when they are entirely against me. Do you wish that the Attorney-General should put down his foot upon my neck and crush me? Certainly not. Then in the *Echo*, last year, it was said that the Attorney-General had gone too far in saying of him that he was "like a loathsome viper, who left his noisome slime upon everybody with whom he came in contact; and that he 'protested' somewhat to much." Was that proper language for the chief law officer of the Crown to use?

Mr. Justice BLACKBURN: But it seems to me that that article is in your favour.

The Claimant: I do not wish to quote one side only. In the *Manchester Courier* of the 22nd inst. were these words:

As to his guilt or innocence of the crime of which he stands accused we do not care to express an opinion; but, by his own showing, he is not a person fit for the friendship of decent people. His expressions in the witness-box—if we believe them—show that he is an unmitigated scoundrel, whether we refer to his dealings with his Australian attorney in the matter of his will, or to his utterly scandalous and gratuitous charges against the honour of Mrs. RADCLIFFE.

Now, it is well known that this charge against Mrs. RADCLIFFE was not gratuitous, but was extorted from me by the Attorney-General, who knew that Mrs. RADCLIFFE meant to come into the box, to swear that I was not her cousin. The *Pall Mall Gazette* said that it was extraordinary that any man who prided himself upon being the debaucher of his young cousin should find gentlemen to consort with. Is this a justifiable comment upon a person who is about to be tried?

Mr. Justice BLACKBURN: It may or it may not be a libel, but it does not come within the class of articles which express contempt of Court.

The Claimant: But surely it would entitle me to go forward to the country and contradict them—that being the only means left to me. Again, the *Morning Post* of the 7th March, 1872, said: "His refusal to go to Australia or Chili, where ARTHUR ORTON was well known, coupled with the fact that the returns to both commissions contained no evidence advancing the Claimant's Case, should, we think, have satisfied any dispassionate person that the probabilities of his being ARTHUR ORTON immensely preponderated over those of his being ROGER TICHBORNE. But, nevertheless, the suit was persisted in, and an innocent family was heavily mulcted, and a case replete with perjury, forgery, and calumny forced during nearly a twelvemonth on the public." The Attorney-General also took upon himself in the House of Commons the functions of both advocate and Judge when he expressed an opinion, and that a very decided opinion, upon a case which is still *sub judice*, in which he declared the case to be an insult upon common-sense. It is sufficient for my purpose to produce these very few extracts to your lordships to show the character of the criticism which has been passed upon me by the press. It would occupy me some days to produce to your lordships the various articles which have from time to time appeared in the public press, and of which I complain, and your lordships will be able to see that, having the whole of the press, with one exception—the *Morning Advertiser*—against me, I have had no other resource left me to contradict these statements, expressed in the press and by the officials of the Government, than by going about from town to town explaining them to my fellow-countrymen. It was, therefore, after mature consideration that I determined to call meetings in the various towns which I have visited with a view of there publicly denying these uncorroborated and prejudiced statements which have been made against me. I further would call your lordships' attention to the fact that I, at every meeting, prefaced my statements by the observation that what I said they must not take as abuse of the other side, and I then proceeded to do what I conceived I had a right to do, namely, to complain of the injuries I had received at the hands of the Attorney-General, and the injustice that I had received at the hands of the prosecution; and surely, my lords, after the violent and unjustifiable language made use of by the Attorney-General, and which was, as you are all aware, so well ventilated, is it to be said that, because I endeavour to put myself right with the public in general, on whom I have to rely, I am to be called before your lordships for contempt of Court? while the Attorney-General not only is not called upon to answer, but was not even called to order by the Lord Chief Justice when he made the observations—observations, I submit to your lordships, that never are made, and are not fairly within the province of a Counsel who is acting in the discharge of a duty to his client. Referring to your lordships' judgment the other day, I submit that I have a perfect right to call meetings for the purpose of enabling me to prosecute my claim, and that the Court has no power to interfere with me in calling such meetings. Your lordships must bear in mind that no opportunity was given to my Counsel in the late Trial of "TICHBORNE *v.* LUSHINGTON" to refute the charges made against me by the Attorney-General, and, up to the present time, the vituperation of the Attorney-General has not been proved against me; that I have been deprived of the advantage of bringing my witnesses forward at the forthcoming Trial at the expense of the Government, through not being taken before a magistrate in the way previously mentioned; that all aid has been refused me by the Government, although £100,000 has been asked for by the Attorney-General to prosecute me; that now I am sure your lordships must see, under these circumstances, that, being a bankrupt, and having no means of procuring my defence, and all aid being refused me by the Government of this country, I had no resource left me but to apply to my fellow-countrymen to assist me, and in order to do that it was necessary for me to go from town to town, and make my grievances known to the people of this nation. Your lordships must also bear in mind that I am innocent even in the eye of the law of this country; that I have already suffered fifty-two days' incarceration in the cell of Newgate. Knowing, as I do, that I am innocent of those base charges brought against me, and suffering as I have suffered, without being convicted by a tribunal of my country, and also taking into consideration that it is as long ago as last March that these charges were brought against me by the Judge who tried the cause between me and my relatives, and that up to the present moment the Government have not thought proper to put me on my trial, I consider that a great injustice has been done me by the Judge who committed me to Newgate as before mentioned, having done so on a charge that was so clear that it takes thirteen months to make a case against me, and, according to the opinion of the adviser to the Crown of this nation, it required six Counsel and £100,000 to prosecute me with. I think your lordships will agree with me that I have just cause for complaint, and that one of two courses was open to me—either to quietly submit to be crushed, and sent into penal servitude by the Attorney-General, assisted by others of the most eminent Counsel at the English Bar, or otherwise to appeal to my countrymen to assist me in my defence against such odds brought to bear against me. And your lordships will also see, as before mentioned, that at the beginning of each address I have delivered in public I have asked the audience not to take as abuse what I was about to state—that I should only state to them facts which occurred during my late Trial and were connected with it. I maintain that what I have stated to the public are facts and facts only. That I felt very much grieved to find the Attorney-General had accepted from the ladies of my family, trees out of my park at Tichborne, which I considered to be my property. That up to the present moment, it is true, I have been unable to prove in a Court of Law my right to that property; but still your lordships must remember that my Mother positively swore to my identity; that her evidence was supported by the evidence of eighty-five other witnesses, who all stood the test of a very severe cross-examination without breaking down. That I myself was twenty-three days under cross-examination by the Attorney-General, assisted by other Counsel, the most eminent at the English Bar; that there were only twelve witnesses examined against me—five of them being my relatives, five French people, and two others. That during part of the examination of these twelve witnesses, one of my Counsel left and went into Wales. How I was represented by the remaining leading Counsel I wish to make no comment on. That your lordships must also bear in mind that the same Counsel engaged against me by my relatives in the late case of "TICHBORNE *v.* LUSHINGTON," were, many of them, engaged by the Government against me in my forthcoming prosecution. That it was after my incarceration in Newgate that the Attorney-General brought the indictment of forgery against me. That notice has been given to my solicitor that it is not at present intended to proceed upon that indictment; therefore showing clearly the Attorney-General brought that indictment against me to prevent my being bailed out, while I was confined in Newgate, by my friends, forgery not being a bailable offence in the eye of the law. All I can say is, if appealing to my countrymen, and making the facts which occurred known to them, was a contempt of this honourable Court, that I was in complete ignorance of it. In fact, looking at the abusive articles which appeared in the press from time to time against me, who have yet to be tried, it was impossible for me to come to any other conclusion than that there was no such thing as contempt of Court, or, if there had been, I cannot understand how they could have been allowed by the Government to write and vilify and abuse me in such articles, and not be interfered with. I have been led to believe that the Government were bound to protect me from being prejudged before the Trial; but, finding the Government took no notice of these scurrilous articles that appeared in the press, and having in the year 1870 brought before Vice-Chancellor STUART the publishers of a paper called the *Echo* for contempt of Court, his Honour the Vice-Chancellor STUART on that occasion stated that no doubt a great libel had been committed, that no doubt a contempt of Court had been committed; and, after hearing the case argued for two days, his Honour decided that the publishers of the *Echo* should pay their own costs, thus leaving me to pay my own costs for doing that which he acknowledged to be correct. From that time until the present, I have not considered it judicious to bring any other publishers up. Since that time I have not had sufficient money to waste to bring up others at my own expense, or I should have troubled this honourable Court to interfere on many occasions since my committal. That, up to the present moment, I am considered innocent in the eye of the law, as aforesaid, and cannot understand how the Government allows its officers and the press of this country to abuse and vilify me in the manner they have done before my Trial. I have attended, at the very least, eighty meetings, and the Government and your lordships have not thought proper to interfere with me before. I made use of the same language at all those meetings as I did on the present occasion. I have never been cautioned against holding such meetings. The matter was prominently brought before one of the Judges in the Court of Chancery on the 12th of December last, and no objection was made on behalf of the officers of the Government against my holding such meetings. I maintain that I have a right of free speech as an Englishman, and that my stating facts in these speeches cannot be looked upon as a contempt of this most honourable Court, which I have never had the slightest desire or intention of doing. Had the Government not deprived me of the advantage of having my witnesses bound over to give evidence in the forthcoming Trial, there would have been no need for me to appeal to the public at large. That I also say and maintain that Mr. HAWKINS, Q.C., the Counsel engaged by the Government to prosecute me, did wrong, and acted indiscreetly in going to the solicitors of Lord RIVERS, one of my bondsmen, and telling them that he could send me into penal servitude as easily as eat his dinner. That it is impossible, after a statement of that description from the Counsel who has the prosecution of me in hand on behalf of the Government, for me to imagine that I can have a fair trial at his hands. That during the whole of my speeches I never even commented on him, but spoke of him with the greatest courtesy in connection with my late Trial, and that I have even stated to the meetings which I have addressed that, had my Counsel worked for me in the manner in which Mr. HAWKINS and other Counsel worked for their client, that I should have been in a different position at this present moment. Asking your lordships to take well into consideration what I have stated here, and asking you to bear in mind that if you order me to be sent to prison for contempt of Court—and I maintain that I have not committed any contempt of Court; if I have done so, I have done so in ignorance, and therefore have not committed a contempt of Court—that you will be doing the very thing for which you have ordered me to appear here to-day, namely prejudicing my forthcoming Trial. If you fine me you will be taking from me what little money I have to defend myself with, and inasmuch as I now state that I never have intentionally offended this most honourable Court, I ask your lordships to overlook anything that I may have said.

The Court then adjourned for luncheon, and, on reassembling,

Mr. HAWKINS, addressing their lordships, said: I have, my lords, but one or two observations to make in this matter. My only object in making observations to your lordships was to call attention to the language uttered by Mr. SKIPWORTH, and to ask him to answer for that language. My sole object on the part of the prosecution was to preserve, as far as it was possible, the due and decorous administration of justice, and to prevent what appeared to me to be a great public scandal and outrage on public decency—that is the discussion of the merits or the demerits of this prosecution previous to the Case being tried before the properly-constituted tribunal. It seems to me that whatever view may be taken of the course pursued by the Defendant in the indictment, if it be proved that great public meetings were held—that inflammatory language was used vilifying all who had taken part in the prosecution—and not only all who had done so, but the witnesses who are about to be called on the part of the prosecution on the coming Trial—if that course, I say, be tolerated, then, my lords, there is no reason why similar meetings should not be held on the part of the prosecution, to discuss the merits of the Case, and to take the sense of a great public meeting upon the question. If such a course were taken, it would be put down with a high hand by your lordships; and if such a proceeding were tolerated, and inflammatory language allowed to be used, it would be a great scandal to the country, and would tend very much to interfere with the impartial administration of justice, and the due discussion before the proper tribunal of the case presented to it. Your lordships have heard Mr. SKIPWORTH's answer to the charge made against him. Your lordships have had the advantage of hearing read those publications which Mr. SKIPWORTH thought right to publish. You have heard Mr. SKIPWORTH's language, and you have witnessed his demeanour. It is not for me to say one syllable in aggravation of the charge. My object is, to take care, if I can, that the proceedings in this Court which are now pending shall not be prejudiced. The public—as your lordships know, and as the sensible, thinking portion of the public know—take a great interest in this Case, in its result, whether that be an acquittal or conviction of the party who stands charged in the indictment; and, taking it to be a matter of so much public interest—whether there be a conviction on the ground of guilt, or an acquittal on account of innocence—my object is to prevent unseemly discussions of the Case in public assemblies. Having done that, I am not anxious to add one word of aggravation to what Mr. SKIPWORTH has said. With regard to the Defendant in the indictment, I propose to say nothing. I did not intend at first that the Defendant should be brought before your lordships, but your lordships thought it right to have him here. He is here, and you have heard his explanation. To that I desire to add nothing; and if I abstain from following him and Mr. SKIPWORTH through the evidence on which they have commented, or the statements they have thought fit to make, not only upon the witnesses, but upon my learned friend the Attorney-General—nay, even upon the Bench itself; if I abstain from noting and making use of these observations, my lords, my silence upon the subject must not be taken as an assent to any of these statements or propositions. I abstain from this for reasons which I am sure your lordships will appreciate, and I am content to leave the whole matter in the hands of your lordships.

After a brief consultation with the other Judges,

Mr. Justice BLACKBURN said: In this case, the question raised before the Court is this—There have been two persons brought before us who were, by the order of the Court, called upon to show cause why they should not be committed for contempt. The first question raised for us is, What, under the circumstances, has taken place to constitute the contempt of Court? Now, the phrase "contempt of Court" has caused persons who are not lawyers to be misled, because they suppose it means some process taken for the purpose of preserving the personal dignity of the Judges as individuals, or something of that sort. Very often contempt is committed by a personal attack upon the Judge, but, as far as the personal dignity of the Judge is concerned, it is a very subordinate affair. Very rarely a Judge would consider that his dignity did not protect him, or think it worth his while to take any steps. But there is another and much more important contempt of Court, in cases which are pending, whether civil or criminal, in which the Court ought to try them in the ordinary course, fairly and impartially. In the present case there is an indictment pending against one of the persons now before us for perjury, and that indictment stands for trial, and will come on in due course for hearing; and, therefore, it ought to be tried fairly and impartially at the time, the Judge and jury deciding the case on the evidence then produced, subject to cross-examination—in the presence of both parties, and in the presence of the Judge. The case should then be fairly and properly tried, but it may happen—and in many cases it does happen—that persons interfere to prevent this impartial trial. Sometimes it has been done, and the decided cases are many. It has been comparatively rarely done by attacking the Judge—sometimes it has been done by attempting to induce the Judge to change his opinion of a case by flattery, and sometimes by offering bribes. There have been attempts made to induce a Judge to change his views in these ways; but most commonly by attacking witnesses, or by commenting upon them, or appealing to the public on *ex parte* statements, no one being heard on the other side, and without the means of testing the accuracy of the statements, such as the law requires—and accordingly the trial has been prejudiced. In all these ways great mischief may be done by interfering with the due and ordinary course of law in cases, whether civil or criminal. When that is the case, there may be libel punishable by the criminal law, or conspiracy or assault punishable by the criminal law, if attempts are made to interfere with the due course of justice; but then we should have to wait for the ordinary process of a criminal indictment and trial by jury, which would be sufficient; but that process is slow, and might not come into play until much mischief was done, and the due administration of justice prevented. For that reason, from the earliest times the Superior Courts at Westminster, including the Courts of Reserve, Equity, and Common Law, had always jurisdiction given them by which, whenever anything was done which had a tendency to obstruct the ordinary course of justice, or to prejudice a trial, they could exercise a summary jurisdiction to prevent any such matter which would interfere with the due course of justice, and that power has been exercised, I believe, from the earliest times, and has always existed, but certainly has been exercised in the manner we exercise it. A Court of Justice being clothed with the power, the duty is imposed upon the Court, in a proper case, where they see it necessary, to interfere to prevent anything which would hinder the due administration of justice. In the present case Mr. HAWKINS said he did not ask to have the Defendant in the indictment brought before us, but we thought there was a case made out, that there was a *primâ-facie* case which required the interposition of the Court to insure the due administration of justice in a case now pending before us, and we did think it right to order the Defendant in the indictments to attend. He has attended. He has defended himself, and, having listened to his defence, I am bound to say he has defended himself with great propriety; and, making proper allowance for the want of technical knowledge, he has brought forward all the points bearing favourably on his case. Now, we have to consider whether this is or is not a contempt of Court. It was decided we ought to allow the case to go to a jury. The question is at present, Has he tried to interfere and to impede justice? Has he, whether innocent or guilty, tried to interfere with the due course of law?—for, however true an allegation may be, any attempt to prejudice a trial is contempt of Court, and one that we must prevent. We make no inquiry whether it is true or false, but is it calculated to prejudice the jurors who come to try the case, or to divert the Judge from pursuing a course he otherwise would? I do not think it necessary to quote authorities on this point, but I will advert to one case for the sake of the language used by Lord COTTENHAM, in which he most clearly explains the law. It appears that there was an attempt to interfere with the administration of justice in the Court of Chancery by writing threatening letters to the Master in Chancery; and Lord COTTENHAM made an order that the Court, having taken notice of these things, directed Mr. LECHMERE CHARLTON to attend. Mr. CHARLTON, relying on his privilege as Member of Parliament, would not come to the Court, and Lord COTTENHAM adjudged him guilty of contempt, and condemned him to imprisonment. After quoting several authorities, Lord COTTENHAM (reported in the 2nd vol. of MILLER and CRAY's Reports, p. 342) said: "All these authorities tend to the same point, and show that it is immaterial what measures are adopted if the object is to taint the source of justice, and to attain a result for legal proceedings different from that which would follow in the ordinary course of law. It is a contempt of the highest order; and although such attempts may be foolish attempts—and if I consulted my own personal feelings I would pass by all these letters as foolish—if I adopted that course I should consider myself guilty of a grave dereliction of duty. I therefore make the order absolute for imprisonment." Now, I quote these words because they express very much the same feelings as I have, and which I am sure my brothers on the Bench have—that there has been an attempt here to influence the course of justice. I think it is impossible not to see that both the defendants have been guilty of trying to change the course of justice, and that both adverted to the Lord Chief Justice in vituperative language, that they attacked witnesses, and attempted to influence the public mind and people to interfere; that they wanted the jury to try the case *ex parte*—that they intended this I cannot doubt. Indeed, Mr. SKIPWORTH said he did intend to do that. He says he thinks he was right, and will do it again if he can. I cannot but think that is decidedly a contempt. Then we have to consider whether it is a "foolish attempt," as Lord COTTENHAM says. I think it is. As far as it concerns the altering the course of justice, it is an attempt utterly foolish. The state of the case is this. Before we heard anything about these meetings, it came to be a question whether the Case was to be tried before a single Judge, or whether it was to be a Trial at Bar. It is known by almost everyone who hears me what a Trial at Bar means. It is a trial by the Court, where the senior, the Lord Chief Justice, will preside, but where the Chief Justice has no more authority in presiding than any of the other judges. Each individual judge has an equal right to express his opinion, and I believe in old times there have been instances—indeed, there was one remarkable instance, that of the Trial of the Seven Bishops—in which each of the four judges took a different view of the law, and gave a contradictory summing-up to the jury. That being the nature of a Trial at Bar, I may state a fact within my own official knowledge, and that of each of my brothers—that an application was made to the Lord Chief Justice, stating the Case was likely to be a case of such magnitude that more than one judge should sit upon it. When we became aware it was to be a Trial at Bar, the Chief Justice thought it was highly desirable it should be so, it being a case of such great magnitude, and accordingly the Attorney-General, exercising the undoubted prerogative of the Crown, had the Case set down for a Trial at Bar. It was the Chief Justice's personal desire that the Case should be tried not before him, but some of his colleagues. Now, when that is pending, we find, among other things, that meetings are held, partly with the intention, by vituperation, to deprive the Chief Justice of sitting upon this Trial. But it will have no such effect. There is not the slightest doubt in the mind—and never has been in the mind of any one in Court—that it would be a great dereliction of duty if we were in the slightest degree to alter the arrangement we have previously made in consequence of these matters. The Chief Justice himself was of opinion it was his duty to have the Trial at Bar, and there could not be a doubt that was the right course. The Case will be tried in the ordinary course of justice, and the Chief Justice and some of my brothers will sit upon it. In the course of all these matters, with the fact of allegations having been made reflecting upon other persons—whether upon Chief Justice BOVILL or others—we have nothing to do. They are not matters of contempt of Court. But there have been vituperative allegations respecting what the Chief Justice has done. I must do the Defendant in the indictment the justice to say he did not make any of these statements—they were principally made by Mr. SKIPWORTH and others. But it is not right for a person occupying the high position of the Chief Justice, when personally attacked, to come forward to explain or to do anything; and, in my mind, when a Judge is attacked in his office for what he does as a Judge, he cannot and ought not to come forward. But the conduct of those who attack the Judge is, to use the mildest term, neither just nor decorous. I say nothing about these imputations, but I may further say without impropriety—as I am not one of the Judges who are to try the Case—that I have, personally, the firmest conviction that when the Trial comes on it will be conducted by those on the Bench as it would have been if nothing of this sort had been said—with absolutely the same impartiality, the same care to see that every point in favour of the Defendant should be fairly and properly considered, and, at the same time, with firmness and attention to see that the interests of justice are done, as it would have been if it were to have gone before a Judge in the ordinary way—before a Judge who had never heard of it before he took his seat on the Bench. Of that I entertain no doubt, nor can I much doubt that every person whose opinion is worth having will be quite of the same opinion, and will not be prevented from entertaining it by anything that may have been said. Considering all this, it seems to me—and I believe I am speaking the opinion of all my brother Judges—that were we, as Lord COTTENHAM said, only consulting our own personal feelings, we could pass it over as an ineffectual attempt to affect the course of justice—an attempt that was incapable of answering the end in view. But we are all agreed that we cannot do that without a dereliction of duty, and I am greatly influenced by this: that though here the attempt to influence popular feeling has been utterly ineffectual, yet that there may be, a some future time, an attempt to do a similar thing, that might not be ineffectual—it might be far from ineffectual, and it might even be a very formidable attempt, and require a strong hand to repress it. We may imagine that a popular person, indicted for sedition or high treason, might go about the country addressing people, and in that case it might require considerable nerve to resist the influence that might be used. So that if we were now to pass over this case, we should be making a precedent which would greatly increase the difficulties of our successors under such circumstances as I have supposed. Besides that, the public scandal is not to be disregarded. It is absolutely essential that these proceedings should be stopped; and, having come to this conclusion, we are clearly of opinion that the two defendants have attended these meetings with the intention of influencing the ordinary course of justice and of prejudicing the course of the approaching Trial. We can really come to no other conclusion. All my brothers agree in it. We are clear that it is a contempt of Court, and we adjudicate both the defendants guilty of that offence. Having come to that conclusion, there come two questions: What should be the amount of sentence to be passed upon each defendant? Is there any reason why the same sentence should not be passed in each case? First, however, there is a matter which might be misunderstood, and which may as well be explained. It is known that in ordinary cases the Lord Chief Justice presides in this Court associated with no puisne Judges, and some of us sit in the other Courts. To-day, however, the Lord Chief Justice is absent, and it might possibly be supposed that what we are about to do is not in accord with his opinion, and it is therefore that I wish to explain why it is that we are determining here the amount of punishment to be awarded for contempt involving personal attacks upon the Lord Chief Justice. Where those attacks are in question there is a risk that feelings might cause him to be vindictive, but, on the other hand, there is a much greater risk that circumstances might operate which would cause him to be too lenient, and therefore it is a matter of importance that judgment should be given by those in whom no such feelings may arise. The Lord Chief Justice was, therefore, of opinion that he should take no part in fixing the sentences, and I may be permitted to say I cordially agree with him. It was his own view, and I think it was the right and dignified view. I explain all this in order to show that the absence of the Lord Chief Justice to-day is not in the slightest degree inconsistent with what I previously stated—that the Trial will come on in the ordinary course, as if these proceedings had never taken place. I now come to consider what shall be done in the two cases, and I will first take the case of Mr. SKIPWORTH. In his case I cannot see any modification in his favour. From the first he has deliberately come forward to try and influence this cause. He asserts that the Claimant is perfectly innocent, and he has tried to arouse the feelings of the people in his favour. Up to last Monday week it might have been supposed that he did not know it was contrary to law to do so, but it is really going a great way to say that. Last Monday week, however, he was present in this very Court when Messrs. ONSLOW and WHALLEY were fined for contempt of Court. Mr. SKIPWORTH heard the judgment of the Court, and he knew that it was a wrong thing to interfere with the course of justice. Having heard this, however, he goes down to Brighton to do the very same thing. The same afternoon he is present at a meeting, and uses terms of abuse—terms not by any means complimentary—to the Lord Chief Justice and to the rest of the Court, and announces his intention to do so again. There was strong language used in the Case—

Mr. SKIPWORTH: Not personal abuse, my lord.

Mr. Justice BLACKBURN: A person who is a barrister ought to have known better, but in this case, although a barrister, Mr. SKIPWORTH does not appear to have been a lawyer. (Laughter.)

Mr. SKIPWORTH: I am much obliged to you, my lord. (Laughter.)

Mr. Justice BLACKBURN: We must, therefore, impose a fine, and we must also impose a sentence of imprisonment. The first question is, what should be the amount of the fine?—not merely for the punishment of this offence, but to show that this Court cannot be treated with disrespect. The fine should be sufficient, and not excessive. Nearer than that we cannot possibly go, and it becomes a matter of discretion what the amount should be. After fully discussing the matter we think the sum should not be less than £500. Further than that, there must be a term of imprisonment—that is, for a prevention of the continuance of the course Mr. SKIPWORTH has adopted. As to the term of imprisonment, we do not wish to make it excessive, and taking into account the fact that the Trial will come on in April, and it will effectually prevent a repetition of this offence, the sentence will be that Mr. SKIPWORTH be imprisoned for a period of three months.

Mr. SKIPWORTH: You called it "SKIPWITH," and that is not correct, my lord.

Mr. Justice BLACKBURN: The sentence, further, is that you be imprisoned until the fine is paid. Though I have not passed the sentence, that is what it will be. Some latitude ought to be given, but here you have gone far beyond it. If you had simply gone to the meetings to protest against the articles inserted in the newspapers, though in one sense it would have been a contempt of Court, yet it might have been thought fit not to invest the case with any punishment. I hope it will be understood that we are not in the least interested in the question of the guilt or innocence of any person. It would be a pity if we were to do anything to prejudice his (the Claimant's) defence. I think it is true that it would deprive him of his means of defence if a heavy fine were imposed, and therefore we will not impose a fine. Again, as he says, imprisonment might prevent him from getting together his witnesses. That, again, would be a pity, as we would not sentence him to imprisonment if we could help it. It is absolutely necessary that this should be stopped, and therefore, under all the circumstances, we think it proper to order him to enter into his own recognizances in the sum of £500, and to find a surety of £500 that he will be of good behaviour, and not be guilty of contempt of this Court for three months. If he can persuade those who have become bail for him for a much larger amount, he will be set at liberty. The sentence is that he find these securities, or be imprisoned until they be obtained. I now leave it to my brothers to state anything they may desire.

The Claimant: One of my bondsmen is here, my lord. If he would guarantee for the £500 would that answer, or do you wish to send me direct to prison?

Mr. Justice BLACKBURN: To whom do you refer?

The Claimant: I refer to Dr. ATTWOOD. He is one of my bail.

Mr. Justice BLACKBURN: You must give notice to the Solicitor to the Treasury, in order that he may make inquiry as to the sufficiency of the bail.

Mr. Justice LUSH: Perhaps he is here.

Mr. Justice BLACKBURN: He is here.

Mr. Justice LUSH: He may be satisfied as to the sufficiency of the bail offered.

Mr. HAWKINS: The Solicitor to the Treasury instructs me to say that he is perfectly content with the suretyship of Dr. ATTWOOD.

Mr. Justice BLACKBURN: If Dr. ATTWOOD is willing to give it.

Mr. HAWKINS: Quite so, my lord. I have no desire that there should be an hour's imprisonment.

Mr. Justice BLACKBURN: The recognizance, it must be remembered, is that the Defendant shall be of good behaviour, and it will be forfeited if there is any renewal of the proceedings now complained of. If Dr. ATTWOOD is content to risk paying £500, and if he enters into the recognizances before the Court rises, of course there will be no necessity to send the Claimant into custody.

Mr. Justice MELLOR: I entirely concur in the view which my brother BLACKBURN has expressed in this matter. I entertain no doubt whatsoever as to the character of the contempt, and I am satisfied that it was one which it was our duty to visit with punishment. I agree, also, in the reasons assigned by my brother BLACKBURN for the judgment he has given, and in the distinction he has drawn between the cases of the two persons charged here.

Mr. Justice LUSH: I am entirely of the same opinion, and have nothing to add to what has fallen from my brothers BLACKBURN and MELLOR.

Mr. Justice QUAIN: I quite concur in what has been stated by the other members of the Court.

Mr. Justice BLACKBURN: It only remains for me to pronounce the sentence of the Court.

The two defendants then rose, and his lordship, addressing Mr. SKIPWORTH, said: You have been adjudged as clearly guilty of contempt of this Court, and the sentence on you is that you be imprisoned for three calendar months in Holloway Gaol, and that you pay a fine to the QUEEN of £500, and that you be further imprisoned in the same prison until the fine is paid. And you (addressing the Claimant), THOMAS CASTRO, or ARTHUR ORTON, or TICHBORNE——

The Claimant: I am Sir ROGER TICHBORNE, my lord.

Mr. Justice BLACKBURN: That is not material, at present. You have heard the reasons for the sentence—and it is a lenient one—which I am about to pronounce. It is that you give security to the Crown, yourself in £500, and one or more sureties in a like sum of £500, that you will be of good behaviour during the space of three months, and not further commit any contempt of the Court of Queen's Bench. On giving that security you wi be freed at once, but unless you do you will be imprisoned once.

The Claimant: Dr. ATTWOOD is here, my lord.

Mr. Justice BLACKBURN: Is he?

Dr. ATTWOOD: I am here, my lord.

Mr. Justice BLACKBURN: Then let the recognizances be at on entered into.

Mr. SKIPWORTH was then removed in the custody of Mr. FRA LING, jun., the tipstaff of the Court.

The Claimant and Dr. ATTWOOD entered into the necessa recognizances, and left the Court. The former was received wi enthusiastic cheering by an immense crowd which had congregate outside the Judges' private entrance. The Claimant's carri was followed down Parliament-street by some hundreds of h admirers, who cheered him loudly.

Mr. SKIPWORTH subsequently followed up his protest, and em bodied his complaint in the following letter and petition, whi we copy from the *Yorkshire Independent* of May 8th, 1875.

THE PETITION OF G. B. SKIPWORTH.

OF MOORTOWN HOUSE, CAISTOR,

SHEWETH, That, on the 25th of January, 1873, your petitione was summoned by Her Majesty's Court of Queen's Bench t answer a charge of contempt of Court for speaking at a publ meeting at Brighton, on behalf of the then Claimant to the Tich borne estates, who was about to take his trial in that Court fo perjury.

That in supporting such cause your petitioner was influence solely by a conviction of its truthfulness and a desire to see jus tice administered according to the laws of the land.

That your petitioner, in simply speaking his honest thought and exercising a strictly conscientious duty, could not be accuse of either acting contumaciously or of disrespect to the Court; an though he certainly acted in defiance of threats of the Judges the consequences of attending any such meetings, and inde purposely to set such threats at defiance, it was from a convicti of their being in total violation and disregard of the rights an liberties of the people and freedom of speech, their nation birthright: and he was compelled to view such threat as tyrannical course of conduct on the part of the Judges, and whic might be made a means of securing obedience to their mandate or of effecting their own designs, objects, or purposes, by intimid tion, and therefore unconstitutional; that, had he not unhes tatingly resisted such threats or attempts at intimidation, h would have felt himself utterly destitute of that British pluc which ought, when his rights are invaded, to inspire every tru born Englishman; and it was for this that he faced fine an imprisonment rather than be deterred from what he believed be a sacred and solemn duty: and in supporting the cause of th accused he submits he was only acting on the well-known rule law, that a man is presumed to be innocent until he is proved be guilty; that, had he, on the other hand, declaimed against hi as guilty before trial, he might have laid himself open, from properly constituted Court, to a charge of that nature, and we merited both fine and imprisonment; but in no other way can h conceive such a charge to have been applicable.

That, nevertheless, your petitioner was, on the 29th of Januar 1873, sentenced by Her Majesty's Court of Queen's Bench t three months' imprisonment and a fine of £500 for contempt Court; that he underwent the full term of imprisonment; an declining, on conscientious grounds, to pay the fine, might hav remained still longer a prisoner, but that a gentleman, unsolicite and contrary to your petitioner's previously expressed declaratio not to pay the same or allow the country to pay it for him, as w kindly offered to be done by voluntary subscriptions, paid th said fine on the day the three months expired.

That the same, whilst in disaccordance with your petitioner prior conscientious declaration, having been paid through philan thropic motives and an anxiety for your petitioner's release fro what was considered an unjust imprisonment, though under promise of repayment, a feeling of honour at least would deman that such should be repaid, which, in fact, has already been do by another party again without your petitioner's previous knowledg and it becomes him seriously to consider how the amount, wit interest, is to be finally paid off consistently with the express conscientious objections of your petitioner to pay the same.

That your petitioner lately addressed a petition to your ho House in some such words, or to the effect hereinbefore stated, an prayed your hon. House to order the amount of the said fine to b refunded, or otherwise advise Her Majesty that such directi might be given; and, further, that your hon. House would d him justice in the premises.

That your petitioner is informed that his said petition was n received by your hon. House, owing to its being at variance wit some rule or order of your hon. House; that no petition contai ing an application for repayment of money can be received unle the consent of Her Majesty's Ministers, some, or one of them, previously given thereto.

That the following is a copy of such petition:—

(COPY PETITION.)

That if your petitioner were guilty of any irregularity informality in the wording or presentation of such last-mentio petition, he humbly apologizes for the same, but he prays yo hon. House, if they will kindly consult the language there-

and consider that mention was made therein of your petitioner's unsuccessful applications to Her Majesty's Government in reference to the subject-matter thereof, and the consequence that thus arose in the mind of your petitioner of an appeal to your hon. House; that, further, your petitioner, during the time of his imprisonment addressed from Holloway Gaol ten letters to Her Majesty's then Secretary of State, Mr. BRUCE; two to Her Majesty's then Prime Minister, Mr. GLADSTONE; two to the then Lord Chancellor, Lord SELBORNE; also one to the QUEEN herself, inclosing a pamphlet on the subject of his imprisonment—and all bearing more or less on the fine and imprisonment to which he had been subjected, and complaining thereof; that he obtained no redress; the answer, through Mr. Secretary BRUCE, to the one addressed to the QUEEN, being to the effect that your petitioner's letter with the inclosures had been laid before the QUEEN, and that her Majesty had not been pleased to signify any command thereon.

That, on your petitioner's return from prison, he wrote to Mr. Secretary BRUCE asking for a return of the fine; but, receiving no reply, he again wrote asking to be informed the course to persue, as when a gentleman friend paid the £500 it was intimated to him at the Home Office that on representation to him it might be returned; and, in reply, your petitioner received a letter from Mr. Secretary BRUCE to the effect that when your petitioner's friend called at that office he was informed that the proper mode of applying for a return of the fine would be to address the Treasury on the subject, which your petitioner accordingly did, but with no satisfactory result; that, since Her Majesty's change of Government, your petitioner has again memorialized the Treasury on the subject—the Lords Commissioners by their reply of the 18th May, 1874, stating that they regretted they were unable to depart from the decision communicated to your petitioner on the 18th June, then last.

That in consequence of your petitioner being unable to obtain any redress, and labouring under a deep sense of injustice of the treatment he had received, he again, on the 28th of June, 1874, addressed a letter to Her Majesty on the subject of the fine and imprisonment, and concluded with a statement that your petitioner held under Her Majesty the office of Deputy-Lieutenant for the County of Lincoln, and unless justice were done him, and due consideration and regard rendered for outraged feelings and honour, he could no longer conscientiously retain the same, but must resign it into her hands.

That Her Majesty's Secretary of State, Mr. CROSS, replied to such letter that he was unable to advise Her Majesty to interfere in the matter; that your petitioner has since written several letters to Mr. Secretary CROSS, both relating to the fine and imprisonment and the TICHBORNE Case generally—your petitioner stating in one that he would sacrifice all if justice were done to the man now languishing in a prison cell, but to none of which has your petitioner received a reply.

That if, therefore, the receipt by your hon. House of your petitioner's application for repayment of the said fine were dependent on the previous consent of even one of Her Majesty's Ministers thereto, his chance of obtaining it might, to say the least, be deemed very precarious; that your petitioner now ventures hereby to pray that your hon. House will be pleased to cause inquiry to be made into the circumstances under which he was so fined and imprisoned, and to afford him such redress as your hon. House may deem justly due.

That, on the bearing of the charge against your petitioner, his solemn appeals to GOD and his conscience (as testified by his own sworn affidavit) in justification of the course he had taken, and in exercise of a strictly conscientious duty, were disregarded and set at nought; that, had the prosecution of the TICHBORNE Trial at Bar been a just and honourable one, such a proceeding under that prosecution against your petitioner, which has the effect of staying the voice of truth and suppressing all action and expression in favour of the defendant, could not have taken place, and the Court would not have presented the unfortunate spectacle of the Judges attempting by threats of fine and imprisonment to extort obedience or submission at the sacrifice of conscience or honour; that your petitioner most unhesitatingly asserts that the whole Trial on the part of the prosecution was corrupt from beginning to end; that the conduct of the Judges was partial both in the reception and construction of evidence, the treatment of the witnesses in their addresses and remarks to the jury, and their final summing-up, all being marked with a strong prejudice against the Defendant; that the Lord Chief Justice who sat upon the Trial had not only prejudged it, but in private assemblages, in course of the Trial, denounced the [illegible]ndant as an impostor; that in numerous instances, whe[illegible] and positive testimony was given in favour of the Defendant's identity, the Lord Chief Justice endeavoured to explain it away, by suppositions altogether, as your petitioner submits, unjustifiable, it being a well-known rule of law that the jury must give their verdict alone upon the evidence; that particularly as regards the old family servant BOGLE, a most important witness for the Defendant, and who distinctly swore to him as his former young master, the Lord Chief Justice endeavoured to throw a doubt on BOGLE's recognition of him in Sydney, and by reasoning of his own to explain away the circumstance of the defendant recognizing BOGLE, if he was not Sir ROGER TICHBORNE, intimating, amongst other things, that the Defendant knowing BOGLE was in Sydney and that he was a valet of Sir EDWARD DOUGHTY, who had been dead some years, and knowing from his Mother's letter (the Lord Chief Justice in that instance using the expression of "Defendant's Mother" in reference to Lady TICHBORNE) that Sir EDWARD DOUGHTY had left him an annuity which would only be given after some years' service, which would only be given after some years' service, he would expect to see an elderly man and a dark man, for he had been so described by Lady TICHBORNE, he sees a negro of a certain age sitting in the courtyard of the hotel, evidently on the look out, it required no great stretch of thought to bring it to the mind of the defendant, "Oh, that must be BOGLE;" at all events, he might have a shot—if the man to whom he addressed the exclamation "Hallon, BOGLE," had said, "I do not know you," he might say, "I beg your pardon, I thought I recognized an old friend;" but if it turned out to be BOGLE, down came the bird, the shot took effect; that he did not see anything wonderful about the defendant's recognizing BOGLE, nor did he see anything very wonderful in BOGLE, under the circumstances, being perfectly satisfied that was his young master;—that such a statement on the part of the Lord Chief Justice, your petitioner submits is of itself enough to prove the unfairness of the Trial, but that your petitioner could, if permitted, adduce numerous instances throughout his summing-up equally biassed and unfair; that during the course of the Trial the Lord Chief Justice was in the habit of frequently dining and visiting with members of the TICHBORNE Family who gave evidence against, or were the known opponents of, the Defendant, in town, or occasionally staying with them or their connections in the country, upon or in the immediate locality of the Tichborne estates, sometimes taking his pastime of shooting with them, of which your petitioner has been informed, and believes the Lord Chief Justice is particularly fond; that the parties with whom he so stayed were notoriously adverse to the cause of the Defendant; that during the Trial the Lord Chief Justice paid a visit to Tichborne House, and in company with Mr. WEBSTER, who married the widow of ALFRED TICHBORNE, and who were then in possession, subject to be dispossessed in the event of the defendant in the said Trial making good his claim as Sir ROGER TICHBORNE, made a tour of part of the Tichborne estates, and afterwards, in his observations from the Bench to the Jury, expressed his own private views about a certain grotto that he had inspected, which had been the subject of discussion during the Trial, as the scene of an alleged occurrence stated by the defendant to have taken place in the year 1852, and upon which he was indicted for perjury, treating its present formation as that of the former period, and making his own observations evidence against the Defendant.

That day by day during the Trial the galleries of the Court were occupied by, and reserved chiefly for the friends and partizans of the prosecution, they for the most part being members and connections of the TICHBORNE Family, the Defendant being scarcely able to obtain admission for his friends at all; that your petitioner has himself applied at the gallery for admission, and been told that the orders of the Lord Chief Justice were not to admit except by ticket, and when he has gained admission he has found it only partially occupied, and for the most part by those whom he had reason to believe were concerned and interested themselves in the prosecution adversely to the defendant; that from the intimacy, constant and close intercourse between the Lord Chief Justice and the members and friends of the TICHBORNE Family, their presence in the galleries of the Court could not fail to have influence over the Judge in his deliberations, and in the conduct of the Case, particularly with a prior evening's entertainment amongst them in recollection, or one by invitation in prospect, and that such influence would operate unfavourably against the Defendant; that the Lord Chief Justice would certainly not be a willing guest (most assuredly not a welcome one) with the avowed enemies of the Defendant, unless he had nailed his colours to their mast and made common cause with them.

That the remarks and line of conduct of the other judges, MELLOR and LUSH, were equally one-sided and prejudicial to the Defendant, coinciding as they did with the Lord Chief Justice; that Mr. Justice BLACKBURN was also on the Bench when your petitioner was sentenced to fine and imprisonment, and so totally disregarded the contents of your petitioner's sworn affidavit, and made charges against him which were utterly false, your petitioner is forced to the conviction that the sentence upon him was a foregone conclusion on the part of the Judges, to stay the popular feeling which was being manifested throughout the country in favour of the Defendant, and which, if displayed by the continuance of such meetings as that at Brighton, would render a conviction of the Defendant, which your petitioner contends and maintains was the aim and scope of the prosecution and of the Judges who sat upon the Trial, a matter of extreme difficulty or impossibility.

That during the Trial a system of jocoseness and familiarity was carried on between the Judges, jury and counsel of the prosecution, leading to the inference that the jury were either tampered with or far from impressed with a serious feeling of responsibility; that, in fact, the court was a scene of merriment and buffoonery throughout the Trial; that the jury were kept in ignorance of the amount of allowance they were to receive until the end of the Trial, implying as it might that their services would be rewarded more or less, according as their verdict was for or against the prosecution, the conductors of which alone had the purse and the distribution of the money, and thus the jury might be considered subjected to at least indirect bribery; that whether or not such had influence, your petitioner submits that the position in which they were thus placed was not one of that perfect independence which should attach to a jury who are expected to give a verdict without fear, favour, or affection, and to which a defendant is also entitled to secure an unsullied verdict at their hands; that he was the more entitled to that security from the extreme in which he was placed with no means of defence (but voluntary subscriptions of the public), whilst arrayed against him was the whole weight of the public purse, the holders of which, nevertheless, paid the jury to give a verdict against him, but refused him the slightest aid in defending himself against such verdict.

That the statements herein contained relating to the conduct of of the judges and the course of proceedings in the TICHBORNE Trial, which your petitioner is prepared to substantiate by proof, and many more of the like nature do, your petitioner submits, materially affect the question raised by your petitioner as to the fine and imprisonment inflicted upon him for alleged contempt of court in relation to that Trial.

And your petitioner humbly prays your hon. House that inquiry may be instituted thereon, and that your hon. House will be pleased to take such steps as to you may seem adequate and necessary, with a view to protect the ancient and constitutional and undoubted rights of the people, to bring under the notice of your hon. House all complaints as to the conduct of Judges in the administration of justice.

And your petitioner will ever pray.

21st April, 1875. G. D. SKIPWORTH.

We insert a specimen of the disgraceful caricatures which the hired newspaper press was base enough to circulate at this time. The centre figure represents Mr. HAWKINS; the others are Mr. WHALLEY and Mr. SKIPWORTH.

This conduct was in accord with the general fury and ferocity which has characterized the proceedings in the TICHBORNE Case from their beginning to their end. In Parliament, the enemies of that unhappy Man made it almost a personal question, and foamed almost with rage at the mere mention of his name. Out of Parliament the Press appeared to go actually rabid with rage, and to have behaved as if the proprietors had been all bitten by so many mad dogs. Broadsides, pamphlets, ballads, caricatures of the most cruel kind were circulated in hundreds, in thousands, in tens of thousands, sent anonymously through the post all over the country, and into every quarter where they would be most likely to influence the approaching Trial, to the evil fate of the Defendant. One of the objects which the Claimant's friends had in holding public meetings was to counteract this malign and diabolical course of conduct; for they were all too proud and high-minded to resort to the system in which their opponents rioted and revelled. The way in which post-cards were used was simply devilish. There was hardly a crime in the calendar of which TICHBORNE, his Friends, his Counsel, his supporters have not been accused by this mode of libel. The whole country seemed, indeed, to swarm with them, like the plague of lice or locusts mentioned in the Old Testament; and this atrocious mode of assault continues to this moment (May, 1875), and hardly a [illegible] passes that does not overwhelm Dr. KENEALY and Mr. Onsl[illegible] with the most frightful letters and abusive pamphlets that [illegible] issued from the printing-press. It is probable that by no other means than the great Jesuit Cabal, and its extensive ramifications throughout the Empire could this universal and persistent sys[illegible] of falsehood, slander, and quasi-assassination be accomplished. Nearly the whole of the Newspaper Press is leagued against TICHBORNE and his supporters. This almost general unanimity on the part of so discordant a body as the penny journalists could never have happened if there had not been at the bottom [illegible] one basis—the Jesuit party—who hold the general Press of [illegible] world in their pay. It was thought at one time that the J[illegible] would rule Rome; but now, by means of the Press, Rome is [illegible]stroying the Earth, and rendering the whole of mankind sub[illegible]vient to its purposes. We alluded, at page 226, to Mr. GLADST[illegible], and sought to explain his hostility to TICHBORNE; but we [illegible] not then aware of the following facts, which go to show an ele[illegible]ut in his Ministry and its surroundings which might well acc[illegible]nt for many of the features of the TICHBORNE persecution and p[illegible]cution. We copy them from a most useful pamphlet, en[illegible] *From Windsor to Rome, through Anglican Sisterhoods*, [illegible]ch

it Evangelical Mission, at 14.
The following section (page
Clewer, for penitent females,
ord (Dr. WILBERFORCE); the
'.

the Appeal for Funds in the
'his penitentiary is in Clewer
nfession, for which they are

appeal for funds for "The
'er," November, 1869, has the

Canterbury . £20
Visitor . . 50
'E 25

Clewer Convent, the Sisters
institutions have "the same
r Confessors, and the same

RTER, Rector of Clewer, in a
ber, 1869,—dated and dis-
t the "Clewer Sisters" have
ach "separate institution" of
ment, as the number of sisters
rease."
e to prepare persons for Con-
The Sister is the pioneer of
there is the Confessional, and
essional is a double ally with

med in the circular soliciting
alescent Hospital:—
ociate the QUEEN's honoured
urch and State, duty to GOD
any longer on this momentous
d introduction of Sisterhoods
e the following disclosures.
the year 1864, Her Majesty,
NA and LOUISE, visited Clewer
eived by Mrs. MONSELL, the
hich is very beautiful, was
party went through the house

d their associates were evi-
n, and to carry on their work
pparent patronage, and thus
icism.
WELLESLEY, wife of the Dean
he QUEEN." Mrs. WELLESLEY
Mercy. She reported to the
OUISE had been so delighted
h to become a Clewer Sister!"
read through the length and
d their friends.
g year, 1863, the Princess of
SLEY, visited Clewer Convent,
the Mother Superior.
of the Hon. and Rev. Canon
Her husband is Warden or
House of Mercy," a branch of
have a house in the Cloisters,
visit them. "Father COURTE-

SELL, widow of the Rev. C.
O'BRIEN, sister-in-law of the
HARRIS, being her sister—
P. for Limerick, and of the
Clewer, and now a Romish
the Bishop of London, and
d, who is visitor of Clewer

Thus the WILBERFORCES, TAITS, O'BRIENS, and MONSELLS, are one family, and seem to have formed a compact against the Church of England.

To indicate what domestic influence might possibly be brought to bear in religious questions on persons in high office and position, a correspondent of *Catholic Opinion* quoted in the "Monthly Letter" of the *Protestant Alliance* for May, 1868, thus wrote:—

"Earl GRANVILLE was President of the Council; Lady GEORGIANA FULLERTON (whom to name is enough) is his lordship's sister. The Duke of ARGYLE was Lord Privy Seal: his Grace's mother is a Catholic. Lord RIPON is a convert to Romanism. CHICHESTER FORTESCUE was returned by the priests. Mr GLADSTONE was Chancellor of the Exchequer; he has a Catholic sister. Sir GEORGE GREY, the Home Secretary of that Ministry, has a Catholic sister-in-law, who is even a nun, and other Catholic relatives. Mr. MONSELL, then Vice-President of the Board of Trade, is a convert himself. Sir ROUNDELL PALMER has (or had) a Catholic brother. Sir ROBERT COLLIER has a Catholic aunt. I deviate a little from the line in adding that Mr. COLERIDGE, law officer *in petto* of the next Liberal Government, has a brother a priest and a Jesuit. So much for the RUSSELL and GLADSTONE Ministry. Others, better acquainted with family connections, would probably extend my list. We now come to the present Ministry. The Duke of Marlborough's sister-in-law, Lady PORTARLINGTON, is a Catholic. Lord STANLEY's sister, Lady EMMA TALBOT, has a brother-in-law a priest, and several other Catholic relatives. Sir STAFFORD NORTHCOTE is, I believe, not distantly related to the Very Rev. President of Oscott. The Earl of Longford had a brother who died a Passionist (and, I may add, a Saint), being also the brother-in law of the present Marquis of Exeter. The Earl of Mayo's brother-in-law, the Hon. W. WYNDHAM, is a recent convert. The Attorney-General, not to be outdone by his old antagonist, Mr. COLERIDGE, has *two* brothers Priests."

Archdeacon HARRIS, now Bishop of Gibraltar, brother-in-law of the Clewer Mother Superior, was *Sub-Warden* or *Father Confessor* of Clewer Convent, and Chaplain to the Bishop of Salisbury.

Mrs. HARRIS was sister to the Superior of Clewer Convent. She died in 1864. Three Masses were offered for the repose of her soul, in the chapel, by the Rev. T. T. CARTER, "Father Confessor to the Sisterhood of St. JOHN the Baptist."

Miss O'BRIEN is sister to Mrs. MONSELL, Superior of the Sisterhood of St. JOHN Baptist, Clewer.

Mrs. MARTINEAU is sister of Mrs. MONSELL. Rev. A. MARTINEAU, a London rector, is her husband.

EDWARD O'BRIEN is nephew of Mrs. MONSELL, and is married to a daughter of SPRING RICE, Lord MONTEAGLE, who is now under the "spiritual guidance" of "Father WHITE," of St. Barnabas, London.

Mrs. TAIT, is wife of Dr. TAIT, Bishop of London—the present Archbishop of Canterbury—is first cousin to the Clewer Mother. She is a frequent visitor at Clewer Convent. Mrs. MONSELL returns these visits by protracted stays at London House and Fulham. Mrs. TAIT's two sisters, Mrs. FORTESCUE, wife of Provost FORTESCUE, of St. Ninian's, Perth, and Miss SPOONER, are frequent residents at Clewer Convent. The former lady, with her only daughter, spends every Lent there, under the guidance of "Father CARTER."*

The Dean of Windsor, Domestic Chaplain to the QUEEN, is a member of the Council of Clewer Convent, and husband of Mrs. WELLESLEY, who is "Associate of the Sisterhood of St. JOHN Baptist," Clewer.

The Rev. T. T. CARTER, Rector of Clewer, is Father Confessor, and "Superior General of the Order of the Confraternity of the Blessed Sacrament of the Body and Blood of CHRIST."

Rev. W. T. GRIEVE, former Curate of Clewer, and Father Confessor in the Convent, an arch-Ritualist, promoted by the Bishop of Oxford to Colnbrook, Bucks, is still a member of the Council of the Convent.

Rev. E. BALSTON, Head Master of Eton College, is brother-in-law to "Father CARTER," and is a member of the Council of the Convent.

Rev. JOHN MONSELL, Vicar of Egham, is brother-in-law of the Clewer Mother Superior, cousin of WILLIAM MONSELL, Romish pervert, M.P. for Limerick, an avowed enemy of Protestantism, and one of Mrs. MONSELL's "advisers."

Rev. C. W. FURSE, married to a niece of Mrs. MONSELL, the Clewer Superior, is Vicar of Staines, near Windsor.

Rev. C. ELLIS, Incumbent of Cranbourne, Berks, is cousin of the Clewer Superior.

Bishop of Oxford is brother-in-law of the Romish Archbishop MANNING, cousin and Father Confessor of "Clewer Mother," cousin of Mrs. TAIT, Mrs. FORTESCUE, and Miss SPOONER. His only daughter, Mrs. PYE, and her husband, and also the Bishop's three brothers, have joined the Church of Rome. He is Almoner to the QUEEN, and Visitor of the Clewer Convent.

The Countess of ERNE and Viscount CRICHTON receive invitations to the Commemoration Festival every July.

- -

gland since JAMES II.'s time, and
Monk, vol. i. p. 29.
herhood" in Bolton, in 1854, pre-
ing it was declared that the death
ished as that of an Irish landlord,
Majesty, a woman, reigning over
liers should shoot their generals
unless the demands of the Priests

re not aware that the Pope has a
ive to madness those who attempt
ure of the Jesuits, whose abject
from Gaeta. A friend of ours who
s us that he heard the dying con-
ns, whose services had been conse-

e examples of the murders, under
tious princes and crowned heads;
PIERCE CONNELLY's "Reasons for
l to "Father LA CHAISE's Letter
e in the Pamphlet, "Oxford and
nish *Idolatry*, and these are the

tion than many a volume. The
Chaplain, the Honourable Canon
onfessors and *Directors*. "*Father*
e "*Oxford and Roman Railway*,"

* [illegible] is now made by Rome and her agents to "beguile the simple," pervert the righteous. The *Standard*, January 29th, 1869, quoting from the *Hants Independent*, says: "The Roman Catholic establishment at Carisbrooke, known as the Convent or Nunnery, was visited by the QUEEN on Wednesday last. Her Majesty was attended by Lady CHURCHILL, and inspected every part of the establishment, accompanied by Lady CLARE, the foundress of the institution."—See "*The Oxford and Roman Railway*."

No doubt Lord CRICHTON, as well as many other honourable men, was misled as to the real character of the Clewer "Settlement." Deception is a prominent feature in the policy of these conspirators.

Lady LOUISA CRICHTON was an annual subscriber. Her governess, AUGUSTA GOERTZ, is a Clewer Sister.

Mr. W. E. GLADSTONE, M.P., is a Trustee of the House of Mercy in Clewer Convent. It will be seen from a pamphlet—"First Five Years of the House of Mercy, at Clewer," that Mr. GLADSTONE has been connected with the Sisterhood of St. JOHN Baptist for the last 17 years—since 1851.

Mrs. GLADSTONE is an "Associate of Clewer." She, Mrs. TAIT, and the Superior of the Sisterhood, frequently visit, together, the so-called "Religious Houses" in London.

Rev. W. HUTCHINGS is Sub-Warden, that is—Father Confessor. He, as well as Mr. CARTER, visits parishes in London and elsewhere to hear confessions.

There are several Houses in London where ladies, married and single, meet these men "by appointment," for *confession*. These "Fathers" also hear confessions in the Boarding School for Daughters of the Clergy and Professional men, at 3, Bloomfield-place, Pimlico.*

Ten of the ladies mentioned in the list of Subscribers have become Sisters. Miss ROBERTSON first became a *Sister*, she then joined the Church of Rome. Her property was kept by the Clewer Sisterhood, and she is now "penniless."

Most of the ladies and gentlemen mentioned in the Circular are "Sister and Brother Associates" of St. JOHN Baptist's Sisterhood. They are received by Mr. CARTER at a solemn service in the chapel of the Convent. They kneel at his feet while they promise what he requires of them. He invests them with the "badge"—a bronze medal—and the ceremony ends by Mr. CARTER placing his hands on their heads, and giving them his benediction.

Lady HELENA and Miss FANNY TRENCH, relatives of the Archbishop of Dublin, also Miss GEORGIANA VERSCHOYLE, relative of the Bishop of Kilmore, are "Associates of Clewer Convent."

An effort was made some years ago to introduce the Bishop of Oxford's Romanizing Sisterhood into Dublin; but the effort failed, as the Sisters would not *then* be sent over unless allowed to wear their peculiar dress. The Sisters are now allowed to divest themselves of their conventual name and dress—*for a purpose*.

Lord JOCELYN is a constant visitor at the "House of Charity," Greek-street, London. It is in charge of Clewer Sisters and "Father CHAMBERS." The Archbishop of Canterbury is patron of this place, and the Bishop of London is Visitor.—The *Times*, Oct. 2, 1869.

Lady ROSA GREVILLE, only child of the Marquis of Westmeath, is warmly interested in the Clewer Sisters. They visit her, she returns their visits, and contributes to their funds.

The Countess of Shrewsbury, then Lady INGESTRE, visited in December, 1867, the Superior of Clewer Convent at a Boarding School belonging to the Sisterhood of St. JOHN the Baptist, 3, Bloomfield-place, Pimlico.

The Archbishop of Canterbury, Dr. TAIT, and Mrs. TAIT, attended the services in the Chapel of Clewer Convent during their last visit to Windsor.

Miss ALICE LEES, grand-daughter of the late Rev. Sir HARCOURT LEES, † is now at Clewer Convent. For some time she was employed by the Sisters as a menial in the laundry at Chiswick. "Though paying handsomely, she had no better accommodation than a share of a small bedroom, while the 'self-denying Sister' appropriated four rooms to her own use."

GERALD GARRETT, a beautiful and intelligent boy, several of whose relatives are Irish Clergymen, is now in charge of a Clewer Sister at Chiswick.

Mrs. WALKER, Superior of St. James's Home, is also a constant visitor at Clewer and its numerous "branch houses" in London. Her daughter, ISABELLA, has been for some years a Clewer Sister.

Mrs. GLADSTONE and Mrs. TAIT had each a large sum of money placed at their disposal, for the use of the orphans of those poor people who died of cholera in London during that epidemic. On August 23, 1866, Mrs. GLADSTONE, accompanied by the Clewer Mother, drove in her carriage to Clapham, to inspect a house in which they intended to place the cholera-orphan boys, while Mrs. TAIT placed the girls in a house at Fulham, under the charge of Sister GEORGIANA, of Clewer Convent.

Sister GEORGIANA was, in 1862, sent on a mission to Wales. Having resumed her surname of IRWIN, and laid aside her conventual dress, she took charge of a Penitentiary in Llandaff, called "Llandaff House of Mercy." She kept up a constant correspondence with the Superiors of Clewer Convent, many of whom visited her in Llandaff. On March 16, 1864, Rev. T. A. WARBURTON, of Iffly, Oxford, a Tractarian priest, and relative of the Mother Superior of Clewer, arrived at Llandaff, and heard Confession in the oratory of the House of Mercy, on two days, viz. March 16 and 17, 1864. The Bishop, the nominal Head of the House, knew nothing of the matter until two months afterwards. He then heard all, but retained the Sister, because the Mother allowed her to stay without salary!

During her stay at Llandaff she always attended the Clewer Retreats in each November—resuming her religious dress and name while at Clewer. On May 1, 1867, Sister GEORGIANA was transferred from Fulham to the "Dalston Refuge for the Destitute," as Miss IRWIN, at a salary of £75, for doing the "Church's work in the Church's way,"—promoting the views of the Bishop of Oxford, and of her confessor, Rev. T. T. CARTER.

Nor were caricatures and broadsides the only means of annoyance to which they resorted. In the course of this history we shall have to allude to, and perhaps copy other caricatures, to which the Family or their agents resorted. But they even went the length of forging post-cards with the Claimant's head (in place of that of Her Majesty) engraved upon them. Strange to say, these passed free through the post. We insert a copy of this post-card—a curiosity in its way—which Sir ROGER handed to Dr. KENEALY; and we transcribe the elegant communications which appeared on the back of two of them now lying before us. It can hardly be matter of surprise, that when they forged post-cards they also forged PITTENDREIGH and ORTON letters; and probably tattoo marks too.

POST CARD No. 1.

St. James's Hotel.

DEAR SIR,—My friends, RIVERS, WHALLEY, ONSLOW, and HUNT, inform me that they had four of the geese of which fifteen hundred were supplied to your Goose Club, last Christmas, and say they never partook of such geese for quality and unequalled flavour. Please add my name to your Club this year, and oblige

Yours truly, R. C. D. TICHBORNE.

P.S.—I have forwarded stamps for the amount.

POST CARD No. 2.

Don't worrit yourself about that Telegram, but come and have a nice fish-dinner (as it is Friday) with me, and BLOCKY, and Young NAPPER. We will have a jolly night. You shall sing, and damn the Pope, and I will dance the *Can-can*.

R. C. D. T., Harley Lodge, Sept. 13, 1872.

G. H. WHALLEY, Esq., Reform Club.

POST CARD

7 JU 12 72

29

BEAR FORBEAR

THE ADDRESS ONLY TO BE WRITTEN ON THIS SIDE

TICHBORNE

To Mr. Jas Chaplin
Red Lion Hotel
Smallbrook St
Birmingham

* "Confession too! that terrible arm of Priestcraft, that diabolical device for seduction, that subtle means of piercing the most sacred domestic secrets, and keeping in chains the superstitious sex!"—*Rule of the Monk*, vol i. p. 77.

† The Rev. Sir HARCOURT LEES was one of the most "faithful and fearless" defenders of our Protestant Constitution. When the Romanists during the reign of WILLIAM IV. boasted of Royal patronage, and no doubt regarded it as "a great encouragement and augury of success," that "Her Royal Highness the Duchess of Kent had, *with characteristic liberality*, subscribed the sum of £20 towards the completion of the Catholic Cathedral of Tuam," Sir HARCOURT "demanded, on the part of the Protestants of this betrayed nation, not only the dismissal of those household confidential advisers of Her Royal Highness, who dared to advise such dangerous liberality, but the immediate withdrawal of the infant princess from the guardianship of a parent whose Popish bias or laxity of religious principle, so perversely exemplified in assisting the growth of Popery, might lead to the most awful and calamitous national results. See *Protestant Confederate*, July 6, 1836.

The worthy Baronet based his observations upon *the Bill of Rights*—a great neglected *National Document* which should again be read by both *Sovereign* and *people*. *The Protestant Evangelical Mission and Electoral Union* has published it in the form of a *Penny Tract*, which may be had at their Office, 14, *Tavistock-street, Covent-garden, London, W.C.*

Mr. Fitz-Norman Ellis, a gentleman who had long taken a most active part in Sir Roger's interest, immediately issued the following:—

ADDRESS TO THE NATION.

On the 29th of January last, England witnessed the humiliating, heartrending spectacle of one of her noblest sons mercilessly torn from the bosom of his family and cast into prison. And what is the crime of which he has been guilty? That of having pleaded the cause of the oppressed:—that of having generously and fearlessly raised his voice in aid of that cruelly maligned and persecuted man, Sir Roger Tichborne. *Right nobly* has he done it, and more than ever by this last sad act, this *heroic* sacrifice of his liberty, has he served the righteous cause for which he has so nobly striven; more than ever has he endeared himself to every *true-born Englishman.*

Any unprejudiced person must now see from the clear and indisputable statement of the Case submitted by Mr. Skipworth on behalf of Sir Roger Tichborne, that for Mr. Hawkins and those who instruct him to talk of his having a "*fair* and *impartial* trial" under existing circumstances, is an *absolute mockery.* How is it possible for a man to have a "fair trial" at the hands of those who have held him up for the past six years as an object of scorn and reproach to the civilized world? Who, having cast him into prison for fifty-two days on a groundless charge, have since for many weary months put off that Trial upon one pretext or another, until having worn him out with anxiety, many of his best friends and witnesses in the meantime having died, and his resources become exhausted, they think to render him an easy prey? Now, what chance has he of a "fair trial," who with the gravest charges impending over his head, having (to their lasting shame it is recorded) been reviled and denounced as an impostor by the press of this country wherever he went, has not only to overcome the prejudice against him thus engendered, but broken in health, bankrupt and penniless, has to contend against the unlimited resources of the Government.

Be it understood that the above statements are made only from a conscientious and fearless sense of public duty, and without the *slightest disrespect* to the Lord Chief Justice or other Judges who may preside in the Court of Queen's Bench; indeed, it is felt that the issue to be *thus* tried is unfair to their lordships as well as to the defendant. The scales of Justice may be *true*, and *impartially* held, but if the weights thrown into them be *false* (unless providentially detected) so will be the result.

Far be it from us to say he will not have justice, but that with such fearful odds against him his Trial can be a fair one (even if triumphantly victorious, as we have faith it will be) we indignantly deny, any more than the trial of David in combat with Goliath was a fair one, although the stripling shepherd-boy conquered the giant warrior.

Let the Government retire, while there is yet time, from this unhallowed endeavour to crush a defenceless man! Or, if they must needs interfere, then for God's sake and the nation's honour, let it be to place him upon an equal footing with his rich and powerful enemies; to assign him Counsel, and the means to produce the witnesses essential to his defence! and so make good their claim to the title they *assume*—that of being the *Liberal* Government of a *freedom-loving people.*

In the *Telegraph* of Jan. 30, it is stated to be "no doubt one of the *awkward features* in the Claimant's Case that a belief in his identity involves as a *necessary sequence* a belief that a vast number of persons of high character and eminent position may be involved in a most monstrous plot to deprive an innocent man of his just rights." A most *logical deduction* this for the *Daily Telegraph*, in which we heartily coincide, and one, moreover, the full significance of whose truly "*awkward features*" a few may live to realize.

The same paper is also good enough to inform us that "opinions are free, and that no legal penalty is incurred by those who prefer the credibility of Baigent and Miss Braine to that of Lord Bellew and Lady Doughty." We did not know before that the *Daily Telegraph* was such a worshipper of titles, and while we do most assuredly prefer the credibility of Mr. Baigent and Miss Braine, and have not a doubt that time will justify that preference, we would remind the editor of that journal of a circumstance he appears to have *conveniently* forgotten, viz., that we also have the evidence of a lady of title, whose relationship to the Claimant was infinitely closer than that of Lady Doughty; and if we have not a "Lord Bellew" we have a *faithful old negro*, an honest Poole fisherman, and a hundred British soldiers, the evidence of any one of whom will shake his lordship into shivers.

Had the Dowager Lady Tichborne and Mr. Hopkins, of Alresford, been alive at the late Trial, would they not have been in court to give evidence in his favour? And in the words of Mr. Guildford Onslow, we would ask "with his Mother by his side, supported by the family Solicitor, where is the Judge in England who would have dared to commit him to a felon's prison? Where is the Counsel who would have dared to vilify him as did the 'chief law officer of the Crown?'" Never did the advisers of the Government,—never did the enemies of Sir Roger Tichborne make a graver mistake than to imagine for one moment that by such *cool, high-handed stifling of common justice* they could suppress the *truth.* For every arm thus rendered powerless a hundred will be raised to vindicate his cause.

As was most ably demonstrated in the dignified defence, or rather justification, offered by Sir Roger Tichborne, the "contempt of Court," if any, was on the part of those who on the occasion of his former Trial had sullied the ermine of the judge,—had dragged the silken robes of the law's majesty in the mire.

OBSERVATIONS ON CONTEMPT.

These proceedings also called forth the following letter:—

To the Editor of the "Daily News."

Sir,—In allegoric sculpture, Justice is shown with bandaged eyes. There are Englishmen who are doubting just now whether she does not see too much. A great speaker of the House of Commons, asked by a foreigner how he managed to govern so large a body with ease, is said to have replied that half his art lay in knowing what to notice and what to let pass. Nothing is more destructive to that dignity which stands in opinion than the excessive sensibility which is betrayed in minute inquiry after supposed matters of offence. There are many things justly censurable in themselves which neither a Speaker nor a Judge could stoop to regard, except at the cost of their moral authority. I am one of those who fear that certain recent proceedings in the Court of Queen's Bench which will not in the long run—say the six months' run—raise the Court in the eyes of those who most need to be impressed with a sense of its august wisdom. Far, indeed, from suggesting that Messrs. Whalley, Onslow, and Skipworth have any right to complain, I fear that the interests of the public have been compromised. Those of us who follow the proceedings of the Law Courts day by day have a perfect confidence in our Judges. Indefatigable, impartial, fearless, they are the pride of the profession, and the glory of the land. But all may not know this, and the greater their merit, the greater the loss when the reputation they deserve is impaired by what seems an unnecessary use of the judicial prerogative to cover the errors of the Bench.

The mischief began when Sir W. Bovill ordered the Claimant into custody—an act that committed not only the learned Judge, but the whole Bench, to an opinion upon Castro alias Tichborne's cause. If this view is correct, the Judge is less to blame than the law, which cast upon him a duty inconsistent with the perfect neutrality and indifference which should always be the characteristic of the Judge. It was bad enough that through the engagement of the principal law officer of the Crown in the cause, and the extent to which he gratuitously identified himself personally and extra-professionally with the interests of his client, the Executive Government should be exhibited to the unreflecting portion of the public as apparently a party to the contest between the Claimant and his opponents.

It was worse when the Ministry undertook the whole expenses of the prosecution of the Claimant. But the worst of all came when the Bench erroneously, as I humbly conceive, felt itself under the obligation to resent the reflections which such conduct was sure to provoke, and engage in a crusade against the right of public criticism. But having resolved to notice the speeches of the excited partizans of the Claimant, the Judges thought proper to do so by a process which Englishmen have always looked on—and will, I trust, always look on—with jealousy. I do not say that every Englishman charged with an offence has a right to an impartial trial before a jury, because it is very doubtful if we have any such privilege; but certainly we have all been taught to think that we ought not to be deprived of our liberty and property except after such an opportunity of defence.

Yet this is what is denied when a person is summoned to the floor of the Court of Queen's Bench to answer for contempt of Court. His judges are precisely those whom he is charged with offending, and a jury of laymen able to take a cool and impartial view of the whole matter is out of the question. And what is the necessity of such a proceeding? To protect the impartiality of the Court, as is said in this morning's papers? As if the spectacle of judges sitting and deciding in their own favour, and sending the delinquent to prison, would produce an impression of impartiality. Or if it be said that the design is to prevent the Trial of the Claimant from being prejudiced, why the explanation is more perplexing than the fact. The truth is that the Claimant has been tried in the newspapers, or some of them, a hundred times within these twelve months, and is being tried still. He has been found to be Orton, Castro, and the real Simon Pure, and a Butcher, and a Baronet, and a persecuted gentleman, and yet justice does not interfere.

I do not say that justice should have interfered. It is too late to expect to stop public discussion by any such assumptions of power. The Courts of Law will have to recognize the liberty of public criticism as the High Court of Parliament has done. Many a public writer has the House of Commons had before it, and many a one has it committed to prison, but the principle contended for was established all the same. Either the Courts select the objects of prosecution arbitrarily, or they are going to proceed much farther than they have done. I have read speeches and resolutions of Trades Unions and Trades Councils on Mr. Justice Brett's sentence on the gas stokers as libellous as anything said by Mr. Skipworth; yet he has not set the machinery of this Court in motion to convict the speakers of contempt, relying on the good sense of the community to counteract the effect of imputations uttered under the influence of momentary passion. I would conclude this too-long letter by asking leave to suggest to some Member of Parliament to take steps by which the law may be so modified that contempt of Court may be made an offence punishable in the fair and constitutional way provided in the case of other trespasses, after a trial by jury. In this way justice will be done to the subject, and the Judges will be protected, both against groundless attacks, and against the more formidable consequences which follow the invidious exercise of a power too apt to betray those who wield it.

AN ENGLISHMAN.

In the same spirit, a most learned member of the Bar published the following in the *Morning Post;* but the whole spirit of the country seemed torpid or dead, and no legislative measures were proposed to check this despotic claim, thus set up; nor did a single man step forth to protest against these acts. The letter in the *Post* was signed, "A Lover of Constitutional Law," and was as follows:—

In your able article on the subject of the recent committal for contempt of Court—in mere words uttered at a distance—you intimated a grave doubt as to the existence of such a formidable power. Careful research has satisfied me that your doubts were more than justified, and that no such power is known to the law. The Lord Chief Justice, when the subject came up again a few days afterwards, suggested that it attached to the Courts, as members of the ancient Curia Regis, where it was incident to the personal presence of the sovereign. But this theory will bear the test neither of history nor law, and is equally inconsistent with both. If it be founded in truth, the power should have been exercised from the first institution of the Courts, and this is the theory propounded by the Judges. It was, they say, coeval with the constitution of the Courts, and has had an immemorial existence. Then, if so, it must have been exercised from the first, and there must have been traces of its exercise. Our ancestors were somewhat rough in their habits, and their character often found expression in unruly words and acts such as must have afforded occasion for the exercise of the power in question, if any such power existed. Yet no trace can be found in our history of the exercise of any such power. Nay, it can be historically shown that no such power was ever exercised by the Courts. In the reign of HENRY II.—the very time the Royal Court was first constituted—a remarkable case of contempt arose. Words of contumely and insult were uttered against the judge, sitting under a royal commission: yet we do not read that the judge committed the offender, but that he was indicted and regularly tried. (LINGARD, vol. ii. c. 3.) Clearly, therefore, at that time there was no idea of the existence of any such power in the Courts, even for contempts in court, and the power, if it exist, must have been acquired by subsequent usurpation. To some extent it was so acquired, but only to the extent required by experience of its necessity. So far from having belonged to the Courts from the beginning, it has been, on the contrary, acquired only by slow degrees and gradual steps. It is not likely that such a power could have existed at the time of the Great Charter, or else, as you very truly observe, what would have been the use of declaring that men should only be fined or imprisoned by the judgment of their peers and the law of the land. And from the age of the Charter to the time of the Commonwealth no trace of the existence or exercising of such a power can be found. Yet contempt was a great head of the law, but it was defined and regulated by law. It meant a disobedience of a lawful mandate of the sovereign in his Courts, or an act of violence or outrage obstructing their process or interrupting proceedings. Numerous instances of contempt are to be found in the "Year Books," but they all range themselves under these heads. Contempts were definite offences, the subject of indictment, and tried, like other offences, by a jury. Our ancestors had no idea of an arbitrary power of fine and imprisonment at the pleasure of the judges for anything that might happen to affront or offend them. Nor had they any idea of constructive contempts; contempts were all actual, and were always indictable. If an act were a real outrage on the Court, or a resistance or disregard of its authority, it was a serious offence, and treated as such by indictment; and if it were short of that, it was no offence at all that could be visited with punishment. Of course, any interruption or disturbance of the proceedings of a Court while sitting could be summarily repressed, but punishment could only be inflicted on indictment and by the judgment of a jury. Not through all the books for the period of three centuries—from the reign of EDWARD I. to the institution of the Star Chamber—can a single instance of summary fine and imprisonment for a supposed contempt be found. Contempts were indictable offences, or they were not offences at all. Contempts meant acts of outrage on the Court, resistance to its process, or violence to jurors, suitors, or witnesses. It was not possible to conceive a case of contempt which was not an indictable offence. And, on the other hand, it would be difficult to conceive of an act not indictable which would be a contempt. Thus, though to assault a juror would be a contempt, to attempt to influence or persuade him would not be, at all events, unless by corrupt and unlawful means. To do so by honest persuasion and argument would certainly never have been deemed a contempt in days when juries judged by hearsay, and found verdicts on the general knowledge of the vicinage. The idea that to address people long before a trial on the subject of the trial could be an unlawful or criminal act would certainly never have occurred to our ancestors. It is doubtful whether to attempt to influence jurors already empanelled was an offence at common law, for ancient statutes were passed to punish it under the name of "embracery" of jurors. These statutes only made it a misdemeanour, so it could hardly have been so before, and if not a misdemeanour, it could not have been punished by fine. Before the statutes no trace can be found of its being treated as an offence, and after the statutes no such offence was ever punished except by indictment thereon. But the statutes only applied to corrupt influence, and not to honest persuasion or reasoning. It is a curious illustration of the results of ignorance of legal history that even lawyers should have brought themselves to fancy that such honest appeals even to jurors empanelled on a trial—still less to people in general before a trial—could possibly have been an offence. Even slander in those days was an offence against secular law, and words not slanderous could be no offence at all. Even assaults on jurors, or suitors, or witnesses, were punished in the regular way, and no one will find in the "Year Books" any mention of summary fine or imprisonment. The idea that such a power has existed "immemorially," as some lawyers are fond of fancying, is a mere chimera. There was no such power known to the law, and that was one of the main reasons for the institution of the Star Chamber. As Sir JAMES MACKINTOSH observes, it was originally instituted for the repression of evils incident to the character of the age, and the worst of them were those which interfered with the administration of justice. The most frequent of them were attempts to influence jurors by means of persuasion which would not come within the ancient statutes of "embracery." The mischief became greater in the sixteenth century, when printed pages could be distributed among the jurors. If there had been a summary power of fine and imprisonment in the Courts of law there could have been no difficulty. But no such power was heard of, and hence the Star Chamber was instituted to redress these offences against justice, and this was one main head of its arbitary jurisdiction. During those ages no instance of such summary exercise of power will be found except in the Star Chamber. When the Star Chamber was abolished, so much of its jurisdiction as was legal, and not arbitrary, passed to the Court of Queen's Bench, and there, if anywhere, this power would be vested. But no instance will be found of its exercise of such a power except in cases of obstruction of its process. By degrees the summary power was exercised in such cases by that and the other superior Courts, but it was never exercised for mere words out of Court except in the case of a party served with its process and treating it with contumely. In cases of words reflecting on the Court or its judges, the remedy, if any, was by criminal information; nor was that available except in case of an imputation of corrupt conduct. Mere words of disrespect at a distance, or attempts to influence jurors, were never treated as a contempt, before or after the Revolution. Half a century later, in 1758 in the time of Lord MANSFIELD, a case occurred, under circumstances curiously resembling those of the TICHBORNE Case. A case was coming on for trial before him at the assizes, when it was found that one of the prosecutors had circulated in the assize town libellous papers intended to influence the jurors. The counsel for the defence loudly complained of it as contempt, but it did not occur to Lord MANSFIELD that he had power to deal with it summarily. He remedied the mischief by putting off the trial, but he did not attempt to punish it. He postponed the trial, and gave time to apply for criminal information, which was tried in the ordinary way. In the time of Lord DENMAN the whole question of contempts arose, and was discussed with infinite learning. Lord DENMAN laid down the true doctrine when he said that the summary power was limited to cases of insult to the Court when sitting, or of obstruction to its process. Moreover, he declared that its exercise could only be justified by a present necessity, to be judged of by the Court at the moment. Thus, when papers reflecting on the Court had been circulated in the Court itself in the presence of the judges, though they might have committed the party at the moment if they had judged it necessary, yet as they did not do so, a warrant of committal afterwards issued was held invalid. What could more clearly or more strongly show that a committal can only be justified on the score of an insult when it is offered to the Court when sitting, and in the face of the Court, and when it is at once and instantly inflicted. It had never occurred to Lord DENMAN that he could send a man to prison for mere words uttered out of Court, and even a hundred miles away, even though uttered against the Court. Criminal information is the proper remedy for defamatory publications which require an extraordinary and speedy redress. If there was not a case for criminal information, there could not be a case for still more summary and arbitrary exercise of authority.

It is true that in the Court of Chancery the summary power has long been exercised to repress publications tending to prejudice the public mind. But this is on peculiar grounds, which do not apply at law, and in applying the precedents of Chancery the Courts have been misled by a false analogy. The Courts of Chancery took evidence by voluntary depositions, and attacks on the parties might prejudice the minds of persons who might be asked to give their evidence as witnesses. By such attacks they might be deterred from giving their evidence, and thus the parties who required such evidence might be deprived of it. This would be a mischief which called for a summary remedy, and no remedy not summary would be really any remedy at all. If the attacks were not stopped at once, irreparable evil might be done without the possibility of a remedy. Therefore a summary power of punishment was held necessary, and has been exercised since the time of Lord HARDWICKE. But no court of law has ever proceeded upon its legality, and its legality is more than doubtful. Its exercise however, has been carefully restricted to cases in which there has been no publication of the evidence, and therefore affords no authority for its exercise in a case where the evidence has already en published to the world, and fully commented on, equally favour of one side and the other. The other cases in Chancery ve all been cases of clear necessity.

In the case of the gentlemen lately dealt with summarily by Court of Queen's Bench, their original offence was the utterce of comments at public meetings for many months previous Michaelmas Term last, which began on the 2nd of November. notice was taken of them all through that Term. The chief mplaint against them related to a meeting held on the 11th of cember. A month afterwards—on the 11th of January—lary Term began, and a criminal information might have been wed and obtained within five days, and could have been tried the course of the Term. Instead of this, Mr. ONSLOW and r. WHALLEY were summarily brought up, threatened with prisonment, and fined. Mr. SKIPWORTH, a gentleman from ncolnshire, at a meeting at Brighton protested against this eatment as arbitrary and unconstitutional, and declared that would not be so intimidated. For that he was summarily ought before the Court, sentenced to fine and imprisonment, d sent to gaol as if he had been guilty of a crime.

If such proceedings are in accordance with the law of this untry, I can only say that I have failed to find any authority r them. In the long annals of our law I venture to say that no ch proceedings will be found. You were right in saying that e exercise of such powers must be regarded with grave apprension, and I for one do not hesitate to say that the late proedings in the Court of Queen's Bench challenge our most serious tention.

Mr. WHALLEY also addressed his constituents in the letter that llows, and subsequently addressed them in Peterborough :—

) THE ELECTORS OF THE CITY OF PETERBOROUGH.

"To sustain, to repair, to beautify this noble pile, is a charge rusted principally to the nobility and such gentlemen of the kingm as are delegated by their country to Parliament. The protection the liberty of Britain is a duty which they owe to themselves, who joy it; to their ancestors, who transmitted it down; and to their serity, who will claim at their hands this, the best birthright and blest inheritance of mankind."—BLACKSTONE'S COMMENTARIES.

Plas Madoc, Ruabon, February, 1873.

GENTLEMEN,—According to usual custom on the commencement the Session I met some of my constituents on Monday, the 10th st., and after stating generally my views on public affairs, tered fully into the question with which I have been lately so entified—The TICHBORNE Prosecution.

The Meeting—not limited to my political friends—thought fit to ree unanimously that I was entitled to the confidence of the nstituency, and I trust it will not be deemed unduly intrusive I now submit, for the information of those who were not preat, the statement on which this vote of confidence rested.

It may perhaps rather deter than induce you to take this ouble when I inform you that it is on general grounds, affecting e administration of justice, that I have taken so deep an interest this Case, and especially that it is from a point of view little cognized by the public. Those who may read the speech will rm their own opinion, but there is one point which I think will generally admitted as giving significance to my public conduct this matter.

On several occasions when unable to make such impressions on e House of Commons as the public interests seemed to me to mand, I have during the last twenty years carried my case as were by appeal to the public, and have attended meetings for e discussion and furtherance of my views. I have always garded this as a legitimate effort to promote what appeared to s to demand public attention; such questions for instance as e Repeal of the Income-tax on trade and labour (Schedule D)—e practice of Parliament in relation to Private Bills—the justice of renewing year by year the Turnpike Toll-tax, and her questions of more or less public interest, have all been scussed at public meetings, and especially have I thus acted in lation to a subject which, in spite of opposition and obloquy, I ll regard as of paramount importance—the agression of the reign power called Popery on our Institutions in Church and ate.

When prevented by clamour and interruption from bringing fore the House of Commons the doctrines and practices of the nfessional, as carried out, not only amongst Roman Catholics, t in a large and growing section of the Established Church of igland, I promoted the publication of a pamphlet well known the title of "The Confessional Unmasked;" and this I did in der to afford to those who might be offended with such dissures the opportunity of stating their views; and I took part organizing the meetings of the late Mr. MURPHY and others r the purpose of justifying such publication, and submitting the hole question to public opinion.

The Court of Queen's Bench thought fit to suppress the publition of "The Confessional Unmasked," on the ground that it s an obscene book within the meaning of an Act of Parliant passed in recent years, and known as Lord CAMPBELL'S t; and several Protestant lecturers, in addition to the penalty the law as thus laid down, were injured by Roman Catholic trage—sent to prison for the riots in which they were the tims—and otherwise suppressed, and Mr. WILLIAM MURPHY s so brutally maltreated that he shortly afterwards died, and Roman Catholics of Whitehaven were afforded a remarkable triumph by the liberation from prison by the Home Secretary of the men who had been tried and convicted of that offence.

When events like these fail to attract public attention, it seems to me to be the duty of those who believe that they can account for such indifference to make known their views, and, so far as their special attention to the subject enables them, to trace to its source this palpable perversion of law and justice.

Nothing can be more unpopular than to preach of dangers unseen by others, and the ridicule which is so skilfully excited against alarmists it is a part of Jesuit education and contrivance to carry out to the utmost their power and influence over the Press; for such purposes can be distinctly traced to special instructions issued from Rome to their priesthood in this country in 1832; and surely it is obvious enough that, as Jesuits are by law prohibited from residing in this country, I am but speaking the language of the law when I say that none but those who make it their special business can trace out and expose the conspiracy which it is the mission of that fraternity to carry out.

If a man takes into his service a professional thief, and knows him to be one, some special detective is required to watch him; and the Jesuits, more numerous now in this country than in any other, are by the law recognized as professional conspirators against our laws and constitution—against social, political, and individual safety—and Dr. MANNING has publicly declared the Jesuits to be the leaders and chief agents in Roman Catholic aggression.

Am I or others to be punished with fine and imprisonment because in the voice of the law—outraged as it is by their presence amongst us—I raise my voice in warning against them; and when I find, as in this TICHBORNE Case, what seems to me to be their track, may I not at least again accept the risk of ridicule and abuse? and if I unconsciously offend against the law and cheerfully submit to its penalties, is there to be no recompense in the recognition by all honest and earnest men of the fact that I am but discharging a plain and paramount public duty?

I am convinced that, so far as you are concerned, knowing me as you have done through many such political storms, I shall not ask for such recompense in vain; and that you will concur with the hundreds of thousands of our countrymen who have declared at the TICHBORNE Meetings that I am justified in my efforts for obtaining for the Claimant a fair trial.

I remain, your faithful servant,

G. H. WHALLEY.

The following is the report of my speech as addressed to a meeting of my constituents on the 10th of February (published in the *Peterborough Times*) as revised and completed:

Mr. WHALLEY met his constituents, by invitation, at The Black Boy and Trumpet Inn on Monday evening. Mr. VERGETTE was called to the chair. Mr. WHALLEY expressed his pleasure at meeting his friends again at the commencement of another Session, and reviewed the measures passed in the last Session and those likely to come forward and occupy attention during the present Session. He also spoke at considerable length on his connection with the TICHBORNE Case, as follows:

It has been our frequent custom to meet in friendly conference on the reassembly of Parliament, and I have found such pleasure and advantage in the practice, that I am unwilling to forego it, even under circumstances that render it doubtful whether I may not be sent to prison for contempt of the Court of Queen's Bench, for attending even such a meeting as this. It is not possible that I can address you without referring to TICHBORNE, and if the Court of Queen's Bench should think fit to construe anything I shall say on that subject as having "the effect of prejudicing the forthcoming Trial," then it would be indeed an aggravation of the wrong which that Court is by many believed to have done to Mr. SKIPWORTH, if with such *warning* I should still remain outside the prison in which he now languishes, as honest and true a gentleman as ever sacrificed himself in defence of the birthright of England—freedom of speech and public meeting.

As to the proceeding in the Court of Queen's Bench my feeling is this, that unless I am free to discuss the conduct of that Court in sending to prison, with a heavy fine added, Mr. SKIPWORTH, and calling public attention to the mode in which it has dealt with Mr. ONSLOW and myself, then there is an end to my public career; and whether my life should henceforth be passed within the walls of a prison or in a private station, matters little to me in comparison with the degradation I should feel in continuing to hold a public position the duties of which I am utterly precluded from discharging to the best of my ability.

There seems to be much misapprehension as to the question on which the Court of Queen's Bench decided to fine Mr. ONSLOW and myself, and to send to prison Mr. SKIPWORTH, and subject to penalties the Claimant.

The question was not whether the TICHBORNE Meetings which have been held through the autumn were decorous, or becoming, or right in any respect, or even legal; nor was it whether I or any of us had been guilty of uttering libels against respectable people, or reviling the Judges, Counsel, Jury and others in the late Trial in the Common Pleas; or whether in any other respect we had been guilty of all or any of the offences described in strong language by the Lord Chief Justice when he addressed Mr. ONSLOW and myself: that was not the question—for it cannot be doubted that for all such offences, if actually committed, the law provides the suitable penalties, providing also that those against whom such charges are made shall be tried by a jury of their countrymen, and not as we were, in our absence and without notice, on statements made by opponents, without an opportunity of reply, explanation, or disproof.

The question was whether we had committed some offence against the Court itself, and the Court itself, being both judge and jury in its own cause, convicted us without hearing us on the 11th of January, of having committed such contempt, and when on the 20th we were called up, it was only to show cause why we should not be punished.

As to the propriety, or otherwise, of the public meetings, I am not here to justify them. I admit that nothing but extreme necessity, the belief not only that the Claimant was innocent, but that his opponents knew it, or might have known it, and that the public money to a large amount was being used to convict him, he was in many respects treated with unprecedented severity—all this having been brought by me before the House of Commons, and explanation or reply being there refused by the Government, I stated then and there the course I felt it a duty to adopt. But for this I do not ask your approval, but only that you will suspend your judgment and wait the result; and though the result may be in accordance with my views, I ask no special credit, but only the admission that I did my duty in resisting the expenditure of public money and public character, in prosecuting to penal servitude or death a man whom it was in no slight degree my own misfortune to know to be innocent. Then as to the vilifying of Judges, Counsel and Jury, I can by no means admit the statements of the Lord Chief Justice; but I say that even if such offences had been committed, either by myself or others at those meetings—the utmost care having been taken to avoid any such expressions—this was no contempt of the Court of Queen's Bench; and as to the Court of Common Pleas, or the Attorney-General, or the Jury, it is incomprehensible how the Court of Queen's Bench should have assumed that they were thereby insulted, and convict us on that supposition without trial, without notice, without a jury, or any opportunity of refuting or replying to the allegations made against us by the Government prosecutors. Also, I have to point out, that even if this conduct of ours could be construed into a contempt of that Court, inasmuch as it was not done in their presence they could only act on evidence; and they had no right to act on that evidence presented by the Government, without giving us notice or affording us an opportunity of being heard in reply and refutation of such evidence. This they did not do, and I leave it to lawyers to say what such a precedent leads to.

Then what was the contempt alleged? Why, that I had three years ago charged the TICHBORNE Family with conspiracy, and it was on this alone that I was convicted on the 11th of January of contempt of Court.

The law of England is, that no man shall be fined or imprisoned, except by the judgment of his peers (trial by jury) and a fair hearing; and the only exception is, that when a man plainly interferes with the course of justice within the sight of the Court, or, if otherwise, in such a way as to make instant punishment essential, then, and in such cases only, the Court is said to be treated with contempt; such summary action being, in fact, necessary in order to carry on its duties. But what did I do—or what was alleged against me? It was not that I attended the meetings, for though that was the offence for which Mr. SKIPWORTH and the Claimant were convicted, the Lord Chief Justice told Mr. ONSLOW and myself that "this was no matter for complaint or punishment;" nor was it for what he chose to call "reviling the Counsel and the Judge," for this we never did, nor was it, so far as I know, alleged against us. No! it was, to use his own words, "because the events of the pending prosecution had been discussed, and the evidence alleged to be false."

And so here it is laid down by the Court of Queen's Bench that any one who shall discuss the events of the TICHBORNE (and of course, any other) prosecution, and who shall assume that evidence given in a previous trial is false, is committing a contempt of the Court of Queen's Bench, and he may thereupon be convicted, without notice, without jury or trial, of such contempt of Court, and be fined and imprisoned at their direction; and if, when called up for judgment he should then attempt to explain and justify his conduct or deny altogether his guilt, as Mr. DIGBY SEYMOUR, my Counsel, did in my case, it is treated as an aggravation of the original offence; for such was the plain inference from the interruption and comments of the Court during my Counsel's addresses. It was also very distinctly intimated that whatever should have the effect, whether in speeches at public meetings, or in writing, "of creating prejudice with reference to the approaching trials, is an offence against the public justice of the Court of Queen's Bench." So here we have it again in this marvellous Case laid down as law—that whoever shall say anything that shall "create prejudice," and of course on one side or the other, may be summarily punished, without jury, or trial, by fine or imprisonment.

It is not for me to dwell upon a decision of the Court which is most undoubtedly at variance with all our notions of the rights of public meeting and of freedom of speech, and utterly subversive of any such rights, and I leave that part of the Case to those, whether lawyers or others, whom it may concern.

What I have now called your attention to being thus rather a question for lawyers than for you and me, I proceed to matters more directly concerning my conduct, apart from its penal results,—namely, as to how far it has been marked by due discretion and a proper regard to the responsibility of my position as a representative in Parliament of this city; and I fully admit that, whatever may be my belief in the justice of the Case, it was my first duty to say and do nothing that would bring discredit upon my constituents, to whom alone any influence that my words might have at these public meetings is attributable; and I assert that I did no more than my duty, and that I discharged that duty, taking every possible precaution against doing injustice either to my constituents or to any person or party whatsoever.

The only words imputed to me as an offence were "that I charged the TICHBORNE Family with Conspiracy" in so far that knowing the Claimant to be their relation, they had resolved to repudiate him for the purpose of retaining possession of his estates. I did not state that charge in these words, but only stated the fact that I had charged them with this offence, and this, or what was equivalent to it, I had so done three years ago in a written correspondence with their solicitors, referring them at the same time to my own solicitors, if they should desire on this or any other account to put me to the proof and justification of my statements. Now, I ask, what could a man do more?—having, as I told their solicitors, carefully investigated this Case in the very district where the best evidence could be got, and becoming convinced that a great public scandal was being perpetrated, and the laws of the country defied by money and in reliance upon political and social influence. I thus declared myself openly and in writing, at the risk of bringing upon myself all the resources of the TICHBORNE Family in legal prosecutions for libel. When these people, so eager for law that they threaten me with prosecution for giving the Claimant £25, took no notice for near three years of this imputation, was I not justified in stating publicly that fact? Whether the Court of Queen's Bench were legally justified in coming to their rescue three years after the offence was committed, and declaring it was an insult or contempt of Court, I again say I leave to lawyers; but it seems to me that the wolf which quarrelled with the lamb because its grandsire muddied the water is, to such common-sense as governs the relations between you and me, something like the treatment I received; for it was in my absence that I was condemned for contempt of Court in respect of an imputation which those concerned had passed over for three years, and which when then uttered in writing, as now verbally, I was prepared to justify before a jury of my countrymen.

But it is said by the Government reporter that I declared that this conspiracy was hatched in a London drawing-room, and rested upon the influence which a certain well-known Ecclesiastical party believed they had in Parliament, on the Judicial Bench, and in Society.

I am not now, any more than in the Queen's Bench, disposed to cavil as to words, but no man could be convicted of the slightest offence in a court of justice before a jury upon such evidence as the Court thought fit to accept, or the Lord Chief Justice to adopt in his address to Mr. ONSLOW and myself. Beyond all possibility of doubt, I did believe, as I do still, that the Claimant is ROGER TICHBORNE, and that his Family who are opposing his claims knew it, or might have known it if they had thought fit to inquire; or what is the same thing, might have exposed or punished him at once if an impostor, and especially if they believed in the tattoo evidence; and this I publicly wrote and stated; and then we all know that the Government were about to spend £100,000 or more in prosecuting him, and would give no information to us in the House of Commons, when called upon to vote this money, nor would they afford to him the information and aid usually given to men charged with such offences. No man in England could or does justify the conduct of the Attorney-General as Counsel in taking upon himself to act for the Government in pledging them to carry on the prosecution. He has admitted himself he was wrong by the fact of his retiring from, and thus so far as possible repudiating all responsibility for, the subsequent proceedings; all this I declared in Parliament, as also my resolve to attend meetings, and to aid in obtaining for the Claimant the means to defend himself. In carrying this out I communicated to Government from time to time the meetings I had attended and was about to attend, and all the evidence that sprung up at the meetings, and at which—one and all—he was declared almost as with one voice to be ROGER TICHBORNE. And, what is still more to the purpose, I had brought to the notice of the Government conclusive evidence that witnesses in his favour had been offered money to suppress or pervert their evidence, with other facts which, if they can be disclosed, will indeed surprise the public; and I ask whether it was not reasonable to infer from all this, that there was a combination or conspiracy to keep in the possession or under the control of the Family in possession the TICHBORNE title and estates. Was it not my duty then, believing this, to make known my suspicions, and how could I do it with less offence than by suggesting as possible that it might have originated in a drawing-room, and that it might have taken into account the well-known influence which the TICHBORNE Family could command in high quarters. If the man should be an impostor, who could be injured by such suggestion but myself?—but if the contrary, surely it will be admitted that my conduct is more in accordance with the Christian example of him who at his own cost and risk rescued the poor man attacked by robbers, than with conduct deserving the treatment of a malefactor brought up to the bar of a British Court of Justice to receive punishment.

And now that I have explained the legal question as to how far I was guilty in strict law of the offence known as contempt of Court; also of the charge of having imputed conspiracy against some persons known or unknown—I come lastly to the most serious charge of all, namely: why should I act the part of Don Quixote, and that too, at the risk of my constituents being involved in the abuse and calumny that inevitably awaits any man that fights against windmills? and this is the view presented by your excellent local paper, *The Standard*, of last week.

I do admit there would be much reason in the complaint that I should spend my time and exhaust my political energies in seeing justice done in some private quarrel about estates in Hampshire, and that although the public money to the extent of £100,000 is thrown away (if so it be) by prosecuting to conviction an innocent man, yet that this is no excuse for such persistency in rushing, in Quixotic fashion, to the relief of "distressed damsels," and I also admit that in a private station there is ample field for the display of whatever may be deserving of encouragement in such adventures.

The answer that I have to offer, not more to you than to myself, is that this Tichborne Case is in itself nothing but a single instance of what, for want of a better word, I call conspiracy. That I firmly believe a conspiracy is thoroughly organized and in active operation in this Empire—striking at the very root of all that constitutes its power and its glory—that every interest social and political—our national independence at home, the future of our fellow-subjects throughout the world, and all that we or they have inherited from our fathers, or would desire to transmit to our children—in a word, all that constitutes the great inheritance of the British name is imperilled by this conspiracy, of which the Tichborne Case is but as the feather driven lightly before that sirocco wind of Jesuitism which never yet failed to wither and destroy every vestige of human liberty and happiness exposed to it. Why do our laws prohibit a Jesuit living in this country? Why has every country in Europe found it necessary to expel and prohibit these professional conspirators from their boundaries? Surely in asking you to believe, with Lord Palmerston, that no country can be safe that allows free action or even a resting-place for Jesuits, and that there cannot even be peace in Europe so long as they are allowed to conspire against the peace and happiness of man-

SIR ALEXANDER COCKBURN.

kind: I may also ask, is it not well that a voice should now and then be raised in Parliament to give warning against such a foe? Is Prince Bismarck, who now, at the risk of civil war, is sending them over here from Germany, a Don Quixote? and why should I be so regarded when I speak but the voice of existing laws, and of all the history of our country, and of Europe, in declaring that these men, now congregated in this country in defiance of the laws, are not idle. Do you ask me what this has to do with Tichborne? I say that so soon as I became satisfied that he was the man, and that his relatives knew or could convince themselves of that fact, I looked upon it as one of those providential warnings of danger sometimes vouchsafed to nations, and which not all the superhuman devices of Jesuitism can prevent cropping up now and then to arouse in time the closed eyes of their victims. This was long before anyone dreamt of the Government taking up the Case on behalf of the infant in possession, but I had only to know the custody and surroundings of this child to foresee that all the resources at the command of Mr. Gladstone would be at their service. Thus it happened that when the Trial in the Common Pleas failed—not, mind you, so much on the part of the Claimant, for he only failed in the means of carrying on his suit against speeches of a month in length, and proceedings heretofore unknown, but on the part of the Tichborne Family—then it was that Government came forward, and, the man being in Newgate with charges of forgery invented for the occasion, and since abandoned, they sought to overwhelm him by public money and arbitrary imprisonment.

Anyone may be excused for sympathizing with a man in such a position, and I did no more on the platform of public meetings than did the thousands who with one voice declared, as they sat and listened to him, that he had not had a fair trial, and that they believed him to be Sir Roger Tichborne; but I always had in my mind an object beyond that of his escape from persecution.

The recovery of his estates no more concerned me than yourselves, but I felt that I should have the eyes and ears of the public to aid in exposing what, firmly believing to be a Jesuit conspiracy, I should be brought into full light by means of this Case, and that as to the perils to which we are exposed from that quarter, the public would see to what extent we can rely for protection upon those whose duty it is to defend us, and also decide whether they are to any and what extent in league with the enemy. This was and continues to be my chief reason for working out this Tichborne Case to the very end.

You would not [illegible] were I to point out how the Jesuit [illegible] to embitter public feeling [illegible] one against the other—so that [illegible] France in fighting for Rome—or [illegible] actions of which the public are as unconscious as are the fish in the sea of the net that is being cast. If the operations of the Jesuits were not all but inscrutable, it would not have been found needful by every country to exclude them bodily from their boundaries; and the fact undoubtedly is that at the present moment there is not a department of the State, nor a single interest of the country, social or political, that is not actively worked "to break," as Dr. MANNING avows his design to be, "the Imperial spirit of England," and bring this Empire into the network of Rome, to do the work which France was unable to accomplish. But of what avail would it be to trouble you or others with my fears on this subject? And if I were to tell public meetings how Jesuit priests are to be found among common labourers of this country organising Unions under all manner of names and with various ostensible objects—all tending to the one purpose of promoting, as they best know how, the grand project of Dr. MANNING, why those who would so speak would meet probably with something more than laughter, clamour, and derision; and, in the exact degree of their success, would incur the risk of fine or imprisonment, or even violent death, as has lately happened even in England to those who have taken up this perilous mission.

But this TICHBORNE Case, as I said before, is to my mind, providential. It has already aroused full public attention by the romance and personal interest of its incidents, and I confidently say that this will not cease until the origin and every feature of the Case is thoroughly exposed to the public gaze.

Whatever you may think of these ulterior objects thus in my mind, they at all events are sufficiently definite and consistent with my known opinions, to relieve me from the charge of Don Quixotism: for whether it be all a delusion or not on my part, it is one which you have yourselves permitted and encouraged me to act upon now for above twenty years, and it is not to be doubted that I stand less alone in this faith than at any former period. Liverpool but yesterday, and every election for the last three years, is evidence how far the Government of Mr. GLADSTONE has in these and other matters lost the confidence of the country; but as to this Case, it is sufficient to say that this man has not had a fair Trial, and that without some aid in public subscriptions and sympathy he cannot expect it, and that, whether acting as a Member of Parliament, or otherwise, I expect you will continue to me your confidence and support in all the efforts I may make to secure it, and that you will regard with indulgence any error that in so difficult and perilous work may be unconsciously committed.

One word, in conclusion, as to my still more unfortunate colleague in Contempt, Mr. SKIPWORTH, and the peculiar line of conduct of the Lord Chief Justice in reference to that gentleman and the Claimant.

It is my hope that some fitting occasion will occur for calling the attention of the House of Commons to the question whether the Court of Queen's Bench has not in these cases carried the rule of arbitrary authority far beyond what has ever before been known to the law, imperilling thereby the ancient liberties of public meeting and freedom of speech, and as a precedent, placing every man at the mercy of a tribunal acting irresponsibly and without appeal, to a degree unknown in this country since the notorious tyrannies of the Star Chamber.

I state here my views the more readily because I desire no such protection for my speech as the walls of the House of Commons are supposed to afford. It will be remembered that the Claimant and Mr. SKIPWORTH were brought before the Court for punishment by the personal action of the Lord Chief Justice, upon reading in some Brighton newspapers the proceedings at a public meeting in that town, and also that it was by the Court, when the Lord Chief Justice was present and presiding, that the Claimant and Mr. SKIPWORTH were condemned for contempt of Court in respect of language reported to have been used by them at that meeting and were then at once peremptorily ordered to appear on the 29th of January less than a week after to receive the punishment for the offences of which in their absence they had been so declared to be guilty.

So far their case was similar to that of Mr. ONSLOW and myself, for we also were convicted in our absence, and upon evidence to which we had no opportunity of reply or contradiction; and I say with confidence that, in the one case, as in the other, this was a [illegible] departure from all that has ever been recognised by the law [illegible] of Court, as has been well argued in the *Law Times* and other journals.

In [illegible] of Court [illegible], as I have [illegible] stated, such conduct [illegible] such as personal insult to the Court in its presence, or interfering with witnesses or suitors, or such other actions as, if not punished summarily, the business of the Court could not proceed; and I say that such being the past practice, clearly intelligible to the common-sense of every one, the action of the Court in treating as contempt words uttered at public meetings, and—as did the Lord Chief Justice—actually prejudging such offence before any parties supposed to be affected thereby had noticed it, is such that every lawyer, I believe, in Westminster Hall will admit is a precedent utterly destructive of the right of public meeting and freedom of speech.

What may be the opinion of lawyers in the House of Commons I will not undertake to say, for I am not without anxiety lest the principles so plainly involved in this question may be frittered away and evaded by lawyers in the House of Commons, under the influence of party, and the privileges which party-feeling often asserts against the public interests and safety.

The case of the Claimant and Mr. SKIPWORTH differs, however, from that of Mr. ONSLOW and myself in this particular. The Claimant, it will be remembered, was alleged to have stated at Brighton that the Lord Chief Justice had gone about abusing him, calling him an impostor, with epithets showing strong personal feelings, and exhibiting these sentiments during the Trial in the Common Pleas—where he was frequently to be seen as a visitor—by the side of Lord Chief Justice BOVILL; and the Claimant had gone so far as to declare that if the Lord Chief Justice should take part in his Trial, he would not expose himself or his witnesses to the indignity and wrong of what he believed would be, on the part of the Lord Chief Justice, a continual exhibition of these antagonistic sentiments.

Now, it is not to be expected that the Lord Chief Justice, any more than others, should have abstained from forming an opinion upon the TICHBORNE Case, and if he expressed that opinion, as I have myself personal reason to believe he has done so, freely and in such strong terms as to influence those who came within his reach against the Claimant, such conduct may be regarded—as was said by him of Mr. ONSLOW and myself—as if not quite in accordance with good taste, yet no one who has any knowledge of the habit and mode of speech of the Lord Chief Justice would be too apt to censure, but would freely give him credit against any such "informality" for the claims he has established to public consideration, by his vast ability and high tone of independence on many important occasions.

But are we to extend this indulgence due to Sir ALEXANDER COCKBURN to the Lord Chief Justice of England, when, ascending to his seat in the full Court of the Queen's Bench, he directs proceedings to be taken against the Claimant and Mr. SKIPWORTH for speeches reported in newspapers to have been delivered by them at Brighton? There may be some who will say that the Lord Chief Justice did not exceed the strict line of his duty, though there seems to be no precedent for such conduct; but all must admit that if the Lord Chief Justice deemed himself sufficiently impartial to give these directions for the prosecution of the Claimant and Mr. SKIPWORTH, he should have been present at their Trial and punishment. Subsequently, indeed, but in their absence, he did join in convicting them unheard, of these offences, and that he should have absented himself from the last stage of these proceedings, when, on the 29th of January, they were brought before the Court to receive their punishment, is the most remarkable.

In the absence of the Lord Chief Justice, wholly unexplained, the Claimant not only repeated his complaint that the Lord Chief Justice had himself committed the offence of "prejudicing the future Trial" far more than could be imputed to Mr. ONSLOW or myself, but submitted to the Court that his brother Judges on the Bench should abstain from adjudicating on a case in which the Lord Chief Justice by his then absence seemed to admit that he was thus personally interested.

The Court, however, did adjudicate, but while sending my unfortunate friend, Mr. SKIPWORTH, to prison for three months, with a fine of £500 added, they not only allowed the Claimant to go free, but, by the voice of Mr. Justice BLACKBURN, paid him a high compliment on the "propriety of his defence."

What, I ask, can the public think of the administration of justice in this most extraordinary Case?

At an early day of the Common Pleas Trial, the Claimant told Lord Chief Justice BOVILL that he was acting the part of Counsel against him, and Lord Chief Justice BOVILL does not regard this as demanding any notice, either by way of contempt of Court, or otherwise. The Claimant then tells the Court of Queen's Bench that the Lord Chief Justice of England is so personally committed against himself, that even his colleagues are not qualified to award punishment for an offence of which they, associated with the Lord Chief Justice, had a few days before, and in his absence, convicted him; and the Court, while punishing Mr. SKIPWORTH with fine and imprisonment, dismiss the Claimant with high compliment on "the propriety of his defence."

This was all that the Claimant did and said at Brighton, and yet the Lord Chief Justice thought fit to treat the remarks upon his own conduct as "contempt" of his Court, and not only ordered the Attorney-General to bring the case before the Court, but actually sat and adjudicated upon it; and without hearing what the Claimant or Mr. SKIPWORTH might have to say in their defence, and upon the mere evidence of what short-hand writers thought fit, or were enabled to report, convicted both of them of having committed a contempt of Court.

Now it is not unusual for a Judge to withdraw from the Bench on account of his personal connection with the parties, or some possible bias that may be supposed to exist in his mind in favour of or against one or other of the litigants; and in this case Mr. Justice ARCHIBALD did so withdraw, because he had been engaged as Counsel in the TICHBORNE Case; and there could have been no contempt in suggesting, as the Claimant did, that the Lord Chief Justice having notoriously gone about expressing a decided opinion, and with a strong feeling, against him, should, in deference to the usage in such cases, not preside at his Trial.

When, however, in pursuance of an order of the Court, to which the Lord Chief Justice had been a party, the Claimant and Mr. SKIPWORTH were brought up to receive punishment, was it not, under these circumstances, reasonable to expect that the Lord Chief Justice would himself have been present to explain to them the nature of their offence, and to accept his share of the responsibility of declaring the punishment due to their offences?

The Lord Chief Justice not being present, and no explanation given for his absence, it is not requisite that I should do more than call your attention to the fact, and ask you to discover, if you can, any reason more probable than that the Lord Chief Justice was not prepared to deny that he had done that which the Claimant imputed to him, namely, "prejudiced" him in respect of his forthcoming Trial, and that he was equally unprepared to reconcile with judicial usage and propriety his subsequent zeal in denouncing and punishing others for "prejudicing" the forthcoming Trial.

Is it too much also to suggest that the Court itself felt the force of these circumstances? That they had no disposition to withdraw from that severity of which Mr. ONSLOW and myself had the foretaste is sufficiently shown by their sentence on Mr. SKIPWORTH—but as to the Claimant, how is it possible to reconcile the high compliment expressed by Mr. Justice BLACKBURN, as the President of the Court, that the Claimant had conducted his defence with "great propriety," when the leading feature in that defence was the public arraignment, in the actual presence of the Court, of the Lord Chief Justice for conduct that should disqualify him for adjudicating upon his case?—for it was for that very offence committed at Brighton that he was convicted of contempt by the Lord Chief Justice himself, and then brought up for punishment.

I leave this, with many other questions arising therefrom, to those who have it in charge to protect from the slightest whisper of impeachment the unsullied honour and integrity of Westminster Hall, and to insure such administration there of the law as shall maintain and perpetuate that instinct of reverence for the law which is alike the Honour and the Safety of our country.

Mr. WHALLEY was repeatedly cheered throughout his speech, and at the conclusion a resolution of entire confidence in him as Member for the Borough was unanimously passed.

Mr. WHALLEY was again imprisoned by order of the Court; we append a report from the select committee on privilege, together with the proceedings of the committee, minutes of evidence, and appendix, ordered by the House of Commons to be printed, 31st March, 1874:—

FRIDAY, 20th MARCH, 1874

Ordered, That the letter of the Lord Chief Justice of England to Mr. Speaker, informing the House of the commitment of Mr. WHALLEY, a member of this House, for contempt of Court, be referred to a Select Committee, for the purpose of considering and reporting whether any of the matters referred to therein demand the further attention of the House.

THURSDAY, 26th MARCH 1874.

Ordered, That the Committee do consist of Seventeen Members.

Committee nominated of—

Mr. DISRAELI.	Sir HENRY JAMES.
Mr. GOSCHEN.	Viscount HOLMESDALE.
Mr. Solicitor-General.	Sir EDWARD COLEBROOKE.
Mr. KNATCHBULL-HUGESSEN.	Sir GRAHAM MONTGOMERY.
Mr. SPENCER WALPOLE.	Mr. MASSEY.
Mr. WHITBREAD.	Viscount CRICHTON.
Mr. STEPHEN CAVE.	Mr. Attorney-General
Mr. CHARLES FORSTER.	Mr. ROEBUCK.
Sir SEYMOUR FITZGERALD.	

Ordered, That the Committee have power to send for Persons, Papers, and Records.

Ordered, That Five be the Quorum of the Committee.

TUESDAY, 31st MARCH, 1874.

Ordered, That the Committee have power to report their observations, together with the Minutes of Evidence taken before them, to the House.

REPORT.

The Select Committee on Privilege, to whom was referred the Letter of the Lord Chief Justice of England to Mr. Speaker, informing the House of the Commitment of Mr. WHALLEY, a Member of this House, for contempt of Court, "for the purpose of considering and reporting whether any of the matters referred to therein demand the further attention of the House";——Have considered the matters to them referred, and have agreed to the following Report:—

1. Your Committee have had before them two orders made by the Court of Queen's Bench in the QUEEN versus CASTRO, with the affidavits and exhibits upon which such orders were founded, the first dated the 21st of January, 1874, and the second dated the 23rd of January in the same year.

2. By the first of these orders, Mr. GEORGE HAMMOND WHALLEY, then and now one of the members for Peterborough, was ordered to attend the Court of Queen's Bench to answer for his contempt in writing a letter and statement, which was printed and published in the newspaper called the *Daily News* of the 21st of Jan., 1874.

3. By the second of these orders, Mr. GEORGE HAMMOND WHALLEY was adjudged to be guilty of contempt in having written such letter and statement, and it was thereupon ordered that he should for such contempt pay a fine to the QUEEN of £250, and be imprisoned in Her Majesty's gaol at Holloway until such fine be paid. These orders, and the affidavits and exhibits upon which they were founded, are printed in the Appendix.

4. Your Committee, having had such orders and affidavits proved before them, proceed to afford to Mr. GEORGE HAMMOND WHALLEY, an opportunity of making such observations on the matters referred to them, as he might desire to offer.

5. Mr. GEORGE HAMMOND WHALLEY has put in a written statement, parts of which appear to your Committee to be irrelevant to the specific object of the present inquiry; but your Committee consider that it would not be expedient to omit any portion of what he deemed essential to lay before them.

6. Under all the circumstances of the case, your committee are of opinion that the matters referred to them do not demand the further attention of the House.

7. And your Committee also desire to express their opinion that the Lord Chief Justice fulfilled his duty in informing the House that a member of the House of Commons had been imprisoned by the Court of Queen's Bench.

31st March, 1874.

PROCEEDINGS OF THE COMMITTEE.

FRIDAY, 27th MARCH, 1874.

Members present:—

Mr. SPENCER WALPOLE.	Mr. Attorney-General.
Mr. ROEBUCK.	Sir CHARLES FORSTER.
Mr. KNATCHBULL-HUGESSEN.	Mr. STEPHEN CAVE.
Mr. Solicitor-General.	Mr. MASSEY.
Sir SEYMOUR FITZGERALD.	Sir EDWARD COLEBROOKE.
Sir HENRY JAMES.	Sir GRAHAM MONTGOMERY.
Mr. WHITBREAD.	Viscount CRICHTON.
Viscount HOLMESDALE.	Mr. GOSCHEN.

Mr. SPENCER WALPOLE was called to the Chair.

The Committee deliberated.

The Letter of the Lord Chief Justice of England to Mr. Speaker was read, as follows:

"SIR, "19 March 1874.

"I take the liberty of troubling you with reference to the facts which I am about to bring under your notice. I am not at all sure that I am not troubling you unnecessarily. Should this be so, I trust that my motive will be deemed a sufficient excuse.

"On the 23rd of January last, Mr. GEORGE HAMMOND WHALLEY, then a Member of the late House of Commons, was adjudged by the Court of Queen's Bench, then sitting on the Trial at Bar in the case of the QUEEN v. CASTRO, to have been guilty of a contempt of that Court in having published certain observations on evidence given on that Trial while it was still pending, and for such his Contempt was sentenced to pay a fine to the QUEEN of £250.

"Having in open Court declared his determination not to pay such fine, Mr. WHALLEY was further ordered to be imprisoned till such fine should be paid.

"In conformity with previous precedents, I should have felt myself called upon, as presiding on the occasion in question, to notify to the House of Commons, in the name of the Court, the fact of one of its Members having been thus imprisoned, as soon as the House, which was at the time prorogued, should have been again sitting. But on Monday the 26th of January, Parliament was dissolved by Her Majesty's Royal Proclamation, and in the meantime, Mr. WHALLEY having paid the fine imposed on him was in due course of law discharged.

"The case does not therefore fall within the existing precedents, in each of which the report was made to the House of which the Member imprisoned for Contempt was an actual Member.

"If I rightly apprehend the principle on which Lord Chancellor BROUGHAM, in the case of Mr. WELLESLEY, and Lord Chancellor COTTENHAM, in the case of Mr. CHARLTON, proceeded in reporting to the House of Commons the imprisonment of one of its Members—and I say so after having consulted very high authorities—it was not that there was any doubt of the power of a Court of Justice to commit a Member of the House of Commons for Contempt, but because it was thought right, out of that deference and respect which every Court of Justice would desire to manifest towards the House of Commons, to inform the House of the arrest of one of its Members, and of the reason why the Member so circumstanced was prevented from appearing in his place and discharging his duties as a Member of the House.

"This reason would not appear to apply to a case in which the House of Commons, of which the Member was a component part at the time of his arrest, had ceased to exist before any report could be made, unless, indeed, the party imprisoned having been again elected a Member of a new House of Commons, the imprisonment should be continued, and the Member should be thus prevented from taking his seat, which, however, is not the case in the present instance.

"I am, therefore, disposed to think that I am unnecessarily

troubling you in reporting the imprisonment of Mr. WHALLEY when a Member of the late House of Commons. It has, however, come to my knowledge that a different view of the matter is taken by several present and former Members of the House of Commons, for whose opinions I entertain the highest respect; and as it would be matter of the deepest concern to me that the Court of Queen's Bench should by any possibility be deemed to have been wanting in respect to the House of Commons, I prefer to run the risk of appearing to do that which may be unnecessary, to the possibility of appearing to be wanting in deference to the House.

"I beg, therefore, under the circumstances, to submit the matter to your judgment; and if you should be of opinion that the fact of Mr. WHALLEY's commitment for contempt by the Court of Queen's Bench, when a Member of the late House of Commons, should be notified to the present House, I beg to leave, through you, to communicate the fact with the expression of my profoundest respect for the House.

"I have, &c.
(signed) "A. E. COCKBURN.

"The Right Honourable
The Speaker of the House of Commons,
&c. &c. &c.

[Adjourned till Monday next, at Eleven o'clock.

MONDAY, 30th MARCH, 1874

Members present:—

Mr. SPENCER WALPOLE in the Chair.

Mr. DISRAELI.	Sir SEYMOUR FITZGERALD.
Mr. GOSCHEN.	Sir HENRY JAMES.
Mr. KNATCHBULL-HUGESSEN.	Sir GRAHAM MONTGOMERY.
Mr. WHITBREAD.	Sir EDWARD COLEBROOKE.
Mr. Attorney-General.	Mr. MASSEY.
Mr. Solicitor-General.	Sir CHARLES FORSTER.
Mr. ROEBUCK.	Viscount HOLMESDALE.
Mr. STEPHEN CAVE.	

The Committee deliberated.

Mr. GEORGE HAMMOND WHALLEY, a Member of the House, was examined.

Mr. LUDLOW HANDCOCK was examined.

Motion made, and Question, "That in the opinion of the Committee, the matters referred to in the Lord Chief Justice's letter in the case of the QUEEN versus CASTRO, do not demand the further attention of the House"—(Mr. ROEBUCK)—put, and agreed to.

The Committee deliberated.

[Adjourned till To-morrow, at Two o'clock.

TUESDAY, 31st MARCH, 1874.

Members present:—

Mr. SPENCER WALPOLE in the Chair.

Mr. ROEBUCK.	Mr. MASSEY.
Mr. STEPHEN CAVE.	Mr. DISRAELI.
Sir HENRY JAMES.	Sir SEYMOUR FITZGERALD.
Sir GRAHAM MONTGOMERY.	Viscount CRICHTON.
Mr. WHITBREAD.	Mr. GOSCHEN.
Mr. Solicitor-General.	Sir CHARLES FORSTER.
Sir EDWARD COLEBROOKE.	Mr. Attorney-General.

DRAFT REPORT proposed by the Chairman, read a first time, as follows:—

"The Select Committee on Privilege, to whom was referred the Letter of the Lord Chief Justice of England to Mr. Speaker, informing the House of the Commitment of Mr. WHALLEY, a Member of this House, for contempt of Court, 'for the purpose of considering and reporting whether any of the matters referred to therein demand the further attention of the House;'—Have considered the matters to them referred, and have agreed to the following Report:—

"1. Your Committee have had before them two orders made by the Court of Queen's Bench in the QUEEN versus CASTRO, with the affidavits and exhibits upon which such orders were founded, the first dated the 21st of January, 1874, and the second dated the 23rd of January in the same year.

"2. By the first of these orders, Mr. GEORGE HAMMOND WHALLEY, then and now one of the Members for Peterborough, was ordered to attend the Court of Queen's Bench to answer for his contempt in writing a certain letter and statement, which was printed and published in the newspaper called the *Daily News* of the 21st of January, 1874.

"3. By the second of these orders, Mr. GEORGE HAMMOND WHALLEY was adjudged to be guilty of contempt in having written such letter and statement, and it was thereupon ordered that he should for such contempt pay a fine to the QUEEN of £250, and be imprisoned in Her Majesty's gaol at Holloway until such fine be paid. These orders, and the affidavits and exhibits upon which they were founded, are printed in the Appendix.

"4. Your Committee, having had such orders and affidavits proved before them, proceeded to afford to Mr. GEORGE HAMMOND WHALLEY an opportunity of making such observations on the matters referred to them as he might desire to offer.

"5. Mr. GEORGE HAMMOND WHALLEY has put in a written statement, parts of which appear to your committee to be irrelevant to the specific object of the present inquiry; but your Committee consider that it would not be expedient to omit any portion of what he deemed essential to lay before them.

"6. Under all the circumstances of the case, your Committee are of opinion that the matters referred to them do not demand the further attention of the House."

Draft Report proposed by the Chairman, read a second time, paragraph by paragraph.

Paragraphs 1—6 agreed to.

Amendment proposed, after paragraph 6, to add the following paragraph—"And your Committee also desire to express their opinion that the Lord Chief Justice fulfilled his duty in informing the House that a Member of the House of Commons had been imprisoned by the Court of Queen's Bench"—(Mr. DISRAELI).—Question, That this paragraph be added to the Draft Report,—put, and agreed to.

Question, That the Draft report, as amended, be the report of the Committee to the House,—put, and agreed to.

Ordered, To Report, together with the Minutes of Evidence, and an Appendix.

MINUTES OF EVIDENCE.

MONDAY, 30th MARCH, 1874.

Members present:—

Mr. Attorney-General.	Sir HENRY JAMES.
Mr. STEPHEN CAVE.	Mr. KNATCHBULL-HUGESSEN.
Sir EDWARD COLEBROOKE.	Mr. MASSEY.
Viscount CRICHTON.	Sir GRAHAM MONTGOMERY.
Mr. DISRAELI.	Mr. ROEBUCK.
Sir SEYMOUR FITZGERALD.	Mr. Solicitor-General.
Mr. CHARLES FORSTER.	Mr. WALPOLE.
Mr. GOSCHEN.	Mr. WHITBREAD.
Viscount HOLMESDALE.	

The Right Hon. SPENCER HORATIO WALPOLE, in the chair.

GEORGE HAMMOND WHALLEY, Esq., a Member of the House, examined.

1. Chairman: The Committee has before it, and will have formally proved before it, an Order of the Court of Queen's Bench made on the 21st of January, 1874, referring to certain affidavits, one by Mr. WILLIAM POLLARD, with an exhibit annexed to it, and the other by Mr. FRANK HARRISON HILL; that was an order, I think, requiring you to attend the Court of Queen's Bench to answer for an alleged contempt?—Yes.

2. We have also before us an order, dated Friday, the 23rd of January, 1874, which is an order adjudging you to be guilty of contempt of Court, and ordering that you for that contempt do pay a fine, and in case the fine is not paid, that you be imprisoned until it is. It concludes with these words, "the said GEORGE HAMMOND WHALLEY is now here in Court, committed to the custody of the said gaol at Holloway until he shall have paid the said fine." That order refers to two affidavits, the one by yourself, and the other by Mr. HENRY HOLLINGSWORTH. Those are the only matters that we have before us, and we are now ready to hear any observations that you, as Member for Peterborough, who, I think, stated in the House of Commons that you wished to call the attention of the House to an alleged breach of privilege, have to make upon the subject. Perhaps I might mention to you, with regard to the terms of our Order of Reference, that the letter of the Lord Chief Justice of the Court of Queen's Bench is referred to us, "informing the House of the commitment of Mr. WHALLEY, a Member of this House, for contempt of Court," and we are ordered to "consider and report whether any of the matters referred to therein demands the further attention of the House"?

Mr. WHALLEY: I must ask the indulgence of the Committee to make a short personal explanation. Since the Committee was constituted, I have made every effort in my power to prepare myself to bring before the Committee all that it can be supposed to be properly within my duty or within my power to bring for the assistance of the Committee in considering the important public and constitutional question which has been referred to them. But this has been attended with considerable difficulty on my part, owing, in the first place, to the circumstance of my Counsel, Mr. MORGAN LLOYD, being at the present time on circuit. I then endeavoured to retain the services of Mr. MONTAGUE CHAMBERS, a gentleman well-known to the members of the Committee, but for the same reason I have not been able to do so; and generally, I may say, that being unable to ascertain precisely what were the issues the Committee would consider that it had to try, I have felt myself under considerable difficulty in preparing myself to appear before them to-day, as by the notice which I received on Friday evening, I was desired to do. Under these circumstances I have written out for my own guidance, as far as I could form for myself an idea of what the Committee desired to be informed upon, a statement which is not very long, and would only occupy a few minutes to read. I therefore ask your permission to read that statement to you.

3. You are quite at liberty to do so?——

Mr. WHALLEY then read the following statement:—

"I attend, by invitation of the Committee, prepared to give them all the information at my command in relation to my commitment to prison, as referred to in the letter of the Lord Chief Justice addressed to the Speaker.

"I do not consider that it is competent for me to urge upon the Committee that a violation of the privileges of Parliament has occurred in my case; of that the Committee itself is alone competent to take cognizance; but I submit respectfully that it is essential that they should be fully informed of all the facts and circumstances connected with or leading to my conviction for contempt of Court, and also with the non-payment of the penalty imposed by the Court, and I regret to have occasion to point out that the statement of the Lord Chief Justice, in his letter to the Speaker, does not state those circumstances with the accuracy that might be anticipated.

"It was not for contempt of Court that I was sent to prison; my offence being deemed by the Court not of sufficient gravity for such punishment, as expressly stated by the Lord Chief Justice in his address communicating to me the opinion and sentence of the Court. It was because the Lord Chief Justice thought fit to assume that I would not pay the penalty of £250; and it is also not the fact that I refused so to pay, as alleged by the Lord Chief Justice 'in open court.'

"One of the Masters of the Court, Mr. COCKBURN, informed the Lord Chief Justice that he overhead a communication made by me privately to my Counsel, Mr. MORGAN LLOYD, M.P., to the effect that I would not pay, and thereupon, and refusing peremptorily to hear the explanation I desired to offer, he added to the sentence, as previously pronounced, the alternative of imprisonment.

"What I so stated to my Counsel was, that I was desirous that the conviction should be so recorded as to afford me the opportunity of submitting the same to a higher Court by way of appeal, and that unless this should be conceded, I was unwilling to pay the penalty; believing at the same time that the same would, in such case, be enforced by levy on goods, and that thus might arise some opportunity of discussing again the right of the Court to impose such penalty.

"It is for the Committee to decide whether this discrepancy between the statement of the Lord Chief Justice and the facts of the Case is entitled to their notice, and whether any and what further information is required in relation thereto.

"As to the circumstances which led to my conviction for contempt of Court, I respectfully submit, and I solicit that the Committee should make full inquiry thereon, and for the following reasons:—

"1. Such was the course adopted in the precedents quoted by the Lord Chief Justice, Mr. LONG WELLESLEY, and Mr. LECHMERE CHARLTON, and inasmuch as in my case the contempt arose out of what I deemed to be a part of my duty as a Member of the House, and as this duty was, by the action of the Court on this as on a previous occasion referred to by the Lord Chief Justice as aggravating the present contempt, prevented from being discharged, I submit that the necessity of investigating fully all the circumstances is apparent.

"2. The offence for which, as I understood the address to me in Court by the Lord Chief Justice, was, that in a letter which had been written by me for the information of my constituents, but which was not, in fact, published at all with my knowledge, or by my authority, I expressed my opinion that a portion of the evidence given by a man who had been convicted to take his trial for perjury was true; such expression of opinion being given incidentally in a letter which, in other respects, the Lord Chief Justice recognized as being called for on my part in vindication of my character and conduct, most falsely and most unjustifiably assailed by statements made in a police court by a detective police officer; and I submit that if this be established to the satisfaction of the Committee, it is entitled to notice, in so far as it is plainly an assumption of authority by the Court of Queen's Bench to fine and imprison, which is utterly inconsistent with, and precludes the possibility of, that freedom of speech which is essential for a Member of the House of Commons in his intercourse with his constituents, or with the public, when his conduct or character may be, as in this instance, falsely and unjustifiably assailed. I may add that, so careful was I not to offend, that before sending my letter for publication I submitted it to, and received the approval of, my solicitor.

"3. It appears by the reports of the proceedings, as given in the newspapers, that the Lord Chief Justice thought fit to allude to my conduct and character in terms of rebuke, and in marked disparagement in relation to a prosecution then pending before them; and inasmuch as my conduct in that respect was well known to them to have been taken in discharge of what I deemed to be my duty as a Member of Parliament, in respect of policy which I had repeatedly in the House of Commons protested against as wrongful on the part of Her Majesty's then Government, and involving large expenditure and waste of public money, and abuse of the powers of the Government, I submit that on this ground also the action of the Court may be entitled to notice, as tending to interfere with, and to subject a Member of the House to penalties or affront by the Court of Queen's Bench for his action in Parliament, and thus restrict his independence there. I beg leave to ask the special notice by the Committee of the comments made by the Lord Chief Justice, and the other Judges, as to the part taken by me on behalf of the Defendant, and I submit that it was calculated to prejudice my position in Parliament, and with my constituents, and was not relevant to the question then before the Court, and I am prepared to prove the following facts:—

"That the Lord Chief Justice had himself taken such action, and exercised such influence against the Defendant in the TICHBORNE Case as to demand on his part—after the public protest of the Defendant in open Court, that he was thereby, by the usage of the Bench, disqualified to preside at this Trial—great care.

"That the Lord Chief Justice knew that the part I had taken was so taken by me on public grounds alone, and that, as shown by the correspondence between the Solicitor of the Treasury and myself, published by order of the House of Commons, that I was most anxious to communicate to the Government all the information that reached me, whether for or against the Defendant, confirmed by me on oath when examined as a witness in the cause.

"That the Lord Chief Justice and the other Judges had allowed Mr. HAWKINS, as Counsel for the prosecution, to impute to me complicity with witnesses, and other discreditable acts, which Mr. HAWKINS undertook to justify by evidence, but did not do so, nor even put any questions to me thereon when I was examined as a witness; thus, as I submit, showing that the object of the Lord Chief Justice, in the remarks made by him, were deliberately intended to disparage me in the estimation of my constituents and the public, and thus interfere most prejudicially, and without any justification from the question on which he had judicially to decide, with the discharge of my duties as a Member of the House of Commons.

"4. What may be the operation in the future, and by way of precedent, of now passing over, without protest, the action of the Court of Queen's Bench, as before mentioned, may best be estimated by ascertaining what has been on the present occasion its operation and effect; and for this reason, therefore, I submit that the circumstances should be fully investigated. The Government having instituted a prosecution, suggested by the late Chief Justice of the Common Pleas, upon the assent of the then Attorney-General, who subsequently, in the House of Commons, admitted that he was not impartial, and withdrew from responsibility for the conduct of such prosecution, and they were therefore in a position that rendered it of political importance to them that the result should, by the conviction of the Defendant, justify the enormous expenditure that they have had to incur.

"The Court of Queen's Bench was then called upon by the Government to exercise powers for suppression of public discussion in speech and writing in reference to this Trial (in itself altogether unprecedented in many of its features), which have never before been exercised by the Court, or even asked for, either in civil or criminal cases, during legal history.

"And further, it will appear that the direct and immediate effect of this suppression of public discussion, so asked for on the part of the Government, and enforced by the Court of Queen's Bench, has been to prevent the Defendant in the said Trial from bringing forward a very large amount of evidence which he would have been enabled to produce if he had not been deprived, as in fact he was, by the action of the Court of Queen's Bench, of the means of paying the costs of witnesses, and other expenses necessary for his defence; and on this point I have to inform the Committee that the number of witnesses which he was then prevented from calling was about 200; and that in other respects his defence was materially impaired by reason of this unprecedented conduct of the Government in asking for suppression of public meetings, and of free discussion in speech or writing, whereby such money as was required up to the time of such suppression was provided, and would, it is reasonable to expect, have continued to be so but for such suppression.

"The appeal to the public for money for the defence was originated and mainly sustained by myself and Mr. ONSLOW, at the time Member for Guildford, and it will appear on my own part that I was acting in the discharge of what I believed to be a paramount public duty, and from no other motive or inducement whatever, and in which I have expended myself a large sum of money, and devoted thereto much time and consideration."

"5. In so far as such inquiry into the circumstances as above suggested may appear to be beyond the question of privilege as raised by the letter of the Lord Chief Justice, I respectfully refer to the terms of reference to this Committee, as also to the fact that this Committee has been specially appointed to consider all that may demand the attention of the House, and that this course was deliberately adopted instead of the ordinary course of referring the matter to a Committee of Privilege; and I submit that this does admit of this Committee extending its inquiry as to circumstances beyond the immediate question of my commitment to prison on the 23rd of January last, and I beg here humbly to express my opinion, founded on an intimate knowledge of those circumstances, that it will be found to be of the utmost public importance that the same should be fully investigated, and if the Committee should think that they are not authorized by the present terms of reference to investigate those circumstances, then, under such amended and additional instruction as this Committee may deem requisite, and that they should for that purpose ask the House for an order to enable it fully to inform the House as to whether the letter of the Lord Chief Justice does or does not demand further attention."

4. *Chairman*: Have you any further observations to make to the Committee?—Yes; I would ask leave to state that I hold in my hand a reprint of an address which I had occasion to make to my constituents in the month of February last; and I refer to it in order to justify, in some degree, some of the suggestions which I have ventured to offer in the paper which I have now read to the Committee. This is a speech which I made to my constituents shortly after my being fined in the month of January for contempt of Court, and it is so far connected with this present inquiry, or with my commitment to prison in February, that the Lord Chief Justice referred to the conduct of the Court, and to my conduct on that occasion, as aggravating very materially the offence for which I was then brought before them. This speech

lays the whole matter before my constituents, as far as I was at liberty to do so, and if I were to read it, or if the Committee would be pleased at their leisure to read it, they would see that I felt it exceedingly difficult to address my constituents on the subject, or to communicate with anybody, in fact, on these public matters, lest I might unwittingly come under the penalties which were so often threatened and so repeatedly enforced by the Court with a view to a complete suppression of discussion, whether in speech or in writing, with reference to this Case; the direct and immediate object and effect being, as I venture to allege with the utmost confidence, and as I shall be able to satisfy the Committee by evidence of the effect there can be no doubt, to prevent the Defendant's obtaining means for his defence. I state that, because I felt it so strongly, that I addressed a letter to the Lord Chief Justice, pointing out exactly how the matter stood in that respect: and I addressed the Government also, offering to them full information with regard to my visit to America, or any other efforts that I made. The fact of my offering to them all the information at my command shows, I think, that I was actuated by no other motive whatever (not even by any personal feeling with regard to the Defendant) except to insure such a fair trial as should be satisfactory to the public mind, and, among others, to my constituents. It may afford some idea of the state of terrorism to which the country has continued to be subjected since the month of February, if I add that, desiring to have this speech reprinted, I could not succeed in obtaining that except by giving security to the amount of £1,500 for any penalties that might result from the republication of a speech which I felt it necessary to address to my constituents; and when it was reprinted, such was the influence of this terrorism, with respect to which it would appear, if it could be made known to the Committee, as I believe I shall be able to make it known to the Committee, that nothing to the same extent has happened within, I may say, recent centuries; I say such was the influence of this terrorism, that after this speech of mine was reprinted, although it was but a fair statement of the facts and of my opinions upon the subject, it was considered to be so attended with risk in the circulation that no one could be induced to sell it. There has been, therefore, a complete suppression of public discussion, whether in speech or in writing, upon this subject. It was known to the Court of Queen's Bench that that suppression had the effect of depriving the Defendant of the means of completing his defence. Those means I am prepared to state, of my own personal knowledge, which he was thus deprived of amounted to at least 200 witnesses.

5. I think you cannot fail to see that that is a matter which we cannot go into here under the terms of the reference now before us?—I felt the danger and difficulty, and I made every endeavour to avoid that rock of entering upon the TICHBORNE Case. I desire only to bring before you what is really within your cognizance. I only refer to this matter, as I stated in my paper, in so far as this, that in this particular case a most grave and serious miscarriage of justice, as I believe, and as millions of other people believe, has resulted from the action of the Court of Queen's Bench in regard to contempt of Court which has reached, fortunately or unfortunately, according to the view which this Committee may take of it, a Member of Parliament, and has therefore brought you into existence as a Court of Appeal from the Court of Queen's Bench on this matter, there being no other Court of Appeal. I mention these circumstances as showing the great danger almost to tranquility, certainly to the public confidence, in the fair administration of justice which may result from the unlicensed and unprecedented exercise by the Court of Queen's Bench of a power which was never asked for until it was asked for by Her Majesty's late Government, and conceded without anything approaching to a precedent by the Court of Queen's Bench. That has been the result in this case, and the circumstance that a Member of Parliament has become involved in these difficulties, affords to this Committee, I humbly submit, an opportunity of taking up the matter and investigating the question, not merely as it regards a Member of their own House, but also as it regards the public at large. I have to thank you for the manner in which you have heard me.

6. You have no further observations which you wish to address to the Committee?—No. I will only add that I have my solicitor in attendance, with all the papers and documents that I could collect at the moment.

Mr. LUDLOW HANBECK, called in, and Examined.

7. Chairman: Are you an officer of the Court of Queen's Bench? I am.

8. What is the character of your office?—I am a clerk in the Crown Office.

9. As a clerk in the Crown Office, I presume you would be in possession of the orders made by the Court?—Yes.

10. Have you an order of the court, or an office copy of an order of the Court, made by the Court of Queen's Bench, in the case of the QUEEN *v.* CASTRO, bearing date 21st of January, 1874?—I have. I produce it (*producing the same*).

11. Is that an order requiring Mr. WHALLEY to appear, and answer for an alleged contempt of Court?—It is.

12. Will you hand it in? (*The same was handed in, vide Appendix.*)

13. Are there any affidavits referred to in that order?—Yes, two.

14. Have you those affidavits?—I have them (*producing the same*).

15. Will you put them in? (*The same were handed in, vide Appendix.*)

16. Have you another order of the Court made on the 23rd of January, 1874?—I have (*producing the same*).

17. Was that an order for the committal of Mr. WHALLEY for contempt of Court to prison?—It was an order to pay a fine of £250, and to be imprisoned until that fine was paid.

18. Will you put it in? (*The same was handed in, vide Appendix.*)

19. Did that order refer to any affidavits?—Yes, to two.

20. Do you produce those affidavits?—Yes, I produce those two affidavits (*producing the same*).

21. Will you hand them in? (*The same were handed in, vide Appendix.*)

22. Where there any exhibits annexed to the affidavits to which these orders of the Court referred?—There were.

23. Will you hand them in?—I have handed in the affidavits with the exhibits annexed to them.

APPENDIX.

Wednesday, the 21st day of January, in the 37th Year of the Reign of QUEEN VICTORIA.

IN THE QUEEN'S BENCH.

Middlesex. The QUEEN *v.* THOMAS CASTRO, otherwise ARTHUR ORTON, otherwise Sir ROGER CHARLES DOUGHTY TICHBORNE, Baronet.

Upon reading the affidavits of WILLIAM HENRY POLLARD, and the exhibits thereto annexed, and FRANK HARRISON HILL, and the exhibits thereto annexed. It is ordered, that GEORGE HAMMOND WHALLEY, Esq., Member of Parliament, do attend this Court on Friday, 23rd day of January instant, by 10 of the clock in the forenoon, peremptorily to answer for his contempt in writing a certain letter and statement which was printed and published in the newspaper called the *Daily News* of the 21st of January 1874.

Upon notice of this rule to be given to the said GEORGE HAMMOND WHALLEY in the meantime.

On the Motion of Mr. HAWKINS,
By the Court.

IN THE QUEEN'S BENCH.

The QUEEN against THOMAS CASTRO otherwise called ARTHUR ORTON, otherwise called Sir ROGER CHARLES DOUGHTY TICHBORNE, Baronet.

I, WILLIAM HENRY POLLARD, one of the Clerks in the Solicitor's Department of the Treasury, make oath, and say,—

1. That the original letter of Mr. WHALLEY to Mr. HENDRICKS (formerly the solicitor for the above Defendant in this prosecution of the 28th August, 1873, a printed copy whereof is hereunto annexed, marked A.), is, I believe, now in the possession of the said Mr. HENDRICKS, who has shown the same to me, and has furnished me with a copy thereof.

2. The said original letter is in the handwriting of Mr. GEORGE HAMMOND WHALLEY, Member of Parliament, of Plas Madoc, Ruabon, as I have been informed and believe.

W. H. POLLARD.

Sworn at Westminster Hall, in the county of Middlesex,
this 21st day of January 1873, before me,
W. E. COE,
A Commissioner, &c.

(A.)

THE TICHBORNE TRIAL.

TO THE EDITOR OF THE "DAILY NEWS."

Sir,—I ask the favour of your insertion of the copy of my letter to the Defendant's solicitor, as written on my way home from America. It was only on Saturday last that I became informed that a copy of this letter has been in the hands of the Solicitor of the Treasury, and the ground on which I now ask for its publication is, that the Lord Chief Justice stated, when I was in the witness-box, that it would be material to show that the prosecution knew the result of my inquiries in America. I was unable, in reply to his Lordship's question, then to say more than that I had from the first pressed upon the Solicitor of the Treasury to accept information of every fact and circumstance that from time to time might come to my knowledge, whether for or against the Defendant, and that he had persistently refused to do so. As the statements of Detective CLARKE of what JEAN LUIE has told him (though denied, as it seems, by LUIE himself) may materially prejudice the Trial, I consider that I am called upon to state that nothing that has occurred in relation to this man affects my belief that his evidence as to the "Osprey" is substantially true.

I am, &c.

London, 20 January, 1874. (signed) G. H. WHALLEY.

COPY.

R.M.S.S. "Scotia," at Sea,
A. HENDRIKS, Esq.— 28 August, 1873.

Dear Sir—I forward to you, with this, a detailed report of the result of my visit to America. It is in a very rough state, having been written out on my voyage (rather a rough one) coming home; but I hope it may be made out for copy. The question, I presume, is, whether JOHN LEWIS's evidence is sufficiently confirmed to justify counsel in calling him at once as a witness, without waiting for such corroborative evidence, as is available in America, and I am most strongly of opinion that he should be so called.

The grounds for this opinion, stated fully in my report, may be summarized thus :—

1. It is not possible to collect or raise and transmit to England any such corroborative evidence, except at a preliminary cost in the employment of lawyers and others agency, involving immediate provision of several hundred pounds.

2. No evidence has been found by me as to the departure of the "Osprey" from Sandy Hook, nor as to her officers and crew, that would meet the requirements specified by Mr. M'Mahon in his memorandum of instructions that would be worth bringing over.

3. There is, however, in a great number of circumstantial facts, sufficient to confirm the story of John Lewis, and to show that he is an honest witness on the main fact of rescuing the "Bella's" crew, and for using his evidence in corroboration of existing testimony as to the arrival of the "Osprey" at Melbourne with "Bella's" crew in 1854, and generally of the other evidence of identity of Defendant.

If the Jury believe this evidence it explains, by sunstroke, the eccentricity of conduct on part of Defendant, and defective memory, and thus disposes of much of the circumstantial evidence against him, and, in fact, settles the question ; and if they do not believe him, it cannot prejudice the defence, unless they also believe that John Lewis has been deliberately suborned to invent a false story ; and apart from the absence of any proof of such conspiracy on part of Defendant and his friends, the fact of my visit to America, and that in many essential particulars Lewis's story is consistent, and in none contradicted (the negative evidence as to "Osprey" admitting of many explanations more reasonable than that John Lewis should have invented such a ship for the purpose of deception), all this is conclusive that the Defendant and his friends have been no party to such invention, and therefore, the defence in other respects would not be prejudiced even though John Lewis should not be believed.

I shall be glad to receive from you, as soon as possible, a fair copy for correction, and am prepared to substantiate and give any further explanation that may be required in my report.

Yours truly,

Address, Plas Madoc, Ruabon. G. H. Whalley.

This is the document marked (A.), mentioned and referred to in the affidavit of William Henry Pollard, sworn before me this 21st day of January, 1874. W. E. Coe,
A Commissioner, &c.

In the Queen's Bench.

The Queen against Thomas Castro, otherwise called Arthur Orton, otherwise called Sir Roger Charles Doughty Tichborne, Baronet.

I, Frank Harrison Hill, of 3, Morpeth-terrace, Victoria-street, Westminster, in the county of Middlesex, Editor of the *Daily News* newspaper, make oath and say,

1. That the printed slip hereunto annexed, marked A, was received by me on Tuesday evening, the 20th January, 1874, at the office of the newspaper, No. 20, Bouverie-street, Fleet-street, London.

2. That it was inclosed in an envelope, which I believe came from Mr. Whalley, and in consequence of that belief I sent the slip forward for publication, having first struck out the first paragraph of the letter, as appears by the said printed slip marked (A.)

3. I had no intention of committing any contempt of this Honourable Court, and if by the publication of it I have committed a contempt, I extremely regret having done so.

Frank H. Hill.

Sworn at Westminster Hall, in the county of Middlesex, this 21st day of Jan. 1874, before me,
W. E. Coe,
A Commissioner, &c.

(A.)

The Tichborne Trial.

To the Editor of the "Daily News."

Sir,—I ask the favour of you insertion of the copy of my letter to the Defendant's solicitor, as written on my way home from America. It was only on Saturday last that I became informed that a copy of this letter has been in the hands of the Solicitor of the Treasury, and the ground on which I now ask for its publication is that the Lord Chief Justice stated when I was in the witness-box, that it would be material to show that the prosecution knew the result of my inquiries in America. I was unable to reply to his Lordship's question then to say more than that I had from the first pressed upon the Solicitor of the Treasury to accept information of every fact and circumstance that from time to time might come to my knowledge whether for or against the Defendant, and that he had persistently refused to do so.

As the statements of Detective Clarke of what Jean Luie has told him, though denied as it seems by Luie himself, may materially prejudice the trial, I consider that I am called upon to state that nothing that has occurred in relation to this man affects my belief that his evidence as to the "Osprey" is substantially true. I am, &c.

London, 20th January, 1874. (Signed) G. H. Whalley.

(Copy.)

A. Hendricks, Esq., R.M.S.S. "Scotia," at Sea.
28th August, 1874.

Dear Sir,—I forward to you with this a detailed report of the result of my visit to America. It is in a very rough state, having been written out on my voyage (rather a rough one) coming home, but I hope it may be made out for copy.

The question, I presume, is whether John Lewis's evidence is sufficiently confirmed to justify Counsel in calling him at once as a witness, without waiting for such corroborative evidence as is available in America, and I am most strongly of opinion that he should be so called.

The grounds for this opinion, stated fully in my report, may be summarized thus :—

1. It is not possible to collect or raise and transmit to England any such corroborative evidence, except at a preliminary cost, in the employment of lawyers and other agency, involving immediate provision of several hundred pounds.

2. No evidence has been found by me as to the departure of the "Osprey" from Sandy Hook, nor as to her officers and crew, that would meet the requirements specified by Mr. M'Mahon in his memorandum of instructions that would be worth bringing over.

3. There is, however, in a great number of circumstantial facts, sufficient to confirm the story of John Lewis, and to show that he is an honest witness on the main fact of rescuing the "Bella's" crew, and for using his evidence in corroboration of existing testimony as to the arrival of the "Osprey" at Melbourne with "Bella's" crew in July, 1854, and generally of the other evidence of identity of Defendant.

4. If jury believe this evidence, it explains, by sunstroke, the eccentricity of conduct on part of Defendant, and defective memory, and thus disposes of much of the circumstantial evidence against him, and in fact settles the question, and if they do not believe him it cannot prejudice the defence unless they also believe that John Lewis has been deliberately suborned to invent a false story, and apart from the absence of any proof of such conspiracy on part of Defendant and his friends, the fact of my visit to America, and that in many essential particulars Lewis's story is consistent, and in none contradicted (the negative evidence as to "Osprey" admitting of many explanations more reasonable than that John Lewis should have *invented* such a ship for the purpose of deception) all this is conclusive that the Defendant and his friends have been no party to such invention, and therefore the defence in other respects would not be prejudiced, even though John Lewis should not be believed.

I shall be glad to receive from you, as soon as possible, a fair copy for correction, and am prepared to substantiate and give any further explanation that may be required in my report. Yours truly,

Address, Plas Madoc, Ruabon. (Signed) G. H. Whalley.

This is the document marked A., mentioned and referred to in the affidavit of Frank Harrison Hill, sworn before me this 21st day of January, 1873. W. E. Coe, Commissioner.

Friday, the 23rd day of January, in the 37th year of the reign of Queen Victoria.

Middlesex.—The Queen v Thomas Castro, otherwise Arthur Orton, otherwise Sir Roger Charles Doughty Tichborne, Baronet.

George Hammond Whalley, Esq., Member of Parliament, being present here in Court, upon reading the several affidavits of the said George Hammond Whalley and Henry Hollingsworth, and upon hearing Mr. Morgan Lloyd of Counsel on his behalf, and Mr. Hawkins of Counsel from the Crown, it is considered and adjudged by this Court here, that he, the said George Hammond Whalley, is guilty of contempt of this Court in having written a certain letter and statement, which was printed and published in the newspaper called the *Daily News*, of the 21st day of January, 1874, and it is thereupon ordered, that he, the said George Hammond Whalley, for the contempt aforesaid, do pay a fine to our Sovereign Lady the Queen of £250 of lawful money of Great Britian, and that he be imprisoned in Her Majesty's goal at Holloway until such fine be paid.

And the said George Hammond Whalley is now here in Court committed to the custody of the said gaol at Holloway until he shall have paid the said fine. By the Court—

The said George Hammond Whalley to be placed in the first class of misdemeanants.

In the Queen's Bench.

In the Matter of George Hammond Whalley, Esq.,
Ex-parte Regina v. Castro.

I, George Hammond Whalley, of Plas Madoc, Ruabon, in the county of Denbigh, Esq., make oath, and say,

1. I have been informed by reading the same in the daily newspapers of the 22nd of January, that on the 21st instant, it was ordered by this honourable Court that a rule should be drawn up calling upon me to appear and answer for a contempt of this Honourable Court, and that such order was made upon a statement by Mr. Hawkins that he had an affidavit of the Editor of the *Daily News*, who produced the original of what was referred to, and declared that the letter was inclosed in an envelope which he believed came from me, and that in consequence of that belief he sent the slip forward for publication,

having first struck out the first paragraph of the letter as appeared by the printed slip marked A, and also an affidavit of Mr. POLLARD, stating that the original letter of Mr. WHALLEY to Mr. HENDRICKS (formerly solicitor for the Defendant), of the 28th day of August, 1873, a printed copy whereof was thereto annexed, marked A, is now in the possession of the said Mr. HENDRICKS, and is in my handwriting.

2. With reference to the aforesaid statement of the Editor of the *Daily News*, I say that I have never sent any letter, or envelope, or slip to the Editor of the *Daily News*, nor did I know of any such being sent to him by any one on my behalf, or by my authority, or at my request, or have I any knowledge whatever as to the letter in the *Daily News* referred to in these proceedings, otherwise or to any other or further extent than is hereinafter set forth.

3. I have this day for the first time read the said letter in the *Daily News*, addressed to the Editor thereof, and also the letter dated the 28th August, 1873, addressed to A. HENDRICKS, formerly solicitor for the Defendant, and I say as to the letter so addressed to the Editor of the *Daily News*, that it is a portion of a letter which was written by me on Tuesday, the 20th January instant, which I delivered to Mr. HENRY HOLLINSWORTH, the publisher of the *Peterborough Times*, for insertion in that newspaper, if on reading the same he saw no objection to such publication.

4. And I further say, that in so far as I may be considered to be responsible for having written the letter dated the 20th instant, or under the circumstances before stated for the same having been published in the *Daily News*, as aforesaid, it was not my intention to prejudice the trial now pending in this honourable Court, nor the trial of JEAN LUIE, nor in any respect whatever to commit any contempt of this Court, but my sole object and purpose in writing such letter and publishing the same, together with my letter to Mr. HENDRICKS, of 28th August, 1873, was to do that which I was advised and believed to be absolutely essential for the vindication of my conduct and character in relation to JEAN LUIE, and the evidence given by him in the cause now pending in this honourable Court, under the circumstances hereinafter set forth.

5. On the 8th of January instant the said JEAN LUIE was brought up on remand at Bow-street Police Court, and evidence was then and there given against him on the charge of perjury, on which he had been committed, and the first witness called, as I believe, was GEORGE CLARKE, the chief officer of the detective police force, and he stated that the said JEAN LUIE had informed him that I had met him in Brussels in the spring of the year 1873, and had then and there suggested to him and requested him to give evidence on behalf of the Defendant in the TICHBORNE Case, and also that I was by such and similar conduct engaged in promoting the defence, it being arranged between the said Defendant and myself that, in the event of his recovering his estates, I was, with others who were named by him, to have a portion of such estates in recompense for my services, and I say that it is not true that I ever met the said JEAN LUIE in Brussels or elsewhere, or ever saw or heard of him until the 7th of July last, when he stated in my presence the evidence he was prepared to give on behalf of the Defendant, and which evidence he did subsequently give in the same words or to the same effect as he so spoke on the said 7th of July, and I say that I never again exchanged one word, as I verily believe, and speaking to the best of my recollection, with the said JEAN LUIE on the subject of his evidence, before the same was given by him in this honourable Court, except on two occasions, namely, on being about to visit New York for the purpose of making inquiry, with a view to the corroboration or contradiction of the said JEAN LUIE, on or about the 26th day of July, when the said JEAN LUIE gave the various names of persons and places whereto such inquiry should be directed, and also letters to some of such persons; and the second occasion was after my return from America, when the only subject spoken of between us was in reference to the port at which, as he alleged, he became one of the crew of the ship "Osprey," and which, as I believe, had been written down by me in the memoranda made at my previous interview as New Bedford, whereas it should have been, as stated to me at this second interview with JEAN LUIE, New Orleans. And I further say that the statement alleged by the said GEORGE CLARKE to have been made by JEAN LUIE, so far as the same refers to me, is utterly untrue.

6. That since the appearance in the newspapers of the report of the said evidence of GEORGE CLARKE, I have been frequently applied to by many of my constituents and others for a public refutation of such statements, and being wholly at a loss how to vindicate my character from the foul aspersions and false charges made against me as aforesaid otherwise than by publishing, for the benefit of my constituents, the said letter of August the 26th, as a proof of my *bona fide* belief, at the time when it was written, that the evidence proposed to be given by the said JEAN LUIE in relation to the "Osprey" was true, and to show that there was no foundation for the accusation made against me in the evidence of the said GEORGE CLARKE, and my said letter, although originally written for the *Times* newspaper, was subsequently, and after consultation with my solicitor, taken by me to the said local paper, with the intention of being there inserted for the information of my constituents.

7. That I desire to express my most sincere regret for anything I may have done in relation to the said matter, which can be construed into a contempt of this honourable Court, and beg to tender to your Lordships my humble apologies for the same.

8. That I have not, and never had, the slightest interest present or prospective, in the issue of the Case now pending in this honourable Court, and all the expenses of and incident to my visit to New York, and every other cost and outlay which I have incurred in relation to this Case for about four years past have been borne solely by myself, and at my own charge.

9. I have been repeatedly referred to in the course of this Trial by Mr. HAWKINS as having tampered with, and improperly procured, evidence on the part of the Defendant, and I say that having submitted myself as a witness, no questions were asked to justify such imputations, or to afford me the opportunity of replying thereto, and on that account also this correspondence complained of appeared to me to be requisite.

G. H. WHALLEY.

Sworn at Westminster Hall, in the county of Middlesex, this 23rd day of January, 1874, before me,
W. E. COE,
A Commissioner, &c.

IN THE QUEEN'S BENCH.

In the Matter of GEORGE HAMMOND WHALLEY, Esq.

Ex-parte REGINA *v.* CASTRO.

I, HENRY HOLLINGSWORTH, of No. 1, High Holborn, in the County of Middlesex, Printer and Publisher, make oath, and say,—

1. That I have for forty years carried on the business of a printer and publisher, and am the printer and publisher, and chief proprietor of the *Peterborough Times* newspaper, which is a weekly newspaper, published on Saturdays, and the business of the said newspaper is carried on at my office and printing establishment, No. 1, High Holborn.

2. On Tuesday, the 20th instant, Mr. WHALLEY called at my office about one o'clock, and handed to me a letter, with a copy of another letter, referred to therein, and asked me to read the same, and if I saw no objection thereto, that he should be much obliged if I would insert the same in the next issue of the *Peterborough Times*.

3. I accordingly printed the said letters for publication in the *Peterborough Times*, and sent a slip proof of same to the Editor of the *Daily News*, and I felt justified in sending a slip proof of such letters to that newspaper, and also, in the event of their not inserting it, to other papers; acting, as I did, on the belief that Mr. WHALLEY would not object to the said letters being published in any one or all of the London papers, though I had no authority or directions from Mr. WHALLEY to do so.

4. I further say, that in sending such slip copies, with a letter of request for insertion, I acted entirely upon my own responsibility and discretion, but I did so under the firm belief that such publication could be no breach of the rules of this honourable Court in relation to contempt, and I had no intention whatever of committing such contempt, either by sending the said slip for publication, as aforesaid, or by the intended publication in the *Peterborough Times*.

5. I further say that having seen a report in the newspapers of what took place in this honourable Court with reference to this matter at the sitting of the Court yesterday, I at once gave orders that the said letters should not be inserted in the *Peterborough Times*, as originally intended, and I desire to express my regret for having been the cause of the said publication, and beg to tender to this honourable Court my humble apologies for the same.

HENRY HOLLINGSWORTH.

Sworn at No. 12, Serjeant's Inn, Fleet-street, in the City of London, this 22nd day of January, 1874, before me,
JAMES PRICE,
A London Commissioner to administer Oaths in the Court of Queen's Bench.

It was soon after these proceedings that the name of Dr. KENEALY was first suggested to the Claimant and Lord RIVERS by persons high in the confidence of each. Dr. KENEALY has given an account of the first introduction of the Claimant to him, in his well known Lecture; and as we shall probably wind up this Report of the TICHBORNE Trial with that Lecture, our readers must defer their curiosity until then. The active hostility perpetually exhibited against Sir ROGER seemed to Dr. KENEALY fitting to be met by no feeble resistance. Accordingly, on the first day of Easter Term (April 16), he made an application to the Court against the publisher of a most harmful book, which the Family, their agents and friends, had circulated, it is said to the amount of 20,000 copies, and which Messrs. SMITH & SON, the extensive Newsagents, had sold at all their bookstalls, though they were not equally liberal to those who represent the Claimant's side. We append the report of

DR. KENEALY'S MOTION FOR CONTEMPT.

COURT OF QUEEN'S BENCH, WESTMINSTER, APRIL 16, 1873.

(Sittings in Banco, before the Lord Chief Justice, Justice BLACKBURN, Justice MELLOR, and Justice QUAIN.)

This being the first day of Term, the above mentioned Judges took their seats upon the Bench.

IN THE MATTER OF THE "TICHBORNE CASE."

An application was made by Counsel on behalf of the Claimant against Mr. GEORGE ROUTLEDGE, of the well-known firm of

ROUTLEDGE & SONS, publishers, to answer for an alleged contempt in publishing a book last year entitled the "Tichborne Romance." The preface begins thus:—

"The TICHBORNE Case forms an epoch in the moral and legal history of England. It has weighed upon the public mind like an incubus. Nobody could make out head or tail of it in its conception and in its progress. It was either a great wrong suffered, or a portentous fraud concocted. Even at the present moment there are some who can't see their way through it. The fact is people had neither the time nor the inclination to wade through the enormous mass of daily reports, and so contented themselves with what they 'heard;' some saying 'He must be the man,' others 'He is an impostor.' This little book is intended to give a succinct account and comprehensive idea of this immense transaction." . . . .

"'Substantially,' as the Lord Chief Justice said, 'the finding of the jury is a verdict for the Defendant. In the opinion of the jury his Lordship entirely concurred, and it appeared to him that the plaintiff had been guilty of wilful and corrupt perjury.' He was therefore committed on that charge and ordered to be prosecuted under the name of THOMAS CASTRO, falsely calling himself Sir ROGER CHARLES TICHBORNE. To those who still believe the prisoner in Newgate is the man we can only address the words of the Attorney-General:—'Is it to be expected in the TICHBORNE Case that people are to take leave of their senses? I never heard a person say you are to believe a thing because it is improbable.' 'You heap monstrous improbability upon monstrous improbability, and the monstrous nature of each of them is the reason why we should swallow them all, though they are beyond the reach of human probability.' The object of this compilation is to establish that proposition for the comprehension of all readers.

"Something of the kind has been rendered necessary by the audacity with which the prisoner has dared to appeal to the nation for assistance! This is an additional outrage on public morality. The man not only acknowledged himself a barefaced liar in the witness-box, not only admitted that he had raised

DR. KENEALY.

money on a fictitious will, and wrote letters which he falsely declared to be forgeries; not only confessed to other evil doings, but also most foully slandered a lady in open Court, standing beside her husband. He has done, according to his motto, what a man 'with plenty brains and no money' can do with 'men who has plenty of money and no brains.'"

Dr. KENEALY, Q. C. (with him Mr. M'MAHON), now moved, he said, that Mr. ROUTLEDGE be called upon peremptorily to answer for contempt committed in the publication of the book.

Justice BLACKBURN: On whose behalf do you apply?

Dr. KENEALY: I hardly know whether I ought to apply on behalf of the Court or on behalf of Sir ROGER TICHBORNE.

Justice BLACKBURN: Surely you know whether you apply only as *amicus curiæ* or on behalf of anyone else?

Dr. KENEALY: I am instructed on behalf of Sir ROGER TICHBORNE. The book was published last year, but he did not become aware of it until February last after the proceedings against him for contempt, and therefore he did not mention it then as he mentioned other publications against him. He complained of it as one of the most scandalous and atrocious libels ever published, and as calculated to make the strongest impression on the minds of the jurors that he is an impostor, and also to deter witnesses from appearing on his behalf.

The Lord Chief Justice: Does it allude to the coming Trial?

Dr. KENEALY: Not expressly.

The Lord Chief Justice: Does it comment upon the past Trial, or enter into the question of perjury to be tried in the ensuing Trial?

Dr. KENEALY: It professes to show that he was an impostor and a perjurer—

The Lord Chief Justice: There is a right of comment upon a trial which has been concluded. There is such a right in public journals for instance; and it may be questioned whether such comments, if not unfair, will amount to libel or contempt. But if, there being a prosecution for perjury arising out of the former trial, comments upon the past trial are made the occasion of observations intended to prejudice the defendants in the coming trial, then that is a contempt.

Dr. KENEALY: That is the way in which we put it. (He then read the preface of the book.)

Justice BLACKBURN: There is a great difference between libel and contempt. We don't interfere on the ground of contempt unless there is an intention to prejudice pending proceedings. There does not yet appear anything of that kind in this publication.

Dr. KENEALY proceeded to read various passages to support his view:—

"The supporters of the Claimant began to wax numerous and apparently important. Carter, an old trooper, joined him, and became a most important auxiliary. A few weeks after CARTER is recognized by another old soldier, who had been ROGER's regimental servant. Previously the Claimant had shirked or blundered about military matters, but now he plunged boldly into ROGER's military history, and converted military witnesses by his wonderful knowledge of minute incidents. He has names, dates, and incidents at his fingers' ends. At first he begins with the privates. CARTER spends a day at Sandhurst, standing beer to his former comrades, gossiping with them about old days and preparing them for a meeting with the Claimant. Separate interviews were arranged; the Claimant received each man as an old friend, and went through the familiar stories. Next there was an expedition to Colchester, with similar proceedings, and afer that visits to various barracks in the North of England. CARTER was an active missionary; there was plenty of beer flowing, and an occasional distribution of half-crowns. One man bought over another; and the Claimant collected not only witnesses but information. When he found that he had got a good hold on the privates, he tackled the officers, and won over four or five who had no idea how the twigs had been limed for them. The interviews were always prearranged. As the ball rolled it gathered bulk. The affidavits of the witnesses who were first secured proved a fruitful nest-egg. They were cleverly concocted, and circulated among people it was desired to catch (207)."

These were observations upon the evidence of the witnesses for the Claimant at the last Trial who would probably be witnesses at the next, and it was on that very ground the Court granted the proceedings against the Claimant and his friend.

Justice MELLOR: It appears as if the sense of the observations were aimed rather at the subscriptions in aid of the Claimant than at the ensuing Trial.

Dr. KENEALY: That was the excuse urged on the last occasion, but it was urged in vain.

Justice MELLOR: These comments were made on the testimony of witnesses.

Dr. KENEALY: So here.

Justice BLACKBURN: There the object was to influence popular opinion, and so to interfere with the course of justice; and if you can show that such is the case here you would make out a case. But it is not a mere libel which will justify our summary interposition.

Justice MELLOR: It is of the utmost importance to draw the distinction between libel and contempt.

Justice QUAIN: Does not your contention come to this—that whenever, after a Trial is over, a prosecution for perjury is pending which has arisen out of it, there can be no right of comment upon the former Trial?

Dr. KENEALY: No, that is not my contention. I admit the right of fair comment.

Justice MELLOR: If it is fair comment it is no libel.

Dr. KENEALY: Surely it is going far beyond fair comment to suggest that a man about to be tried for perjury is an impostor and a perjurer.

Justice BLACKBURN said he found from the affidavits that the publication was at an end. That being so, though there might be ground for a prosecution for libel, what ground was there for a proceeding for contempt? A proceeding for contempt was necessary to protect some proceeding which was pending, but that protection could hardly be required against a publication which had ceased.

Dr. KENEALY urged that the contempt already committed had not been purged.

The Lord Chief Justice: When was the book published?

Dr. KENEALY: We do not know. But it was evidently after the committal for Trial.

Justice MELLOR: What passages are directed at the coming Trial.

Dr. KENEALY: There is no allusion to it in terms; neither was there any in the last proceeding.

Justice BLACKBURN: It is impossible to comment on the past Trial without in that way indirectly alluding to the one ensuing, but that is not enough to justify a proceeding for contempt.

The Lord Chief Justice: You must bear in mind that the writer refers to the appeal for public support made on behalf of the Claimant. Then it is not competent for any one to say that the appeal ought not to be responded to, because of the incidents and events of the last Trial? If that were the real purpose of the publication it does not fall within the principle laid down last Term. The Court will not, indeed, allow persons, by publications or public speeches, to interfere with the course of justice on a proceeding which is pending, but you must show that there is an intention to interfere with the coming Trial, and the difficulty we have is in seeing that intention.

Dr. KENEALY observed that no doubt the author was too cunning to express and avow that intention, but surely the evidence of it was as strong in this case as in the last. In this case the reflections on the Claimant and on the witnesses at the last Trial were as strong as anything could possibly be, and the Court said on the last occasion that such reflections necessarily indicated an intention to prejudice the coming Trial. He then read the following passage, and asked if anything could be stronger:—

"Whether the Claimant took any of his various advisers and backers into his full confidence is a question upon which some light may perhaps be thrown by the criminal proceedings which have now been commenced. It is scarcely possible to doubt that some of his associates must have known not only that he was quite scoundrel enough to be an impostor—for that, of course, they all knew after a little while—but that he was actually an impostor."

This was quoted from the *Saturday Review*, but it was none the less strong for that.

Mr. Justice MELLOR: The object was to discourage public subscriptions in support of the Claimant.

Dr. KENEALY: But is not its natural tendency also (as the Court said on a former occasion) to excite prejudice against him, and so to prejudice the ensuing Trial? And so as to the reflection on his "backers"—that is, his witnesses. But that was not the worst. The book contained the following passage:—

"The person who for the greater part of a year has borne the ancient name of that great house, has concentrated upon himself the attention of the civilized world, has monopolised an entire Court of Law, and kept an army of barristers at work, with a river of gold and silver flowing to support them, now stands as THOMAS CASTRO, indicted for wilful perjury and committed to Newgate. On the day—if it shall arrive—when he stands convicted of building his lost suit upon false oaths and baseless calumnies, the day will also have arrived to affirm that no more dangerous or shameless rascal ever stood to hear the sentence of the law thundered in wrath upon his wickedness."—(Quoted from the *Daily Telegraph*.)

Mr. Justice BLACKBURN: That appears to be quoted from a newspaper.

Dr. KENEALY: No doubt, but it is none the less injurious for that.

Mr. Justice BLACKBURN: Still that may have a bearing upon the probability of an intention to interfere with the coming Trial. Why did you not proceed against the newspaper editors?

Dr. KENEALY: We were not aware of the publication until lately, and then we naturally proceeded against the publishers, who had probably made a great deal of money by it.

Mr. Justice BLACKBURN: That is extremely unlikely. —(Laughter).

The Lord Chief Justice (after conferring with his learned brethren) said the passage last read certainly did appear to be pointed to the coming Trial, and, therefore, the learned Counsel might, if he pleased, take a rule. But the Court thought that such a discussion as this on the very eve of the Trial was very inopportune.

Dr. KENEALY asked that the rule might be made returnable at once.

Mr. Justice BLACKBURN: Why should it be so?

Dr. KENEALY: That it may be disposed of before the Trial, which begins on Monday.

Mr. Justice BLACKBURN: But why should it be so?

Dr. KENEALY: That a great moral lesson may be read to the jury, as to the importance of disregarding these publications.

Mr. Justice BLACKBURN: In other words, that they may be influenced.

Dr. KENEALY: No; rather to prevent an improper influence upon their minds. It would have a most wholesome effect upon them if the publisher of this book should be called up to receive the admonition of the Court.

The Lord Chief Justice observed that any comments on the evidence, on one side or the other, before the jury are empanelled, should be avoided.

Dr. KENEALY urged that the rule should be disposed of before the Trial came on.

The Lord Chief Justice: Certainly not; and I only hope that the application was not made with that view.

Dr. KENEALY: My Lord, it certainly was made with the object that the jury should be admonished to disregard such publications.

The Lord Chief Justice: We cannot admonish a jury before they are empanelled.

Dr. KENEALY continued to urge that the admonition of the publisher would have a good moral effect upon the minds of the jurors; but—

The Lord Chief Justice observed that the Court could not help the observations made on one side or the other; and added that the pertinacity of the learned Counsel rather raised doubts in their minds as to the propriety of granting the rule at all. (A laugh.) It was a premature and inopportune discussion of the merits of the Trial.

Dr. KENEALY: The object was to stop the publication.

Mr. Justice BLACKBURN: Then we ought not to grant the rule, for it appears the publication is stopped already.

Dr. KENEALY said he would take the rule without further observation, adding that it had been attempted to get at the author, but without effect, as, though his name is known, he could not be found.—Rule *nisi*.

The Claimant's Counsel and his advisers were so little satisfied with the reception which this application met with, that we believe they never served the Rule; they certainly abandoned the whole proceeding.

On the following day, April 17, Dr. KENEALY made another effort for justice, but in a different direction. We append the report:—

THE TICHBORNE CASE.

At the sittings of the Court of Queen's Bench yesterday in Banco, before the Lord Chief Justice, Mr. Justice MELLOR, Mr. Justice LUSH, and Mr. Justice QUAIN, another application was made in the TICHBORNE Case – another preliminary "skirmish" before the main encounter. It was an application on the part of the Defendant for certain information as necessary to his defence with which the Counsel for the Crown had refused to furnish him. To understand the nature and object of the application, it is necessary to explain, as was explained by counsel on making the application, how the matter stands. The Defendant was committed for Trial for perjury at the close of the civil Trial, and three indictments were afterwards preferred against him—two for perjury, which is a misdemeanour, and one for forgery, which is a felony. The indictments for perjury proceed upon his evidence at the Trial, and also on an affidavit in a Chancery suit. The indictment for perjury proceeds upon the signature to what are called "The TICHBORNE bonds." The committal for trial proceeded upon the evidence at the Trial, and of this, of course, both parties are equally in possession. It has, indeed, been printed and published, and is in the possession of the entire community. But, as is well known, the Trial was postponed avowedly for the purpose of obtaining additional evidence, and it has transpired that there are new witnesses to be called, added to which there is a certain correspondence which is deemed of importance, and has for that reason been printed on the part of the Crown. The Counsel for the Defendant, under these circumstances, applied to the Crown for copies of the examinations of the new witnesses, and also for copies of the printed letters. These applications, however, were not acceded to—at all events beyond a delivery of one copy of the correspondence; another being refused, it was said, except on condition of payment of £35. Moreover, for some reason or other, the prosecution, it was believed, intended to proceed upon the indictment for perjury, and not on the indictment for forgery, though that is the graver charge; and the prisoner's counsel rather desired that the forgery case should be tried first. Under these circumstances there was a summons at Judge's Chambers, calling upon the agents for the prosecution to show cause why the indictment for felony should not in the ordinary case be tried before the indictments for perjury: why the solicitor for the prosecution should not supply the Defendant with a copy of the evidence of the several witnesses whom he intends to call, with the exception of those who were examined on the Nisi Prius trial, and also why the solicitor for the prosecution should not supply without charge a second copy of the printed correspondence put in evidence at the Nisi Prius trial. This summons came on to be heard before Baron MARTIN, and though he refused to make any order thereon, because, he said, he had no authority to do so, yet, with reference to that part of the summons which related to a copy of the evidence of the witnesses proposed to be called for the prosecution, the learned Baron said, addressing the Counsel who appeared for the Crown, "of course you will do this;" adding that if he were the Judge to try the Case he would not proceed with the Trial until copies of the evidence had been supplied to the Defendant. There was now an affidavit in support of the present application by Mr. ALFRED HENDRICKS, the attorney for the Defendant, that if copies of the evidence be not furnished he "verily believed that the Defendant would be greatly damaged in making his defence, and the ends of justice will be liable to be defeated," and that the application was made solely for the *bonâ fide* purpose of the proper conduct of the defence. And he further stated that the issue tried on the trial in the Court of Common Pleas was as to the identity of Sir ROGER CHARLES TICHBORNE, and that, in fact, there was no other material issue; and that while the indictment for perjury raised numerous issues, more or less material, the trial of the indictment for forgery would raise the main and substantial issue of identity. On these materials,

Dr. KENEALY, Q.C. (with him Mr. MCMAHON), moved on the part of the Defendant that the counsel for the Crown might be directed either to enter a *nolle prosequi* upon the indictment for forgery, or to proceed upon it first, and also that they might be directed to furnish the agent for the defence with copies of the evidence of the new witnesses, and with a second copy of the correspondence. He pressed in support of the former part of the application the obvious convenience of first trying the indictment which raised the broad substantial question whether the Defendant was or was not Sir ROGER TICHBORNE, especially as that was the graver charge, and ordinarily the graver charge was tried first, unless it was intended to be abandoned, in which case it ought to be distinctly withdrawn, and not kept hanging over the head of the Defendant, thereby creating a prejudice against him; while he also pressed the obvious fairness of the other part of his application, and the necessity of it for the purposes of justice.

The Lord Chief Justice: It is quite impossible for the Court to interfere as asked. The prosecution can proceed with which they think best.

Dr. KENEALY: I apprehend I shall be able to produce authorities to show that from a very early period it has been the uniform practice in the procedure of our Courts to order indictments to be first taken or to be quashed.

Mr. Justice MELLOR: It is a matter of convenience with the prosecution which shall be taken first.

Dr. KENEALY: I am here to contend that it is not. My second application is for the Solicitor for the prosecution to supply the Defendant with a copy of the evidence of each of the witnesses it is intended to call, except that taken by commission, and given in Court in the Ejectment Case in the Court of Common Pleas. We want a copy, or something like an idea, of the evidence to be given by the fresh witnesses intended to be called on the forthcoming Trial.

The Lord Chief Justice: Have you applied to the prosecution for it?

Dr. KENEALY: Yes; and have been refused. We then went to Chambers, and when the summons came on to be heard before Mr. Baron MARTIN, that learned Judge said it was not for him to prescribe what this Court should do in the matter, but he expressed an opinion that if he had to try the Case he would not allow it to be tried until the prosecution had supplied the evidence to the Defendant.

The Lord Chief Justice: What authority have we sitting in Banco to make the order?

Dr. KENEALY: I think I have several authorities. There are twenty-six assignments of perjury, but the main and substantial question for the Trial, both in the perjury and the felony, is the same, viz., whether the Defendant is Sir ROGER TICHBORNE or not; and that can be raised and decided as well on the forgery as on the perjury indictment. The Crown by this proceeding could not possibly suffer any substantial injury, and the Defendant ought not to suffer from having to defend himself from a number of charges if, on the forgery indictment, he shows that he is Sir R. C. TICHBORNE.

Mr. Justice MELLOR: It is raised incidentally in the forgery and directly in the perjury.

Dr. KENEALY: No. Because in the forgery it alleges that the Defendant issued certain bonds in the name of Sir ROGER TICHBORNE, whom he is not. The question really and substantially then is whether the Defendant is Sir ROGER TICHBORNE or not.

Mr. Justice QUAIN: Have you received notice that fresh witnesses are to be called?

Dr. KENEALY: I cannot answer the question offhand. I have not been able to compare the voluminous list of witnesses that have been handed to me. I confine my motion to the evidence of those witnesses only of which we have had no notice.

The Lord Chief Justice: I quite agree that the case may be summed up in the question whether the Defendant is Sir ROGER TICHBORNE or not, of which all the assignments of perjury are component parts.

Dr. KENEALY: And can be tried equally as well on the indictment for forgery.

The Lord Chief Justice: No; because we should have to lock up the jury probably for three months.

Dr. KENEALY: Although I apprehend that, as a general principle, a person tried on a criminal charge cannot consent to certain things being done, yet it might be done in permitting the jury to separate each day.

The Lord Chief Justice: There is a fixed rule that it cannot be done. The Attorney-General purposes in his Jury Bill to alter it.

(The Defendant here came into Court, and sat just under the Bar.)

Dr. KENEALY: The only effect of locking up a jury is for the protection of the prisoner.

The Lord Chief Justice: No; for the protection of both sides. A jury was just as likely to be meddled with by a prisoner, if he has means to do so, as by a prosecutor. It is for the protection of both, by securing a purer administration of justice. I quite agree that the distinction between felony and a misdemeanour cannot justify the locking up a jury in one case more that the other, but it is the law that it shall be done. Whether the Attorney-General will be able in the Legislature to alter it is another matter.

Dr. KENEALY: If that is an insuperable objection to the felony being tried first, I would ask, in accordance with precedents, to have the indictment for felony quashed.

The Lord Chief Justice: That is another and totally different application. If the defendant were acquitted of the perjury I should think the prosecution would not think of proceeding on the felony, because they involve substantially the same question.

Dr. KENEALY: It might prejudice the jury when trying the perjury to know that a case of felony was looming in the background.

Mr. Justice MELLOR: It is not the practice at assizes to order felonies to be taken before misdemeanours, except for the convenience of the prosecution in relieving witnesses from continued attendance. It is a pure matter of convenience.

Dr. KENEALY: It is a pity that the Court should have to be engaged on the perjury case of inquiring whether the Defendant had answered truly the time when he came over from Paris to attend a funeral and other similar matters, when the main and substantial question can be raised better on the indictment for felony.

The Lord Chief Justice: All that is fair matter for observation before a jury, but I don't see how we can interfere and say these assignments of perjury ought to be omitted.

Dr. KENEALY: Then in that case I will ask your lordships to call on the Crown to abandon the charge of felony, because, if acquitted on the perjury, it will be useless to try the forgery.

Mr. Justice MELLOR: We cannot quash an indictment that is good on the face of it.

Dr. KENEALY: It can be withdrawn, or a *nolle prosequi* entered.

The Lord Chief Justice: We can only suggest it. A very nice point of law arises on the felony, whether the signing of the bonds amounts to forgery. The issue, as you point out, is the same in both cases, and the jury need not be prejudiced, because they may easily be made to understand that it is the same issue, though in another form. My impression is, that if the charge of perjury is first taken nothing will be said by the prosecution about the felony.

Dr. KENEALY: That might be so, but we cannot prevent the usual channels of information diffusing all over England that the Defendant has to be tried for forgery, and a jury of commercial men will look upon it as a serious matter.

The Lord Chief Justice: Only if the Defendant is not Sir ROGER TICHBORNE. If he is Sir ROGER TICHBORNE he has done nothing more than he was entitled to do. If the jury are men of intelligence, as I hope they will be, they will see it in a moment.

Mr. Justice MELLOR: The point of law on the forgery, if decided in favour of the Defendant, might prevent effect being given to a verdict of Guilty; and why should we proceed and take it out of its course and against the consent of the Crown? It is not desirable that we should waste a moment of time by taking a case that might result in making the whole of the proceedings fruitless.

Dr. KENEALY: The answer to that is, Why subject the Defendant to so great a hardship?

Mr. Justice MELLOR: No more than in the case of any other Defendant.

Dr. KENEALY: Yes.

Mr. Justice MELLOR: No; not at all.

Dr. KENEALY: If there is a doubt in your lordships' minds as to the forgery, it is a great hardship that the Defendant should have such an indictment kept hanging over him like the sword of DAMOCLES.

The Lord Chief Justice: If such an application as this had been made to me at the assizes, I should say that, as the charges are substantially the same, take that which is the most convenient to the prosecution. I cannot suppose that the Counsel for the Crown in this case, if a verdict of acquittal is returned on the charge of perjury, will think of trying the case over again in another form.

Dr. KENEALY: After that intimation I will not further proceed with that portion of my application, although I have strong authority for showing that, from the time of Sir MICHAEL FOSTER downwards, the Crown had been put to its election to proceed or enter a *nolle prosequi.*

The Lord Chief Justice: I should deprecate, unless under very special circumstances, the necessity for a second trial, after a full investigation and an impartial verdict by the jury in another form.

Mr. Justice LUSH: It is an analogous case to that of an indictment and a coroner's inquisition. We never try on both. If the indictment ends in an acquittal we never try on the coroner's inquisition.

The Lord Chief Justice: Did the Crown give any reason for not supplying copies of the evidence required?

Dr. KENEALY: When we applied they refused to give it, and then we went to Chambers.

Mr. Justice LUSH: It is usually given on application.

Mr. Justice MELLOR: I never knew of an order being made that it should be done. A Judge may postpone a trial in order that it may be done. What direct authority has a Judge to say that the prosecution shall give copies of evidence obtained on its own behalf and at its own cost?

The Lord Chief Justice: If instead of making this motion you were to make the application on the Trial at Bar, we should then put pressure on the prosecution, without absolute authority to say that it shall be done, to give you what you require. I think you ought to have opportunity of knowing substantially what the additional witnesses, if any, are going to state. A party accused before a magistrate is entitled to know what the witnesses are going to state on the trial, in order that he might be able to cross-examine them and bring counter-evidence in order to meet it. I think it is but reasonable that it should be done in this case. There may be special circumstances why it should not be done, but we cannot know that until we have Counsel before us. I think you may trust to us when the Case comes on for trial to put reasonable pressure on the prosecution to give you what you ought to have. Hear the opening of the Counsel for the Crown as to the evidence he intends to produce, and then if there are any witnesses mentioned of whom you have no knowledge, I, for one, think, and I have no doubt the other Judges will agree with me, that subject to what might be said on the other side, you ought to have what you require. But I doubt if this Court, sitting in Banco, has any right to dictate to the prosecution what shall be done.

Dr. KENEALY: The only objection to that is that it might possibly cause the delay of the Trial, and that we have no desire should occur.

The Lord Chief Justice: In what way?

Dr. KENEALY: In copying the evidence; for unless pressure be put upon the clerks, several days' delay might occur.

Mr. Justice MELLOR: In civil cases we have express power to grant a discovery, but we have no power over evidence got up in a criminal case at the trouble and expense of the prosecution.

The Lord Chief Justice: I never knew an instance where a Judge has ordered copies of fresh evidence to be supplied to a defendant.

Dr. KENEALY: Probably what has been said by your lordships to-day will be brought to the attention of the prosecution, and they may do something before the Trial comes on; but it would have been more gracious if they had done it before pressure had been put on them by the Bench.

Mr. Justice MELLOR: I wish not to express a decided opinion on the point. I have great doubt what power the Court has under the circumstances. The question is whether the circumstances are such that the Court might put pressure on the prosecution by saying that if it is not given we will adjourn.

The Lord Chief Justice: I have no doubt that in this case, as in all others, the Counsel for the prosecution will listen to the suggestions of the Court and act upon them.

Dr. KENEALY: I cannot echo that expression, because although the evidence impounded in the Court of Common Pleas had been printed at the expense of the country, the prosecution refused to give a second copy except on the payment of £35, and it was only by applying to Mr. Baron MARTIN at Chambers that it was obtained.

The Lord Chief Justice: Justice must be done to all parties by putting the saddle on the right horse. The Master informs me that it was the Treasury who insisted on the payment of the money. I should be sorry, in the interest of Justice, that anything should be done contrary to the suggestion of the Court.

Dr. KENEALY said he was satisfied, and would not further press his motion.

EX-PARTE THE CLAIMANT V. ROUTLEDGE.

Later in the day Mr. CHANNELL said that in the case moved yesterday the first intimation the firm had of it was that morning through the newspapers. One of the members of the firm, which consisted of GEORGE ROUTLEDGE and Sons, had arranged some months ago to go to America on business, and yesterday he took his passage for that purpose. The rule had not been served upon him, and he was anxious that his going to America should not be considered an aggravation of the contempt with which he had been charged.

The Lord Chief Justice said it was unanimously agreed by the Judges that cause should not be shown against the rule whilst the trial was pending, and the rule was granted because the passage quoted in the book might possibly bear the construction of contempt, for which, when the proper time arrived, the defendants might be made responsible. Agreeing that it was a case that should not be argued on the eve of the trial that was coming on, they might enlarge it until next Term.

Mr. CHANNELL said Mr. ROUTLEDGE wished it to be understood that in going to America he was not leaving the country to evade the rule.

The Lord Chief Justice said that in all probability the rule would not be argued until next Term, but Mr. ROUTLEDGE was not to understand that he would not be called on hereafter.

THE LUIE EPISODE.

The LUIE Episode in the Trial at Bar was so wonderful that it would be wrong to close this Introduction to the Report without adverting to it. At the present moment, notwithstanding all that has elapsed, we are unable to decide whether LUIE was really the witness of truth, or whether he was what is vulgarly called a "plant;" that is, a person put upon the Defendant for the purpose of leading him into a trap. If he were the latter, his selection was admirable; for there was a time when he thoroughly deceived even the Lord Chief Justice; and when he so persuaded Dr. KENEALY of his integrity that he forced his whole case before the Court, for the purpose of vindicating LUIE's character from what he then believed to be the false suspicions of Mr. POLLARD, one of the assistant solicitors, and getting the latter committed for contempt.

LUIE first appeared upon the scene on the 7th of July, 1873, when he left the following letter at the residence of the Defendant. It was handed to the latter, who refused to see him, but told him to go to Poets-corner and see the lawyer if he liked; but he declined to admit him at all, though LUIE pressed it very much. We copy from the original manuscript now before us; handed to his Counsel by Sir ROGER.

July 7, 1873.

SIR,—Since my arrival in London did I learn of your Trial, and as I was the Steward on board the "Osprey," belonging to New Bedford, U.S., and shall be very glad to give you such information and testimony what will ultimately lead to your acquital. I therefore deliver this my ownself, and am waiting your answer, as soon as you got this to hand. I have something very particular to tel you; and no one knows anything about this or that.—Yours obt.,

JOHN LEWIS.

LUIE, it appears, found his way to Poets-corner, and was seen there by Mr. WHALLEY who brought him to the Defendant. There are conflicting statements as to what took place during that interview; one being that the Claimant recognized LUIE. The other alleging only a partial or guarded recognition, founded on the facts that he related. We have no knowledge either way.

We transcribe from the original manuscript of LUIE, the first account of himself, which he gave to the solicitor.

"I left Ballaratt in May, 1855, Engaged at the "Prinz Carl" at Sydney for £90 a run to Chincas Island; loaded guano, and when she cleared at Calao I left. Stayed at Calao for nine or ten months: took engagement on board "Charlotta Letitia" at £20 a month; discharged myself at Queenstown; got on board the "Blue Jacket" for New York; the remainder four years entered different coasting vessels, and river boats. Went to Chicago, Bishopville; stayed as boarding-house keeper for three years; went to Buffalo, and as Steward entered the Erie Boat Company down to New York; afterwards was in the blockade run between Nassau, Charleston, Wilmington and Bermuda: at '65 went to Melbourne for New York; from there to Newcastle, Australia—coals for Hong Kong—Tea, coffee, rice and arrack for Stockholm; and to Gothenburg by the steamer "Western," over Lake Maeler, and remained six months; went over to New York as passenger; from '67 to '71, was on board the "Toledo" as Steward; from '72 to May '73, Steward on board the "Ironsides" in Lake Michigan, and am now here."

We transcribe also from the original manuscript of LUIE, now lying before us, and which is excellently well written, the following fuller account of himself:—

I was born in Bornholm, an island belonging to Denmark, in 1825. I am 48 years old, and went over to Helsingver 1838, where I got a berth as cabin-boy on board "Christian VII." We sailed for St. Thomas, and back again to Copenhagen; and took trips afterwards with different vessels from Gefle, Hernosand, and Memel, with cargoes of deals and timber for Marseilles, Algiers, Oran. In 1840 I left "Audacia" in Barcelona, and joined the "Carlos" for Havanah, caught the yellow fever, and was laid up for three months in the hospital. After, went coasting voyages with different coasting schooners on the American coast, and the West India Islands, and the Mexican coast, during the war in 1848 with Mexico, and stayed afterwards in New Orleans for one year. Engaged myself again, entered a schooner ship commanded by Captain SCHNEIDAN, and made trips between the West India Islands; joined the "Osprey" in the latter part of '52, and was trading to Cardenas, Cape Verd Islands; took salt for Buenos Ayres; loaded carne seca for Rio and Pernambuco; coursed for Cape de Verd Island; loaded salt for Rio Grande; took carne seca for Musco and Paraiba; in ballast for New York; brought to an anchor at Staten Island; after a vile (while) began loading bricks, bread-stuff, butts for washing-tubs, lumbers for huts, and digging implements; sailed for Melbourne in the month of February, 1854; and in April, somewhere in lat. 19 and 20 south, picked up the "Bella" crew—the Defendant, HENRY, DOCKTOR, JARVIS, LEWIS—one name forgoten—six in number, and landed them in Melbourne the same year, in the month of July. I left the "Osprey" same day we arived, and with others went in shore, and proceeded to Ballarat, where I remained ten months.

JOHN LUIE.

The following is a draft of LUIE's evidence, as given to Counsel:

JEAN LUIE, at present residing at 12, Churchyard-row, Newington-butts, Mariner, of Newberry-avenue, Seventh-street, Chicago.

I was born in Bornholm, an island belonging to Denmark, in 1825, am 48 years old, and went over to Helsingfors in 1838, when I got a berth as cabin-boy on board "Christian VII." We sailed for St. Thomas and back again to Copenhagen, and took trips afterwards with different vessels from Gefle, Hernosand, and Memel, with cargoes of deals and timber for Marseilles, Algiers, and Oram. In 1840 I left "Audacia," in Barcelona, and joined the "Carlos" for Havanna; caught the yellow fever, and was laid up for three months in the hospital. After went coasting voyages with different coasting schooners on the American coast and the West India Islands, and the Mexican coast, during the War in 1848 with Mexico, and stayed afterwards in New Orleans for one year; engaged myself again on board a schooner ship, commanded by Captain SCHNEIDAN, and made trips between the West India Islands.

I joined the "Osprey" in the latter part of 1852, and was trading to Cardinas, Cape Verde Island; took salt for Buenos Ayres; loaded carne seca, &c., for Rio and Pernambuco; coursed for Cape de Verds Island; loaded salt for Rio Grande; took carne seca for Maseo and Paraiba; in ballast for New York; brought to an anchor at Staten Island, after a while loading bricks, bread-stuff, butts for washing tubs, lumbers for huts, and digging implements. Sailed for Melbourne in the month of February, 1854.

I was steward of the "Osprey" from the year 1852 till I, with other men, deserted her in Melbourne, in July, 1854.

The "Osprey" hailed from New Bedford, United States. She was a Swedish-built vessel, of the same style as the American clippers, between 500 and 600 tons burden, and barque-rigged. She carried a cabin on deck, and the mizzen-mast ran through the middle of the table. The brokers of the "Osprey" were FUNCKE and MEINKE, of New York. At this time there was no register for classes.

In February, 1854, we left Staten Island, New Jersey, carrying a cargo of bread-stuff, timber and spars, agricultural implements, and bricks for ballast.

We proceeded on our voyage, across the Line about the middle of March, I think, and got a very favourable south-east trade wind.

When in latitude 19 or 20, off the coast of Brazil, distance some 300 miles, we saw in the morning a boat, with a signal up, on the port bow. This was about the middle of April.

We stayed and made for the boat. On getting alongside we found six men lying helpless, and apparently dying. The heat was most intense, and the men seemed delirious. We took them on board at once, and used every means to restore them.

I soon perceived that one of the six men was not a sailor, and I placed him in my own berth. What struck me about him was, his hands were particularly small and fine—not the hands of a seafaring man. His hair was dark brown, his eyes blue, and lips a little protruding. He had a little twitching about the eyes, and he had a peculiar walk. He was ill all the time until we landed in Melbourne. I think he was suffering from sunstroke. I have often seen people ill from sunstroke, and have had sunstroke myself.

I washed him every day, and saw him naked frequently. I can positively swear he was not tattooed. I cannot speak to his personal formation.

He had a cut in the back of his head, and a mark on his side.

We often chatted in French and broken Spanish. He was deficient in French, I think, and spoke English better.

He told me his name was ROGER, and had been a long time away from home.

His description of the loss of the "Bella" was different from the description of the other men. As a seafaring man, I do not think his description was correct. The other men told me that the "Bella" went down head foremost; and the leak was caused by the rats eating through her, and all her seams were open for want of caulking. The vessel was, in other respects, not quite fit for sea.

The men told me that the "Bella" was a barque hailing from Liverpool.

We arrived at Melbourne Heads in July, 1854, very late in the evening: about seven or eight o'clock. We were laying to and fro at the Heads that night, and got into Williamstown at eight o'clock the following morning.

After breakfast the Captain went ashore. Pilot and the young gentleman went ashore to report the vessel. Whilst the Captain was away every one of us left the ship.

I remember the names of some of the "Bella" men: they were LEWIS, JARVIS, we called one the Doctor, and another JEMMY and HARRIS.

After deserting the "Osprey," I with four of the crew and two of the "Bella" men went to Ballarat. I parted with the "Bella" men at Ballarat, and never saw them afterwards.

JARVIS and LEWIS were the names of the "Bella" men who accompanied me to Ballarat.

The name of the "Bella" was not written on the boat—we took the boat on board and rowed her on shore when we arrived at Melbourne.

The "Bella" men used to work with us during the voyage.

I met the Defendant on the 7th July last, and identified him as the person whom we picked up with others from the boat of the "Bella." I remembered him by his forehead, his nose, and general appearance. I cannot be mistaken. I cut his hair when he was on board the "Osprey," and I noticed the mark on the back of his head. I talked a little Spanish with him.

The young gentleman whom we picked up in the boat of the "Bella," and whom I now recognize in the person of the Defendant, was scarcely sensible during the whole time he was on board the "Osprey," and when we left him in Melbourne he was suffering from sunstroke. I saw nothing of him after he went ashore.

The log-book of the "Osprey" was kept by the mate and second mate. I should suppose it would be mentioned in the log-book that these men were picked up—the first mate would be the person who would most likely enter it, as it would be an important thing.

The log-books at that time were generally destroyed at the end of the voyage by four twelve or fifteen years—they have been asked for scientific purposes, such as laying out Wind Charts, and Barometrical Observations in different latitude and longitude.

I left Ballarat in May 1855. Engaged in the "Prinz Carl" at Sydney for £90 a run to Chinca's Island loaded guano and when she cleared at Callao I left. Stayed at Callao for nine or ten months; took engagement on board "Charlotte Letitia" at £20 a month; discharged myself at Queenstown; got on board the "Blue Jacket" for New York; the remainder four years on board different coasting vessels and run boats; went to Chicago, Bishopsville; stayed as boarding-house keeper for three years; went to Buffalo, and as steward on board the Erie Boat Company run to New York, afterwards was in the blockade run between Nassau, Charlestown, Wilmington, and and Bermuda.

In 1865 went to Melbourne from New York; whilst there I saw the "Osprey" converted into a barge for stores. From there to Newcastle, Australia, coals for Hong Kong, tea, coffee, rice and arrac for Stockholm, went to Gothenburg by the steamer "Western" over Lake Maeler and remained six months; went over to New York as passenger from '67 to '71 was on board the "Toledo" as Steward, from '72 to '73, Steward on board the "Ironside" in Lake Michigan, and am now here.

There are some of the crew of the "Osprey" now in New York, viz., ANDERSON, living, eighteen months ago, 19 street, Brooklyn, keeping a grog-shop; a man whom I knew as HARRY, (I forget his other name), but he is a sail-maker, living at the East River.

I never afterwards saw or heard of the crew of the "Bella." I think they could not stand long at the work of the diggings after the rattling they got in the "Bella's" boat.

Undoubtedly they would never be well again after what they went through in that wreck.

I don't know anything of a claim by the Captain of the "Osprey" for maintenance of the "Bella" men. It is not like the custom of Americans to do so, and we had plenty of bread stuff, and we did it for humanity.

The captain was named BANNATT. I saw him in 1862, and after that he joined the Southerners in the war, and I believe he was killed.

I came to London from Ostend at Saturday the 5th of July last. The same evening, after landing, I went into a public-house in St. George's-in-the-East for a glass of ale, and whilst there I heard a conversation on the TICHBORNE Case. I did not understand it: I did not know who the man ORTON was. They then told me about the TICHBORNE Trial, and during the conversation that ensued they said the Claimant was an impostor, and after a little time the name of the "Bella" was mentioned. It then struck me that as the crew of the "Bella" were saved by us, that perhaps this (the Defendant), was the man we picked up with the five other men in the "Bella's" whale boat.

Upon reading over this evidence, Dr. KENEALY and Mr. McMAHON had two or three long consultations upon the matter. To the latter it seemed doubtful, but Dr. KENEALY was inclined to believe it in its entirety. The Claimant himself was sent for, and the whole matter was discussed for a couple of hours, there being present only Dr. KENEALY, Sir ROGER TICHBORNE, and Mr. McMAHON. The Claimant, without absolutely pledging himself to a personal recognition of LUIE—though he very nearly did so—expressed the fullest conviction that he was a true witness; the more especially as he had reminded them of matters which only the mate of the "Osprey" could have known.

Mr. McMAHON still was doubtful, and accordingly it was resolved to apply a test, which it was supposed could hardly mislead; and that test was to get LUIE himself examined, and cross-examined, for the purpose of ascertaining whether he could be found tripping in his narrative. This was done at Mr. McMAHON's suggestion, principally. As Dr. KENEALY, from the very beginning of the Case, was so scrupulous, that he never saw a single witness, and refused to hold any communication, personally or otherwise, even with Mr. BAIGENT, it was proposed by Mr. McMAHON that two eminent Chancery Counsel should see and examine LUIE. This was done accordingly. Lord RIVERS, Sir ROGER TICHBORNE, and Mr. ONSLOW, met Mr. E. K. KARSLAKE, Q.C., and Mr. LOCOCK WEBB, both of the Chancery Bar, and LUIE having come with Sir ROGER's lawyer, was carefully examined, for upwards of an hour, by the two last-named Counsel, who brought all their skill, experience, and deeply-founded knowledge of the Case, to bear, in testing the truth of LUIE's story. They both reported to Dr. KENEALY and Mr. McMAHON that there could be no doubt of his truthfulness, and almost pledged themselves for the accuracy of his narrative. They expressed themselves strongly upon this, and declared that Counsel for the Claimant could not venture to abstain from placing LUIE in the witness-box without incurring a most serious, nay, even a most terrible responsibility. Lord RIVERS and Mr. ONSLOW joined in their expression of the same views, and Mr. WHALLEY, at a later period, was so convinced by LUIE, that he even went the length of saying, that if Dr. KENEALY did not call LUIE, he would summon public meetings all through the country, and denounce Dr. KENEALY from every platform in the land.

He wrote as follows:—

MR. WHALLEY TO DR. KENEALY.

Plas Madoc, 20th July, 1873.

DEAR KENEALY,—Just one word. LOCOCK WEBB strongly feels that the Steward should be relied on, and for the following reasons. I *intensely* feel that before opening your speech you should ask that he may give his evidence.

First: The man who has him in charge (PULLEYN) says he is dying to get away home, and it is to be feared he may give us the slip, it being impossible to make him feel an interest in the case greater than his desire to get home. Second: He himself says, the best plan would be for him to go to New York and look up the witnesses and evidence in support. Third: If the Court *refuse*, it will bring in money at once. Fourth: If he is examined, I will start with him at once to New York to bring over the sailors. Yours ever,

G. H. WHALLEY.

The reasons above suggested made Dr. KENEALY advise that someone should proceed to New York, to ascertain, personally, whether LUIE could be corroborated by any evidence existing there. Mr. WHALLEY at once, in the most noble and generous manner, volunteered to go at his own expense; and it was agreed that LUIE should not be called until Mr. WHALLEY's report had been made. The member for Peterborough lost no time in sailing for New York, and we append the letter and report which he wrote, so far as they relate to LUIE. A copy of this report he sent to the Treasury, so that the Prosecutors, if they thought fit, might inquire for themselves.

Mr. McMAHON having been now called upon to state his objections to LUIE in writing, did so, and Mr. ONSLOW gave the answers that follow. The nature of the objections will be apparent from Mr. ONSLOW's answers, but we have never seen, and cannot procure a copy of the objections themselves.

MR. ONSLOW'S REPLIES TO MR. McMAHON'S OBJECTIONS.

Reply 1st.—A three-masted barque, with her yards down, according to custom, riding at anchor, might, and possibly would, be taken for a three-masted schooner, by nine men out ten, especially as she was known to be a Yankee, the country that builds three-masted schooners.

Reply 2nd.—It is perfectly true that she had yards to her masts, or she could not be called a barque, and every landsman would call a barque ship-rigged; I have repeatedly done so myself.

Mr. ACKER's "Brilliant," of about 600 tons burden, three-masted, I have often heard called ship-rigged, barque-rigged, and brig-rigged; she is, in fact, a three masted brig.

Reply 3rd.—The Defendant states to having eight saved with him from the "Bella." Remember the Claimant was insensible all, or nearly all, the time he was on board the "Osprey," and his statement, as regards those that were saved from the "Bella," ought not to be taken as being a bit more accurate than the many mis-statements (according to Dr. KENEALY's speech), he has made, especially considering the wrong statement he had made to LUIE respecting the loss of the "Bella," when he came on board the "Osprey," thus showing the fearful wreck of his mind, owing to the sunstroke.

Reply 4th.—It is true others have corroborated Defendant's statement by stating they saw eight or ten seamen, supposed to be the crew of the "Bella," on board the "Osprey," but they don't say or mean that all these men they saw were absolutely "Bella's" men, for in all probability, they were, several of them, the crew of the "Osprey," who went on shore and deserted their ship.

Reply 5th.—Some say she was about 400 tons, LUIE says 500, measurement. Any seafaring man looking at a low-sided vessel deep in the water, could easily make the mistake, even so far as the difference of 200 tons.

Reply 6th.—Some say she was an American in build and trim; LUIE says she was built in Norway. All Norwegian vessels especially, and most English yacht builders, copy to the utmost extent, Yankee build and rig, even to the fiddle figure-head and hollow bow, and lacing the sails to the yards.

Reply 7th.—Defendant states, he and those saved with him rowed towards the "Osprey," hoisting a red shirt on an oar. Defendant also stated he was insensible when taken on board the "Osprey," therefore he could not have rowed alongside. LUIE states they were all down with sunstroke when they sailed alongside, and they were taken on board in this condition.

No doubt the Defendant rowed towards the "Osprey" under this tropical sun, and was struck by the sun, thus corroborating both LUIE's statement and the Defendant's.

Reply 8th.—Forty miles from the Heads to Melbourne, could, with a clipper, be done easily, with a fair wind, in four hours, at ten miles an hour, and therefore there is nothing inconsistent in LUIE's statement on this point.

Reply 9th.—Defendant states there were passengers on board the "Osprey;" LUIE, I believe, says there were none. Now, considering the large crew on board the "Osprey" of mixed nationalities, and consider the diseased state of the brain of Defendant, owing to the sunstroke spoken of by LUIE, and admitted by the Defendant, great allowance must be made as to the Defendant's statement of there having been passengers on board; and assuming LUIE's story to be the correct one, it would fully account for our never having heard from any passengers said to have been on board that ship.

Reply 10th.—Mr. WHALLEY distinctly reports, from information he gained in New York, that vessels could at that period have sailed from New York or New Bedford, or New Jersey, without being recorded, he having ascertained that LUIE's statement may be correct; refer to Mr. WHALLEY's written statement.

Reply 11th.—LUIE positively stated that FUNCKE and MEINKE were the "Osprey's" *brokers*, and not her *owners*, but that Baron FALKENBERG and Captain BANNATT, who commanded her, were the real owners, both since dead.

Reply 12th.—Remember that LUIE offered to go to New York to find part of the crew of the "Osprey," and thus to verify his statement, but Dr. KENEALY refused to let him go, therefore you must not blame him. LUIE wrote a letter, a *bona fide* one, which we produce, to ANDERSON, mate of the "Osprey," who, we have ascertained through Mr. WHALLEY, did keep a "grog-shop" in Brooklyn, but has since removed, and cannot, up to the present time, be discovered. LUIE's daughter is now in New York, and I presume Mr. WHALLEY has seen her, as he had those instructions.

Reply 13th.—LUIE told me GUILDFORD ONSLOW, in his first interview with me, that the Swedish name of the "Osprey" was, he believed, the "Helvetia," that he (LUIE) suspects the name was changed in New Orleans. Mr. RUSSELL, of the firm of RUSSELL and Company, of No. 1, London-street, City, who will be in the box, is prepared to swear he purchased the Australian "Osprey" that laid alongside the three-masted American "Osprey," and therefore the hulk spoken of by LUIE six years ago as being laid up in Melbourne Harbour, cannot be the Australian "Osprey" purchased by Mr. RUSSELL, and of which he can give good account.

A telegram to Melbourne will settle the question whether there is, or was, within the past six years, a hulk in existence, used as a stone-ship, having once borne the name of "Osprey."

Luie is perfectly willing to give an account of the whole of his life, as far back as he can remember, as to when he sailed, and what he has done; as he truly says, he has never been asked for this.

After Luie's evidence, and during the adjournment, the following questions put by Mr. Onslow, received the subjoined answers from Luie.

JEAN LUIE.

Questions by Mr. Onslow; Answers by Jean Luie.

Jean Luie stated he had a daughter in New York, living with a friend. Where does she reside? What is the friend's name? and how came it this friend's name and the daughter's were not given to Mr. Whalley, to call upon and communicate with on his arrival in New York?

Answer.—His daughter is living with Mrs. Kindberg, in his own house in Caroline-street, New Jersey, New York. Mr. Whalley was duly informed of this by Luie.

Has Jean Luie ever written to his daughter or friend, or has he ever received letters from them during his stay in London, and if not, *why?*

Answer.—Has written several times to his daughter, and received at least one reply from her. Thinks other replies may have been intercepted.

Has Jean Luie ever held any communication by letter with anyone in the United States since he has been in England—if so, with whom—will he show the letter—if not, *why not?*

Answer.—He wrote to Anderson and the letter was in time returned with the postmark on it—"Not Claimed." He has this letter, which was read by the Lord Chief Justice. He has also the letter which he received from his daughter, which he can produce.

Jean Luie stated that when he first arrived in England (London), that he had *only recently* left New York, where he had been residing. How came it then when talking of Anderson, of 19, Street, Brooklyn, he stated he *had not seen him for* 18 *months*, and yet he writes to him as "My dear Boy?" How came it, having so recently left New York, he had never seen Anderson or the sail-maker for some months?

Answer.—He had been for some time in the employ of the Lake Ironsides Co., and had been in New York very little, and had never chanced for a long time to come across Anderson. In writing to him the recollection of former intimacy and friendship would cause him to use such a term as "My dear Old Boy," regard also being had to the fact that he was writing from a distant land, and in the genuine feeling of a warm-hearted man. The same remark would apply as to the sail-maker.

Who knows Jean Luie in New York who knew him in New Orleans?

Answer.—Possibly some of those who are coming to give evidence against him may have known him in both places. A gentleman has just come over who lived near him, and knew him very well in York.

Who were the "Osprey's" brokers in New York, or does he remember a man of the name of Casey there?

Answer.—He had little to do with her there, and does not remember the brokers; nor Casey.

Has Jean Luie ever corresponded with his relatives in Bornholm, and if so, did any of them know he picked up the "Bella's" crew?

Answer.—He left them after the death of his father and mother, and has not corresponded with anyone there for more than 25 years.

If Jean Luie were to start for New York to-morrow, upon whom would he call, who were his friends?

Answer.—Upon his own daughter, and the other inmates of his house in the first place.

Cannot he name one living in New York who was cognizant of the "Osprey" picking up the "Bella's" crew?

Answer.—Yes, Harry or Anderson (for he does not know that they are dead), and Mr. Funcke, the ship-chandler.

Can he furnish us with the names and addresses of any of the relatives of Capt. Bannatt, or any people in the United States who can tell us about Capt. Bannatt?

Answer.—Robinson, the proprietor of the Scandinavian Hotel, was a great friend of Bannatt. Also Johnny Peterson, the carpenter.

Did the United States Government supply Capt. Bannatt with legal papers when he left New York in the "Osprey," in 1854?

Answer.—Probably not, as the cargo was of such a nature as to necessitate his going to the Custom House at that time.

In what year did the "Helvetia" change her name to "Osprey," and why?

Answer.—In 1852, and "for reasons best known to" Bannatt, or Falkenberg, and probably to Funcke.

Does Jean Luie remember any tradesmen's names who are now alive in New York, who supplied goods to the "Osprey" in 1854?

Answer.—Ship-chandlers generally supplied all goods for vessels. The ship-chandlers of the "Osprey" were Larson or Peterson. The sail-maker married the sister of Robinson, who kept the Scandinavian Hotel.

Had the "Osprey" chronometers on board—if so, does he remember anyone by name who came on board to rectify them and adjust the compasses?

Answer.—Chronometers were on board, and required, so far as Luie remembers, no adjusting.

Does he remember any land-carpenter or butcher, or baker, coming on board?

Answer.—No occasion for land-carpenters; and butchers or bakers were superseded by the ship-chandlers.

Where in New York were his two houses?

Answer.—One house was in Caroline-street, New Jersey, New York; and the other in Newbury Avenue, Chicago. He rented them. The one in New Jersey is in the management of a responsible person. That in Chicago is in the management of his wife's sister's husband.

Where did he lodge the time he left New York?

Answer.—At his own house in Caroline-street, New Jersey.

Mr. Whalley lost no time on his arrival in New York, in making such inquiries as he thought necessary. He wrote the following letter to Mr. Onslow, but before it reached England, a telegram was received from him, of which this is a copy:—LUIE'S EVIDENCE IS TRUE: EXAMINE AND SEND HIM HERE. REPLY.

A few days afterwards we received this—

LETTER FROM G. H. WHALLEY, ESQ., M.P., TO GUILDFORD ONSLOW, ESQ., M.P.

Perth Amboy, 30 miles from New York: Aug. 9th, 1873.

My dear Onslow,—I have not telegraphed as yet, because I had nothing definite to say. Now all the progress I have made has been satisfactory, and in all respects confirmatory of Lewis' statement. I have had incessant labours, and there seems to be good work for a month of such work from early morning till twelve and one o'clock at night, and this is what I have had since I arrived at New York, mid-day on Wednesday.

I am writing this at a Ferry, 10th August, Sunday. I resume my report broken off yesterday by the Ferry Bell, and purpose to give it you in chronological order—first premising that from the time of my arrival, noon on Wednesday, till now I have never worked so incessantly in my life, never out of the streets and avenues and alleys of this oven of a town, from about 8 a.m. to 12 or 1 o'clock at night. The telegram I sent you this morning gives the shown result, viz., that Lewis is a true man, and I am now working up into legal form the evidence in support of his statement as detailed generally as follows:—

Wednesday, 6th August, arrived, and reached the British Consulate at two. The Consul, being absent, as is almost everybody at this fever season, I wrote appointing to meet him at 12 on the following day, and with such information as I could get from the Secretary, went out to Funcke and Edye, formerly Funcke and Meinke, the brokers of Lewis' ship "Osprey." All the principals also on the spree, but appointed to meet Mr. Funcke the following day. Found they had, at the instances of Belmont and Co., my Rothschild correspondent, been making search for their books of 1854, but without effect, and were afraid they had all been made away with about five years ago, when by fire and removal there was a general combustion, and loss of old books and papers. Hearing of a Mr. Mackie, the agent of Lloyd's, as likely to possess information, went and found him at home, and obtained obtained important facts. It appeared that a paper, *The New York Journal of Commerce*, had, on the 30th of July, published an article showing that an "Osprey" left New York on 6th June, 1854, and as they said for Melbourne, and they pointed out with great glee, how the ship, having been filched by Claimant as his rescuer, was by their diligence to have left New York not earlier than 1st June, and therefore could not have saved him on 26th April.

Mr. Mackie and I at once proceeded to trace out this "Osprey," and found that she did not go to Melbourne at all, but to St. Stephen's and to Bristol, returning again to New York, whence she again cleared out 24th May, 1855. This was a settler for the *Journal of Commerce*, and I at once proceeded to their office. Editor, as usual, not in, but appointed to see him on following day, and with wry faces, and the most ingenious efforts to sustain his case, I *forced* upon him my letter in reply to his article, and which duly appeared the following day, Friday, as per copy inclosed. In support of this letter I got a letter from the agents of the "Osprey" that left on the 1st June, 1854, and other evidence, showing that she never went to Melbourne at all; and when the editor of the *Journal of Commerce* showed me in triumph, a *Melbourne Argus* of 4th December, 1854, stating that "Osprey" was up, so sailing to Sydney, I turned the tables upon him, and called upon him to explain where that "Osprey" came from, if not from New York in February, seeing that she clearly was not the "Osprey" that left on the 1st June, 1854, and I put it to him, that if he, with his world-wide means of information, could not otherwise account for the appearance of this "Osprey" in Melbourne waters on 1st December, 1854, we had a right to put in our own evidence, and demand its acceptance that this was the vessel that left, as Lewis says, in February, 1854.

My letter, as it appeared, has had a great effect upon opinion in New York, which I was told by all was as one to amillion against the Claimant. Thursday, 7th, met Mr. Archibald, the Consul, by appointment, and received from him an extract from Custom House Register of the "Osprey" that left on 1st June, 1854, and again 24th May, 1855, and a positive statement that no other vessel of that name had left New York in those years. Went to Custom House and verified by my own search that this was so, and being received with much courtesy, the Chief Collector complied with my request, that all old books showing the entry to New York should be looked up and searched, so that the probability which suggested that she might have been shipped away unregistered, might be disposed of.

Went to the Norwegian Consul and searched with him their books from 1850 to 1855, but could find no such vessel. Again visited Mr. MACKIE my best friend, and with him to Mr. COOK the Broker of the "Osprey" of 1st June, 1854, and got his certificate, and to various other offices and agencies, but with no trace found of the "Osprey" of Feb., 1854.

Calling again, saw Mr. FUNCKE who offered all possible aid. He read and verified as quite exact LEWIS' statement in his evidence and letter of PETERSON, DALSTROM, BROCKMAN, VOLCKER, and others, and had no doubt that LEWIS was giving a true account in every particular; but every one of these men were dead: his partner also, who attended to such business, was dead, and his books, so far as he knew, all were burnt or destroyed.

Remembering one old man, then in his employ, and now living on pension, he promised to try to get him there to meet me on the following day, Friday.

Friday. Again at Custom House, and searched through all their books and memoranda for 1854, but could find nothing. I then got out the fact that there were two other places in connection with New York, Perth Amboy and Newark, where by a bare possibility a ship might have cleared out. And I yesterday went to Perth Amboy, some thirty miles out on the coast; searched them: no result, but left instructions for further search, the result of which I shall learn after to-morrow.

The old man called in by Mr. FUNCKE met me, and going through all the letters of LEWIS, and quietly rummaging up his memory, he confirmed all that LEWIS had said, in every particular, and possessed a glimmer of a recollection of having seen in the handwriting of FALKENBERG, who was a clerk or manager of FUNCKE and MEINKE, a manifest of a ship "Osprey." He had one or two persons in view whom he would consult, and appointed to meet me again on Saturday. I could not get back from Perth Amboy before he had gone away, and I am now going to his house this afternoon in Hobbach, a great distance, as places are here, to hear the result.

Saturday. Went to Perth Ambor, starting at 8 a.m., and returning at 5. There saw Mr. FUNCKE and others, also Mr. MACKIE, but no practical progress in identifying the "Osprey" of 1850—1854 at Melbourne with the "Osprey" of Feb. 1854 in New York.

Interrupted by two gentlemen of Perth, who follow the waiter, walk in, as a matter of course, sit down and question.

The papers are full of the results of these interviews with me.

To proceed, I believe as to the "Osprey" that she *did* sail from New York; how it happens that there is no record, it is beyond anyone's power, at present, to say; and how it is that we can get no more specific information from the agents can be explained by the lapse of time and the death of every single person to whom LEWIS in his letter refers.

I hope, however, to get more information.

And now as to the men ANDERSON and HARRY: no words can express the toil I have gone through in search of ANDERSON. He is not now in 19 Street, Brooklyn, and I can only find such account of him in the neighbourhood as induces the belief that such a man was there, or thereabouts; but where he is now I have not been able to find. I see there are nearly 200 men of this name in Brooklyn, and as very few people are more than a year in the same house, you may guess the difficulty of tracing a sailor. I have been about this district, a sort of Wapping, for five hours, walking my legs off after each will-o'-the-wisp, till I have almost dropped from fatigue.

I have now found a very respectable man to aid me, have inserted in the papers an advertisement offering twenty dollars reward for the discovery of ANDERSON, and the same for HARRY.

I have been so completely absorbed with those labours, physically and mentally, with the heat at 85°, that I could not write before, having in fact, nothing definite to say, but of this I am confident, LEWIS' story is true. To get up the evidence here to support him will take a month, and at the least £500, and how this is to be done I must leave it to you in London, but I think all this at needed is to put in LEWIS and *defy them to contradict him.*

It will be simply to sacrifice the Case if you do not put in LEWIS.

I am now preparing the formal depositions of witnesses, and I hope to be able to get away from here on Wednesday.

My son who came with me has been laid up with New York fever, as is almost every new-comer. I have no time to think of that.—Yours,

T. H. WHALLEY.

This letter was inclosed in the following, from

MR. ONSLOW TO DR. KENEALY.

The Grove, Ropley, Thursday.

My dear Dr. KENEALY,—I wrote a hurried letter to you to save the post last night about JEAN LUIE. I now inclose his letter to me this morning. *Depend upon it he is right and correct.* EVELYN LIARDET, his brother, the Mail conductor, at Melbourne LONGLAND, LOCKHART, THOMPSON, KING, BATTEN, RICHARDS, all swear to have been on board the three-masted "Osprey" in July 1854, and saw the shipwrecked crew of the "Bella," picked up by the "Osprey," on board. See LIARDET's, LONGLAND's, LOCKART and SHARPE's evidence in the late Trial. Refer to my book on the evidence. * * * * JEAN LUTZ is determined to see the rights of this, and will prove he is telling the truth and nothing but the truth—don't ignore him. I wish you had seen him when I brought him to your house; the extraordinary circumstances of the case would have justified a breach of etiquette. Please don't ignore a single Tichborne Park witness; although their depositions are vague, they are honest, truthful men I vouch.—Yours,

GUILDFORD ONSLOW.

After this came Mr. WHALLEY himself who handed to Dr. KENEALY his

REPORT FROM NEW YORK.

Mr. WHALLEY's Report on the result of his visit to America to obtain information in corroboration of the evidence of JOHN LEWIS.

In pursuance of Mr. MCMAHON's instructions of 25th July, that I should, on my arrival at New York, "at once put myself in communication with some eminent Counsel or Attorney, who would see that all the various matters previously detailed should be done in strict conformity with American law," I was introduced to Mr. H. T. WING, a Counsel and Attorney of high standing, by Mr. ROBERT MACKIE, for above twenty years the agent for LLOYD's in New York, as a person most qualified of any known to him for such duties; Mr. WING being also the solicitor for Messrs. FUNCKE and EDYE, the firm to whom JOHN LEWIS referred as having been connected with the "Osprey."

Before consulting Mr. WING, I made every effort in my power, and by incessant labour—continued from early morning to late at night, from Wednesday, the 6th August, the day of my arrival at New York, to the 12th, the day of my departure for New Bedford and for Quebec—to collect all the information possible on the matters specified in Mr. MCMAHON's Memorandum of Instructions—namely, all the particulars relative to the ship "Osprey," in which JOHN LEWIS states he sailed from Sandy Hook, in February, 1854, and rescued the Claimant from the wreck-boat of the "Bella," in April following.

On submitting to Mr. WING the result of my labours, and after taking a day to go through the papers laid by me before him, he gave me generally his opinion that no evidence could be got ready for use in the present Trial, except by means of inquiry and investigation that would occupy a very considerable space of time, and be attended with much actual outlay of money and labour; that before he could enter upon such duty it would be essential he should receive as a retaining fee 250 dollars, and security for the payment of such outlay and costs as might be incurred by him in carrying out the business.

In the Memorandum of Instructions handed to me by Mr. MCMAHON, he limits the inquiry to the simple question of the "Osprey," stating as many of the officers and crew of that vessel as could be got should be sent over without delay; also any owners or charterers, together with the ship's register, and all proper documents, according to American law, to prove all details respecting the vessel.

I found it impossible, by all the efforts I could make, to obtain such information in regard to the "Osprey" as would meet the requirements of Mr. MCMAHON; and, having regard to the result of the inquiry, of which a full detail will be hereafter given, I did not see any such prospect of Mr. WING's being enabled, without the personal aid of JOHN LEWIS himself, as would justify my retaining and giving general instructions to Mr. WING on the terms suggested by him.

With every aid and facility that could be rendered to me by the British Consul, Mr. ARCHIBALD, by the Chief Collector of Customs, General ARTHUR, and the Deputy-Collector, I prosecuted for two days successively—the 7th and 8th the most careful search through all the registers and official records of the port of New York, but without succeeding in finding any trace whatever of any ship of that name having entered or left that port corresponding with the date given by JOHN LEWIS. A ship named the "Osprey" did leave New York on the 1st of June, 1854, but this vessel could not have rescued the "Bella" boat in April preceding.

I also made search at the Custom House of Perth Amboy, a port which has a register independent of New York, and at which vessels sailing from the Hudson River, and from Sandy Hook, do, under certain special circumstances, obtain clearances, and I could find no trace there of such vessel.

I had also made careful search at the office of the Norwegian Consul, through the year 1854, and some years preceding, for any vessel bearing this name, and for any vessel having a captain of the name of BANNATT, but without discovering any trace thereof.

Also I consulted various persons of long experience in such matters, and, amongst others, Captain HARDING, the agent of the French LLOYD's, by whom is issued the Shipping List called the *French Veritas*, mentioned by JOHN LEWIS. The agency for this not having been established in New York previous to 1857, I could get no information as to 1854, except by application to the central office, 188, Rue Royale, Brussels.

My notes and memoranda will show specifically the inquiries made by me, and the result, which may be summed up in the fact that I could find no official record of any ship called the "Osprey" leaving New York in February, 1854; and as no definite information as to any such ship could be obtained from the firm of FUNCKE and EDYE, to whom JOHN LEWIS referred as the owners or agents for such ship, under the circumstances to be after mentioned, I had no instructions to give to Mr. WING other than to pursue an indefinite inquiry as to this ship "Osprey," which might be endless, and most costly, but was not likely to lead to any practical result without further information, and the personal presence and aid of JOHN LEWIS himself.

Although I could not see my way to retaining Mr. WING generally for the carrying out of the Memorandum of Instructions, as prepared by Mr. McMAHON, I did retain him, with suitable fees, for the purpose of advising myself periodically as to the course which, under the circumstances, it was advisable for me to adopt; and it was in pursuance of his advice that I proceeded on the 12th August to New Bedford, 400 miles from New York, and thence to Quebec, about 500 further still, in search of traces of the ship "Osprey."

After these journeys which, for the reasons stated in my notes, were attended with no results so far as obtaining definite information as to such a ship "Osprey" as JOHN LEWIS speaks of, I returned to New York on the 19th August; and having again conferred with Mr. WING as to the result of my journeys, left the matter in his hands to await such instructions as might be remitted to him from London, either with or without the personal assistance of JOHN LEWIS. And in explanation of this, I refer to the notes and memoranda as to the "Osprey" and of the efforts made by me in search of CARL ANDERSON and HARRY named by JOHN LEWIS.

In the mean time, and subject to such further explanation as JOHN LEWIS may afford as a basis for instruction for further inquiry for the "Osprey" and her officers and crew, I proceed to point out those features in JOHN LEWIS' statement which confirm the belief that his evidence as to the rescue of the Defendant from the wreck boat of the "Bella" is true, notwithstanding that, by reason of the lapse of nearly twenty years and from other at present inscrutable causes, the history of the ship itself cannot be recovered.

JEAN LUIE.

Before I left, however, JOHN LEWIS gave me various names of persons to see, with description of their positions and relations to the ship "Osprey"; and he also gave me letters of introduction to two of such persons.

One of the persons referred to was Mr. FUNCKE, of the firm of FUNCKE and EDYE, formerly and in 1854 FUNCKE and MEINKE, and so described by JOHN LEWIS.

Mr. FUNCKE, who, I was informed by our Consul, is one of the leading merchants in New York, entered into the affair with the utmost kindness and desire to aid me in the inquiry, and stated the references made by JOHN LEWIS in the statement which I had taken down in writing from him, also in the letters of introduction he had given me, were quite correct in so far as he described the duties and the position of the various persons so referred to: and that it appeared to him that no one could possibly make mention or write letters as JOHN LEWIS had done, without having a thorough acquaintance with the persons referred to, and with the mode in which the business of their firm was carried on in 1854.

CLERK was one, and PETERSON—also DALSTROM the cashier. VOLCKERT, the clerk to Messrs. THOMSON, was dead, and the firm broken up. BIORCKMAN, who shipped men for service, was dead, as also ROBINSON, who kept the Scandinavian Hotel, where they resorted; but the mode in which JOHN LEWIS refers to all these persons was, according to Mr. FUNCKE and various other persons whom he called in to assist him in recalling the events of 1854, quite conclusive as to the fact that JOHN LEWIS was intimately connected with them and their duties, in relation to the shipping business of FUNCKE and MEINKE.

It appeared that such business would have been attended to by Mr. MEINKE, who died in 1860, and all the books relating to the firm of 1854 had been destroyed by fire or were otherwise not to be found. Mr. FUNCKE, had caused a careful search to be made as to this, previous to my visit, and in consequence of my telegram through ROTHSCHILD, and BELMONT and Co., but without effect, and although he had some recollection of the name of the "Osprey," he could not recollect any particulars.

The only person now surviving, who was in their employ in

1854, was a man named GODECKE, who is retired under a pension for old age and long service to the firm, and this person being sent for, stated that he had a recollection of having seen the name of the "Osprey" in the manifest books of Messrs. FUNCKE and MEINKE, and in the handwriting of Baron FALKENBERG, who was at that time in the employment of FUNCKE and MEINKE; and he also remembered the name of Capt. BANNATT, and on a subsequent day Mr. GODECKE brought to meet me at the office of Messrs. FUNCKE and MEINKE an old boatman named MATHESON, and he had also some recollection of a ship called the "Osprey," with which FUNCKE and MEINKE were connected in 1854.

With reference to Baron FALKENBERG, of whom JOHN LEWIS speaks as being the owner, or otherwise connected with the "Osprey," it appears that he was at that time in the employment of FUNCKE and MEINKE, and had a separate establishment or agency at Quebec, which continued till his death about six months ago; and JOHN LEWIS refers to him as having been the owner of other ships at New Bedford, and it appeared on inquiry there, that this was so, and that about 1854 he purchased a new ship built at New Bedford, and gave it his own name, "Falkenberg."

I refer to my notes and memoranda for such more exact information as to all these details as may enable Counsel to decide whether they could, without prejudice to the defence, put JOHN LEWIS into the witness-box, leaving it to the prosecution to contradict his statement.

It is my opinion that there is abundant corroboration of the fact that JOHN LEWIS is speaking the truth when he states that the Defendant is the man he saved from the "Bella's" boat, and nursed for three months for sunstroke; and that, without further expenditure which it is not in fact in the Defendant's power to incur, the jury may with confidence be expected to give weight to his evidence as being in itself corroborative of other evidence given on the Trial in the Common Pleas, and also consistent in itself, and that it would be most unjust towards the Defendant to expect him to establish by evidence, to be collected from all parts of the world, all the details respecting a vessel that reached Melbourne in 1854; and the following are the grounds for that opinion:—

1st. Unless all the evidence given in the Common Pleas as to the arrival at Melbourne in July, 1854, of the ship "Osprey" is to go for nothing, and to be set aside as concocted, and forming part of the Defendant's conspiracy, then the evidence now offered by JOHN LEWIS is corroborated by all that evidence, and in return corroborates the evidence so given in the Common Pleas. The "Osprey" evidence, as extracted in the pamphlet published by Mr. ONSLOW, is as little broken down by cross-examination as any such evidence could be, and is in itself as conclusive as that of JOHN LEWIS, that a boat's crew was rescued from the "Bella."

Nothing can be more certain to myself, and to all who take an active interest in this Case, that no one can have offered to JOHN LEWIS any inducement, by money or otherwise, to invent such a story as he gave to myself on his first appearance; and if the idea ever occurred to him of gaining something by voluntarily presenting to us such a fabrication, there have been time and efforts enough to detect it: whereas, on the contrary, all who have been in personal communication with LEWIS are thoroughly convinced of his honesty and truth, and I, who have examined his references at New York, retain fully the opinion that he is a true and honest witness.

The difficulty as to the "Osprey" not being traceable in the official records of New York admits of several possible explanations.

The Custom House records at Perth Amboy, where she might have cleared out, are kept in an irregular and loose way, not being entered in any book or register, but merely vouched for by the retention of a copy of the certificate of charter, of which another copy is sent to Washington; and it will give some idea of the state of these records that a copy of a certificate granted to a ship in 1854 is indorsed upon a copy of a certificate granted in 1851; and, so far as we could discover by these records, there had been none granted in the interval between that of 1851 and 1854, although the collector told me that at certain periods there would be a great number of ships entered and cleared at Perth Amboy instead of at New York. Then there is another port of clearance, at which, as I was informed, a ship might possibly have cleared out—namely, Newark, but as to which there seemed to be no means whatever of arriving at any certain knowledge of what might have occurred in 1854.

Another possible explanation was that the "Osprey" might have merely called at Sandy Hook, as many ships do, without going within the limits either of the port of New York or of Perth Amboy; and in that case she might have sailed, as JOHN LEWIS says, from Sandy Hook without any notice being taken in any official records of either of those ports. Another possible explanation is that she might have stolen away surreptitiously, and without having her papers properly verified, and reasons are not wanting to prove that this was, in fact, what did actually occur.

JOHN LEWIS says there was a disputed ownership in the case, and Captain BANNATT had claims upon the vessel, which were disputed by his owners in Norway, and he and FALKENBERG had, as it would appear, dealt with the ship as their own.

If for this or any other reason she had left New York surreptitiously, it would account for the fact of her not being duly verified at Melbourne, as deposed to by Mr. CHILDERS; and the following fact, brought to light at New York, lends some support to this suggestion:—

On the 30th of July a leading article appeared in the *New York Journal of Commerce* exposing, as was therein alleged, the TICHBORNE imposition, by tracing a vessel called the "Osprey" from New York to Melbourne, under dates inconsistent with the Defendant's story. It was shown in this article that there was at Melbourne on the 1st December, 1854, a vessel called the "Osprey;" of this there is no doubt, as it was recorded in the shipping list of the *Melbourne Argus*, of 4th December, 1854, which was shown to me. It was also certain that a ship called the "Osprey" did leave New York on 1st June, 1854, and the article in the *Journal of Commerce* stated that this vessel which so left New York on the 1st of June was the same as was in the port of Melbourne on the 1st December.

By very close and difficult inquiry, I ascertained that the vessel which so left New York on the 1st of June could not have been the vessel that was in Melbourne on the 1st December. I traced the course of that vessel of 1st June to St. Stephen's, in New Brunswick, and thence to Bristol, and back again to New York on the 7th of May, 1855, and I succeeded with difficulty in obtaining the insertion by the editor in the *Journal of Commerce* of a letter from myself, completely exposing the error he had committed, and calling upon him to acknowledge his error, and to explain, if he could, where the "Osprey" which was in Melbourne in December, 1854, came from, if it were not that which is alleged to have rescued the "Bella's" boat. The Editor of the paper could not, or did not give any reply, and he admitted to me that it was not impossible that the "Osprey" might have left New York surreptitiously without any notice on the official records, and that he had known many instances of ships having done so.

2nd. Another ground for relying upon JOHN LEWIS' statement is the intrinsic evidence of its veracity, from various incidents, one of which being entirely within my own personal knowledge, is quite conclusive; for instance, JOHN LEWIS, in reply to my question, told me that the Defendant, whom he had not then seen, if he was the man whom he saved from the "Bella," and nursed for three months, would recognize him by reason of a crooked finger which caused annoyance to TICHBORNE whilst being rubbed at the back of his head, as he used to be by LEWIS.

At the interview between JOHN LEWIS and the Defendant, the former recognized the Defendant almost immediately, but the Defendant did not recognize him until he noticed, by shaking hands with him, this crooked finger—and this he did without being informed of what JOHN LEWIS had told me.

The prosecution may of course allege that this is all collusion, and a part of some conspiracy to which I and others, they may suggest, are parties; but so far as the friends and professional advisers of the Defendant are concerned it does not seem necessary that we should hesitate to act upon what to us is certain knowledge, because as to conspiracy collusion, not one tittle of evidence exists, or has been even suggested in the case for the prosecution.

3rd. The statement of JOHN LEWIS that the Defendant was suffering from sunstroke for the three months' voyage to Melbourne, supported by the medical evidence, is corroborated by the eccentric career which the Defendant entered upon from the moment of his arrival at Melbourne, all through his Australian life, and explains also the loss and defect of memory.

His mother seems to have instinctively anticipated this evidence of JOHN LEWIS, when in her letter to GIBBES she said that her son ROGER's mind must have been affected by what he had gone through; and so in fact it was, and LEWIS' story gives the clue to the entire mystery of the Defendant's career.

For these reasons I think JOHN LEWIS should be at once examined.

I proceed to give details of my inquiries and interviews with various parties on which the foregoing report is based, and from which instructions can readily be prepared for such further inquiry as may be deemed material.

It will be obvious that if JOHN LEWIS had invented this tale amongst his associates at the Mahogany Bar at Wapping or elsewhere, he would not have given the names of eminent ship-brokers and others at New York, who he must have known would at once contradict him; and if such a scheme of deception can be imagined to have moved him at first, he would certainly have shifted his ground when examined by myself on the eve of my departure for New York; but, on the contrary, his statement throughout has been completely consistent and the same.

That all these people should be dead Mr. FUNCKE said was not unlikely: they were Swedes, and much given to drink, for which the temptation was great in their business of visiting vessels; but some of them may have left the books and memoranda which may yet be looked for and examined for what occurred to them in 1854, and having regard to the difficulty of tracing out such matters in New York, where everything changes in seven years more than in three times that period in England, and at this season men of business are away from New York, and the difficulty of following up an inquiry as I did with hundreds of miles intervening between each step, it cannot be asserted that the Defendant, in putting in JOHN LEWIS has failed in any possible effort to corroborate and support him.

JOHN LEWIS stated that FUNCKE and MEINKE, of New York, were the ship-brokers, agents, or owners of the ship "Osprey."

Mr. ARCHIBALD, the British Consul, informed me that the firm of FUNCKE and MEINKE had ceased to exist under that name, Mr.

MEINKE having died, but that it was continued under the firm of FUNCKE and EDYE, and was one of the leading ship-brokers in New York. I called at this office, 27, South William-street, on the 6th August, and Mr. FUNCKE not being in, I was informed by his cashier, Mr. PRECHT, that in consequence of an application from Messrs. BELMONT, the agents of ROTHSCHILD, they had made search for any books or records of the year 1854, but without effect, and that he believed they had all been destroyed by fire or lost, but that he would make further search and report to me on the following day, when I could see Mr. FUNCKE himself.

On the 7th I called and saw Mr. FUNCKE, and he expressed his regret to find that he had no books or documents whatever of that period.

He offered every aid in his power, and the following is the substance of his statement.

In the year 1854 I was in partnership with Mr. MEINKE, who has since died, and my firm might have been the agents and brokers for a ship named the "Osprey" which is referred to in the letter of JOHN LEWIS dated the 25th July, 1873, and addressed to Mr. VOLCKERT, and now shown to me, although I have no personal recollections on the subject.

I have no books to which I can refer as to the business done by my firm at that date, all such books having been, to the best of my belief, burnt or lost; and the death of Mr. MEINKE and the change of firm and the removal of our business from one place to another no less than six times, being sufficient to account for my want of recollection as to any particular ship of which we may in 1854 have been the brokers.

I have read the letters of JOHN LEWIS to Mr. VOLCKERT and to Mr. PETERSON, and the same seem to have been written by a person who had a knowledge of those who were, in 1854, in our employ, and with whom, as steward of the "Osprey," he would have been in communication; and unless he had such business with our firm I do not believe that he could have written letters containing so many facts, and referred, as he does correctly, to persons in our employment, as by the said letters he does.

I am well acquainted with AXELL GODECKE as having been for twenty-one years in the employment of my firm, and now receiving a pension from us.

I am certain that the said AXELL GODECKE would not make any statement on the subject of the ship "Osprey," or otherwise, that he did not verily believe to be true.

Mr. FUNCKE further stated that he would continue to make such search and inquiry as he could, and if he found anything bearing on the subject would communicate it to Mr. WING, the solicitor whom I have retained to collect and arrange any such further evidence; but Mr. FUNCKE repeatedly expressed his belief in the substantial truth of JOHN LEWIS's evidence in so far as that, by giving him and others as a reference, he must have been aware that if his story were untrue it could not be confirmed by them, but would in all reasonable probability have been open to positive and plain contradiction. The only person he could call to mind who would be likely to have some recollection of those times was an old pensioner of their firm, named AXELL GODECKE, and he appointed him to meet me on the following day, the 7th August.

On the 7th day of August I met, at the office of Messrs FUNCKE and EDYE, the said AXELL GODECKE, an elderly person, and somewhat infirm.

He confirmed what had been stated by Mr. FUNCKE, as to the various persons referred to by JOHN LEWIS, and his statement made on that and subsequent occasions was substantially as follows:—

I, AXELL GODECKE, now residing at 192, Park-avenue, Hoboken, New York, state:—

1st.—I was in the employ of Messrs. FUNCKE and MEINKE in the year of 1854, it the capacity of water clerk, and for other duties connected with the ships, for which that firm were brokers and agents. I have now retired from their service on a pension granted to me by one of that firm.

2nd.—Mr. MEINKE, then a member of the firm, is dead, and also many of the persons who were at that time employed by them in and about the duties connected with their business, and amongst others, Mr. FALKENBERG, Mr. PETERSON, Mr. DALSTROM, Mr. BIORCKMAN, and Mr. VOLCKERT.

3rd.—Have read the letter signed JOHN LUIE, steward of the "Osprey," 1854, addressed to Mr. VOLCKERT, also the letter signed by him, and addressed to Mr. PETERSON, and dated July 25th, 1873, and in so far as such letters refer to events and persons connected with the firm of FUNCKE and MEINKE in 1854, the writer's statements are quite in accordance with what happened, or might have happened. In his letter to Mr. VOLCKERT he mentions a Captain BANNATT, and I have a recollection of having heard of such a person in connection with some ship of which FUNCKE and MEINKE were brokers. He also mentions in the same letter Mr. M. PETERSON's brother-in-law, as being the shipping master, and I remember that the brother-in-law of Mr. M. PETERSON was a shipping master, employed by FUNCKE and MEINKE, and his name was BIORCKMAN.

I also well knew Mr. VOLCKERT, to whom the letter is addressed, as late in the employment of Messrs. THOMSON, shipbrokers, and I know that he was employed by that firm.

4th.—I have a recollection of having seen the name "Osprey" in FUNCKE and MEINKE's manifest books, and it was in the handwriting of Baron FALKENBERG, who was in 1854 in the employment of FUNCKE and MEINKE. The manifest book being a book that contains a written description of the cargo of ships. The letters of JOHN LUTE to PETERSON and VOLCKERT are evidently written by a person who knows the parts spoken of, which are all true. He refers to the brother-in-law who was shipping master, and his name, BIORCKMAN. All he says in both letters is perfectly true about those persons.

Remembers two Captain BANNATTS—one a Swede, the other a Norwegian; thinks he can find a person who, if this one was a Swede, knew him. It was his (GODECKE's) business to go round the vessels and wait upon the captains.

There is an old stevedore, named CRUSOE, who may know something about it, and I will see him on the subject. I remember ROBINSON, who kept the "Scandinavian Arms;" he is dead, and all these people used to frequent his house, whilst they were engaged in clearing out any vessel at Perth Amboy.

Mr. GODECKE further promised to make inquiry, and he subsequently brought to me, at Messrs. FUNCKE's office, an old boatman who had been in the year 1854 employed by that firm, and the following was the statement of this man:—

JOHN MATHESON, of No. 7, Third-street, Hoboken. Am a boatman employed by brokers in carrying to and from ships. Was employed by FUNCKE and MEINKE for about 16 years, and was so employed in 1854. I have some recollection of a ship named the "Osprey" about 1854, of which FUNCKE and MEINKE were brokers. Have no distinct recollection, and fear I may have lost the books in which there would be the names entered. Will search all my papers for "Osprey" and let you know. And as to names mentioned by him in his letters, I remember them all.

BIORCKMAN, the shipping master, had a partner whose name I now forget. He will perhaps remember the "Osprey." Will inquire and let Mr. WING know the result.

With reference to the various persons named by JOHN LEWIS, viz., PETERSON, DALSTROM, VOLCKERT, and FALKENBERG, it would be expedient to follow up the inquiry by seeing their relations, and those connected with them in business or otherwise, and endeavour to discover, by entries in old books or otherwise, their transactions in 1854, and from some or other of them information might be got; but this is a task requiring much time and considerable cost. I did what I could in this respect, and I saw the brother of PETERSON, referred to by JOHN LEWIS, who confirmed generally the statement of LEWIS, as to his brother's positions and dates in connection with the shipping, and also that of BIORCKMAN and others, but could only say that he would endeavour to find, in old books and papers, whether he was in February, 1854, connected with the "Osprey." Also as to Baron FALKENBERG, referred to by LEWIS as part owner of the "Osprey," I thought it worth while to go to Quebec, where he had carried on business for many years till his death a few months since. He was Consul for Sweden and Norway, and has since been succeeded by his son, who, when I reached Quebec, was absent, and I was referred by his wife to Mr. JOHNSON, his manager.

Mr. JOHNSON knew nothing, but would cause a search to be made amongst old books, and would communicate the result to Mr. THORN, the editor of the *Quebec Morning Chronicle*, whose statement was as follows:—

At Quebec: August, 1873.

I have been Acting Consul for about five months since the death of Baron FALKENBERG, who was my predecessor since 1855. Baron FALKENBERG was in partnership with FUNCKE, MEINKE, and Company, of New York and Quebec. Do not remember his being connected with New Bedford, nor of his being connected with a ship called the "Osprey." I had no connection with Baron FALKENBERG till 1858. His son, who now carries on his business, is only twenty-two years of age, and is now absent from Quebec. There are, or may be, a few old books (letter books) of the date of 1854, but as he only commenced business at Quebec that year it is not likely there are. Will make inquiry, considering it to be of great importance to obtain information from Baron FALKENBERG's books. I left the matter in the hands of Mr. THORN, to see the widow of Baron FALKENBERG, also a person who was an intimate friend, and might remember or be able to obtain information, and being obliged myself to leave Quebec I left my son there to follow up this inquiry.

JOHN LEWIS stated that this Baron FALKENBERG was the owner of other ships at New Bedford, and I found on visiting New Bedford that in 1854 he bought, and gave his own name, FALKENBERG, to a ship of 419 tons burden, which for some years traded from Boston.

In searching the Custom House Register at New Bedford, found a ship named the "Osprey," of which the captain was THURSTON MACOMBER. This was a whaling ship, and sailed on June 3rd, 1851, and did not return till October 2nd, 1854.

In 1852 and 1853 she seems to have been engaged in the fishing trade in the Indian Ocean, in the vicinity of the Seychelles Islands and Mauritius, and in 1854 she was at a place called Tohaurah, and sailed from Table Bay, Cape of Good Hope, on April 22nd, 1854, but was not in the latitude of the "Bella" at the time she is supposed to have been lost.

Found in Register of Sailors in New Bedford: No LUIE, but many LEWISES.

The following is a copy of letter in reply to application to Mr. FALKENBERG:—

Mrs. FALKENBERG's compliments to Mr. WHALLEY. She begs to say her son is out of town; he may not return until Tuesday.

Mrs. FALKENBERG is sure he will give any information he may possess, or Mr. WHALLEY might call at the office, Peter-street. And Mr. JOHNSON, who was for many years with Baron FALKENBERG, might perhaps know something more concerning it.

4, Clapham-terrace, Sunday morning.

AS TO THE "OSPREY" AT NEW YORK.

The British Consul, on my calling on him on the 7th day of August, handed me the following as the result of his search of the Custom House Registers, and which he had made in anticipation of my visit, and in consequence of application of ROTHSCHILD'S agents, BELMONT and Co.

"7th August, 1873.

"A return made to him from Custom House.

"Ship 'Osprey.'

"JOHN TOMLINSON, master, cleared May 31st, 1854. In ballast for St. Stephen's.

"Ship 'Osprey.'

"JOHN TOMLINSON, master, cleared May 24th, 1855. W 787, B Basin, 1874, for St. Stehpen's."

I made careful search myself on the 7th, and again, in old books containing the entries of ships, on the 8th August, but could find no "Osprey" sailing in February, 1854.

In addition to the "Osprey" which sailed 31st May, Captain TOMLINSON, I found the following:—

"'Osprey' of E —— G ——, British; arrived 21st May, 1855."

The collector of customs, and also the deputy-collector, afforded me every facility, and looked up, at great trouble, old registers, and it is suggested she might have cleared out for the Port of Perth Amboy, near Sandy Hook, about forty miles distant. Visited that place and inspected all the records the collector of customs had in his charge.

The only record kept at this port of vessels that have cleared out there consists in the actual counterpart of their register or license, and as the same is not entered in any book, but kept loosely in a cover, it might easily happen that it would be lost or disappear, being, in fact, nothing more than a loose document kept with a great number of other miscellaneous papers, of little or no value.

A copy of this, as was stated by Mr. McNIGHT, sent to the Department at Washington, made it of less importance to keep the copy safely at this outlying port, the history and course of business at which is very eccentric.

I could not visit Washington, and Mr. McNIGHT promised to give me any further information he might obtain by further search amongst the papers of this office, but I did not hear from him. He is a very respectable gentleman, who combines the business of a physician in good practice with that of collector of customs, and depended chiefly on his deputy, who was absent when I was there.

Newark is another outlying or branch port, at which I was told the "Osprey" might possibly have cleared out, and thus account for the name not appearing in the New York register; but from inquiry I made, there is no authentic record of the shipping of that period, 1854, to be found there, nor even such as I met with at Perth Amboy.

As to the possibility of the "Osprey" having sailed, as JOHN LEWIS says, from Sandy Hook without entering any port, either Amboy or New York, I was informed by the collector at Amboy that this might have happened, and that ships did frequently call in and sail again without coming within the limits of the port.

As to the possibility or the degree of probability of a ship such as the "Osprey" leaving the port, either of Amboy or Newark, or New York, surreptitiously, I was informed by Mr. STONE, the editor of the *New York Journal of Commerce*, that this had occurred on many occasions within his own recollection, and there would in that case be no official record.

AS TO THE 1ST OF JUNE "OSPREY."

If JOHN LEWIS' statement was untrue he might have been quite certain that it would be contradicted by positive evidence forthcoming at New York, and as an instance of this the case of the "Osprey" which left New York on the 1st June, according to the Custom House Register before quoted, is worthy of attention.

On the 30th July last there appeared in the *New York Journal of Commerce*—the paper of the highest authority in the United States on all that relates to ships and shipping, the following leading article in which it will be seen they state as a fact that this was the "Osprey" that went to Melbourne in that year, and to which the "Osprey" evidence on the part of Defendant referred.

If this statement were true, namely, that a ship named the "Osprey" did sail from NewYork to St. Stephen's and thence to Melbourne, it would be not unreasonable to infer that this was the ship that arrived at Melbourne towards the end of that year, and to which the Defendant's witnesses in the Common Pleas referred, and that it was also the same ship that was at Melbourne on 1st December, 1854, as appears in the *Melbourne Argus* of December.

On reading this article I instituted inquiry as to the ship, and succeeded at length in obtaining the certificate of the broker Mr. COOK, also of Mr. ROBERT MACKIE, the agent of LLOYD'S at New York, that this ship did not go to Melbourne in that year as stated in the *New York Journal*; but that after reaching St. Stephen's she loaded with timber for England and made the voyage to Bristol, and that she again returned from Bristol to New York on the 7th of May in the following year, after a passage from Bristol of thirty-one days.

The agents at New York were Messrs. COOK and SMITH, and I annex the letter of Mr. COOK, the surviving partner. And any further evidence that may be required may be got from Messrs. WILKINS, of Bristol, the agents there.

New York, August 8th, 1873.

Mr. WHALLEY.

DEAR SIR,—I find in reference to my books, that COOK and SMITH chartered the British ship "Osprey" on the 31st May, 1854, to load deals at St. Stephen's, N.B., for Bristol, England, and have no doubt of her having performed the voyage.—Respectfully yours,

GEORGE E. COOK,
(formerly of the firm of COOK and SMITH.)

The following is substantially the statement on this point of Mr. ROBERT MACKIE, of 24, Beaver-street, New York, merchant. He has been the agent of LLOYD'S in New York since the year 1856, and well acquainted with all that relates to the shipping business of that port since 1849. Have made inquiry respecting the ship "Osprey," which appears on the register of Customs to have left the port of New York on the 31st of May for St. Stephen's, and find that she reached St. Stephen's in New Brunswick in due course and left that port for Bristol, England, loaded with timber. That she returned to New York on 7th May, 1855, and again cleared out from that port for St. Stephen's on the 24th May. That the Custom House register for St. Stephen's should contain entries of her arrival there, also the books of Messrs. COOK and SMITH, the brokers. There she cleared out for St. Stephen's to go thence to Bristol. And the Custom House Register of New York shows her return to that port and that she again cleared out for St. Stephen's on 24th May, 1855. That having regard to these dates, she could not have been at Melbourne on 1st December in the year 1854. That it appears by the *Melbourne Argus* newspaper of 4th December, 1854, that a ship named the "Osprey" was up for sailing on the 1st December for Sydney. That this could not have been the same ship which left New York on 1st June, 1854, and again on the 24th May, 1855.

The ship "Osprey" which was at Melbourne on 1st December, 1855, might have sailed from Sandy Hook in February, 1854, without having been recorded in the New York Custom register. She might possibly have cleared out from Perth Amboy, or from Newark, near New York, or from some other port, and merely called at New York or Sandy Hook without discharging or embarking cargo, and in that case on showing papers she would be free to sail without being registered in the Custom House books of New York.

Having ascertained these facts, I addressed a letter to the *New York Journal of Commerce*, which they inserted, as annexed; and, as they omitted to make any apology or contradiction of their previous article, I again wrote asking them to explain, if they could, from their world-wide sources of information, where the "Osprey" that was in Melbourne on 1st December, 1854, came from, unless it was the "Osprey" spoken of by JOHN LEWIS; but they would not insert it.

As to various "Ospreys":—

The name "Osprey" seems to be a favourite amongst shipowners, and this may afford some mode of clearing up the mystery as to what particular ship of that name rescued the crew of the "Bella."

It is certain that on the 1st of December, 1854, there was in Melbourne Harbour an "Osprey" which is not accounted for; and this seems to be a reasonable answer to the evidence of Mr. CHILDERS, for although no such ship is recorded as having entered that harbour, it is clear that the ship advertised in the *Melbourne Argus* of 4th December as being up for sailing to Sydney on the 1st, must have entered the port as before stated. Mr. STONE, the Editor of the *New York Journal of Commerce*, who claims for his paper the most complete shipping intelligence, can give no account for it.

The French Veritas, in which JOHN LEWIS suggested it might be found, I searched, so far as copies of it are to be found in New York, and found no less than four ships named "Osprey"—this is in the List for 1870—the Lists for 1854 can only be got at the head office in Brussels, No. 188, Rue Royale.

In *New York Register* for 1854, I found more than one "Osprey," and at New Bedford two, but none that answer to our "Osprey," and a paragraph referring to an "Osprey" at Baltimore appeared in the papers.

Almost the only register in which I failed to find an "Osprey," or "Ospray," was in the registers of the Norwegian Consulate, which I searched most carefully from 1851 to 1855, and as "Osprey" is not a Norwegian word, it seems likely that if she was built in Norway or Sweden, the name might have been changed either before LEWIS joined her or afterwards, and this may have resulted from the disputed ownership he refers to.

There is another point on which JOHN LEWIS may be enabled to give further explanation. He says the "Osprey" traded coastwise between New Bedford and New York. This I find she could not do, as a foreign-built vessel, unless rebuilt to the extent of two-thirds in America, could not become entitled to trade coastwise if purchased by an American citizen.

AS TO SAILORS—ANDERSON AND HARRY.

My adventures in search of these men would be more amusing than profitable to narrate, and I have only to say as to CARL

ANDERSON, of 19th Street, Brooklyn, that no such person could be found there now, though I heard of several, and that having followed up one after the other at great cost of time, labour, and money, I at last gave it up, when I found that in Brooklyn Directory there were no less than about 200 persons of the name of ANDERSON, and as to HARRY, all I can say is that there are several sail-makers at the East River, and I believe scores of persons named HARRY have been and are employed by them but; it would be a work of months in a district like this where people appear to change their residence habitually every month (a year is looked upon as an old inhabitant) to find these persons.

I at length advertised for them with a reward, got several replies, of which the annexed is a specimen:—

Naval Hospital, Brooklyn, L.I., August 11th, 1873.

SIR,—Having seen a personal notice in the *New York Sun* of this day in reference to CARL ANDERSON, a sailor who sailed in the ship "Osprey" in February, 1854,

I would respectfully inform you that I have been a shipmate of the said CARL ANDERSON for the last two years, and by your calling or sending to the above place at any convenient time, the desired information of his whereabouts can be obtained from me. —Very respectfully yours, &c.,

JOHN SLATTERY.

I called on the writer, whom I found to be a sailor in the Naval Hospital, and the account he gave was that the man in question was now serving on board the U.S.S. "Ticonderoga," on the Brazil station, and I attach no importance to it.

I annex a copy of my advertisement, and if it be deemed requisite to make further inquiry, I suggest that some such person as the writer of the letter, which I also annex, should be employed.

TICHBORNE CLAIMANT.

"Twenty dollars reward to anyone who will find CARL ANDERSON, a sailor in the ship "Osprey," that left Sandy Hook for Melbourne in February, 1854. He is supposed to have kept a liquor-shop, in or near 19 Street, Brooklyn, about eighteen months ago.

"Also the like reward to a sailor known by the name of HARRY, who about that time worked in a sailmaker's yard near the East River."

To following letter I reply, to make an appointment for 6 p.m. on the following day, but was unfortunately prevented from reaching the hotel in time, and found that the writer of the letter and Mr. WILCOX referred to therein had left, and I had not again the means of meeting them, as no address is given. This is an instance of the time and difficulties involved in these investigations.

August, 11th 1873.

SIR,—Seeing it reported in the papers that you are seeking information relative to the ship "Osprey," I take great pleasure in informing you that HUBERT WILSON Esq., of that city, is in possession of the log-book of that vessel covering the period of time that is referred to in the TICHBORNE Trial. Out of admiration for you and the noble cause of which you are the champion, at my solicitations Mr. WILSON has consented to submit the book to your inspection to take therefrom anything that would be of use to you in prosecution of what I and all Americans consider a just claim.

This log-book is a much-prized family relic, and Mr. WILSON would very justly refuse to let it out of his possession.

But believing it contains valuable information, he will bring it you himself. So if you name any hour at your convenience on to-morrow (Tuesday) evening we will call at your hotel.

I send this by special messenger, to whom you will favour a reply.—I have the honor to be, yours &c.,

T. W. GOFF.

HON. G. H. WHALLEY.

AS TO AMERICAN EVIDENCE AND THE COST OF IT.

If further reasons were required for examining JOHN LEWIS without waiting for corroborative evidence from America, it should be found in the enormous cost and difficulty of collecting and bringing witnesses thence to Westminster.

As before stated, it cannot be collected except through the agency of lawyers, and they must be aided by persons such as are employed in similar cases, as explained in the letter before quoted of Mr. KIMBER. And it may be observed that every sort of professional service in America is by much more than double the cost to what it is in England.

That it is from no desire to take credit for such evidence without having a good excuse for not producing it in Court, I will now refer to the state of public opinion in New York and elsewhere, showing, as it does, that by the suppression of public discussion, and by the circulation through the press of these summaries—so called—of the evidence by the *Daily News*, the *Telegraph*, the *Times*, and others, all of which, as is known to those who read or hear the evidence as given in Court, being unfair to the Defendant, there is not, so far as I could find, one single newspaper in New York, or in America, that has not long since treated the question as settled against the Defendant, and their observations on the case are merely those of amazement that an imposition so gross and palpable has not been punished years ago; but it does suggest inquiry why so much money should be spent by the Government, and such anxiety and efforts exhibited by the Court of Queen's Bench to suppress public discussion. I was much beset by interviewers, and some of the remarks which appeared in the newspapers, as the same chanced to be seen by me, I have extracted and annexed. And these, as also the meetings I attended at Montreal, left the impression on my mind that if time and attention were given to it, public sympathy in America might be aroused by showing the extent to which the press in England had lent itself, by mis-report or by silence, to the designs of the Prosecution. On one point, however, there can be no doubt whatever that the only possible means of arousing again any interest in a question of which people in America had become thoroughly weary, is to present it, as I believe it can be so truly represented, as a Jesuit conspiracy to "kill the heir and keep the inheritance." I have had very many communications and letters to this effect, of which the following is a specimen:—

Steel's Hotel, New York: Aug. 7th, 1873.

SIR,—I was one of the supporters of the Claimant in London, and still believe in him. I have frequently spoken in public in his favour. I have been in this country about 12 months, and have mixed myself up with the politics, the business, and the society of this town, and might be of service to you in your very difficult mission. As the Irish element is very strong here, and the opposition to Roman Catholic aggression also strong, I think your visit might be hailed by the latter party, and upon the real arguments in favour of Sir ROGER being known, some assistance might be forthcoming out of personal respect for you.

I once had the pleasure of hearing you speak in the House of Commons, and should you wish to see me I should be happy to wait upon you for the sake of the good old times in the dear old country.—I am, Sir, yours respectfully,

HENRY S. PRICE.

My address is Steel's Hotel, Greenwich-street.

The main point for consideration being whether JOHN LEWIS should be examined without being first prepared with specific evidence to be produced in Court, corroborative of the leading features of his story, I submit that it is not more incumbent on the Defendant to remove all possible grounds of doubt or suspicion in regard to the assertion that he is TICHBORNE, than it is for the Prosecution to remove the doubts and suspicions which surround their proposition that he is not TICHBORNE, and the various circumstantial items of evidence which have been brought forward by them in support of it, and this will lead at once to the question of conspiracy. The direct testimony on the one side and the other consists of those who say he is not TICHBORNE, and those who say he is. And it may be said on behalf of the latter, speaking as all have done, and so far as they can be brought forward will again do, from personal intercourse with him, that they are less likely to be mistaken than those who speak only from seeing him as he sits in Court or otherwise, with much less opportunity of satisfying themselves as to his non-identity than they could if so disposed, avail themselves of, such as talking to him and so forth.

The evidence of JOHN LEWIS is "circumstantial," like that of the tattoo marks, and the Wapping evidence; but it is far less open to suspicion.

It may be impossible to corroborate his account of the ownership and other features of the voyage of the ship by which the Claimant was saved, for want of money or otherwise; but while there is nothing in it contradictory in itself, or which might have not reasonably occurred, there is in the tattoo and Wapping evidence such contradiction as not only forbids belief, but suggests wilful conspiracy in support of the prosecution.

So far from JOHN LEWIS's evidence being in itself improbable, it exactly corresponds with and accounts for all the leading features of Defendant's Case, and Defendant's own story.

It corresponds with the evidence given in Common Pleas as to the "Osprey's" arrival at Melbourne, which is further confirmed by the fact of an "Osprey" being at Melbourne on 1st December, and not otherwise accounted for, as it would have been by the *Journal of Commerce* and others who have become involved in false theories, as to this fact. And above all, JOHN LEWIS, in his description of the condition in which he found the "Bella" crew and the Defendant, accounts in some degree for their not having turned up for twenty years, and for eccentricities of Defendant and loss of memory. In order to make out the Claimant to be ORTON, it is shown that he is the most astute and accomplished swindler that was ever known, and at the same time the most unmitigated fool that ever embarked on such a scheme. When the Defendant is asked to prove the Registers, &c., of the "Osprey," may not he reply by demanding explanation how ORTON could know anything about the "Osprey," and why he should invent a story of being saved by that particular ship? It will be seen that the Editor of the *Journal of Commerce* supplies a theory as to this, but when that is disposed of, neither he nor anyone else can suggest any conceivable reason why ORTON should invent such a story of his escape; nor can one tittle of the corroboration of that story by persons who saw the "Osprey" come into Melbourne and saw the rescued men—the unaccounted-for presence in the port of an "Osprey" on 1st December, and now JOHN LEWIS, be met except by the theory that all these persons, with others, have been in collusion and conspiracy upon this point. How, again, do they account for the fact that ORTON did not take the pains to learn the name of TICHBORNE's mother? nor to use as names of executors persons who identify the fraud? or such extravagant folly as to speak of 66th Dragoons? and that he omitted to get, at the least, a smattering of French, and to get his arms tattooed *à la* TICHBORNE? When it is remembered that he did collect, as is alleged, enough information to baffle the

Attorney-General's Cross-Examination for twenty-six days, at the end of which the Jury and the Court could not discover any perjury—is not all this more wanting in all that claims belief than the story of JOHN LEWIS?

On the other hand, is it not reasonable to ask for an explanation why the Family, all well knowing of the tattoo marks, as they allege, should have kept the secret till after they had expended hundreds of thousands in resisting a civil claim when, by the tattoo alone, if it were true, he could have been stopped by a Criminal prosecution at the outset of his career? And in the absence of this explanation, I now repeat what in 1870 I publicly charged the Family with—viz., a wilful conspiracy then to keep possession of the property, and now to convict an innocent man of perjury and forgery.

In the disclosures as to the PITTENDREIGH letters, the Daguerreotype, the publication of the lithograph letters, and the efforts of the Government to suppress all discussion, there are grounds for the belief that the Defendant is the victim of conspiracy.

What is there in the Defendant's Case to suggest conspiracy on the part of himself or others of the like significance?—If nothing, then every part of the evidence for the prosecution is tainted by such *primâ facie* presumption of conspiracy, whereas every part of the Defendant's evidence is, as well in itself as by comparison with the Prosecution, free from any such suspicion, and may fairly claim to be considered entirely upon its own merits as presented to the Court, and so far as I or anyone can form an opinion by the ordinary tests, JOHN LEWIS is as true a witness as ever stood before a Court.

28 August, 1873. G. H. WHALLEY.

GENERAL EVIDENCE FOR DEFENDANT.

In America, as in England, the agitation of this question brings forward constantly fresh offers of evidence, and some which has come to light in America and Canada seems well entitled to notice.

At Montreal a Mr. HOLBROW called on me and made the following statement, and he subsequently attended a public meeting prepared to repeat it in public if required; but I did not deem it expedient he should do so. He had been for about twenty years in the Army, and for the whole of that period had been attached to the mess service, in which he appeared, by his testimonials he produced to me, to have obtained the confidence and respect of the officers, and to have been treated by them as a man of superior claims to their consideration and friendship. Being a Hampshire man, he had, when at Winchester with the 22nd Regiment, satisfied himself that the Defendant was TICHBORNE, having a personal recollection and a local knowledge that enabled him to be quite certain on that point, and he accordingly risked all his savings, about £300, in bets upon the result of the Trial in the Common Pleas, and by his representations or otherwise, had induced others to do so. While at Dublin, shortly before the Trial in the Common Pleas, he was much in communication with the Honourable ———, an officer in the ——— Regiment, and he had been employed by Captain ——— to make bets for him to the extent of about £9,000. Mr. ——— was the brother-in-law of ——— and was at or about the time when ——— left Dublin for London to give his evidence in the Common Pleas in daily and constant intercourse with him, and he has reason to believe that up to a short time previous to ——— so going to London, he had himself many large bets in favour of the Claimant's identity. That a few days previous to ——— leaving Dublin for London to give his evidence as to the tattoo marks, Mr. ——— told him (HOLBROW) that ——— had made up his mind to give such evidence, and that in consequence thereof the Claimant would surely be defeated, and that they would all lose their bets. That he, Mr. ——— told him, in answer to his inquiries, that he had been told this by ———, and he urged him (HOLBROW) to set to work at once and hedge the bets of him (Mr. ———) and his own, and he did so as far at it was in his power. That he told Mr. ——— at the time, and he firmly believes, that the evidence as to the tattoo marks was only an after-thought, and that it was absolutely false and was concocted during the Trial in the Common Pleas. This person also stated that he was well acquainted with Colonel WILLIAMSON, the brother of Mr. HEDWORTH WILLIAMSON, M.P., and that speaking to him on the subject of the evidence he had given as to the Claimant not being TICHBORNE, he reminded him of the fact that on the occasion when he said that TICHBORNE dined at the mess, and that he met him there, and from so meeting him he could say that the Claimant was not TICHBORNE, that in fact he (Col. WILLIAMSON) did not dine at the mess on the day that TICHBORNE was there, owing to an accident that occurred to Col. WILLIAMSON on that day, and that on being reminded, Col. WILLIAMSON said it was so, but that he thought he must have seen him later in the evening after dinner, but HOLBROW states positively that Col. WILLIAMSON was not present during any part of the time when TICHBORNE was at the mess, and that his evidence must have been given under a total mis-recollection or misapprehension.

Annexed is an extract from a newspaper sent to me—the *Daily Mercury*, New Bedford, of the 15th August, and the following is a copy of a letter which I addressed to the Mr. CROWLEY named therein:—

SIR,—A letter from you to some person in Chicago, and published in the newspaper, has been brought to my notice, and I should feel obliged by your giving me such recollections as to the personal appearance of Mr. TICHBORNE as known to you, by which his identity would be recognized, such as his height, and whether you could speak as to his not being tattooed on his arms. Agents of his opponents, in order to mislead, stated to persons who knew TICHBORNE that the Claimant is upwards of six feet in height, whereas he is only five feet eight and a half inches.—Yours, &c.,

G. H. WHALLEY.

To another letter received by me, and of which a copy is annexed, I have addressed the following reply.

DEAR SIR,—In reply to yours of the 10th of August, I shall feel greatly obliged if you will forward to me, signed by the person you refer to, such a description as his memory will enable him to give of ARTHUR ORTON, the son of GEORGE ORTON, the butcher, of Wapping—viz., his height, whether he was marked with small-pox, or wore earrings, or was tattooed, and any general features he can call to mind.—I am, yours faithfully and obliged,

G. H. WHALLEY.

On board "Scotia," 29th August, 1873.

In addition to the foregoing statement of what appears to me material for the information of Counsel in considering again the question of examining JOHN LEWIS at once, and without the further delay of searching for and bringing evidence from America, I have many letters and notes, and memoranda, of my doings in America and in Canada which may be useful for reference, but which I need not now press on their attention, and the result of the whole, that I earnestly repeat my opinion that JOHN LEWIS should be at once examined.

Nothing has come to my knowledge to impair my confidence in his statement that he was present when the Defendant was rescued from the "Bella" boat, and that he did nurse him for sunstroke during the voyage to Melbourne, while much has occurred to justify the opinion that no man would, or could, have invented such a story, with details that would, if untrue, have brought about its inevitable exposure.

G. H. WHALLEY.

We supplement this report with a copy of the letter which LUIE gave to Mr. WHALLEY, addressed to his friend, C. ANDERSON.

12, Churchyard-row, Newington-butts, London,
10th July, 1873.

MY OLD BOY,—You will be surprised to hear from me in this quarter, but the reason is that I am accidentally detained here as a witness, on account of the fellows we picked up when we was bound for Melbourne. The young fellow I had in my berth is turning up to be a nobleman of immence property, and you will be, as well as HARRY, required over here to give evidence; of course you will be paid expenses, and I think you are in duty bound to come, as a true man, when a trial of such importance are pending. They are sending a telegram to some one to call on you and HARRY, so you will, before you get this, know something. I wish for you to call on KINDBERG and tell him that I have had no success in finding the old woman, and that he will be so kind to let JANE be kind to my poor girl. I will be back in a fortnight's time, and let them know all about it. I have seen the young fellow once, but he is so fat you would hardly know him; he seems to be on the last board. Please write me by return, and let me know all. I wish to GOD I was back, as this place here is no place at all, and being a stranger can't find any place like home.—Yours very,

C. ANDERSON, JOHN LUIE.
19, Street, Brooklyn.

Of the general accuracy of Mr. WHALLEY'S research, the letter that follows may be taken as some proof:—

To THE EDITOR OF THE "ENGLISHMAN."

SIR,—Referring to the testimony of LUIE in the TICHBORNE case, I will state the following facts, which in the newspapers reports are not exactly stated:—

The broker's firm in New York is (or rather was in 1854) FUNCH and MEINCKE, spelt as I now spell the names. Their office then was in Wall Street, corner of Water Street upstairs. They had in their employ a Baron ALFRED FALKENBERG, a Swede by birth, a nobleman in fact, but very poor, and whom in 1855 or 1856 FUNCH and MEINCKE sent to Quebec, where he established himself as a shipbroker (in connection with the New York firm), got appointed Swedish and Norwegian Consul at Quebec, and died there in or about 1869. Mr. MEINCKE died in New York about 1866. Mr. FUNCH removed his office to No. 27, South Williams Street (not Williamson Street), where I know he still carries on the business of a Swedish and Norwegian shipbroker under the firm of FUNCH, EDYE, and Co.

When Mr. WHALLEY was in New York he should have gone to the Swedish and Norwegian Consulate, and he would have found the old officer BROOKS, where the "Osprey" and Captain BENNETT (not BANNATT) pronounced BEN-NETTE, would have been found. The writer distinctly remembers a Captain BENNETT; also a vessel, the "Osprey," but cannot give any date. In the Consular Books of 1853-54-55-56 and up to 1858 all the names of the sailors, cooks, stewards, &c., are noted down; in short, any changes in the crews.

This is mentioned in case it can be of any use to you. A. C.

We transcribe, from the original manuscript of LUIE, the following letter addressed by him to Sir ROGER, before Mr. WHALLEY returned home. It is evident from it that LUIE spared no pains to impress on the mind of TICHBORNE that he was genuine and true in all respects.

Wednesday, 6th August, 1873.

SIR,—I have stated that FALKENBERG and Capt. BANNETE was the owners of the "Osprey;" they came into possession of her by some means unknown to me in 1853, and I joined her then in New Orleans, when the name she had under the Norwegian owners was changed to the present one in 1854. In the month of February we commenced loading in New York with the cargo, I have described in the proof, and FUNCK and MEINKE was acting for FALKENBERG or BANNET. As to our advances, if Mr. FUNCK look over his books he will find that Mr. DAHLSTROM who was then cashier in their employ, has undoubtedly acknowledged the pay and receipt of seamen's advances, and amongst them the crew of the "Osprey." Respecting Mr. FUNCKE not remembering my name stands to good reason, as to the length of time passed, and also thousands of men he has had under his notice: besides no ship-broker has to do anything *with a ship's crew*. You will please bear in mind that I stated, that although the ship was to have hailed from New Bedford, baron FALKENBERG was residing at Quebec, and the letter you have received from New York confirms that as true. The information Mr. WHALLEY has got from me will in all probability assist to get sufficient evidence, as the shipping master and stevedor, undoubtedly [are] in existence.

I think if you allow me to see you to-morrow, and give you a mutual information of these things, which was made up in the fraudulent transaction between FALKENBERG and BANNET. How is it that MEINKE is dead, when according to the latest news you had, he was in Germany?—Your humble servant,

JOHN LEWIS.

Meanwhile Mr. ONSLOW was active in his inquiries. Knowing all, or nearly all the witnesses who were at Melbourne in 1854, when the "Osprey" arrived with the shipwrecked crew, he thought it would be well to test by them, as well as he could, LUIE's description of the "Osprey." He accordingly asked that individual one day to give him a sketch of the "Osprey" as she appeared in 1854: but he did not communicate to LUIE what was the object that he had in view. LUIE, without a moment's hesitation, sat down and sketched the rough outlines of the "Osprey," as she lay at anchor, and in full sail. These outlines appear in page 281. We append to them a sketch of the figure-head of the "Osprey," drawn by the Claimant, and handed by him to his Counsel in Court.

Mr. ONSLOW subsequently showed them to some of the witnesses, who all stated that this sketch exactly resembled the "Osprey" as they remembered her: none of them having been made acquainted by him with the fact of LUIE having been the draughtsman.

The following letter was sent to Lord RIVERS by Mr. WHALLEY, very soon after his return from the United States.

MR. WHALLEY TO LORD RIVERS.

Reform Club, Sept. 4th, 1873.

DEAR LORD RIVERS,—The result of my visit to America has been that Dr. KENEALY is now satisfied that the man who states he saved TICHBORNE from the "Bella" is a true witness, and should be cross-examined, and that, so far as I understand from your letter, was the object for which you were good enough to express your wish for my journey. It was my opinion that he should have been cross-examined at once, and so be free to go himself to get whatever corroborative evidence might be deemed essential. This was refused by Counsel—also they refused to act on the telegram I instantly sent on my arrival and inquiries at New York. FALKENBERG was an owner of ships at New Bedford. The "Osprey" not known there—BANNATT probably told him she hailed from New Bedford for some reason connected with FALKENBERG.

And now, when Mr. WHALLEY's report became generally known, the greatest pressure was brought to bear upon Dr. KENEALY to put LUIE into the witness-box without further delay. The following extracts from letters addressed to him by Lord RIVERS, Mr. ONSLOW, and Mr. WHALLEY show the strong feeling which TICHBORNE's friends evinced upon this point. In effect Dr. KENEALY was compelled to call LUIE by a pressure which could not be resisted. At the same time we are bound to state that this reluctance was not caused by any disbelief of LUIE's evidence; but Dr. KENEALY hoped to have been able to do without him, expecting (alas! how vainly) that after the mighty mass of testimony which he produced the jury would have stopped the case. And under this delusion he laboured almost to the end. But it was not to be.

LORD RIVERS TO DR. KENEALY.

A letter this morning from ONSLOW begs me to implore you to put LEWIS (the "Osprey" man) in the box, whether there is corroborative evidence or not. KARSLAKE and LOCOCK WEBB both wish it also, and although I never wish to thrust my suggestions unpalatably before you, I cannot see what harm it can do, whilst it cannot fail to show the public the grounds on which I and others found their belief. . . . If LEWIS's evidence is backed up by the production of the two other "Osprey" men, or books proving that ship to have existed, as described by LEWIS, I think you will even get a verdict. . . . I was obliged to come up on Monday for a division in the House, and saw ONSLOW on Tuesday, before returning. At his request I telegraphed to WHALLEY, urging him to come up at once and go with LEWIS to America, to bring back the two men and any other corroborative testimony he could obtain. If he does this at once they could be back before the Wapping witnesses were done with. . . . I bow to your judgment as to the witnesses, but felt bound to inform you of the wishes of KARSLAKE, WEBB, and ONSLOW. . . . Alluding to some conversation which he had with a party of gentlemen at a dinner, Lord RIVERS writes:—You get great credit from them for your conduct of the case, with an exception that you ought to have put LEWIS (your trump card) into the box at the outset. . . .

MR. ONSLOW TO DR. KENEALY.

I am as convinced as I am of my own existence, after you have called the two LIARDETS, LOCKHART, LONGLAND, RUSSELL, SHARPEN, GOODYEAR, RICHARDS—all "Osprey" witnesses, who can swear they saw her—we shall so fix public opinion that money will flow into our coffers in all directions. Put in LUIE they say, and we will send up large cheques to help you on. Stand or fall by JEAN LUIE. If that don't make an impression, nothing will. Close the case and sit down. Let me beg of you, as the least personal favour, to arrange to call the "Osprey" witnesses and JEAN LUIE; then call who you please—all will be second rate after that. . . . I say we are bound to put JEAN LUIE in the witness-box at once. We are now without funds to continue tha case for witnesses' expenses, and if you put JEAN LUIE in *first*, there will be such a revulsion of feeling that money will come in from all quarters. TICHBORNE himself, knowing LUIE's statement to be correct, wishes you to put him in. Indeed, I see no alternative to get money. Please give it your serious consideration. JEAN LUIE is still here, but he may be gone at any moment.—Yours ever,

GUILDFORD ONSLOW.

So convinced, indeed, was Mr. KARSLAKE, Q.C., of the perfect identity of LUIE with the steward of the "Osprey," that he wrote the following exordium for Dr. KENEALY, which we copy from the original manuscript, headed,

KARSLAKE'S DREAM.

"My Lords and Gentlemen of the jury, it is now my duty to address you for the defence in this most remarkable Case;—well may I say this remarkable Case!—for fifty-five days elapsed before the very able and eminent Counsel for the Crown considered that they had presented to you such a Case as could be safely relied on entitling them to a verdict. In great and celebrated causes, such as this, it has been in ancient as well as in modern times the custom of the Advocate to introduce to the Court his client's defence, by an elaborate, if not an eloquent exordium. But I have too much respect for the time of the Court and of the jury to adopt this usage, time-honoured tho' it be—I shall prefer to begin my address in a very simple and inartistic manner. I shall commence by telling you the name and the description of the first witness whom I propose to call. His name is JEAN LUIE. He is forty-eight years of age. He was steward of the "Osprey" in the spring of 1854. (*Here the proof of* LUIE *will be briefly stated.*) The evidence of this witness will, before my Case is concluded, be corroborated by the depositions of several other witnesses and of some important documentary evidence. When you have heard the witnesses on this part of the defence (the part which, as you will all feel is the most important) you will judge what reliance is to be placed on that portion of the Case of the Crown which is the very Head and Front of their attack, namely, that no one was saved from the wreck of the "Bella," and that there never was any such ship as the "Osprey"! Much, I wish, my Lords and gentlemen, that there was more elasticity in our course of procedure, and that I cannot, before I proceed with my address for the defence, call this one witness, JEAN LUIE, and submit him to the hands of my learned friend for cross-examination. This, I should much prefer, but unfortunately it cannot be. And therefore, I shall for the present say no more as to this portion of my defence. I shall simply remind you that I stand here, representing an individual who has to struggle for his liberty as well as for his honour, against some of the ablest members of the English, indeed, of any Bar; and against that which is still far more powerful and dangerous, the purse of the entire English nation. I do not conceal from myself, or attempt to disguise the difficulty which the elaborate address of my learned friend, and the evidence of the witnesses whom he has called must, until they are met and answered, have necessarily raised against me, and of the prejudice which must have necessarily been created in your mind against my client. But, at present all that I ask from you is your careful and intelligent attention. You will remember that in ancient times a celebrated man, when in the course of a momentous discussion, he was threatened with a blow by an equally celebrated opponent, merely exclaimed "Strike, but hear me!" I, addressing you, on behalf of my client, shall content myself with asking you to listen, first to my opening the case for the Defendant, and then to the witnesses whom I shall call, and to suspend your decision until this most wonderful cause shall have come to a conclusion. In a word, I only ask of you this kind indulgence, that you will not prejudge my client's case, and that, not even in your thoughts, not even in the inmost recesses of your minds, you will think it proper or becoming to strike before you hear.

And now, gentlemen, what have the Counsel for the Crown to oppose to this mass of evidence. They told you many weeks ago, that they would prove to you, beyond all doubt, that my client is ARTHUR ORTON. Yet so little confidence had they in their case, that they spent day after day in calling witnesses of every variety, to lead you to think it improbable that the man who, as they say, is clearly ARTHUR ORTON, is also, and at the same time, Sir R. TICHBORNE. Improbable! Why, if you balance the probabilities on each side of the case, improbable as they are, I freely admit, many features of the view which I present to you, they are far less glaring than the improbabilities of that which is presented to you by the Crown. How improbable, for instance, it is, say the Counsel for the Crown, that Sir ROGER TICHBORNE would immediately after his arrival in England, go to Wapping to make inquiries as to the ORTON family. But how far more improbable is it, say I with confidence, that the supposed clever and crafty villain, my client, who had long been studying and maturing his nefarious plans, should deliberately address himself to do that which he must have well known would be most calculated to raise a serious suspicion and a grave argument against himself. On the other hand, a genuine Sir ROGER, conscious of his own identity, and having nothing to conceal, would not be influenced by any notion of the possible consequence of a visit to Wapping.

Again, what impossibility have I to contend with, which, in any degree, equals that arising out of the conduct of the late Mr. HOPKINS—an example which I select out of many? According to the case presented to you by the Crown, either that gentleman, who was, up to the day of his death, looked upon as one of the most able men of business, and one of the most honest persons in the County of Hants, was unable, in the course of continuous and intimate communications, extending over a period of several days at a time, to find out whether the man whose identity, so far as it could be collected from the mere expression of his features, he, to the last, failed to recognize his former client and friend, with whom, and for whom he had transacted many important matters of business, or else this same Mr. HOPKINS turned rogue and liar in his old age, and deliberately determined to hand over to a perfect stranger, a butcher, forsooth, from Wapping, the patrimony of a family which had for many years been among his most valued clients. If you adopt this latter alternative, you must believe that this aged and highly respectable gentleman, when he was approaching his grave, threw away all the honour, and all the reminiscences of a well-spent life, and without a motive; yet, with his eyes open, cheerfully consigned himself to perdition and infamy!

But it is a very old saying, well embodied in the often quoted lines of a celebrated Greek poet, that there is no greater probability in human life than the existence of many things which appear to be utterly improbable. In moderate times, we Englishmen have rendered the same idea into a briefer form of expression. "Truth," we say, "is stranger that fiction." But whether my client is Sir ROGER TICHBORNE or ARTHUR ORTON, the story which, in the one case, he tells of himself, and that which, in the other, is told of him by the Counsel for the Crown, is full of the most glaring improbabilities. Place yourselves, gentlemen, in the position of the supposed Wapping butcher, when he determined to start from the antipodes to personate Sir ROGER TICHBORNE, knowing that he must be prepared to brave the united efforts of the English aristocracy, the rigour of the English criminal law, and the purse of the entire English nation. What story has ever been read by any of you, either in the "Arabian Nights," or in any other of the wildest works of fiction, which involved such monstrous improbabilities as the supposed history of ARTHUR ORTON, such as it is presented to you on behalf of the Crown.

But you are told "he *must* be ARTHUR ORTON, for many persons who cannot be mistaken, since they knew ARTHUR ORTON well, have positively sworn to the defendant's identity." Gentlemen, if there be any one thing in human life which is deceptive and treacherous, it is the recognition, or the non-recognition of one whom you have not seen for many years; by his features, his expression, his general appearance. This is not a truth impressed upon you by me for the first time. It must have been long since engraved on your minds by the events of real life, and by the stories of the most accomplished authors of works of fiction, whose celebrity could never have been attained if they had not, in their works, closely imitated the events which the ever-changing kaleidoscope of human life produces from time to time. You will, I have no doubt, bear in mind one remarkable instance of a recent date, which was mentioned in our daily papers not many months ago. Two French persons were convicted of murder, on evidence which was treated as conclusive of their identity with the murderers. And two other persons were convicted of perjury in swearing to an alibi of the supposed criminals. Of these four persons, two died in the hulks, the other two completed their time of imprisonment. But an old man on his death-bed confessed that he, and not the persons who were unjustly convicted, had committed the murder. Again, take an instance from a deservedly celebrated work of fiction, "Les Misérables" of VICTOR HUGO, which all of you have probably read. The Chief Justice has, I feel sure, often read it with the pleasure which, in spite of its eccentricity, its prolixity, and other numerous and grave faults, it cannot fail to cause. There, an innocent man is identified by three witnesses as the person who was a fellow-convict with them in the hulks. They are absolutely positive; they cannot possibly be mistaken as to the identity. The hero of the tale, nevertheless, asserts that *he* is the man; they are recalled, they are warned, and they do not falter for a moment. Then that noble Christian, JEAN VALJEAN, who was really the convict in question, and who had determined to surrender himself to justice to save the innocent men, reminds each of the three witnesses of a circumstance which occurred at the hulks, within the common knowledge of the hero himself and the respective deponents. In an instant, the recognition, clear and unhesitating as it was by mere features and expression, is nullified, and the identity of the hero with the convict is conclusively established.

Discard, therefore, from your minds the evidence of all the numerous witnesses who merely say "We knew ARTHUR ORTON many years ago, and though we have not put a single question to the Defendant, we believe him to be the same man"; and listen to the testimony of those who have, in repeated conversations with my client, been reminded by him of a mass of circumstances which would be, ought to be, nay, *must* be, in them, the common knowledge of the witnesses, and the real Sir ROGER TICHBORNE, and which circumstances have been accurately detailed by my client; whereas it is, humanly speaking, impossible that they should have come to the knowledge of the impostor, ARTHUR ORTON. And here let me beg you to suspend your judgment, and to prepare your minds for the reception of such a body of evidence as no guilty man since the beginning of the world ever adduced in his favour. And while I beseech you not for one moment to forget that it is for the Crown to prove clearly, and beyond all doubt, that my client is not Sir ROGER TICHBORNE, and that if you have the slightest doubt as to the defendant's identity, you are bound to give a verdict in his favour, I, for my part, shall not be satisfied with merely exciting doubts in your minds; I shall, I feel confident, before I complete the evidence for the Defence, show you conclusively that my client is not, and cannot be, any other person in the world than Sir ROGER CHARLES DOUGHTY TICHBORNE, Bart., that long-lost and ill-used man, who has now for nearly seven years engaged the attention of the entire English nation, and who has confronted, without flinching, the most powerful combination which any one human being, alone and single-handed, was ever called on to resist."

LUIE was eventually called. We refer our readers to his examination, which took place on Tuesday and Wednesday, October 14 and 15.

He appeared to have made a profound impression on the mind even of Sir ALEXANDER COCKBURN, but this, it should be added, is a matter of deep mystery. His testimony is reported to have convinced Sir W. BOVILL of the injustice he had done to TICHBORNE in the Common Pleas. A near connection of his asked him what he thought of LUIE'S testimony. He answered: "Don't talk of it—it weighs on me; it weighs on me;" and he pressed his head uneasily. Six weeks afterwards he died of paralysis. If his compunction killed him, it was the one solitary good spot in his career.

When the Court adjourned, in order to give the Prosecution an opportunity of getting evidence from New York and elsewhere, for the purpose of contradicting LUIE, Dr. KENEALY gave the most positive directions that he should never be lost sight of, being determined not to allow him an opportunity to abscond, if he should be persuaded to do so. To this he was moved by the following

LETTER FROM SIR ROGER TICHBORNE.

31, Bessborough-street, S. W.

LUIE called on me on Saturday night, and told me somebody put his hand on his shoulder and said, You are wanted at the Treasury. When he got there, he says, he was introduced to the Duke of Newcastle, and Mr. SEYMOUR, and another M.P., and that they told him he could go, that they would not require him. This is too bad to tell the man he could go, without acquainting me that he would not be required. It could not have been the Duke of Newcastle, because he said he was an old man with grey hair, whereas the Duke of Newcastle is only about thirty-five years of age; so they have made use of his name.

It is a positive and certain fact, that at this time, the greatest vigilance was used by the Claimant and his friends, so that LUIE should not leave the country. They all thought the agents for the Family would make him do so, in order that they might use his flight as a proof of perjury, and as powerful evidence that he had been brought forward as a false witness, whom the agents for the Defence knew to be false. But LUIE was so closely watched by the Claimant's agents that he could not get away without being stopped, and Dr. KENEALY gave orders that if he was found attempting to escape, he should be instantly given into custody.

And now a curious question arises: Why did LUIE remain in England, being conscious that he was a ticket-of-leave man, and having, at least in many things, committed perjury, without an attempt at escape, when he knew that the evidence likely to be produced would reveal his true character? Did he so remain there in the interest of the Defendant or of the Prosecution? With his extraordinary cleverness and tact, he must have known that the discovery of his true character must have been almost a fatal blow to the cause which he advocated. Was that the reason why he was employed to remain? Did the detectives all along know who he was? And was the adjournment for evidence from America all a sham and a pretence? That a ticket-of-leave man could walk about London, and appear at public meetings as he did, without being at once found out by the police, seems incredible. And if the police *did* find him out, why the necessity for an expedition to America, when, then and there, without a moment's delay, his true character could be unveiled? All this is a mystery of mysteries. Dr. KENEALY wanted the Royal Commission to inquire into it, and clear it up, but he failed. Now, we suppose, the enigma can never be elucidated. LUIE was born in the Lutheran religion, which he professed for the greatest part of his

The fiddle-head, No. 1, is from a rough sketch, drawn in Court by TICHBORNE; the ship sketches are by LUIE—No. 2 lying at anchor, No. 3 under weigh. See page 279.

lie, he became a convert to Romanism when in gaol. This is a fact not unworthy of note. *Who set him upon the Claimant?* If any one connected with this unhappy man did so, how is it that we have had no confession of the fact from LUIE? Why has he not revealed the means by which the Claimant's agents inveigled and "coached" him up in the evidence that he should give? Why has he not made a clean breast of it, and unmasked the whole intrigue, by which and by whom he was induced to give false testimony on behalf of SIR ROGER? It is evident that if the Claimant had ever used any means to put him forward as a false witness, the Crown would only be too glad to furnish the world with information of those means, given by LUIE himself, if, indeed, they could bear the test of inquiry. The Crown now has him—if, indeed, as some allege, he has not been secretly set free—and could do as it pleases with him in getting a confession, if a confession could be had. Mr. HAWKINS, in his summing up to the jury, over and over again insinuated, and we fear with immense effect, that Mr. BAIGENT, Lord RIVERS, and others had suborned and "coached" up LUIE. If that were so, why has not LUIE come forward, and revealed the fact? Why have not those who were guilty of the crime been prosecuted and convicted as they deserve? Why does the Crown allow such guilty wretches to escape? Why, indeed! These are questions not easily answered. We may be quite sure that from the *animus*, the malignity, the virulence of passion and hate, which have ever been shown against all the friends and supporters of TICHBORNE, this forbearance of the Crown is owing in no measure to any feeling of mercy. Why, then, does it exist? The Family have it in their power, if it is true, conclusively to prove by evidence, of time and place and person, whether LUIE was brought forward by the agents of the Claimant; and why do they not do so? Is it not absolute *proof* that all such statements and insinuations are positively, wilfully, and most wickedly false? We have always regarded it as strong evidence in favour of LUIE being the true steward of the "Osprey," and in that respect, a faithful witness, that he has never been induced or constrained to come forward with a false accusation of subornation against the Claimant, or any of his friends. Admit him to be a false witness, if you please; yet there are certain lengths of falsehood to which, perhaps, not even the most wicked may go. And this would appear to be so in this case; for LUIE has certainly never made any accusation against a single person connected with the Defendant.

LUIE was a ticket-of-leave man, and must have guessed that he would be found out; and if found out, that he would be remitted to Chatham prison. Yet, as far as we know, he made no effort to get away. How can this be explained? We know that it was not until after Dr. KENEALY had made the most strenuous exertions to get Mr. POLLARD committed for contempt of Court, and when the Court had really—according to their own rulings—no means of avoiding that committal; that then it was that Mr. HAWKINS gave evidence—much against his will apparently—of the whole preceding career of LUIE, which was as pat in his mouth as the alphabet itself. Could it be that LUIE had been promised by some one that if he remained in London, none of the past would be disclosed, and thus no pretext given for his remission to gaol? He must have had some motive to remain. He never could have imagined that he could derive any benefit from the Defendant, for he could have no doubt that he must speedily be detected. From whom, then, did he anticipate some gain? It clearly must have been from the Prosecution, who he knew held his fate in their hands, able to execute that fate at any moment. No other tribunal could ever have satisfactorily cleared up these mysteries but the Royal Commission for which DR. KENEALY, in his place in Parliament, on the 23rd April, 1875, asked; and the world will never know how or why it was that LUIE so unexpectedly appeared, when the Claimant's case was almost won—as far as outsiders could judge.

The following memorandum of LUIE's proceedings during the adjournment indicate certain features of suspicion:—

JEAN LUIE AND THE TREASURY.

Memorandum of my having this day accompanied JEAN LUIE to the Treasury, to be present with him on his application for his expenditure, arising from his detention in England by command of the Lord Chief Justice. We arrived there at one o'clock and were left waiting twenty minutes. On LUIE stating that he had an engagement for 1.30 and could not wait longer, he was called to the solicitor's room, and I went to go with him, but was prevented entering the room by Mr. STEPHENSON shutting the door in my face, and saying, "You are not a solicitor, nor a solicitor's clerk, and we can't admit you here. We want to speak to LUIE only." I waited, therefore, for LUIE in the outer office from ten to fifteen minutes, and, on descending the stairs with him, was called by one of the clerks to come back, but, acting under the advice of LUIE, I did not go back. LUIE informed me that they had refused to pay him until the Trial was over, and that they would expect him to be living at the Sailors' Home. Also that they questioned him as to the witnesses, and asked him who or what witnesses were to be called on Monday next.

LUIE refused to tell me all that passed between the solicitors at the Treasury and himself, but he said that he told them nothing would separate him from Sir ROGER's interest, and that they said he could make application in Court on Monday for his money.

October 25th, 1873.

H. B. H.

Taken in conjunction with the note from SIR ROGER, both are well worthy of reflection.

When Mr. WHALLEY was put into the box, Mr. HAWKINS having everywhere announced that when he caught him there, "he would skin him alive," the Counsel for the Prosecution, who had been furnished by the Treasury with a copy or at least the purport of the report which Mr. WHALLEY had sent to that department, did not venture to ask him a single question upon the subject of his mission. By the rules of evidence, Dr. KENEALY could not do so. They afterwards called Mr. PURCELL to contradict Mr. WHALLEY: who thereupon made the following affidavit, now lying before us. There were no means, however, of bringing its important statements before the Court.

AFFIDAVIT OF GEORGE HAMMOND WHALLEY, SWORN 28TH NOVEMBER, 1873.

1. That I was present in the Court of Queen's Bench on the 27th of November inst., during the trial of this Case, and heard the evidence given in the said trial by Mr. PURCELL and others.

2. The said Mr. PURCELL stated that Mr. FUNCKE, a ship-broker, carrying on business at New York, in the United States of America, informed him that he believed the story given by JEAN LUIE as a witness in this Trial, to the effect that a ship called the "Osprey" left the port of New York in February, 1854, was untrue, or to that effect; and I say that in the month of August last I had several interviews with the said Mr. FUNCKE on that subject, and the said Mr. FUNCKE expressed to me his opinion thereon, and the same was entirely inconsistent with and at variance with that so attributed to him by the said Mr. PURCELL, and in confirmation thereof refer to the following statement which I took down in writing of the said Mr. FUNCKE in relation to the said JEAN LUIE, and the evidence given by him in this Trial and which as so written by me, I read over to the said Mr. FUNCKE, and he expressed his full assent thereto. "In the year 1854 I was in partnership with Mr. MEINKE, who has since died, and my firm might have been the agents and brokers of a ship named the 'Osprey,' which is referred to in the letter of JEAN LUIE, dated the 25th of July, 1873, addressed to Mr. VOLCKERT, and now shown to me, although I have no personal recollection on the subject. I have no books to which I can refer as to the business done by my firm at that date, all books to the best of my belief are burnt or lost, and the death of Mr. MEINKE and the change of firm and removal of our business from one place to another no less than six times being sufficient to account for my want of recollection as to any particular ship of which we may in 1854 have been the brokers. I have read the letter of JEAN LUIE to Mr. VOLCKERT and to Mr. PETERSON, and the same seems to have been written by a person who had a knowledge of those who were in 1854 in our employ, and with whom as steward of the 'Osprey' he would have been in communication, and unless he had such business with our firm, I don't believe he could have written letters containing so many facts, and referred as he does correctly to persons in our employment, as by the said letters he does. I am well acquainted with AXELL GODECKE as having been for 21 years in the employment of my firm and now receiving a pension from us. I am certain that the said AXELL GODECKE would not make any statement on the subject of the ship 'Osprey' that he did not verily believe to be true."

The said Mr. FUNCKE further stated that the only person he could call to mind who would be likely to have recollection of those times was the said AXELL GODECKE.

And I further say that I had several interviews with the said AXELL GODECKE on this subject, and that he made and signed the following statement in relation thereto.

"I, AXELL GODECKE, now residing at 192, Park Avenue, Hoboken, New York, state: 1st, I was in the employ of Messrs. FUNCKE and MEINKE in the year 1854, in the capacity of water clerk, and for other duties connected with the ships for which that firm were brokers and agents. I have now retired from their service on a pension granted to me by one of that firm. 2nd, Mr. MEINKE, then a member of the firm, is dead, and also many of the persons who were at that time employed by them in and about the duties connected with their business, and amongst others Mr. FALKENBERG, Mr. PETERSON, Mr. DALSTROM, Mr. BIORCKMAN, and Mr. VOLCKERT. 3rd, Have read the letter signed JEAN LUIE, steward of the 'Osprey,' 1854, addressed to Mr. VOLCKERT, also the letter signed by him and addressed to Mr. PETERSON, and dated July 25th, 1873, and in so far as such letters refer to events and persons connected with the firm of FUNCKE and MEINKE in 1854, the written statements are quite in accordance with what happened, or might have happened. In his letter to Mr. VOLCKERT, he mentions a Capt. BANNATT, and I have a recollection of having heard of such a person in connection with some ship of which FUNCKE and MEINKE were brokers. He also mentions in the same letter Mr. M. PETERSON's brother-in-law as being the shipping master, and I remember that the brother-in-law of Mr. M. PETERSON was a shipping master employed by Mr. FUNCKE and MEINKE, and his name was BIORCKMAN. I also well knew Mr. VOLCKERT, to whom the letter is addressed as late in the employment of Messrs. THOMPSON, ship brokers, and I know that he was employed by the firm. 4th, I have a recollection of having seen the name 'Osprey' in FUNCKE and MEINKE'S manifest books, and it was in the handwriting of Baron FALKENBERG, who was in 1854 in the employment of FUNCKE and MEINKE—the manifest book being a book that contains a written description of the cargo of ships. The letters of JEAN LUIE to PETERSON and VOLCKERT are evidently written by a person who knew the parties spoken of, which are all true. He refers to the brother-in-law who was shipping master, and his name BIORCKMAN. All he says in both letters is perfectly true about those persons. Remembers two Capts. BANNATT'S, one a Swede, the other a Norwegian. Thinks he can find a person, who if this one was a Swede, will know him. It was his (GODECKE'S) business to go round the vessels and wait upon the captains. There is an old Stevedore named CRUSOE, who may know something about it. I remember ROBINSON who kept the Scandinavian Arms, he is dead and all people who used to frequent his house, and were engaged in clearing out any vessel at Perth Amboy."

And I further say that the said AXELL GODECKE subsequently brought to me at Messrs. FUNCKE'S office a boatman who in 1854 had been employed by that firm, named JOHN MATHESON, and he made the following statement, as written down by me at the time. "I JOHN MATHESON, of No. 7, Third-street, Hoboken, am a boatman employed by brokers carrying to and from ships. Was employed by FUNCKE and MEINKE for about 16 years, and was so employed in 1854. I have some recollection of a ship named the 'Osprey,' about 1854, of which FUNCKE and MEINKE were brokers. I have no distinct recollection, and fear I may have lost the books in which there would be the name entered. Will search all my papers for the 'Osprey,' and let you know. As to names mentioned in JEAN LUIE'S letter, remember them all. BIORCKMAN, the shipping master had a partner, whose name I now forget. He will perhaps remember the 'Osprey.' Will inquire and let Mr. WING know."

3. In reference to the evidence given by the said Mr. PURCELL as to a Baron FALKENBERG, referred to by the said JEAN LUIE in his evidence given on this Trial, I say the said Mr. FUNCKE informed me that the said Baron FALKENBERG was at the time mentioned by the said JEAN LUIE in the employ of his firm, in a responsible position, and that he subsequently established himself as a ship broker and merchant at Quebec, and that the account given of him by JEAN LUIE was not inconsistent with the position and pursuits of the said Baron FALKENBERG. At New Bedford I was informed by the Chief Officer of the Customs that the said Baron FALKENBERG did, in or about the year 1854, purchase a ship then building at New Bedford, of about 400 tons burthen as I believe, and gave to the said ship the name of "Falkenberg," and the same is to be found as I believe in the Register of Ships, belonging to or connected with the port of New Bedford.

The said Baron FALKENBERG was subsequently for many years a Consul at Quebec, and carried on business as a ship broker and merchant until his death, about six months before my visit there, and his son had then succeeded him in his business and consulate.

4. Although I visited Quebec for the purpose, I could not obtain any information, owing to the absence at the time of the son of the said late Baron FALKENBERG, but I verily believe if time be allowed for further inquiry as to this and other statements of the said JEAN LUIE, the same will be in all respects substantially confirmed.

5. In confirmation of my statement that the evidence of the said JEAN LUIE would by full and impartial investigation be found to be substantially true, I say that having visited the United States for the express purpose of ascertaining how far the information given by him to the Defendant and his advisers was correct, I made every effort in my power for that purpose, and I did so impartially and with no other desire than to promote the ends of Justice in this Trial, and having on my return home made a full report of all the facts and circumstances that came to my knowledge and also the grounds on which, and the direction to be given to such further inquiry as might be deemed requisite. I refer to such report marked "A," and I say that the statements contained in the same are in all respects true to the best of my knowledge and belief.

6. I further say that I have this day received from New York the two letters marked "B" and annexed to this affidavit, and which I believe to have been written by Mr. WING, the Solicitor with whom I consulted on the occasion of my visit in reference to the inquiry as to JEAN LUIE.

7. And I further say that I have been in attendance on this Trial, with the exception of the time during which I was absent in America, in obedience to writs of subpœna duces tecum, served upon me on the part of the Prosecution, and that I have been prepared to produce all the notes and memoranda and other documents made by me, or that came into my possession in relation to my said visit to America; and with reference thereto, I say that the same were entrusted by me for safe keeping to Mr. HARCOURT, the Solicitor for the Defendant, and were, as I believed, deposited in the office lately used used for the purposes of the Defence at No. 2, Poets-corner, and that I am now informed that all such papers have disappeared, and cannot anywhere be found, and I have also been informed by Mr. HARDING, the Secretary or Agent of the Defendant, that two of the clerks lately employed in that office in the service of the Defendant have, since their leaving that service, been in communication with the officers of the Government in charge of, or taking an active part in carrying on, this prosecution.

8. I further say that on the 12th of October last I addressed a letter to Mr. JOHN GRAY, the Solicitor of the Treasury, in reference to the subpœna duces tecum, with which I have been so as aforesaid served, and a copy of such letter, together with his reply thereto, is annexed to this affidavit, and is marked "C."

The letters marked "A" and "B," and alluded to above, do not seem to be very important, but we think the Correspondence marked "C," is. We therefore insert it.

CORRESPONDENCE.

To JOHN GRAY, Esq., Solicitor to the Treasury.

Oct. 12, 1873.

SIR,—I submit for your perusal a copy of correspondence by which you will be further informed of the imminent prospect of the Defence being cut short by the inability of the Defendant to pay the expenses of the witnesses essential to the full disclosure of all the circumstances of the Case.

Your reply to the last application of his Solicitor seems conclusive. I understand that the consequences of an inconclusive and unsatisfactory result of the pending Trial are fully recognized and accepted by the Government, but I have to remind you that about three months since I was served with a subpœna duces tecum, requiring me, on the part of the Prosecution, to be in attendance at the Court as a witness. On several occasions I observe that my name has been brought before the Court by your Counsel, so as to call forth a remonstrance from the Defendant's Counsel, and that the Court have allowed it to be suggested that I, as also Mr. ONSLOW, have been tampering with witnesses, or improperly seeking for evidence, and holding similar relations to the Defence as the Detective officers, WHICHER and CLARKE, do to the Prosecution. Under these circumstances I consider that I am entitled to require you to afford your Counsel the means of justifying such allusions by calling me on my subpœna, and I have to request that you will inform me whether it is your intention to do so and when.

I have communicated with the Defendant's Solicitor on this subject and he is prepared to afford every facility for my being called as a witness without further delay.

With reference to the allusions of Mr. HAWKINS to which I have referred, I have to ask you specifically to inform me whether the same have been made in pursuance of instructions from you.—I am, Sir, Your obedient servant,

G. H. WHALLEY.

Treasury, Whitehall: Oct. 14, 1873.

SIR,—I acknowledge the receipt of your letter of the 14th inst., together with a copy of a correspondence, which, however, as yet I have not read. With respect to your letter, my answer is that I decline to answer its inquiries or comply with its requests.

Your letter throws upon WHICHER and CLARKE the imputation of tampering with witnesses in the Case. In their justification I feel bound to say that I have never heard or seen the least evidence of any impropriety in the conduct of either of these men in reference to the Case. As it is not in any way my duty to defend or censure you, I gladly abstain from any remark upon the comparison you have made between yourself and them.—I am, Sir, your obedient servant,

G. H. WHALLEY, Esq. JOHN GRAY.

Putney House, Putney, S.W.

The following is the Correspondence referred to in the foregoing letter:—

To the Lord Chief Justice of England.

Plas Madoc, Ruabon: Oct, 5, 1873.

MY LORD,—In consequence of the prohibition to the Defendant in the TICHBORNE Case to attend meetings—following previous restrictions on appeals by his friends for money for his Defence, I considered it my duty to make a renewed effort to give effect to the concession by the late Chancellor of the Exchequer, Mr. LOWE, and the late Home Secretary, Mr. BRUCE, in the House of Commons, in respect of such appeal, and I find it to be essential, in support of it, to state the nature of the evidence that the Defendant desires to bring before the Court. As such statement might be construed as disparaging or contradicting the evidence for the Prosecution, I am at a loss to know whether your lordship and the Court might deem me precluded from publishing any such statement, on account of what took place on the former appearance in Court of Mr. ONSLOW and myself, or otherwise, and I have thus no other means of discharging an imperative public duty, free from risk of fine and imprisonment, than by soliciting the expression of your lordship's views on this subject.

The correspondence of Mr. GRAY, of the Treasury, and myself, published by order of the House of Commons, makes known that I entertain the belief that the Defendant is the victim of a conspiracy of unexampled atrocity; and also that the Government refuse to aid in such inquiry as may confirm or disprove the facts on which it rests; and it also appears that I have repeatedly desired to bring before the authorities all the information that has reached me, and to afford the utmost facilities for testing its accuracy.

In the House of Commons I have given notice that I shall at the proper time submit for consideration the conduct of the Government in relation to this prosecution; and I submit, respectfully, that it is of the utmost public importance that the investigation should not be cut short by the destitution of the Defendant, and that any means of preventing this are entitled to the favourable consideration of your lordship.—I have the honour to be, my Lord, Your most obedient humble servant.

G. H. WHALLEY.

Court of Queen's Bench: Oct. 6, 1873.

SIR,—I have the honour to acknowledge the receipt of your letter of the 4th inst.

In reply to your inquiry whether certain statements, which you desire to make publicly, relative to evidence given, or proposed to be given, on the pending Trial in the Court of Queen's Bench, would, or would not, amount to a contempt of Court; I beg to say that my learned brothers and myself must altogether decline to express any opinion on the question.

It is not the practice of English Courts of Justice, nor of English Judges, to deliver opinions on speculative questions, or to advise individuals as to whether a proposed line of conduct would, or would not, amount to a violation of the law.

That the Court of Queen's Bench should not only be asked to do this, but, what is still more extraordinary, be asked to do so extra-judicially, in the way of correspondence, cause us, we must say, infinite astonishment. Such an application is altogether unprecedented and unwarranted, and we have a difficulty in supposing it to have been made with any serious expectation of its being complied with.

All we can do to relieve you from difficulty is to refer you to the recent judgments of the Court on the subject of contempt. In these the law has been fully and clearly laid down so as to leave no room for ambiguity or doubt as to what may, or may not, be said or done with reference to the pending Trial. The rule, as so laid down, we intend to uphold and enforce. Having said which, we must leave you to act on your own responsibility.—I have the honour to be, Your obedient humble Servant,

A. E. COCKBURN.

G. H. WHALLEY, Esq., M.P.

Putney House, Putney, S.W.
Oct. 9, 1873.

MY LORD,—The reply which your lordship does me the honour to make to my letter of the 4th inst., leaves me in doubt as to whether I can state the nature of the evidence for which money is now required, without being subjected to further fine and imprisonment, or both, and I, therefore, consider myself precluded from doing so.

In so far as this restriction further tends to deprive the Defendant of the means of bringing forward evidence in his defence, any verdict but that of Acquittal may, of course be regarded as inconclusive and unsatisfactory, and I beg leave to assure your lordship that for this reason, as also from assuming that your lordship and the Court would yourselves desire a full investigation of a case that has demanded such exceptionable exercise of the powers of the Court, I did expect a favourable consideration of my application.—I have the honour to be, My Lord, Your Lordship's most obedient and humble Servant,

G. H. WHALLEY.

To the Lord Chief Justice of England.

Upon the rebutting testimony offered, Mr. WHALLEY sent Dr. KENEALY, the following

MEMORANDUM.

Nov., 1873.

LUIE wished Dr. KENEALY to be informed as follows:—

1. The "Ironsides" on which I served on Lake Michigan blew up a few months ago, since I have been in London; was in her three months: it was last May when I left this vessel, and I believe the captain was the same as was in her when blown up.

2. As to the house which I said I occupied in Newbery avenue, Chicago, 6th and 7th street, is now burnt down. It happened about two months ago, since I have been here. From what I can learn my house was not burnt down, but have not been able to get any correct information.

3. As to clearing out, there is another explanation why there may be no record, namely, that she may have cleared out in her old name of "Helvetia," as that name would be in her papers. The name was changed while I was on board at New Orleans; we painted the name "Osprey" on the quarter at New Orleans. Do not remember where the other name was shown.

4. JEAN LUIE states:—

He slept last night at the house of Mr. RIMELL at Finchley. Came to town this morning by rail to M. R.'s place of business, 29, Golden-square, about 9 o'clock.

5. Went out to get shaved, and a man came up to me and said, "Good morning LUIE, take my advice and don't go near the Court to day; you are sure to be sent to prison." I said, "That's a d——d bad job."

6. He then left and I proceeded to Reform Club and saw Mr. WHALLEY, and told him what had occurred. I do not know the man, but I think I have seen his face before; I may have spoken to him, and I think I shall know him again.

7. The police have been following me about ever since I have been in town, both before and after I gave my evidence, and I complained at Scotland Yard, and there saw Mr. CLARKE, the chief Detective, he promised me I should not be molested until this morning.

He sent also the following

LETTER TO MR. WHALLEY, M.P.

29, Golden-square, London, W.: 23 Nov., 1874.

MY MOST HONOURABLE AND LEARNED GENTLEMAN,—I am very greived to learn that Sir ROGER has not met your great kindness towards him, with such acknowledgement as is justly due to you for all the pains and expenses that has involved you in his defence, but I have no doubt your generous and good heart will soon forgive the poor man.

I saw Dr. KENEALY yesterday and Captain ANDERSON, of Cunard steamer was there with me and substantiated me in all points regarding two vessels loading at Staten island, also respecting Custom House produce and it as regarding cargoes of the "Osprey" description. I don't think in my own mind that Mr. HAWKINS will profit anything should he call any rebutting evidence against me.

I hope that Mr. ONSLOW, M.P., are getting well and that yourself my noble gentleman is in perfect health,—I beg to remain, Sir, your humble and obedient

JEAN LUIE.

G. H. WHALLEY, Esq. M.P.

LUIE also made the following

AFFIDAVIT.

IN THE QUEEN'S BENCH.

The QUEEN against THOMAS CASTRO, otherwise called ARTHUR ORTON, otherwise called Sir ROGER CHARLES DOUGHTY TICHBORNE, Baronet.

I, JEAN LUIE, of Rosebank, Finchley, in the county of Middlesex, Mariner, make oath and say as follows:—

1. I have read the evidence of Mr. JOSEPH DE ROSIER given in this matter on the 27th day of November, 1873, and I say that with reference to the statement of the said JOSEPH DE ROSIER, that the names and addresses of the persons I have referred to in my examination as HARRY the sailmaker, and CARL ANDERSON, are false, I say if time be afforded me I can produce to this honourable Court (if now living) the said person named, HARRY, then working as a sailmaker, and CARL ANDERSON, and I can also produce evidence that I kept a grog-shop at Chicago.

2. I can also produce evidence to prove that a vessel called the "Ironsides" did ply on Lake Michigan, at the period referred to in my evidence given in this matter, and that I was steward on board of the said vessel.

3. I have also read the evidence of PAUL CORNELL given in this matter on the 27th day of November, 1873, and in reference to the statements of the said PAUL CORNELL that ordinary vessels did not load at Staten island, I say that if time be afforded, I can produce witnesses who will prove how vessels were loaded at Staten Island many years ago, and down to a very recent period.

4. I also say that if sufficient time be afforded me I can produce to this honourable Court (if now living), MACCARTHY, one of the crew of the "Osprey" at the time that vessel picked up the shipwrecked crew of the "Bella."

Sworn at Westminster Hall in the county of Middlesex this 28th day of November, 1873. JEAN LUIE.

N. E. COE,
A Commissioner, &c.

When LUIE'S evidence was sworn to be false, and he was committed to prison, while lying there he wrote the following letters. It should be stated that it was at LUIE'S own particular desire and entreaty, urged even with tears in his eyes, that Dr. KENEALY brought Mr. POLLARD'S case before the Court, so that LUIE'S "character might be set free from all charge." These are the words he used, when begging Dr. KENEALY—who then for the *first time* came into communication with him—to bring his case before the Court.

Holloway Prison.

DR. KENEALY,—I am most greatful to you for the able manner you cross-examined the witness to-day and thereby beg leave to inform you what I overheard this morning of the Chatam Warders, before the Court opened, there was one who said that the man they were going to swear to, was *ruptured* and that he came from Millbank Prison, ruptured and that he had seen it in the Doctor's book in Chatham, pray remember this to-morrow, ask them, or any one else that comes against us that *question*, also if the man they knew had worn ear-rings, did he walk lame and had any complaints of walking.

DR. KENEALY, I heard several people talking about this matter when I was waiting for two hours in the waiting-room.

I saw two women who was to recognize me, but they seemed to me to be ——. You obedient and humble

JEAN LUIE.

P.S. Ask if they open the mouths of prisoners to see if they have any tobacco in their mouth and if they discover if there is any lost teeth and how many. J. L.

I was told this now, after finishing my letter.

Friday evening.

DEAR SIR,—This evening has been here to see me a man who is an officer from some prison, and he called me by a name of some description, and asked me if I did not know him. I told him no. The governor was with him, and they examined my hands, they looked at me twice, and I asked what it meant. They said I should know in a day or so. Ascertain to-morrow the first thing, what is the meaning of it, and lose no time. I am afraid Dr. KENEALY has spoiled the Case by calling upon POLLARD for the affair in the Court on Friday last.—Your obedient servant,

JEAN LUIE.

December 5th, 1873.

DR. KENEALY,—This morning was I brought up by CLARK and the Governor into a private room, Westminster Hall, and a lot of people was put in front of me, and before I came to the door, a man put his hand on me and said I am very sorry for you I told him I don't know you then another said I know him and shall prove 2 convictions against him, I declare I never saw any of these men, it appears from what I learnt that this knowledge of me should have been in 1862. Another was called to see, he spoke to me in Danish (how do you do), and what I learnt, he should have known me in 1854 and 1855, and that I was married to some Woman, who he says he knew, and Mrs. CLARKE told me his name was BRAMMER, what was that Woman's name and where is she. The warder from Clapham said the monkey jacket I have on now was given me on my discharge from Clapham, and he examined my boots, but did not think they were the same. I think it most unjust in a way of identification, to bring me before men *alone*, they well knowing who they were expected to see, and I at the same time not being allowed to have a single individual on my side.

But I think in the position I am now I shall take my *own counsel*, for it seems to me the extraordinary excitement all ROGER's supporters are in now will be of nothing but ruin to the Case.—Your obedient servant,

JEAN LUIE.

DR. KENEALY,—All the case now is thrown upon my shoulders, and, as my advice has never been taken any notice of, and it now being at the eleventh hour, I tell you sir, I am still in power to save your cause and Sir ROGER, and that is in this way: you must keep up your speech for five or six weeks, get a bailsman for me, and I and PULLEYN will go to New York immediately, no one to know it, and will return with evidence of such a nature that the verdict shall immediately be given for ROGER, if you go on with telegrams, and pay expenses in that way, why not lessen the expenditure and have a genuine result. Every hour from now is of the greatest importance for your honour and Sir ROGER's liberty.—Your most obedient servant,

JEAN LUIE.

At this period appeared the annexed Correspondence, which we think it well to preserve:—

MR. WHALLEY AND THE TICHBORNE CASE.

(From the *Peterborough Times*.)

Plas Madoc, Dec. 18, 1873.

SIR,—I trust you may consider yourself at liberty to publish, for the information of my constituents, the correspondence I now forward to you.—I am, your obedient servant.

G. H. WHALLEY.

Liverpool, Dec. 17, 1873.

DEAR MR. WHALLEY,—Having long looked upon you as the *beau ideal* Protestant champion, the determined foe to Jesuitism and the kindred schemes of Rome, I am constrained to write and tell you, that your conduct about "LUIE" has quite shaken my confidence in you, and I am beginning to think that even you may be an S. J. agent. You do not know what I have had to endure from friends of mine, who know how I have maintained my faith in you until this has happened; and now there is that charge that he, LUIE, brought against somebody having "made up" his work for him. Now we do know that you went over to America, and must have known what a liar he was. How will you explain it? I have looked in the papers, thinking you would, but so far nothing has appeared. For the sake of the Protestantism you were once the champion of, do let us know that you are still pure, if you are so, or manfully tell us you have thrown us over altogether. TICHBORNE is nothing to me, but WHALLEY is something yet, I will fain hope. Perhaps you may notice this; but I have been faithful to myself.—Yours obediently,

15, Newstead-road, Liverpool. JOHN PETERS,

Plas Madoc, Ruabon,

JOHN PETERS, Esq. 18th Dec., 1873.

DEAR SIR,—I am happy to relieve you from further endurance on my account in respect of JEAN LUIE by repeating the evidence I gave in Court that, neither as to him or any other witness, have I "made up his work," or in any degree whatever influenced his testimony, and as to your suggestion about "the Papers," you seem to forget that it may be deemed a criminal offence to offer any public explanation in this TICHBORNE Case, not only by those who offer it, but by the publishers of such explanation.

The report of my inquiries in America having been confirmed by an affidavit tendered in evidence to the Court, is accessible I presume to everyone, and I may therefore quote from it as follows:—

"It is my opinion that there is abundant corroboration of the fact that JEAN LUIE is speaking the truth when he states that the Defendant is the man he saved from the "Bella's" boat and nursed for three months for sunstroke, and that without further expenditure, which it is not in fact in the Defendant's power to incur (all the cost of my journey and otherwise in relation to this TICHBORNE Case having been from the first wholly borne by myself), the Jury may with confidence be expected to give weight to his evidence as being in itself corroboration of other given in the Trial in the Common Pleas and also consistent in itself. Is it not possible that if a hundred witnesses (more or less) have, by error or design, been mistaken in the identity of ORTON and TICHBORNE, half that number might fall into the like infirmity in regard to LUIE and LUNDGREN, or that the man himself, a foreigner and unacquainted with the ultimate strength of public opinion in England, might have less faith in such protection as the Defendant can afford him, than in what to him appears the irresistible power of the Government, with the Exchequer and the entire legal resources of the Treasury, and the Detective force of Scotland-yard on the other side.

The following copy of a letter addressed by LUIE (or LUNDGREN) to a gentleman of high respectability seems to express what might naturally occur to an honest man. The letter to which he refers, as addressed to me, expresses more forcibly, if possible, his desire to do what is right; but it might be deemed a contempt of Court in the present stage of the affair to communicate it to any one. The Government is aware that every document that has ever come into my possession, and every fact and circumstance within my knowledge relating to this TICHBORNE Case, I have repeatedly requested permission to place at their service; and it throws a strong light on, as it seems to me, the conduct of the Case, that their Counsel should be instructed to deter me from doing what they well know is regarded by me as a public duty to my constituents and the public.

I am, dear Sir,

Your very obedient Servant,

G. H. WHALLEY.

City Prison, Holloway, Dec. 12, 1873.

DEAR SIR,—I have not heard from any one of you, and I fear that all are inclined to believe me to be the scoundrel LUNDGREN, as is mentioned by all these monstrous witnesses. This is a hard thing for me to bear, and you know very well that if I can have no assistance given me to bring LUNDGREN's relatives here, as well as JANES, the two American ladies, and the two men now in England, who know both the "Osprey" and myself, as well as a proper and independent medical man to examine me respecting rupture, I must be in a hopless state. But this I mean to tell you, let the matter take what course it will, I shall declare openly in Court that no one connected with the Case, or anybody else, has ever used any influence on me, nor attempted such a thing, to make me tell the fate and circumstances with Sir ROGER. It is a truth, and nothing but the truth, and that it seems to me villany is practised all over the world against both ROGER and myself. HARCOURT asked me if I will defend myself What does he mean? I wrote you last night a letter. I wrote also to Mr. WHALLEY. Perhaps you have not received it. What am I to do?—I am shut out from the world, and am starving. I must go to the criminal side to-night. as I have no means. See what Sir ROGER says. I am willing to undergo any medical operation, to prove that I am not ruptured, or I have any cause with me.

I am, your obedient servant,

JEAN LUIE.

If I am rendered assistance, Sir ROGER and all of you are saved.

We extract one or two further passages from the Letters of LORD RIVERS, written about this time; as they help to throw some light upon this inexplicable transaction.

LORD RIVERS TO DR. KENEALY, Q.C.

Had I been present at your councils, I should not have known what advice to offer, or what was the best course to pursue—you are so surrounded by difficulties that it appears to me whatever line you adopt and follow must get you into trouble. By sticking to and fighting for LUIE, you make yourself the advocate of a man who I fear is too unmistakeably proved to have been for years a swindler and a scoundrel—and if you throw up the sponge so far as he is concerned, you tacitly admit he is a scoundrel—that his "Osprey" story was got up for money, and that your client was a party to the fraud. My belief in his identity is not in the least shaken—that he is not ORTON the evidence and various facts in the whole Case prove beyond a doubt. He must be someone, and therefore, taking all things into consideration, I am as sure as I can be of anything he is the man he pretends to be. But as on two if not three occasions I have myself seen him cross-examine a voluntary witness and discard his evidence, because, although on material points they were right, they were wrong on some minor details, which in his opinion would damage them if discovered, I cannot reconcile to myself how he should be such an ass—if nothing else, as to pretend to a recognition of LUIE, when he could never have seen him before. But for LUIE, I am sure there would have been no conviction, and, perhaps, through your able advocacy and eloquence there might have been an acquittal; now the latter is an impossibility, and the former almost hopeless. I cannot believe in the mistakes or the rognery of all those witnesses who swear to LUNDGREN; as they also prove he was engaged in an office the very year of the "Osprey" story. LUIE's whole statement must have been a cleverly concocted lie—who paid him for it, and who got it up? The whole thing is a mystery beyond my powers of solution. Before I write this you will have made up your mind how to act, but had I been able to attend your consultations I think I should have advised your giving up all defence of LUIE, or belief in his story, after the evidence brought against him—that your best argument would be the mistake your client made in the recognition of a man he evidently never saw before, and which was another proof of the many extraordinary mistakes and follies you had started by calling attention to—that the existence of the "Osprey" in Melbourne having been so conclusively proved, his story ought not to be entirely discredited, because he had foolishly been led to believe after 20 years that the man's story was true as to being the man who saved him, and that as you had proved him not to be ORTON he was entitled to an acquittal. But this *fiasco* appears to have so poisoned the minds of everyone, that I fear TICHBORNE has not the ghost of a chance. You have worked like a Trojan for him, because you honestly believed and I think still believe, as I do, that your cause was a just one—but although both as a Counsel and a conscientious man, you may feel both bound and disposed to do all in your great power for your client, I don't want to see you degrade yourself by fighting a battle for a man not your client, and of whose guilt and rascality you must be as convinced as I am. I send you up some game, and only wish I could send you more substantial comfort. My dear KENEALY, I inclose you TICH's answer received this morning, and confess I think he speaks the truth. As to LUIE it looks very ugly, but still there is nothing to disprove his "Osprey" story, and no reason why the steward of that vessel should not have got into prison. Still of course the lies he has told as to his subsequent life, fairly entitle both Judge and Jury to discredit any statement of his—but I feel convinced he did pick him up, and that the recognition was genuine on both sides. If he can prove his "Osprey" existence to be true, I think the rest don't signify."

The following was received about the same time from Mr. E. K. KARSLAKE, Q.C., to Dr. KENEALY, Q.C.

It is not unfortunate that I came to the meetings at your chambers, where I saw you for the first time. I shall be able to testify that certainly Lord RIVERS, Mr. ONSLOW, and the legal advisers, and as I firmly believe, WHALLEY, had nothing to do with LUIE's evidence. What a liar that scoundrel has proved himself to be! You have certainly shown wonderful pluck and stamina in keeping poor T. out of gaol.

We subjoin TICHBORNE's account of this man, and of the impression which he made upon him, when all had been discovered:—

SIR ROGER TICHBORNE'S ACCOUNT OF JEAN LUIE.

Although I have no remembrance of the features of the steward of the "Osprey," still from what LUIE told me about that ship and different things he had done for me, I did firmly believe, and do believe, notwithstanding all the evidence I have heard against him, that he is the late steward of that vessel. My reasons for still believing him to be that person: In the first place, the length of his beard, which my medical man, now sitting beside me, tells me never took less than two years to grow. Second, had he been a prisoner out on license, he would not have had his photograph taken and distributed all over the world. Thirdly, I cannot bring my mind to believe a prisoner out on licence would show or present himself at the Treasury, and walk about with detective officers, and show himself on a stage, as he did at St. James's Hall about a month before, before hundreds of persons; then again, this man was on parole, and could if he had thought proper, have left the country; he had money to do so, because Mr. ONSLOW and Mr. WHALLEY each gave him a £5 note. It must also be remembered that on the day of his examination (the last day) he was not told he would be required again, and he could, if he had thought proper, have gone away that night; because, when he came down to my chambers with PULLEYN, I asked him (LUIE) what he was now going to do, when he replied "I intend to get back to America, as soon as possible, to join my family." I said "How are you going?" He replied, "I will go to the docks and get a ship, and work my passage back." I then said, "Oh, no; I will pay your passage. I shall give you £25, and you can have the money to-night if you wish it." He replied "Oh, no; I will not take it until I am ready to go." And he has never from that day asked or received money from me except five shillings when in Holloway prison, through Mr. HARDING. On looking at the two photographs, I cannot believe they are one and the same person. The Chatham photo looks to me ten or fifteen years older. As regards the evidence of his supposed wife, I think it very unfair to LUIE, that she should be allowed to swear to him, without speaking to him.

Written at the Court of Queen's Bench, to Dr. KENEALY, Q. C.

Dec. 10th. R. C. D. TICHBORNE.

The following Notes throw some additional light upon this abstruse question:—

TICHBORNE ON LUIE.

SIR ROGER TICHBORNE TO DR. KENEALY, Q.C.

34, Bessborough-street, S.W.

I hear that you blame me for putting LUIE into the box; before doing so, I wish you to remember that when LUIE called at my chambers I refused to see him, and it was not until WHALLEY came and read his (LUIE's) statement to me that I consented to see him. From his statement I believed him to be the man. As I had no remembrance of the features of the Steward of the "Osprey," I could form no opinion for myself.

Dec. 11, 1873.

SIR ROGER TICHBORNE TO MR. GUILDFORD ONSLOW.

34, Bessborough-street, S.W.; Dec 11, 1873.

DEAR ONSLOW,—I think there is no doubt of LUIE being the person all these witnesses have sworn to. We had him examined last night, which leaves no doubt he is a convict. The Judges have ordered him to be taken before a magistrate and prosecuted for perjury. I consider WHALLEY has entirely deceived us regarding this man. If you remember, when LUIE first called on me I refused to see him, and he was sent by my servant to Poets-corner. In the afternoon WHALLEY came to my chambers, and read to me LUIE's statement. After hearing it I consented to see him. He (LUIE), who was outside in a cab with Mr. O'BRIEN came in. As I had not any recollection of the features of the "Osprey" steward, I could form no judgment from memory, but I refused to give my consent for him to be put into the box until some inquiry had been made. WHALLEY went to America, he telegraphed back, "All correct, examine LUIE, and send him on to me." I did not even then consent, and it was not until WHALLEY came back, and his statement laid before Counsel; what his statement was I don't know. I was treated as so insignificant a person that it was not necessary to acquaint me, I suppose.

I have so much to say, I can't possibly put it to paper.

Hoping yourself and Mrs. ONSLOW are well,—Yours sincerely,

R. C. D. TICHBORNE.

LETTER FROM MR. WHALLEY, M.P.

TO THE EDITOR OF THE "ENGLISHMAN."

SIR,—Your insertion of a letter from Sir ROGER TICHBORNE to Mr. ONSLOW, stating "WHALLEY has entirely deceived us as regards this man," demands some explanation, notwithstanding what you say as to its being written under an angry feeling, and that the word "deceived," should be read as "misled." I neither deceived nor misled anyone in this matter.

Sir ROGER TICHBORNE, as you know, did repeatedly declare that LUIE was the man who saved and nursed him on board the "Osprey," and the letter you publish is the first intimation I have received that he doubted the truth of LUIE's story. I should no more think of finding fault with Sir ROGER TICHBORNE now than I would speak ill of the dead, and can well understand that the astounding disclosures of the subsequent career of LUIE may have bewildered him as they did others, and any want of memory disclosed in his letter to Mr. ONSLOW merely tends to prove the lasting influence in this, as in other cases, on his mind of "sunstroke;" and as to angry feeling, you are aware that zealous as I was and still am to rescue an innocent man from prison and death, I could not and did not hold any personal communication with him for months before the Case closed. I was of opinion that LUIE should have been put into the box as the very first witness, and you are aware that my journey to America was undertaken at the joint and urgent solicitation of the friends and advisers of the Defendant, with a view on the part of all of us to prevent the possibility of such imputations as have since been so groundlessly and unjustifiably suggested. With best wishes for the success of your admirable paper, I am, your obedient servant,

G. H. WHALLEY.

London, April 25th.

NOTE ON THE ABOVE.

Sir ROGER TICHBORNE wrote the first of these Notes in consequence of his Counsel's angry remonstrance with him about LUIE. The statement is correct that TICHBORNE never professed to recognize LUIE, except by what he told him had occurred. With reference to the expression about Mr. WHALLEY in the letter to Mr. ONSLOW, Sir ROGER TICHBORNE wrote it under an angry feeling, and without having properly weighed his words. Instead of "deceived" he should have said "misled," which was probably the idea that was in his mind. Mr. WHALLEY's Report sets forth the main grounds on which he trusted LUIE's statements, and it was not until every word of that Report had been well considered that, in compliance with the most urgent desire, LUIE was called.

We append the newspaper Report of the proceedings against LUIE at Bow-street and at the Central Criminal Court:—

JEAN LUIE AT BOW STREET.

JEAN LUIE, the notorious witness for the Claimant in the TICHBORNE Case, appeared yesterday, before Sir THOMAS HENRY, at Bow Street Police-court, to answer charges of perjury. Much public interest was evinced in the proceedings. Long before the Court was opened a crowd of persons had congregated in front of the building, eager to effect an entrance, or even to catch a glimpse of LUIE, and some time before Sir THOMAS HENRY took his seat on the Bench the interior of the Court was crammed. Notable among those present were:—Mr. GUILDFORD ONSLOW, M.P., Mr. GRAY, Q.C. (Solicitor to the Treasury), Mr. BOWKER, Mr. HENDRIKS (formerly solicitor to the Claimant), and Mr. HARDING (the Claimant's secretary). When LUIE entered the dock there was a buzz of astonishment at the great change in his appearance since last he was seen in the Court of Queen's Bench. His head and face were closely shaven, and he wore the dress of a convict. He was handcuffed when he entered the Court, but before the proceedings commenced this restraint was removed.

Mr. POLAND, instructed by the Solicitor to the Treasury, prosecuted; and Mr. EDWARD LEWIS defended.

Mr. POLAND was about to open the case, when

Mr. LEWIS, addressing Sir THOMAS HENRY, said: I am instructed by certain friends of the prisoner to appear on his behalf; but I do not feel justified in undertaking the duty until I have an interview with, and a personal retainer from, the prisoner. I have no doubt that the prisoner will readily approve of what his friends have done for him. Although no impediment has been thrown in the way by the police superintendent to my having a private interview with the prisoner, I have been told by Mr. CLARKE, the superintendent at Scotland-yard, that I must have an order from you to effect my purpose. I therefore, Sir THOMAS, apply to you for the necessary order.

Sir T. HENRY: You can have the order, of course. How long do you want?

Mr. LEWIS: Only a few minutes.

Mr. LEWIS and the prisoner then retired to an adjoining room, and remained absent about five minutes. On their return into Court,

Sir T. HENRY (to prisoner): What is your name?

Prisoner: My name is JEAN LUIE.

Sir T. HENRY: Do you wish to be defended by Mr. LEWIS?

Prisoner: Yes, if you please.

Mr. POLAND then proceeded to open the Case for the prosecution. He said: I am instructed, Sir THOMAS, by the Court of Queen's Bench to prosecute the defendant on a charge of perjury, and a charge of bigamy also. It will not be necessary for me just now to prefer formally the charge of bigamy, but I shall have occasion to show you in the course of the evidence in substantiation of the charge of perjury that the defendant has committed bigamy. You will, doubtless, remember that the defendant was examined as a witness in the Court of Queen's Bench on the 14th and 15th of October last. He was first called on the 14th of October, and was partly cross-examined on that day, and he was again examined on the following day. The prisoner had been in this country from the 5th of July, and his evidence was taken down on the 7th of July, yet he was not called till the 14th of October. That was, no doubt, an arrangement whereby it was believed that after giving his evidence he might be able to leave England and go to America. It appeared, however, for reasons which I shall detail, he was unable to do this. In consequence of something which occurred in the Court of Queen's Bench on the 14th of October, my learned friend Mr. HAWKINS stated that it was probable that he should have to ask permission to recall this witness, in order to question him further. Thus the matter rested till the 16th of October, when Dr. KENEALY announced that it had come to his knowledge that the defendant was about to leave the country, and added that he considered it his duty to make the piece of news known to the Court. In consequence of that statement the defendant was directed to attend before the Court of Queen's Bench on the following day. The defendant did attend the following day, and admitted that he intended to leave the country, alleging that he had an attack of blood-spitting. He acknowledged that he intended to leave England on Saturday, the 18th, but agreed to remain here if the Court so desired. He was not then obliged to enter into any recognizance, but care was taken that he should be forthcoming whenever his presence was required. He was further examined on the 16th, and further facts had been gleaned respecting him. It is beyond doubt doubt, therefore, that he intended at that time to leave the country. Indeed, a letter was found at his lodgings addressed to the Dock Master at the Southampton Docks, and signed by Mr. GUILDFORD ONSLOW, which read thus:—

"DEAR SIR,—The bearer of this is JEAN LUIE. I need hardly ask you to do all you can for him to help him on to America. He will telegraph from New York."

What I have just referred to as having occurred in the Court of Queen's Bench, took place on October 16th, and this letter was found in the defendant's lodgings the day after. This shows that even on the 17th it was his intention to leave the country as soon as possible. After that date a learned friend of mine, Mr. PURCELL, was sent to America for the purpose of testing the truth of defendant's story. Mr. PURCELL made full inquiries, and, in the end of November and in December, rebutting evidence was produced, the result of which was the defendant was recognized, and the Court of Queen's Bench ordered, on December 11, that he should be charged with wilful and corrupt perjury. It is now plain enough that, from the beginning to the end of his statements, there was perjury in almost every sentence. Indeed, he has admitted to the officer who has had him in charge that his evidence was false. His statement of how he became connected with the case was this. He alleged that he joined a vessel called the "Osprey" at New Orleans in 1852; that he was steward of that vessel; that he was in Rio and other places in 1853, and that in Feburary, 1854, he sailed from Staten Island, New York, to Melbourne in that vessel. He even mentioned the names of the agents of the vessel, so as to show conclusively that such a vessel existed. He stated that about April he saw a boat paddled by two men, JARVIS and LEWIS, and that four others were lying in it delirious. That the six persons were taken on board, and that they had been saved from the "Bella." One of them, who was known as ROGERS, was afterwards identified as the Claimant to the Tichborne estates. The prisoner stated that this man was under his care for three months, till the vessel arrived at Melbourne; that he saw a brown or olive mark about the left hip of the man ROGERS, and was able to identify him. The "Osprey," he said, arrived at Melbourne in July; the prisoner went on shore in the "Bella's" boat, and the man ROGERS in another boat, when he lost sight of him. After that time the prisoner stated that he remained at the diggings till May, 1855, when he left for Sydney. He gave an account of the ships he was in from the time he left Sydney, and gave a history of himself up to April, 1861. He stated that the captain of the "Osprey," Captain BANNATT, whom he saw in 1864, joined the Southern army, and was killed, and that in 1865 he saw the "Osprey" dismantled at Melbourne. He gave an account of himself as having kept a grog-shop in Chicago until he had a reason for coming to England, which was to find his wife, who had left him, and taken some papers with her. He said he came over in the "Circassia" from New York to Liverpool. At first he said he came from Belgium, but afterwards said he came direct to Liverpool on the 8th of June, 1873, and that he took a through ticket to Folkestone, and went from there to Ostend, being unable to find his wife. He came back to London on the 5th of July, 1873, and according to his statement, this was his first arrival in London. He then told the remarkable story that on his arrival in London he heard in a public house there was a great deal talked about a man who had been saved from the "Bella" by the "Osprey." He made up his mind to go to the West-end to see the Claimant. On the 16th of July he endeavoured to find the Claimant, but could not, and for some reason he went down to Brighton, and on coming back on the Sunday night he walked about till five in the morning, endeavouring to find the Claimant. Ultimately he went to 31, Bessborough-gardens, where the Claimant lived, but did not see him. He then went to Poets-corner, to the solicitor's office which Mr. WHALLEY and Mr. ONSLOW were in the habit of frequenting, and thence in a cab to 34, Bessborough-gardens, with Mr. GUILDFORD ONSLOW, when he saw the Claimant, and identified him. It is not necessary, Sir THOMAS, to trouble you with a relation of all the various reasons the defendant has given for recognizing the person who is called the Claimant. All his statements have been already taken down. When called as a witness on the 14th of October, he was asked had he ever gone by another name, and had he ever been in trouble. He replied to both questions that he had not. We shall see that. I now come to deal with the question as to who the defendant really is, and where he really has been from 1852 up to the present day. The real facts of the case, so far as the defendant is concerned, are these: He was in Hull, in this country, in May or June, 1853, till the end of 1854. There was no mistake about that, as the evidence was overwhelming. He then left Hull and went to Cardiff, where he stayed at the Scandinavian Hall, and formed the acquaintance of a person of the name of SARAH COLBURN, whom he married at Melksham in Wilts, in the name of CARL PETER LUNDGREN. In September, 1852, he was taken into custody at Bristol for stealing a bill of exchange. In October, 1862, he was tried and sentenced to three years' penal servitude, and was in prison till April, 1865, so that it was impossible that he could have been at Melbourne in the spring of 1865. In January, 1866, he was tried at Newcastle, and sentenced to six months' imprisonment under the name of PETERSEN for obtaining money under false pretences. In March, 1867, he appeared at a coffee-house in Star-street, Edgware-road, as JOHN SMITH, and he lived at this coffee-house, which was kept by HARRIET ARHEND, and there he was from March till April, 1867, and then he, as JOHN SMITH, married the keeper of the coffee-house. He lived there till the 6th of June, and then it appeared that he assaulted this woman. He was bound over at the Marylebone Police-court to keep the peace, and was released from custody on the 15th of June. This, then, is a clear case of bigamy. The next that was proved was that in the same year he was arrested at Cardiff, and in October, 1867, was sentenced to seven years' penal servitude, and was in various convict prisons till the 25th of March, 1873. After that date he passed in the East-end of London as Captain SORENSEN. But on the 27th of May last year he went back to Paddington, and was recognized by Mr. and Mrs. MILLER, who kept a beer-shop, and who knew him when he lived in Paddington formerly. He had to account for himself, and he did so by saying he had just returned from sea, and wished to know where Mrs. ARHEND was. He stayed at MILLER's till the 4th of July, and on the 5th of July he borrowed half a sovereign. He was not seen again till he was recognized as the convict JEAN LUIE, *alias* JOHN LUNDGREN *alias* CARL LUNDGREN. They found him to be their old friend JOHN SMITH. Mrs. MILLER lent him one of her husband's shirts, which was afterwards found at his lodgings. If necessary, numerous witnesses can be brought to prove that he is the same man as JOHN SMITH. This man, therefore, was directed to be prosecuted. There was a desire on the part of the Prosecution that the fullest inquiry should be made. The result of the delay had been the discovery of this JOHN SMITH's history and the case of bigamy. He had called GOD to witness the truth of his asseverations, and when the real facts became known it was enough to make one's blood run cold. When brought before the magistrate on a previous occasion he had said that it would not have occurred if he had not been led into it, and he was sorry for it. He stated to the officer who had him in charge that on the 4th or 5th of July he met BAIGENT, and got into conversation, and he appears to have seen young BOGLE, and the crooked finger was shown to BOGLE. Afterwards he went on to state that the Claimant mentioned the crooked finger to him after he had shown it to BOGLE. He told the officer that he would tell him all about it; but the officer said he had better make the statement to the solicitor. Ultimately he said he had been desired to hold his tongue, and would not say anything. He, however, made the admission that he had never been in America or Australia in his life. He said he had his Australian information from JAMES, and the "Osprey" information from Captain BROWN. Inspector CLARKE found a rough drawing of Hobson's Bay at the prisoner's lodgings, and on the same piece of paper is a short account of his going to Australia and his picking up. Notwithstanding this remarkable history, it appears that this man has still some good friends, who have instructed Mr. LEWIS to appear for him and defend him. But this matter cannot end here. Not only has this man committed perjury, but he has been making statements to the officers who had him in charge which show the mode in which he originally became connected with this case, and which reflect strongly upon the characters of certain persons who have figured in it. All these things will have to be inquired into before we are entirely done with the matter. When brought before Sir THOMAS HENRY, by direction of the Crown, the defendant said: "I am sorry for what I have done. It would not have happened if I had not been made up to do it." He told one of the officers that he went to Poets-corner in July, and had conversations with Mr. BAIGENT and young BOGLE; and you will also hear of subsequent conversations which he had with Mr. WHALLEY, Mr. ONSLOW, and the Claimant, and how the latter recognized in JEAN LUIE the person who had saved his life so miraculously, who had nursed him in the "Osprey," who spoke to him in Spanish, whom he knew by his voice, and remembered that LUIE's crooked fingers hurt him when he used to be washed, the prisoner having previously shown his fingers to BOGLE. It will be shown that soon after this the prisoner expressed a wish to make a full statement to one of the officers, and that the officer advised him not to do it, except in the presence of a solicitor. Meanwhile the prisoner appears to have been visited by his friends, for when called upon for his proffered statement, he said he had altered his mind, and declined to make any statement. The learned Counsel was about to read a letter written by the prisoner, and which had been copied by the prison officials, when

Mr. LEWIS interposed, and appealed to Sir THOMAS HENRY to know whether he would allow such a document as this to be put in evidence. He contended that a private letter such as this should not be admissible.

Sir THOMAS HENRY: I think that a prisoner's handwriting can be received as evidence in a court of justice. Such letters as these have been received as evidence hundreds of times. Unless you can cite a case to the contrary, I cannot allow your objection.

Mr. LEWIS: I cannot immediately cite any case; but if you postpone your decision on the point I'll look for one. I think it is very hard upon the Defendant to be dealt with in this way. Ever since his committal he has been subjected to all sorts of threats and intimidation.

Sir THOMAS HENRY: You are now irregular, Mr. LEWIS.

Mr. LEWIS: All I want is that nothing may be put in that will prejudice the prisoner in the eyes of the public until, at all events, I am in a position to cross-examine the witnesses, and until I am fully instructed. These letters and statements ought not to be admitted, because I am told that they have been elicited from him by means of threats. I submit that the copying of the letter to which I now object is an improper act.

Sir T. HENRY: These letters are, I think, evidence, and I will not stop their being read.

Mr. POLAND continued: If Mr. LEWIS really appears for the defendant he should not object to this letter at all; for it is more serviceable to the defendant than anything else. It is surely to the interest of the defendant, if he has any excuse for his crime, that it should be made known.

The letter in question was addressed to Mr. J. RIMELL, 29, Golden-square, and was dated Dec. 22, 1873. It was as follows:

DEAR SIR,—By this I beg to acquaint you all that I am here retained, and have heard nothing. This is a miserable life, and to suffer such all for not being allowed to have my own way. [Here Mr. POLAND explained that the prisoner had objected to be examined, and if this referred to his objection it was to the interest of the prisoner that it should be known.] But what is done can't be altered. I refer you to my last from House of Detention. I had a letter from Plas Madox [explained by Mr. POLAND as the residence of Mr. WHALLEY], wherein was stated that £5 had been sent to HARDING.

The letter concluded by wishing "Merry Christmas to W., at Plas Madox, and all friends."

Mr. LEWIS: Have you read the original letter?

Mr. POLAND: I am reading from my brief.

Mr. LEWIS: There may be no original to this letter.

Mr. POLAND: If the original letter is not put in I shall prove either it was lost or destroyed, and will produce a person who has seen it. Now, if this man of whom I have been speaking had succeeded in getting out of the country, and nobody had come forward to identify him, it is easy to imagine what might have occurred; but by a fortunate accident, he was not able to leave the country. And all this information respecting him has since been ascertained. When Dr. KENEALY himself was obliged to sever his case from this man, it was pretty conclusive that there was no doubt about the genuineness of all this information. As I have already told you, the man admitted himself that he has never been in America or Australia; that he has never wished to go into the witness-box; that it would not have occurred had he not been made up to do it, and that it was all through his not being allowed to have his own way. This is the case for the prosecution, put into as narrow a compass as I can manage it. In the evidence to be brought forward in support of my case, I shall narrow the whole matter as much as possible, and at the same time endeavour to bring out all the salient points. I am bound to say, at the same time, that no expense or trouble will be spared in having evidence produced of persons from all parts of the country to prove the full history of the defendant from 1853 up to the present time. Before sitting down I wish to state that in August, 1873, Mr. HENDRIKS was not the solicitor at Poets-corner.

WILLIAM AISH DAVIS, examined by Mr. POLAND: I am a shorthand-writer. I was present during the Trial of the Claimant at the Court of Queen's Bench, on the 14th and 15th October, when the prisoner was giving evidence. I produce a printed copy of the notes I took on these two occasions.

Mr. LEWIS contended that the original notes, and not the printed copy, should be produced and sworn to.

By Mr. Poland: I can get my original notes easily enough, and compare them with the printed copy, if that should be considered necessary.

GEORGE CLARKE, examined by Mr. POLAND: I am Chief Inspector of the Detective Department at Scotland-yard. I was in Court on the 11th December, when the prisoner was ordered to be prosecuted. I took him into custody, and afterwards made a search of his lodgings at No. 12, Churchyard-row, Newington-butts. I went with PULLEYN, who was the occupier of the house. I was introduced to PULLEYN's wife. The house in question is a small one. Mrs. PULLEYN took me upstairs to a bedroom. She showed me a striped shirt, a flannel shirt, flannel drawers, a sailor's blue suit of clothes, and a cap with a peak. I took possession of these articles. I found several papers there also, including an unopened letter. The papers produced are those shown me by Mrs. PULLEYN. One is a letter addressed to "Mr. E. C. GREY, the Docks, Southampton." The letter found in the envelope is signed "GUILDFORD ONSLOW, 2, Poets-corner." There was a paper signed "JOHN LUIE." On the back of that there is a rough sketch.

Mr. LEWIS submitted that unless this was in the Defendant's handwriting it was not evidence, and urged that the document referred to might have been written by somebody else, and placed in LUIE's room.

Mr. POLAND contended that as LUIE gave this house as the one in which he had lodged, what was found in the room occupied by him might be taken as evidence.

Sir T. HENRY: Of course it is possible that these papers may have been placed by somebody other than the prisoner, but I think that these documents are admissible.

Examination continued: On the sketch on the back of this paper was the word "Melbourne." There appeared to be the word "Sandridge," but it was not very plain. There was the word "Williamstown." There were some crosses on it. Those appeared to be in different handwriting to that in the ink in which "JOHN LUIE" was signed. There was also written on the same paper what was meant to be an account of LUIE's life. It was as follows:

"I was born in Bornholm, an iland beloning to Danmark. Am 48 years old, and at 13 or 14 years old went over to Helsingen, where I engaged myself as cabin-boy ombord the 'Christian VII.' We saild for St. Thomas, and back again to Kjobenham (Copenhagen), and again took several trips with different vessels, and the places being Marselles, Algiers, and Oran, with cargoes of Deals from Gefle, Hornisand, and Memel. My first sea voyage was 1838. In 1846, I left the "Audacia" in Barcelona, and joyned the "Carlos" for Havana. Was staying in the hospital for yellow fever for three months, and went on coasting voyages. Then went to the Mexican war, 1848. 1852, in latter part, I joyned the "Osprey," Captain BANNETT, and we was trading to Cordenas, Cape de Verds Islands, took salt for Buenos Ayres, loaded carne secas (dryed meat by the sun) for Rio Pernambuco, crosed over for Cape de Verds, took salt for Rio Grand, loaded carne secas for Musio and Paraiba. In ballast to New York, brought to an anchor at Staten Island. 1854, in February, after taking in bricks, breadstuff, butts (half puncheons sawed in two) for washing-tubs, lumbers for huts, and digging implements, sailed for Melbourne in April (the middle); somewhere in lat. 19 or 20, picked upp the "Bella's" crew (one not a sailor), HENRY DOCHTOR (DOGLAS), JARVIS LEWIS, and one not known. Took them overboard, and landed them in Melbourne, July, the same year. Two of the men in the boat was Portugeos, and had shipped in Rio. X JOHN LUIE.

"Stayed in New Orleans one years engaged with SCHNEDAN."

Other papers and letters were also found. One was a returned registered letter from America, addressed to Mr. C. ANDERSON, Nineteenth-street, Brooklyn, New York. The letter was signed "JOHN LUIE," and dated "12, Churchyard-row, Newington-butts, London, July 10, 1873." This was one of the letters given to me by Mrs. PULLEYN. The letters and papers I now produce and hand in are the same that I found at LUIE's lodgings.

Mr. POLAND read the letter addressed to Brooklyn, which appears on p. 278, and stated that it was carefully registered before being sent to America, and that it, of course, came back to England, as was the case with all registered letters which did not reach the places to which they were addressed.

Examination continued: I brought the prisoner to Bow-street on the 13th December. I had a conversation with him in the cab from Holloway Prison to this court. He asked me what he had better do in the matter. I said, "You are old enough to advise yourself, LUIE." I do not recollect that he then said anything particular to me. But on leaving court he said, "I wish you would advise me." I said, "You ought to think over what you had better do yourself." LUIE then said, "I was first spoken to on the matter in the spring of the year in Brussels, by Mr. WHALLEY, who was stopping there with his daughter. I got into conversation with him and he told me there was a trial pending in his country which made him ashamed of it. Seeing that I was a sailor, Mr. WHALLEY said, 'We have never been able to find any of the crew of a shipwrecked vessel whom it was important we should find.' I said to Mr. WHALLEY, 'I do not think it would be very difficult, as I have been a sailor myself.'" LUIE added, "I saw him two or three times afterwards, but nothing particular was arranged. I first went to Poets-corner about the 4th or 5th July. I met a man there with something the matter with his eye. I found subsequently that was BAIGENT. BAIGENT asked me who I was, and I said 'JEAN LUIE.' BAIGENT said, 'Oh, yes; I know all about it.' This was on Monday, the 7th. BAIGENT said it was all arranged, and he knew I was coming. I showed my fingers to the little black fellow BOGLE, who ran into the inner room to, I believe, tell 'Sir ROGER.' When Sir ROGER first came into the outer office he spoke loud and said, 'If you are the man who saved me your little fingers are crooked.'" When we got to the House of Detention I again saw LUIE at his own request before I left the prison. He said, "If I thought they wouldn't prosecute me I'd tell all particulars." Witness said, "I can make no promise about that; but, if you wish to do so, I'd rather you would do it before the solicitors." LUIE said, "Very well, then; let them come on Monday." That was on Saturday, the 13th. I then left the prison. After communicating with the Solicitor to the Treasury I went to the House of Detention on Monday. I saw the prisoner in a private room. I said "Here are Inspector CLARKE and Mr. POLLARD. Do you wish to see them?" He followed me to a corner of the room, and said in an under tone, "No, not now. I have been advised to hold my tongue." Mr. POLLARD and I then left the prison. On the following day I went there with an order to bring LUIE to this Court. On our way to the Court he said to me, "Since I saw you last I have had a visit from Captain NICHOLSON. He brought me a letter from Mr. WHALLEY, saying that he would get me remanded from time to time, that I should not go to a convict prison, and that he had sent £5 to HARDING to keep me; that he had a private letter for me from Mr. WHALLEY, but as the warder of the prison was present the whole time he could not give it to me." LUIE said, "I should not have got into

SIR THOMAS HENRY.

this trouble at all if it had not been for the folly of Dr. KENEALY, by forcing Mr. HAWKINS to call the rebutting evidence. It is not all my fault. I begged of them scores of times not to put me in the witness-box; but Mr. ONSLOW is a very violent man, and would not listen to me. He gave me a book of the evidence of the last trial, with different passages marked, which he gave me to learn at night time, and I frequently sat up all night to do so. Mr. ONSLOW told me about the brown mark on the side, and drew with his finger the size and shape of it. Mr. ONSLOW put his hand on my side to show where the brown mark was situated. Mr. ONSLOW wanted me to prove the malformation. I was frightened, and refused to do it. I did not know what he meant at first, and asked Sergeant-Major MARKS. I mentioned this to Mr. ONSLOW when I saw him again. I was afraid to get into a mess, and I said I should have nothing to do in it. Before the day of the examination I got a good deal of my Australian information from the man JANES, of Holloway, and all about the 'Osprey' from Captain BROWN. I had to see Captain BROWN frequently for the purpose of arranging the evidence."

Mr. POLAND: Did you say anything to him about Australia?

Witness: Yes. He told me he had never been in Australia in his life. I said, "You do surprise me. I can't believe Mr. WHALLEY would have gone to America unless on some good information." LUIE said, "It is all a 'barney.' It was all part of the same scheme which had been arranged upon." He added, "It speaks for itself. I could not have given information myself if I had never been there." Witness said, "You must have been to Australia, because I found some drawings on a paper in your lodging of Hobson's Bay." LUIE said, "What paper?" I said, "A piece of paper whereon you have written a short account of your life." LUIE said, "Oh, yes; I did that, I recollect; but I did not do the back. That was done by Mr. ONSLOW. If you look you will see it was not the same handwriting." LUIE said, further, "ONSLOW was a most violent man, and was to have the largest share of the property, and I was to be his steward. Capt. BROWN was to be dock-superintendent of Southampton. Mr. ONSLOW was to get him that berth. JANES, of Holloway, was to have a public-house. Mr. WHALLEY was to have some of the property, and Mr. Baigent some more." Luie said, with regard to giving evidence, that he never intended giving evidence, but to make some money, and that they forced him to do it. Luie said, "I was never allowed out by myself, but one or the other of them was with me. I thought that if they knew all, they would do nothing for me when I came out. I should have been put into the box before only that I could not learn my story correctly." I had altogether about three hours' conversation with Luie. A good deal of it took place in the yard of the police-station and going backwards and forwards in the cab. Luie told me frequently that he would make a clean breast of it, and tell the Solicitor to the Treasury everything. Another thing said by Luie to me was that he would have told all this long ago, but that he did not like to injure Mr. Whalley. I know No. 2, Poets-corner. I knew it to have been the office of the attorney for the Claimant for months. I have seen Baigent, Mr. Whalley, Mr. Onslow, and Jane there. Sergeant-Major Marks is a person who attended meetings of the Claimant. I have seen him at Poets-corner several times. I do not know Captain Nicholson. I knew Mr. Rimell, of Golden-square, well. I have seen him frequently with Luie at the Poets-corner, and in conversation with the Claimant. Rose Bank, Ballard's-lane, Finchley, is the private address of Mr. Rimell. I have never seen the prisoner there.

Mr. Lewis intimated that, in consequence of having been instructed only very recently, and having had only a few minutes' conversation with the prisoner, he was not prepared to commence to cross-examine any witness to-day.

Sir Thomas Henry: There is other business to be got through here to-day, and I am afraid I shall have to stop this case.

Mr. Poland begged that two witnesses from Bristol be heard. After that he was ready to consent to an adjournment of the case. The evidence of these would not take long.

Sir Thomas Henry assented, and the hearing of the case was continued.

Eliza Golledge was then called, and examined by Mr. Poland: I reside in Sophia-street, Bute-street, Cardiff. I have resided there since 1851. I knew the prisoner. I knew him in Cardiff and in Bristol as Carl Lundgren. I became first acquainted with him in the latter part of the year 1854 at Cardiff. I knew a person named Sarah Colborne. She was living with her brother William at that time, in Bute-road. Her sister lived with us, and because she was keeping company with the prisoner she was turned out by her brother. The "Scandinavian" was the name of the hotel we kept. The prisoner used to meet foreign captains there. Sarah Colborne and the prisoner left our house to be married. They were married in April, 1855. [Certificate of marriage handed in.] They came back to Cardiff, and passed as Mr. and Mrs. Lundgren. They returned to Cardiff in about a fortnight after the marriage. This was, I believe, in April, 1855. I saw the prisoner nearly every day after, till they left for London. They did not remain long in Cardiff. They went from London to Bristol. I saw them in Bristol. I knew them living in three different places in Bristol for five or six years. Mrs. Lundgren had three children during that time. Lundgren was taken into custody whilst in Bristol. I never saw him afterwards till I saw him in Westminster, when I was examined there, on the 9th December. The prisoner's wife was then alive. I saw her at Westminster. I also saw them in Bristol. I was there on business when I saw them. My sister Emma is now living at Woolwich. She is married to Sergeant-Major Bleach, and is known in Woolwich as Mrs. Bleach.

Mr. Poland read a marriage certificate, which stated that Carl Lundgren, age 34, a bachelor and a ship-broker, son of Elias Lundgren, deceased, was married by license, on the 2nd April, 1855, at Melksham, to Sarah Colborne, age 21, spinster, whose residence was given as Melksham, and who was represented to be the daughter of Wm. Colborne, a plasterer.

John Nicholls, a police-constable in the City of Bristol, examined by Mr Poland: I have been nearly 17 years a policeman in Bristol. I knew the prisoner by the name of Charles Lundgren. I took him into custody in October, 1862. That was at Bristol. He was afterwards tried at the Bristol Quarter Sessions, under the name of Charles Lundgren, for stealing a bill of exchange. He was sentenced to three years' penal servitude. I have got the certificate of conviction, and hand it in. I knew the prisoner for 18 months before that time, living at Bristol with his wife. She is still living. I saw her at one o'clock yesterday. I was present in 1867 at the October Sessions at Cardiff, when the prisoner was tried, convicted, and sentenced to seven years' penal servitude. I was there to prove the previous conviction.

A Gentleman, who refused to give his name, said that he appeared for Mr. Whalley, M.P., and for Mr. Onslow, M.P., and was desirous of making a statement on behalf of these hon. gentlemen, but he was interrupted by

Sir Thomas Henry, who declared that he could not allow it on any account.

Mr. Poland: These gentlemen will have to come here and appear for themselves.

The further hearing of the case was, at four o'clock, adjourned till the next Saturday week at eleven o'clock.

Mr. Lewis made an application for the privilege of having free access to the prisoner during the time which would elapse between then and the resumption of the hearing of the case.

Sir Thomas Henry acceded to the application without hesitation, and issued instructions which gave Mr. Lewis all the facilities which he might require.

The prisoner was then remanded.

We are requested by Mr. Guildford Onslow, M.P., to publish the following statement: "On my arrival in London, some days after the appearance of Jean Luie, and his identification of the Claimant, I was first told of the circumstance, and a few days afterwards I met Jean Luie at the Claimant's office, No. 2, Poets-corner, Westminster, when I had two hours' conversation with him, and subjected him to a severe cross-examination regarding the "Osprey," testing him by the evidence given in the late Trial, and I could not shake him in a single point. I was much struck at his vehemence in declaring the "Osprey" a barque, and not a three-masted schooner, and his decided opinion she had a square stern, instead of a round one. I was in the habit of meeting him from time to time at No. 2, Poets-corner and sometimes in Court, when I had frequent conversations on the Case, chiefly regarding the "Osprey." On one occasion I asked him if he could draw. He said he could. I asked him to sketch me the "Osprey" as he had known her. He made a very fair rough sketch of a barque, with three masts, with two cabins on deck, with the remarkable circumstance of making the mizzenmast pass right through the cabin. The sketch he made was in full sail. I have it by me. Some time after Luie had given his evidence I happened to be in the office, and spoke to a man—the mate, I believe, of the "Queen of the South," who gave evidence on the Trial as having seen the "Osprey" in Melbourne Harbour in 1854. I asked him if he knew Jean Luie. He told me he did not, and had never read his evidence. I asked him if he could draw. He said "Yes." I begged him to sketch me the "Osprey" as he remembered her; upon which he drew me a most artistic sketch of a vessel at anchor, very like Jean Luie's sketch, with the same remarkable circumstance of making the mizzenmast pass through the main cabin on deck, precisely in the same position as Jean Luie had sketched it. I never showed this man Luie's sketch, nor did I tell Luie of it.

"Both sketches are in my possession. Jean Luie went into the witness-box, and gave his evidence in a most clear and satisfactory manner. About two o'clock, after he came out, and whilst a number of people in the office were congratulating him on the way he had acted, I asked him what his intentions were. Would he go to New York? He said his intention was to leave by the Saturday's boat from Southampton to New York. I strongly commended this intention, and told him if he would start by the next train (five o'clock) I would give him a letter of introduction to Mr. Grey, of the docks at Southampton, asking that gentleman, as a personal favour, to help and aid him in starting for New York, where he agreed to telegraph to me when he had found Anderson, the mate of the "Osprey," and Harry, the sailmaker; and, having found them, to telegraph two words to save expense, viz., "Found—coming," which I was to understand meant, found Anderson and Harry, and that they were on their way to England. I gave him a cheque on my bankers for £5, and said, if I could afford it, I would give him £500 for all the trouble he had been put to, and for having been kept in England so long from his family and friends in New York. Mr. Whalley also gave him £5, and I understood the Claimant, Sir Roger Tichborne, would give him £20; this would be sufficient to go to New York. I wished him good-bye, but before he left Mr. Whalley drew up a sort of acknowledgment of the straightforward manner in which he had so truthfully (as we thought) given his evidence. This paper was written on the hurry of the moment to save the train, and was signed by Mr. Whalley and myself. After this happened I was much surprised to find Jean Luie had never left for New York as he promised; but as he was brought up before the Court, and gave his promise not to leave, I thought no more about it until I heard he had been sent to Holloway Prison as a convict. I then went to London to ask Mr. Pulleyn, with whom Luie had been living, not to give up his papers, but to return me the paper Mr. Whalley and I had signed, and my letter to Mr. Grey, of Southampton. Mr. Pulleyn informed me he had in his possession the paper we both signed, and which he should hand over to Mr. Whalley himself, and that my letter to Mr. Grey was, with other papers of Luie's, handed to the police. From that day to this I have never seen or communicated with Jean Luie.

"I will add, I always understood Jean Luie recognized the Claimant, but that the Claimant never recognized him, except from the truthful statement he made regarding the "Osprey," and from the fact that Jean Luie, like the *real* steward of the "Osprey," spoke both Spanish and French. The Claimant, having tested him in both languages, believed him to be the man who saved him, and, therefore, did not hesitate to put him in the witness-box.

(Signed) "Guildford Onslow.

"Jan. 1, 1874."

JEAN LUIE AT BOW STREET

On Saturday morning, at a quarter-past eleven o'clock, Jean Luie, the notorious witness for the Claimant in the Tichborne Case, was brought up at Bow-street, on remand before Sir Thomas Henry, to answer a charge of perjury. A good deal of public interest was again displayed in the inquiry. More than an hour before the commencement of the proceedings many persons had assembled in front of the entrance to Bow-street Police-court, in the hope of effecting an entrance, or, failing that, catching a glimpse of the prisoner; and during the whole day the interior of the court and corridors leading thereto were inconveniently crammed with people. Mr. POLLARD and Mr. POLAND appeared for the prosecution, and Mr. EDWARD LEWIS for the defence. Mr. WHALLEY, M.P., was early in attendance. After having a private conversation with Mr. LEWIS, the hon. gentleman squeezed himself into a seat in the attorneys' box, which was already pretty well packed with the learned gentlemen and the shorthand-writers engaged in the case. When LUIE made his appearance in the dock, attired as a convict, Mr. WHALLEY looked up at him with an appearance of much surprise. On each side of Sir THOMAS HENRY sat several gentlemen whose names did not transpire. Near to the witness-box stood Mr. HARDING, secretary to the Claimant. Except during the time HARRIET ARRENDS was giving her evidence, the prisoner displayed the utmost indifference to what was being said respecting him. Some of the evidence given by HARRIET ARRENDS seemed to afford him no small amount of amusement.

CHARLES BENNETT, examined by Mr. POLAND: I am a shorthand writer. I was present in the Court of Queen's Bench on the 14th of October last, when the prisoner LUIE was examined as a witness. I took down parts of his evidence on that day. I have them with me. I have compared them with the printed copy or transcript, and have found them to be accurate.

MATTHIAS LEVY, examined by Mr. POLAND: I am a shorthand-writer. I was present in the Court of Queen's Bench when the prisoner was examined. I took down his evidence on the 14th and 15th October. The printed transcript of my report produced is an accurate account of what the prisoner said on those two occasions.

Inspector CLARKE having been recalled for cross-examination.

Mr. LEWIS rose, and, addressing the Bench, said: Sir THOMAS, I have now to apply to you to have all witnesses, except those who have been already examined and will not be called again, and who may have only to speak to facts, ordered out of court.

Sir. THOMAS HENRY: Certainly; all those who have evidence to give, except, I suppose, the shorthand-writers.

Mr. LEWIS: Yes, sir.

Mr. POLAND: I think, Mr. LEWIS, that two of your witnesses (Mr. HARDING and another) should leave also.

Sir. THOMAS HENRY: They must do so, but they will have to wait.

Mr. POLAND: The usher will see that the witnesses remain. Perhaps Mr. WHALLEY should also leave. Do you, Mr. LEWIS, intend to call him as a witness?

Mr. LEWIS: I do not know what I shall do yet.

Sir THOMAS HENRY: In that case Mr. WHALLEY had better leave.

Mr. WHALLEY, Mr. HARDING, and several other persons then left the court, and were, it was understood, kept in waiting outside during the remainder of the day.

Inspector CLARKE, cross-examined by Mr. LEWIS: How long have you been connected with the TICHBORNE Trial?—Only since the commencement of the present inquiry.

You have been engaged in prosecuting inquiry respecting it ever since, down to the present time?—I have.

You take, I presume, a very great interest in the Trial of the Claimant?—None whatever: except so far as my duties as an officer are concerned.

Did you make any statement before this man was taken into custody to the effect that he had been coached up by Mr. ONSLOW and Mr. WHALLEY?—I did not.

I ask you in the most general way possible—and I warn you to be careful in your answer—whether, long before any statement was made to you by the defendant, you did not make imputations to the effect that Mr. ONSLOW, Mr. WHALLEY, and Mr. BAIGENT had coached up the prisoner?—No: I have made no such imputation. I may have spoken confidentially in the office.

What do you mean by that?—Simply that I made verbal reports. I never mentioned anything about his being coached up in my written reports.

You mean to say that you have never made any imputations of this description with regard to these gentlemen?—I cannot say just now what I may have said confidentially to my superintendent or my brother-inspectors at my office; but know I never said anything of this description outside my office.

I do not care whether it was outside or inside your office. I ask you whether you have ever cast imputations on the gentlemen I have named?—No.

Have you had conversations on the subject?—Yes; I have had private conversations. I have frequently conversed for hours about the subject to my brother-officers, but I have never cast any imputation upon the gentlemen you have named.

Did you take the prisoner into custody at the Court of Queen's Bench?—No, he was taken back by the warders.

Were you not appointed to bring him from the House of Detention?—I was not appointed. It was my duty to do so, and I did so.

You acted on some instructions?—I received instructions from Sir THOMAS HENRY to bring him here, and to take him back to prison.

Mr. LEWIS: But who directed you to bring him here?—SIR THOMAS HENRY: He has told you. The warrant from this Court.

Mr. LEWIS: Very well, Sir THOMAS. I did not know that. Was there one of the warders in the cab in which you conveyed the defendant?—Yes.

When was that?—I think it was on the 13th December.

You have stated that the prisoner said something to you on your way to the Court? Did he make a statement then?—Not much of a statement on that occasion. He put his head towards me and said something about Mr. W. I understood that he meant Mr. WHALLEY. I cannot remember all he said on that day, as I paid little attention to him, but as well as I remember, he said that Mr. WHALLEY had seen him respecting the matter.

Was that all that passed between you?—When he made use of the expression "Mr. W.," I asked him what he meant, and he replied "Mr. WHALLEY." It was he who first spoke to me about the matter. He spoke to me at intervals in a low tone, to the effect that there were certain persons who knew something of the matter, and that Mr. WHALLEY was one of them.

Who was the warder with you at the time?—I do not know his name.

Sir THOMAS HENRY: His name can be easily ascertained.

Mr. LEWIS: Mr. CLARKE, you have given us a long and clear account of what he said when there was no one with you; do you mean to say that you cannot remember this?—I have tried to remember.

Do you know if the warder heard what he said?—I do not. He spoke in a low tone. I should think that he did hear some of it; but when a cab is rattling along you cannot hear all that is said. When I took him back Sergeant BUTCHER was with me. He was on the outside of the cab.

By whose orders?—By my orders.

Was that arrangement made so that you might be alone with the prisoner?—No; I did it as a matter of caution. I should take such a course with any other prisoner, for the purpose of seeing that the cabman went right.

I understand you have summarized what the prisoner said to you on the two occasions?—Yes. And in doing so I followed his words as well as I could recollect them.

And I think you have said that what you stated was not a hundredth part of what the prisoner said to you?—That was so. He was very communicative indeed.

Mr. LEWIS: And you encouraged him to be as communicative as possible?—I did not.

You did not discourage him?—No. He told me he should make a statement to the solicitor. He said that a score of times at least, and that was the reason why I took less notice of it than I otherwise should have done.

When you were going to the House of Detention with the prisoner, did you tell him that Sergeant-Major MARKS had opened his breast and made a full confession?—I did not.

Have you said anything of that nature upon any occasion? I had a statement of Sergeant-Major MARKS in my possession, and I may have spoken about it.

Did you say so to the prisoner?—I did not.

Have you upon that or any other occasion said that if he would make a full confession to Mr. POLLARD, the evidence would not be used against him, and he would not be prosecuted?—No. On the contrary, I told him I could not promise.

I will come to that presently. You told him you could not promise?—He said, "What good could it do me to get any one else into trouble? I should not benefit by it." I did not answer, and after a short time he said, "What do you think of that?" Then I said I had no control, and I could not promise in any way. I explained to him that I was merely a policeman in the matter, and so on.

And then did you advise him to make a statement to Mr. POLLARD?—Yes; I told him that Mr. POLLARD was the proper person to make such a statement to.

Sir T. HENRY: You were asked if you advised him. Did you advise him?—Certainly not. I did not advise him. I answered him in the way I have stated several times when he appealed to me.

Mr. LEWIS: Did you not go one step further, and recommend that as the best course?—No, sir.

You thought it would be the best course?

Sir T. HENRY: Anything which was passing in his mind is not evidence.

Mr. LEWIS: At all events, you accompanied Mr. POLLARD to the House of Detention in order that LUIE might make a statement?—I did.

You told us on the last occasion that the prisoner said he had been advised not to make any statement?—I did.

And you led it to be inferred that he had seen Captain NICHOLSON?—He told me he had.

Don't you know that the visit of Captain NICHOLSON was not till some days afterwards?—I don't know.

Did you learn from any of the officials at the House of Detention that Captain NICHOLSON had been there?—I am not sure.

Did you not make it your business to inquire who had seen the prisoner?—I did not. I went to make inquiries on one occasion. I was only there twice. The first occasion I was there with Mr. POLLARD. I saw no one separate from him. On the second occasion I fetched the prisoner.

Was that the occasion when you inquired?—No; I went to see about a letter.

Did you not say that you had been to make inquiry as to who had visited the prisoner?—I did not. I said I went to make inquiries.

Don't you know as a fact that between the 13th, when you took the prisoner to the House of Detention, and the time that you went with Mr. POLLARD, the prisoner had seen no one but the prison officials?—I do not.

Mr. POLAND: Do you know anything about that?—No.

Mr. LEWIS: I will now take you to the interview in the cab. Did you use these words to the prisoner, "You must take that as from myself; I have no authority to tell you so, but there is no doubt you will not be prosecuted if you make a clean breast of it"?—I did not.

Nothing of the kind?—Nothing of the kind.

Is there anything more in that written statement than what you stated here last week?—No, I think not. I think it is about the same.

Now, upon any occasion has the prisoner mentioned the name of any one other than those you gave as having instigated him?—No. I don't recollect any other names. He mentioned Mr. WHALLEY, Mr. ONSLOW, Mr. BAIGENT, HARDING, young BOGLE, JANES, and Captain BROWN.

Those are the only names in your written report to the Treasury?

Sir T. HENRY: You can't make that evidence.

Mr. LEWIS: Those are the only names you recollect?—Yes.

Have you stated to any one whatever that the prisoner had said Lord RIVERS was one of the persons who had coached him?—Never.

Have you made an imputation to any person against Lord RIVERS? Never.

Mr. LEWIS: I propose to call for that written report.

Mr. POLAND: I don't produce it.

Sir T. HENRY: It is not evidence.

Mr. Lewis (to witness): You had a conversation with the prisoner as to New York, among other things?—Yes.

Have you been in New York?—Yes.

Do you know the city?—Yes.

Did you tell the prisoner so?—Yes.

Did he ask you where you had been staying?—No.

Did he not mention Astor House to you?—I cannot say. I do not recollect.

Did you say, "No; I was stopping in the Broadway?"—I did not. I was not stopping in the Broadway.

Did he not say something to you about BARNUM's Museum?—No.

In conversation with the prisoner in reference to New York, did he not show a familiarity with the city?—No; he mentioned one or two places which would have induced me to believe he had been there.

Did you put test questions to him about Australia?—No, I am not acquainted with Australia.

Did the prisoner, in reply to some questions about Australia, say, "How could I know a place if I have not been there?"—No.

Sir THOMAS HENRY (to Mr. LEWIS): Do you suggest that the prisoner used that expression to Mr. CLARKE

Mr. LEWIS: I do, sir.

Mr. LEWIS (to witness): Did the prisoner say, in reply to further questions, "Well then, I have not been there"?—No.

Did he say that when he first met Mr. WHALLEY that hon. gentleman said to him, "It seems a providence that you should turn up, because none of the crew of either vessel have ever been heard of"?—No.

You adhere to that?—I do. He never told me that on any occasion.

Did the prisoner say, "Some of your fellows have been down to JANES, and offered him a purse of money to say he had never seen me in Australia; but JANES refused to do so"?—He did not.

Did he at all refer to an attempt to bribe JANES?—No.

And did you say, "Mr. JANES came to me, and said so himself"?—No.

Did you ask the prisoner whether he had been to Rio?—He told me he had been there. I did not ask him.

Did not the prisoner say, "If I had never been at Rio, how could I know people there, and know Rio? I knew Rio before Captain OATES went to sea"?—No; he only said he had been to Rio.

Did he say "JANES, of Holloway, has gone away now. I think he has taken a public-house"?—No; he said he was to have a public-house.

Now, upon the occasion that you went with Mr. POLLARD to see the prisoner, did you see him alone?—No.

Did you take him to a corner of the room?—No; he beckoned me.

Did you not converse in tones that could not be overheard by Mr. POLLARD?—I am not sure; it was not a loud tone, but it was not a whisper.

Is it not a fact that upon that occasion you urged him to make a statement to Mr. POLLARD?—I did not.

In the various conversations with the prisoner had he not conveyed the impression that, whatever was said about his late history, the whole of the evidence as to the "Osprey" was true?—No; quite the contrary.

On any occasion did the prisoner ever say to you, "I dare say you are cunning enough to have heard the tales made up by your side, that I and WHALLEY had made the tale up in Brussels in the spring"?—No; never.

Before he was in custody, did you ever have conversation with him?—Yes; he came to my office. His tone then seemed to ridicule the idea of his story being believed. He threw out the idea that nobody could be fool enough to believe in him.

Sir THOMAS HENRY: Am I to understand from you that he came to Scotland-yard?—Yes, sir.

Sir THOMAS HENRY: When was that?—After he had given his evidence; before the rebutting evidence was called.

Sir THOMAS HENRY: That ought to be taken down.

Mr. POLAND: What did he come to Scotland-yard about?—I cannot say. I found him in the passage. I do not know the date. He had been drinking freely, and he invited me to drink.

Mr. LEWIS: At what time in the day was that? What date?—About six o'clock in the evening. I do not remember the date. I have the entry in my diary.

Mr. POLAND: Some money was promised him if he stayed in this country, I believe?—Yes.

Sir THOMAS HENRY: But he would not go to Scotland-yard for that.

Mr. LEWIS: These are all the questions I have to put to Inspector CLARKE.

EMMA BLEACH, examined by Mr. Poland: I am the wife of WILLIAM BLEACH, a clerk in the Pension Department, Woolwich Dockyard. In April, 1855, I was living at Melksham, in the county of Wilts. I was living there with my father, WM. COLNORNE. He was a plasterer by trade. SARAH COLNORNE is my sister. I knew the prisoner, and he married my sister on the 2nd April, 1855, in the parish-church of Melksham. I was present at the marriage, and signed the register. I knew him by the name of CARL PETER LUNDGREN. He came from Cardiff to be married. My sister had been staying at Cardiff for a short time at the Scandinavian Hotel, kept by my brother WILLIAM. She came home about a month previously to her marriage. The prisoner came to the house to see my sister, and my father wished the marriage postponed for six months. Prisoner would not agree to that, and was afterwards married. He said he was a native of Gothenburg, in Sweden; that his mother, sister, and brother were living at Gothenburg; that his mother kept a small baker's shop, and that his sister was living at a minister's house at Gothenburg. I never heard of any ships the prisoner had been in. He said he had once been captain of a ship, but he did not mention its name. The second day after the marriage they came to London, and lived at No. 1, Tichborne-street. (Laughter.) They went back to Cardiff to see my father, and prisoner was afterward clerk to a firm of ship-brokers in Cardiff. I remember his living at Bristol, and his being arrested and tried. I was living at Bristol at that time with my brother, who kept a public-house there. It was, I believe, in 1862 when prisoner was convicted. He asked me to take care of some money for him, but my brother would not let me. The prisoner did not say what money it was. It was soon after that he was arrested and sentenced to three years' penal servitude. I never saw him afterwards. My sister is still alive, at Bristol.

Cross-examined by Mr. LEWIS: The first time I ever saw the prisoner was when he came to Melksham some time before his marriage. I am pretty certain it was about a month, but I may make a mistake in regard to the exact time.

Mr. POLAND: You have not the remotest doubt that he is the same man?

Witness (looking at the prisoner): Oh, sir, I am certain he is the same person.

HARRIETT ARHEND, examined by Mr. POLAND: I was a widow—(laughter)—but I suppose I am now—(Loud laughter, which drowned the remainder of the sentence). In 1867 I kept the Star Coffee-house, in Edgware-road. I knew the prisoner in that year as Captain JOHN SMITH. He stayed at my house.

Mr. POLAND: What did he say about himself?—He came in and asked for a bed. My servant answered him, and said we hadn't a very good one, only one at the bottom of the house. He said it didn't matter much, as he was going to Bristol the next day, and wanted to catch the six o'clock train. The next morning I came down at eight o'clock, and found he was not up. I sent the servant again to call him, but he didn't get up. He was not called any more, and he got up about eleven o'clock.

Did he go to Bristol?—I suppose not, for he came back the same night and slept in my house. He said he was Captain JOHN SMITH, one of the partners of GREEN and SMITH, shipowners, of East India-road. He stayed in the house. He courted me, and I was married to him on the 11th April, 1867. I was married at Pimlico, and the prisoner was described as "JOHN SMITH, bachelor, master mariner." I think it was in February that he first came to the coffee-house. I had some money, and had a marriage settlement from that man (looking towards LUIE) before the marriage. We had linen, and he marked it all "H. SMITH." He said that he had made it all over to me, and that I should have everything. It was not all my own. He paid for some, but when we went out shopping what he didn't pay for I did. He talked about opening a public-house, and said he had taken a house in the East India-road. We lived together as man and wife for seven or eight weeks. He talked continually about the marriage settlement.

I had taken it to Somerset House when he executed it, and I paid 36s. for a stamp. He often asked me if he should fetch it. I said, "No; I will fetch it myself." He told me it was not worth a farthing, because the names were wrong. I said I should keep it, and he said, "If there is anything wrong with it I can see and alter it." I would not give it up. He said, "I see you are an artful woman." "Artful or not," I said, "I don't mean to give you it up. If you are sorry for the property you have made over to me, you can have it back, but you don't have mine." I threw the lease of the house in East India-road to him, and told him I thought he was a blackleg, and wished him to walk off. He asked what I meant, and tore up the lease of the place he said he had taken for a public-house. After some more words he went out. I told my servant to pick up the pieces of the lease and bring them to me. The next day he asked me what I was afraid of, and said he would take me to a solicitor's to ask his opinion respecting the genuineness of the lease. We went to Mr. LEWIS's, in Ely-place, Holborn. Some statement was made there, and the solicitor tried to reconcile us. He said, "She won't even show it," and I refused, because I was afraid he would give it up to him. The next day he began again, and followed me about the streets for two hours, and struck me. I said I would go into the Marlborough-street Police-station, which was close by, and I did so. The next day I went to a solicitor, Mr. DOLMAN, of Jewin-street, and when I came back he said, "You fool; where have you been? I might have saved you all this expense." Then he threatened to go upstairs and break all the furniture, and a new piano I had had in. I dared him to do it, and we had words. I went to St. Mary's Hospital, to see my little boy, who had met with an accident. On the 5th of June my little boy died, and the prisoner entered with a black band reaching up to the top of his hat. He said he was going to have a Freemason's funeral for my child. I said, "What do you mean, you villain? I dare you to have a funeral, or to put a hatband on your hat." He replied, "I shall; so don't put yourself out for an infant." He then asked, "Will you give me that marriage settlement?" I said, "No; I never will." He swore, and said, "If you do not give it to me, I'll murder you." He pitched me through a glass door. My hand was cut, and I had to have my wrist dressed. He took up a poker to me, and when people came he took up a knife to me. I charged him at the John-street Police-station. He was afterwards charged before the magistrate at the Marylebone Police-court, and ordered to find sureties in £50 each, and was sent to prison, as he was unable to find them. He was bailed out on the 15th June, 1867. He paid somebody £5 to bail him out. He came back again then to the Star Coffee-house. By this time I had applied for a judicial separation, and had left the Coffee-house with my family. The lease had just been renewed, and he sold it. I had had it renewed for seven years three months before my marriage with this man. I also insured my life for my children. He sold the furniture and fixtures as well, and I never saw him until I identified him at Millbank. He spent about £70 or £80 of my money. I went on one occasion with the prisoner to the East India-road, and he showed me a house which he said was to be granted to him. He afterwards tore up the lease, which he said referred to that house. I did not know what had become of him after he sold the things, and did not care. I got my judicial separation in April of the following year. I knew a Mr. GEORGE MILLER and his wife. They were living in Praed-street, Paddington, in 1867. I have been there with the prisoner, and they have been to our house.

ALEXANDER GOSS, examined by Mr. POLAND: I am a licensed victualler. I am not now in business. My present address is 102, Bingfield-street, Caledonian-road. In 1867 I was manager of the Carlton Tavern, Kilburn. I knew Mrs. ARREND, who kept the Star Coffee-house. I know the prisoner as JOHN SMITH. I was present at the parish-church of the district of St. Peter, Paddington, on April 14th, 1867, and saw the prisoner married to Mrs. ARREND. I was one of the witnesses to the marriage, and signed the register. I knew him first in the early part of the previous March. He was staying at Mrs. ARREND's coffee-house. He told me he was a captain. I first saw him at the Carlton Tavern. He came there with Mrs. ARREND respecting a public-house in the East India-road, which he said he was going to open. Soon after the marriage I lost sight of him. I believe he was given into custody. I had a letter from him last June. He signed the letter JOHN SMITH. He wrote a good hand. It was addressed to me, at the "Crown," York-road, King's-cross, and was dated from the Carlton Tavern. He wished me to forward a letter which he had inclosed to his wife. His letter stated that he had been at sea for several years, and had saved some money, which he wished to invest for his children. He said nothing further. I wrote to Mrs. SMITH, but I did not give the letter up to her, and she never called for it. The prisoner called at the "Crown" on June 2nd last year, and I returned the inclosure to him. He said he did not care, and that he could soon find her. He read the letter to me. It was to the same effect as the one he sent me.

Mr. POLAND: Is that the man (pointing to LUIE) you know as JOHN SMITH?—That is the man, sir.

ELIZABETH MILLER, examined by Mr. POLAND: I live at No. 2, Cardigan-road, Cambridge-road, Kilburn. My husband is an invalid, and cannot attend the court. In 1867 my husband kept a public-house in Praed-street, Paddington. I knew the prisoner then as JOHN SMITH. I used to see him daily at my husband's beer-shop. I saw him after the assault case in July or August, 1867. I do not know what became of him after that. I knew he had married Mrs ARREND, and I heard of the assault case. Mrs. ARREND is a friend of mine, and he was living with her. I saw the prisoner again May, 1873, at 2, Cardigan-road. He was then dressed as a sailor. He said he had been cruising about the seas for the last six years, chiefly on the lakes of America. He was then going by the name of JOHN SMITH.

Mr. POLAND: Your old friend?

Witness: Yes; he said he hadn't been near London for five years, so that he could not come and see anybody. He asked where his wife was. He said he should like to see her. I told him I did not know where she was. He stayed with me about seven weeks. On the night of the 4th of July he was out till morning. I let him in about six o'clock in the morning of the 5th July, and he went to bed. He got up about ten o'clock. He had been robbed of his purse. I remarked, "I suppose you have no money, then, SMITH?" and he said, No, but he would have some later in the day. My husband told me to put 10s. on the mantel-shelf, which I did. He went out, and took the 10s. with him. He said he was going to the bank to draw money, but he never came back. I never saw him till the end of December, when I found him at Millbank. I lent him a shirt of my husband's, and a shirt has been shown me by Inspector CLARKE (found at the lodging in Churchyard-row, Newington Butts), and I identify it as the one I lent him.

WILLIAM SMALL, examined by Mr. POLAND: I am the manager of the Carlton Tavern, Carlton-road, Kilburn. I knew the prisoner as JOHN SMITH. Last year he came to the Carlton Tavern on the 27th of May, and asked for Mr. and Mrs. MILLER's address. I gave it to him. He used to come there as a customer. I knew him as Captain JOHN SMITH. He used to come there day after day up to the 26th June, and was not away more than two days at a time. He used to read the newspaper at the bar, and speak about the Claimant there to the customers as they became acquainted. I used to hear him say occasionally to customers, "What do you think of the Claimant now? How is he getting on?" At the time when Captain OATES's evidence was being given, he used to get very excited, and he said he was telling falsehoods. He said to me one day, "SMALL, I'll go and see KENEALY myself. I believe I can do the Claimant some good yet." On one occasion he drew a map of the port of Rio, and showed it to me. I tore it up and threw it over the bar. He said Captain OATES was out several miles in his reckoning, and explained where they used to camp. He used to write, and I gave him notepaper. I lost sight of him for a long time, and did not see him till I was taken to Millbank Prison.

WILLIAM GEORGE WOOD, examined by Mr. POLAND: I am one of the warders of the Chatham Convict Prison. I knew the prisoner by the name of JOHN LUNDGREN.

Mr. POLAND: Was he received into the prison on the 7th December, 1868?—On the 7th of August, I think, sir.

And was he discharged on 25th March, 1873, on a license?—Yes. I saw him frequently in the prison, sometimes 200 or 300 times during the day. He told me he was a Belgian. He worked part of the time in the tailors' shop, and afterwards with the drivers. He said he had been mate of a vessel several years.

GEORGE BONTNGE, examined by Mr. POLAND: I am a tailor warder of the Chatham Convict Prison. I joined there on the 26th February, 1870. I know the prisoner. He was under my superintendence from that time till April, 1872. Then he was transferred to the drivers. On the 24th March, 1873, I provided him with "liberty clothes" before he was discharged. He was discharged on the 25th. He said he wanted a sailor's suit, and I provided it for him. The clothes shown to me by Inspector CLARKE I find are the pattern clothes supplied to the prisoner, shirt, drawers, and jacket.

Mr. POLAND: I now, Sir THOMAS, call upon Mr. RIMELL to produce any letters he has received from the prisoner. He attends here upon subpœna.

Mr. RIMELL having stepped into the witness-box,

Mr. POLAND said: I call upon you, Mr. RIMELL, to produce all letters received from the prisoner—the one received on the 22nd, and the one from the House of Detention. I call upon you to produce also one received on the 13th of December.

Mr. RIMELL: I have only two, the one written on the 22nd December, and the previous letter written from the House of Detention. I now produce them and their envelopes. I have not got the other letter.

Mr. POLAND: Then I must call upon you to produce it on the next occasion, Mr. RIMELL.

The two letters were then handed to Mr. POLAND.

JOHN M'MANUS, examined by Mr. POLAND: I am one of the warders at Millbank Prison. On Monday, December 22, I was in charge of the ward where JOHN LUNDGREN was confined. I gave to the prisoner paper, pen, and ink on that day. It was the ordinary prison paper. He wrote a letter, and gave it to me. I read it. That (looking carefully at a letter handed to him) is the letter. It is dated December 22, and addressed to Mr. RIMELL, 29, Golden-square, Regent-street.

Mr. POLAND then read the two letters. They were both addressed to Mr. J. RIMELL, 29, Golden-square. The one dated December 22, 1873, was as follows:—

"Dear Sir,—By this I beg to acquaint you all that I am here retained, and have heard nothing. This is a miserable life, and to suffer such all for not being allowed to have my own way. But what is done can't be altered. I refer you to my last from the House of Detention. I had a letter from Plas Madoc, wherein was stated that £5 had been sent to HARDING."

The letter concluded by wishing "Merry Christmas to W., at Plas Madoc, and all friends."

Mr. POLAND: In that letter he refers to "my last." That letter is now produced by Mr. RIMELL, and I propose to read it. Mr. POLAND then read:—

"House of Detention, Clerkenwell, Saturday, Dec. 13, 1873.

"Dear Mr. RIMELL,—I have now been sent to this place until next Thursday, and as I heard yesterday that you was ill, I could not expect to see you. Mr. CLARK brought me down here, and will himself bring me back to Bow-street. I should like to see Mr. HARDING, as he would be able to let me know about the American and the other witnesses. I saw in the morning paper that M'MAHON and WILD had left KENEALY alone yesterday to do the work, and that they were not in court. I hope Mrs. RIMELL and Miss FANNY are well, and that they be pleased to accept my compliment. HARDING told me that you had seen the man who is so like me, and who has caused me all this trouble. The only thing would be to get his brothers over here, so that this affair may be settled. I hope Sir ROGER TICHBORNE keeps up his spirit, although the amount of adversaries are numerous. Just think what amount of persecutors I have. My dear RIMELL, I should like to see you on Monday, as I have something important to ask you.—Yours respectfully, JEAN LUIE.

Mr. POLAND: That is as far as I propose to go to-day, Sir. I hope to be able to finish the case at the next hearing. I have, however, to ask for another remand. There is some other evidence to be produced. After what has occurred I do not, however, propose to bring any more witnesses up from the country.

Sir THOMAS HENRY: You know that remands are very inconvenient to us here. I am quite ready to go on and complete the case to-day.

Mr. POLAND: I cannot go further to-day, sir.

Sir THOMAS HENRY: Why not? You have already produced ample evidence for a committal.

Mr. POLAND: I am not prepared to complete the case to-day. I think it desirable that there should be another remand. I do not know that there will be any additional evidence of importance, but there is a certain matter which it may be necessary to bring before you.

Sir THOMAS HENRY: Oh! well, if you think so, it is better there should be another remand.

Mr. LEWIS: I have one question to ask the last witness.

Sir THOMAS HENRY: Certainly.

Mr. LEWIS: Did you keep copies of those letters?

Witness: No, sir.

Did you see anybody make a copy of them?—No.

The further hearing of the case was then adjourned till Thursday next, at eleven o'clock.

MR. WHALLEY, M.P., AND THE CONVICT LUIE.

JEAN LUIE was brought up yesterday morning at Bow-street, and remanded formally by Sir THOMAS HENRY, as previously arranged, until to-morrow. Shortly afterwards Mr. WHALLEY entered the Court, and occupying the place allotted to persons summoned to the Court, addressed Sir THOMAS HENRY, saying—May I address the Court, sir?

Sir THOMAS HENRY: What do you wish to say?

Mr. WHALLEY: I am Mr. WHALLEY, the Member of Parliament, whose name has—

Sir THOMAS HENRY: If it has anything to do with the LUIE case I really cannot enter into that now.

Mr. WHALLEY: No, Sir THOMAS. I wish to pass through the hands of the Court these papers to the prisoner LUIE. I find the prisoner has already been brought up. If I had arrived in time I would have handed them over to him here.

Sir THOMAS HENRY: I could not have allowed that. He has Mr. EDWARD LEWIS for his solicitor, and all papers and evidence must be given to him.

Mr. WHALLEY: I wish to have no communication with either LUIE, his friends, or solicitors, but I wish to offer myself as a witness on his behalf. These papers are the results of my inquiries in America and elsewhere.

Sir THOMAS HENRY: You must see Mr. LEWIS, and give them to him. He will know what to do with them. Everything must be done through him.

Mr. WHALLEY then referred to a correspondence that had taken place between him and Mr. GRAY, Q.C., the Solicitor to the Treasury.

Sir THOMAS HENRY: I would rather not go into any matter connected with the case in the absence of the parties. You can see Mr. LEWIS and tell him anything you may have to say.

Mr. WHALLEY: Thank you, Sir THOMAS.

Mr. WHALLEY handed to the reporters' desk the following copies of the correspondence with Mr. GRAY, the Treasury Solicitor:

Plas Madoc, Ruabon, 13th January, 1874.

To JOHN GRAY, Esq.

Sir,—It is my intention to be present at Bow-street on Thursday, when, as I am informed, LUIE will again be on trial; and I have to suggest to you the propriety of informing me what further imputations, if any, are then to be made against me by your witnesses, and also that you should afford all practical support for immediate reply and refutation in open court. In one of your letters to me, published by order of the House of Commons, you put a series of questions tending to the conclusion that the defendant in the TICHBORNE prosecution is ARTHUR ORTON; and it occurs to me that you may be glad of the opportunity to answer two or three questions as to LUIE. 1st. How does it happen, if LUIE has been for above twenty years under the eye or in the custody of the police—mainly Metropolitan—that he was allowed to carry on this alleged imposture from July to December—attending public meetings, and in frequent communication with Scotland-yard and the Home Office, to complain of being watched and beset by police and detectives? 2ndly. Have you any evidence beyond that of LUIE's statement to Detective CLARKE, of my having tampered with witnesses contrary to my positive statement in the witness-box; and, if so, why was I not examined thereon; and will you now concur in my being again examined as a witness?—I am, sir, your obedient servant, G. H. WHALLEY.

Treasury, 14th January, 1874.

Sir,—As you are not the attorney of the man LUIE, I think it proper to decline any correspondence with you on the case, or on anything relating to it. You will please not to infer from this that I have no other reasons for my determination.—Your obedient servant, JOHN GRAY.

G. H. WHALLEY, Esq., M.P., Reform Club.

JEAN LUIE AT BOW STREET.

On Saturday, shortly after half-past eleven, JEAN LUIE, the notorious witness in the TICHBORNE Case, was brought up for the fourth time at the Bow-street Police-court, before Sir THOMAS HENRY, to answer the charge of perjury.

Mr. POLLARD and Mr. POLAND prosecuted on behalf of the Crown, and the prisoner was defended by Mr. LEWIS, of Marlborough-street. The court was again crowded.

Mr. LEWIS: I feel bound, sir, in justice to my client, to make some observations in introducing the evidence which I intend submitting to you in defence of the charge which has been preferred against him. I cannot help feeling that the accused has been called upon to undergo a preliminary examination under very great disadvantages. Indeed, I do not know of any case in which a prisoner has been placed under so many disadvantages as the person now before you. He has not only to contend against disadvantages in connection with a celebrated Trial still pending, but he has also to contend against much public prejudice resulting from certain statements which have been made in connection with that Trial. The evidence given by the prisoner in connection with the Trial to which I refer has called forth comments from the public press and from other quarters, which materially affect the position of the prisoner——

Sir THOMAS HENRY: I have nothing to do with that. I have merely to consider if there is sufficient evidence for trial. The comments of the public press have nothing to do with me.

Mr. LEWIS: I want to clear away some of the prejudice.

Sir THOMAS HENRY: I have no prejudice.

Mr. LEWIS: Of course not. I do not mean to say so.

Sir THOMAS HENRY: Well, then, you need not address me upon the matter of the prejudice of other people.

Mr. LEWIS: The prisoner has not been actually committed by the Judges, to do which they had power. They have only directed that the prosecution should be made. If they had tried him the prejudice would not have been so great.

Sir THOMAS HENRY: On the contrary.

Mr. LEWIS: I will give my reason for that statement. If the Judges had tried him, the prisoner would have been admitted to bail, and would have had every opportunity of getting up evidence and of preparing his case, which cannot be done whilst he is in prison.

Sir THOMAS HENRY: You find fault, then, with what the Court of Queen's Bench has done?

Mr. LEWIS: Yes.

Sir THOMAS HENRY: Do you think it right to find fault with that Court here?

Mr. LEWIS: I am about to show you that there are three distinct courses taken against this man. He is first charged with contempt of Court.

Sir THOMAS HENRY: That has not been proved before me. What have I to do with this?

Mr. LEWIS: Well, the prisoner is charged with perjury in connection with a Trial still pending, which, in itself, is a great hardship. If that Trial were concluded—and it may be in a few weeks—and if the verdict were given in favour of the Claimant, he could then be called to give evidence in favour of the prisoner.

Sir THOMAS HENRY: There is nothing to prevent that being done now.

Mr. LEWIS: It would be a disadvantage; for he would have to admit that he himself was being charged with perjury. There were other witnesses who, in the great Trial, had corroborated the prisoner's evidence in many points, and upon whom, including LUIE, the jury had expressed an opinion. There was no reason why this investigation should not have been postponed until the end of the Trial of the Claimant. There were but two reasons why this should not be done. Firstly, because the prisoner might escape. He could not do that, however; for he was sent to prison to undergo the remainder of his sentence. The other reason was that something might happen to the witnesses.

Sir THOMAS HENRY: That is the only reason that I know of.

Mr. LEWIS: The evidence required against the prisoner is that of the prison warders, and there are plenty of those who could be called. There is no reason, therefore, why this investigation should have been forced on. The matter does not rest here. A charge of bigamy has been preferred by the Crown, a charge which should have been left to the aggrieved wives themselves, and with regard to which, as well as the charge of perjury, the accused, according to English law, is considered innocent as long as he is not proved guilty. It is, in my opinion, unfair, under these circumstances, to enter into the whole life of Mrs. ARREND.

Mr. POLAND: It was necessary, both as to the evidence and identification, and in support of the charge of perjury.

Mr. LEWIS: Perhaps the most important feature of the case before you, sir, is the evidence which has been given by Inspector CLARKE. It was, I think, a great wrong that an officer so interested in the Trial of the Claimant should have been selected to take charge of the present case.

Sir THOMAS HENRY: What do you say to the prisoner's own confession at this Court on his first examination? What CLARKE has said seems to me to be only a confirmation of that.

Mr. LEWIS: As he had no one else to consult, he asked CLARKE what he should do. Even in his letter to Mr. RIMELL he denies that he had ever been tampered with, and he adheres to the facts connected with the "Osprey" and the "Bella."

Sir THOMAS HENRY: What is the date of that letter?

Mr. LEWIS: The letter is dated, "City Prison, Holloway, Dec. 12, 1873," and the postscript is, "If I am rendered assistance, Sir ROGER and all will be saved." As regards his evidence respecting the "Osprey" and the "Bella," I am instructed to maintain that he has told the perfect and the accurate truth. I do not think there has been any evidence of value to prove that this man was in England in 1852 and 1853. Inasmuch as it has not been proved, I take it for granted it cannot be proved. He arrived in Melbourne with the men who had been wrecked, and had been picked up. After that he went to Ballarat, and was there ten months. I admit that his statements about being so long at Ballarat cannot be maintained. I contend that he may have been at Ballarat some considerable time, and yet have been back and married at Cardiff in 1855. Besides, Mrs. GOLLEDGE may have been mistaken in her date. She said that the father of SARAH COLBORNE disapproved of the match, and wished them to wait six months, and that strongly bears out my presumption that the marriage did not take place so soon as is here represented. I cannot ask you to acquit this man, but the question whether he gave evidence wilfully or only to conceal his other crime (if he had committed bigamy), all the rest of the evidence as to the main facts being substantially correct, or whether he wilfully concocted the whole story to support the case of the Claimant, are two very different questions. I refer to the evidence of a witness as to the prisoner being at a public-house at Paddington, where he is described as reading in a newspaper the account given by Captain OATES, and throwing down the paper in indignation, declaring the statement to be untrue, and showing great excitement. This is the conduct of a man desiring to speak the truth about a certain matter of which he had some personal knowledge, and goes far to support his subsequent statements. But if the graver aspect of the matter is assumed, and the prisoner is supposed to have wilfully related the story prepared for the purpose (and I can hardly believe that such depravity could exist), why was not Mr. O'BRIEN, who took down his statement, subpœnaed instead of Mr. HENDRIKS, who could only speak to the facts at second-hand, and had produced a document said to have been sent from FUNCKE, EDYE, and Co., without there being any evidence of this being a *bona-fide* letter, or as to whether such a firm ever existed.

Mr. POLAND: The prisoner himself has admitted that the whole of the Australian story was a sham.

Sir THOMAS HENRY: I am quite aware of that, but it is obvious that Mr. LEWIS is not addressing these observations to me.

Mr. LEWIS: I do not withdraw anything I have said about this illegal document being produced to destroy the assertion of the prisoner as to his connection with the Osprey, but I maintain that there has been no legal evidence given to rebut his account of this transaction. I am quite aware of his having made other misstatements, and that he denied his having ever been convicted, and it is most unfortunate that the proved misstatements on these points have prejudiced the man's integrity with regard to other portions of his story. I hope to call evidence to prove that that story was true. Before I conclude I desire to say a few word in justification of this man (pointing to the prisoner). It may be said that the "Osprey" evidence is extraordinary. It is not more extraordinary than that which I intend to bring forward in support of the observations I have made with regard to the prisoner. That man is the son of a wealthy ship-owner, now dead. That man once occupied the position of a gentleman. He has instructed me to say that he adheres to perfect truth in all he has said about the "Osprey" and the "Bella," which I myself have no reason to doubt. I hope that when the case passes away from this court the class of persons from whom jurors are drawn——

Sir THOMAS HENRY: They are not here.

Mr. LEWIS: I know that. They may hear what I say, however. I hope that those persons will suspend their judgment respecting the prisoner until they hear what remains to be said in favour of the unhappy LUIE. I now proceed to call my witnesses.

Sir THOMAS HENRY: Whom do you call first?

Mr. LEWIS: Captain BROWN. (Laughter, and some commotion).

Captain BROWN was several times called for in vain.

Mr. LEWIS: Then I call Mr. JANES.

CHARLES JANES, examined by Mr. LEWIS: I am a fruiterer and greengrocer; I live at 16, Cornwall-road, Upper Holloway. I went to Australia in 1851. I have been to Melbourne and Ballarat. I was in Ballarat in 1853 and 1854. I know the prisoner. I first met him at Ballarat. I have no doubt he is the same man. As near as I can guess I met him in winter time—in June or July, 1854. I met him first at Golden point, Ballarat. He came there with two or three others. I was keeping a butcher's shop and was grog-selling. One day in the middle of July, as well as I can recollect, the prisoner came into my shop. He said he had just come from Melbourne. We wanted a cook at the time. There were five of us engaged in digging; I butchered, and they dug for gold. We engaged him as a cook. I believe he remained with us several weeks. During my absence for some days I found he had left. We used to call him "Doctor," on account of his being our cook; but he was known by the name of LUIE. In July or August of last year I saw him in Westminster for the first time since I saw him in Australia. I went to a public-house opposite Westminster Abbey, and I saw the prisoner at the public bar. Some other man was with him. I met the prisoner afterwards several times. We walked from one end of the Park to the other (St. James's, it was understood). I said "Your face is familiar to me. You are a seafaring man, are you not? I think you have been to Victoria, haven't you?" He said "Yes, I have." I said "Yes, and Ballarat." He said "Yes," and I said "Do you know Butcher CHARLIE?" He said "Yes; and I believe you are the same man." I said, "Well, I am. Do you know anything about the fat in the damper?" He said "Yes, I do; and that was on my birthday." I asked, "Why did you leave before I came back?" He said it was a fit of his, and that something prevented him. I said, "Are you just home, then?" He said, "Yes; I have been some little time here now." I said, "What is your business here?" He said, "I am on the TICHBORNE Trial." I said, "Well, then, so am I. It is curious that we should meet like this." We had two glasses of drink, and went to Poets-corner. I never saw him from the time I saw him at Ballarat till I saw him at Westminster. He told me something about some men who had been wrecked; but sailors' "yarns" used to run about the diggings so much that we used not to take much notice of him.

Cross-examined by Mr. POLAND: He says in his evidence, "JANES was living in my tent at Ballarat." Is that true?—It is not. He had a tent next mine, but I did not live in it with him.

Mr. POLAND: Perhaps we shall have more cases of perjury. Did he tell you at Ballarat that he was steward of the "Osprey?"—I do not remember. He said that he was steward of some vessel. I could not swear that he did.

Mr. POLAND continued to read from LUIE's evidence in the Court of Queen's Bench: "I dare say you told JANES that you were steward of the 'Osprey.'—I did; and he must have known it." Is that true?

Sir THOMAS HENRY: Did you hear of the "Osprey" at that time?—I did hear of the "Osprey."

Mr. POLAND: What did you hear of the "Osprey?"—I heard nothing about it but what was mentioned by my mates.

Did you understand that this man was steward of the "Osprey?"—I did.

Speaking of you, LUIE says: "I was a month with JANES when I went away, and then came back again." Is that true?—I went backwards and forwards three times during that time. I was in Ballarat in April, 1855. I did not see him then.

He says, further, that you came back one time in April, 1855, and that he left in May, 1855?—I never saw him then.

Is it true?—It is not true.

Did you say one word about this man from the beginning to the end of your examination in Court?—No, sir.

Or the "Osprey?" Did you mention the "Osprey" from the beginning to the end of your evidence?—No, sir.

Were you asked one word about the "Osprey" or LUIE?—I do not know that I was.

Are you positive?—I am not positive.

This is rather remarkable. I suppose you used to see the prisoner daily?—I saw him altogether about six times—once at the public-house, once at Holloway, and four times at Poets-corner. I went to Australia in 1851, and I remained there till 1861. Before I went to Australia I was engaged at farming at Lewisham, Kent. I left England with the intention of improving my position. I was then going by the name of JANES, and I went to Australia in that name with my family.

Who told you to come here to give evidence?—Mr. RIMELL.

Mr. RIMELL, of Golden-square and of Finchley?—Yes I do not know him very well. I never visited him but once; that was about three weeks ago.

Captain BROWN was here again called to give evidence, but he did not answer to his name.

Mr. LEWIS: I have eleven other witnesses to call, and they live in different parts of the country. I must, therefore, ask for a further remand.

Sir THOMAS HENRY: What I should like to know is, whether

these witnesses are really to be produced. I hope you will supply us with a list of the names and addresses of the witnesses you intend to call.

Mr. LEWIS: That I certainly shall do. One of those witnesses will be the Claimant who, as you know, I cannot bring before you except on a habeas corpus. I submit that the peculiar circumstances of his position are in themselves sufficient to require a remand, as I am instructed to state that Mr. WHALLEY is prepared to give some very material evidence having a bearing upon the case, and I intend to examine him at some length.

Sir THOMAS HENRY: If you state as a professional man that you intend to call Mr. WHALLEY, and that he has evidence to give material to the case, I am bound to grant a further remand.

Mr. LEWIS: I shall pledge myself to call Mr. WHALLEY and to examine him, and eleven witnesses besides.

Sir THOMAS HENRY: Well, then, you will give us their names and addresses.

Mr. LEWIS: I will hand in their names and addresses to the Treasurer before the day is out.

Sir THOMAS HENRY: Then under all the circumstances, I will agree to a further remand till next Thursday, at eleven o'clock.

JEAN LUIE AT BOW STREET.

The further investigation of the charges of perjury and bigamy against JEAN LUIE was resumed before Sir THOMAS HENRY.

Mr. POLAND prosecuted, and Mr. EDWARD LEWIS, of Great Marlborough-street, defended.

Mr. LEWIS called and examined the following witnesses:

Mr. GEORGE HAMMOND WHALLEY: I reside at 10, Suffolk-street, Pall-mall. My country seat is at Plas Madoc, Wales. I have represented Peterborough in the House of Commons for twenty-two years. I am a magistrate of three counties. I am also High Sheriff of Carnarvonshire. I first became acquainted with LUIE on the 7th July last year, at the office of the Claimant's solicitor, 2, Poets-corner. I think it was between ten and eleven in the morning. The prisoner arrived first. When I arrived, Mr. O'BRIEN, the law student, was also present. There were others in the room—two or three clerks. I observed Mr. O'BRIEN was taking down the statement made by the prisoner when I arrived. Up to that moment I had never seen the prisoner. It is not true that I met him at Brussels, in the spring of that year. Until that morning when I went to Poets-corner I was unaware of the existence of such a man as JEAN LUIE. I did not take any part in the taking down of that statement beyond listening. I had no knowledge whatever that such a statement was going to be made. I had been in the habit of going occasionally to Poets-corner. When I went to Westminster on account of the Trial, I always visited Poets-corner. After the statement was taken I think the prisoner said he should like to see the Claimant. While arrangements were being made for that purpose, such as getting a cab and packing up the papers, I asked the prisoner whether he thought the Claimant would recognize him. He replied, "I should think he ought to do, considering that I nursed him for three months." After a pause, he broke out, "Yes, I'll tell you how he'll recognize me—by my crooked finger." He held out his hand. In reply to my question, "Why?" he said, "That crooked finger used to drive him nearly mad, as I used to rub the back of his neck for sunstroke." He explained that the finger scratched him. The cab arrived, and Mr. O'BRIEN, the prisoner, and I got into the cab. We then proceeded to Bessborough-street, to the house of the Claimant. I did not hear LUIE say he had been there before. When we arrived I went into the Claimant's house first. I found the Claimant very unwell. He was suffering from erysipelas, and was reclining. I having told him we had brought an important witness to identify him, the Claimant expressed reluctance to see any one on account of his severe indisposition, but, on my urging the importance of it, he consented, and Mr. O'BRIEN and the prisoner came in. On the prisoner's entering the room he walked up to within about three or four yards where the Claimant was reclining, and looked very steadily at him for some time. The first words I remember the prisoner to have said were "Yes; that is the man," or words to that effect. Upon that some exchange of conversation, which I cannot call to mind, took place between the prisoner and the Claimant, and the former went over to the other direct, and with great show of feeling—tears coming into his eyes, in fact—shook hands with him, asserting that he was as certain as of his life that he was the man, and he would stand by him and do all he could on his behalf.

Mr. LEWIS: Was the recognition mutual?

Witness: I could not possibly say if the Claimant recognized him then. He recognized him as he had other witnesses—with caution and reticence, with no warmth of feeling. LUIE then resumed his seat, and he and the Claimant began to converse with perfect freedom and familiarity about the Claimant's illness and eccentricities, and about the incidents of the voyage. The prisoner mentioned various names which appeared to be familiar to both.

Mr. LEWIS: Names of whom?

Witness: Sailors on board the "Osprey." Especially I remember the Claimant asking if the prisoner recollected driving him back into his berth when he had come out in a state of nakedness. The prisoner not remembering, I put the question to him myself. The prisoner replied, "Oh, yes, that is nothing; that happened often enough, and he knows well enough the trouble I had with him." The Claimant smiled, and assented to that as a sufficient answer. Mr. O'BRIEN took notes, and so did I, of what struck us at the interview. That interview lasted from half-an-hour to three-quarters. In speaking of some of the companions of the wreck, who were Spaniards, there was some reference made to language; and, to the best of my recollection, it was in respect to that part of the conversation that the Claimant said, "Como esta, LUIE?" I know the Claimant did address to him these words, but I won't swear it was under those circumstances. I was present at only one interview. I cannot say how it was that the Claimant remembered his name, but most likely it was because I told him. I have no doubt that the statement taken by Mr. O'BRIEN was taken to the house, and read on that occasion. Subsequently, on the evening of that day, I called on the Claimant and asked him if he was certain that the prisoner was whom he described himself to be, and he said that he had no doubt whatever.

Sir THOMAS HENRY: I don't think we can have all the conversation.

Mr. LEWIS: With respect to the charge of conspiracy——

Sir THOMAS HENRY: There is no charge of conspiracy.

Mr. LEWIS: But I apprehend if there is a charge of perjury the Claimant must have been concerned in it.

Sir THOMAS HENRY: But we cannot have evidence of a conversation which took place when the prisoner was not present.

Examination continued: The effect of the conversation was that the Claimant recognized the prisoner, partly by his looks and partly by his crooked finger.

Sir THOMAS HENRY: That is not strictly evidence.

Mr. LEWIS: I am asking his impression of the Claimant at the interview.

Sir THOMAS HENRY: You did not put it in that way.

Examination continued: The Claimant did not recognize the prisoner thoroughly until the last part of the interview, when the conversation that took place left in my mind no possibility of a doubt that they had met. Subsequently I went to America on this matter, at the request of the Claimant's Counsel, Lord RIVERS, and other friends. I left London about the 26th or 27th of July. It was on a Saturday. I returned after about five weeks. I prosecuted inquiries in America and Canada with a view to getting confirmatory evidence with regard to the prisoner's statement. I made a report to the Claimant's solicitor as to the result of my inquiries. I first went to New York. I put myself into communication with the British Consul there, and was introduced to Mr. WING by the agent of LLOYD's at New York. Mr. WING is counsel and attorney in New York. Before leaving I received certain names from the prisoner—the names of VOLCKERT DALSTROM, to whom letters were addressed by the prisoner, and about seven or eight other names, who, as well as VOLCKERT and DALSTROM, were in some way or another connected with FUNCKE and MEINKE, ship brokers, of New York, and with the ship "Osprey" in the year 1854. I gave Mr. WING certain instructions, and took his advice from time to time. I was in New York about a week, from Wednesday till the following Tuesday. I prosecuted inquiries all the time. I took the instructions furnished by Mr. M'MAHON, one of the Claimant's Counsel. I pursued inquiries in reference to the whole of the matters in connection with the statement. I communicated with the chief collector of Customs. I also inquired at Perth Amboy, a port independent of New York. This is a port at which vessels from Sandy Hook call. The prisoner referred me to an agent at LLOYD's. I communicated with him also, and afterwards proceeded to New Bedford and then to Quebec. I communicated with FUNCKE and MEINKE, now FUNCKE and EDYE. I saw Mr. FUNCKE, and showed him the prisoner's letters to VOLCKERT and DALSTROM, and also his statement. I ascertained as a fact that the prisoner had given an exact account of the persons and positions of which he had spoken. I also discovered that VOLCKERT was dead. Mr. FUNCKE made a statement to me. He sent for a person named GOLDECKER, and I had an interview with him in FUNCKE's presence, and took down his deposition in writing. That statement I can produce if the Counsel for the Prosecution wishes it. I searched for Baron FALKENBERG. In consequence of the inquiries I made at Quebec and New York, I addressed a letter to the solicitor for the Claimant. That letter has appeared in the newspapers, and for it I have had to suffer some inconvenience.

Sir THOMAS HENRY: Be good enough, Mr. WHALLEY, not to make any observations in the witness-box.

Witness continued: I obtained information as to the clearance of vessels, and communicated that also to the Claimant's solicitor. I corresponded with other persons, and can state what it was if I am asked.

Mr. POLAND objected to all this as not being evidence.

Sir THOMAS HENRY: It is not evidence; it is only waste of time. You keep repeating, Mr. LEWIS, what you are not allowed to do, and keep asking the same questions over and over again.

Cross-examined by Mr. POLAND: Before I went to America I was not in the constant habit of visiting LUIE. I only had two interviews with him to the best of my recollection. I attested the first statement taken by Mr. O'BRIEN. I think the name at the beginning is "JOHN LEWIS," but it is illegible. The prisoner said that he was called "JOHN LEWIS," but that his name was "JEAN LUIE." I never attested statements taken down before at Poets-corner. I attested this one because it seemed so important, and I was impressed with its clearness and truth. I never took that statement to America, nor copies or notes of it. I swear, to the best of my recollection, that I was not furnished with a copy of that statement. The only statement I had was the one I took myself. The second statement is signed "JOHN LEWIS." I went to America to satisfy the Counsel that LUIE was an honest witness, for they refused to put him into the box until some inquiries were made about him. I was at the Court of Queen's Bench only a short time while the prisoner was being examined. I read his evidence. I am not aware that any arrangement was made before he gave his evidence that he should return to New York. It was my advice that he should do so without delay. The testimonial is in my handwriting, and signed by Mr. ONSLOW. I don't know when I wrote it. I wrote out the certificate of character, and Mr. ONSLOW wrote the introduction to Mr. GREY, the dockmaster at Southampton. I think I saw him write it. No one had greater grounds for writing that testimonial at the time than I had. I put "M.P." after my name. My reason for writing it was this: In every instance, to the best of my belief, of a witness examined on the part of the Claimant, the antecedents had become completely known to the Prosecution. I said to Mr. ONSLOW, "I think we may now certify to his whole career, seeing that his evidence has not been shaken." This man has been followed and watched, to our knowledge, from the 7th July up to the time he was examined. He complained to the Home Office——

Sir THOMAS HENRY: You do not know that.

Witness: He was cross-examined as to his character by the Crown, and, with all the efforts of the Prosecution, nothing was found out against him.

By Mr. POLAND: I do not know if notice of his being called was given to the Crown Counsel. I considered it a perfect certifi-

MR. JUSTICE BRETT.

cate of character, his leaving the box as he did. I did not know how he was being supported. I knew he was living with Mr. PULLEYN, and being taken by him to the meetings. I did not see him at the meetings. I was told he had money about him. I was not aware that the Claimant was supporting him. I was not in Court when the prisoner said he supported himself entirely. I do not know he swore he was never called LEWIS.

Mr. POLAND read the portion of the prisoner's evidence when he swore he was never called LEWIS.

Witness: I give him £5 once, and so did Mr. ONSLOW. That was after he was examined, and that was the time when I wrote out his certificate with the intention of his leaving for America.

Mr. POLAND: Look at that plan of Melbourne, Sandridge Town, &c.?

Witness: I have no recollection of this. I observe the names and writing on the plain at Williamstown, but I am unable to say that it is in the writing of Mr. ONSLOW. I have no opinion about it. I should rather say it is not. I was in Brussels in the spring of last year with my daughter. I think I saw LUIE only once after my return from America. He came to me at the Reform Club once only. I was in court when the rebutting evidence was called. After he was in custody I sent my nephew, Mr. NICHOLSON, to him with a private note. The note was returned to me. I sent £5 to be given to LUIE. It was to enable him to get evidence. I am not paying the expenses of the prisoner's defence, and I have not had any communication with him or his solicitor on the subject.

Re-examined: Did you say it was your desire that LUIE should return to New York as soon as he had given his evidence?—Yes.

For what reason?—So that he might continue the inquiries I had made as to HARRY, the sail-maker, and others. I had found out certain things——

Was that the sole reason?—It was.

And was it with that view that the letter of Mr. ONSLOW and yourself was given?—It was to expedite his journey.

Was there any concealment about it?—No.

Do you remember the statement made by Dr. KENEALY to the Court?—No.

Well, with regard to the certificate of character you gave LUIE—were you influenced by the inquiries you had made?—Yes.

Had he given you certain references?—Yes.

And you found them correct?—Yes. It was not however the references so much as the inquiries I made. Mr. FUNCKE stated to me——

Mr. POLAND: That is not evidence.

Mr. LEWIS: Well, you felt yourself justified in giving him the certificate?—Yes: I did not make any inquiries as to his personal character, only to confirm his story.

Can you explain his not being called before the 16th of August?—Yes: he gave me certain statements which I inquired into, and was satisfied. I was in New York, and telegraphed over to SIR——

Mr. POLAND: If you produce the telegram it can be admitted. If not, can you give us the words?—I don't know. I think, "The story of the 'Osprey' is true: let the man be examined."

Mr. POLAND: And was it added, "and then send him over to me"?—No, it was not. Mr. FUNCKE told me certain things which satisfied me.

By Mr. LEWIS: I cannot say if it was a well-known fact that I was in Brussels in the spring of the year. I was only there about twelve hours, and went to take my daughter to school. I went on Saturday night and came back on the Monday. I never saw LUIE in Brussels. I said nothing to the Claimant, when I saw him, about the crooked finger. When I returned from America I asked the prisoner what he meant by sending me on this mission to New Bedford. He said the captain used to say, that the ship sailed from New Bedford and he knew that FALKENBERG had ships there. I saw Mr. FUNCKE, and he referred me to the oldest person who had been in his office. I was able from him to trace the "Osprey," but not the "Osprey" of New Bedford, from New York.

Sir THOMAS HENRY: That cannot be evidence. You must prove how you traced it.—By the memory of the oldest survivor in his office, who had seen the ship's manifest in the writing of FALKENBERG. It was the prisoner's wish on all occasions that I should go to FUNCKE, MEINKE, and Co. I went there through LLOYD's agent.

By Mr. POLAND: I telegraphed to Mr. ONSLOW. I think to the Reform Club. I think soon after my arrival—about 48 hours after.

Mr. LEWIS: I have now to apply, Sir THOMAS HENRY, that this case may now be adjourned till after the jury have given their verdict in the Trial in the Court of Queen's Bench, and for this reason I have applied to the Judges on that Trial to grant a writ of Habeas, so that I may have the defendant in that case here, or to excuse his attendance on some day from the Court at Westminster. The learned Judge, however, thought that he should not be examined here until after that Trial had concluded.

Sir THOMAS HENRY: When was that application made?

Mr. LEWIS: It should have been made yesterday afternoon, but, owing to an accident, was not made till this morning.

Mr. POLAND: I did not know of this application, Sir THOMAS; but as Mr. LEWIS states that it is his intention to call the Claimant, I feel some difficulty in opposing his application. But Mr. LEWIS has given us a list of ten or twelve witnesses.

Mr. LEWIS: Which will be further supplemented.

Mr. POLAND: I think we might go on with the evidence, so that it will not go over another session of the Central Criminal Court. I may say that the prisoner was committed by the judges, and ordered to be brought before you, Sir THOMAS, in order that a *prima facie* case should be made out, and some of the witnesses be allowed their expenses.

Mr. LEWIS: One reason why I desire to have it adjourned at this stage is that I may have an opportunity of speaking to him, which I have not had yet.

Sir T. HENRY: You might have had; he has been at large.

Mr. LEWIS: When I have examined the Claimant, I may have to put questions to other witnesses to corroborate his story, and, with the small amount of money at my disposal for the defence of this man, I do not desire to rush into expense by bringing witnesses here over and over again.

Sir T. HENRY: Then, in fact, you desire to make the Claimant your principal witness. Under the Recorder's Act, you, of course, have a right to do that.

It was then decided that the prisoner should be formally remanded for a week, and so on from time to time until the Claimant was present, Mr. LEWIS pledging himself to call him.

THE TRIAL OF JEAN LUIE.

The Claimant not having been called, LUIE was finally committed for trial at the Old Bailey. We give the newspaper report of his trial.

The trial of JEAN LUIE for wilful and corrupt perjury in the evidence given by him in the TICHBORNE Case was commenced at the Central Criminal Court, Old Bailey, yesterday, there being also a second indictment against him for bigamy. The trial excited more than ordinary interest. The gallery and the other portions of the court to which the public had free access were filled at the commencement of the proceedings, and the body of the court was soon afterwards densely crowded, and continued so during the whole day. Precisely at ten o'clock Mr. Justice BRETT, who was to try the case, came into court, accompanied by Alderman Sir T. DAKIN and Mr. Sheriff WHETHAM. The prisoner was then placed at the bar. He had lost the flowing beard which he had so complacently and so assiduously stroked during the many days he was present at the trial of the Claimant, and when, sitting by his side, he ostentatiously extended to him his support, and took so warm an interest in the proceedings. Moreover, his hair had been closely cropped, and he wore the grey dress in which convicts are ordinarily clad, so that altogether he had a very different appearance indeed from the JEAN LUIE in the Tyrolese hat, as represented in the published photographs with the extract printed underneath from his evidence, "Before mein GOTT I declare that what I state is the truth." Shortly after the commencement of the proceedings Mr. WHALLEY, M.P., came into court and conversed for some time with the prisoner's attorney. He then seated himself for a short time amongst the counsel, and afterwards sat at the attorneys' table, where he continued the remainder of the day. During a portion of the day, Sir C. REED, M.P., and Mr. GURNEY, M.P., the Recorder, occupied seats on the bench. As will be seen from the detailed report which follows, the Court refused an application to postpone the trial, and thereupon Mr. WARNER SLEIGH, who made the application for postponement, withdrew from the case and the prisoner was not defended by counsel. Left thus as he was to his own resources, he evinced considerable shrewdness in watching the evidence, in detecting what he conceived to be a weak point, and in cross-examining the witnesses.

Immediately on the Judge taking his seat,

Mr. WARNER SLEIGH rose and said he had to renew the application which he made yesterday on the part of the prisoner for a postponement of this trial. There appeared to be a misapprehension, not of what he said yesterday, but of what he intended to convey. What he intended to convey was that there should be a postponement at least until Friday, in order that Mr. LEWIS might have an opportunity of consulting with his client, and that then an application might be made for a postponement until the next session. The solicitor for the defence had instructed him to say that it was absolutely necessary he should have instructions from the prisoner, and that without them he was utterly unable to instruct Counsel. An affidavit had been filed, in which it was stated that there were a number of witnesses, of whom notice had been given by Mr. LEWIS to the Treasury, and that he had not had an adequate opportunity up to the present time of ascertaining the evidence which they would be able to give, that he believed it would be necessary to subpœna various witnesses, amounting to nearly twenty in number, and that as to several of these he had given notice to the Solicitor to the Treasury. The fifth paragraph of the affidavit stated that several of the assignments of perjury were of a complex character, extending over a period of twenty years, and that it was impossible to do justice to the prisoner's defence without having an adequate opportunity of carefully considering the whole case, and that it was impossible for the prisoner to have a fair trial if he were tried at the present sessions. The observations, said the learned counsel, which he had to make on this affidavit were, that the prisoner was a foreigner, and he ought to have as fair a trial and as much indulgence as if he were an Englishman, and he submitted that the prisoner ought not to be deprived of the opportunity of having a fair trial and of being defended by Counsel, and that he would not have the opportunity unless Counsel was furnished with the requisite instructions. The facts of the case were very voluminous and complex, while the issues were of the gravest importance. With regard to himself, he knew nothing of the case beyond what he had derived from a very cursory glance at the papers which he was enabled to take on the previous day, when he was instructed, and he could not possibly, in justice to his client and himself, undertake to defend him if he were tried that day. No harm could be done by postponing the trial to next session; the indictment was not preferred till the previous day, and the solicitor for the defence had not been able to obtain a copy of it till the afternoon, and therefore he asked, even now, at the eleventh hour, for that indulgence which he was sure the Court would grant if it possibly could, by postponing the case until the next sessions.

Mr. POLAND was about to rise in reply, when

The Judge said—You need not trouble yourself, Mr. POLAND. According to the ordinary law of this country, and the ordinary course of procedure, this trial ought to take place to-day, and the question is whether sufficient ground has been shown to me for postponing it. Now a request was made yesterday that an attorney should speak to the prisoner before he pleaded. This, which was an unusual request, was granted, and in the sight of everybody in the court, we saw what the result was—that a boy of eighteen or some such age, spoke two or three words to the prisoner, probably three were sufficient for the purpose, and that was all that he required to say to him. I asked at the time whether the attorney who was alleged to have been instructed for the defence was instructed, and I was told that the attorney had been instructed by the prisoner, not for his defence, but to appear for him at the police-court. On looking at this affidavit, there is no allegation that he was instructed before yesterday to defend him on the present indictment. Either, therefore, he was not so instructed by those who are represented to be the prisoner's friends, or he was. If he were, what he says is this—

Since that date I have received no instructions as to any defence but as to employing Counsel on his behalf or otherwise in relation to his defence, until the morning of Wednesday, the 8th inst. If, therefore, he was retained, there is no allegation that any further step was taken until yesterday morning, although they must have known that the trial would come on at these sittings. They therefore left the prisoner practically undefended, and it seems to me that that is of itself a manifest demonstration that this application is not bonâ fide, and that those who call themselves his friends are no real protectors of this unhappy man. As I said yesterday, it is an attempt to mislead one from one's duty made by those who pretend to be the friends and protectors of this man. If there have been no instructions given to Counsel, it is entirely the fault of those who come here pretending to be the prisoner's friends. There is no fact in the case which is not known to those who assume the duty of defending the prisoner, and which might not be brought forward just as well now as it would be at the next sessions. I shall not interfere on any such grounds as those stated in this affidavit. The same affidavit might be used at the next sessions, and the one after that, and so on, so that the man would never be tried at all. If he is innocent, let him be cleared—if he is guilty, let the law take its course.

Mr. POLAND appeared, with Mr. BEASLEY, for the prosecution, and stated the case on the part of the Crown. He said they had heard from the officer of the Court that the prisoner was arraigned on the serious charge of wilful and corrupt perjury at the Court of Queen's Bench, when he was examined as a witness on the 14th and 15th October, and in December last. He would state the facts connected with the case as briefly as he could. A person of the name of ARTHUR ORTON appeared to have claimed to be Sir ROGER CHARLES DOUGHTY TICHBORNE, Bart., and to have claimed the Tichborne estates. In May, 1871, an action brought by him was tried in the Court of Common Pleas at Westminster, when ORTON was examined as a witness at great length, and among other things it was proved beyond all question that ROGER TICHBORNE was at Rio in April, 1854; that on the 21st of that month he sailed in a vessel called the "Bella" for New York; that that vessel was wrecked, and no human being on board of her was ever seen alive afterwards. This person, ARTHUR ORTON, stated that after the wreck he was picked up by a vessel called the "Osprey." Now there was no doubt whatever that, according to the evidence of Captain OATES, who was at Rio at the time the "Bella" sailed, that ROGER TICHBORNE was on board the "Bella." The Trial in the Court of Common Pleas came to an end by the Plaintiff being nonsuited, and ARTHUR ORTON was directed by the judge to be prosecuted for perjury, and his Trial for perjury was commenced in the Court of Queen's Bench on the 23rd of April last. After the case for the prosecution had been closed the prisoner was called as a witness on the 14th of October, on the part of the Defendant, and he then stated that he was steward of a vessel called the "Osprey," which he had joined in 1852; that he was at Rio in 1853, and that he there saw a Captain BROWN; that after sailing about in the "Osprey," he in February, 1854, sailed in her from Staten Island, New York, on a voyage to Melbourne, and that while on that voyage he saw a boat in which there were six men, four of whom were delirious, that two of them, of the name of JERVIS and LEWIS, were plying the oars, and that on a red shirt being hoisted as a signal the boat was picked up, and the persons on board of her were taken on board the "Osprey." He also stated that among the four persons who were delirious was a person who was not a sailor at all, but a nobleman, whom he took into his own cabin and attended to during the voyage. This person he described as Mr. ROGERS. The "Osprey," he stated, arrived at Melbourne in July, 1854, and then he lost sight of Mr. ROGERS, and he and JERVIS and LEWIS, and two of the crew of the "Osprey," went to the diggings; and he remained there about ten months. He further stated that he left Australia in 1855, and that, being in New York in 1864, he saw Captain BANNATY, the captain of the "Osprey." He also said that in 1863 he returned to Australia; and at Williamstown, which was part of the port of Melbourne, he saw the "Osprey" dismantled. He further stated that he was afterwards in America and various places; and that he did not return to this country until June, 1873; that he came over in a ship called the "Circassia," arriving at Liverpool in June; that he then went to Belgium to look after his wife, who had run away from him; and that on the 5th of July he came to London, and that on that day he was at the bar of a public-house in the east of London when he heard that an impostor was claiming some estates, and he also heard the name of the "Bella" mentioned; and it occurred to him that the person he had picked up in the "Osprey" and had been wrecked in the "Bella" in 1854 was the person who was claiming the estates, and that he would try and find him; and he stated that he went to Paddington, and walked about all night, and found the next morning that the Claimant was living at Bessborough-gardens; that he was not allowed to see him, but the servant directed him to go to 2, Poets-corner, where the attorney's office was; and that on the 7th July he went there and his statement was taken down by a Mr. O'BRIEN, who took him to the Claimant, who at once recognized him and said "Como esta LUIE—How do you do, LUIE?" This was in July, but the prisoner was not called into the witness-box till the 14th of October. He was then asked some questions about himself and he said JEAN LUIE was the only name he had ever gone by, and that he had never been in trouble all his life. At that time nothing was known of this man, and his cross-examination was put off till inquiries could be made about him. On the 1st of December he was called into the witness-box again, and he was cross-examined with a view to test the credibility of his story. It had been ascertained that instead of being JEAN LUIE, his name was CARL LUNDGREN, or CARL PETER LUNDGREN. He had stated that he was a native of Denmark, but the fact was that he was a native of Gothenburg, in Sweden. In 1852 or 1853 he was master of a vessel called the "Isabella," and in 1853 he went to Hull and became water-clerk to a person of the name of JOHN LUNDGREN, who was no relation whatever to the prisoner. He should call Mr. JOHN LUNDGREN himself, his partner, and other witnesses, who would show beyond all question that in the greater part of the year 1853, and down to so late as October, 1854, the whole time that this man had represented himself as being the steward of the "Osprey," he was at Hull. He then appeared to have gone to Cardiff, where he entered the service of Messrs. CORBY, and while in their service he made the acquaintance of a young woman of the name of SARAH COLBORNE. Her father lived at Melksham, in Wiltshire, and it was arranged that they should be married there, and they were married in the parish-church there on the 2nd April, 1855, at the very time he had stated he was in Australia. He should call two witnesses who were present at the marriage. The prisoner lived with his wife five or six years, and in October, 1862, he was taken into custody at Bristol, and charged with a criminal offence. He was convicted, and he remained in prison undergoing his sentence until April, 1863. Those were important dates, as he had sworn to have seen the captain of the "Osprey" in New York in 1865; and he had also stated that he went to Australia again in 1865. The next date was also important. In October, 1865, he was taken into custody at Newcastle, and was sentenced to six months' imprisonment. In March, 1867, they found him in London. He presented himself, under the name of JOHN SMITH, at 2, Star-street, Edgware-road, at a coffee-house kept by a Mrs. ARREND. He represented himself as a partner in a shipping firm, and said he was about to start a public-house. He married Mrs. ARREND on the 14th April, 1867, and lived with her till about the following June, when he assaulted her and was taken to a police-court. He sold off her property, and disappeared from Paddington in June or July, 1867. After that he appeared to have gone back to Cardiff. On the 16th September he was taken into custody again for some criminal offence, and was sentenced to seven years' penal servitude, and he remained in prison undergoing that sentence until the 25th of March, 1873, when he was discharged on ticket-of-leave. He then appeared to have come to London, and to have repaired to his old quarters at Paddington. Mrs. ARREND had gone away, but he stayed at a coffee-house kept by a Mrs. MILLER till the morning of the 7th of July, when he said he had got no money, and he borrowed 10s. and disappeared from Paddington. On the same morning he presented himself at the office of the Claimant's solicitor, at 2, Poets-corner, and stated that his name was JEAN LUIE, and that he was steward of the "Osprey," and that he could give important information with regard to the Claimant, which he afterwards swore to in Court, and for which he was now indicted. The Court of Queen's Bench, on the 11th of December, directed that the prisoner should be tried for perjury, but instead of committing him for trial at once, as in the case of ARTHUR ORTON, they directed that he should be examined at Bow-street, in order that any witnesses he might call should be bound over to appear at the trial. Inquiries were made, and Inspector CLARKE went to his lodgings and found that he had been living with a Mr. PULLEYN, somewhere in Newington. The prisoner stated in his evidence that he maintained himself, in the interests of truth and justice, while waiting to be examined. So far from this being true, it would be shown that ARTHUR ORTON paid for his keep, supplied him with clothes, gave him pocket-money, and, in fact, entirely maintained him from the 7th of July till he was called at the trial. His lodgings at PULLEYN's were searched after his arrest, and there were found the clothes given him when he was discharged at Chatham, in 1873—it being the custom at that prison to give discharged convicts "liberty clothes"—and also a shirt lent to him by Mrs. MILLER during his visit to Paddington some few months before. Of course, when all this evidence was brought against the prisoner, his testimony before the Court of Queen's Bench was robbed of all value, and there was an end of it, for no one could doubt that his story was a tissue of lies from beginning to end. When before Sir THOMAS HENRY he said, "All I have to say is that I am very sorry for what has happened; it would not have happened if I had not been encouraged and made up to do it." At Millbank also, where he was taken to see if the officers could recognize him, and where he was at once known, POWER, a warder, said to him, "Well LUNDGREN, you have come back," and in reply, the prisoner said, "I would not have gone into the witness-box, only Mr. ONSLOW and the rest persuaded me to do it." The prisoner afterwards made a similar statement to the same effect, viz., that "BAIGENT and ONSLOW had urged him to do it." He told Inspector CLARKE that he would like to make a statement, and if he thought they would not prosecute him he would tell all about it. The inspector said that the statement had better be taken down by a solicitor, if he wished of his own accord to make one, and it was arranged that a solicitor's clerk should see him in prison for the purpose. Before the time came, however, the prisoner was advised not to make a statement, but he said to the inspector, "I did not want to go into the witness-box, but I was urged to do it." He further told the officer that he never was in America or Australia in his life, and he (Mr. POLAND) should prove that he never was there, or at any rate certainly not at the material dates to which reference had been made in his evidence. CLARKE said to the prisoner that he was surprised at this, for among other things which he found when searching his lodgings was a plan of the port of Melbourne, and he replied that he did not make it, and the names of the places would show that it was in the handwriting of some other person. While in custody the prisoner wrote certain letters to a friend of his, Mr. RIMELL, who was very active indeed in defending ARTHUR ORTON. In one, written on December 12, he said that he should declare in open court that nobody had anything to do with the false evidence—that he alone was responsible, and this was followed by a most remarkable expression—"If I am rendered assistance Sir ROGER and all of you are saved." Writing again on the 22nd of December, he said, "By this I beg to acquaint all of you that I am here retained and have heard nothing. This is a miserable life to suffer such, all for not being allowed to have my own way." The meaning of that expression was explained by something the prisoner told Inspector CLARKE. He said he originally intended to humbug and deceive the persons conducting the Defence and to get money out of them, but not to give evidence; that he asked them scores and scores of times not to put him into the witness-box, but that Mr. ONSLOW became very violent, and forced him to come forward. He did not at first intend to do more, he said, than to defraud and cheat these persons by pretending to give material evidence. This statement to Inspector CLARKE explained the passage in the letter about his not being allowed to have his own way. When the prisoner's evidence was taken in July, 1873, by Mr. HENDRIKS, who was then the solicitor for the Defence, the prisoner, in answer to questions about the "Osprey," told him that Messrs. FUNCKE and MEINKE, of New York, were the agents for the ship. Mr. HENDRIKS at once telegraphed to America, and in addition wrote to the firm on the 10th of July, in order to get from them evidence confirmatory of the prisoner's statement. They replied in a letter, dated the 22nd of July, received in London on the 5th of August, in substance stating that they had no vessel named the "Osprey," and knew nothing about her, or about a man named LUIE. Mr. HENDRIKS read the letter to the prisoner, and he replied that it was all very well for them to say that; but the fact was, the "Osprey" was a filibuster; the firm had become possessed of her in a way very much like stealing, and therefore they would not know anything about the matter. Mr. HENDRIKS was not likely to believe a story of that kind, and it was only fair to him to state that on the 11th of August he ceased to be the attorney for the Defence. Notwithstanding that, on the 14th October the prisoner was put into the witness-box, and gave evidence. After its termination, it appeared to have been arranged that he should return to America, and he received £5 from Mr. WHALLEY, and £5 from Mr. ONSLOW, a certificate of character signed by those two gentlemen, and a letter of introduction to the dockmaster at Southampton. Dr. KENEALY having mentioned in Court that LUIE was about to return to America, steps were taken to prevent his doing so, and on the 11th December he was committed to prison, his evidence having been shown to be a tissue of falsehoods. He (Mr. POLAND) should prove conclusively that all the salient points of the prisoner's story in the Court of Queen's Bench were false, that he had told falsehoods as to his name, his country, his life, his never having been convicted, and his having been in America and Australia at certain periods. Mr. POLAND closed his speech, which had lasted more than a hour, by briefly pointing out how important it was to the administration of justice in this country, that evidence given on oath should be such as could be relied on; in this case he should be able to show conclusively that in every answer the prisoner gave, he committed wilful and corrupt perjury.

The Judge: Does any one appear for the prisoner?

No answer was given for some time to the question, and then Mr. POLAND observed, "It appears not." Mr. WARNER SLEIGH had previously left the Court.

Mr. POLAND put in the certificate of the conviction of THOMAS CASTRO in the Court of Queen's Bench, dated 2nd April, 1874, and signed by Master COCKBURN.

Mr. W. AISH DAVIS, Mr. CHARLES BENNETT, and Mr. MATTHIAS LEVY, shorthand-writers, employed in the TICHBORNE Trial, produced their notes of the evidence given by the prisoner during that Trial on the 14th, 15th, and 17th October, and the 1st December. Each had revised the printed transcript by his notes, and pronounced it correct.

His Lordship asked the prisoner whether he had any questions to put to any of the witnesses, and he replied in each case in the negative.

The evidence was then read by the Clerk of Arraigns (Mr. AVORY). A printed copy was furnished to the prisoner, and he first followed the reading very attentively, but after reading a few minutes he closed the copy, and remained with his arms resting on the front of the dock and his hands clasped, occasionally glancing round the Court.

Mr. AVORY had proceeded for a little over an hour with his reading of the evidence, up to a point in the cross-examination of LUIE by Mr. HAWKINS, respecting his meeting Mr. WHALLEY at Poets-corner, when

Mr. Justice BRETT interposed, and said he did not see what this part of the evidence had to do with what they had to try. The circumstances which the prisoner related took place on board the "Osprey," and the question they had to consider was whether he was on board the "Osprey" or not.

Mr. POLAND: It is so difficult to omit the circumstances under which the prisoner first gave information.

Mr. Justice BRETT: It is difficult to omit, no doubt; but you might just as well read this at Charing-cross for any good it can do.

Mr. POLAND: I always thought that on a charge of perjury the prisoner is entitled to have the whole of the evidence read.

Mr. Justice BRETT: The prisoner is entitled to have it all read if he so desires.

Mr. POLAND: The difficulty is to eliminate the material passages in this evidence, because such of it as relates to the circumstances of the "Osprey" and her ownership has yet to come.

Mr. Justice BRETT: Where is there any assignment about who is the owner of the "Osprey"?

Mr. POLAND: That question arises; the prisoner gave the name of the brokers as the owners.

Mr. Justice BRETT: Go on.

Mr. POLAND: I am afraid, my lord, there is no option.

Mr. Justice BRETT: I would only say that it appears to me to be utterly useless to read all this evidence; but if you think it must be read, I will not interfere to prevent it.

Mr. POLAND: The difficulty is to pick out the questions and answers which should be read.

Mr. Justice BRETT: Why not point out attention to certain things which are material? There are yet many hundred pages of this evidence which really goes for nothing so far as the issues into which we have to inquire are concerned. (To the prisoner): You do not wish every word which has been taken down here to be read?

The Prisoner: No, my lord.

Mr. Justice BRETT: I would ask you, then, Mr. POLAND, to point out the passages material upon this indictment.

Mr. POLAND: I have got the evidence indexed, and I will endeavour to do so.

Mr. AVORY then went on to read such portions of the evidence as were deemed by Mr. POLAND to be material to his case.

The learned Judge again interposed, and suggested that as Mr. POLAND had stated certain perjuries, he should call his witnesses, and point out to them those parts of the evidence upon which the Jury were asked to convict.

Mr. POLAND said that the reading of the chief points would not take up very much time.

Mr. AVORY once more resumed the reading of the evidence; and on its conclusion,

HERMON THEODORE TRANA was called up and examined by Mr. BEASLEY. He said: I am in the service of Messrs. MONTGOMERY and Co., provision merchants, of Liverpool. In the years 1850 and 1851 I was in the service of Messrs. HEALD and Co., of Newcastle. They were ship-brokers. At that time I knew a vessel called the "Isabella."

Were Messrs. HEALD the brokers of that vessel?—No.

But you knew the vessel?—Yes; I went on board of her.

Did you see any person on board whom you are able now to recognize?—I saw the prisoner there, who went by the name of CARL LUNDGREN.

Did you go on board about business?—Yes.

Mr. Justice BRETT: What business?—I was offering to become agent for the ship.

But you were not accepted?—No.

Mr. BEASLEY: How long afterwards was it that you saw him at Hull?—In 1853 or 1854.

Mr. Justice BRETT: How came you to be at Hull—had you changed your service?—Yes.

Who were you with then?—JOHN LUNDGREN and Co., ship-brokers

By Mr. BEASLEY.—I was their corresponding clerk. I first went to them in 1853 or 1854, and I suppose I remained there six or seven months. Whilst I was there I saw the prisoner almost daily. He was clerk in the same office. I do not remember whether he was there all the time I was there.

Mr. Justice BRETT—How long was he there?—That I can't tell.

Was he there for a month or two months?—Yes. After that I went to Liverpool. I next saw the prisoner at Bristol in 1862 or 1863, when I was trying to charter a Russian vessel. I saw him on board a Russian vessel, the "Arcoot." He was going backwards and forwards, and seemed to belong to the ship. I spoke to him in Swedish. He is a Swede, and I am also one. I think he belonged to Gothenburg, but he did not tell me so. I saw him at the Queen's Bench.

The Judge: Now, prisoner, do you wish to ask him anything?

Prisoner: No, my lord; I don't know the man; I don't want to ask him anything.

The Judge (to the witness): You say you were corresponding clerk to LUNDGREN and Co., at Hull, for six or seven months?—Yes.

Was the prisoner a water-clerk when you went there?—Yes.

How long was he in the office with you?—Six or seven months.

Nearly all the time you were there?—Yes.

Do you know where he went when he left?—No.

Where did you go to from Hull?—To Liverpool.

Have you ever been at Liverpool with Messrs. MONTGOMERY and Co., ever since?—I commenced as corresponding clerk in a French house. I was then with Messrs. PILKINGTON Brothers, and I am now with Messrs. MONTGOMERY.

You have been a corresponding clerk, I suppose, because of your knowledge of languages?—Yes.

You say that you found this man at Bristol. You don't know in whose employ he was, but he was going backwards and forwards to the ship?—Yes.

At Hull, you say you saw him every day for six or seven months?

A Juryman: When you saw him at Bristol, which of you knew the other first?

Witness: I recognized him at once.

The Judge: And did he recognize you?—We spoke together.

Did you talk together about Hull?—We talked together in Swedish.

Had you been accustomed to talk together before in Swedish?—Oh, Yes.

JAMES COOPER, examined by Mr. POLAND: I am clerk to a firm of ship-brokers at Hull, named HUMPHREY and Son. I commenced with them in 1856. I first went to Hull in 1849.

The Judge: Have you been there ever since?—No, I left in 1852, and went back in 1853.

By Mr. Poland: In 1853 I knew a firm in Hull named JOHN LUNDGREN and Co. I also knew their clerks. I knew TRANA, the last witness. I also knew the prisoner. I knew him by the name of LUNDGREN, the same name as that of his employers, JOHN LUNDGREN and Co. He was in their service when I first knew him. I knew him in Hull from the latter part of 1853 till about the middle of 1854. He was a Swede, and I often used to see him. I saw him almost every day up to the middle of 1854. I was then in the employment of a firm of carriers at Hull.

By the Judge: I was acquainted with TRANA, and it was through him I became acquainted with the prisoner LUNDGREN. We first met at an hotel, where we drank together. I went there to see TRANA, and so became acquainted with the prisoner.

Mr. POLAND: You are a Swede, I think, yourself?

Witness: Yes.

Have you any doubt whatever that the prisoner is the same man?—He is the same man.

You saw him at the Queen's Bench, I think, in December last?—Yes.

The Judge (to prisoner): Do you wish to ask him anything? You hear what he says.

Prisoner: Yes, I hear what he says, my lord. I don't know the man; I don't know what to ask him.

The Judge: Yes, I understand that is your case. You don't know him?

Prisoner: No.

FRANCIS MORRIS FOSTER, the next witness, was so deaf that the questions put to him by Mr. POLAND had to be shouted close to his ear by the usher of the Court. He said—I am a doctor of medicine and a member of the Royal College of Surgeons, and practise at Hull. I was practising there in 1854. I then knew the prisoner by the name of CARL P. LUNDGREN or CARL LUNDGREN. He was in the service of JOHN LUNDGREN and Co., ship-brokers, and I knew him for six or eight months. In October, 1854, I lent him 30s. [A small, discoloured-looking bit of paper was here handed to the witness.] This receipt was written and signed by the prisoner.

By the Judge: I saw him write it.

By Mr. POLAND: I did not see him after that time.

The Judge then read the receipt, which was as follows:—"Received from Mr. FOSTER the sum of 30s. Hull, 7th October, 1854.—CARL LUNDGREN."

The Judge (to prisoner): Do you wish to look at this?

The Prisoner: Yes, if you please, my lord.

The paper was then handed to the prisoner, and after looking at it he muttered, "That is not my writing."

By Mr. POLAND: He was in the service of JOHN LUNDGREN and Co. as water-side clerk, or clerk on board ship.

The Judge (to prisoner): He says that is your handwriting; that he saw you write it. Do you wish to ask him anything?

The prisoner: It is not my writing, my lord. I don't think the man swears anything against me wilfully; but the man is mistaken in me by another man.

The Judge: Then you don't wish to ask him anything?

The prisoner: No, my lord. I can't ask him anything; I don't know him.

After the witness had retired he was recalled, and further examined by the Judge, at the suggestion of the jury, as follows:

Why did you lend the prisoner 30s.?—I thought I was lending it to his employers. I had been accustomed to see him from time to time. On a Saturday evening, between 7 and 8 o'clock, he came to me and said that two ships had arrived that night, the offices were closed, and the captains, being foreigners, wished for some English money. He said that if I would lend him some money he would return it on Monday morning. I at once gave him 30s., and I handed him a piece of paper, and he wrote a receipt.

The Judge: Was the 30s. ever repaid?—It was never repaid.

Did you apply to his employers for it?—I asked COOPER, one of the witnesses, the following week—

You can only say "Yes" or "No." Did you apply to his employers? Say "Yes" or "No."—No, I did not; but I got information that he had left Messrs. LUNDGREN's employ, and therefore I knew I had lost my money. I thought I was lending the money to his employer. When I went to their office on Monday I found that he had left them, and then I knew that I had lost my money.

Dr. JOHN HARE GIBSON, examined by Mr. POLAND: I am a general practitioner in Hull, and was practising there in the years 1853 and 1854. I knew the firm of JOHN LUNDGREN and Co. at Hull, and I attended Mr. LUNDGREN, the head of that firm. I knew the prisoner by the name of CARL LUNDGREN, and was under the impression that he was a brother. I saw him many times. I have here my book. He consulted me, I think, at my house, from the 1st to 13th of April. I knew him as being at JOHN LUNDGREN and Co.'s. That was all I knew about him. I thought he was a brother of the head of the firm, in consequence of the name being the same. There is an entry in my ledger, "brother so called," made by a partner of mine who is dead.

By the Judge: It was entered first to JOHN LUNDGREN, and the entries continued to be made in that way till the 13th April, when we discovered that he was not actually a brother. The amount against the prisoner was £3. 15s.

Were you paid?—In 1860 I was paid by the firm.

The Judge: They paid the whole?—Yes.

Why?—I applied to Mr. JOHN LUNDGREN, and he paid it; he was then living in London.

Was that done on the ground that you attended the man as one of the firm?—I had no understanding with him at the time.

Then did you make the division when the account was made out?—I applied to my partner.

Who entered all this?—My late partner. My partner had entered the whole, and before the account went in I divided it.

Did you apply to the man for his share?—No, I lost sight of him.

Then in 1860 you applied to the firm and they paid the whole?

Mr. POLAND: Are you quite sure this (pointing to the prisoner) is the man?

Witness: I am sure of it.

[The Judge here handed the witness's ledger to the jury for examination.]

Did you attend the clerks generally?—No.

The Judge (to prisoner): Do you wish to ask him anything, prisoner?

Prisoner (to witness): What illness had that man that you attended?

Witness: I cannot tell you; my memory does not serve me. That is the ledger (alluding to the book produced). If I had had the day-book I might have formed some idea.

The Judge (to witness): Could you tell the medicine itself?—I could if I had the prescription-book, but that is destroyed.

The Judge (to prisoner): Anything else?

Prisoner—No; I don't want to ask him anything.

The Court then adjourned for a quarter of an hour. Just as Mr. Justice BRETT was leaving, the prisoner attempted to address him, but the words, "My lord" were uttered in too low a tone to reach his lordship.

When the court had reassembled, SAMUEL SHIELDS was examined by Mr. POLAND. He said: I am a ship-broker at Hull, and a member of the firm of SAMUEL SHIELDS and Co. I was in Hull in 1852. I joined the firm of JOHN LUNDGREN and Co. in that year, and remained in it till the latter part of that year. While I was a member of it I knew the prisoner by the name of CARL P. LUNDGREN. He was a water-clerk. He first entered the service in the early part of 1853, and he remained during all the time I was connected with them, and for some time afterwards, about 18 months altogether. I used to see him almost daily, and after I left the firm I still knew him as being in the service of JOHN LUNDGREN and Co. I missed him in the latter part of 1854. I don't know where he went to.

The prisoner is the man?—Yes, he is the same man.

A Swede?—A Swede.

The Judge (to prisoner): Do you wish to ask him anything.

Prisoner: How do you know that he was a Swede?

Witness: I know you perfectly well.

Prisoner: How do you know me? By what do you know me?

The Judge: How do you know he was a Swede?

Witness: He spoke Swedish with me.

The Prisoner: When did you speak to me last?—Not till I saw you in court.

The Prisoner: Do you know every person you have ever seen twenty years ago?

Witness: I know you perfectly well.

The Prisoner: Well, I don't know you.

The Judge (to witness): Answer his question—Do you know every person whom you saw twenty years ago?

The Prisoner: How do you know me?

Witness: By your general appearance and your nose.

The Prisoner: There are many persons with a nose like me.

Witness: I know you by your voice, even now. I knew you the first time I heard you speak.

The Prisoner: Had that man a beard when you saw him in 1853 and 1854, or any whiskers?

Witness: Yes; he was not so bald as you are at present; but he was slightly bald.

The Judge: You saw the prisoner at the Queen's Bench?

Witness: Yes.

And then he had a beard?—I think he had.

Did you see him write?—Yes, my lord.

Prisoner: Bear in mind that I am a marked man; that is the cause of it.

The Judge (to witness): You have not the slightest doubt about him?—None, my lord.

Did you see him write ?—Yes, my lord.

A paper was here handed to the witness, and after looking at it he said: It is some time ago since I saw him write, and I could not swear that this is his writing. I believe it to be his writing.

JOHN LUNDGREN, examined by Mr. BEASLEY: I am a native of Finland, and have been in this country since 1848. From 1851 to 1857 I was a ship-owner at Hull, and during that period I knew a Mr. CHANDLER, who was my corresponding clerk. He was a Swede. I had also a man in my service named LUNDGREN, who likewise was a Swede. I saw the same person in the Court of Queen's Bench. The prisoner is the man. At that time I had some conversation with him in English, and he remarked, "Even thou knowest me." He was first in my employment in the beginning of 1853, and remained until the end of 1854. I met him frequently. I afterwards saw him at Bristol. He left there at the time the Crimean war broke out in 1852. I have seen him in the company of some foreign captains.

The Judge: Did he dine with you ?

Witness: No, no; certainly not. (Laughter.)

Cross examined by the Prisoner: What time of the year was it when you spoke to me at Bristol ?

Witness: It might have been when the pears were getting ripe in this country. (Laughter.) It was when I was going to the Lakes of Killarney.

The Judge: That would be in August or September—just when you were going on your holidays ?

Witness: I have no holidays.

The Judge: In that respect you are not unlike the judges. (Laughter.)

Prisoner: Who were the Swedish captains at Bristol at the time you speak of ?

Witness: You have no right to ask me that question.

The Judge: Oh yes, he has.

Witness: Well, I knew Captain SNELMORE, of the ship "Sophia," and Captain DENMAN, the name of whose ship I cannot at present recollect.

Mr. BEASLEY: Do you recognize the prisoner as your former clerk ?

Witness: I do positively.

JOHANN NICHOLAS SCHERLING, examined by Mr. POLAND: I am a tailor and outfitter in Hull, and lived there in April, 1854. Two years afterwards the prisoner was a wharf-clerk to JOHN LUNDGREN and Co. I saw him almost daily at the place where we used to have luncheon, along with other Swedes. I have not the slightest doubt about the prisoner's identity.

FREDERICK GRANBERG, examined by Mr. BEASLEY: I am a native of Finland, and came over to Hull as a ship-broker in 1853. At the time I knew the firm of JOHN LUNDGREN and Co., who had a water-clerk named LUNDGREN. I believe the prisoner is the same man.

JOHANN LINSTRONN, examined by Mr. POLAND: I am a native of Gothenburg. I recollect when the prisoner was master of a ship called the "Wilhelm," and he was afterwards master of another vessel called the "Isabella." I knew him as a schoolfellow, and met him every day.

The Judge: Where did you last see him ?

Witness: In Gothenburg. I have not seen him for 22 years. His father had a share in the "Isabella."

SINGER STOKES, examined by Mr. POLAND: I am the parish-clerk of a town in the county of Wilts, and held that office in 1855. I knew SARAH COLBORNE, and I produce the original register of her marriage, in 1855, with CARL PETER LUNDGREN. He is described as a ship-broker, and his father as ELIAS LUNDGREN, deceased. I believe the prisoner is the identical man. I saw him in the Court of Queen's Bench in July last, but could not identify him in consequence of his having so much hair on his face, but seeing him now close-shaven I am able to recognize him. I saw Mrs. LUNDGREN (SARAH COLBORNE) in the Court of Queen's Bench. She is the same who was married to the prisoner.

Mr. LINSTRONN was here recalled, at the request of the judge, for the purpose of verifying a date. A young man who sat beside Mr. WHALLEY, and who was understood to be Mr. EDWARD LEWIS's clerk, wished to put a question to the witness, but his lordship ruled that he had no *locus standi.*)

EMMA BLEACH, examined by Mr. BEASLEY: I am the wife of WILLIAM BLEACH, who is a clerk in the pension department of the Woolwich Dockyard. I am sister to SARAH COLBORNE. I knew the prisoner, who was married to my sister. After the wedding they came to London and lived at No. 1, Tichborne-street. (Laughter.) They lived together in London as man and wife for nearly six months. They afterwards went to Cardiff and Bristol, at which latter place I often visted them. My sister is still alive, and resides at Bristol.

Cross-examined by Prisoner: Are you married ?

Witness: I am. I was married in London.

Prisoner: Where is your sister now living ?

Witness: I am not supposed to know her address at present.

Prisoner: What name does she now go under ?

Witness: She goes under the name of HAWKINS. (Laughter.)

The Judge: Has your sister married again ?

Witness: No.

ELIZA GOLLEDGE, examined by Mr. POLAND: I live at Cardiff, and know the prisoner and SARAH COLBORNE. After his marriage with that woman I saw him daily in Cardiff.

Cross-examined by Prisoner: At what time did you see me last ?

Witness: The latter part of April, 1854.

Prisoner: I know you very well; but you are wrong as to the year.

Witness: No, sir, I am not.

JOHN NICHOLLS, police-constable at Bristol, proved that the prisoner had been convicted at the Quarter Sessions there for felony in October, 1862, and sentenced to three years' penal servitude, and that he was afterwards convicted for felony at Cardiff in October, 1867, and sentenced to seven years' penal servitude. He has no doubt as to the prisoner's identity.

Prisoner: It is quite correct that I was sentenced to three years' penal servitude at Bristol, but I was convicted on the oath of a single person of having stolen a bill of exchange for £200 which was entrusted to me by my master. A lady was mixed up in the affair.

WILLIAM MATHWIN was examined by Mr. POLAND. He said—I am a member of the firm of S. HEAL and Co., Newcastle. In 1867 I was living there. I knew the prisoner. I was present at the Quarter Sessions at Newcastle in January, 1866. I gave evidence against the prisoner, who was on his trial.

[The certificate was produced. It was dated the 3rd of January, 1866, and stated that the prisoner had, by falsely representing himself to be PETER PETERSON, captain of a certain ship lying at Lowestoft, wrongfully obtained the sum of £30, and was sentenced to six months' imprisonment.]

Mr. POLAND: Is the prisoner the person who was so convicted ? He is the same man. I saw him in the Court of Queen's Bench.

Prisoner, on being asked if he had any questions to put to this witness, said: That is all entirely wrong. As I am deprived of the means of proving it, I ask the Press to be kind enough to take notice that the evidence is entirely false and impossible, because I joined the ship the "Great St James" in June, 1866. I shipped on board of her at Deptford, and we were loaded with Government stores for Ascension. We arrived at Ascension in December, and discharged there. We then took ballast and went to Pernambuco; from thence to Demerara and Belize, and thence to St. Thomas. Last we went to Jamaica, where we loaded with pimento, logwood, and condemned Government stores. We finished completing the cargo in Black River, and arrived in London in February, 1867. The reason I ask the press to take notice of this is that the people who were connected with the ship and knew me, well know that I signed my name in the ship's books as JOHN SMIDT. Secondly, I say that I never could have been at Newcastle at the time mentioned.

Mr. Justice BRETT: If that is true then the other certificate must be incorrect of your being tried at Cardiff.

The Prisoner: This was in 1866.

The witness: I gave him into custody myself on 14th of October, 1865, and he remained in Newcastle Prison until January, 1866, when he was sentenced.

DENIS POWER, examined by Mr. Poland, said: I am chief warder at Millbank Prison. In December last the prisoner was brought there. When he came in I knew him. I said to him, "LUNDGREN, are you come back again ?" He said, "Yes, Mr. Power, I am." He said "It is not my fault. I would have not gone into the witness-box only for Mr. ONSLOW and the others at the office."

The Prisoner here ejaculated, "Good God Almighty !"

The Witness: He said, "They persuaded me to do it, Mr. ONSLOW and Mr. BAIGENT;" but he said Mr. WHALLEY knew nothing about it at all. He then asked to be allowed to see any one from the Treasury who might call, and I said, "If they do you shall see them."

Prisoner here again muttered, "GOD Almighty !" and throughout this witness's evidence laughed and made gestures of apparent amazement.

Witness: I then conducted him to his cell, and ordered him his supper.

When had you known him before ?—I knew him in 1863. I received him from Bristol. He came to me on the 28th May, 1863. He was removed to Portsmouth on the 8th of July, 1863, and came back to Millbank Prison in 1865. On the 13th of April, 1865, he was discharged on license. I have the book with his signature in.

Mr. Justice BRETT (to prisoner): Do you wish to ask this witness any questions ?

Prisoner: I do not see any use in asking him. I never said such words to him.

Mr. Justice BRETT: But he says you were in Millbank Prison under sentence.

Prisoner: Oh, I have never disputed it. (Laughter.)

WILLIAM GEORGE WOOD, examined by Mr. POLAND, said: I am one of the principal warders at Chatham Convict Prison. I know the prisoner by the name of JOHN LUNDGREN. He was received at Chatham Prison on the 7th of August, 1868, for seven years. He was discharged on the 25th of March, 1873, on a license. I knew him well, and saw him every day.

The prisoner did not cross-examine this witness.

Inspector CLARKE, examined by Mr. POLAND, said: I am inspector of the detective police force at Scotland-yard. I was present at the Court of Queen's Bench on the 11th of December, 1873, when the prisoner was ordered to be prosecuted.

Did you afterwards go to GEORGE PULLEYN's ?—Yes, at 12,

Churchyard-row, Newington Butts. PULLEYN was present in Court. I knew the prisoner lived there. I searched PULLEYN's lodging-house, and he accompanied me. I found there some clothes, which are in Court. Amongst other things there was a striped shirt, which has been shown to Mrs. MILLER. I took possession of some papers, which I produce. I saw the prisoner after this at Holloway Prison. I went there in order to bring him to the Court of Queen's Bench. I had some conversation with him going from Bow-street to the House of Detention on Saturday, the 13th of December.

What passed between you and the prisoner?—He had previously asked me to advise him, and asked me what he had better do. I said, "I cannot advise you, LUIE; you are old enough to advise yourself." He said, "I was first spoken to on this matter by Mr. WHALLEY in the spring of the year at Brussels. I was in a house of ill-fame, and I saw Mr. WHALLEY in Brussels, stopping there with his daughter. He was speaking of a case that had happened in England, that, he said, made him ashamed of his country. He said, 'The difficulty is that we cannot find any one who saved the boat of the shipwrecked crew.' I said 'That would not be very difficult. I have been a sailor myself.' But nothing was particularly arranged on that occasion, or at Brussels at all. I saw Mr. WHALLEY a time or two after that, and I had communication with him. I first saw the Claimant about the 1st of July, at Poets-corner. I went early in the morning, and saw a man standing at the door, who asked me my name. He had something the matter with one eye, and I afterwards found it was BAIGENT. I told him my name was JEAN LUIE, and he said, 'Oh! yes. I know all about it.' He said it had all been arranged. He said BOGLE, the little black fellow, was there, and I showed my fingers to him. He went into a little inner room, I believe to tell the Claimant, who came out shortly after. The Claimant said, 'If you are the man that saved me, your little fingers are crooked.'" I don't think there was any other conversation on that occasion; but I had a further conversation with the prisoner on the following Tuesday, and he said, "Since I saw you I have had a visit from Mr. WHALLEY's nephew, Captain NICHOLSON. He said he had brought a letter from Mr. WHALLEY to say that he had given £5 to Mr. HARDING for my support, and that he had got a private letter for me, but as the warders were present he could not give it to me." I told him that anything he had to tell me had better be told to the Treasury, and he said that if one of them would come with me he would do so. I said that if he wished it I would inform Mr. POLLARD, and I went to Mr. POLLARD on the following day. We went into LUIE's cell, but he said then that he had been advised to hold his tongue.

Did he make some further statements to you as to how he went into the witness-box?—He said he should never have gone into the box if it had not been for Mr. ONSLOW. He said he never intended to give evidence, but only to make money, and he should not have gone into the box had it not been for the violence of Mr. ONSLOW, who was a very violent man. He said, "I begged of him scores of times not to put me in the box. The reason I was not put in the box before was that I had not learnt my lessons sufficiently." [The prisoner here laughed incredulously.] He said, "Mr. ONSLOW gave me a book of the evidence upon the former Trial, and pointed out certain passages with reference to the shipwreck which I was to learn. I have sat up many a night studying the book. He also put his hand on his side to show me the position of the brown mark on the Claimant. He also wanted me to prove the malformation, but I refused to do that, as I was afraid of getting into a mess. I also had to see JANES, from whom I got the information about Australia, and Captain BROWN I had to see frequently to arrange about the Rio evidence." The prisoner said that Captain BROWN was to be the dock superintendent at Southampton for his trouble, Mr. ONSLOW was to have the greater share of the property, and LUIE was to be his steward. (Laughter.) The witness JANES was to be put into a public-house, and Mr. WHALLEY was to have some property. Prisoner said, "I was very reluctant to give evidence because I had never been in Australia or America in my life." I said, "You astonish me, LUIE. I should not have supposed Mr. WHALLEY would have gone to America except upon some information of yours," and he replied that it was all a "barney" and part of the piece. He said, "The thing speaks for itself; if I had not been there I could not have told him." When he said he had not been in Australia, I asked him how it was I had seen some plan of the harbour of Melbourne amongst his papers. He asked what papers I meant, and I told him the short history of his life which I had found at his lodgings. He said, "Yes, I wrote that when I had nothing to do. The drawing at the back you will see is in a different hand." He said that it was done by Mr. ONSLOW. He went on talking for hours, and said that he had been at PULLEYN's, and at RINELL's, at Finchley.

When you found that paper with the drawing at the back did you also find these letters (produced)?—I found two letters—one in an envelope addressed "Mr. JEAN LUIE, late steward of the 'Osprey,'" and signed in the corner "G. H. WHALLEY," and inside there was a paper purporting to be signed by Mr. ONSLOW and Mr. WHALLEY.

The paper, which was signed G. H. WHALLEY and G. ONSLOW, was then read by the Clerk of Arraigns. It was as follows: "This is to certify on our part, and on the part of all who know JEAN LUIE, that he is a man of thorough honesty and of great intelligence. He has borne himself throughout his life as a man entitled to confidence and respect. He has been exposed to great difficulties, harassment, and temptation, but he has remained staunch and true, and has rendered great service to Sir ROGER TICHBORNE."

The letter was addressed to Mr. E. C. GREY, Southampton, and was signed G. ONSLOW. It was produced and read upon the Trial at the Court of Queen's Bench, and was as follows:—

"DEAR SIR,—The bearer of this is JEAN LUIE. I need hardly ask you to do all you can for him, and help him on board a ship for New York. He will telegraph from New York."

The Judge (to the prisoner): You have heard this witness. Have you anything to ask him?

Prisoner (to witness): Have you got those letters with you that you took away from me?—No, I have not had them.

Oh yes, you took it. I am speaking about the letter which asks me to make a confession, and promises that I shall receive a pardon and a reward from the TICHBORNE Family, and also from the Lord Chief Justice. (Laughter.)

Witness: I have not the letter.

Prisoner: Yes, you have; the letter was given to me in the City prison, and all the warders there knew it. Where is that letter?

These are the only other writings I have in my possession [produced].

One of these proved to be the letter the prisoner was inquiring for. The writer said, "As you are now committed for perjury, I would strongly advise you to make a clean breast of the matter, and disclose all you know about the evidence, and also mention the names of the individuals at whose instance you came into Court. I may inform you that one of the Judges who tried the Case is related to the TICHBORNE Family, and is strongly biassed against the Defendant. Should you make a full disclosure, you will not only receive a free pardon, but also a large sum of money. On the part of the Treasury, and of the Judges, there is a strong feeling against the Claimant, and this will have a great effect upon your case. Write to the Solicitor of the Treasury. . . When you are at liberty you can assume another name, say WILLIAM SMITH, and with the money you will get you can easily regain your position in life by going to some distant quarter of the globe with a good sum of money which you will obtain from the Family. And in this matter the Judge, who is related to the TICHBORNE Family, will give you every assistance. Write also to Mr. HAWKINS."

This letter was signed "One who knows of the relationship alluded to and a member of the Family." It was addressed "To JEAN LUIE, now in the Prison of Holloway," and the post-mark was Charing-cross.

Witness: I had no means of making any inquiries about that letter, as it bore no address.

The second communication was written on a post-card and ran as follows:—"The kindness you have shown to those half-dozen men is recorded in Heaven. (Laughter.) Keep up your heart, notwithstanding the array of the Prosecution's witnesses. We have a strong belief in your evidence, and consider you may have been sent by Providence to aid Sir ROGER. Ps. xxxvii., verse 38."

Prisoner: There was another letter, asking me to come to the Marble Arch.

Witness: He told me he had been written to, asking him to meet a person at the Marble Arch.

Letter produced, saying, that if LUIE would be at the Marble Arch at 1 p.m. the next day, something beneficial for his future should be ——, the next word being unintelligible.

Prisoner: Well, Mr. CLARKE, you don't mean to say I told you all those things?—Yes, you told me you wished you had known me before you got into trouble.

Prisoner: Why, you said that to me.

Witness: He said to me, "Do you recollect my calling at your office in Scotland-yard on the 13th November?" He did call, and I saw him in my office. I could not tell what he wanted. I had some conversation with him. I cannot tell what he called for.

Prisoner: It was about the men who were hanging about after me.

The Judge: Was he being watched?

Witness: No, but he did complain to me that some one was watching him.

Prisoner: You say that I told you respecting Captain NICHOLSON?—Yes.

But you already knew that before I knew you was in the House of Detention. You were talking to the warders when I came down to you?—Yes; I was in the passage. I did not know that Captain NICHOLSON had been there before prisoner told me.

Now, Mr. CLARKE, do you remember what you told me in the cab respecting Dr. KENEALY?—No. You said, "I should not have been in this fix had it not been for the folly of Dr. KENEALY in forcing Mr. HAWKINS to call rebutting evidence."

But did not you allude to his turning me overboard?—No. I did show you a newspaper in the cab. It was a report of some part of the Trial.

You remember telling me that if I should make a disclosure, in your own mind you thought they would not prosecute me?—No, you asked me, and I said I could not tell you. You said, "It is no good my getting other people into trouble without my benefiting by it." You said you did not wish to get Mr. WHALLEY into trouble.

Prisoner: You told me to say: "I am sorry for what has happened, but I was made and compelled to do it."

Witness: No, I did not. He asked me, and said he did not know what to do, and I said, "You must consider what is best for yourself."

Prisoner: Respecting that observation I made, on "being made and compelled to do it," was nothing else than I was made to tell my life by the order of the Lord Chief Justice. That was all.

Mr. JOHN GRANVILLE LAYARD, Assistant Clerk at the Bow-street Police-court, stated that when prisoner was brought up at Bow-street on the 16th December, he was asked what he had to say in reply to the charge, and he said, "I am very sorry for what has happened. It would not have occurred if I had not been encouraged and made up to do it. That is all I wish to say at present."

Prisoner: That must be a mistake, because I said compelled, made and compelled.

GEORGE PULLEYN deposed: I live at 12, Churchyard-row, Newington Butts. I was business manager for ARTHUR ORTON before and during his Trial, and I attended meetings. The first time I ever saw the prisoner was on the 7th of July. I was at Poets-corner one morning, and I saw this man standing there. It was afterwards arranged by the lawyer, Mr. HENDRIKS, and the Claimant, that he should come and live at my house. The arrangement was that they were to pay me, independent of attending meetings, a sum of £3. 10s. a week for the prisoner's board and lodging, and he was to have what pocket-money in reason he thought proper. The Claimant was to pay me, and he holds three receipts from me. The Claimant made me four payments. Prisoner came to my house on the 7th of July, and he lived with me till he gave his evidence. I took him about the country with me, and I paid his expenses. I also paid £3. 5s. for his clothes. Altogether my charges came to about £60 or £70. I was paid all but £11. The prisoner never paid me a single penny.

Prisoner: You charged £8 a week for me.

Witness: I never charged £8 a week: I should have been very sorry.

How much pocket-money did you give me?—Sometimes a pound a week, sometimes 30s.

Never thirty shillings. I got a pound a week when I was in London. When I was in the country I collected the tickets and that sort of thing. I did work for it, did I not?—Yes, you did work.

You never told me that you were paid £3. 10s. a week for me.

That was, for everything—spirits and all.

Lord bless my soul!—two bottles of rum and one bottle of gin. (Laughter.)

MARY ANN PULLEYN, wife of the last witness, said—On two occasion I went to Bessborough-gardens to get some money for the prisoner's lodging. I inquired for the Claimant. An envelope directed to my husband was brought out. It contained a £5 note; and on a second occasion I got another £5 in the same way.

ELIZABETH MILLER: I live at 2, Cardigan-road, Kilburn. In 1867 I was living at Paddington, and at the time I knew the prisoner as JOHN SMITH. He married HARRIET ARREND, and lived with her a few weeks. After he left I lost sight of him for five or six years. He came back last year, the day before the Derby-day. He lived in my house on the 5th of July, passing by the name of Captain JOHN SMITH. I lent him some money, and he left, and I saw no more of him.

The Prisoner: I do not know whether the bigamy is to be gone into. If it is, I should like to ask this witness some questions.

The Judge: If they do, this woman may be a material witness, and she will be called again. You gave an account of having come from Australia to London. This woman says that is not true.

Prisoner: Then I have no question to ask her.

HARRIET ARREND said: In 1867 I was keeping a coffee-house at Paddington, being a widow at the time. In the latter part of February prisoner came to lodge with me, stating that his name was Captain JOHN SMITH, and that he was a ship-owner at the East-end. He courted me, and we were married on the 14th April at St. Peter's, Pimlico. He lived with me till the 6th of June.

Mr. POLAND: Did he leave you then?—Yes; I put him in prison for assaulting me. (Laughter.)

The Judge: You have no doubt that the prisoner is the man?—Oh dear, no.

The Judge (to the prisoner): She says you are the man she knew. Do you wish to ask her anything?

Prisoner: Oh, that will do. I have no question to ask her.

Mr. ALFRED HENDRIKS said: I was the Defendant's attorney during part of the Trial in the Court of Queen's Bench. I first saw the prisoner on the 7th of July, at my office, in Poets-corner. He told me his name was JOHN LUIE, and that he wished to make a very important statement. I asked my friend Mr. O'BRIEN to take it, and he did so. I afterwards saw the prisoner sign it, and Mr. WHALLEY attested it, having been present while the statement was being made. [The statement, with the prisoner's signature, was put in.] After it was taken I read it, and the prisoner went by my direction, with Mr. WHALLEY and Mr. O'BRIEN, to see the Claimant, and he afterwards made further statements and signed them. [These were also put in.] I both telegraphed and wrote to New York, to FUNCKE, EDYE and Co., the present representatives of FUNCKE and MEINKE, and on the 5th of August I received their reply. I read it to the prisoner. The letter dated July 26, 1873, from Messrs. FUNCKE, EDYE and Co., was put in, and after acknowledging the receipt of the letter, and "previous cable" stated that Mr. FUNCKE never owned any vessel named the "Osprey," nor did Mr. MEINKE or Mr. FALKENBERG, both of whom were dead. In accordance with request, they had examined the Custom-house records for 1854, and also a newspaper file from January to July, 1854, and no record of any vessel so named appeared. It added that their Mr. FUNCKE did not remember anyone of the name of JEAN LUIE.] Mr. HENDRIKS continued: When I read the letter to the prisoner he said that the firm had motives for disclaiming any knowledge of the "Osprey"—that they had filibustered her, and that that was why they had denied all knowledge of the vessel or himself.

Mr. POLAND: Did you say anything to that?—No; I did not say anything. We afterwards had some further conversation about the matter, and he urged me to make inquiries and so on.

Mr. POLAND: On the 11th August I believe you retired from the case?—I ceased to act for the Claimant from the 15th of August. The two letters shown to me (from the prisoner to Mr. RIMELL) are, I believe, in the prisoner's handwriting. [Mr. RIMELL was a supporter of the Claimant, and was frequently at Poets-corner.

The letters were put in and read as follows:—

City Prison, Holloway, 12th December, 1873.

Mr. RIMELL.—DEAR SIR,—I have not heard from any one of you, and I feare that all are inclined to believe me to be the scoundrel LUNDGREN, as is mentioned by all those monstrosse witniss. It is a hard thing for me to baer, and you know very well that if I can have no assistances given me to bring LUNDGREN's relations here as well as JEAN's, the two American ladies, and they two men now in England, who knows both the "Osprey" and myself, independent of that villian woman, who is a——, and living with another man than her husband LUNDGREN, as well as proper and independent medical men to examine me respecting rupture, I must be in a hopeless state. But this I mean to tell you: let the matter take what course it will, I shall declare openly in court that no one connected with the case, or any one else, has ever used any influence on me, nor attempted such a thing as to make me tel the fate and circumstances with Sir ROGER. It is the truth, and nothing but the truth, and that it seems to me villany is practised all over the world against both ROGER and myself. HARCOURT asked me if I could defend myself. What does he mean? I wrote you last night a letter. I wrote also to Mr. W. Perhaps you have not received it. What am I to do? I am shut out from the world, and am starving. I must go to the criminal side to-night, as I have no means. See what Sir ROGER says. I am willing to undergo any medical operation to prove that I am not ruptured, or have any cause with me.—I am, obt. fd.,

JEAN LUIE.

P.S.—If I am rendered assistance Sir ROGER and all of you are saved.

Mr. G. RIMELL, 29, Golden-square. December 22, 1873.

DEAR SIR,—By this I beg to acquaint all of you that I am here retained, and have heard nothing. This is a miserable life, and to suffer such—all for not being allowed to have my own way. But what is done cannot be altered. I refer you to my last from House of Detention. I had letter from Plas Madoc, wherein was stated that £5 had been sent to HARDING. If the same is not returned please take charge of it for me, as you will see in the printed form. I don't want to have any letters unless of the greatest importance. I conclude by wishing yourself and family a merry Christmas, and with respect to W——, in Plas Madoc, and all friends.—Your obedient, J. L.

N.B.—None of you would know me now if you was to see me.

In answer to Mr. POLAND, Mr. HENDRIKS said that Mr. WHALLEY lived at Plas Madoc.

Mr. POLAND said that that evidence closed the case for the Prosecution.

The Judge: Now, prisoner, do you wish to call any witnesses, or to make any statement?

Prisoner: I am deprived of the means to call witnesses, my lord.

The Judge: That I can't help. I only ask if you wish to call any?

Mr. WHALLEY, who was sitting at the attorneys' table, rose and said: I beg to offer myself——

The Judge: Prisoner, do you wish to ask Mr. HENDRIKS any question.

Prisoner: No. I don't see there is any necessity in asking Mr. HENDRIKS any question, except I don't believe I mentioned filibuster or anything of that sort.

The Judge: Now you may call witnesses if you have any to call; if not, you had better tell your own story to the jury.

Prisoner: I don't see any to call.

Mr. WHALLEY: I am in attendance, my lord, under an order from Bow-street, to——

The Judge: I can hear nobody but the prisoner.

Prisoner: I have lots of witnessess to call, but I have not got them here.

Mr. WHALLEY: I am here.

Prisoner: There is only one gentleman here, Mr. WHALLEY, who has been over to New York, and ascertained some facts.

The Judge: Do you wish Mr. WHALLEY to be called?

Prisoner: I do so.

The Judge: You do. Follow your own course, and don't be advised by anybody. You are defending yourself now.

Prisoner: That is the worst of it—the position in which I am placed. No man was ever placed in an equal position.

The Judge: Oh, yes, a great many men have been. You are defending yourself, and don't be ill-advised. Do you wish Mr. WHALLEY to be called or not?

Prisoner: Yes, I wish him to be called.

Mr. WHALLEY then entered the box, and having been sworn,

The Judge (addressing the prisoner) said: What do you wish to ask him?

Prisoner: You went over to New York expressly on the purpose to ascertain whether what I had stated were facts, Mr. WHALLEY, I believe?

Mr. WHALLEY: I did.

Did you call upon Mr. FUNCKE?—I did.

Was it correct, respecting that firm, that there had been a Baron FALKENBERG in the year 1854?—It was.

Mr. POLAND: I object, my lord, to leading questions.

The Judge (to prisoner): What this witness heard in America cannot be received in evidence, because here it is not legal. If there were any evidence to be had in America, seeing he went over on your account, and if he meant to assist you, he ought to have brought these witnesses from America to speak here. It is of no use coming here to say what was said in America, because I am unable to listen to it.

Mr. WHALLEY: I wish to explain. I did not go on his account.

The Judge: "I went to New York to ascertain whether what the prisoner stated were facts," is your answer. If any evidence existed in America which could do you any good, it ought to have been brought here. I cannot listen to what is not brought here.

Prisoner: Yes, that's just what it is.

Mr. WHALLEY: From the statement which he made to me I satisfied—

ALFRED TICHBORNE ("BELLE TÊTE") WHEN A CHILD.

The Judge: No, no, Mr. WHALLEY.

Mr. POLAND: No opinion, Mr. WHALLEY; you are a barrister.

The Judge: I cannot help you to do that which is contrary to the law.

The Prisoner: No, my lord.

The Judge: Is there anything Mr. WHALLEY knows himself about the questions in issue here that you wish to ask him?

Prisoner (to witness): Did you go down to Staten Island to ascertain whether there had been any vessel of the name of "Osprey" loading there?

Mr. WHALLEY: I went to Staten Island, but I did not go there for that purpose. I went to a Custom-house which has connection with Staten Island to see the register.

Prisoner: And you found it correct that FALKENBERG was the ship-owner.

Mr. POLAND: You cannot ask that.

The Judge: You may ask him anything that was in the register, because it cannot be brought here. You may ask him whether he found anything in the register.

Prisoner: Did you find any registry at New Bedford of a ship of FALKENBERG.

The Judge: He says he went to Staten Island, where vessels loading might probably clear out.

Prisoner: Did you examine the register at Perth Amboy.

Mr. WHALLEY: I did, and did not find the clearance of an "Osprey," but I had such an explanation at Perth Amboy on the subject as accounted——

The Judge: No, no.

Prisoner: You ascertained from the Custom-house that no vessels were clearing out?

The Judge: What he has stated is that he did not find the clearing out of an "Osprey" in the register.

Prisoner: No, because there is no necessity for finding it out.

That might be. Do you wish to ask anything about New Bedford?

Prisoner: Yes.

Mr. WHALLEY: I found by the Custom-house register at New Bedford——

The Judge: What entry did you find, sir?
Mr. WHALLEY. I went to New Bedford——
The Judge: Did you examine the register there?
Mr. WHALLEY: I did.
The Judge: Well?
Mr. WHALLEY: I found there a confirmation——
The Judge: No, no. I told you before, sir, that all you could say was what you saw in the register.
Mr. WHALLEY: I found two ships registered as belonging to Baron FALKENBERG.
The Judge: Well, go on. What were their names?
Mr. WHALLEY: One was called the "Falkenberg." I forget the other one. It was not the "Osprey."
Prisoner: There is the man who wrote out the manifest for the "Osprey"—you spoke to him in New York?
The Judge: You cannot answer that. (To prisoner.) You can only ask as to the contents of the book that cannot be brought here.
Mr. WHALLEY: May I be allowed to suggest to him a question?
The Judge: Certainly not.
Prisoner: Did you find the existence of a Mr. FUNCKE there?
Mr. WHALLEY: Certainly. I found full confirmation there.
The Judge: No, no.
Prisoner: The letters I sent with you, Mr. WHALLEY, you delivered to Mr. FUNCKE?
Mr. WHALLEY: Yes. He gave me certain letters, but they were not to Mr. FUNCKE. They were to two servants of Mr. FUNCKE, both of whom were dead—(a laugh)—but they were handed to me by Mr. FUNCKE, and the contents of those letters were verified.
The Judge: No, no.
Prisoner: I am in that position that I cannot ask questions.
Cross-examined by Mr. POLAND: Were you in the Queen's Bench when this man was examined?
The Judge: You had better consider, Mr. POLAND, whether you may not let in one matter. Of course I do not object.
Mr. POLAND (to witness): After this man had been examined did you give him £5?—Yes.
On that day?—I think it was the day after he had given his evidence.
Did Mr. ONSLOW give him £5?—Yes. Both of us gave him £5. I think it must have been on the 16th, on the day we signed that testimonial.
Was that testimonial written by you?—It was.
Have you been in Court while this Trial has been going on?—For the most part of the time.
You wrote to certify that he has borne himself through all his life as a man entitled to confidence and respect?—I did, and I ask to be allowed to explain explicitly the reasons why I did write it.
The Judge: As the question has been asked, I think he must be permitted to explain.
Mr. WHALLEY: They were written with great deliberation under these circumstances. We knew that the Crown had in their service a great number of detectives engaged in following up, investigating, and ascertaining the character of every person that was connected with or about to be called on the part of the Defence: that every circumstance of their life was in the hands of the cross-examining Counsel; and we came to the conclusion that if anything whatever could be found against this man, unless he was a plant by the Government, and unless he was put forward knowingly as the man he turns out to be, that that undoubtedly would have become known to the Government, and would have been disclosed in the cross-examination; and therefore Mr. ONSLOW and myself, in considering what was due to the man, deliberately stated that we believed, having passed through the cross-examination as he did, that his character was by that circumstance well established. That was the reason, and it was a matter of full consideration.
Mr. POLAND: You signed yourself G. H. WHALLEY, M.P., and Mr. ONSLOW appeared as M.P. too?
Mr. WHALLEY: Yes.
The Judge: You say you knew the Government had had detectives who knew the whole life of every witness. How did you know that?
Mr. WHALLEY: By complaints made by those witnesses of the extent to which they were personally harassed previous to being called. One person committed suicide in consequence. (Laughter.) So we were told.
Mr. POLAND: I think you are a magistrate of three counties?—That is so.
And you live at Plas Madoc?—Yes.
And because this man in cross-examination did not admit the circumstances of his life, you gave him a certificate of character covering his whole life?—That is so. I have given you the reason why we certified.
The Judge: Is that the reason why you certified that he has borne himself through all his life as a man entitled to confidence and respect?—That was the best of our belief.
The Judge: That is not your belief. You certified it?—We certified that to best of our belief.
Mr. POLAND: Did you not give him that certificate and put "M.P." after your name in order that he might take it with him to America?—We had the further object that in going to America he was to look up such evidence as he could collect and telegraph to us, so that his evidence might be further corroborated.

Did you know he was going to leave for America on the 16th, after his two days' examination?
No answer.
Question repeated.
Mr. WHALLEY: I had no further knowledge than that Mr. ONSLOW and myself requested that he should go immediately—with as little delay as possible.
But did you know that Mr. ONSLOW gave him a letter of introduction to the dock-master of Southampton, to give him every assistance to get away?—Yes; I concurred in that.
After he was in custody did you send your nephew, Captain W. NICHOLSON, to the House of Detention to see him?—I did.
Did you send him £5?—I send £5 to another person for him if he was in the state I was told.
For the benefit of this man?—Certainly.
The Judge: Do I understand that this certificate was signed after the examination in the Queen's Bench?
Mr. POLAND: Yes.
The Judge: After the Counsel for the then Defendant had thrown over the evidence of this man?
Mr. POLAND: No, my lord. He is examined on the 14th and 15th of October, and that is signed on the 16th—the same date as Mr. ONSLOW'S letter to the dock-master; then something occurs, and he remains in this country, and is recalled on the 1st of December. (To witness, handing him the plan of Melbourne Harbour)—Just look at the writing on that plan. Do you know the writing?
Mr. WHALLEY: Melbourne?
Mr. POLAND: Yes, and Sandridge and Williamstown.
Mr. WHALLEY: No.
Do you know Mr. ONSLOW'S handwriting?—I am almost sure it is not his handwriting.
You are not quite sure?—I could not be quite sure, but the words "Sandridge" and "Williamstown" I do not recognize at all as the writing of Mr. ONSLOW.
Will you undertake to swear that it is not in the handwriting of Mr. ONSLOW?—No, I will not undertake to swear that.
The Judge: The question of the handwriting is as to belief.
Mr. POLAND: Do you believe that is the handwriting of the prisoner?—I do not; but before I give a final answer to that question I should like to see the letters put in.
The Judge: No. It is a question of belief.
Mr. WHALLEY: I believe that is not his handwriting. It certainly is not Mr. ONSLOW'S. To the best of my belief it is not.
Mr. POLAND: Did you go with this man in a cab to see the Claimant and Mr. O'BRIEN?—I did.
Did you know after that date where he was living?—I heard in a general way that he was put in the charge of PULLEYN.
Did you know he was being maintained by the Claimant?—I had no knowledge of any of these matters.
You knew PULLEYN very well yourself?—I knew him as one attached to the Claimant, in his service more or less.
Mr. WHALLEY, are you defending this man? Did you pay his expenses yesterday?
Mr. WHALLEY: Yesterday!
Mr. POLAND: Did you communicate with his attorney on his behalf?
Mr. WHALLEY: I had no communication with him in any shape or form before yesterday morning; but finding then that he was undefended, I immediately sent for Mr. LEWIS, and said "Let him be defended."
The Judge: You mean that so far as you are concerned, yesterday was the first time that Mr. LEWIS was retained for the defence.
Mr. WHALLEY: Yes. I have not had any communication with this man, directly or indirectly, since I was bail for him. I was bail for him some time alone.
Mr. POLAND: You mean since he was in the police-court?
Mr. WHALLEY: Yes.
The Judge: Were you in court when the clerk said that Mr. LEWIS, who was retained for the prisoner's defence in the police-court, had been retained for his defence here?—I was in court when the clerk said what he did say. I understood him to say that.
Did you hear him state here yesterday that Mr. LEWIS had been retained for the defence?—I was in court during what transpired. What I understood and wished was that Mr. LEWIS, who was retained at the police-court, should be retained yesterday.
The Judge: Unfortunately, your understanding is very different from mine. I asked you a plain question.
Mr. WHALLEY: May I read the evidence which I gave in the police-court?
The Judge: No. (To prisoner) Do you wish to ask Mr. WHALLEY anything more?
Prisoner: No, my lord; it won't be legal it won't be right. (Laughter.)
The Judge: Have you any other witnesses to call?
Prisoner: Yes, I have a lot of witnesses.
The Judge: What are their names?
Prisoner: Well, I want JANES.
The Judge: Is JANES here?
The Usher: Yes, my lord.
The Usher then called loudly two or three times for CHARLES JANES, but there was no response.
The Judge: Does he not answer?

The Usher: No, my lord.

Inspector CLARKE: I have seen him here, my lord, this afternoon.

The Judge (to prisoner): Is there anybody else?

Prisoner: Well, that is the only one I had that was bailed over in the police-court. The others were to be brought up here. I had twelve or thirteen of them. There is Mr. GOODRIDGE.

By the direction of the Judge, the Usher then called out several times the name "GOODRIDGE!" but again there was no answer.

The Judge (to prisoner): Well, your witnesses are not here, you see.

Prisoner: No, my lord; I don't suppose they are, their names having been called.

The Judge: Now tell your own story. The great charge against you is that you swore that you were on board the "Osprey," and that you picked up the boat. It is said that that is untrue, and of course if it were untrue you knew that it was so. They (the Prosecution) have proved that it was untrue, because they have proved that you were in England at the time. That is the first great charge against you. The next charge is that you gave evidence that you were not in England till shortly before the Trial, whereas they have proved that you were in England for many years before. Those charges are what you have to answer for before the jury.

Prisoner: Well, my lord, during my cross-examination in the Court of Queen's Bench I objected to questions of Mr. HAWKINS respecting the latest period of my life in consequence of a misfortune that I was really led into; but the Lord Chief Justice ordered me to answer the questions. I was compelled to do so, and I did it as it came into my mind at the time. Numbers of witnesses have been called here against me as to the period of 1853 and 1854, one, according to his account, being himself a schoolfellow of mine. How is it possible for me to contradict these men when I am void entirely of assistance, either legal assistance, or assistance of people whom I should have been able to bring forward? If I had time I should prove that they are mistaken—entirely mistaken—in the identity. It requires in fact a wonderful memory for any one to distinguish one man from another after a period of over twenty years' time, and especially when you have a man only just come into court to discern an individual. Had I been able to be defended, and produced witnesses, it would certainly have substantiated my story to a great extent. Of course in the later periods of 1862 and 1867 misfortunes have fallen to my lot. That undoubtedly is true, but respecting the time of 1852, or 1853, and 1854, there is no truth whatever in what has been said. I don't say that people have perjured themselves, because if they have perjured themselves a vast number of witnesses who have been brought against ROGER TICHBORNE must be as bad as they are in respect. But I say I have been the sole victim of prosecution from a number of people amounting to nearly 300. I think it is very hard indeed that I should suffer the inconvenience in which I am placed. It can be proved, and will in time come out, that the "Osprey" which I joined at New Orleans in 1852, and was with her up to the end of 1854, is a fact undoubtedly, and will be found to be true. Time will tell that, and it should have been proved satisfactorily both to your lordship and the jury if I had had that ample means given me which I now stand in need of. Had it not been for the misfortune of this bigamy affair of mine, I certainly should never have given the account which I have given, because I stood in the position that whatever turn I took, when it came to the period 1855 to 1867, whether I admitted that or made any false statement or not, it would have fallen to my lot to be punished. I am very sorry that this has taken up the time so long, keeping your lordship and the jury for such a length of time through the calling of all these witnesses, since I am not in a position now to bring forward evidence in support of my story. Very sorry, indeed, I am, but I trust that the time will come soon enough to prove my story and the fact of the "Osprey" in 1854. (For some seconds before this the prisoner spoke with considerable apparent emotion, the signs of which gradually increased towards the close of his remarks.) At the same time, I beg his lordship to be as lenient in his punishment towards me as possible, bearing in mind that I have still 18 or 19 months to be under servitude. (Here the prisoner seemed to be actually crying, and he applied a handkerchief to his eyes.)

It being now about a quarter past five, Mr. Justice BRETT asked the jury whether it would be most convenient to them for him to sum up then, or to wait till the morning, observing that he did not think it would take long.

The Foreman, after consulting the other jurymen, replied that they would prefer the latter course; and the Judge, having cautioned them against talking to anyone about the trial in the interval, the Court ajourned.

CENTRAL CRIMINAL COURT.—*April* 10.

(Before Mr. Justice BRETT.)

The trial of CARL PETER LUNDGREN, alias JEAN LUIE, was proceeded with this morning at the sitting of the Court.

As the learned Judge entered the Court, Mr. EDWARD LEWIS stood up in the front of the dock, and was about to speak to the prisoner, when

Mr. Justice BRETT said it is not right that anybody should interfere with the proceedings in a court of justice unless they are engaged in the case being inquired into.

Mr. EDWARD LEWIS: I am the solicitor of this man, and I have applied for permission to see him.

Mr. Justice BRETT: You are his solicitor, and that is enough.

Mr. LEWIS: Will your lordship allow me to have a few words—?

Mr. Justice BRETT: Certainly not.

Mr. LEWIS: My lord——

Mr. Justice BRETT: I say certainly not. I will listen to no one but counsel.

Mr. LEWIS here exchanged a few words with the prisoner in the dock from the gangway below the attorneys' seat.

Prisoner: Can I have the witness JANES, my lord? May I be permitted to call him?

Mr. Justice BRETT: If you wish it.

The witness JANES was called by the usher, but he did not answer to his name.

Inspector CLARKE: I have searched everywhere about the Court for JANES, but I cannot find him here.

Prisoner: Then call Captain BROWN.

Mr. Justice BRETT (to prisoner): Just let me advise you. I see people suggesting things to you. Just beware of what they are doing. They are pretended friends. Now, exercise your own judgment. You are quick and intelligent enough; then don't be made the tool of other people. Now, do you wish of your own accord, that Captain BROWN should be called? If you do, he shall be summoned—if you think he would do you any good.

Prisoner: I think he can do me some good.

Mr. Justice BRETT: You think he can? Then let him be called. Let the man BROWN, who is in prison here, be called. Is there any other "Captain" BROWN.

Mr. POLAND: No, he is the only Captain BROWN in the Case.

Mr. Justice BRETT (to prisoner): I presume you mean to call the man who was examined as a witness in the TICHBORNE Trial, and who is now in custody charged with perjury.

Prisoner: Yes, my lord.

Mr. Justice BRETT: Then let him be called.

Prisoner: I did not know the man was charged with perjury.

Mr. Justice BRETT: But he is, and he will be tried here after you.

Prisoner: What use will it be for me to call him, then? I did not know about this.

Mr. Justice BRETT: It is for you to decide. You must exercise your own intelligence, which seems to me to be quite as great as that of other people. Do you wish Captain BROWN called?

Prisoner: Yes, my lord. I suppose I could not call the Claimant, my lord?

Mr. Justice BRETT: Has it been suggested to you to call the Claimant?

Prisoner hesitated to reply.

Mr. Justice BRETT: I ask you whether this has been suggested to you?

Prisoner: Yes, my lord.

Mr. Justice BRETT: I will explain it to you. It is suggested to you to call a man who has been convicted of perjury, and whose word, therefore, will not be believed by anyone who hears what he has to say. It has been suggested to you to call a man who has been before the public in a particular character, and under a particular appearance, and who is now in the midst of his ignominy and degradation, in order to make a show of him. Unless you think that that man can do you any good, I say, advisedly, that to call him would be an act of the most wicked cruelty which could be devised towards him. Now I leave it to you to say whether you will adopt the suggestion of the people who are pretending to advise you. What do you say?

Prisoner: No, my lord.

Mr. Justice BRETT: That you will not call him?

Prisoner: Yes, my lord.

Mr. Justice BRETT: Then you are a man!!!

[Mr. LEWIS here went up to the dock, and handed a slip of paper to the prisoner.]

Mr. Justice BRETT: You be quiet, sir.

Mr. LEWIS: My lord, I submit I have a right to advise this man.

Mr. Justice BRETT: You be quiet, and do nothing without my leave.

Prisoner: My lord, I will call no witnesses.

Mr. Justice BRETT: Very well.

Gentlemen of the Jury—Before I enter into this case, let us reflect for a moment upon that which has been the chief complaint of this unhappy prisoner. His chief complaint has been that he has not had assistance in this trial; that he has not had pecuniary help to enable him to call witnesses. If there had been no interference in this case—if the matter had been left to the ordinary course of law, and the prisoner had suggested to me that he wished for legal assistance—I should have asked some gentleman at the Bar to give him his services gratuitously, and according to the tradition of the Bar, which has never yet in my experience failed, there is not a barrister, however eminent, who, if I asked him to defend this man, would have refused to do it. There is not one who would have thought for a moment whether or not, by undertaking the defence without ample consideration, he would be damaging his own reputation. No such cowardly feeling ever existed in the mind of a barrister at the Bar of England. Over and over again they undertake the most hopeless cases, when asked by the Judge, on the spur of the moment; they do their best for the prisoner at the bar without a thought of themselves. I was prevented from so acting because there are people in this country who have interfered with the ordinary course of justice; who have undertaken, at least in appearance, to assist this man; who have professed a feeling of superior love of justice to the people; who have given certificates to this man; who have instructed an attorney to make a simulated defence, and who have so far instructed Counsel as to induce him to come forward and make a temporary show of defending the prisoner. These are persons who, if they really intended to defend the prisoner, if they really intended to assist him, and if they really had that love of justice which would lead them to seek for witnesses, have had ample opportunity, and have ample means, to enable them to do so. They are persons who knew that this man was charged weeks, nay months, ago with the offence for which he is now on his trial, who knew that he would be tried at these sessions, who knew that he was helpless, who knew that he had no money, who—if they intended to assist him at all—had knowledge of every piece of evidence which was to be brought against him, but who never moved a finger or spent a shilling in his behalf until the day when the man was brought here in Court to plead to this indictment. Then they came forward and pretended that they were anxious to assist him. Gentlemen, I will be no party to this mean attempt at gaining popularity. Let us now cast these people away, if you agree with me in what I have said, with the contempt which all this pretence inspires. Let us take care, however, in forming our opinion in this case, that this pretended sympathy of his friends does not hurt him. The learned Judge, after a pause, then continued. The prisoner was charged with wilful and corrupt perjury, which offence consisted in his having in a court of justice stated things that were false, things that he knew to be false, and things that were material to the question then at issue. He was examined upon a Trial when a person named ARTHUR ORTON was being tried for perjury in a cause in which he swore that he was Sir ROGER TICHBORNE. By evidence which satisfied four judges and two juries it was proved that ARTHUR ORTON was guilty of perjury, and no person of common-sense could doubt that the man was not Sir ROGER TICHBORNE, but that he was ARTHUR ORTON. It was admitted that ROGER TICHBORNE was at Rio, and that he sailed from thence in the "Bella," and it was necessary to make out his claim that he had been saved from the "Bella" when she was lost, and he swore that he was picked up by a vessel called the "Osprey," and he stated where he was taken to. One fatal blot among the hundreds of others in his case was that until he came forward no one had ever heard either of such a vessel as the "Osprey," or of the other persons who were represented to have been saved. In order to remedy this the prisoner came forward to swear that he was on board the "Osprey," and that he assisted in saving the Defendant ORTON, and that he went with him to Melbourne. He was examined, and he swore positively to these facts, and it became of vital importance to know who he was, and what his previous character had been, and in reference to these matters he was alleged to have sworn to matters which were false, and which he must have known to be false. Again, it was most material that he should explain why he had not come forward before, and his explanation was that he had only arrived in England immediately before, and if this was false, and he knew it to be false, in his opinion it was a material matter, and was properly made the subject of an allegation of wilful and corrupt perjury against the prisoner. There were some minor matters, but these were the most important questions for the consideration of the jury. The learned judge then proceeded to observe that the prisoner had given a great deal of evidence in support of his statement, which was that from the year 1853 he was in Australia, South America, and other parts of the world, during all the interval down to the year 1873, whereas the evidence for the Prosecution went to show that during the whole of this period the prisoner was in England, and for a considerable portion of the time that he was in prison for different offences that he had committed. Of course, if this evidence was relied on—and there did not appear to be any reason why it should not be—it was manifest that the story told by the prisoner about saving the people in the boat from the "Bella" must have been false, and the prisoner must have known that it was false. The prisoner, by the questions he had put to some of the witnesses, seemed to be desirous of showing that they were mistaken as to his identity; but it would be for the jury to say whether this was possible, particularly after what had been stated by the witness LINSTRONN, a native of Gothenburg, who had known the prisoner from his childhood, when he was a schoolboy, apprentice, mate, and master of the vessel the "Isabella." He asked the jury whether it was possible this man ever could have made a mistake with regard to the identity of the prisoner. His evidence was confirmed in a very extraordinary manner by the fact that in the prisoner's marriage certificate the name of his father was stated to be JOHANN ELIAS LUNDGREN, and the witness he referred to proved that this was the name of the prisoner's father. The learned judge next referred to the evidence given by the other witnesses with regard to the identity of the defendant, some of whom were fellow-clerks to the defendant, and his employers, all of whom spoke positively to the fact, and he asked the jury whether any reasonable person could doubt that the prisoner was the same man. The whole of these witnesses appeared to be most respectable persons, and they gave their evidence in the most positive manner, and he reminded the jury that with regard to one of them the prisoner appeared to have almost admitted that he was not JEAN LUIE, and that he was CARL LUNDGREN. His lordship called the attention of the jury at some length to this part of the case, and said that if the prisoner's suggestion was correct, every one of these witnesses must have made a mistake. These appeared to him to be the most material witnesses with regard to this part of the case, and he now came to another portion of the inquiry, which related to the marriage of the prisoner at Cardiff in the year 1855. All the witnesses to the marriage swore positively as to the identity of the prisoner, and here again the jury would have to consider whether it was possible that these witnesses were mistaken or that they were saying what they did not believe to be true. The sister of the woman the prisoner was married to, who had seen him constantly for a long period afterwards, could hardly be mistaken, and it was for the jury to consider whether there was anything in relation to her conduct that ought to induce them to doubt the truth of her testimony. His lordship next referred to the evidence of the Bristol constable, NICHOLS, that the prisoner was convicted of stealing a bill of exchange and sentenced to three years' penal servitude in 1862, and in 1867 the same witness proved his conviction upon another charge, and he was sentenced upon this charge to seven years' penal servitude. Evidence was then given that the prisoner had been convicted at Newcastle of obtaining money by falsely pretending that he was the captain of a ship, and for this offence he was sentenced to six months' hard labour. If this evidence were correct, it was perfectly clear that the prisoner could not have been at the places abroad that he had mentioned, and the evidence he had given was clearly false. His lordship then referred to the evidence of POWER, the warder at Millbank, and to the admissions that were made to him by the prisoner. Upon this evidence could the jury have any doubt that the prisoner swore falsely when he stated that he had never been in trouble? His lordship said there was no doubt that the prisoner, like the Claimant, had many persons about him who, either from folly or wickedness, were doing all they could to tempt him to commit perjury. He then referred to the evidence given by Inspector CLARKE, and he said that the prisoner appeared to have made a good many rambling statements to him, but the effect of what he stated certainly appeared to be that he admitted that the statements he had made were false. The prisoner also represented that Mr. WHALLEY had said to him at Brussels that a trial was going on in England which made him ashamed of his country. Why he should be ashamed of his country on this account he certainly could not see. (A laugh.) The learned judge further said he also represented that Mr. WHALLEY said that one difficulty they had to contend with was that they could not find any man who had picked up a shipwrecked crew. Sitting on that bench, he had no hesitation in saying that if Mr. WHALLEY, either from folly or wickedness, or both, really did make this statement, he was giving an incitement to perjury. (Sensation.) He then referred to the statements of the prisoner with regard to Mr. WHALLEY and Mr. ONSLOW, and his representation that he should not not have gone into the witness-box if Mr. ONSLOW had not compelled him to do so. He did not say that this story was true, but all he could say was that if it was true, the prisoner was not the only person who ought to be put on his trial, as a conspiracy evidently existed to commit a serious offence. If the prisoner's story was true, it amounted to an admission that he was guilty of perjury, and if it was not true, and he had made these false statements against other parties, what could they think of a man who could act in such a manner? His lordship said he had now arrived at what was a painful part of the case, and which satisfied him, with the other matters, that there never was any real intention on the part of those who were called the prisoner's friends to defend him. He had no hesitation in saying that Mr. WHALLEY had obtruded himself as a witness for the prisoner. He was asked in derision by the learned counsel for the Prosecution whether he was not a magistrate of three counties and also a barrister; and if he had had the slightest knowledge of even the elements of law he must have known perfectly well that he could not give any evidence that would be of the slightest benefit to the prisoner. It might have the effect of showing sympathy. It might have afforded an opportunity for giving an explanation upon any public matter, but he must have known that he could not say anything that was likely to be of use to the prisoner, and it gave the Counsel for the Prosecution a right to reply. If any evidence of importance could have been obtained in America, the witnesses might have been brought forward; but nothing of the sort was done, and a child could see through the proceeding that was attempted to be carried out. His lordship then referred to the certificate of character that had been given by Mr. ONSLOW and Mr. WHALLEY to the prisoner, and said that it was as false as anything possibly could be; it represented that the prisoner, the wretched man at the bar, had borne himself through all his life in such a manner as entitled him to confidence and respect. Mr. WHALLEY had endeavoured to explain this proceeding by stating that as the witness had come out of his cross-examination without any imputation upon his character, he had a right to believe that he was a man of good character. The fact was, however, that he knew nothing whatever about him; and his statement in the certificate was entirely unfounded. He said that, to his mind, it was really shocking to see such things done. His lordship, in conclusion, recapitulated the material questions that would have to be decided by the jury, and left the question in their hands.

ANOTHER REPORT.

The learned Judge's observations on Mr. WHALLEY appear thus in another newspaper.

As I told you before, gentlemen, if you think the prisoner has perjured himself it does not do to accept what he said about Mr. WHALLEY, or Mr. ONSLOW, or Mr. anybody else. The inspector says further that the prisoner said to him that Mr. WHALLEY had told him that there was a difficulty in the fact of their not being able to find anyone who had picked up a shipwrecked crew. If Mr. WHALLEY ever did say such a thing—I say it sitting here, and I am no respecter of persons—then Mr. WHALLEY, prompted either by folly, mischief, or obstinacy, or what you please, suggested a perjury; but I don't accept it as true because this man says it. The witness goes on to say, "Prisoner told me that the reason he was not put into the box earlier was because he had not learnt his lesson." Now, I tell you, you must not accept this as true. If it is true, however, the prisoner is not the only man who should be on his trial, for this would show a conspiracy—a wicked conspiracy. I am sorry now to have to point out to you that the prisoner was encouraged to believe that he was to be defended, and has been led into a false position. To my mind it never was really intended that he should be defended, because if his friends had meant it, there is no reason why they should not have instructed Counsel. You recollect what happened yesterday. I asked him whether he intended calling witnesses, when Mr. WHALLEY—and I say it advisedly—obtruded himself upon the prisoner as a witness. He was asked in cross-examination whether he was not a magistrate of three counties and a barrister, to which he replied in the affirmative. The meaning of that question is obvious. It meant, "Could you, a magistrate and a barrister, who should at least know some of the elements of law—could you believe that what you wished to state would be of any use to the prisoner? It might be of use to you to enable you to exhibit your alleged sympathy, and to explain something: but of what use could it be to the prisoner? If you are acquainted with the merest elements of law, you must knows that you could not force upon the Court what you heard or saw in America. The merest novice in legal matters knows that such would not be evidence, and could not be admitted. Ought you not to know that by suggesting to the prisoner to call you as a witness you could not do him good, but might do him harm?" The evidence which Mr. WHALLEY gave, you heard, gentlemen. He tried to put in that what he had heard in America had satisfied him that this man's story was true. Well, there are two views of that matter. If he found witnesses to facts who could prove this man's statements, where was Mr. WHALLEY's pretended philanthropy? Why were not those witnesses produced? Could not one of them have been brought here? or, at least, could not an affidavit giving his name have been prepared? Of course Mr. WHALLEY, and Mr. ONSLOW, or anybody else, was not bound to interfere if there really were witnesses in America who could have helped this man; but if these gentlemen had never interfered in this case it would not have been necessary for me to make these observations. When Mr. WHALLEY gets into the box, and says, "I believe this prisoner is innocent. I have been to America, and I have instructed Counsel to make an application in his behalf," why does he not go further, and do what would be of real advantage to him—namely, bring those witnesses from America, if they exist, who could do the prisoner a substantial good? Mr. WHALLEY says he is satisfied of the prisoner's integrity. Well, could that be evidence? Could anyone, after hearing Mr. WHALLEY, declare, "I could act upon what Mr. WHALLEY says?" Mr. WHALLEY and Mr. ONSLOW have signed a certificate which, in the hands of any person who did not know the circumstances, would mislead them as surely as any certificate did. They have signed a certificate which, in point of fact, is as false as it can be—a certificate which, in effect, says that this wretched man has borne himself through all his life as a man entitled to confidence and respect. That is false in fact, as you must see. What does Mr. WHALLEY say about it? Why, that when he signed it he believed it to be true; and that he is assured of the man's innocence because he was not broken down in cross-examination, which was conducted after the most searching inquiries had been made into the character of all the witnesses for the Defendant in the TICHBORNE Trial. How does he know what inquiries were made? He does not say that he ever saw the detectives at work. He says "I know it because the man told me it was so." I say such incidents in this case as these I have felt it my duty to mention are shocking to see. No one could act upon Mr. WHALLEY's opinion—he is not cautious enough.

The jury retired at twelve o'clock to deliberate, and after being absent a very short time they returned into court and found the prisoner Guilty.

Mr. Justice BRETT said he should not pass sentence at present.

Captain BROWN was then put upon his trial, and found guilty of perjury: and immediately after LUIE and BROWN were brought up together.

THE SENTENCE.

Mr. Justice BRETT, addressing them, said they had both been convicted upon evidence equally as clear as that upon which ARTHUR ORTON had been convicted of the crime of wilful and corrupt perjury. Nothing was more essential to the administration of the law than that it should be kept free from perjured testimony; and although some people entertained the opinion that false testimony was almost certain to be detected by cross-examination, still his experience led him to come to a contrary opinion, which was supported by what had taken place in reference to the extraordinary Trial with which the present charge was connected. It was absolutely necessary for the due administration of the law that where perjury was detected it should be visited with most severe punishment. The crime no doubt varied to a considerable extent. In the case where a witness, suddenly introduced into a trial in which he had no interest, upon cross-examination, concealed events in his life, although it would undoubtedly amount to perjury in the eye of the law, for his own part he should be very sorry to pass a severe sentence upon such a person. When, however, the perjury was deliberate, and calculated to inflict serious injury upon innocent persons, the case was very different, and it was the duty of a judge to pass a sentence that would mark his sense of the enormity of the offence that had been committed. Although in this case the false evidence that had been given would not have affected the interests of the family whom ARTHUR ORTON had attempted to plunder, there was very little doubt that the object they had in view in giving false evidence upon the trial of that man was in the hope that he would escape a conviction, and he thereby enabled to renew his claims, and possibly obtain possession of the property he claimed, in which case they would have expected to receive some benefit. After some further observations his lordship said that in the case of LUIE there was the additional aggravation that he had been previously convicted of other offences, and although he had at the last exhibited some symptoms of contrition, and had certainly acted properly in refraining from calling the wretched man ARTHUR ORTON as a witness, still, under all the circumstances, he felt compelled to pass a severe sentence upon him, which was that he be imprisoned for one day, and that he be afterwards kept in penal servitude for seven years. With respect to the other prisoner, JAMES BROWN, the observations he had made equally applied to him; but, as he had not been before convicted, he should only sentence him to be imprisoned for one day, and to be kept in penal servitude for five years.

The prisoner LUIE heard the sentence without exhibiting any, or very little, emotion. The other prisoner, BROWN, was a good deal affected, and cried bitterly both before and after the sentence was pronounced.

Upon these convictions of LUIE and BROWN, we cut the following out of the *Leicester Evening News*, April 15th, 1874:—

Those persons who would fain believe in all the proceedings which have been instituted against ROGER TICHBORNE and his Counsel as they do in the Gospel, betray, after all that is said, a wavering faith in their anxiety to call up additional evidence to prove that pure and simple justice has been done. The conviction of JEAN LUIE and Captain BROWN for having committed wilful and corrupt perjury in the evidence they gave in the Claimant's favour, is claimed as another unanswerable proof that the late Defendant is an impostor. We admit that the testimony which these men, as the professed friends of the Defendant, gave at the late trial was most unfortunate; but regarding them as the perjurers they are alleged to be, collusion with the Defendant and some of his responsible friends must be established before their crime can be cited as a corroborative proof of the Defendant's guilt. This has not been done. We may rest certain that all that money and police espionage could do has been done to supply this link; nevertheless, the Prosecution, unscrupulous as they have shown themselves to be, have failed to show that either money or promises were given these men to act the part for which they are doomed to suffer. On the other hand, Mr. WHALLEY, who espoused the Claimant's cause in the public interest, was so determined to test the truth of the story, that he took a voyage to America to ascertain the accuracy of LUIE's references, and from all his inquiries found no reason to doubt them. If Mr. WHALLEY was deceived by the Dane, so was the Lord Chief Justice himself. The best evidence we can have that he regarded LUIE as a truthful man was allowing him full liberty on his promise to appear in court again when he was wanted. JEAN LUIE has deceived Mr. WHALLEY and Dr. KENEALY as effectually as he did the judges and the detectives, and there is no more evidence to show that the friends of the Claimant were privy to the false part he had resolved to take at the Trial, than that the judges and prosecution connived at his perjury, knew him to be a ticket-of-leave man, and suspended his recognition until he had played out his false purpose. To reason that as LUIE is an impostor, therefore the Defendant is one, is most illogical. The diversified and abundant evidence in favour of the Defendant's identity as ROGER TICHBORNE stands altogether apart from the evidence of JEAN LUIE and Captain BROWN, and is not invalidated by their perjury. Their conviction does not explain or clear away the facts in the Claimant's favour, ignored by the judges, and considered irrelevant by the jury. The supplementary testimony of that respectable man CHARLES ORTON, the conviction of LUIE and Captain BROWN, the persecution of Dr. KENEALY, are all intended to strengthen the justice of the verdict found by the jury. If not open to doubt, wherefore this anxiety? A final judgment pronounced by three judges after a hearing extending over 180 days should be so complete as to defy suspicion. But there are facts evaded in this Trial which not only give rise to doubt, but positive dissent, and every attempt to remove it made by the press in publishing CHARLES ORTON's letters, by the law in sentencing LUIE and BROWN, and by the Benchers in persecuting Dr. KENEALY, only serve to increase the uneasiness which gathers strength every day.

The following Letter appeared shortly after LUIE's conviction:—

THE CASE OF JEAN LUIE IN THE TICHBORNE LITIGATION — THE TICKET-OF-LEAVE SYSTEM — THE CLAIMANT.

To THE EDITOR OF THE "JOHN O'GROAT JOURNAL."

SIR,—I wish to make a few observations suggested by the extraordinary case of JEAN LUIE in the TICHBORNE litigation. It will be recollected that this man alleged that he was steward of a vessel called the "Osprey," trading from the United States to Melbourne, and that on the passage he encountered the "Bella"—a vessel which had become a wreck—from which he brought several passengers, among whom was the individual now known as the Claimant. The story was found to be false; and further it transpired that the deponent was a convict at large on what is called a "ticket-of-leave." In consequence of the discovery, the man's license was revoked, and he subjected to a criminal prosecution for perjury.

At this point, I find cause for interposing some strictures on the conduct of the Case. By our law a man is treated as innocent till proved guilty. Many outside may be so assured of the guilt of the individual, that no proof at bar can have the effect of corroborating a previous certainty; and this state of mind might not be altered by even acquittal. Notwithstanding, the law has no knowledge of an offender till after proof. But it was not after proof that the ticket-of-leave was revoked in LUIE's case, and the forfeiture was, in reality, a penalty attached to a crime not forensically established. That this was the real state of matters is demonstrated by the after prosecution of the party at a police office, preliminary to a subsequent and final criminal trial. Why this proceeding, if what was simply gathered up in the court dealing with another case could become a ground of punishment? It is here to be kept in view that precedents of a bad and arbitrary kind are most readily made where the forlorn and obnoxious are dealt by. The case of JOHN WILKES and "General Warrants" may be suggested as admonitory. Even the prosecution of LUIE for bigamy has its unseemliness; for there is no propriety whatever in mixing up the crime with another and different, and that more properly of a public nature. The first wife who was deserted might have here taken action against the bigamist; and by the law of England she is the legitimate and proper promoter of such an action. The prosecutors of the Claimant have concern with the perjury of LUIE—a material witness for the Defence—but not with LUIE for having a plurality of wives. If the Crown was concerned in this imbroglio, the worse for its representatives.

The ticket-of-leave shortens punishment to the *detenue* held to deserve the concession; but it leaves him exposed to future bitter consequences—he must from time to time report himself at a police-office, and for most offences may be thrust out from society to his old experience of penal severities. Accused, the whole feeling of a criminal court is likely to be against him; and how the police can act in cases *ex voluntate*, or is earwigged by chums and others, we can guess where we do not know contemporary facts. But reverting to the case under notice, if I hold a constitutional doctrine to have been invaded, I would question the soundness of the ticket-of-leave system, so apt to become illusory in the hands of public justice. Agreeably to the Bill of Rights—our more recent Magna Charta—the citizen is protected from "all barbarous and unusual punishments," which, however, could hardly have been applied in the case of the horrid press-yard of Newgate, where the accused might have been put to the torture till he pleaded guilty or not guilty—an enormity but recently abolished, I believe, by one of Mr. PEEL's bills. Now imprisonment with hard labour is not a barbarous, and certainly not an "unusual punishment." But it is, our legal code being witness, "unusual" to punish a man for a crime unproved by law, and which the law is but engaged in investigating initially. This is the state of the case as respects the ex-convict LUIE.

I do not intend to go over the case of the Claimant, now so far settled by a criminal court—if the result may divide opinion, and circumstances may well do so. Were disquisition expedient, I might advert to hypotheses hurled against the convict, as those about the loss of language, and his repudiating, as it were, rank and property. I might also censure the condemnation improperly launched from the Bench against Dr. KENEALY, the able, faithful, indefatigable Counsel of the accused. It has been said that here the quarrels betwixt the Lord Chief Justice and that great barrister could not have occurred. But under the (divisional) sway of Lord Justice CLERK JOHN HOPE such contendings might have occurred, and the *Scotsman* was besieged with letters complaining of the conduct of that judge. However, I wish to notice how twice the claimant was refused permission to speak in court. This was an exercise of high-handed severity. If the accused might have had more Counsel than one at bar, why might he not have been one for himself as it were, if some say that he who conducts his own cause in court has a "fool for his client." The party principally concerned might say something more effective than his advocate. But chiefly would I condemn the harsh refusal to allow the man to speak after verdict. BURKE, the West Port murderer, in the same situation, asked leave to address the Court, and the venerable Lord Justice CLERK BOYLE replied that he saw nothing to hinder him. Supposing the claimant guilty, as alleged, he was severely treated, as a thief may be robbed. Vile as the man represented his conduct in the case of Lady Radcliffe, I do not see that the Court was bound to avenge her cause. That was her own look out.—I am, &c.,

S.

The present impression contains two portraits—one of ALFRED TICHBORNE, Sir ROGER's younger brother, when a child: the other is the copy photograph of HENRIETTE FELICITE, the youngest daughter of Sir ROGER. Great judges of physiognomy pronounce the features of both to be wonderfully alike. See pp. 305, 313.

The letters that follow represent the antagonistic views on the vexed subject of JEAN LUIE.

MR. ONSLOW, M.P., ON LUIE.

SIR,—When I had the pleasure of addressing my Guildford friends, on the 16th of December, I much regret I had not time to give them my version regarding the individual "JEAN LUIE," especially as my name has been connected with his in the TICHBORNE Trial; I shall, therefore, be extremely obliged if you will give publication to this letter in your next journal. The following is entirely my own theory, and, therefore, your readers can take it for what it is worth.

Several days after JEAN LUIE had appeared on the scene, and had acknowledged the Claimant as the man he had saved from the "Bella," I went up to London, and for the first time in my life I heard of this man, "JEAN LUIE," and his story. Some days after, I happened to call in at 2, Poets-corner, the office of the Claimant's Solicitor in Westminster, and there I saw the man whom I was told was "JEAN LUIE," the steward of the "Osprey." I had several conversations with him, but always in the presence of other people, and I subjected him to a close and searching examination.

He told me so many things I knew to be true, and replied to all the questions I put to him, that I became, like the Lord Chief Justice, much inclined to believe in him. The Claimant also believed in him for the same reasons, but always declared, *by word of mouth and in writing, that he never recognized him.* I heard from Mr. WHALLEY and Mr. O'BRIEN, that the Claimant never acknowledged him, that is, recognized him as the steward of the "Osprey." Time went on, and JEAN LUIE was called by Dr. KENEALY, when one of the solicitors *for the Prosecution* was distinctly heard to say in Court, "We have won the case."

JEAN LUIE came out of the witness-box, after having been complimented by the Lord Chief Justice for the straightforward manner in which he gave his evidence. (Here I may remark the curious coincidence that JEAN LUIE's cross-examination took but a short time, although if his evidence was believed the Claimant had won his case, whilst the cross-examination of Mr. BAIGENT, in the first Trial, took nearly as long as the Claimant himself).

JEAN LUIE came out of the witness-box in the forenoon of Friday, and called at the Solicitors' office, 2, Poets-corner, where I met him by chance. I immediately asked what he was going to do. He instantly said, "Why, to go home to America." I commended his intention, and said, "Don't lose a moment; take the train to-day at five o'clock, for Southampton; there is, I hear, a steamer that sails for New York to-morrow. Do you go by that, as no one can tell how soon this Trial may be over. Find out your friends, ANDERSON, the mate of the "Osprey," and HARRY, the sailmaker, and bring them over to this country at once, and telegraph to me, 'Found so many.' Here is a check on my banker for £5." To all this he assented, and Mr. WHALLEY, who was present, gave him another £5, and the Claimant promised to give him £20. I then wrote him a letter of introduction to Mr. GREY, of the Docks of Southampton, begging that gentleman to facilitate his voyage to America on the following day. Now, assuming for a moment that JEAN LUIE was a plant of the Claimant's, would he not have instantly started for America? and the case was won for the Claimant; for no power on earth could then have convicted him. But what did this man do? He took our money and, according to Mr. CLARKE's, the detective's diary, he went straight to Scotland-yard, and offered to "liquor up" with CLARKE and WHICHER on the event, and added, "What fools they are to believe me!" This evidence was wrung out of CLARKE, the detective officer, by that clever solicitor, Mr. LEWIS, at Bow-street, and immediately attracted the attention of the magistrate, Sir THOMAS HENRY, who instantly said to the clerk of the Court in Bow-street Police-office "*Take special note of that.*"

So here we have this JEAN LUIE, the most important witness for the Defence, instead of acting under the advice of the Defendant, he goes into Scotland-yard, *into the teeth of the detective officers and police*, whose business it was to have known he was a ticket-of-leave man, and proffering his offer of "liquoring up" in a semi-drunken state, expressing his surprise at having been believed; and yet not one word of this is re-reported to the Judges, and never would have been known to the world had it not been wormed out of CLARKE, the head of the Detective Department in Scotland-yard, whose duty it was to have reported it at Bow-street Police-office himself.

JEAN LUIE was tried at the Old Bailey, and condemned to seven years' penal servitude for perjury. How was it, I ask that this special note, made by Sir THOMAS HENRY, and to which so much importance was attached, was not forthcoming, and why did Judge BRETT (the same Judge that refused to accept bail for the Claimant in the first Trial) why did he recommend JEAN LUIE not to call the Claimant as a witness when he wished to do so?

JEAN LUIE stated *absolute truths.* All about the "Osprey" was true, down to a pot of tamarind jam on her decks; he gave her real history. She did sail from New York, FUNCKE, MEINS and Co. were her brokers, Baron FALKENBERG was her proprietor, this was all found out by Mr. WHALLEY, in America. The question arises, How came LUIE, a convict, to know all this? Why, he was coached; he was *a trap baited with truth*, which the Claimant was bound to fall into, and when his name was called out in Court, it caused the solicitor to forget himself, and say, "We have won the case!" That same solicitor, on the Monday following, was met by one of the witnesses for the Defence in Winchester, and the witness said, "Well, what do think of your LUIE's evidence?" The reply was, "Oh, nothing; we shall prove him a convict."

Yes, they all knew about JEAN LUIE; he was the plant of the Prosecution. Some one not difficult to name found out all about the "Osprey" and the saving of the "Bella" in Australia, and coached JEAN LUIE to carry the trap to the poor unfortunate Claimant, into which he fell and lost his case.

How come it, I should ask, that this convict LUNDGREN came to change his name from JEAN LUIE, but to fit it with OWEN LEWIS or LEWIS OWEN? How came it he was not known to the police, in the four months before he was called by Dr. KENEALY, he being only just out of Chatham Prison; and how came it, if it were his own invention, or the plant of the Claimant, that he did not go at once to America, and then drain a fortune from Sir ROGER TICHBORNE?

There was a person deeply interested in the Case for the Prosecution, who attended the court daily, and took a prominent part in the Case on both Trials: how came it that he disappeared from the scene when JEAN LUIE appeared upon it, and how is it that that person has never been heard of since?

There has been a great deal said about the Claimant accosting JEAN LUIE with "*Como esta* LUIE?" but the fact related by those *who were present* at the interview was, that the Claimant, towards the close, and not at the beginning, said, "*Como esta* LUIE?" to test his knowledge of Spanish, as the man who saved him spoke that language.

The whole history of this man JEAN LUIE points to the conclusion I have arrived at: that he was the *plant of the Prosecution*: and as they found they could not convict the Claimant by fair means, they tried foul, and the villain that carried the trap, baited with truth, to the Claimant, is in prison, and the biter bit, and thus the case was lost.—Your obedient servant,

Dec. 21, 1873. GUILDFORD ONSLOW

MR. WHALLEY, M.P., ON LUIE.

SIR,—As my friend Mr. ONSLOW has made known, through your columns, his theory as to JEAN LUIE, it may be expected, and you will at all events perhaps permit me to state mine—mixed up as I have so specially been with that witness. JEAN LUIE is but a common instance of the fate which attends those who deviate in any respect from the truth, viz.:—to be wholly disbelieved, even when he speaks truly.

He told the Court, as he himself very plainly suggested in his first examination, a "pack of lies" as to his antecedents, but he did not fail to suggest that his being thus called upon to disclose such antecedents might, in his view, justify him in such concealment or misrepresentation.

Beyond the possibility of a doubt, to my mind, JEAN LUIE *was* the steward of the "Osprey," and was in that ship when it picked up the wreck-boat of the "Bella,"—and of this I was prepared to give proof within my own knowledge, when examined as a witness on his trial, had I not been prevented from doing so by Mr. Justice BRETT.

On the conduct of that Judge on that occasion I abstain from comment here, because I have already brought the same to the notice of the Secretary of State for the Home Department, and he has sent my letter to Mr. Justice BRETT, with the usual understanding, that a letter so sent demanded a reply. No such reply has been given, and I need not further refer to it, than to say that the trial of JEAN LUIE, so far as Mr. Justice BRETT was concerned, was, if possible, a greater scandal to the administration of Justice than that of the Claimant himself, and that I look forward in the public interest to have the opportunity of justifying this statement, as well in respect of the one trial as of the other.

When Mr. ONSLOW states that the Claimant did not recognize and, to the utmost possible extent, admit and assert that JEAN LUIE was the man who attended him when on board the "Osprey," he endeavoured—as it seems to me needlessly—to exonerate the Claimant from responsibility for what he deems to be "a plant." I know that the Claimant did, in the most emphatic manner, declare that JEAN LUIE's account of what occurred on board the "Osprey" was true,—that it was absolutely impossible that any man could have known what LUIE recounted of the "Osprey" and her doings, but one who had been there; and though I will not so positively assert that the Claimant did expressly recognize the features of the man, it is not possible for me to forget that the Claimant assured me, when I revisited him in the evening of the day on which he first saw LUIE, that he was undoubtedly the man who nursed him while ill with sunstroke, on his voyage in the "Osprey," to Melbourne.

I also take this opportunity of saying that a more truthful man than the Claimant, in regard to his identification of witnesses, or anyone more careful not to accept any testimony on his behalf that had the slightest tinge of being invented or even exaggerated, it would not be possible to imagine; many witnesses that would have passed well through cross-examination having been, to my knowledge, rejected and repudiated by him on account of some undue zeal exhibited by them on his behalf.

It may be, as Mr. ONSLOW states, that after LUIE's exposure as a ticket-of-leave man, the Claimant might have given way to the general feeling of repugnance against the man and have persuaded himself that he was "a plant."

The Claimant was himself always regarded by me as "eccentric" to a degree that, long before the close of the proceedings, prevented my holding any intercourse with him, and as this was very satisfactorily explained by medical men as the possible and probable results of a severe sunstroke, it ought to be accepted as at least a possible explanation of his whole career from the day he was landed in Melbourne, till he disappeared from public view within the walls of Millbank,—the victim of Jesuitism and the scandal of British Justice; but if he did repudiate LUIE thus, it would not alter the facts ascertained by myself in New York, or diminish by one iota the cumulative evidence that I believe could be brought forward—if for such a purpose there yet remains in England a fair Tribunal to prove the truth of his story about the "Osprey."

I will not further trespass on your space now; but if my friend Mr. ONSLOW, with whom I can cordially agree to differ on this subject, desires to pursue the discussion, I shall be ready to reply by facts and arguments which will, I believe, ultimately satisfy himself that LUIE was not "a plant" by the police.

How it could happen that a ticket-of-leave man could have been for near six months in and about the Court, attending public meetings and otherwise, as notorious as JEAN LUIE, without being recognized and apprehended as such, or, at all events, cross-examined, is, I fully admit, utterly beyond my power of comprehension or explanation. It was from my knowledge of the fact that the witnesses of the Claimant were one and all well-known to the police long before they appeared, and that in many instances they were subjected to temptations, such as bribery; in others to threats and other inducements—in one case, ending in suicide—and in very many others in their absconding, or refusing to give evidence—induced me to certify that JEAN LUIE was as deserving from me of good words as from the Lord Chief Justice; and is the *one* mystery to me in this case how it happened that he was not cross-examined effectively.—I am, Sir, your obedient servant,

G. H. WHALLEY.

NOTE.

Soon after Dr. KENEALY was returned to Parliament, a Mr. EVELYN ASHLEY, M.P. for Poole, accused Dr. KENEALY of having put LUIE into the box, knowing him to be a False Witness. Dr. KENEALY brought the matter before the House on Thursday, March 4th, 1875, but obtained no redress. See *Englishman*, No. 49. The following correspondence was the result.

Dr. KENEALY to Mr. M'MAHON, his Junior in the TICHBORNE Case:—

March 4, 1875.

MY DEAR M'MAHON,—ASHLEY, to-night, in the House, intimated that you were guilty of the baseness, falsehood, and treachery of conveying to *his* mind that I called LUIE, knowing him to be a false witness. I think this places you in a most odious position before the world; because *you know* that both KARSLAKE and WEBB took on themselves the responsibility of vouching for him as a truthful witness, and told us so distinctly. I must hear from you on this without delay. It is a fearful imputation on you.—Yours truly, E. V. K.

To this letter Mr. M'MAHON never sent any reply; so we suppose he is guilty.

MR. GUILDFORD ONSLOW TO MR. ASHLEY.

The Grove, Ropley: March 6th, 1875.

MY DEAR MR. ASHLEY,—As an act of common justice to my friend Dr. KENEALY, seeing, as I do, that your charge against him emanated from conviction on your mind, I feel bound to tell you the exact truth of the matter in question. Dr. KENEALY never set eyes on JEAN LUIE in his lifetime until he called him as a witness in the Court of Queen's Bench, on the TICHBORNE Trial. It was only by the advice of two of the most eminent Counsel (not engaged in the Case), who had cross-examined JEAN LUIE, together with the earnest request of Lord RIVERS and myself, that Dr. KENEALY consented to put him in the box. My friend Sir ROGER TICHBORNE admitted, that while every word JEAN LUIE said was perfectly correct, and therefore he wished him to be called, *he did not recognize his personal appearance as the man who saved him*; and I do not hesitate to say, from all I can learn, that JEAN LUIE was a plant got up by someone interested against the Claimant—that he acted as a trap baited with absolute truth, into which the unfortunate Claimant was bound to fall. A gentleman was sitting near one of the solicitors for the *Prosecution* when Dr. KENEALY called JEAN LUIE, and he was seen and heard to slap his knee with joy, and say, "Now we have won the case, because we shall prove him a convict." The same solicitor met a friend of mine within a few hours afterwards, and said, "We shall prove JEAN LUIE to be a convict," thereby showing they well knew who he was: a convict and a plant. Had he been an accomplice of the Claimant's, or a rogue on his own account, would he not too gladly have taken our money and proceeded immediately to America, and thus have won the case, and made his fortune? Instead of which, he left the Court—complimented by the Judge—for Scotland-yard, where he was well known, and went at once to Detectives WHICHER and CLARKE, as they stated, "to liquor up," and said "What fools they are to believe in me!" and the officers neglected to inform the Lord Chief Justice of this occurrence—proved at Bow-street.

If ever there was a man in this world who was less to blame, or more innocent of the charges you have brought against him, *it is* Dr. KENEALY; and I know him to be one of the most truthful and honest gentlemen in England, and well worthy of an ample apology on your part.

Please excuse the liberty I have taken in presuming on our short but agreeable acquaintance at Guildford in 1869, and believe me, my dear Mr. ASHLEY,—Yours faithfully,

GUILDFORD ONSLOW.

The Hon. EVELYN ASHLEY, M.P.

MR. WHALLEY, M.P., ON JEAN LUIE.

TO THE EDITOR OF THE "ENGLISHMAN."

SIR,— I was, unfortunately, absent when the discussion on Mr. ASHLEY'S proceedings at Ryde took place, and shall feel obliged by your allowing me to state in your columns the testimony which, if present, I should have given as to your action in relation to the witness LUIE.

Mr. ASHLEY, it appears, imputed to you that, knowing that LUIE was not the steward of the "Osprey," and that his story as to the rescue of the "Bella" men was a fabrication, you nevertheless put him into the witness-box.

If anyone is responsible for LUIE being called as a witness it is myself; and I am prepared to justify that step whenever the opportunity may occur; but, as well with respect to LUIE as to every other witness called by you, I know of nothing more remarkable in the TICHBORNE Trial than the extraordinary efforts made by you to test the integrity and truth of every single witness, before you would permit him to be called.

This precaution, which to myself and others appeared to be carried to excess, is the main exception that the friends of the Defendant took to your conduct of the Case, and, as I remember with pain, greatly added, by the differences of opinion thence arising, to the difficulties and labour you had to meet throughout the Trial.

It was my opinion that LUIE should have been the first witness called, being firmly convinced, as was everyone else except the Junior Counsel, that his story of the "Osprey" was true; and it was owing to my insisting so strongly on this course that I felt called upon to accede to the request to visit America.

The result of that visit, as my report tendered to the Government shows, was to confirm the opinion that he should, without an hour's delay, be called as a witness; and, as you are also aware, nothing has occurred to shake in the slightest degree my belief that he was the steward of the "Osprey," and did take part in saving ROGER TICHBORNE from the wreck-boat of the "Bella."

The Trial of LUIE for this perjury was, if possible, a more gross outrage than even that of TICHBORNE; and I am convinced that the result of any inquiry would be to release not only TICHBORNE, but also LUIE and BROWN, for all these cases stand together, and ROGER TICHBORNE, if saved, must have been so as stated by LUIE and declared by himself.

In a letter addressed by me to the Home Office, I so charged Mr. Justice BRETT with deliberate partiality and injustice as to place in issue, on the one hand my own position as a magistrate for three counties, deputy-lieutenant, &c. &c., and his fitness as a Judge in the Superior Courts; and this letter, being forwarded to him, he has not replied to.

Had LUIE been fairly tried, I have not a doubt he would have been acquitted; and as this would have at once reopened the whole TICHBORNE Case, it was a vital point with the TICHBORNE prosecutors to convict both LUIE and BROWN; and hence the scandal of the Trial over which Mr. Justice BRETT presided.

This will be, if at all, a remote episode in the renewed inquiry which the public mind is, I trust, steadily maturing up to a firm and irrevocable determination; but meanwhile it is desirable to clear away the mist through which the *educated* classes view this question, by giving them the benefit of accurate information as to those "parrot cries" with which they go about, deluding themselves and others; and by your most judicious and manly course in relation to Mr. ASHLEY you have done much to save others from exhibiting themselves in public under the like ridiculous aspect.—I am, yours, &c.,

Plas Madoc: 7th March, 1875. G. H. WHALLEY.

We have now brought our Introduction to the TICHBORNE Trial to a close, and shall simply supplement it by republishing a short pamphlet written at the time by two most accomplished persons; one of whom had devoted no less than two months to the drawings from life, taken day by day from the Claimant's face, which appear in the large sheet published with this number. The title of the Pamphlet, was "TICHBORNE OR ORTON." It can now be had at the ENGLISHMAN Office. The large sheet, which is a splendid lithographic plate, should be had with this number.

"THE 'CRUCIAL TEST' TESTED."

This pamphlet and its accompanying drawings originated through its authors having seen, in October last (1873), similar drawings, with explanatory letterpress, by an artist who proposed photography as a crucial test in cases of disputed identity, he having then in view its especial application to the embarrassing Trial at that time proceeding in the Court of Queen's Bench. The immediate publication of the "Crucial Test" had been announced, not only by public advertisements, but on the cover of the circular of its intending publisher, with an illustrative example of the eyes. This publication was restrained by the legal advisers for the Defence, not, however, before the said drawings had been shown to many persons in the artist's studio, and one, if not more, or several copies had got into private circulation. We had the good fortune to become possessed of a copy whilst, as a matter of scientific curiosity, we were ourselves examining the reliability of the photographic test. At a very early stage of our investigations, having discovered that there was inaccuracy somewhere, we procured various new photographs. For these we are indebted to the kind assistance and liberality of the well-known photographer, Mr. MAULL, Piccadilly. We are not aware to what extent the drawings referred to were circulated, and the effect they might have produced upon the minds of those favoured with an inspection of them. We felt the question to be of serious import, because it might affect human interest hereafter in the cause of justice and truth. So we pursued our investigations, and concluded that the deductions in the pamphlet were based upon erroneous premises.

The author, in his pamphlet "The Crucial Test" speaks of "dissimilarities" as the first points to be observed. But we would suggest that to take either "similarities" or "dissimilarities" for a starting point on occasions like the present, would not be likely to keep the mind of the investigator entirely free from bias. The correct method for mathematically testing a supposed likeness between two pictures is, to take ascertained proportions as the basis. Should the proportions for length prove totally different, there would be no necessity to proceed further. Assuming them correct, you should examine the outlines, and look for "dissimilarities." Should any be found, it may fairly be taken into consideration whether they may not be the natural result of circumstances, such as lapse of time, difference of size, disease, accident, or mode of life. Should the result be satisfactory, pass on to similarities, and if these can be proved to exist, then, and not till then, it may be assumed that the likeness also exists.

These investigations have been submitted to the criticism of the well-known and talented artist, Mr. F. HAVILL, of "The Willows," Kensington, who has compared the measurements, and pronounced them to be correct; and, as truth can be the only object in view, we do not hesitate to lay before the public "The 'Crucial Test' Tested." *

Now let us proceed to criticize separately the pamphleteer's remarks upon the features; we will comment upon our own illustrations, and append quotations from eminent medical men confirming our views.

EARS.

The enlarged "left ear" marked "Chili," and given as an example by the Author of "The Crucial Test," is contrasted by him with an ear copied from a photograph by Mr. MAULL. These respective ears are not enlarged to the same focus. The "Chili" ear is attached to a face which shows a three-quarter front, and is foreshortened,—presenting, therefore, no fair contrast to the ear in the other picture, which ear, being attached to a face much further inclined to profile, presents nearly its broadside to the beholder, causing the "Chili" ear to appear narrow by comparison. It should also be noted that the artist appears to have misunderstood the angular effect caused by the way in which the hair falls over the youthful ear.

We now direct the attention of the reader to the examples given in our accompanying illustrations on Plate II. Observe the lines drawn from *A* to *A*, which in each instance cut the top of the ear and the base, that is, where the lobe is attached to the cheek; also the lines *B* to *B* from the outer corner of the eye to just above the commencement of the helix around the outer rim of the ear; also the lines *D D* and *E E*. It will be found that all these measurements are the same, allowing for a slight increase or breadth to the rim of the English ear, which is proper to greater age, as *C*. We would call attention to the similarity in the upper parts of the ears, and particularly in the points of the left ear.

On the subject of the lobes we quote the great authority of the late Dr. CONOLLY, of Hanwell, and M. FOVILLE, chief physician to the asylum of Charenton. Allied with different brain disorders, such as epilepsy, paralysis, *sunstroke*, &c., there is a known alteration in the form of the ear. This consists of general inflammation, and slow enlargement by thickness and effusion. In some instances, flattening or thickening of the ears, and disproportionate enlargement and *pendulosity* of the lobes are strikingly noticeable. This disfigurement in its origin being dependent upon the brain, is frequently accompanied by a weakness of the mental faculties. For instance, should the brain become deteriorated in quality from any exciting causes, such as the abuse of alcoholic beverages, or tobacco in excess, the inward defection will begin to show itself by some outward sign, the gradual enlargement of the lobes already mentioned being not uncommon, as M. FOVILLE first discovered. If the exciting causes be not removed, the enlargement will grow into a deformity, the faculties of the mind, at the same time, continuing to deteriorate. The hair is also affected through the agency of the brain, heavy, smooth masses being a common characteristic of the melancholy temperament, whilst the more mercurial spirit induces a corresponding tendency in the hair to lie lightly.

* Copies of the Chili daguerreotypes were obtained from Mr. SAVAGE, of Winchester; and the English photographs, and the life-size enlargements of both, were taken by Messrs. MAULL and Co., 187A, Piccadilly.

EYES.

The original Chili daguerreotype represents ROGER TICHBORNE with his eyes almost entirely open, and slightly shifted. The Birmingham photograph, used by the author of the "Test" as a contrast, represents the eyes partially closed, and slightly lowered. To meet this difference in position, he has dropped the "Chili" eyelids; but observe that the outer corners of the eyes are retained in their original position, although the action of the levator, or muscle that raises the lid, would be relaxed.

Dissimilarities.—If the reader turns to our examples of eyes, given on page 1 of plate III., the dissimilarity to be noticed appears to lie in those very outer corners, those in the English photograph drooping, whilst those in the other are slightly raised. The "Chili" picture represents a young man full of vigour; consequently, the muscles of the face are firm, the angles of the features are raised, and the eyebrows inclined to an arch. In more advanced life the muscles would become relaxed and enfeebled, and cause a depression of the features, more noticeable in some cases than in others, perhaps, but in all perceptible, and occasionally exaggerated by the enervating consequences of a reckless life, or the undue use of stimulants.

By drawing lines through the outer and inner corners of the eyes, as from *a a*, we perceive that in our "Chili" example they form an angle by joining at the root of the nose, whilst in our English example, No. 1, they present a straight line, and in No. 2 another distinct angle. Hence we may fairly assume that these eyes were raised at the corners in youth, as, had they been originally straight, they would now be depressed by the relaxing of the muscles. In No. 2 the eyes are drawn as they appear when in repose, or under the dreamy influence of the cigar. Note here the effect of the orbicularis muscle, *b* and *c*, upon the eyelid when enfeebled and relaxed. Observe also that the eyeball appears smaller by the drooping of the eyelid over the outer corner, which thus would seem to be placed lower down in the face. In the "Chili" eyelids is seen a marked tendency to droop at the corners, although the eyeball is raised.

SIR ROGER'S YOUNGEST DAUGHTER (IN WHOM "BELLE TÊTE" IS REVIVED).

On page 2, plate III., we give an example of three distinct expressions, taken from the eyes of a sitter, who was at the time engaged by the artist in conversation, for the purpose of noting the changes that might occur through the action of the muscles.

Similarities.—The width of the foreheads and their shape as on plate I. The length of the eyeballs, and the distance between the eyes. The marked angles between the eyebrows as *(f)*, narrowed in the elder man by reason of the drawing together and uplifting of the corrugator muscle, the natural consequence of added years and mental anxiety, but still quite visible. There is also the lengthened sweep of the upper eyelids towards the nose, and the very peculiar form of the eyebrows, especially at the outer corners, as *(e)*. That the habit of taking stimulants has such an effect upon the brain as to influence the muscles of the eyes is supported by the highest authority, Sir CHARLES BELL, who says "that the voluntary muscles of the eyeball resign their action to the oblique muscles, which instinctively revolve the eye upward. At the same time the muscle which elevates the upper lid yields, in sympathy with the oblique muscles, to the action of the orbicularis, which closes the eyes, and the lids droop. This sometimes causes a puzzled expression, from the forcible elevation of the eyebrow to counteract the dropping of the upper eyelid, when yielding to the paralyzing influences of tobacco and stimulants."

NOSE.

In the "Crucial Test" attention is called to the difference of the nose in the two pictures; but the artist has omitted to mark the sharply defined curve and flatness at the end of the nose, everywhere observable in the English photographs.

Dissimilarities.—Turning to plate I. By measurement we perceive an increase of breadth in the middle of the end of the nose *g* at forty-five, as compared with that of the younger man. The narrowness and elevation of the nostrils in our English photograph as contrasted with the width and sweep of the nostril in the Chili daguerreotype.

The first point hardly requires comment, as it is the natural accompaniment of years. The second may be accounted for in various ways, which cannot fairly be overlooked. For instance, ROGER TICHBORNE was constantly widening or dilating his nostrils by playing wind instruments; and, were such practice discontinued, the nostrils would in after life resume their natural dimensions. Also, we must remember that extreme fat will press the nostrils together. There is another and unusual reason for this difference, which consists in an ascertained injury to the part of the nose (*h*), which has been broken, and new bone thrown out, according to Sir WILLIAM FERGUSSON. This would have the permanent effect of tightening the skin, and so drawing up the nostrils, naturally causing them to appear narrower than before. That such an accident should have so slightly altered the natural configuration is almost a miracle, as any one may satisfy themselves by looking at the plates of that organ to be seen in popular works on physiology and human anatomy. Neither must it be forgotten, that in addition to such a serious accident, the constant habit of jerking up the skin and muscles of the brow and forehead, would, with the advance of years, materially tend to retract the nostrils upwards, and thus alter, to a considerable extent, the youthful configuration. In fact, a cursory inspection of an anatomical plate, displaying all the minute muscles of the face, would show that it is wonderful that the jerking of brows has not wrought greater changes in the expression.

Similarities.—The peculiarity of the curved form of the rather flat end of the nose, which in both instances presents the appearance of an arc, thus ‿. The shape of the nostrils in both cases is angular, but the injury to the nose has caused the angle to appear more acute in the case of the elder man. The length of the nose is the same in both cases.

MOUTHS AND CHINS.

The example given in the "Crucial Test" from the Chili picture shows the mouth closed, whilst the mouth in the other is open. By this accident the shape and expression of the latter is changed, and the distance between the lips and the nose is slightly altered.

Dissimilarities.—In our English picture we perceive a narrow and well-defined groove perpendicular from the middle of the nose to the mouth (*i*), whereas in the youthful face there is the ordinary delicately articulated mark. A contracted or pinched look of the former mouth, whilst the latter presents a flowing curve. A hole or dimple in the chin of the elder man, whilst in that of the younger there is but a slight shade (*k*).

The Author of the "Crucial Test," in giving illustrations of his own mouth at different periods of life, distinctly says: "The only alteration is on the left side of the lower lip, which is slightly altered and the line straightened, but this is a speciality in my own case, and is accounted for by a dragging of the muscles at the corner of the mouth, the result of a spinal accident nine years ago." Thus he admits that the appearance of a feature is capable of being altered by accident, that such an alteration may remain after several years, and that the muscles act upon the features. These are truisms we must not forget. Not only would the drawing up of the nostrils by an injury have a tightening effect upon the part immediately below, but the known loss of three front teeth in the elder man readily accounts for the contraction both of the groove and of the upper lip. The remarks made previously as to the effect of playing wind instruments might also apply here, as such practice invariably produces distension, that is, flattening and widening the centre of the lip. Discontinue the practice and contraction will follow.

Similarities.—The curve of the upper lip, the well-defined under lip, and the holes at the corners of each mouth, see Plate I.

The distances from the end of the nose to the centre of the upper lip, again from the centre of the upper lip to the bottom of the lower lip, and from thence to the bottom of the chin are the same. In taking these measurements on the English picture, we must remember that fat causes deeper indentations, and therefore deeper shadows, causing the light to appear smaller. It is right, therefore, to measure a little within the outer edge of such shadows (*l*).

On Plate IV. we have given circle (*o*) within circle (*n*), to show that the actual difference in the width of the grooves below the nose is small, and may be fairly attributed to the causes previously assigned. The mouth has also an inclination to open slightly, or to be drawn up in the centre by the straightening of the muscles. Here let it be noted that the triangularis muscle (*m* Plate I. and those immediately connected with it, being not only enfeebled by years and the cares which years bring with them, but also weighted with fat, would exercise a very considerable influence in drawing down the corners of the mouth. In respect to the dimple, observe carefully the heavy form of chin, as shown in the Chili picture, Plate I. The reader will perceive a slight shade or compression in the centre, which is caused by the adhesion of the muscle to the bone. It can be easily understood that this, amidst surrounding fat, would become more strongly marked.

On page 1 of Plate IV., we give in outline the features of ROGER TICHBORNE, from the Chili daguerreotype, showing the result of deepening the lines of the shadows, increasing the breadth of the cheek, and adding wrinkles below and around the eyes.

We would observe that, although the author of the "Crucial Test" has pointed out every apparent, though not real, discrepancy between the English and Chili pictures, *he has omitted to notice many points of similarity.*

SHOULDERS.

On page 2 of Plate IV. we have placed outlines of two smaller photographs *in the same focus*, for the purpose of showing the corresponding *width of the shoulders.* Taking the artistic rule of measurement, that the length of the whole face is equal to that of three times the nose, and the width from shoulder to shoulder equal to twice the length of the face, or three times the width of the skull, it will be evident that instead of ROGER TICHBORNE's shoulders being narrow, they were in fact, broad. In this example, the artist has placed the Chili ear upon the English outline, for the purpose of showing the size of the head.

THE MALFORMED THUMB.

The drawing of the "Chili" *thumb*, given on page 2 of Plate IV., is enlarged from the photograph copied by Mr. SAVAGE in 1868 from one taken by MAYALL from the original daguerreotype.—This thumb, as well as the Paris example, is drawn on a larger scale than the tracing taken from the recent photograph. It will be seen that the nail is in character the same as that in the Paris and English examples. An unusual distance is apparent between the nail and the end of the thumb, and the thumb itself is different in shape from that on the right hand.

In conclusion, the authors of this pamphlet *seriously invite the most earnest attention of scientific artists to the suggestion of the Photographic Test.* This, when honestly worked out in mathematical detail, may be found to be a satisfactory and reliable test of identity, in this, as well as in all similar instances in respect of which there might be any dispute or question.

NOTE.

We must add that, for the thorough understanding of this most able, argumentative, and conclusive Pamphlet (of which we wish that we could give the writers' names), a study of the large and beautiful Lithographic Plate is absolutely essential.

This admirable pamphlet was made the subject of a review and a letter that appeared in the *Morning Advertiser* of April 2, 1874, and April 10, 1874. We reprint both here.

THE PHOTOGRAPHIC TEST APPLIED TO THE TICHBORNE CASE.*

A REVIEW AND LETTER REPRINTED FROM THE "MORNING ADVERTISER" OF APRIL 2ND AND 10TH.

There is a scarcely suspected danger in absolute reliance upon photography as a means of identification. The obvious value of a sun picture as a means of recognizing and verifying individuals, and the unprejudiced trustworthiness of a "mirror with a memory," as the photograph has been phrased, may easily lead to obliviousness of the limits of that trustworthiness, and to the conditions which surround it. Photography, with a natural inclination to the truth, can be made to lie. A frame of twenty portraits, exhibited some time ago by a Berlin artist, strikingly illustrated this. The head was that of a pretty girl photographed under twenty varying conditions of light, position, *entourage*, and expression, giving a presentation of twenty different persons, of whom at least half appeared so diverse in every way from each other, that it would have been impossible to identify them as portraits of the same person. The camera was truthful in recording that which was presented to it, but the varied conditions presented entirely different images to the lens, which hence produced entirely different pictures. Either sinister design or accidental conditions may so mar the accuracy of the autotypic presentment of the camera, that recognition may be rendered difficult and doubtful, and absolute indentification impossible. But whilst modifications in the light and shadow, the expression, and the make-up may thus militate against familiar likeness, and may not be anything like aids to recognition, there are certain other qualities inherent in the photograph which remain unchanged in varying conditions, and are of importance, in conjunction with other evidence, in establishing identity. The expression of a face may vary, but its contour will remain the same. The eye may be made light or dark in the photograph, at the will of the photographer; but the shape of the eye, the size, the position, the character of the eyebrow, will (unless fraudulently modified) within certain limits, retain the same character in all photographs of the same face. So with the ears, nose, mouth, and chin; whilst easily capable of modification in detail sufficient to destroy familiar likeness, they will retain certain specific elements of form, size, and proportion, which, on submission to suitable tests, possess almost overwhelming weight in establishing or disproving identity.

Viewed in this aspect, the pamphlet just issued, on the application of the photographic test to the Claimant to the Tichborne estates, possesses an especial interest. During the course of the late Trial, one of the many amateur and volunteer advocates for the Prosecution, an artist, prepared a series of drawings from the Chili daguerreotypes of ROGER TICHBORNE, consisting of eyes, ears, and other features, on the scale of life, with similar drawings for comparison of recent portraits of the *soi-disant* ROGER then under trial. These drawings, with explanatory text, were intended for publication, the professed aim being the recommendation of the use of photography as a crucial test in cases of disputed identity. The especial object of the drawings was to illustrate dissimilarities between the features of the daguerreotypes of the undoubted ROGER and those of the Claimant. Produced by an artist whose skill was not inferior to his manifest bias against Dr. KENEALY's client, these drawings formed a practical argument of

* TICHBORNE or ORTON? The "Crucial Test" tested. By A. L. L. C. Being a review of the photographic test suggested in a recent pamphlet for use in cases of disputed identity.

no mean order for the Prosecution, and the artist knowing their tendency, evidently had no fear of committal for Contempt before his eyes in taking steps for their publication.

The legal advisers for the Defence took steps in time to prevent actual publication; but to what extent the drawings went into private circulation and what influence they had on the final result it is impossible to say. The writer of the pamphlet just issued having seen the drawings, arrived at the conviction that the legitimate conclusion to be deduced from an honest and discriminating comparison of all the points in the portraits was irresistibly in the favour of the Claimant, the cardinal qualities of the face in all the portraits being essentially the same, the variations to be found being not only such as might be produced by the various modifying conditions, but such as are the legitimate result of the known modifying circumstances in operation. The state of terror produced by the unprecedented committals for Contempt of Court—terrible whether strictly within the sanction of the English law and Constitution or not—having now subsided, the writer of the present pamphlet issues it as having an interest on the general tests for disputed identity, as well as on the TICHBORNE inquiry which as a question of abstract justice must continue to possess public interest, although it may have no influence on the fate of the Claimant.

The chief value of the pamphlet consists in the completeness of the illustrations, which present the whole of the Claimant's features in detail for comparison with the same features in detail taken from the Chilian daguerreotypes, and sagacious comments thereon pointing out similarities and dissimilarities, with their bearing on the question of identity.

In relation to the ears, for example, the pendent lobe, which, as compared with the Chilian portrait, was a strong point with the recent Prosecution, the similarity of form and measurement in the general structure are shown beyond a question, the pendent lobe alone forming a point of variation. As explanatory of the latter fact, we find that the late Dr. CONOLLY, of Hanwell, and Dr. FOVILLE, of Charenton, agree in indicating this pendulosity as one of the results of brain disorder, arising from sunstroke and other of the vicissitudes to which the Claimant has beyond a question been subject. Other features examined in detail afford similar argument, and demonstrate that if the refusal to admit the Defendant's claims to the TICHBORNE baronetcy rest on no better grounds than the alleged dissimilarity *au fond* between himself and the ROGER TICHBORNE whose Chilian daguerreotypes remained the only tangible aids to his identification, then the unfortunate Claimant, who has just commenced a term of imprisonment from which it is probable death alone will release him, *is the victim of terrible misfortune, if not absolute injustice.*

WHAT CONSTITUTES "CONTEMPT OF COURT" IN THE NINETEENTH CENTURY.

To THE EDITOR OF THE "MORNING ADVERTISER."

SIR,—In your able review of the "Crucial Test Tested," you make this pertinent suggestion, *à propos* of the illustrations to the pamphlet which it was intended to meet—"Produced by an artist whose skill was not inferior to his manifest bias against Dr. KENEALY'S client, these drawings formed a practical argument of no mean order for the Prosecution; and the artist knowing their tendency, evidently had no fear of committal for Contempt before his eyes in taking steps for their publication. The legal advisers for the Defence took steps in time to prevent actual publication; but to what extent the drawings went into circulation and what influence they had on the final result it is impossible to say." In this paragraph you have touched the vital point of the question, and we feel impelled to ask you to admit a more detailed account of the circumstances under which our pamphlet originated. The first intimation we had that such a "crucial test" was proposed was in the autumn of last year, when the artist voluntarily showed to casual visitors to his studio the life-sized negatives he had made from the Chili daguerreotype, and a Birmingham photograph of the Defendant. The artist also states in his text "that nothing that has been published gives anything but a misleading idea of the two beautiful daguerreotypes taken in Chili twenty years ago." It is evident, therefore, that he had had excess to the pictures actually at that time in the custody of the Court. Although it was pointed out to him that his negatives exhibited a striking likeness, notwithstanding the unsatisfactory character of the English one that had been used, the artist still adhered to his opinion that his "test" was conclusive, and pointed out what he considered unmistakable dissimilarities. At the same time, he made no secret of the fact that it was regarded with great favour at the Treasury, and also that correspondence had been exchanged between himself and the advisers to the Crown, who assured him that "the judges had examined, with very great care, his clever drawings, in which they took a deep interest, but the Court regretted that they had no power to compel the Defendant to sit for a photograph in the position he required." Visiting the artist's studio shortly afterwards, we found that he was on the eve of publishing the detailed drawings which he showed us. Having remonstrated with him on the unfair way in which his subjects were treated, we deemed it only right, in the interests of justice, that information should be given to the Defence. The publication was thereupon stopped, but not before a copy came into our possession. Notwithstanding the prohibition he was under, we are aware that the artist subsequently showed the negatives to many persons who visited his studio, making comments thereon, and denouncing the Claimant as a barefaced impostor. In the preface to the "Crucial Test," the pamphleteer suggests that it was set forth simply as a matter of scientific inquiry. We were, therefore, surprised that on the conclusion of the trial, the artist did not publish the 2,000 copies which he had acknowledged were ready printed. It would appear as though he were satisfied that the drawings had been used privately as incidental and collateral evidence. The artist also said that the Defendant "would not dare to submit himself to the life-size crucial test." Nevertheless, it is obvious that the Defendant was not reluctant to sit for ordinary photographs, as was proved by the numerous copies in every shop-window. Beyond this, we can with truth assert that on his being made acquainted with our desire of publishing drawings on a life-size scale, with the express object of meeting the other pamphlet when it should be published, the Defendant willingly submitted to several tedious sittings at Mr. MAULL'S studio, and to the most minute and searching investigations and measurements. It is also just to the Defendant to take this opportunity of saying, that whereas his enemies have described him as "coarse, brutal, and vulgar," our experience has been quite the reverse, and we have on all occasions found him most courteous, agreeable, and intelligent. It further appears to us a subject for inquiry, whether the power so freely exercised of committal for Contempt of Court did not tend to stifle much evidence which would have materially assisted in throwing light upon difficult parts of the Case, particularly upon the conflicting medical testimony, and which, in the desire for truthful investigation, ought, one would think, to have been welcome to both sides. We have always been of opinion that the Claimant was unfairly treated in being denied the last examination to which he willingly offered to submit, with a view to the corroboration of the medical evidence as to the marks on his person, &c. Fearing that we have already trespassed too largely on your space,—We are, sir, yours, &c.,

THE AUTHORS OF "THE CRUCIAL TEST TESTED."

In the ENGLISHMAN of May 28, 1871, the following criticism also appeared:—

THE PHOTOGRAPHIC TEST.

Two pamphlets on this subject have been recently published, one entitled "A Crucial Test in Cases of Disputed Identity," and the other "Tichborne or Orton? The Crucial Test Tested," bearing directly upon a question lately at issue in our Courts of law, and whilst professing to use the same method for discovering the identity or non-identity of the Claimant with ROGER TICHBORNE, shows forth totally opposite results. The author of "A Crucial Test" assumes a tone of decided partisanship in stating at once his opinion that the original of the Birmingham photograph used by him is "ARTHUR ORTON." He also states that "there is no portrait of ARTHUR ORTON extant in identically the same position as that of ROGER CHARLES TICHBORNE. Perhaps he has not seen the rival pamphlet, "TICHBORNE or ORTON," wherein the English drawings bear date 1873 and 1874, and are traced from photographs taken of the Claimant by Mr. MAULL, of Piccadilly. This work purports to be a review of the "Crucial Test," and from the quotations occurring in it we conclude that the letterpress of the original pamphlet (the publication of which during the Trial was stopped by the Defence) must have been different to that now accompanying the illustrations, although evidently manifesting the same bias.

We note with surprise that the author of "A Crucial Test" acknowledges having communicated with the Judges* on the subject; as we should have imagined that any attempt to influence their judgment would have been treated as Contempt of Court. It appears strange that a portrait painter, accustomed to depict the different phases of the human countenance, should ignore the wonderful mobility of the muscles of the face, and the changes that befall its complexion, tissue, and size, in the course of years, and through the action of those "various ills that flesh is heir to." It was hardly justifiable on the part of the artist to lower the eyes in the "Chili" portrait, in order to bring them nearer to a level with those in the English picture, at the same time retaining the elevated position of the outer corners of the eyelids; thus making the expression and even the drawing of the eyes unlike the daguerreotype. We have seen the English photograph used for comparison, and it is our opinion that, although the general effect of the face is given, the minor details of the features are passed over, the result being simply that of a clever, but rather coarse, caricature. This is an unfair way of treating a serious subject, involving truth or falsehood. Nothwithstanding, if the proportion for length, such as the width of the eyes, &c., are measured on the two drawings, with compasses, they will be found startlingly alike. The author of the "Crucial Test" has also apparently forgotten to notice the peculiar outline of the Defendant's left ear, as there is a marked difference between his drawing and the left ear in the photographs of Mr. MAULL. If amongst the numerous likenesses to be seen everywhere of the

* The Pamphlet here mentioned was written by a gentleman advocating the ORTON theory, and strongly in the interest of the Prosecution. "I made my photographic enlargements," he says, "and *sent them to the Judges*, with the suggestion that they might order such things to be supplied for the use of the Jury. Very much to my regret, I was told that the Judges could not interfere"!! (page 7). Is this really true? And is it certain that copies of this partisan Pamphlet did not, by some means, reach the Jury also?

Defendant, the artist could select none better than the one he has chosen upon which to found his comparisons, we submit he should either have refrained from such a difficult task, or have stated all the circumstances that might fairly be taken into account. The authors of "TICHBORNE or ORTON?" appear to have adopted a more painstaking method, entering minutely into "similarities" and "dissimilarities," even to the direction taken by the hairs of the eyebrows, arguing dispassionately from cause to effect, and founding their investigation upon the discovery of the same proportions for length of features in both faces. We would suggest that the "eminent anatomists and medical men" whose opinion is quoted in the "Crucial Test," would do well to criticize honestly both the pamphlets, and follow carefully these minute investigations, before pronouncing judgment upon the case in point.

In connection with the foregoing observations, we beg the attention of our readers to the heads that follow, in which we present four different views of ROGER TICHBORNE, as a young and as a middle-aged man. It will be seen by those who carefully observe that the four faces are one. We direct particular attention to—

1. Width and shape of the forehead.
2. Shape of the eyebrows. *The direction in which the hairs of the eyebrows lie.*
3. Width between the eyes. Length and shape of the eyes. The line of white showing below the iris.
4. Distance from the eye to the ear. The outline of the tops of the ears.
5. Length of nose. *Shape of the end of the nose*, and the nostrils.
6. The curve of the lips.
7. The shape and size of the chin. *The heavy form of chin in R.C.T.*, made heavier by fat in the Claimant.
8. The smooth hair, slightly turned at the ends.

The above outlines are simply offered as "suggestions." Any-one who will take the trouble to compare correct photographs of ROGER TICHBORNE and the Claimant, will see the wonderful likeness that exists in all the *small details* of the features. As no two leaves from off the same tree would fit to an absolute nicety if laid one on the other, so no two faces *can be* absolutely alike. Is it probable that ROGER CHARLES TICHBORNE and ARTHUR ORTON should possess faces *so exactly the same in every point*, as to allow of no differences but those caused by age, fat, and a broken nose?

The figure on the left represents ROGER TICHBORNE as he appears in the Chili photograph of 1851. In the original, the lobe of the ear appears to have been tampered with in some way, so as to cut it off, or hide it. Dr. KENEALY called the attention of the Jury to this; but they all shook their heads, and would not see it. In the photograph taken from the original, a black artificial line is drawn so as to conceal and cut off this lobe. All the TICHBORNE Family have lobes to their ears. Lady DORMER and Lady RADCLIFFE have large lobes, exactly the same as the lobe that appears in the second head, which is that of TICHBORNE, as he appeared at the Trial. Both likenesses are, in effect, one and the same; they are most faithfully copied. The reader is requested to place a piece of paper across the page, a short distance below the eyes of the figures, and it will be manifest in a moment that they represent the same man. The expression of the eyes and eyebrows, and the shape of the head are identical.

In the above we see the head of ROGER TICHBORNE as he was daguerreotyped at Chili; the lobe of the ear is artfully cut off in the Photo by a black line behind it; which when Dr. KENEALY pointed out to the jury as being perfectly self-evident, Mr. Justice MELLOR, and after him the Chief Justice, kindly informed them that this black line "represented the hair." It is impossible for the hair to have been daguerreotyped from the position of the sitter; it was simply a fraud to draw such a line so as to disguise and hide the lobe, which it was pretended ROGER had not, but which every TICHBORNE has. Hundreds of persons, and of medical men in particular, have been misled by this artifice of the Prosecution. Here also may be seen the same expression in the two faces, modified only by the effect of years and fat. The formation of the mouth in each is exactly the same. The chin also is alike. The muscles of the eyelids in the older appear to be relaxed from the excessive use of stimulants. As an addendum to the above, we may add that if our readers look at the portrait of Mr. BIDDULPH (ROGER's cousin), which appears, *ante* page 103, they will see the large kangaroo ears for which all the family are noted, and which the Claimant himself possessed. The head also is of the same shape. And when we publish the portrait of Mr. SEYMOUR, &c., the kangaroo ears will again be seen. The TICHBORNE and SEYMOUR family are noted for the kangaroo ear. In the Portraits, which we shall publish, of old Mrs. SEYMOUR and of Lady TICHBORNE, the Claimant's mother, taken when the latter was very young, the large ears are concealed by the artistic device of full ringlets, and plaits of hair under a full-laced cap. In the portrait of the present (so-called) Baronet, which appears *ante* p. 57, the enormous ears which all knew that he possessed, are artfully concealed by the photographer of the family under lumps of hair.

The above outlines are simply offered as "suggestions," and do not pretend to be conclusive. Should any one desire to make closer photographic investigation, we give a list of the principal points to be observed.

1. The general proportions of the features.
2. Width and shape of the forehead.
3. Shape of the eyebrows. *The direction in which the hairs of the eyebrows lie.*
4. Width between the eyes. Length and shape of the eyes. The line of white showing below the iris.
5. Distance from the eye to the top of the ear. The outline of the tops of the ears.
6. Length of nose. *Shape of the end of the nose, and the nostrils.* Effect of broken nose upon the nostrils and mouth The twist of the nose to the right, said to have belonged to ROGER TICHBORNE.
7. The curve of the lips. The shape and size of the chin. *The heavy form of chin in R. C. T.* made heavier by fat in the Claimant.
8. The natural effects of age and fat upon all the facial muscles.
9. The smooth hair, slightly turned at the ends.

Whilst writing on the subject of likenesses, we would call attention to the Lord Chief Justice's remarks on page 5 of the "summing up." We would then ask our readers if they can understand how the "highly trained and intelligent jurymen" satisfactorily accounted for the rash way in which a man of unusual size, with dark brown hair and hazel eyes, came forward to represent a person advertised as "of a delicate constitution, rather tall, with very light brown hair, and blue eyes." He must also, if the theory of the Prosecution be correct, that ROGER TICHBORNE was drowned in the "Bella," have had no possible opportunity of knowing that he in any way resembled the lost heir of the TICHBORNES. The *Illustrated News* and the *Peerage* could give him no portraits in which he could trace a likeness to himself, and fortify his mind with the idea that the resemblance was sufficiently strong to enable him to confront the scrutiny of his family. The advertisement was so vaguely worded, that he would indeed be a bold impostor who should have risked the liberty on the chance of possessing features of the same shape and size as those of ROGER TICHBORNE.

In page 5, the L. C. J. says, "In addition to this, there is another matter of inquiry equally important. One man may resemble another. There have been such instances in the world, or imposture would never have been attempted. No man attempts to personate another who does not more or less resemble him. If a fair man represented himself as a dark one, if a tall man came to take the place of a short man, or a stout man to take place of a lean man, if a man with a turned up nose sought to represent a man with an aquiline nose, without being able to give an account for the change, in such case such a person would be repudiated with scorn."

In page 210, of the L. C. J's. summing up, he says "It is just possible that those who only see in the Defendant an impostor would persuade themselves that there is not the likeness which, in point of fact, there is. For I cannot help believing, whether the Defendant is, or is not ROGER TICHBORNE, that there must have been many points of resemblance between the two. I do not suppose that honest people would come forward to say, 'That is ROGER TICHBORNE,' unless there was some great likeness between the Defendant and ROGER TICHBORNE. It is impossible."

Page 120, the L. C. J., commenting on the evidence of JAMES MORLEY, says, "Like many of the witnesses (and this is remarkable) he does not speak of the Defendant's likeness to ROGER, but of his likeness to some member of the TICHBORNE family."

The outlines above were drawn as an interesting experiment, curiosity being felt as to the result of placing the Claimant's features within Lady TICHBORNE's bonnet. Our readers will perceive the likeness thus brought out. The smile upon the mother's lips is, however, replaced by a gravity in the son which is hardly surprising under the circumstances.

After these sketches have been carefully scrutinized, we refer the investigator to the larger heads engraved on preceding page.

INDEX.

A

Aberdeen, Lady, acknowledged her son by the identification of his handwriting before she saw him, 118

Account of Jean Luie, Sir Roger's, 286

Accoutrements, Roger's made for him by Mr. Andrews, of Pall Mall, 11

Adams, Jno. Fras., a commissioner to administer oaths in Chancery, 10, 223

"Address to the Nation," by Mr. Fitz-Norman Ellis, a gentleman who has long taken a most active part in Sir Roger's interest, 253

Advertisement in an Australian newspaper to discover Tichborne, 45; and in the *Sydney Morning Herald* offering a £1,000 reward to any person who would prove the relationship to the Claimant otherwise than Tichborne, 178

Advice to a Judge (a poem by Dr. Kenealy), 6

Affecting meeting of Lady Tichborne and her son in Paris, 24

Affidavits:—Baigent, 29; Biddulph, 11; Bishop, 42; Bogle, 18; Braine, 12; Cater, 40; Cherrett, 38; Constable, 11; Custance, 12; Herriott, 198; Hingston, 174; Holmes and Leete, 26, 27; Hopkins, 32; Hnggius, 103; Jury and Tredgett, 48; Lipscomb, 10; Long, 18; Lousada, 23; Luie, 284; Lushington, 34; Marx, 38; McCann, 14; McCourt, 39; Mc Eleny, 39; Morley, 20; Noble, Henry, 223; Noble, Ann, 223; Norbury, 12; Olliffe and Shrimpton, 24; Onslow, 235; O'Ryan, 39; Rous, 21; Scott, 15; Skipworth, 242; Tichborne, 80; Tichborne, the Dowager Lady, 24; Waddington, 39; Whalley (allusion to by Mr. Digby Seymour,) 236; affidavit, 263, 282; Wheeler, 109.

Aguardiente, a fiery liquor, a kind of white brandy, on which Roger got intoxicated at the time he went on board the "Bella," 16

Alexander, Mrs. Anna Maria, Dry Creek, Red Jacket, Australia—letters from, 165, 166

Alfred, King, 5

Alfred Tichborne, death of, 46; habits of life, 46; belief that his brother Roger was alive, 195; mentioned by Mr. Giffard, 231

Aliases given to Tichborne, 37

Allen, George (butler to Mr. Robert Tichborne) witness in Common Pleas, 76

Allport and Sedgfield, the Claimant's agent at Melbourne, 174

Alresford Meeting—letter from Mr. Joseph Knowles, 90

Alresford, Mr. Herriott's recognition of the Claimant at, 198; went to the Swan Hotel, 202

Alresford, Tichborne at, and his Contemplated tour—*Morning Advertiser*, 102

America, South, 15, 184, 185; Tichborne in, 191; evidence of Sir Talbot Constable concerning, 203

America, detailed report of Mr. Whalley's visit to, 263; letter from Mr. Whalley to Mr. Onslow, 271

American view of the Great Tichborne Case, 99

Amiens, Claudius, 154

Amphilis Tichborne, wife of Sir Benjamin Tichborne, 7

Analysis of the Tattoo evidence, 86

Anderson, Professor, testimony in favour of the Claimant, 195

Anderson, Carl, a friend of Jean Luie, to whom the latter wrote a letter 10th July, 1873, 278

Anderson, Harry, a friend of Jean Luie's, 271

Andrews, James (Australian witness in favour of the Claimant), 136, 147

Andrews, Mary (Australian witness in favour of the Claimant), 139

Andrews, Mr. William, of Pall Mall, military accoutrement maker, (witness in Common Pleas), 11, 77

Andrews, Mr. William, junr., 78

Anglo-Saxon Charta to Tichborne, 8

Anidjah, Mr. a renegade friend of the Claimant's—who first professed to assist and afterwards persecuted him—alluded to by the *Morning Advertiser*, 219

Animosity of the Attorney-General against the Claimant, 213

Ankle-marks on the Claimant, found by Dr. Lipscomb to be the same as those on Roger Tichborne, 219

Anne Tichborne, wife of Sir Henry Joseph Tichborne, the eighth Baronet, 7

Another Report of the observations made by Judge Brett on Mr. Whalley and Mr. Onslow, 309

Answer given by the Claimant at the meeting in St. James's Hall to twelve questions in writing which were handed up to him from some bitter unbeliever in his identity, 227

Anxiety of Roger to get away from the scenes of contention in his family, 9

Appeal for aid from the Secretary of the Christian Knowledge Society;—Mr. Skipworth's reply, justly censuring their un-Christian conduct in allowing an innocent man to be persecuted and imprisoned as well as a nation's rights to be violated, while they remained looking on with the utmost apathy, 243

Appendix to the Report of the Select Committee on Privilege on the Lord Chief Justice's letter respecting Mr. Whalley's case of Contempt of Court, 262

Appleby, the name of a person well-known to Tichborne and John Moore at Santiago de Chili, 189

Application for bail, 98

Application against Mr. Whalley, M.P., and Mr. Guildford Onslow, M.P., in the Court of Queen's Bench, *Daily Telegraph*, Jany. 13th, 1873, 232

Application made by the Family in the Court of Common Pleas before Chief Justice Bovill, and Justices Byles, Keating, and Brett, to stop an action under the title of "Tichborne, Bart., *v.* Mostyn, Bart., and another," until the costs of the Tichborne Trial had been paid by the plaintiff, 230

Archæological Journal, contributed to by Mr. Francis Joseph Baigent, 29

Archbishop of Canterbury gave £20 to "the House of Mercy, Clewer" (a Puseyite Convent), 251

Archibald, Mr., the British Consul at New York, alluded to by Mr. Whalley in his Report of his visit to America, 272

Archibald, Mr., Counsel for Crown, cross-examination of, Lord Rivers G. Onslow, Esq., Dr. Atwood, Mr. J. Lamont, 98; retired from the Bench when a Judge, when the application for Contempt of Court was made against Mr. Whalley and Mr. Onslow, because he had previously been a Counsel engaged on the side of the Prosecution, 232

Archives of the Court—letter headed "Arthur Orton to his Sister," abstracted from the, 149

Argyle, Duke of, late Lord Privy seal—alluded to in *Catholic Opinion* on account of his mother being a Roman Catholic, 25

Arica, a place at which the Claimant said that the second mate of the "Pauline" left that vessel, 192, 200

Arm round Serjeant Ballantine's neck—the Attorney-General, 244

Arrend, Harriet, the second wife of Jean Luie, who gave evidence against him at Bow-st., 292; at the Old Bailey, 304

Arrest of Tichborne after the nonsuit in Common Pleas, 75

Arrival in Bristol, Tichborne's — *Western Telegraph*, 110

Arrival at Stonyhurst, July 1st, 1845, 199

Arrival of ships in Australia from 1852 to 1857, 135

Arthur, the butcher, 136, 137

Arthur, General, a gentleman mentioned by Mr. Whalley as having rendered him great assistance in searching records at New York, when striving to obtain information in corroboration of Jean Luie's statement, 272

Arundell, Lord, 8, 9, 11, 193

Ashley, Mr. Evelyn, M.P. for Poole, accused Dr. Kenealy of having put Luie into the box knowing him to be a False Witness. Dr. Kenealy brought the matter before the House of Commons on Thursday, March 4th, 1875; and fully refuted the accusation of Mr. Ashley, but obtained no redress, 211; Mr. Guildford Onslow's reply to Mr. Ashley, 311; Dr. Kenealy's letter to Mr. McMahon, his junior in the Tichborne Case, respecting the statements of Mr. Ashley, 311

"Asia," the ship, extract from the *Illustrated London News* of April 22nd, 1854, 116

As to the "Osprey" at New York, 276

As to the 1st June "Osprey," 276

As to the Sailors—Anderson and Harry, 276

As to American Evidence and the cost of it, 277

Aske, Falconer, Her Britannic Majesty's Consul in Paris, before whom Doctors Olliffe and Shrimpton signed their affidavit, 24

Astounding influence brought to bear against Sir Roger—a letter to the *Englishman* from Mr. Onslow, Decr. 5th, 1874, 35

Attorney General, ode to the, 91; the 95, 96, 161, 162, 164; mentioned by the Claimant at Leeds; at Birmingham, 171; vilified Thomas Carter, a Carabineer witness, 173; and the Tattoo, 174, 175; bet of some bottles of wine on the Tichborne Case, 175; asserted that British Soldiers were to be bought for pots of beer, 177; assured the jury that it was not necessary for his purpose to show who the Claimant was, 195; rancour against the Claimant, 213; reply to Mr. Neville Granville, M.P., respecting the Claimant, 213; asserted that he would prove the Claimant Arthur Orton in twenty minutes, 225; demands a Trial at Bar against the Claimant, 229; Mr. Onslow's accusation of 234; instructed by Lord Chief Justice Cockburn to prosecute Mr. Skipworth for Contempt of Court, 240; failed to prove one word of his accusations against the Plaintiff—affidavit of Mr. Skipworth, 242; Attorney-General, the, with his arm round Serjeant Balantine's neck, 244; called the Claimant a conspirator, a perjurer, a forger, a villain, an impostor, an Australian thief, a loathsome reptile which left his slime upon everybody and everything with whom he came in contact, and said if he could find stronger words in the English language against the Claimant he would use them, 244

Atwood, Dr. William Alban, Cross-examination of, as to bail, 98; mentioned by the Claimant, 248

Austen, Thomas (coachman to Mr. Bowyer,) witness in Common Pleas, 76

Australian Commission, transcript from, 133; brief summary of the, 146

Australian evidence in favour of the Claimant, 135

Australian navvy, the Prosecution tried to make Sir Roger to be, 242; also an Australian prizefighter, 242

Australia, Tichborne in, letter from Mr. George Ross, the Mayor of Sale, Gippsland, and Justice of the Peace, 168; Tichborne in, 198

Avory, Mr., Clerk of Arraigns at the Old Bailey, 330

Ayrton, Mr., M.P., allusion to by the *Morning Advertiser*, 218

B.

Bad spelling: the Dowager Lady Tichborne made use of the same bad spelling as her son, a most remarkable circumstance in proof of his identity, 206, 207, 208

Baigent, Mr. Francis Joseph—affidavit, 29; Lady Doughty to, 20; and Mrs. Greenwood, 31; evidence in Common Pleas, 80; questions concerning, 161, 162, 163; broken down in health and spirits through the Trial, 171; sees the daguerreotype with the thumb rubbed out, 178; alluded to in the cross-examination of Sir Talbot Constable in the Common Pleas, 208; alluded to by Jean Luie, 289

Baigent, Mr. Richard (affidavit), 31

Bail: threat to increase the amount of the, 95;

application for, 98, 147; ten thousand pounds bail entered into for Sir Roger, referred to by him at the meeting at Leicester, 224; Dr. Atwood, 248

Bailey, William, landlord of the Anchor Inn, Ropley, the first person that recognized the Claimant in England, witness in Common Pleas, 79, 202

Baines, Mr. Edward, M.P.—letter in reply to Mr. Onslow respecting the attacks of the *Leeds Mercury* on the Claimant, 176

Baker, a gentleman mentioned in the affidavit of Mrs. Ann Noble, a witness in favour of Tichborne, 223

Ball given to the Tichborne tenantry on Roger coming of age, 5th January, 1850, 12

Ballads, of the most cruel kind, were circulated in legions by the friends of the Prosecution, and sent anonymously by post all over the country to prejudice the minds of the jury and the public against the Claimant at the forthcoming trial, 250

Batanger, C., letter respecting Arthur Orton, 122

Ballantine, Mr. Serjeant: 51—68, 72, 73, 74, 75, 91, 95, 155, 156, 157, 159, 160, 161, 162, 163, 182, 184, 209; the last time he appeared as counsel for Sir Roger Tichborne, and the reason for it, 230; mentioned by Judge Brett, 231; by Lord Chief Justice Bovill, 231, 232; the Attorney-General with his arm round Serjeant Ballantine's neck, 244

Ballarat, Australia, 167, 168

Ballarat Harry, a man mentioned in connection with the Australian evidence relating to the Claimant, 137, 145

Balston, Rev. E., Head Master of Eton College, is brother-in-law to "Father Carter," and is a member of the Council of the Puseyite Convent at Clewer, to which Mr. Gladstone subscribed, 251

Banco, sittings in, before the Lord Chief Justice, and Justices Blackburn, Lush, and Quain, 95; before Lord Chief Justice Cockburn, Mr. Justice Blackburn, and Mr. Justice Mellor, 228; before the Lord Chief Justice and Justices Blackburn, Mellor, and Lush. Observations by the Lord Chief Justice upon what had occurred at the passing of the sentence on Messrs. Onslow and Whalley in the Court of Queen's Bench, Jany. 21st, 1873.—*Standard*, Jany. 22nd, 239; before the Lord Chief Justice and Justices Blackburn, Mellor, and Quain. The Tichborne Case again.—More Contempt (Mr. Whalley), 240

Bank Holidays Bill — Lord Chief Justice Bovill wished to see it, 204

Bannatt, Captain, a gentleman mentioned by Mr. Onslow in his questions to Jean Luie, 271

Banquet to Sir Roger at Leeds, 125

Baptized, Tichborne, Jany. 6th, 1829, 199

Bar, Trial at of Sir Roger Tichborne, Court of Queen's Bench, November 22, sittings in Banco, at Westminster, before Lord Chief Justice Cockburn, Mr. Justice Blackburn, and Mr. Justice Mellor, 229; the meaning of Trial at Bar explained by Mr. Justice Blackburn, 247

Barber, Mr. Chapman, one of the cross-examining Counsel employed against Tichborne, whose cross-examination was remarkable for its unfair spirit, 50—64, 67, 68

Bardwell, Mr. William, photographer at Ballarat, statement respecting the "Osprey," 167

Barney Woods (splitter in Australia), 136

Baronetcy, the Tichborne, letters between Dobinson, Geare, and Holmes, 37; *Hobart Town Mercury* on the, 134

Barrant, Jules, Tichborne's servant, and formerly manager at the Globe d'Or, Lima, 15, 16, 192, 200; discharged by Sir Roger for stealing his luggage, 221

Barry, Patrick (Carabineer witness in Common Pleas), 78; testimony in behalf of the Claimant at Leeds, 171; testimony in behalf of the Claimant at Bradford, 179

Bartlett, Mr. William, letter to the *Birmingham Post* respecting the "Osprey," 165

Baxter, Rose and Norton, the Claimant's Attorneys, great quarrel between, 90; letter concerning Tichborne's thumb, 111; questions concerning, 161, 162, 164; reference to in letter of Mr. William Bartlett, 165; retaining the Claimant's documents, 175

Bayford, Mr (lawyer in the Court of Probate), 71

Beaken (police-sergeant, witness in Common Pleas), 80

Beaken, James (sergeant 8th Hussars), witness in Common Pleas, 80

Beasley, Mr., one of the Liverpool reporters who verified the transcript of speeches delivered by Mr. Skipworth and the Claimant, at a meeting held at the Royal Amphitheatre, Liverpool, when they were arraigned before the Court of Queen's Bench for Contempt of Court, 210

Beasley, one of the Counsel employed against Luie at his Trial at the Old Bailey for perjury, 300, 302

Bed, Sir Roger lying on when the interview with his mother took place in Paris, 24, 26

Beddit, Frank U., a commissioner for affidavits in Queensland, 147

Bedrooms at Burton Constable, the Claimant's knowledge of them, 204

Bedwell, Frederick, the gentleman before whom the affidavit of the Dowager Lady Tichborne was taken, 26

Beeby, Isaac B., letter to the *Englishman*, showing that Orton and Castro are two distinct persons, 164

Believers in the Claimant—educated persons—a list of, 176

"Bella," the, 15, 16, 18, 25, 44, 68; discovery of one of the crew, 129, 133; John Gray, Esq., respecting the, 130; reference to by Mr. Whalley, 132; the Tichborne Claimant and the crew of the, 132; mysterious proceedings at Swansea, 152; questions concerning, 161, 162, 163; reference to by Mr. William Bartlett, 165; reference to by Henry F. Michell, Esq., 165; reference to by Mrs. Alexander, 166; statement of W. Craikshank, Esq., on the, 168; mention of by Chief Justice Bovill, 186; allusion to by the Claimant, 197

Bellew, Lord, and the Tattoo, 86, 174; alluded to by Sir Roger at a meeting at Leicester, 224

Belmont and Co., alluded to in relation to the statement of Jean Luie, 273

Bendigo, a place in Australia at which Castro stayed, 201

Benjamin Tichborne, a knight who proclaimed James VI. of Scotland as King James I. of England, 7, 8

Bennett, Charles, a shorthand writer, who appeared as a witness against Jean Luie at Bow-street, 291

Benson, Mrs. (landlady of Morgan Harris's father), declaration of, 129

Berthier, Paul, the Parisian photographer who took Sir Roger's likeness, 28

Betty, William T., Lieut. Colonel, Carabineers, 87

Bickerstaff, Robert, Lieut.-Colonel, Carabineers, 87, 173

Biddulph, Anthony, Esq., Justice of the Peace (Affidavit) 11; witness in Common Pleas, 76; asked to bet on the Claimant's case, 173, 178; speech at Guildford, 194; identified his cousin at Croydon, 203; godfather to his eldest son, 203

Biggenden, John, a London Commissioner to administer oaths in Chancery, 24

Bill in Chancery, filed by Sir James Tichborne for the purpose of setting aside Messrs. Gosford and Slaughter as Trustees of Roger's Will, 13

Bill, the landlord of the Clarendon Hotel, Gravesend, demands immediate payment of from the Claimant in consequence of the underhand conduct of Gosford, 45, 202

Bilton, a place referred to in the evidence of Sir Talbot Constable, 201

Bingley, George (resident for many years in S. America, witness in Common Pleas), 77

Biographical sketch of Sir R. Tichborne, 42

Bird-skinning, a favourite pastime of Roger's, 187

Birds, pictures, spurs, and stirrups sent by the Claimant to the Dowager Lady—his perfect recollection of, 26

Birmingham Morning News, its abominable scurrility read by Captain Hunt in the Town Hall, Birmingham, 172

Birmingham Post, letter from Mr. William Bartlett, concerning the "Osprey," 165

Birmingham, Sir Roger at, 171; dinner at, 171; meetings at the Town Hall, 172, 173

Birth of Claimant's second child—Roger Joseph Doughty Tichborne, 37

Bishop, Rev. Mr. Alfred Cæsar, perpetual curate of Tichborne, and afterwards rector of Bramdean, letter on Tichborne, 40; affidavit, 12

Bismarck, Prince, allusion to by the *Morning Advertiser*, 218; allusion to by Mr. Skipworth, 243

Blackburn, Mr. Justice, 95, 96; sittings in Banco before, 228; trial at Bar of Sir Roger Tichborne, Court of Queen's Bench, November 18, sittings in Banco, 228; sittings in Banco, 229; and Mr. Skipworth, 240; tried the Claimant for Contempt of Court, 244; judgment in the case of Contempt of Court by the Claimant and Mr. Skipworth, 246; complimented the Claimant on his excellent defence, 247

Blackstone, allusion to by the *Morning Advertiser*, 218; Blackstone's Commentaries, quoted from in Mr. Whalley's address to the Electors of the City of Peterborough, 255

Blagden, Mr. Richard, a Commissioner to administer oaths in Chancery in England, 11

Bleach, Emma, sister to Sarah Colborne, Jean Luie's wife, and the wife of William Bleach, a Clerk in the Pension Department, Woolwich Dockyard, 292, 302

Bleeding of Tichborne in the army, 14

Blissett, a gun-maker of whom Roger purchased his firearms, 187

"Blecky" and "young Napper," two persons mentioned in one of the forged post-cards which some of the friends of the Prosecution circulated during the Trial in order to prejudice the minds of the jury and the public against the Claimant, 252

Blount, Mr., a banker at Paris, mentioned by the Claimant to Mr. Leete, 23

Bloxam, 134

"Bob Bell, the cabman," a man who was matched to fight with Orton for £10 a side, 216

Body-mark on the Claimant—Would anyone but a son have ventured to mention it in a letter to his mother? 219; that very mark identified on the Claimant by Roger's nurse as the one on his body when born, 219

Bogle, Andrew, formerly valet to Sir Edward Doughty, recognized by the Claimant, 17; pension stopped, 18; affidavit, 18; letter to Lady Doughty, 19; letter, 21; and Mrs. Greenwood, 22, 45; evidence in Common Pleas, 78; mentioned by Mr. George Ross, the Mayor of Sale, Australia, 169; mentioned by Mr. Giffard in the Common Pleas, 231

Dogle, Andrew, son of Sir Edward Doughty's valet, 142, 147

"Bogota" the ship on board of which Roger left Lima, 200

Boisdale, a place in Australia frequently alluded to in the history of the Claimant, 145, 146, 200, 201

Bonds, Tichborne, 193; Mr. Skipworth had none, nor had ever seen any, 242

Bonynge, George, Tailor-warder of Chatham Convict Prison, one of the witness who gave evidence against Jean Luie, 293

Boree, a place in Australia at which Castro stayed, 201; alluded to by Mr. Madden, in his letter to Tichborne, 222

Borgia, 148

Born at Paris, Tichborne, January 5th, 1829, 199

Bott, Thomas, Major Carabineers, 87

Bovill, Lord Chief Justice of the Court of Common Pleas, application made to postpone the Trial, 74, 131; remarks on Tichborne being nonsuited, 75; killed by the Tichborne Case, 170; allusion to by Sir Roger at Bradford meeting, 177; remarks of respecting the evidence given by John Moore, 82, 183, 184, 185, 186, 188, 189, 190, 191; two brothers betting against the Claimant winning his case, 196; appeared in Court with documents signed for the committal of the Claimant before he knew he was about to be nonsuited, 196; denounced the Claimant at the Lord Mayor's dinner as the greatest of impostors, 196; remarks in the Common Pleas during the examination and cross-examination of Sir T. Constable, 201, 205; application before, by the Family, to stop an action under the title of "Tichborne, Bar v. Mostyn, Bart., and another," until the costs of the Tichborne Trial had been paid to the Plaintiff, 230; Tichborne bitterly complained of Bovill's partiality in ordering him to pay £60,000 before he would allow him to commence a suit in his Court again, 242

Bowen, Mr., a counsel who appeared against Mr. Onslow in the case of Contempt of Court, 235

Bowker's, Mr., insulting behaviour to Tichborne, 22; taking home the daguerreotype, which appeared again with thumb rubbed out 78; alluded to by Mr. Giffard in the Common Pleas, 206

Bow-street, 193; Jean Luie at, before Sir Thomas Henry, 286; brought up on remand, 290; brought up for the third time, 291 for the fourth time, 294; for the fifth time 296

Boxes of the Dowager Lady opened by order of Gosford, and her papers abstracted, 21

Boyd, Mr., 154
Boyle, Clerk, Lord Justice, greatly to his credit as a Judge, when a prisoner asked leave to address the Court after the verdict, replied that he saw nothing to hinder him, 310
Bradford, Sir Roger Tichborne at, 177; *Bradford Chronicle*—an interesting account of the Claimant at the Bradford meeting, 179
Braine: Miss Anna Mary, governess to Miss Doughty in 1850, 12; affidavit, 12; evidence in Common Pleas, 76, 131
Brandy flask, a small flat-sided pewter one, carried by Tichborne, and on which he wrote his name in Australia, as positively stated by Mr. Madden in a letter to Mr. Onslow, 222; "Brandy tears! brandy tears!!" (verses said to be written by Mr. Shirley Brooks), 103
Bravery of the Claimant, 195
Brett: Mr. Justice, one of the Judges of the Common Pleas, 230; 298; who tried Jean Luie at the Old Bailey for perjury, 298; summing up of, in Luie's case, 307; sentence on Luie, and Captain Brown, 309; another report of the observations made by Judge Brett on Mr. Onslow and Mr. Whalley, 309
Brief summary of the Australian Commission, 146
Bright, John, 3; letter of the Rev. W. Buckingham to, 167
Brighton, the Claimant at, and there recognized by Colonel Sawyer, 203
Bristol, arrival of the Claimant at, 110
Brittany, a place in France where Roger and Chatillon took a tour when he was about 14 years old, 9
Brittlebank, Sergeant-Major, testimony in behalf of the Claimant at the Town Hall, Birmingham, 173
Broad, Mr. Charles, the senior emigration officer stationed at Williamstown, Australia, 163
Broadmead Rooms, Bristol, meeting of the Claimant's friends, 110
Broadsides, pamphlets, ballads, caricatures of the most cruel kind, were circulated in tens of thousands and sent anonymously by post all over the country to prejudice the minds of the jury and the public against the Claimant at the forthcoming trial, 250
Bromby, Robert (custom-house officer—witness in Common Pleas), 79
Bromley, Mr. E., a solicitor who instructed Sir John Karslake, Q.C., and Mr. A. L. Smith, counsel on behalf of Mr. Onslow, in the case of Contempt of Court, 235
Brompton Hospital, the place where Thomas Carter, a most staunch Carabineer witness in favour of Tichborne, died a pauper, 222
Bromwell, Colonel, 154
Brookwood, the residence of Roger's cousin, Mrs. Greenwood, 21
Brougham, Lord Chancellor, alluded to in the Lord Chief Justice's letter respecting Mr. Whalley's case of Contempt of Court, 259
Brown: Mr. Horace, one of the Counsel in behalf of the Claimant in the Court of Queen's Bench, during Mr. Hawkins's application for a trial, 228, 229; Captain; a witness connected with the Luie evidence, 289; sentence passed on Brown by Mr. Justice Brett, 309
Bruce: Right Hon. H. A., Secretary, under Mr. Gladstone, in reference to the Leeds petition in behalf of the Claimant, 149; allusion to by Sir Roger, 181; fierce opposition to Mr. Whalley's motion on behalf of the Claimant, 217, 218; mentioned by Sir Roger in his speech at St. James's Hall, 227
Bryant, Mary Ann (marriage to Tichborne), 17, 142
Buckingham, the Rev. William, a letter to the Right Hon. John Bright, M.P., 167
Buckley: a man who was found among the natives in Australia, 162; had forgotten the English language, 197
Buenos Ayres, Tichborne at, 15, 200
Buffoonery and merriment, in the Court of Queen's Bench, during the Tichborne Trial, 249
Bulpett, William Whitear, Esq., banker (witness in Common Pleas), 79
Burden, John (witness in Common Pleas), 79
Burdon, a man who called upon McCann at Maidstone and tried to prevent him acknowledging the Claimant as Roger Tichborne, 11
Burke: 154; Martin (Carabineer witness in Common Pleas), 78
Burney, Miss, 151
Burrows: Mr. Frederick, Castro's partner in Australia, 44, 198; Mr. John, Castro's master in Australia, 198
Burton Constable, a place in Yorkshire, the residence of Sir Talbot Constable, 203, 207, 208, 210
Butcher of Wapping, the Claimant is not. *Morning Advertiser*, 229
Bute, Lord, 4; allusion to by Mr. Whalley, 195
Butts: Stephen, hotel-keeper in Sydney, evidence of, 140, 147, 162; Butts, Truth William Palmer (son of the hotel-keeper, at Sydney and Secretary to Tichborne), 21, 16; evidence of, 141, 142, 147
Byles, Mr. Justice, one of the judges of the Common Pleas, 98, 230

C.

CABINET the (Gladstone) consented to squander the public money for the Tichborne Trial, 196
Cahir, a place in Ireland where Roger was stationed with a troop of his regiment, 13, 199
Cairns: James, sergt., Carabineers, witness in Common Pleas, 78; Mary Ann, wife of James, witness in Common Pleas, 78
Callao, a place where Roger was robbed of his watch, chain, tobacco-box, and about £3 in money, 192
Cambridge Music-Hall, Commercial-street, Bishopsgate, a place where the Claimant received an enthusiastic reception from the inhabitants of East London, 175
Campbell, Captain, Chairman of the meeting at Greenock, 197; Campbell, Major, a Carabineer officer, 151; Campbell, Councillor, president of a meeting at Grimsby, 181
Canterbury, a city where Roger was stationed with his regiment, 13; seen there stripped by Thomas Carter, and was not tattooed, 171
Canute, King, 3
Carabineers, Tichborne gazetted as a Cornet in, July 13th, 1849, 199; officers, a letter concerning, by Mr. Gorton to the *Standard*, 87; Carabineers, memorandum showing the official movements of Tichborne in the army, 13
Carden, Captain, captain of the "Comet," 165
Caricatures which the newspaper press basely circulated tending to prejudice the minds of the jury and the public before the trial, 250
Caroline, Queen, 4
Carroll, Michael, Carabineer, witness in Common Pleas, 77
Carter, Rev. T. T., Rector of Clewer, and one of the heads of the Puseyite Convent there, 251; Carter, Thomas, witness in Common Pleas, 76; letter to the Editor of the *Tichborne Gazette*, 173; knew that Tichborne was never tattooed, 171; died a pauper in the hospital at Brompton, 222
Carysfort, Lord, 154
Case, David, three men brought forward to prove the Claimant that person, 37; Case of Jean Luie in the Tichborne Litigation—the Ticket-of-leave system—the Claimant—a letter to *John o'Groat's Journal*, by "S.," 310
Castro, Don Tomas, of Melipilla, Chili, 171; Castro, Tomas de, 133, 134, 135, 142, 143, 144, 145, 146, 151, 161, 165; letters of Mrs. Alexander concerning, 165, 166; declaration of Mrs. Alexander, 166; Castro and Orton, 167; recollections of Mr. George Ross, Mayor of Sale, concerning, 168
Cater, John, Wyatt (affidavit), 40
Catholic Opinion, a journal that gave an account of the family connections existing between members of the English aristocracy who favour Puseyism and Romanism, 251
Cawley, William Wilkes, a commissioner to administer oaths in Chancery, 12
"Cella," the steamer in which the Claimant and his family arrived in the Victoria Docks in 1866, 21; 171
Chabot, Mons., the expert, handsomely paid for his evidence, 118, 154, 155
Chambers, Mr. Montague, a gentleman alluded to before the Select Committee on Privilege by Mr. Whalley, 260
Chancellor of the Exchequer (Mr. Robert Lowe) replies to Mr. Onslow and Mr. Mellor respecting the expenditure of the public money by Government in the Tichborne Case, 213, 211
Character and personal appearance of young Roger, 15
Charges against the Claimant, the graver of the two abandoned by the Prosecution, 229
Charles the Second, 4
Charlton, Mr. Lechmere, a gentleman alluded to by Lord Chief Justice Cockburn, who was committed for Contempt of Court, but in whose behalf the House of Commons declined to interfere, 239; alluded to by Mr. Justice Blackburn, 247
Charsley, a solicitor at Melbourne, 135
Chatham, Lady, 154
Chatillon: and Roger, 9, 10, 27, 28, 86, 209; Madame and Roger, 86, 177; the tattoo and Madame, the *Geelong Advertiser*, an Australian newspaper, on, 215
Cheer, Sergeant-Major, of the Yeomanry Cavalry, a supporter of Tichborne at the Wolverhampton meeting, 175
Cheques for £500, editors of newspapers are said to receive when a great trial is pending, 244
Cheriton, a place which forms part of the Tichborne estate, 8
Cherrett, Robert (affidavit), 30
Chess-players, the Claimant asserted by Mr. Onslow to be one of the best, 227
Chichester, Major, a cousin of Sir Talbot Constable, alluded to by him in his cross-examination by the Solicitor-General, 209
Chick, Mr. Peter—recognition of the Claimant at Southsea, 116
Childers, Mr. Hugh Eardley, one of Mr. Gladstone's Cabinet, 147
Children of the Dowager Lady Tichborne—their names, 21
Chili witnesses, alluded to by John Gray, Esq., Solicitor to the Treasury, 150
Chili daguerreotype, the, in which Tichborne's thumb was rubbed out, 113, 174
Chili, a place visited by Roger Tichborne, 189
Christian Knowledge, the Society for Promoting—Mr. Skipworth's letter on their un-Christian conduct in allowing an innocent man to be persecuted and imprisoned, 213
Christmas-box of twenty guineas presented by a lady for Sir Roger's little children, 223; Christmas-day, 1866, the time when Tichborne arrived in London after his long absence abroad, 20
Chydioke Tichborne, executed for participation in the Babington conspiracy against Queen Elizabeth, 8
Claimant, the:—Places visited by him on his tour, &c.—Alresford, 101; Australia, 198; Birmingham, 172; Bradford, 177; Bristol, *Western Telegraph*, 110; Dewsbury, 175; Dundee, 198; East London, 130; Gravesend, 23; Greenock, 198; Grimsby, 180, 181; Leeds, 121; Leicester and Loughborough, 130; Leicester, 223; Newgate, *Daily Telegraph*, 84; release from, 99; Paris, 23; Preston, 197; Southampton, 104, 196; Southsea, 114; St. James's Hall, 226; Sunderland, 123; Swansea, 116; Wolverhampton, 171; his defective education, as proved by his French and English letters and Mr. South's report thereon, 219; and his friends, a letter by Mr. Onslow to Mr. Edward Baines, M.P., 176; his handwriting does not prove him to be Arthur Orton—a letter by Mr. Gurnell, 153; writing, observations on the, 153; bail, 147; complimented by Mr. Justice Blackburn on his excellent defence, 247; his daughter, Teresa Mary Agnes Tichborne, 17; maintained his right of free speech as an Englishman before the Judges of the Court of Queen's Bench, 246; his poverty, 100; recognition of him by Mrs. Radcliffe according to the statement of Gosford, 219; his recollection of the birds, pictures, spurs, and stirrups that he sent to the Dowager Lady Tichborne, 26; his life in South America, 191; his tenants—*Morning Advertiser*, 100; Trial at Bar of the Claimant, Court of Queen's Bench, November 22, sittings in Banco at Westminster, before Lord Chief Justice Cockburn, Mr. Justice Blackburn, and Mr. Justice Mellor, 229; Contempt of Court, the Claimant's trial before Justices Blackburn, Mellor, and Quain, 241; speeches delivered by him at Alresford, 101; Birmingham, 172; Bradford, 177; Broadmead Rooms, Bristol, 112, Dewsbury, 175; Greenock, 198; Grimsby, 180; Leeds, 125; banquet at Leeds, 126; speech at Leicester and Loughborough, 130; Leicester, 223; Southampton, 197; Southsea, 116; St. James's Hall, 227; Sunderland, 123; Swansea, 117, 119; Wolverhampton, 171; his speeches exposing the conduct of the Prosecution construed into Contempt of Court, 240
Clamber, a large farmer and breeder of horses, alluded to by Sir Talbot Constable in his cross-examination by the Solicitor-General, 210
Clarendon Hotel, New York, the Claimant at, 202; Clarendon Hotel, Gravesend, the Claimant at, and Gosford's rude behaviour, 23, 26, 45
Clarke, Mr. John James, statutory declaration that the Claimant is not Arthur Orton, 168; Clarke, chief-inspector of the police—one of the officers who arrested Tichborne after his

D.

Davy, R. M., a commissioner to administer oaths in Chancery, 12
Dawson, George, the supposed writer of a vile article in the *Birmingham Morning News* against the Claimant, 172
Death's-head pipe that Roger used to smoke, 10
Death of Alfred Tichborne, 46; of Mr. John Gray, Q.C., 170; of Thomas Carter, a witness in the Tichborne Case, 174; of Lady Tichborne, 37; a poem on the, 199
Debts of Alfred Tichborne, 46
Deceit of Gosford towards the Claimant; shaking hands with him at the London-bridge station, saying "Good-bye, Sir Roger," and afterwards turning out one of the bitterest enemies he had in the world, 23
Deception practised by a lady on Tichborne at the instigation of his Family, 36
Declaration of Mrs. Benson, landlady of Morgan Harris's father, 129; of Morgan Harris, senr., 129; of George Jones respecting Morgan Harris, 130; of John Clay, of Fitzroy, Australia, respecting the "Osprey," 164; of Mrs. Anna Maria Alexander, of Dry Creek, Red Jacket, Australia, 166; statutory, of Mr. John James Clarke, of Melbourne, that the Claimant is not Arthur Orton, 168
Dedication to the Queen of the Report of the Trial, by Dr. Kenealy, 3
Deeds drafted by Mr. Hopkins which Roger refused to sign, 12
Defective education; the Claimant's as proved by his English and French letters and Mr. South's report thereon, 219
Defence of the Claimant when charged with having committed Contempt of Court, 244
Defiance of the threat held out to Messrs. Onslow and Whalley in Westminster Hall, Mr. Skipworth's, 243
Delay of the Tichborne Trial contrary to Magna Charta, as stated by himself in St. James's Hall, 227
Deliberate refusal of the Family to find out the fact of Tichborne being alive, 195
De Lolme, 154
Deniliquin, a place in Australia at which Castro resided, 142, 143, 144, 145, 147, 198, 200
Denison, Sir William, succeeded Sir Charles Fitzroy as Governor of New South Wales, 165
Denman, Mr., a counsel who took part in the proceedings at the Trial in Common Pleas, 204; Lord, a celebrated Judge referred to by the *Morning Post* in a letter by a most learned member of the Bar—signed "A Lover of Constitutional Law," 254
Denning, inspector of police, one of the officers who arrested Tichborne after his nonsuit in the Common Pleas, 75
Denounced publicly as an impostor—the Claimant asserted he was, and also in the presence of a lady friend of his by Lord Chief Justice Cockburn before the Trial began, 240
Deputy Lieutenant for the county of Lincoln—Mr. Skipworth, who told the Government that unless justice were done him (referring to his fine and imprisonment), and due consideration and regard for outraged feelings and honour, he could no longer conscientiously retain his office, but must resign it into Her Majesty's hands, 249
Descent of the Tichborne family, 8
Desertion of ships' crews at Melbourne in 1854, 146
Dewsbury, the Claimant at, 175
Different persons the Claimant was asserted to be, 170; 178
Digby Seymour, Mr., Q.C., a Counsel who appeared in behalf of Mr. Whalley in the case of Contempt of Court, 235; alluded to by Mr. Whalley in his address to the Electors of the City of Peterborough, 256
Dining with the Tichborne Family during the Trial, the Lord Chief Justice, 249
Dinner at the Royal Hotel, Birmingham, 171
Discovery of one of the "Bella's" crew, 129
Discussion among all classes respecting the identity of the Claimant from the time that he made his first claim, 235
"Disgrace to mention the Claimant's name in decent society;" these words the Claimant declared were uttered to a lady friend of his by Lord Chief Justice Cockburn in a company of ladies before the Trial in the Court of Queen's Bench commenced, 240; "Dishonour and disgrace to the land in which we live," was the judgment passed upon Mr. Onslow and Mr. Whalley for so-called "Contempt of Court"; affidavit of Mr. Skipworth, 242
Dislike of a civilized life, Roger's reasons for, 13
Disraeli, 5; one of the Special Committee on Privilege on the Lord Chief Justice's letter respecting Mr. Whalley's case of Contempt of Court, 259
Dobinson and Geare's impudent denial of the identity of the Claimant, 28; letter on the Tichborne baronetcy, 37; letter on the funeral of Lady Tichborne, 69; the way they got up the evidence, 49; trying to intimidate the friends of Tichborne before the first trial commenced, 92; and Mackenzie, 135
Documents, the Claimant's, impounded by order of the Solicitor of the Treasury, 175; Documents mentioned by Mr. Whalley, as giving two letters signed Arthur Orton and Roger Tichborne, issued by the enemies of the Claimant, 227
"Doe dem. Bather v. Brain," a law-book mentioned by Chief Justice Bovill, 232
Dole, the Tichborne, 8
Donaldson—a person referred to by the Claimant in connection with the forged letters, 131
Don Quixote, alluded to by Mr. Whalley in his address to the electors of the City of Peterborough, 257
Dorney, Thomas, hairdresser, witness in Common Pleas, 80
Doughty, Sir Edward, 9, 11; estates, 8; Doughty estate entail, contemplation of cutting it off on Roger coming of age, 12; Kate, 13; Lady, refusal to see Bogle, 18; to Mr. Baigent, 20; and the tattoo, 86; Doughtys the, Mr. Whalley's opinion respecting them, 284; Doughty Tichborne, the, howled out, *Hobart Town Mercury*, 184
Dowager Lady Tichborne, descent, 7; marriage 8; affidavit, 24; the names of her children, 24; leaves Croydon, 34; inquest, 37; funeral, 68; letter to Teresa Tichborne, 28, 45, 148
Dream of Mr. Karslake, Q.C., concerning Luie, 279
Drowning the mate of the "Bella," 168
Dublin, one of the places where Roger was stationed with his regiment, 13
Dugget, Mr, a person mentioned by Sir John Karslake as having made an affidavit in order to obtain a rule against Messrs. Onslow and Whalley for Contempt of Court, 235
"Duke of Cornwall," the steamer from which Roger disembarked at Herne Bay, 13
Du Moulin, an overseer of Mr. Johnson's in Australia, 139
Dumb-bells used by Orton, 216
Dunchy, a stockrider in Australia, 136
Dundee, the Tichborne Claimant at, 198; *Dundee Courier*, a paper mentioned by the *Morning Advertiser*, which showed that the Claimant made friends and converts wherever he went; and this not only amongst the "rabble" as his enemies would call them—that is, the honest men and artisans of Great Britain, but in intellectual and educated coteries as well, 229
Dunne, Thomas, sergeant in the Carabineers, witness in Common Pleas, 76
Dyke, John—letter confirming Dr. Wheeler's statement that the Claimant is not Orton, 121

E

EARL Grey, 5
Ears (Tichborne's) remarks on, by the author of the "Crucial Test Tested," as taken from the copies of the Chilian daguerreotypes, 312
Easeman, a person in Chili alluded to by John Moore in his evidence, 190
East London, the Claimant at, 130; speech of, 131; speech of Mr. Whalley at, 132; the Claimant at, 175
East, Esq., W. Quartermaine, letter on Pierre Feron, Boatswain of the "Pauline," 192
Ecarte players, the Claimant asserted by Mr Onslow to be one of the best, 227
Echo, alluded to by the Claimant in his defence when charged with Contempt of Court before Justices Blackburn, Mellor, and Quain, 245; the Claimant, in 1870, brought the publishers of the *Echo* before Vice-Chancellor Stuart for Contempt of Court; his honour stated that no doubt a great libel had been committed, as well as a Contempt of Court, but decided that the publishers should pay their own costs, and thereby inflicted the hardship on the Claimant of making him pay his own costs for doing that which he acknowledged to be correct, 246
Edgar, a Saxon King who made a grant of land to the Bishops and Church of Winchester, which is positive evidence of the existence of a place called Tichborne in the Anglo-Saxon days, 8
Editors of newspapers are said to receive cheques for £500 when great trials are pending, 241
Educated people who believe in the identity of the Claimant—list of—176
Education defective—the Claimant's as proved by his French and English letters and Mr. South's report thereon—Mr. Onslow to the *Hampshire Chronicle*, June 18th, 1872, 219
Edward Tichborne, Mr., afterwards Sir Edward Doughty, 7, 9
Edward Orton, the Prosecution tried to make out Sir Roger to be, 242
Electors of the City of Peterborough, Mr. Whalley's address to the, 255
Elizabeth Tichborne, wife of Sir Henry Tichborne, the seventh baronet, 7
Elizabeth Tudor, 5
Endeavour of Messrs. Cullington and Gosford to prevent the Claimant obtaining access to his Mother in Paris, 23
Engine of the Law set in motion against a penniless individual; that engine got jammed and blocked—*Morning Advertiser*, 229
England, Roger's Mother refused to allow him to go to, for his education, although both his father and grandfather Seymour continually urged it. It was afterwards accomplished by a stratagem, 10
Enlargement of the Claimant's instep the same as that of Roger Tichborne, 219
Englishman, the Jesuit and Tichborne's Mother, 31; Mrs. Vansittart and Tichborne, communicated by Mr. Onslow, 35; letter by Mr. Gurnell, the "Handwriting of the Claimant does not prove him to be Arthur Orton," 153; letter by Mr. Isaac B. Beeby showing that the Claimant and Orton are two distinct persons, 164; letter by Mr. Onslow stating why Mr. Serjeant Ballantine was not engaged as Counsel for Sir Roger Tichborne at the last Trial, 230, letter from Mr. Whalley, M.P. respecting Luie, 286
Epaulettes, Tichborne's, mentioned by the Dowager Lady in her affidavit, 26
Episode in the Tichborne Case (Sealed packet), 112; the Luie, 268
Epithets, the Attorney General only used them when he wished to win a bad case, 220; epithets which he applied to the Claimant, 241
Equity, a Court alluded to by Mr. Justice Blackburn in his judgment against the Claimant and Mr. Skipworth for Contempt of Court, 246
Essex, Lodge, Croydon, the residence of Roger Tichborne, and where the Dowager Lady stayed with him after her return from France, 202; mention of in a letter of the Dowager Lady, 208
Estates, the Doughty, 8; the Tichborne, 8; value of, 175
Evans, T. M. Esq., High Bailiff of Leicester, Chairman of the meeting in the Claimant's favour at Leicester, 223
Every encouragement given in public and private to scandalize the Claimant, affidavit of Mr. Skipworth, 242
Evidence: the way it was got up by Dobinson and Geare, 49; summary of in the Court of Common Pleas, 75—82; analysis of the Tattoo, 86; in Australia in favour of the Claimant, 135; not produced in Australia, 161; of William Brougham Penny on the "Osprey," 168; of John Moore, 182; evidence of Sir Talbot Constable in the Common Pleas, 203
Ewens, Mr., speech at the Broadmead rooms, Bristol, 110
Examination of Roger (military); subjects in which he did and did not pass, 11
Examiner, the, in the Court of Chancery, 50—68
Exhibition at Paris, Sir Talbot Constable at, 205
Ex-Parte, the Claimant v. Routledge, 268.
Expenses incurred by the Tichborne Family in prosecuting Roger, 195
Extract from Dr. Kenealy's Lecture respecting Tichborne's thumb, 111
Eyes, twitching of Tichborne's, 204; eyes as taken from the copies of the Chili daguerreotypes, remarks on by the author of the "Crucial Test Tested," 313; Eyes, eyebrows, and upper part of the Claimant's face recognized by Mrs. Radcliffe as Roger Tichborne, according to the statement of Gosford, 219
Eyelid, fish-hook run through Roger's 186

F.

"FACING-BOTH-WAYS" (letter to the *Daily News* after Tichborne's committal to Newgate), 82

G.

H.

I.

J.

K.

L.

LETTERS.

M.

N.

O.

P.

Q.

ford, 13. 199; Wellington, New Zealand, 202. ——LEGAL MATTERS: Affidavit of Tichborne extracts from as read by Mr. Hawkins in Common Pleas, 88. Application to postpone the Trial, *Hampshire Chronicle*, 74. Arrest after the nonsuit, 75. Astounding influence brought to bear against Sir Roger, 35. Australian evidence respecting Tichborne, 135. Baronetcy, the Tichborne, letters between Dobinson, Geare, and Holmes, 37; *Hobart Town Mercury*, 134. Common Pleas, —arrest of Tichborne after the Trial, 75; summary of evidence, 75—82; indecent behaviour of the Judge and spectators during the Trial, 89; names of the jurors in the Tichborne Trial, 91; evidence of Sir Talbot Constable in favour of Tichborne in the Common Pleas, 203. Cross-examination in Chancery, 60. Episode in the Tichborne Case, 112. Estates, the Tichborne, 8. Holmes, Mr., and Tichborne, 23; and Mr. Leete, affidavit of, 26, 27; letter to the *Times* respecting the funeral of Lady Tichborne, 69; reply to Higgins, 70; meeting of Sir Roger at the office of Mr. Holmes, 173. Hopkins, Mr. Edward, Roger's solicitor, first visit of Tichborne to Mr. Hopkins's house, 10; communication with, 12; Tichborne's letter to, 28; Mr. Hopkins and Mr. Baigent, Tichborne and Mr. Hopkins, 31; affidavit of Mr. Hopkins in favour of Tichborne, 32; letter from Mr. Hopkins to the Commissioner of the London Police respecting Tichborne, 34; Holmes and Mr. Hopkins, 46; wrote to Lord Arundell and Mr. Danby Seymour informing them that the Claimant was indeed his former client Roger Charles Tichborne; refused to see Gosford, 203. Inquest on the Dowager Lady Tichborne, 37. Insulting behaviour of Bowker to Tichborne, 22. Jocelyn, Major, letter to the *Standard*, 87; Leete, Mr., and Tichborne, 22. Persons—the various, the Claimant was asserted to be by the Prosecution before they said he was Arthur Orton, 37. Probate, Court of, transcript of Mr. Tolcher's short-hand notes, 70; probate of Lady Tichborne's Will, 70. Threat held out to Messrs. Onslow and Whalley in Westminster Hall—Mr. Skipworth's noble defiance of, 213. Thumb of Sir Roger Tichborne—the *Englishman*, 113. Tichborne and the Australian evidence, 135. Tichborne Claimant and the crew of the "Bella," 152. Tichborne succession, 68. Tichborne Case, the, letter from Mr. Whalley, 148; letter from Mrs. Alexander, 166; account of the punishment awarded in the Court of Queen's Bench to Mr. Onslow and Mr. Whalley, 235. "Tichborne-cum-Orton case."—*Geelong Advertiser*, Friday, June 28th, 1872, 215. Tichborne v. Lushington,—a letter from Mr. Karslake, Q.C., stating his belief in the identity of the Claimant, 170, 230. Tichborne remembered his own room after his long absence abroad, 210; remembered things he could not have been told, 211; the twitching of his eyes a confirmation of his identity, 211. Tichborne, Trial at Bar of Sir Roger, Court of Queen's Bench, November 22, sittings in Banco at Westminster before Lord Chief Justice Cockburn, Mr. Justice Blackburn, and Mr. Justice Mellor, 229. Tichborne Case: the, an application by Dr. Kenealy for certain information as necessary to his defence, with which the Counsel for the Crown had refused to furnish him, 267; the, and Mr. Whalley, from the *Peterborough Times*, 285; "Twenty dollars reward to anyone who will find Carl Anderson, a sailor in the ship 'Osprey,'" 277; letter from Sir Roger, concerning Luie, 280; Tichborne's account of Luie, 286.——LETTERS: To his mother concerning Gosford, 22; to Mr. Hopkins, 28; from Newgate, March 25th, 1872, the *Standard*, 88; to Mr. Spofforth concerning Mr. Rose, May 28th, 1872, the *Standard*, 90; respecting his release from Newgate to the *Daily Telegraph*, 99; French epistle written by him on his arrival at Stonyhurst, 153; on Lord Penzance's successor, to the *Morning Advertiser*, 196; to Sir Talbot Constable, 207; to his mother respecting Holmes and Sir Talbot Constable, 211; to his mother respecting his adherents, 212; to the *Morning Advertiser* denying that he had said that the Jury in the Trial in the Common Pleas were bribed, 219. ——MEETINGS at Alresford, 100, 101; Birmingham, 171, 172; Bradford, 177; Broadmead Rooms, 110; Dewsbury, 175; Dundee, 198; East London, 130; Greenwich, 138; Grimsby, 180, 181; Leeds, 121; Leicester and Loughborough, 130; Leicester, 223; Preston, 197; Southampton, 104, 196; Southsea, 114; St. James Hall, 226; Sunderland, 123; Swansea, 116, 119; Wolverhampton, 174.——PERSECUTIONS: Application to postpone the Trial, 74; Arrest after the non-suit, 75; Astounding influence brought to bear against Sir Roger, 35; Attorney-General bet some bottles of wine on the Tichborne Case, 175; Bail, threat to increase the amount of, 93; Bovill denounced the Claimant as an impostor at the Lord Mayor's dinner, 196; his two brothers betted against the Claimant winning his case, 196; and Bovill himself appeared in Court with documents signed for the committal of the Claimant before he knew he was to be non-suited, 196; Bowker's insulting behaviour to Tichborne, 22; Cockburn, he asserted, denounced him publicly as an impostor and also in the presence of a lady friend of his, 210; Dobinson and Geare's impudent denial of the identity of the Claimant, 29; the way they got up the evidence, 49; trying to intimidate the friends of Tichborne before the first Trial commenced, 92; Gosford's treacherous behaviour to Tichborne at the Clarendon Hotel, Gravesend, 23, 26, 45; ordered the Dowager Lady's boxes to be opened, 203; Hoax practised on Tichborne's friends at Swansea, 118; insinuations of the Lord Chief Justice, 163; insolent conduct of Mr. Robert Lowe (Chancellor of the Exchequer), respecting questions put to him by various Members of Parliament respecting the expenditure of the public money in the Tichborne Case, 213, 214; Radcliffe, Mr., censurable behaviour, 36; Rous stated by Tichborne to have taken copies of the evidence in his favour and to have sold them to the other side, 178; Ruse practised by a lady on, 36.——RELATIVES AND ANCESTORS: Alfred Joseph, second and youngest son of Sir James Francis Tichborne, afterwards tenth Baronet of Tichborne, and of Henriette Felicité, his wife, born at Paris on September 4th, and died 22nd February, 1866, aged twenty-six, 7; death of, 46; habits of life, 46; belief that his brother Roger was alive, 193. Alice Mary Perpetua, daughter of Alfred Joseph Tichborne and of Teresa Mary, his wife, born on the 4th October, 1837, and died 20th October, 1839, 7. Amphilis, wife of Sir Benjamin Tichborne, and daughter of Richard Weston, of Skrynes, in Roxwell, co. Essex, Esq., one of the justices of the Common Pleas, 7. Ann, wife of White Tichborne, Esq., daughter of James Supple, of the parish of St. James, Westminster, buried at Frimley, 14th October, 1681, 7. Anna Maria, wife of Henry Doughty, of Snarford Hall, Esq., and sole heiress of Gregory Byrne, of Hatton Garden, in the parish of St. Andrew, Holborn, Esq., married in 1762, 7. Anne, wife of Sir Henry Joseph Tichborne, eighth Baronet of Tichborne, and daughter of Sir Thomas Burke, of Marble Hill, co. Galway, Ireland, Baronet, married on the 23rd April, 1806; resided after her husband's death at Grove House, Brompton, died at Woodstock, co. Oxford on the 12th August, 1853, 7. Benjamin Tichborne, Sir, Knight, Lord of Tichborne in the county of Hants, created a Baronet on the 8th of March, 1620, aged 93, 7. This Knight proclaimed, at Winchester, James the VI. of Scotland as James I. King of England, 8. Benjamin Tichborne, Sir, Knight, third son of Richard, of West Tisted, in the county of Hants, died without issue on the 21st August, 1665, 7. Benjamin Edmund Tichborne, the second son of Sir Henry Joseph Tichborne, the eighth Baronet, and of Anne his wife, a captain in the service of the East India Company, died unmarried in China, on the 8th October, 1810, 7. Catherine Caroline Tichborne, daughter of Sir Henry Joseph Tichborne, eighth Baronet, and of Anne his wife, born on the 21st April, 1814, married on the 22nd April 1817, to William Greenwood, late Colonel of Grenadier Guards; issue one son and two daughters, 7, 31. Chydioke Tichborne, executed in the year 1586 in Lincoln's Inn Fields for participation in the Babington conspiracy against Queen Elizabeth, 8. Edward Tichborne, third but second surviving son of Sir Henry Joseph Tichborne, eighth Baronet, and of Anne his wife; born on 27th March, 1782, assumed the name of Doughty only by royal license, dated on the 29th May, 1826, succeeded his brother as ninth Baronet on the 3rd June, 1845, and died on the 5th March, 1853, 7 Elizabeth Doughty, only daughter and sole heiress of Henry Doughty, of Snarford Hall, Esq., and of Anna Maria his wife; born on the 9th of June, 1793, and died unmarried on the 8th of May, 1826, aged 63. She bequeathed her estates to her cousin, Edward Tichborne, Esq., as the second surviving son of Sir Henry Tichborne, the seventh Baronet, who assumed by royal license the name and arms of Doughty, 7. Elizabeth Tichborne, wife of Sir Henry Tichborne, seventh Baronet of Tichborne, and daughter of Edmund Plowden, of Plowden, co. Salop, Esq., born in 1757, married in 1778, and died on the 24th Jan., 1829, aged 72, 7; Elizabeth Ann Tichborne, daughter of Sir Henry Joseph Tichborne, the eighth Baronet, and of Anne his wife, born the 28th May, 1807; married, 5th May, 1829, to Joseph Thadeus, eleventh Lord Dormer, both living in March, 1867, having surviving issue three sons and one daughter, 7; Emily Blanche Tichborne, daughter of Sir Henry Joseph Tichborne, eighth Baronet, and of Anne his wife, born 18th June, 1818, married on the 25th July, 1836, to John Benett, Esq., who died the 26th December, 1843. She married, secondly, on 2nd July, 1850, Matthew James Higgins, Esq., of Lowndes-square, London, no issue, 7; Francis Tichborne, of Aldershot and Frimley, Esq., son of Sir Walter Tichborne, Knt., and of Mary his wife, baptized on the 5th Dec., 1602, and died July 12th, 1671, aged 69, 7. Frances Cecily Tichborne, wife of George Brownlow Doughty, of Snarford Hall, Lincoln, Esq., married in 1721, and died the 20th August, 1765, 7. Frances Catherine Tichborne, daughter of Sir Henry Joseph Tichborne, eighth Baronet, and of Anne his wife, born 18th March, 1809, married 22nd September, 1829, Henry Benedict, eleventh Lord Arundell of Wardour. She died 19th April, 1836, and her husband on the 19th Oct., 1862, leaving issue by this marriage two sons, 7. George Brownlow Doughty, of Snarford Hall, co. Lincoln, Esq., born in 1685, and died the 24th September, 1743, 7. Henry Tichborne, Sir, Knight, fourth and youngest son of Sir Benjamin Tichborne, Knight, Lord of Tichborne in the county of Hants, and of Amphilis his wife, born in 1582, and died in 1667, aged 85, ancestor of Sir Henry Tichborne, Bart., created Baron Ferrard, of Ireland, in 1715, all issue extinct, 7; Henry Tichborne, Sir, eldest surviving son and heir of Sir Richard Tichborne, second Baronet of Tichborne, and of Susan his wife, baptized on the 24th May, 1624, and died in 1689, aged 65, 7. Henry Joseph Tichborne, Sir, eldest son and heir of Sir Henry Tichborne, third Baronet of Tichborne and Mary his wife—fourth Baronet of Tichborne, died without male issue on the 15th July, 1743, 7; Henry Doughty, Esq., son and heir of George Brownlow Doughty, of Snarford Hall, co. Lincoln, Esq., and of Frances Cecily his wife, born on 14th March, 1723, and died on the 28th August, 1795, and 73, 7; Henry Tichborne, of Aldershot and Frimley, Esq., son of Sir James Tichborne, of Aldershot and Frimley, and of Mary his wife, baptized at Frimley on the 14th Oct., 1710, succeeded to the estates of Sir Henry Joseph Tichborne, fourth Baronet, under his will, proved the 14th January, 1743-4, and to the baronetcy on the death of the Rev. Sir John Hermengild Tichborne, of the Society of Jesus, on the 5th May, 1748, died 16th July, 1785, aged 75, 7; Henry Tichborne, Sir, seventh Baronet of Tichborne, Aldershot and Frimley, only son and heir, born September 6th, 1756, and died on the 14th June, 1821, aged 65, 7; Henry Joseph Tichborne, Sir, eldest son and heir of Sir Henry Tichborne and of Elizabeth his wife, and eighth Baronet of Tichborne, born on 5th January, 1779, and died on the 3rd June, 1845, High Sheriff of Hants in 1831, 7; the first Roman Catholic who was made High Sheriff after the passing of the Emancipation Act, 9; Henriette Felicité Tichborne, daughter of Henry Seymour, Esq., of Knoyle, co. Wilts, married James Francis Tichborne on 1st of August, 1827, who afterwards became the tenth Baronet. She was the mother of Roger Tichborne and Alfred Tichborne; died on the 12th March, 1868, and buried at Tichborne, 7; marriage, 8; affidavit, 21; the names of her children, 21; leaves Croydon, 31; inquest, 37; funeral, 68; letter to Teresa Tichborne, 29, 15, 148; Henriette

Felicité Tichborne, daughter of Sir Roger Charles Doughty Tichborne and of Mary Ann his wife, born at Brompton, Middlesex, January, 1870, 7; Henry Alfred Joseph Tichborne, a posthumous son and heir of Alfred Joseph Tichborne; born 28th of May, 1866. His mother is Teresa Mary Tichborne, eldest daughter of Henry Benedict, eleventh Lord Arundell of Wardour, 7; James Tichborne, of Aldershot and Frimley, Esq., eldest son and heir of White Tichborne, Esq., and of Ann his wife, baptized on the 30th May, 1674, and died in 1735, 7; James Francis Tichborne, succeeded his brother, Sir Edward Doughty, as tenth Baronet, on 5th March, 1853, and died on the 11th June, 1862. He was father to Roger Charles Doughty Tichborne and Alfred Tichborne, 7, 8, 9; James Francis D. Tichborne, second son of Sir Roger Charles Doughty Tichborne and Mary Ann his wife, born at Alresford, 30th June, 1868, 7; John Hermengild Tichborne, Sir, second and youngest son of Sir Henry Tichborne, the third Baronet of Tichborne, and of Mary his wife. He was a priest of the Society of Jesus. He became fifth Baronet on the death of his brother, Sir Henry Joseph Tichborne, and died at Ghent on the 5th May, 1748, 7; Julia Tichborne, third daughter of Sir Henry Joseph Tichborne, the eighth Baronet, and of Anne his wife. Born 15th July, 1810, married on 2nd July, 1830, Colonel Charles Thomas Talbot, who died 30th April, 1838. She married, secondly, on the 10th January, 1839, Washington Hibbert, Esq., issue by both marriages, 7; Katherine Doughty, wife of Sir Edward Doughty, and daughter of Everard Arundell, ninth Lord Arundell, of Wardour, county Wilts, born 23th August, 1795, married 26th June, 1827. Mother of "Kate Doughty," afterwards Lady Radcliffe, 7; Katherine Mary Elizabeth Doughty, only daughter and surviving issue of Sir Edward Doughty and Katherine his wife, born 30th April, 1834, married 18th October, 1854, to Joseph Percival Pickford Radcliffe, eldest son of Joseph Radcliffe, Bart., and has issue, 7; treacherous interview with Tichborne, 35; Mrs. and the tattoo, 86; Mrs. and Sir Roger, 107, 131; Mrs. and Gosford, 171, 219. Lucy Mary Tichborne, born on 22nd March, 1803, married in April, 1823, George Naugle, a lieutenant on half-pay, and had issue four sons and two daughters, 7; Lucy Ellen Tichborne, sixth daughter of Sir Henry Joseph Tichborne, the eighth Baronet, and of Anne his wife, born 21st December, 1817, married 28th October, 1840, to John Towneley, Esq., second son of Peregrine Towneley, of Towneley, county Lancaster, issue one son and four daughters, 7, 11; Mabella, the wife of Sir Roger Tycheburne, and foundress of the Tichborne Dole, 8; Mabella Tichborne, third and youngest daughter of Sir Henry Joseph Tichborne, the fourth Baronet, and of Mary his wife, and one of the co-heiresses, married Sir John Webb, Bart., and had issue two daughters, who both died unmarried, 7; Mabella Louisa, daughter of Alfred Joseph Tichborne, and of Teresa Mary his wife, born 8th July, 1832, died on the 22nd March, 1833, 7; Mary Tichborne, wife of Sir Walter Tichborne, Knt., and second daughter and co-heir of Robert White, of Aldershot, Esq., married 7th May, 1597, and died January 31st, 1620-1, 7; Mary Tichborne, wife of Sir Henry Tichborne, the third Baronet, and daughter of the Hon. William Arundell, of Horningsham, county Wilts, second son of Thomas, the first Lord Arundell, of Wardour, in the same county, died on the 24th December, 1698, 7; Mary Tichborne, wife of Sir Henry Joseph Tichborne, the fourth Baronet, and daughter of Anthony Kemp, of Slindon, county Sussex, Esq., married in 1689, and died in 1753, 7; Mary Agnes Tichborne, eldest daughter of Sir Henry Joseph Tichborne, the fourth Baronet, and of Mary his wife, and one of the co-heiresses, born in 1695, married 1715 to Michael Blount, of Mapel Durham, in the county of Oxford, and died the 19th May, 1777, aged 82, 7; Mary Tichborne, wife of James Tichborne, of Aldershot and Frimley, Esq., and daughter of Benjamin Rudyerd, of Winchfield, in the county of Hants, Esq., married at Frimley, on the 30th October, 1694, and died in December, 1746, 7; Mary Blount, eldest daughter of Michael Blount, Esq., by his wife Mary Agnes, eldest daughter, and one of the co-heiresses of Sir Henry Joseph Tichborne, Bart., born 9th November, 1716, married 22nd April, 1743, and died 10th February, 1799; aged 82, 7; Mary Tichborne, fourth daughter of Sir Henry Joseph Tichborne, the eighth Baronet, and of Anne his wife, born on the 28th May, 1812, and died unmarried 29th Aug., 1827, 7; Mary Ann Bryant, married at Wagga-Wagga, Australia, 29th January, 1865, to Sir Roger Charles Doughty Tichborne, the eldest son and heir of Sir James Francis Tichborne, and of Henriette Felicité, his wife, and the eleventh Baronet of Tichborne, 7; Richard Tichborne, Sir, Knight, eldest son and heir of Sir Benjamin Tichborne, Knight, Lord of Tichborne in the county of Hants, and of Amphilis his wife; Richard was second Baronet of Tichborne, and died in April, 1652, aged 76; Roger Robert Tichborne, youngest son of Sir Henry Tichborne, the seventh Baronet, and of Elizabeth his wife, born 15th February, 1792, died without issue on 3rd November, 1849, married Rebecca, daughter of Aaron Fernandis Nunez, of Belmont Park, co. Hants, died on 26th January, 1859, 7; Roger Charles Doughty Tichborne, Sir, the eldest son and heir of Sir James Francis Tichborne, and of Henriette Felicité his wife, born at Paris on 5th of January, 1829, eleventh Baronet of Tichborne, and married Mary Ann Bryant, of Wagga-Wagga, Australia, on 29th January, 1865, 7; Roger Joseph D. Tichborne, eldest son of Sir Roger Charles Doughty Tichborne, and of Mary Ann his wife, born at Croydon, 20th Mar, 1867, 7; Susan Tichborne, wife of Sir Richard Tichborne, second Baronet of Tichborne, and second daughter and co-heir of William Waller, of Stoke Charity, in the county of Hants, Esq., born in 1597, and living in 1659, 7; Susanna Tichborne, wife of Francis Tichborne, of Aldershot and Frimley, Esq., and daughter of William Haws, of Brumley Hall, co. Essex, Esq., died on 21st December, 1687, aged 77, 7; Teresa Mary Tichborne, wife of Alfred Joseph Tichborne, and eldest daughter of Henry Benedict, eleventh Lord Arundell of Wardour, by his third wife, born in 1840, married 17th April, 1861, 7; Teresa Mary Agnes, eldest daughter of Sir Roger Charles Doughty Tichborne, Bart., and of Mary Ann his wife, born at Wagga-Wagga, Australia, 18th March, 1866, 7; Tycheburne, Sir Roger de, a Crusader, 8; Walter Tichborne, Sir, Knight, of Aldershot, second son of Sir Benjamin Tichborne, Knight, Lord of Tichborne, in the county of Hants, died in 1640, 7; White Tichborne, Esq., son of Francis Tichborne, of Aldershot and Frimley, Esq., baptized on the 5th December, 16—, and buried on 30th August, 1700, 7.—SPEECHES DELIVERED BY TICHBORNE:—At Alresford, 101; Birmingham, 172; Bradford, 177; Broadmead Rooms, Bristol, 110; Dewsbury, 175; Gravesend, 123; Greenock, 198; Grimsby, 180; Leeds, 125, 126; Leicester and Loughborough, 130; Leicester, 223; Southampton, 197; Southsea, 116; St. James's Hall, 227; Sunderland, 123; Swansea, 117, 119; Wolverhampton, 174.

"Tidd's Practice," a law-book mentioned by Chief Justice Bovill, 232

Tilbury, Giles, an eminent Flemish artist, who painted the celebrated picture of the "Tichborne Dole," 8

Tilt, Mr., the priest of Tichborne, 11

"Tissie Tichborne," a letter from, to the Dowager Lady Tichborne, and the Dowager Lady's reply to the same, 28, 45, 148

Tom Toke, a servant of Mr. Johnson's of Mewburn Park, Australia, 136

Tour, the Claimant's contemplated—*Morning Advertiser*, 103

Towneley Mr., 11

Trana, Herman Theodore, a witness against Luie, in his trial for perjury at the Old Bailey, 300.

Transcript: of letter written by Roger Charles Tichborne in July, 1845, on his arrival at Stonyhurst College, 153; from the Australian Commission, 133, 134

Treasury: correspondence between the Solicitor of and Mr. Whalley, 149—150; the, and Luie, 282

Tredgett, Mary Ann, one of Arthur Orton's sisters (affidavit), 48

Trench, Lady Helena and Miss Fanny, relatives of the Archbishop of Dublin, are "Associates" of the Puseyite Convent at Clewer, 252

Trial: evidence not produced at the, 164; at Bar of Sir Roger Tichborne, Court of Queen's Bench, November 22nd, sittings in Banco, at Westminster, before Lord Chief Justice Cockburn, Mr. Justice Blackburn, and Mr. Justice Mellor, 229; the, of Jean Luie, at the Old Bailey, 298

Tristram, Dr., Counsel for Tichborne in the Court of Probate, Westminster Hall, 70—72

"Troubadour," the Attorney-General asked the Claimant what the word meant, and he not only gave a definition of it, but pointed out an important fact in connection with it in his own family which no one but the undoubted Sir Roger Tichborne could have done, 224

True Bills found against the Claimant for perjury and forgery, mentioned by Mr. Onslow in his affidavit, 235

"Truth stranger than fiction," a letter from Mr. East on Pierre Feron, boatswain of the "Pauline," 191

Tucker, Alderman, Chairman of the meeting at Southampton, 101

Tumut, a place in Australia where Castro stayed, 201

Turville: Mr., saw Roger in Australia, 12; going abroad necessitates the appointment of another trustee to Roger's will, 13; has no doubt whatever of the Claimant's being Roger Tichborne, 18; Mr., letter from, 20; gave Tichborne the address of a London solicitor, 23

Twelve questions in writing handed up to the Claimant, at St. James's Hall, from some bitter unbeliever in his identity, which were completely answered by the Claimant, 227

Tycheburne, Sir Roger de, a Crusader, 8

U.

ULTRAMONTANE party—Mr. Whalley the butt of their ridicule—*Morning Advertiser*, 218

Unfair distinction made by the tribunals of Justice between the cases of Mr. Onslow and Mr. Whalley for Contempt of Court and the editors and writers in newspapers, on the other side, for the same offence—pointed out by Sir John Karslake, 236

Union Bank, at Sydney, the establishment from which Bogle received from Lady Doughty the £50 a year which Sir Edward Doughty promised to leave him, 19

"Unsolicited Questions"—a poem, 179

Upper part of the Claimant's face, eyes and eyebrows recognized by Mrs. Radcliffe as being those of Roger Tichborne, according to the statement of Gosford, 219

Upton Park, in the county of Dorset, part of the Tichborne property inherited from Elizabeth Doughty, 9

V.

VACCINATION MARK (French) the same on the Claimant as on Roger Tichborne, 219

Valparaiso, Tichborne at, 15, 185, 191, 192, 200

Value of the Tichborne estates, 175

Van Den Bergh, Mr. J. R., Consul at Portsmouth to several different countries, Chairman of the Southsea meeting in behalf of the Claimant, 115

Vansittart, Mrs. and Tichborne, an extraordinary incident, communicated to the *Englishman* by Mr. Onslow, 35

Vasseur, Abbé, the Dowager Lady Tichborne's confessor, 63

Verschoyle, Miss, relative of the Bishop of Kilmore, an "Associate" of the Puseyite Convent at Clewer, 252

Vinkel, a place at which Roger Tichborne used secretly to take arsenic, 192

Vice-Chancellor Stuart, — before him the Claimant brought, in 1870, the publishers of the *Echo* for Contempt of Court; his Honour stated that no doubt a great libel had been committed, as well as a Contempt of Court, but decided that the publishers should pay their own costs, and thereby inflicted the hardship on the Claimant of making him pay his own costs for doing that which he acknowledged to be correct, 216

Victoria, Queen, 6

Villany of the Press in keeping out the news in favour of Tichborne, 196

Virgil, the celebrated Roman poet, 6

Visit of Sir Roger to Tichborne, 21; of the Lord Chief Justice to Tichborne House, during the Trial, in company with Mr. Webster who had married the widow of Alfred Tichborne, 219

Vituperation and foul language of the Attorney-General, for which he was never called to order by the Lord Chief Justice, bitterly complained of by the Claimant in the Court of Queen's Bench before Justices Blackburn, Mellor, and Quain, 215

Volckert, the clerk to Messrs. Thompson alluded to in relation to the statement o Jean Luie, 273

W.

Y.

www.ingramcontent.com/pod-product-compliance
Lightning Source LLC
Chambersburg PA
CBHW031856220426
43663CB00006B/654

* 9 7 8 3 3 3 7 3 2 5 2 6 8 *